ECONOMICS

ECONOMICS
PRINCIPLES, PROBLEMS, AND POLICIES
THIRTEENTH EDITION

CAMPBELL R. McCONNELL

Professor of Economics, Emeritus
University of Nebraska

STANLEY L. BRUE

Professor of Economics
Pacific Lutheran University

McGRAW-HILL, INC.

New York • St. Louis • San Francisco • Auckland
Bogotá • Caracas • Lisbon • London • Madrid
Mexico City • Milan • Montreal • New Delhi
San Juan • Singapore • Sydney • Tokyo • Toronto

ECONOMICS
Principles, Problems, and Policies

Copyright © 1996, 1993, 1990, 1987, 1984, 1981, 1978, 1975, 1972, 1969, 1966, 1963 by McGraw-Hill, Inc.
All rights reserved. Previously published under the title of *Elementary Economics: Principles, Problems, and Policies.* Copyright © 1960 by McGraw-Hill, Inc. All rights reserved. Printed in the United States of America. Except as permitted under the United States Copyright Act of 1976, no part of this publication may be reproduced or distributed in any form or by any means, or stored in a data base or retrieval system, without the prior written permission of the publisher.

This book is printed on acid-free paper.

1 2 3 4 5 6 7 8 9 0 VNH VNH 9 0 9 8 7 6 5

ISBN 0-07-046814-1

This book was set in Century Oldstyle by York Graphic Services, Inc.
The editors were Michael R. Elia, Lucille H. Sutton, and Edwin Hanson;
the designer was Joseph A. Piliero;
the production supervisor was Annette Mayeski.
Illustrations were done by Cathy Hull and Roy Wiemann.
Technical drawings were done by Vantage Art.
Von Hoffmann Press, Inc., was printer and binder.

Library of Congress Cataloging-in-Publication Data

McConnell, Campbell R.
    Economics—principles, problems, and policies / Campbell R.
McConnell, Stanley L. Brue.—13th ed.
        p.   cm.
    Includes index.
    ISBN 0-07-046814-1
    1. Economics.   I. Brue, Stanley L., (date).
HB171.5.M139   1996
    330—dc20   95-13487

ABOUT THE AUTHORS

Campbell R. McConnell earned his Ph.D. from the University of Iowa after receiving degrees from Cornell College and the University of Illinois. He taught at the University of Nebraska—Lincoln from 1953 until his retirement in 1990. He is also coauthor of *Contemporary Labor Economics,* 4th ed. (McGraw-

Hill) and has edited readers for the principles and labor economics courses. He is a recipient of both the University of Nebraska Distinguished Teaching Award and the James A. Lake Academic Freedom Award and is past-president of the Midwest Economics Association. Professor McConnell was awarded an honorary Doctor of Laws degree from Cornell College in 1973 and received its Distinguished Achievement Award in 1994. His primary areas of interest are labor economics and economic education. He has an extensive collection of jazz recordings and enjoys reading jazz history.

Stanley L. Brue did his undergraduate work at Augustana College (S.D.) and received his Ph.D. from the University of Nebraska—Lincoln. He teaches at Pacific Lutheran University, where he has been honored as a recipient of the Burlington Northern Faculty Achievement Award. He has also received the na-

tional Leavey Award for excellence in economic education. Professor Brue is national President and member of the International Executive Board of Omicron Delta Epsilon International Economics Honorary. He is coauthor of *Economic Scenes,* 5th ed. (Prentice-Hall) and *Contemporary Labor Economics,* 4th ed. (McGraw-Hill) and author of *The Evolution of Economic Thought,* 5th ed. (HB/Dryden). For relaxation, he enjoys boating on Puget Sound and skiing trips with his family.

To Mem
and to Terri and Craig

CONTENTS IN BRIEF

CONTENTS

ix

The "Big Picture"

LAST WORD For the Fed, Life Is a Metaphor

LIST OF KEY GRAPHS

PREFACE

We are pleased to present the thirteenth edition of *Economics* (and its companion editions *Macroeconomics* and *Microeconomics*). *Economics* continues to be the top-selling economics text in the United States —with an expanded market share in the twelfth edition. Moreover, the Russian-language version of *Economics* is the leading economics text in Russia. More than 1 million Russians have learned about market economics from it since the fall of communism. The Canadian and Australian adaptations of this book and its translations into French, Spanish, and other languages have further extended its reach.

Capitalism in Russia, interest-rate hikes, GATT and NAFTA, pollution rights, the balanced budget amendment—what a remarkable time for teaching and learning economics! More than ever before it is clear that people who comprehend economic principles will be better able to make sense of the emerging world and have an advantage functioning in it. We thank each of you using *Economics,* wherever you are in this rapidly changing world, for granting us a modest role in your efforts to teach or learn this vital subject.

WHAT'S NEW?

This edition has been thoroughly revised, polished, and updated. Many of the changes have been motivated by the comments of 43 reviewers, 10 participants in focus groups and 124 respondents to a questionnaire. We sincerely thank each of these contributors and have acknowledged them at the end of this preface.

Here, we strive only for an overview of the changes in the thirteenth edition; chapter-by-chapter details are provided in the *Instructor's Resource Manual.*

New Chapters

We have written two new chapters for this edition.
- *The United States in the Global Economy.* The material throughout Part 1 has been condensed and rearranged to allow for an early and comprehensive new chapter (Chapter 6) on the global economy. This chapter contains not only descriptive material (volume and pattern of world trade), but also essential theory (comparative advantage, exchange rates) and institutional features (trade barriers, GATT, EU, NAFTA). By providing the basics of international trade and finance, the chapter is a springboard for the instructor who wishes to fully integrate micro and macro materials into a global framework.
- *Economics of Health Care.* A new chapter (Chapter 35) presents the economics of health care, an issue that has dominated and will continue to dominate national debates. The twin problems of rising costs of health care and unequal access to health care are presented, as is a demand and supply model explaining cost increases. The chapter applies and reinforces a host of economic concepts, including asymmetric information, spillovers, tax subsidies, income and price elasticities, the moral hazard problem, optimal health care, and more. The chapter concludes with a discussion of reform options. To make room for this new chapter, we have deleted the twelfth-edition's chapter on general equilibrium analysis.

New Features

The thirteenth edition contains two new features— one adding another global dimension to *Economics,* the other making the book more interactive
- *Global Perspectives.* We have added 43 Global Perspective sections—most containing charts— throughout the book to compare the United States economy with other nations. To merely state, for example, United States' rates of inflation, unemployment, or taxes, the size of American farm subsidies, or health care spending, without international comparisons denies students the context needed for meaningful comparisons

- *Key Questions (with Answers).* In each chapter we have designated two to five end-of-chapter questions as "Key Questions," providing answers in the back of the text. Many of these questions are quantitative and are designed to help the student work through and understand basic concepts. The student is alerted within the chapters as to when a particular Key Question is relevant. Students wanting to immediately test their understanding can turn to the specially marked Key Question, checking their answer against the end-of-book answer. Others may want to wait until they have read the full chapter before answering the Key Questions. Either way, the Key Questions make this edition of *Economics* more interactive.

Reconstituted Macroeconomics

The macro analysis has been carefully rethought and restructured for logical development of the ideas and to provide greater flexibility for instructors. Because these changes are extensive, we describe them more fully.

- *Chapters 7 and 8* on national income accounting and macroeconomic instability have undergone only minor revision.
- *Chapter 9* addresses the components of the private, closed aggregate expenditures (AE) model and examines equilibrium GDP. We have abridged the discussion of classical economics, quickly getting the student into the AE model. We present the AE theory as part of integrated modern macro rather than emphasizing disputes between "camps." Comparison of schools of macroeconomic thought is deferred to Chapter 16 on alternative perspectives.
- *Chapter 10* examines changes in equilibrium GDP and the multiplier in the private, closed economy. It then brings in the net export and government components of the aggregate expenditures model, the latter from the previous edition's chapter on fiscal policy. Then, recessionary and inflationary gaps are considered, along with historical applications of these concepts (the Great Depression and Vietnam inflation).
- *Chapter 11* develops the aggregate demand–aggregate supply (AD-AS) model, with two optional sections which (1) derive the AD curve from the AE model, and (2) show how shifts in the AD curve and AE curve are related. We anticipate that most instructors will assign the AE chapters, but instructors wishing to use only AD-AS can delete the AE chap-

ters along with these optional sections in Chapter 11. With in-class supplementation, Chapter 11's section on the multiplier with inflation could serve as a springboard for instructors to develop the concepts of the MPC, MPS, and multiplier (the latter in an AD-AS framework).

- *Chapter 12* on fiscal policy has been recast entirely in terms of AD-AS.

We believe the new organization of the macroeconomics chapters accomplishes three goals.

Most importantly, by eliminating all "jumping" between models, the AE and AD-AS models are better integrated for the majority of professors who teach both. The new progression is: National income accounting, macroeconomic instability, the AE model, derivation of AD from the AE model, addition of AS, and application of the AD-AS model to fiscal policy (and later to monetary policy).

Second, the new organization provides an exclusive AD-AS option (Chapters 11 and 12 and beyond) for those desiring it.

Finally, the two AE chapters are now unencumbered with AD-AS sections for instructors wishing to emphasize the AE model.

Consolidated Introductory Chapters

We have consolidated the introductory chapters for clearer focus and to make room for the new Chapter 6 on the global economy. The two twelfth-edition chapters on the private and public sectors are combined into new Chapter 5 (The Mixed Economy) in this edition. Also, new Chapter 4 (previously Chapter 5) now meshes the former Chapter 3 discussion of pure capitalism with analysis of the market system. This is facilitated by relocating supply and demand analysis as Chapter 3 in this edition.

The Economic Perspective

We have placed greater emphasis on the economic way of thinking. In Chapter 1 we have greatly expanded the section on the economic perspective, discussing scarcity and choice, rational behavior, and marginal analysis. In Chapter 2 we use the ideas of marginal benefits and marginal costs (Figure 2-2) to determine the optimal position on the production possibilities curve. We then take opportunities to reinforce the economic perspective in the remainder of the book.

Culling and Tightening

Our considerable culling and tightening in the twelfth edition has been well received by instructors and, of course, students. Buoyed by that response, we have again looked to delete the archaic, remove redundancy, tighten sentences, and reduce formality. In further economizing on words, we were careful *not* to reduce the thoroughness of our explanations. Where needed, the "extra sentence of explanation" remains a distinguishing characteristic of *Economics*.

Other New Topics and Revised Discussions

Along with the changes just discussed, there are many other revisions.

• *Part 1. Chapter 1:* Reorganization of the "policy" section; new discussion of the correlation-causation fallacy. *Chapter 2:* Clarification of productive versus allocative efficiency; new application on lumber versus owls. *Chapter 3:* New examples: increased demand for broccoli, carrots, guns; reduced supply of haddock. *Chapter 4:* Expanded discussion of property rights. *Chapter 5:* New discussions on growth of transfer payments and lottery revenues.

• *Part 2. Chapter 8:* Revised Figure 8-7 to allow for output beyond the full-employment output; new Figure 8-8 on nominal versus real interest rate. *Chapter 10:* Major new aggregate expenditure applications: the Great Depression and Vietnam inflation. *Chapter 11:* Removal of "Keynesian" and "classical" labels from the horizontal and vertical ranges of AS; new distinction between full-employment GDP and full-capacity GDP. *Chapter 12:* New presentation of fiscal policy in the AD-AS framework (Figures 12-1 and 12-2); revised discussion of the full-employment budget (new Figure 12-4).

• *Part 3. Chapter 13:* New discussions on the relative decline of bank and thrift assets and globalization of financial activity. *Chapter 15:* New AD-AS presentation of monetary policy (Figure 15-2); new discussions of recent successes of monetary policy; the "loss of control" issue; the effect of interest-rate changes on interest income; and the recent policy focus on the Federal funds rate. New Figure 15-3 provides an extended AD-AS "overview" of macro theory and policy.

• *Part 4. Chapter 16:* New title: "Alternative Views of Macro Theory and Policy"; AD-AS comparison of classical and Keynesian analysis (from twelfth-edition Chapter 10). *Chapter 17:* New discussion of employ-

ment and training policy. *Chapter 18:* New topics: entitlements; ownership of the public debt (Figure 18-1); debt as a curb on fiscal policy; Deficit Reduction Act of 1993. *Chapter 19:* Clarification of demand and efficiency factors in growth (Figure 19-1); new Figure 19-4 on the educational attainment of the population; discussions of slow growth of median family income (new Figure 19-5) and the new resurrection of Doomsday models (Figure 19-6).

• *Part 5. Chapter 20:* New price elasticity example on the excise tax on luxury boats; fuller discussions of cross and income elasticity of demand; *Chapter 21:* Clearer delineation of the total utility–marginal utility relationship (Figure 22-1); new applications: compact discs, transfers and gifts, medical care. *Chapter 22:* New numerical example of the difference between accounting and economic profits; new examples of scale economies, including the prices of introductory versus advanced textbooks and bank mergers. *Chapter 24:* Improved discussion of economies of scale as an entry barrier (Figure 24-1); new graphical comparison of a single-price monopolist versus price-discriminating monopolist (Figure 24-7). *Chapter 25:* Revised discussion of long-run equilibrium in monopolistic competition; new Figure 25-4 on advertising and economies of scale. *Chapter 26:* Revision of the "causes of oligopoly" section; updating in the case study of autos.

• *Part 6. Chapter 27:* New applications of the determinants of labor demand: auto workers, fast-food workers, impact of personal computers, defense cutbacks, contingent workers. *Chapter 28:* Discussions of real wage stagnation and failed pay-for-performance plans. *Chapter 29:* New application: usury laws.

• *Part 7. Chapter 30:* Graphical analysis of spillovers (from twelfth-edition Chapter 6); updates on pollution credits and the Superfund. *Chapter 31:* Discussion of the "reinventing government" effort and the Deficit Reduction Act of 1993. *Chapter 32:* New section on the tradeoffs between antitrust and other goals (balance of trade, desired consolidation in the defense industry, and promoting new technologies); new examples of price-fixing cases; major new section on industrial policy. *Chapter 33:* New Figure 33-3 showing volatility and long-run decline in farm prices; new discussions of rent-seeking in agriculture and environmental impacts of price supports. *Chapter 34:* New discussions on causes of increasing inequality; decomposed poverty rates (Figure 34-5); the Earned Income Tax Credit; and welfare reform proposals. *Chapter 36:*

Greatly tightened sections on union history and union impacts; new discussion of immigrants' use of welfare programs.

• *Part 8. Chapter 37:* New topics: supply and demand analysis of exports and imports (Figures 37-3, 37-4, and 37-5); government export promotion policies; renewal of China's most-favored-nation status; and negotiations with Japan. *Chapter 38:* Revised discussion of the managed float; updated discussion of recent American trade deficits. *Chapter 39:* New table on the distribution of world income (Table 39-1); a reworked and extended discussion of population problems; new discussion of the difficulties associated with foreign aid; reworked discussion of the debt crisis; new section on the "New Global Compact." *Chapter 40:* Progress report on the Russian transition to capitalism.

New Last Words

Reviewers have indicated they appreciate the "Last Word" minireadings and their placement toward the conclusion of each chapter. These selections serve several purposes: Some provide current or historical real-world applications of economic concepts; others reveal human interest aspects of economic problems; some present contrasting or nonmainstream points of view; and stll others present economic concepts or issues in a global context. Sixteen of the Last Words are new and others have been revised and updated.

The new topics are: Cuba's declining production possibilities (Chapter 2); ticket scalping (Chapter 3); alternative views on why Europe's unemployment rate is so high (Chapter 11); the use of the dollar around the world (Chapter 13); the problem of entitlements (Chapter 18); pros and cons of economic growth (Chapter 19); market forces and the rising value of education (Chapter 20); the inefficiency of Christmas gift giving (Chapter 21); creative destruction as a competitive force (Chapter 23); the De Beers diamond monopoly (Chapter 24); news accounts of public sector failure (Chapter 31); the impact of airline deregulation (Chapter 32); welfare for the rich (Chapter 34); physicians versus economists on health care reform (Chapter 35); speculation in currency markets (Chapter 38); and China as an emerging economic power (Chapter 40).

New Software and Multimedia Materials

The extensive ancillaries available with the thirteenth edition for either students or instructors are describ-

ed later in the Preface. Three new items are described here.

PowerPoint Presentation/Tutorial Software for Windows

C. Norman Hollingsworth of Dekalb College, North Campus, Dunwoody, Georgia, has prepared a multi-slide presentation for every chapter in the thirteenth edition (2000 slides in all). This Windows software includes a full run-time version of PowerPoint, allowing instructors to use these presentations "right out of the box" without having to purchase the PowerPoint software program. Owners of PowerPoint software can edit any slide in the set or add additional slides to the set to more closely match their classroom needs. This software is interactive, flexible, and in full color. While designed to enhance the instructor's classroom lecture/discussion, it can also be used in a computer lab for tutorial/review purposes.

Interactive Key Graphs Presentation/Tutorial Software for Windows

The 21 Key Graphs in the thirteenth edition are critical for student understanding of the concepts in introductory economics. With this Key Graphs Tutorial Software students will be able to study and review critical concepts in the IBM-PC/Windows environment in a computer lab or on their own PC. Instructors may also use this software in class, manipulating the full-color graphs to dynamically illustrate concepts in ways that a book or overhead transparencies never can.

Multimedia: Principles of Economics on CD-ROM

Charles Link, Jeffrey Miller, and Fred Hofstetter of the University of Delaware have prepared a stand-alone multmedia CD-ROM for principles of economics that contains both an instructor and a tutorial component. The CD-ROM, with sound, video, and animation, includes substantial interactive tutorial material for creative learning. There are eight content modules covering the topics in macroeconomics and eight modules covering microeconomics.

In addition we continue to provide *Concept Master,* a DOS-based student tutorial by William and Irene Gunther, updated to reflect the changes in the thirteenth edition, *Macroeconomics: A Lab Course* by Norris Peterson, for use with IBM-PCs, and *DiscoverEcon* by Gerald Nelson and Wesley Seitz, for use with the Macintosh computer.

FUNDAMENTAL GOALS

Although the thirteenth edition bears only a modest resemblance to the first, the basic purpose remains the same—to introduce the beginning economics student to principles essential in understanding the basic economizing problem, specific economic issues, and the policy alternatives available for dealing with them. We hope that an ability to reason accurately and objectively about economic matters and a lasting interest in economics will be two byproducts of this basic objective. Our intention remains to present the principles and problems of economics in a straightforward, logical fashion. Therefore, we continue to stress clarity of presentation and organization.

PRODUCT DIFFERENTIATION

This text embraces a number of distinguishing features.

- *Comprehensive explanations at an appropriate level.* We have attempted to craft a comprehensive, analytical text which is challenging to better students, yet accessible—with appropriate diligence—to average students. We think the thoroughness and accessibility of *Economics* enables the instructor to select topics for special classroom emphasis with confidence that students can independently read and comprehend other assigned material in the book.

- *Comprehensive definition of economics.* The principles course sometimes fails to provide students with a comprehensive and meaningful definition of economics. To avoid this shortcoming, all of Chapter 2 is devoted to a careful statement and development of the economizing problem and an exploration of its implications. This foundation should be helpful in putting the many particular subject areas of economics in proper perspective.

- *Fundamentals of the market system.* Economies the world over are making the difficult transition from planning to markets. Our detailed description of the institutions and operation of the market *system* in Chapter 4 is even more relevant than before. Property rights, freedom of enterprise and choice, competition, the role of profits—these and related concepts are poorly understood by the typical student. We think we have accorded them the elaboration they require.

- *Early integration of international economics.* The principles and institutions of the global economy are given early treatment. Chapter 6 examines the growth of world trade, the major participants in world trade, specialization and comparative advantage, the foreign exchange market, tariffs and subsidies, and various trade agreements. This strong introduction to international economics permits "globalization" of later discussions of macroeconomics and microeconomics.

- *Early and extensive treatment of government.* Government is an integral component of modern capitalism. Its economic role, therefore, should not be treated piecemeal or as an afterthought. This text introduces the economic functions of government early and accords them systematic treatment in Chapter 5. Chapter 30 examines government and market failure in further detail, and Chapter 31 looks at salient facets of public choice theory and public finance. Both the macroeconomics and the microeconomics sections of the text have problem- and policy-oriented chapters.

- *Emphasis on economic growth.* This volume continues to emphasize economic growth. Chapter 2 employs the production possibilities curve to show the basic ingredients of growth. Chapter 19 discusses the rate and causes of American growth, in addition to some of the controversies surrounding it. Chapter 39 focuses on the less-developed countries and the growth obstacles they confront. A segment of Chapter 40 concerns the stalling of growth in the former Soviet Union. Beyond these the chapters on price theory pay special attention to the implications that the various market structures have for technological progress.

- *Emphasis on the theory of the firm.* We have given much attention to microeconomics in general and to the theory of the firm in particular, for two reasons. First, the concepts of microeconomics are difficult for most beginning students. Short expositions usually compound these difficulties by raising more questions than they answer. Second, we have coupled analysis of the various market structures with a discussion of the impact of each market arrangement on price, output levels, resource allocation, and the rate of technological advance.

- *Chapters on economic issues.* As most students see it, Part 4 on macroeconomic issues and

Part 7 on micro-oriented problems are where the action is. We have sought to guide the action along logical lines through the application of appropriate analytical tools. Our bias favors inclusiveness; each instructor can effectively counter this bias by omitting those chapters felt to be less relevant for a particular group of students.

ORGANIZATION AND CONTENT

The prerequisite of an understandable economics text is the logical arrangement and clear exposition of subject matter. This book has been organized so the exposition of each particular topic and concept is directly related to the level of difficulty which the average student is likely to encounter. For this reason we have given microeconomics and macro employment theory comprehensive and careful treatments. Simplicity here is correlated with comprehensiveness, not brevity.

Furthermore, our experience suggests that in treating each basic topic—aggregate demand and aggregate supply, money and banking, theory of the firm, and international economics—it is desirable to couple analysis with policy. Generally, a three-step development of analytical tools is employed: (1) verbal descriptions and illustrations, (2) numerical examples, and (3) graphical presentation based on these numerical illustrations.

The material in this book is organized into eight parts: Part 1: An Introduction to Economics and the Economy; Part 2: National Income, Employment, and Fiscal Policy; Part 3: Money, Banking, and Monetary Policy; Part 4: Problems and Controversies in Macroeconomics; Part 5: Microeconomics of Product Markets; Part 6: Microeconomics of Resource Markets; Part 7: Government and Current Economic Problems; and Part 8: International Economics and the World Economy. The Contents lists the specific chapters in each part and the topics within each chapter.

ORGANIZATION ALTERNATIVES

Although instructors generally agree as to the content of a principles of economics course, there are differences of opinion on what particular arrangement of material is best. The structure of this book provides considerable organizational flexibility. Users of prior editions tell us they accomplish substantial rearrangements of chapters with little sacrifice of continuity.

We have chosen to move from macro- to microeconomics, but the introductory material of Part 1 can be followed immediately by the micro analysis of Parts 5 and 6. Similarly, the AD-AS model appears after, rather than before, aggregate expenditures analysis. Those who disagree with this reorganization will encounter no special problems by covering Chapter 11 before Chapters 9 and 10.

Furthermore, some instructors will prefer to intersperse the microeconomics of Parts 5 and 6 with the problems chapters of Part 7. This is easily accomplished. Chapter 33 on agriculture may follow Chapter 23 on pure competition; Chapter 32 on antitrust, regulation, and industrial policy may follow Chapters 24 to 26 on imperfect competition. Chapter 36 on labor market issues may follow Chapter 28 on wages; and Chapter 34 on income inequality may follow Chapters 28 and 29 on distributive shares of national income.

Those who teach the typical two-semester course and who feel comfortable with the books' organization will find that, by putting the first four parts in the first semester and Parts 5 through 8 in the second, the material is divided both logically in terms of content and satisfactorily in terms of quantity and level of difficulty between the two semesters. For those instructors who choose to emphasize international economics, Parts 1, 2, 3, and 8 may be treated in the first semester and Parts 4 through 7 in the second.

For a course based on three quarters of work we would suggest Chapters 1 through 12 for the first quarter, 13 through 29 for the second, and 31 through 40 for the third.

Those interested in the one-semester course will discern several possible groups of chapters appropriate for such a course. Tentative outlines for three one-semester courses, emphasizing macroeconomics, microeconomics, or a survey of micro and macro theory, follow this preface. Also included are several one-quarter course options.

PEDAGOGICAL AIDS

As in previous editions, *Economics* is highly student-oriented. The new "To the Student" statement at the beginning of Part 1 details the many pedagogical aids.

SUPPLEMENTS

The thirteenth edition is accompanied by a variety of high-quality supplements.

Study Guide

Professor William Walstad—one of the nation's foremost experts on economic education—has prepared the thirteenth edition of the *Study Guide,* which many students find to be indispensable. It contains for each chapter an introductory statement, a checklist of behavioral objectives, an outline, a list of important terms, hints and tips, fill-in questions, problems and projects, objective questions, and discussion questions. The glossary found at the end of *Economics* also appears in the *Study Guide.*

The *Guide* is a superb "portable tutor" for the principles student. Separate *Study Guides* have been prepared to correspond with the individual macro and micro paperback editions of the text.

Instructors' Resource Manual

Professor Joyce Gleason of Nebraska Wesleyan University has revised and updated the *Instructor's Resource Manual.* It comprises chapter summaries, listings of "what's new" in each chapter, teaching tips and suggestions, learning objectives, chapter outlines, data and visual aid sources with suggestions for classroom use, and questions and problems. Answers to the text's end-of-chapter questions are also found in the manual (with the exception of the answers to the Key Questions, which are found at the end of *Economics*).

Available again in this edition is a computerized version of the *Manual,* suitable for use with IBM-PC compatibles and Macintosh computers. Users of *Economics* can print out portions of the *Manual's* contents, complete with their own additions and alterations, for use as student handouts or in whatever ways they might wish. This capability includes printing out answers to the end-of-chapter questions not answered in the textbook.

Three Test Banks

This edition of *Economics* is supplemented by two test banks of objective, predominantly multiple-choice questions and a third test bank of short-answer essay questions and problems.
- *Test Bank I* now comprises about 5200 questions, all written by the text authors.
- *Test Bank II* by Professor Walstad, contains over 4700 questions.
- *Test Bank III,* also prepared by Professor Walstad, contains "constructive response" testing to evaluate student understanding in a manner different from conventional multiple-choice and true-false questions. Suggested answers to the essay and problem questions are included.

For all test items in Test Banks I and II, the nature of each question is identified (for example, G = graphical; C = conceptual, etc.) as are the page numbers in the text containing the material that is the basis for each question. Also, each chapter in Test Banks I and II begins with a list that groups questions by topics. Text adopters can use this sizable number of questions, organized into three test banks of equal quality, with maximum flexibility. The fact that the text authors and *Study Guide* authors have prepared all the test items assures the fullest possible correlation with the text content.

Additional Supplements

- *Computerized testing.* Test Banks I, II, and III are available in computerized versions, both for IBM-PC and compatibles and for Macintosh computers. These systems include test generation, capable of producing high-quality graphs from the test banks. They also can generate multiple tests, with versions "scrambled" to be distinctive, and other useful features. This software will meet the various needs of the widest spectrum of computer users. Separate versions of the Computerized Test Banks have been prepared to correspond with the individual macro and micro editions of the text.
- *Color transparencies (figures and tables).* Over 250 new full-color transparencies for overhead projectors have been prepared especially for the thirteenth edition. They encompass all the figures appearing in *Economics* and are available on request to adopters. New to this edition are overhead transparencies for the tables in the book. As with the Computerized Test Banks, the transparencies are also available in versions corresponding to *Macroeconomics* and *Microeconomics.*
- *Student software. Concept Master III,* a student software package, has been prepared for users of IBM-PCs and compatibles by William Gunther of the University of Alabama and Irene Gunther. The previous version of this software was widely praised by its users. It provides extensive and varied computer-assisted study material.

More than twenty graphic-based tutorial programs provide an opportunity for students to study key topics in the book in an interactive way. The tutorial programs are linked to the text. Selected end-of-chapter questions relating to the content of one of the tutorial programs are highlighted by a floppy disk symbol ( ). The questions themselves are not necessarily contained within the tutorial program, but the tutorial does contain material relating directly to the concepts underlying the highlighted questions.

In addition to the tutorial programs, students can quiz themselves with a self-testing program accompanying each text chapter. The package also features eight simulation games, divided between macroeconomics and microeconomics. Some of the simulations are elementary, others are more complex. Wherever possible, they include a global perspective. Also included in the package are a list of key terms, a pop-up calculator for computations, and a section using the Key Graphs in the text to direct students to the appropriate tutorial lesson.

- *Macroeconomics: A Lab Course.* Professor Norris Peterson of Pacific Lutheran University, working with the talented staff of Intellipro, Inc., has created the software package *Macroeconomics: A Lab Course,* to be used in macroeconomics courses. It builds the basic macroeconomic framework in sequential, "building block" laboratory simulations that allow students to grasp the fundamental concepts of macroeconomics in a dynamic and creative manner.

- *DiscoverEcon.* For users of MacIntosh computers, there is an exciting tutorial program, *DiscoverEcon.* Developed by Professors Gerald Nelson and Wesley Seitz of the University of Illinois, this innovative package uses Apple's HYPERCARD programming environment to produce an extremely interactive learning experience. Dynamic shifts of curves, screen animation, sound effects, and simple-to-use command keys are features of this program.

- *Videos.* New videotape materials have been assembled for this edition to illustrate fundamental concepts and economic issues in a manner that will be equally effective in classroom settings or media resource centers. Among these materials are numerous videos selected from "Adam Smith's Money World" that may be used when covering such topics as production possibilities, the role of government, the labor market, monopolistic competition and international economics. Your local McGraw-Hill representative can provide details on all video ancillaries for the text.

DEBTS

The publication of this thirteenth edition will extend the life of *Economics* well into its fourth decade. This gracious acceptance has no doubt been fostered by the many teachers and students kind enough to provide their suggestions and criticisms.

Our colleagues at the University of Nebraska—Lincoln and Pacific Lutheran University have generously shared knowledge of their specialties with us and have provided encouragement. We are especially indebted to Jerry Petr, Dave Palm, and Norris Peterson, who have been most helpful in offsetting our comparative ignorance in their areas of specialty.

As indicated, the thirteenth edition has benefited from a number of perceptive reviews. In both quantity and quality, they provided us the richest possible source of suggestions for this revision. These contributors are listed at the end of this Preface.

Professor Thomas Barbiero of Ryerson Polytechnic Institute in his role as coauthor of the Canadian edition of *Economics* has provided helpful ideas. Also, we are most appreciative of several good suggestions for improvement provided by Professor Walstad, the author of the *Study Guide.* Thanks also goes to Professor Mark Lovewell, who coded the new Test Bank items by type of question and identified the corresponding text page numbers for all the items.

We are greatly indebted to the many professionals at McGraw-Hill—and in particular Lucille Sutton, Mike Elia, Edwin Hanson, Joseph Murphy, Joe Piliero, Victoria Richardson, Annette Mayeski, and Jonathan Hulbert, for their expertise in the production and distribution of the book. Cathy Hull and Roy Wiemann provided the creative illustrations for the Last Word readings. The positive contributions of these highly skilled professionals are gratefully acknowledged.

With this much assistance, we see no compelling reason why the authors should assume full responsibility for errors of omission or commission. But we bow to tradition.

Campbell R. McConnell
Stanley L. Brue

CONTRIBUTORS

REVIEWERS

Mamhoud Arya, Edison Community College
Noel Bennett, Metro Community College
Trent Bogges, Plymouth State College
Frank Bonello, University of Notre Dame
Mark Chopin, Louisiana Tech University
Chris Colburn, Old Dominion University
Gordon Crocker, Community College of Allegheny
    County
John Dorsey, University of Maryland
Paul Farnham, Georgia State University
Rashi Fein, Harvard Medical School
Paul Feldstein, University of California—Irvine
Arthur Friedberg, Mohawk Valley Community
    College
Nicholas Grunt, Tarrant County College
Will Harris, University of Delaware
Yu Hsing, Southern Louisiana University
Mark Huston, San Diego Mesa College
Leo Kahane, California State University
Charles Link, University of Delaware
Patrick Litzinger, Robert Morris College
Ray Mack, Community College of Allegheny County
Drew Mattson, Anoka-Ramsey Community College
Frank Musgrave, Ithaca College
Asghan Nazemzadeh, University of Houston
Kathy Parkison, Indiana University—Kokomo
Martin Perliene, Wichita State University
Mary Pitts, Onondaga Community College
Jeff Pliskin, Hamilton College
Joseph Prizginger, Lynchburg College
Chris Rhoden, Solano College
Philip Rothman, East Carolina University
John Saussy, Harrisburg Area Community College
Carol Scott, West Georgia College
David Shorow, Richland College
Jerry Swartz, Broward Community College
Phil Smith, DeKalb College
Jeff Summers, Lynnfield College
Donna Thompson, Brookdale Community College
Ted Tsukahara, St. Mary's College

Percy Vera, Sinclair Community College
Harold Warren, East Tennessee State University
Art Welsh, Pennsylvania State University
Janet West, University of Nebraska—Omaha
Dieter Zschock, SUNY—Stony Brook

FOCUS GROUP PARTICIPANTS

Joseph Barr, Framingham State College
Marc C. Chopin, Louisiana Tech University
Sharon Ehrenburg, Eastern Michigan University
Paul Farnham, Georgia State University
David E. R. Gay, University of Arkansas
Paul W. Grimes, Mississippi State University
Michael N. Hayes, Radford University
Delores Linton, Tarrant County College
Kathy Parkison, Indiana University—Kokomo
Ted Tsukahara, St. Mary's College

QUESTIONNAIRE RESPONDENTS

Steve Ahn, Mercer Community College
A.K. Barakeh, University of Southern Alabama
Doris Beuttenmuller, Webster University
Jerry Bodily, School of Business
Bernard Bogar, Indiana University—Indianapolis
George Bohler, Florida Community College
R. Bohm, University of Tennessee—Knoxville
Barry Bombay, J. Sargent Reynolds Community
    College
Joseph Brandt, Incarnate Word College
Robert Brooker, Gannon University
Louis Buda, Nassau Community College
Norman Caldwell, Iowa Central Community College
Jack Chambless, Valencia Community College
Arshad Chawdhry, California University
    of Pennsylvania
Jane Clary, College of Charleston
Don Coffin, Indiana University Northwest
Tom Cole, Amarillo College

George Collier, Southeastern Oklahoma State University
John Connelly, Corning Community College
Jerry Crawford, Arkansas State University
Norman Cure, Macomb Community College
Maria DaCosta, University of Wisconsin—Eau Claire
Cynthia Dempster, Pellissippi State Technical Community College
Bruce Donelson, Bellevue College
Michael Doyle, Dana College
Robert Eggleston, Shippensburg University
Bernice Evans, Morgan State University
John Ewing-Smith, Burlington County College
Loretta Fairchild, Nebraska Wesleyan University
William Foeller, State University of New York—Fredonia
Kaya Ford, North Virginia Community College
Thomas Fox, Pennsylvania State University
Julie Granthen, Oakland Community College—Auburn Hills
Ron Gunderson, Northern Arizona University
Ron Hansen, Muscatine Community College
Paul Harris, Camden County College
Will Harris, University of Delaware
Mark Healy, William Rainey Harper College
Alfred Herschede, Indiana University South Bend
Charles Hiatt, Delta College
Cal Hoerneman, Delta College
Brad Hoppes, Southwest Missouri State University
Pat Hunston, Bee County College
Bruce Hutchinson, University of Tennessee—Chattanooga
Eric Jacobsen, University of Delaware
Wayne Jesswein, University of Minnesota—Duluth
Chuck Jewell, Charles County Community College
Kay Johnson, Pennsylvania State University at Erie—Behrend
Mary Ann Keating, Valparaiso University
John Kinworthy, Concordia College
Andrew Kliman, New York Institute of Technology
Peter Kressler, Rowan College of New Jersey
Jim Kyle, Indiana State University
William Laughlin, Fairmont State University

Nancy Lawler, Oakton Community College
Molly Lee, New York Institute of Technology
Secunderabad Leela, Millersville University of Pennsylvania
Delores Linton, Tarrant County College
Louis McClain, Texas Wesleyan University
Michael McGuire, Incarnate Word College
Eugene McKibbins, Fullerton College
John Manzer, Indiana/Purdue at Fort Wayne
David Martin, State University of New York at Geneseo
Saul Mekies, Kirkwook Community College
Ed Mills, Clackamas College
John Muth, Regis University
Ron Noreen, Camden County College
Gerard O'Boyle, St. Johns University
Dennis O'Connor, Loras College
Alex Obiya, San Diego City College
Duane Oyen, University of Wisconsin—Eau Claire
Deborah Paige, McHenry County College
Young Park, California University of Pennsylvania
Kathy Parkison, Indiana University—Kokomo
John Peck, Indiana University South Bend
Hilda Pope, Jones County Junior College
Gary Rourke, Lakewood Community College
Noel Rozells, San Diego Miramar College
Paul Schmitt, St. Clair County Community College
Ken Seidenstricker, Regis University
Jack Sheeks, Broward Community College—Central Campus
Dorothy Siden, Salem State College
Donald Sparks, The Citadel
Theresa Spencer, Meredith College
Gerald Stollman, Oakland Community College—Auburn Hills
Roger Traver, Johnson County Community College
John Walgreen, Wheaton College
Irvin Weintraub, Towson State University
Janet West, University of Nebraska at Omaha
Howard Yergan, Southwest Texas State University

Other respondents wished to remain anonymous.

SUGGESTED ONE-SEMESTER AND ONE-QUARTER COURSE OUTLINES
(Core chapters are indicated by "c"; optional chapters by "o")

Chapter	One-semester course Macro emphasis	Micro emphasis	Macro-micro survey	One-quarter course Macro emphasis	Micro emphasis
1	c	c	c	c	c
2	c	c	c	c	c
3	c	c	c	c	c
4	c	c	c	c	c
5	c	c		c	c
6	c	c		c	c
7	c		c	c	
8	c		c	c	
9	c		c	c	
10	c		c	c	
11	c		c	c	
12	c		c	c	
13	c		c	c	
14	c		c	c	
15	c		c	c	
16	c		c	o	
17	c		o	o	
18	c		o		
19	c		o		
20		c	c		c
21		o			
22		c	c		c
23		c	c		c
24		c	c		c
25		c	o		c
26		c	o		c
27		c			c
28		c			c
29		c			c
30		o			o
31		o			
32		o[1]			
33		o[2]			
34		o[3]			
35		o			
36		o[4]			
37	o	o			
38	o	o			
39	o				
40	o				

[1] If used, Chapter 32 may follow Chapter 26.

[2] If used, Chapter 33 may follow Chapter 23.

[3] If used, Chapter 34 may follow Chapter 28 or 29.

[4] If used, Chapter 36 may follow Chapter 28.

An Introduction to Economics and the Economy

TO THE STUDENT

Economics is concerned with efficiency—accomplishing goals using the best methods. Therefore, we offer some brief introductory comments on how to improve your efficiency—and your understanding and grade—in studying economics. Several features of this book will aid your learning.

- **Appendix on graphs** Being comfortable with graphical analysis and a few related quantitative concepts will be a big advantage to you in understanding principles of economics. The appendix to Chapter 1 reviews graphing, line slopes, and linear equations. Be sure not to skip it!

- **Introductions** The introductory paragraphs of each chapter are designed to stimulate interest, state the main objectives, and present an organizational overview of the chapter.

- **Terminology** A significant portion of any introductory course is terminology. To designate key terms, we have put them in **boldface type,** listed them at the end of each chapter, and provided a glossary at the end of the book.

- **Reviews** Important things should be said more than once. You will find a chapter summary at the conclusion of every chapter plus two or three "Quick Reviews" within each chapter. These review statements will help you focus on the essential ideas of each chapter and also to study for exams. If any of these statements are unclear, you should reread the appropriate section of the text.

- **Key Graphs** We have labeled graphs having special relevance as "Key Graphs." Your instructor may or may not emphasize each of these figures, but pay special attention to those your instructor discusses in class. You can bet there will be exam questions on them!

- **Figure legends** Economics is known for its many graphs. The legends accompanying the diagrams in this book are self-contained analyses of the concepts shown. Study these legends carefully —they are quick synopses of important ideas.

- **Globalization** Each nation functions increasingly in a global economy. To gain appreciation of this wider economic environment, be sure to take a look at the "Global Perspectives" which compare the United States to other selected nations.

- **Last Words** Each chapter concludes with a "Last Word" minireading. While it is tempting to ignore these sections, doing so is a mistake. Some of them are revealing applications of economic concepts; others are short case studies; still others present views which contrast with mainstream thinking; some are easy and delightful to read. All will deepen and broaden your grasp of economics.

- **Questions** A comprehensive list of questions is located at the end of each chapter. The old cliché that you "learn by doing" is very relevant to economics. Use of these questions will enhance your understanding. We designate several of them as "Key Questions" and answer them at the end of the book. You can immediately turn to these particular questions when they are cited in each chapter, or later, after you have read the full chapter.

- **Software** Many of the end-of-chapter questions deal with subject matter reinforced by the computerized tutorial, *Concept Master III,* which complements this text. A floppy disk symbol ⌷ identifies questions whose content correlates to a lesson in the tutorial program.

- **Study Guide** We enthusiastically recommend the *Study Guide* accompanying this text. This "portable tutor" contains not only a broad sampling of various kinds of questions, but a host of useful learning aids.

You will find in Chapter 1 that economics involves a special way of thinking—a unique approach to analyzing problems. The overriding goal of this book is to help you acquire that skill. If our cooperative efforts—yours, ours, and your instructor's—are successful, you will be able to comprehend a whole range of economic, social, and political problems which otherwise would have remained murky and elusive.

So much for the pep talk! Let's get on with the show.

THE NATURE AND METHOD OF ECONOMICS

Human beings, unfortunate creatures, are plagued with wants. We want, among other things, love, social recognition, and the material necessities and comforts of life. Our striving to improve our material well-being, to "make a living," is the concern of economics. Economics is the study of our behavior in producing, distributing, and consuming material goods and services in a world of scarce resources.

Humans are characterized by both biologically and socially determined wants. We seek food, clothing, shelter, and the many goods and services associated with a comfortable or affluent standard of living. We are also blessed with aptitudes and surrounded by quantities of property resources—both natural and manufactured. We use available human and property resources—labor and managerial talents, tools and machinery, land and mineral deposits—to produce goods and services which satisfy material wants. This is done through the organizational mechanism we call the *economic system*.

Quantitative considerations, however, rule out an ideal solution. The blunt fact is that the total of all our material wants is beyond the productive capacity of available resources. Thus, absolute material abundance is not possible. This unyielding fact is the basis for our definition of economics: *Economics is concerned with the efficient use or management of limited productive resources to achieve maximum satisfaction of human material wants.* Though it may not be self-evident, all the headline-grabbing issues of the day—inflation, unemployment, health care problems, government and international trade deficits, free-trade agreements among nations, poverty and inequality, pollution, and government regulation of business—are rooted in the one issue of using limited resources efficiently.

In this first chapter, however, we will not plunge into problems and issues. Our immediate concern is with some basic preliminary questions: (1) Of what importance or consequence is the study of economics? (2) How should we study economics—what are the proper procedures? What is the methodology of this subject? (3) What specific problems, limitations, and pitfalls might we encounter in studying economics? (4) How do economists think about problems? What is the "economic perspective"?

THE AGE OF THE ECONOMIST

Is studying economics worth your time and effort? Half a century ago John Maynard Keynes (1883–1946)—the most influential economist of this century—said this:

> The ideas of economists and political philosophers, both when they are right and when they are wrong, are more powerful than is commonly understood. Indeed the world is ruled by little else. Practical men, who believe themselves to be quite exempt from any intellectual influences, are usually the slaves of some defunct economist.

Most of the ideologies of the modern world have been shaped by the great economists of the past—Adam Smith, David Ricardo, John Stuart Mill, Karl Marx, and John Maynard Keynes. And it is currently common for world leaders to receive and invoke the advice and policy prescriptions of economists.

For example: The President of the United States benefits from the ongoing counsel of his Council of Economic Advisers. The broad spectrum of economic issues facing political leaders is suggested by the contents of the annual *Economic Report of the President.* Areas covered include unemployment and inflation, economic growth and productivity, taxation and public expenditures, poverty and income maintenance, the balance of payments and the international monetary system, labor-management relations, health care, pollution, discrimination, immigration, and competition and industrial regulation, among others.

Economics for Citizenship

A basic understanding of economics is essential if we are to be well-informed citizens. Most of today's problems have important economic aspects, and as voters we can influence the decisions of our political leaders in coping with these problems. What are the causes and consequences of the "twin deficits"—the Federal budget deficit and the international trade deficit—that are constantly reported by the news media? What of the depressing stories of homeless street people? Why is inflation undesirable? What can be done to reduce unemployment? Are existing welfare programs effective and justifiable? Should we continue to subsidize farmers? Do we need further reform of our tax system? Does America need to "reindustrialize" to reassert its dominant position in world trade and finance?

Since responses to such questions are determined largely by our elected officials, intelligence at the polls depends on a basic working knowledge of economics. Needless to say, a sound grasp of economics is more than helpful to politicians themselves!

A recent survey by the National Center for Research in Economic Education suggests economic illiteracy is widespread. The American public, high school seniors, and college seniors show widespread ignorance of basic economics that is needed to understand economic events and changes in the national economy. When asked questions about fundamental economics, only 35 percent of high school seniors, 39 percent of the general public, and 51 percent of college seniors gave correct answers.

Personal Applications

Economics is also vital in business. An understanding of the overall operation of the economic system enables the business executive to better formulate policies. The executive who understands the causes and consequences of inflation can make more intelligent business decisions during inflationary periods. That's why economists are on the payrolls of most large corporations. Their job is to gather and interpret economic information on which rational business decisions can be made.

Economics also gives the individual as a consumer and worker insights on how to make wiser buying and employment decisions. How can you "hedge" against the reduction in the dollar's purchasing power which accompanies inflation? Which occupations pay well; which are most immune to unemployment? Should you buy or lease a car? Should you use a credit card or pay cash? Similarly, someone who understands the relationship between budget and trade deficits, on the one hand, and security (stock and bond) values, on the other, can make more enlightened personal investment decisions.

In spite of its practical benefits, you must be forewarned that economics is mainly an academic, not a vocational, subject. Unlike accounting, advertising, corporation finance, and marketing, economics is not primarily a how-to-make-money area of study. A knowledge of economics will help you run a business or manage personal finances, but this is not its primary objective. In economics, problems are usually examined from the *social,* rather than the *personal,* point of view. The production, exchange, and consumption of goods and services are discussed from the viewpoint of society as a whole, rather than from the standpoint of one's own bankbook.

METHODOLOGY

What do economists do? What are their goals? What procedures do they employ? The subtitle of this textbook—*Principles, Problems, and Policies*—contains a thumbnail answer to the first two questions. Economists formulate economic *principles* useful in the establishment of *policies* designed to solve economic *problems*.

The procedures employed by the economist are summarized in Figure 1-1. The economist ascertains and gathers facts relevant to a specific economic problem. This task is sometimes called **descriptive** or **empirical economics** (box 1). The economist also states economic principles, that is, generalizes about the way individuals and institutions actually behave. Deriving principles is called **economic theory** or "economic analysis" (box 2).

As we see in Figure 1-1, economists are as likely to move from theory to facts in studying economic behavior as they are to move from facts to theory. Stated more formally, economists use both deductive and inductive methods. **Induction** distills or creates principles from facts. Here an accumulation of facts is arranged systematically and analyzed to permit the derivation of a generalization or principle. Induction moves from facts to theory, from the particular to the general. The inductive method is suggested by the left upward arrow from box 1 to box 2 in the figure.

Generalizations may also be created through *deduction* or the hypothetical method. Here economists draw upon casual observation, insight, logic, or intuition to frame a tentative, untested principle called an **hypothesis.** For example, they may conjecture, on the basis of "armchair logic," that it is rational for consumers to buy more of a product when its price falls.

To test the validity of the hypothesis they have deduced, economists must subject it to systematic and repeated examination of relevant facts. Do "real-world" data in fact reveal a negative or inverse relationship between price and the amount purchased? This testing process is suggested by the right downward arrow from box 2 to box 1 in Figure 1-1.

Deduction and induction are complementary, rather than opposing, techniques of investigation. Hypotheses formulated by deduction provide guidelines for the economist in gathering and systematizing em-

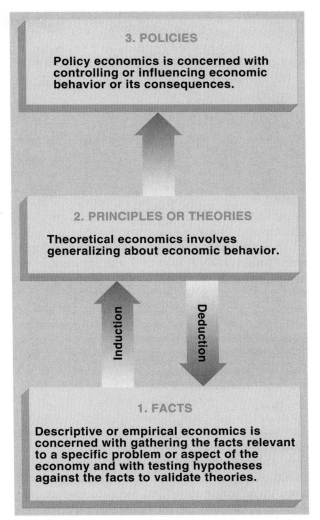

FIGURE 1-1 The relationship between facts, principles, and policies in economics
In analyzing problems or aspects of the economy, economists may use the inductive method whereby they gather, systematically arrange, and generalize on facts. Alternatively, the deductive method entails the development of hypotheses which are then tested against facts. Generalizations derived from either method of inquiry are useful not only in explaining economic behavior, but also as a basis for formulating economic policies.

pirical data. Conversely, some understanding of factual evidence—of the "real world"—is prerequisite to formulation of meaningful hypotheses.

Finally, the general knowledge of economic behavior which economic principles provides can then be used in formulating policies, that is, remedies or solutions, for correcting or avoiding the problem under scrutiny. This final aspect of economics is sometimes called "applied economics" or **policy economics** (box 3).

Continuing to use Figure 1-1 as a reference, we now examine the economist's methodology in more detail.

Descriptive Economics

All sciences are empirical; they are based on facts, that is, on observable and verifiable behavior of certain data or subject matter. In the physical sciences the factual data are inorganic. As a social science, economics examines the behavior of individuals and institutions engaged in the production, exchange, and consumption of goods and services.

Fact-gathering can be a complex task. Because the world of reality is cluttered with innumerable interrelated facts, economists must use discretion in gathering them. They must distinguish economic from noneconomic facts and then determine which economic facts are relevant and which irrelevant for the problem under consideration. But even when this sorting process is complete, the relevant economic facts may appear diverse and unrelated.

Economic Theory

The task of economic theory or analysis is to systematically arrange, interpret, and generalize upon facts. Principles and theories—the end result of economic analysis—bring order and meaning to facts by tying them together, putting them in correct relationship to one another, and generalizing upon them. "Theories without facts may be barren, but facts without theories are meaningless."[1]

Principles and theories are meaningful statements drawn from facts, but facts, in turn, serve as a check on the validity of principles already established. Facts—how individuals and institutions actually behave in producing, exchanging, and consuming goods and services—may change with time. This is why economists must continually check principles and theories against the changing economic environment.

Terminology Economists talk about "laws," "principles," "theories," and "models." These terms all mean essentially the same thing: generalizations, or statements of regularity, concerning the economic behav-

---

[1]Kenneth E. Boulding, *Economic Analysis: Microeconomics,* 4th ed. (New York: Harper & Row, Publishers, Incorporated, 1966), p. 5.

ior of individuals and institutions. The term "economic law" is a bit misleading because it implies a high degree of exactness, universal application, and even moral rightness. So, to a lesser degree, does the term **principle.** And some people incorrectly believe "theory" has nothing to do with the facts and realities of the world. The term "model" has much to commend it. A model is a simplified picture of reality, an abstract generalization of how relevant data actually behave.

In this book these four terms will be used synonymously. The choice of terms in labeling any particular generalization will be governed by custom or convenience. Thus, the relationship between the price of a product and the quantity consumers purchase will be called the "law" of demand, rather than the theory or principle of demand, simply because this is the customary designation.

Several other points regarding the character and derivation of economic principles are in order.

Generalizations Economic principles are **generalizations** and, as the term implies, characterized by somewhat imprecise quantitative statement. Economic facts are usually diverse; some individuals and institutions act one way and some another way. Economic principles are therefore frequently stated as averages or statistical probabilities. For example, when economists say that the average family earned an income of about $37,000 in 1993, they are generalizing. It is recognized that some families earned much more and a good many others much less. Yet this generalization, properly handled and interpreted, can be very meaningful and useful.

Similarly, economic generalizations are often stated in terms of probabilities. A researcher may tell us there is a 95 percent probability that every $1.00 reduction in personal income taxes will result in a $.92 increase in consumer spending.

"Other Things Equal" Assumption Like other scientists, economists use the *ceteris paribus* or **other things equal assumption** to construct their generalizations. They assume all other variables except those under immediate consideration are held constant. This simplifies the reasoning process by isolating the relationship under consideration. For example, in considering the relationship between the price of Pepsi and the amount purchased, it helps to assume that, of all the factors which might influence the amount of Pepsi purchased (for example, the price of Pepsi, the prices of other goods such as Coke, consumer incomes and preferences), only the price of Pepsi varies. The economist can then focus on the "price of Pepsi–purchases of Pepsi" relationship without reasoning being blurred or confused by intrusion of other variables.

In the natural sciences controlled experiments usually can be performed where "all other things" are in fact held constant or virtually so. Thus, scientists can test the assumed relationship between two variables with great precision. But economics is not a laboratory science. The economist's process of empirical verification is based on "real-world" data generated by the actual operation of the economy. In this rather bewildering environment "other things" *do* change. Despite the development of complex statistical techniques designed to hold other things equal, such controls are less than perfect. As a result, economic principles are less certain and less precise in application than those of laboratory sciences.

Abstractions   Economic principles, or theories, are necessarily abstractions. They do not mirror the full complexity of reality. The very process of sorting out noneconomic and irrelevant facts in the fact-gathering process involves abstracting from reality. Unfortunately, the abstractness of economic theory prompts the uninformed to identify theory as impractical and unrealistic. This is nonsense! Economic theories are practical simply because they are abstractions. The level of reality is too complex and bewildering to be very meaningful. Economists theorize to give meaning to a maze of facts which would otherwise be confusing and useless, and to put facts into a more usable, practical form. Thus, to generalize is to abstract or purposely simplify; generalization for this purpose is practical, and therefore so is abstraction.

An economic theory is a model—a simplified picture or map—of some segment of the economy. This model helps us understand reality better *because* it avoids the confusing details of reality. Theories—*good* theories—are grounded on facts and therefore are realistic. Theories which do not fit the facts are simply not good theories.

Macro and Micro   There are two levels of analysis at which the economist may derive laws concerning economic behavior. **Macroeconomics** deals either with the economy as a whole or with the basic subdivisions or aggregates—such as the government, household, and business sectors—making up the

economy. An aggregate is a collection of specific economic units treated *as if* they were one unit. Thus, we might find it convenient to lump together the over twenty million businesses in our economy and treat them as if they were one huge unit.

In dealing with aggregates, macroeconomics is concerned with obtaining an overview, or general outline, of the structure of the economy and the relationships among the major aggregates constituting the economy. No attention is given to specific units making up the various aggregates. Macroeconomics speaks of such magnitudes as *total* output, *total* level of employment, *total* income, *aggregate* expenditures, the *general* level of prices, and so forth, in analyzing various economic problems. Macroeconomics examines the forest, not the trees. It gives us a bird's-eye view of the economy.

Microeconomics deals with *specific* economic units and a *detailed* consideration of these individual units. At this level of analysis, the economist figuratively puts an economic unit, or very small segment of the economy, under the microscope to observe details of its operation. Here we talk of an individual industry, firm, or household, and concentrate on such magnitudes as the output or price of a specific product, the number of workers employed by a single firm, the revenue or income of a particular firm or household, or the expenditures of a given firm or family. In microeconomics we examine the trees, not the forest. Microeconomics is useful in achieving a worm's-eye view of some specific component of our economic system.

The macro–micro distinction does not mean that the subject matter of economics is so highly compartmentalized that each topic can be readily labeled as "macro" or "micro"; many topics and subdivisions of economics are rooted in both. There has been a convergence of macro- and microeconomics in important areas in recent years. While the problem of unemployment was treated as a macroeconomic topic some twenty or twenty-five years ago ("unemployment depends on *aggregate* spending"), economists now recognize that decisions made by *individual* workers in searching for jobs and the way specific product and labor markets function are also critical in determining the unemployment rate. *(Key Question 5)*

Graphical Expression   Many of the economic models or principles in this book will be expressed graphically. The most important of these models are labeled "Key Graphs." You should read the appendix to this chapter to review graphing and other relevant quantitative relationships.

Policy Economics

Economic theories are the basis for **economic policy.** Our understanding of economic principles can be applied in resolving or alleviating specific problems and in furthering the realization of society's overall goals (box 3 of Figure 1-1). Economic principles are valuable as predictive devices. And accurate prediction is required if we want to alter some event or outcome. If some undesirable event such as unemployment or inflation can be predicted or understood through economic theory, we may then be able to influence or control that event.

Formulating Economic Policy The creation of policies designed to achieve specific goals is no simple matter. Here's a brief examination of the basic steps in policy formulation.

1 Stating Goals The first step is to make a clear statement of a goal. If we say that we want "full employment," do we mean that everyone between, say, 16 and 65 years of age should have a job? Or do we mean that everyone who wants to work should have a job? Should we allow for some "normal" unemployment caused by inevitable changes in the structure of industry and workers' voluntarily changing jobs?

2 Policy Options Next, we must state and recognize the possible effects of alternative policies designed to achieve the goal. This requires a clear un-

derstanding of the economic impact, benefits, costs, and political feasibility of alternative programs. For example, economists debate the relative merits and demerits of fiscal policy (which involves changing government spending and taxes) and monetary policy (which entails altering the supply of money) as alternative means of achieving and maintaining full employment.

3 Evaluation We are obligated to ourselves and future generations to review our experiences with chosen policies and evaluate their effectiveness; it is only through this evaluation that we can hope to improve policy applications. Did a specific change in taxes or the supply of money alter the level of employment to the extent originally predicted? Did deregulation of a particular industry (for example, the airlines) yield the predicted beneficial results? If not, why not? *(Key Question 1)*

Economic Goals If economic policies are designed to achieve certain **economic goals,** then we need to recognize a number of goals which are widely accepted in our own and many other societies. They include:

1 Economic Growth The production of more and better goods and services, or, more simply, a higher standard of living, is desired.

2 Full Employment Suitable jobs should be available for all willing and able to work.

3 Economic Efficiency We want maximum benefits at minimum cost from the limited productive resources available.

4 Price Level Stability Sizable upswings or downswings in the general price level, that is, inflation and deflation, should be avoided.

5 Economic Freedom Business executives, workers, and consumers should enjoy a high degree of freedom in their economic activities.

6 An Equitable Distribution of Income No group of citizens should face stark poverty while others enjoy extreme luxury.

7 Economic Security Provision should be made for those who are chronically ill, disabled, handicapped, laid off, aged, or otherwise unable to earn minimal levels of income.

8 Balance of Trade   We seek a reasonable balance in our international trade and financial transactions.

This list of goals is the basis for several significant points.

1 Interpretation   This or any other statement of basic economic goals inevitably involves problems of interpretation. What are "sizable" changes in the price level? What is a "high degree" of economic freedom? What is an "equitable" distribution of income? Although most of us might accept these goals as generally stated, we might also disagree substantially on their specific meanings and hence the types of policies needed to attain them. Although goals 1 to 4 and 8 are subject to reasonably accurate measurements, the inability to quantify goals 5 to 7 contributes to controversy over their precise meaning.

2 Complementary   Certain of these goals are complementary in that when one goal is achieved, some other goal or goals will also be realized. For example, achieving full employment (goal 2) means eliminating unemployment, a basic cause of low incomes (goal 6) and economic insecurity (goal 7). Comparing goals 1 and 6, a particular degree of income inequality is more acceptable if economic growth is raising all incomes absolutely.

3 Conflicting   Some goals may be conflicting or mutually exclusive. They entail **tradeoffs,** meaning that to achieve one goal we must sacrifice some other goal. For example, goals 1 and 6 may be in conflict. Efforts to achieve greater equality in the distribution of income may weaken incentives to work, invest, innovate, and take business risks, all of which promote rapid economic growth. If government tries to equalize the distribution of income by taxing high-income people heavily and transferring those tax revenues to low-income people, the incentives of a high-income individual may diminish because taxation reduces income rewards. Similarly, a low-income person may be less motivated to work and engage in other productive activities when government stands ready to subsidize that individual.

International example: In the former Soviet Union, central planning virtually eliminated unemployment so that this source of worker insecurity disappeared. With little fear of losing their jobs, Soviet workers were quite cavalier regarding work effort and therefore productivity and efficiency in the Soviet Union were quite low. Here we have a conflict between goal 7, economic security, and goal 1, the growth of worker productivity.

4 Priorities   When goals conflict, society must develop a system of priorities for the objectives it seeks. If full employment and price stability are to some extent mutually exclusive, that is, if full employment is accompanied by some inflation *and* price stability entails some unemployment, society must decide on the relative importance of these two goals. There is clearly ample room for disagreement here. But society must assess the tradeoffs and make decisions.

Positive and Normative   As we move from the fact and principles levels (boxes 1 and 2) of Figure 1-1 to the policy level (box 3) we make a critical leap from positive to normative economics.

Positive economics deals with facts (once removed at the level of theory) and avoids value judgments. Positive economics attempts to set forth scientific statements about economic behavior.

Normative economics, in contrast, involves someone's value judgments about what the economy should be like or what particular policy action should be recommended based on a given economic generalization or relationship.

Positive economics concerns *what is,* while normative economics embodies subjective feelings about *what ought to be.* Positive economics deals with what the economy is actually like; normative economics examines whether certain conditions or aspects of the economy are desirable or not.

Examples: Positive statement: "Unemployment is 7 percent of the labor force." Normative statement: "Unemployment ought to be reduced." Second positive statement: "Other things being the same, if tuition is increased, enrollment at Gigantic State University will fall." Normative statement: "Tuition should be lowered at GSU so that more students can obtain an education." Whenever words such as "ought" or "should" appear in a sentence, there is a strong chance you are dealing with a normative statement.

Most of the apparent disagreement among economists involves normative, value-based policy questions. To be sure, various economists present and support different theories or models of the economy and its component parts. But by far most economic controversy reflects differing opinions or value judgments as to what our society should be like. For example, there is greater agreement about the actual distribution of income in our society than how income should be distributed. The point we reemphasize is that value judgments or normative statements come into play at the level of policy economics. *(Key Question 6)*

QUICK REVIEW 1-2

■ Policy economics entails the clear statement of goals, the assessing of policy options, and the evaluation of policy results.

■ Some of society's economic goals are complementary while others are conflicting.

■ Positive economics deals with factual statements ("what is"), while normative economics concerns value judgments ("what ought to be").

PITFALLS TO OBJECTIVE THINKING

Our discussion of the economist's procedure has skirted some specific problems and pitfalls which frequently hinder our thinking objectively about economic problems. Consider the following impediments to valid economic reasoning.

Bias

In contrast to a neophyte physicist or chemist, the budding economist ordinarily brings into economics a bundle of biases and preconceptions about the field. For example, you might be suspicious of business profits or feel that deficit spending is evil. Biases may cloud your thinking and interfere with objective analysis. The beginning economics student must be willing to shed biases and preconceptions not warranted by facts.

Loaded Terminology

The economic terminology in newspapers and popular magazines is sometimes emotionally loaded. The writer—or the interest group he or she represents—may have a cause to further or an ax to grind, and terms will be slanted to solicit the support of the reader. A governmental flood-control project in the Great Plains region may be called "creeping social-

ism" by its opponents and "intelligent democratic planning" by its proponents. We must be prepared to discount such terminology to objectively understand economic issues.

Definitions

No scientist is obligated to use popularized or immediately understandable definitions of his or her terms. The economist may find it convenient and essential to define terms in such a way that they are at odds with the definitions held by most people in everyday speech. No problem, so long as the economist is explicit and consistent in these definitions. For example, the term "investment" to the average citizen is associated with the buying of bonds and stocks in the securities market. How often have we heard someone talk of "investing" in General Motors stock or government bonds? But to the economist, "investment" means the purchase of real capital assets such as machinery and equipment, or the construction of a new factory building, not the purely financial transaction of swapping cash or part of a bank balance for a neatly engraved piece of paper.

Fallacy of Composition

Another pitfall in economic thinking is assuming "what is true for the individual or part of a group is necessarily true for the group or whole." This is a logical **fallacy of composition;** it is *not* correct. The validity of a particular generalization for an individual or part does *not* necessarily ensure its accuracy for the group or whole.

A noneconomic example: You are watching a football game and the home team executes an outstanding play. In the excitement, you leap to your feet to get a better view. Generalization: "If you, *an individual,* stand, then your view of the game is improved." But does this also hold true for the group—for everyone watching the game? Not necessarily! If everyone stands to watch the play, everyone—including you—will probably have the same or worse view than when seated.

Consider two examples from economics: A wage increase for Smith is desirable because, with constant product prices, it increases Smith's purchasing power and standard of living. But if everyone gets a wage increase, product prices may rise, that is, inflation might occur. Therefore, Smith's standard of living may be unchanged as higher prices offset her larger salary.

Second illustration: An *individual* farmer fortunate enough to reap a bumper (particularly large) crop is likely to realize a sharp gain in income. But this generalization does not apply to farmers as a *group*. For the individual farmer, crop prices will not be influenced (reduced) by this bumper crop, because each farmer produces a negligible fraction of the total farm output. But to farmers as a group, prices vary inversely with total output. Thus, as *all* farmers realize bumper crops, the total output of farm products rises, thereby depressing crop prices. If price declines are relatively greater than the increased output, farm incomes will *fall*.

Recalling our earlier discussion between macroeconomics and microeconomics, the fallacy of composition reminds us that *generalizations valid at one of these levels of analysis may or may not be valid at the other.*

Causation Fallacies

Causation is sometimes difficult to discern in economics. Consider these two fallacies.

Post Hoc Fallacy You must be very careful before concluding that because event A precedes event B, A is the cause of B. This kind of faulty reasoning is known as the **post hoc, ergo propter hoc,** or **after this, therefore because of this, fallacy.**

Example: Suppose early each spring the medicine man of a tribe performs his ritual by cavorting around the village in a green costume. A week or so later the trees and grass turn green. Can we safely conclude that event A, the medicine man's gyrations, has caused event B, the landscape's turning green? Obviously not. The rooster crows before dawn, but this doesn't mean the rooster is responsible for the sunrise!

Gigantic State University hires a new basketball coach and the team's record improves. Is the new coach the cause? Maybe. But perhaps the presence of more experienced players, an easier schedule, or the violation of NCAA recruiting rules is the true cause.

Correlation versus Causation We must not confuse **correlation** with **causation.** *Correlation* is a technical term indicating that two sets of data are associated in some systematic and dependable way. For example, we may find that when X increases, Y also increases. But this does not necessarily mean that X is the cause of Y. The relationship could be purely coincidental or determined by some other factor, Z, not included in the analysis.

Example: Economists have found a positive correlation between education and income. In general, people with more education earn higher incomes than people with less education. Common sense suggests education is the cause and higher incomes are the effect; more education suggests a more productive worker and such workers receive larger monetary rewards.

But might not causation run the other way? Do people with higher incomes buy more education, just as they buy more automobiles and steaks? Or is the relationship explainable in terms of still other factors? Are education and income positively correlated because the bundle of characteristics—ability, motivation, personal habits—required to succeed in education are the same characteristics required to be a productive and highly paid worker? *(Key Question 9)*

THE ECONOMIC PERSPECTIVE

The methodology used by economists is common to all the natural and social sciences. And all scholars try to avoid the reasoning errors just discussed. Thus, economists do *not* think in a special way, but they *do* view things from a special perspective.

The **economic perspective** entails several critical and closely interrelated features, including scarcity, rational behavior, and benefit-cost comparisons.

Scarcity and Choice

From our definition of economics, it is easy to see why economists view the world from the vantage point of scarcity. Human and property resources are scarce. It follows that outputs of goods and services must be scarce or limited, and scarcity limits our options and necessitates choices. We "can't have it all." If not, what should we choose to have?

At the core of economics is the idea that "there is no free lunch." Someone may treat you to lunch, making it "free" to you, but there is a cost to someone—ultimately to society. Scarce inputs of farm products and the labor of cooks and waiters are required. These resources could have been used in alternative productive activities, and those activities—those other goods and services—are sacrificed in providing your lunch.

LAST WORD

FAST-FOOD LINES: AN ECONOMIC PERSPECTIVE

How might the economic perspective help us understand the behavior of fast-food consumers?

You enter a fast-food restaurant. Which line will move fastest? What do you do when you are in the middle of a long line and a new station opens? Have you ever gone to a fast-food restaurant, only to see long lines, and then leave? Have you ever had someone in front of you in a fast-food line place an order which takes a long time to fill?

The economic perspective is useful in analyzing the behavior of fast-food customers. These customers are at the restaurant because they expect the marginal benefit or satisfaction from the food they buy to match or exceed its marginal cost. When customers enter the restaurant they scurry to the *shortest* line, believing that the shortest line will reduce their time cost of obtaining their food. They are acting purposefully; time is limited and most people would prefer using it in some way other than standing in line.

All fast-food lines normally are of roughly equal lengths. If one line is temporarily shorter than other

lines, some people will move toward that line. These movers apparently view the time saving associated with the shorter line to exceed the cost of moving from their present line. Line changing normally results in an equilibrium line length. No further movement of customers between lines will occur once all lines are of equal length.

Fast-food customers face another cost-benefit decision when a clerk opens a new station at the counter.

Rational Behavior

Economics is grounded on the assumption of "rational self-interest." Individuals make rational decisions to achieve the greatest satisfaction or maximum fulfillment of their goals. Thus, consumers seek to spend their incomes rationally to get the greatest benefit or satisfaction from the goods and services their incomes allow them to buy.

Rational behavior means people will make different choices, because their circumstances (constraints) and available information differ. You may have decided that it is in your self-interest to attend college before entering the labor force, but a high school classmate has decided to forgo additional schooling and take a job. Why the different choices? Your academic abilities, along with your family's income, may be greater than those of your classmate. You may also be better informed, realizing that college-educated workers make much higher incomes and are less likely to be unemployed than workers

with a high school education. Thus, you opt for college while your high school classmate with fewer human and financial resources and less information chooses a job. Both are rational choices, but based on differing constraints and information.

Of course, rational decisions may change as circumstances change. Suppose the Federal government decides it is in the national interest to increase the supply of college-educated workers. As a result, government policy changes to provide greater financial assistance to college students. Under these new conditions, your high school classmate may opt for college rather than a job after graduating from high school.

Rational self-interest is not the same as being selfish. People make personal sacrifices to help family members or friends and contribute to charities because they derive pleasure from doing so. Parents contribute financially to their childrens' educations because they derive satisfaction from that choice.

Should you move to the new station or stay put? Those who do shift to the new line decide that the benefit of the time savings from the move exceeds the extra cost of physically moving. In so deciding, customers must also consider just how quickly they can get to the new station compared to others who may be contemplating the same move. (Those who hesitate in this situation are lost!)

Customers at the fast-food establishment select lines without having perfect information. For example, they do not first survey those in the lines to determine what they are ordering before deciding on which line to enter. There are two reasons for this. First, most customers would tell them "It is none of your business," and therefore no information would be forthcoming. Second, even if they could obtain the information, the amount of time necessary to get it (cost) would most likely exceed any time saving associated with finding the best line (benefit). Because information is costly to obtain, fast-food patrons select lines on the basis of imperfect information. Thus, not all decisions turn out to be as expected. For example, some people may enter a line in which the person in front of them is ordering hamburgers and fries for the forty people in the Greyhound bus parked out back! Nevertheless, at the time the customer made the decision, he or she thought that it was optimal.

Imperfect information also explains why some people who arrive at a fast-food restaurant and observe long lines decide to leave. These people conclude that the marginal cost (monetary plus time costs) of obtaining the fast food is too large relative to the marginal benefit. They would not have come to the restaurant in the first place had they known the lines were so long. But, getting that information by, say, employing an advance scout with a cellular phone would cost more than the perceived benefit.

Finally, customers must decide what to order when they arrive at the counter. In making these choices they again compare marginal costs and marginal benefits in attempting to obtain the greatest personal satisfaction or well-being.

Economists believe that what is true for the behavior of customers at fast-food restaurants is true for economic behavior in general. Faced with an array of choices, consumers, workers, and businesses rationally compare marginal costs and marginal benefits in making decisions.

Marginalism: Benefits and Costs

The economic perspective focuses largely on **marginal analysis**—decisions which compare marginal benefits and marginal costs. *Marginal* means "extra," "additional," or "a change in." Most economic choices or decisions entail changes in the status quo. When you graduated from high school you faced the question of whether you should get *additional* education. Similarly, businesses are continuously deciding whether to employ more or fewer workers or to produce more or less output.

In making such choices rationally, we must compare marginal benefits and marginal costs. Because of scarcity, any option or choice will entail both extra benefits and additional costs. Example: Your time is scarce. What will you do with, say, two "free" hours on a Saturday afternoon? Option: Watch Gigantic State University's Fighting Aardvarks play basketball on television. Marginal benefit: The pleasure of seeing the game. Marginal cost: Any of the other things you sacrifice by spending an extra two hours in front of the tube, including studying (economics, hopefully), jogging, or taking a nap. If the marginal benefit exceeds the marginal cost, then it is rational to watch the game. But if you perceive the marginal cost of watching the game to exceed its marginal benefits, then one of the other options should be chosen.

On the national level government is continuously making decisions involving marginal benefits and costs. More spending on health care may mean less spending on homeless shelters, aid for the poor, or military security. Lesson: In a world of scarcity the decision to obtain the marginal benefit with some specific choice includes the marginal cost of forgoing something else. Again, there's no free lunch.

One implication of decisions based on marginal analysis is that there *can* be too much of a "good thing." Although certain goods and services seem inherently desirable—education, health care, a clean environment—we can in fact have too much of them. "Too much" occurs when we push their production to some point where their marginal cost (the value of the forgone options) exceeds their marginal benefit. If we choose to produce health care to the extent that its marginal cost exceeds its marginal benefit, we are providing "too much" health care even though health care is a good thing. If the marginal cost of health care is greater than its marginal benefit, then we are sacrificing alternative products (for example, education and pollution reduction) which are more valuable than health care at the margin. *(Key Question 13)*

The accompanying Last Word provides an everyday application of the economic perspective.

> ### QUICK REVIEW 1-3
>
> ■ Beware of logical errors such as the fallacy of composition, the post hoc fallacy, and confusing correlation with causation when engaging in economic reasoning.
>
> ■ The economic perspective stresses *a* resource scarcity and the necessity of making choices; *b* the assumption of rational behavior; and *c* marginal analysis.

CHAPTER SUMMARY

1 Economics deals with the efficient use of scarce resources in the production of goods and services to satisfy material wants.

2 A knowledge of economics contributes to effective citizenship and provides useful insights for consumers and businesspersons.

3 The tasks of descriptive or empirical economics are **a** gathering those economic facts relevant to a particular problem or specific segment of the economy, and **b** testing hypotheses against facts to validate theories.

4 Generalizations stated by economists are called "principles," "theories," "laws," or "models." The derivation of these principles is the task of economic theory.

5 Induction distills theories from facts; deduction uses logic to derive hypotheses which are then tested against facts.

6 Some economic principles deal with macroeconomics (the economy as a whole or major aggregates); others pertain to microeconomics (specific economic units or institutions).

7 Economic principles are valuable as predictive devices; they are the bases for the formulation of economic policy designed to solve problems and control undesirable events.

8 Economic growth, full employment, economic efficiency, price level stability, economic freedom, equity in the distribution of income, economic security, and reasonable balance in our international trade and finance are all widely accepted economic goals in our society. Some of these goals are complementary; others are mutually exclusive.

9 Positive statements deal with facts ("what is"), while normative statements express value judgments ("what ought to be").

10 In studying economics the beginner may encounter pitfalls, such as **a** biases and preconceptions, **b** terminological difficulties, **c** the fallacy of composition, and **d** the difficulty of establishing clear cause-effect relationships.

11 The economic perspective envisions individuals and institutions making rational decisions based on marginal costs and marginal benefits.

TERMS AND CONCEPTS

economics	hypothesis	economic goals	post hoc, ergo propter
descriptive or	*ceteris paribus* or	tradeoffs	hoc or "after this,
empirical economics	"other things equal"	positive and normative	therefore because of
economic theory	assumption	economics	this" fallacy
induction and	policy economics	correlation and	economic perspective
deduction	macroeconomics and	causation	marginal analysis
principles or	microeconomics	fallacy of composition	
generalizations			

QUESTIONS AND STUDY SUGGESTIONS

1 *Key Question* *Explain in detail the interrelationships between economic facts, theory, and policy. Critically evaluate: "The trouble with economics is that it is not practical. It* *has too much to say about theory and not enough to say about facts."*

2 Analyze and explain the following quotation.[2]

Facts are seldom simple and usually complicated; theoretical analysis is needed to unravel the complications and interpret the facts before we can understand them . . . the opposition of facts and theory is a false one; the true relationship is complementary. We cannot in practice consider a fact without relating it to other facts, and the relation is a theory. Facts by themselves are dumb; before they will tell us anything we have to arrange them, and the arrangement is a theory. Theory is simply the unavoidable arrangement and interpretation of facts, which gives us generalizations on which we can argue and act, in the place of a mass of disjointed particulars.

3 Of what significance is the fact that economics is not a laboratory science? What problems may be involved in deriving and applying economic principles?

4 Explain each of the following statements:

a "Like all scientific laws, economic laws are established in order to make successful prediction of the outcome of human actions."[3]

b "Abstraction . . . is the inevitable price of generality . . . indeed abstraction and generality are virtually synonyms."[4]

c "Numbers serve to discipline rhetoric."[5]

5 *Key Question   Indicate whether each of the following statements pertains to microeconomics or macroeconomics:*

a *The unemployment rate in the United States was 5.9 percent in September of 1994.*

b *The Alpo dogfood plant in Bowser, Iowa, laid off 15 workers last month.*

c *An unexpected freeze in central Florida reduced the citrus crop and caused the price of oranges to rise.*

d *Our national output, adjusted for inflation, grew by about 3.1 percent in 1993.*

e *Last week Manhattan Chemical Bank lowered its interest rate on business loans by one-half of 1 percentage point.*

f *The consumer price index rose by 2.7 percent in 1993.*

6 *Key Question   Identify each of the following as either a positive or a normative statement:*

a *The high temperature today was 89 degrees.*

b *It was too hot today.*

c *The general price level rose by 4.4 percent last year.*

d *Inflation eroded living standards last year and should be reduced by government policies.*

7 To what extent would you accept the eight economic goals stated and described in this chapter? What priorities would you assign to them? It has been said that we seek only four goals: progress, stability, justice, and freedom. Is this list of goals compatible with that given in the chapter?

8 Analyze each of the following specific goals in terms of the eight general goals stated on pages 6 and 7, and note points of conflict and compatibility: **a** the lessening of environmental pollution;   **b** increasing leisure; and   **c** protection of American producers from foreign competition. Indicate which of these specific goals you favor and justify your position.

9 *Key Question   Explain and give an illustration of* **a** *the fallacy of composition, and* **b** *the "after this, therefore because of this" fallacy. Why are cause-and-effect relationships difficult to isolate in the social sciences?*

10 Suppose empirical studies show that students who study more hours receive higher grades, as suggested by the graph accompanying question 4 in this chapter's appendix. Does this relationship guarantee that any particular student who studies longer will get higher grades?

11 A recent psychiatric study found that there is a positive correlation between the amount of time children and youth spend watching television and mental depression. Speculate on possible cause-effect relationships.

12 "Economists should never be popular; men who afflict the comfortable serve equally with those who comfort the afflicted and one cannot suppose that American capitalism would long prosper without the critics its leaders find such a profound source of annoyance."[6] Interpret and evaluate.

13 *Key Question   Use the economic perspective to explain why someone who normally is a light eater at a standard restaurant may become somewhat of a glutton at a buffet-style restaurant which charges a single price for all you can eat.*

14 (Last Word)   Explain how the economic perspective can be used to explain the behavior of customers in fast-food restaurants.

[2]Henry Clay, *Economics for the General Reader* (New York: The Macmillan Company, 1925), pp. 10–11.

[3]Oskar Lange, "The Scope and Method of Economics," *Review of Economic Studies,* vol. 13, 1945–1946, p. 20.

[4]George J. Stigler, *The Theory of Price* (New York: The Macmillan Company, 1947), p. 10.

[5]Victor R. Fuchs, *How We Live* (Cambridge, Mass.: Harvard University Press, 1983), p. 5.

[6]John Kenneth Galbraith, *American Capitalism,* rev. ed. (Boston: Houghton Mifflin Company, 1956), p. 49.

GRAPHS AND THEIR MEANING

If you glance quickly through this text, you will find graphs. Some seem simple, while others seem more formidable. Contrary to student folklore, graphs are *not* designed by economists to confuse students! Graphs are employed to help you visualize and understand important economic relationships. The physicist and chemist sometimes illustrate their theories by building TinkerToy arrangements of multicolored wooden balls representing protons, neutrons, and so forth, held in proper relation to one another by wires or sticks. Economists often use graphs to illustrate their models. By understanding these "pictures" you can more readily comprehend what economists are saying.

Most of our principles or models will explain the relationship between just two sets of economic facts, which can be conveniently represented with two-dimensional graphs.

Constructing a Graph

A graph is a visual representation of the relationship between two variables. Table 1 is a hypothetical illustration showing the relationship between income and consumption. Without ever having studied economics, you would expect intuitively that high-income people would consume more than low-income people. Thus we are not surprised to find in Table 1 that consumption increases as income increases.

How can the information in Table 1 be expressed graphically? Glance at the graph shown in Figure 1.

Now look back at the information in Table 1 and we will explain how to represent it in a meaningful way by constructing the graph you just examined.

What we want to show visually, or graphically, is how consumption changes as income changes. Since income is the determining factor, we represent it on the horizontal axis of the graph, as is customary. And, because consumption depends on income, we represent it on the vertical axis of the graph, as is also customary. Actually, what we are doing is representing the independent variable on the horizontal axis and the dependent variable on the vertical axis.

Now we must arrange the vertical and horizontal scales of the graph to reflect the range of values of consumption and income, as well as mark the steps in convenient graphic increments. As you can see, the ranges in the graph cover the ranges of values in Table 1. The increments on both scales are $100 for approximately each half-inch.

Next, we must locate for each consumption value, and the income value that it depends on, a single point which reflects the same information graphically. Our five income–consumption combinations are plotted by drawing perpendiculars from the appropriate points on the **vertical** and **horizontal axes.** For example, in plotting point *c*—the $200 income–$150 consumption point—perpendiculars must be drawn up from the horizontal (income) axis at $200 and across from the vertical (consumption) axis at $150. These perpendiculars intersect at point *c,* which locates this particular income–consumption combination. You should

TABLE 1 The relationship between income and consumption

Income (per week)	Consumption (per week)	Point
$ 0	$ 50	a
100	100	b
200	150	c
300	200	d
400	250	e

TABLE 2 The relationship between ticket prices and attendance

Ticket price	Attendance (thousands)	Point
$25	0	a
20	4	b
15	8	c
10	12	d
5	16	e
0	20	f

verify that the other income–consumption combinations shown in Table 1 are properly located in Figure 1. By assuming that the same general relationship between income and consumption prevails at all other points between the five points graphed, a line or curve can be drawn to connect these points.

Using Figure 1 as a benchmark, we can make several additional comments.

Direct and Inverse Relationships

Our upsloping line depicts a direct relationship between income and consumption. By a positive or **direct relationship** we mean that the two variables—in this case consumption and income—change in the *same* direction. An increase in consumption is associated with an increase in income; a decrease in consumption accompanies a decrease in income. When

two sets of data are positively or directly related, they will always graph as an *upsloping* line as in Figure 1.

In contrast, two sets of data may be inversely related. Consider Table 2, which shows the relationship between the price of basketball tickets and game attendance at Gigantic State University. We observe a negative or **inverse relationship** between ticket prices and attendance; these two variables change in *opposite* directions. When ticket prices decrease, attendance increases. When ticket prices increase, attendance decreases. In Figure 2 the six data points of Table 2 are plotted following the same procedure outlined before. Observe that an inverse relationship will always graph as a *downsloping* line.

FIGURE 1 Graphing the direct relationship between consumption and income
Two sets of data which are positively or directly related, such as consumption and income, graph as an upsloping line. In this case the vertical intercept is 50 and the slope of the line is $+\frac{1}{2}$.

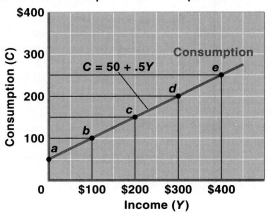

FIGURE 2 Graphing the inverse relationship between ticket prices and game attendance
Two sets of data which are negatively or inversely related, such as ticket price and the attendance at basketball games, graph as a downsloping line. The slope of this line is $-1\frac{1}{4}$.

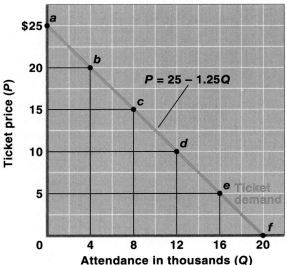

Dependent and Independent Variables

Although it is not always easy, economists seek to determine which variable is "cause" and which "effect." Or, more formally, we want to ascertain the independent and the dependent variable. By definition, the **dependent variable** is the "effect" or outcome; it is the variable which changes because of a change in another (independent) variable.

The **independent variable** is the "cause"; it is the variable which causes the change in the dependent variable. As noted in our income–consumption example, generally, income is the independent variable and consumption the dependent variable. Income causes consumption to be what it is rather than the other way around. Similarly, ticket prices determine attendance at GSU basketball games; attendance does not determine ticket prices. Ticket price is the independent variable and the quantity purchased is the dependent variable.

You may recall from your high school courses that mathematicians always put the independent variable (cause) on the horizontal axis and the dependent variable (effect) on the vertical axis. Economists are less tidy; their graphing of independent and dependent variables is more arbitrary. Thus, their conventional graphing of the income–consumption relationship is consistent with mathematical presentation. But economists put price and cost data on the vertical axis. Hence, economists' graphing of GSU's ticket price–attendance data conflicts with normal mathematical procedure.

Other Variables Held Constant

Our simple two-variable graphs ignore many other factors which might affect the amount of consumption occurring at each income level or the number of people who attend GSU basketball games at each possible ticket price. When economists plot the relationship between any two variables, they invoke the *ceteris paribus* or "other things equal" assumption. Thus, in Figure 1 all other factors (that is, all factors other than income) which might affect the amount of consumption are presumed to be constant or unchanged. Similarly, in Figure 2 all factors other than ticket price which might influence attendance at GSU basketball games are assumed constant. In reality, we know "other things" often change, and when they do, the specific relationships presented in our two tables and graphs will change. Specifically, we

would expect the lines we have plotted to shift to new locations.

For example, what might happen to the income–consumption relationship if a stock market "crash" such as that of October 1987 occurred? The expected impact of this dramatic fall in the value of stocks would be to make people feel less wealthy and therefore less willing to consume at each income level. We would anticipate a downward shift of the consumption line in Figure 1. You should plot a new consumption line, assuming that consumption is, say, $20 less at each income level. Note that the relationship remains direct, but the line has merely shifted to reflect less consumer spending at each level of income.

Similarly, factors other than ticket prices might affect GSU game attendance. If the government abandoned its program of student loans, GSU enrollment and hence attendance at games might be less at each ticket price. You should redraw Figure 2, assuming that 2000 fewer students attend GSU games at each ticket price. *(Key Appendix Questions 1 and 2)*

Slope of a Line

Lines can be described in terms of their slopes. The **slope of a straight line** between any two points is defined as the ratio of the vertical change (the rise or fall) to the horizontal change (the run) involved in moving between those points.

Positive Slope   In moving from point b to point c in Figure 1 the rise or vertical change (the change in consumption) is +$50 and the run or horizontal change (the change in income) is +$100. Therefore:

$$\text{Slope} = \frac{\text{vertical change}}{\text{horizontal change}} = \frac{+50}{+100} = +\frac{1}{2}$$

Note that our slope of $\frac{1}{2}$ is positive because consumption and income change in the same direction, that is, consumption and income are directly or positively related.

This slope of $+\frac{1}{2}$ tells us that there will be a $1 increase in consumption for every $2 increase in income. Similarly, it indicates that for every $2 decrease in income there will be a $1 decrease in consumption.

Negative Slope   For our ticket price–attendance data the relationship is negative or inverse with the result that the slope of Figure 2's line is negative. In particular, the vertical change or fall is 5 and the horizontal change or run is 4. Therefore:

$$\text{Slope} = \frac{\text{vertical change}}{\text{horizontal change}} = \frac{-5}{+4} = -1\frac{1}{4}$$

This slope of $-5/+4$ or $-1\frac{1}{4}$ means that lowering the price of a ticket by \$5 will increase attendance by 4000 people—which is the same as saying that a \$1 price reduction will increase attendance by 800 persons.

Three Addenda Our discussion of line slopes needs three additional comments.

1 Measurement Units The slope of a line will be affected by the choice of units for either variable. If, in our ticket price illustration we had chosen to measure prices in dimes rather than dollars, our vertical change for a price cut would be -50 (dimes) instead of -5 (dollars) and the slope would be $-12\frac{1}{2}$ ($= -50 \div 4$) rather than $-1\frac{1}{4}$. The measurement of slope depends on the way the relevant variables are denominated.

2 Marginal Analysis Economics is largely concerned with *marginal* or incremental changes—changes from the status quo. Should you work an hour more or an hour less each day on your part-time job? Should you buy one more or one less GSU basketball ticket? Should a fast-food restaurant, now employing eight workers, hire an extra or marginal worker?

This is relevant because the slopes of lines measure marginal changes. For example, in Figure 1, the slope shows that \$50 of extra or marginal consumption is associated with each \$100 increase in income. Consumers will spend half of any increase in their income and reduce their consumption by half of any decline in income. The concept of slope is important in economics because it reflects marginal changes.

3 Infinite and Zero Slopes Many variables are unrelated or independent of one another. We would not expect the price of bananas to be related to the quantity of wristwatches purchased. If we put the price of bananas on the vertical axis and the quantity demanded of watches on the horizontal axis, the absence of a relationship between them would be described by a line parallel to the vertical axis, indicating that changes in the price of bananas have no impact on watch purchases. The slope of such a line is *infinite*. Similarly, if aggregate consumption was completely unrelated to, say, the quantity of rainfall and we put consumption on the vertical axis and rainfall on the horizontal axis, this unrelatedness would be represented by a line parallel to the horizontal axis. This line has a slope of *zero*.

Intercept

In addition to its slope, the only other information needed in locating a line on a graph is the vertical intercept. The **vertical intercept** is the point where the line meets the vertical axis. For Figure 1 the intercept is \$50. This means that, if current income were zero, consumers would still spend \$50. How might they manage to consume when they have no current income? Answer: By borrowing or by selling off some of their assets. Similarly, the vertical intercept in Figure 2 shows us that at a \$25 ticket price GSU's basketball team would be playing in an empty auditorium.

Equation Form

With a specific intercept and slope, our consumption line can be succinctly described in equation form. In general, a linear equation is written as $y = a + bx$, where y is the dependent variable, a is the vertical intercept, b is the slope of the line, and x is the independent variable. For our income–consumption example, if C represents consumption (the dependent variable) and Y represents income (the independent variable), we can write $C = a + bY$. By substituting the values of the intercept and the slope for our specific data, we have $C = 50 + .5Y$. This equation allows us to determine consumption at *any* level of income. At the \$300 income level (point d in Figure 1), our equation predicts that consumption will be \$200 [$= \$50 + (.5 \times \$300)$]. You should confirm that at the \$250 income level consumption will be \$175.

When economists reverse mathematical convention by putting the independent variable on the vertical axis and the dependent variable on the horizontal axis, the standard linear equation solves for the independent, rather than the dependent, variable. We noted earlier that this case is relevant for our GSU ticket price–attendance data. If P represents the ticket price and Q represents attendance, our relevant equation is $P = 25 - 1.25Q$, where the vertical intercept is 25 and the negative slope is $-1\frac{1}{4}$ or -1.25. But knowing the value for P lets us solve for Q, which is actually our dependent variable. For example, if $P = 15$, then the values in our equation become: $15 = 25 - 1.25(Q)$, or $1.25Q = 10$, or $Q = 8$. You should check this answer against Figure 2 and also use this equation to predict GSU ticket sales when price is $7.50. *(Key Appendix Question 3)*

Slope of a Nonlinear Curve

We now move from the simple world of linear relationships (straight lines) to the more complex world of nonlinear relationships (curves). By definition, the slope of a straight line is constant at every point on it. The slope of a curve changes as we move from one point to another on the curve.

For example, consider the downsloping curve in Figure 3. Although its slope is negative throughout, it diminishes or flattens as we move southeast along the curve. Because the slope is constantly changing, we can only measure the slope at some particular point on the curve.

We begin by drawing a straight line which is tangent to the curve at that point where we want to measure its slope. A line is **tangent** at that point where it touches, but does not intersect, the curve. Thus, line *aa* is tangent to the curve at point *A* in Figure 3. Having done this, we can measure the slope of the curve at point *A* by measuring the slope of the straight tangent line *aa*. Specifically, in Figure 3 the vertical change (fall) in *aa* is −20 and the horizontal change (run) is +5. Thus the slope of the tangent *aa* line is −20/+5 or −4 and therefore the slope of the curve at *A* is also −4.

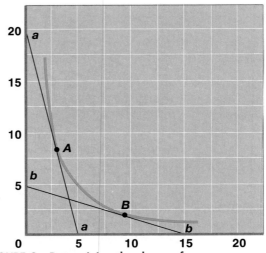

FIGURE 3   Determining the slopes of curves
The slope of a nonlinear curve changes as one moves from point to point on the curve. The slope at any point can be determined by drawing a straight line tangent to that point and calculating the slope of that straight line.

We can now draw line *bb* tangent to a flatter part of the curve at point *B*. Following the same procedure, we find the negative slope to be smaller, specifically −5/+15 or −$\frac{1}{3}$. Similar analysis applies to upsloping curves. *(Key Appendix Question 6)*

APPENDIX SUMMARY

1   Graphs are a convenient and revealing means of presenting economic relationships or principles.

2   Two variables are positively or directly related when their values change in the same direction. Two directly related variables will plot as an upsloping line on a graph.

3   Two variables are negatively or inversely related when their values change in opposite directions. Two variables which are inversely related will graph as a downsloping line.

4   The value of the dependent variable ("effect") is determined by the value of the independent variable ("cause").

5   When "other factors" which might affect a two-variable relationship are allowed to change, the plotted relationship will likely shift to a new location.

6   The slope of a straight line is the ratio of the vertical change to the horizontal change in moving between any two points. The slope of an upsloping line is positive; the slope of a downsloping line is negative.

7   The slope of a line   a depends on the choice of units in denominating the variables and   b are especially relevant for economics because they measure marginal changes.

8   The slope of a horizontal line is zero; the slope of a vertical line is infinite.

9   The vertical intercept and the slope of a line establish its location and are used in expressing the relationship between two variables as an equation.

10   The slope of a curve at any point is determined by calculating the slope of a straight line drawn tangent to that point.

APPENDIX TERMS AND CONCEPTS

vertical and horizontal axes	direct and inverse relationships	dependent and independent variables	vertical intercept
slope of a straight line			tangent

APPENDIX QUESTIONS AND STUDY SUGGESTIONS

💾 *1 Briefly explain the use of graphs as a means of presenting economic principles. What is an inverse relationship? How does it graph? What is a direct relationship? How does it graph? Graph and explain the relationships one would expect to find between **a** the number of inches of rainfall per month and the sale of umbrellas, **b** the amount of tuition and the level of enrollment at a university, and **c** the size of a university's athletic scholarships and the number of games won by its football team.

In each case cite and explain how considerations other than those specifically mentioned might upset the expected relationship. Is your second generalization consistent with the fact that, historically, enrollments and tuition have both increased? If not, explain any difference.

💾 2 *Key Appendix Question* *Indicate how each of the following might affect the data shown in Table 2 and Figure 2 of this appendix.*

  a *GSU's athletic director schedules higher-quality opponents.*

  b *GSU's Fighting Aardvarks experience three losing seasons.*

  c *GSU contracts to have all its home games televised.*

💾 3 *Key Appendix Question* *The following table contains data on the relationship between saving and income. Rearrange these data as required and graph the data on the accompanying grid. What is the slope of the line? The vertical intercept? Interpret the meaning of both the slope and the intercept. Write the equation which represents this line. What would you predict saving to be at the $12,500 level of income?*

Income (per year)	Saving (per year)
$15,000	$1,000
0	−500
10,000	500
5,000	0
20,000	1,500

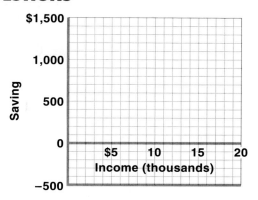

💾 4 Construct a table from the data shown on the graph below. Which is the dependent and which the independent variable? Summarize the data in equation form.

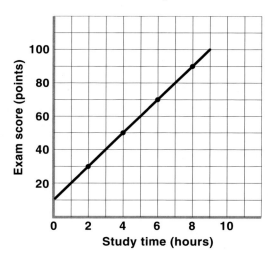

💾 5 Suppose that when the interest rate which must be paid to borrow funds is 16 percent, businesses find it unprofitable to invest in machinery and equipment. However, when the interest rate is 14 percent, $5 billion worth of investment is profitable. At 12 percent, a total of $10 billion of investment is profitable. Similarly, total investment increases by $5 billion for each successive 2 percentage point decline in the interest rate. Indicate the relevant relationship between the interest rate and investment verbally, tabularly, graphically, and as an equation. Put the interest rate on the vertical axis and investment on the horizontal axis. In your equation use the form $i = a - bI$, where i is the interest rate, a is the vertical intercept, b is the slope of the line, and I is the level of investment. Comment on advantages and disadvantages of verbal, tabular, graphical, and equation forms of presentation.

---

*Note to the reader: A floppy disk symbol 💾 precedes each of the questions in this appendix. This icon is used throughout the text to indicate that a particular question relates to the content of one of the tutorial programs in the student software which accompanies this book. Please refer to the Preface for more detail about this software.

6 *Key Appendix Question* The accompanying diagram shows curve XX and three tangents at points A, B, and C. Calculate the slope of the curve at these three points.

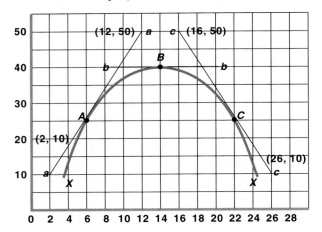

7 In the accompanying diagram, is the slope of curve AA' positive or negative? Does the slope increase or decrease as we move from A to A'? Answer the same two questions for curve BB'.

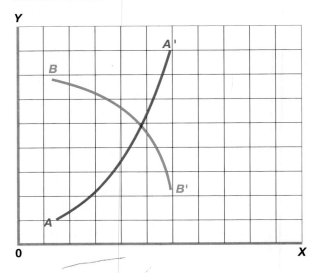

THE ECONOMIZING PROBLEM

You make decisions every day which capture the essence of economics. Suppose you have $30 and are deciding how to spend it. Should you buy a new pair of jeans? A couple of compact discs? A ticket for a rock concert? Similarly, what to do with your time between three and six o'clock on, say, a Thursday afternoon? Should you work extra hours on your part-time job? Do research on a term project? Prepare for an economics quiz? Watch TV? Take a nap? Money and time are both scarce and making decisions in the context of scarcity implies costs. If you choose the jeans, the cost is the forgone CDs or concert. If you nap or watch TV, the cost might be a low grade on your quiz. Scarcity, choices, and costs—these are the building blocks of this chapter.

Here we introduce and explore the fundamentals of economic science. We expand on the definition of economics introduced in Chapter 1 and explore the essence of the economizing problem. We will illustrate, extend, and modify our definition by using production possibilities tables and curves. Next, we will briefly survey different ways by which institutionally and ideologically diverse economies respond to the economizing problem. Finally, we present an overview of the market system in the form of the circular flow model.

THE FOUNDATION OF ECONOMICS

Two fundamental facts which constitute the **economizing problem** provide a foundation for the field of economics. We must carefully state and fully understand these two facts, because everything that follows depends directly or indirectly on them.

1 *Society's material wants, that is, the material wants of its citizens and institutions, are virtually unlimited or insatiable.*

2 *Economic resources—the means of producing goods and services—are limited or scarce.*

Unlimited Wants

In the first statement, what do we mean by "material wants"? We mean, first, the desires of consumers to obtain and use various *goods* and *services* which provide **utility,** the economist's term for pleasure or satisfaction.[1] An amazingly wide range of products fills the bill in this respect: houses, automobiles, toothpaste, compact-disc players, pizzas, sweaters, and the like. Innumerable products sometimes classified as

---

[1]This definition leaves a variety of wants—recognition, status, love, and so forth—for the other social sciences to worry about.

necessities (food, shelter, clothing) and *luxuries* (perfumes, yachts, mink coats) all can satisfy human wants. Of course, what is a luxury to Smith may be a necessity to Jones, and what is a common necessity today may have been a luxury a few years ago.

Services satisfy our wants as much as products. Repair work on our car, the removal of our appendix, a haircut, and legal advice also satisfy human wants. On reflection, we realize that we buy many goods, for example, automobiles and washing machines, for the services they render. The differences between goods and services are often less than they first appear.

Businesses and units of government also seek to satisfy material wants. Businesses want factory buildings, machinery, trucks, warehouses, communications systems, and other things that help them realize their production goals. Government, reflecting the collective wants of its citizenry or goals of its own, seeks highways, schools, hospitals, and military hardware.

As a group, these material wants are *insatiable,* or *unlimited,* meaning material wants for goods and services cannot be completely satisfied. Our wants for a *particular* good or service can be satisfied; over a short period of time we can get enough toothpaste or beer. Certainly one appendicitis operation is par for the course.

But goods *in general* are another story. We do not, and presumably cannot, get enough. A simple experiment will help verify this. Suppose all members of society are asked to list those goods and services they want but do not now possess. Chances are this list will be impressive!

Furthermore, over time, wants multiply. As we fill some of the wants on the list, we add new ones. Material wants, like rabbits, have a high reproduction rate. The rapid introduction of new products whets our appetites, and extensive advertising persuades us that we need items we might not otherwise buy. Not long ago, we didn't want personal computers, light beer, video recorders, fax machines, and compact discs because they didn't exist. Furthermore, we often cannot stop with simple satisfaction: The acquisition of an Escort or Geo has been known to whet the appetite for a Porsche or Mercedes.

At any specific time the individuals and institutions constituting society have innumerable unfulfilled material wants. Some—food, clothing, shelter—have biological roots. But some are also influenced by the conventions and customs of society: The specific kinds of food, clothing, and shelter we seek are fre-

quently determined by the general social and cultural environment in which we live. Over time, wants change and multiply, fueled by development of new products and extensive advertising and sales promotion.

The overall objective of all economic activity is the attempt to satisfy all these diverse material wants.

Scarce Resources

In considering the second fundamental fact—*economic resources are limited or scarce*—what do we mean by **economic resources?** In general, we mean all natural, human, and manufactured resources that go into the production of goods and services. This covers a lot of ground: factory and farm buildings and all equipment, tools, and machinery used to produce manufactured goods and agricultural products; transportation and communication facilities; innumerable types of labor; and land and mineral resources of all kinds. Economists broadly classify these as either (1) *property* resources—land or raw materials and capital; or (2) *human* resources—labor and entrepreneurial ability.

Resource Categories Let's examine these various resource categories.

Land **Land** means much more to the economist than to most people. Land is all natural resources—all "gifts of nature"—usable in the productive process. Such resources as arable land, forests, mineral and oil deposits, and water resources come under this classification.

Capital **Capital,** or investment goods, is all manufactured aids to production, that is, all tools, machinery, equipment, and factory, storage, transportation, and distribution facilities used in producing goods and services and getting them to the ultimate consumer. The process of producing and purchasing capital goods is known as **investment.**

Two other points are pertinent. First, *capital goods* ("tools") differ from *consumer goods* in that the latter satisfy wants directly, whereas the former do so indirectly by facilitating production of consumable goods. Second, the term "capital" as here defined does *not* refer to money. True, business executives and economists often talk of "money capital," meaning money available to purchase machinery, equipment, and other productive facilities. But money, as such, produces nothing; hence, it is not considered an economic resource. *Real capital*—tools, machinery, and other productive equipment—is an economic resource; *money* or *financial capital* is not.

Labor   **Labor** is a broad term the economist uses for all the physical and mental talents of men and women available and usable in producing goods and services. (This excludes a special set of talents—entrepreneurial ability—which, because of their special significance in a capitalistic economy, we consider separately.) The services of a logger, retail clerk, machinist, teacher, professional football player, and nuclear physicist all fall under the general heading of labor.

Entrepreneurial Ability   Finally, there is the special human resource we label **entrepreneurial ability,** or, simply, *enterprise.* We can assign four related functions to the entrepreneur.

1   The entrepreneur takes the *initiative* in combining the resources of land, capital, and labor to produce a good or service. Both a sparkplug and a catalyst, the entrepreneur is the driving force behind production and the agent who combines the other resources in what is hoped will be a profitable venture.

2   The entrepreneur makes basic *business-policy decisions,* that is, those nonroutine decisions which set the course of a business enterprise.

3   The entrepreneur is an *innovator*—the one who attempts to introduce on a commercial basis new products, new productive techniques, or even new forms of business organization.

4   The entrepreneur is a *risk bearer.* This is apparent from a close examination of the other three entrepreneurial functions. The entrepreneur in a capitalistic system has no guarantee of profit. The reward for his or her time, efforts, and abilities may be profits *or* losses and eventual bankruptcy. The entrepreneur risks not only time, effort, and business reputation, but his or her invested funds and those of associates or stockholders.

Resource Payments   The income received from supplying property resources—raw materials and capital equipment—is called *rental* and *interest income,* respectively. The income accruing to those who supply labor is called *wages* which includes salaries and various wage and salary supplements in the form of bonuses, commissions, royalties, and so forth. En-

trepreneurial income is called *profits,* which may be a negative figure—that is, losses.

These four broad categories of economic resources, or *factors of production* or *inputs* as they are often called, leave room for debate when it comes to classifying specific resources. For example, suppose you receive a dividend on some newly issued Exxon stock which you own. Is this an interest return for the capital equipment the company bought with the money you provided in buying Exxon stock? Or is this return a profit which compensates you for the risks involved in purchasing corporate stock? What about the earnings of a one-person consulting firm where the owner is both entrepreneur and labor force? Are the owner's earnings considered wages or profit income? The answer in both examples is "some of each." The point is that while we might quibble about classifying a particular flow of income as wages, rent, interest, or profits, all income can be fitted under one of these general headings.

Relative Scarcity   Economic resources, or factors of production, have one fundamental characteristic in common: *They are scarce or limited in supply.* Our "spaceship earth" contains only limited amounts of resources to use in producing goods and services. Quantities of arable land, mineral deposits, capital equipment, and labor (time) are all limited; they are available only in finite amounts. Because of the scarcity of productive resources and the constraint this scarcity puts on productive activity, output will necessarily be limited. Society will *not* be able to produce and consume all the goods and services it might want. Thus, in the United States—one of the most affluent nations—output per person was limited to $25,847 in 1994. In the poorest nations, annual output per person is as low as $200 or $300!

ECONOMICS: EMPLOYMENT AND EFFICIENCY

Restating the basic definition of economics: *Economics is the social science concerned with the problem of using or administering scarce resources (the means of producing) to attain the greatest or maximum fulfillment of society's unlimited wants (the goal of producing).* Economics is concerned with "doing the best with what we have." If our resources are scarce, we cannot satisfy all of our unlimited material wants. The next best thing is to achieve the greatest possible satisfaction of these wants.

Economics is a science of efficiency—efficiency in the use of scarce resources. Society wants to use its limited resources efficiently; it wants to get the maximum amount of useful goods and services produced with its available resources. To achieve this desirable outcome it must realize both full employment and full production.

Full Employment: Using Available Resources

By **full employment** we mean all available resources should be employed. No workers should be involuntarily out of work; the economy should provide employment for all who are willing and able to work. Nor should capital equipment or arable land sit idle. Note we say all *available* resources should be employed. Each society has certain customs and practices which determine what particular resources are available for employment. For example, legislation and custom provide that children and the very aged should not be employed. Similarly, it is desirable for productivity to allow farmland to lie fallow periodically. And it is desirable to "conserve" some resources for use by future generations.

Full Production: Using Resources Efficiently

But the employment of all available resources is insufficient to achieve efficiency. Full production must also be realized. By **full production** we mean that all employed resources should be used so that they provide the maximum possible satisfaction of our material wants. If we fail to realize full production, economists say our resources are *underemployed*.

Full production implies two kinds of efficiency—allocative and productive efficiency.

Allocative Efficiency   **Allocative efficiency** means that resources are being devoted to that combination of goods and services most wanted by society. It is obtained when we produce the best or optimal output-mix. For example, society wants resources allocated to compact discs and cassettes, rather than 45 rpm or long-playing records. We prefer word processors and personal computers, not manual typewriters. Xerox copiers are desired, not mimeograph machines.

Productive Efficiency   **Productive efficiency** is realized when desired goods and services are produced in the least costly ways. When we produce, say, compact discs at the lowest achievable unit cost, this means we are expending the smallest amount of resources to produce CDs and therefore making available the largest amount of resources for the production of other wanted products. Suppose society has only $100 worth of resources available. If we can produce a CD with only $5 of resources, then $95 of resources would be available to produce other goods. This is clearly better than producing the CD for $10 and only having $90 of resources for alternative uses.

In real-world terms, productive efficiency requires that Tauruses and Grand Ams be produced with computerized and roboticized assembly techniques rather than with the primitive assembly lines of the 1920s. Nor do we want our farmers harvesting wheat with scythes or picking corn by hand when elaborate harvesting equipment will do the job at a much lower cost per bushel.

In summary, allocative efficiency means resources are apportioned among firms and industries to obtain the particular mix of products society wants the most. Productive efficiency means each good or service in this optimal product-mix is produced in the least costly fashion. Full production means producing the "right" goods (allocative efficiency) in the "right" way (productive efficiency). *(Key Question 5)*

QUICK REVIEW 2-1

■ Human material wants are virtually unlimited.

■ Economic resources—land, capital, labor, and entrepreneurial ability—are scarce or limited.

■ Economics is concerned with the efficient management of scarce resources to achieve the maximum fulfillment of our material wants.

■ Economics entails the pursuit of full employment and full production, the latter involving both allocative and productive efficiency.

Production Possibilities Table

We can clarify the economizing problem through the use of a production possibilities table. This device reveals the core of the economizing problem: *Because resources are scarce, a full-employment, full-production economy cannot have an unlimited output of goods and services. As a result, people must choose which goods and services to produce and which to forgo.*

Assumptions   Several assumptions will set the stage for our illustration.

1 Efficiency The economy is operating at full employment and achieving productive efficiency. (We will consider allocative efficiency later.)

2 Fixed Resources The available supplies of the factors of production are fixed in both quantity and quality. But they can be shifted or reallocated, within limits, among different uses; for example, a relatively unskilled laborer can work on a farm, at a fast-food restaurant, or as a gas station attendant.

3 Fixed Technology The state of the technological arts is constant; that is, technology does not change during our analysis. Assumptions 2 and 3 are another way of saying that we are looking at our economy at a specific point in time, or over a very short period of time. Over a relatively long period it would be unrealistic to rule out technological advances and the possibility that resource supplies might vary.

4 Two Products To further simplify, suppose our economy is producing just two products—industrial robots and pizza—instead of the innumerable goods and services actually produced. Pizza is symbolic of **consumer goods,** those goods which directly satisfy our wants; industrial robots are symbolic of **capital goods,** those goods which satisfy our wants *indirectly* by permitting more efficient production of consumer goods.

Necessity of Choice From our assumptions we see that a choice must be made among alternatives. Available resources are limited. Consequently, the total amounts of robots and pizza that our economy can produce are limited. *Limited resources mean a limited output.* Since resources are limited in supply and fully employed, any increase in the production of robots will mean shifting resources away from the production of pizza. And the reverse holds true: If we step up the production of pizza, needed resources must come at the expense of robot production. *Society cannot have its cake and eat it, too.* Facetiously put, there's no such thing as a "free lunch." This is the essence of the economizing problem.

Let's generalize by noting in Table 2-1 alternative combinations of robots and pizza which our economy might choose. Though the data in this and the following **production possibilities tables** are hypothetical, the points illustrated have tremendous practical significance. At alternative A, our economy would be devoting all its resources to the production of ro-

TABLE 2-1 Production possibilities of pizza and robots with full employment and productive efficiency, 1996

Type of product	Production alternatives				
	A	B	C	D	E
Pizza (in hundred thousands)	0	1	2	3	4
Robots (in thousands)	10	9	7	4	0

bots (capital goods). At alternative E, all available resources would go to pizza production (consumer goods). Both these alternatives are unrealistic extremes; any economy typically strikes a balance in dividing its total output between capital and consumer goods. As we move from alternative A to E, we step up the production of consumer goods (pizza), by shifting resources away from capital goods (robot) production.

Remembering that consumer goods directly satisfy our wants, any movement toward E—producing more pizza—looks tempting. In making this move, society increases the current satisfaction of its wants. But there is a cost—fewer robots. This shift of resources catches up with society over time as its stock of capital goods dwindles—or at least ceases to expand at the current rate—with the result that the potential for greater future production is impaired. In moving from alternative A toward E, society chooses "more now" at the expense of "much more later."

In moving from E toward A, society chooses to forgo current consumption. This sacrifice of current consumption frees resources which can be used to increase production of capital goods. By building up its stock of capital in this way, society can anticipate greater production and, therefore, greater consumption in the future. In moving from E toward A, society is choosing "more later" at the cost of "less now."

At any point in time, an economy which is achieving full employment and productive efficiency must sacrifice some of product X to obtain more of product Y. The basic fact that economic resources are scarce prohibits such an economy from having more of both X and Y.

Production Possibilities Curve

To ensure our understanding of the production possibilities table, let's view these data graphically. We employ a simple two-dimensional graph, arbitrarily

KEY GRAPH

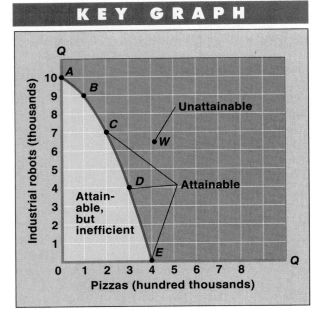

FIGURE 2-1   The production possibilities curve
Each point on the curve represents some maximum combination of any two products which can be achieved if full employment and full production are realized. When operating on the curve, more robots mean less pizza, and vice versa. Limited resources and a fixed technology make any combination of robots and pizza lying outside the curve, such as *W*, unattainable. Points inside the curve are attainable, but indicate that full employment and productive efficiency are not being realized.

putting the output of robots (capital goods) on the vertical axis and the output of pizza (consumer goods) on the horizontal axis, as in Figure 2-1 (Key Graph). Following the plotting procedure in the appendix to Chapter 1, we can locate the "production possibilities" curve, as shown in Figure 2-1.

Each point on the production possibilities curve represents some maximum output of the two products. Thus the curve is a *frontier.* To realize the various combinations of pizza and robots which fall *on* the production possibilities curve, society must achieve both full employment and productive efficiency. Points lying *inside* the curve are also attainable, but are not as desirable as points on the curve. These interior points imply a failure to achieve full employment and productive efficiency. Points lying *outside* the production possibilities curve, like point *W*, would represent greater output than at any point on the curve; but such points are unattainable with the current supplies of resources and technology. The production barrier of limited resources and existing technological knowl-

edge prohibits production of any combination of capital and consumer goods lying outside the production possibilities curve.

Law of Increasing Opportunity Costs

Because resources are scarce relative to the virtually unlimited wants which these resources can be used to satisfy, people must choose among alternatives. More of X (pizza) means less of Y (robots). *The amount of other products which must be forgone or sacrificed to obtain some amount of a specific product is called the* **opportunity cost** *of that good.* In our case the amount of Y (robots) which must be forgone or given up to get another unit of X (pizza) is the *opportunity cost,* or simply the *cost,* of that unit of X.

In moving from possibility A to B in Table 2-1, we find that the cost of 1 additional unit of pizza is 1 less unit of robots. But, as we now pursue the concept of cost through the additional production possibilities— B to C, C to D, and D to E—an important economic principle is revealed. In shifting from alternative A to alternative E, the sacrifice or extra cost of robots involved in getting each additional unit of pizza *increases.* In moving from A to B, just 1 unit of robots is sacrificed for 1 more unit of pizza; but going from B to C sacrifices 2 additional units of robots for 1 more unit of pizza; then 3 more of robots for 1 more of pizza; and finally 4 for 1. Conversely, you should confirm that in moving from E to A the cost of an additional robot is $\frac{1}{4}, \frac{1}{3}, \frac{1}{2}$, and 1 unit of pizza, respectively, for each of the four shifts.

Note two points about opportunity costs:
1   The analysis is in *real* or physical terms. We will shift to monetary comparisons in a moment.
2   Our explanation also is in terms of *marginal* (meaning "added" or "extra") cost, rather than cumulative or *total* opportunity cost. For example, the marginal opportunity cost of the third unit of pizza in Table 2-1 is 3 units of robots (= 7 − 4). But the total opportunity cost of 3 units of pizza is 6 units of robots (= 10 − 4 or 1 + 2 + 3).

Concavity   Graphically, the **law of increasing opportunity costs** is reflected in the shape of the production possibilities curve. The curve is *concave* or bowed out from the origin. As verified in Figure 2-1, when the economy moves from *A* toward *E,* it must give up successively larger amounts of robots (1, 2, 3, 4) as shown on the vertical axis to acquire equal increments of pizza (1, 1, 1, 1) as shown on the horizontal axis. The slope of the production possibilities curve becomes steeper as we move from *A* to *E* and such a curve, by definition, is concave as viewed from the origin.

Rationale   What is the economic rationale for the law of increasing opportunity costs? *Why* does the sacrifice of robots increase as we get more pizza? The answer is that *economic resources are not completely adaptable to alternative uses.* As we step up pizza production, resources which are less and less adaptable to making pizza must be induced, or "pushed," into pizza production. If we start at *A* and move to *B,* we can first pick resources whose productivity of pizza is greatest in relation to their productivity of robots. But as we move from *B* to *C, C* to *D,* and so on, resources highly productive of pizza become increasingly scarce. To get more pizza, resources whose productivity in robots is great in relation to their productivity in pizza will be needed. It will take more and more of such resources—and hence a greater sacrifice of robots—to achieve each increase of 1 unit in the production of pizza. This lack of perfect flexibility, or interchangeability, on the part of resources and the resulting increase in the sacrifice of one good that must be made in acquiring more and more units of another good is the rationale for the law of increasing opportunity costs. In this case, these costs are stated as sacrifices of goods and not in terms of dollars and cents. *(Key Question 6)*

Allocative Efficiency Revisited

Our analysis has purposely stressed full employment and productive efficiency, the realization of which allows society to achieve *any point* on its production possibilities curve. We now focus again on allocative efficiency, the question of determining the most-valued or *optimal point* on the production possibilities curve. Of all the attainable combinations of pizza and robots on Figure 2-1's curve, which is optimal or "best"? That is, what quantities of resources should be allocated to pizza and what quantities to robots?

Our discussion of the "economic perspective" in Chapter 1 puts us on the right track. Recall that economic decisions center on comparisons of marginal benefits and marginal costs. Any economic activity—for example, production or consumption—should be expanded so long as marginal benefits exceed marginal costs and should be reduced if marginal costs are greater than marginal benefits.

Consider pizza. We already know from the law of increasing opportunity costs that the marginal cost

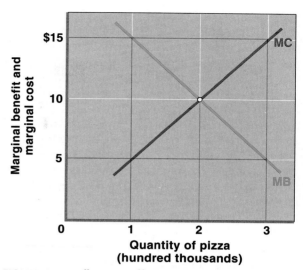

FIGURE 2-2   Allocative efficiency: MB = MC
Resources are efficiently allocated to any product when its output is such that marginal benefits equal marginal costs.

(MC) of additional units of pizza will rise as more units are produced. This is shown by the upsloping MC curve in Figure 2-2. We are also aware that we obtain extra or marginal benefits (MB) from additional units of pizza. However, although material wants *in the aggregate* are insatiable, the consumption of each *particular* product yields less and less extra satisfaction or, in other words, less MB. A consumer can become relatively saturated with a specific product. A second pizza provides less additional utility or benefit to you than the first. And a third will provide even less MB than the second. So it is for society as a whole. Hence, we can portray the marginal benefits from pizza by the downsloping MB line in Figure 2-2.

The optimal amount of pizza to produce is 200,000 units as indicated by the intersection of the MB and MC curves. Why is this optimal? If only 100,000 pizzas were produced, the MB of pizzas would be greater than their MC. In money terms the MB of a pizza here might be $15 while its MC is only $5. This suggests that society is *underallocating* resources to pizza production.

Why? Because society values an additional pizza as being worth $15, while the alternative products or services the required resources could have produced are only worth $5 as indicated by MC. Society will benefit—it will be better off in the sense of having a larger total output to enjoy—whenever it can gain something worth $15 by giving up or forgoing something (alternative goods and services) worth only $5. A reallocating of resources from other products to pizza means society is using its resources more efficiently. Each additional pizza up to 200,000 provides such gains, indicating that allocative efficiency is improved by this production. But when MB = MC the value of producing pizza or alternative products with available resources is the same. Allocative efficiency is achieved where MB = MC.

The production of 300,000 pizzas would represent an *overallocation* of resources to their production. Here the MC of pizza is $15 and MB is only $5. This means a unit of pizza is worth only $5 to society while the alternative products the resources required for its production could have otherwise produced are valued at $15. By producing one less unit society loses a pizza worth $5, but by reallocating the freed resources it gains other products worth $15. When society can gain something worth $15 by forgoing something (a pizza) worth only $5, it has realized a net gain. The net gain in this instance is $10 worth of total output. In Figure 2-2 net gains can be realized so long as pizza production is reduced from 300,000 back to 200,000. A more valued output from the same aggregate amount of inputs means greater allocative efficiency.

Generalization: Resources are being efficiently allocated to any product when its output is such that its marginal benefit equals its marginal cost (MB = MC). Suppose that by applying the same analysis to robots we find that 7000 is their optimal or MB = MC output. This would mean that alternative C on our production possibilities curve—200,000 pizzas and 7000 robots—would result in allocative efficiency for our hypothetical economy. *(Key Question 9)*

QUICK REVIEW 2-2

■ The production possibilities curve illustrates four concepts: *a* the *scarcity* of resources is implicit in that all combinations of output lying outside the production possibilities curve are unattainable; *b* *choice* is reflected in the need for society to select among the various attainable combinations of goods lying on the curve; *c* the downward slope of the curve implies the notion of *opportunity cost;* *d* the concavity of the curve reveals *increasing opportunity costs.*

■ Full employment and productive efficiency must be realized for the economy to operate on its production possibilities curve.

■ A comparison of marginal benefits and marginal costs is needed to determine allocative efficiency— the best or optimal output-mix on the curve.

UNEMPLOYMENT, GROWTH, AND THE FUTURE

Let's now release the first three assumptions underlying the production possibilities curve to see what happens.

Unemployment and Productive Inefficiency

The first assumption was that our economy is characterized by full employment and productive efficiency. How would our analysis and conclusions be altered if idle resources were available (unemployment) or if least-cost production was not realized? With full employment and productive efficiency, our five alternatives in Table 2-1 represent a series of maximum outputs; they illustrate combinations of robots and pizzas which might be produced when the economy is operating at full capacity. With unemployment or inefficient production, the economy would produce less than each alternative shown in the table.

Graphically, a situation of unemployment or productive inefficiency can be illustrated by a point *inside* the original production possibilities curve, reproduced in Figure 2-3. Point *U* is such a point. Here the economy is falling short of the various maximum combinations of pizza and robots reflected by all the points

FIGURE 2-3 **Unemployment and the production possibilities curve**
Any point inside the production possibilities curve, such as *U*, indicates unemployment or a failure to achieve productive efficiency. By realizing full employment and productive efficiency, the economy can produce more of either or both of the two products, as the arrows indicate.

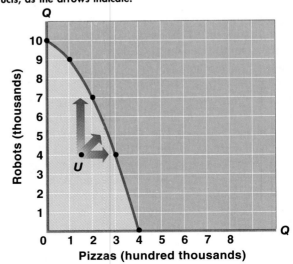

on the production possibilities curve. The arrows in Figure 2-3 indicate three of the possible paths back to full employment and least-cost production. A move toward full employment and productive efficiency will entail a greater output of one or both products.

A Growing Economy

When we drop the remaining assumptions that the quantity and quality of resources and technology are fixed, the production possibilities curve will shift position; that is, the potential total output of the economy will change.

Expanding Resource Supplies   Let's abandon the assumption that total supplies of land, labor, capital, and entrepreneurial ability are fixed in both quantity and quality. Common sense tells us that over time a nation's growing population will bring about increases in supplies of labor and enterpreneurial ability.[2] Also, labor quality usually improves over time. Historically, our stock of capital has increased at a significant, though unsteady, rate. And although we are depleting some of our energy and mineral resources, new sources are being discovered. The drainage of swamps and the development of irrigation programs add to our supply of arable land.

The net result of these increased supplies of the factors of production will be the ability to produce more of both robots and pizza. Thus, in the year 2016, the production possibilities of Table 2-1 for 1996 may be obsolete, having given way to those shown in Table 2-2. The greater abundance of resources results in a greater potential output of one or both products at each alternative. Economic growth, in the sense of an expanded potential output, has occurred.

But such a favorable shift in the production possibilities curve does not guarantee the economy will actually operate at a point on that new curve. The economy might fail to realize fully its new potentialities. Some 125 million jobs will give us full employment now, but ten or twenty years from now our labor force, because of a growing population, will be larger, and 125 million jobs will not be sufficient for full employment. The production possibilities curve

---

[2]This does not mean that population growth as such is always desirable. Overpopulation can be a constant drag on the living standards of many less developed countries. In advanced countries overpopulation can have adverse effects on the environment and the quality of life.

TABLE 2-2   Production possibilities of pizza and robots with full employment and productive efficiency, 2016

Type of product	Production alternatives				
	A′	B′	C′	D′	E′
Pizza (in hundred thousands)	0	2	4	6	8
Robots (in thousands)	14	12	9	5	0

may shift, but the economy may fail to produce at a point on that new curve.

Technological Advance   Our other assumption is a constant or unchanging technology. We know that technology has progressed remarkably over a long period. An advancing technology involves new and better goods *and* improved ways of producing them. For now, let's think of technological advance as comprising merely improvements in capital facilities—more efficient machinery and equipment. Such technological advance alters our earlier discussion of the economizing problem by improving productive efficiency, allowing society to produce more goods with fixed resources. As with increases in resource supplies, technological advance permits the production or more robots *and* more pizza.

When the supplies of resources increase or an improvement in technology occurs, the production possibilities curve of Figure 2-3 shifts outward and to the right, as illustrated by the A′B′C′D′E′ curve in Figure 2-4. **Economic growth**—*the ability to produce a larger total output—is reflected in a rightward shift of the production possibilities curve; it is the result of increases in resource supplies, improvements in resource quality, and technological progress.* The consequence of growth is that our full-employment economy can enjoy a greater output of *both* robots and pizza. While a static, no-growth economy must sacrifice some of X to get more Y, a dynamic, growing economy can have larger quantities of both X and Y.

Economic growth does *not* typically mean proportionate increases in a nation's capacity to produce various products. Note in Figure 2-4 that, while the economy can produce twice as much pizza, the increase in robot production is only 40 percent. You should pencil in two new production possibilities curves: one to show the situation where a better technique for producing robots has been developed, the

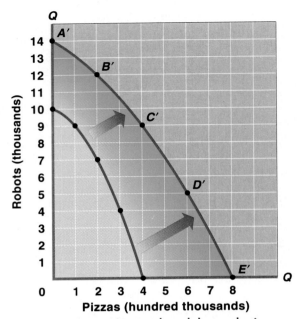

FIGURE 2-4 Economic growth and the production possibilities curve

The expanding resource supplies, improved resource quality, and technological advances which characterize a growing economy move the production possibilities curve outward and to the right. This permits the economy to enjoy larger quantities of both types of goods.

technology for producing pizza being unchanged, and the other to illustrate an improved technology for pizza, the technology for producing robots being constant.

Present Choices and Future Possibilities *An economy's current choice of position on its production possibilities curve is a basic determinant of the future location of that curve.* Let's designate the two axes of the production possibilities curve as "goods for the future" and "goods for the present," as in Figures 2-5a and b. "Goods for the future" are such things as capital goods, research and education, and preventive medicine, which increase the quantity and quality of property resources, enlarge the stock of technological information, and improve the quality of human resources. As we have already seen, "goods for the future" are the ingredients of economic growth. "Goods for the present" are pure consumer goods such as foods, clothing, "boom boxes," and automobiles.

Now suppose there are two economies, Alphania and Betania, which are initially identical in every respect except that Alphania's current (1996) choice of position on its production possibilities curve strongly favors "present goods" as opposed to "future goods." The dot in Figure 2-5a indicates this choice. Betania,

FIGURE 2-5 An economy's present choice of position on its production possibilities curve helps determine the curve's future location

A current choice favoring "present goods," as made by Alphania in (a), will cause a modest rightward shift of the curve. A current choice favoring "future goods," as made by Betania in (b), will result in a greater rightward (outward) shift of the curve.

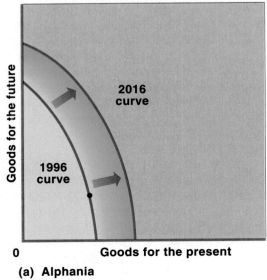

(a) Alphania

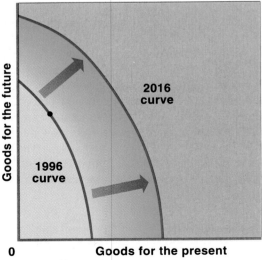

(b) Betania

on the other hand, makes a current (1996) choice which stresses large amounts of "future goods" and lesser amounts of "present goods" as shown by the dot in Figure 2-5b.

Now, all other things the same, we can expect the future (2016) production possibilities curve of Betania to be farther to the right than Alphania's curve. By currently choosing an output more conducive to technological advance and to increases in the quantity and quality of property and human resources, Betania will tend to achieve greater economic growth than Alphania, whose current choice of output places less emphasis on those goods and services which cause the production possibilities curve to shift rightward. In terms of capital goods, Betania is choosing to make larger current additions to its "national factory"—to invest more of its current output—than Alphania. The payoff from this choice is more rapid growth—greater future productive capacity—for Betania. The opportunity cost is fewer consumer goods in the present. *(Key Questions 10 and 11)*

QUICK REVIEW 2-3

■ Unemployment and the failure to realize productive efficiency cause the economy to operate at a point inside its production possibilities curve.

■ Expanding resource supplies, improvements in resource quality, and technological progress cause economic growth, depicted as an outward shift of the production possibilities curve.

■ An economy's present choice of output—particularly of capital and consumer goods—helps determine the future location of its production possibilities curve.

Applications

There are many possible applications of the production possibilities curve.

1 Microeconomic Budgeting While our discussion is in macroeconomic terms—in terms of the output of the entire economy—the concepts of scarcity, choice, and opportunity cost also apply at the microeconomic level. You should reread the first paragraph of this chapter.

2 Going to War In beginning to produce war goods for World War II (1939–1945), the United States

GLOBAL PERSPECTIVE 2-1

Investment and economic growth, selected countries

Nations which invest large proportions of their national outputs enjoy high growth rates, measured here by output per person. Additional capital goods make workers more productive and this means greater output per person.

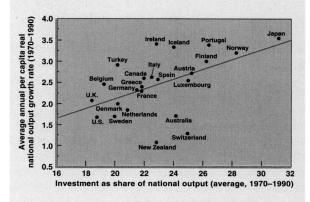

Source: International Monetary Fund data, as reported in *Economic Report of the President, 1994,* p. 37.

found itself with considerable unemployment. Our economy was able to produce an almost unbelievably large quantity of war goods and at the same time increase the output of consumer goods (Figure 2-3). The Soviet Union, on the other hand, entered World War II at almost capacity production; it was operating close to full employment. Its military preparations required considerable shifting of resources from production of civilian goods with a drop in the standard of living.

The United States' position during the Vietnam War was similar to that of the Soviet Union during World War II. Our economy was at full employment in the mid-1960s and the government accelerated military spending for Vietnam while simultaneously increasing expenditures on domestic "war on poverty" programs. This attempt to achieve simultaneously more pizza and more robots—or, more guns and more butter—in a full-employment economy was doomed to failure. The attempt to spend beyond our capacity to produce—to realize a point like *W* in Figure 2-1—contributed to the double-digit inflation of the 1970s.

3 Discrimination Discrimination based on race, gender, age, or ethnic background impedes the efficient employment of human resources, keeping the economy operating at some point inside its production possibilities curve. Discrimination prevents blacks, women, and others from obtaining jobs in which society can use efficiently their skills and talents. Elimination of discrimination would help move the economy from some point inside the production possibilities curve toward a point on the curve.

4 Lumber versus Owls The tradeoffs portrayed in the production possibilities curve occur regularly in environmental issues. An example is the much-publicized conflict between the logging industry of the Pacific Northwest and environmentalists. Envision a production possibilities curve with "lumber production" on one axis and "environmental quality" or "biodiversity" on the other. It so happens that the spotted owl depends on the mature or old-growth trees of that region for survival. Increasing the output of lumber limits the owl's habitat, destroys the species, and thus reduces environmental quality. Maintaining the old-growth forests preserves the owl, but destroys thousands of jobs in the logging and lumber industries. The production possibilities curve is an informative context within which to grasp the many difficult environmental decisions confronting society.

5 Productivity Slowdown Since the mid-1960s the United States has experienced an alarming decline in the rate of growth of labor productivity, defined as output per worker-hour. One cause of this decline is that the rate of increase in the mechanization of labor has slowed because of reduced investment relative to total output. One remedy is to increase investment as compared to consumption—a D to C type of shift in Figure 2-1. Special tax incentives to make business investment more profitable might be an appropriate policy to facilitate this shift. The expectation is that the restoration of a more rapid rate of productivity growth will accelerate the growth of the economy (the rightward shifting of the production possibilities curve) through time.

6 Growth: Japan versus United States The growth impact of a nation's decision on how much of its domestic output will be devoted to investment and

how much to consumption is illustrated vividly in comparing Japan and the United States. Japan has been investing over 25 percent of its domestic output in productive machinery and equipment compared to only about 10 percent for the United States. The consequences are in accord with our earlier discussion. Over the 1960–1990 period Japan's domestic output expanded at about 6.4 percent per year compared to only 3.2 percent for the United States. Japan's production possibilities curve shifted outward more rapidly than the United States' curve. This is reflected in living standards. In 1980 the per capita output of Japan was $16,711 as compared to $17,643 for the United States. By 1992 these figures had changed to $28,190 and $23,240, respectively.

7 International Trade Aspects The message of the production possibilities curve is that a nation cannot live beyond its means or production potential. When the possibility of international trade is taken into account, this statement must be modified in two ways.

Trade and Growth We will discover in later chapters that a nation can circumvent the output constraint imposed by its domestic production possibilities curve through international specialization and trade. International specialization and trade have the same impact as having more and better resources or discovering improved production techniques. Both increase the quantities of capital and consumer goods available to society. The output gains from international specialization and trade are the equivalent of economic growth.

Trade Deficits Within the context of international trade, a nation can achieve a combination of goods outside its domestic production possibilities curve (such as point W in Figure 2-1) by incurring a *trade deficit*. A nation may buy and receive an amount of imported goods from other nations which exceeds the amount of goods it exports. The United States has been doing just that recently. In 1993 the United States had a trade deficit of approximately $133 billion. We imported $133 billion more worth of goods than we exported. The net result was that in 1993 we enjoyed some $133 billion of output over what we produced domestically.

This looks like a favorable state of affairs. Unfortunately, there is a catch. To finance its deficit—to pay for its excess of imports over exports—the United

States must go into debt to its international trading partners *or* it must give up ownership of some of its assets to those other nations. Analogy: How can you live beyond your current income? Answer: Borrow from your parents, the sellers of goods, or a financial institution. Or sell some of the real assets (your car or stereo) or financial assets (stocks or bonds) you own. This is what the United States has been doing.

A major consequence of our large and persistent trade deficits is that foreign nationals hold larger portions of American private and public debt and own larger amounts of our business corporations, agricultural land, and real estate. To pay our debts and repurchase those assets we must in the future live well *within* our means. We must settle for some combination of goods within our production possibilities curve so that we can export more than we import—incur a *trade surplus*—to pay off our world debts and reacquire ownership of those assets. On the other hand, to the extent that some of our imports are capital goods, our future production possibilities curve will be farther rightward than it might otherwise be.

8   Famine in Africa   Modern industrial societies take economic growth—more-or-less continuous rightward shifts of the production possibilities curve—for granted. But, as the recent catastrophic famines in Somalia and other sub-Saharan nations of Africa indicate, in some circumstances the production possibilities curve may shift leftward. In addition to drought, a cause of African famines is ecological degradation—poor land-use practices. Land has been deforested, overfarmed, and overgrazed, causing the production possibilities of these highly agriculturally oriented countries to diminish. In fact the per capita national outputs of most of these nations declined in the last decade or so.

9   Castro's Cuba   This chapter's Last Word chronicles how the inefficiencies inherent in central planning, along with an American trade embargo and the loss of foreign aid, have diminished Cuba's production possibilities.

THE "ISMS"

A society can use many different institutional arrangements and coordinating mechanisms to respond to the economizing problem. Historically, the industrially advanced economies of the world have differed essentially in two ways: (1) the ownership of the means of production, and (2) the method of coordinating and directing economic activity. Let's examine the main characteristics of two "polar" types of economic systems.

Pure Capitalism

Pure, or **laissez faire, capitalism** is characterized by the private ownership of resources and the use of a system of markets and prices to coordinate and direct economic activity. In such a system each participant is motivated by his or her own self-interests; each economic unit seeks to maximize its income through individual decision making. The market system communicates and coordinates individual decisions and preferences. Because goods and services are produced and resources are supplied under competitive conditions, there are many independently acting buyers and sellers of each product and resource. As a result, economic power is widely dispersed. Advocates of pure capitalism argue that such an economy is conducive to efficiency in the use of resources, output and employment stability, and rapid economic growth. Hence, there is little or no need for government planning, control, or intervention. The term *laissez faire* means "let it be," that is, keep government from interfering with the economy, because such interference will disturb the efficient working of the market system. Government's role is therefore limited to protecting private property and establishing an appropriate legal framework for free markets.

The Command Economy

The polar alternative to pure capitalism has been the **command economy** or **communism,** characterized by public ownership of virtually all property resources and the rendering of economic decisions through central economic planning. All major decisions concerning the level of resource use, the composition and distribution of output, and the organization of production are determined by a central planning board. Business firms are governmentally owned and produce according to state directives. Production targets are determined by the planning board for each enterprise and the plan specifies the amounts of resources to be allocated to each enterprise so that it might realize its production goals. The division of output between capital and consumer goods is centrally decided and capital goods are allocated among industries in terms of the central planning board's long-term priorities.

Mixed Systems

Real-world economies fall between the extremes of pure capitalism and the command economy. The United States economy leans toward pure capitalism, but with important differences. Government plays an active role in our economy in promoting economic stability and growth, in providing certain goods and services which would be underproduced or not produced at all by the market system, and in modifying the distribution of income. In contrast to the wide dispersion of economic power among many small units which characterizes pure capitalism, American capitalism has spawned powerful economic organizations in the form of large corporations and labor unions. The ability of these power blocs to manipulate and distort the functioning of the market system to their advantage is a further reason for governmental involvement in the economy.

While the former Soviet Union historically approximated the command economy, it relied to some extent on market-determined prices and had some vestiges of private ownership. Recent reforms in the former Soviet Union, China, and most of the eastern European nations are designed to move these command economies toward more capitalistic, market-oriented systems. North Korea and Cuba are the best remaining examples of centrally planned economies.

But private ownership and reliance on the market system do not always go together, nor do public ownership and central planning. For example, the *fascism* of Hitler's Nazi Germany has been dubbed **authoritarian capitalism** because the economy had a high degree of governmental control and direction, but property was privately owned. In contrast, the former Yugoslavian economy of the 1980s was **market socialism,** characterized by public ownership of resources coupled with considerable reliance on free markets to organize and coordinate economic activity. The Swedish economy is also a hybrid system. Although over 90 percent of business activity is in private hands, government is deeply involved in achieving economic stability and in redistributing income. Similarly, the capitalistic Japanese economy entails a great deal of planning and "coordination" between government and the business sector.

The Traditional Economy

Many less developed countries have **traditional** or **customary economies.** Production methods, exchange, and distribution of income are all sanctioned by custom. Heredity and caste circumscribe economic roles of individuals and socioeconomic immobility is pronounced. Technological change and innovation may be closely constrained because they clash with tradition and threaten the social fabric. Economic activity is often secondary to religious and cultural values and society's desire to perpetuate the status quo.

The point is that there is no unique or universally accepted way to respond to the economizing problem. Various societies, having different cultural and historical backgrounds, different mores and customs, and contrasting ideological frameworks—not to mention resources which differ both quantitatively and qualitatively—use different institutions in dealing with the reality of relative scarcity. China, the United States, and Great Britain, for example, are all—in terms of their accepted goals, ideology, technologies, resources, and culture—attempting to achieve efficiency in the use of their respective resources. The best method for responding to the unlimited wants–scarce resources dilemma in one economy may be inappropriate for another economic system.

THE CIRCULAR FLOW MODEL

Market-oriented systems now dominate the world scene. Thus, our focus in the remainder of this chapter and in the following two chapters is on how nations use markets to respond to the economizing problem. Our goal in this last section is modest; we want to identify the major groups of decision makers and the major markets in the market system. Our point of reference is the circular flow diagram.

Resource and Product Markets

Figure 2-6 (Key Graph) shows two groups of *decision makers*—households and businesses. (Government will be added as a third decision maker in Chapter 5.) The *coordinating mechanism* which brings the decisions of households and businesses into alignment with one another is the market system, in particular resource and product markets.

The upper half of the diagram portrays the **resource market.** Here, households, which directly or indirectly (through their ownership of business corporations) own all economic resources, *supply* these

KEY GRAPH

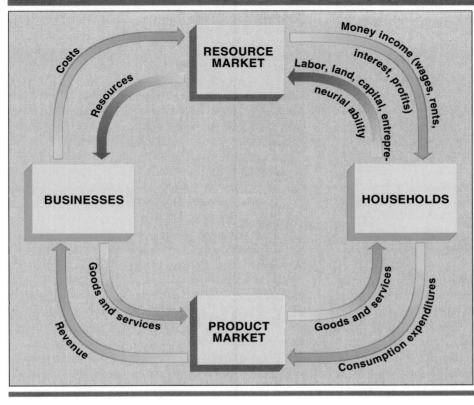

FIGURE 2-6 The circular flow of output and income The prices paid for the use of land, labor, capital, and entrepreneurial ability are determined in the resource market shown in the upper loop. Businesses are on the demand side and households on the supply side of this market. The prices of finished goods and services are determined in the product market located in the lower loop. Households are on the demand side and businesses on the supply side of this market.

resources to businesses.[3] Businesses will *demand* resources because they are the means by which firms produce goods and services. The interaction of demand and supply for the immense variety of human and property resources establishes the price of each. The payments which businesses make in obtaining resources are costs to businesses, but simultaneously constitute flows of wage, rent, interest, and profit income to the households supplying these resources.

Now consider the **product market** shown in the bottom half of the diagram. The money income received by households from the sale of resources does not, as such, have real value. Consumers cannot eat or wear coins and paper money. Thus, through the expenditure of money income, households express

their *demand* for a vast array of goods and services. Simultaneously, businesses combine the resources they have obtained to produce and *supply* goods and services in these same markets. The interaction of these demand and supply decisions determines product prices (Chapter 3). Note, too, that the flow of consumer expenditures for goods and services constitutes sales revenues or receipts from the viewpoint of businesses.

The **circular flow model** implies a complex, interrelated web of decision making and economic activity. Note that households and businesses participate in both basic markets, but on different sides of each. Businesses are on the buying or demand side of resource markets, and households, as resource owners and suppliers, are on the selling or supply side. In the product market, these positions are reversed; households, as consumers, are on the buying or demand side, and businesses are on the selling or supply side. Each group of economic units both buys and sells.

[3]For present purposes think of businesses simply as organizational charts, that is, institutions on paper apart from the capital, raw materials, labor, and entrepreneurial ability which breathe life into them and make them "going concerns."

LAST WORD

THE DIMINISHING PRODUCTION POSSIBILITIES OF CASTRO'S CUBA

Inefficiencies associated with its command economy, a thirty-year United States trade embargo, and the recent loss of Soviet aid are causing the Cuban economy to collapse.

The fortieth anniversary of Cuba's communist revolution in 1993 was overshadowed by a collapsing economy. Shortages of essential goods began to appear on the island by mid-1989 and have since become widespread and severe. Long lines are common as consumers attempt to buy rationed goods such as eggs, fish, meat, and soap. Some 50,000 Cubans have been diagnosed as having optic neuritis, a disease causing gradual blindness from malnutrition and vitamin deficiencies. Energy shortages have closed factories and disrupted construction projects. Shortages of gasoline and spare parts have idled automobiles, buses, and farm tractors. Ox carts are being substituted for tractors in agriculture and hundreds of thousands of bicycles are being imported from China as substitutes for autos and buses.

There are three reasons behind the collapse of Fidel Castro's Cuban economy. First, the Cuban economy has suffered increasingly from the kinds of central planning problems which brought about the fall of the command economies of eastern Europe and the former Soviet Union. Central planning has simply failed to (a) accurately assess consumer wants, (b) provide the market signals needed to minimize production costs, and (c) furnish adequate economic incentives for workers and business managers.

The second factor in Cuba's economic decline is an American trade embargo. Although Cuba is only 90 miles from the vast American market, that market has been denied to Cuba for some thirty years, causing a substantial decline in and distortion of Cuba's world trade.

Third, Soviet patronage has ended. For decades the Soviet Union heavily subsidized its communist partner in the Western Hemisphere. The Soviets bought Cuban exports (primarily sugar) at inflated

prices and sold oil and other goods to Cuba at low prices. Best estimates suggest Soviet economic and military aid averaged about $5 billion per year. The decline of the Soviet economy and the subsequent political breakup of the Soviet Union has brought an end to these subsidies and dealt a very damaging blow to the Cuban economy.

Estimates of the decline in Cuba's production possibilities vary. Some suggest that in recent years the domestic output has fallen by one-half; others indicate a three-quarters decline. In either case this decline in output is not simply a temporary move to a point inside Cuba's production possibilities curve, but rather a significant inward shift of the curve itself.

Castro has attempted to rejuvenate the Cuban economy in several ways. First, an attempt is being made to revitalize the tourist industry through joint ventures—for example, hotel and resort construction —with foreign firms. Second, Cuba has invited foreign companies to explore the island for oil. Third, Cuba is making a concerted effort to cultivate trade relations with new trading partners such as China and Japan. Whether such efforts will be successful is doubtful and most experts predict the economic crisis in Cuba to spark either widespread reforms toward a market economy or the overthrow of the Castro regime.

Furthermore, the specter of scarcity haunts these transactions. Because households have only limited amounts of resources to supply to businesses, the money incomes of consumers will be limited. This means that each consumer's income will go only so far. A limited number of dollars clearly will not permit the purchase of all the goods and services the consumer might like to buy. Similarly, because resources are scarce, the output of finished goods and services is also necessarily limited. Scarcity and choice permeate our entire discussion.

To summarize: In a monetary economy, households, as resource owners, sell their resources to businesses and, as consumers, spend the money income received buying goods and services. Businesses must buy resources to produce goods and services; their finished products are then sold to households in exchange for consumption expenditures or, as businesses view it, revenues. The net result is a counterclockwise *real* flow of economic resources and finished goods and services, and a clockwise *money* flow of income and consumption expenditures. These flows are simultaneous and repetitive.

Limitations

Our model simplifies in many ways. Intrahousehold and intrabusiness transactions are concealed. Government and the "rest of the world" are ignored as decision makers. The model subtly implies constant flows of output and income, while in fact these flows are unstable over time. Nor is the circular flow a perpetual motion machine; production exhausts human energies and absorbs physical resources, the latter giving rise to problems of environmental pollution. Finally, our model does not explain how product and resource prices are actually determined, which is examined in Chapter 3.

CHAPTER SUMMARY

1   Economics centers on two basic facts: first, human material wants are virtually unlimited; second, economic resources are scarce.

2   Economic resources may be classified as property resources—raw materials and capital—or as human resources—labor and entrepreneurial ability.

3   Economics is concerned with the problem of administering scarce resources in the production of goods and services to fulfill the material wants of society. Both full employment and full production of available resources are essential if this administration is to be efficient.

4   Full production consists of productive efficiency—producing any output in the least costly way—and allocative efficiency—producing the specific output-mix most desired by society.

5   An economy which is achieving full employment and productive efficiency—that is, operating *on* its production possibilities curve—must sacrifice the output of some types of goods and services to achieve increased production of others. Because resources are not equally productive in all possible uses, shifting resources from one use to another yields the law of increasing opportunity costs; that is, the production of additional units of product X entails the sacrifice of increasing amounts of product Y.

6   Allocative efficiency means achieving the optimal or most desired point on the production possibilities curve. It is determined by comparing marginal benefits and marginal costs.

7   Over time, technological advance and increases in the quantity and quality of human and property resources permit the economy to produce more of all goods and services. Society's choice as to the composition of current output is a determinant of the future location of the production possibilities curve.

8   The various economic systems of the world differ in their ideologies and also in their responses to the economizing problem. Critical differences have centered on **a** private versus public ownership of resources, and **b** the use of the market system versus central planning as a coordinating mechanism.

9   An overview of the operation of the capitalistic system can be gained through the circular flow of income. This simplified model locates the product and resource markets and presents the major income-expenditure flows and resources-output flows which constitute the lifeblood of the capitalistic economy.

TERMS AND CONCEPTS

economizing problem	full production	law of increasing	authoritarian
utility	allocative efficiency	opportunity costs	capitalism
economic resources	productive efficiency	economic growth	traditional or
land, capital, labor,	consumer goods	pure or laissez faire	customary
and entrepreneurial	capital goods	capitalism	economies
ability	production possibilities	command economy or	resource market
investment	table (curve)	communism	product market
full employment	opportunity cost	market socialism	circular flow model

ing finance major interviews with Citicorp or Chase Manhattan at the university placement office.

All these situations which link potential buyers with potential sellers constitute markets. As our ex-

DEMAND

Demand is *a schedule which shows the various amounts of a product consumers are willing and able*

QUESTIONS AND STUDY SUGGESTIONS

to purchase at each price in a series of possible prices during a specified period of time.[1] Demand portrays a series of alternative possibilities which can be set down in tabular form. It shows the quantities of a product which will be demanded at various possible prices, *all other things equal.*

We usually view demand by looking at price; that is, we read demand as showing the amounts consumers will buy at various possible prices. It is equally correct and sometimes more useful to view demand by looking at quantity. Instead of asking what quantities can be sold at various prices, we ask what prices can be gotten from consumers for various quantities of a good. Table 3-1 is a hypothetical **demand schedule** for a single consumer purchasing bushels of corn.

This tabular portrayal of demand reflects the relationship between the price of corn and the quantity the consumer would be willing and able to purchase at each of these prices. We say willing and *able,* because willingness alone is not effective in the market. I may be willing to buy a Porsche, but if this willingness is not backed by the necessary dollars, it will not be effective and, therefore, not reflected in the market. In Table 3-1, if the price of corn were $5 per bushel, our consumer would be willing and able to buy 10 bushels per week; if it were $4, the consumer would be willing and able to buy 20 bushels per week; and so forth.

The demand schedule does not tell us which of the five possible prices will actually exist in the corn market. This depends on demand *and supply.* Demand is simply a tabular statement of a buyer's plans, or intentions, with respect to the purchase of a product.

To be meaningful the quantities demanded at each price must relate to a specific period—a day, a week, a month. To say "a consumer will buy 10 bushels of corn at $5 per bushel" is meaningless. To say "a consumer will buy 10 bushels of corn *per week* at $5 per bushel" is clear and meaningful. Without a specific time period we would not know whether demand for a product was large or small.

Law of Demand

A fundamental characteristic of demand is this: *All else being constant, as price falls, the quantity demanded rises. Or, other things being equal, as price increases, the corresponding quantity demanded falls.* In short,

TABLE 3-1   An individual buyer's demand for corn

Price per bushel	Quantity demanded per week
$5	10
4	20
3	35
2	55
1	80

there is a negative or *inverse* relationship between price and quantity demanded. Economists call this inverse relationship the **law of demand.**

The "other things being constant" assumption is critical here. Many factors other than the price of the product under consideration affect the amount purchased. The quantity of Nikes purchased will depend not only on the price of Nikes, but also on the prices of such substitutes as Reeboks, Adidas, and L.A. Gear. The law of demand in this case says that fewer Nikes will be purchased if the price of Nikes rises *and the prices of Reeboks, Adidas, and L.A. Gear all remain constant.* In short, if the *relative price* of Nikes increases, fewer Nikes will be bought. However, if the price of Nikes and all other competing shoes increase by some amount—say $5—consumers might buy more, less, or the same amount of Nikes.

What is the foundation for the law of demand? There are several levels of analysis on which to argue the case.

1   Common sense and simple observation are consistent with the law of demand. People ordinarily *do* buy more of a product at a low price than they do at a high price. Price is an obstacle which deters consumers from buying. The higher this obstacle, the less of a product they will buy; the lower the price obstacle, the more they will buy. A high price discourages consumers from buying; a low price encourages them to buy. The fact that businesses have "sales" is evidence of their belief in the law of demand. "Bargain days" are based on the law of demand. Businesses reduce their inventories by lowering prices, not by raising them.

2   In any given time period each buyer of a product will derive less satisfaction or benefit or utility from each successive unit consumed. The second "Big Mac" will yield less satisfaction to the consumer than the first; and the third still less added benefit or utility than the second. Because consumption is subject to **diminishing marginal utility**—consuming successive units of a particular product yields less and

---

[1]In adjusting this definition to the resource market, substitute the word "resource" for "product" and "businesses" for "consumers."

less extra satisfaction—consumers will only buy additional units if price is reduced.

3   The law of demand also can be explained in terms of income and substitution effects. The **income effect** indicates that, at a lower price, you can afford more of the good without giving up other goods. A decline in the price of a product will increase the purchasing power of your money income, enabling you to buy more of the product than before. A higher price will have the opposite effect.

The **substitution effect** suggests that, at a lower price, you have the incentive to substitute the cheaper good for similar goods which are now relatively more expensive. Consumers tend to substitute cheap products for dear products.

For example, a decline in the price of beef will increase the purchasing power of consumer incomes, enabling them to buy more beef (the income effect). At a lower price, beef is relatively more attractive and is substituted for pork, mutton, chicken, and fish (the substitution effect). The income and substitution effects combine to make consumers able and willing to buy more of a product at a low price than at a high price.

The Demand Curve

This inverse relationship between product price and quantity demanded can be represented on a simple graph where, by convention, we measure quantity demanded on the horizontal axis and price on the vertical axis. To graph those five price–quantity possibilities in Table 3-1 we draw perpendiculars from the appropriate points on the two axes. In plotting the "$5-price–10-quantity-demanded" possibility, we draw a perpendicular from the horizontal (quantity) axis at 10 to meet a perpendicular drawn from the vertical (price) axis at $5. If this is done for all five possibilities, the result is a series of points as shown in Figure 3-1. Each point represents a specific price and the corresponding quantity the consumer will purchase at that price.

Now, assuming the same inverse relationship between price and quantity demanded at all points between the ones graphed, we can generalize on the inverse relationship between price and quantity demanded by drawing a curve to represent *all* price–quantity-demanded possibilities within the limits shown on the graph. The resulting curve is called a **demand curve,** labeled *DD* in Figure 3-1. It slopes downward and to the right because the relationship it portrays between price and quantity demanded is negative or inverse. The law of demand—people buy more at a low price than at a high price—is reflected in the downward slope of the demand curve.

What is the advantage of graphing our demand schedule? After all, Table 3-1 and Figure 3-1 contain exactly the same data and reflect the same relationship between price and quantity demanded. The advantage of graphing is that we can represent clearly a given relationship—in this case the law of demand—more simply than if we relied on verbal and tabu-

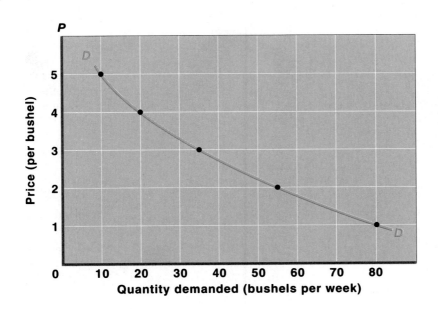

FIGURE 3-1   An individual buyer's demand curve for corn
An individual's demand schedule graphs as a downsloping curve such as *DD*, because price and quantity demanded are inversely related. Specifically, the law of demand generalizes that consumers will buy more of a product as its price declines.

TABLE 3-2   Market demand for corn, three buyers

Price per bushel	Quantity demanded			Total quantity demanded per week
	First buyer	Second buyer	Third buyer	
$5	10 +	12 +	8 =	30
4	20 +	23 +	17 =	60
3	35 +	39 +	26 =	100
2	55 +	60 +	39 =	154
1	80 +	87 +	54 =	221

lar presentation. A single curve on a graph, if understood, is simpler to state *and manipulate* than tables and lengthy verbal descriptions. Graphs are invaluable tools in economic analysis. They permit clear expression and handling of sometimes complex relationships.

Individual and Market Demand

Until now we have assumed just one consumer. Competition assumes many buyers are in the market. We can get from an *individual* to a *market* demand schedule by summing the quantities demanded by each consumer at the various possible prices. If there were just three buyers in the market, as is shown in Table 3-2, it would be easy to determine the total quantities demanded at each price. Figure 3-2 shows the same summing procedure graphically, using only the $3 price to illustrate the adding-up process. Note that we are simply summing the three individual demand curves *horizontally* to derive the total demand curve.

Competition, of course, entails many more than three buyers of a product. So—to avoid a lengthy addition process—suppose there are 200 buyers of corn in the market, each choosing to buy the same amount at each of the various prices as our original consumer. Thus, we can determine total or market demand by multiplying the quantity-demanded data of Table 3-1 by 200, as in Table 3-3. Curve D_1 in Figure 3-3 indicates this market demand curve for the 200 buyers.

Determinants of Demand

An economist constructing a demand curve such as D_1 in Figure 3-3 assumes that price is the most important influence on the amount of any product purchased. But the economist knows that other factors can and do affect purchases. In locating a specific demand curve such as D_1, it must be assumed that "other things are equal"; that is, certain *determinants* of the amount demanded are assumed to be constant. When any of these determinants change, the location of the demand curve will shift to the right or left of D_1. For this reason determinants of demand are referred to as *demand shifters*.

The basic determinants of market demand are: (1) the tastes or preferences of consumers, (2) the number of consumers in the market, (3) the money incomes of consumers, (4) prices of related goods, and (5) consumer expectations about future prices and incomes.

Changes in Demand

A change in one or more of the determinants of de-

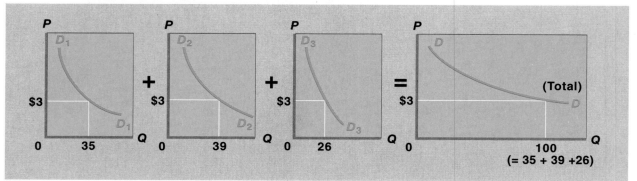

FIGURE 3-2   The market demand curve is the sum of the individual demand curves
Graphically the market demand curve (D total) is found by summing horizontally the individual demand curves (D_1, D_2, and D_3) of all consumers in the market.

TABLE 3-3 Market demand for corn, 200 buyers

(1) Price per bushel	(2) Quantity demanded per week, single buyer		(3) Number of buyers in the market		(4) Total quantity demanded per week
$5	10	×	200	=	2,000
4	20	×	200	=	4,000
3	35	×	200	=	7,000
2	55	×	200	=	11,000
1	80	×	200	=	16,000

mand will change the demand schedule data in Table 3-3 and therefore the location of the demand curve in Figure 3-3. A change in the demand schedule data, or, graphically, a shift in the location of the demand curve, is called a *change in demand.*

If consumers become willing and able to buy more corn at each possible price than is reflected in column 4 of Table 3-3, the result will be an *increase in demand.* In Figure 3-3, this increase in demand is reflected in a shift of the demand curve to the *right,* as from D_1 to D_2. Conversely, a *decrease in demand* occurs when, because of a change in one or more of the determinants, consumers buy less corn at each possible price than indicated in column 4 of Table 3-3. Graphically, a decrease in demand is shown as a shift of the demand curve to the *left,* for example, from D_1 to D_3 in Figure 3-3.

Let's now examine how changes in each determinant affect demand.

1 Tastes A change in consumer tastes or preferences favorable to a product—possibly prompted by advertising or fashion changes—will mean that more will be demanded at each price; that is, demand will increase. An unfavorable change in consumer preferences will decrease demand, shifting the curve to the left. Technological change in the form of a new product may affect consumer tastes. For example, the introduction of compact discs has greatly decreased the demand for long-playing records. Consumer concerns over the health hazards posed by cholesterol and obesity have increased the demands for broccoli, low-calorie sweeteners, and fresh fruits, while decreasing the demands for beef, veal, eggs, and whole milk. Medical studies linking beta carotene to the prevention of heart attacks, strokes, and some types of cancer have greatly boosted the demand for carrots.

FIGURE 3-3 Changes in the demand for corn
A change in one or more of the determinants of demand—consumer tastes, the number of buyers in the market, money incomes, the prices of other goods, or consumer expectations—will cause a change in demand. An increase in demand shifts the demand curve to the right, as from D_1 to D_2. A decrease in demand shifts the demand curve to the left, as from D_1 to D_3. A change in the quantity demanded is caused by a change in the price of the product, and is shown by a movement from one point to another—as from a to b—on a fixed demand curve.

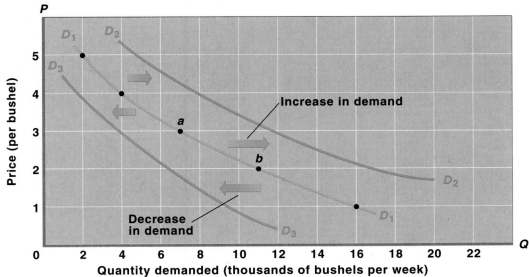

2 Number of Buyers An increase in the number of consumers in a market will increase demand. Fewer consumers will decrease demand. For example, improvements in communications have given financial markets international range, increasing demand for stocks and bonds. And the "baby boom" after World War II increased demand for diapers, baby lotion, and services of obstetricians. When the "baby boomers" reached their twenties in the 1970s, the demand for housing increased. Conversely, the aging of the baby boomers in the 1980s and 1990s has been a factor in the recent "slump" in housing demand. Also, increasing life expectancy has increased demands for medical care, retirement communities, and nursing homes. And recent international trade agreements such as the North American Free Trade Agreement (NAFTA) and the General Agreement on Tariffs and Trade (GATT) have reduced foreign trade barriers to American farm products, increasing demands for those products.

3 Income How changes in money income affect demand is more complex. For most commodities, a rise in income will cause an increase in demand. Consumers typically buy more steaks, sunscreen, and stereos as their incomes increase. Conversely, the demand for such products will decline as incomes fall. Commodities whose demand varies *directly* with money income are called **superior,** or **normal, goods.**

Although most products are normal goods, there are a few exceptions. As incomes increase beyond some point, the amounts of bread or lard or cabbages purchased at each price may diminish because higher incomes allow consumers to buy more high-protein foods, such as dairy products and meat. Rising incomes may also decrease demands for used clothing and third-hand automobiles. Similarly, rising incomes may cause demands for hamburger and margarine to decline as wealthier consumers switch to T-bones and butter. Goods whose demand varies *inversely* with a change in money income are called **inferior goods.**

4 Prices of Related Goods Whether a particular change in the price of a related good will increase or decrease the demand for a product will depend on whether the related good is a substitute for it or a complement to it. A substitute is a good which can be used in place of another good. A complement is a good used in conjunction with another good.

Substitutes Butter and margarine are examples of **substitute goods.** When the price of butter rises, consumers buy less butter, increasing the demand for margarine.[2] Conversely, as the price of butter falls, consumers will buy more butter, decreasing the demand for margarine. *When two products are substitutes, the price of one good and the demand for the other are directly related.* So it is with Nikes and Reeboks, sugar and Nutrasweet, Toyotas and Hondas, and Coke and Pepsi.

Complements Other products are related and are **complementary goods;** they "go together" in that they are used in tandem and jointly demanded. If the price of gasoline falls and, as a result, you drive your car more, this extra driving will increase your demand for motor oil. Conversely, an increase in the price of gasoline will diminish the demand for motor oil.[3] Thus gas and oil are jointly demanded; they are complements. So it is with ham and eggs, tuition and textbooks, movies and popcorn, VCRs and video cassettes, golf clubs and golf balls, cameras and film. *When two commodities are complements, the price of one good and the demand for the other are inversely related.*

Many goods are not related to one another—they are *independent* goods. For example, with such pairs as butter and golf balls, potatoes and automobiles, bananas and wristwatches, a change in the price of one would have little or no impact on the demand for the other.

5 Expectations Consumer expectations about future product prices, product availability, and future income can shift demand. Consumer expectations of higher future prices may prompt them to buy now to "beat" anticipated price rises; similarly, the expectation of rising incomes may induce consumers to be freer in current spending. Conversely, expectations of falling prices and income will decrease current demand for products.

---

[2]Note that the consumer is moving up a stable demand curve for butter. But the demand curve for margarine shifts to the right (increases). Given the supply of margarine, this rightward shift in demand means more margarine will be purchased and that its price will also rise.

[3]While the buyer is moving up a stable demand curve for gasoline, the demand for motor oil shifts to the left (decreases). Given the supply of motor oil, this decline in the demand for motor oil will reduce both the amount purchased and its price.

First example: If freezing weather destroys much of Florida's citrus crop, consumers may reason that forthcoming shortages of frozen orange juice will escalate its price. They may stock up on orange juice by purchasing large quantities now.

Second example: In late 1993 there was a substantial increase in the demand for guns. Reason? The expectation of Congress passing more stringent gun control laws.

Third example: A first-round NFL draft choice might splurge for a new Mercedes in anticipation of a lucrative professional football contract.

Final example: Additional Federal excise taxes imposed on beer, wine, and distilled liquor on January 1, 1991, sharply increased demand in December of 1990 as consumers "bought early" to beat anticipated price increases.

In summary, an *increase* in demand—the decision by consumers to buy larger quantities of a product at each possible price—can be caused by:

1 A favorable change in consumer tastes
2 An increase in the number of buyers
3 Rising incomes if the product is a normal good
4 Falling incomes if the product is an inferior good
5 An increase in the price of a substitute good
6 A decrease in the price of a complementary good
7 Consumer expectations of higher future prices and incomes

Be sure you can "reverse" these generalizations to explain a *decrease* in demand. Table 3-4 provides additional illustrations to reinforce your understanding of the determinants of demand. *(Key Question 2)*

Changes in Quantity Demanded

A "change in demand" must not be confused with a "change in quantity demanded." A **change in demand** is a shift in the entire demand curve either to the right (an increase in demand) or to the left (a decrease in demand). The consumer's state of mind concerning purchases of this product has been altered. The cause: a change in one or more of the determinants of demand. The term "demand" refers to a schedule or curve; therefore, a "change in demand" means that the entire schedule has changed and that graphically the curve has shifted its position.

In contrast, a **change in the quantity demanded** designates the movement from one point to another point—from one price-quantity combination to another—on a fixed demand curve. The cause of a change in quantity demanded is a change in the

TABLE 3-4 Determinants of demand: factors that shift the demand curve

1 **Change in buyer tastes   Example:** Physical fitness increases in popularity, increasing the demand for jogging shoes and bicycles
2 **Change in number of buyers   Examples:** Japanese reduce import quotas on American telecommunications equipment, increasing the demand for it; a birthrate decline reduces the demand for education
3 **Change in income   Examples:** An increase in incomes increases the demand for such normal goods as butter, lobster, and filet mignon, while reducing the demand for such inferior goods as cabbage, turnips, retreaded tires, and used clothing
4 **Change in the prices of related goods   Examples:** A reduction in airfares reduces the demand for bus transportation (substitute goods); a decline in the price of compact disc players increases the demand for compact discs (complementary goods)
5 **Change in expectations   Example:** Inclement weather in South America causes the expectation of higher future coffee prices, thereby increasing the current demand for coffee

price of the product under consideration. In Table 3-3 a decline in the price from $5 to $4 will increase the quantity of corn demanded from 2000 to 4000 bushels.

In Figure 3-3 the shift of the demand curve D_1 to either D_2 or D_3 is a "change in demand." But the movement from point *a* to point *b* on curve D_1 is a "change in the quantity demanded."

Is a change in demand or a change in quantity demanded illustrated in each of the following?

1 Consumer incomes rise, with the result that more jewelry is purchased.
2 A barber raises the price of haircuts and experiences a decline in volume of business.
3 The price of Toyotas goes up, and, as a consequence, the sales of Chevrolets increase.

QUICK REVIEW 3-1

■ A market is any arrangement which facilitates purchase and sale of goods, services, or resources.

■ The law of demand indicates that, other things being constant, the quantity of a good purchased will vary inversely with its price.

■ The demand curve will shift because of changes in *a* consumer tastes, *b* the number of buyers in the market, *c* incomes, *d* the prices of substitute or complementary goods, and *e* expectations.

■ A "change in quantity demanded" refers to a movement from one point to another on a stable demand curve; a "change in demand" designates a shift in the entire demand curve.

SUPPLY

Supply is *a schedule which shows the amounts of a product a producer is willing and able to produce and make available for sale at each price in a series of possible prices during a specified period.*[4] This **supply schedule** portrays a series of alternative possibilities, such as shown in Table 3-5, for a single producer of corn. Supply tells us the quantities of a product which will be supplied at various prices, all other factors held constant.

Our definition of supply indicates that supply is usually viewed from the vantage point of price. That is, we read supply as showing the amounts producers will offer at various prices. It is equally correct and more useful in some instances to view supply from the reference point of quantity. Instead of asking what quantities will be offered at various prices, we can ask what prices will induce producers to offer various quantities of a good.

Law of Supply

Table 3-5 shows a positive or *direct* relationship between price and quantity supplied. As price rises, the corresponding quantity supplied rises; as price falls, the quantity supplied also falls. This particular relationship is called the **law of supply.** Producers will produce and offer for sale more of their product at a high price than at a low price. This again is basically a commonsense matter.

Price is a deterrent from the consumer's standpoint. A high price means that the consumer, being on the paying end of this price, will buy a relatively small amount of the product; the lower the price obstacle, the more the consumer will buy. The supplier is on the receiving end of the product's price. To a supplier, price is revenue per unit and therefore an inducement or incentive to produce and sell a product. Given production costs, a higher product price means

---

[4]In talking of the resource market, our definition of supply reads: a schedule which shows the various amounts of a resource which its owners are willing to supply in the market at each possible price in a series of prices during a specified time.

TABLE 3-5 An individual producer's supply of corn

Price per bushel	Quantity supplied per week
$5	60
4	50
3	35
2	20
1	5

greater profits and thus an incentive to increase the quantity supplied.

Consider a farmer who can shift resources among alternative products. As price moves up in Table 3-5, the farmer will find it profitable to take land out of wheat, oats, and soybean production and put it into corn. Furthermore, higher corn prices will make it possible for the farmer to cover the costs associated with more intensive cultivation and the use of larger quantities of fertilizers and pesticides. The result is more corn.

Now consider a manufacturer. Beyond some point manufacturers usually encounter increasing production costs per added unit of output. Therefore, a higher product price is necessary to cover these rising costs. Costs rise because certain productive resources — in particular, the firm's plant and machinery — cannot be expanded quickly. As the firm increases the amounts of more readily variable resources such a labor, materials, and component parts, the fixed plant will at some point become crowded or congested. Productive efficiency will decline and the cost of successive units of output will increase. Producers must receive a higher price to produce these more costly units. Price and quantity supplied are directly related.

The Supply Curve

As with demand, it is convenient to represent graphically the concept of supply. Our axes in Figure 3-4 are the same as those in Figure 3-3, except for the change of "quantity demanded" to "quantity supplied" on the horizontal axis. The graphing procedure is the same, but the quantity data and relationship involved are different. The market supply data graphed in Figure 3-4 as S_1 are shown in Table 3-6, which assumes there are 200 suppliers in the market having the same supply schedules as the producer previously portrayed in Table 3-5.

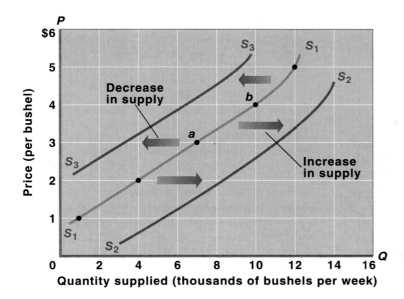

FIGURE 3-4 Changes in the supply of corn
A change in one or more of the determinants of supply—resource prices, productive techniques, the prices of other goods, taxes and subsidies, price expectations, or the number of sellers in the market—will cause a change in supply. An increase in supply shifts the supply curve to the right, as from S_1 to S_2. A decrease in supply is shown graphically as a shift of the curve to the left, as from S_1 to S_3. A change in the quantity supplied is caused by a change in the price of the product and is shown by a movement from one point to another—as from a to b—on a fixed supply curve.

Determinants of Supply

In constructing a supply curve, the economist assumes that price is the most significant influence on the quantity supplied of any product. But, as with the demand curve, the supply curve is anchored on the "other things are equal" assumption. The supply curve is drawn assuming that certain determinants of the amount supplied are given and do not change. If any of these determinants of supply do change, the supply curve will shift.

The basic determinants of supply are (1) resource prices, (2) the technique of production, (3) taxes and subsidies, (4) prices of other goods, (5) price expectations, and (6) the number of sellers in the market. A change in any one or more of these determinants or *supply shifters* will cause the supply curve for a product to shift either to the right or the left. A shift to the

right, from S_1 to S_2 in Figure 3-4, designates an *increase in supply:* Producers will supply larger quantities of the product at each possible price. A shift to the *left,* S_1 to S_3 in Figure 3-4, indicates a *decrease in supply:* Suppliers offer less at each price.

Changes in Supply

Let's consider how changes in each of these determinants affect supply.

1 Resource Prices The relationship between production costs and supply is an intimate one. A firm's supply curve is based on production costs; a firm must receive higher prices for additional units of output because those extra units cost more to produce. It follows that a decrease in resource prices will lower production costs and increase supply, shifting the supply curve to the right. If prices of seed and fertilizer decrease, we can expect the supply of corn to increase. Conversely, an increase in resource prices will raise production costs and reduce supply, shifting the supply curve to the left. Increases in the prices of iron ore and coke will increase the cost of producing steel and reduce its supply.

2 Technology A technological improvement means new knowledge permits us to produce a unit of output with fewer resources. Given the prices of these resources, this will lower production costs and increase supply. Recent breakthroughs in supercon-

TABLE 3-6 Market supply of corn, 200 producers

(1) Price per bushel	(2) Quantity supplied per week, single producer		(3) Number of sellers in the market		(4) Total quantity supplied per week
$5	60	×	200	=	12,000
4	50	×	200	=	10,000
3	35	×	200	=	7,000
2	20	×	200	=	4,000
1	5	×	200	=	1,000

ductivity portend the possibility of transporting electric power with little or no loss. Currently, about 30 percent of electric power transmitted by copper cable is lost. Consequence? Significant cost reductions and supply increases might occur in a wide range of products where electricity is an important input.

3 Taxes and Subsidies Businesses treat most taxes as costs. An increase in sales or property taxes will increase costs and reduce supply. Conversely, subsidies are "taxes in reverse." If government subsidizes the production of a good, it in effect lowers costs and increases supply.

4 Prices of Other Goods Changes in the prices of other goods can also shift the supply curve for a product. A decline in the price of wheat may cause a farmer to produce and offer more oats at each possible price. Conversely, a rise in the price of wheat may make farmers less willing to produce and offer oats in the market. A firm making athletic equipment might reduce its supply of basketballs in response to a rise in the price of soccer balls.

5 Expectations Expectations concerning the future price of a product can affect a producer's current willingness to supply that product. It is difficult, however, to generalize how the expectation of higher prices will affect the present supply of a product. Farmers might withhold some of their current corn harvest from the market, anticipating a higher corn price in the future. This will cause a decrease in the current supply of corn. Similarly, if the price of IBM stock is expected to rise significantly in the near future, the supply offered today for sale might decrease. On the other hand, in many types of manufacturing, expected price increases may induce firms to add another shift of workers or expand their production facilities, causing supply to increase.

6 Number of Sellers Given the scale of operations of each firm, the larger the number of suppliers, the greater the market supply. As more firms enter an industry, the supply curve will shift to the right. The smaller the number of firms in an industry, the less the market supply will be. This means that as firms leave an industry, the supply curve will shift to the left. Example: The United States and Canada recently imposed restrictions on haddock fishing to replenish dwindling stocks. The requirement that every haddock fishing boat remain in dock 80 days a year

TABLE 3-7 Determinants of supply: factors that shift the supply curve

1 **Change in resource prices** Examples: A decline in the price of fertilizer increases the supply of wheat; an increase in the price of irrigation equipment reduces the supply of corn

2 **Change in technology** Example: The development of a more effective insecticide for corn rootworm increases the supply of corn

3 **Changes in taxes and subsidies** Examples: An increase in the excise tax on cigarettes reduces the supply of cigarettes; a decline in subsidies to state universities reduces the supply of higher education

4 **Change in prices of other goods** Example: A decline in the prices of mutton and pork increases the supply of beef

5 **Change in expectations** Example: Expectations of substantial declines in future oil prices cause oil companies to increase current supply

6 **Change in number of suppliers** Examples: An increase in the number of firms producing personal computers increases the supply of personal computers; formation of a new professional football league increases the supply of professional football games

put a number of fishermen out of business and reduced the supply of haddock.

Table 3-7 provides a checklist of the determinants of supply; the accompanying illustrations deserve careful study. *(Key Question 5)*

Changes in Quantity Supplied

The distinction between a "change in supply" and a "change in quantity supplied" parallels that between a change in demand and a change in quantity demanded. A **change in supply** means the entire supply curve shifts. An increase in supply shifts the curve to the right; a decrease in supply shifts it to the left. The cause of a change in supply is a change in one or more of the determinants of supply. The term "supply" refers to a schedule or curve. A "change in supply" therefore must mean that the entire schedule has changed and that the curve has shifted.

A **change in the quantity supplied** refers to the movement from one point to another on a stable supply curve. The cause of such a movement is a change in the price of the specific product under consideration. In Table 3-6 a decline in the price of corn from $5 to $4 decreases the quantity of corn supplied from 12,000 to 10,000 bushels.

Shifting the supply curve from S_1 to S_2 or S_3 in Figure 3-4 entails "changes in supply." The movement from point *a* to point *b* on S_1, however, is a "change in quantity supplied."

You should determine which of the following involves a change in supply and which a change in quantity supplied:

1   Because production costs decline, producers sell more automobiles.

2   The price of wheat declines, causing the number of bushels of corn sold per month to increase.

3   Fewer oranges are offered for sale because their price has decreased in retail markets.

4   The Federal government doubles its excise tax on liquor.

QUICK REVIEW 3-2

■ The law of supply states that, other things being unchanged, the quantity of a good supplied varies directly with its price.

■ The supply curve will shift because of changes in *a* resource prices, *b* technology, *c* taxes or subsidies, *d* prices of other goods, *e* expectations regarding future product prices, and *f* the number of suppliers.

■ A "change in supply" means a shift in the supply curve; a "change in quantity supplied" designates the movement from one point to another on a given supply curve.

SUPPLY AND DEMAND: MARKET EQUILIBRIUM

We may now bring supply and demand together to see how interaction of the buying decisions of households and the selling decisions of producers deter-

mines the price of a product and the quantity actually bought and sold. In Table 3-8, columns 1 and 2 reproduce the market supply schedule for corn (from Table 3-6), and columns 2 and 3, the market demand schedule for corn (from Table 3-3). Note that in column 2 we are using a common set of prices. We assume competition—a large number of buyers and sellers.

Surpluses

Of the five[5] possible prices at which corn might sell in this market, which will actually prevail as the market price? Let's derive our answer through the process of trial and error. For no particular reason, we start with $5. Could this be the prevailing market price for corn? The answer is "No," because producers are willing to produce and offer in the market some 12,000 bushels of corn at this price while buyers are willing to buy only 2000 bushels at this price. The $5 price encourages farmers to produce a great deal of corn, but discourages most consumers from buying it. Other products appear as "better buys" when corn is high-priced. The result here is a 10,000-bushel **surplus** or *excess supply* of corn. This surplus, shown in column 4, is the excess of quantity supplied over quantity demanded at $5. Corn farmers find themselves with unwanted inventories of output.

A price of $5—even if it existed temporarily in the corn market—could not persist over a period of time. The very large surplus of corn would prompt competing sellers to bid down the price to encourage buyers to take this surplus off their hands.

Suppose price goes down to $4. The lower price has encouraged buyers to take more of this product off the market and, at the same time, has induced farmers to use a smaller amount of resources in producing corn. The surplus has diminished to 6000 bushels. However, a surplus or excess supply still exists and competition among sellers will once again bid down the price of corn. We can conclude, then, that prices of $5 and $4 will be unstable because they are "too high." The market price for corn must be less than $4.

Shortages

Let's jump to $1 as the possible market price for corn. Observe in column 4 that at this price, quantity de-

TABLE 3-8   Market supply and demand for corn

(1) Total quantity supplied per week	(2) Price per bushel	(3) Total quantity demanded per week	(4) Surplus (+) or shortage (−) (arrows indicate effect on price)
12,000	$5	2,000	+10,000 ↓
10,000	4	4,000	+ 6,000 ↓
7,000	3	7,000	0
4,000	2	11,000	− 7,000 ↑
1,000	1	16,000	−15,000 ↑

---

[5]There are many possible prices; our example shows only five.

manded exceeds quantity supplied by 15,000 units. This price discourages farmers from devoting resources to corn production and encourages consumers to attempt to buy more than is available. The result is a 15,000-bushel **shortage** of, or *excess demand* for, corn. The $1 price cannot persist as the market price. Competition among buyers will bid up the price to something greater than $1. At $1, many consumers who are willing and able to buy at this price will be left out in the cold. Many potential consumers will express a willingness to pay a price above $1 to ensure getting some of the available corn.

Suppose competitive bidding by buyers boosts the price of corn to $2. This higher price has reduced, but not eliminated, the shortage of corn. For $2, farmers will devote more resources to corn production, and some buyers who were willing to pay $1 for a bushel of corn will choose not to buy at $2. But a shortage of 7000 bushels still exists at $2. We can conclude that competitive bidding among buyers will push the market price above $2.

Equilibrium

By trial and error we have eliminated every price but $3. At $3, *and only at this price,* the quantity farmers are willing to produce and supply in the market is identical with the amount consumers are willing and able to buy. As a result, there is neither a shortage nor a surplus. A surplus causes price to decline and a shortage causes price to rise.

With neither a shortage nor a surplus at $3, there is no reason for the price of corn to change. The economist calls this price the *market-clearing* or **equilibrium price,** equilibrium meaning "in balance" or "at rest." At $3, quantity supplied and quantity demanded are in balance; that is, **equilibrium quantity** is 7000 bushels. Hence $3 is the only stable price of corn under the supply and demand conditions shown in Table 3-8. The price of corn will be established where the supply decisions of producers and the demand decisions of buyers are mutually consistent. Such decisions are consistent with one another only at a price of $3. At any higher price, suppliers want to sell more than consumers want to buy and a surplus will result; at any lower price, consumers want to buy more than producers are willing to offer for sale, as shown by the consequent shortage. Discrepancies between supply and demand intentions of sellers and buyers will prompt price changes which will bring these two sets of plans into accord with one another.

A graphical analysis of supply and demand should yield the same conclusions. Figure 3-5 (Key Graph) puts the market supply and market demand curves for corn on the same graph, the horizontal axis now measuring both quantity demanded and quantity supplied.

At any price above the equilibrium price of $3, quantity supplied will exceed quantity demanded. This surplus will cause a competitive bidding down of price by sellers eager to rid themselves of their surplus. The falling price will cause less corn to be offered and will simultaneously encourage consumers to buy more.

Any price below the equilibrium price will entail a shortage; quantity demanded will exceed quantity supplied. Competitive bidding by buyers will push the price up toward the equilibrium level. This rising price will simultaneously cause producers to increase the quantity supplied and ration buyers out of the market, eliminating the shortage. *Graphically, the intersection of the supply curve and the demand curve for the product will indicate the equilibrium point.* In this case equilibrium price and quantity are $3 per bushel and 7000 bushels.

Rationing Function of Prices

The ability of the competitive forces of supply and demand to establish a price where selling and buying decisions are synchronized or coordinated is called the **rationing function of prices.** In this case, the equilibrium price of $3 "clears the market," leaving no burdensome surplus for sellers and no inconvenient shortage for potential buyers. The composite of freely made individual buying and selling decisions sets this price which clears the market. In effect, the market mechanism of supply and demand says that any buyer willing and able to pay $3 for a bushel of corn will be able to acquire one; those who are not, will not. Similarly, any seller willing and able to produce bushels of corn and offer them for sale at $3 will be able to do so; those who are not, will not. *(Key Question 7)*

Changes in Supply and Demand

We know demand might change because of fluctuations in consumer tastes or incomes, changes in consumer expectations, or variations in the prices of related goods. Supply might vary in response to changes in technology, resource prices, or taxes. Now we are ready to consider the effect of changes

KEY GRAPH

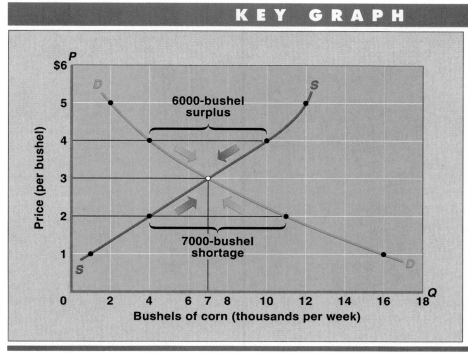

FIGURE 3-5 The equilibrium price and quantity for corn as determined by market demand and supply
The intersection of the downsloping demand curve *D* and the upsloping supply curve *S* indicates the equilibrium price and quantity, $3 and 7000 bushels in this instance. The shortages of corn which would exist at below-equilibrium prices, for example, 7000 bushels at $2, drive price up, and in so doing, increase the quantity supplied and reduce the quantity demanded until equilibrium is achieved. The surpluses which above-equilibrium prices would entail, for example, 6000 bushels at $4, push price down and thereby increase the quantity demanded and reduce the quantity supplied until equilibrium is achieved.

in supply and demand on equilibrium price and quantity.

Changing Demand   First, we analyze the effects of a change in demand, assuming supply is constant. Suppose demand *increases,* as shown in Figure 3-6a. What is the effect on price? Since the new intersection of the supply and demand curves is at a higher point on both the price and quantity axes, an increase in demand, other things (supply) equal, will have a *price-increasing effect* and a *quantity-increasing effect.* (The value of graphical analysis is now apparent; we need not fumble with columns of figures in determining the effect on price and quantity but only compare the new with the old point of intersection on the graph.)

A *decrease* in demand, shown in Figure 3-6b, reveals both *price-decreasing* and *quantity-decreasing effects.* Price falls and so does quantity. *In brief, we find a direct relationship between a change in demand and resulting changes in both equilibrium price and quantity.*

Changing Supply   Let's now see how a change in supply affects price, assuming demand is constant. If supply increases, as in Figure 3-6c, the new intersection of supply and demand is located at a lower equilibrium price. Equilibrium quantity, however, increases. If supply decreases, product price will rise, but quantity declines. Figure 3-6d illustrates this situation.

An increase in supply has a *price-decreasing* and a *quantity-increasing effect.* A decrease in supply has a *price-increasing* and a *quantity-decreasing effect. There is an inverse relationship between a change in supply and the resulting change in equilibrium price, but the relationship between a change in supply and the resulting change in equilibrium quantity is direct.*

Complex Cases   Many complex cases might arise, involving changes in both supply and demand.

1 Supply Increase; Demand Decrease   Assume first that supply increases and demand decreases. What effect does this have on equilibrium price? This example couples two price-decreasing effects, and the net result will be a price fall greater than what would result from either change alone.

How about equilibrium quantity? Here the effects of the changes in supply and demand are opposed:

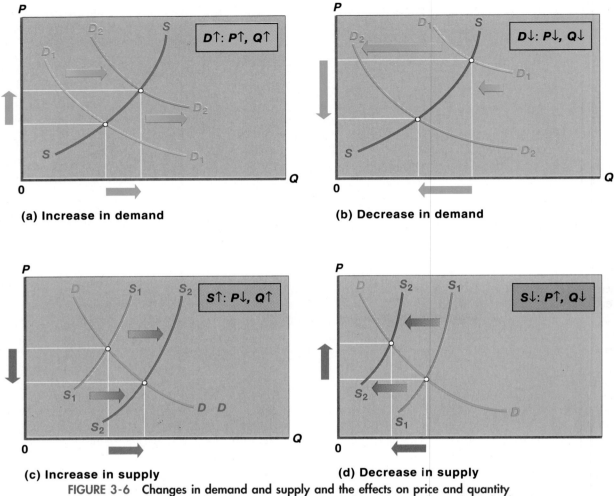

FIGURE 3-6 Changes in demand and supply and the effects on price and quantity
The increase in demand of (a) and the decrease in demand of (b) indicate a direct relationship between a change in demand and the resulting changes in equilibrium price and quantity. The increase in supply of (c) and the decrease in supply of (d) show an inverse relationship between a change in supply and the resulting change in equilibrium price, but a direct relationship between a change in supply and the accompanying change in equilibrium quantity.

The increase in supply increases equilibrium quantity, but the decrease in demand reduces the equilibrium quantity. The direction of the change in quantity depends on the relative sizes of the changes in supply and demand. If the increase in supply is larger than the decrease in demand, the equilibrium quantity will be larger than it was originally. But if the increase in supply is relatively smaller than the decrease in demand, equilibrium quantity will decrease. You should use graphs to verify these results.

2   Supply Decrease; Demand Increase   Another possibility is for supply to decrease and demand to increase. Two price-increasing effects are involved here. We can predict an increase in equilibrium price greater than that caused by either change separately. The effect on equilibrium quantity is again indeterminate, depending on the relative size of the changes in supply and demand. If the decrease in supply is relatively larger than the increase in demand, the equilibrium quantity will be less than initially. But if the decrease in supply is relatively smaller than the increase in demand, the equilibrium quantity will increase. You should trace through these two cases graphically to verify these conclusions.

3 Supply Increase; Demand Increase What if supply and demand both increase? What is the effect on equilibrium price? It depends. Here we must compare two conflicting effects on price—the price-decreasing effect of the increase in supply and the price-increasing effect of the increase in demand. If the increase in supply is greater than the increase in demand, the equilibrium price will decrease. If the opposite holds, equilibrium price will increase.

The effect on equilibrium quantity is certain: Increases in supply and in demand both have quantity-increasing effects. This means that equilibrium quantity will increase by an amount greater than either change alone.

4 Supply Decrease; Demand Decrease A decrease in both supply and demand can be similarly analyzed. If the decrease in supply is greater than the decrease in demand, equilibrium price will rise. If the reverse holds true, equilibrium price will fall. Because decreases in supply and demand both have quantity-decreasing effects, we can predict with certainty that equilibrium quantity will be less than it was initially.

Table 3-9 summarizes these four cases. You should draw a supply and demand diagram for each case to confirm the effects on equilibrium price and quantity indicated in the table.

Special cases might arise where a decrease in demand and a decrease in supply, on the one hand, and an increase in demand and an increase in supply, on the other, exactly cancel out. In both these cases, the net effect on equilibrium price will be zero; price will not change. *(Key Question 8)*

The Resource Market

As in the product market, resource supply curves are typically upsloping, and resource demand curves are downsloping.

TABLE 3-9 Effects of changes in both supply and demand

Change in supply	Change in demand	Effect on equilibrium price	Effect on equilibrium quantity
1 increase	decrease	decrease	indeterminate
2 decrease	increase	increase	indeterminate
3 increase	increase	indeterminate	increase
4 decrease	decrease	indeterminate	decrease

Resource supply curves reflect a *direct* relationship between resource price and quantity supplied, because it is in the interest of resource owners to supply more of a particular resource at a high price than at a low price. High income payments in a particular occupation or industry encourage households to supply more human and property resources. Low income payments discourage resource owners from supplying resources in this occupation or industry and encourage them to supply their resources elsewhere.

On the demand side, businesses buy less of a given resource as its price rises, and they substitute other relatively low-priced resources for it. Entrepreneurs will find it profitable to substitute low- for high-priced resources as they try to minimize costs. More of a particular resource will be demanded at a low price than at a high price. The result? A downsloping demand curve for the various resources.

Just as supply decisions of businesses and the demand decisions of consumers determine prices in the product market, so the supply decisions of households and demand decisions of businesses set prices in the resource market.

"Other Things Equal"

In Chapter 1 we explained that because economists cannot conduct controlled experiments, they assume "other things are equal" in their analyses. We have seen in this chapter that a number of forces bear on both demand and supply. Therefore, in locating specific supply and demand curves, such as D_1 and S in Figure 3-6a, economists isolate the impact of what they judge to be the most important influence on the amounts supplied and demanded—the price of the specific product under consideration. In thus representing the laws of demand and supply by downsloping and upsloping curves, respectively, the economist assumes that the determinants of demand (incomes, tastes, and so forth) and of supply (resource prices, technology, and other factors) are constant or unchanging. That is, price and quantity demanded are inversely related, *other things equal.* And price and quantity supplied are directly related, *other things equal.*

If you forget the "other things equal" assumption, you can encounter situations which *seem* to be in conflict with the laws of demand and supply. For example, suppose Ford sells 200,000 Escorts in 1993 at $10,000; 300,000 at $11,000 in 1994; and 400,000 in 1995 at $12,000. Price and the number purchased vary *directly,* and these real-world data seem to be at odds

TICKET SCALPING: A BUM RAP?

Some market transactions get a bad name which is unwarranted.

Tickets to athletic and artistic events are sometimes resold at higher-than-original prices—a market transaction known by the unsavory term "scalping." For example, a $40 ticket to a college bowl game may be resold by the original buyer for $200, $250, or more. The media often denounces scalpers for "ripping off" buyers by charging "exorbitant" prices. Scalping and extortion are synonymous in some people's minds.

But is scalping really sinful? We must first recognize that such ticket resales are voluntary, not coerced, transactions. This correctly implies that both buyer and seller gain from the exchange or it would not occur. The seller must value the $200 more than seeing the game and the buyer must value seeing the game more than the $200. There are no losers or victims here; both buyer and seller benefit from the transaction. The "scalping" market simply redistributes assets (game tickets) from those who value them less to those who value them more.

Does scalping impose losses or injury on other parties—in particular, the sponsors of the event? If the sponsors are injured, it is because they initially priced tickets below the equilibrium level. In so doing they suffer an economic loss in the form of less revenue and profit than they might have otherwise received. But the loss is self-inflicted because of their pricing error. That mistake is quite separate and distinct from the fact that some tickets were later resold at a higher price.

What about spectators? Does scalping somehow impose losses by deteriorating the quality of the game's audience? No! People who most want to see the game—generally those with the greatest interest in and understanding of the game—will pay the scalper's high prices. Ticket scalping will benefit athletic teams and performing artists—they will appear before more understanding and appreciative audiences.

So, is ticket scalping undesirable? Not on economic grounds. Both seller and buyer of a "scalped" ticket benefit and a more interested and appreciative audience results. Game sponsors may sacrifice revenue and profits, but that derives from their own misjudgment of equilibrium price.

---

with the law of demand. But there is really not a conflict here; these data do *not* refute the law of demand. The catch is that the law of demand's "other things equal" assumption has been violated over the three years in the example. Specifically, because of, for example, growing incomes, population growth, and relatively high gasoline prices, all increasing the attractiveness of compact cars, the demand curve for Escorts has increased over the years—shifted to the right as from D_1 to D_2 in Figure 3-6a—causing price to rise and, simultaneously, a larger quantity to be purchased.

Conversely, consider Figure 3-6d. Comparing the original S_1D and the new S_2D equilibrium positions, *less* of the product is being sold or supplied at a higher price; that is, price and quantity supplied seem to be *inversely* related, rather than *directly* related as the law of supply indicates. The catch again is that the "other things equal" assumption underlying the upsloping supply curve has been violated. Perhaps production costs have gone up or a specific tax has been levied on this product, shifting the supply curve from S_1 to S_2.

These examples also emphasize the importance of our earlier distinction between a "change in quantity demanded (or supplied)" and a "change in demand (supply)." In Figure 3-6a a "change in demand" has caused a "change in the quantity supplied." In Figure 3-6d a "change in supply" has caused a "change in the quantity demanded."

QUICK REVIEW 3-3

■ In competitive markets price adjusts to the equilibrium level at which quantity demanded equals quantity supplied.

■ A change in demand alters both equilibrium price and equilibrium quantity in the same direction as the change in demand.

■ A change in supply causes equilibrium price to change in the opposite direction, but equilibrium quantity to change in the same direction, as the change in supply.

■ Over time equilibrium price and quantity may change in directions which seem at odds with the laws of demand and supply because the "other things equal" assumption is violated.

CHAPTER SUMMARY

1 A market is any institution or arrangement which brings together buyers and sellers of some product or service.

2 Demand refers to a schedule representing the willingness of buyers to purchase a given product during a specific time period at each of the various prices at which it might be sold. According to the law of demand, consumers will ordinarily buy more of a product at a low price than they will at a high price. Therefore, other things equal, the relationship between price and quantity demanded is negative or inverse and demand graphs as a downsloping curve.

3 Changes in one or more of the basic determinants of demand—consumer tastes, the number of buyers in the market, the money incomes of consumers, the prices of related goods, and consumer expectations—will cause the market demand curve to shift. A shift to the right is an increase in demand; a shift to the left, a decrease in demand. A "change in demand" is distinguished from a "change in the quantity demanded," the latter involving movement from one point to another point on a fixed demand curve because of a change in the price of the product under consideration.

4 Supply is a schedule showing the amounts of a product which producers would be willing to offer in the market during a given period at each possible price. The law of supply says that, other things equal, producers will offer more of a product at a high price than they will at a low price. As a result, the relationship between price and quantity supplied is a direct one, and the supply curve is upsloping.

5 A change in resource prices, production techniques, taxes or subsidies, the prices of other goods, price expectations, or the number of sellers in the market will cause the supply curve of a product to shift. A shift to the right is an increase in supply; a shift to the left, a decrease in supply. In contrast, a change in the price of the product under consideration will result in a change in the quantity supplied, that is, a movement from one point to another on a fixed supply curve.

6 Under competition, the interaction of market demand and market supply will adjust price to that point where quantity demanded and quantity supplied are equal. This is the equilibrium price. The corresponding quantity is the equilibrium quantity.

7 The ability of market forces to synchronize selling and buying decisions to eliminate potential surpluses or shortages is termed the "rationing function" of prices.

8 A change in either demand or supply will cause equilibrium price and quantity to change. There is a positive or direct relationship between a change in demand and the resulting changes in equilibrium price and quantity. Though the relationship between a change in supply and resulting change in equilibrium price is inverse, the relationship between a change in supply and equilibrium quantity is direct.

9 The concepts of supply and demand also apply to the resource market.

TERMS AND CONCEPTS

market
demand
demand schedule (curve)
law of demand
diminishing marginal utility

income and substitution effects
normal (superior) good
inferior good
substitute goods
complementary goods

change in demand (supply) versus change in the quantity demanded (supplied)
supply
supply schedule (curve)

law of supply
surplus
shortage
equilibrium price and quantity
rationing function of prices

QUESTIONS AND STUDY SUGGESTIONS

1 Explain the law of demand. Why does a demand curve slope downward? What are the determinants of demand? What happens to the demand curve when each of these determinants changes? Distinguish between a change in demand and a change in the quantity demanded, noting the cause(s) of each.

2 *Key Question   What effect will each of the following have on the demand for product B?*
  a *Product B becomes more fashionable*
  b *The price of substitute product C falls*
  c *A decline in incomes if B is an inferior good*
  d *Consumers anticipate the price of B will be lower in the near future*
  e *The price of complementary product D falls*
  f *Foreign tariff barriers on B are eliminated*

3 Explain the following news dispatch from Hull, England: "The fish market here slumped today to what local commentators called 'a disastrous level'—all because of a shortage of potatoes. The potatoes are one of the main ingredients in a dish that figures on almost every café-menu —fish and chips."

4 Explain the law of supply. Why does the supply curve slope upward? What are the determinants of supply? What happens to the supply curve when each of these determinants changes? Distinguish between a change in supply and a change in the quantity supplied, noting the cause(s) of each.

5 *Key Question   What effect will each of the following have on the supply of product B?*
  a *A technological advance in the methods of producing B*
  b *A decline in the number of firms in industry B*
  c *An increase in the prices of resources required in the production of B*
  d *The expectation that the equilibrium price of B will be lower in the future than it is currently*
  e *A decline in the price of product A, a good whose production requires substantially the same techniques and resources as does the production of B*
  f *The levying of a specific sales tax on B*
  g *The granting of a 50-cent per unit subsidy for each unit of B produced*

6 "In the corn market, demand often exceeds supply and supply sometimes exceeds demand." "The price of corn rises and falls in response to changes in supply and demand." In which of these two statements are the terms "supply" and "demand" used correctly? Explain.

7 *Key Question   Suppose the total demand for wheat and the total supply of wheat per month in the Kansas City grain market are as follows:*

Thousands of bushels demanded	Price per bushel	Thousands of bushels supplied	Surplus (+) or shortage (−)
85	$3.40	72	_____
80	3.70	73	_____
75	4.00	75	_____
70	4.30	77	_____
65	4.60	79	_____
60	4.90	81	_____

  a *What will be the market or equilibrium price? What is the equilibrium quantity? Using the surplus-shortage column, explain why your answers are correct.*

  b *Using the above data, graph the demand for wheat and the supply of wheat. Be sure to label the axes of your graph correctly. Label equilibrium price "P" and equilibrium quantity "Q."*

  c *Why will $3.40 not be the equilibrium price in this market? Why not $4.90? "Surpluses drive prices up; shortages drive them down." Do you agree?*

  d *Now suppose that the government establishes a ceiling (maximum legal) price of, say, $3.70 for wheat. Explain carefully the effects of this ceiling price. Demonstrate your answer graphically. What might prompt government to establish a ceiling price?*

8 *Key Question   How will each of the following changes in demand and/or supply affect equilibrium price and equilibrium quantity in a competitive market; that is, do price and quantity rise, fall, remain unchanged, or are the answers indeterminate, depending on the magnitudes of the shifts in supply and demand? You should rely on a supply and demand diagram to verify answers.*
  a *Supply decreases and demand remains constant*
  b *Demand decreases and supply remains constant*
  c *Supply increases and demand is constant*
  d *Demand increases and supply increases*
  e *Demand increases and supply is constant*
  f *Supply increases and demand decreases*
  g *Demand increases and supply decreases*
  h *Demand decreases and supply decreases*

9 "Prices are the automatic regulator that tends to keep production and consumption in line with each other." Explain.

10 Explain: "Even though parking meters may yield little or no net revenue, they should nevertheless be retained because of the rationing function they perform."

11 Use two market diagrams to explain how an increase in state subsidies to public colleges might affect tuition and enrollments in both public and private colleges.

12 Critically evaluate: "In comparing the two equilibrium positions in Figure 3-6a, I note that a larger amount is actually purchased at a higher price. This refutes the law of demand."

13 Suppose you go to a recycling center and are paid 25 cents per pound for your aluminum cans. However, the recycler charges you 20 cents per bundle to accept your old newspapers. Use demand and supply diagrams to portray both markets. Can you explain how different government policies with respect to the recycling of aluminum and paper might account for these different market outcomes?

14 **Advanced analysis:** Assume that demand for a commodity is represented by the equation $P = 10 - .2Q_d$ and supply by the equation $P = 2 + .2Q_s$, where Q_d and Q_s are quantity demanded and quantity supplied, respectively, and P is price. Using the equilibrium condition $Q_s = Q_d$, solve the equations to determine equilibrium price. Now determine equilibrium quantity. Graph the two equations to substantiate your answers.

15 (Last Word) Discuss the economic aspects of ticket scalping, specifying gainers and losers.

4

PURE CAPITALISM
AND THE
MARKET SYSTEM

In Chapter 3 we saw how equilibrium prices and quantities are established in *individual* product and resource markets. We now widen our focus to take in all product and resource markets—the *competitive market system*, also known as the private enterprise system or capitalism. In the past few years, the press and television have regularly reported how Russia and other centrally planned economies are trying to shift toward capitalism. Precisely what are the features and institutions of capitalism which these nations are trying to emulate?

First we will describe the capitalist ideology and explain how pure, or laissez faire, capitalism would function. Although pure capitalism has never existed, describing it provides a useful approximation of how the economies of the United States and many other industrially advanced nations function. We will modify our model of pure capitalism in later chapters to correspond more closely to the reality of modern capitalism.

In explaining pure capitalism, we will discuss: (1) the institutional framework and basic assumptions which make up the capitalist ideology; (2) certain institutions and practices common to all modern economies; and (3) how a market system can coordinate economic activity and contribute to the efficient use of scarce resources. In achieving this third goal we will rely heavily on Chapter 3's explanation of how individual markets work.

CAPITALIST IDEOLOGY

There is no neat, universally accepted definition of capitalism. We therefore must examine in some detail the basic tenets of pure capitalism to understand what it entails. In short, the framework of capitalism embraces the following institutions and assumptions: (1) private property, (2) freedom of enterprise and choice, (3) self-interest as the dominant motive, (4) competition, (5) reliance on the price or market system, and (6) a limited role for government.

Private Property

Under a capitalistic system, property resources are owned by private individuals and private institutions, not by government. **Private property,** coupled with the freedom to negotiate binding legal contracts, permits private persons or businesses to obtain, control, employ, and dispose of property resources as they see fit. The institution of private property is sustained over time by the *right to bequeath*—the right of a property owner to designate who receives his or her property at the time of death.

Property rights—rights to own, use, and dispose of property—are significant because they encourage investment, innovation, exchange, and economic growth. Why would anyone build a house, construct a factory, or clear land for farming if someone or some institution (for example, government) could confiscate that property for their own benefit?

Property rights also apply to "intellectual property" and function similarly. Patents and copyrights exist to encourage individuals to write books, music, and computer programs and to invent new products and production processes without fear that others will expropriate them along with the associated economic rewards.

Another important role of property rights is that they facilitate exchange. A title to an automobile or a deed to a house assures the buyer that the seller is the legitimate owner. Finally, without property rights people would have to devote considerable energy and resources simply to protect and retain the property they have produced or acquired.

There are broad legal limits to this right of private ownership. For example, the use of resources to produce illicit drugs is prohibited. Nor is public ownership nonexistent. Even in pure capitalism, public ownership of certain "natural monopolies" may be essential to realize efficiency in the use of resources.

Freedom of Enterprise and Choice

Closely related to private ownership of property is freedom of enterprise and choice. Capitalism charges its component economic units with the responsibility of making certain choices, which are registered and made effective through the free markets of the economy.

Freedom of enterprise means that private business enterprises are free to obtain economic resources, to organize these resources in the production of a good or service of the firm's own choosing, and to sell it in the markets of their choice. In pure capitalism no artificial obstacles or restrictions imposed by government or other producers block an entrepreneur's choice to enter or leave a particular industry.

Freedom of choice means that owners of property and money can employ or dispose of them as they see fit. It also means that laborers are free to enter any lines of work for which they are qualified. Finally, it means that consumers are at liberty, within the limits of their incomes, to buy that collection of goods and services most appropriate in satisfying their wants.

Freedom of *consumer* choice is perhaps the most profound of these freedoms. The consumer is in a particularly strategic position in a capitalistic economy; in a sense, the consumer is sovereign. The range of free choices for suppliers of human and property resources depends on the choices of consumers. The consumer ultimately decides what the capitalistic economy should produce, and resource suppliers must make their free choices within these constraints. Resource suppliers and businesses are not really "free" to produce goods and services consumers do not desire because producing them would be unprofitable.

Again, broad legal limitations prevail in the expression of all these free choices.

Role of Self-Interest

The primary driving force of capitalism is **self-interest.** Each economic unit attempts to do what is best for itself. Entrepreneurs aim to maximize their firm's profits or, as the case might be, minimize losses. And, other things equal, property owners attempt to get the highest price for the rent or sale of these resources. Given the amount and irksomeness of the effort involved, those who supply human resources will also try to obtain the highest possible incomes from their employment. Consumers, in purchasing a specific product, will seek to obtain it at the lowest price. Consumers also apportion their expenditures to maximize their utility or satisfaction. In short, capitalism presumes self-interest as the fundamental *modus operandi* for the various economic units as they express their free choices. The motive of self-interest gives direction and consistency to what might otherwise be an extremely chaotic economy.

Pursuit of economic self-interest should not be confused with selfishness. A stockholder may invest to receive the best available corporate dividends and then may contribute a portion to the United Way or leave bequests to grandchildren.

Competition

Freedom of choice exercised in terms of promoting one's own monetary returns is the basis for **competition,** or economic rivalry, as a fundamental feature of capitalism. Competition entails:

1   Large numbers of independently acting buyers

and sellers operating in the market for any particular product or resource.

2 Freedom of buyers and sellers to enter or leave particular markets.

Large Numbers The essence of competition is the widespread diffusion of economic power within the two major aggregates—businesses and households —which comprise the economy. When many buyers and sellers are in a particular market, no one buyer or seller will be able to demand or offer a quantity of the product sufficiently large to noticeably influence its price. Let's examine this statement in terms of the selling or supply side of the product market.

We know that when a product becomes unusually scarce, its price will rise. An unseasonable frost in Florida may seriously curtail the supply of citrus crops and sharply increase the price of oranges. Similarly, *if* a single producer, or a small group of producers acting together, can somehow control or restrict the total supply of a product, then price can be raised to the seller's advantage. By controlling supply, the producer can "rig the market" on his or her own behalf. The idea of pure competition is that there are so many independently acting sellers that each, *because he or she is contributing an almost negligible fraction of the total supply,* has virtually no influence over the supply or, therefore, over product price.

Suppose there are 10,000 farmers, each supplying 100 bushels of corn in the Kansas City grain market when the price of corn is $4 per bushel. Could a single farmer who feels dissatisfied with that price cause an artificial scarcity of corn and thereby boost the price above $4? The answer clearly is "No." Farmer Jones, by restricting output from 100 to 75 bushels, exerts virtually no effect on the total supply of corn. The total amount supplied is reduced only from 1,000,000 to 999,975 bushels. This is not much of a shortage! Supply is virtually unchanged, and, therefore, the $4 price persists.

Competition means that each seller is providing a drop in the bucket of total supply. Individual sellers can make no noticeable dent in total supply; thus, a seller cannot *as an individual producer* manipulate product price. This is what is meant when it is said that an individual competitive seller is "at the mercy of the market."

The same rationale applies to the demand side of the market. Buyers are plentiful and act independently. Thus single buyers cannot manipulate the market to their advantage.

The widespread diffusion of economic power underlying competition controls the use and limits the potential abuse of that power. Economic rivalry prevents economic units from wreaking havoc on one another as they attempt to further their self-interests. Competition imposes limits on expressions of self-interest by buyers and sellers. It is a basic regulatory force in capitalism.

Entry and Exit Competition also implies it is simple for producers to enter or leave an industry; there are no artificial legal or institutional obstacles to prohibit expansion or contraction of specific industries. This freedom of an industry to expand or contract provides a competitive economy with the flexibility it needs to remain efficient over time. Freedom of entry and exit is necessary for the economy to adjust appropriately to changes in consumer tastes, technology, or resource supplies.

Markets and Prices

The basic coordinating mechanism of a capitalist economy is the market or price system. *Capitalism is a market economy.* Decisions rendered by buyers and sellers of products and resources are made effective through a system of markets. We know from Chapter 3 that a **market** is a mechanism or arrangement which brings buyers or "demanders" and sellers or "suppliers" of a good or service into contact with one another. A McDonald's, a gas station, a grocery supermarket, a Sotheby's art auction, the New York Stock Exchange, and worldwide foreign exchange markets are illustrations. The preferences of sellers and buyers are registered on the supply and demand sides of various markets, and the outcome of these choices is a system of product and resource prices. These prices are guideposts on which resource owners, entrepreneurs, and consumers make and revise their free choices in furthering their self-interests.

Just as competition is the controlling mechanism, so a system of markets and prices is a basic organizing force. The market system is an elaborate communication system through which innumerable individual free choices are recorded, summarized, and balanced against one another. Those who obey the dictates of the market system are rewarded; those who ignore them are penalized by the system. Through this communication system, society decides what the economy should produce, how production can be efficiently organized, and how the fruits of productive endeavor are distributed among the individual economic units which make up capitalism.

Not only is the market system the mechanism through which society decides how it allocates its resources and distributes the resulting output, but it is through the market system that these decisions are carried out. All of this will be detailed in the final sections of this chapter.

Limited Government

A competitive capitalist economy promotes a high degree of efficiency in the use of its resources. There is allegedly little need for governmental intervention in the operation of such an economy beyond its role of imposing broad legal limits on the exercise of individual choices and the use of private property. The concept of pure capitalism as a self-regulating and self-adjusting economy precludes any extensive economic role for government. However, as we will find in Chapter 5, a number of limitations and potentially undesirable outcomes associated with capitalism and the market system have resulted in an active economic role for government.

QUICK REVIEW 4-1

■ Pure capitalism rests on the private ownership of property and freedom of enterprise and choice.

■ Economic entities—businesses, resource suppliers, and consumers—seek to further their own self-interest.

■ The coordinating mechanism of capitalism is a competitive system of prices or markets.

■ The efficient functioning of the market system under capitalism allegedly precludes significant government intervention.

OTHER CHARACTERISTICS

Private property, freedom of enterprise and choice, self-interest as a motivating force, competition, and reliance on a market system are all institutions and assumptions more or less exclusively associated with pure capitalism.

In addition, there are certain institutions and practices which are characteristic of all modern economies: (1) the use of advanced technology and large amounts of capital goods, (2) specialization, and (3)

the use of money. Specialization and an advanced technology are prerequisites to efficient employment of any economy's resources. The use of money is a mechanism which allows society more easily to practice and reap the benefits of specialization and advanced productive techniques.

Extensive Use of Capital Goods

All modern or "industrially advanced" economies are based on state-of-the-art technology and the extensive use of capital goods. Under pure capitalism it is competition, coupled with freedom of choice and the motivation of self-interest, which create the opportunities for achieving technological advance. The capitalistic framework is highly effective in harnessing incentives to develop new products and improved techniques of production, because monetary rewards accrue directly to the innovator. Pure capitalism therefore presupposes extensive use and rapid development of complex capital goods: tools, machinery, large-scale factories, and facilities for storage, communication, transportation, and marketing.

Why are advanced technology and capital goods important? Because the most direct method of producing a product is usually the least efficient.[1] Even Robinson Crusoe avoided the inefficiencies of direct production in favor of **roundabout production.** It would be ridiculous for a farmer—even a backyard farmer—to go at production with bare hands. It pays huge dividends in terms of more efficient production and, therefore, a more abundant output, to create tools of production—capital equipment—to aid in the productive process. There is a better way of getting water out of a well than to dive in after it!

But there is a catch. Recall our discussion of the production possibilities curve and the basic nature of the economizing problem. For any economy operating on its production possibilities curve, resources must be diverted from the production of consumer goods to be used in the production of capital goods. We must currently tighten our belts as consumers to free resources for the production of capital goods which will give us a greater output of consumer goods in the future. Greater abundance tomorrow requires sacrifice today. *(Key Question 2)*

---

[1]Remember that consumer goods satisfy wants directly, while capital goods do so indirectly through the more efficient future production of consumer goods.

Specialization and Efficiency

The extent to which society relies on **specialization** is astounding. The vast majority of consumers produce virtually none of the goods and services they consume and consume little or nothing of what they produce. The worker who spends a lifetime stamping out parts for jet engines may never "consume" an airplane trip. The worker who devotes 8 hours a day to installing windows in Fords may own a Honda. Few households seriously consider any extensive production of their own food, shelter, and clothing. Many farmers sell their milk to the local dairy and then buy margarine at the local general store. Society learned long ago that self-sufficiency breeds inefficiency. The jack-of-all-trades may be a very colorful individual, but is certainly not efficient.

Division of Labor   In what ways might human specialization—the **division of labor**—enhance a society's output?

1   Ability Differences   Specialization permits individuals to take advantage of existing differences in their abilities and skills. If caveman A is strong, swift, and accurate with a spear, and caveman B is weak and slow, but patient, this distribution of talents can be most efficiently used if A hunts and B fishes.

2   Learning by Doing   Even if the abilities of A and B are identical, specialization may be advantageous. By devoting all your time to a single task, you are more likely to develop the appropriate skills and to discover improved techniques than when apportioning your time among a number of diverse tasks. You learn to be a good hunter by hunting!

3   Saving Time   Specialization—devoting all one's time to, say, a single task—avoids the loss of time involved in shifting from one job to another.

For all these reasons the division of labor results in greater total output from society's limited human resources.

Geographic Specialization   Specialization also works on a regional and international basis. Oranges could be grown in Nebraska, but because of the unsuitability of the land, rainfall, and temperature, the costs would be very high. Florida could achieve some success in the production of wheat, but for similar reasons such production would be costly. That's why Nebraskans produce those products—wheat in particular—for which their resources are best adapted, and Floridians do the same, producing oranges and other citrus fruits. In so doing, both produce surpluses of their specialties. Then, very sensibly, Nebraskans and Floridians swap some of their surpluses. Specialization permits each area to turn out those goods which its resources can most efficiently produce. In this way both Nebraska and Florida can enjoy a larger amount of both wheat and oranges than would otherwise be the case.

Similarly, on an international basis the United States specializes in such items as commercial aircraft and computers which it sells abroad in exchange for video recorders from Japan, bananas from Honduras, shoes from Italy, and woven baskets from Thailand. In short, human and geographical specialization are both essential in achieving efficiency in the use of resources.

Use of Money

Virtually all economies, advanced or primitive, use money. Money performs several functions, but first and foremost it is a **medium of exchange.**

In our example, Nebraskans must trade or exchange wheat for Florida's oranges if both states are to share in the benefits of specialization. If trade was highly inconvenient or prohibited for some reason, gains from specializing would be lost to society. Consumers want a wide variety of products and, without trade, would devote their human and material resources to many diverse types of production. If exchange could not occur or was very inconvenient to transact, Nebraska and Florida would be forced to be more self-sufficient, and the advantages of specialization would not occur. *A convenient means of exchanging goods is a prerequisite of specialization.*

Exchange can, and sometimes does, occur on the basis of **bartering,** that is, swapping goods for goods. But bartering as a means of exchange can pose serious problems for the economy. Exchange by barter requires a *coincidence of wants* between the two transactors. In our example, we assumed that Nebraskans had excess wheat to trade and that they wanted oranges. And we assumed Floridians had excess oranges to swap and that they wanted wheat. So exchange occurred. But if this coincidence of wants did not exist, trade would be stymied.

Suppose Nebraska does not want any of Florida's oranges but is interested in buying potatoes from Idaho. Ironically, Idaho wants Florida's oranges but

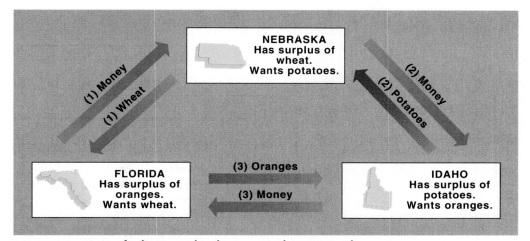

FIGURE 4-1   Money facilitates trade where wants do not coincide
By the use of money as a medium of exchange, trade can be accomplished, as indicated by the arrows, despite a noncoincidence of wants. By facilitating exchange, the use of money permits an economy to realize the efficiencies of specialization.

not Nebraska's wheat. And, to complicate matters, suppose that Florida wants some of Nebraska's wheat but none of Idaho's potatoes. The situation is summarized in Figure 4-1.

In no case do we find a coincidence of wants. Trade by barter clearly would be difficult. To overcome such a stalemate, economies use *money,* which is simply a convenient social invention to facilitate exchange of goods and services. Historically, cattle, cigarettes, shells, stones, pieces of metal, and many other commodities have been used, with varying degrees of success, as a medium for facilitating exchange. But to be money, an item needs to pass only one test: *It must be generally acceptable by buyers and sellers in exchange.* Money is socially defined; whatever society accepts as a medium of exchange *is* money.

Most economies use pieces of paper as money. This is the case with the Nebraska–Florida–Idaho economy; they use pieces of paper called "dollars" as money. Can the use of paper dollars as a medium of exchange overcome our stalemate?

Yes, with trade occurring as shown in Figure 4-1:
1   Floridians can exchange money for some of Nebraska's wheat.
2   Nebraskans use the money from the sale of wheat and exchange it for some of Idaho's potatoes.
3   Idahoans exchange the money received from the sale of potatoes for some of Florida's surplus oranges.

The willingness to accept paper money (or any other kind of money) as a medium of exchange has permitted a three-way trade which allows each state to specialize in one product and obtain the other product(s) its residents desire, despite the absence of a coincidence of wants between any two of the parties. Barter, resting as it does on a coincidence of wants, would have impeded this exchange and in so doing would have induced the three states not to specialize. Of course, the efficiencies of specialization would then have been lost to those states. Strange as it may first seem, two exchanges—surplus product for money and then money for a wanted product—are simpler than the single product-for-product exchange which bartering entails. In this example, product-for-product exchange would likely not occur.

On a global basis the fact that different nations have different currencies complicates international specialization and exchange. However, foreign exchange markets permit Americans, Japanese, Germans, Britons, and Mexicans to exchange dollars, yen, marks, pounds, and pesos for one another to complete international exchanges of goods and services.

A final example: Imagine a Detroit laborer producing crankshafts for Oldsmobiles. At the end of the week, instead of receiving a piece of paper endorsed by the company comptroller, or a few pieces of paper engraved in green and black, the worker receives from the company paymaster four Oldsmobile crankshafts. Inconvenient as this is, and with no desire to hoard crankshafts, the worker ventures into the Detroit business district to spend this income on a bag of groceries, a pair of jeans, and a movie. Obviously, the worker is faced with some inconvenient and time-consuming trading, and may not be able to negotiate any exchanges at all. Finding a clothier with jeans who happens to be in the market for an Oldsmobile crankshaft can be a formidable task. And, if the jeans do not trade evenly for crankshafts, how do the transactors "make change"? It is fair to say that money is one of the great social inventions of civilization.

QUICK REVIEW 4-2

■ Advanced economies achieve greater efficiency in production through the use of large quantities of capital goods.

■ Specialization enhances efficiency by having individuals, regions, and nations produce those goods and services for which their resources are best suited.

■ The use of money facilitates the exchange of goods which specialization entails.

THE COMPETITIVE MARKET SYSTEM

We noted earlier that a fundamental feature of capitalism is its reliance on a market system. We have also stressed that a capitalistic system is characterized by freedom of enterprise and choice. Consumers are free to buy what they choose; businesses, to produce and sell what they choose; and resource suppliers, to make their property and human resources available in whatever occupations they choose. We may wonder why such an economy does not collapse in chaos. If consumers want breakfast cereal, businesses choose to produce aerobic shoes, and resource suppliers want to offer their services in manufacturing computer software, production would seem to be deadlocked because of the apparent inconsistency of these free choices.

In reality, the millions of decisions made by households and businesses are highly consistent with one another. Firms do produce those particular goods and services consumers want. Households provide the kinds of labor businesses want to hire. Here we will see how a competitive market system constitutes a coordinating mechanism which overcomes the potential chaos suggested by freedom of enterprise and

choice. The competitive market system is a mechanism both for communicating decisions of consumers, producers, and resource suppliers to one another and for synchronizing those decisions toward consistent production objectives.

THE FIVE FUNDAMENTAL QUESTIONS

To understand the operation of a market economy we must first recognize that there are **Five Fundamental Questions** to which *every* economy must respond:

1 *How much* is to be produced? At what level—to what degree—should available resources be employed or used in the production process?

2 *What* is to be produced? What collection of goods and services will best satisfy society's material wants?

3 *How* is that output to be produced? How should production be organized? What firms should do the producing and what productive techniques should they use?

4 *Who* is to receive the output? How should the output of the economy be shared by consumers?

5 Can the system *adapt* to change? Can it appropriately adjust to changes that occur in consumer wants, resource supplies, and technology?

Two points are relevant. First, we will defer the "how much" question for now. Macroeconomics deals in detail with the complex question of the level of resource employment.

Second, the Five Fundamental Questions are merely an elaboration of the choices underlying Chapter 2's production possibilities curve. These questions would be irrelevant were it not for the economizing problem.

THE MARKET SYSTEM AT WORK

Chapter 2's circular flow diagram (Figure 2-6) provides the setting for our discussion. In examining how the market system answers the Fundamental Questions, we must add demand and supply diagrams as developed in Chapter 3 to represent the various product and resource markets embodied in the circular flow model.

Determining What Is to Be Produced

Given the product and resource prices established by

competing buyers and sellers in both the product and resource markets, how would a purely capitalistic economy decide the types and quantities of goods to be produced? Remembering that businesses seek profits and want to avoid losses, we can generalize that those goods and services which can be produced at a profit will be produced and those whose production entails a loss will not. Two things determine profits or losses.

1 The total revenue a firm receives when it sells a product.

2 The total costs of producing the product.

Both total revenue and total costs are price-times-quantity figures. Total revenue is found by multiplying product price by the quantity of the product sold. Total costs are found by multiplying the price of each resource used by the amount employed and summing the costs of each.

Economic Costs and Profits

To say that those products which can be produced profitably will be produced and those which cannot will not is only an accurate generalization if the meaning of **economic costs** is clearly understood.

Let's again think of businesses as simply organizational charts, that is, businesses "on paper," distinct from the capital, raw materials, labor, and entrepreneurial ability which make them going concerns. To become actual producing firms, these "on paper" businesses must secure all four types of resources. *Economic costs are the payments which must be made to secure and retain the needed amounts of these resources.* The per unit size of these costs—that is, resource prices—will be determined by supply and demand in the resource market. Like land, labor, and capital, entrepreneurial ability is a scarce resource and has a price tag on it. Costs therefore must include not only wage and salary payments to labor and interest and rental payments for capital and land, but also payments to the entrepreneur for the functions he or she performs in organizing and combining the other resources in the production of a commodity. The cost payment for these contributions by the entrepreneur is called a **normal profit.**

A product will be produced only when total revenue is large enough to pay wage, interest, rental, *and* normal profit costs. Now if total revenues from the sale of a product exceed all production costs, including a normal profit, the remainder will go to the entrepreneur as the risk taker and organizing force. This return above all costs is called a **pure,** or **economic,** **profit.** It is *not* an economic cost, because it need not be realized for the business to acquire and retain entrepreneurial ability.

Profits and Expanding Industries

A few examples will explain how the market system determines what to produce. Suppose the most favorable relationship between total revenue and total cost in producing product X occurs when the firm's output is 15 units. Assume, too, that the least-cost combination of resources to use in producing 15 units of X is 2 units of labor, 3 units of land, 1 of capital, and 1 of entrepreneurial ability, selling at prices of $2, $1, $3, and $3, respectively. Finally, suppose that the 15 units of X which these resources produce can be sold for $1 per unit. Will firms produce X? Yes, because the firm will be able to pay wage, rent, interest, and normal profit costs of $13 [= (2 × $2) + (3 × $1) + (1 × $3) + (1 × $3)]. The difference between total revenue of $15 and total costs of $13 will be an economic profit of $2.

This economic profit is evidence that industry X is a prosperous one. It will become an **expanding industry** as new firms, attracted by these above-normal profits, are created or shift from less profitable industries.

But the entry of new firms will be self-limiting. As new firms enter industry X, the market supply of X will increase relative to the market demand. This will lower the market price of X (Figure 3-6c) and economic profits will in time be competed away. The market supply and demand condition prevailing when economic profits become zero will determine the total amount of X produced. At this point the industry will be at its "equilibrium size," at least until a further change in market demand or supply upsets that equilibrium.

Losses and Declining Industries

But what if the initial market situation for product X were less favorable? Suppose conditions in the product market were such that the firm could sell the 15 units of X at a price of just 75 cents per unit. Total revenue would be $11.25 (= 15 × 75 cents). After paying wage, rental, and interest costs of $10, the firm would obtain a below-normal profit of $1.25. In other words, *losses* of $1.75 (= $11.25 − $13) would be incurred.

Certainly, firms would not be attracted to this unprosperous **declining industry.** On the contrary, if these losses persisted, entrepreneurs would seek the normal profits or possibly even the economic profits offered by more prosperous industries. In time existing firms in industry X would go out of business or migrate to other industries where normal or better profits prevail. However, as this happens, the market supply of X will fall relative to the market demand. Product price will rise (Figure 3-6d) and losses will eventually disappear. Industry X will then stabilize itself in size. The supply and demand situation that prevails at that point where economic profits are zero will determine the total output of product X. Again, the industry for the moment will have reached its equilibrium size.

"Dollar Votes" Consumer demand is crucial in determining the types and quantities of goods produced. Consumers, unrestrained by government and with money incomes from the sale of their resources, spend their dollars on those goods they are most willing and able to buy. These expenditures are **dollar votes** by which consumers register their wants through the demand side of the product market. If these votes for a product are great enough to provide a normal profit, businesses will produce it. An increase in consumer demand, that is, an increase in the dollar votes cast for a product, will mean economic profits for the industry producing it. These profits will signal expansion of that industry and increases in the output of the product.

Conversely, a decrease in consumer demand, that is, fewer votes cast for the product, will result in losses and, in time, contraction of the industry. As firms leave the industry, the output of the product declines. Indeed, the industry may cease to exist. The dollar votes of consumers play a key role in determining what products profit-seeking businesses will produce. The capitalistic system is characterized by **consumer sovereignty** because of the strategic role consumers have in determining the types and quantities of goods produced.

Illustration: In 1991, responding to doctors and nutritionists, McDonald's introduced its low-fat McLean burger. Good idea? Not really. Most consumers have found the new product "too dry" and "not tasty" so sales have been meager. While the McLean burger remains on McDonald's menu, it is there largely for public relations reasons and not as a source of significant profits. Hardee's, Burger King, and other fast-food franchises have also found that consumers have rejected their low-fat products.

Market Restraints on Freedom From the viewpoint of businesses, we now see that firms are not really "free" to produce what they wish. The demand decisions of consumers, by making production of some products profitable and others not, restrict the choice of businesses in deciding what to produce. Businesses must match their production choices with consumer choices or face losses and eventual bankruptcy.

It's the same for resource suppliers. The demand for resources is a **derived demand**—derived, that is, from the demand for the goods and services which the resources help produce. There is a demand for autoworkers only because there is a demand for automobiles. Resource suppliers will not be "free" to allocate their resources to the production of goods which consumers do not value highly. Firms will not produce such products, because consumer demand is not sufficient to make it profitable.

In brief: Consumers register their preferences on the demand side of the product market; producers and resource suppliers respond appropriately in seeking to further their own self-interests. The market system communicates the wants of consumers to businesses and resource suppliers and elicits appropriate responses.

Organizing Production

How is production to be organized in a market economy? This Fundamental Question is composed of three subquestions:
1 How should resources be allocated among specific industries?
2 What specific firms should do the producing in each industry?
3 What combinations of resources—what technology—should each firm employ?

Production and Profits The preceding section has answered the first subquestion. The market system steers resources to those industries whose products consumers want badly enough to make their production profitable. It simultaneously deprives unprofitable industries of scarce resources.

The second and third subquestions are closely intertwined. In a competitive market economy, the firms which do the producing are the ones willing and able to employ the economically most efficient technique

TABLE 4-1   Techniques for producing $15 worth of product X

Resource	Price per unit of resource	Units of resource		
		Technique no. 1	Technique no. 2	Technique no. 3
Labor	$2	4	2	1
Land	1	1	3	4
Capital	3	1	1	2
Entrepreneurial ability	3	1	1	1
Total cost of $15 worth of X		$15	$13	$15

of production. And the most efficient technique depends on:

1   Available technology, that is, the alternative combinations of resources of inputs which will produce the desired output.

2   The prices of needed resources.

Least-Cost Production   The combination of resources which is most efficient economically depends not only on the physical or engineering data provided by available technology but also on the relative worth of the required resources as measured by their market prices. A technique which requires just a few physical inputs of resources to produce a given output may be highly *in*efficient economically *if* the required resources are valued very highly in the market. *Economic efficiency entails getting a given output of product with the smallest input of scarce resources, when both output and resource inputs are measured in dollars-and-cents.* That combination of resources which will produce, say, $15 worth of product X at the lowest possible money cost is the most efficient.

Suppose there are three possible techniques to produce the desired $15 worth of product X. The quantity of each resource required by each production technology and the prices of the required resources are shown in Table 4-1. By multiplying the quantities of each resource required by its price in each of the three techniques, the total cost of producing $15 worth of X by each technique can be determined.

Technique No. 2 is economically the most efficient because it is the least costly. It permits society to obtain $15 worth of output by using a smaller amount of resources—$13 worth—than the $15 worth required by the two other techniques.

But will firms actually use technique No. 2? The answer is "Yes." Firms will want to use the most efficient technique because it yields the greatest profit.

A change in *either* technology *or* resource prices may cause the firm to shift from the technology it is using. If the price of labor falls to 50 cents, technique No. 1 will now be superior to technique No. 2. Businesses will find they can lower their costs by shifting to a technology which uses more of that resource whose price has fallen. You should verify that a new technique involving 1 unit of labor, 4 of land, 1 of capital, and 1 of entrepreneurial ability will be preferable to all three techniques listed in Table 4-1, assuming the resource prices given there. *(Key Question 8)*

Distributing Total Output

The market system enters the picture in two ways in solving the problem of distributing total output. Generally, any given product will be distributed to consumers on the basis of their ability and willingness to pay the existing market price for it. If the price of X is $1 per unit, those buyers who are able and willing to pay that price will get a unit of this product; those who are not, will not. This is the rationing function of equilibrium prices.

The size of consumers' money incomes determines their abilities to pay the equilibrium price for X and other products. And money income depends on the quantities of the various property and human resources which the income receiver supplies and their prices in the resource market. Thus, resource prices play a key role in determining the size of each household's income claim against the total output of society. Within the limits of a consumer's money income, his or her willingness to pay the equilibrium price for

X determines whether or not some of this product is distributed to that person. And this willingness to buy X will depend on one's preference for X compared to available close substitutes for X and their relative prices. Thus, product prices play a key role in determining spending patterns of consumers.

There is nothing particularly ethical about the market system as a mechanism for distributing output. Households which accumulate large amounts of property resources by inheritance, through hard work and frugality, through business acumen, or by crook will receive large incomes and thus command large shares of the economy's total output. Others, offering unskilled and relatively unproductive labor resources which elicit low wages, will receive meager money incomes and small portions of total output.

Accommodating Change

Industrial societies are dynamic: Consumer preferences, technology, and resource supplies all change. This means that the particular allocation of resources which is *now* the most efficient for a *given* pattern of consumer tastes, for a *given* range of technological alternatives, and for *given* supplies of resources will become obsolete and inefficient as consumer preferences change, new techniques of production are discovered, and resource supplies change over time. Can the market economy adjust to these changes so that resources are still used efficiently?

Guiding Function of Prices Suppose consumer tastes change. Specifically, assume that, because of greater health consciousness, consumers decide they want more exercise bikes and fewer cigarettes than the economy currently provides. This change in consumers' tastes will be communicated to producers through an increase in demand for bikes and a decline in demand for cigarettes. Bike prices will rise and cigarette prices will fall. Now, assuming firms in both industries were enjoying precisely normal profits before these changes in consumer demand, higher exercise bike prices mean economic profits for the bike industry, and lower cigarette prices mean losses for the cigarette industry. Self-interest induces new competitors to enter the prosperous bike industry. Losses will in time force firms to leave the depressed cigarette industry.

These adjustments in the business sector are appropriate to changes in consumer tastes. Society—

meaning consumers—wants more exercise bikes and fewer cigarettes, and that is precisely what it is getting as the bike industry expands and the cigarette industry contracts. These adjustments portray the concept of consumer sovereignty at work.

This analysis assumes resource suppliers are agreeable to these adjustments. Will the market system prompt resource suppliers to reallocate their human and property resources from the cigarette to the bike industry, permitting the output of bikes to expand at the expense of cigarette production? The answer is "Yes."

The economic profits which initially follow the increase in demand for bikes will not only induce that industry to expand but will also give it the revenue needed to obtain the resources essential to its growth. Higher bike prices will permit firms in that industry to pay higher prices for resources, increasing resource demand and drawing resources from less urgent alternative employments.

The reverse occurs in the adversely affected cigarette industry. The losses following the decline in consumer demand will cause a decline in the demand for resources in that industry. Workers and other resources released from the shrinking cigarette industry can now find employment in the expanding bike industry. Furthermore, the increased demand for resources in the bike industry will mean higher resource prices in that industry than those being paid in the cigarette industry, where declines in resource demand have lowered resource prices. The resulting differential in resource prices will provide the incentive for resource owners to further their self-interests by reallocating their resources from the cigarette to the bike industry. And this is the precise shift needed to permit the bike industry to expand and the cigarette industry to contract.

The ability of the market system to communicate changes in such basic data as consumer tastes and to elicit appropriate responses from businesses and resource suppliers is called the **directing** or **guiding function of prices.** By affecting product prices and profits, changes in consumer tastes direct the expansion of some industries and the contraction of others. These adjustments carry through to the resource market as expanding industries demand more resources and contracting industries demand fewer. The resulting changes in resource prices guide resources from the contracting to the expanding industries. Without a market system, some administrative agency, presumably a governmental planning board, would have to direct businesses and resources into specific lines of production.

Similar analysis would indicate that the market system would adjust to other fundamental changes—for example, to changes in technology and in the relative supplies of various resources.

Initiating Progress Adjusting to changes is one thing; initiating changes, particularly desirable changes, is something else. Is the competitive market system congenial to technological improvements and capital accumulation—the interrelated changes which lead to greater productivity and a higher level of material well-being for society?

Technological Advance The competitive market system contains the incentive for technological advance. A firm developing new cost-cutting techniques has a temporary advantage over its rivals. Lower production costs mean economic profits for the innovating firm. By passing part of its cost reduction to the consumer through a lower product price, the firm can increase sales and obtain economic profits at the expense of rival firms. Furthermore, the competitive market system provides an environment favorable to the rapid spread of a technological advance throughout the industry. Rivals *must* follow the lead of the most progressive firm or suffer immediate losses and eventual bankruptcy.

The lower product price which technological advance permits will cause the innovating industry to expand. This expansion may be the result of existing firms' expanding their rates of output or of new firms entering the industry lured by the economic profits initially created by technological advance. This expansion, that is, the diversion of resources from less progressive to more progressive industries, is as it should be. Sustained efficiency in the use of scarce resources demands that resources be continually reallocated from industries whose productive techniques are relatively less efficient to those whose techniques are relatively more efficient.

Capital Accumulation But technological advance typically requires more capital goods. The entrepreneur as an innovator can command through the market system the resources necessary to produce the machinery and equipment upon which technological advance depends.

If society registers dollar votes for capital goods, the product market and the resource market will adjust to these votes by producing capital goods. The market system acknowledges dollar voting for both consumer and capital goods.

But who will register votes for capital goods? First, the entrepreneur as a receiver of profit income can be expected to apportion part of that income to accumulation of capital goods. By doing so, an even greater profit income can be achieved in the future if innovation is successful. Furthermore, by paying interest, entrepreneurs can borrow portions of the incomes of households and use these borrowed funds in casting dollar votes for the production of more capital goods.

Competition and Control

In pure capitalism the market system is the organizing mechanism and competition is the mechanism of control. Supply and demand communicate the wants of consumers (society) to businesses and through businesses to resource suppliers. It is competition, however, which forces businesses and resource suppliers to make appropriate responses.

To illustrate: We have seen that an increase in consumer demand for some product will raise that good's price and generate economic profits. These profits signal producers that society wants more of the product. It is competition—new firms entering the industry—that simultaneously brings an expansion of output and a lowering of price back to a level just consistent with production costs. However, if the industry was dominated by, say, one huge firm (a monopolist) which was able to prohibit entry of potential competitors, that firm could continue to enjoy economic profits.

But competition does more than guarantee responses appropriate to the wishes of society. It also forces firms to adopt the most efficient productive techniques. In a competitive market, a firm that fails to use the least costly production technique will eventually be eliminated by more efficient firms. And we have seen that competition provides an environment conducive to technological advance.

The "Invisible Hand"

The operation and adjustments of a competitive market system create a curious and important identity—

the identity of private and social interests. Firms and resource suppliers, seeking to further their own self-interest and operating within the framework of a highly competitive market system, will simultaneously, as though guided by an **"invisible hand,"**[2] promote the public or social interest. For example, we have seen that given a competitive environment, business firms use the least costly combination of resources in producing a given output because it is in their private self-interest to do so. To act otherwise would be to forgo profits or even to risk bankruptcy. But, at the same time, it is clearly also in the social interest to use scarce resources in the least costly, that is, most efficient, manner. Not to do so would be to produce a given output at a greater cost or sacrifice of alternative goods than is necessary.

In our more-bikes–fewer-cigarettes illustration, it is self-interest, awakened and guided by the competitive market system, which induces responses appropriate to the change in society's wants. Businesses seeking to make higher profits and to avoid losses, on the one hand, and resource suppliers pursuing greater monetary rewards, on the other, negotiate the changes in the allocation of resources and therefore the composition of output society demands. The force of competition controls or guides the self-interest motive in such a way that it automatically, and quite unintentionally, furthers the best interests of society. The "invisible hand" tells us that when firms maximize their profits, society's domestic output is also maximized.

The Case for the Market System

The virtues of the market system are implicit in our discussion of its operation. Three merit emphasis.

Efficiency The basic economic argument for the market system is that it promotes the efficient use of resources. The competitive market system guides re-sources into production of those goods and services most wanted by society. It forces use of the most efficient techniques in organizing resources for production, and leads to the development and adoption of new and more efficient production techniques.

Incentives The market system effectively harnesses incentives. Greater work effort means higher money incomes which can be translated into a higher standard of living. Similarly, the assuming of risks by entrepreneurs can result in substantial profit incomes. Successful innovations may also generate economic rewards.

Freedom The major noneconomic argument for the market system is its great emphasis on personal freedom. In contrast to central planning, the market system can coordinate economic activity without coercion. The market system permits—indeed, it thrives on—freedom of enterprise and choice. Entrepreneurs and workers are not herded from industry to industry by government directives to meet production targets established by some governmental agency. On the contrary, they are free to further their own self-interests, subject to the rewards and penalties imposed by the market system itself.

> ### QUICK REVIEW 4-3
>
> ■ The output mix of the competitive market system is determined by profits. Profits cause industries to expand; losses cause them to contract.
>
> ■ Competition forces firms to use the least costly (most efficient) production methods.
>
> ■ The distribution of output in a market economy is determined by consumer incomes and product prices.
>
> ■ Competitive markets reallocate resources in response to changes in consumer tastes, technological progress, and changes in resource supplies.

CHAPTER SUMMARY

1 The capitalistic system is characterized by private ownership of resources and the freedom of individuals to engage in economic activities of their choice to advance their material well-being. Self-interest is the driving force of such an economy, and competition functions as a regulatory or control mechanism.

2 Capitalistic production is not organized in terms of a government plan, but rather features the market system as a means of organizing and making effective the many millions of individual decisions which determine what is pro-

---

[2]Adam Smith, *The Wealth of Nations* (New York: Modern Library, Inc., originally published in 1776), p. 423.

LAST WORD

BACK TO BARTER

Despite the advantages of using money, there is evidence that bartering is a "growth industry."

Because money facilitates exchange, it may seem odd that a considerable and growing volume of both domestic and international trade occurs through barter.

Suppose you own a small firm selling equipment to television stations. The economy is in recession; business is slow; your cash flow is down; and your inventories are much higher than desired. What do you do? You approach a local TV station which needs new equipment. But it, too, is feeling the effects of recession. Its advertising revenues are down and it also faces a cash-flow crunch. So a deal is struck. You provide $50,000 worth of equipment in exchange for $50,000 worth of "free" advertising. Advantage to seller: You move unwanted inventory, eliminating warehousing and insurance costs. You also receive valuable advertising time. The TV station gets needed equipment and pays for it with advertising time slots which would otherwise be unfilled. Both parties gain and no money changes hands.

Internationally, a firm might encounter an obstacle in selling its goods to a nation which does not have "hard" (exchangeable) currencies such as dollars, marks, or yen. Barter circumvents this problem. Example: Arcon Manufacturing of North Carolina sold its grain silos to a Nicaraguan firm, knowing that the buyer had no hard currency for making payment. Arcon took payment in sesame seeds, which it delivered to a Middle Eastern food manufacturer which was able to pay Arcon in hard currency. PepsiCo swaps cola syrup for Russian vodka. Coca-Cola has traded its syrup for Egyptian oranges, Turkish tomato paste, Polish beer, and Hungarian soft-drink bottles. Recently, large American oil companies such as Chevron and Amoco have negotiated "joint ventures" with the former Soviet Union based on barter. The Russians get updated capital equipment, new technologies, and increased oil production; American oil companies take their earnings in oil rather than currency.

Estimates differ on the volume of barter transactions within the United States. One estimate is that 175,000 businesses engaged in barter transactions of almost $1 billion in 1990, a fivefold increase in dollar volume since 1980. Other estimates put the dollar value of barter transactions as high as $6 billion per year.

The increasing popularity of barter has partly resulted from the development of "exchange companies" which coordinate barter transactions. The exchange company provides trade credits to members who make goods or services available; these accounts are debited when members make purchases. For its services the exchange company charges a membership fee and receives a percentage of the value of each transaction. At present there are over 400 barter exchanges in America.

Barter does involve time-consuming negotiation and it could undermine and distort the flow of open multilateral trade (Figure 4-1). Yet, as our illustrations make clear, barter is sometimes a means of bringing about mutually advantageous transactions which otherwise would not have occurred.

---

duced, the methods of production, and the sharing of output. The capitalist ideology envisions government playing a minor and relatively passive economic role.

3 Specialization and an advanced technology based on the extensive use of capital goods are common to all modern economies.

4 Functioning as a medium of exchange, money circumvents problems of bartering and thereby permits greater specialization both domestically and internationally.

5 Every economy faces Five Fundamental Questions: **a** At what level should available resources be employed? **b** What goods and services are to be produced? **c** How is that output to be produced? **d** To whom should the out-

put be distributed?   **e** Can the system adapt to changes in consumer tastes, resource supplies, and technology?

6   In a market economy those products whose production and sale yield total revenue sufficient to cover all costs, including a normal profit, will be produced. Those whose production will not yield a normal profit will not be produced.

7   Economic profits designate an industry as prosperous and signal its expansion. Losses mean an industry is unprosperous and result in contraction of that industry.

8   Consumer sovereignty means that both businesses and resource suppliers channel their efforts in accordance with the wants of consumers.

9   Competition forces firms to use the least costly, and therefore the most economically efficient, productive techniques.

10   The prices commanded by the quantities and types of resources supplied by each household will determine the number of dollar claims against the economy's output which each household receives. Within the limits of each household's money income, consumer preferences and the relative prices of products determine the distribution of total output.

11   The competitive market system can communicate changes in consumer tastes to resource suppliers and entrepreneurs, thereby prompting appropriate adjustments in the allocation of the economy's resources. The competitive market system also provides an environment conducive to technological advance and capital accumulation.

12   Competition, the primary mechanism of control in the market economy, will foster an identity of private and social interests; as though directed by an "invisible hand," competition harnesses the self-interest motives of businesses and resource suppliers to simultaneously further the social interest in using scarce resources efficiently.

TERMS AND CONCEPTS

private property	**specialization and**	**economic costs**	**dollar votes**
freedom of enterprise	**division of labor**	**normal versus**	**consumer sovereignty**
freedom of choice	**medium of exchange**	**economic profits**	**derived demand**
self-interest	**bartering**	**expanding industry**	**directing (guiding)**
competition	**Five Fundamental**	**versus declining**	**function of prices**
market	**Questions**	**industry**	**"invisible hand"**
roundabout production			

QUESTIONS AND STUDY SUGGESTIONS

1   "Capitalism may be characterized as an automatic self-regulating system motivated by the self-interest of individuals and regulated by competition."[3] Explain and evaluate.

2   *Key Question   What advantages result from "round-about" production? What problem is involved in increasing a full-employment economy's stock of capital goods? Illustrate this problem in terms of the production possibilities curve. Does an economy with unemployed resources face the same problem?*

3   What are the advantages of specialization in the use of human and material resources? Explain: "Exchange is the necessary consequence of specialization."

4   What problems does barter entail? Indicate the economic significance of money as a medium of exchange. "Money is the only commodity that is good for nothing but to be gotten rid of. It will not feed you, clothe you, shelter you, or amuse you unless you spend or invest it. It imparts value only in parting."[4] Explain this statement.

5   Describe in detail how the market system answers the Fundamental Questions. Why must economic choices be made?

6   Evaluate and explain the following statements:
   a "The capitalistic system is a profit and loss economy."

   b "Competition is the indispensable disciplinarian of the market economy."

   c "Production methods which are inferior in the engineering sense may be the most efficient methods in the economic sense."

---

[3]Howard R. Bowen, *Toward Social Economy* (New York: Holt, Rinehart and Winston, Inc., 1948), p. 249.

[4]Federal Reserve Bank of Philadelphia, "Creeping Inflation," *Business Review,* August 1957, p. 3.

7 Explain fully the meaning and implications of the following quotation.

> The beautiful consequence of the market is that it is its own guardian. If output prices or certain kinds of remuneration stray away from their socially ordained levels, forces are set into motion to bring them back to the fold. It is a curious paradox which thus ensues: the market, which is the acme of individual economic freedom, is the strictest taskmaster of all. One may appeal the ruling of a planning board or win the dispensation of a minister; but there is no appeal, no dispensation, from the anonymous pressures of the market mechanism. Economic freedom is thus more illusory than at first appears. One can do as one pleases in the market. But if one pleases to do what the market disapproves, the price of individual freedom is economic ruination.[5]

8 *Key Question* *Assume that a business firm finds that its profits will be at maximum when it produces $40 worth of product A. Suppose also that each of the three techniques shown in the following table will produce the desired output.*

Resource	Price per unit of resource	Technique no. 1	Technique no. 2	Technique no. 3
Labor	$3	5	2	3
Land	4	2	4	2
Capital	2	2	4	5
Entrepreneurial ability	2	4	2	4

a *Given the resource prices shown, which technique will the firm choose? Why? Will production entail profits or losses? Will the industry expand or contract? When is a new equilibrium output achieved?*

b *Assume now that a new technique, technique No. 4, is developed. It entails the use of 2 units of labor, 2 of land, 6 of capital, and 3 of entrepreneurial ability. Given the resource prices in the table, will the firm adopt the new technique? Explain your answer.*

c *Suppose now that an increase in labor supply causes the price of labor to fall to $1.50 per unit, all other resource prices being unchanged. Which technique will the producer now choose? Explain.*

d *"The market system causes the economy to conserve most in the use of those resources which are particularly scarce in supply. Resources which are scarcest relative to the demand for them have the highest prices. As a result, producers use these resources as sparingly as is possible." Evaluate this statement. Does your answer to question 8c bear out this contention? Explain.*

9 (Last Word) What considerations have increased the popularity of barter in recent years?

[5]Robert L. Heilbroner, *The Worldly Philosophers,* 3d ed. (New York: Simon & Schuster, Inc., 1967), p. 42.

5

THE MIXED ECONOMY: PRIVATE AND PUBLIC SECTORS

This chapter will put meat on the bear-bones model of capitalism developed thus far. Here we will provide some descriptive detail about the private sector (households and businesses) and introduce and analyze the public sector (government) of the economy. Because government is new to our discussion, it will receive most of our attention. Our goal is to understand households, businesses, and governmental units as the primary *decision makers* of our economy.

HOUSEHOLDS AS INCOME RECEIVERS

The household sector is currently composed of some 96 million households. They are the ultimate suppliers of all economic resources and simultaneously the major spenders in the economy. We will consider households first as income receivers and second as spenders.

There are two related approaches to studying income distribution.

1   The **functional distribution** of income indicates how society's money income is divided among wages, rents, interest, and profits. Here total income is distributed according to the function performed by the income receiver. Wages are paid to labor, rents and interest compensate property resources, and profits flow to the owners of corporations and unincorporated businesses.

2   The **personal distribution** of income shows the

way total money income of society is apportioned among individual households.

The Functional Distribution of Income

The functional distribution of the nation's total earned income for 1994 is shown in Figure 5-1. The largest source of income for households is the wages and salaries paid to workers by the businesses and governmental units hiring them. In our capitalist system the bulk of total income goes to labor, not to "capital." Proprietors' income—the incomes of doctors, lawyers, small business owners, farmers, and other unincorporated enterprises—is in fact a combination of wage, profit, rent, and interest incomes. The other three sources of earnings are self-defining. Some households own corporate stock and receive dividend income on their holdings. Many households also own bonds and savings accounts which yield interest income. Rental income results from households pro-

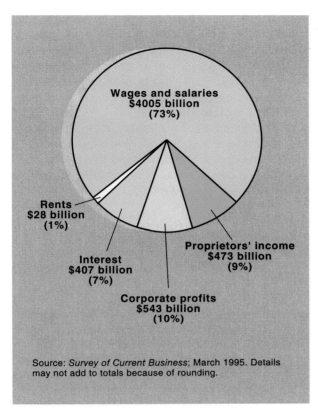

FIGURE 5-1 The functional distribution of income, 1994
Almost three-fourths of national income is received as wages and salaries. Capitalist income—corporate profits, interest, and rents—only account for less than one-fifth of total income.

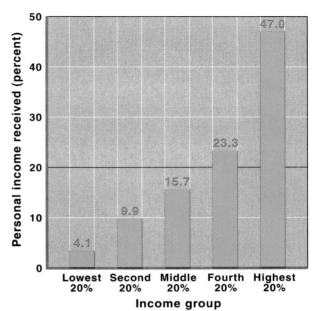

FIGURE 5-2 The distribution of income among families, 1993
Personal income is quite unequally distributed in the United States. An equal distribution would mean that all vertical bars would be equal to the horizontal line drawn at 20 percent; each 20 percent of the families would get 20 percent of total personal income. In fact, the richest fifth of the families gets over eleven times as much income as does the poorest fifth.

viding buildings, land, and other natural resources to businesses.

Personal Distribution of Income

Figure 5-2 is an overall view of how total income is distributed among households. Here we divide families into five numerically equal groups or *quintiles* and show the percentage of total income received by each group. In 1993 the poorest 20 percent of all families received about 4 percent of total personal income in contrast to the 20 percent they would have received if income were equally distributed. In comparison the richest 20 percent of all families received over 47 percent of personal income. The richest fifth of the population received over eleven times as much income as the poorest fifth. Most economists agree

there is considerable inequality in the distribution of income. *(Key Question 2)*

HOUSEHOLDS AS SPENDERS

How do households dispose of their income? Part flows to government as personal taxes, and the rest is divided between personal consumption expenditures and personal saving. In 1994, households disposed of their total personal income as shown in Figure 5-3.[1]

Personal Taxes

Personal taxes, of which the Federal personal income tax is the major component, have risen in both absolute and relative terms since World War II. In 1941,

[1]The income concepts used in Figures 5-1 and 5-3 are different, accounting for the quantitative discrepancy between "total income" in the two figures.

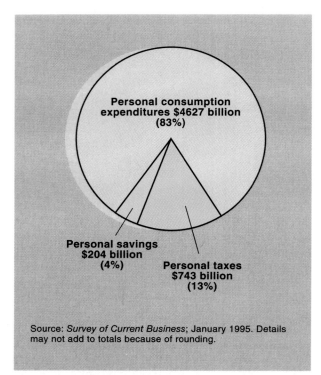

Source: *Survey of Current Business*; January 1995. Details may not add to totals because of rounding.

FIGURE 5-3   The disposition of household income, 1994 Household income is apportioned between taxes, saving, and consumption, with consumption being the dominant use of income.

households paid $3.3 billion, or 3 percent of their $95.3 billion total income, in personal taxes, compared to $743 billion, or 13 percent of $5574 billion total income in 1994.

Personal Saving

Economists define saving as "that part of after-tax income which is *not* consumed"; hence, households have just two choices with their incomes after taxes —to consume or to save. Saving is that portion of current (this year's) income not paid in taxes nor used in the purchase of consumer goods, but which flows into bank accounts, insurance policies, bonds and stocks, and other financial assets.

Reasons for saving center around *security* and *speculation.* Households save to provide a nest egg for unforeseen contingencies—sickness, accident, unemployment—for retirement from the work force, to finance the education of children, or simply for financial security. Also, people save for speculation. You might channel part of your income to purchase securities, speculating they will increase in value.

The desire or willingness to save is not enough. You must be *able* to save, which depends on the size of your income. If your income is very low, you may *dissave;* that is, you may consume in excess of your after-tax income. You do this by borrowing and by digging into savings you may have accumulated in years when your income was higher.

Both saving and consumption vary directly with income; as households get more income, they divide it between saving and consumption. In fact, the top 10 percent of income receivers account for most of the personal saving in our society.

Personal Consumption Expenditures

Figure 5-3 shows that over four-fifths of total income flows from income receivers back into the business sector as personal consumption expenditures.

The size and composition of the economy's total output depend on the size and composition of the flow of consumer spending. So we must examine how households divide their expenditures among the various goods and services competing for their dollars. Consumer spending is classified as (1) expenditures on durables, (2) expenditures on nondurables, and (3) expenditures on services.

If a product generally has an expected life of three years or more, it is called a **durable good;** if its life is less than three years, it is labeled **nondurable.** Automobiles, video recorders, washing machines, personal computers, and most furniture are durables. Most food and clothing items are nondurables. **Services** refer to the work done by lawyers, barbers, doctors, mechanics, and others for consumers. Note in Table 5-1 that *ours is a service-oriented economy in that over one-half of consumer outlays are for services.*

QUICK REVIEW 5-1

■ The functional distribution of income indicates how income is divided among wages, rents, interest, and profits; the personal distribution of income shows how income is apportioned among households.

■ Wages and salaries are the major component of the functional distribution of income. The personal distribution reveals considerable inequality

■ Over 80 percent of household income is consumed; the rest is saved or paid in taxes.

■ Over half of consumer spending is for services.

TABLE 5-1   The composition of personal consumption expenditures, 1994*

Types of consumption	Amount (billions of dollars)	Percent of total
Durable goods	$ 591	13
Motor vehicles and parts	$251	5
Furniture and household equipment	229	5
All others	111	2
Nondurable goods	1394	30
Food	679	15
Clothing and shoes	247	5
Gasoline and oil	107	2
Fuel oil and coal	14	0
All others	347	8
Services	2642	57
Housing	660	14
Household operations	264	6
Medical care	727	16
Transportation	180	4
Personal services recreation, and others	811	18
Personal consumption expenditures	$4627	100

*Excludes interest paid to businesses.
Source: Survey of Current Business, January 1995. Details may not add to totals because of rounding.

THE BUSINESS POPULATION

Businesses constitute the second major aggregate of the private sector. To avoid confusion, we first explain some terms. In particular, we distinguish among a plant, a firm, and an industry.

1   A **plant** is a physical establishment—a factory, farm, mine, retail or wholesale store, or warehouse which performs one or more functions in the fabrication and distribution of goods and services.

2   A business **firm** is the business organization which owns and operates these plants. Most firms operate only one plant, but many own and operate a number of plants. Multiplant firms may be "horizontal," "vertical," or "conglomerate" combinations. For example, every large steel firm—USX Corporation (United States Steel), Bethlehem Steel, Republic Steel, and the others—are **vertical combinations** of plants; that is, each company owns plants at various stages of the production process. Each steelmaker owns ore and coal mines, limestone quarries, coke

ovens, blast furnaces, rolling mills, forge shops, foundries, and, in some cases, fabricating shops.

The large chain stores in the retail field—A&P, Kroger, Safeway, J.C. Penney—are **horizontal combinations** in that each plant is at the same stage of production.

Other firms are **conglomerates;** they comprise plants which operate across many different markets and industries. For example, International Telephone and Telegraph, apart from operations implied by its name, is involved through affiliated plants on a large-scale basis in such diverse fields as hotels, baking products, educational materials, and insurance.

3   An **industry** is a group of firms producing the same, or similar, products. Though an apparently uncomplicated concept, industries are usually difficult to identify in practice. For example, how do we identify the automobile industry? The simplest answer is, "All firms producing automobiles." But automobiles are heterogeneous products. While Cadillacs and Buicks are similar products, and Buicks and Fords are similar, and Fords and Geos are similar, it is clear that Geos and Cadillacs are very dissimilar. At least most buyers think so. And what about trucks? Certainly, small pickup trucks are similar in some respects to vans and station wagons. Is it better to speak of the "motor vehicle industry" rather than of the "automobile industry"?

Delineating an industry becomes even more complex because most enterprises are multiproduct firms. American automobile manufacturers also make such diverse products as diesel locomotives, buses, refrigerators, guided missiles, and air conditioners. For these reasons, industry classifications are usually somewhat arbitrary.

LEGAL FORMS OF BUSINESSES

The business population is extremely diverse, ranging from giant corporations like General Motors with 1993 sales of $134 billion and 711,000 employees to neighborhood speciality shops and "mom and pop" groceries with one or two employees and sales of only $100 or $150 per day. This diversity makes it necessary to classify business firms by some criterion such as legal structure, industry or product, or size. Figure 5-4a shows how the business population is distributed among the three major legal forms: (1) the sole proprietorship, (2) the partnership, and (3) the corporation.

Percentage of firms   **Percentage of sales**

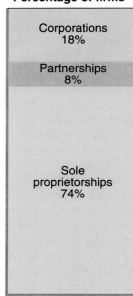

The business population by form
of legal organization

Form	Number of firms
Sole proprietorships*	14,783,000
Partnerships	1,554,000
Corporations	3,717,000
Total	20,054,000

*Excludes farmers.

FIGURE 5-4   The business population and shares of
domestic output
Although sole proprietorships dominate the business population
numerically, corporations account for 90 percent of total sales.

Sole Proprietorship

A **sole proprietorship** is an individual in business for himself or herself. The proprietor owns or obtains the materials and equipment needed by the business and personally supervises its operation.

Advantages   This simple type of business organization has certain advantages:

1   A sole proprietorship is easy to organize—there is virtually no legal red tape or expense.

2   The proprietor is his or her own boss and has substantial freedom of action. Since the proprietor's profit income depends on the enterprise's success, there is a strong and immediate incentive to manage the business efficiently.

Disadvantages   But the disadvantages of this form of business organization are great.

1   With rare exceptions, the financial resources of a sole proprietorship are insufficient to permit the firm to grow into a large enterprise. Finances are usually limited to what the proprietor has in the bank and to what he or she can borrow. Since proprietorships often fail, commercial banks are not eager to extend them credit.

2   Being in complete control of an enterprise forces the proprietor to carry out all management functions. A proprietor must make decisions concerning buying, selling, and the hiring and training of personnel, not to mention the technical aspects involved in producing, advertising, and distributing the product. In short, the potential benefits of specialization in business management are usually inaccessible to the typical small-scale proprietorship.

3   Most important, the proprietor is subject to *unlimited liability*. Individuals in business for themselves risk not only the assets of the firm but also their personal assets. If assets of an unsuccessful proprietorship are insufficient to satisfy the claims of creditors, claims can be filed by creditors against the proprietor's personal property.

Partnership

The **partnership** form of business organization is a natural outgrowth of the sole proprietorship. Partnerships were developed to overcome some of the shortcomings of proprietorships. In a partnership, two or more individuals agree to own and operate a business. Usually they pool their financial resources and business skills. Similarly, they share the risks and the profits or losses.

Advantages   What are the advantages of a partnership?

1   Like the sole proprietorship, it is easy to organize. Although a written agreement is almost invariably involved, legal red tape is not great.

2   Greater specialization in management is possible because there are more participants.

3   Because there are several participants, the odds are that the financial resources of a partnership should be greater than those of a sole proprietorship. Partners can pool their money capital and are usually

somewhat better risks in the eyes of lending institutions.

Disadvantages   The partnership may not overcome the shortcomings of the proprietorship as expected, and may raise some potential problems the sole proprietorship does not have.

1   Whenever several people participate in management, this division of authority can lead to inconsistent policies or to inaction when action is required. Worse yet, partners may disagree on basic policy.

2   The finances of partnerships are still limited, although generally superior to those of a sole proprietorship. But the financial resources of three or four partners may still not be enough for the growth of a successful enterprise.

3   The continuity of a partnership is precarious. The withdrawal or death of a partner generally means dissolution and complete reorganization of the firm, disrupting its operations.

4   Unlimited liability plagues a partnership, just as it does a proprietorship. In fact, each partner is liable for all business debts incurred, not only as a result of each partner's own management decisions, but also as a consequence of the actions of any other partner. A wealthy partner risks money on the prudence of less affluent partners.

Corporation

Corporations are legal entities, distinct and separate from the individuals who own them. These governmentally designated "legal persons" can acquire resources, own assets, produce and sell products, incur debts, extend credit, sue and be sued, and carry on all those functions any other type of enterprise performs.

Advantages   The advantages of the corporate form of business enterprise have catapulted it into a dominant position in modern American capitalism. Although corporations are relatively small in number, they are frequently large in size and scale of operations. As Figure 5-4 indicates, less than 20 percent of all businesses are corporations, but they account for roughly 90 percent of all business sales.

1   The corporation is by far the most effective form of business organization for raising money capital. As this chapter's Last Word reveals, the corporation features unique methods of finance—the selling of stocks and bonds—which allow the firm to tap the savings of untold thousands of households. Through the securities market, corporations can pool the financial resources of extremely large numbers of people.

Financing by the sale of securities also has advantages from the viewpoint of the purchasers of these securities. First, households can now participate in enterprise and share the expected monetary reward without assuming an active part in management. In addition, an individual can spread any risks by buying the securities of several corporations. Finally, it is usually easy for the holder of corporate securities to sell those holdings. Organized stock exchanges make it easy to transfer securities among buyers and sellers, which increases the willingness of savers to buy corporate securities.

Corporations have easier access to bank credit than other types of business organizations. Corporations are better risks and are more likely to provide banks with profitable accounts.

2   Corporations have the distinct advantage of **limited liability.** The owners (stockholders) of a corporation risk *only* what they paid for their stock. Their personal assets are not at stake if the corporation suffers bankruptcy. Creditors can sue the corporation as a legal person, but cannot sue the owners of the corporation as individuals. Limited liability clearly eases the corporation's task in acquiring money capital.

3   Because of their advantage in attracting money capital, successful corporations find it easier to expand the size and scope of their operations and to realize the benefits of expansion. They can take advantage of mass-production technologies and greater specialization in the use of human resources. While the manager of a sole proprietorship may be forced to share her time among production, accounting, and marketing functions, a corporation can hire specialized personnel in these areas and achieve greater efficiency.

4   As a legal entity, the corporation has a life independent of its owners and its officers. Proprietorships are subject to sudden and unpredictable demise, but, legally at least, corporations are immortal. The transfer of corporate ownership through the sale of stock will not disrupt the continuity of the corporation. Corporations have a permanence, lacking in other forms of business organization, which is conducive to long-range planning and growth.

Disadvantages   The corporation's advantages are of tremendous significance and typically override any accompanying disadvantages. Yet there are drawbacks of the corporate form.

1   There are some red tape and legal expense in obtaining a corporate charter.

2   From the social point of view, the corporate form of enterprise lends itself to certain abuses. Because the corporation is a legal entity, unscrupulous business owners sometimes can avoid personal responsibility for questionable business activities by adopting the corporate form of enterprise.

3   A further disadvantage of corporations is the **double taxation** of corporate income. That part of corporate income paid out as dividends to stockholders is taxed twice—once as part of corporate profits and again as part of stockholders' personal incomes.

4   In sole proprietorships and partnerships, the owners of the real and financial assets of the firm also directly manage or control those assets. In large corporations where ownership is widely diffused over tens or hundreds of thousands of stockholders, there is **separation of ownership and control.**

The roots of this cleavage lie in the lethargy of the typical stockholder. Most stockholders do not vote, or, if they do, merely delegate their votes to the corporation's present officers. Not voting, or the automatic signing over of proxy votes to current corporate officials, makes those officials self-perpetuating.

The separation of ownership and control is of no consequence so long as the actions of the control (management) group and the wishes of the ownership (stockholder) group are in accord. But the interests of the two groups are not always identical. Management, seeking the power and prestige which accompany control over a *large* enterprise, may favor unprofitable expansion of the firm's operations. Or a conflict of interest can develop over dividend policies. What portion of corporate earnings after taxes should be paid out as dividends, and what amount should be retained by the firm as undistributed profits? And corporation officials may vote themselves large salaries, pensions, bonuses, and so forth, out of corporate earnings which might otherwise be used for increased dividend payments.

Postscript: A number of states have passed legislation authorizing **limited-liability companies** (LLCs) which seeks to make the corporate advantage of limited liability available to a partnership. The LLC is like an ordinary partnership for tax purposes, but resembles a corporation on liability issues. Like a partnership, a LLC distributes income directly to owners and investors which is treated as personal income for tax purposes. But like a corporation, a LLC shields the personal assets of participants from liability claims.

LLCs have a limited life, typically 30 or 40 years. *(Key Question 4)*

Incorporate or Not?

The need for money capital is critical to whether or not a firm incorporates. The money capital required to establish and operate a barbershop, a shoeshine stand, or a small gift shop is modest, making incorporation unnecessary. In contrast, modern technology and a much larger dollar volume of business make incorporation imperative in many lines of production. In most branches of manufacturing—automobiles, steel, fabricated metal products, electrical equipment, and household appliances—substantial amounts of money are needed for investment in fixed assets and working capital. Here, there is no choice but to incorporate.

Big Business

A glance back at Figure 5-4 reminds us that, although relatively small in number, corporations are the major source of production in our economy. Many of our major industries are dominated by corporate giants which enjoy assets and annual sales revenues of billions of dollars, employ hundreds of thousands of workers, have a hundred thousand or more stockholders, and earn annual profits after taxes running into hundreds of millions of dollars. We have already cited the vital statistics of General Motors, America's largest corporation, for 1993: sales, about $134 *billion;* assets, about $188 *billion;* employees, about 711,000. Remarkably, there are only 20 or so nations in the world whose annual domestic outputs are more than GM's annual sales!

In 1993 some 20 industrial corporations had annual sales over $20 billion; 47 industrial firms realized sales over $10 billion. Realizing that corporations constitute less than 20 percent of the business population, yet produce 90 percent of total business output, suggests the dominant role of large corporations in our economy.

But the influence of large corporations varies significantly from industry to industry. Big business dominates manufacturing and is pronounced in the transportation, communications, power utilities, and banking and financial industries. At the other extreme are some 2 million farmers whose total sales in 1993 were less than the economy's two largest industrial corporations! In between are a variety of retail and service industries characterized by relatively small firms.

Nevertheless, large corporations dominate the American business landscape and grounds exist for labeling the United States a "big business" economy.

ECONOMIC FUNCTIONS OF GOVERNMENT

All economies in the real world are "mixed"; government and the market system share the responsibility of responding to the Five Fundamental Questions. Our economy is predominantly a market economy, yet the economic activities of government are of great significance. Here we want to (1) state and illustrate the major economic functions of the public sector; (2) add government to Chapter 2's circular flow model; and (3) examine the major expenditures and sources of tax revenue for Federal, state, and local governments.

Some economic functions of government strengthen and facilitate the operation of the market system; others supplement and modify pure capitalism.

LEGAL AND SOCIAL FRAMEWORK

Government provides the legal framework and the services needed for a market economy to operate effectively. The legal framework provides the legal status of business enterprises, defines the rights of private ownership, and makes it possible to provide for enforcement of contracts. Government also establishes legal "rules of the game" governing the relationships of businesses, resource suppliers, and consumers with one another. Through legislation, government can referee economic relationships, detect foul play, and exercise authority in imposing appropriate penalties.

Services provided by government include police powers to maintain internal order, a system of standards for measuring the weight and quality of products, and a monetary system to facilitate exchange of goods and services.

The Pure Food and Drug Act of 1906 is an example of how government has strengthened the market system. This act sets rules of conduct governing producers in their relationships with consumers. It prohibits the sale of adulterated and misbranded foods and drugs, requires net weights and ingredients of products to be specified on their containers, establishes quality standards which must be stated on labels of canned foods, and prohibits deceptive claims on patent-medicine labels. These measures are designed to prevent fraudulent activities by producers and to increase the public's confidence in the integrity of the market system. Similar legislation pertains to labor-management relations and relations of business firms to one another.

This type of government activity is presumed to improve resource allocation. Supplying a medium of exchange, ensuring product quality, defining ownership rights, and enforcing contracts increase the volume of exchange. This widens markets and permits greater specialization in the use of property and human resources. Such specialization means a more efficient allocation of resources. However, some argue that government overregulates interactions of businesses, consumers, and workers, stifling economic incentives and impairing productive efficiency.

MAINTAINING COMPETITION

Competition is the basic regulatory mechanism in a capitalistic economy. It is the force which subjects producers and resource suppliers to the dictates of consumer sovereignty. With competition, buyers are the boss, the market is their agent, and businesses are their servants.

It's completely different with **monopoly.** *Monopoly exists when the number of sellers becomes small enough for each seller to influence total supply and therefore the price of the commodity being sold.*

In a monopoly sellers can influence, or "rig," the market in their own self-interests, to the detriment of society as a whole. Through their ability to influence total supply, monopolists can restrict the output of products and enjoy higher prices and, frequently, persistent economic profits. These above-competitive prices and profits directly conflict with the interests of consumers. Monopolists are not regulated by the will of society as are competitive sellers. Producer sovereignty supplants consumer sovereignty to the degree that monopoly supplants competition. In a monopoly resources are allocated in terms of the profit-seeking interests of sellers rather than in terms of the wants of society as a whole. Monopoly causes a misallocation of economic resources.

In the United States, government has attempted to control monopoly primarily in two ways.

1   Regulation and Ownership   In the case of "natural monopolies"—industries in which technological and economic realities rule out competitive markets—government has created public commissions to regulate prices and service standards. Transportation, communications, and electric and other utilities are industries which are regulated in varying degrees. At local levels of government, public ownership of electric and water utilities is common.

2 Antimonopoly Laws In nearly all markets, efficient production can be attained with a high degree of competition. The Federal government has therefore enacted a series of antimonopoly or antitrust laws, beginning with the Sherman Act of 1890, to maintain and strengthen competition as a regulator of business behavior.

Even if the legal foundation of capitalistic institutions is assured and competition is maintained, there is still a need for certain additional economic functions on the part of government. *The market economy has certain biases and shortcomings which compel government to supplement and modify its operation.*

REDISTRIBUTION OF INCOME

The market system is impersonal. It may distribute income with more inequality than society desires. The market system yields very large incomes to those whose labor, by virtue of inherent ability and acquired education and skills, commands high wages. Similarly, those who possess—through hard work or easy inheritance—valuable capital and land receive large property incomes.

But others in our society have less ability, have received modest amounts of education and training, and have accumulated or inherited no property resources. Thus, their incomes are very low. Furthermore, many of the aged, the physically and mentally handicapped, and female-headed families earn only very small incomes or, like the unemployed, no incomes at all through the market system. In the market system there is considerable inequality in the distribution of money income (recall Figure 5-2) and therefore in the distribution of total output among individual households. Poverty amidst overall plenty in our economy persists as a major economic and political issue.

Government's role in ameliorating income inequality is reflected in a variety of policies and programs.

1 Transfers *Transfer payments* provide relief to the destitute, aid to the dependent and handicapped, and unemployment compensation to the unemployed. Social security and Medicare programs provide financial support for the retired and aged sick. These programs transfer income from government to households which would otherwise have little or none.

2 Market Intervention Government also alters the distribution of income by *market intervention,* that is, by modifying the prices established by market forces. Price supports for farmers and minimum-wage legislation are illustrations of government price fixing designed to raise incomes of specific groups.

3 Taxation The personal income tax has been used historically to take a larger proportion of the incomes of the rich than the poor.

REALLOCATION OF RESOURCES

Economists recognize *market failure* occurs when the competitive market system either (1) produces the "wrong" amounts of certain goods and services, or (2) fails to allocate any resources whatsoever to the production of certain goods and services whose output is economically justified. The first case involves "spillovers" or "externalities," the second "public" or "social" goods.

Spillovers or Externalities

The idea that competitive markets automatically bring about efficient resource use rests on the assumption that *all* the benefits and costs of production and consumption of each product are fully reflected in the market demand and supply curves respectively. It is assumed that there are no *spillovers* or *externalities* associated with the production or consumption of any good or service.

A *spillover* occurs when some of the benefits or costs of production or consumption of a good "spillover" onto parties other than the immediate buyer or seller. Spillovers are also called *externalities* because they are benefits and costs accruing to some third party external to the market transaction.

Spillover Costs When production or consumption of a commodity inflicts costs on a third party without compensation, these costs are **spillover costs.** Examples of spillover costs include environmental pollution. When a chemical manufacturer or meat-packing plant dumps its wastes into a lake or river, swimmers, fishermen, and boaters—not to mention communities' water supplies—suffer spillover costs. Human health hazards may arise and wildlife may be damaged or destroyed. When a petroleum refinery pollutes the air with smoke or a paint factory creates distressing odors, the community bears spillover costs for which it is not compensated. Acid rain and global warming are spillover costs which receive almost daily media attention.

What are the economic effects? Recall that costs underlie the firm's supply curve. When a firm avoids some costs by polluting, its supply curve will lie further to the right than when it bears the full costs of production. This results in a larger output and causes an *overallocation* of resources to the production of this good.

Correcting for Spillover Costs   Government can do two things to correct this overallocation of resources. Both are designed to *internalize* the external costs, that is, to make the offending firm pay these costs rather than shift them to society.

1   Legislation   In our examples of air and water pollution, the most direct action is *legislation* prohibiting or limiting pollution. Such legislation forces potential polluters to bear costs of properly disposing of industrial wastes. Firms must buy and install smoke-abatement equipment or facilities to purify water contaminated by manufacturing processes. The idea is to force potential offenders, under the threat of legal action, to bear *all* costs associated with their production.

2   Specific Taxes   A less direct action is based on the fact that taxes are a cost and therefore a determinant of a firm's supply curve (Chapter 3). Government might levy a *specific tax* which equals or approximates the spillover costs per unit of output. Through this tax, government attempts to shove back onto the offending firm those external or spillover costs—which private industry would otherwise avoid—and thus eliminate the overallocation of resources.

Spillover Benefits   But spillovers may also appear as benefits. Production or consumption of certain goods and services may confer spillover or external benefits on third parties or the community at large for which payment of compensation is not required. Measles and polio immunization shots result in direct benefits to the immediate consumer. But immunization against these contagious diseases yields widespread and substantial spillover benefits to the entire community. Discovery of an AIDS vaccine would benefit society far beyond those vaccinated. Unvaccinated individuals would clearly benefit by the slowing of the spread of the disease.

Education is another example of **spillover benefits.** Education benefits individual consumers: "More educated" people generally achieve higher incomes than "less educated" people. But education also provides benefits to society. The economy as a whole benefits from a more versatile and more productive labor force, on the one hand, and smaller outlays on crime prevention, law enforcement, and welfare programs, on the other. There is evidence indicating that any worker with a *given* educational or skill level will be more productive if associated workers have more education. In other words, worker X becomes more productive simply because fellow-workers Y and Z are more educated. Significant, too, is the fact that political participation correlates positively with the level of education in that the percentage of persons who vote increases with educational attainment.

Spillover benefits mean the market demand curve, which reflects only private benefits, understates total benefits. The demand curve for the product lies further to the left than if all benefits were taken into account by the market. This means that a smaller amount is produced or, alternatively stated, there is an *underallocation* of resources to the product.

Correcting for Spillover Benefits   How might the underallocation of resources associated with spillover benefits be corrected? The answer is to either subsidize consumers (increase demand), subsidize producers (increase supply), or, in the extreme, have government produce the product.

1   Increase Demand   In the case of higher education, government provides low-interest student loans and grants to provide student employment. Second example: Our food stamp program is designed to improve the diets of low-income families. The food stamps which government provides can be spent only on food. Stores accepting food stamps are reimbursed with money by the government. Part of the rationale for this program is that improved nutrition will help disadvantaged children perform better in school and disadvantaged adults to be better employees. In helping disadvantaged people become productive participants in the economy, society as a whole benefits.

2 Increase Supply In some cases government might find it more convenient and administratively simpler to subsidize producers. This is also true with higher education where state governments provide substantial portions of the budgets of public colleges and universities. These subsidies lower costs to students and increase educational supply. Public subsidization of immunization programs, hospitals, and medical research are additional examples.

3 Government Provision A third policy option arises if spillover benefits are extremely large: Government may simply choose to finance or, in the extreme, to own and operate such industries. This option leads us into a discussion of public goods and services.

Public Goods and Services

Private goods, which are produced through the market system, are *divisible* in that they come in units small enough to be afforded by individual buyers. Also, private goods are subject to the **exclusion principle,** the idea that those willing and able to pay the equilibrium price get the product, but those unable or unwilling to pay are excluded from the benefits provided by that product.

Certain goods and services—**public** or **social goods**—would not be produced by the market system because their characteristics are opposite those of private goods. Public goods are *indivisible,* involving such large units that they cannot ordinarily be sold to individual buyers. Individuals can buy hamburgers, computers, and automobiles through the market, but not Patriot missiles, highways, space telescopes, and air-traffic control.

More importantly, the exclusion principle does *not* apply to public goods; there is no effective way of excluding individuals from their benefits once those goods come into existence. Obtaining the benefits of private goods is predicated on *purchase;* benefits from public goods accrue to society from the *production* of such goods.

Illustrations The classic public goods example is a lighthouse on a treacherous coast. The construction of a lighthouse would be economically justified if benefits (fewer shipwrecks) exceed production costs. But the benefit accruing to each individual user would not justify the purchase of such a large and indivisible product. But once in operation, its warning light is a guide to *all* ships. There is no practical way to exclude certain ships from its benefits. Therefore, why should any ship owner voluntarily pay for the benefits received from the light? The light is there for all to see, and a ship captain cannot be excluded from seeing it if the ship owner chooses not to pay. Economists call this the **free-rider problem;** *people can receive benefits from a good without contributing to its costs.*

Because the exclusion principle does not apply, there is no economic incentive for private enterprises to supply lighthouses. If the services of the lighthouse cannot be priced and sold, it will be unprofitable for private firms to devote resources to lighthouses. Here is a service which yields substantial benefits but for which the market would allocate no resources. National defense, flood-control, public health, satellite navigation systems, and insect-abatement programs are other public goods. If society is to enjoy such goods and services, they must be provided by the public sector and financed by compulsory charges in the form of taxes.

Large Spillover Benefits While the inapplicability of the exclusion principle distinguishes public from private goods, many other goods and services are provided by government even though the exclusion principle *could* be applied. Such goods and services as education, streets and highways, police and fire protection, libraries and museums, preventive medicine, and sewage disposal could be subject to the exclusion principle. All could be priced and provided by private producers through the market system. But, as noted earlier, these are all services with substantial spillover benefits and would be underproduced by the market system. Therefore, government provides them to avoid the underallocation of resources which would otherwise occur. Such goods and services are called *quasi-public goods.* One can understand the long-standing controversies surrounding the status of medical care and housing. Are these private goods to be provided through the market system, or are they quasi-public goods to be provided by government?

Allocating Resources to Public Goods

The price system will fail to allocate resources for public goods and will underallocate resources for quasi-public goods. What, then, is the mechanism by which such goods get produced?

Public goods are purchased through the government on the basis of group, or collective, choices, in contrast to private goods, which are purchased from private enterprises on the basis of individual choices. The types and quantities of public goods produced are determined in a democracy by political voting. The quantities of the various public goods consumed are a matter of public policy.[2] These group decisions, made in the political arena, supplement the choices of households and businesses in answering the Five Fundamental Questions.

How are resources reallocated from production of private goods to production of public goods? In a full-employment economy, government must free resources from private employment to make them available for production of public goods. The means of releasing resources from private uses is to reduce private demand for them. This is accomplished by levying taxes on businesses and households, diverting some of their incomes—some of their potential purchasing power—out of the income-expenditure stream. With lower incomes, businesses and households must curtail their investment and consumption spending. *Taxes diminish private demands for goods and services, which in turn prompts a drop in the private demand for resources.* By diverting purchasing power from private spenders to government, taxes free resources from private uses.

Government expenditure of the tax proceeds can then reabsorb these resources in the provision of public goods and services. Corporation and personal income taxes release resources from production of investment goods—printing presses, boxcars, warehouses—and consumer goods—food, clothing, and television sets. Government expenditures can reabsorb these resources in production of post offices, military aircraft, and new schools and highways. Government purposely reallocates resources to bring about significant changes in the composition of the economy's total output. *(Key Questions 9 and 10)*

Stabilization

Historically, the most recent function of government is that of stabilizing the economy—assisting the private economy to achieve the full employment of resources and a stable price level. Here we will only outline (rather than fully explain) how government tries to do this.

The level of output depends directly on total or aggregate expenditures. A high level of total spending means it will be profitable for industries to produce large outputs. This means that both property and human resources will be employed at high levels. But aggregate spending may either fall short of, or exceed, that particular level which will provide for full employment and price stability. Two possibilities, unemployment or inflation, may then occur.

1   Unemployment   The level of total spending in the private sector may be too low for full employment. Thus, the government may choose to augment private spending so that total spending—private *and* public—will be sufficient to generate full employment. Government can do this by using the same techniques—government spending and taxes—as it uses to reallocate resources to production of public goods. Specifically, government might increase its own spending on public goods and services on the one hand, and reduce taxes to stimulate private spending on the other.[3]

2   Inflation   The economy may attempt to spend more than its capacity to produce. If aggregate spending exceeds the full-capacity output, the price level will rise. Excessive aggregate spending is inflationary. Government's obligation here is to eliminate the excess spending. It can do this by cutting its own expenditures and by raising taxes to curtail private spending.

---

[2]There are differences between *dollar voting*, which dictates output in the private sector of the economy, and *political voting*, which determines output in the public sector. The rich person has many more votes to cast in the private sector than does the poor person. In the public sector, each—at least in theory—has an equal say. Furthermore, the children who cast their votes for bubble gum and comic books in the private sector are banned by virtue of their age from the registering of social choices.

---

[3]In macroeconomics we learn that government can also use monetary policy—changes in the nation's money supply and interest rates—to help achieve economic stability.

THE CIRCULAR FLOW REVISITED

Government is thoroughly integrated into the real and monetary flows comprising our economy. Let's reexamine the redistributional, allocative, and stabilization functions of government in terms of Chapter 2's circular flow model. In Figure 5-5 flows (1) through (4) restate Figure 2-6. Flows (1) and (2) show business expenditures for the resources provided by households. These expenditures are costs to businesses, but represent wage, rent, interest, and profit income to households. Flows (3) and (4) portray households making consumer expenditures for the goods and services produced by businesses.

Now consider the modifications resulting from the addition of government. Flows (5) through (8) tell us that government makes purchases in both product and resource markets. Specifically, flows (5) and (6) represent government purchasing such things as paper, computers, and military hardware from private businesses. Flows (7) and (8) reflect government purchases of resources. The Federal government employs and pays salaries to members of Congress, the armed forces, Justice Department lawyers, various bureaucrats, and so on. State and local governments hire teachers, bus drivers, police, and firefighters. The Federal government might lease or purchase land to expand a military base; a city may buy land to build a new elementary school.

Government then provides public goods and services to both households and businesses as shown by flows (9) and (10). Financing public goods and services require tax payments by businesses and households as reflected in flows (11) and (12). We have labeled these flows as *net* taxes to acknowledge that they also include "taxes in reverse" in the form of transfer payments to households and subsidies to businesses. Thus, flow (11) entails not merely corporate income, sales, and excise taxes flowing from businesses to government, but also various subsidies to farmers, shipbuilders, and some airlines. Most business subsidies are "concealed" in the form of low-interest loans, loan guarantees, tax concessions, or public facilities provided at prices less than costs. Similarly, government also collects taxes (personal income taxes, payroll taxes) directly from households and makes available transfer payments, for example, welfare payments and social security benefits as shown by flow (12).

Our circular flow model clearly shows how government can alter the distribution of income, reallocate resources, and change the level of economic activity. The structure of taxes and transfer payments can have a significant impact on income distribution. In flow (12) a tax structure which draws tax revenues primarily from well-to-do households combined with a system of transfer payments to low-income households will result in greater equality in the distribution of income.

Flows (6) and (8) imply an allocation of resources different from that of a purely private economy. Government buys goods and labor services which differ from those purchased by households.

Finally, all governmental flows suggest ways government might try to stabilize the economy. If the economy was experiencing unemployment, an increase in government spending with taxes and transfers held constant would increase aggregate spending, output, and employment. Similarly, given the level of government expenditures, a decline in taxes or an increase in transfer payments would increase spendable incomes and boost private spending. Conversely, with inflation the opposite government policies would be in order: reduced government spending, increased taxes, and reduced transfers.

GOVERNMENT FINANCE

How large is the public sector? What are the main economic programs of Federal, state, and local governments? How are these programs financed?

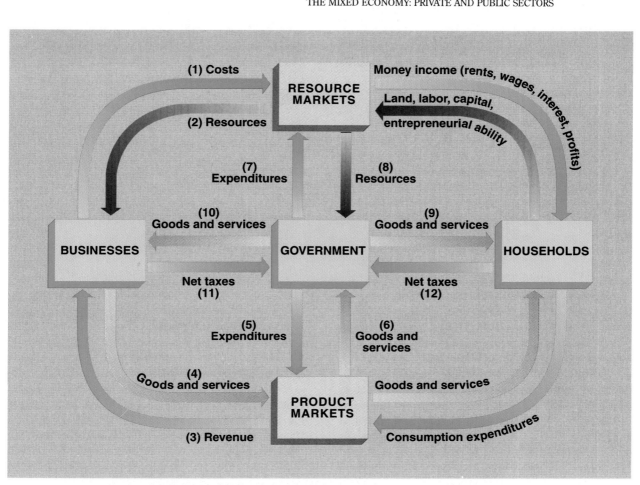

FIGURE 5-5 The circular flow and the public sector
Government expenditures, taxes, and transfer payments affect the distribution of income, the allocation
of resources, and the level of economic activity.

Government Growth: Purchases and Transfers

We can get a general impression of the size and growth of government's economic role by examining government purchases of goods and services and government transfer payments. The distinction between these two kinds of outlays is significant.

1   Government purchases are "exhaustive"; they directly absorb or employ resources and the resulting production is part of the domestic output. For example, the purchase of a missile absorbs the labor of physicists and engineers along with steel, explosives, and a host of other inputs.

2   Transfer payments are "nonexhaustive"; they do not directly absorb resources or account for production. Social security benefits, welfare payments,

veterans' benefits, and unemployment compensation are examples of transfer payments. Their key characteristic is that recipients make no current contribution to output in return for these payments.

Figure 5-6 shows that *government purchases* of goods and services have been approximately 20 percent of domestic output over the past 45 years. Of course, domestic output has increased greatly during that time so that the *absolute* volume of government purchases has increased substantially. Government purchases were $75 billion in 1955 as compared to $1,175 billion in 1994.

But if we now look at *transfer payments* we get a different impression of government's role and growth. As Figure 5-6 reveals, transfers have grown significantly since the 1960s, rising from 5 percent of do-

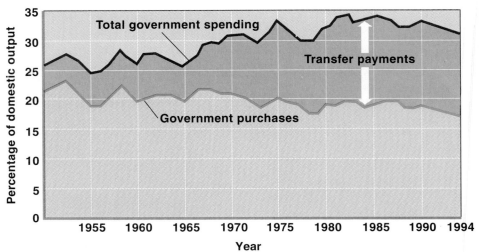

FIGURE 5-6 Government purchases, transfers, and total spending as a percentage of domestic output, 1950–1994
Government purchases have tightly fluctuated around 20 percent of domestic output since 1950. Transfer payments, however, have increased as a percentage of domestic output so that total government spending (purchases plus transfers) have grown and are now about one-third of domestic output.

mestic output in 1960 to over 14 percent in 1994. The net result is that tax revenues required to finance total government spending—purchases plus transfers —are equal to about one-third of domestic output. In 1994 the average taxpayer spent about 2 hours and 45 minutes of each 8-hour workday to pay taxes.

FEDERAL FINANCE

Now let's look separately at the Federal, state, and local units of government to compare their expenditures and taxes. Figure 5-7 tells the story for the Federal government.

FIGURE 5-7 Federal expenditures and tax revenues, 1993
Federal spending is largely on pensions and income security, national defense, health, and interest payments on the public debt. Major revenue sources are the personal income tax, payroll taxes, and the corporate income tax.

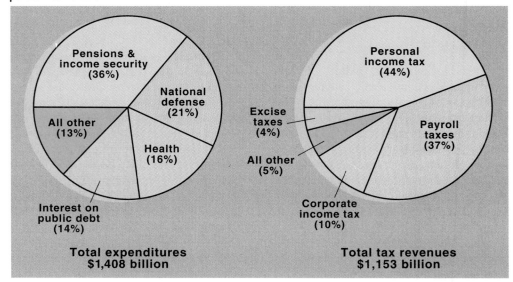

Federal Expenditures

Four important areas of Federal spending stand out: (1) pensions and income security, (2) national defense, (3) health, and (4) interest on the public debt. The *pensions and income security* category reflects the myriad income-maintenance programs for the aged, the disabled, the unemployed, the handicapped, and families with no breadwinner. *National defense* constitutes about one-fifth of the Federal budget and underscores the high costs of military preparedness. *Health* reflects dramatic increases in costs of government health programs for the retired and poor. *Interest on the public debt* has grown dramatically in recent years because the public debt itself has grown.

Federal Tax Revenues

The revenue side of Figure 5-7 clearly shows that the personal income tax, payroll taxes, and the corporate income tax are the basic revenue getters, accounting for 44, 37, and 10 cents of each dollar collected.

Personal Income Tax   The **personal income tax** is the kingpin of our national tax system and merits special comment. This tax is levied on *taxable income,* that is, on the incomes of households and unincorporated businesses after certain exemptions ($2,450 for each household member) and deductions (business expenses, charitable contributions, home mortgage interest payments, certain state and local taxes) are taken into account.

The Federal personal income tax is a *progressive tax,* meaning that people with higher incomes pay a larger percentage of their income as taxes than do persons with lower incomes. The progressivity is achieved through a system of higher tax rates which apply to successive layers or brackets of income.

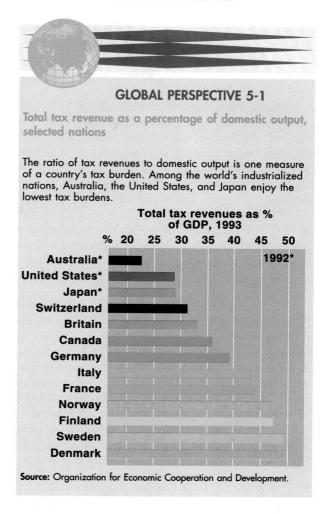

GLOBAL PERSPECTIVE 5-1

Total tax revenue as a percentage of domestic output, selected nations

The ratio of tax revenues to domestic output is one measure of a country's tax burden. Among the world's industrialized nations, Australia, the United States, and Japan enjoy the lowest tax burdens.

Total tax revenues as % of GDP, 1993

Source: Organization for Economic Cooperation and Development.

Columns 1 and 2 of Table 5-2 portray the mechanics of the income tax for a married couple filing a joint return. Note that the 15 percent rate applies to all taxable income up to $36,900, at which point any *additional* income up to $89,150 is taxable at the 28

TABLE 5-2   Federal personal income tax rates, 1995*

(1) Total taxable income	(2) Marginal tax rate (4) ÷ (3)	(3) Change in income Δ(1)	(4) Change in taxes Δ(5)	(5) Total tax	(6) Average tax rate (5) ÷ (1)
$ 0	0%	—	—	—	—
36,900	15	$ 36,900	$ 5,535	$ 5,535	15%
89,150	28	52,250	14,630	20,165	22.6
140,000	31	50,850	15,764	35,929	25.7
250,000	36	110,000	39,600	75,529	30.2
Over 250,000	39.6	—	—	—	

*Data are for a married couple filing a joint return.

percent rate. Additional income between $89,150 and $140,000 is taxed at 31 percent with a 36 percent rate applying to income in the $140,000–$250,000 range. All taxable income above $250,000 is taxed at 39.6 percent.

The tax rates shown in column 2 of Table 5-2 are marginal tax rates. A **marginal tax rate** is the tax paid on additional or incremental income. By definition, it is the *increase* in taxes paid (column 4) divided by the *increase* in income (column 3). Thus, if our couple's taxable income increased from $0 to $36,900, the increase in taxes paid would be $5,535 (= .15 × $36,900) as shown in column 4. If the couple's taxable income rose by an additional $52,250 (column 3)—that is, from $36,900 to $89,150—a higher marginal tax rate of 28 percent would apply so an additional tax of $14,630 (= .28 × $52,250) would have to be paid (column 4).

The marginal tax rates of column 2 overstate the personal income tax bite because the rising rates apply only to income falling within each successive tax bracket. To get a better picture of the tax burden we must consider average tax rates. The **average tax rate** is the total tax paid divided by total taxable income. In column 6 of Table 5-2 for the $0 to $36,900 tax bracket, the average tax rate is $5,535 (column 4) divided by $36,900 (column 1) or 15 percent, the same as the marginal tax rate. But the couple earning $89,150 does *not* pay 28 percent of its income as taxes as the marginal tax rate would suggest. Rather, its average tax rate is only about 22.6 percent (= $20,165 ÷ $89,150). The reason is that the first $36,900 of income is taxed at 15 percent and only the next $52,250 is subject to the 28 percent rate. You should calculate the average tax rate for a couple earning $350,000. What we observe here is that, if the marginal tax rate is higher than the average tax rate, the average tax rate will rise. The arithmetic is the same as what you may have encountered in school. You must get a score on an additional or "marginal" examination higher than your existing average grade to pull your average up!

A tax whose average tax rate rises as income increases is called a *progressive tax.* Such a tax claims both a larger absolute amount and a larger proportion of income as income rises. Thus we can say that our current personal income tax is modestly progressive. *(Key Question 15)*

Payroll Taxes Social security contributions, or **payroll taxes,** are the premiums paid on the compulsory insurance plans—old age insurance and Medicare—provided under social security legislation. These taxes are paid by both employers and employees. Improvements in, and extensions of, our social security programs, plus growth of the labor force, have resulted in very significant increases in payroll taxes in recent years. In 1995 employees and employers each paid a tax of 7.65 percent on the first $61,200 of an employee's annual earnings. Also, employers and employees each pay a 1.45 percent tax on all wages to finance Medicare.

Corporate Income Tax The Federal government also taxes corporate income. This **corporate income tax** is levied on a corporation's profits—the difference between its total revenue and its total expenses. The basic rate is 35 percent, which applies to annual profits above $10 million. A firm with profits of $15 million would pay corporate income taxes of $1,750,000 (= $5 million × .35). Firms making annual profits less than $10 million are taxed at lower rates.

Excise Taxes Commodity or consumption taxes may take the form of **sales taxes** or **excise taxes.** The difference between the two is basically one of coverage. Sales taxes fall on a wide range of products, whereas excises are taxes on a small, select list of commodities. As Figure 5-7 suggests, the Federal government collects excise taxes (on such commodities as alcoholic beverages, tobacco, and gasoline). The Federal government does *not* levy a general sales tax; sales taxes are the bread and butter of most state governments.

STATE AND LOCAL FINANCE

Note in Figure 5-8 that the basic sources of tax revenue at the state level are sales and excise taxes, which account for about 49 percent of all sales tax revenues. State personal income taxes, which entail much more modest rates than those of the Federal income taxes are the second most important source of revenue. Taxes on corporate income, property, inheritances, and licenses and permits constitute the remainder of state tax revenue.

The major outlays of state governments are for (1) public welfare, (2) education, (3) health and hospitals, and (4) highway maintenance and construction.

Figure 5-8 contains aggregated data, telling us little about the finances of individual states. States vary

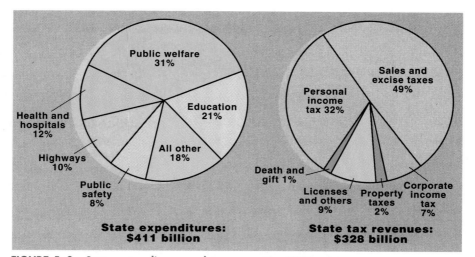

FIGURE 5-8 State expenditures and tax revenues, 1992
State governments spend mainly on public welfare and education. Their primary source of tax revenue comes from sales and excise taxes.

significantly in the types of taxes employed. Thus, although personal income taxes are a major source of revenue for all state governments combined, six states do not use the personal income tax. Furthermore, great variations in the size of tax receipts and disbursements exist among the states.

The receipts and expenditures shown in Figure 5-9 are for all units of local government, including not only cities and towns but also counties, municipalities, townships, and school districts. One source of revenue and one use of revenue stand out: The bulk of

the revenue received by local government comes from **property taxes.** And most local revenue is spent for education.

The gaping deficit found by comparing revenue and expenditure in Figure 5-9 is largely removed when nontax resources of income are taken into account: In 1992 the tax revenues of local governments were supplemented by some $216 billion in intergovernmental grants from Federal and state governments. Furthermore, local governments received an additional $56 billion as proprietary income, that is,

FIGURE 5-9 Local expenditures and tax revenues, 1992
The expenditures of local governments are largely for education and are financed mostly by property taxes.

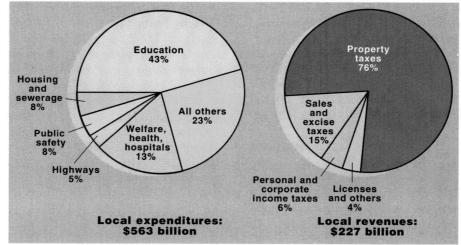

LAST WORD

THE FINANCING OF CORPORATE ACTIVITY

One of the advantages of corporations is their ability to finance their operations through the sale of stocks and bonds. It is informative to examine the nature of corporate finance in more detail.

Generally speaking, corporations finance their activities in three different ways. First, a very large portion of a corporation's activity is financed internally out of undistributed corporate profits. Second, like individuals or unincorporated businesses, corporations may borrow from financial institutions. For example, a small corporation planning to build a new plant may obtain the funds from a commercial bank, a savings and loan association, or an insurance company. Third, unique to corporations, they can issue common stocks and bonds.

Stocks versus Bonds A common stock is an ownership share. The purchaser of a stock certificate has the right to vote for corporate officers and to share in dividends. If you buy 1000 of the 100,000 shares issued by Specific Motors, Inc. (hereafter SM), then you own 1 percent of the company, are entitled to 1 percent of any dividends declared by the board of directors, and control 1 percent of the votes in the annual election of corporate officials.

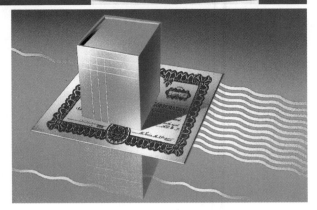

In contrast, a bond is not an ownership share. A bond purchaser is simply lending money to a corporation. A bond is merely an IOU, in acknowledgment of a loan, whereby the corporation promises to pay the holder a fixed amount at some specified future date and other fixed amounts (interest payments) every year up to the bond's maturity date. For example, you might purchase a ten-year SM bond with a face value of $1000 with a 10 percent stated rate of interest. This means that in exchange for your $1000 SM guarantees you a $100 interest payment

---

as revenue from government-owned hospitals and utilities.

QUICK REVIEW 5-3

■ Government purchases are about 20 percent of the domestic output; the addition of transfers increases government spending to almost one-third of domestic output.

■ Income security and national defense are the main Federal expenditures; personal income, payroll, and corporate income taxes are the primary sources of revenue.

■ States rely on sales and excise taxes for revenue; their spending is largely for public welfare, education, health, and highways.

■ Education is the main expenditure for local governments and most of their revenue comes from property taxes.

Fiscal Federalism

Historically, the tax collections of both state and local governments have fallen substantially short of their expenditures. These revenue shortfalls are largely filled by Federal transfers or grants. It is not uncommon for 15 to 20 percent of all revenue received by state and local governments to come from the Federal government. In addition to Federal grants to state and local governments, the states also make grants to local governmental units. This system of intergovernmental transfers is called **fiscal federalism.** Because the Federal budget has suffered large and persistent deficits, Federal grants in recent years have declined. That's why state and local governments have increased tax rates, imposed new taxes, and restrained expenditures.

Lotteries

Both state and local governments have increasingly

for each of the next ten years and then to repay your $1000 principal at the end of that period.

Differences   There are clearly important differences between stocks and bonds. First, as noted, the bondholder is not an owner of the company, but is only a lender. Second, bonds are considered to be less risky than stocks for two reasons. On the one hand, bondholders have a "legally prior claim" upon a corporation's earnings. Dividends cannot be paid to stockholders until all interest payments that are due to bondholders have been paid. On the other hand, holders of SM stock do not know how much their dividends will be or how much they might obtain for their stock if they decide to sell. If Specific Motors falls on hard times, stockholders may receive no dividends at all and the value of their stock may plummet. Provided the corporation does not go bankrupt, the holder of an SM bond is guaranteed a $100 interest payment each year and the return of his or her $1000 at the end of ten years.

Bond Risks   But this is not to imply that the purchase of corporate bonds is riskless. The market value of your SM bond may vary over time in accordance with the financial health of the corporation. If SM encounters economic misfortunes which raise questions about its financial integrity, the market value of your bond may fall. Should you sell the bond prior to maturity you may receive only $600 or $700 for it (rather than $1000) and thereby incur a capital loss.

Changes in interest rates also affect the market prices of bonds. Specifically, increases in interest rates cause bond prices to fall and vice versa. Assume you purchase a $1000 ten-year SM bond this year (1996) when the interest rate is 10 percent. This obviously means that your bond provides a $100 fixed interest payment each year. But now suppose that by next year the interest rate has jumped to 15 percent and SM must now guarantee a $150 fixed annual payment on its new 1997 $1000 ten-year bonds. Clearly, no sensible person will pay you $1000 for your bond which pays only $100 of interest income per year when new bonds can be purchased for $1000 which pay the holder $150 per year. Hence, if you sell your 1993 bond before maturity, you will suffer a capital loss.

Bondholders face another element of risk due to inflation. If substantial inflation occurs over the ten-year period you hold a SM bond, the $1000 principal repaid to you at the end of that period will represent substantially less purchasing power than the $1000 you loaned to SM ten years earlier. You will have lent "dear" dollars, but will be repaid in "cheap" dollars.

turned to **lotteries** as a means of closing the gaps between their tax receipts and expenditures. In 1993 some 37 states had lotteries which sold $25 billion of tickets.

Lotteries are controversial. Critics argue that (1) it is morally wrong for states to sponsor gambling; (2) lotteries generate compulsive gamblers who impoverish themselves and their families; (3) low-income families spend a larger proportion of their incomes on lotteries than do high-income families; (4) as a cash business, lotteries attract criminals and other undesirables; and, (5) lotteries send the message that luck and fate—rather than education, hard work, and saving and investing—are the route to wealth.

Defenders contend that (1) lotteries are preferable to taxes because they are voluntary rather than compulsory; (2) they are a painless way to finance government services such as education, medical care, and welfare; and (3) lotteries are competitive with illegal gambling and thus socially beneficial in curtailing organized crime.

CHAPTER SUMMARY

1   The functional distribution of income shows how society's total income is divided among wages, rents, interest, and profits; the personal distribution of income shows how total income is divided among individual households.

2   Households divide their total incomes among personal taxes, saving, and consumer goods. Over half of consumption expenditures are for services.

3   Sole proprietorships, partnerships, and corporations are the major legal forms of business enterprises. Corporations dominate the business sector because they   a have limited liability, and **b** can acquire money capital for expansion more easily than other firms.

4 Government enhances the operation of the market system by **a** providing an appropriate legal and social framework, and **b** acting to maintain competition.

5 Government alters the distribution of income by direct market intervention and through the tax-transfer system.

6 Spillovers or externalities cause the equilibrium output of certain goods to vary from the optimal output. Spillover costs result in an overallocation of resources which can be corrected by legislation or specific taxes. Spillover benefits are accompanied by an underallocation of resources which can be corrected by subsidies to either consumers or producers.

7 Government must provide public goods because such goods are indivisible and entail benefits from which nonpaying consumers cannot be excluded.

8 The manipulation of taxes and its expenditures is one way by which government can reduce unemployment and inflation.

9 The circular flow model helps us envision how government performs its redistributional, allocative, and stabilizing functions.

10 Government purchases exhaust or absorb resources; transfer payments do not. Government purchases have been about 20 percent of domestic output since 1950. However, transfers have grown significantly, so total government spending is now about one-third of domestic output.

11 The main categories of Federal spending are for pensions and income security, national defense, health, and interest on the public debt; revenues come primarily from personal income, payroll, and corporate income taxes.

12 The primary sources of revenue for the states are sales and excise taxes; public welfare, education, health and hospitals, and highways are the major state expenditures.

13 At the local level, most revenue comes from the property tax, and education is the most important expenditure.

14 Under our system of fiscal federalism, state and local tax revenues are supplemented by sizable revenue grants from the Federal government.

TERMS AND CONCEPTS

functional and personal distribution of income	conglomerates	limited-liability companies	personal income tax
durable and nondurable goods	industry	monopoly	marginal and average tax rates
services	sole proprietorship	spillover costs and spillover benefits	payroll taxes
plant	partnership	exclusion principle	corporate income tax
firm	corporation	public or social goods	sales and excise taxes
horizontal and vertical combinations	limited liability	free-rider problem	property taxes
	separation of ownership and control	government purchases	fiscal federalism
	double taxation	transfer payments	lotteries

QUESTIONS AND STUDY SUGGESTIONS

1 Distinguish between functional and personal distributions of income.

2 *Key Question* *Assume the five residents of Econoville receive incomes of $50, $75, $125, $250, and $500. Present the resulting personal distribution of income as a graph similar to Figure 5-2. Compare the incomes of the lowest and highest fifth of the income receivers.*

3 Distinguish clearly between a plant, a firm, and an industry. Why is an "industry" often difficult to define in practice?

4 *Key Question* *What are the major legal forms of business organization? Briefly state the advantages and disadvantages of each. How do you account for the dominant role of corporations in our economy?*

5 "The legal form which an enterprise assumes is dictated primarily by the financial requirements of its particular line of production." Do you agree?

6 Enumerate and briefly discuss the main economic functions of government.

7 What divergencies arise between equilibrium and an efficient output when **a** spillover costs and **b** spillover benefits are present? How might government correct for these discrepancies? "The presence of spillover costs suggests underallocation of resources to that product and the need for governmental subsidies." Do you agree? Explain how zoning and seat belt laws might be used to deal with a problem of spillover costs.

8 UCLA researchers have concluded that injuries caused

by firearms cost about $429 million a year in hospital expenses alone. Because the majority of those shot are poor and without insurance, almost 86 percent of hospital costs must be borne by taxpayers. Use your understanding of externalities to recommend appropriate policies.

9 *Key Question What are the basic characteristics of public goods? Explain the significance of the exclusion principle. By what means does government provide public goods?*

10 *Key Question Draw a production possibilities curve with public goods on the vertical axis and private goods on the horizontal axis. Assuming the economy is initially operating on the curve, indicate the means by which the production of public goods might be increased. How might the output of public goods be increased if the economy is initially functioning at a point inside the curve?*

11 Use your understanding of the characteristics of private and public goods to determine whether the following should be produced through the market system or provided by government: a bread; b street lighting; c bridges; d parks; e swimming pools; f medical care; g mail delivery; h housing; i air traffic control; j libraries.

12 Explain how government might manipulate its expenditures and tax revenues to reduce a unemployment and b the rate of inflation.

13 "Most governmental actions simultaneously affect the distribution of income, the allocation of resources, and the levels of unemployment and prices." Use the circular flow model to confirm this assertion for each of the following: a the construction of a new high school in Blackhawk County; b a 2 percent reduction in the corporate income tax; c an expansion of preschool programs for disadvantaged children; d a $50 million increase in spending for space research; e the levying of a tax on air polluters; and f a $1 increase in the minimum wage.

14 What is the most important source of revenue and the major type of expenditure at the Federal level? At the state level? At the local level?

15 *Key Question Suppose in Fiscalville there is no tax on the first $10,000 of income, but earnings between $10,000 and $20,000 are taxed at 20 percent and income between $20,000 and $30,000 at 30 percent. Any income above $30,000 is taxed at 40 percent. If your income is $50,000, how much in taxes will you pay? Determine your marginal and average tax rates. Is this a progressive tax?*

6

THE UNITED STATES IN THE GLOBAL ECONOMY

Backpackers in the wilderness like to think they are "leaving the world behind," but, like Atlas, they carry the world on their shoulders. Much of their backpacking equipment is imported—knives from Switzerland, rain gear from South Korea, cameras from Japan, aluminum pots made in England, miniature stoves from Sweden, sleeping bags from China, and compasses from Finland. Some backpackers wear hiking boots from Italy, sunglasses made in France, and watches from Japan or Switzerland. Moreover, they may drive to the trailheads in Japanese-made Toyotas or Swedish-made Volvos, sipping coffee from Brazil or snacking on bananas from Honduras.

International trade and the global economy affect all of us daily, whether we are hiking in the wilderness, driving our cars, listening to music, or working at our jobs. We cannot "leave the world behind." We are enmeshed with the rest of the world in a complex web of economic relationships—trade of goods and services, multinational corporations, cooperative ventures among the world's firms, and ties among the world's financial markets. This web is so complex that it is difficult to determine just what is—or isn't—an American product! RCA television sets are made by a company based in France; a Canadian company owns Tropicana Orange Juice; and the parent company of Gerber baby food is Swiss. The Chevrolet Lumina sedan is manufactured in Canada and a British corporation owns Burger King. Many "American" products are made with components from abroad. For example, international firms supply major components of the new "American" Boeing 777 airplane (see Figure 6-1), and, conversely, many "foreign" products contain numerous American-produced parts.

This chapter will introduce the basic principles underlying the global economy (a more advanced discussion of international economics is found in the last Part). We first look at the growth of world trade, the United States' role in it, and factors causing the growth. Next, Chapter 5's circular flow diagram is modified to account for international trade flows. We then explore the basis for world trade, focusing on the concept of comparative advantage. Foreign currencies and exchange rates are discussed. Next, some restrictive trade practices implemented by nations are examined, leading to a discussion of multilateral trade agreements and free-trade regions of the globe. We conclude with some answers to the question: "Can American firms compete?"

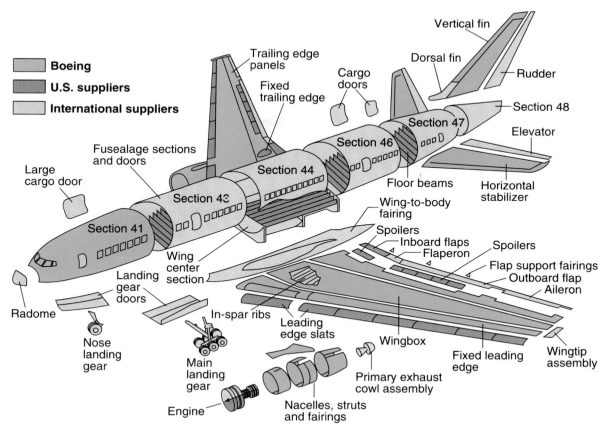

FIGURE 6-1 The Boeing 777: who supplies the parts?
International firms supply major components of the "American" Boeing 777 aircraft. (*Seattle Post Intelligencer.* Reprinted by permission.)

GROWTH OF WORLD TRADE

The volume of world trade is so large and its characteristics so unique that it requires special consideration.

Volume and Pattern

Table 6-1 provides a rough index of the importance of world trade for several representative countries. Many nations with restricted resource bases and limited domestic markets cannot produce with reasonable efficiency the variety of goods they want to consume. For such countries, exports—sales abroad—are the route for obtaining imported goods they de-

TABLE 6-1 Exports of goods and services as a percentage of GDP, selected countries, 1993

Country	Exports as percentage of GDP
The Netherlands	52
Germany	37
New Zealand	33
Canada	30
United Kingdom	27
France	23
Italy	22
United States	11
Japan	9

Source: IMF, *International Financial Statistics,* 1994.

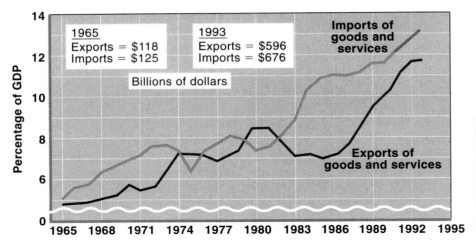

FIGURE 6-2   United States trade as percentage of GDP American imports and exports have increased in volume and have more than doubled as a percentage of GDP since 1965. [*Economic Report of the President, 1994*. Data are from the national income accounts and are adjusted for inflation (1987 dollars).]

sire. Therefore, exports may run from 25 to 35 percent of their domestic outputs. Other countries, the United States, for example, have rich and diversified resource bases and vast internal markets. They are less dependent on world trade.

Volume   For the United States and the world the volume of international trade has been increasing both absolutely and relatively. A comparison of the boxed data in Figure 6-2 reveals the substantial growth in the absolute dollar volume of both American exports and imports over the past several decades. The lines in the figure show the growth of exports and imports of goods and services as a percentage of gross domestic product (GDP)—the dollar value of all goods and services produced within the United States. Exports and imports currently are 11 to 13 percent of GDP, more than double their percentages in 1965.

However, the United States accounts for a diminishing percentage of total world trade. In 1947 it supplied about one-third of the world's total exports compared to about one-eighth today. World trade has increased more rapidly for other nations than it has for the United States. *But in terms of absolute volumes of imports and exports the United States is the world's leading trading nation.*

Dependence   There can be no question as to the United States' dependence on the world economy. We are almost entirely dependent on other countries for bananas, cocoa, coffee, spices, tea, raw silk, nickel, tin, natural rubber, and diamonds. Casual observation suggests that imported goods compete in many of our domestic markets: Japanese cameras and video

recorders, French and Italian wines, Swiss and Austrian snow skis, and Japanese motorcycles and autos are a few examples. Foreign cars now account for about 33 percent of the total car sales in the United States. Even the great American pastime—baseball—relies heavily on imported gloves and baseballs.

But world trade is a two-way street, and many American industries are highly dependent on foreign markets. Almost all segments of agriculture rely on foreign markets—rice, wheat, cotton, and tobacco exports vary from one-fourth to more than one-half of total output. The chemical, aircraft, automobile, machine tool, coal, and computer industries are only a few of many American industries which sell significant portions of their output in international markets. Table 6-2 shows some of the major commodity exports and imports of the United States.

Trade Patterns   Tables 6-2 and 6-3 provide an overall picture of the pattern of United States merchandise trade. Note the following:
1   In 1993 our imports of goods exceeded our exports by $133 billion. (Not shown, our exports of services, however, exceeded our imports by $57 billion.)
2   Most of our export and import trade is with other industrially advanced nations, not with the less developed nations or the countries of eastern Europe.
3   Canada is our most important trading partner quantitatively. Twenty-two percent of our exports are sold to Canadians, who in turn provide us with 19 percent of our imports.
4   There is a sizable imbalance in our trade with Japan ($60 billion); our imports greatly exceed our exports. Large American imports of Japanese autos

TABLE 6-2 Principal commodity exports and imports of the United States, 1993 (dollars in billions)

Exports	Amount	Imports	Amount
Chemicals	$30.1	Automobiles	$52.2
Computers	29.3	Petroleum	51.5
Consumer durables	26.6	Computers	38.0
Aircraft	20.1	Clothing	31.7
Semiconductors	19.1	Household appliances	22.5
Generating equipment	17.0	Semiconductors	19.5
Nonferrous metals	14.6	Chemicals	18.1
Automobiles	14.5	Toys and sporting goods	12.4
Grains	14.4	Iron and steel	11.8
Telecommunications	13.5	Telecommunications	11.3

Source: Consolidated from Department of Commerce data.

and electronic goods explain most of this trade imbalance.

5 Our dependence on foreign oil is reflected in the excess of imports in our trade with countries belonging to the Organization of Petroleum Exporting Countries (OPEC).

6 We import some of the same categories of goods that we export (specifically, automobiles, computers, chemicals, semiconductors, and telecommunications equipment).

Linkages Table 6-3 also implies complex financial linkages among nations. How is the $133 billion trade deficit reported in Table 6-3 financed? How does a nation—or an individual—obtain more goods from others than it provides to them? The answer is by either borrowing from them or by giving up ownership of some of your assets or wealth. This is what has been happening to the United States. We have financed our trade deficits by borrowing from (selling securities to) other nations. The United States is now the world's largest debtor nation. Moreover, nations with which we have large trade deficits, such as Japan, are acquiring assets in America. CBS Records and Firestone Tire now are owned by Japanese firms; Doubleday publishing and RCA are owned by German firms;

TABLE 6-3 United States merchandise exports and imports by area, 1993

Export to	Value (in billions of dollars)		Percent-age of total		Import from	Value (in billions of dollars)		Percent-age of total	
Industrial countries	$267		58		Industrial countries	$345		58	
Canada		101		22	Canada		113		19
Japan		47		10	Japan		107		18
Western Europe		111		24	Western Europe		121		21
Australia		8		2	Australia		3		1
Developing countries	183		40		Developing countries	241		41	
Mexico		41		9	Mexico		40		7
OPEC		14		3	OPEC		24		4
Other		128		28	Other		181		31
Eastern Europe	6		1		Eastern Europe	4		1	
Total	$457		100			$590		100	

Note: Data are on an international transactions basis and exclude military shipments. Data will not add to totals because of rounding.
Source: Survey of Current Business, September 1994.

and Standard Oil and Holiday Inns are in British hands.

Facilitating Factors

Several factors have facilitated the rapid growth of international trade since World War II.

Transportation Technology   High transportation costs are a barrier to any type of trade, particularly trade between distant places. But improvements in transportation have shrunk the globe, fostering world trade. Airplanes now transport low-weight, high-value items such as diamonds and semiconductors quickly from one nation to another. We now routinely transport oil in massive tankers, greatly reducing the cost of transportation per barrel. Grain is loaded onto ocean-going ships at modern, efficient grain silos at Great Lakes and coastal ports. Container ships transport self-contained railroad boxes directly to foreign ports, where cranes place the containers onto railroad cars for internal shipment. Natural gas flows through large-diameter pipelines from exporting to importing countries—for instance, from Russia to Germany and Canada to the United States. Workers clean fish on large processing ships directly on the fishing grounds. Refrigerated vessels then transport the fish to overseas ports. Commercial airplane manufacturers deliver new aircraft within a matter of hours by simply flying them directly to their foreign customers.

Communications Technology   World trade has expanded as well due to dramatic improvements in communications technology. Telephones, fax (facsimile) machines, and computers now directly link traders around the world, allowing exporters to assess the potential for selling products abroad and consummate trade deals. New communications methods enable us to move money around the world in the blink of an eye. Exchange rates, stock prices, and interest rates flash onto computer screens nearly simultaneously in Los Angeles, London, and Lisbon.

In short, exporters and importers today can as easily communicate between Sweden and Australia as between San Francisco and Oakland. A distributor in Florida can get a price quote on 1000 woven baskets in Thailand as quickly as a quotation on 1000 bottles of bourbon in Kentucky.

General Decline in Tariffs   Tariffs—excise taxes or duties on imported products—have had their ups and downs, but since 1940 have generally fallen worldwide. A glance ahead to Figure 6-6 shows that United States' tariff duties as a percentage of dutiable imports are now about 5 percent, down from 40 percent in 1940. Many nations still have barriers to free trade, but, on average, tariffs have fallen greatly, increasing international trade.

Peace   During World War II powerful industrial countries fought one another, certainly disrupting international trade. Not only has trade since been restored, it has been bolstered by peaceful relations and by trade-conducive institutions linking most industrial nations. In particular, Japan and Germany—two defeated World War II powers—now are major participants in world trade.

Participants

All nations of the world participate to some extent in international trade.

United States, Japan, and western Europe   As shown in Global Perspective 6-1, the top participants in world trade are the United States, Germany, and Japan. In 1993 these three nations had combined exports of $1.2 trillion. Along with Germany, other western European nations such as France, Britain, and Italy are major exporters and importers. In fact, three major "players"—the United States, Japan, and the western European nations—now dominate world trade. These three areas also form the heart of the world's financial system and headquarter most of the world's large **multinational corporations**—firms with sizable foreign production and distribution assets. Among the world's top twenty-five multinationals are Royal Dutch Shell and Unilever (Britain/Netherlands); Ford Motor, General Motors, and IBM (United States); British Petroleum (Britain); Nestlé (Switzerland); Fiat (Italy); Siemens and Bayer Chemicals (Germany); Mitsubishi and Mitsui (Japan); and Alcatel Alstrom (France).

New Players   New, important participants have arrived on the world trade scene. One such group of nations is the newly industrializing Asian economies of Hong Kong, Singapore, South Korea, and Taiwan. These **"Asian tigers"** have expanded their share of world exports from about 3 percent in 1972 to more than 9 percent today. Together, they export about as much as Japan and much more than either France,

Britain, or Italy. Other countries in southeast Asia, particularly Malaysia and Indonesia, have also expanded their international trade.

China, with its increasing reliance on the market system, is another emerging trading power. Since initiating market reforms in 1979, its annual growth of output has averaged nearly 10 percent (compared to 2 to 3 percent annually in the United States). At this remarkable rate, China's total output nearly doubles every seven years! An upsurge of exports and imports has accompanied this expansion of output. In 1989 Chinese exports and imports each were about $50 billion. In 1994 they each topped $90 billion, with 30 percent of China's exports going to the United States. Also, China has been attracting much foreign investment. In 1993 alone, it contracted for about $100 billion of foreign-produced capital to be delivered during the next several years. Experts predict China will become one of the world's leading trade nations.

The collapse of communism in eastern Europe and the former Soviet Union has also altered world trade patterns. Before this collapse, the eastern European nations of Poland, Hungary, Czechoslovakia, and East Germany mainly traded with the Soviet Union and its political allies such as North Korea and Cuba. Today, East Germany is reunited with West Germany, and Poland, Hungary, and the Czech Republic have established new trade relationships with Europe and America.

Russia itself has initiated far-reaching market reforms, including widespread privatization of industry, and has consummated major trade deals with firms from across the globe. Although its transition to capitalism has not been smooth, no doubt Russia can be a major trading power. Other former Soviet republics —now independent nations—such as Ukraine and Estonia also are opening their economies to international trade and finance.

BACK TO THE CIRCULAR FLOW

Now that we have an idea of the size and growth of world trade, we need to represent it as "the Rest of the World" in Chapter 5's circular flow model. In Figure 6-3 we make two adjustments to Figure 5-5:

1 Our previous "Resource Markets" and "Product Markets" now become "U.S. Resource Markets" and "U.S. Product Markets." Similarly, we add the modifier "U.S." to the "Businesses," "Government," and "Households" sectors.

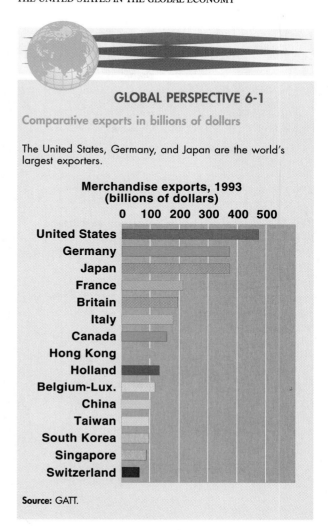

GLOBAL PERSPECTIVE 6-1

Comparative exports in billions of dollars

The United States, Germany, and Japan are the world's largest exporters.

**Merchandise exports, 1993
(billions of dollars)**

	0	100	200	300	400	500
United States						
Germany						
Japan						
France						
Britain						
Italy						
Canada						
Hong Kong						
Holland						
Belgium-Lux.						
China						
Taiwan						
South Korea						
Singapore						
Switzerland						

Source: GATT.

2 We place the foreign sector—the "Rest of the World"—at the bottom of the circular flow diagram. This sector designates all foreign nations with which we deal and the individuals, businesses, and governments comprising them.

Flow (13) shows that people, businesses, and governments abroad buy American products—our exports—from our product market. This real flow of American exports to foreign nations is accompanied by a monetary revenue flow (14) from the rest of the world to us. In response to these revenues from abroad, American businesses demand more domestic resources to produce the goods for export; they are on the demand side of the resource market. Thus, the domestic flow (1) of money income (rents, wages, interest, and profits) to American households rises.

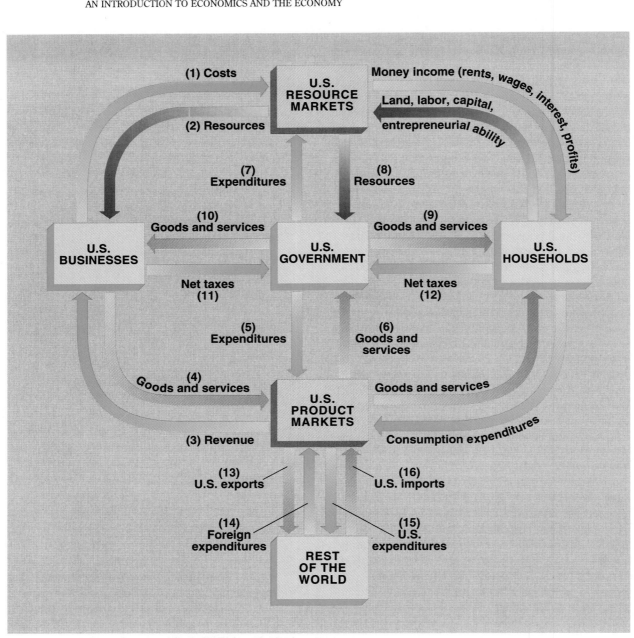

FIGURE 6-3   **The circular flow with the foreign sector**
Flows 13–16 in the lower portion of the diagram show how the United States economy interacts with the "Rest of the World." People abroad buy American exports, contributing to our business revenues and money incomes. Americans, in turn, spend part of their incomes to buy imports from abroad. Income from a nation's exports helps pay for its imports.

But U.S. exports are only half the picture. Flow (15) shows that American households, businesses, and government spend some of their income on foreign products. These products, of course, are our imports—flow (16)—in the circular flow. Purchases of imports, say, autos and electronics, contribute to foreign output and income, which in turn enable foreign households to buy U.S. exports.

Our circular flow model is a simplification which emphasizes product market effects, but a few other

United States–Rest of the World relationships also merit mention. Specifically, there are linkages between the U.S. resource market and the rest of the world.

America imports and exports not only products but resources as well. For example, we import crude oil and export raw logs. Moreover, some American firms engage in "offshore" production, which diverts spending on capital from our domestic resource market to resource markets in other nations. For instance, General Motors might build an auto assembly plant in Canada or Germany. Or, flowing in the other direction, Sony might construct a plant for manufacturing CD players in the United States.

There are also international flows of labor. About 1 million legal and illegal immigrants enter the United States each year, expanding the availability of labor resources in the United States and raising our total output and income. On the other hand, immigration increases labor supply in specific American labor markets, pulling down wage rates for some types of American labor.

The expanded circular flow model (Figure 6-3) also demonstrates that a nation engaged in world trade risks instability which would not affect a "closed" nation (Figure 5-5). For example, recessions and inflation can be highly contagious among trading nations. Suppose that the nations of western Europe experience a severe recession. As their incomes decline, they would purchase fewer American exports. As a result, flows (13) and (14) in Figure 6-3 would decline and inventories of unsold American goods would rise. American firms would respond by reducing their production and employment, which diminishes the flow of money income to American households [flow (1)]. Recession in Europe might contribute to a recession in the United States.

Figure 6-3 also helps us see that the foreign sector alters resource allocation and incomes in the U.S. economy. With a foreign sector, we produce more of some goods (our exports) and fewer of others (our imports) than we would otherwise. Thus, American labor and other productive resources are shifted toward export industries and away from import industries. We use more of our resources to make commercial aircraft and to grow wheat and less to make autos and clothing. So we ask: "Do these shifts of resources make any economic sense? Do they enhance our total output and thus our standard of living?" We look at some answers next. *(Key Question 3)*

SPECIALIZATION AND COMPARATIVE ADVANTAGE

Specialization and trade increase the productivity of a nation's resources and allow for larger total output than otherwise. This notion is not new! According to Adam Smith in 1776:

> It is the maxim of every prudent master of a family, never to attempt to make at home what it will cost him more to make than to buy. The taylor does not attempt to make his own shoes, but buys them from the shoemaker. The shoemaker does not attempt to make his own clothes, but employs a taylor. The farmer attempts to make neither the one or the other, but employs those different artificers. . . .
>
> What is prudence in the conduct of every private family, can scarce be folly in that of a great kingdom. If a foreign country can supply us with a commodity cheaper than we can make it, better buy it of them with some part of the produce of our own industry, employed in a way in which we have some advantage.[1]

Nations specialize and trade for the same reasons as individuals: Specialization and exchange among in-

---

[1]Adam Smith, *The Wealth of Nations* (New York: Modern Library, Inc., 1937), p. 424. (Originally published in 1776.)

dividuals, regions, and nations result in greater over-all output and income.

Basic Principle

In the early 1800s British economist David Ricardo expanded Smith's idea, correctly observing that it pays for a person or a country to specialize and exchange even if that person or nation is more productive than a potential trading partner in *all* economic activities.

Consider the certified public accountant (CPA) who is also a skilled house painter. Suppose the CPA can paint her house in less time than the professional painter she is thinking of hiring. Also suppose the CPA can earn $50 per hour doing her accounting and must pay the painter $15 per hour. Let's say that it will take the accountant 30 hours to paint her house; the painter, 40 hours.

Should the CPA take time from her accounting to paint her own house or should she hire the painter? The CPA's opportunity cost of painting her house is $1500 (= 30 hours × $50 per hour of sacrificed income). The cost of hiring the painter is only $600 (= 40 hours × $15 per hour paid to the painter). Although the CPA is better at both accounting and painting, her relative or comparative advantage lies in accounting. She will *lower the cost of getting her house painted* by specializing in accounting and using some of the earnings from accounting to hire a house painter.

Similarly, the house painter can reduce his cost of obtaining accounting services by specializing in painting and using some of his income to hire the CPA to prepare his income tax forms. Suppose that it would take the painter 10 hours to prepare his tax return, while the CPA could handle this task in 2 hours. The house painter would sacrifice $150 of income (= 10 hours × $15 per hour of sacrificed time) to accomplish a task which he could hire the CPA to do for $100 (= 2 hours × $50 per hour of the CPA's time).

By using the CPA to prepare his tax return, the painter *lowers his cost of getting the tax return completed*.

What is true for our CPA and house painter is also true for nations. Countries can reduce their cost of obtaining desirable goods by specializing in production where they have comparative advantages.

Comparative Costs

Our simple example clearly shows that specialization is economically desirable because it results in more efficient production. To understand the global economy, let's now put specialization in the context of trading nations, employing the familiar concept of the production possibilities table for our analysis. Suppose production possibilities for Mexico and the United States are as shown in Tables 6-4 and 6-5. In these tables we assume constant costs. Each country must give up a constant amount of one product in securing constant increments of the other product. (This assumption will simplify our discussion without impairing the validity of our conclusions.)

Specialization and trade are mutually beneficial or "profitable" to the two nations if the comparative costs of the two products within the two nations differ. What are the domestic comparative costs of avocados and soybeans in Mexico? Comparing production alternatives A and B in Table 6-4, we see that 5 tons of soybeans (= 15 − 10) must be sacrificed to produce 20 tons of avocados (= 20 − 0). Or, more simply, in Mexico it costs 1 ton of soybeans to produce 4 tons of avocados—that is, $1S = 4A$. Because we assumed constant costs, this domestic comparative-cost relationship will not change as Mexico expands the output of either product. This is evident from production possibilities B and C, where we see that 4 more tons of avocados (= 24 − 20) cost 1 unit of soybeans (= 10 − 9).

Similarly, in Table 6-5, comparing production alternatives R and S reveals that at a domestic opportunity cost of 10 tons of soybeans (= 30 − 20),

TABLE 6-4 Mexico's production possibilities table (in tons)

Product	Production alternatives				
	A	B	C	D	E
Avocados	0	20	24	40	60
Soybeans	15	10	9	5	0

TABLE 6-5 United States' production possibilities table (in tons)

Product	Production alternatives				
	R	S	T	U	V
Avocados	0	30	33	60	90
Soybeans	30	20	19	10	0

Americans can obtain 30 tons of avocados (= 30 − 0). That is, the domestic comparative-cost ratio for the two products in the United States is $1S = 3A$. Comparing production alternatives S and T demonstrates this clearly. Note that an extra 3 tons of avocados (= 33 − 30) comes at the direct sacrifice of 1 ton of soybeans (= 20 − 19).

The comparative cost of the two products within the two nations is clearly different. Economists say that the United States has a domestic comparative-cost advantage or, simply, a **comparative advantage,** in soybeans. The United States must forgo fewer avocados—3 tons—to get 1 ton of soybeans than in Mexico where 1 ton of soybeans costs 4 tons of avocados. In terms of domestic opportunity costs, soybeans are relatively cheaper in the United States. *A nation has a comparative advantage in some product when it can produce that product at a lower domestic opportunity cost than can a potential trading partner.* Mexico, on the other hand, has a comparative advantage in avocados. While it costs $\frac{1}{3}$ ton of soybeans to get 1 ton of avocados in the United States, by comparison 1 ton of avocados only costs $\frac{1}{4}$ ton of soybeans in Mexico. Comparatively speaking, avocados are cheaper in Mexico. In summary: Mexico's domestic cost conditions: $1S = 4A$; United States' domestic cost conditions: $1S = 3A$.

Because of these differences in domestic opportunity costs, if both nations specialize, each according to its comparative advantage, each can achieve a larger total output with the same total input of resources. Together, they will be using their scarce resources more efficiently.

Terms of Trade

Since the United States' cost ratio of $1S$ equals $3A$, it makes sense that Americans would specialize in soybeans, if they could obtain *more than* 3 tons of avocados for a ton of soybeans through trade with Mexico. Similarly, recalling Mexico's $1S$ equals $4A$ cost ratio, it will be advantageous to Mexicans to specialize in avocados, provided they can get 1 ton of soybeans for *less than* 4 tons of avocados.

Suppose through negotiation the two nations agree on an exchange rate of 1 ton of soybeans for $3\frac{1}{2}$ tons of avocados. These **terms of trade** will be mutually beneficial to both countries since each can "do better" through trade than by domestic production alone. Americans get $3\frac{1}{2}$ tons of avocados by sending 1 ton of soybeans to Mexico, while they can get only 3 tons of avocados by shifting resources domestically from soybeans to avocados. It would cost Mexicans 4 tons of avocados to obtain 1 ton of soybeans by shifting their domestic resources. Instead, they can obtain 1 ton of soybeans through trade with the United States at the lower cost of $3\frac{1}{2}$ tons of avocados.

Gains from Specialization and Trade

Let's pinpoint the size of the gains in total output from specialization and trade. Suppose that, before specialization and trade, production alternative C in Table 6-4 and alternative T in 6-5 were the optimal product-mixes for each country. These outputs are shown in column 1 of Table 6-6. That is, Mexicans preferred 24 tons of avocados and 9 tons of soybeans (Table 6-4) and Americans preferred 33 tons of avocados and 19 tons of soybeans (Table 6-5) to all other alternatives available within their respective domestic economies.

Now assume both nations specialize according to comparative advantage, Mexico producing 60 tons of avocados and no soybeans (alternative E) and the United States producing no avocados and 30 tons of soybeans (alternative R) as reflected in column 2 of Table 6-6. Using our $1S = 3\frac{1}{2}$ terms of trade, assume Mexico exchanges 35 tons of avocados for 10 tons of American soybeans. Column 3 of Table 6-6 shows quantities exchanged in this trade. As observed in column 4, Mexicans will now have 25 tons of avocados and 10 tons of soybeans, while Americans will obtain

TABLE 6-6   Specialization according to comparative advantage and the gains from trade (in tons)

Country	(1) Outputs before specialization	(2) Outputs after specialization	(3) Amounts traded	(4) Outputs available after trade	(5) = (4) − (1) Gains from specialization and trade
Mexico	24 avocados	60 avocados	−35 avocados	25 avocados	1 avocados
	9 soybeans	0 soybeans	+10 soybeans	10 soybeans	1 soybeans
United States	33 avocados	0 avocados	+35 avocados	35 avocados	2 avocados
	19 soybeans	30 soybeans	−10 soybeans	20 soybeans	1 soybeans

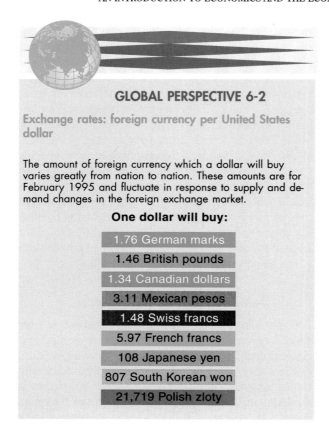

Exchange rates: foreign currency per United States dollar

The amount of foreign currency which a dollar will buy varies greatly from nation to nation. These amounts are for February 1995 and fluctuate in response to supply and demand changes in the foreign exchange market.

One dollar will buy:

1.76 German marks
1.46 British pounds
1.34 Canadian dollars
3.11 Mexican pesos
1.48 Swiss francs
5.97 French francs
108 Japanese yen
807 South Korean won
21,719 Polish zloty

35 tons of avocados and 20 tons of soybeans. Compared with their optimum product-mixes before specialization and trade (column 1), *both* nations now enjoy more avocados and more soybeans! Specifically, Mexico will gain 1 ton of avocados and 1 ton of soybeans. The United States will gain 2 tons of avocados and 1 ton of soybeans. These gains are shown in column 5 where we have subtracted the *before*-specialization outputs of column 1 from the outputs realized *after*-specialization in column 4.

Specialization according to comparative advantage improves global resource allocation. The same total inputs of world resources and technology have resulted in a larger global output. If Mexico and the United States allocate all their resources to avocados and soybeans respectively, the same total inputs of resources have produced more output between them, indicating that resources are being more efficiently used or allocated.

We saw in Chapter 2 that through specialization and international trade a nation can overcome the production constraints imposed by its domestic production possibilities curve. Although the domestic production possibilities frontiers of the two countries have not been pushed outward, specialization and trade have circumvented the constraints of the production possibilities curve. The economic effects of specialization and trade between two nations are tantamount to having more or better resources or to having achieved technological progress. The national self-interest of trading partners is the foundation of the world economy. Such trade provides mutual gains in consumable output and thus higher domestic standards of living. *(Key Question 4)*

FOREIGN EXCHANGE MARKET

People, firms, or nations specializing in the production of specific goods or services exchange those products for money and then use the money to buy other products or to pay for the use of resources. Within an economy—for example, Mexico—prices are stated in pesos and buyers use pesos to purchase domestic products. The buyers possess pesos, exactly the currency sellers want.

International markets are different. How many dollars does it take to buy a truckload of Mexican avocados selling for 3000 pesos, a German automobile selling for 90,000 marks, or a Japanese motorcycle priced at 300,000 yen? Producers in Mexico, Germany, and Japan want payment in pesos, marks, and yen, respectively, so they can pay their wages, rent, interest, dividends, and taxes. This need is served by a **foreign exchange market,** *the market where various national currencies are exchanged for one another.* (See Global Perspective 6-2.) Two points about this market require emphasis.

1 A Competitive Market Real-world foreign exchange markets conform closely to the kinds of markets studied in Chapter 3. These are competitive markets characterized by large numbers of buyers and sellers dealing in a standardized "product" such as the American dollar, the German mark, the British pound, Swedish krona, or the Japanese yen.

2 Linkage to All Domestic and Foreign Prices The price or exchange value of a nation's currency is an unusual price; it links all domestic (say, United States) prices with all foreign (say, Japanese or German) prices. Exchange rates enable consumers in one country to translate prices of foreign goods into units of their own currency—just multiply the foreign product price by the exchange rate. If the dollar–yen exchange rate is $.01 (1 cent) per yen, a Sony cassette player priced at ¥20,000 will cost an American $200 (= 20,000 × $.01). If the exchange rate is $.02 per yen, it would cost an American $400 (= 20,000 × $.02). Similarly, all other Japanese products will double in price to American buyers. As we will see, a change in exchange rates has important implications for a nation's levels of domestic production and employment.

Dollar–Yen Market

How does the foreign exchange market for dollars and yen work? (We defer technical details until later.) When nations trade, they must exchange their currencies. American exporters want to be paid in dollars, not yen; but Japanese importers of American goods possess yen, not dollars. This problem is resolved by Japanese importers who offer to supply their yen in exchange for dollars. Conversely, there are American importers who need to pay Japanese exporters with yen, not dollars. So these Americans go to the foreign exchange market as demanders of yen.

Figure 6-4 shows Japanese importers as suppliers of yen and American importers as demanders of yen. The intersection of the demand for yen curve D_y and the supply of yen curve S_y establishes the equilibrium dollar price of yen. Note that the equilibrium dollar price of 1 yen—the dollar–yen exchange rate—is $.01 = ¥1, or $1 = ¥100. At this price, the yen market clears; there is neither a shortage nor a surplus of yen. The equilibrium $.01 price of 1 yen means that $1 will buy 100 yen and therefore 100 yen worth of Japanese goods. Conversely, 100 yen will buy $1 worth of American goods.

Changing Rates: Depreciation and Appreciation

What might cause the exchange rate to change? The determinants of the demand for and the supply of yen are similar to the determinants of supply and demand discussed in Chapter 3. In the United States, several things might increase the demand for—and therefore the dollar price of—yen. Incomes might rise in the United States, enabling Americans to buy not only more domestic goods, but also more Sony televisions, Nikon cameras, and Nissan automobiles from Japan. So Americans need more yen and the demand for yen increases. Or, a change in American tastes may enhance our preferences for Japanese goods. When gas prices soared in the 1970s, many American auto buyers shifted their demands from gas-guzzling domestic cars to gas-efficient Japanese compact cars. The result? An increased demand for yen.

An increase in the American demand for Japanese goods will increase the demand for yen and raise the dollar price of yen. Suppose the dollar price of yen rises from $.01 = ¥1 (or $1 = ¥100) to $.02 = ¥1 (or $2 = ¥100). When the dollar price of yen increases, a **depreciation** of the dollar relative to the yen has occurred: It takes more dollars (pennies in this case) to

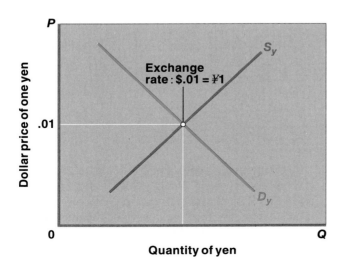

FIGURE 6-4 The market for foreign exchange
American imports from Japan create a demand for yen, while American exports to Japan create a supply of yen. The dollar price of one yen—the exchange rate—is determined at the intersection of the supply and demand curves. In this case the equilibrium price is $.01, meaning that 1 cent will buy 1 yen (or $1 will buy 100 yen).

buy a single unit of a foreign currency (the yen). A dollar is worth less because it will buy fewer yen and therefore fewer Japanese goods; the yen and therefore all Japanese goods become more expensive to Americans. Result: American consumers shift their expenditures from Japanese to American goods. The Ford Taurus becomes relatively more attractive than the Honda Accord to American consumers. Conversely, because each yen will buy more dollars, American goods become cheaper to people in Japan and our exports to them rise.

If opposite events occurred—if incomes rose in Japan and Japanese preferred more American goods —then the supply of yen in the foreign exchange market would increase. This increase in the supply of yen relative to demand would decrease the equilibrium dollar price of yen. For example, yen supply might increase, causing the dollar price of yen to decline from $.01 = ¥1 (or $1 = ¥100) to $.005 = ¥1 (or $1 = ¥200). This decrease in the dollar price of yen means there has been an **appreciation** of the dollar relative to the

yen. It now takes fewer dollars (or pennies) to buy a single yen; the dollar is worth more because it can purchase more yen and therefore more Japanese goods. Each Sony Walkman becomes less expensive in terms of dollars, so Americans purchase more of them. In general, American imports rise. Meanwhile, because it takes more yen to get a dollar, American exports to Japan fall.

We summarize these currency relationships in Figure 6-5, which you should examine closely. *(Key Question 6)*

QUICK REVIEW 6-2

■ A country has a comparative advantage in some product when it can produce it at a lower domestic opportunity cost than can a potential trading partner.

■ Specialization based on comparative advantage increases the total output available for nations which trade with one another.

■ The foreign exchange market is the market where the currency of one nation is exchanged for that of another nation.

■ Appreciation of the dollar is an increase in the international value of the dollar relative to the currency of some other nation; a dollar now buys more units of another currency. Depreciation of the dollar is a decrease in the international value of the dollar relative to other currencies; a dollar now buys fewer units of another currency.

GOVERNMENT AND TRADE

If people and nations benefit from specialization and international exchange, why do governments sometimes try to restrict the free flow of imports or to subsidize exports? What kinds of world trade barriers exist? And what is the rationale for them?

Trade Impediments and Subsidies

The major government interferences with free trade are fourfold:

1 **Protective tariffs** are excise taxes or duties placed on imported goods. Most are designed to shield domestic producers from foreign competition. They impede free trade by increasing the prices of imported goods, shifting demand toward domestic products.

FIGURE 6-5 Currency appreciation and depreciation
An increase in the dollar price of foreign currency is equivalent to a decline in the international value of the dollar (dollar depreciation). An increase in the dollar price of foreign currency also implies a decline in the foreign currency price of dollars. That is, the international value of foreign currency rises relative to the dollar (foreign currency appreciates).

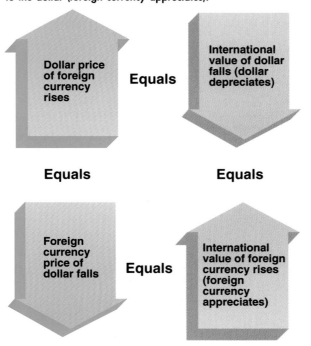

2 **Import quotas** are maximum limits on the quantity or total value of specific imported items. Once quotas are "filled," they choke off imports which domestic consumers might prefer to domestic goods. Import quotas can be more effective in retarding international commerce than tariffs. A particular product might be imported in large quantities despite high tariffs; low import quotas completely prohibit imports once quotas are filled.

3 **Nontariff barriers** include licensing requirements, unreasonable standards pertaining to product quality, or simply unnecessary bureaucratic red tape in customs procedures. Some nations require their domestic importers of foreign goods to obtain licenses. By restricting the issuance of licenses, imports can be effectively impeded. Great Britain bars coal importation in this way. Also, some nations impede imports of fruit by insisting that each crate be inspected for worms and insects.

4 **Export subsidies** consist of governmental payments to domestic producers to reduce their production costs. With lower production costs, domestic producers can charge lower prices and thus sell more exports in world markets. Two examples: Participating European governments have heavily subsidized Airbus Industries, which produces commercial aircraft. These subsidies have helped Airbus compete against two American firms, Boeing and McDonnell Douglas. The United States and other nations have subsidized domestic farmers, boosting domestic food supply. This has reduced the market price of food, artificially decreasing export prices on agricultural produce.

Why Government Trade Interventions?

Why would a nation want to send more of its output for consumption abroad than it gains as imported output in return? Why the impulse to impede imports or boost exports through government policy when free trade is beneficial to a nation? There are several reasons—some legitimate, most not. We will look at two here, and examine others in a later chapter.

1 **Misunderstanding of the Gains from Trade** It is a commonly accepted myth that the fundamental benefit of international trade is larger domestic employment in the export sector. This suggests that exports are "good" because they increase domestic employment, whereas imports are "bad" since they deprive people of jobs at home. In reality, the true ben-

efit from international trade is the *overall* increase in output obtained through specialization and exchange. A nation can fully employ its resources, including labor, with or without international trade. International trade, however, enables society to use its resources in ways that increase its total output and therefore its overall well-being.

A nation does not need international trade to locate *on* its production possibilities curve. A closed (nontrading) national economy can have full employment without international trade. But through world trade an economy can reach a point *beyond* its domestic production possibilities curve. The gain from trade is the extra output obtained from abroad—the imports gotten for less cost than if they were produced using domestic resources. The only valid reason for exporting part of our domestic output is to obtain imports of greater value to us. Specialization and international exchange make this possible.

2 **Political Considerations** While a nation as a whole gains from trade, trade may harm particular domestic industries and groups of resource suppliers. In our example of comparative advantage, specialization and trade adversely affected the American avocado industry and the Mexican soybean industry. These industries may seek to preserve or improve their economic positions by persuading their respective governments to impose tariffs or quotas to protect them from harm.

> The direct beneficiaries of import relief or export subsidy are usually few in number, but each has a large individual stake in the outcome. Thus, their incentive for vigorous political activity is strong.
>
> But the costs of such policies may far exceed the benefits. It may cost the public [$60,000–$80,000] a year to protect a domestic job that might otherwise pay an employee only half that amount in wages and benefits. Furthermore, the costs of protection are widely diffused—in the United States, among 50 states and [263] million citizens. Since the cost borne by any one citizen is likely to be quite small, and may even go unnoticed, resistance at the grass-roots level to protectionist measures often is considerably less than pressures for their adoption.[2]

Also, the costs of protectionism are hidden because tariffs and quotas are embedded in the prices of goods. Thus policy makers face fewer political restraints in responding positively to demands for pro-

---

[2]*Economic Report of the President, 1982*, p. 177. Updated.

tectionism. Indeed, the public may be won over, not only by the vigor of the arguments for trade barriers, but also by the apparent plausibility ("Cut imports and prevent domestic unemployment") and patriotic ring ("Buy American!") of the protectionists. Alleged tariff benefits are immediate and clear-cut to the public. The adverse effects cited by economists are obscure and dispersed over the economy. Then, too, the public is likely to stumble on the fallacy of composition: "If a quota on Japanese automobiles will preserve profits and employment in the American automobile industry, how can it be detrimental to the economy as a whole?" When political considerations are added in— "You back tariffs for the apparel industry in my state and I'll back tariffs for the auto industry in your state" —the sum can be protective tariffs, import quotas, and export subsidies.

Costs to Society

Tariffs and quotas benefit domestic firms in the protected industries, but hurt American consumers who must pay higher than world prices. The cost of trade protection to American consumers exceeds the gain to American producers, resulting in a *net* cost to Americans. In the early 1990s this net cost exceeded $21 billion annually. Removing trade barriers, on average, would reduce product prices in protected industries by 3 percent. Prices of apparel products would fall by 11.4 percent, luggage prices by 9.1 percent, and sugar prices by 8.3 percent. Prices would also decline for footwear, watches, roller bearings, pressed and blown glass, costume jewelry, machine tools, frozen fruit and vegetables, ceramic tiles, and leather goods.[3]

Tariffs and quotas on textiles and apparel cost our economy about $16 billion annually. Other net costs of trade protection, by industry, include $3 billion in maritime transport, $850 million in dairy products, $657 million in sugar, $353 million in peanuts, $177 million in meat, $170 million in nonrubber footwear, and $101 million in watches and clocks.

MULTILATERAL AGREEMENTS AND FREE-TRADE ZONES

When one nation enacts barriers against imports, the nations whose exports suffer may retaliate with trade barriers of their own. In a "trade war" tariffs escalate,

---

[3]United States International Trade Commission.

choking off world trade and reducing everyone's economic well-being. The **Smoot-Hawley Tariff Act of 1930** is a classic example. Rather than reducing imports and stimulating domestic production, its high tariffs prompted affected nations to retaliate with equally high tariffs. International trade across the globe fell, lowering the output, income, and employment levels of all nations. Economic historians generally agree that the Smoot-Hawley tariff was a contributing cause of the Great Depression. In view of this fact, the world's nations have worked to lower tariffs worldwide. This pursuit of free trade has been aided by the expansion of powerful domestic interest groups. Specifically, exporters of goods and services, importers of foreign components used in "domestic" products, and domestic sellers of imported products all strongly support lower tariffs worldwide.

Figure 6-6 makes clear that the United States has been a high tariff nation over much of its history. But it also demonstrates that, in general, American tariffs have declined during the past half-century.[4]

Reciprocal Trade Agreements Act and GATT

The **Reciprocal Trade Agreements Act of 1934** started the downward trend of tariffs. Specifically aimed at reducing tariffs, this act had two main features:

1 *Negotiating Authority*   It authorized the President to negotiate with foreign nations agreements reducing American tariffs up to 50 percent of the existing rates. Tariff reductions hinged on other nations reciprocating by lowering tariffs on American exports.
2 *Generalized Reductions*   By incorporating **most-favored-nation clauses** in these agreements, the reduced tariffs would not only apply to the specific nation negotiating with the United States, but to all nations previously granted most-favored-nation status.

But the Reciprocal Trade Act gave rise to only bilateral (between-two-nations) negotiations. This approach was broadened in 1947 when twenty-three nations, including the United States, signed a **General Agreement on Tariffs and Trade (GATT)**. GATT is based on three cardinal principles: (1) equal, nondiscriminatory treatment for all member nations;

---

[4]Average tariff-rate figures understate the importance of tariffs, however, by not accounting for the fact that some goods are excluded from American markets because of existing tariffs. Also, average figures conceal the high tariffs on particular items.

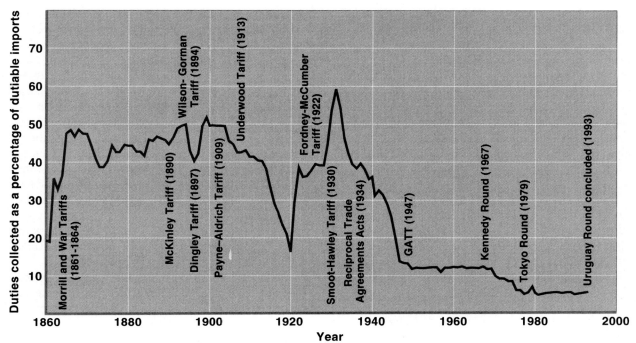

FIGURE 6-6 United States tariff rates, 1860–1994
American tariff rates have fluctuated historically. But beginning with the Reciprocal Trade Agreements
Act of 1934, the trend has been downward. (U.S. Department of Commerce data.)

(2) the reduction of tariffs by multilateral negotiations; and (3) the elimination of import quotas.

Basically, GATT is a forum to negotiate reductions in trade barriers on a multilateral basis among nations. More than 120 nations now belong to GATT, and there is little doubt that it has been a positive force in the trend toward liberalized trade. Under its sponsorship, member nations have completed eight "rounds" of negotiations to reduce trade barriers in the post-World War II period.

Uruguay Round The eighth "round" of GATT negotiations began in Uruguay in 1986. After seven years of wrangling, in 1993 the 124 participant nations reached a new agreement. This new agreement took effect on January 1, 1995 and its provisions will be phased in through 2005.

The major provisions of the new GATT agreement are:

1   *Tariff Reduction* Tariffs will be eliminated or reduced on thousands of products, including construction equipment, medical equipment, paper, steel, chemicals, wood, memory chips, and aluminum. Overall, tariffs will drop by about 33 percent.

2   *Inclusion of Services* Services are now a $900 billion segment of world trade and GATT will apply to them for the first time. The GATT accord will liberalize governmental rules which in the past have impeded the global market for advertising, insurance, consulting, accounting, legal, tourist, financial, and other services.

3   *Agriculture* All member nations together agree to cut agricultural subsidies they pay to farmers, reducing the collective total subsidy by about 21 percent, or $300 billion annually. The agreement lifts Japanese and South Korean bans on rice importation and phases out American quotas on sugar, dairy products, and peanuts. These quotas will be replaced with tariffs.

4   *Intellectual Property* International protection against piracy is provided for intellectual property such as patents, trademarks, and copyrights. This protection will greatly benefit American book publishers, music producers, and software firms.

5   *Phased Reduction of Quotas on Textiles and Apparel* Quotas on imported textiles and apparel will be phased out over a ten-year period, to be replaced with tariffs. These quotas have choked off apparel and clothing imports to the industrial nations. Eliminating them will benefit developing countries having comparative advantages in these areas.

6 *World Trade Organization* GATT creates the World Trade Organization with judicial powers to mediate among members disputing the new rules.

When fully implemented, the GATT agreement will boost the world's GDP by an estimated $6 trillion, or 8 percent! Consumers in the United States will gain about $30 billion annually.

European Union

Countries have also sought to reduce tariffs by creating regional free-trade zones or trade blocs. The most dramatic example is the **European Union (EU),** formerly called the European Economic Community. Initiated as the Common Market in 1958, the EU now comprises fifteen western European nations—France, Germany, Italy, Belgium, the Netherlands, Luxembourg, Denmark, Ireland, United Kingdom, Greece, Spain, Portugal, Austria, Finland, and Sweden.

Goals The original Common Market called for (1) gradual abolition of tariffs and import quotas on all products traded among the participating nations; (2) establishment of a common system of tariffs applicable to all goods received from nations outside the EU; (3) free movement of capital and labor within the Common Market; and (4) creation of common policies in other economic matters of joint concern, such as agriculture, transportation, and restrictive business practices. The EU has achieved most of these goals and is now a strong **trade bloc.**

Results Motives for creating the European Union were both political and economic. The main economic motive was freer trade for members. While it is difficult to determine how much of EU prosperity and growth has resulted from economic integration, integration clearly has created the mass markets essential to EU industries. The economies of large-scale production have enabled European industries to achieve the lower costs historically denied them by small, localized markets.

Effects on nonmember nations, such as the United States, are less certain. On the one hand, a peaceful and increasingly prosperous EU makes its member nations better customers for American exports. On the other, American and other nonmember

firms encounter tariffs which make it difficult to compete against firms within the EU trade bloc. For example, before the establishment of the EU, American German, and French automobile manufacturers all faced the same tariff selling their products in, say, Belgium. However, with the establishment of internal trading among EU members, Belgian tariffs on German Volkswagens and French Renaults fell to zero, but an external tariff still applies to American Chevrolets and Fords. This puts American firms at a serious disadvantage. Similarly, EU trade restrictions hamper eastern European exports of metals, textiles, and farm products, goods which the eastern Europeans produce in abundance.

By giving preferences to other countries within their free-trade zone, trade blocs such as the EU may reduce their trade with nonbloc members. Thus, the world loses some of the benefits of a completely open global trading system. Eliminating this disadvantage has been one of the motivations for promoting freer global trade through GATT.

North American Free Trade Agreement

In 1993 Canada, Mexico, and the United States formed a trade bloc. The **North American Free Trade Agreement (NAFTA)** established a free-trade zone having about the same combined output as the EU, but a much larger geographical area. A 1989 free-trade agreement between the United States and Canada preceded NAFTA. Through this United States–Canada accord, Canadian producers have gained increased access to a market ten times the size of Canada; United States' consumers have gained advantage of lower-price Canadian goods. Eliminating the high Canadian tariffs has helped American producers and Canadian consumers. Because Canada is the United States' largest trade partner, there have been large gains to each country from the United States–Canadian accord. When fully implemented in 1999, the agreement is expected to generate $1 billion to $3 billion of annual gains for each nation.

Free trade with Mexico is more controversial in the United States than is free trade with Canada. NAFTA will eliminate tariffs and other trade barriers between Mexico and the United States and Canada over a fifteen-year period. Critics of the agreement fear a loss of American jobs as firms move to Mexico to take advantage of lower wages and less stringent regulations on pollution and workplace safety. Also, there is concern that Japan and South Korea will build plants in Mexico to transport goods duty-free to the United States, further hurting American firms and workers.

Defenders of NAFTA reject these concerns and cite several strong arguments in its favor:

1 Specialization according to comparative advantage will enable the United States to obtain more total output from its scarce resources.

2 The reduction of high Mexican tariffs will greatly increase American exports to Mexico.

3 This free-trade zone will encourage worldwide investment in Mexico, enhancing Mexican productivity and national income. Mexican consumers will use some of that increased income to buy United States exports.

4 A higher standard of living in Mexico eventually will help stem the flow of illegal immigrants to the United States.

5 The higher standard of living in Mexico will enable Mexico to afford more pollution control equipment and to provide safer workplaces.

6 The loss of specific American jobs to Mexico may have occurred anyway to low-wage countries such as South Korea, Taiwan, and Hong Kong. NAFTA will enable and encourage American firms to be more efficient, enhancing their long-term competitiveness with firms in Japan and the European Union.

7 By binding Mexico to an international agreement, NAFTA will lock in the politically fragile free-market reforms already implemented by Mexico.

It may appear that the world's nations are combining into potentially hostile trade blocs. But NAFTA constitutes a vehicle to negotiate reductions in trade barriers with the EU, Japan, and other trading countries. Access to the vast North American market is as important to the EU and Japan as is access to their markets by the United States, Canada, and Mexico. NAFTA gives the United States a lever in future trade negotiations with the EU and Japan. Conceivably, direct negotiations between NAFTA and the EU could eventually link the two free-trade zones. Japan and other major trading nations, not wishing to be left out of the world's wealthiest trade markets, would be forced to eliminate their high trade barriers—to open their domestic markets to additional imports. Nor do other nations and trade blocs want to be excluded from free-trade zones. Examples:

1 *APEC* In late 1994 the United States and seventeen other members of the Asia-Pacific Economic Cooperation (APEC) nations agreed to establish freer trade and more open investment over the next few decades. APEC nations are Australia, Brunei, Canada,

Chile, Hong Kong, Indonesia, Japan, Malaysia, Mexico, New Zealand, the Philippines, Papua New Guinea, Singapore, South Korea, Taiwan, Thailand, and the United States.

2 *Admission of Chile into NAFTA* At the invitation of Canada, Mexico, and the United States, Chile has agreed to become the fourth partner in NAFTA.

3 *Mercosur* The free-trade area encompassing Brazil, Argentina, Uruguay, and Paraguay—called *Mercosur*—is interested in linking up with NAFTA. So are other South American countries. In late 1994 President Clinton and thirty-three other presidents and prime ministers of Western hemisphere nations agreed to begin negotiations on a free-trade area from "Alaska to Argentina."

Economists agree that the *ideal* free-trade area would be the world. *(Key Question 10)*

QUICK REVIEW 6-3

■ Governments promote exports and reduce imports through tariffs, quotas, nontariff barriers, and export subsidies.

■ The various "rounds" of the General Agreement on Tariffs and Trade (GATT) have established multinational reductions in tariffs and import quotas among the more than 120 member nations.

■ The Uruguay Round of GATT which went into effect in 1995: *a* reduced tariffs worldwide; *b* liberalized rules impeding barriers to trade in services; *c* reduced agricultural subsidies; *d* created new protections for intellectual property; *e* phased out quotas on textiles and apparel; and *f* set up the World Trade Organization, the successor to GATT.

■ The European Union (EU) and the North American Free Trade Agreement (NAFTA) have reduced internal trade barriers by establishing large free-trade zones.

CAN AMERICAN FIRMS COMPETE?

Freer international trade has brought with it intense competition in a number of product markets in the United States and the world. Not long ago three large domestic producers dominated our automobile industry. Imported autos were an oddity, accounting for a minuscule portion of auto sales. But General Motors, Ford, and Chrysler now face intense competition as they struggle for sales against Nissan, Honda, Toyota, Hyundai, BMW, and others. Similarly, imports

LAST WORD

BUY AMERICAN: THE GLOBAL REFRIGERATOR

Humorist Art Buchwald looks at the logic of the "Buy American" campaign.

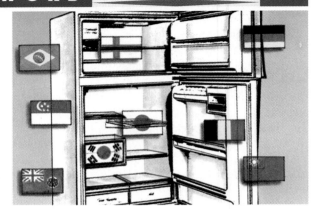

"There is only one way the country is going to get on its feet," said Baleful.

"How's that?" I asked, as we drank coffee in his office at the Baleful Refrigerator Company.

"The consumer has to start buying American," he said, slamming his fist down on the desk. "Every time an American buys a foreign refrigerator it costs one of my people his job. And every time one of my people is out of work it means he or she can't buy refrigerators."

"It's a vicious circle," I said.

Baleful's secretary came in. "Mr. Thompson, the steel broker is on the phone."

My friend grabbed the receiver. "Thompson, where is that steel shipment from Japan that was supposed to be in last weekend? . . . I don't care about weather. We're almost out of steel, and I'll have to close down the refrigerator assembly line next week. If you can't deliver when you promise, I'll find myself another broker."

"You get your steel from Japan?" I asked Baleful.

"Even with shipping costs, their price is still lower than steel made in Europe. We used to get all our sheets from Belgium, but the Japanese are now giving them a run for their money."

The buzzer on the phone alerted Baleful. He listened for a few moments and then said, "Excuse me, I have a call from Taiwan. Mark Four? Look, R&D designed a new push-button door handle and we're going to send the specs to you. Tell Mr. Chow if his people send us a sample of one and can make it for us at the same price as the old handle, we'll give his company the order."

---

have gained major market shares in automobile tires, clothing, sporting goods, electronics, motorcycles, outboard motors, and toys.

Nevertheless, thousands of American firms—large and small—have thrived and prospered in the global marketplace. Boeing, McDonald's, Dow Chemicals, Intel, Coca-Cola, 3M, Microsoft, AT&T, Monsanto, Procter & Gamble, and Hewlett-Packard are just a few cases. These and many other firms have continued to retain high market shares at home and have dramatically expanded their sales abroad. Of course, not all firms have been so successful. Some corporations simply have not been able to compete; their international competitors make better-quality products, have lower production costs, or both. Not surprisingly, the American firms which have been most vulnerable to foreign competition are precisely those which have enjoyed long periods of trade protection via tariffs and quotas. These barriers to imports have artificially limited competition, dampening incentives to innovate, reduce costs, and improve

products. Also, trade barriers have shielded some domestic firms from the usual consequences of national shifts in comparative advantages over time. As trade protection declines under GATT and NAFTA, some American firms will surely discover that they are producing goods for which America clearly has a comparative *dis*advantage (apparel, for example).

Is the greater competition accompanying the global economy a good thing? Although some domestic producers and their workers do not like it, foreign competition clearly benefits consumers. Imports reduce product prices and provide consumers with a greater variety of goods. Foreign competition also forces domestic producers to become more efficient and to improve product quality—precisely the outcome in several American industries, including autos and steel. Evidence shows that most—clearly not all—American firms *can* and *do* compete successfully in the global economy.

What about American firms which cannot successfully compete in open markets? The harsh reality

A man came in with a plastic container and said, "Mr. Baleful, you said you wanted to see one of these before we ordered them. They are the containers for the ice maker in the refrigerator."

Baleful inspected it carefully and banged it on the floor a couple of times. "What's the price on it?"

"Hong Kong can deliver it at $2 a tray, and Dong-Fu Plastics in South Korea said they can make it for $1.70."

"It's just a plastic tray. Take the South Korea bid. We'll let Hong Kong supply us with the shelves for the freezer. Any word on the motors?"

"There's a German company in Brazil that just came out with a new motor, and it's passed all our tests, so Johnson has ordered 50,000."

"Call Cleveland Motors and tell them we're sorry, but the price they quoted us was just too high."

"Yes, sir," the man said and departed.

The secretary came in again and said, "Harry telephoned and wanted to let you know the defroster just arrived from Finland. They're unloading the box cars now."

"Good. Any word on the wooden crates from Singapore?"

"They're at the dock in Hoboken."

"Thank heaven. Cancel the order from Boise Cascade."

"What excuse should I give them?"

"Tell them we made a mistake in our inventory, or we're switching to plastic. I don't care what you tell them."

Baleful turned to me. "Where were we?"

"You were saying that if the consumer doesn't start buying American, this country is going to be in a lot of trouble."

"Right. It's not only his patriotic duty, but his livelihood that's at stake. I'm going to Washington next week to tell the Senate Commerce Committee that if they don't get on the stick, there isn't going to be a domestic refrigerator left in this country. We're not going to stay in business for our health."

"Pour it to them," I urged him.

Baleful said, "Come out with me into the showroom."

I followed him. He went to his latest model, and opened the door. "This is an American refrigerator made by the American worker, for the American consumer. What do you have to say to that?"

"It's beautiful," I said. "It puts foreign imports to shame.

Source: Art Buchwald, "Being Bullish on Buying American." Reprinted by permission. We discovered this article in *Master Curriculum Guide in Economics: Teaching Strategies for International Trade* (New York: Joint Council on Economic Education, 1988).

---

is that they should go out of business, much like an unsuccessful corner boutique. Persistent economic losses mean valuable scarce resources are not being used efficiently. Shifting these resources to alternative, profitable uses will increase the total value of American output.

CHAPTER SUMMARY

1   International trade is growing in importance globally and for the United States. World trade is vital to the United States in two respects.   a The absolute volumes of American imports and exports exceed those of any other single nation.   b The United States is completely dependent on trade for certain commodities and materials which cannot be obtained domestically.

2   Our principal exports include chemicals, computers, consumer durables, aircraft, and grain; our major imports are petroleum, automobiles, clothing, computers, and household appliances. Quantitatively, Canada is our most important trading partner.

3   Global trade has been greatly facilitated by   a improvements in transportation technology;   b improvements in communications technology;   c general declines

in tariffs; and   d peaceful relations among major industrial nations. The United States, Japan, and the western European nations dominate the global economy. But the total volume of trade has been increased by several new trade participants, including the "Asian tigers" (Hong Kong, Singapore, South Korea, and Taiwan), China, the eastern European countries, and the new independent countries of the former Soviet Union.

4   The open-economy circular flow model connects the domestic U.S. economy to the rest of the world. Customers from abroad enter our product market to buy some of our output. These American exports create business revenues and generate income in the United States. American households spend some of their money income on products made abroad and imported to the United States.

5 Specialization according to comparative advantage permits nations to achieve higher standards of living through exchange with other countries. A trading partner should specialize in products and services where its domestic opportunity costs are lowest. The terms of trade must be such that both nations can get more of a particular output via trade than they can at home.

6 The foreign exchange market sets exchange rates between nations' currencies. Foreign importers are suppliers of their currencies and American importers are demanders of foreign currencies. The resulting equilibrium exchange rates link the price levels of all nations. Depreciation of the dollar reduces our imports and increases our exports; dollar appreciation increases our imports and reduces our exports.

7 Governments shape trade flows through a protective tariffs; b quotas; c nontariff barriers; and d export subsidies. These are impediments to free trade; they result from misunderstanding about the gains from trade and from political considerations. By driving up product prices, trade barriers cost American consumers billions of dollars annually.

8 The Reciprocal Trade Agreements Act of 1934 marked the beginning of a trend toward lower American tariffs. In 1947 the General Agreement on Tariffs and Trade (GATT) was formed to a encourage nondiscriminatory treatment for all trading nations; b reduce tariffs; and c eliminate import quotas.

9 The Uruguay Round of GATT negotiations, completed in 1993: a reduced tariffs; b liberalized trade in services; c reduced agricultural subsidies; d reduced pirating of intellectual property; e phased out import quotas on textiles and apparel; and f established the World Trade Organization, which replaces GATT.

10 Free-trade zones (trade blocs) may liberalize trade within regions but may also impede trade with nonbloc members. Two examples of free-trade arrangements are a the European Union (EU), formerly the European Community or "Common Market"; and b the North American Free Trade Agreement (NAFTA), comprising Canada, Mexico, the United States, and later, Chile.

11 The global economy has created intense foreign competition in many American product markets.

TERMS AND CONCEPTS

multinational corporations	appreciation	Reciprocal Trade Agreements Act of 1934	European Union (EU)
"Asian tigers"	protective tariffs		trade bloc
comparative advantage	import quotas	most-favored-nation clauses	North American Free Trade Agreement (NAFTA)
terms of trade	nontariff barriers	General Agreement on Tariffs and Trade (GATT)	
foreign exchange market	export subsidies		
depreciation	Smoot-Hawley Tariff Act of 1930		

QUESTIONS AND STUDY SUGGESTIONS

1 What is the quantitative importance of world trade to the United States? Who is the United States' most important trade partner, quantitatively? How have persistent United States trade deficits been financed? "Trade deficits mean we get more merchandise from the rest of the world than we provide them in return. Therefore, trade deficits are economically desirable." Do you agree?

2 Account for the rapid growth of world trade since World War II. Who are the major players in international trade? Who are the "Asian tigers" and how important are they in world trade?

3 *Key Question Use the circular flow model (Figure 6-3) to explain how an increase in exports would affect revenues of domestic firms, money income of domestic households, and imports from abroad. Use Table 6-3 to find the exact* *amounts (1993) of United States exports (flow 13) and imports (flow 16) in the circular flow model. What do these amounts imply for flows 14 and 15?*

💾 4 *Key Question The following are production possibilities tables for South Korea and the United States. Assume that before specialization and trade the optimal product-mix for South Korea is alternative B and for the United States alternative U.*

Product	South Korea's production possibilities					
	A	B	C	D	E	F
Radios (in thousands)	30	24	18	12	6	0
Chemicals (in tons)	0	6	12	18	24	30

Product	U.S. production possibilities					
	R	S	T	U	V	W
Radios (in thousands)	10	8	6	4	2	0
Chemicals (in tons)	0	4	8	12	16	20

a *Are comparative-cost conditions such that the two areas should specialize? If so, what product should each produce?*

b *What is the total gain in radio and chemical output which results from this specialization?*

c *What are the limits of the terms of trade? Suppose actual terms of trade are 1 unit of radios for $1\frac{1}{2}$ units of chemicals and that 4 units of radios are exchanged for 6 units of chemicals. What are the gains from specialization and trade for each area?*

d *Can you conclude from this illustration that specialization according to comparative advantage results in more efficient use of world resources? Explain.*

5 Suppose that the comparative-cost ratios of two products—baby formula and tuna fish—are as follows in the hypothetical nations of Canswicki and Tunata.

Canswicki: 1 can baby formula = 2 cans tuna fish

Tunata: 1 can baby formula = 4 cans tuna fish

In what product should each nation specialize? Explain why terms of trade of 1 can baby formula = $2\frac{1}{2}$ cans tuna fish would be acceptable to both nations.

6 *Key Question   "Our exports create a demand for foreign currencies; foreign imports of our goods generate supplies of foreign currencies." Do you agree? Would a decline in American incomes or a weakening of American preferences for foreign products cause the dollar to depreciate or appreciate? What would be the effects of that depreciation or appreciation on our exports and imports?*

7 If the French franc declines in value (depreciates) in the foreign exchange market, will it be easier or harder for the French to sell their wine in the United States? Suppose you were planning a trip to Paris. How would the depreciation of the franc change the dollar price of this trip?

8 True or False? "An increase in the American dollar price of the German mark implies that the German mark has depreciated in value." Explain.

9 What tools do governments use to promote exports and restrict imports? What are the benefits and the costs of protectionist policies? What is the net outcome for society?

10 *Key Question   What is GATT? How does it affect nearly every person in the world? What were the major outcomes of the Uruguay Round of GATT? How is GATT related to the European Union (EU) and the North American Free Trade Agreement (NAFTA)?*

11 Explain: "Free-trade zones such as the EU and NAFTA lead a double life: They can promote free trade among members, but pose serious trade obstacles for nonmembers." Do you think the net effects of these trade blocs are good or bad for world trade?

12 Do you think American firms will be able to compete with foreign firms in world trade during the next twenty years? What do you see as the competitive strengths of American firms? Competitive weaknesses? Explain: "Even if Japan captured the entire worldwide auto market, that simply would mean that Japan would have to buy a whole lot of other products from abroad. Thus, the United States and other industrial nations would necessarily experience an increase in exports to Japan."

13 (Last Word) What point is Art Buchwald making in his humorous essay on the Baleful Refrigerator Company? Why might Mr. Baleful *oppose* tariffs on imported goods, even though he wants consumers to buy "American" refrigerators?

PART TWO

National Income, Employment, and Fiscal Policy

MEASURING DOMESTIC OUTPUT, NATIONAL INCOME, AND THE PRICE LEVEL

"**D**isposable Income Flat"; "Personal Consumption Surges"; "Domestic Investment Stagnates"; "Japan Suffers GDP Decline"; "GDP Deflator Rises Less Rapidly Than CPI"

Typical headlines in the business and economics news. Gibberish—unless you know the language of macroeconomics and national income accounting. This chapter will help you learn this language and understand the ideas it communicates.

There are two substantial payoffs from carefully studying this chapter. One is an understanding of the basics of how government statisticians and accountants measure and record the levels of domestic output, national income, and prices for the economy. Second, knowledge of the terms and ideas examined in this chapter—for example, consumption, investment, government purchases, net exports, real GDP, national income, and the price level—will help you comprehend material in subsequent chapters.

In the present chapter we will first explain why it is important to measure the performance of the economy. Second, we define the key measure of total output—gross domestic product (GDP)—and show how it is measured. We then derive and explain several other important measures of output and income. Next, measurement of the overall level of prices —the price level—is examined. We then demonstrate how GDP is adjusted for inflation or deflation so that changes in the physical amount of a nation's production are more accurately reflected. Finally, some limitations of the measures of domestic output and national income are listed and explained.

MACROECONOMIC MEASUREMENT

Our first goal is to explain the ways the overall production performance of the economy is measured. This comes under the heading of national income accounting, which does for the economy as a whole what private accounting does for the individual business enterprise or, for that matter, for the household. The

business executive must know how well his or her firm is doing, but that is not always immediately discernible.

A firm measures its flows of income and expenditures to assess its operations, usually for a three-month period or for the current year. With this information in hand the firm can gauge its economic health. If things are going well, the accounting data can be used to explain this success. Costs might be down or output or prices up, resulting in large profits. If things are going badly, accounting measures can help discover why. And by examining the accounts over a specific period, the firm can detect growth or decline of profits and what caused the change. All this information helps the firm's managers make intelligent business decisions.

National income accounting operates in much the same way for the economy.

1   It allows us to keep a finger on the economic pulse of the nation. Our national income accounting system permits us to measure the level of production in the economy at some point in time and explain why it's at that level.

2   By comparing national income accounts over a number of years, we can track the long-run course of the economy and see whether it has grown, been steady, or stagnated.

3   Information supplied by national income accounts provides a basis for formulating and applying public policies to improve the performance of the economy. Without national income accounts, economic policy would be based on guesswork. *National income accounting allows us to keep tabs on the health of the economy and formulate polices which will maintain and improve that health.*

GROSS DOMESTIC PRODUCT

There are many measures of the economic well-being of society. But the best available measure is its annual total output of goods and services or, as it is sometimes called, the economy's aggregate output. There are two ways of measuring an economy's total output of goods and services: gross national product and gross domestic product. Both measure *the total market value of all final goods and services produced in the economy in one year.* They are closely related, differing only in how the "economy" is defined.

Gross national product (GNP) consists of the total output produced by land, labor, capital, and entrepreneurial talent supplied by Americans, *whether these resources are located in the United States or abroad.* For example, the share of output (income) produced by an American working in France or Saudi Arabia is included in our GNP. Conversely, the share of output (income) produced in the United States by foreign-owned resources is excluded from our GNP.

Gross domestic product (GDP) is slightly different. It comprises the value of the total goods and services *produced within the boundaries of the United States,* whether by American or foreign-supplied resources. For instance, the value of the autos produced at a Japanese-owned Nissan factory in the United States, including profits, is a part of American GDP. Conversely, profits earned by an American-owned IBM plant in France are excluded from our GDP.

Specifically, the difference between GDP and GNP consists of *net foreign factor income earned (output produced) in the United States.* This amount is found by subtracting receipts of factor (resource) income *from* the rest of the world from payments of factor income *to* the rest of the world. Net foreign factor income earned in the United States can be positive or negative. In 1994 it was a *positive* $12 billion, meaning that foreign-owned resources produced and earned more in the United States than American-supplied resources produced and earned abroad.

	Billions
Factor payments to the rest of the world	$178
Less: Factor receipts from the rest of the world .	166
Net foreign factor income earned in the U.S. . . .	$12

Since net foreign factor income earned in the United States is positive, GDP in the United States exceeds GNP. The total value of output produced within the borders of the United States (GDP) is greater than the total value of output produced by Americans, wherever located (GNP):

	Billions
Gross national product	$6725
Plus: Net foreign factor income earned in the U.S.	12
Gross domestic product	$6737

Because most nations, including the United States, use GDP as the measure of their output, our focus will be on GDP. *(Key Question 2)*

A Monetary Measure

If the economy produces three oranges and two apples in year 1 and two oranges and three apples in year 2, in which year is output greater? We cannot answer this question until price tags are attached to the various products as indicators of society's evaluation of their relative worth.

That's what GDP does. It measures the market value of annual output; it is a monetary measure. In-

TABLE 7-1   Comparing heterogeneous outputs by using money prices

Year	Annual outputs	Market values
1	3 oranges and 2 apples	3 at 20 cents + 2 at 30 cents = $1.20
2	2 oranges and 3 apples	2 at 20 cents + 3 at 30 cents = $1.30

deed, it must be if we are to compare the heterogeneous collections of goods and services produced in different years and get a meaningful idea of their relative worth.

In Table 7-1 the money price of oranges is 20 cents and the price of apples is 30 cents. Year 2's output is greater than year 1's, because society values year 2's output more highly; society is willing to pay $.10 more for the collection of goods produced in year 2 than for goods produced in year 1.

Avoiding Double Counting

To measure total output accurately, all goods and services produced in any specific year must be counted once, but not more than once. Most products go through a series of production stages before reaching a market. As a result, parts or components of most products are bought and sold many times. To avoid counting several times the parts of products that are sold and resold, GDP includes only the market value of final goods and ignores transactions involving intermediate goods.

By **final goods** we mean goods and services being purchased for final use and not for resale or further processing or manufacturing. *They are "purchases not resold."* Transactions involving **intermediate**

goods refer to purchases of goods and services for further processing and manufacturing or for resale.

The sale of *final goods is included* and the sale of *intermediate goods is excluded* from GDP. Why? Because the value of final goods already includes all intermediate transactions involved in producing those final goods. To count intermediate transactions separately would be **double counting** and exaggerating the value of GDP.

To clarify this, suppose there are five stages of production in getting a wool suit manufactured and to the consumer—the ultimate or final user. As Table 7-2 indicates, firm A, a sheep ranch, provides $120 worth of wool to firm B, a wool processor. Firm A pays out the $120 it receives in wages, rents, interest, and profits. Firm B processes the wool and sells it to firm C, a suit manufacturer, for $180. What does firm B do with this $180? As noted, $120 goes to firm A, and the remaining $60 is used by B to pay wages, rents, interest, and profits for the resources needed in processing the wool. The manufacturer sells the suit to firm D, a clothing wholesaler, who sells it to firm E, a retailer, and then, at last, it is bought for $350 by a consumer, the final user.

At each stage, the difference between what a firm has paid for the product and what it receives for its sale is paid out as wages, rent, interest, and profits for

TABLE 7-2   Value added in a five-stage production process

(1) Stage of production	(2) Sales value of materials or product	(3) Value added
	0	
Firm A, sheep ranch	$ 120	$120 (= $120 − $ 0)
Firm B, wool processor	180	60 (= 180 − 120)
Firm C, suit manufacturer	220	40 (= 220 − 180)
Firm D, clothing wholesaler	270	50 (= 270 − 220)
Firm E, retail clothier	350	80 (= 350 − 270)
Total sales values	$1140	
Value added (total income)		$350

the resources used by that firm in helping to produce and distribute the suit.

How much should we include in GDP in accounting for the production of this suit? Just $350, the value of the final product. This figure includes all the intermediate transactions leading up to the product's final sale. It would be a gross distortion to sum all the intermediate sales figures and the final sales value of the product in column 2 and include the entire amount, $1140, in GDP. This would be double counting: counting the final product *and* the sale and resale of its various parts in the multistage productive process. The production and sale of the suit has generated $350, *not* $1140, worth of output and income.

To avoid double counting, national income accountants are careful to calculate only the *value added* by each firm. **Value added** is the market value of a firm's output *less* the value of the inputs which it has purchased from others. In column 3 of Table 7-2 the value added of firm B is $60, the difference between the $180 value of its output and the $120 it paid for the inputs provided by firm A. By adding together the values added by the five firms in Table 7-2, the total value of the suit can be accurately determined. Similarly, by calculating and summing the values added by all firms in the economy, we can determine the GDP—the market value of total output.

GDP Excludes Nonproduction Transactions

GDP measures the annual production of the economy. The many nonproduction transactions which occur each year must be excluded. *Nonproduction transactions* are of two major types: (1) purely financial transactions, and (2) secondhand sales.

Financial Transactions Purely financial transactions are of three general kinds.

1 Public Transfer Payments These are the social security payments, welfare payments, and veterans' payments which government makes to particular households. The basic characteristic of public transfer payments is that recipients make no contribution to *current* production in return for them. To include them in GDP would be to overstate this year's production.

2 Private Transfer Payments These payments, for example, a university student's monthly subsidy from home or an occasional gift from a wealthy relative, do not entail production but simply the transfer of funds from one private individual to another.

3 Security Transactions Buying and selling of stocks and bonds are also excluded from GDP. Stock market transactions involve swapping paper assets. The amount spent on these assets does not directly create current production. Only the services provided by the security broker are included in GDP. However, sales of *new* issues of stocks and bonds transfer money from savers to businesses which often spend the proceeds on capital goods. Thus, these transactions may indirectly contribute to spending, which does account for output and hence add to GDP.

Secondhand Sales Secondhand sales are excluded from GDP because they either reflect no *current* production, or involve double counting. If you sell your 1965 Ford Mustang to a friend, this transaction would be excluded in determining GDP because no current production is involved. Including the sales of goods produced some years ago in this year's GDP would be an exaggeration of this year's output. Similarly, if you purchased a brand new Mustang and resold it a week later to your neighbor, we would still exclude the resale transaction from the current GDP. When you originally bought the new car, that's when its value was included in GDP. To include its resale value at a later time would be to count it twice.

Two Sides to GDP: Spending and Income

We now must consider how the market value of total output—or for that matter, any single unit of output—is measured. Returning to Table 7-2, how can we measure the market value of a suit?

We can determine how much a consumer, the final user, pays for it. Or we can add up all the wage, rental, interest, and profit incomes created in its production. This second approach is the value-added technique discussed in Table 7-2.

The final-product and value-added approaches are two ways of looking at the same thing. *What is spent on a product is received as income by those who contributed to its production.* Chapter 2's circular flow model demonstrated this. If $350 is spent on the suit, then $350 is the total amount of income derived from its production. You can verify this by looking at the incomes generated by firms A, B, C, D, and E in Table 7-2—$120, $60, $40, $50, and $80—which total $350.

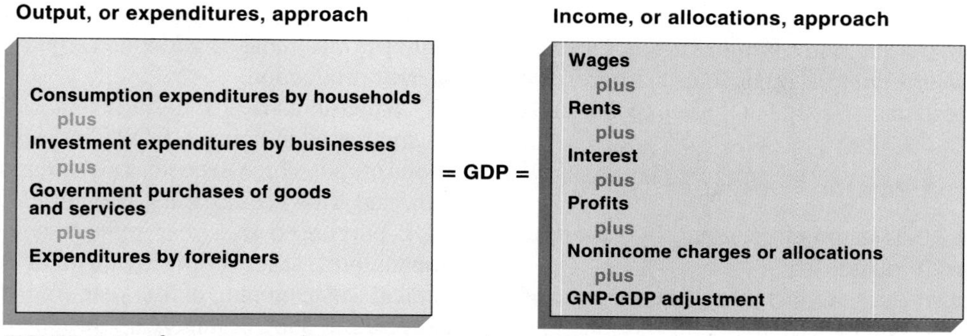

Output, or expenditures, approach   **Income, or allocations, approach**

Consumption expenditures by households		Wages
plus		plus
Investment expenditures by businesses		Rents
plus	**= GDP =**	plus
Government purchases of goods and services		Interest
plus		plus
Expenditures by foreigners		Profits
		plus
		Nonincome charges or allocations
		plus
		GNP-GDP adjustment

FIGURE 7-1   The output and income approaches to GDP
There are two general approaches to measuring gross domestic product. We can determine the value of output by summing the expenditures on that output. Alternatively, with some modifications, we can determine GDP by adding up the components of income arising from producing that output.

This equality of the expenditure for a product and the income derived from its production is guaranteed, because profit income is a balancing item. Profit—or loss—is the income remaining after wage, rent, and interest incomes have been paid by the producer. If the wage, rent, and interest incomes the firm must pay in getting the suit produced are less than the $350 expenditure for the suit, the difference will be the firm's profits.[1] Conversely, if wage, rent, and interest incomes exceed $350, profits will be negative. That is, losses will be realized, to balance the expenditure on the product and the income derived from its production.

It is the same for the output of the economy as a whole. There are two ways of looking at GDP: One is to see GDP as the sum of all the expenditures in buying that total output. This is the *output,* or **expenditures, approach.** The other views GDP in terms of the income derived or created from producing it. This is the *earnings,* or *allocations,* or **income, approach.**

GDP can be determined either by adding up all that is spent to buy this year's total output or by summing up all the incomes derived from the production of this year's output. Putting this as an equation, we can say

$$\text{Amount spent to purchase this year's total output} = \left\{ \begin{array}{l} \text{money income} \\ \text{derived from} \\ \text{production of} \\ \text{this year's output} \end{array} \right.$$

This is more than an equation: It is an identity. Buying (spending money) and selling (receiving money

income) are two aspects of the same transaction. *What is spent on a product is income to those who have contributed their human and property resources in getting that product produced and to market.*

For the economy as a whole, we can expand our identity to read as in Figure 7-1. Considered as output, all final goods produced in the American economy are purchased by the three domestic sectors—households, businesses, and government—and by foreign buyers. On the income side of GDP, this figure shows that (aside from a few complicating factors, discussed later) the total receipts businesses acquire from the sale of total output are allocated among resource suppliers as wage, rent, interest, and profit income. Using this diagram as a point of reference, we next examine the types of expenditures and the incomes derived from them.

EXPENDITURES APPROACH

To determine GDP through expenditures, we add up all types of spending on finished or final goods and services. But national income accountants have more precise terms for the different types of spending than those in Figure 7-1.

Personal Consumption Expenditures (C)

What we have called "consumption expenditures by households" is **personal consumption expenditures** to national income accountants. It includes expenditures by households on *durable consumer goods* (automobiles, refrigerators, video recorders), *non-*

---

[1]The term "profits" is used here in the accounting sense to include both normal profits and economic profits as defined in Chapter 4.

durable consumer goods (bread, milk, vitamins, pencils, shirts, toothpaste), and *consumer expenditures for services* (of lawyers, doctors, mechanics, barbers). We will use *C* to designate the total of these expenditures.

Gross Private Domestic Investment (I_g)

This refers to all investment spending by American business firms. It includes:

1 All final purchases of machinery, equipment, and tools by business enterprises
2 All construction
3 Changes in inventories

This is more than we have meant by "investment" thus far. We therefore must explain why each of these three items is included under the general heading of gross private domestic investment.

The first group simply restates our definition of investment spending as the purchase of tools, machinery, and equipment.

The second—all construction—such as building a new factory, warehouse, or grain elevator is also a form of investment. But why include residential construction as investment rather than consumption? Because apartment buildings are investment goods which, like factories and grain elevators, are income-earning assets. Other residential units which are rented are for the same reason investment goods. Owner-occupied houses are investment goods because they could be rented out to yield a money income return, even though the owner may not do so. For these reasons all residential construction is considered as investment.

Finally, changes in inventories are counted as investment because an increase in inventories is, in effect, "unconsumed output." And that precisely is what investment is!

Inventory Changes as Investment Because GDP measures total current output, we must include in GDP any products produced this year even though *not sold* this year. To be an accurate measure of total production, GDP must include the market value of any additions to inventories accruing during the year. A tube of lipstick produced in 1995 must be counted as GDP in 1995, even though it remains unsold as of February of 1996. If we excluded an increase in inventories, GDP would understate the current year's total production. If businesses have more goods on their shelves and in warehouses at year's end than they had at the start, the economy has produced more

than it has purchased during this year. This increase in inventories must be added to GDP as a measure of *current* production.

What about a decline in inventories? This must be subtracted in figuring GDP. The economy can sell a total output which exceeds its production by dipping into, and thus reducing its inventories. Some of the GDP purchased this year reflects not current production but, rather, a drawing down of inventories on hand at the beginning of this year. And inventories on hand at the start of any year's production represent the production of previous years. The tube of lipstick produced in 1995, but sold in 1996, cannot be counted as 1996 GDP. Consequently, a decline in inventories in any specific year means the economy has purchased more than it has produced during that year. This means society has purchased all of that year's output plus some of the inventories inherited from the previous year's production. Because GDP is a measure of the *current* year's output, we must omit any purchases of past production, that is, any drawing down of inventories, in determining GDP.[2]

Noninvestment Transactions We have discussed what investment is. Now we need to emphasize what it isn't. Investment does *not* refer to the transfer of paper assets or secondhand tangible assets. Economists exclude the buying of stocks and bonds from their definition of investment, because such purchases merely transfer the ownership of existing assets. It's the same for the resale of existing assets.

Investment is the construction or manufacture of *new* capital assets. The production of these assets creates jobs and income; the exchange of claims to existing capital goods does not.

Gross versus Net Investment Our concepts of investment and investment goods include purchases of machinery and equipment, all construction, and changes in inventories. Let's now focus on the modifiers, "gross," "private," and "domestic," which describe investment. "Private" and "domestic" tell us we are talking about spending by private business enterprises as opposed to governmental (public) agencies, and that the investment is in America—rather than abroad.

---

[2]Both *planned* and *unplanned* changes in inventories are included as part of investment. In the former, firms may intentionally increase their inventories because aggregate sales are growing. In the latter, an unexpected drop in sales may leave firms with more unsold goods (larger inventories) than intended.

"Gross" is not as simple. **Gross private domestic investment** includes production of *all* investment goods—those which replace machinery, equipment, and buildings used up to produce the current year's output *plus* any net additions to the economy's stock of capital. Gross investment includes both replacement and added investment. **Net private domestic investment** refers only to the added investment in the current year.

To make the distinction clear: In 1994 our economy produced about $1038 billion of capital goods. However, in producing the GDP in 1994, the economy used up $716 billion of machinery and equipment. Thus, our economy added $322 (or $1038 minus $716) billion to its stock of capital in 1994. Gross investment was $1038 billion in 1994; net investment was only $322 billion. The difference is the value of the capital used up or depreciated in the production of 1994's GDP.

Net Investment and Economic Growth The relationship between gross investment and *depreciation* —the amount of the nation's capital worn out or used up in a particular year—indicates whether our economy is expanding, static, or declining. Figure 7-2 illustrates these cases.

1 Expanding Economy When gross investment exceeds depreciation (Figure 7-2a), the economy is expanding since its production capacity—measured by its stock of capital goods—is growing. Net investment is a positive figure in an expanding economy. For example, in 1994 gross investment was $1038 billion, and $716 billion of capital goods was consumed in producing that year's GDP. Our economy ended 1994 with $322 billion more capital goods than it had on hand at the start of the year. Bluntly stated, we added $322 billion to our "national factory" in 1994.

Increasing the supply of capital goods is a basic means of expanding the productive capacity of the economy (Chapter 2).

2 Static Economy In a stationary or static economy gross investment and depreciation are equal (Figure 7-2b). The economy is standing pat; it produces just enough capital to replace what is consumed in producing the year's output—no more, no less. Example: During World War II, the Federal government purposely restricted private investment to free resources to produce war goods. In 1942 gross private investment and depreciation (replacement investment) were each about $10 billion. Thus net invest-

ment was about zero. At the end of 1942 our stock of capital was roughly the same as at the start of that year. Our economy was stationary; its production facilities failed to expand.

3 Declining Economy An economy declines when gross investment is less than depreciation, that is, when the economy uses up more capital in a year than it produces (Figure 7-2c). When this happens net investment will be negative—the economy will be *disinvesting*. Depressions foster such circumstances. During bad times, when production and employment are low, the nation has a greater productive capacity than it is currently using. There is no incentive to replace depreciated capital equipment, much less add to the existing stock. Depreciation is likely to exceed gross investment, with the result that the nation's stock of capital is less at the end of the year than it was at the start.

This was the case during the Great Depression. In 1933 gross investment was only $1.6 billion, while the capital consumed during that year was $7.6 billion. Net disinvestment was therefore $6 billion. That is, net investment was a minus $6 billion, indicating that the size of our "national factory" shrunk during that year.

We will use I for domestic investment spending and attach the subscript g when referring to gross and n when referring to net investment. *(Key Question 5)*

Government Purchases (G)

Government purchases *include* all governmental spending (Federal, state, and local) on the finished products of businesses and all direct purchases of resources—labor, in particular. It *excludes* all government transfer payments, because such outlays do not reflect any current production but merely transfer governmental receipts to certain specific households. We'll use G to indicate **government purchases.**

Net Exports (Xₙ)

Do American international trade transactions enter into national income accounting? They do, and in this way: On the one hand, we include all spending in American markets accounting for or inducing the production of goods and services in the American economy. Spending by people abroad on American goods will account for American output just as will spending by Americans. Thus, we must add in what the rest of

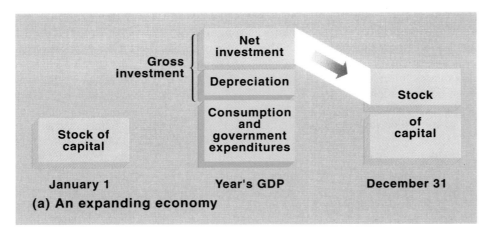

(a) An expanding economy

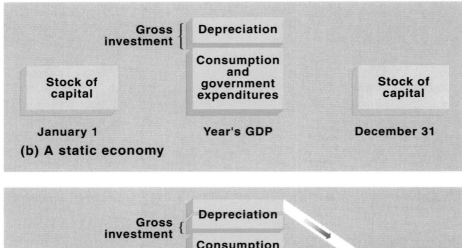

(b) A static economy

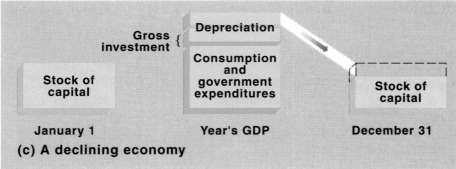

(c) A declining economy

FIGURE 7-2 Expanding, static, and declining economies

In an expanding economy (a), gross investment exceeds depreciation, which means that the economy is making a net addition to its stock of capital facilities. In a static economy (b), gross investment precisely replaces the capital facilities depreciated in producing the year's output, leaving the stock of capital goods unchanged. In a declining economy (c), gross investment is insufficient to replace the capital goods depreciated by the year's production. As a result, the economy's stock of capital declines.

the world spends on American goods and services—we must add in the value of American exports—in determining GDP by the expenditures approach.

On the other hand, we know that part of consumption, investment, and government purchases is for imports, meaning goods and services produced abroad. This spending does *not* reflect production activity in the United States. The value of imports is subtracted to avoid overstating total production in the United States.

Rather than treat American exports and imports separately, our national income accountants take the difference between them. Thus, net exports of goods and services, or **net exports,** *is the amount by which foreign spending on American goods and services exceeds American spending on foreign goods and services.*

If people abroad buy $45 billion worth of American exports and Americans buy $35 billion worth of foreign imports in a year, net exports would be *plus*

TABLE 7-3 The income statement for the economy, 1994 *(in billions of dollars)*

Receipts: expenditures approach		Allocations: income approach	
Personal consumption expenditures (C).......	$4627	Compensation of employees...	$4005
Gross private domestic investment (I_g)........	1038	Rents...	28
Government purchases (G).........................	1174	Interest..	407
Net exports (X_n).....................................	−102	Proprietors' income	473
		Corporate income taxes	203
		Dividends...	205
		Undistributed corporate profits	135
		National income	5456
		Indirect business taxes	553
		Consumption of fixed capital......................................	716
		Gross national product	6725
		Plus: Net foreign factor income earned in the U.S.	12
Gross domestic product	$6737	Gross domestic product	$6737

Source: U.S. Department of Commerce data. Because of rounding, details may not add up to totals.

$10 billion. Our definition of net exports might result in a negative figure. If the rest of the world spends $30 billion on American exports and Americans spend $40 billion on foreign imports, our "excess" of foreign spending over American spending is *minus* $10 billion.

Note in Table 7-3 that in 1994 Americans spent $102 billion more on foreign goods and services than the rest of the world spent on American goods and services, a matter which will receive our attention in later chapters.

The letter X_n will designate net exports.

$C + I_g + G + X_n = GDP$

These four categories of expenditures—personal consumption expenditures *(C)*, gross private domestic investment *(I_g)*, government purchases *(G)*, and net exports *(X_n)*—are comprehensive. They include all possible types of spending. Added together, they measure the market value of the year's output or, in other words, the GDP. That is,

$C + I_g + G + X_n = GDP$

For 1994 (Table 7-3):

$4627 + $1038 + $1174 − $102 = $6737

Global Perspective 7-1 compares GDPs for selected nations.

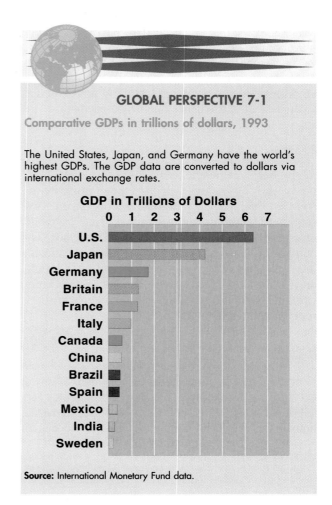

GLOBAL PERSPECTIVE 7-1

Comparative GDPs in trillions of dollars, 1993

The United States, Japan, and Germany have the world's highest GDPs. The GDP data are converted to dollars via international exchange rates.

GDP in Trillions of Dollars

U.S.
Japan
Germany
Britain
France
Italy
Canada
China
Brazil
Spain
Mexico
India
Sweden

Source: International Monetary Fund data.

INCOME APPROACH[3]

How was this $6737 billion of expenditure allocated or distributed as income? It would be simple if we could say that all total expenditures on the economy's annual output flowed to American households as wage, rent, interest, and profit incomes. But the picture is complicated by two *nonincome charges* against the value of total output (GDP). These are (1) consumption of fixed capital and (2) indirect business taxes. Also, a complication arises because some of the wage, rent, interest, and profit income flows to foreigners. But let's first look at the national income elements of GDP in Table 7–3.

Compensation of Employees

This largest income category comprises primarily the wages and salaries paid by businesses and government to suppliers of labor. It also includes wage and salary supplements, in particular, payments by employers into social insurance and into a variety of private pension, health, and welfare funds for workers. These wage and salary supplements are part of the employer's cost of obtaining labor and are treated as a component of the firm's total wage payments.

Rents

Rents consist of income payments received by households and businesses which supply property resources. Examples include the monthly payments of renters to landlords and the annual lease payments by corporate tenants for the use of office space. The number in Table 7-3 is *net* rent—gross rental income minus depreciation of rental property. It is the rental income which remains after allowable depreciation (wearing out of the property) is subtracted from gross rental revenues.

Interest

Interest refers to money income payments flowing from private businesses to the suppliers of money capital. It includes items such as the interest payments households receive on saving deposits, certificates of

deposits (CDs), and corporate bonds. For reasons we will soon discuss, interest payments made by government are excluded from interest income.

Proprietors' Income

What we have loosely termed "profits" is broken into two basic accounts: *proprietors' income* or income of unincorporated businesses, and *corporate profits*. Proprietors' income refers to the net income of sole proprietorships and partnerships. Corporate profits cannot be dismissed so easily, because corporate earnings may be distributed in several ways.

Corporate Profits

Generally, three things happen with corporate profits:

1 *Corporate Income Taxes* A portion will be claimed by, and therefore flow to, government as *corporate income taxes.*

2 *Dividends* A part of the remaining corporate profits will be paid out to stockholders as *dividends.* Such payments flow to households, which are the ultimate owners of all corporations.

3 *Undistributed Corporate Profits* What remains of corporate profits after both corporate income taxes and dividends have been paid is called *undistributed corporate profits.* These retained corporate earnings, along with consumption of fixed capital, are invested currently or in the future in new plants and equipment, increasing the real assets of the investing businesses.

Indirect Business Taxes

When we add employee compensation, rents, interest, proprietors' income, and corporate profits we get *national income*—all income earned by American-supplied resources, whether here or abroad. To move from national income to GDP we need to consider two nonincome charges against the value of total output. We also must move from "national" to "domestic" via the GNP-GDP adjustment discussed previously.

The first nonincome charge arises because government levies certain taxes, called **indirect business taxes,** which business firms treat as costs of production and therefore add to the prices of the products they sell. Such taxes include general sales taxes, excises, business property taxes, license fees, and customs duties. Assume a firm produces a product selling at $1. Production of this item creates an equal

---

[3]Some instructors may choose to omit this section because the expenditures approach is more relevant for the analysis of Chapters 9–12.

amount of wages, rental, interest, and profit income. But now government imposes a 5 percent sales tax on all products sold at retail. The retailer adds this 5 percent to the price of the product, raising its price from $1 to $1.05 and thus shifting the sales tax to consumers.

This $.05 of tax must be paid to government before the remaining $1 can be paid to households as wage, rent, interest, and profit incomes. Furthermore, this flow of indirect business taxes to government is not earned income, because government contributes nothing directly to the production of the good in return for these tax receipts. For this reason we must exclude indirect business taxes when figuring the total income earned by the factors of production. Part of the value of the annual output reflects the indirect business taxes passed along to consumers as higher product prices. This part of the value of the nation's output is *not* available as either wages, rents, interest, or profits.

Depreciation: Consumption of Fixed Capital

The second nonincome charge against the value of total output is depreciation. The useful life of capital equipment extends far beyond the year of purchase. Actual expenditures for capital goods and their productive life are not synchronized in the same accounting period. To avoid gross understatement of profit and therefore of total income in the year of purchase and overstatement of profit and total income in succeeding years, individual businesses estimate the useful life of their capital goods and allocate the total cost of such goods over the life of the machinery. The annual charge which estimates the amount of capital equipment used up in each year's production is called "depreciation." Depreciation is a bookkeeping entry designed to yield a more accurate statement of profit income and hence total income of a firm in each year.

If profits and total income for the economy are to be stated accurately, a gigantic depreciation charge must be made against the total receipts of the business sector. This depreciation charge is called **consumption of fixed capital**—the allowance for capital goods "consumed" in producing this year's GDP. This depreciation charge constitutes the difference between gross and net investment (I_g and I_n). That is,

$$I_n = I_g - \text{consumption of fixed capital}$$

For present purposes, the significance of this charge is that part of the business sector's receipts is

not available for income payments to resource suppliers. Part of the receipts—some of the value of production—is a cost of production which reduces business profits. But, unlike other costs of production, depreciation does not add to anyone's income. In terms of physical goods and services, the consumption of fixed capital tells us that a portion of this year's GDP must be set aside to replace the machinery and equipment used up in its production. Not all of GDP can be consumed as income by society without impairing the economy's stock of production facilities.

Net Foreign Factor Income Earned in the United States

Our last step is to make the GNP-GDP adjustment discussed earlier. The sum of wages, rents, interest, and profits yields *national* income. Adding the two nonincome charges—indirect business taxes and consumption of fixed capital—gives us gross *national* product (GNP). To convert GNP to gross *domestic* product, we add to GNP net foreign factor income earned (output produced) in the United States. Recall that this amount was positive in 1994, making GDP slightly larger than GNP.

Table 7-3 summarizes our discussions of the expenditure and income approaches to GDP. This table is an income statement for the economy as a whole. The left side shows what the economy produced in 1994 and the total revenue derived from that production. The right side indicates how the income derived from the production of 1994's GDP was allocated.

QUICK REVIEW 7-1

■ Gross domestic product (GDP) measures the total market value of all final goods and services produced within the economy in a specific year.

■ The expenditures approach to GDP sums total spending on final goods and services: $C + I_g + G + X_n$.

■ When net investment is positive, the economy's production capacity expands; when net investment is negative, the economy's production capacity erodes.

■ The income approach to GDP sums the total income earned by American resource suppliers, adds two nonincome charges (depreciation and indirect business taxes), and adds net foreign factor income earned in the United States.

OTHER SOCIAL ACCOUNTS

Our discussion has centered on GDP as a measure of the economy's annual output. But there are related social accounting concepts of equal importance which can be derived from GDP. In identifying these concepts, let's start with GDP and make adjustments—subtractions and additions—necessary to derive the related social accounts.

Net Domestic Product (NDP)

GDP as a measure of total output has a defect: It gives an exaggerated sense of output available for consumption and new capital. *It fails to make allowance for that part of this year's output needed to replace the capital goods used up in the year's production.*

Example: Using hypothetical figures, suppose that on January 1, 1996, the economy had $100 billion of capital goods on hand. Assume also that during 1996, $40 billion of this equipment and machinery is used up in producing a GDP of $800 billion. Thus, on December 31, 1996, the stock of capital goods on hand stands at only $60 billion.

Does the GDP figure of $800 billion measure what this year's production adds to society's well-being? In fact, it would be much more accurate to subtract from the year's GDP the $40 billion worth of capital goods used to replace the machinery and equipment consumed in producing that GDP. This leaves a *net* output figure of $800 minus $40, or $760 billion.

Net output is a better measure of the production available for consumption and additions to the capital stock than is *gross* output. In our system of social accounting, we derive **net domestic product** (NDP) by subtracting from GDP the consumption of fixed capital. Recall this measures replacement investment or the value of the capital used up in a year's production. In 1994:

	Billions
Gross domestic product	$6737
Consumption of fixed capital	−716
Net domestic product	$6021

NDP is GDP adjusted for depreciation. It measures the total annual output the entire economy—households, businesses, governments, and foreigners—

might consume without impairing our capacity to produce in ensuing years.

Adjusting Table 7-3 from GDP to NDP is easy. On the income side, we strike consumption of fixed capital. The other items should add up to a NDP of $6021 billion. On the expenditure side, we adjust *gross* private domestic investment to *net* private domestic investment by subtracting replacement investment as measured by the consumption of fixed capital. In 1994, a gross investment figure of $1038 billion less a depreciation charge of $716 billion results in a net private domestic investment figure of $322 billion and therefore a NDP of $6021 billion.

National Income (NI)

In analyzing some problems, it is useful to know how much American resource suppliers earned for their contributions of land, labor, capital, and entrepreneurial talent. As already noted, **national income** is all income *earned* by American-owned resources, whether located here or abroad. To determine national income, we must make two adjustments to NDP.

1 Net output produced (net income earned) by foreign-supplied resources in the United States must be *subtracted* from NDP. That is, we want a measure of all factor income earned by Americans. We need to *exclude* the net income earned in the United States by foreigners.

2 Indirect business taxes also must be *subtracted* from NDP. Government contributes nothing directly to production in return for the indirect business tax revenues it receives; government is not an economic resource. Indirect taxes are not part of payments to resources, and thus not part of national income.

In 1994:

	Billions
Net domestic product	$6021
Net foreign factor income earned in the U.S.	−12
Indirect business taxes	−553
National income	$5456

National income can be thought of as how much it costs society to obtain its *national* output. We know that NI can be obtained through the income approach by directly adding up employee compensation, rent, interest, proprietors' income, and corporate profits (Table 7-3).

$$\text{GDP price index}_{1993} = \frac{\$64}{\$50} \times 100 = 128$$

The price index for 1996 is 128. This index value may be thought of as the price level for 1996.

These steps can be used to calculate the price level for all years in a series of years. For example, the price index in the 1987 base year is found by discovering the price of the particular collection of goods and services produced in 1987 and comparing this price to the price of that same market basket in the base year. However, in this special case, the "specific year" and the "reference year" are the same. That is,

$$\frac{\text{GDP}}{\text{price}}_{\text{index}_{1987}} = \frac{\text{price of market basket}_{1987}}{\text{price of market basket}_{1987}} \times 100$$

The GDP price index for the 1987 base year therefore is 100. In effect, we automatically set the price index at 100 in the base year.

Likewise, if we wanted to know the GDP price index for 1950, we would determine 1950 output and then estimate what that same or a similar collection of goods and services would have cost in the 1987 base year. If prices on the 1950 output had quadrupled between 1950 and 1987, the price ratio of the market basket would be $\frac{1}{4}$ (= .25) and the 1950 GDP price index would be 25 (= .25 $\times$ 100).

Once a GDP price index has been constructed for each year in a series of years, comparisons of price levels between years is possible. Examples:

1 If the price indexes for 1996 and 1987 are 128 and 100, respectively, we can calculate that the price level increased by 28 percent [= (128 − 100)/100] between the two years.

2 If, as suggested by our previous illustration, the price index for 1950 is 25, we can say that the price level rose by 412 percent [(128 − 25)/25] between 1950 and 1993.

3 If the price index fell from 100 in 1987 to 98 in 1988, we would know that the price level declined by 2 percent [= (98 − 100)/100].

Conclusions: The GDP price index or deflator compares the price of each year's output to the price of that same output in the base year or reference year. A series of price indexes for various years enables us to compare price levels among years. An increase in the GDP price index from one year to the next constitutes *inflation*; a decrease in the price index constitutes *deflation*. *(Key Question 10)*

NOMINAL AND REAL GDP

Inflation or deflation complicates GDP because GDP is a price-times-quantity figure. The data from which the national income accountants estimate GDP are the total sales revenues of business firms; however, these revenue figures include changes in *both* the quantity of output *and* the level of prices. This means that a change in either the quantity of total physical output or the price level will affect the size of GDP. However, it is the quantity of goods produced and distributed to households which affects their standard of living, not the size of the price tags on these goods. The hamburger of 1970 which sold for 65 cents yielded the same satisfaction as will an identical hamburger selling for $2.00 in 1996.

The situation facing government accountants is this: In gathering statistics from financial reports of businesses and deriving GDP in various years, they get nominal GDP figures. They do *not* know directly to what extent changes in price and changes in quantity of output have accounted for the changes in nominal GDP. For example, they would not know directly if a 4 percent increase in nominal GDP resulted from a 4 percent rise in output and zero inflation, from a zero percent change in output and 4 percent inflation, or some other combination of changes in output and the price level, say, a 2 percent increase in output and 2 percent inflation. The problem is adjusting a price-times-quantity figure so it will accurately reflect changes in physical output or quantity, not changes in prices.

As we will soon see, this problem is resolved by *deflating* GDP for rising prices and *inflating* it when prices are falling. These adjustments give us a picture of GDP for various years *as if* prices and the value of the dollar were constant. A GDP figure which reflects current prices, that is, *not* adjusted for changes in the price level, is called *unadjusted, current dollar, money,* or nominal GDP. Similarly, GDP figures which are inflated or deflated for price level changes measure *adjusted, constant dollar,* or **real GDP.**

The Adjustment Process

The process for adjusting current dollar or nominal GDP for inflation or deflation is straightforward. The GDP deflator for a specific year tells us the ratio of that year's prices to the prices of the same goods in the base year. The GDP deflator or GDP price index therefore can be used to inflate or deflate nominal GDP figures for each year to express them in real terms—in other words, *as if* base year prices prevailed. *The simplest and most direct method of deflating or inflating a year's nominal GDP is to express that year's index number in decimal form, and divide it into the nominal GDP.* This yields the same result as the more complex procedure of dividing nominal GDP by the corresponding index number and multiplying the quotient by 100. In equation form:

$$\frac{\text{Nominal GDP}}{\text{Price index (in hundredths)}} = \text{real GDP}$$

To illustrate in Table 7-5, in 1996 nominal GDP is $64 and the price index for that year is 128 (= 1.28 in hundredths). Real GDP in 1996, therefore, is:

$$\frac{\$64}{1.28} = \$50$$

In summary, the real GDP figures measure the value of total output *as if* the prices of the products had been constant from the reference or base year throughout all the years being considered. Real GDP thus shows the market value of each year's output measured in dollars of the same value, or purchasing power, as the base year.

Real GDP is clearly superior to nominal GDP as an indicator of the economy's production performance.

Inflating and Deflating

Table 7-6 illustrates the **inflating** and **deflating** process. Here we are taking actual nominal GDP figures for selected years and adjusting them with the GDP deflator for these years to obtain real GDP. Note the base year is 1987.

Because the long-run trend has been for the price level to rise, we need to increase, or *inflate,* the pre-1987 figures. This upward revision of nominal GDP acknowledges that prices were lower in years before 1987 and, as a result, nominal GDP figures understated the real output of those years. Column 4 reveals what GDP would have been had the 1987 price level prevailed.

The rising price level has caused the nominal GDP figures for the post-1987 years to overstate real output. These figures must be reduced, or *deflated,* as in column 4, to gauge what GDP would have been in 1988, 1991, and so on, if 1987 prices had prevailed.

In short, while the *nominal* GDP figures reflect both output and price changes, the *real* GDP figures

TABLE 7-6 Adjusting GDP for changes in the price level *(selected years, in billions of dollars)*

(1) Year	(2) Nominal, or unadjusted, GDP	÷	(3) Price level index,* percent (1987 = 100)	=	(4) Real, or adjusted, GDP, 1987 dollars
1960	$ 513.4		26.0		$1974.6 (= 513.4 ÷ 0.260)
1965	702.7		28.4		_____
1970	1010.7		35.1		$2879.5 (= 1010.7 ÷ 0.351)
1975	1585.9		49.2		_____
1980	2708.0		71.7		$3776.8 (= 2708.0 ÷ 0.717)
1983	3405.0		87.2		$3904.8 (= 3405.0 ÷ 0.872)
1985	4038.7		94.4		_____
1986	4268.6		96.9		$4405.2 (= 4268.6 ÷ 0.969)
1987	4539.9		100.0		$4539.9 (= 4539.9 ÷ 1.000)
1988	4900.4		103.9		_____
1989	5250.8		108.5		$4839.4 (= 5250.8 ÷ 1.085)
1991	5724.8		117.6		$4893.0 (= 5724.8 ÷ 1.170)
1994	6736.9		126.1		$5342.5 (= 6736.9 ÷ 1.261)

*U.S. Department of Commerce implicit price deflators.
Source: U.S. Department of Commerce data.

allow us to estimate changes in real output, because the real GDP figures, in effect, hold the price level constant.

Example: For 1994 nominal GDP was $6736.9 billion and the price index was 126.1 or 26.1 percent higher than 1987. To compare 1994's GDP with 1987's we express the 1994 index in hundredths (1.261) and divide it into the nominal GDP of $6736.9 as shown in column 4. The resulting real GDP of $5342.5 is directly comparable to the 1987 base year's GDP because both reflect only changes in output and *not* price level changes. You should trace through the computations involved in deriving the real GDP figures given in Table 7-6 and also determine real GDP for years 1965, 1975, 1985, and 1988, for which the figures have been purposely omitted. *(Key Question 11)*

QUICK REVIEW 7-3

■ A price index compares the combined price of a specific market basket of goods and services in a particular year to the combined price of the same basket in a base year.

■ Nominal GDP is output valued at current prices; real GDP is output valued at constant prices (base year prices).

■ A year's nominal GDP can be adjusted to real GDP by dividing nominal GDP by the GDP price index (expressed in hundredths).

GDP AND SOCIAL WELFARE

GDP is a reasonably accurate and extremely useful measure of domestic economic performance. It is not, and was never intended to be, an index of social welfare. GDP is merely a measure of the annual volume of market-oriented activity.

> . . . any number of things could make the Nation better off without raising its real [GDP] as measured today: we might start the list with peace, equality of opportunity, the elimination of injustice and violence, greater brotherhood among Americans of different racial and ethnic backgrounds, better understanding between parents and children and between husbands and wives, and we could go on endlessly.[5]

---

[5]Arthur M. Okun, "Social Welfare Has No Price Tag," *The Economic Accounts of the United States: Retrospect and Prospect* (U.S. Department of Commerce, July 1971), p. 129.

Nevertheless, it is widely held that there should be a strong positive correlation between real GDP and social welfare, that is, greater production should move society toward "the good life." Thus, we must understand some of the shortcomings of GDP—why it might understate or overstate real output and why more output will not necessarily make society better off.

Nonmarket Transactions

Certain production transactions do not appear in the market. Thus, GDP as a measure of the market value of output fails to include them. Examples include the production services of a homemaker, the work of the carpenter who repairs his or her own home, or the work of the professor who writes a scholarly article. Such transactions are *not* reflected in the profit and loss statements of business firms and therefore escape the national income accountants, causing GDP to be understated. However, some large nonmarket transactions, such as that part of farmers' output which farmers consume themselves, are estimated by national income accountants.

Leisure

Over many years, leisure has increased significantly. The workweek declined from about 53 hours at the turn of the century to approximately 40 hours by the end of World War II. Since then the average workweek has declined more slowly and is currently about 35 hours. Also, the expanded availability of paid vacations, holidays, and leave time has reduced the work year. This increased leisure has had a positive effect on our well-being. Our system of social accounting understates our well-being by not directly recognizing this. Nor do the accounts reflect the satisfaction—the "psychic income"—which people derive from their work.

Improved Product Quality

GDP is a quantitative, not a qualitative, measure. It does not accurately reflect improvements in product quality. For example, there is a fundamental qualitative difference between a $3000 personal computer purchased today and a computer for that same amount bought just a few years ago. Today's $3000 computer has far more speed and storage capacity, as

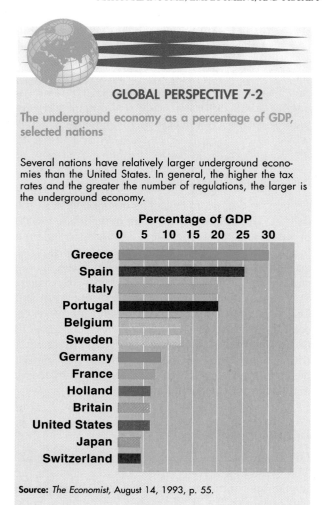

GLOBAL PERSPECTIVE 7-2

The underground economy as a percentage of GDP, selected nations

Several nations have relatively larger underground economies than the United States. In general, the higher the tax rates and the greater the number of regulations, the larger is the underground economy.

Percentage of GDP

Greece
Spain
Italy
Portugal
Belgium
Sweden
Germany
France
Holland
Britain
United States
Japan
Switzerland

Source: *The Economist,* August 14, 1993, p. 55.

well as a clearer monitor and improved multimedia capabilities.

Failure to account for quality improvement is a shortcoming of GDP accounting: Quality improvements clearly affects economic well-being as much as does the quantity of goods. Because product quality has improved over time, GDP understates improvement in our material well-being.

Composition and Distribution of Output

Changes in the composition and the allocation of total output among specific households may influence economic welfare. GDP, however, reflects only the size of output and tells us nothing about whether this collection of goods is "right" for society. A hand gun and a set of encyclopedias, both selling for $350, are weighted equally in the GDP. And some economists feel that a more equal distribution of total output would increase national economic well-being. If they are correct, a future trend toward a less unequal distribution of GDP would enhance the economic welfare of society. A more unequal distribution—which appears to be occurring—would have the reverse effect.

Conclusion: GDP measures the size of the total output but does not reflect changes in the composition and distribution of output which might also affect the economic well-being of society.

Per Capita Output

For many purposes the most meaningful measure of economic well-being is per capita output. Because GDP measures the size of total output, it may conceal or misrepresent changes in the standard of living of individual households. GDP may rise, but if population is also growing rapidly, the per capita standard of living may be constant or even declining.

This is the plight of many of the less developed countries. Ethiopia's domestic output grew at 1.2 percent per year in 1980–1992. But annual population growth exceeded 3 percent, resulting in a yearly decrease in per capita output of 1.9 percent.

GDP and the Environment

There are undesirable and much publicized "gross domestic by-products" accompanying the production and growth of the GDP such as dirty air and water, automobile junkyards, congestion, noise, and other forms of environmental pollution. The costs of pollution reduce our economic well-being. These spillover costs associated with the production of the GDP are not now deducted from total output and, thus, GDP overstates our national economic welfare.

Ironically, the final physical product of economic production and consumption is garbage. A rising GDP means more garbage, and may mean more pollution and a greater divergence between GDP and economic well-being. In fact, under existing accounting procedures, when a manufacturer pollutes a river and government spends to clean it up, the cleanup expense is added to the GDP while the pollution is not subtracted!

The Underground Economy

Economists agree there is a large underground or subterranean sector in our economy. Some participants in this sector engage in illegal activities such as gambling, loansharking, prostitution, and the narcotics trade. These may well be "growth industries." Obviously, persons receiving income from illegal businesses choose to conceal their incomes.

Most participants in the underground economy are in legal activities, but do not fully report their incomes to the Internal Revenue Service (IRS). A waiter or waitress may underreport tips from customers. A businessperson may record only a portion of sales receipts for the tax collector. A worker who wants to retain unemployment compensation or welfare benefits may obtain an "off the books" or "cash only" job so there is no record of his or her work activities. A nanny who is an illegal immigrant may wish to be paid in cash, so as not to be detected by the immigration service, and her employer may acquiesce, as a way to avoid paying social security taxes.

Although there is no consensus on the size of the underground economy, estimates suggest it is between 7 to 12 percent of the recorded GDP. In 1994, that meant GDP was understated by between $472 and $808 billion. If this additional income had been taxed at a 20 percent average tax rate, the Federal budget deficit for 1994 would have declined from $203 billion to between a $109 billion and a $41 billion deficit.

Global Perspective 7-2 indicates the relative sizes of underground economies of selected nations.

CHAPTER SUMMARY

1 Gross domestic product (GDP), a basic measure of society's economic performance, is the market value of all final goods and services produced within the borders of the United States in a year. It is more than GNP—output produced by Americans, regardless of where located—by the amount of net foreign factor income earned (output produced) in the United States.

2 Intermediate goods, nonproduction transactions, and secondhand sales are purposely excluded in calculating GDP.

3 GDP may be calculated by summing total expenditures on all final output or by summing the income derived from the production of that output.

4 By the expenditures approach GDP is determined by adding consumer purchases of goods and services, gross investment spending by businesses, government purchases, and net exports; GDP = $C + I_g + G + X_n$.

5 Gross investment can be divided into **a** replacement investment (required to maintain the nation's stock of capital at its existing level), and **b** net investment (the net increase in the stock of capital). Positive net investment is associated with a growing economy; negative net investment with a declining economy.

6 By the income or allocations approach GDP is calculated as the sum of compensation to employees, rents, interest, proprietors' income, corporate income taxes, dividends, undistributed corporate profits, *plus* the two nonincome charges (indirect business taxes and capital consumption allowance) and *plus* net foreign factor income earned in the United States.

7 Other national income accounting measures are derived from GDP. Net domestic product (NDP) is GDP less the consumption of fixed capital. National income (NI) is total income earned by American resource suppliers; it is found by subtracting both net foreign factor income earned in the United States and indirect business taxes from NDP. Personal income (PI) is the total income paid to households prior to any allowance for personal taxes. Disposable income (DI) is personal income after personal taxes have been paid. DI measures the amount of income households have available to consume or save.

8 Price indexes are computed by comparing the price of a specific collection or "market basket" of output in a particular period to the price (cost) of the same market basket in a base period and multiplying the outcome (quotient) by 100. The GDP deflator is the price index associated with adjusting nominal GDP to account for inflation or deflation and thereby obtaining real GDP.

9 Nominal (current dollar) GDP measures each year's output valued in terms of the prices prevailing in that year. Real (constant dollar) GDP measures each year's output in terms of the prices which prevailed in a selected base year. Because it is adjusted for price level changes, real GDP measures the level of production activity.

10 National income accounting measures exclude nonmarket and illegal transactions, changes in leisure and product quality, the composition and distribution of output, and the environmental effects of production. Nevertheless, these measures are reasonably accurate and very useful indicators of the nation's economic performance.

LAST WORD

THE CPI: DOES IT OVERSTATE INFLATION?

The consumer price index is the most widely reported measure of inflation; therefore, we should become familiar with its characteristics and limitations.

The consumer price index (CPI) measures changes in the prices of a "market basket" of some 300 goods and services purchased by urban consumers. The present composition of the market basket was determined from a survey of the spending patterns of urban consumers in the 1982–1984 period. Unlike the GDP deflator, the CPI is a historical, fixed-weight price index. In each year, the composition or "weight" of the items in the market basket remains the same as in the base period (1982–1984). If 20 percent of consumer spending was on housing in 1982–1984, it is assumed that 20 percent of consumer spending is still spent on housing in 1990 and 1996. The base period is changed roughly every ten years, with a new base period scheduled to appear soon. The idea behind the historical, fixed-weight approach is to measure changes in the cost of a constant standard of living. These changes supposedly measure the rate of inflation facing consumers.

But here are four problems with the CPI which cause it to overstate the true rate of inflation, according to critics.

1   Changed Spending Patterns   Although the composition of the market basket is assumed to remain unchanged, in fact, consumers do change their spending patterns. In particular, they shift their purchases

in response to changes in relative prices. When the price of beef rises while fish and chicken prices are steady, consumers substitute away from beef and buy fish or chicken instead. This means that over time consumers are buying a market basket which contains more of the relatively low-priced and less of the relatively high-priced goods and services. The fixed-weight CPI assumes that these substitutions have not occurred. Therefore the index overstates the actual cost of living.

2   New Products   Many new consumer goods and services such as fax machines, multimedia computers, and cellular phone service either are not included or are severely underweighted in the market basket used to construct the CPI. Often prices of new products drop following their introductions. The CPI, with

TERMS AND CONCEPTS

national income
   accounting
gross national product
gross domestic product
final and intermediate
   goods
double counting
value added

expenditures and
   income approaches
personal consumption
   expenditures
gross and net private
   domestic investment
government purchases

net exports
indirect business taxes
consumption of fixed
   capital
net domestic product
national income
personal income

disposable income
price index
consumer price index
GDP deflator
nominal GDP
real GDP
inflating and deflating

QUESTIONS AND STUDY SUGGESTIONS

1   "National income statistics are a powerful tool of economic understanding and analysis." Explain this statement. "An economy's output is its income." Do you agree?

2   *Key Question*   *Why do national income accountants include only final goods in measuring total output? How do GNP and GDP differ? How do GDP and NDP differ?*

its historical, fixed-weight market basket fails to pick up these price changes and thus overstates inflation.

3 Quality Improvements The CPI does not take quality improvements into account. To the extent that product quality has improved since the base year, prices should be higher. We ought to pay more for medical care today than in a decade ago because it is generally of higher quality. Its the same for automobiles, automobile tires, electronic equipment, and many other items. But the CPI assumes that all of the increases in the nominal value of the market basket arises solely from inflation, not quality improvements. Again the CPI overstates the rate of inflation.

4 Price Discounting In calculating the CPI, the Federal government continually rotates the stores they check for prices. But once a set of stores is selected, the price survey only picks up price changes on a same-store basis. If Kmart raises its price on footwear, then this price increase is picked up in the CPI. But the CPI survey does not fully account for price discounts on footwear that Kmart may have offered during a particular period. If people increasingly shop for discounts and special sales to buy footwear—and other products—the CPI will overstate the true increase in the cost of living.

In general, economists conclude that the CPI overstates the rate of inflation, perhaps by as much as 0.5 percentage points a year. So what? The problem is that the CPI affects nearly everyone. Examples abound: Government payments to social security receivers are indexed to the CPI; when the CPI rises, social security payments automatically rise in lockstep. Millions of unionized workers have cost-of-living adjustment clauses (COLAs) in their labor contracts. Moreover, the wage demands of virtually all workers—union or nonunion, blue- or white-collar—are linked to the rate of inflation as measured by the CPI. Also, interest rates are often linked to the rate of inflation, as measured by the CPI. When the CPI rises, lenders raise their nominal interest rates to keep their real interest rates constant. And, the Federal Reserve bases its monetary policy (Chapter 15) on the CPI.

Another consequence of an overstated CPI stems from the indexing of personal income tax brackets. This adjusting of tax brackets upward to account for the rate of inflation was begun in 1985 to resolve an inequity in the personal income tax. The intent of indexing is to prevent inflation from pushing households into higher tax brackets even though their real incomes have not increased. For example, a 10 percent increase in your *nominal* income might put you in a higher marginal tax bracket and increase the proportion of your income paid in taxes. But if product prices are also rising by 10 percent, your *real* or inflation-adjusted income has remained constant. The result would be an unintended redistribution of real income from taxpayers to the Federal government. The purpose of indexing tax brackets was to prevent this redistribution. However, to the extent that the CPI *overstates* inflation, indexing will reduce government's tax share. The Federal government will be deprived of substantial tax revenues and real income will be redistributed from government to taxpayers.

3 What is the difference between gross private domestic investment and net private domestic investment? If you were to determine net domestic product through the expenditures approach, which of these two measures of investment spending would be appropriate? Explain.

4 Why are changes in inventories included as part of investment spending? Suppose inventories declined by $1 billion during 1996. How would this affect the size of gross private domestic investment and gross domestic product in 1996? Explain.

5 *Key Question* Use the concepts of gross and net investment to distinguish between an expanding, a static, and a declining economy. "In 1933 net private domestic investment was minus $6 billion. This means in that particular year the economy produced no capital goods at all." Do you

agree? Explain: "Though net investment can be positive, negative, or zero, it is quite impossible for gross investment to be less than zero."

6 Define net exports. Explain how the United States' exports and imports each affect domestic production. Suppose foreigners spend $7 billion on American exports in a given year and Americans spend $5 billion on imports from abroad in the same year. What is the amount of America's net exports? Explain how net exports might be a negative amount.

7 *Key Question* The following is a list of domestic output and national income figures for a given year. All figures are in billions. The ensuing questions ask you to determine the major national income measures by both the expenditure and income methods. Answers derived by each approach should be the same.

Personal consumption expenditures	$245
Net foreign factor income earned in the U.S.	4
Transfer payments	12
Rents	14
Consumption of fixed capital (depreciation)	27
Social security contributions	20
Interest	13
Proprietors' income	33
Net exports	11
Dividends	16
Compensation of employees	223
Indirect business taxes	18
Undistributed corporate profits	21
Personal taxes	26
Corporate income taxes	19
Corporate profits	56
Government purchases	72
Net private domestic investment	33
Personal saving	20

a *Using the above data, determine GDP and NDP by both the expenditure and income methods.*

b *Now determine NI (1) by making the required additions and subtractions from GDP, and (2) by adding up the types of income which comprise NI.*

c *Make those adjustments of NI required in deriving PI.*

d *Make the required adjustments from PI (as determined in 7c) to obtain DI.*

8   Given the following national income accounting data, compute   a GDP,   b NDP, and   c NI. All figures are in billions.

Compensation of employees	$194.2
U.S. exports of goods and services	17.8
Consumption of fixed capital	11.8
Government purchases	59.4
Indirect business taxes	14.4
Net private domestic investment	52.1
Transfer payments	13.9
U.S. imports of goods and services	16.5
Personal taxes	40.5
Net foreign factor income earned in the U.S.	2.2
Personal consumption expenditures	219.1

9   Why do national income accountants compare the market value of the total outputs in various years rather than actual physical volumes of production? Explain. What problem is posed by any comparison over time of the market

values of various total outputs? How is this problem resolved?

10   *Key Question*   *Suppose that in 1974 the total output of a hypothetical economy consisted of three goods—X, Y, and Z—produced in the following quantities: X = 4, Y = 1, Z = 3. Also suppose that in 1974 the prices of X, Y, and Z were as follows: X = $3, Y = $12, and Z = $5. Finally, assume that in 1987 the prices of these goods were X = $5, Y = $10, and Z = $10. Determine the GDP price index for 1974, using 1987 as the base year. By what percent did the price level rise between 1974 and 1987?*

11   *Key Question*   *The following table shows nominal GDP and an appropriate price index for a group of selected years. Compute real GDP. Indicate in each calculation whether you are inflating or deflating the nominal GDP data.*

Year	Nominal GDP, billions	Price level index, percent (1987 = 100)	Real GDP, billions
1959	$ 494.2	25.6	$_____
1964	648.0	27.7	$_____
1967	814.3	30.3	$_____
1973	1349.6	41.3	$_____
1978	2232.7	60.3	$_____
1988	4900.4	103.9	$_____

12   Which of the following are included in deriving this year's GDP? Explain your answer in each case.

   a   Interest on an AT&T bond

   b   Social security payments received by a retired factory worker

   c   The services of a painter in painting the family home

   d   The income of a dentist

   e   The money received by Smith when he sells a 1983 Chevrolet to Jones

   f   The monthly allowance which a college student receives from home

   g   Rent received on a two-bedroom apartment

   h   The money received by Mac when he resells this year's model Plymouth to Ed

   i   Interest received on government bonds

   j   A 2-hour decline in the length of the workweek

   k   The purchase of an AT&T bond

   l   A $2 billion increase in business inventories

   m   The purchase of 100 shares of GM common stock

   n   The purchase of an insurance policy

13   (Last Word) What is the CPI? How does it differ from the GDP deflator? What are the shortcomings of the CPI in accurately measuring inflation?

8

MACROECONOMIC INSTABILITY: UNEMPLOYMENT AND INFLATION

In an ideal economy, real GDP would expand over time at a brisk, steady pace. Additionally, the price level, as measured by the GDP deflator or the consumer price index, would remain constant or only rise slowly. The result would be neither significant unemployment nor inflation. Several periods of U.S. history fit this pattern. But experience shows that steady economic growth, full employment, and a stable price level cannot be taken for granted. Recent examples: (1) The inflation rate skyrocketed to 13.5 percent in 1980. (2) During a sixteen-month period in the early 1980s, real output fell by 3.3 percent. (3) Three million more people were unemployed in 1982 than in 1980. (4) The annual inflation rate rose from 1.9 percent in 1986 to 4.8 percent in 1989. (5) In 1990–1991, output in the U.S. economy turned downward for the eighth time since 1950.

In this and the next several chapters we explore the problem of achieving macroeconomic stability—steady economic growth, full employment, and price stability. The present chapter proceeds as follows: First, we establish an overview of the business cycle—the periodic fluctuations in output, employment, and price level characterizing our economy. Then we look in detail at unemployment: What are the various types of unemployment? How is unemployment measured? Why is unemployment an economic problem? Finally, we examine inflation—a problem which plagued us throughout the 1970s and into the early 1980s. What are inflation's causes and consequences?

THE BUSINESS CYCLE

Our society seeks economic growth *and* full employment *and* price level stability along with other less quantifiable goals (Chapter 1). American economic history reflects remarkable economic growth. Technological progress, rapid increases in productive capacity, and a standard of living among the highest in the world are major facets of the dynamic character of our economy.

The Historical Record

But our long-run economic growth has not been steady; it has been interrupted by periods of economic instability as Figure 8-1 reveals. Periods of rapid economic expansion have sometimes been marred by inflation. At other times, expansion has given way to recession and depression, that is, falling levels of employment and output. On a few occasions—as in the 1970s and early 1980s—we have experienced a

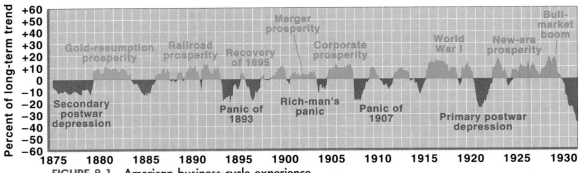

FIGURE 8-1 American business-cycle experience
As indicated by this chart which shows deviations from the long-run trend line of economic activity, the American economy has had periods of prosperity and depression. (AmeriTrust Company, Cleveland. Updated.)

rising price level and abnormally high unemployment simultaneously. In short, both unemployment and inflation have interrupted and complicated the long-term trend of economic growth.

Phases of the Cycle

The term **business cycle** refers to the recurrent ups and downs in the level of economic activity extending over several years. Individual business cycles vary substantially in duration and intensity. Yet all display common phases which are variously labeled by different economists. Figure 8-2 shows the several phases of a stylized business cycle.

1 Peak We begin our explanation with a **peak** at which business activity has reached a temporary maximum such as the middle peak in Figure 8-2. Here the economy is at full employment and the domestic output is also at or very close to capacity. The price level is likely to rise during this phase.

2 Recession The peak is followed by a **recession** —a period of decline in total output, income, employment, and trade, lasting six months or longer. This downturn is marked by widespread contractions of business in many sectors of the economy. But, because many prices are downwardly inflexible, the price level is likely to fall only if the recession is severe and prolonged—that is, if a depression occurs. An old one-liner is: "When your neighbor loses his job, it's a recession; when you lose your job it's a depression."

3 Trough The **trough** of the recession or depression is where output and employment "bottom out" at their lowest levels. The trough phase of the cycle may be short-lived or quite long.

4 Recovery In the **recovery** phase, output and employment expand toward full employment. As recovery intensifies, the price level may begin to rise before there is full employment and full capacity production.

Despite common phases, business cycles vary greatly in duration and intensity. Some economists

FIGURE 8-2 The business cycle
Economists distinguish between four phases of the business cycle and recognize the duration and strength of each phase is highly variable. A recession, for example, need not always entail serious and prolonged unemployment. Nor need a cyclical peak always entail full employment or inflation.

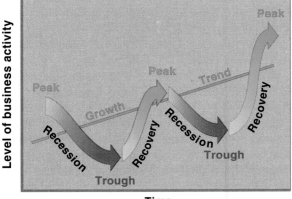

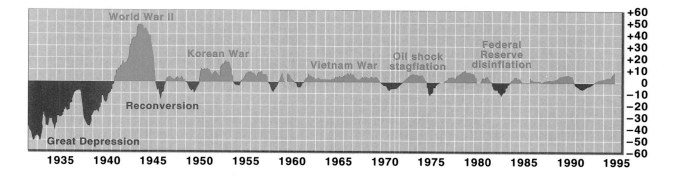

prefer to talk of business *fluctuations,* rather than *cycles,* because cycles imply regularity while fluctuations do not. The Great Depression of the 1930s resulted in a 40 percent decline in real GDP over a three-year period and seriously undermined business activity for a decade. By comparison, our more recent recessions —detailed in Table 8-1—have been minor in both intensity and duration.

Causation: A First Glance

Historically, economists have suggested many theories to explain fluctuations in business activity. Some contend that major innovations, such as the railroad, the automobile, or synthetic fibers have great impact on investment and consumption spending and therefore on output, employment, and the price level. But these major innovations occur irregularly and thus contribute to the variability of economic activity.

Other economists have explained the business cycle in terms of political and random events, as suggested by some of the labeling in Figure 8-1. Wars, for example, can be economically disruptive. A virtu-

ally insatiable demand for war goods during hostilities can generate a period of overfull employment and sharp inflation, followed by an economic slump when peace returns and military spending plummets.

Still other economists view the cycle as a purely monetary phenomenon. When government creates too much money, an inflationary boom is generated; too little money will precipitate a declining output and unemployment.

Despite their diverse opinions, most economists agree that the immediate determinant of the levels of domestic output and employment is the level of total or aggregate expenditures. In a market economy, businesses produce goods and services only if they can be sold profitably. If total spending is low, most businesses will not find it profitable to produce a large volume of goods and services. Hence, output, employment, and the level of incomes will all be low. A higher level of total spending will mean more production will be profitable; thus, output, employment, and incomes will all be higher also. Once the economy approaches full employment, further real output gains become more difficult to achieve and added spending begins to pull up the price level.

Noncyclical Fluctuations

Not all changes in business activity result from the business cycle. There can be **seasonal variations** in business activity. Pre-Christmas and pre-Easter buying rushes cause considerable fluctuations each year in the tempo of business activity, particularly in the retail industry. Agriculture, the automobile industry, and construction—all are subject to some degree of seasonality.

Business activity also displays a **secular trend** —expansion or contraction over a long period of

TABLE 8-1   United States recessions since 1950

Period	Duration in months	Depth (decline in real output)
1953–54	10	−3.7%
1957–58	8	−3.9
1960–61	10	−1.6
1969–70	11	−1.0
1973–75	16	−4.9
1980	6	−2.3
1981–82	16	−3.3
1990–91	8	−1.6

Source: Economic Report of the President, 1993. Updated.

years, for example, 25, 50, or 100 years. The long-run secular trend for American capitalism has been remarkable expansion (Chapter 19). For present purposes, the importance of this long-run expansion is that the business cycle fluctuates around a long-run growth trend. Note that in Figure 8-1 cyclical fluctuations are measured as deviations from the secular growth trend and that the stylized cycle of Figure 8-2 is drawn against a trend of growth.

Cyclical Impact: Durables and Nondurables

The business cycle is felt in every nook and cranny of the economy. The elements of the economy are related in such a way that few, if any, escape the negative effects of depression or surging inflation. However, the business cycle affects various individuals and segments of the economy in different ways and degrees.

Insofar as production and employment are concerned, service industries and industries producing nondurable consumer goods are somewhat insulated from the most severe effects of recession. And, of course, recession actually helps some firms such as pawnbrokers and law firms specializing in bankruptcies! Who is hit hardest by recession? Those firms and industries producing capital goods and consumer durables. The construction industry is particularly vulnerable. Industries and workers producing housing and commercial buildings, heavy capital goods, farm implements, automobiles, refrigerators, gas ranges, and similar products bear the brunt of bad times. Conversely, these "hard goods" industries are stimulated most by expansion.

Two facts help explain the vulnerability of these industries to the business cycle.

1 Postponability Within limits, purchase of hard goods is postponable. As the economy slips into bad times, producers frequently defer the acquisition of more modern production facilities and construction of new plants. The business outlook simply does not warrant increases in the stock of capital goods. The firm's present capital facilities and buildings will likely still be usable and in excess supply. In good times, capital goods are usually replaced before they completely depreciate. When recession strikes, however, business firms patch up their outmoded equipment and make it do. As a result, investment in capital goods will decline sharply. Some firms, having excess plant capacity, may not even bother to replace all the capi-

tal they are currently consuming. Net investment for them may be negative.

It's the same for consumer durables. When recession occurs and the family must trim its budget, plans for the purchases of durables such as major appliances and automobiles first feel the ax. People repair their old appliances and cars rather than buy new models. Food and clothing—consumer nondurables—are a different story. A family must eat and clothe itself. These purchases are much less postponable. To some extent the quantity and quality of these purchases will decline, but not so much as with durables.

2 Monopoly Power Most industries producing capital goods and consumer durables are industries of high concentration, where a small number of large firms dominate the market. These firms have sufficient monopoly power to temporarily resist lowering prices by restricting output in the face of a declining demand. Therefore, the impact of a fall in demand centers primarily on production and employment. The reverse is true in nondurable, or soft, goods industries, which are highly competitive and have low concentration. Firms are unable to resist price declines in such industries, and the declining demand reduces prices more than the levels of production.

Figure 8-3 provides historical evidence from the Great Depression on this point. It shows the percentage declines in price and quantity in ten selected industries as the economy fell from peak prosperity in 1929 to the depth of depression in 1933. Generally, high-concentration industries make up the top half of the table and low-concentration industries the bottom half. Note the drastic production declines and relatively modest price declines of the high-concentration industries. Contrast those outcomes to the large price declines and relatively small output declines which occurred in the low-concentration industries. *(Key Question 1)*

QUICK REVIEW 8-1

■ The long-term secular trend of real domestic output has been upward in the United States.

■ The typical business cycle has four phases: peak, recession, trough, and recovery.

■ Industries producing capital goods and consumer durables normally suffer greater output and employment declines during recession than do service and nondurable consumer goods industries.

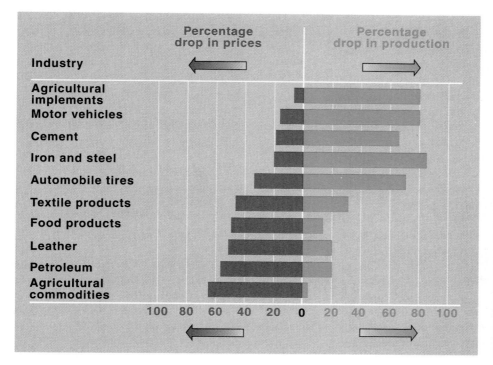

FIGURE 8-3 Relative price and production declines in ten industries, 1929–1933 The high-concentration industries shown in the top half had relatively small price declines and large declines in output during the early years of the Great Depression. In the low-concentration industries of the bottom half, price declines were relatively large, and production fell by relatively small amounts. [Gardiner C. Means, *Industrial Prices and Their Relative Flexibility* (Washington, 1953), p. 8.]

UNEMPLOYMENT

"Full employment" is hard to define. A person might think it means that everyone in the labor market—100 percent of the labor force—is employed. But that's not so; some unemployment is normal or warranted.

Types of Unemployment

Before defining full employment, we first need to know about three types of unemployment: frictional, structural, and cyclical.

Frictional Unemployment With freedom to choose occupations and jobs, at any time some workers will be "between jobs." Some will be voluntarily switching jobs. Others will have been fired and are seeking reemployment. Still others will be temporarily laid off from their jobs because of seasonality, for example, bad weather in the construction industry. And there will be some particularly young workers searching for their first jobs.

As these unemployed people find jobs or are called back from temporary layoffs, other job seekers and temporarily laid-off workers will replace them in the "unemployment pool." Therefore, even though the specific individuals who are unemployed for these reasons change from month to month, this type of unemployment persists.

Economists use the term **frictional unemployment**—consisting of *search unemployment* and *wait unemployment*—for workers who are either searching for jobs or waiting to take jobs in the near future. "Frictional" correctly implies that the labor market does not operate perfectly nor instantaneously—without friction—in matching workers and jobs.

Frictional unemployment is inevitable and, at least in part, desirable. Many workers who are voluntarily "between jobs" are moving from low-paying, low-productivity jobs to higher-paying, higher-productivity positions. This means more income for workers and a better allocation of labor resources—and therefore a larger real output—for the economy as a whole.

Structural Unemployment Frictional unemployment blurs into a category called **structural unemployment.** Here, economists mean "structural" in the sense of "compositional." Changes occur over time in the "structure" of consumer demand and in technology, which alter the "structure" of the total demand for labor. Because of such changes, some skills will be in less demand or may even become obsolete. Demand for other skills will expand, including skills which did not exist. Unemployment results because the composition of the labor force does not respond quickly or completely to the new structure of job opportunities. Some workers therefore find they have no readily marketable talents; their skills and experience become obsolete and unwanted by changes in technology and consumer demand. Similarly, the geographic distribution of jobs constantly changes. The migration of industry and employment opportunities from the Snow Belt to the Sun Belt over the past few decades is an example.

We can cite many illustrations of structural unemployment.

1 Many years ago, highly skilled glass blowers were thrown out of work by the invention of bottle-making machines.

2 Historically, mechanization of agriculture in the South dislodged thousands of low-skilled, poorly educated blacks from their jobs. Many migrated to northern cities and suffered prolonged unemployment because of racial bias and insufficient skills.

3 Many oil-field workers in the American "oil-patch" states found themselves structurally unemployed when the world price of oil nosedived in the 1980s. Less drilling and oil-related activity took place, resulting in widespread layoffs.

4 In the 1980s many pilots, mechanics, flight attendants, and other airline employees became structurally unemployed as a result of mergers following deregulation of the airline industry.

5 Recently, "corporate downsizing" has occurred in several major American manufacturing industries. Many people losing their jobs have been corporate managers, who have found it difficult to find new work.

6 Recent closures of military bases and other defense cutbacks have displaced many workers, adding them to the roles of the structurally unemployed.

The distinction between frictional and structural unemployment is hazy, however. The key difference is that frictionally unemployed workers have salable skills, while structurally unemployed workers are not readily reemployable without retraining, additional education, and possibly geographic relocation. Frictional unemployment is short-term; structural unemployment is more long-term, and therefore regarded as more serious.

Cyclical Unemployment **Cyclical unemployment** is caused by the recession phase of the business cycle, that is, by a deficiency of total spending. As the overall demand for goods and services decreases, employment falls and unemployment rises. For this reason, cyclical unemployment is sometimes called *deficient-demand unemployment.* During the recession year 1982, for example, the unemployment rate rose to 9.7 percent. This compares to a 6.7 percent unemployment rate in the recession year 1991. Cyclical unemployment at the depth of the Great Depression in 1933 was about 25 percent of the labor force.

Defining "Full Employment"

Full employment does *not* mean zero unemployment. Economists regard frictional and structural unemployment as essentially unavoidable. Thus, "full employment" is defined as something less than 100 percent employment of the labor force. Specifically, the **full-employment unemployment rate** is equal to the total of frictional and structural unemployment. Stated differently, the full-employment unemployment rate is achieved when cyclical unemployment is zero. The full-employment rate of unemployment is also referred to as the **natural rate of unemployment.** The real level of domestic output associated with the natural rate of unemployment is called the economy's **potential output.** The economy's potential output is the real output forthcoming when the economy is "fully employed."

From a slightly different vantage point the full or natural rate of unemployment results when labor markets are in balance in the sense that the number of job seekers equals the number of job vacancies. The natural rate of unemployment is some positive amount because it takes time for frictionally unemployed job seekers to find open jobs they can fill. Also, regarding the structurally unemployed, it takes time to achieve the skills and geographic relocation needed for reemployment. If the number of job seekers exceeds available vacancies, labor markets are not in balance; there is a deficiency of aggregate demand and cyclical unemployment is present. But if aggregate demand is excessive a "shortage" of labor will arise; the number of job vacancies will exceed the number of workers seeking employment. In this situation the actual rate of unemployment is below the natural rate. Unusually "tight" labor markets such as this are associated with inflation.

The concept of the natural rate of unemployment merits elaboration in two respects.

1 Not Automatic "Natural" does *not* mean the economy will always operate at the natural rate and realize its potential output. Our brief discussion of the business cycle demonstrated that the economy frequently operates at an unemployment rate higher than the natural rate. On the other hand, the economy may on some occasions achieve an unemployment rate lower than the natural rate. For example, during World War II, when the natural rate was about 4 percent, the pressure of wartime production resulted in an almost unlimited demand for labor. Overtime work was common as was "moonlighting" (working at more than one job). The government also froze some people working in "essential" industries in their jobs, reducing frictional unemployment. The actual rate of unemployment was below 2 percent in 1943–1945 and dropped to 1.2 percent in 1944. The economy was producing beyond its potential output, but incurred considerable inflationary pressure in the process.

2 Not Immutable The natural rate of unemployment itself is *not* immutable. It is subject to periodic revision because of the shifting demographics of the labor force or institutional changes (changes in society's laws and customs). In the 1960s this unavoidable minimum of frictional and structural unemployment was about 4 percent of the labor force. That is, full employment meant 96 percent of the labor force was employed. But today, economists generally agree that the natural rate of unemployment is about 5.5 to 6 percent.

Why is the natural rate of unemployment higher today than in the 1960s? First, the demographic makeup of the labor force has changed. Young workers—who traditionally have high unemployment rates—have become relatively more important in the labor force. Second, laws and customs have changed. For example, our unemployment compensation program has been expanded both in terms of numbers of workers covered and size of benefits. By cushioning the economic impact of unemployment, unemployment compensation permits unemployed workers to engage in a more deliberate, lengthy job search, increasing frictional unemployment and the overall unemployment rate.

Measuring Unemployment

Defining the full employment rate of unemployment is complicated by problems in measuring unemployment. Figure 8-4 is a helpful starting point. The total

Total population	260,991,000
Less: Under 16 and institutionalized	−64,177,000
Not in labor force	−65,758,000
Equals: Labor force	131,056,000
Employed	123,060,000
Unemployed	7,996,000

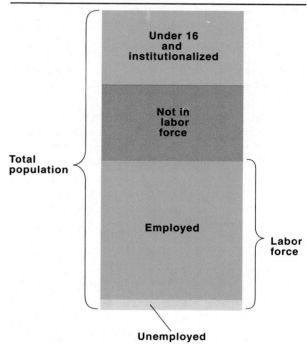

FIGURE 8-4 The labor force, employment, and unemployment, 1994
The labor force consists of persons sixteen years of age or older who are not in institutions and who are employed or unemployed.

population is divided into three groups. One comprises people under 16 years of age and people who are institutionalized, for example, in mental hospitals or correctional institutions. These people are not considered potential members of the labor force.

A second group, labeled "not in labor force," are adults who are potential workers, but for some reason—they are homemakers, in school, or retired—are not employed and are not seeking work.

The third group is the **labor force,** which constituted about 50 percent of the total population in 1994. The labor force is all people who are able and willing to work. Both those who are employed and those who are unemployed but actively seeking work are counted as being in the labor force. The *unemployment rate* is the percentage of the labor force which is unemployed:

$$\frac{\text{Unemployment}}{\text{rate}} = \frac{\text{unemployed}}{\text{labor force}} \times 100$$

In 1994 the unemployment rate was

$$6.1\% = \frac{7,996,000}{131,056,000} \times 100$$

Unemployment rates for selected years between 1929 and 1994 are provided on the inside covers of this book.

The Bureau of Labor Statistics (BLS) determines who is employed and who is not by a nationwide random survey of some 60,000 households each month. A series of questions is asked as to which members of the household are working, unemployed and looking for work, not looking for work, and so on. Despite the careful sampling and interview techniques used, the data collected from this survey are subject to a number of criticisms.

1 Part-time Employment The official data include all part-time workers as fully employed. In 1994 about 17.5 million people worked part time because of personal choice. Another 6.5 million part-timer workers either wanted to work full time, but could not find suitable full-time work, or worked fewer hours because of a temporary slack in consumer demand. These last two groups were, in effect, partially employed and partially unemployed. By counting them as fully employed the official BLS data *understate* the unemployment rate.

2 Discouraged Workers You must be actively seeking work to be counted as unemployed. An unemployed individual who is not actively seeking employment is classified as "not in the labor force." The problem is there are numerous workers who, after unsuccessfully seeking employment for a time, become discouraged and drop out of the labor force. The number of **discouraged workers** is larger during recession than prosperity; an estimated 1.25 million people fell into this category in recession-year 1991. By not counting discouraged workers as unemployed, official data *understate* the unemployment rate.

3 False Information Alternatively, the unemployment rate may be *overstated*. Some respondents who are not working may claim they are looking for work, even though they are not. These individuals will be classified as "unemployed," rather than "not in the labor force." A person's motivation for giving this false information is that unemployment compensation or welfare benefits may depend on professed job pursuit. The underground economy (Chapter 7) may also cause the official unemployment rate to be overstated. Someone fully employed in the South Florida drug traffic or "running numbers" for the Chicago Mafia may identify himself as "unemployed."

The point is that, although the unemployment rate is a basic consideration in policy making, it has certain shortcomings. And, while the unemployment rate is one of the best measures of the economic condition of the nation, it is not an infallible barometer. *(Key Question 5)*

Economic Cost of Unemployment

Problems in measuring the unemployment rate and defining the full-employment unemployment rate do not negate the fact that above-normal unemployment involves great economic and social costs.

GDP Gap and Okun's Law The basic economic cost of unemployment is forgone output. *When the economy fails to generate enough jobs for all who are able and willing to work, potential production of goods and services is irretrievably lost.* In Chapter 2's analysis, unemployment keeps society from moving to its production possibilities curve. Economists measure this sacrificed output in terms of the **GDP gap**—the amount by which *actual GDP* falls short of *potential GDP*.

Potential GDP is determined by assuming the natural rate of unemployment exists and projecting the economy's "normal" growth rate. Figure 8-5 shows the GDP gap for recent years and the close correlation between the actual unemployment rate (Figure 8-5b) and the GDP gap (Figure 8-5a). The higher the unemployment rate, the larger the GDP gap.

Macroeconomist Arthur Okun quantified the relationship between the unemployment rate and the GDP gap. **Okun's law** indicates that *for every 1 percent that the actual unemployment rate exceeds the natural rate, a $2\frac{1}{2}$ percent GDP gap occurs.* With this $1:2\frac{1}{2}$, or $1:2.5$, unemployment rate–GDP gap link, we can calculate the absolute loss of output associated with any unemployment rate. For example, in 1992 the unemployment rate was 7.4 percent, or 1.6 per-

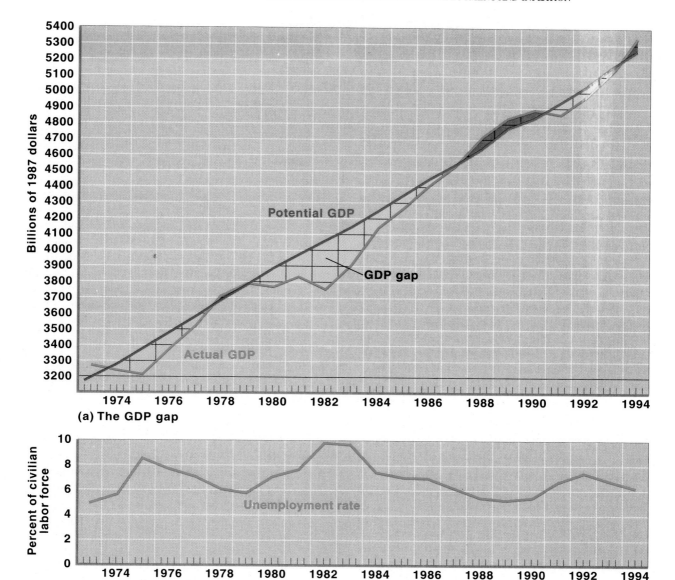

FIGURE 8-5   Potential and actual GDP (a) and the unemployment rate (b)
The difference between potential GDP and actual GDP is the GDP gap. The GDP gap measures the output the economy sacrifices because it fails to use fully its productive potential. A high unemployment rate means a large GDP gap. [*Economic Report of the President* and Robert J. Gordon, *Macroeconomics*, 6th ed. (New York: HarperCollins, 1993). Updated.]

centage points above an assumed 6 percent natural rate. Multiplying this 1.6 percent by Okun's 2.5 figure indicates that 1992's GDP gap was 4 percent. Stated differently, 1992's GDP would have been 4 percent larger than it actually was had the economy realized its full employment rate of unemployment. Applying this 4 percent loss to 1992's $6020 billion

nominal GDP, we find that the economy sacrificed almost $241 billion (= $6020 × 4 percent) of output because the natural rate of unemployment was not achieved. *(Key Question 3)*

As you see in Figure 8-5, sometimes the economy's actual output can exceed its potential output. We have already mentioned that this happened during World War II when unemployment rates fell below 2 percent. Extra shifts of workers were employed, capital equipment was used beyond its designed capacity, and overtime work and moonlighting were common. We observe in Figure 8-5 that an economic expansion caused actual GDP to exceed potential GDP in 1989, creating a "negative" GDP gap. Potential GDP can occasionally be exceeded, but the excess of actual over potential GDP cannot be sustained indefinitely.

Unequal Burdens Aggregate figures conceal the fact that the cost of unemployment is unequally distributed. An increase in the unemployment rate from 6 to, say, 9 or 10 percent might be more tolerable to society if every worker's hours of work and wage income were reduced proportionally. But this is not the case.

Table 8-2 contrasts unemployment rates for various labor market groups for two years. The economy achieved full employment in 1989, with a 5.3 percent unemployment rate, while the 1990–1991 recession pushed the 1992 unemployment rate to 7.4 percent. By observing the large variance in the rates of un-

TABLE 8-2 Unemployment rates by demographic group: full employment (1989) and recession (1992)*

Demographic group	Unemployment rate, 1989 (%)	Unemployment rate, 1992 (%)
Overall	5.3	7.4
Occupation		
Blue-collar	7.3	9.3
White-collar	3.9	4.6
Age		
16–19	15.0	20.2
Black, 16–19	32.4	39.8
White, 16–19	12.7	17.1
Males, 20+	4.5	7.0
Females, 20+	4.7	6.3
Race		
Black	11.4	14.1
White	4.5	6.5
Gender		
Female	5.4	6.9
Male	5.2	7.8
Duration		
15 weeks or more	1.1	2.6

*Civilian labor force data. In 1992 the economy was suffering the lingering unemployment effects of the 1990–1991 recession.
Source: Economic Report of the President; Employment and Earnings.

employment for the different categories *within each year* and comparing the rates *between the two years* we can make several generalizations.

1 Occupation White-collar workers enjoy lower unemployment rates than blue-collar workers. White-collar workers generally are employed in less cyclically vulnerable industries (services and nondurable goods) or are self-employed. Also, white-collar workers are usually less subject to unemployment during recession than blue-collar workers. Businesses want to retain their more-skilled white-collar workers in whom they have invested the expense of training. But its not always this way. During the 1990–1991 recession, many firms "downsized" their management structures, discharging more white-collar workers than ever before. The unemployment rate of white-collar workers increased more rapidly than for blue-collar laborers. Nevertheless, the unemployment rate of white-collar workers remained far below that of blue-collar workers.

2 Age Teenagers incur much higher unemployment rates than adults. Teenagers have low skill levels, more frequently quit their jobs, are more frequently discharged from jobs, and have little geographic mobility. Many unemployed teenagers are new in the labor market, searching for their first job.

3 Race The unemployment rate for blacks—adults and teenagers—has been roughly *twice* that of whites. Factors explaining this discrepancy include: discrimination in education and the labor market; the concentration of blacks in less-skilled (blue-collar) occupations; and the geographic isolation of blacks in central-city areas where employment opportunities for new labor-market entrants are minimal.

4 Gender Male and female unemployment rates are comparable. The lower unemployment rate for women in 1992 reflects the fact there are more male than female workers in such cyclically vulnerable hard-goods industries as automobiles, steel, and construction.

5 Duration The number of persons unemployed for long periods—fifteen weeks or more—as a percentage of the labor force is much less than the overall unemployment rate. This figure rises significantly during recessions. The "long-term" unemployed were only 1.1 percent of the labor force in 1989 compared to the overall 5.3 percent unemployment rate. A large proportion of unemployment is of relatively short duration. But also observe that the "long-term" unemployed were 2.6 percent of the labor force in 1992, implying more economic hardship.

Noneconomic Costs

Severe cyclical unemployment is more than an economic malady; it is a social catastrophe. Depression means idleness. And idleness means loss of skills, loss of self-respect, a plummeting of morale, family disintegration, and sociopolitical unrest. A job:

> . . . gives hope for material and social advancement. It is a way of providing one's children a better start in life. It may mean the only honorable way of escape from the poverty of one's parents. It helps to overcome racial and other social barriers. In short . . . a job is the passport to freedom and to a better life. To deprive people of jobs is to read them out of our society.[1]

History demonstrates that severe unemployment leads to rapid and sometimes violent social and political change. The movement to the left of American political philosophy during the Depression of the 1930s is an example. The Depression-inspired New Deal was a revolution in American political and economic thinking. Witness also Hitler's ascent to power against a background of unemployment. Furthermore, the high unemployment among blacks and other minorities unquestionably has been a cause of the unrest and violence periodically plaguing cities in America and elsewhere. At a more mundane level, research links increases in suicides, homicides, cardiovascular mortality, and mental illness to high unemployment.

International Comparisons

Unemployment rates vary greatly among nations over specific periods. The major reason for these differences is that nations have different natural rates of unemployment and also may be in different phases of their business cycles. Global Perspective 8-1 shows unemployment rates approximating U.S. measurement concepts for five industrialized nations for recent years. Historically, the United States has had

---

[1]Henry R. Reuss, *The Critical Decade* (New York: McGraw-Hill Book Company, 1964), p. 133.

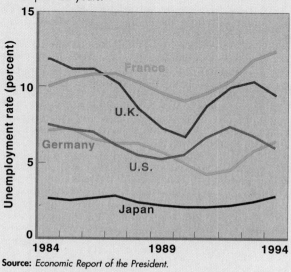

GLOBAL PERSPECTIVE 8-1

Unemployment rates in five industrial nations, 1984–1994

The unemployment rate in the United States has been below that in France, the United Kingdom, and Germany in several of the past ten years.

Source: *Economic Report of the President.*

higher unemployment rates than most industrially advanced nations. But this general pattern changed in the 1980s. Observe that the U.S. unemployment rate has been below the rates in the United Kingdom, Germany, and France in several years since 1983.

QUICK REVIEW 8-2

■ Unemployment is of three general types: frictional, structural, and cyclical.

■ The natural unemployment rate is estimated to be between 5.5 and 6 percent.

■ Society loses domestic output—goods and services—when cyclical unemployment occurs.

■ Blue-collar workers, teenagers, and blacks bear a disproportionate burden of unemployment.

INFLATION: DEFINED AND MEASURED

We now turn to inflation as an aspect of macroeconomic instability. The problems posed by inflation are more subtle than those of unemployment.

The Meaning of Inflation

Inflation is a rising general level of prices. This does not mean that *all* prices are rising. Even during periods of rapid inflation, some prices may be relatively constant and others falling. For example, although the United States experienced high rates of inflation in the 1970s and early 1980s, the prices of video recorders, digital watches, and personal computers declined. As we will see, one of the troublesome aspects of inflation is that prices rise unevenly. Some streak upward; others ascend leisurely; others do not rise.

Measuring Inflation

Inflation is measured by price index numbers such as those introduced in Chapter 7. Recall that a price index measures the general level of prices in reference to a base period.

To illustrate, the consumer price index uses 1982–1984 as the base period, meaning that period's price level is set equal to 100. In 1994 the price index was approximately 148. This means that prices were 48 percent higher in 1994 than in 1982–1984, or that a set of goods which cost $100 in 1982–1984 cost $148 in 1994.

The *rate* of inflation can be calculated for any specific year by subtracting last year's (1993) price index from this year's (1994) index, dividing that difference by the prior year's (1993) index, and multiplying by 100 to express it as a percentage. For example, the consumer price index was 144.5 in 1993 and 148.2 in 1994. The rate of inflation for 1994 is calculated as follows:

$$\frac{\text{Rate of}}{\text{inflation}} = \frac{148.2 - 144.5}{144.5} \times 100 = 2.6\%$$

The so-called **rule of 70** provides a quantitative appreciation of inflation. It permits quick calculation of the number of years it takes the price level to double. We divide the number 70 by the annual rate of inflation:

$$\frac{\text{Approximate number of years required to double}}{} = \frac{70}{\text{percentage annual rate of increase}}$$

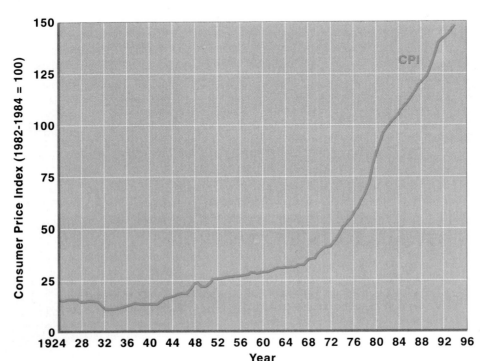

FIGURE 8-6   Price level behavior in the United States since 1924
The price stability of the 1920s and the deflation of the 1930s gave way to sharp inflation in the immediate post–World War II period. The 1951–1965 period had a reasonably stable price level, but the period since 1965 has clearly been an "age of inflation." (Bureau of Labor Statistics.)

For instance, a 3 percent annual rate of inflation will double the price level in about 23(= 70 ÷ 3) years. Inflation of 8 percent per year will double the price level in about 9(= 70 ÷ 8) years. Inflation at 12 percent will double the price level in only about 6 years. The rule of 70 is generally applicable. This rule will allow you, for example, to estimate how long it will take for real GDP *or* your savings account to double. *(Key Question 7)*

The Facts of Inflation

Figure 8-6 surveys inflation in the United States since 1924. The CPI curve represents annual increases in the consumer price index, which is constructed using a base period of 1982–1984. That is, the CPI for the 1982–1984 period is arbitrarily set at 100.

Although most of you have grown up in an "age of inflation," our economy has not always been inflation-prone. The price level was stable in the prosperous 1920s and declined—*deflation* occurred—during the early years of the Great Depression of the 1930s. Prices then rose sharply in the immediate post–World War II period (1945–1948). However, overall price stability characterized the 1951–1965 period in which the average annual increase in the price level was less than $1\frac{1}{2}$ percent. But the inflation starting in the late 1960s and then surging in the 1970s introduced Americans to double-digit inflation. In 1979 and 1980 the price level rose at 12 to 13 percent annual rates. By the 1990s, the inflation rate had settled into a 2–4 percent annual range. Historical annual rates of inflation can be found on the inside covers of this textbook.

Inflation is not distinctly American. All industrial nations have experienced this problem. Global Perspective 8-2 traces the post-1983 annual inflation rates of the United States, the United Kingdom, Japan, France, and Germany. Observe that inflation in the United States has been neither unusually high nor low relative to inflation in these other industrial countries.

Some nations have had double-digit, triple-digit, or still higher annual rates of inflation in recent years. In 1993, for example, the annual inflation rate in Hungary was 23 percent; in Turkey, 66 percent; and in Romania, 256 percent. A few nations experienced astronomical rates of inflation in 1993: Zaire, 1,987 percent; and Brazil, 2,148 percent!

Causes: Theories of Inflation

Economists distinguish between two types of inflation.

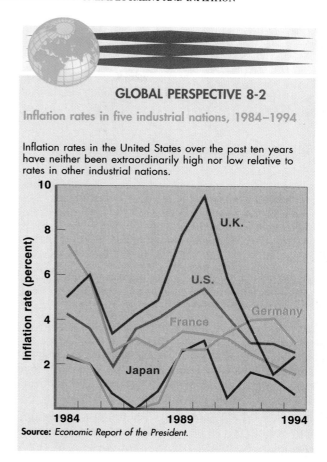

GLOBAL PERSPECTIVE 8-2

Inflation rates in five industrial nations, 1984–1994

Inflation rates in the United States over the past ten years have neither been extraordinarily high nor low relative to rates in other industrial nations.

Source: *Economic Report of the President.*

1 Demand-Pull Inflation Traditionally, changes in the price level have been attributed to an excess of total demand. The economy may attempt to spend beyond its capacity to produce; it may seek some point beyond its production possibilities curve. The business sector cannot respond to this excess demand by expanding real output because all available resources are already fully employed. This excess demand will bid up the prices of the fixed real output, causing **demand-pull inflation.** The essence of demand-pull inflation is "too much money chasing too few goods."

But the relationship between the total demand, on the one hand, and output, employment, and the price level, on the other, is not so simple. Figure 8-7 will help unravel the complications.

Range 1 In *range 1* total spending—the sum of consumption, investment, government, and net export spending—is so low that domestic output is far short of its maximum full-employment level. That means there's a substantial GDP gap. Unemployment rates

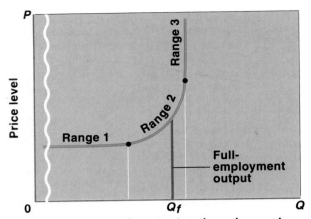

FIGURE 8-7 The price level and the level of employment

As aggregate expenditures increase, the price level generally begins to rise before full employment is reached. At some point, additional spending is purely inflationary.

are high and businesses have much idle production capacity. Now assume total demand increases. Real domestic output will rise and the unemployment rate will fall. But there will be little or no increase in the price level. Large amounts of idle human and property resources can be put back to work at their *existing* prices. An unemployed worker does not ask for a wage increase when called back to a job!

Range 2 As demand continues to rise, the economy enters *range 2* where it approaches—and then surpasses—full employment. Before full employment is achieved, the price level may begin to rise. As production expands, supplies of idle resources do not vanish simultaneously in all sectors and industries of the economy. Bottlenecks develop in some industries even though most have excess production capacity. Some industries are using fully their production capacity before others and cannot respond to further increases in demand for their products by increasing output. So their prices rise. As still more labor is hired, workplaces become increasingly congested and each added worker contributes less to output. Labor costs thus rise, forcing up product prices. As full employment is approached many firms hire less qualified workers and this, too, contributes to rising costs and prices. The inflation which occurs in this portion of range 2 is sometimes called *premature inflation* because it occurs before the economy reaches full employment.

Once the economy achieves full employment, additional spending and still higher prices in range 2 may induce some businesses to demand—and some households to supply—resources beyond the full-employment level of output. Firms may employ additional work shifts and use overtime to achieve greater output. Households may supply secondary workers such as teenagers and spouses, who normally would not choose to enter the labor force. In this part of range 2, the rate of unemployment falls below the natural rate of unemployment and actual GDP exceeds potential GDP. Here, the pace of inflation usually quickens.

Range 3 As total spending increases into *range 3*, the economy simply cannot supply more resources. Firms cannot respond to increases in demand by increasing output. Real domestic output is at an absolute maximum so that further increases in demand do only one thing—raise the price level. The rate of inflation may be high and growing because total demand greatly exceeds society's absolute capacity to produce. The demand-pull inflation of range 2 becomes the *pure* demand-pull inflation of range 3. There is no increase in real output to absorb some of the increased spending.

Reprise: Chapter 7's distinction between nominal and real GDP is helpful at this point. So long as the price level is constant (range 1), increases in nominal and real GDP are identical. But with inflation in range 2, nominal GDP is rising faster than real GDP, so nominal GDP must be "deflated" to measure changes in physical output. In range 3, nominal GDP is rising—perhaps rapidly due to high inflation—but real GDP is constant. In brief, the demand-pull inflation of ranges 2 and 3 breaks the link between nominal and real GDP.

2 Cost-Push or Supply-Side Inflation Inflation may also arise on the supply or cost side of the market. During several periods in our recent economic history the price level has risen even though aggregate demand was not excessive. These were periods when output and employment were both *declining* (evidence of a deficiency of total demand), while at the same time the general price level was *increasing*.

The theory of **cost-push inflation** explains rising prices in terms of factors which raise **per unit production cost**. Per unit production cost is the average cost of a particular level of output. This average cost is found by dividing the total cost of resource inputs by the amount of output produced. That is,

$$\text{Per unit production cost} = \frac{\text{total input cost}}{\text{units of output}}$$

Rising per unit production costs squeeze profits and reduce the amount of output firms are willing to supply at the existing price level. As a result, the economywide supply of goods and services declines. This decline in supply drives up the price level. Under this scenario, costs are *pushing* the price level upward, rather than demand *pulling* it upward, as with demand-pull inflation.

Two sources of cost-push inflation are increases in nominal wages and increases in the prices of nonwage inputs such as raw materials and energy.

Wage-Push Variant This theory of cost-push inflation suggests that, under some circumstances, unions may be a source of inflation. That is, unions exert some control over nominal wage rates through collective bargaining. Suppose large unions demand and receive large increases in wages. Let's also assume that these wage gains set the standard for wage increases paid to nonunion workers. If the economywide wage gains are excessive relative to any offsetting factors such as rises in output per hour, then producers' per unit production costs will rise. Firms will respond by reducing the amount of goods and services offered for sale. Assuming no change in demand, this decline in supply will increase the price level. Because the culprit is an excessive increase in nominal wages, this type of inflation is called the *wage-push variant* of cost-push inflation.

Supply-Shock Variant The *supply-shock* theory of cost-push inflation traces rising production costs—and therefore product prices—to abrupt, unanticipated increases in the costs of raw materials or energy inputs. The rocketing prices of imported oil in 1973–1974 and again in 1979–1980 are good illustrations. As energy prices rose during these periods, the costs of producing and transporting virtually every product in the economy increased. Rapid cost-push inflation ensued.

Complexities

The real world is more complex than our distinction between demand-pull and cost-push inflation suggests. Usually, it is difficult to distinguish between the two types of inflation. For example, suppose a boost in health care spending occurs which increases total spending, causing demand-pull inflation. As the demand-pull stimulus works its way through product and resource markets, individual firms find their wage costs, material costs, and fuel prices rising. From their perspective they must raise their prices because production costs have risen. Although this inflation is clearly demand-pull, it appears to be cost-push to business firms. It is not easy to label inflation as demand-side or supply-side without knowing the original cause of price and wage increases.

Cost-push and demand-pull inflation differ in another respect. Demand-pull inflation will continue so long as there is excess total spending. Cost-push inflation automatically is self-limiting; it will die out or cure itself. Reduced supply will decrease real domestic output and employment and these declines will constrain further cost increases. Cost-push inflation generates a recession and the recession inhibits additional cost increases. We'll see this in more detail in Chapter 17.

QUICK REVIEW 8-3

■ Inflation is a rising general level of prices, measured as a percentage change in a price index.

■ The United States' inflation rate has been within the middle range of rates of other advanced industrial nations, and far below the rates experienced by some nations.

■ Demand-pull inflation occurs when total spending exceeds the economy's ability to provide goods and services at the existing price level; total spending *pulls* the price level upward.

■ Cost-push inflation occurs when factors such as excessive wage increases and rapid increases in raw material prices drive up per unit production costs; higher costs *push* the price level upward.

REDISTRIBUTIVE EFFECTS OF INFLATION

Shifting from what causes inflation, we now look at its effects. We first consider how inflation redistributes income; then we examine possible effects on domestic output.

The relationship between the price level and the domestic output is ambiguous. Historically, real output and the price level have risen and fallen together.

In the past two decades, however, there have been times when real output has fallen while prices have continued to rise. We will dodge this matter for a moment by assuming that real output is constant and at the full-employment level. By holding real output and income constant we can isolate the effects of inflation on the distribution of that income. With a fixed national income pie, how does inflation affect the size of the slices going to different incomes receivers?

Nominal and Real Income To answer this question we must understand the difference between money income or nominal income and real income.[2] *Money* income or **nominal income** is the number of dollars received as wages, rent, interest, or profits. **Real income** measures the amount of goods and services nominal income can buy.

If your nominal income increases faster than the price level, your real income will rise. If the price level increases faster than your nominal income, your real income will decline. We can approximate a change in real income through this formula:

$$\begin{matrix} \text{Percentage} & & \text{percentage} & & \text{percentage} \\ \text{change in} & = & \text{change in} & - & \text{change in} \\ \text{real income} & & \text{nominal income} & & \text{price level} \end{matrix}$$

If your nominal income rises by 10 percent and the price level rises by 5 percent in the same period, your real income will *increase* by about 5 percent. Conversely, a 5 percent increase in nominal income accompanied by 10 percent inflation will *decrease* your real income by approximately 5 percent.[3]

The point is this: While inflation reduces the purchasing power of the dollar—the amount of goods and services each dollar will buy—it does not neces-

sarily follow that a person's real income will fall. The purchasing power of the dollar declines whenever inflation occurs; a decline in your real income or standard of living occurs only when your nominal income fails to keep pace with inflation.

Anticipations The redistribution effects of inflation depend on whether or not it is expected. With **anticipated inflation,** an income receiver *may* be able to take steps to avoid or lessen the adverse effects inflation would otherwise have on real income. The generalizations which immediately follow assume **unanticipated inflation.** We will then modify our generalizations to reflect the anticipation of inflation.

Fixed-Nominal-Income Receivers

Our distinction between nominal and real incomes shows that *inflation penalizes people who receive fixed nominal incomes.* Inflation redistributes income away from fixed income receivers toward others in the economy. The classic case is the elderly couple living on a private pension or annuity providing a fixed amount of nominal income each month. The pensioner who retired in 1980 on what appeared to be an adequate pension finds by 1995 that the purchasing power of that pension had been cut by one-half.

Similarly, landlords who receive lease payments of fixed dollar amounts will be hurt by inflation as they receive dollars of declining value over time. To a lesser extent some white-collar workers, some public sector employees whose incomes are dictated by fixed pay scales, and families living on fixed levels of welfare will be victims of inflation. Note, however, that Congress has *indexed* social security benefits; social security payments are tied to the consumer price index to prevent erosion from inflation.

Some people living on flexible incomes *may* benefit from inflation. The nominal incomes of such households may spurt ahead of the price level, or cost of living, with the result that their real incomes are enhanced. Workers in expanding industries and represented by aggressive unions may keep their nominal wages apace with, or ahead of, the rate of inflation.

Some wage earners are hurt by inflation. Those in declining industries or without strong unions may find that the price level skips ahead of their money incomes.

Business executives and other profit receivers might benefit from inflation. If product prices rise

---

[2]Chapter 7's distinction between nominal and real GDP is pertinent and you may want to review the "inflating" and "deflating" process involved in converting nominal GDP to real GDP (Table 7-6).

[3]A more precise calculation follows Chapter 7's process for changing nominal GDP to real GDP. Thus,

$$\text{Real income} = \frac{\text{nominal income}}{\text{price index (in hundredths)}}$$

In our first illustration, if nominal income rises by 10 percent from $100 to $110 and the price level (index) increases by 5 percent from 100 to 105, then real income has increased as follows:

$$\frac{\$110}{1.05} = \$104.76$$

The 5 percent increase in real income shown by the simple formula in the text is a good approximation of the 4.76 percent yielded by our more complex formula.

faster than resource prices, business receipts will grow at a faster rate than costs. Thus some—but not necessarily all—profit incomes will outdistance the rising tide of inflation.

Savers

Inflation hurts savers. *As prices rise, the real value, or purchasing power, of a nest egg of savings will deteriorate.* Savings accounts, insurance policies, annuities, and other fixed-value paper assets once adequate to meet rainy-day contingencies or provide for a comfortable retirement decline in real value during inflation. The simplest case is the individual who hoards money as a cash balance. A $1000 cash balance would have lost one-half its real value between 1980 and 1995. Of course, most forms of savings earn interest. But the value of savings will still decline if the rate of inflation exceeds the rate of interest.

Example: A household may save $1000 in a certificate of deposit (CD) in a commercial bank or savings and loan association at 6 percent annual interest. But if inflation is 13 percent (as in 1980), the real value or purchasing power of that $1000 will be cut to about $938 at the end of the year. That is, the saver will receive $1060 (equal to $1000 plus $60 of interest), but deflating that $1060 for 13 percent inflation means that the real value of $1060 is only about $938 (equal to $1060 divided by 1.13).

Debtors and Creditors

Inflation redistributes income by altering the relationship between debtors and creditors. *Unanticipated inflation benefits debtors (borrowers) at the expense of creditors (lenders).* Suppose you borrow $1000 from a bank, to be repaid in two years. If in that time the general level of prices were to double, the $1000 which you repay will have only half the purchasing power of the $1000 originally borrowed. True, if we ignore interest charges, the same number of dollars is repaid as was borrowed. But because of inflation, each of these dollars will now buy only half as much as it did when the loan was negotiated. As prices go up, the value of the dollar comes down. Thus, because of inflation, the borrower is given "dear" dollars but pays back "cheap" dollars.

The inflation of the past several decades has been a windfall to those who purchased homes in, say, the mid-1960s with fixed-interest-rate mortgages. Inflation has greatly reduced the real burden of their mortgage indebtedness. Also, until very recently the nominal value of housing has increased more rapidly than the overall price level.

The Federal government, which has amassed $4600 billion of public debt over the decades, has also been a beneficiary of inflation. Historically, the Federal government has regularly paid off its loans by taking out new ones. Inflation has permitted the Treasury to pay off its loans with dollars which have less purchasing power than the dollars it originally borrowed. Nominal national income and therefore tax collections rise with inflation; the amount of public debt owed does not. Thus, inflation reduces the real burden of the public debt to the Federal government. Because inflation benefits the Federal government in this way, some economists have questioned whether society can really expect government to be zealous in its efforts to halt inflation.

In fact, some nations such as Brazil once used inflation so extensively to reduce the real value of their debts that lenders forced them to borrow money in U.S. dollars or in some other relatively stable currency instead of their own currency. This prevents them from using domestic inflation as a means of subtly "defaulting" on their debt. Any inflation which they generate will reduce the value of their own currencies, but not the value of the dollar-denominated debt they must pay back.

Anticipated Inflation

The redistributive effects of inflation will be less severe or eliminated if people (1) anticipate inflation and (2) can adjust their nominal incomes to reflect expected price level changes. The prolonged inflation which began in the late 1960s prompted many unions in the 1970s to insist on labor contracts with **cost-of-living adjustment (COLA)** clauses to automatically adjust workers incomes for inflation.

Similarly, the redistribution of income from lender to borrower might be altered if inflation is anticipated. Suppose a lender (perhaps a commercial bank or savings and loan) and a borrower (a household) both agree that 5 percent is a fair rate of interest on a one-year loan, *provided* the price level is stable. But assume inflation has been occurring and is expected to be 6 percent over the next year. If the bank lends the household $100 at 5 percent, the bank will be paid back $105 at the end of the year. But if 6 percent inflation does occur during the year, the purchasing power of that $105 will have been reduced to about $99. The *lender* will in effect have paid the *borrower* $1 to use the lender's money for a year.

The lender can avoid this subsidy by charging an **inflation premium,** which means increasing the interest rate by the amount of the 6 percent anticipated inflation. By charging 11 percent the lender will receive back $111 at the end of the year which, adjusted for the 6 percent inflation, has the real value or purchasing power of about $105. Here there is a mutually agreeable transfer of purchasing power from borrower to lender of $5, or 5 percent, for the use of $100 for one year. Note that financial institutions have developed variable-interest-rate mortgages to protect themselves from the adverse effects of inflation. Incidentally, these examples imply that, rather than being a cause of inflation, high nominal interest rates are a consequence of inflation.

Our illustration shows the difference between the real rate of interest and the money or nominal rate of interest. The **real interest rate** *is the percentage increase in purchasing power that the lender receives from the borrower.* In our example the real interest rate is 5 percent. The **nominal interest rate** *is the percentage increase in money that the lender receives.* The nominal rate of interest is 11 percent in our example. The difference in these two concepts is that the real interest rate is adjusted or "deflated" for the rate of inflation while the nominal interest rate is not. The nominal interest rate is the sum of the real interest rate plus the premium paid to offset the expected rate of inflation. These distinctions are illustrated in Figure 8-8.

FIGURE 8-8 **The inflation premium and nominal and real interest rates**
The inflation premium—the expected rate of inflation—gets built into the nominal interest rate. Here, the real interest rate of 5 percent plus the inflation premium of 6 percent equals the nominal interest rate of 11 percent.

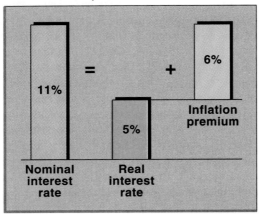

Addenda

Three final points must be mentioned.

1 Deflation The effects of unanticipated deflation are substantially the reverse of those of inflation. *Assuming no change in total output,* people with fixed money incomes will find their real incomes enhanced. Creditors will benefit at the expense of debtors. And savers will discover the purchasing power of their savings has grown because of falling prices.

2 Mixed Effects The fact that any family may be an income earner, a holder of financial assets, and an owner of real assets simultaneously will likely cushion the redistributive impact of inflation. If the family owns fixed-value monetary assets (savings accounts, bonds, and insurance policies), inflation will lessen their real value. But that same inflation may increase the real value of any property assets (a house, land) which the family owns.

In short, many families are simultaneously hurt and benefited by inflation. All these effects must be considered before we can conclude that the family's net position is better or worse because of inflation.

3 Arbitrariness The redistributive effects of inflation are *arbitrary;* they occur regardless of society's goals and values. Inflation lacks a social conscience and takes from some and gives to others, whether they be rich, poor, young, old, healthy, or infirm.

QUICK REVIEW 8-4

■ Inflation arbitrarily "taxes" those who receive relatively fixed nominal incomes and "subsidizes" some people who receive flexible nominal incomes.

■ Unanticipated inflation arbitrarily penalizes savers and it benefits debtors at the expense of creditors.

■ The nominal interest rate exceeds the real interest rate by the expected rate of inflation.

OUTPUT EFFECTS OF INFLATION

We have assumed thus far that the economy's real output is fixed at the full-employment level. As a result, the redistributive effects of inflation and deflation have been in terms of some groups gaining absolutely at the expense of others. *If* the size of the pie is fixed and inflation causes some groups to get larger slices, other groups get smaller slices. But, in fact, the level of domestic output—the size of the pie—may vary as the price level changes.

There is uncertainty and disagreement as to whether inflation will be accompanied by a rising or a falling real output. We will consider three scenarios, the first associating inflation with an expanding output and two with a declining output.

Stimulus of Demand-Pull Inflation

Some economists argue that full employment can only be achieved if some modest amount of inflation is tolerated. They base their reasoning on Figure 8-7. We know that the levels of real output and employment depend on aggregate spending.

If spending is low, the economy will operate in range 1. In this range there is price level stability, but real output is substantially below its potential and the unemployment rate is high.

If aggregate spending increases so that the economy moves into range 2, society must accept a higher price level—some amount of inflation—to achieve these higher levels of real output and the accompanying lower unemployment rates.

If further increases in aggregate spending pull the economy into range 3, that spending will be purely inflationary because the absolute capacity level of real output will have been reached.

The critical point is that in range 2 there appears to be a tradeoff between output (and thus employment) and inflation. Some moderate amount of inflation must be accepted if we are to realize high levels of output and employment. The high levels of spending which give us higher levels of output and low unemployment rates also cause some inflation. That means there is an inverse relationship between the inflation rate and the unemployment rate.

This scenario has been criticized in recent years. Many economists feel that any tradeoff between the inflation rate and the unemployment rate is transitory and there is no such tradeoff in the long run. This controversy will be explored in Chapter 17.

Cost-Push Inflation and Unemployment

There is an equally plausible set of circumstances in which inflation might reduce both output and employment. Suppose the level of total spending is initially such that the economy is enjoying full employment *and* price level stability. If cost-push inflation occurs, the existing level of total demand will now buy less real output. A specific level of total spending will only be capable of taking a smaller real output off the market because of the higher price level. Thus, real output will fall and unemployment will rise.

Economic events of the 1970s support this scenario. In late 1973 the Organization of Petroleum Exporting Countries (OPEC) became effective and exerted its market power to quadruple the price of oil. The cost-push inflationary effects generated rapid price level increases in the 1973–1975 period. At the same time the unemployment rate rose from slightly less than 5 percent in 1973 to 8.5 percent in 1975. Similar outcomes occurred in 1979–1980 in response to a second OPEC oil price shock.

Hyperinflation and Breakdown

Some economists express anxiety over our first scenario. They are fearful that the mild, "creeping" inflation which might initially accompany economic recovery may snowball into a severe **hyperinflation.** This is an extremely rapid inflation whose impact on real output and employment can be devastating. The contention is that, as prices persist in creeping upward, households and businesses will expect them to rise further. So, rather than let their idle savings and current incomes depreciate, people "spend now" to beat anticipated price rises. Businesses do the same in buying capital goods. Action based on this "inflationary psychosis" intensifies pressure on prices, and inflation feeds on itself.

Wage-Price Inflationary Spiral Furthermore, as the cost of living rises, labor demands higher nominal wages and gets them. Unions may seek wage increases sufficient not only to cover last year's price level increase but also to compensate for inflation anticipated during the future life of their new collective bargaining agreement. Prosperity is not a good time for business firms to risk strikes by resisting such demands. Business managers recoup their rising labor costs by boosting the prices they charge consumers. And for good measure, businesses may jack prices up an extra notch or two to be sure their profits keep abreast or ahead of the inflationary parade. As the cost of living rises as a result of these price increases, labor once again has an excellent reason to demand another round of substantial wage increases. But this triggers another round of price increases. The net effect is a cumulative *wage-price inflationary spiral.* Nominal-wage and price rises feed on each other, and this creeping inflation bursts into galloping inflation.

Potential Economic Collapse Aside from disruptive redistributive effects, hyperinflation can cause economic collapse. Severe inflation encourages speculative activity. Businesses may find it increasingly profitable to hoard both materials and finished products, anticipating further price increases. But restricting the availability of materials and products relative to the demand for them will intensify inflationary pressures. Rather than invest in capital equipment, businesses and individual savers may purchase nonproductive wealth—jewels, gold and other precious metals, real estate, and so forth—as hedges against inflation.

In the extreme, as prices shoot up sharply and unevenly, normal economic relationships are disrupted. Business owners do not know what to charge for their products. Consumers do not know what to pay. Resource suppliers will want to be paid with actual output, rather than with rapidly depreciating money. Creditors will avoid debtors to escape the repayment of debts with cheap money. Money becomes virtually worthless and ceases to do its job as a measure of value and medium of exchange. The economy may be thrown into a state of barter. Production and exchange grind toward a halt, and the net result is economic, social, and possibly political chaos. Hyperinflation has precipitated monetary collapse, depression, and sociopolitical disorder.

Examples History reveals a number of examples which fits this scenario. Consider the effects of World War II on price levels in Hungary and Japan:

> The inflation in Hungary exceeded all known records of the past. In August, 1946, 828 octillion (1 followed by 27 zeros) depreciated pengös equaled the value of 1 prewar pengö. The price of the American dollar reached a value of 3×10^{22} (3 followed by 22 zeros) pengös. Fishermen and farmers in 1947 Japan used scales to weigh currency and change, rather than bothering to count it. Prices rose some 116 times in Japan, 1938 to 1948.[4]

The German inflation of the 1920s was also catastrophic:

> The German Weimar Republic is an extreme example of a weak government which survived for some time through inflationary finance. On April 27, 1921, the German government was presented with a staggering bill for reparations payments to the Allies of 132 billion gold marks. This sum was far greater than what the Weimar Republic could reasonably expect to raise in taxes. Faced with huge budget deficits, the Weimar government simply ran the printing press to meet its bills.
>
> During 1922, the German price level went up 5,470 percent. In 1923, the situation worsened; the German price level rose 1,300,000,000,000 times. By October of 1923, the postage on the lightest letter sent from Germany to the United States was 200,000 marks. Butter cost 1.5 million marks per pound, meat 2 million marks, a loaf of bread 200,000 marks, and an egg 60,000 marks. Prices increased so rapidly that waiters changed the prices on the menu several times during the course of a lunch. Sometimes customers had to pay double the price listed on the menu when they ordered.[5]

A closing word of caution: Dramatic hyperinflations like these are almost invariably the consequence of imprudent expansion of the money supply by government. With appropriate public policies, mild inflation need not become hyperinflation.

CHAPTER SUMMARY

1 Our economy has been characterized by fluctuations in domestic output, employment, and the price level. Although having common phases—peak, recession, trough, recovery—business cycles vary greatly in duration and intensity.

2 Although economists explain the business cycle in terms of such ultimate causal factors as innovations, political events, and money creation, they generally agree that the level of total spending is the immediate determinant of real output and employment.

3 The business cycle affects all sectors of the economy,

but in varying ways and degrees. The cycle has greater output and employment ramifications in the capital goods and durable consumer goods industries than it does in services and nondurable goods industries. Over the cycle, price fluctuations are greater in competitive than in monopolistic industries.

[4]Theodore Morgan, *Income and Employment,* 2d ed. (Englewood Cliffs, N.J.: Prentice-Hall, Inc., 1952), p. 361.

[5]Raburn M. Williams, *Inflation! Money, Jobs, and Politicians* (Arlington Heights, Ill.: AHM Publishing Corporation, 1980), p. 2.

LAST WORD

THE STOCK MARKET AND MACROECONOMIC INSTABILITY

How, if at all, do changes in stock prices relate to the macroeconomy?

Financial investors daily buy and sell the stock certificates of thousands of corporations. These corporations pay dividends—a portion of their profits—to the owners of their stock shares. The price of a particular company's stock is determined by supply and demand. Individual stock prices generally rise and fall in concert with the collective expectations for each firm's profits. Greater profits normally result in higher dividends to the owners of the stock, and in anticipation of these higher dividends, financial investors are willing to pay more for the stock.

Stock market averages such as the Dow Jones industrial average—the average price of the stocks of a selected list of major United States industrial firms—are closely watched and reported. It is common for these price averages to change over time, or even to rise or fall sharply during a single day. On "Black Monday," October 19, 1987, the Dow Jones industrial average experienced a record one-day fall of 20 percent. About $500 billion in stock market wealth evaporated in a single day!

The volatility of the stock market raises this question: Do changes in stock price averages *cause* macroeconomic instability? There are linkages between the stock market and the economy which might lead us to think the answer is "Yes." Consider a sharp decline in stock prices. Feeling poorer, owners of stock may respond by reducing their spending on goods and services. Because it is less attractive to raise funds by issuing new shares of stock, firms may react by cutting back on their purchases of new capital goods.

Research studies find, however, that the consumption and investment impacts of stock price changes are relatively mild. Therefore, although stock price averages do influence total spending, the stock market is *not* a major cause of recession or inflation.

A related question emerges: Even though changes in stock prices do not *cause* significant changes in domestic output and the price level, might they *predict* such changes? That is, if stock market values are based on expected profits, wouldn't we expect rapid changes in stock price averages to forecast changes in future business conditions? Indeed, stock prices often *do* fall prior to recessions and rise prior to expansions. For this reason stock prices are among a group of eleven variables which constitute an index of leading indicators (Last Word, Chapter 12). This index often provides a useful clue to the future direction of the economy. But taken alone, stock market prices are not a reliable predictor of changes in domestic output. Stock prices have fallen rapidly in some instances with no recession following. Black Monday itself did not produce a recession during the following two years. In other instances, recessions have occurred with no prior decline in stock market prices.

In summary, the relationship between stock market prices and the macroeconomy is quite loose. Changes in stock prices are not a major source of macroeconomic instability nor are they reliable in forecasting business recessions or expansions.

---

4 Economists distinguish between frictional, structural, and cyclical unemployment. The full-employment or natural rate of unemployment is currently between 5.5 and 6 percent. Part-time and discouraged workers complicate the accurate measurement of unemployment.

5 The economic cost of unemployment, as measured by the GDP gap, consists of the goods and services which so-

ciety forgoes when its resources are involuntarily idle. Okun's law suggests that every 1 percent increase in unemployment above the natural rate causes a $2\frac{1}{2}$ percent GDP gap.

6 Unemployment rates and inflation rates vary greatly among nations. Unemployment rates differ because nations have different natural rates of unemployment and often are in different phases of their business cycles. Inflation and unemployment rates in the United States recently have been in the middle range compared to rates in other industrial nations.

7 Economists discern both demand-pull and cost-push (supply-side) inflation. Two variants of cost-push inflation are wage-push inflation and inflation caused by supply shocks.

8 Unanticipated inflation arbitrarily redistributes income at the expense of fixed-income receivers, creditors, and savers. If inflation is anticipated, individuals and businesses may be able to take steps to lessen or eliminate adverse redistributive effects.

9 The demand-pull theory of inflation suggests that some inflation may be necessary if the economy is to realize high levels of output and employment. However, the cost-push theory of inflation indicates that inflation may be accompanied by declines in real output and employment. Hyperinflation, usually associated with injudicious government policy, might undermine the monetary system and precipitate economic collapse.

TERMS AND CONCEPTS

business cycle

peak, recession, trough, and recovery phases

seasonal variations

secular trend

frictional, structural, and cycle unemployment

full-employment unemployment rate

natural rate of unemployment

potential output

labor force

discouraged workers

GDP gap

Okun's law

rule of 70

demand-pull and cost-push inflation

per unit production cost

nominal and real income

anticipated versus unanticipated inflation

cost-of-living adjustment (COLA)

inflation premium

nominal and real interest rates

hyperinflation

QUESTIONS AND STUDY SUGGESTIONS

1 *Key Question* What are the major phases of the business cycle? How long do business cycles last? How do seasonal variations and secular trends complicate measurement of the business cycle? Why does the business cycle affect output and employment in durable goods industries more severely than in industries producing nondurables?

2 Why is it difficult to determine the full-employment unemployment rate? Why is it difficult to distinguish between frictional, structural, and cyclical unemployment? Why is unemployment an economic problem? What are the consequences of the "GDP gap"? What are the noneconomic effects of unemployment?

3 *Key Question* Assume that in a given year the natural rate of unemployment is 5 percent and the actual rate of unemployment is 9 percent. Use Okun's law to determine the size of the GDP gap in percentage point terms. If the nominal GDP is $500 billion in that year, how much output is being forgone because of unemployment?

4 Given that there exists an unemployment compensation program which provides income for those out of work, why worry about unemployment?

5 *Key Question* Use the following data to calculate **a** the size of the labor force and **b** the official unemployment rate. Total population, 500; population under 16 years of age and institutionalized, 120; not in labor force, 150; unemployed, 23; part-time workers looking for full-time jobs, 10.

6 Explain how an *increase* in your nominal income and a *decrease* in your real income might occur simultaneously. Who loses from inflation? From unemployment? If you had to choose between **a** full employment with a 6 percent annual rate of inflation or **b** price stability with an 8 percent unemployment rate, which would you select? Why?

7 *Key Question* If the price index was 110 last year and is 121 this year, what was this year's rate of inflation? What is the "rule of 70"? How long would it take for the price level to double if inflation persisted at **a** 2, **b** 5, and **c** 10 percent per year?

8 Carefully describe the relationship between total spending and the levels of output and employment. Explain the relationship between the price level and increases in total spending as the economy moves from substantial unemployment to moderate unemployment, to full employment, and, finally, to absolute capacity.

9 Explain how "hyperinflation" might lead to a depression.

10 Evaluate as accurately as you can how each of the following individuals would be affected by unanticipated inflation of 10 percent per year:

    a A pensioned railroad worker

    b A department-store clerk

    c A UAW assembly-line worker

    d A heavily indebted farmer

    e A retired business executive whose current income comes entirely from interest on government bonds

    f The owner of an independent small-town department store

11 A noted television comedian once defined inflation as follows: "Inflation? That means your money today won't buy as much as it would have during the depression when you didn't have any." Is his definition accurate?

12 (Last Word) Suppose that stock prices fall by 10 percent in the stock market. All else equal, are these lower stock prices likely to *cause* a decrease in real GDP? How might these lower prices forecast a decline in real GDP? Are stock prices always reliable predictors of recessions?

BUILDING THE AGGREGATE EXPENDITURES MODEL

Sometime in your lifetime you or a member of your family may be permanently discharged or temporarily laid off from work during a recession. Total spending will not be sufficient to buy all the goods produced and services offered. You may also live through boom periods in which total spending surges, sharply increasing employment, real GDP, and national income.

In this chapter and Chapter 10, we shift from description to analysis by building on the definitions and facts of Chapter 7 (national income accounting) and Chapter 8 (macroeconomic instability). Using an aggregate expenditures model, we explain how the economy's equilibrium real GDP relates to total spending and how a change in total spending affects the level of real GDP. First, we establish the historical backdrop of the aggregate expenditures model. Next, we focus on the consumption-income and saving-income relationships which are part of the model. Third, investment—specifically, how businesses choose the amounts of capital goods to buy—is examined. Finally, consumption, saving, and investment concepts are combined to explain the equilibrium levels of output, income, and employment in a private (no government), closed (no foreign sector) economy.

In this chapter and the next a *model* of the economy is developed to clarify the basic determinants of the levels of output and employment. The specific numbers employed are not intended to measure the real world. Also, note that, while the aggregate expenditures model provides valuable insights about the macroeconomy, for the most part it assumes a constant price level. In Chapter 11 we therefore develop a complementary model allowing for changes in real GDP *and* the price level.

HISTORICAL BACKDROP

Let's gain some historical perspective on the aggregate expenditures model.

Classical Economics and Say's Law

Until the Great Depression of the 1930s, many economists of the nineteenth and early twentieth centuries —now called classical economists[1]—believed the market system would ensure full employment of the economy's resources. They acknowledged that now and then abnormal circumstances such as wars, political upheavals, droughts, speculative crises, and gold rushes would occur, deflecting the economy from the path of full employment (review Figure 8-1). But when these deviations occurred, automatic adjustments in prices, wages, and interest rates within the market would soon restore the economy to the full-employment level of output. A slump in output and employment would reduce prices, wages, and interest rates. Lower prices would increase consumer

[1]The most prominent classical economists were David Ricardo, John Stuart Mill, F. Y. Edgeworth, Alfred Marshall, and A. C. Pigou.

spending, lower wages would increase employment, and lower interest rates would boost investment spending. Any excess supply of goods and workers soon would be eliminated.

Classical macroeconomists denied the possibility of long-term underspending—a level of spending insufficient to purchase a full-employment output. This denial was based in part on **Say's law,** attributed to the nineteenth-century French economist J. B. Say. Say's law is the disarming notion that the very act of producing goods generates an amount of income equal to the value of the goods produced. The production of any output automatically provides the income needed to take that output off the market—the income needed to buy what's produced. *Supply creates its own demand.*

Say's law can best be understood in terms of a barter economy. A shoemaker, for example, produces or *supplies* shoes as a means of buying or *demanding* the shirts and stockings produced by other workers. The shoemaker's supply of shoes is his demand for other goods. And so it allegedly is for other producers and for the entire economy. Demand must be the same as supply! The circular flow model of the economy and national income accounting both suggest something of this sort. Income generated from the production of any level of output would, when spent, be just sufficient to provide a matching total demand. Assuming the composition of output is in accord with consumer preferences, all markets would be cleared of their outputs. It would seem that all business owners need to do to sell a full-employment output is to produce that output; Say's law guarantees there will be sufficient consumption spending to buy it all.

Say's law and classical macroeconomics is not simply an historical curiosity. A few modern economists have reformulated, revitalized, and extended the work of these nineteenth- and twentieth-century economists to generate a "new" classical economics. (We will examine its modern reincarnation, the new classical economics, in later chapters.)

The Great Depression and Keynes

Two events undermined the theory that supply creates its own demand (Say's law) and led to the emergence of the theory that underspending or overspending can occur (the aggregate expenditures theory).

1 The Great Depression The Depression of the 1930s was worldwide. In the United States, it plummeted real GDP by 40 percent and skyrocketed the unemployment rate to nearly 25 percent. Much the same occurred in other industrial nations. The negative effects of the Depression lingered for a decade. There is a blatant inconsistency between a theory which says that unemployment is virtually impossible and the actual occurrence of a ten-year siege of very substantial unemployment.

2 Keynes and Keynesian Economics In 1936 the English economist John Maynard Keynes (pronounced "Caines") explained why there was cyclical employment in capitalistic economies. In his *General Theory of Employment, Interest, and Money,* Keynes attacked the foundations of classical theory and touched off a major revolution in economic thinking on macroeconomic questions. Keynes disputed Say's law, pointing out that in some periods not all income will get spent on the output produced. When widespread underspending occurs, unsold goods will accumulate in producers' warehouses. Producers will respond to rising inventories by reducing their output and cutting their employment. A recession or depression will follow.

Keynes initiated modern employment theory, but many others have since refined and extended his work. The modern aggregate expenditures model reflects **Keynesian economics,** not just the economics of Keynes. In the aggregate expenditures model, the macroeconomy is inherently unstable; it is subject to periods of recession and inflation. Keynesian economics says that capitalism is not a self-regulating system capable of uninterrupted prosperity. While it is an excellent engine of long-term economic growth, we cannot always depend on it to "run itself."

Furthermore, economic fluctuations are not associated exclusively with external forces such as wars, droughts, and similar abnormalities. Rather, the Keynesian view sees the causes of unemployment and inflation as the failure of certain fundamental economic decisions—in particular, saving and investment decisions—to be completely synchronized. In addition, product prices and wages are downwardly inflexible, meaning that extended and costly periods of recession or depression will prevail before significant declines in prices and wages occur. Internal factors, in addition to external forces (wars and droughts), contribute to economic instability.

SIMPLIFICATIONS

Four assumptions will help us build the aggregate expenditures model.

1 Initially we will assume a "closed economy" where there are no international trade transactions. Complications arising from exports and imports in the "open economy" will be deferred to Chapter 10.

2 We will also ignore government until Chapter 10, permitting us first to demonstrate that at times laissez faire capitalism may not achieve and maintain full employment. For now we will deal with a "private" closed economy.

3 Although both businesses and households save, we will for convenience speak as if all saving were personal saving.

4 To keep things simple, we will assume that depreciation and *net* foreign factor income earned in the United States are zero.

We should tell you about two implications of these assumptions. First, recall from Chapter 7 there are four components of aggregate spending: consumption, investment, government purchases, and net exports. Assumptions 1 and 2 mean that, for now, we are concerned only with consumption and investment.

Second, assumptions 2 through 4 permit us to treat gross domestic product (GDP), national income (NI), personal income (PI), and disposable income (DI) as being equal to each other. All the items which in practice distinguish them from one another result from depreciation, net American income earned abroad, government (taxes and transfer payments), and business saving (see Table 7-4). Our assumptions mean if $500 billion of goods and services is produced as GDP, exactly $500 billion of DI is received by households to use as either consumption or saving.

TOOLS OF THE AGGREGATE EXPENDITURES THEORY

How are the levels of output and employment determined in modern capitalism? *The amount of goods and services produced and therefore the level of employment depend directly on the level of total or aggregate expenditures.* Businesses will produce a level of output they can profitably sell. Workers and machinery are idled when there are no markets for the goods and services they can produce. Total output and employment vary directly with aggregate expenditures.

Our strategy in this chapter is to analyze the consumption and investment components of aggregate expenditures and derive a private sector model of equilibrium GDP and employment. Chapter 10 examines changes in real GDP and adds net exports and government expenditures (along with taxes) to the model.

Be sure you understand as we begin our discussion that unless specified otherwise we assume the economy has substantial excess production capacity and unemployed labor. An increase in aggregate expenditures thus will increase real output and employment, but *not* the price level.

CONSUMPTION AND SAVING

In terms of absolute size, consumption is the largest component of aggregate expenditures (Chapter 7). We therefore need to understand the determinants of consumption spending. Recall that economists define personal saving as "not spending" or "that part of disposable income (DI) not consumed." In other words, disposable income equals consumption plus saving. Thus, in examining the determinants of consumption we are also simultaneously exploring the determinants of saving.

Income-Consumption and Income-Saving Relationships

Many considerations influence the level of consumer spending. But the most significant determinant is income—in particular, disposable income. And, since saving is that part of disposable income not consumed, DI is also the basic determinant of personal saving.

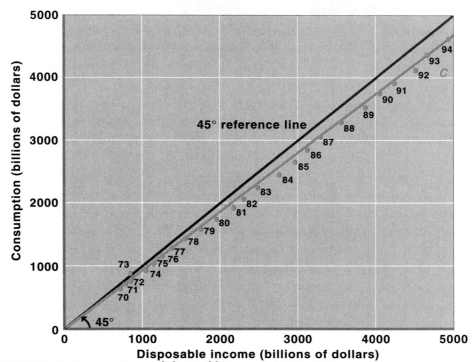

FIGURE 9-1   Consumption and disposable income, 1970–1994
Each dot in this figure shows consumption and disposable income in a given year. The *C* line generalizes on the relationship between consumption and disposable income. It indicates a direct relationship
and that households consume the bulk of their incomes.

Consider some recent historical data. In Figure 9-1 each dot indicates the consumption–disposable income relationship for each year since 1970 and the green line is fitted to these points. Consumption is directly related to disposable income and, indeed, households clearly spend most of their income.

But we can say more. The gray 45-degree line is added to the diagram for reference purposes. Because the 90-degree angle formed by the vertical and horizontal axes of the graph is bisected by this 45-degree line, each point on it must be equidistant from the two axes. We can therefore regard the vertical distance from any point on the horizontal axis to the 45-degree line as either consumption *or* disposable income. If we regard it as disposable income, then the amount (the vertical distance) by which the actual amount consumed in any year falls short of the 45-degree guideline indicates the amount of saving in that year. For example, in 1994 consumption was $4627 billion, and disposable income was $4959 billion; hence, saving in 1994 was $332 billion. Disposable income less

consumption equals saving. By observing these vertical distances as we move to the right in Figure 9-1, we see that saving also varies directly with the level of disposable income.

Figure 9-1 suggests (1) households consume most of their disposable income and (2) both consumption and saving are directly related to the income level.

The Consumption Schedule

The dots in Figure 9-1 represent historical data—how much households *actually did consume* (and save) at various levels of DI over a period of years. To analyze what the data can tell us, we need to show an income-consumption relationship—a consumption schedule —indicating the various amounts households *plan* to consume at various levels of disposable income which might prevail at some specific *point in time.* A hypothetical **consumption schedule** of the type we require for analysis is shown in columns 1 and 2 of Table

TABLE 9-1   Consumption and saving schedules *(columns 1 through 3 in billions)*

(1) Level of output and income (GDP = DI)	(2) Consumption, C	(3) Saving, S (1) − (2)	(4) Average propensity to consume (APC) (2)/(1)	(5) Average propensity to save (APS) (3)/(1)	(6) Marginal propensity to consume (MPC) Δ(2)/Δ(1)*	(7) Marginal propensity to save (MPS) Δ(3)/Δ(1)*
(1) $370	$375	$−5	1.01	−.01		
					.75	.25
(2) 390	390	0	1.00	.00		
					.75	.25
(3) 410	405	5	.99	.01		
					.75	.25
(4) 430	420	10	.98	.02		
					.75	.25
(5) 450	435	15	.97	.03		
					.75	.25
(6) 470	450	20	.96	.04		
					.75	.25
(7) 490	465	25	.95	.05		
					.75	.25
(8) 510	480	30	.94	.06		
					.75	.25
(9) 530	495	35	.93	.07		
					.75	.25
(10) 550	510	40	.93	.07		

*The Greek letter **Δ**, delta, means "a change in."

9-1 and is plotted in Figure 9-2a (Key Graph). This consumption schedule reflects the consumption–disposable income relationship suggested by the empirical data of Figure 9-1, and is consistent with many empirical family budget studies. The relationship is direct—as common sense would suggest—and we note that households will spend a *larger proportion* of a small disposable income than of a large disposable income.

The Saving Schedule

It is simple to derive a **saving schedule.** Because disposable income equals consumption plus saving (DI = C + S), we need only subtract consumption (Table 9-1, column 2) from disposable income (column 1) to find the amount saved (column 3) at each level of DI. That is, DI − C = S. Thus, columns 1 and 3 of Table 9-1 constitute the saving schedule, plotted in Figure 9-2b. Note there is a direct relationship between saving and DI but that saving is a smaller proportion (fraction) of a small DI than of a large DI. If households consume a smaller and smaller proportion of DI as DI goes up (column 4), they must save a larger and larger proportion (column 5).

Remembering that at each point on the 45-degree line DI equals consumption, we see that dissaving would occur at the relatively low DI of, say, $370 billion (column 1, row 1), where consumption is actually $375 billion. Households will consume more than their current incomes by liquidating (selling for cash)

accumulated wealth or by borrowing. Graphically, the vertical distance of the consumption schedule *above* the 45-degree line is equal to the vertical distance of the saving schedule *below* the horizontal axis at the $370 billion level of output and income (see Figure 9-2a and b). In this instance, each of these two vertical distances measures the $5 billion of *dissaving* occurring at the $370 billion income level.

The **break-even income** is at the $390 billion income level (row 2). This is the level where households consume their entire incomes. Graphically, the consumption schedule cuts the 45-degree line, and the saving schedule cuts the horizontal axis (saving is zero) at the break-even income level.

At all higher incomes, households will plan to save part of their income. The vertical distance of the consumption schedule *below* the 45-degree line measures this saving, as does the vertical distance of the saving schedule *above* the horizontal axis. For example, at the $410 billion level of income (row 3), both these distances indicate $5 billion worth of saving (see Figure 9-2a and b).

Average and Marginal Propensities

Columns 4 to 7 of Table 9-1 show additional characteristics of the consumption and saving schedules.

APC and APS   That fraction, or percentage, of any total income which is consumed is called the **average propensity to consume** (APC). That fraction of any

KEY GRAPH

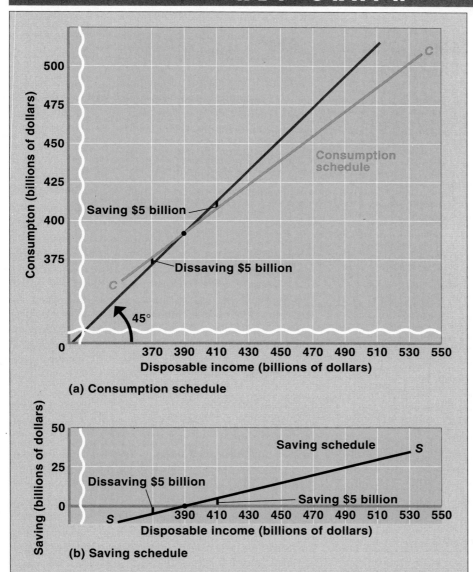

(a) Consumption schedule

(b) Saving schedule

FIGURE 9-2   Consumption (a) and saving (b) schedules The two parts of this figure show the income-consumption and income-saving relationships graphically. Each point on the 45-degree line in (a) indicates a point where DI equals consumption. Therefore, because saving equals DI minus consumption, the saving schedule in (b) is found by subtracting the consumption schedule vertically from the 45-degree guideline. Consumption equals DI (and saving therefore equals zero) at $390 billion for these hypothetical data.

total income which is saved is the **average propensity to save** (APS). That is,

$$APC = \frac{\text{consumption}}{\text{income}}$$

and

$$APS = \frac{\text{saving}}{\text{income}}$$

For example, at the $470 billion level of income (row 6) in Table 9-1, the APC is $\frac{450}{470} = \frac{45}{47}$, or about 96 percent, while the APS is $\frac{20}{470} = \frac{2}{47}$, or about 4 percent. By calculating the APC and APS at each of the ten levels of DI shown in Table 9-1, we find that the APC falls and the APS rises as DI increases. This quantifies a point just made: The fraction of total DI which is consumed declines as DI

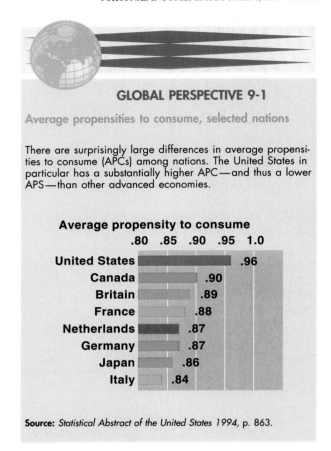

There are surprisingly large differences in average propensities to consume (APCs) among nations. The United States in particular has a substantially higher APC—and thus a lower APS—than other advanced economies.

Average propensity to consume

	.80	.85	.90	.95	1.0
United States					.96
Canada			.90		
Britain			.89		
France			.88		
Netherlands		.87			
Germany		.87			
Japan		.86			
Italy	.84				

Source: *Statistical Abstract of the United States 1994*, p. 863.

rises, and the fraction of DI which is saved rises as DI increases.

Because disposable income is either consumed or saved, the sum of the fraction of any level of DI consumed plus the fraction saved (not consumed) must exhaust that level of income. Mathematically, APC + APS = 1. Columns 4 and 5 of Table 9-1 illustrate this.

Global Perspective 9-1 shows APCs for several countries.

MPC and MPS   The fact that households consume a certain portion of some total income—for example, $\frac{45}{47}$ of a $470 billion disposable income—does not guarantee they will consume the same proportion of any *change* in income they might receive. The proportion, or fraction, of any change in income consumed is called the **marginal propensity to consume** (MPC), marginal meaning "extra" or "a change in." Or, the MPC is the ratio of a *change* in consumption

to the *change* in income which caused that change in consumption:

$$MPC = \frac{\text{change in consumption}}{\text{change in income}}$$

Similarly, the fraction of any change in income saved is the **marginal propensity to save** (MPS). The MPS is the ratio of a *change* in saving to the *change* in income bringing it about:

$$MPS = \frac{\text{change in saving}}{\text{change in income}}$$

If disposable income is $470 billion (row 6) and household incomes rise by $20 billion to $490 billion (row 7), they will consume $\frac{15}{20}$, or $\frac{3}{4}$, and save $\frac{5}{20}$, or $\frac{1}{4}$, of that *increase in income* (see columns 6 and 7 of Table 9-1). In other words, the MPC is $\frac{3}{4}$, or .75, and the MPS is $\frac{1}{4}$, or .25.

The sum of the MPC and the MPS for any change in disposable income must always be 1. Consuming and saving out of extra income is an either-or proposition; that fraction of any change in income which is not consumed is, by definition, saved. Therefore the fraction consumed (MPC) plus the fraction saved (MPS) must exhaust the whole increase in income:

$$MPC + MPS = 1$$

In our example .75 plus .25 equals 1.

MPC and MPS as Slopes   The MPC is the numerical value of the slope of the consumption schedule and the MPS is the numerical value of the slope of the saving schedule. We know from the appendix to Chapter 1 that the slope of any line can be measured by the ratio of the vertical change to horizontal change involved in moving from one point to another on that line.

In Figure 9-3 we highlight the slopes of the consumption and saving lines derived from Table 9-1 by enlarging relevant portions of Figures 9-2a and 9-2b. Observe that consumption changes by $15 billion (vertical change) for each $20 billion change in disposable income (horizontal change); the slope of the consumption line is .75 (=$15/$20)—the value of the MPC. Saving changes by $5 billion (vertical change) for every $20 billion change in disposable income (horizontal change). The slope of the saving line therefore is .25 (=$5/$20), which is the value of the MPS. *(Key Question 6)*

Nonincome Determinants of Consumption and Saving

The level of disposable income is the basic determinant of the amounts households will consume and save, just as price is the basic determinant of the quantity demanded of a single product. Recall that changes in determinants other than price, such as consumer tastes, incomes, and so forth (Chapter 3), will shift the demand curve for a given product. Similarly, certain determinants might cause households to consume more or less at each possible level of DI and thereby change the locations of the consumption and saving schedules.

1 Wealth Generally, the greater the amount of wealth households have accumulated, the larger will be the amount of consumption and the smaller the amount of saving out of any level of current income. By *wealth* we mean both real assets (a house, automobiles, television sets, and other durables) and financial assets (cash, savings accounts, stocks, bonds, insurance policies, pensions) which households own. Households save—refrain from consumption—to accumulate wealth. The more wealth households have accumulated, the weaker the incentive to save in order to accumulate additional wealth. An increase in wealth shifts the saving schedule downward and the consumption schedule upward.

Examples: The dramatic stock market crash of 1929 significantly decreased the financial wealth of many families almost overnight and was a factor in the low levels of consumption in the depressed 1930s. More recently: The general decline in real estate values during 1989 and 1990 eroded household wealth and contributed to a retrenchment of consumer spending.

For the most part, however, the amount of wealth held by households only changes modestly from year to year and therefore does not account for large shifts in the consumption and saving schedules.

2 Expectations Household expectations concerning future prices, money incomes, and the availability of goods may significantly affect current spending and saving. Expectations of rising prices and product shortages trigger more spending and less saving currently. This shifts the consumption schedule upward and the saving schedule downward.

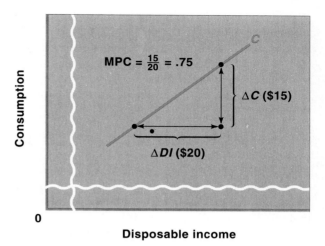

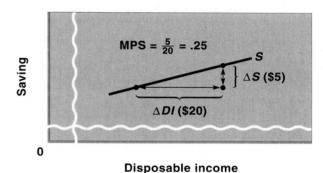

FIGURE 9-3   The marginal propensity to consume and the marginal propensity to save
The MPC is the slope of the consumption schedule and the MPS is the slope of the saving schedule.

It is natural for consumers to seek to avoid paying higher prices or having to "do without." Expected inflation and expected shortages induce people to "buy now" to escape higher future prices and bare shelves. The expectation of rising money incomes in the future also makes consumers freer in their current spending. Conversely, expected price declines, anticipations of shrinking incomes, and the feeling that goods will be abundantly available may induce consumers to retrench on consumption and build up savings.

3 Consumer Indebtedness The level of consumer debt can also affect the willingness of households to consume and save out of current income. If households are in debt to the degree that, say, 20 or

25 percent of their current incomes are committed to installment payments on previous purchases, consumers may well retrench on current consumption to reduce indebtedness. Conversely, if consumer indebtedness is relatively low, households may consume at an unusually high rate by increasing this indebtedness.

4 Taxation In Chapter 10, we will find that changes in taxes will shift the consumption and saving schedules. Taxes are paid partly at the expense of consumption *and* partly at the expense of saving. Therefore, an *increase* in taxes will shift *both* the consumption and saving schedules *downward*. Conversely, a tax reduction will be partly consumed and partly saved by households. A tax *decrease* will shift *both* the consumption and saving schedules *upward*.

Shifts and Stability

Three final, related points are relevant to our discussion of the consumption and saving schedules.

1 Terminology The movement from one point to another on a stable consumption schedule (for example, *a* to *b* on C_0 in Figure 9-4a) is called a *change in the amount consumed*. The sole cause of this change in consumption is a change in disposable income. On the other hand, a *change in the consumption schedule* refers to an upward or downward shift of the entire schedule—for example, a shift from C_0 to C_1 or to C_2 in Figure 9-4a. A relocation of the consumption schedule is caused by changes in any one or more of the four nonincome determinants just discussed.

A similar distinction in terminology applies to the saving schedule in Figure 9-4b.

2 Schedule Shifts The first three nonincome determinants of consumption will shift the consumption and saving schedules in opposite directions. If households decide to consume *more* at each possible level of disposable income, they want to save *less,* and vice versa. Graphically, if the consumption schedule shifts upward from C_0 to C_1 in Figure 9-4, the saving schedule will shift downward from S_0 to S_1. Similarly, a downshift in the consumption schedule from C_0 to C_2 means an upshift in the saving schedule from S_0 to S_2. The exception to this is the fourth nonincome determinant—taxation. Households will consume less *and* save less to pay higher taxes. Thus, a tax increase

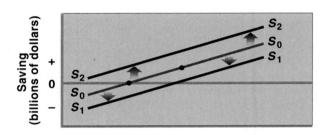

(a) Consumption schedule

(b) Saving schedule

FIGURE 9-4 Shifts in the consumption (a) and saving (b) schedules

A change in any one or more of the nonincome determinants will cause the consumption and saving schedules to shift. If households consume more at each level of DI, they are necessarily saving less. Graphically this means that an upshift in the consumption schedule (C_0 to C_1) entails a downshift in the saving schedule (S_0 to S_1). If households consume less at each level of DI, they are saving more. A downshift in the consumption schedule (C_0 to C_2) is reflected in an upshift of the saving schedule (S_0 to S_2).

will lower *both* consumption and saving schedules, while a tax cut will shift *both* schedules upward.

3 Stability Economists generally agree that, aside from deliberate governmental actions designed to shift them, the consumption and saving schedules are generally stable. This may be because consumption-saving decisions are strongly influenced by habit or because the nonincome determinants are diverse and changes in them frequently work in opposite directions and therefore may be self-canceling.

INVESTMENT

We now turn to investment, the second component of private spending. Recall that investment consists of expenditures on new plants, capital equipment, machinery, and so on. The investment decision is a marginal benefit–marginal cost decision (Chapters 1 and 2). The marginal benefit from investment is the expected rate of net profits businesses hope to realize. The marginal cost is the interest rate—the cost of borrowing. We will see that businesses will invest in all projects for which expected net profits exceed the interest rate. Expected net profits and the interest rate therefore are the two basic determinants of investment spending.

Expected Rate of Net Profit, r

Investment spending is guided by the profit motive; businesses buy capital goods only when they expect such purchases to be profitable. Suppose the owner of a small cabinetmaking shop is considering investing in a new sanding machine costing $1000 and having a useful life of only one year. The new machine will presumably increase the firm's output and sales revenue. Suppose the *net* expected revenue (that is, net of such operating costs as power, lumber, labor, certain taxes, and so forth) from the machine is $1100.

In other words, after operating costs have been accounted for, the remaining expected net revenue is sufficient to cover the $1000 cost of the machine and leave a profit of $100. Comparing this $100 profit with the $1000 cost of the machine, we find that the expected *rate* of net profit, r, on the machine is 10 percent (= $100/$1000). Businesses sometimes refer to the "return" on an investment, meaning the profits that resulted from the investment. Thus, our use of r for this "return" or "profit."

The Real Interest Rate, i

One important cost associated with investing which our example has ignored is the interest rate—the financial cost the firm must pay to borrow the *money* capital required to purchase the *real* capital (the sanding machine).

We can consider the interest rate in the context of an investment and its expected return with the following generalization: If the expected rate of net profits (10 percent) exceeds the interest rate (say, 7 percent), it will be profitable to invest. But if the interest rate (say, 12 percent) exceeds the expected rate of net profits (10 percent), it will be unprofitable to invest.

But what if the firm does *not* borrow, instead financing the investment internally out of funds saved from past profits? The role of the interest rate as a cost in investing in real capital doesn't change. By using money from savings to invest in the sander, the firm incurs an opportunity cost (Chapter 2) because it forgoes the interest income it could have realized by lending the funds to someone else.

The *real* rate of interest, rather than the nominal rate, is crucial in making investment decisions. Recall from Chapter 8 that the nominal interest rate is expressed in dollars of current value, while the real interest rate is stated in dollars of constant or inflation-adjusted value. The real interest rate is the nominal rate less the rate of inflation. In our sanding machine illustration we implicitly assumed a constant price level so that all our data, including the interest rate, were in real terms.

But what if inflation is occurring? Suppose a $1000 investment is estimated to yield a real (inflation-adjusted) expected rate of net profits of 10 percent and the nominal interest rate is 15 percent. At first, we would say the investment will be unprofitable. But assume there is ongoing inflation of 10 percent per year. This means the investor will pay back dollars with approximately 10 percent less in purchasing power. While the nominal interest rate is 15 percent, the real rate is only 5 percent (= 15 percent − 10 percent). Comparing this 5 percent real interest rate with the 10 percent expected real rate of net profits, we find that the investment *is* profitable and should be undertaken.

Investment-Demand Curve

We now move from a single firm's investment decision to total demand for investment goods by the entire business sector. Assume every firm has estimated the expected rate of net profits from all investment projects and these data have been collected. These estimates can be *cumulated*—successively summed—by asking: How many dollars' worth of investment projects have an expected rate of net profit of, say, 16 percent or more? Of 14 percent or more? Of 12 percent or more? And so on.

Suppose there are no prospective investments yielding an expected net profit of 16 percent or more. But there are $5 billion of investment opportunities with an expected rate of net profits between 14 and 16 percent; an *additional* $5 billion yielding between 12 and 14 percent; still an *additional* $5 billion yielding between 10 and 12 percent; and an *additional* $5 billion in each successive 2 percent range of yield down to and including the 0 to 2 percent range.

By *cumulating* these figures we obtain the data of Table 9-2, shown graphically by the economy's **investment-demand curve** in Figure 9-5. In Table 9-2 the number opposite 12 percent, for example, tells us there are $10 billion of investment opportunities which will yield an expected net profit of 12 percent *or more;* the $10 billion includes the $5 billion of investment yielding an expected return of 14 percent or

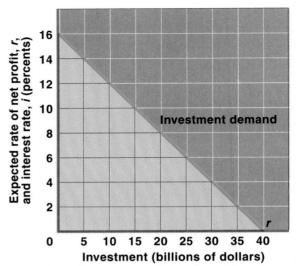

FIGURE 9-5   The investment-demand curve
The investment-demand curve for the economy is derived by arraying all relevant investment projects in descending order of their expected rate of net profitability and applying the rule that investment should be undertaken up to the point at which the interest rate, *i*, is equal to the expected rate of net profit, *r*. The investment-demand curve is downsloping, reflecting an inverse relationship between the interest rate (the financial price of investing) and the aggregate quantity of capital goods demanded.

more *plus* the $5 billion which is expected to yield between 12 and 14 percent.

With this cumulated information on expected net profit rates of all possible investment projects, we introduce the real interest rate or financial cost of investing. We know from our sanding machine example that an investment project will be undertaken if its expected net profit rate, *r*, exceeds the real interest rate, *i*.

Let's apply this reasoning to Figure 9-5. If we assume that rate of interest is 12 percent, we find that $10 billion of investment spending will be profitable, that is, $10 billion worth of investment projects have an expected net profit rate of 12 percent or more. At a financial "price" of 12 percent, $10 billion of investment goods will be demanded. If the interest rate were lower, say, 10 percent, an additional $5 billion of investment projects would become profitable and the total amount of investment goods demanded would be $15 billion (= $10 + $5). At 8 percent, a further $5 billion of investment would become profitable and the total demand for investment goods would be $20 billion. At 6 percent, investment would be $25 billion.

By applying the marginal benefit–marginal cost rule that all investment projects should be undertaken

TABLE 9-2   Profit expectations and investment

Expected rate of net profit, r (in percent)	Amount of investment (billions of dollars per year)
16%	$ 0
14	5
12	10
10	15
8	20
6	25
4	30
2	35
0	40

up to the point where the expected rate of net profit equals the interest rate (r = i), we discover that the curve of Figure 9-5 is the investment-demand curve. Various possible financial prices of investing (various real interest rates) are shown on the vertical axis and the corresponding quantities of investment goods demanded are revealed on the horizontal axis. Any line or curve embodying such data is the investment-demand curve. Consistent with our product and resource demand curves of Chapter 3, observe the *inverse* relationship between the interest rate (price) and the amount of spending on investment goods (quantity demanded).

This conception of the investment decision allows us to anticipate an important aspect of macroeconomic policy. We will find in our discussion of monetary policy in Chapter 15 that by changing the supply of money, government can alter the interest rate. It does this primarily to change the level of investment spending. At any point in time, business firms in the aggregate have a variety of investment projects under consideration. If interest rates are high, only projects with the highest expected rate of net profit will be undertaken. Thus, the level of investment will be small. As the interest rate is lowered, projects whose expected rate of net profit is less will also become commercially feasible and the level of investment will rise. *(Key Question 8)*

Shifts in Investment Demand

In discussing the consumption schedule, we noted that, although disposable income is the key determinant of the amount consumed, other factors affect consumption. These "nonincome determinants" shift the consumption schedule. So it also is with the investment-demand schedule. In view of the expected rates of net profit of various possible investments, Figure 9-5 portrays the interest rate as the main determinant of investment.

But other factors determine the location of the investment-demand curve. Any factor which increases the expected net profitability of investment will shift the investment-demand curve to the right. Anything decreasing the expected net profitability of investment will shift the investment-demand curve to the left.

1   Acquisition, Maintenance, and Operating Costs   As our sanding machine example revealed, the initial costs of capital goods, along with the estimated costs of operating and maintaining those

goods, must be considered in gauging the expected rate of net profitability of any investment. When these costs rise, the expected rate of *net* profit from prospective investment projects will fall, shifting the investment-demand curve to the left. Conversely, when these costs decline, expected net profit rates will rise, shifting the investment-demand curve to the right. Example: Higher wages or electricity costs would shift the investment demand curve to the left.

2   Business Taxes   Business owners look to expected profits *after taxes* in making their investment decisions. An increase in business taxes will lower profitability and shift the investment-demand curve to the left; a tax reduction will shift it to the right.

3   Technological Change   Technological progress —the development of new products, improvements in existing products, the creation of new machinery and production processes—stimulates investment. The development of a more efficient machine, for example, will lower production costs or improve product quality, increasing the expected rate of net profit from investing in the machine. Profitable new products—mountain bikes, sports utility vehicles, high-resolution television, legal drugs, and so on—induce a flurry of investment as firms tool up for expanded production. A rapid rate of technological progress shifts the investment-demand curve to the right.

4   The Stock of Capital Goods on Hand   Just as the stock of consumer goods on hand affects household consumption-saving decisions, so the stock of capital goods on hand influences the expected profit rate from additional investment in industry. When a specific industry is well stocked with productive facilities and inventories of finished goods, investment will be retarded in that industry. Such an industry will be amply equipped to fulfill present and future market demand at prices which yield mediocre profits. If an industry has enough, or even excessive, production capacity, the expected rate of profit from further investment in the industry will be low, and therefore little or no investment will occur. Excess production capacity shifts the investment-demand curve to the left; a relative scarcity of capital goods shifts it to the right.

5   Expectations   We noted earlier that business investment is based on *expected* profits. Capital goods are durable—they may have a life expectancy of ten

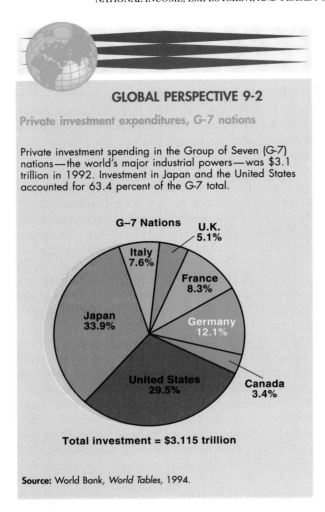

GLOBAL PERSPECTIVE 9-2

Private investment expenditures, G-7 nations

Private investment spending in the Group of Seven (G-7) nations—the world's major industrial powers—was $3.1 trillion in 1992. Investment in Japan and the United States accounted for 63.4 percent of the G-7 total.

G–7 Nations

U.K. 5.1%
Italy 7.6%
France 8.3%
Germany 12.1%
Japan 33.9%
United States 29.5%
Canada 3.4%

Total investment = $3.115 trillion

Source: World Bank, *World Tables,* 1994.

Investment and Income

To add the investment decisions of businesses to the consumption plans of households, we must express investment plans in terms of the level of disposable income (DI), or GDP. That is, we need to construct an **investment schedule** showing the amounts business firms as a group plan or intend to invest at each possible level of income or output. Such a schedule will mirror the investment plans or intentions of business owners and managers in the same way the consumption and saving schedules reflect the consumption and saving plans of households.

We assume that business investment is geared to long-term profit expectations as influenced by technological progress, population growth, and so forth, and therefore is *autonomous* or independent of the level of current disposable income or real output. Suppose the investment-demand curve is as shown in Figure 9-5 *and* the current rate of interest is 8 percent. This means that the business sector will find it profitable to spend $20 billion on investment goods. In Table 9-3, columns 1 and 2, we are assuming that this level of investment will occur at every level of income. The I_g line in Figure 9-6 shows this graphically.

This assumed independence of investment and income is admittedly simplified. A higher level of business activity may *induce* additional spending on capital facilities, as suggested by columns 1 and 3 of Table 9-3 and I'_g in Figure 9-6. There are at least two reasons why investment might vary directly with income.

1 Investment is related to profits; much investment is financed internally out of business profits. Therefore, it is plausible that as disposable income and GDP

or twenty years—and thus the profitability of any capital investment will depend on business planners' expectations of the *future* sales and *future* profitability of the product which the capital helps produce. Business expectations may be based on elaborate forecasts of future business conditions. In addition, such elusive and difficult-to-predict factors as changes in the domestic political climate, the thrust of foreign affairs, population growth, and stock market conditions must be taken into account on a subjective or intuitive basis. If business executives become more optimistic about future business conditions, the investment-demand curve will shift to the right; a pessimistic outlook will shift it to the left.

The amount of investment spending is enormous globally. The seven leading industrial nations alone invest more than $3 trillion annually (Global Perspective 9-2).

TABLE 9-3   The investment schedule *(in billions)*

(1) Level of real output and income	(2) Investment, I_g	(3) Investment, I'_g
$370	$20	$10
390	20	12
410	20	14
430	20	16
450	20	18
470	20	20
490	20	22
510	20	24
530	20	26
550	20	28

rise, so will business profits and therefore the level of investment.

2   At low levels of income and output, the business sector will have excess production capacity; many industries will have idle machinery and equipment and therefore little incentive to purchase additional capital goods. But, as the level of income rises, this excess capacity disappears and firms are inclined to add to their stock of capital goods.

Our simplification, however, is not too unrealistic and will greatly facilitate later analysis.

Instability of Investment

In contrast to the consumption schedule, the investment schedule is unstable; it shifts significantly upward or downward quite often. Proportionately, investment is the most volatile component of total spending. Figure 9-7 shows the volatility of investment and that its swings are greater than GDP. These data also suggest that our simplified treatment of investment as being independent of GDP (Figure 9-6) is essentially realistic; investment spending does not closely follow GDP.

Factors explaining the variability of investment follow:

1   Durability   Because of their durability, capital goods have an indefinite useful life. Within limits, purchases of capital goods are discretionary and therefore postponable. Older equipment or buildings can be scrapped and entirely replaced or patched up and used for a few more years. Optimism about the future may prompt business planners to replace their older facilities; modernizing their plants will call for a high level of investment. A less optimistic view, however, may lead to very small amounts of investment as older facilities are repaired and kept in use.

2   Irregularity of Innovation   We know that technological progress is a major determinant of investment. New products and processes provide a stimulus to investment. But history suggests that major innovations—railroads, electricity, automobiles, fiber optics, and computers—occur quite irregularly, and when they do occur, they induce a vast upsurge or "wave" of investment spending which in time recedes.

A classic illustration is the widespread acceptance of the automobile in the 1920s. This event not only substantially increased investment in the automobile industry itself, but also induced tremendous amounts of investment in such related industries as steel, pe-

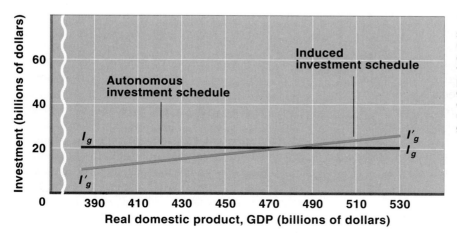

FIGURE 9-6   **The investment schedule: two possibilities**   Our discussion will be facilitated by employing the investment schedule I_g, which assumes that the investment plans of businesses are independent or autonomous of the current level of income. Actually, the investment schedule may be slightly upsloping, as suggested by I'_g.

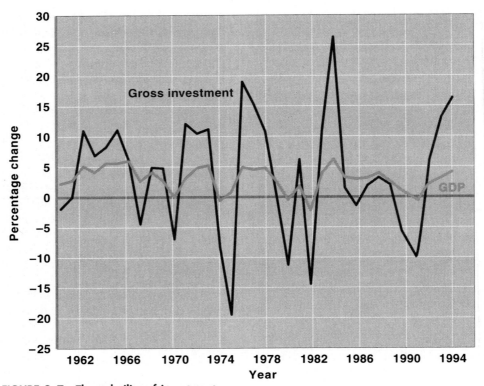

FIGURE 9-7 **The volatility of investment**
Investment spending is highly volatile. In comparing changes in real investment and real GDP, we observe that the annual percentage changes in investment are greater than the percentage changes in GDP.

troleum, glass, and rubber, not to mention public investment in streets and highways. But when investment in these related industries was ultimately "completed"—when enough capital facilities had been created to meet the needs of the automobile industry —total investment leveled off.

3 Variability of Profits Business owners and managers invest only when they think it will be profitable and, to a significant degree, the expectation of future profitability is influenced by the size of current profits. Current profits, however, are themselves highly variable (line 13 of the table on the inside covers provides information on undistributed corporate profits). Thus, the variability of profits contributes to the volatile nature of the incentive to invest.

Furthermore, the instability of profits may also cause investment fluctuations, because profits are a major source of funds for business investment. American businesses often prefer this internal source of fi-

nancing to increases in external debt or stock issue.

In short, expanding profits give business planners both greater *incentives* and greater *means* to invest; declining profits have the reverse effects. The fact that actual profits are variable adds to the instability of investment.

4 Variability of Expectations While business firms often project current business conditions into the future, it is equally true that expectations are sometimes subject to radical revision when some event suggests a significant change in future business conditions. Changes in the domestic political climate, changes in exchange rates, changes in population growth and therefore in anticipated market demand, court decisions in key labor or antitrust cases, legislative actions, changes in trade barriers, changes in governmental economic policies, and a host of similar considerations may cause substantial shifts in business optimism or pessimism.

The stock market requires specific comment in this regard. Business planners frequently look to the stock market as an index or barometer of the overall confidence of society in future business conditions; a rising "bull" market signifies public confidence in the business future, while a falling "bear" market implies a lack of confidence. The stock market, however, is a highly speculative market, and initially modest changes in stock prices can be seriously intensified by participants who jump in by buying when prices begin to rise and by selling when stock prices start to fall. Also, by affecting the amount of proceeds gained through offerings of new stock, upsurges and slumps in stock values affect the level of investment—the amount of capital goods purchased.

For these and similar reasons, changes in investment cause most fluctuations in output and employment. In Figure 9-6, we can think of this volatility as being reflected in frequent and substantial upward and downward shifts in the investment schedule.

EQUILIBRIUM GDP: EXPENDITURES-OUTPUT APPROACH

Now let's use the consumption, saving, and investment schedules to explain the equilibrium levels of output, income, and employment. We'll begin with the aggregate expenditures–domestic output (or $C + I_g = $ GDP) approach.

Tabular Analysis

Table 9-4 combines the income-consumption and income-saving data of Table 9-1 and the simplified income-investment data of columns 1 and 2 in Table 9-3.

Real Domestic Output   Column 2 of Table 9-4 is the total or real output schedule for the economy. It indicates the various possible levels of total output—the various possible real GDPs—which the business sector might produce. *Producers are willing to offer each of these ten levels of output on the expectation that they will receive an identical amount of receipts of income from its sale.* For example, the business sector will produce $370 billion of output, incurring $370 billion of costs (wages, rents, interest, and profit), only if businesses believe this output can be sold for $370 billion of receipts. Some $390 billion of output will be offered if businesses think this output can be sold for $390 billion. And so it is for all the other possible levels of output.

Aggregate Expenditures   The total, or aggregate, expenditures schedule is shown in column 6 of Table 9-4. It shows the total amount which will be spent at each possible output-income level. In the closed pri-

TABLE 9-4   Determination of the equilibrium levels of employment, output, and income: the closed private sector

(1) Possible levels of employment, millions	(2) Real domestic output (and income) (GDP = DI),* billions	(3) Consumption, C, billions	(4) Saving, S, billions	(5) Investment, I_g, billions	(6) Aggregate expenditures (C + I_g), billions	(7) Unintended investment (+) or disinvestment (−) in inventories	(8) Tendency of employment, output, and incomes
(1) 40	$370	$375	$−5	$20	$395	$−25	Increase
(2) 45	390	390	0	20	410	−20	Increase
(3) 50	410	405	5	20	425	−15	Increase
(4) 55	430	420	10	20	440	−10	Increase
(5) 60	450	435	15	20	455	−5	Increase
(6) 65	470	450	20	20	470	0	Equilibrium
(7) 70	490	465	25	20	485	+5	Decrease
(8) 75	510	480	30	20	500	+10	Decrease
(9) 80	530	495	35	20	515	+15	Decrease
(10) 85	550	510	40	20	530	+20	Decrease

*If depreciation and net American income earned abroad are zero, government is ignored, and it is assumed that all saving occurs in the household sector of the economy, GDP as a measure of domestic output is equal to NI, PI, and DI. This means that households receive a DI equal to the value of total output.

vate sector of the economy, the aggregate expenditures schedule shows the combined amount of consumption and planned gross investment spending $(C + I_g)$ forthcoming at each output-income level. Aggregate expenditures are the sum of columns 3 and 5 at each level of GDP.

We'll start by focusing on *planned* or intended investment in column 5 of Table 9-4. Later we'll see that imbalances in aggregate expenditures and real output will result in unplanned or unintended investment in the form of inventory changes (column 7).

Equilibrium GDP   Of the ten possible levels of GDP in Table 9-4, which will be the equilibrium level? Which level of total output will the economy be capable of sustaining?

The equilibrium level of output is that output whose production will create total spending just sufficient to purchase that output. The equilibrium level of GDP is where the total quantity of goods produced (GDP) equals the total quantity of goods purchased $(C + I_g)$. Look at the domestic output schedule of column 2 and the aggregate expenditures schedule of column 6 and you see that this equality exists only at $470 billion of GDP (row 6). This is the only output at which the economy is willing to spend precisely the amount necessary to take that output off the market. Here the annual rates of production and spending are in balance. There is no overproduction, which would result in a piling up of unsold goods and therefore cutbacks in the production rate. Nor is there an excess of total spending, which would draw down inventories and prompt increases in the rate of production. In short, there is no reason for businesses to alter this rate of production; $470 billion is therefore the **equilibrium GDP.**

Disequilibrium   To understand better the meaning of the equilibrium level of GDP, let's examine other levels of GDP to see why they cannot be sustained.

At the $410 billion level of GDP (row 3), businesses would find that if they produced this output, the income created would produce $405 billion in consumer spending. Supplemented by $20 billion of planned investment, total expenditures $(C + I_g)$ would be $425 billion, as shown in column 6. The economy provides an annual rate of spending more than sufficient to purchase the current $410 billion rate of production. Because businesses are producing at a lower rate than buyers are taking goods off the shelves, an unintended decline in business inventories of $15 billion would occur (column 7) if this situation were sus-

tained. But businesses will adjust to this imbalance between aggregate expenditures and real output by stepping up production. A higher rate of output will mean more jobs and a higher level of total income. In brief, if aggregate expenditures exceed the domestic output, those expenditures will drive domestic output upward.

By making the same comparisons of GDP (column 2) and $C + I_g$ (column 6) at all other levels of GDP below the $470 billion equilibrium level, we find that the economy wants to spend in excess of the level at which businesses are willing to produce. The excess of total spending at all these levels of GDP will drive GDP upward to the $470 billion level.

The reverse is true at all levels of GDP above the $470 billion equilibrium level. Businesses will find that the production of these total outputs fails to generate the levels of spending needed to take them off the market. Being unable to recover their costs, businesses will cut back on production.

To illustrate: At the $510 billion level of output (row 8), business managers will find there is insufficient spending to permit the sale of that output. Of the $510 billion of income which this output creates, $480 billion is received back by businesses as consumption spending. Though supplemented by $20 billion of planned investment spending, total expenditures ($500 billion) fall $10 billion short of the $510 billion quantity produced. If this imbalance persisted, $10 billion of inventories would pile up (column 7). But businesses will react to this unintended accumulation of unsold goods by cutting back on the rate of production. This decline in GDP will mean fewer jobs and a decline in total income. You should verify that deficiencies of total spending exist at all other levels of GDP above the $470 billion level.

The equilibrium level of GDP occurs where the total output, measured by GDP, and aggregate expenditures, $C + I_g$, are equal. Any excess of total spending over total output will drive GDP upward. Any deficiency of total spending will pull GDP downward.

Graphical Analysis

The same analysis can be shown in a graph. In Figure 9-8 (Key Graph) the **45-degree line** now takes on increased significance. Recall that the special property of this line is that at any point on it, the value of what is being measured on the horizontal axis (in this case GDP) is equal to the value of what is being measured on the vertical axis (here, aggregate expendi-

KEY GRAPH

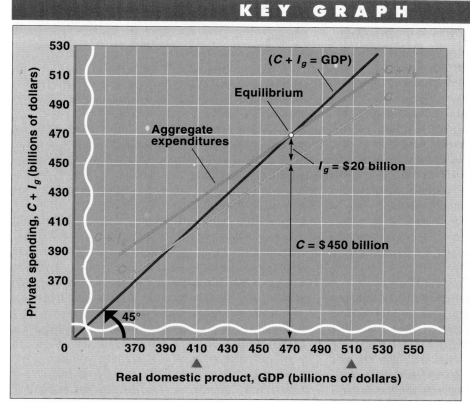

FIGURE 9-8 The aggregate expenditures–domestic output approach to the equilibrium GDP
The aggregate expenditures schedule, $C + I_g$, is determined by adding a fixed amount of investment to the upsloping consumption schedule. The equilibrium level of GDP is determined where the aggregate expenditures schedule intersects the 45-degree line, in this case at $470 billion.

tures or $C + I_g$). Having discovered in our tabular analysis that the equilibrium level of domestic output is determined where $C + I_g$ equals GDP, we can say that the 45-degree line in Figure 9-8 is a graphical statement of this equilibrium condition.

Next, we must add the aggregate expenditures schedule to Figure 9-8. To do this we graph the consumption schedule of Figure 9-2a and add to it *vertically* the constant $20 billion amount I_g from Figure 9-6, which, we assume, businesses plan to invest at each possible level of GDP. More directly, we can plot the $C + I_g$ data of column 6 in Table 9-4.

Observe that the aggregate expenditures line $C + I_g$ shows total spending rising with output and income, but not as much as income rises. This is because the marginal propensity to consume—the slope of line C—is less than 1. Because the aggregate expenditures line $C + I_g$ is parallel to the consumption line, the slope of the aggregate expenditures line equals the MPC and is also less than 1. A part of any increase in disposable income will *not* be spent; it will

be saved. For our particular data, aggregate expenditures rise by $15 billion for every $20 billion increase in real output and income because $5 billion of each $20 billion income increment is saved.

The equilibrium level of GDP is that GDP level corresponding to the intersection of the aggregate expenditures schedule and the 45-degree line. This intersection locates the only point at which aggregate expenditures (on the vertical axis) are equal to GDP (on the horizontal axis). Because our aggregate expenditures schedule is based on the data of Table 9-4, we once again find that equilibrium output is $470 billion. Observe that consumption at this output is $450 billion and investment is $20 billion.

It is evident from Figure 9-8 that no levels of GDP above the equilibrium level are sustainable, because $C + I_g$ falls short of GDP. Graphically, the aggregate expenditures schedule lies *below* the 45-degree line. At the $510 billion GDP level, $C + I_g$ is only $500 billion. Inventories of unsold goods rise to undesired levels, prompting businesses to readjust production sights downward in the direction of the $470 billion output level.

Conversely, at all possible levels of GDP less than $470 billion, the economy wants to spend in excess of what businesses are producing. $C + I_g$ exceeds the value of the corresponding output. Graphically, the aggregate expenditures schedule lies *above* the 45-degree line. At the $410 billion GDP, for example, $C + I_g$ totals $425 billion. Inventories decline as the rate of spending exceeds the rate of production, prompting businesses to raise production toward the $470 billion GDP. Unless there is some change in the location of the aggregate expenditures line, the $470 billion level of GDP will be sustained indefinitely.

EQUILIBRIUM GDP: LEAKAGES-INJECTIONS APPROACH

The expenditures-output approach to determining GDP spotlights total spending as the immediate determinant of the levels of output, employment, and income. Though the **leakages-injections** ($S = I_g$) **approach** is less direct, it does have the advantage of underscoring the reason $C + I_g$ and GDP are unequal at all levels of output except the equilibrium level.

The idea of the leakages-injections approach is this: Under our simplifying assumptions we know that the production of any level of real output will generate an identical amount of disposable income. But we also know a part of that income may be saved—*not* consumed—by households. Saving therefore represents a *leakage* or withdrawal of spending from the income-expenditures stream. Saving is what keeps consumption short of total output or GDP; thus, by itself consumption is insufficient to take the domestic output off the market, setting the stage, it would seem, for a decline in total output.

However, the business sector does not intend to sell its entire output to consumers; some domestic output will consist of capital or investment goods sold within the business sector. Investment can therefore be thought of as an *injection* of spending into the income-expenditures stream which supplements consumption. Investment is a potential offset to, or replacement for, the leakage of saving.

If the leakage of saving exceeds the injection of investment, then $C + I_g$ will fall short of GDP and this level of GDP will be too high to be sustained. Any GDP where saving exceeds investment will be an above-equilibrium GDP. Conversely, if the injection of

investment exceeds the leakage of saving, then $C + I_g$ will be greater than GDP and GDP will be driven upward. Any GDP where investment exceeds saving will be a below-equilibrium GDP.

Only where $S = I_g$—where the leakage of saving is exactly offset by the injection of investment—will aggregate expenditures equal real output. And we know this equality defines the equilibrium GDP.

In the closed private economy assumed here, there are only one leakage (saving) and one injection (investment). In general terms, a *leakage* is any use of income other than its expenditure on domestically produced output. In the more realistic models which follow (in Chapter 10), we will need to incorporate the additional leakages of imports and taxes into our analysis.

Similarly, an *injection* is any supplement to consumer spending on domestic production. Again, in later models we must add injections of exports and government purchases to our discussion. But for now we need only compare the single leakage of saving with the sole injection of investment to assess the impact on GDP.

Tabular Analysis

Our $C + I_g$ = GDP approach has led us to conclude that all levels of GDP less than $470 billion are unstable because the corresponding $C + I_g$ exceeds these GDPs, driving GDP upward. Now let's look at the saving schedule (columns 2 and 4) and the investment schedule (columns 2 and 5) of Table 9-4. Comparing the amounts households and businesses want to save and invest at each of the below-equilibrium GDP levels explains the excesses of total spending. At each of these lower GDP levels, businesses plan to invest more than households want to save.

For example, at the $410 billion level of GDP (row 3), households will save only $5 billion, spending $405 of their $410 billion incomes. Supplemented by $20 billion of business investment, aggregate expenditures ($C + I_g$) are $425 billion. Aggregate expenditures exceed GDP by $15 billion (= $425 − $410) *because* the amount businesses plan to invest at this level of GDP exceeds the amounts households save by $15 billion. The fact is that a very small leakage of saving at this relatively low income level will be more than compensated for by the relatively large injection of investment spending which causes $C + I_g$ to exceed GDP and induce GDP upward.

Similarly, all levels of GDP above the $470 billion level are also unstable, because they exceed $C + I_g$. The reason for this insufficiency of aggregate expenditures is that at all GDP levels above $470 billion, households will want to save more than businesses plan to invest. The saving leakage is not compensated for by the injection of investment.

For example, households will choose to save at the high rate of $30 billion at the $510 billion GDP (row 8). Businesses, however, will plan to invest only $20 billion. This $10 billion excess of saving over planned investment will reduce total spending to $10 billion below the value of total output. Specifically, aggregate expenditures are $500 billion and real GDP is $510 billion. This spending deficiency will reduce GDP.

Again we verify that the equilibrium GDP is $470 billion. Only at this level are the saving desires of households and the investment plans of businesses equal. Only when businesses and households attempt to invest and save at the same rate—where the leakages and injections are equal—will $C + I_g = $ GDP. Only here will the annual rates of production and spending be in balance; only here will there be no unplanned changes in inventories.

Think of it this way: If saving were zero, consumer spending would always be sufficient to clear the market of any GDP; consumption would equal GDP. But saving can and does occur, causing consumption to fall short of GDP. Only when businesses are willing to invest at the same rate at which households save

will the amount by which consumption falls short of GDP be precisely counterbalanced.

Graphical Analysis

The leakages-injections approach to determining the equilibrium GDP can be demonstrated graphically, as in Figure 9-9. Here we have combined the saving schedule of Figure 9-2b and the investment schedule of Figure 9-6. The numerical data for these schedules are in columns 2, 4, and 5 of Table 9-4. We see the equilibrium level of GDP is at $470 billion, where the saving and investment schedules intersect. Only here do businesses and households invest and save at the same rates; therefore, only here will GDP and $C + I_g$ be equal.

At all higher levels of GDP, households will save at a higher rate than businesses plan to invest. The saving leakage exceeds the investment injection which causes $C + I_g$ to fall short of GDP, driving GDP downward. At the $510 billion GDP, for example, saving of $30 billion will exceed investment of $20 billion by $10 billion, with the result that $C + I_g$ is $500 billion, $10 billion short of GDP.

At all levels of GDP below the $470 billion equilibrium level, businesses will plan to invest more than households save. Here the injection of investment exceeds the leakage of saving so that $C + I_g$ exceeds GDP, driving GDP upward. To illustrate: At the $410 billion level of GDP the $5 billion leakage of saving is more than compensated for by the $20 billion that

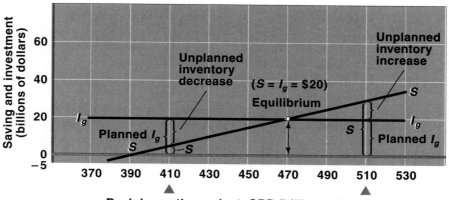

FIGURE 9-9   The leakages-injections approach to the equilibrium GDP
A second approach is to view the equilibrium GDP as determined by the intersection of the saving (S) and the planned investment (I_g) schedules. Only at the point of equilibrium will households plan to save the amount businesses want to invest. It is the consistency of these plans which equates GDP and $C + I_g$.

JOHN MAYNARD KEYNES (1883–1946)

The English economist John Maynard Keynes is regarded as the originator of modern macroeconomics.

1935 George Bernard Shaw received a letter from n Maynard Keynes in which Keynes asserted, "I lieve myself to be writing a book on economic the- y which will largely revolutionize . . . the way the orld thinks about economic problems." And, in fact, ynes's *The General Theory of Employment, Inter- , and Money* (1936) did revolutionize economic alysis and established Keynes as one of the most luential economists of all time.

The son of an eminent English economist, Keynes s educated at Eton and Cambridge. While his early erests were in mathematics and probability theory, nes ultimately turned to economics.

Keynes was far more than an economist: He was an incredibly active, many-sided man who also played such diverse roles as principal rep-

resentative of the Treasury at the World War I Paris Peace Conference, deputy for the Chancellor of the Exchequer, a director of the Bank of England, trustee of the National Gallery, chairman of the Council for the Encouragement of

businesses plan to invest. The result is that $C + I_g$ exceeds GDP by $15 billion, inducing businesses to produce a larger GDP. *(Key Question 10)*

PLANNED VERSUS ACTUAL INVESTMENT

We have emphasized that discrepancies in saving and investment can occur and bring about changes in the equilibrium GDP. Now we must recognize that, in another sense, saving and investment must always be equal! This apparent contradiction concerning the equality of saving and investment is resolved when we distinguish between **planned investment** and saving (which need not be equal) and **actual investment** and saving (which by definition must be equal). The catch is that *actual investment consists of both planned and unplanned investment (unplanned changes in inventory investment), and unplanned investment acts as a balancing item which always equates the actual amounts saved and invested in any period of time.*

Disequilibrium and Inventories

Consider, for example, the $490 billion above-equilibrium GDP (row 7 of Table 9-4). What would happen if businesses produced this output, thinking they could sell it? At this level, households save $25 billion of their $490 billion DI, so consumption is only $465 billion. *Planned* investment (column 5) is $20 billion; businesses plan or desire to buy $20 billion worth of capital goods. This means aggregate expenditures $(C + I_g)$ are $485 billion, and sales therefore fall short of production by $5 billion. This extra $5 billion of goods is retained by businesses as an *unintended* or *unplanned* increase in inventories (column 7). It is unintended because it results from the failure of total spending to take total output off the market. Remembering that, by definition, changes in inventories are a part of investment, we note that *actual* investment of $25 billion ($20 planned *plus* $5 unintended or unplanned) equals saving of $25 billion, even though saving exceeds *planned* investment by $5 billion. Businesses, being unwilling to accumulate un-

Music and the Arts, bursar of King's College, Cambridge, editor of the *Economic Journal,* chairman of the *Nation* and later the *New Statesman* magazines, and chairman of the National Mutual Life Assurance Society. He also ran an investment company, organized the Camargo Ballet (his wife, Lydia Lopokova, was a renowned star of the Russian Imperial Ballet), and built (profitably) the Arts Theatre at Cambridge.*

In addition, Keynes found time to amass a $2 million personal fortune by speculating in stocks, international currencies, and commodities. He was also a leading figure in the "Bloomsbury group," an *avant-garde* group of intellectual luminaries who greatly influenced the artistic and literary standards of England.

Most importantly, Keynes was a prolific scholar.

*E. Ray Canterbery, *The Making of Economics,* 3d ed. (Belmont, Calif.: Wadsworth Publishing Company, 1987), p. 126.

His books encompassed such widely ranging topics as probability theory, monetary economics, and the economic consequences of the World War I peace treaty. His *magnum opus,* however, was the *General Theory,* which has been described by John Kenneth Galbraith as "a work of profound obscurity, badly written and prematurely published." Yet the *General Theory* attacked the classical economists' contention that recession will automatically cure itself. Keynes' analysis suggested that recession could easily spiral downward into a depression. Keynes claimed that modern capitalism contained no automatic mechanism which would propel the economy back toward full employment. The economy might languish for many years in depression. Indeed, the massive unemployment of the worldwide depression of the 1930s seemed to provide sufficient evidence that Keynes was right. His basic policy recommendation—a startling one in view of the balanced-budget sentiment at the time—was for government in these circumstances to increase its spending to induce more production and put the unemployed back to work.

wanted inventories at this annual rate, will cut back production.

Now look at the below-equilibrium $450 billion output (row 5 of Table 9-4). Because households save only $15 billion of their $450 billion DI, consumption is $435 billion. Planned investment by businesses is $20 billion, so aggregate expenditures are $455 billion. Sales exceed production by $5 billion. This is so because an unplanned decline in business inventories has occurred. Businesses have unintentionally *dis*invested $5 billion in inventories (column 7). Note once again that *actual* investment is $15 billion ($20 planned *minus* $5 unintended or unplanned) and equal to saving of $15 billion, even though *planned* investment exceeds saving by $5 billion. This unplanned decline in investment in inventories due to the excess of sales over production will induce businesses to increase the GDP by expanding production.

To summarize:

At all *above-equilibrium* levels of GDP (where saving exceeds planned investment), actual investment and saving are equal because of unintended increases in inventories which are a part of actual investment. Graphically (Figure 9-9), the unintended inventory increase is measured by the vertical distance by which the saving schedule lies above the (planned) investment schedule.

At all *below-equilibrium* levels of GDP (where planned investment exceeds saving), actual investment will be equal to saving because of unintended decreases in inventories which must be subtracted from planned investment to determine actual investment. These unintended inventory declines are shown graphically as the vertical distance by which the (planned) investment schedule lies above the saving schedule.

Achieving Equilibrium

These distinctions are important because they mean that *it is the equality of planned investment and saving which determines the equilibrium level of GDP.* We can think of the process by which equilibrium is achieved as follows:

1 A difference between saving and planned investment causes a difference between the production and spending plans of the economy as a whole.

2 This difference between aggregate production and spending plans results in unintended investment or disinvestment in inventories.

3 As long as unintended investment in inventories persists, businesses will revise their production plans downward and reduce GDP. Conversely, as long as unintended disinvestment in inventories exists, firms will revise their production plans upward and increase GDP. Both movements in GDP are toward equilibrium because they bring about the equality of planned investment and saving.

4 Only where planned investment and saving are equal will the level of GDP be in equilibrium. Only where planned investment equals saving will there be no unintended investment or disinvestment in inven-

tories to drive the GDP downward or upward. Note in column 7 of Table 9-4 that only at the $470 billion equilibrium GDP is there no unintended investment or disinvestment in inventories. *(Key Question 11)*

QUICK REVIEW 9-4

■ In a private closed economy, equilibrium GDP occurs where aggregate expenditures equal real domestic output $(C + I_g = \text{GDP})$.

■ Alternatively, equilibrium GDP is established where saving equals planned investment $(S = I_g)$.

■ Actual investment consists of planned investment plus unplanned changes in inventories and is always equal to saving.

■ At equilibrium GDP, changes in inventories are zero; no unintended investment or disinvestment occurs.

CHAPTER SUMMARY

1 Classical economists argued that because supply creates its own demand (Say's law), general underspending was improbable. Thus the economy would provide virtually continuous full employment. Even if temporary declines in total spending occurred, these declines would be compensated for by downward price-wage adjustments which would boost spending and employment, restoring the economy to its full-employment level of output.

2 The Great Depression and Keynes's *General Theory* undermined classical macroeconomics. The Great Depression challenged the classical precept that full employment was the norm in a capitalist economy. Keynes's aggregate expenditures analysis showed how periods of underspending or overspending could occur.

3 The basic tools of the aggregate expenditures model are the consumption, saving, and investment schedules, which show the various amounts households intend to consume and save and businesses plan to invest at the various income-output levels, assuming a fixed price level.

4 The *average* propensities to consume and save show the fraction of any level of *total* income consumed and saved. The *marginal* propensities to consume and save show the fraction of any *change* in total income consumed or saved.

5 The locations of the consumption and saving schedules are determined by **a** the amount of wealth owned by households; **b** expectations of future income, future prices, and product availability; **c** the relative size of consumer indebtedness; and **d** taxation. The consumption

and saving schedules are relatively stable.

6 The immediate determinants of investment are **a** the expected rate of net profit and **b** the real rate of interest. The economy's investment-demand curve can be determined by cumulating investment projects and arraying them in descending order according to their expected net profitability and applying the rule that investment will be profitable up to the point at which the real interest rate, i, equals the expected rate of net profit, r. The investment-demand curve reveals an inverse relationship between the interest rate and the level of aggregate investment.

7 Shifts in the investment-demand curve can occur as the result of changes in **a** the acquisition, maintenance, and operating costs of capital goods; **b** business taxes; **c** technology; **d** the stocks of capital goods on hand; and **e** expectations.

8 For simplicity we assume the level of investment determined by the current interest rate and the investment-demand curve does not vary with the level of real GDP.

9 The durability of capital goods, the irregular occurrence of major innovations, profit volatility, and the variability of expectations all contribute to the instability of investment spending.

10 For a private closed economy the equilibrium level of GDP is where aggregate expenditures and real output are equal or, graphically, where the $C + I_g$ line intersects the 45-degree line. At any GDP greater than equilibrium GDP, real output will exceed aggregate spending, resulting in unintended investment in inventories, depressed profits, and eventual declines in output, employment, and income. At any below-equilibrium GDP, aggregate expenditures will exceed real output, resulting in unintended disinvestment in inventories, substantial profits, and eventual increases in GDP.

11 The leakages-injections approach determines equilibrium GDP at the point where the amount households save and the amount businesses plan to invest are equal. This is at the point where the saving and planned investment schedules intersect. Any excess of saving over planned investment will cause a shortage of total spending, forcing GDP

to fall. Any excess of planned investment over saving will cause an excess of total spending, inducing GDP to rise. These changes in GDP will in both cases correct the indicated discrepancies in saving and planned investment.

12 Actual investment consists of planned investment and unplanned changes in inventories. When planned investment diverges from planned saving, unintended investment or disinvestment in inventories occur which equate actual investment and saving. At equilibrium GDP, planned investment equals saving; inventory levels are constant (there is no unplanned investment or disinvestment).

TERMS AND CONCEPTS

Say's law	average propensities to	investment schedule	45-degree line
Keynesian economics	consume and save	aggregate	leakages-injections
consumption and	marginal propensities	expenditures–	approach
saving schedules	to consume and save	domestic output	planned versus actual
break-even income	investment-demand	approach	investment
	curve	equilibrium GDP	

QUESTIONS AND STUDY SUGGESTIONS

1 Relate Say's law to the perspective held by classical economists that the economy generally will operate at a position *on* its production possibilities curve (Chapter 2). Use production possibilities analysis to demonstrate the Keynesian perspective on this matter.

2 Explain what relationships are shown by   **a** the consumption schedule,   **b** the saving schedule,   **c** the investment-demand curve, and   **d** the investment schedule.

3 Precisely how are the APC and the MPC different? Why must the sum of the MPC and the MPS equal 1? What are the basic determinants of the consumption and saving schedules? Of your own level of consumption?

4 Explain how each of the following will affect the consumption and saving schedules or the investment schedule:

   a A decline in the amount of government bonds which consumers are holding

   b The threat of limited, nonnuclear war, leading the public to expect future shortages of consumer durables

   c A decline in the real interest rate

   d A sharp decline in stock prices

   e An increase in the rate of population growth

   f The development of a cheaper method of manufacturing pig iron from ore

   g The announcement that the social security program is to be restricted in size of benefits

   h The expectation that mild inflation will persist in the next decade

   i An increase in the Federal personal income tax

5 Explain why an upshift in the consumption schedule typically involves an equal downshift in the saving schedule. What is the exception?

6 *Key Question   Complete the accompanying table.*

Level of output and income (GDP = DI)	Consumption	Saving	APC	APS	MPC	MPS
$240	$_____	$−4	__ __			
260	_____	0	__ __	__ __		
280	_____	4	__ __	__ __		
300	_____	8	__ __	__ __		
320	_____	12	__ __	__ __		
340	_____	16	__ __	__ __		
360	_____	20	__ __	__ __		
380	_____	24	__ __	__ __		
400	_____	28	__ __	__ __		

   a *Show the consumption and saving schedules graphically.*

   b *Locate the break-even level of income. How is it possible for households to dissave at very low income levels?*

   c *If the proportion of total income consumed decreases and the proportion saved increases as income rises, explain both verbally and graphically how the MPC and MPS can be constant at various levels of income.*

7 What are the basic determinants of investment? Explain the relationship between the real interest rate and the level of investment. Why is the investment schedule less stable than the consumption and saving schedules?

8 Key Question Assume there are no investment projects in the economy which yield an expected rate of net profit of 25 percent or more. But suppose there are $10 billion of investment projects yielding expected net profit of between 20 and 25 percent; another $10 billion yielding between 15 and 20 percent; another $10 billion between 10 and 15 percent; and so forth. Cumulate these data and present them graphically, putting the expected rate of net profit on the vertical axis and the amount of investment on the horizontal axis. What will be the equilibrium level of aggregate investment if the real interest rate is   **a** 15 percent,   **b** 10 percent, and   **c** 5 percent? Explain why this curve is the investment-demand curve.

9 Explain graphically the determination of the equilibrium GDP by   **a** the aggregate expenditures–domestic output approach and   **b** the leakages-injections approach for a private closed economy. Why must these two approaches always yield the same equilibrium GDP? Explain why the intersection of the aggregate expenditures schedule and the 45-degree line determines the equilibrium GDP.

10 Key Question Assuming the level of investment is $16 billion and independent of the level of total output, complete the following table and determine the equilibrium levels of output and employment which this private closed economy would provide. What are the sizes of the MPC and MPS?

Possible levels of employment, millions	Real domestic output (GDP = DI), billions	Consumption, billions	Saving, billions
40	$240	$244	$____
45	260	260	____
50	280	276	____
55	300	292	____
60	320	308	____
65	340	324	____
70	360	340	____
75	380	356	____
80	400	372	____

11 Key Question Using the consumption and saving data given in question 10 and assuming the level of investment is $16 billion, what are the levels of saving and planned investment at the $380 billion level of domestic output? What are the levels of saving and actual investment? What are saving and planned investment at the $300 billion level of domestic output? What are the levels of saving and actual investment? Use the concept of unintended investment to explain adjustments toward equilibrium from both the $380 and $300 billion levels of domestic output.

12 "Planned investment is equal to saving at all levels of GDP; actual investment equals saving only at the equilibrium GDP." Do you agree? Explain. Critically evaluate: "The fact that households may save more than businesses want to invest is of no consequence, because events will in time force households and businesses to save and invest at the same rates."

13 Advanced analysis: Linear equations (see appendix to Chapter 1) for the consumption and saving schedules take the general form $C = a + bY$ and $S = -a + (1 - b)Y$, where C, S, and Y are consumption, saving, and national income, respectively. The constant a represents the vertical intercept, and b is the slope of the consumption schedule.

   a Use the following data to substitute specific numerical values into the consumption and saving equations.

National income (Y)	Consumption (C)
$ 0	$ 80
100	140
200	200
300	260
400	320

   b What is the economic meaning of b? Of $(1 - b)$?

   c Suppose the amount of saving which occurs at each level of national income falls by $20, but that the values for b and $(1 - b)$ remain unchanged. Restate the saving and consumption equations for the new numerical values and cite a factor which might have caused the change.

14 Advanced analysis: Suppose that the linear equation for consumption in a hypothetical economy is $C = 40 + .8Y$. Also suppose that income (Y) is $400. Determine   **a** the marginal propensity to consume,   **b** the marginal propensity to save,   **c** the level of consumption,   **d** the average propensity to consume,   **e** the level of saving, and   **f** the average propensity to save.

15 Advanced analysis: Assume that the linear equation for consumption in a hypothetical private closed economy is $C = 10 + .9Y$, where Y is total real income (output). Also suppose that the equation for investment is $I_g = I_{g0} = 40$, meaning that I_g is 40 at all levels of real income (output). Using the equation $Y = C + I_g$, determine the equilibrium level of Y. What are the total amounts of consumption, saving, and investment at equilibrium Y?

16 (Last Word) What is the significance of John Maynard Keynes's book, *The General Theory*, published in 1936?

10

AGGREGATE EXPENDITURES: THE MULTIPLIER, NET EXPORTS, AND GOVERNMENT

We have seen why a particular level of real GDP exists, specifically in a private closed economy. Now we want to see why and how that level might change, as it often does in the real economy. Also, we gain realism by adding the foreign sector and government to our aggregate expenditures model.

First, we analyze changes in investment spending and how they affect real GDP, income, and employment, finding that a change in investment creates a multiple change in output and incomes. Then we "open" our simplified "closed" economy to show how exports and imports affect it. Government—with its expenditures and taxes—is next brought into the model; the "private" economy becomes the "mixed" economy. Finally, we apply our model to two historical periods and consider some of its deficiencies. We continue to assume the price level remains constant unless stated otherwise. Our focus therefore remains on real GDP.

CHANGES IN EQUILIBRIUM GDP AND THE MULTIPLIER

Thus far, we have been concerned with using the aggregate expenditures model to explain the equilibrium levels of total output and income. But we saw in Chapter 8 that the GDP of American capitalism is seldom stable; rather, it is characterized by long-run growth and punctuated by cyclical fluctuations. Let's see *why* and *how* the equilibrium level of real GDP fluctuates.

The equilibrium level of GDP will change in response to changes in the investment schedule or the saving-consumption schedules. Because investment spending generally is less stable than the consump-

tion-saving schedules, we will assume the investment schedule changes.

The impact of changes in investment can be seen through Figure 10-1a and b. Suppose the expected rate of net profit on investment rises (shifting the investment-demand curve of Figure 9-5 to the right) *or* the interest rate falls (the investment-demand curve in Fig. 9-5 doesn't shift; we move down the stable curve). As a result, investment spending increases by, say, $5 billion. This is indicated in Figure 10-1a by an upward shift in the aggregate expenditures schedule from $(C + I_g)_0$ to $(C + I_g)_1$, and in Figure 10-1b by an upward shift in the investment schedule from I_{g0} to I_{g1}. In each graph the consequence is a rise in the equilibrium GDP from $470 to $490 billion.

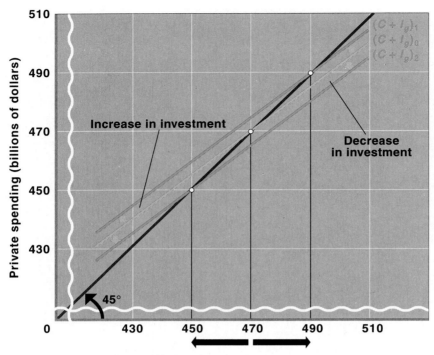

(a) Change in aggregate expenditures schedule

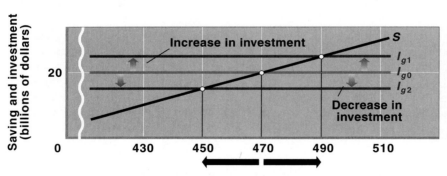

(b) Change in investment schedule

FIGURE 10-1 Changes in the equilibrium GDP caused by shifts in (a) the aggregate expenditures schedule and (b) the investment schedule
An upshift in the aggregate expenditures schedule from $(C + I_g)_0$ to $(C + I_g)_1$ will increase the equilibrium GDP. Conversely, a downshift in the aggregate expenditures schedule from $(C + I_g)_0$ to $(C + I_g)_2$ will lower the equilibrium GDP. In the saving-investment figure an upshift in the investment schedule $(I_{g0}$ to $I_{g1})$ will raise, and a downshift $(I_{g0}$ to $I_{g2})$ will lower, the equilibrium GDP.

If the expected rate of net profit from investment decreases *or* the interest rate rises, the result is a decline in investment spending of, say, $5 billion. This is shown by the downward shift of the investment schedule from I_{g0} to I_{g2} in Figure 10-1b and the aggregate expenditures schedule from $(C + I_g)_0$ to $(C + I_g)_2$ in Figure 10-1a. In each case, these shifts reduce the equilibrium GDP from the original $470 billion level to $450 billion.

You should verify these conclusions in terms of Table 9-4 by substituting $25 billion and then $15 billion for the $20 billion planned investment figure in column 5 of the table.

At the risk of getting ahead of ourselves, we note the $5 billion changes in investment may be the direct result of economic policy. Looking back at Table 9-3, we see the initial $20 billion level of investment is associated with an 8 percent interest rate. *If* the economy is in recession, monetary authorities may purposely reduce the interest rate to 6 percent (by increasing the money supply), causing a $5 billion increase in investment and thereby in aggregate expenditures to stimulate the economy.

Conversely, *if,* with the initial $20 billion of investment, the economy faces a demand-pull inflation problem, the monetary authorities may increase the interest rate to 10 percent (by reducing the money supply), reducing investment and aggregate expenditures to constrain the inflation. Monetary policy—changing the money supply to alter interest rates and aggregate expenditures—is the subject of Chapter 15.

Changes in the consumption-saving schedules will have similar effects. If households consume more (save less) at each level of GDP, the aggregate expenditures schedule will shift upward and the saving schedule downward in Figure 10-1a and b, respectively. Either of these shifts will increase the equilibrium GDP. If households consume less (save more) at each possible GDP, the resulting drop in the consumption schedule and the increase in the saving schedule will reduce the equilibrium GDP.

The Multiplier Effect

You may have noticed in these examples that a $5 billion change in investment spending led to a $20 billion change in the output-income level. This surprising result is called the **multiplier effect** or, simply, the *multiplier.* The multiplier is the ratio of a change in equilibrium GDP to the change in (investment) spending which caused that change in GDP. Stated generally,

$$\text{Multiplier} = \frac{\text{change in real GDP}}{\text{initial change in spending}}$$

Here the multiplier is 4 (change of GDP of $20 ÷ change in investment of $5). Or, by rearranging our equation, we can say that:

$$\text{Change in GDP} = \text{multiplier} \times \frac{\text{initial change in}}{\text{spending}}$$

Three points about the multiplier must be made here.
1   The "initial change in spending" is usually associated with investment spending because investment is the most volatile component of aggregate expenditures (Figure 9-7). But changes in consumption, exports, or government purchases also are subject to the multiplier effect.

2   The "initial change in spending" refers to an up-shift or downshift in the aggregate expenditures schedule due to an upshift or downshift in one of its components. In Figure 10-1b we find that real GDP has increased by $20 billion because the investment schedule has shifted upward by $5 billion from I_{g0} to I_{g1}.
3   Implicit in our second point is that the multiplier works in both directions. A small increase in spending can create a multiple increase in GDP, or a small decrease in spending can be multiplied into a much larger decrease in GDP. Note carefully the effects of the shift in $(C + I_g)_0$ to $(C + I_g)_1$ or to $(C + I_g)_2$ and I_{g0} to I_{g1} or to I_{g2} in Figure 10-1a and b.

Rationale   The multiplier is based on two facts.
1   The economy has repetitive, continuous flows of expenditures and income through which dollars spent by Smith are received as income by Jones.
2   Any change in income will cause both consumption and saving to vary in the same direction as, and by a fraction of, the change in income.

It follows that an initial change in the rate of spending will cause a spending chain reaction which, although of diminishing importance at each successive step, will cumulate to a multiple change in GDP.

The rationale underlying the multiplier effect is illustrated numerically in Table 10-1. Suppose a $5 billion increase in investment spending occurs. This is an upshift of the aggregate expenditures schedule by $5 billion in Figure 10-1a and the upshift of the investment schedule from $20 to $25 billion in Figure 10-1b. We continue to assume that the MPC is .75 and the MPS is .25. Also, we suppose that the economy is initially in equilibrium at $470 billion.

The initial increase in investment spending generates an equal amount of wage, rent, interest, and profit income because spending income and receiving income are two sides of the same transaction. How much consumption will be induced by this $5 billion increase in the incomes of households? The answer is found by applying the marginal propensity to consume of .75 to this change in income. Thus, the $5 billion increase in income raises consumption by $3.75 (= .75 × $5) billion and saving by $1.25 (= .25 × $5) billion, as shown in columns 2 and 3 of Table 10-1.

The $3.75 billion spent is received by other households as income (second round). These households consume .75 of this $3.75 billion, or $2.81 billion, and save .25 of it, or $0.94 billion. The $2.81 billion con-

TABLE 10-1   The multiplier: a tabular illustration *(in billions)*

	(1) Change in income	(2) Change in consumption (MPC = .75)	(3) Change in saving (MPS = .25)
Assumed increase in investment	$ 5.00	$ 3.75	$1.25
Second round	3.75	2.81	0.94
Third round	2.81	2.11	0.70
Fourth round	2.11	1.58	0.53
Fifth round	1.58	1.19	0.39
All other rounds	4.75	3.56	1.19
Totals	$20.00	$15.00	$5.00

sumed flows to still other households as income (third round). This process continues.

Figure 10-2, derived from Table 10-1, shows the cumulative effects of the rounds of the multiplier process. Each round *adds* the orange blocks to national income and GDP. The cumulation of the additional income in each round—the sum of the orange blocks—is the total change in income or GDP. Though the spending and respending effects of the

FIGURE 10-2   The multiplier process (MPC = .75)
An initial change in investment spending of $5 billion creates an equal $5 billion of new income in round 1. Households spend $3.75 (= .75 × $5) billion of this new income, creating $3.75 of added income in round 2. Of this $3.75 of new income, households spend $2.81 (= .75 × $3.75) billion and income rises by that amount in round 3. The cumulation of such income increments over the entire process eventually results in a total change of income and GDP of $20 billion. The multiplier therefore is 4 (= $20 billion ÷ $5 billion).

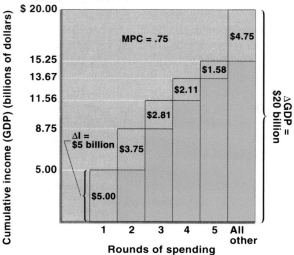

increase in investment diminish with each successive round of spending, the cumulative increase in the output-income level will be $20 billion if the process is carried through to the last dollar. The $5 billion increase in investment will therefore increase the equilibrium GDP by $20 billion, from $470 to $490 billion. Thus, the multiplier is 4 (= $20 billion ÷ $5 billion).

It is no coincidence that the multiplier effect ends at the point where exactly enough saving has been generated to offset the initial $5 billion increase in investment spending. Only then will the disequilibrium created by the investment increase be corrected. GDP and total incomes must rise by $20 billion to create $5 billion in additional saving to match the $5 billion increase in investment spending. Income must increase by four times the initial excess of investment over saving, because households save one-fourth of any increase in their incomes (that is, the MPS is .25). In this example the multiplier—the number of times the ultimate increase in income exceeds the initial increase in investment spending—is 4.

The Multiplier and the Marginal Propensities
You may have sensed from Table 10-1 a relationship between the MPS and the size of the multiplier. The fraction of an increase in income saved—the MPS—determines the cumulative respending effects of any initial change in I_g, G, X_n or C, and therefore the multiplier. *The size of the MPS and the size of the multiplier are inversely related.* The smaller the fraction of any change in income saved, the greater the respending at each round and, therefore, the greater the multiplier. If the MPS is .25, as in our example, the multiplier is 4. If the MPS were .33, the multiplier would be 3. If the MPS were .2, the multiplier would be 5.

Look again at Table 9-4 and Figure 10-1b. Initially the economy is in equilibrium at the $470 billion level of GDP. Now businesses increase investment by $5 billion so that planned investment of $25 billion exceeds saving of $20 billion at the $470 billion level. This means $470 billion is no longer the equilibrium GDP. By how much must GDP or national income rise to restore equilibrium? By enough to generate $5 billion of additional saving to offset the $5 billion increase in investment. Because households save $1 out of every $4 of additional income they receive (MPS = .25), GDP must rise by $20 billion—four times the increase in investment—to create the $5 billion of extra saving necessary to restore equilibrium. Thus, the multiplier is 4.

If the MPS were .33, GDP would only have to rise by $15 billion (three times the increase in investment) to generate $5 billion of additional saving and restore equilibrium, and the multiplier therefore would be 3. But if the MPS were .20, GDP would have to rise by $25 billion for people to save an extra $5 billion and equilibrium to be restored, yielding a multiplier of 5.

Also, recall the MPS measures the slope of the saving schedule. In the leakages-injections ($S = I_g$) approach, this means that if the MPS is relatively large (say, .5) and the slope of the saving schedule is therefore relatively steep (.5), any upward shift in investment spending will be subject to a relatively small multiplier. A $5 billion increase in investment will entail a new point of intersection of the S and I_g schedules only $10 billion to the right of the original equilibrium GDP. The multiplier is only 2.

But if the MPS is relatively small (say, .10), the slope of the saving schedule will be relatively gentle. Therefore, the same $5 billion upward shift in the investment schedule will provide a new intersection point $50 billion to the right of the original equilibrium GDP. The multiplier is 10 in this case. You should verify these two examples by drawing appropriate saving and investment diagrams.

We can summarize by saying *the multiplier is equal to the reciprocal of the MPS*. The reciprocal of any number is the quotient you obtain by dividing 1 by that number:

$$\text{The multiplier} = \frac{1}{\text{MPS}}$$

This formula is a shorthand way to determine the multiplier. All you need to know is the MPS to calculate the size of the multiplier.

Recall, too, from Chapter 9 that since MPC + MPS = 1, it follows that MPS = 1 − MPC. Therefore, we can also write our multiplier formula as

$$\text{The multiplier} = \frac{1}{1 - \text{MPC}}$$

Significance of the Multiplier   The significance of the multiplier is that a small change in the investment plans of businesses or the consumption-saving plans of households can trigger a larger change in the equilibrium level of GDP. The multiplier magnifies the fluctuations in business activity initiated by changes in spending.

As illustrated in Figure 10-3, the larger the MPC (the smaller the MPS), the greater will be the multiplier. If the MPC is .75, the multiplier is 4, a $10 billion decline in planned investment will reduce the equilibrium GDP by $40 billion. But if the MPC is only .67, the multiplier is 3, the same $10 billion drop in investment will reduce the equilibrium GDP by only $30 billion. This makes sense intuitively: A large MPC means the chain of induced consumption shown in Figure 10-2 dampens down slowly and thereby cumulates to a large change in income. Conversely, a small MPC (a large MPS) causes induced consumption to decline quickly so the cumulative change in income is small.

Generalizing the Multiplier   The multiplier we have presented here is called the *simple multiplier* because it is based on a simple model of the economy. In terms of $\frac{1}{\text{MPS}}$, the simple multiplier reflects only

FIGURE 10-3   The MPC and the multiplier
The larger the MPC (the smaller the MPS), the greater is the size of the multiplier.

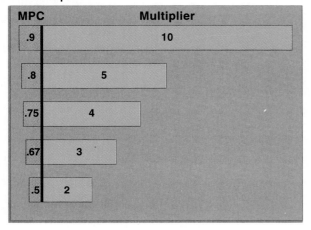

MPC	Multiplier
.9	10
.8	5
.75	4
.67	3
.5	2

the leakage of saving. In the real world successive rounds of income and spending can also be dampened down by other leakages from imports and taxes. As with the leakage into saving, some part of income at each round would be siphoned off as additional taxes, and another part would be used to purchase additional goods from abroad. The result of these added leakages is that the $\frac{1}{\text{MPS}}$ statement of the multiplier can be generalized by changing the denominator to read "fraction of the change in income which is not spent on domestic output" or "fraction of the change in income which leaks, or is diverted, from the income-expenditure stream." The more realistic multiplier which results when all leakages—saving, taxes, and imports—are included is called the *complex multiplier.* The Council of Economic Advisers, which advises the President on economic matters, has estimated the complex multiplier for the United States to be about 2. *(Key Question 2)*

INTERNATIONAL TRADE AND EQUILIBRIUM OUTPUT

Our aggregate expenditures model has ignored international trade by assuming a closed economy. We now acknowledge exports and imports and that **net exports** (exports minus imports) may be either positive or negative. Line 4 on the inside covers of this book reveals that net exports in some years have been positive (exports > imports) and in other years negative (imports > exports). Observe that net exports in 1975 were a *positive* $14 billion, for example, while in 1987 they were a *negative* $143 billion.

How do net exports—exports *minus* imports—relate to aggregate expenditures?

Net Exports and Aggregate Expenditures

Like consumption and investment, exports (X) create domestic production, income, and employment. Even though goods and services produced in response to such spending are sent abroad, foreign spending on American goods increases production and creates jobs and incomes in the United States. Exports must therefore be added as a component of aggregate expenditures.

Conversely, when an economy is open to international trade, part of its consumption and investment spending will be for imports (M)—goods and

services produced abroad rather than in the United States. So as not to overstate the value of domestic production, we must reduce the sum of consumption and investment expenditures by the amount expended on imported goods. In measuring aggregate expenditures for domestic goods and services, we must subtract expenditures on imports.

In short, for a private closed economy, aggregate expenditures are $C + I_g$. But for an open economy with international trade, aggregate spending is $C + I_g + (X - M)$. Or, recalling that net exports (X_n) equals $(X - M)$, we can say that aggregate expenditures for a private open economy are $C + I_g + X_n$.

The Net Export Schedule

Table 10-2 shows two potential net export schedules for the hypothetical economy characterized by the data presented previously in Table 9-4. Similar to consumption and investment schedules, a net export schedule lists the amount of a particular expenditure —in this case net exports—which will occur at each level of GDP. The net export schedule X_{n1} (columns 1 and 2) reveals that exports exceed imports by $5 billion at each level of GDP. Perhaps exports are $15 billion while imports are $10 billion. The schedule X_{n2} (columns 1 and 3) shows that imports are $5 billion higher than exports. Perhaps imports are $20 billion while exports are $15 billion. To simplify our discussion we assume in both cases that net exports are autonomous or independent of GDP.[1]

The two net export schedules from Table 10-2 are plotted in Figure 10-4b. Schedule X_{n1} reveals that a *positive* $5 billion of net exports are associated with each level of GDP. Conversely, X_{n2} is below the horizontal axis and shows net exports of *negative* $5 billion.

Net Exports and Equilibrium GDP

The aggregate expenditures schedule labeled $C + I_g$ in Figure 10-4a is identical to that in Table 9-4 and Figure 9-8. That is, $C + I_g$ reflects the combined con-

---

[1]Although our *exports* depend on *foreign* incomes and are thus independent of American GDP, our *imports* do vary directly with our own *domestic* national income. Just as our domestic consumption varies directly with our GDP, so do our purchases of foreign goods. As our GDP rises, American households buy not only more Pontiacs and more Pepsi but also Porsches and Perrier. However, for now we will ignore the resulting complications of the positive relationship between imports and American GDP.

TABLE 10-2 **Two net export schedules** *(in billions)*

(1) Level of GDP	(2) Net exports X_{n1} (X $=$ M)	(3) Net exports X_{n2} (X $<$ M)
$370	$+5	$-5
390	+5	-5
410	+5	-5
430	+5	-5
450	+5	-5
470	+5	-5
490	+5	-5
510	+5	-5
530	+5	-5
550	+5	-5

sumption and gross investment expenditures occurring at each level of GDP. With no foreign sector, the equilibrium level of GDP will be $470 billion. This equilibrium level of output is determined at the intersection of the $C + I_g$ schedule and the 45-degree reference line. Only there will aggregate expenditures equal GDP.

But net exports can be either positive or negative. Let's see how each of the net export schedules presented in Figure 10-4b affect equilibrium GDP.

Positive Net Exports Suppose the net export schedule is X_{n1}. The $5 billion of additional net export expenditures by the rest of the world are accounted

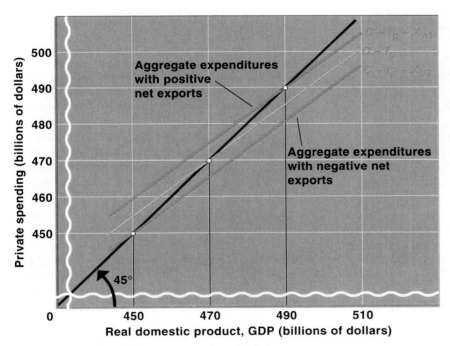

(a) Aggregate expenditures schedule

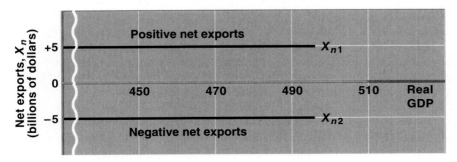

(b) Net export schedule, X_n

FIGURE 10-4 **Net exports and the equilibrium GDP**
Positive net exports such as shown by the net export schedule X_{n1} in (b) elevate the aggregate expenditures schedule in (a) from the closed-economy level of $C + I_g$ to the open-economy level of $C + I_g + X_{n1}$. Negative net exports such as depicted by the net export schedule X_{n2} in (b) lower the aggregate expenditures schedule in (a) from the closed-economy level of $C + I_g$ to the open-economy level of $C + I_g + X_{n2}$.

for by adding $5 billion to the $C + I_g$ schedule in Figure 10-4a. Aggregate expenditures at each level of GDP are $5 billion higher than represented by the $C + I_g$ schedule alone. The aggregate expenditures schedule for the open economy thus becomes $C + I_g + X_{n1}$. International trade has increased equilibrium GDP from $470 billion in the private closed economy to $490 billion in the more realistic private open economy.

You should verify that the new equilibrium GDP is $490 billion by adding $5 billion to each level of aggregate expenditures in Table 9-4 and then determining where $C + I_g + X_n$ equals GDP.

Generalization: *Positive net exports increase aggregate expenditures beyond what they would be in a closed economy and thus have an expansionary effect on domestic GDP.* Adding net exports of $5 billion has increased GDP by $20 billion, in this case implying a multiplier of 4.

Negative Net Exports An extension of our reasoning enables us to determine the impact of negative net exports on equilibrium GDP. If net exports are X_{n2} as shown in Figure 10-4b, $5 billion of net export spending by the rest of the world must be subtracted from the aggregate expenditure schedule $C + I_g$ to establish aggregate expenditures for the private open economy. The $5 billion of negative net exports mean that our hypothetical economy is importing $5 billion more of goods than it is selling abroad. The aggregate expenditures schedule shown as $C + I_g$ in Figure 10-4a therefore has overstated the expenditures on *domestic* output at each level of GDP. We must reduce the sum of consumption and investment expenditures by the $5 billion net amount expended on imported goods. If imports are $15 billion and exports are $10 billion, we must subtract the $5 billion of *net* imports (= − $5 billion of net exports) from the combined domestic consumption and investment expenditures.

After we subtract $5 billion from the $C + I_g$ schedule in Figure 10-4a, the relevant aggregate expenditures schedule becomes $C + I_g + X_{n2}$ and equilibrium GDP falls from $470 to $450. Again, a change in net exports of $5 billion has resulted in a fourfold change in GDP, reminding us that the multiplier is 4. Confirmation of the new equilibrium GDP can be obtained by subtracting $5 billion from aggregate expenditures at each level of GDP in Table 9-4 and ascertaining the new equilibrium GDP.

A corollary to our first generalization emerges: *Negative net exports reduce aggregate expenditures relative to what they would be in the closed economy and therefore have a contractionary effect on domestic GDP.* Imports add to the stock of goods available in the economy, but they diminish real GDP by reducing expenditures on domestically produced products.

Our generalizations concerning positive and negative net exports and equilibrium GDP mean that a decline in net exports—a decrease in exports or an increase in imports—decreases aggregate expenditures and contracts domestic GDP. Conversely, an increase in net exports—the result of either an increase in exports or a decrease in imports—increases aggregate expenditures and expands domestic GDP.

Net exports vary greatly among the major industrial nations, as shown in Global Perspective 10-1. *(Key Question 5)*

International Economic Linkages

Our analysis of net exports and real GDP reveals how circumstances or policies abroad can affect our GDP.

Prosperity Abroad A rising level of national income among our trading partners permits us to sell more goods abroad, thus raising our net exports and increasing our real GDP. We should be interested in the prosperity of our trading partners because their good fortune enables them to buy more of our exports and transfer some of their prosperity to us.

Tariffs Suppose our trading partners impose high tariffs on American goods to reduce their imports and stimulate production in their economies. But their imports are our exports. When they restrict their imports to stimulate *their* economies, they are reducing our exports and depressing *our* economy. We may retaliate by imposing trade barriers on their products. If so, their exports will decline and their net exports may be unchanged or even fall. In the Great Depression of the 1930s various nations, including the United States, imposed trade barriers as a way to reduce domestic unemployment. But rounds of retaliation simply throttled world trade, worsened the depression, and increased unemployment.

Exchange Rates Depreciation of the dollar relative to other currencies (Chapter 6) will permit people abroad to obtain more dollars per unit of their currencies. The price of American goods in terms of these currencies will fall, stimulating purchases of our exports. Also, American consumers will find they need more dollars to buy foreign goods and consequently will reduce their sending on imports. Higher American exports and lower imports will result, increasing our net exports and expanding our GDP.

Whether depreciation of the dollar raises real GDP or produces inflation depends on the initial position of the economy relative to its full-employment level of output. If the economy is operating below its production capacity, the depreciation of the dollar and the resulting rise in net exports will increase real GDP. But if the economy is fully employed, the depreciation of the dollar and higher level of net exports will cause domestic inflation.

Finally, while this last example has been cast in terms of a depreciation of the dollar, you should think through the impact that an *appreciation* of the dollar will have on net exports and equilibrium GDP.

QUICK REVIEW 10-1

■ The multiplier is the principle that initial changes in spending can cause magnified changes in national income and GDP.

■ The higher the marginal propensity to consume (the lower the marginal propensity to save), the larger is the simple multiplier.

■ Positive net exports increase aggregate expenditures on domestic output and increase equilibrium GDP; negative net exports decrease aggregate expenditures on domestic output and reduce equilibrium GDP.

ADDING THE PUBLIC SECTOR

Our final step in constructing the aggregate expenditures model is to move the analysis from that of a private (no government) open economy to a mixed economy having a public sector. Unlike private expenditures, government expenditures and taxes are subject to direct public control. Government can manipulate them to counter private underspending or overspending, thereby promote economic stability.

Simplifying Assumptions

For clarity, the following simplifying assumptions are made.

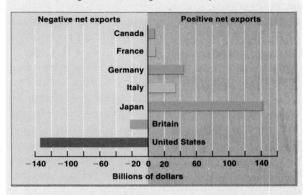

GLOBAL PERSPECTIVE 10-1

Merchandise net exports, selected nations

Some nations, such as Japan and Germany, have positive net exports; other countries, such as the United States and the United Kingdom, have negative net exports.

Source: *Organization for Economic Cooperation and Development. Data are for 1993.*

1   We continue to use the simplified investment and net export schedules, where levels of investment and net exports are independent of the level of GDP.

2   We suppose government purchases neither depress nor stimulate private spending. They do not cause any upward or downward shifts in consumption and investment schedules.

3   We assume government's net tax revenues—total tax revenues less "negative taxes" in the form of transfer payments—are derived entirely from personal taxes. Although DI will fall short of PI by the amount of government's tax revenues, GDP, NI, and PI will remain equal.

4   We assume that a fixed amount of taxes is collected regardless of the level of GDP.

5   We continue to suppose that, unless otherwise indicated, the price level is constant.

These assumptions will give us a simple and uncluttered view of how government spending and taxes fit within the aggregate expenditures model. Most of these assumptions will be dropped in Chapter 12 when we discuss how government uses changes in its expenditures and taxes to alter equilibrium GDP and the rate of inflation.

Government Purchases and Equilibrium GDP

Suppose government decides to purchase $20 billion of goods and services regardless of the level of GDP.

Tabular Example Table 10-3 shows the impact on the equilibrium GDP. Columns 1 through 4 are carried over from Table 9-4 for the private closed economy, in which the equilibrium GDP was $470 billion. The only new wrinkles are the additions of net exports (exports minus imports) in column 5 and government purchases in column 6. (Observe in column 5 that net exports are zero). By adding government purchases to private spending $(C + I_g + X_n)$, we get a new, higher level of aggregate expenditures as shown in column 7. Comparing columns 1 and 7, we find that aggregate expenditures and real output are equal at a higher level of GDP. Without government spending equilibrium GDP was $470 (row 6); with government spending, aggregate expenditures and real output are equal at $550 billion (row 10). *Increases in public spending, like increases in private spending, will boost the aggregate expenditures schedule and result in a higher equilibrium GDP.*

Note, too, that government spending is subject to the multiplier. A $20 billion increase in government purchases has increased equilibrium GDP by $80 billion (from $470 billion to $550 billion). The multiplier in this example is 4.

This $20 billion increase in government spending is *not* financed by increased tax revenues. In a moment we will find that increased taxes reduce equilibrium GDP.

In the leakages-injections approach, government purchases—like investment and exports—are an injection of spending. Leakages of savings and imports cause consumption of real output to fall short of disposable income, creating a potential spending gap. This gap may be filled by injections of investment, exports, and government purchases. In Table 10-3 the $550 billion equilibrium level of GDP (row 10) occurs where $S + M = I_g + X + G$. That is, when taxes are zero, $40 + 10 = 20 + 10 + 20$.

Graphical Analysis In Figure 10-5a we add government purchases, G, vertically to the level of private spending, $C + I_g + X_n$. That increases the aggregate expenditures schedule (private plus public) to $C + I_g + X_n + G$, resulting in the $80 billion increase in equilibrium GDP shown on the horizontal axis.

Figure 10-5b shows the same change in the equilibrium GDP in the leakages-injections approach. Like investment and exports, government spending is an offset to the leakage of saving and imports. With G added to our economy, the equilibrium level of GDP is determined where the amount households save and import is offset exactly by the amount businesses plan to invest and export *plus* the amount government spends on goods and services. Assuming no taxes, the equilibrium GDP is determined by the intersection of the $S + M$ schedule and the $I_g + X + G$ schedule.

Both the aggregate expenditures and leakages-injections approaches indicate the same new $550 billion equilibrium GDP.

TABLE 10-3 The impact of government purchases on equilibrium GDP

(1) Real domestic output and income (GDP = DI), billions	(2) Consumption, C, billions	(3) Saving, S, billions	(4) Investment, I_g, billions	(5) Net exports, X_n, billions — Exports, X	(5) Imports, M	(6) Government purchases, G, billions	(7) Aggregate expenditures $(C + I_g + X_n + G)$, billions, or (2) + (4) + (5) + (6)
(1) $370	$375	$−5	$20	$10	$10	$20	$415
(2) 390	390	0	20	10	10	20	430
(3) 410	405	5	20	10	10	20	445
(4) 430	420	10	20	10	10	20	460
(5) 450	435	15	20	10	10	20	475
(6) 470	450	20	20	10	10	20	490
(7) 490	465	25	20	10	10	20	505
(8) 510	480	30	20	10	10	20	520
(9) 530	495	35	20	10	10	20	535
(10) 550	510	40	20	10	10	20	550

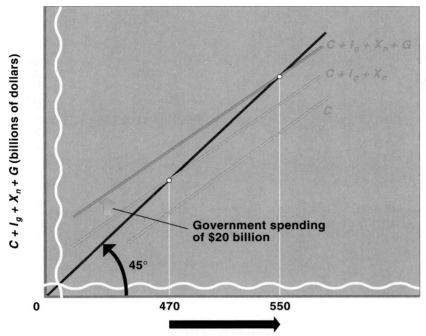

(a) Aggregate expenditures-domestic output approach

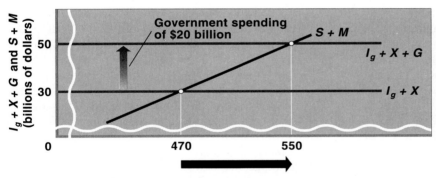

(b) Leakages-injections approach

FIGURE 10-5 Government spending and the equilibrium GDP
(a) *The aggregate expenditures–domestic output approach.* The addition of government expenditures of *G* to our analysis raises the aggregate expenditures ($C + I_g + X_n + G$) schedule and increases the equilibrium level of GDP as would an increase in *C, I_g,* or X_n. Note that changes in government spending are subject to the multiplier effect. (b) *Leakages-injections approach.* In terms of the leakages-injections approach, government spending supplements private investment and export spending ($I_g + X + G$), increasing the equilibrium GDP.

A *decline* in government spending *G* will cause the aggregate expenditures schedule to fall in Figure 10-5a and the $I_g + X + G$ schedule to fall in Figure 10-5b. In either case the result is a multiple *decline* in the equilibrium GDP. You should verify that, if government spending were to decline from $20 to $10 billion, the equilibrium GDP would fall by $40 billion, that is, from $550 to $510 billion, implying a multiplier of 4.

Taxation and Equilibrium GDP

But government also collects tax revenues. Suppose government imposes a **lump-sum tax** which is *a tax of a constant amount or, more precisely, a tax yielding the same amount of tax revenue at each level of GDP.* Also, assume the lump-sum tax is $20 billion so that government obtains $20 billion of tax revenue at each level of GDP. What is the impact?

TABLE 10-4 Determination of the equilibrium levels of employment, output, and income: private and public sectors

(1) Real domestic output and income (GDP = NI = PI), billions	(2) Taxes, T, billions	(3) Disposable income, DI, billions, or (1) − (2)	(4) Consumption, C_a, billions	(5) Saving, S_a, billions, or (3) − (4)	(6) Investment, I_g, billions	(7) Net exports, X_n, billions		(8) Government purchases, G, billions	(9) Aggregate expenditures $(C_a + I_g + X_n + G)$, billions, or (4) + (6) + (7) + (8)
						Exports, X	Imports, M		
(1) $370	$20	$350	$360	$−10	$20	$10	$10	$20	$400
(2) 390	20	370	375	−5	20	10	10	20	415
(3) 410	20	390	390	0	20	10	10	20	430
(4) 430	20	410	405	5	20	10	10	20	445
(5) 450	20	430	420	10	20	10	10	20	460
(6) 470	20	450	435	15	20	10	10	20	475
(7) 490	20	470	450	20	20	10	10	20	490
(8) 510	20	490	465	25	20	10	10	20	505
(9) 530	20	510	480	30	20	10	10	20	520
(10) 550	20	530	495	35	20	10	10	20	535

Tabular Example In Table 10-4 we find taxes in column 2 and we see in column 3 that disposable (after-tax) income is reduced by $20 billion—the amount of the taxes—at each level of GDP. Because DI consists of consumer spending and saving, a decline in DI will lower both consumption and saving. But by how much will each decline as a result of taxes? The MPC and MPS hold the answer: The MPC tells us what fraction of a decline in DI will be at the expense of consumption, and the MPS indicates what fraction of a drop in DI will be at the expense of saving. Since the MPC equals .75 (= 15/20) and the MPS equals .25 (= 5/20), if government collects $20 billion in taxes at each possible level of GDP, the amount of consumption at each level of GDP will drop by $15 billion (.75 × $20 billion), and the amount of saving at each level of GDP will fall by $5 billion (.25 × $20 billion).

In columns 4 and 5 of Table 10-4 the amounts of consumption and saving *at each level of GDP* are $15 and $5 billion smaller, respectively, than in Table 10-3. For example, before taxes, where GDP equaled DI, consumption was $420 billion and saving $10 billion at the $430 billion level of GDP (row 4 of Table 10-3). After taxes are imposed, DI is $410 billion, $20 billion short of the $430 billion GDP, with the result that consumption is only $405 billion and saving is $5 billion (columns 4 and 5 of Table 10-4).

Taxes cause DI to fall short of GDP by the amount of the taxes. This decline in DI reduces both consumption and saving at each level of GDP. The sizes of the declines in C and S are determined by MPC and MPS.

What is the effect of taxes on equilibrium GDP? We calculate aggregate expenditures again as shown in column 9 of Table 10-4. Note that aggregate spending is $15 billion less at each level of real output than it was in Table 10-3. The reason is that after-tax consumption, designated by C_a, is $15 billion less at each level of GDP. Comparing real output and aggregate expenditures in columns 1 and 9, we see the aggregate amounts produced and purchased are equal only at $490 billion of GDP (row 7). The $20 billion lump-sum tax has caused equilibrium GDP to fall by $60 billion from $550 billion (row 10 in Table 10-3) to $490 billion (row 7 in Table 10-4).

Our alternative leakages-injections approach confirms this result. Taxes, like saving and imports, are a leakage from the domestic income-expenditures stream. Saving, importing, and paying taxes are all uses of income which do not involve domestic consumption. Consumption will now fall short of domestic output—creating a potential spending gap—in the amount of after-tax saving and imports *plus* taxes. This gap may be filled by planned investment, exports, and government purchases. Thus, our new equilibrium condition for the leakages-injections approach is: After-tax saving, S_a, plus imports plus taxes equals planned investment plus exports plus government purchases. Symbolically, $S_a + M + T = I_g + X + G$. You should verify in Table 10-4 that this equality of leakages and injections is fulfilled *only* at the $490 billion GDP (row 7).

Graphical Analysis In Figure 10-6a the $20 billion *increase* in taxes shows up as a $15 (*not* $20) billion *decline* in the aggregate expenditures $(C_a + I_g + X_n + G)$ schedule. Under our continuing assumption

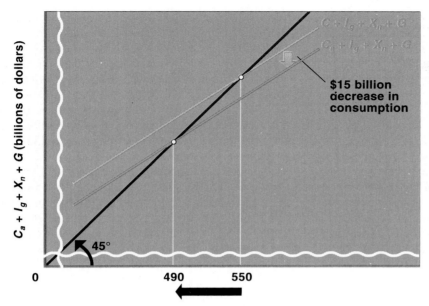

Real domestic product, GDP (billions of dollars)

(a) Aggregate expenditures-domestic output approach

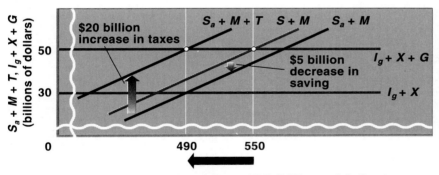

Real domestic product, GDP (billions of dollars)

(b) Leakages-injections approach

FIGURE 10-6 Taxes and the equilibrium GDP
(a) *The aggregate expenditures–domestic output approach.* If the MPC is .75, the imposition of $20 billion of taxes will lower the consumption schedule by $15 billion and cause a decline in the equilibrium GDP. (b) *The leakages-injections approach.* Here taxes have a twofold effect. First, with an MPS of .25, the imposition of taxes of $20 billion will reduce disposable income by $20 billion and saving by $5 billion at each level of GDP. This is shown by the shift from S (saving before taxes) + M to S_a (saving after taxes) + M. Second, the $20 billion of taxes is an additional $20 billion leakage at each GDP level, giving us $S_a + M + T$. By adding government, the equilibrium condition changes from $S + M = I_g + X$ to $S_a + M + T = I_g + X + G$.

that all taxes are personal income taxes, this decline in aggregate expenditures solely results from a decline in the consumption component of the aggregate expenditures schedule. The equilibrium GDP shifts from $550 billion to $490 billion because of this tax-caused drop in consumption. *Increases in taxes will lower the aggregate expenditures schedule relative to the 45-degree line and reduce the equilibrium GDP.*

Consider now the leakages-injections approach: The analysis here is slightly more complex because the $20 billion in taxes has a twofold effect in Figure 10-6b.

1 The taxes reduce DI by $20 billion and, with the MPS at .25, cause saving to fall by $5 billion at each level of GDP. In Figure 10-6b this is shown as a shift from $S + M$ (saving before taxes plus imports) to $S_a + M$ (saving after taxes plus imports).

2 The $20 billion in taxes is a $20 billion leakage at each GDP level which must be added to $S_a + M$ (not $S + M$), giving us $S_a + M + T$.

Equilibrium now exists at the $490 billion GDP, where the total amount which households save plus imports plus the amount of taxes government intends to collect are equal to the total amount businesses plan to invest plus exports plus the amount of government purchases. The equilibrium condition for the leakages-injections approach is $S_a + M + T = I_g + X + G$. Graphically, the intersection of the $S_a + M + T$ and the $I_g + X + G$ schedules determines the equilibrium GDP.

A *decrease* in existing taxes will increase the aggregate expenditures schedule as a result of an upward shift in the consumption schedule in Figure 10-6a. In Figure 10-6b a tax cut will lower the $S_a + M + T$ schedule. The result in either case is a multiple *increase* in the equilibrium GDP. You should employ both the expenditures-output and the leakages-injections approaches to confirm that a tax reduction of $10 billion (from the present $20 to $10 billion) will increase the equilibrium GDP from $490 to $520 billion. *(Key Question 8)*

Balanced-Budget Multiplier

There is an important and curious thing about our tabular and graphical illustrations. *Equal increases in gov-ernment spending and taxation increase the equilibrium GDP. If G and T are each increased by a particular amount, the equilibrium level of real output will rise by that same amount.* In our example the $20 billion increase in G and $20 billion rise in T increase the equilibrium GDP by $20 billion (from $470 to $490 billion).

The rationale for this **balanced-budget multiplier** is revealed in our example. A change in government spending more powerfully affects aggregate expenditures than does a tax change of the same size.

Government spending has a *direct* and unadulterated impact on aggregate expenditures. Government spending is a component of aggregate expenditures and, when government purchases increase by $20 billion as in our example, the aggregate expenditures schedule shifts upward by the entire $20 billion.

But a change in taxes affects aggregate expenditures *indirectly* by changing disposable income and thereby changing consumption. Specifically, our lump-sum tax increase shifts the aggregate expenditures schedule downward only by the amount of the tax *times* the MPC. A $20 billion tax increase shifts

FIGURE 10-7 The balanced-budget multiplier
The balanced-budget multiplier is 1. An equal increase in taxes and government expenditures will increase GDP by an amount equal to the increase in the amount of government expenditures and taxes. Given an MPC of .75, a tax increase of $20 billion will reduce disposable income by $20 billion and lower consumption expenditures by $15 billion. Because the multiplier is 4, GDP will therefore decline by $60 billion. The $20 billion increase in government expenditures, however, will produce a more than offsetting increase in GDP of $80 billion. The net increase in GDP will be $20 billion, which equals the amount of the increase in government expenditures and taxes.

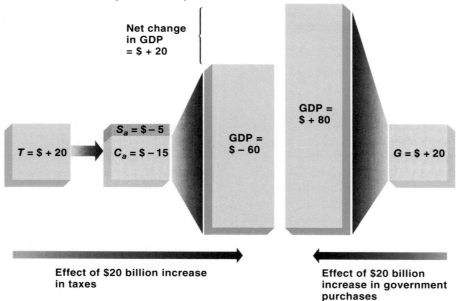

Net change in GDP = $ + 20

$T = $ + 20$

$S_a = $ - 5$
$C_a = $ - 15$

GDP = $ - 60

GDP = $ + 80

$G = $ + 20$

Effect of $20 billion increase in taxes

Effect of $20 billion increase in government purchases

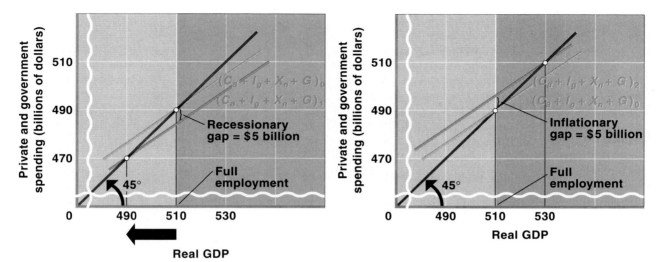

(a) Recessionary gap   **(b) Inflationary gap**

FIGURE 10-8   Recessionary and inflationary gaps
The equilibrium and full-employment GDPs may not coincide. A recessionary gap, shown in (a), is the amount by which aggregate expenditures fall short of the aggregate expenditures needed to produce the noninflationary full-employment GDP. A recessionary gap will cause a multiple decline in real GDP. The inflationary gap in (b) is the amount by which aggregate expenditures exceed the aggregate expenditures consistent with the noninflationary full-employment level of GDP. This gap will cause demand-pull inflation.

the aggregate expenditures schedule downward by $15 billion (= $20 billion × .75).

The overall result is a *net* upward shift of the aggregate expenditures schedule of $5 billion which, subject to a multiplier of 4, boosts GDP by $20 billion. This $20 billion increase in GDP is equal to the size of the initial increase in government expenditures and taxes. *The balanced budget multiplier is 1.*

The fact that the balanced budget multiplier is 1 is shown in Figure 10-7. With an MPC of .75, the tax increase of $20 billion reduces disposable income by $20 billion and decreases consumption expenditures by $15 billion. The $15 billion decline in consumption expenditures *reduces* GDP by $60 billion (= $15 billion × the multiplier of 4). But observe in Figure 10-7 that the increase in government expenditures of $20 billion *increases* GDP by $80 billion (= $20 billion × the multiplier of 4). The equal increases of taxes and government expenditures of $20 billion thus yield a *net* increase of GDP of $20 billion (= $80 billion − $60 billion). *Equal increases in G and T expand GDP by an amount equal to that increase.*

You should experiment with different MPCs and MPSs to verify that the balanced-budget multiplier is valid regardless of their sizes.

EQUILIBRIUM VERSUS FULL-EMPLOYMENT GDP

Now that we have the full aggregate expenditures model at our disposal, we can use it to evaluate the equilibrium GDP.

The $490 billion equilibrium GDP in our complete analysis (Table 10-4 and Figure 10-6) may or may not entail full employment. The aggregate expenditures schedule might lie above or below where it would intersect the 45-degree line at the full-employment level of output. Indeed, our assumption thus far has been that the economy is operating at less than full employment.

Recessionary Gap

Assume in Figure 10-8a that the full-employment level of domestic output is $510 billion and the aggregate expenditures schedule is at $(C_a + I_g + X_n + G)_1$. This schedule intersects the 45-degree line to the left of the full-employment output, causing the economy's aggregate production of $490 billion to fall $20 billion short of its full-employment output of $510 billion. In Chapter 9's Table 9-4, column 1, the economy depicted in Figure 10-8a is failing to employ 5 million of its 75 million full-employment labor force and, as a result, is sacrificing $20 billion of output.

The amount by which aggregate expenditures fall short of those required to achieve the full-employment level of GDP is called the **recessionary gap,** since this deficiency of spending has a contractionary or depressing impact on the economy. In Table 10-4, assuming the full-employment GDP is $510 billion (column 1), the corresponding level of total expenditures is only $505 billion (column 9). The recessionary gap is $5 billion, the amount by which the aggregate expenditures schedule would have to shift upward to realize the full-employment GDP. Graphically, the recessionary gap is the *vertical* distance by which the aggregate expenditures schedule $(C_a + I_g + X_n + G)_1$ lies below the full-employment point on the 45-degree line. Because the multiplier is 4, we observe a $20 billion differential (the recessionary gap, $5 billion, *times* the multiplier of 4) between the equilibrium GDP and the full-employment GDP. This $20 billion gap is the GDP gap which we encountered in Figure 8-5.

Inflationary Gap

If aggregate expenditures are at $(C_a + I_g + X_n + G)_2$ in Figure 10-8b, a demand-pull inflationary gap will exist. The amount by which aggregate spending exceeds that necessary to achieve the full-employment level of GDP is called an **inflationary gap.** In this case, there is a $5 billion inflationary gap, shown by the *vertical* distance between $(C_a + I_g + X_n + G)_2$ and the full-employment point on the 45-degree line. The inflationary gap is the amount by which the aggregate expenditures schedule would have to shift downward to realize the full-employment noninflationary GDP.

The effect of this inflationary gap—this excess demand—will be to pull up the prices of the economy's output. In this model, businesses as a whole cannot respond to the $5 billion in excess demand by expanding their real outputs, so pure *demand-pull inflation* will occur. Nominal GDP will rise, but real GDP will not. (*Key Question 10*)

HISTORICAL APPLICATIONS

Let's see how these concepts of recessionary and inflationary gaps apply to two economic events.

Great Depression

In October 1929 the stock market collapsed. At the same time the most severe and prolonged depression of modern times began. In the United States real GDP (1987 dollars) plummeted from $822 billion in 1929 to a low of $587 billion in 1933. The unemployment rate rose from 3.2 percent in 1929 to 24.9 percent in the same period. As late as 1939, real GDP was only slightly above its level of ten years earlier and the unemployment rate still was 17.2 percent! (As shown in Global Perspective 10-2, the Great Depression was worldwide.)

A sagging level of investment spending was the major weight that pulled American capitalism into the economic chaos of the 1930s. In real terms, gross investment spending shrunk from $153 billion in 1929 to $27 billion in 1933—an 82 percent decline. In Figure 10-8, we would depict this decline in investment as a large downward shift in the nation's aggregate expenditure schedule. The outcome in the 1930s was a severe recessionary (depressionary) gap and an historic decline in real GDP.

What factors caused this steep decline in investment?

1   Overcapacity and Business Indebtedness Flush with the prosperity of the 1920s, businesses overexpanded their production capacity. In particular, the tremendous expansion of the automobile industry—and the related petroleum, rubber, steel, glass, and textile industries—ended as the market for new autos became saturated. Business indebtedness also increased rapidly during the 1920s. Furthermore, by the late 1920s much of the income of businesses was committed for the payment of interest and principal on past purchases, and thus was not available for current expenditures on new capital.

2   Decline in Residential Construction The 1920s experienced a boom in residential construction in response to population growth and housing demand deferred because of World War I. This investment spending began to level off as early as 1926, and by the late 1920s the construction industry had virtually collapsed.

3   Stock Market Crash The most striking aspect of the Great Depression was the stock market crash of October 1929. The optimism of the prosperous

1920s had elevated stock market speculation to something of a national pastime. This speculation had bid up stock prices to the point where they did not reflect financial reality—stock prices were far beyond the profit-making potentials of the firms they represented. A downward adjustment was necessary and it came suddenly and quickly in 1929.

The stock market crash had significant secondary effects. Most important were the psychological repercussions. The buoyant optimism of the 1920s gave way to a wave of crippling pessimism, and the crashing of stock prices created highly unfavorable conditions for acquiring additional money for investment.

4 Shrinking Money Supply The nation's money supply plummeted in the early years of the Great Depression, from $27 billion in 1929 down to $20 billion by 1933 (Last Word, Chapter 14). This shrinkage resulted from forces operating both abroad and at home, including inappropriate policies of the Federal Reserve Banks (Chapters 14–16). It was this drastic reduction of the money supply that contributed to the sharp decline in the volume of aggregate expenditures which characterized the early 1930s.

Vietnam War Inflation

The 1960s was a period of prolonged economic expansion, fueled by increases in consumption spending and investment. Perhaps the major factor in this long expansion was the revolution in economic policy which occurred under the Kennedy–Johnson administrations. This policy called for government to manipulate its tax collections and expenditures in such a way to increase aggregate demand, increasing employment and real GDP. For example, in 1962 legislation was enacted which provided for a 7 percent tax credit on investment in new machinery and equipment, thus strengthening the incentives of businesses to invest. In 1964 the government cut personal and corporate income taxes, boosting consumption spending and further increasing investment spending. The unemployment rate fell from 5.2 percent in 1964 to 4.5 percent in 1965.

At this time another expansionary force came into play. The escalation of the war in Vietnam resulted in a 40 percent increase in government spending on national defense between 1965 and 1967. Another 15 percent increase in war-related spending occurred in

GLOBAL PERSPECTIVE 10-2

Changes in industrial production, selected countries, 1929–1930 and 1937–1938

The Great Depression of the 1930s was global, with large declines in industrial output occurring in most countries. The Depression began in 1929–1930 for many countries. Precipitous declines in industrial output again occurred in some nations in 1937–1938.

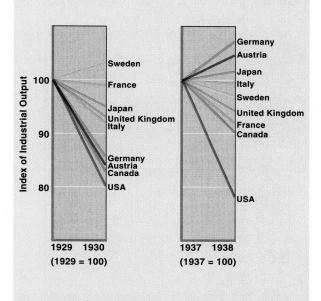

Source: *League of Nations, World Economic Survey, 1938–1939*, p. 107.

1968. Simultaneously, the draft claimed more and more young people from the ranks of the unemployed.

Remarkably, the unemployment rate fell below 4 percent during the entire 1966–1969 period. But the increased government expenditures, imposed on an already booming economy, also brought about the worse inflation in two decades. Inflation jumped from 1.6 percent in 1965 to 5.7 percent by 1970. In terms of Figure 10-8, the booming investment expenditures and the added government expenditures shifted the aggregate expenditures schedule sharply upward, creating a sizable inflationary gap.

LAST WORD

SQUARING THE ECONOMIC CIRCLE

Humorist Art Buchwald examines the multiplier.

WASHINGTON—The recession hit so fast that nobody knows exactly how it happened. One day we were the land of milk and honey and the next day we were the land of sour cream and food stamps.

This is one explanation.

Hofberger, the Chevy salesman in Tomcat, Va., a suburb of Washington, called up Littleton, of Littleton Menswear & Haberdashery, and said, "Good news, the new Novas have just come in and I've put one aside for you and your wife."

Littleton said, "I can't, Hofberger, my wife and I are getting a divorce."

"I'm sorry," Littleton said, "but I can't afford a new car this year. After I settle with my wife, I'll be lucky to buy a bicycle."

Hofberger hung up. His phone rang a few minutes later.

"This is Bedcheck the painter," the voice on the other end said. "When do you want us to start painting your house?"

"I changed my mind," said Hofberger, "I'm not going to paint the house."

"But I ordered the paint," Bedcheck said. "Why did you change your mind?"

"Because Littleton is getting a divorce and he can't afford a new car."

QUICK REVIEW 10-2

■ Government purchases shift the aggregate expenditures schedule upward and raise equilibrium GDP.

■ Taxes reduce disposable income, lower consumption spending and saving, shift the aggregate expenditures schedule downward, and reduce equilibrium GDP.

■ The balanced budget multiplier is 1.

■ A recessionary gap is the amount by which the aggregate expenditures line must be increased for the economy to realize full-employment GDP; the inflationary gap is the amount by which the aggregate expenditures line must decrease for the economy to eliminate demand-pull inflation.

■ The Great Depression of the 1930s was a period characterized by a large recessionary (depressionary) gap; the years of the Vietnam War (the late 1960s) represent a period having a sizable inflationary gap.

CRITIQUE AND PREVIEW

Our analysis and examples demonstrate the power of the aggregate expenditures model to help us understand how the economy works, how recessions or depressions can occur, and how demand-pull inflation can arise. But all models are only approximations of what really happens—they have shortcomings. The aggregate expenditures theory has four limitations.

1 Price Level Changes This model can account for demand-pull inflation, as in Figure 10-8b, but it does not indicate how *much* the price level will rise when aggregate expenditures are excessive relative to the economy's capacity. Will the $5 billion inflationary gap of Figure 10-8b cause a 3 percent, 5 percent, 10 percent, or some other rate of inflation? By how much will the GDP price deflator of Chapter 7 rise when there is a particular inflationary gap? The aggregate expenditures model has no price level axis; it has no way of measuring the rate of inflation.

That evening when Bedcheck came home his wife said, "The new color television set arrived from Gladstone's TV Shop."

"Take it back," Bedcheck told his wife.

"Why?" she demanded.

"Because Hofberger isn't going to have his house painted now that the Littletons are getting a divorce."

The next day Mrs. Bedcheck dragged the TV set in its carton back to Gladstone. "We don't want it."

Gladstone's face dropped. He immediately called his travel agent, Sandstorm. "You know that trip you had scheduled for me to the Virgin Islands?"

"Right, the tickets are all written up."

"Cancel it. I can't go. Bedcheck just sent back the color TV set because Hofberger didn't sell a car to Littleton because they're going to get a divorce and she wants all his money."

Sandstorm tore up the airline tickets and went over to see his banker, Gripsholm. "I can't pay back the loan this month because Gladstone isn't going to the Virgin Islands."

Gripsholm was furious. When Rudemaker came in to borrow money for a new kitchen he needed for his restaurant, Gripsholm turned him down cold.

"How can I loan you money when Sandstorm hasn't repaid the money he borrowed?"

Rudemaker called up the contractor, Eagleton, and said he couldn't put in a new kitchen. Eagleton laid off eight men.

Meanwhile, General Motors announced it was giving a rebate on its new models. Hofberger called up Littleton immediately. "Good news," he said, "even if you are getting a divorce, you can afford a new car."

"I'm not getting a divorce," Littleton said. "It was all a misunderstanding and we've made up."

"That's great," Hofberger said. "Now you can buy the Nova."

"No way," said Littleton. "My business has been so lousy I don't know why I keep the doors open."

"I didn't realize that," Hofberger said.

"Do you realize I haven't seen Bedcheck, Gladstone, Sandstorm, Gripsholm, Rudemaker or Eagleton for more than a month? How can I stay in business if they don't patronize my store?"

Source: Art Buchwald, "Squaring the Economic Circle," *Cleveland Plain Dealer,* February 22, 1975. Reprinted by permission.

2 Premature Demand-Pull Inflation In Chapter 8, specifically Figure 8-7, we noted that demand-pull inflation can occur *before* the economy reaches its full-employment level of output. The aggregate expenditures model does not explain why this can happen. In Figure 10-8 the economy moves from $490 billion of expenditures and real GDP to the $510 billion full-employment level of GDP without inflation occurring. In the aggregate expenditures model inflation occurs only after the economy reaches its full-employment level of output—not what happens in reality.

3 Real GDP Beyond the Full-Employment Level of Output We also know from our earlier discussions surrounding Figures 8-5 and 8-7 that for a time the economy can expand beyond its full-employment level of real GDP. The aggregate expenditures model does not explain this possibility. In Figure 10-8b, the economy's real output cannot expand beyond $510 billion, even though the aggregate expenditures schedule is $(C_a + I_g + X_n + G)_2$. This high level of spending does *not* generate additional real output; in this model, spending simply drives up inflation.

4 Cost-Push Inflation We know from Chapter 8 there are two general types of inflation: demand-pull inflation and cost-push inflation. The aggregate expenditures model does not address cost-push inflation.

In Chapter 11, we remedy these deficiencies, while preserving the insights of the aggregate expenditures model. We use the model to derive aggregate demand—a schedule or curve relating various price levels to corresponding amounts of real GDP which will be demanded. When this aggregate demand curve is combined with an aggregate supply curve, we obtain an aggregate expenditures-based model which overcomes the shortcomings just discussed. The better you understand the aggregate expenditures model, the easier it will be to grasp Chapter 11's aggregate demand–aggregate supply model.

CHAPTER SUMMARY

1 Shifts in the saving-consumption schedules or in the investment schedule will change the equilibrium output–income level by several times the amount of the initial change in spending. This multiplier effect accompanies both increases and decreases in aggregate expenditures.

2 The multiplier is equal to the reciprocal of the marginal propensity to save: The higher the marginal propensity to save, the smaller the size of the multiplier; the higher the marginal propensity to consume, the greater the multiplier.

3 The net export schedule relates net exports (exports minus imports) to levels of real GDP. We have assumed in our model that the level of net exports is the same at all levels of real GDP.

4 Positive net exports increase aggregate expenditures above their level in a private closed economy, raising American real GDP by a multiple amount; negative net exports decrease aggregate expenditures below their level in a private closed economy, decreasing American real GDP by a multiple amount. Increases in exports or decreases in imports have an expansionary effect on real GDP, while decreases in exports or increases in imports have a contractionary effect.

5 Government purchases shift the aggregate expenditures schedule upward and raise equilibrium GDP.

6 Taxation reduces disposable income, lowers both consumption spending and saving, shifts the aggregate expenditures schedule downward, and reduces equilibrium GDP.

7 The balanced-budget multiplier is 1, meaning that equal increases in government spending and taxation will increase the equilibrium real GDP by the amount of the increases in government expenditures and taxes.

8 The equilibrium level of real GDP and the full-employment GDP need not coincide. The amount by which aggregate expenditures fall short of the aggregate expenditures consistent with the full-employment GDP is called the recessionary gap; this gap prompts a multiple decline in real GDP. The amount by which aggregate expenditures exceed the aggregate expenditures consistent with the full-employment GDP is the inflationary gap; it causes demand-pull inflation.

9 The Great Depression of the 1930s resulted from a precipitous decline in aggregate expenditures which produced a severe and long-lasting recessionary (depressionary) gap. The Vietnam war period provides a good example of an inflationary gap. An abrupt increase in aggregate demand caused by war spending led to a sizable inflationary gap, with its accompanying demand-pull inflation.

10 The aggregate expenditures model provides many insights about the macroeconomy, but does not **a** show price level changes, **b** account for premature demand-pull inflation, **c** allow for real GDP to temporarily expand beyond the full-employment level of output, or **d** account for cost-push inflation.

TERMS AND CONCEPTS

multiplier effect	balanced-budget	recessionary gap
net exports	multiplier	inflationary gap
lump-sum tax		

QUESTIONS AND STUDY SUGGESTIONS

1 What effect will each of the changes designated in question 4 at the end of Chapter 9 have on the equilibrium level of GDP? Explain your answers.

2 *Key Question* *What is the multiplier effect? What relationship does the MPC bear to the size of the multiplier? The MPS? What will the multiplier be when the MPS is 0, .4, .6, and 1? When the MPC is 1, .90, .67, .50, and 0? How much of a change in GDP will result if businesses increase their level of investment by \$8 billion and the MPC in the economy is .80? If the MPC is .67? Explain the difference between the simple and the complex multiplier.*

3 Graphically depict the aggregate expenditures model for a private closed economy. Next, show a decrease in the aggregate expenditures schedule and explain why the decrease in real GDP in your diagram is greater than the initial decline in aggregate expenditures. What would be the ratio of a decline in real GDP to the initial drop in aggregate expenditures if the slope of your aggregate expenditures schedule were .8?

4 Speculate on why a planned increase in saving by households, unaccompanied by an increase in investment spending by businesses, might result in a decline in real GDP and *no* increase in actual saving. Demonstrate this point graphically, using the leakages-injections approach to equilibrium real GDP. Now assume in your diagram that investment instead increases to match the initial increase in desired saving. Using your knowledge from Chapter 2, explain why these joint increases in saving and investment might be desirable for a society.

5 Key Question *The data in columns 1 and 2 of the table below are for a private closed economy.*

(1) Real domestic output (GDP = DI), billions	(2) Aggregate expenditures, private closed economy, billions	(3) Exports, billions	(4) Imports, billions	(5) Net exports, billions	(6) Aggregate expenditures, private open economy, billions
$200	$240	$20	$30	$_____	$_____
250	280	20	30	_____	_____
300	320	20	30	_____	_____
350	360	20	30	_____	_____
400	400	20	30	_____	_____
450	440	20	30	_____	_____
500	480	20	30	_____	_____
550	520	20	30	_____	_____

a Use columns 1 and 2 to determine the equilibrium GDP for this hypothetical economy.

b Now open this economy for international trade by including the export and import figures of columns 3 and 4. Calculate net exports and determine the equilibrium GDP for the open economy. Explain why equilibrium GDP differs from the closed economy.

c Given the original $20 billion level of exports, what would be the equilibrium GDP if imports were $10 billion larger at each level of GDP? Or $10 billion smaller at each level of GDP? What generalization concerning the level of imports and the equilibrium GDP is illustrated by these examples?

d What is the size of the multiplier in these examples?

6 Assume that, without taxes, the consumption schedule of an economy is as shown below:

GDP, billions	Consumption, billions
$100	$120
200	200
300	280
400	360
500	440
600	520
700	600

a Graph this consumption schedule and note the size of the MPC.

b Assume now a lump-sum tax system is imposed such that the government collects $10 billion in taxes at all levels of GDP. Graph the resulting consumption schedule and compare the MPC and the multiplier with that of the pretax consumption schedule.

7 Explain graphically the determination of equilibrium GDP through both the aggregate expenditures–domestic output approach and the leakages-injections approach for the private sector. Now add government spending and taxation, showing the impact of each on the equilibrium GDP.

8 Key Question Refer to columns 1 and 6 of the tabular data for question 5. Incorporate government into the table by assuming that it plans to tax and spend $20 billion at each possible level of GDP. Also assume that all taxes are personal taxes and that government spending does not induce a shift in the private aggregate expenditures schedule. Explain the changes in the equilibrium GDP which the addition of government entails.

9 What is the balanced-budget multiplier? Demonstrate the balanced-budget multiplier in terms of your answer to question 8. Explain: "Equal increases in government spending and tax revenues of *n* dollars will increase the equilibrium GDP by *n* dollars." Does this hold true regardless of the size of the MPS?

10 Key Question Refer to the accompanying table in answering the questions which follow.

(1) Possible levels of employment, millions	(2) Real domestic output, billions	(3) Aggregate expenditures, $C_a + I_g + X_n + G$, billions
90	$500	$520
100	550	560
110	600	600
120	650	640
130	700	680

a If full employment in this economy is 130 million, will there be an inflationary or a recessionary gap? What will be the consequence of this gap? By how much would aggregate expenditures in column 3 have to change at each level of GDP to eliminate the inflationary or recessionary gap? Explain.

b Will there be an inflationary or recessionary gap if the full-employment level of output is $500 billion? Explain the consequences. By how much would aggregate expenditures in column 3 have to change at each level of GDP to eliminate the inflationary or recessionary gap? Explain.

c *Assuming that investment, net exports, and government expenditures do not change with changes in real
GDP, what are the sizes of the MPC, the MPS, and the
multiplier?*

11 Which of the two situations in question 10—the one
described in 10a or 10b—is consistent with the realities of
the Great Depression? With the Vietnam war era? Explain
your answers.

12 **Advanced analysis:** Assume the consumption schedule for a private open economy is such that $C = 50 + 0.8Y$.
Assume further that investment and net exports are autonomous (indicated by I_{g0} and X_{n0}); that is, planned investment and net exports are independent of the level of
real GDP in the amount $I_g = I_{g0} = 30$ and $X_n = X_{n0} = 10$.
Recall also that in equilibrium the amount of domestic output produced (Y) is equal to aggregate expenditures $(C +
I_g + X_n)$, or $Y = C + I_g + X_n$.

a Calculate the equilibrium level of income or real
GDP for this economy. Check your work by putting the

consumption, investment, and net export schedules in
tabular form and determining the equilibrium GDP.

b What will happen to equilibrium Y if $I_g = I_{g0} = 10$?
What does this tell you about the size of the multiplier?

13 **Advanced analysis:** We can add the public sector to
the private economy of question 12 as follows. Assume $G =
G_0 = 28$ and $T = T_0 = 30$. Because of the taxes, the con-
sumption schedule, $C = 50 + 0.8Y$, must be modified to
read $C_a = 50 + 0.8(Y - T)$, where the term $(Y - T)$ is disposable (after-tax) income. Assuming all taxes are on personal income, investment remains $I_g = I_{g0} = 30$. Net exports are again independent of the level of income, that is,
$X_n = X_{n0} = 10$. Using the equilibrium condition $Y = C_a +
I_g + X_n + G$, determine the equilibrium level of income. Ex-
plain why the addition of the public budget with a slight surplus *increases* the equilibrium income.

14 (Last Word) What is the central economic idea hu-
morously illustrated in Art Buchwald's piece, "Squaring the
Economic Circle"?

AGGREGATE DEMAND AND AGGREGATE SUPPLY

The aggregate expenditures model developed in Chapters 9 and 10 is a *fixed-price-level model*—its focus is on changes in real GDP, not on changes in the price level. Moving closer to the real world, we now develop a *variable-price-level model* so that we can simultaneously analyze changes in real GDP *and* the price level. To do this we need to combine—or aggregate—all individual markets in the economy into a single market. We must combine the thousands of individual equilibrium prices—of pizzas, robots, corn, computers, crankshafts, donuts, diamonds, oil, perfume, and lipstick—into an aggregate price level. Similarly, we must merge the equilibrium quantities of individual products and services into real GDP, which is already familiar to us. Thus, our new graphical model measures the price level on the vertical axis and real domestic output, or "real GDP" or "real output" on the horizontal axis.

What you learn in this chapter will help organize your thinking about equilibrium GDP, the price level, and government macroeconomic policies. The tools learned here will also help you in later chapters, where we contrast differing views on macroeconomic theory and policy.

In the present chapter we introduce the concepts of aggregate demand and aggregate supply, explaining the shapes of the aggregate demand and aggregate supply curves and the forces causing them to shift. Next, we consider the equilibrium levels of prices and real GDP. Finally, we explore the effects of shifts in the aggregate demand and aggregate supply curves on the price level and the size of real GDP.

AGGREGATE DEMAND

Aggregate demand *is a schedule, graphically represented as a curve, showing the various amounts of goods and services—the amounts of real output—that domestic consumers, businesses, government, and foreign buyers collectively desire to purchase at each possible price level.* Other things equal, the lower the price level, the larger will be the real GDP these buyers will purchase. Conversely, the higher the price level, the smaller will be the real output they buy. Thus, the relationship between the price level and the amount of real GDP demanded is inverse or negative.

Aggregate Demand Curve

The inverse relationship between the price level and real output is shown in Figure 11-1 where the aggregate demand curve slopes downward, as does the demand curve for an individual product.

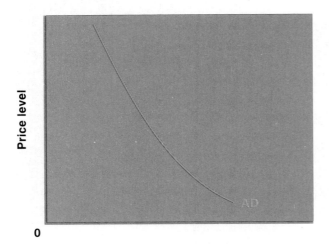

FIGURE 11-1 The aggregate demand curve
The downsloping aggregate demand curve indicates an inverse relationship between the price level and the amount of real domestic output purchased.

Why? The rationale is *not* the same as it is for the demand for a single product. That explanation centered on income and substitution effects. When the price of an individual product falls, the consumer's (constant) nominal income will enable him or her to purchase more of the product (the income effect). And, as price falls, the consumer wants to buy more of the product because it becomes relatively less expensive than other goods (the substitution effect).

But these explanations do not work for aggregates. In Figure 11-1 prices in general are falling as we move down the aggregate demand curve so the rationale for the substitution effect (a product becoming cheaper relative to all other products) is not applicable. Similarly, while an individual's demand curve for a specific product assumes the consumer's nominal income is fixed, the aggregate demand curve implies differing levels of aggregate incomes. As we move up the aggregate demand curve we move to higher price levels. But, recalling our circular flow model, higher prices paid for goods and services will flow to resources suppliers as expanded wage, rent, interest, and profit incomes. As a result, an increase in the price level does *not* necessarily mean a decline in the nominal income of the economy as a whole.

If substitution and income effects do not explain the downsloping aggregate demand curve, what does? The rationale rests on the following three factors.

1 Wealth Effect The first reason why the aggregate demand curve is downsloping involves the **wealth** or **real balances effect.** A higher price level reduces the real value or purchasing power of the public's accumulated financial assets. In particular, the real value of assets with fixed money values such as savings accounts or bonds diminish. Because of the erosion of purchasing power of such assets, the public is poorer in real terms and will retrench on its spending. A household might buy a new car or a sailboat if the purchasing power of its financial asset balances is, say, $50,000. But if inflation erodes the purchasing power of these asset balances to $30,000, the family may defer its purchase.

Conversely, a decline in the price level will increase the real value or purchasing power of a person's wealth and increase spending.

2 Interest-Rate Effect The **interest-rate effect** suggests that the rationale for the downsloping aggregate demand curve lies in the impact of the changing price level on interest rates and in turn on consumption and investment spending. As the price level rises so do interest rates, and rising interest rates reduce certain kinds of consumption and investment spending.

Elaboration: *The aggregate demand curve assumes the supply of money in the economy is fixed.* When the price level increases, consumers need more money for purchases and businesses similarly require more money to meet their payrolls and to buy other needed inputs. In short, a higher price level increases the demand for money.

With a fixed supply of money, this increase in demand for money drives up the price paid for its use. That price is the interest rate. Higher interest rates curtail interest-sensitive expenditures by businesses and households. A firm expecting a 10 percent return on a potential purchase of capital will find that purchase profitable when the interest rate is, say, only 7 percent. But the purchase is unprofitable and will not be made when the interest rate has risen to, say, 12 percent. Similarly, some consumers will decide *not* to purchase houses or automobiles because of the rise in the interest rate.

Conclusion: A higher price level—by increasing the demand for money and the interest rate—reduces the amount of real output demanded.

3 Foreign Purchases Effect We found in Chapter 7's discussion of national income accounting that im-

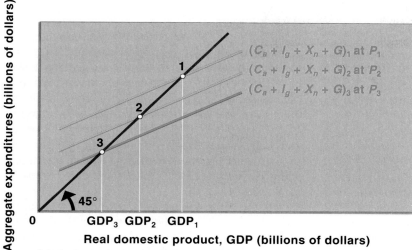

(a) Aggregate expenditures model

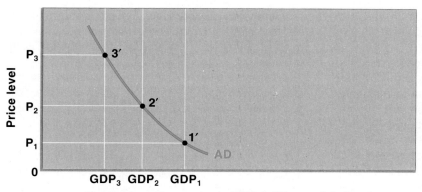

(b) Aggregate demand–aggregate supply model

FIGURE 11-2 Deriving the aggregate demand curve from the expenditures-output model
Through the wealth, interest-rate, and foreign purchases effects, the consumption, investment, and net exports schedules and therefore the aggregate expenditures schedule will rise when the price level declines and fall when the price level increases. If the aggregate expenditure schedule is at $(C_a + I_g + X_n + G)_2$ when the price level is P_2, we can combine that price level and the equilibrium output, GDP_2, to determine one point (2′) on the aggregate demand curve. A lower price level such as P_1 increases aggregate expenditures to $(C_a + I_g + X_n + G)_1$, providing point 1′ on the aggregate demand curve. Similarly, a higher price level at P_3 shifts aggregate expenditures down to $(C_a + I_g + X_n + G)_3$ so P_3 and GDP_3 yield another point on the aggregate demand curve at 3′.

ports and exports are components of total spending. The volumes of our imports and exports depend on, among other things, relative price levels here and abroad. If the price level rises in the United States relative to foreign countries, American buyers will purchase more imports and fewer American goods. Similarly, the rest of the world will buy fewer American goods, reducing American exports. In brief, a rise in our price level will increase our imports and reduce our exports, reducing the amount of net export (export minus import) spending on American-produced products.

Conclusion: The **foreign purchases effect** of a price-level increase results in a decline in the aggregate amount of American output demanded. Conversely, a relative decline in our price level reduces our imports and increases our exports, increasing the

net exports component of American aggregate demand.

Deriving the Aggregate Demand Curve from the Aggregate Expenditures Model[1]

We can directly derive the downsloping aggregate demand curve shown in Figure 11-1 from the aggregate expenditures model developed in Chapters 9 and 10. The aggregate demand curve in Figure 11-1 merely relates the various possible price levels to corresponding GDPs. Note in Figure 11-2 that we can stack the aggregate expenditures model of Figure 11-2a and

---

[1]This section presumes knowledge of the aggregate expenditures model discussed in Chapters 9 and 10 and can be skipped by readers who are not assigned those chapters.

the aggregate demand curve of Figure 11-2b vertically because real output is measured on the horizontal axis of both models. Now we can start at the top with the aggregate expenditures schedule $(C_a + I_g + X_n + G)_2$. The price level relevant to this schedule is P_2, as shown in the graph to remind us of that fact. From this information we can plot the equilibrium real output, GDP_2, and the corresponding price level P_2. This gives us one point—namely $2'$—on Figure 11-2b's aggregate demand curve.

Let's now assume the price level is P_1. Other things equal, this lower price level will: (1) increase the value of wealth, boosting consumption expenditures; (2) reduce the interest rate, promoting investment expenditures; and (3) reduce imports and increase exports, increasing net export expenditures. The aggregate expenditures schedule will rise from $(C_a + I_g + X_n + G)_2$ to, say, $(C_a + I_g + X_n + G)_1$, giving us equilibrium at GDP_1. In Figure 11-2b we locate this new price level–real output combination, P_1 and GDP_1, at point $1'$.

Now suppose the price level increases from the original P_2 level to P_3. The real value of wealth falls, the interest rate rises, exports fall, and imports rise. Consequently, the consumption, investment, and net export schedules fall, shifting the aggregate expenditures schedule downward from $(C_a + I_g + X_n + G)_2$ to $(C_a + I_g + X_n + G)_3$ where real output is GDP_3. This lets us locate a third point on Figure 11-2b's aggregate demand curve, namely point $3'$ where the price level is P_3 and real output is GDP_3.

In summary, a decrease in the price level shifts the aggregate expenditures schedule upward and increases real GDP. An increase in the price level shifts the aggregate expenditures schedule downward, reducing real GDP. The resulting price level–real GDP combinations yield various points such as $1'$, $2'$, and $3'$, which locate a specific downsloping aggregate demand curve.

Determinants of Aggregate Demand

Thus far we have found that changes in the price level change the level of spending by domestic consumers, businesses, government, and foreign buyers such that we can predict changes in the amount of real GDP. That is, an increase in the price level, *other things equal,* will decrease the quantity of real GDP demanded; a decrease in the price level will increase the amount of real GDP desired. This relationship is represented graphically as movements along a stable ag-

gregate demand curve. However, if one or more of those "other things" change, the entire aggregate demand curve shifts. We refer to those "other things" as **determinants of aggregate demand;** they "determine" the location of the aggregate demand curve.

To understand what causes changes in real output, you must distinguish between *changes in the quantity of real output demanded* caused by changes in the price level and *changes in aggregate demand* caused by changes in one or more of the determinants of aggregate demand. We made a similar distinction when discussing single-product demand curves in Chapter 3.

As shown in Figure 11-3, an increase in aggregate demand is depicted by the rightward movement of the curve from AD_1 to AD_2. This shift indicates that, at each price level, the desired amount of real goods and services is larger than before.

A decrease in aggregate demand is shown as the leftward shift of the curve from AD_1 to AD_3, indicating that people desire to buy less real output at each price level.

To reemphasize: The changes in aggregate demand shown in the graph occur when changes happen in one or more of the factors previously assumed

FIGURE 11-3   Changes in aggregate demand
A change in one or more of the determinants of aggregate demand listed in Table 11-1 will change aggregate demand. An increase in aggregate demand is shown as the rightward shift of the AD curve from AD_1 to AD_2; a decrease in aggregate demand, as a leftward shift from AD_1 to AD_3.

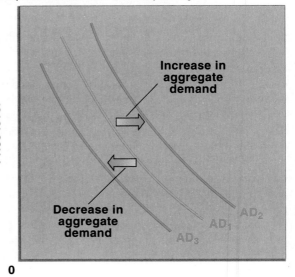

TABLE 11-1 Determinants of aggregate demand: factors that shift the aggregate demand curve

1 Change in consumer spending
   a Consumer wealth
   b Consumer expectations
   c Consumer indebtedness
   d Taxes
2 Change in investment spending
   a Interest rates
   b Profit expectations on investment projects
   c Business taxes
   d Technology
   e Degree of excess capacity
3 Change in government spending
4 Change in net export spending
   a National income abroad
   b Exchange rates

to be constant. These determinants of aggregate demand, or *aggregate demand shifters,* are listed in Table 11-1. Let's examine each element of the table.

Consumer Spending Independently of changes in the price level, domestic consumers collectively may alter their purchases of American-produced real output. When this happens the entire aggregate demand curve shifts. It shifts leftward as from AD_1 to AD_3 in Figure 11-3 when consumers buy less output than before at each possible price level; it moves rightward as from AD_1 to AD_2 when they buy more at each possible price level.

Changes in one or more of several non-price-level factors may change consumer spending, shifting the aggregate demand curve. As indicated in Table 11-1, these factors are real consumer wealth, consumer expectations, consumer indebtedness, and taxes.

Consumer Wealth Consumer wealth comprises all consumer assets, including financial assets such as stocks and bonds and physical assets such as houses and land. A sharp decline in the real value of consumer assets encourages people to save more (buy fewer products) to restore their wealth. The resulting decline in consumer spending will decrease aggregate demand—shift the aggregate demand curve leftward. An increase in the real value of consumer wealth will increase consumption spending at each price level; the aggregate demand curve will shift rightward.

Warning: We are *not* referring here to the previously discussed "wealth effect" or "real balances effect." It assumes a fixed aggregate demand curve and

results from a change in the price level. In contrast, the change in real wealth addressed here is independent of a change in the price level; it is a *non-price-level factor* which shifts the entire aggregate demand curve. An example would be a rocketing boost in stock prices which increases consumer wealth, even though the price level has not changed. Similarly, a sharp decline in the real value of houses and land reduces consumer wealth, independent of changes in the general price level.

Consumer Expectations Changes in expectations about the future may alter consumer spending. When people expect their future real income to rise, they spend more of their current income. Present consumption spending increases (present saving falls), and the aggregate demand curve shifts rightward. An expectation that real income will decline in the future reduces present consumption spending and therefore reduces aggregate demand.

Similarly, a widely held expectation of surging future inflation increases aggregate demand today, because consumers buy products before prices escalate. Just the opposite, expectations of lower price levels in the near future may reduce present consumption since people may postpone some of their present consumption to take advantage of the future lower prices.

Consumer Indebtedness Consumers with high levels of indebtedness from past buying financed by installment loans may be forced to cut present spending to pay off their existing debt. The result is a decline in consumption spending and a leftward shift of the aggregate demand curve. When consumers' indebtedness is low, their present consumption spending increases. This produces an increase in aggregate demand.

Taxes A reduction in personal income tax rates raises take-home income and increases consumer purchases at each possible price level. Tax cuts shift the aggregate demand curve rightward. Tax increases reduce consumption spending and shift the aggregate demand curve to the left.

Investment Spending Investment spending—the purchase of capital goods—is a second determinant of aggregate demand. A decline in the amount of new capital goods desired by businesses at each price level will shift the aggregate demand curve leftward. An increase in the desired amount of investment goods will increase aggregate demand. Let's consider the factors which can alter the level of investment spending as listed in Table 11-1.

Interest Rates All else equal, an increase in the interest rate caused by a factor other than a change in the price level will lower investment spending and reduce aggregate demand. We are *not* referring here to the so-called "interest-rate effect" due to a change in the price level. Instead, we are identifying a change in the interest rate resulting from, say, a change in the nation's money supply. An increase in the money supply reduces the interest rate, increasing investment. A decrease in the supply of money increases the interest rate and reduces investment.

Profit Expectations on Investment Projects Improved profit expectations on investment projects will increase the demand for capital goods and shift the aggregate demand curve rightward. For example, an anticipated rise in spending by consumers may improve the profit expectations of possible investment projects. Alternatively, if the profit outlook on possible investment projects dims because of an expected decline in consumer spending, investment spending will decline. Consequently, aggregate demand will also decline.

Business Taxes An increase in business taxes reduces after-tax profits from corporate investment and reduces investment spending and aggregate demand. Conversely, tax reductions increase after-tax profits from corporate investment, boost investment spending, and push the aggregate demand curve rightward.

Technology New and improved technologies stimulate investment spending and increase aggregate demand. Example: Recent advances in microbiology and electronics have spawned new labs and production facilities to exploit the new technologies.

Degree of Excess Capacity A rise in excess capacity—unused existing capital—will retard the demand for new capital goods and reduce aggregate demand. Firms operating factories at well below capacity have little incentive to build new factories. But when firms collectively discover their excess capacity is dwindling, they build new factories and buy more equipment. Thus, investment spending rises and the aggregate demand curve shifts to the right.

Government Spending Government's desire to buy goods and services is a third determinant of aggregate demand. An increase in government purchases of real output at each price level will increase aggregate demand so long as tax collections and interest rates do not change as a result. An example would be a decision by government to expand the interstate highway system. A reduction in government spending, such as a cutback in orders for military hardware, will reduce aggregate demand.

Net Export Spending The final determinant of aggregate demand is net export spending. When foreign consumers change their purchases of U.S. goods independently of changes in our price level, the American aggregate demand curve shifts. We again specify "independent of changes in our price level" to distinguish clearly from changes in spending arising from the foreign purchases effect. That effect helps explain why a change in the American price level moves the economy *along* its existing AD curve.

In discussing aggregate demand shifters we instead address changes in net exports caused by factors other than changes in the price level. Increases in net exports (exports minus imports) caused by these other factors push our aggregate demand curve rightward. The logic is as follows. First, a higher level of American exports constitutes an increased *foreign demand* for American goods. Second, a reduction of our imports implies an increased *domestic demand* for American-produced products.

The non-price-level factors which alter net exports are primarily national income abroad and exchange rates.

National Income Abroad Rising national income in a foreign nation increases the foreign demand for United States goods, increasing aggregate demand in America. As income levels rise in a foreign nation, its citizens can afford to buy both more products made at home *and* made in the United States. Our exports therefore rise in step with increases in the national income levels of our trading partners. Declines in national income abroad have the opposite effect: Our net exports decline, shifting the aggregate demand curve leftward.

Exchange Rates A change in the exchange rate (Chapter 6) between the dollar and other currencies also affects net exports and hence aggregate demand. Suppose the dollar price of yen rises, meaning the *dol-*

lar depreciates in terms of the yen. This is the same as saying the yen price of dollars falls—the *yen appreciates.* The new relative values of dollars and yen means consumers in Japan can obtain *more* dollars with any particular number of yen and that consumers in the United States will obtain *fewer* yen for each dollar. Japanese consumers will therefore discover that American goods are cheaper in terms of yen. American consumers will find that fewer Japanese products can be purchased with a set number of dollars.

With respect to our *exports,* a $30 pair of American-made blue jeans now might be bought for 2880 yen compared to 3600 yen. And in terms of our *imports,* a Japanese watch might now cost $225 rather than $180. In these circumstances our exports will rise and imports will fall. This increase in net exports translates into an increase in American aggregate demand.

You are urged to think through the opposite scenario in which the dollar appreciates (yen depreciates).

Aggregate Demand Shifts and the Aggregate Expenditures Model[2]

The determinants of aggregate demand in Table 11-1 are the components of Chapter 10's aggregate expenditures model. When one of these determinants changes, so does the location of the aggregate expenditures schedule. We can easily link shifts in the

aggregate expenditures schedule to shifts in the aggregate demand curve.

Let's suppose that the price level is constant. In Figure 11-4 we begin with the aggregate expenditures schedule at $(C_a + I_g + X_n + G)_1$ in the top diagram, yielding real output of GDP_1. Assume now that more optimistic business expectations increase investment so the aggregate expenditures schedule rises from $(C_a + I_g + X_n + G)_1$ to $(C_a + I_g + X_n + G)_2$. (The P_1 labels remind us that the price level is assumed to be constant.) The result will be a multiplied increase in real output from GDP_1 to GDP_2.

FIGURE 11-4   Shifts in the aggregate expenditures schedule and in the aggregate demand curve
In (a) we assume that some determinant of consumption, investment, or net exports other than the price level shifts the aggregate expenditures schedule from $(C_a + I_g + X_n + G)_1$ to $(C_a + I_g + X_n + G)_2$, increasing real GDP from GDP_1 to GDP_2. In (b) we find that the aggregate demand counterpart of this is a rightward shift of the aggregate demand curve from AD_1 to AD_2 which is just sufficient to show the same increase in real output as in the expenditures-output model. The "aggregate demand shifters" are summarized in Table 11-1.

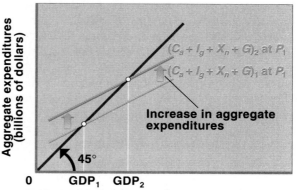

(a) Aggregate expenditures model

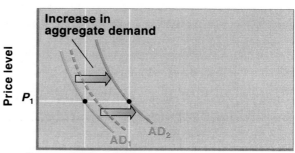

(b) Aggregate demand-aggregate supply model

[2]This section presumes knowledge of the aggregate expenditures model (Chapters 9 and 10). It may be skipped by instructors who wish to rely exclusively on the aggregate demand–aggregate supply framework.

In the lower graph the initial increase in investment spending is reflected in the horizontal distance between AD_1 and the broken line to its right. The immediate effect of the increase in investment is to increase aggregate demand by the amount of this new spending. The multiplier process then magnifies the initial change in investment into successive rounds of consumption spending and an ultimate increase in aggregate demand from AD_1 to AD_2. Equilibrium real output rises from GDP_1 to GDP_2, the same multiplied increase in real GDP as in the top graph. *The initial increase in investment in the top graph has shifted the AD curve in the lower graph by a horizontal distance equal to the change in investment times the multiplier.* In this case, the change in real GDP is associated with the constant price level P_1. To generalize,

$$\frac{\text{Shift in AD}}{\text{curve}} = \text{initial change in spending} \times \text{multiplier}$$

AGGREGATE SUPPLY

Aggregate supply *is a schedule, graphically represented by a curve, showing the level of real domestic output which will be produced at each price level.* Higher price levels create an incentive for enterprises to produce and sell additional output, while lower price levels reduce output. As a result, the relationship between the price level and the amount of real output businesses offer for sale is direct or positive.

Aggregate Supply Curve

For now let's think of the aggregate supply curve as comprising three distinct segments or ranges. Also assume the aggregate supply curve itself does not shift when the price level changes.

The three segments of the aggregate supply curve are identified as (1) the horizontal, (2) the intermediate (upsloping), and (3) the vertical range. Let's examine these three ranges and explain what each represents. You are already familiar with our explanations from our discussion of Figure 8-7. The shape of the aggregate supply curve reflects what happens to per unit production costs as GDP expands or contracts. We know from Chapter 8 that per unit production cost is found by dividing the total cost of the inputs (resources) used by the quantity of output. That is, the per unit production cost of a particular level of output is the average cost of that output.

Horizontal Range   In Figure 11-5 Q_f designates the full-employment or potential level of real output. Recall from Chapter 8 that the natural rate of unemployment occurs at this output. Observe that the **horizontal range** (*ab*) of aggregate supply comprises real levels of output substantially less than the full-employment output Q_f. Thus, the horizontal range implies the economy is in a severe recession or depression and that large amounts of unused machinery and equipment and unemployed workers are available for production. These idle resources—both human and property—can be put back to work with little or no upward pressure on the price level. As output expands over this *ab* range, no shortages or production bottlenecks will be incurred to raise prices. Workers unemployed for two or three months will hardly expect a wage increase when recalled to their jobs. Because producers can acquire labor and other inputs at stable prices, production costs will not rise as output is expanded and so there is no reason to raise product prices.

This horizontal range also implies that, if real output falls, product and resource prices will be downwardly inflexible. That means real output and employment will fall, but product prices and wages will remain rigid. Indeed, real output and employment will decline in this range *because* prices and wages are inflexible.

Vertical Range   At the other extreme, we find that the economy reaches its absolute full-capacity level of real output at Q_c. Any increase in the price level in this **vertical range** (*cd*) will fail to elicit additional real output because the economy is operating at full capacity. Individual firms may try to expand production by bidding resources away from other firms. But the resources and additional production one firm gains will be lost by some other firm. This will raise resource prices (costs) and ultimately product prices, but real output will remain unchanged.

Intermediate (Upsloping) Range   Finally, in the *bc* **intermediate range** between Q_u and Q_c, an expansion of real output is accompanied by a rising price level. The aggregate economy is comprised of innumerable product and resource markets, and full employment is not reached evenly or simultaneously in various sectors or industries. As the economy expands in the Q_uQ_f real output range, the high-tech computer industry may encounter shortages of skilled workers while the automobile or steel indus-

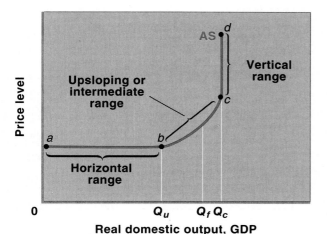

FIGURE 11-5   The aggregate supply curve
The aggregate supply curve shows the level of real domestic output which will be produced at various price levels. It comprises three ranges: (a) a horizontal range where the price level remains constant as domestic output varies; (b) a vertical range where real domestic output is constant at the absolute full-capacity level and only the price level can vary; and (c) an intermediate range where both real output and the price level are variable.

tries still face substantial unemployment. Similarly, in certain industries raw-material shortages or other production bottlenecks may begin to appear. Expansion also means some firms will be forced to use older and less efficient machinery as they approach capacity production. Additional employees will create congestion in workplaces and productivity will decline, increasing per unit costs and product prices. Also, less capable workers may be hired as output expands.

Once the full-employment level of GDP is reached at Q_f, for a time further price level increases may bring forth added real output. We know from Chapter 8 that employment and real GDP can expand beyond the full-employment level of output until the economy reaches its absolute maximum capacity. Recall from Figure 8-5 that periodically actual GDP exceeds full-employment or potential GDP. In a prosperous economy the size of the labor force, daily working hours, and the workweek can be extended. Workers can also "moonlight"—hold more than one job. But once the economy's absolute full capacity is reached at Q_c, the aggregate supply curve becomes vertical.

In the intermediate range of aggregate supply, per unit production costs rise and firms must receive higher product prices for their output to be profitable. In this range a rising real output is accompanied by a higher price level.

Determinants of Aggregate Supply

Our discussion of the shape of the aggregate supply curve revealed that real output increases as the economy moves from left to right through the horizontal and intermediate ranges of aggregate supply. These changes in output result from *movements along* the aggregate supply curve and must be distinguished from *shifts* in the curve itself. An existing aggregate supply curve identifies the relationship between the price level and real output, *other things being equal.* But when one or more of these "other things" change, the curve itself shifts.

The shift of the curve from AS_1 to AS_2 in Figure 11-6 shows an *increase* in aggregate supply. Over the intermediate and vertical ranges this shift is rightward, indicating that businesses collectively will produce more output at each price level. Over the horizontal range of the aggregate supply curve, an increase in aggregate supply can be thought of as a decline in the price level at each level of output (a downward shift of aggregate supply). We will refer to an increase in aggregate supply as a "rightward" shift of the curve. Also, the shift of the curve from AS_1 to AS_3 is a "leftward" shift, depicting a *decrease* in ag-

FIGURE 11-6   Changes in aggregate supply
A change in one or more of the determinants of aggregate supply listed in Table 11-2 will cause a change in aggregate supply. An increase in aggregate supply is shown as a rightward shift of the AS curve from AS_1 to AS_2; a decrease in aggregate supply, as a leftward shift from AS_1 to AS_3.

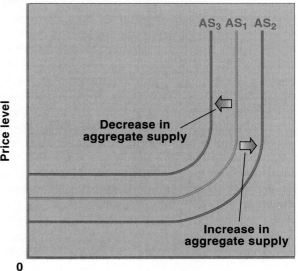

gregate supply. That means businesses now will produce less output at each price level than before (or charge higher prices at each level of output).

Table 11-2 lists the "other things" which shift the aggregate supply curve when they change. Called the **determinants of aggregate supply,** they collectively "determine" or establish the location of the aggregate supply curve. These determinants have one thing in common: When they change, per unit production costs also change. We saw earlier that supply decisions of businesses are based on production costs and revenues. Businesses are profit seekers and profits arise from the difference between product prices and per unit production costs. Producers respond to higher prices for their products—to higher price levels—by increasing their real output. And, production bottlenecks mean that per unit production costs rise as output expands toward—and beyond—full employment. For this reason the aggregate supply curve slopes upward in its intermediate range.

But there are factors *other than changes in real output* which alter per unit production costs (see Table 11-2). When one or more change, per unit production costs change *at each price level* and the aggregate supply curve shifts. Decreases in per unit production costs of this type shift the aggregate supply curve rightward; increases in per unit production costs shift it leftward. *When per unit production costs change for reasons other than a change in real output, firms collectively alter the amount of output they produce at each price level.*

Let's examine how changes in the aggregate supply shifters listed in Table 11-2 affect per unit production costs and shift the aggregate supply curve.

Input Prices Input or resource prices—to be distinguished from the output prices comprising the price level—are a major determinant of aggregate supply. All else equal, higher input prices increase per unit production costs and reduce aggregate supply. Lower input prices do just the opposite. A number of factors influence input prices.

Domestic Resource Availability We noted in Chapter 2 that a society's production possibilities curve shifts outward when the resources available to it increase. Rightward shifts in the production possibilities curve translate to rightward shifts of our aggregate supply curve. Increases in the supply of domestic resources lower input prices and decrease per unit production costs. At any specific price level, firms col-

TABLE 11-2 Determinants of aggregate supply: factors that shift the aggregate supply curve

1 **Change in input prices**
  a **Domestic resource availability**
    a_1 **Land**
    a_2 **Labor**
    a_3 **Capital**
    a_4 **Entrepreneurial ability**
  b **Prices of imported resources**
  c **Market power**
2 **Change in productivity**
3 **Change in legal-institutional environment**
  a **Business taxes and subsidies**
  b **Government regulation**

lectively will produce and offer for sale more real output than before. Declines in resource supplies increase input prices and shift the aggregate supply curve to the left.

How might changes in the availability of land, labor, capital, and entrepreneurial resources work to shift the aggregate supply curve? Let's look at several examples.

Land Land resources might expand through discoveries of mineral deposits, irrigation of land, or technical innovations, permitting us to transform what were previously "nonresources" into valuable factors of production. An increase in the supply of land resources lowers the price of land inputs, lowering per unit production costs. For example, the recent discovery that widely available materials at low temperatures can act as superconductors of electricity is expected eventually to reduce per unit production costs by reducing electricity loss during transmission. This lower price of electricity will increase aggregate supply.

Two examples of reductions in land resources availability may also be cited: (1) the widespread depletion of the nation's underground water through irrigation, and (2) the nation's loss of topsoil through intensive farming. Eventually, these problems may increase input prices and shift the aggregate supply curve leftward.

Labor About 75 percent of all business costs are wages or salaries. All else being equal, changes in wages have a significant impact on per unit production costs and on the location of the aggregate supply curve. An increase in the availability of labor resources reduces the price of labor; a decrease raises labor's price. Examples: The influx of women into the labor force during the past two decades placed a downward pressure on wages and expanded American aggregate supply. Emigration of employable workers from abroad also has historically increased the availability of labor in the United States.

The great loss of life during World War II greatly diminished the postwar availability of labor in the United States, raising per unit production costs. Currently, the AIDS epidemic threatens to reduce the supply of labor and thus diminish the nation's aggregate supply of real output.

Capital Aggregate supply usually increases when society adds to its stock of capital. Such an addition would happen if society saved more of its income and directed the savings toward purchase of capital goods. In much the same way, an improvement in the quality of capital reduces production costs and increases aggregate supply. For example, businesses over the years have replaced poor quality equipment with new, superior equipment.

On the other hand, aggregate supply declines when the quantity and quality of the nation's stock of capital diminishes. Example: In the depths of the Great Depression of the 1930s, our capital stock deteriorated because new purchases of capital were insufficient to offset the normal wearing out and obsolescence of plant and equipment.

Entrepreneurial Ability Finally, the amount of entrepreneurial ability available to the economy can occasionally change and shift the aggregate supply curve. Recent media focus on individuals such as Ted Turner and Bill Gates who have amassed fortunes through entrepreneurial efforts might conceivably increase the number of people who have entrepreneurial aspirations. If so, the aggregate supply curve might shift rightward.

Prices of Imported Resources Just as foreign demand for American goods contributes to our aggregate demand, resources imported from abroad add to our aggregate supply. Resources, whether domestic or imported, boost our production capacity. Imported resources reduce input prices and decrease the per unit cost of producing American real output. Generally, a decrease in the prices of imported resources expands our aggregate supply; an increase in the prices of these resources reduces our aggregate supply.

Exchange rate fluctuations alter the price of imported resources. Suppose the dollar price of foreign currency falls—the dollar appreciates—enabling American firms to obtain more foreign currency with each American dollar. This means that American producers face a lower dollar price of imported resources. Under these conditions, American firms would expand their imports of foreign resources and realize reductions in per unit production costs at each level of output. Falling per unit production costs of this type shift the American aggregate supply curve to the right.

Also, an increase in the dollar price of foreign currency—dollar depreciation—raises the prices of imported resources. Our imports of these resources fall, our per unit production costs jump upward, and our aggregate supply curve moves leftward.

Market Power A change in the degree of market power or monopoly power held by sellers of resources can also affect input prices and aggregate supply. *Market power* is the ability to set a price above the price that would occur in a competitive situation. The rise and fall of market power held by the Organization of Petroleum Exporting Countries (OPEC) during the past three decades is a good illustration. The tenfold increase in the price of oil OPEC achieved during the 1970s permeated our economy, drove up per unit production costs, and jolted the American aggregate supply curve leftward. But then a steep reduction in OPEC's market power during the mid-1980s reduced the cost of manufacturing and transporting products, and as a direct result, increased American aggregate supply.

A change in labor union market power also can affect the location of the aggregate supply curve. Some observers believe that unions experienced growing market power in the 1970s, resulting in union wage increases which widened the gap between union and nonunion workers. This higher pay may have increased per unit production costs and produced leftward shifts of aggregate supply. But union market power greatly waned during the 1980s. The price of union labor fell in many industries, resulting in lower per unit production costs. The outcome was an increase in aggregate supply.

Productivity Productivity relates a nation's level of real output to the quantity of input used to produce that output. In other words, **productivity** is a measure of average output, or of real output per unit of input:

$$\text{Productivity} = \frac{\text{real output}}{\text{input}}$$

An increase in productivity means the economy can obtain more real output from its resources—or inputs.

How does an increase in productivity affect the aggregate supply curve? We first need to see how a change in productivity alters per unit production costs. Suppose real output is 10 units, the input quantity needed to produce that quantity is 5, and the price of each input unit is $2. Productivity—output per input—is 2 (= 10/5). The per unit cost of output would be found as follows:

$$\text{Per unit production cost} = \frac{\text{total input cost}}{\text{units of output}}$$

Per unit cost is $1, found by dividing $10 of input cost (= $2 × 5 units of input) by 10 units of output.

Now suppose real output doubles to 20 units, while the input price and quantity remain constant at $2 and 5 units. That means productivity rises from 2 (= 10/5) to 4 (= 20/5). Because the total cost of the inputs stays at $10 (= $2 × 5 units of input), the per unit cost of the output falls from $1 to $.50 (= $10 of input cost/20 units of output).

By reducing per unit production costs, an increase in productivity shifts the aggregate supply curve rightward; a decline in productivity increases per unit production costs and shifts the aggregate supply curve leftward.

We will see in Chapter 19 that productivity growth is a major factor explaining the long-term expansion of aggregate supply in the United States and the corresponding growth of real GDP. More machinery and equipment per worker, improved production technology, a better-educated and trained labor force, and improved forms of business enterprises have raised productivity and increased aggregate supply.

Legal-Institutional Environment

Changes in the legal-institutional setting in which businesses collectively operate may alter per unit costs of output and shift the aggregate supply curve. Two changes of this type are (1) changes in taxes and subsidies, and (2) changes in the extent of regulation.

Business Taxes and Subsidies   Higher business taxes, such as sales, excise, and payroll taxes, increase per unit costs and reduce aggregate supply in much the same way as a wage increase. Example: An increase in payroll taxes paid by businesses will increase production costs and reduce aggregate supply.

Similarly, a business subsidy—a payment or tax break by government to firms—reduces production costs and increases aggregate supply. Example: During the 1970s, the government subsidized producers of energy from alternative sources such as wind, oil shale, and solar power. The purpose was to reduce production costs and encourage development of energy sources which might substitute for oil and natural gas. To the extent that these subsidies were successful, the aggregate supply curve moved rightward.

Government Regulation   It is usually costly for businesses to comply with government regulations. Thus, regulation increases per unit production costs and shifts the aggregate supply curve leftward. "Supply-side" proponents of deregulation of the economy have argued forcefully that, by increasing efficiency and reducing paperwork associated with complex regulations, deregulation will reduce per unit costs. In this way, the aggregate supply curve purportedly will shift rightward. Conversely, increases in regulation raise production costs and reduce aggregate supply. *(Key Question 5)*

QUICK REVIEW 11-2

■ The aggregate supply curve has three distinct ranges: the horizontal range, the upsloping intermediate range, and the vertical range.

■ In the intermediate range, per unit production costs and therefore the price level rise as output expands toward—and beyond—its full-employment level.

■ By altering per unit production cost independent of changes in the level of output, changes in one or more of the determinants of aggregate supply (Table 11-2) shift the location of the aggregate supply curve.

■ An increase in aggregate supply is shown as a rightward shift of the aggregate supply curve, a decrease by a leftward shift of the curve.

KEY GRAPH

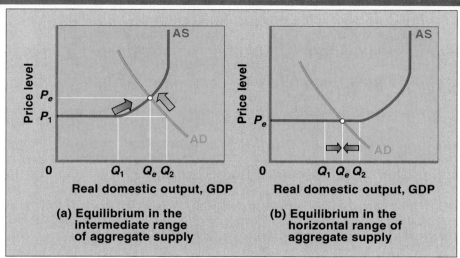

(a) Equilibrium in the intermediate range of aggregate supply

(b) Equilibrium in the horizontal range of aggregate supply

FIGURE 11-7   The equilibrium price level and equilibrium real GDP
The intersection of the aggregate demand and supply curves determines the equilibrium price level and equilibrium real output. In (a) where aggregate demand intersects aggregate supply in its intermediate range, the price level will change to eliminate underproduction or overproduction of output; in (b) where the aggregate demand curve intersects the aggregate supply curve in its horizontal range, no change in the price level accompanies the move toward equilibrium real output.

EQUILIBRIUM: REAL OUTPUT AND THE PRICE LEVEL

We found in Chapter 3 that the intersection of the demand for and supply of a particular product will determine its equilibrium price and output. Similarly, as we see in Figure 11-7a and b (Key Graph), the intersection of the aggregate demand and aggregate supply curves determines the **equilibrium price level** and **equilibrium real domestic output.**

In Figure 11-7a, where aggregate demand crosses aggregate supply in its intermediate range, the equilibrium price level and level of real output are P_e and Q_e, respectively. To illustrate why P_e is the equilibrium price and Q_e is the equilibrium level of output, suppose the price level were P_1 rather than P_e. We observe from the aggregate supply curve that price level P_1 would entice businesses to produce (at most) real output level Q_1. How much real output would domestic consumers, businesses, government, and foreign buyers want to purchase at P_1? The aggregate

demand curve tells us the answer is Q_2. Competition among buyers to purchase the available real output of Q_1 will drive up the price level to P_e.

As arrows in Figure 11-7a indicate, the rise in the price level from P_1 to P_e encourages *producers* to increase their real output from Q_1 to Q_e and simultaneously causes *buyers* to scale back their purchases from Q_2 to Q_e. When equality occurs between the amount of real output produced and the amount purchased, as it does at P_e, the economy has achieved equilibrium.

In Figure 11-7b aggregate demand intersects aggregate supply in the range where aggregate supply is perfectly horizontal. Here, the price level does *not* play a role in bringing about the equilibrium level of real output. To understand why, first observe that the equilibrium price and real output levels in Figure 11-7b are P_e and Q_e. If the business sector had produced a larger output, such as Q_2, it could not dispose of it. Aggregate demand would be insufficient to take the output off the market. Faced with unwanted inventories of goods, businesses would reduce their production to Q_e—shown by the leftward pointing arrow—and the market would clear.

If firms had only produced output of Q_1, businesses would find their inventories of goods would quickly diminish because sales would exceed production. Businesses would react by increasing production, and output would rise to its equilibrium as shown by the rightward pointing arrow. *(Key Questions 4 and 7)*

CHANGES IN EQUILIBRIUM

Let's shift the aggregate demand and aggregate supply curves and see the effects on equilibrium real output and the price level.

Shifting Aggregate Demand

Suppose households, businesses, and government decide to increase their spending, shifting the aggregate demand curve to the right. Our list of determinants of aggregate demand (Table 11-1) provides several reasons why this could occur. Perhaps consumers become more optimistic about future economic conditions. These favorable expectations might stem from new American technological advances which promise to increase the competitiveness of our products in

both domestic and world markets and therefore to increase future real income. As a result, consumers would consume more (save less) of their current incomes. Similarly, firms anticipate that future business conditions will enhance profits from current investments in new capital. They increase their investment spending to enlarge their production capacities.

As shown in Figure 11-8, the precise effects of an *increase* in aggregate demand depend on whether the economy is currently in the horizontal, intermediate, or vertical range of the aggregate supply curve.

In the horizontal range of Figure 11-8a, where there is high unemployment and much unused production capacity, the increase in aggregate demand (AD_1 to AD_2) creates a large increase in real output (Q_1 to Q_2) and employment with no increase in the price level (P_1).

In the vertical range of Figure 11-8b, where labor and capital are at their absolute full capacities, an increase in aggregate demand (AD_5 to AD_6) will affect the price level only, increasing it from P_5 to P_6. Real output will remain at Q_c.

In the intermediate range of Figure 11-8c an increase in aggregate demand (AD_3 to AD_4) will raise both real output (Q_3 to Q_4) *and* the price level (P_3 to P_4).

The price level increases associated with aggregate demand increases in both the vertical and intermediate ranges of the aggregate supply curve con-

FIGURE 11-8 The effects of increases in aggregate demand
The effects of an increase in aggregate demand depend on the range of the aggregate supply curve in which it occurs. (a) An increase in aggregate demand in the horizontal range will increase real output, but leave the price level unaffected. (b) In the vertical range, an increase in aggregate demand will increase the price level, but real output cannot increase beyond the absolute full-capacity level. (c) An increase in demand in the intermediate range will increase both real output and the level of prices. The increases in aggregate demand shown in (b) and (c) depict demand-pull inflation.

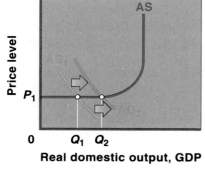

(a) Increasing demand in the horizontal range

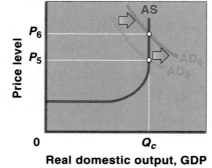

(b) Increasing demand in the vertical range

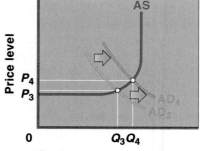

(c) Increasing demand in the intermediate range

stitute **demand-pull inflation** because shifts in aggregate demand are pulling up the price level.

Multiplier with Price Level Changes[3]

Close inspection reveals that real GDP does not increase as much in Figure 11-8c as it does in Figure 11-8a, even though the shifts in aggregate demand are of equal magnitudes. In Figure 11-9, which combines Figures 11-8a and 11-8b, we see the shift in aggregate demand from AD_1 to AD_2 occurs in the horizontal range of aggregate supply. In other words, the economy is in recession with excess production capacity and a high unemployment rate. Businesses are willing to produce more output *at existing prices.* Any initial change in spending and resulting multiple change in aggregate demand over this range is translated fully into a change in real GDP and employment while the price level remains constant. In the horizontal range of aggregate supply a "full-strength" multiplier is at work.

If the economy is in either the intermediate or vertical range of the aggregate supply curve, part or all of any initial increase in aggregate demand will be dissipated in inflation and therefore *not* reflected in increased real output and employment. In Figure 11-9 the shift of aggregate demand from AD_2 to AD_3 is of the same magnitude as the AD_1 to AD_2 shift, but look what happens. Because we are now in the intermediate range of the aggregate supply curve, a portion of the increase in aggregate demand is absorbed as inflation as the price level rises from P_1 to P_2. Real GDP rises to only GDP'. If the aggregate supply curve had been horizontal, then the AD_2 to AD_3 shift would have increased real output to GDP_3. But inflation has reduced the multiplier so that the actual increase is to GDP' which is only about half as much.

Our conclusion is that, *for any initial increase in aggregate demand, the resulting increase in real GDP will be smaller the larger the increase in the price level.* Price level increases weaken the multiplier.

You should sketch an increase in demand equal to the AD_2 to AD_3 shift in the vertical range to confirm that this increase in spending would be entirely absorbed as inflation. The multiplier would be zero because real GDP would be unchanged.

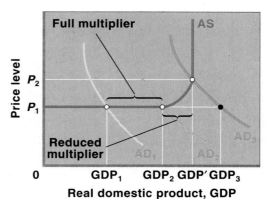

FIGURE 11-9   Inflation and the multiplier
The aggregate demand–aggregate supply model shows how inflation reduces the size of the multiplier. For the AD_1 to AD_2 increase in aggregate demand the price level is constant and the multiplier is at full strength. Although the increase in aggregate demand from AD_2 to AD_3 is of equal magnitude, it is partly dissipated in inflation (P_1 to P_2) and real output only increases from GDP_2 to GDP'.

A Ratchet Effect?

What of *decreases* in aggregate demand? Our model predicts that in the horizontal range of aggregate supply real GDP will fall and the price level will remain unchanged. In the vertical range prices fall and real output remains at the absolute full-capacity level. In the intermediate range the model suggests that both real output and the price level will diminish.

But a complicating factor raises doubts about the predicted effects of declines in aggregate demand in the vertical and intermediate ranges. The reverse movements of aggregate demand—from AD_6 to AD_5 in Figure 11-8b and from AD_4 to AD_3 in Figure 11-8c —may *not* restore the initial equilibrium positions, at least in the short term. The complication is that many prices—both of products and resources—are "sticky" or inflexible in a downward direction. Some economists envision a **ratchet effect** at work (a ratchet is a mechanism which cranks a wheel forward but not backward).

Graphical Depiction   The workings of the ratchet effect are shown in Figure 11-10. If aggregate demand increases from AD_1 to AD_2, the economy moves from the P_1Q_1 equilibrium at *a* in the horizontal range to the P_2Q_c equilibrium at *b* in the vertical range. But while prices readily move up, they do not easily come down, at least not in the short term. If aggregate demand should reverse itself and decrease from AD_2 to

---

[3]Instructors who do not assign Chapters 9 and 10 may want to use this section as a springboard for introducing the MPC, MPS, and multiplier concepts.

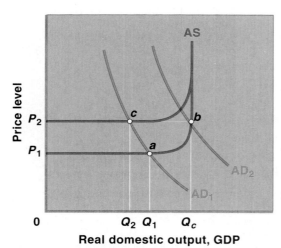

FIGURE 11-10   The ratchet effect
An increase in aggregate demand from AD₁ to AD₂ will move the equilibrium position from *a* to *b* with real domestic output rising from Q₁ to Q_c and the price level from P₁ to P₂. But if prices are inflexible downward, then a decline in aggregate demand from AD₂ to AD₁ will not return the economy to its original equilibrium at *a*. Rather, the new equilibrium will be at *c* with the price level remaining at P₂ and real output falling below the original level to Q₂. The ratchet effect means that the aggregate supply curve has changed from P₁abAS to P₂cAS.

AD₁, the economy will *not* return to the original equilibrium position at *a*. Rather, the higher price level of P₂ will persist—prices have been ratcheted up from P₁ to P₂—and the decline in aggregate demand will move the economy to equilibrium at *c*. The price level remains at P₂ and real output has fallen all the way to Q₂.

The initial increase in aggregate demand and the downward inflexibility of prices have ratcheted the horizontal range of the aggregate supply curve up from the P₁ to the P₂ price level. The original aggregate supply curve was P₁abAS; the new aggregate supply curve is P₂cAS. There is an asymmetry in the aggregate supply schedule because its horizontal range shifts upward readily and rapidly when aggregate demand is expanding, but shifts downward slowly or not at all when aggregate demand declines.

Causes   The reasons for downward price inflexibility are numerous.

1   Wage Contracts   Wages—which typically constitute 75 percent or more of a firm's total costs—often are inflexible downward, at least temporarily. It

is therefore difficult for firms to reduce their prices and remain profitable. But why are wages inflexible? One reason is that part of the labor force works under contracts prohibiting wage cuts for the duration of the contract. It is not uncommon for collective bargaining agreements in major industries to run for three years. Similarly, wages and salaries of nonunion workers are usually adjusted once a year, rather than quarterly or monthly.

2   Morale and Productivity   Wage inflexibility is reinforced because employers may *not* want to reduce wage rates. The reasons are at least twofold. Lower wages may reduce worker morale and labor productivity (output per worker). While lower wages lower labor cost per unit of output, lower worker productivity increases unit labor costs. An employer might fear that the latter might more than counterbalance the former so that a lower wage rate increases, rather than reduces, labor cost per unit of production.

3   Training Investments   Also, most employers have an "investment" in the training and experience of their present labor forces. If they cut wages in the face of a decline in aggregate demand, they may lose workers more or less randomly—both some highly trained and some relatively unskilled workers may quit. When highly trained workers find jobs with other firms, the present employer forgoes any chance of getting a return on the investment made in their training. A better option might be to maintain wages and lay off workers on the basis of seniority. Generally, workers with less seniority who are laid off will also be the less skilled workers in whom the employer's training investment is least.

4   Minimum Wage   The minimum wage imposes a legal floor under the wages of the least skilled workers.

5   Monopoly Power   In many industries firms have sufficient monopolistic power to resist price cuts for a time when demand declines. Firms often incur *menu costs* when they change their prices. These costs are named after their most obvious example: the cost of printing new restaurant menus. But there are other such costs of changing prices: estimating the magnitude and duration of the shift in demand; repricing items held in inventory; entering new price lists into computers; printing and mailing new catalogs; and communicating new prices to customers, perhaps through advertising. Where these menu costs are high, firms may retain current prices, even though demand has declined. Also, some firms may be concerned that a price reduction may set off a "price war," where rivals cut prices even deeper. Thus, declines in aggregate demand may for a time reduce output and employment, not prices.

A glance back at Figure 8-3 will reveal the extent of downward price inflexibility at the beginning of the Great Depression. Despite the catastrophic decline in aggregate demand that occurred between 1929 and 1933, monopolistic firms in the agricultural implements, motor vehicle, cement, iron and steel, and similar industries had a remarkable capacity to resist price cuts, accepting large declines in production and employment as an alternative.

Controversy   Not all economists are persuaded that the ratchet effect is relevant today. They point to declining power of unions in the United States and large wage cuts in several basic industries following the 1981–1982 recession as evidence of increased downward wage flexibility. They also note that growing foreign competition has undermined monopoly power and the accompanying ability of firms to resist price cuts when faced with falling demand. But defenders of the ratchet effect question whether these recent institutional changes have altered the basic historical pattern. Since 1950 the price level has fallen in only a single year—1955. Meanwhile, in this period the economy has experienced eight recessions (Table 8-1).

Shifting Aggregate Supply

Two hypothetical situations will help illustrate the effects of a change in aggregate supply on the equilibrium price level and level of real output.

First, suppose that foreign suppliers impose steep increases in the prices of our imported oil as OPEC did in 1973–1974 and again in 1979–1980. The higher energy prices spread through the world economy, driving up the cost of producing and distributing virtually every domestically produced product and imported resource. Thus, domestic per unit costs of production rise at each output level. The American aggregate supply curve shifts leftward, from AS_1 to AS_2 in Figure 11-11. The price level increase here is clearly **cost-push inflation** (Chapter 8).

The effects of a leftward shift in aggregate supply are doubly bad. When aggregate supply shifts from AS_1 to AS_2, real output will decline from Q_1 to

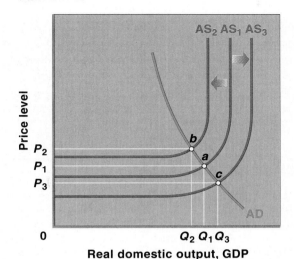

FIGURE 11-11   The effects of changes in aggregate supply
A leftward shift in aggregate supply from AS_1 to AS_2 will cause cost-push inflation in that the price level increases from P_1 to P_2. Real output will fall from Q_1 to Q_2. A rightward shift of aggregate supply from AS_1 to AS_3 will increase real output from Q_1 to Q_3 and reduce the price level from P_1 to P_3.

Q_2 *and* the price level will rise from P_1 to P_2. That means the economy will move from a to b, employment will fall, and inflation will occur.

Now suppose one of the factors in Table 11-2 changes so that aggregate supply increases. Assume the economy experiences a sharp increase in productivity which is not matched by higher paychecks for workers. Or perhaps a liberalization of immigration laws increases the supply of labor and pulls wage rates down. Or maybe lower business excise tax rates reduce per unit costs (an excise tax is a cost as viewed by a business), shifting the aggregate supply curve rightward. In Figure 11-11 the shift in the aggregate supply from AS_1 to AS_3 increases real output from Q_1 to Q_3 and assuming downward price and wage flexibility, a simultaneous decline in the price level from P_1 to P_3. In brief, the economy moves from a to c.

The AS_1 to AS_3 shift in the aggregate supply curve involves a change in the full-employment and absolute capacity levels of real output. In particular, this shift signifies economic growth and indicates that the economy's potential output has increased. In terms of Chapter 2, the economy's production possibilities curve has moved outward, reflected in the rightward shift of the aggregate supply curve in Figure 11-11. *(Key Question 9)*

QUICK REVIEW 11-3

■ The equilibrium price level and amount of real output are determined at the intersection of the aggregate demand and aggregate supply curves.

■ Increases in aggregate demand in the upsloping and vertical ranges of aggregate supply cause demand-pull inflation.

■ The price level is "sticky" or inflexible in a downward direction in the short run.

■ Decreases in aggregate supply cause cost-push inflation.

■ Increases in aggregate supply expand real output; they result in economic growth.

CHAPTER SUMMARY

1   For purposes of analysis we consolidate—or aggregate—the outcomes from the enormous number of individual product markets into a composite market in which there are two variables—the price level and the level of real output. This is accomplished through an aggregate demand–aggregate supply model.

2   The aggregate demand curve shows the level of real output which the economy will purchase at each price level.

3   The rationale for the downsloping aggregate demand curve is based on the wealth or real balances effect, the interest-rate effect, and the foreign purchases effect. The wealth or real balances effect indicates that inflation will reduce the real value or purchasing power of fixed-value financial assets held by households, causing them to retrench on their consumer spending. The interest-rate effect means that, with a specific supply of money, a higher price level will increase the demand for money, raising the interest rate and reducing consumption and investment purchases. The foreign purchases effect suggests that an increase in the United States' price level relative to other countries will reduce the net exports component of American aggregate demand.

*4   A change in the price level alters the location of the aggregate expenditures schedule through the wealth, interest rate, and foreign purchases effects. The aggregate demand curve is derived from the aggregate expenditures model by allowing the price level to change and observing the effect on the aggregate expenditures schedule and thus on equilibrium GDP.

5   The determinants of aggregate demand are spending by domestic consumers, businesses, government, and foreign buyers. Changes in the factors listed in Table 11-1 cause changes in spending by these groups and shift the aggregate demand curve.

*6   Holding the price level constant, increases in consumption, investment, and net export expenditures shift the aggregate expenditures schedule upward and the aggregate demand curve to the right. Decreases in these spending components produce the opposite effects.

7   The aggregate supply curve shows the levels of real output which businesses will produce at various possible price levels.

8   The shape of the aggregate supply curve depends on what happens to per unit production costs—and therefore to the prices which businesses must receive to cover costs and make a profit—as real output expands. In the horizontal range of aggregate supply, there is substantial unemployment and thus production can be increased without raising per unit cost or prices. In the intermediate range, per unit costs increase as production bottlenecks appear and less efficient equipment and workers are employed. Prices must therefore rise as real output is expanded. The vertical range coincides with absolute full capacity; real output is at a maximum and cannot be increased, but the price level will rise in response to an increase in aggregate demand.

9   As indicated in Table 11-2, the determinants of aggregate supply are input prices, productivity, and the legal-institutional environment. A change in one of these factors will change per unit production costs at each level of output and therefore alter the location of the aggregate supply curve.

10   The intersection of the aggregate demand and aggregate supply curves determines the equilibrium price level and real GDP.

11   Increases in aggregate demand will a increase real output and employment but not alter the price level in the horizontal range of aggregate supply; b increase both real output and the price level in the intermediate range; and c increase the price level but not change real output in the vertical range.

12   In the intermediate and vertical ranges of the aggregate supply curve, the aggregate demand–aggregate supply model shows that the multiplier will be weakened because a portion of any increase in aggregate demand will be dissipated in inflation.

13   The ratchet effect is at work when prices are flexible upward, but inflexible downward. An increase in aggregate demand will raise the price level, but in the short term, the price level cannot be expected to fall when aggregate demand decreases.

14   Leftward shifts of the aggregate supply curve reflect

---

*This summary point presumes knowledge of the aggregate expenditures model presented in Chapters 9 and 10.

WHY IS UNEMPLOYMENT IN EUROPE SO HIGH?

Are the high unemployment rates in Europe the result of structural problems or deficient aggregate demand?

Several European economies have had high rates of unemployment in the past several years. For example, in 1994 France had an unemployment rate of 12.4 percent; Great Britain, 9.5 percent; Italy, 11.6 percent; and all of Germany, 10.2 percent.

There is little dispute that recessions in Europe in the early 1990s contributed to these high rates. Declines in aggregate demand reduced real GDP and increased unemployment. Nevertheless, a mystery remains: Why were unemployment rates in many European nations so high even *before* their recessions? In 1990 the unemployment rate in France was 9.1 percent; in Great Britain, 6.9 percent; and in Italy, 7.0 percent (compared to only 5.5 percent in the United States). And why have European unemployment rates remained far higher than in the United States during economic recovery? There are two views on these questions:

1 High Natural Rates of Unemployment Many economists believe the high unemployment rates in Europe largely reflect high natural rates of unemployment. They envision a situation as in Figure 11-7a, where aggregate demand and aggregate supply have produced the full-employment level of real output Q_e. But high levels of frictional and structural unemployment accompany this level of output. In this view, the recent extensive unemployment in Europe has resulted from a high natural rate of unemployment, not from deficient aggregate demand. An increase in aggregate demand would push these economies beyond their full-employment levels of output, causing demand-pull inflation.

The alleged sources of the high natural rates of unemployment are government policies and union contracts which have increased the costs of hiring workers and reduced the cost of being unemployed. Examples: High minimum wages have discouraged employers from hiring low-skilled workers; generous welfare benefits have weakened incentives for people to take available jobs; restrictions against firings have discouraged firms from employing workers; thirty to forty days per year of paid vacations and holidays have boosted the cost of hiring workers; high worker absenteeism has reduced productivity; and high employer costs of health, pension, disability, and other benefits have discouraged hiring.

2 Deficient Aggregate Demand Not all economists agree that government and union policies have ratcheted up Europe's natural rate of unemployment. Instead, they point to insufficient aggregate demand as the culprit. They see the European economies in terms of Figure 11-7b, where the Q_e real output is less than it would be if aggregate demand were stronger. The argument is that the European governments have been so fearful of inflation that they have not undertaken appropriate fiscal and monetary policies (Chapters 12 and 15) to increase aggregate demand. In this view, increases in aggregate demand would not be inflationary, since these economies have considerable excess capacity. If they are operating in the horizontal range of their aggregate supply curves, a rightward shift in aggregate demand curves would expand output and employment, without increasing inflation.

Conclusion: The debate over high unemployment in Europe reflects disagreement on where European aggregate demand curves lie relative to full-employment levels of output. If these curves are *at* the full-employment real GDP, as in Figure 11-7a, then the high levels of unemployment are "natural." Public policies should focus on lowering minimum wages, reducing vacation time, reducing welfare benefits, easing restrictions on layoffs, and so on. But if the aggregate demand curves in the European nations lie to the left of their full-employment levels of output, as in Figure 11-7b, then expansionary government policies such as reduced interest rates or tax cuts may be in order.

increases in per unit product costs and cause cost-push inflation. Rightward shifts in the aggregate supply curve result from decreases in per unit production costs and entail an expansion of real output.

TERMS AND CONCEPTS

aggregate demand	determinants of	horizontal, vertical,	equilibrium real
wealth or real balances	aggregate demand	and intermediate	domestic output
effect	aggregate supply	ranges of the	demand-pull inflation
interest-rate effect	determinants of	aggregate supply	ratchet effect
foreign purchases	aggregate supply	curve	cost-push inflation
effect	productivity	equilibrium price level	

QUESTIONS AND STUDY SUGGESTIONS

1 Why is the aggregate demand curve downsloping? Specify how your explanation differs from the rationale for the downsloping demand curve for a single product.

2 Explain the shape of the aggregate supply curve, accounting for the differences between the horizontal, intermediate, and vertical ranges of the curve.

*3 Explain carefully: "A change in the price level shifts the aggregate expenditures curve, but not the aggregate demand curve."

4 *Key Question* *Suppose that the aggregate demand and supply schedules for a hypothetical economy are as shown below:*

Amount of real domestic output demanded, billions	Price level (price index)	Amount of real domestic output supplied, billions
$100	300	$400
200	250	400
300	200	300
400	150	200
500	150	100

a *Use these sets of data to graph the aggregate demand and supply curves. What is the equilibrium price level and level of real output in this hypothetical economy? Is the equilibrium real output also the absolute full-capacity real output? Explain.*

b *Why will a price level of 150 not be an equilibrium price level in this economy? Why not 250?*

c *Suppose that buyers desire to purchase $200 billion of extra real output at each price level. What factors might cause this change in aggregate demand? What is the new equilibrium price level and level of real output? Over*

which range of the aggregate supply curve—horizontal, intermediate, or vertical—has equilibrium changed?

5 *Key Question* *Suppose that the hypothetical economy in question 4 had the following relationship between its real output and the input quantities necessary for producing that output:*

Input quantity	Real domestic output
150.0	400
112.5	300
75.0	200

a *What is the level of productivity in this economy?*

b *What is the per unit cost of production if the price of each input is $2?*

c *Assume that the input price increases from $2 to $3 with no accompanying change in productivity. What is the new per unit cost of production? In what direction would the $1 increase in input price push the aggregate supply curve? What effect would this shift in aggregate supply have on the price level and the level of real output?*

d *Suppose that the increase in input price had not occurred but instead that productivity had increased by 100 percent. What would be the new per unit cost of production? What effect would this change in per unit production cost have on the aggregate supply curve? What effect would this shift in aggregate supply have on the price level and the level of real output?*

6 Will an increase in the American price level relative to price levels in other nations shift our aggregate demand curve? If so, in what direction? Explain. Will a decline in the dollar price of foreign currencies shift the American aggregate supply curve rightward or simply move the economy along an existing aggregate supply curve? Explain.

---

*Questions designated with an asterisk presume knowledge of the aggregate expenditures model (Chapters 9 and 10).

7 *Key Question* *What effects would each of the following have on aggregate demand or aggregate supply? In each case use a diagram to show the expected effects on the equilibrium price level and level of real output. Assume all other things remain constant.*

  a *A widespread fear of depression on the part of consumers*

  b *A large purchase of wheat by Russia*

  c *A $1 increase in the excise tax on cigarettes*

  d *A reduction in interest rates at each price level*

  e *A cut in Federal spending for health care*

  f *The expectation of a rapid rise in the price level*

  g *The complete disintegration of OPEC, causing oil prices to fall by one-half*

  h *A 10 percent reduction in personal income tax rates*

  i *An increase in labor productivity*

  j *A 12 percent increase in nominal wages*

  k *Depreciation in the international value of the dollar*

  l *A sharp decline in the national incomes of our western European trading partners*

  m *A decline in the percentage of the American labor force which is unionized*

8 What is the relationship between the production possibilities curve discussed in Chapter 2 and the aggregate supply curve discussed in this chapter?

9 *Key Question* *Other things equal, what effect will each of the following have on the equilibrium price level and level of real output:*

  a *An increase in aggregate demand in the vertical range of aggregate supply*

  b *An increase in aggregate supply (assume prices and wages are flexible)*

  c *An equal increase in both aggregate demand and aggregate supply*

  d *A reduction in aggregate demand in the horizontal range of aggregate supply*

  e *An increase in aggregate demand and a decrease in aggregate supply*

  f *A decrease in aggregate demand in the intermediate range of aggregate supply (assume prices and wages are inflexible downward)*

*** 10** Suppose that the price level is constant and investment spending increases sharply. How would you show this increase in the aggregate expenditures model? What would be the outcome? How would you show this rise in investment in the aggregate demand–aggregate supply model? What range of the aggregate supply curve is involved?

*** 11** Explain how an upsloping aggregate supply curve might weaken the multiplier.

12 In the accompanying diagram assume that the aggregate demand curve shifts from AD_1 in year 1 to AD_2 in year 2, only to fall back to AD_1 in year 3. Locate the new year 3 equilibrium position on the assumption that prices and wages are **a** completely flexible and **b** completely rigid downward. Which of the two equilibrium positions is more desirable? Which is more realistic? Explain why the price level might be ratcheted upward when aggregate demand increases.

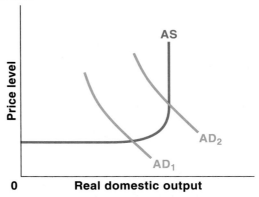

13 "Unemployment can be caused by a leftward shift of aggregate demand or a leftward shift of aggregate supply." Do you agree? Explain. In each case, specify price level effects.

14 (Last Word) What are the alternative views on why unemployment in Europe has recently been so high? Discuss the policy implications of each view.

12

FISCAL POLICY

In 1962 the Kennedy administration initiated legislation to cut tax rates without simultaneously reducing government spending. The Johnson administration implemented these cuts two years later.

During the Vietnam war, the Johnson administration convinced Congress to place a 10 percent surcharge—a tax added to taxes otherwise owed—on corporate and individual income taxes.

In 1990 the Bush administration put in place a tax-spending package designed to reduce the Federal budget deficit by $500 billion over a five-year period.

Just three years later, the Clinton administration raised the top personal income tax rate from 31 percent to 39.6 percent. The purpose, again, was deficit reduction.

What is the logic of such fiscal actions? Shouldn't government always match any increase in its spending with an increase in taxes, or match tax cuts with government spending cuts? Under what circumstances might government want to purposely create a budget deficit or a budget surplus?

Recall that consumption, investment, and import-export decisions of households and businesses are based on private self-interest and that outcomes of these decisions may be either recession or inflation. In contrast, government is an instrument of society as a whole. Within limits (and admitting several complications), government's decisions on spending and taxing can be altered to influence the equilibrium real GDP in terms of the general welfare. In particular, we saw in Chapter 5 that a fundamental function of government is to stabilize the economy. Stabilization is achieved in part through manipulating the public budget—government spending and tax collections—to increase output and employment or to reduce the rate of inflation.

This chapter briefly looks at the legislative mandates given government to pursue stabilization, then explores the tools of government stabilization policy in terms of the aggregate demand–aggregate supply model. Next, some factors that automatically adjust government expenditures and tax revenues as the economy moves through the business cycle are examined. Finally, problems, criticisms, and complications of government stabilization policy are addressed.

LEGISLATIVE MANDATES

The idea that government fiscal actions can exert a stabilizing influence on the economy began in the Depression of the 1930s. Macroeconomic theory has since played a major role in the design of remedial fiscal measures.

Employment Act of 1946   In 1946, when the end of World War II recreated the specter of unemployment, the Federal government formalized its area of responsibility in promoting economic stability. The **Employment Act of 1946** proclaims:

> The Congress hereby declares that it is the continuing policy and responsibility of the Federal Government to use all practicable means consistent with its needs and obligations and other essential considerations of national policy, with assistance and cooperation of industry, agriculture, labor and State and local governments, to coordinate and utilize all its plans, functions, and resources for the purpose of creating and maintaining, in a manner calculated to foster and promote free competitive enterprise and the general welfare, conditions under which there will be afforded useful employment opportunities, including self-employment, for those able, willing, and seeking to work and to promote maximum employment, production, and purchasing power.

The Employment Act of 1946 is a landmark in American socioeconomic legislation because it commits the Federal government to take action through monetary and fiscal policy to maintain economic stability.

CEA and JEC   Responsibility for fulfilling the purposes of the act rests with the executive branch; the President must submit an annual Economic Report describing the current state of the economy and making policy recommendations to stabilize the economy. The act also established a **Council of Economic Advisors** (CEA) to assist and advise the President on economic matters, and a *Joint Economic Committee* (JEC) of the Congress, which has investigated a wide range of economic problems of national interest. In its advisory capacity as "the President's intelligence arm in the war against the business cycle," the three-member CEA and its staff gather and analyze relevant economic data and use them to make forecasts; to formulate programs and policies designed to fulfill the

goals of the Employment Act; and to "educate" the President, the Congress, and the general public on problems and policies relevant to the nation's economic health.

DISCRETIONARY FISCAL POLICY

Discretionary fiscal policy is the deliberate manipulation of taxes and government spending by Congress to alter real GDP and employment, control inflation, and stimulate economic growth. "Discretionary" means changes in taxes and government spending are *at the option of* the Federal government. These changes do not occur automatically, independent of specific congressional action.

For clarity, we assume government purchases neither depress nor stimulate private spending. Also, we assume fiscal policy affects only the aggregate demand side of the macroeconomy; it has no intended or unintended effects on aggregate supply. Both assumptions will be dropped as we examine the complications and shortcomings of fiscal policy in the real world.

First, we'll examine fiscal policy in two situations: (1) recession and (2) demand-pull inflation.

Expansionary Fiscal Policy

When recession occurs, an **expansionary fiscal policy** may be in order. Consider Figure 12-1 where we suppose a sharp decline in investment spending has shifted the economy's aggregate demand curve leftward from AD_1 to AD_2. (Disregard the arrows and the dashed, downsloping line for now.) Perhaps profit expectations on investment projects have dimmed, curtailing much investment spending and reducing aggregate demand. Consequently, real GDP has fallen to $485 billion from its near full-employment level of $505 billion. Accompanying this $20 billion decline in real output is an increase in unemployment, since fewer workers are needed to produce the diminished output. This economy is experiencing recession and cyclical unemployment.

What should the Federal government do? It has three main fiscal policy options: (1) increase government spending, (2) reduce taxes, or (3) some combination of the two. If the Federal budget is balanced at the offset, fiscal policy during a recession or depres-

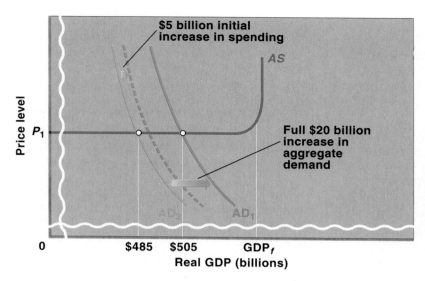

FIGURE 12-1   Expansionary fiscal policy

Expansionary fiscal policy is aimed at lessening or correcting recessions and comprises an increase in aggregate demand brought about by an increase in government spending, a decrease in taxes which raises private spending, or some combination of the two. Here, a $5 billion increase in government spending or a $6.67 billion decrease in personal taxes (= $5 billion increase in consumption) expands aggregate demand from AD_2 to AD_1 and increases real GDP by $20 billion.

sion should create a government **budget deficit**—government spending in excess of tax revenues.

Increased Government Spending   All else equal, an increase in government spending will shift an economy's aggregate demand curve to the right, as from AD_2 to AD_1 in Figure 12-1. To see why let's suppose that in response to the recession government initiates $5 billion of new spending on highways, satellite communications systems, and Federal prisons. We represent this new $5 billion of government spending as the horizontal distance between AD_2 and the dashed, downsloping line immediately to its right. At *each* price level the amount of real output demanded is $5 billion greater than before the increase in government spending.

But the aggregate demand curve shifts rightward to AD_1; it increases by more than the $5 billion increase in government purchases. This occurs because the multiplier process magnifies the initial change in spending into successive rounds of new consumption spending. If the economy's MPC is .75, then the simple multiplier is 4. The aggregate demand curve will shift rightward by four times the distance representing the $5 billion increase in government spending. This particular increase in aggregate demand occurs within the horizontal range of aggregate supply and therefore real output will rise by the full extent of the multiplier. Observe that real output jumps to $505 billion, up $20 billion from its recessionary level of $485 billion. Concurrently, unemployment will fall as firms call back workers laid off during the recession.

Tax Reductions   Alternatively, government could reduce taxes to shift the aggregate demand curve rightward, as from AD_2 to AD_1. Suppose government cuts personal income taxes by $6.7 billion, which increases disposable income by the same amount. Consumption will rise by $5 billion (= MPC of .75 × $6.67 billion) and saving will go up by $1.67 billion (= MPS of .25 × $6.67 billion). In this case the horizontal distance between AD_2 and the dashed, downsloping line in Figure 12-1 represents a $5 billion initial increase in consumption spending. Again, we say "initial" consumption spending because via the multiplier process it adds rounds of increased consumption spending. The aggregate demand curve will shift rightward by four times the $5 billion initial increase in consumption produced by the tax cut. Real GDP will rise by $20 billion, from $485 billion to $505 billion, implying a multiplier of 4. Employment will also increase accordingly.

Undoubtedly you have noted that a larger tax cut than an increase in government spending is required to achieve the same amount of rightward shift in the aggregate demand curve. This is because part of a tax reduction boosts *saving*, not consumption. *To increase initial consumption by a specific amount, government must reduce taxes by more than that amount.* With an MPC of .75, taxes must fall by $6.67 billion for $5 billion of new consumption to be forthcoming because $1.67 billion is saved (not consumed). If the MPC instead had been, say, .6, an $8.33 billion reduction in tax collections would have been necessary to increase initial consumption by $5 billion. The

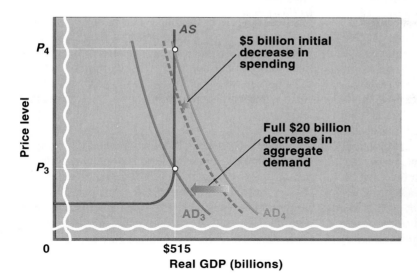

FIGURE 12-2 Contractionary fiscal policy Contractionary fiscal policy is aimed at demand-pull inflation and consists of a decrease in aggregate demand brought about by a decrease in government spending, an increase in taxes, or some combination of the two. In this case a $5 billion decline in government spending or a $6.67 billion tax increase (= $5 billion decrease in consumption) halts the demand-pull inflation.

smaller the MPC, the greater the tax cut needed to accomplish a specific increase in consumption and a specific shift in the aggregate demand curve.

Combined Government Spending Increases and Tax Reductions   Government can combine spending increases and tax cuts to produce the desired initial increase in spending and the eventual increase in aggregate demand and real GDP. In the economy depicted in Figure 12-1, government might increase its spending by $1.25 billion while reducing taxes by $5 billion. You should ascertain why this combination will produce the targeted $5 billion initial increase in new spending.

If you were assigned Chapters 9 and 10, you should think through these three fiscal policy options in terms of the recessionary gap analysis associated with the aggregate expenditures model (Figure 10-8). Recall from Chapter 11 that rightward shifts of the aggregate demand curve relate directly to upshifts in the aggregate expenditures schedule. *(Key Question 2)*

Contractionary Fiscal Policy

When demand-pull inflation occurs, a restrictive or **contractionary fiscal policy** may help control it. Figure 12-2 emphasizes the vertical range of aggregate supply. First, suppose that an AD_3 to AD_4 shift in the aggregate demand curve in the vertical range of aggregate supply has boosted the price level from P_3 to P_4. (Ignore the leftward arrows and dashed line for

now.) This increase in aggregate demand might have resulted from a sharp increase in, say, investment or net export spending. If government looks to fiscal policy to control this inflation, its options are opposite those used to combat recession. It can (1) decrease government spending, (2) raise taxes, or (3) use some combination of these two policies. When the economy faces demand-pull inflation, fiscal policy should move toward a government **budget surplus**—tax revenues in excess of government spending.

Decreased Government Spending   Government can reduce its spending to slow or eliminate demand-pull inflation, as seen in Figure 12-2 where the horizontal distance between AD_4 and the dashed line shows a $5 billion reduction in government spending. This spending cut will shift the aggregate demand curve leftward from AD_4 all the way to AD_3 once the multiplier process is complete. Assuming downward price flexibility, the price level returns to P_3 where it was before demand-pull inflation occurred. Real output remains at its absolute full-capacity level of $515 billion of real GDP.

In the real world prices are "sticky" downward so stopping inflation is a matter of halting the rise in the price level, not reducing it to some previous level. Demand-pull inflation usually is a continuously shifting aggregate demand curve to the right. Fiscal policy is designed to stop these shifts, not to restore a lower previous price level. Nevertheless, Figure 12-2 displays the basic principle: Reductions in government expenditures can halt demand-pull inflation.

Increased Taxes   Just as government can use tax cuts to increase consumption spending, it can use tax increases to reduce it. If the economy in Figure 12-2 has an MPC of .75, government must raise taxes by $6.67 billion to reduce consumption by $5. The $6.67 tax will reduce saving by $1.67 (= the MPS of .25 × $6.67 billion) and this $1.67 billion reduction in saving, by definition, is not a spending reduction. But the $6.67 billion tax increase *will* reduce consumption spending by $5 billion (= the MPC of .75 × $6.67), as shown by the distance between AD_4 and the dashed line to its left. After the multiplier process, aggregate demand will shift leftward by $20 billion at each price level (= multiplier of 4 × $5 billion) and the price level will fall from P_4 to P_3. Demand-pull inflation will have been controlled.

Combined Government Spending Decreases and Tax Increases   Government can combine spending decreases and tax increases to reduce aggregate demand and check inflation. To test your understanding you should determine why a $2 billion decline in government spending *paired* with a $4 billion increase in taxes would shift the aggregate demand curve from AD_4 to AD_3.

Also, if you were assigned Chapters 9 and 10, you should be able to explain the three fiscal policy options for fighting inflation in terms of the inflationary gap concept developed in the aggregate expenditures model (Figure 10-8). Recall from Chapter 11 that leftward shifts in the aggregate demand curve are associated with downshifts in the aggregate expenditures schedule. *(Key Question 3)*

Financing Deficits and Disposing of Surpluses

The expansionary effect of a specific budget deficit on the economy will depend on the method used to finance it. Similarly, the deflationary impact of a particular budget surplus will depend on what is done with it.

Borrowing versus New Money   There are two ways the Federal government can finance a deficit: borrowing from (selling interest-bearing bonds to) the public, or issuing new money to its creditors. The impact on aggregate demand will be different in each case.

1   **Borrowing**   If the government enters the money market and borrows, it will be competing with private business borrowers for funds. This added demand for funds may drive up the equilibrium interest rate. Investment spending is inversely related to the interest rate. Government borrowing therefore may increase the interest rate and "crowd out" some private investment spending and interest-sensitive consumer spending.

2   **Money Creation**   If deficit spending is financed by issuing new money, crowding out of private expenditures can be avoided. Federal spending can increase without any adverse effect on investment or consumption. *The creation of new money is a more expansionary way of financing deficit spending than is borrowing.*

Debt Retirement versus Idle Surplus   Demand-pull inflation calls for fiscal action which will result in a budget surplus. But the anti-inflationary effect of this surplus depends on what government does with it.

1   **Debt Reduction**   Since the Federal government has an outstanding debt of $4.6 trillion, it is logical that government should use a surplus to retire outstanding debt. The anti-inflationary impact of a surplus, however, may be reduced by paying off debt. In retiring debt held by the general public, the government transfers its surplus tax revenues back into the money market. This causes the interest rate to fall, stimulating investment and consumption.

2   **Impounding**   On the other hand, government can realize a greater anti-inflationary impact from its budgetary surplus by impounding the surplus funds, meaning to allow them to stand idle. An impounded surplus means that the government is extracting and withholding purchasing power from the economy. If surplus tax revenues are not reinjected into the economy, there is no possibility of some portion of that surplus being spent. There is no chance that the funds will create inflationary pressure to offset the deflationary impact of the surplus itself. We conclude that *the impounding of a budgetary surplus is more contractionary than the use of the surplus to retire public debt.*

Policy Options: *G* or *T*?

Is it preferable to use government spending or taxes to eliminate recession and inflation? The answer depends largely on one's view as to whether the public sector is too large or too small.

"Liberal" economists, who think the public sector needs to be enlarged to meet various failures of the market system (Chapter 5), can recommend that aggregate demand be expanded during recessions by increasing government purchases *and* that aggregate demand should be constrained during inflationary periods by increasing taxes. Both actions either expand or preserve the absolute size of government.

"Conservative" economists, who think the public sector is too large and inefficient, can advocate that aggregate demand be increased during recessions by cutting taxes *and* that aggregate demand be reduced during inflation by cutting government spending.

An active fiscal policy designed to stabilize the economy can be associated with either an expanding or a contracting public sector.

QUICK REVIEW 12-1

■ The Employment Act of 1946 commits the Federal government to promote "maximum employment, production, and purchasing power."

■ Fiscal policy is the purposeful manipulation of government expenditures and tax collections by Congress to promote full employment, price stability, and economic growth.

■ Government uses expansionary fiscal policy— shown as a rightward shift of the aggregate demand curve—to stimulate spending and expand real output. It involves increases in government spending, reductions in taxes, or some combination of the two.

■ Contractionary fiscal policy—shown as a leftward shift of the aggregate demand curve—is aimed at demand-pull inflation. It entails reductions in government expenditures, tax increases, or some combination of each.

■ The expansionary effect of fiscal policy depends on how the budget deficit is financed; the contractionary effect of fiscal policy depends on the disposition of the budget surplus.

NONDISCRETIONARY FISCAL POLICY: BUILT-IN STABILIZERS

To some degree appropriate changes in the levels of government expenditures and taxes occur automatically. This automatic or *built-in stability* is not included in our discussion of discretionary fiscal policy because

we implicitly assumed a simple lump-sum tax where the same amount of tax revenue was collected at each level of GDP. Built-in stability arises because in reality our net tax system (net taxes equal taxes minus transfers and subsidies) is such that *net tax revenues*[1] *vary directly with GDP.*

Virtually all taxes will yield more tax revenues as GDP rises. In particular, personal income taxes have progressive rates and result in more than proportionate increases in tax collections as GDP expands. Furthermore, as GDP increases and more goods and services are purchased, revenues from corporate income taxes and sales and excise taxes will increase. And, similarly, payroll tax payments increase as economic expansion creates more jobs. Conversely, when GDP declines, tax receipts from all these sources will decline.

Transfer payments (or "negative taxes") behave in the opposite way as tax collections. Unemployment compensation payments, welfare payments, and subsidies to farmers all *decrease* during economic expansion and *increase* during a contraction.

Automatic or Built-In Stabilizers

Figure 12-3 helps us understand how the tax system creates built-in stability. Government expenditures G are fixed and assumed to be independent of the level of GDP; expenditures are decided on at some specific level by Congress. But Congress does *not* determine the *level* of tax revenues; rather, it establishes tax *rates.* Tax revenues then vary directly with the level of GDP which the economy actually realizes. The direct relationship between tax revenues and GDP is shown in the upsloping T line.

Economic Importance   The economic importance of this direct relationship between tax receipts and GDP comes into focus when we consider two things.
1   Taxes reduce spending and aggregate demand.
2   It is desirable from the standpoint of stability to reduce spending when the economy is moving toward inflation and to increase spending when the economy is slumping.

In other words, the tax system portrayed in Figure 12-3 builds some stability into the economy. It automatically brings about changes in tax revenues and

---

[1]From now on, we will use the term "taxes" in referring to net taxes.

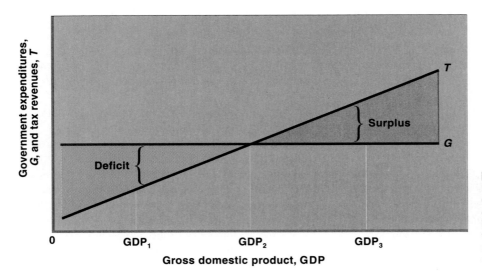

FIGURE 12-3 Built-in stability
If tax revenues vary directly with GDP the deficits which will occur automatically during recession will help alleviate that recession. Also, the surpluses which occur automatically during expansion will assist in offsetting possible inflation.

therefore in the public budget which counter both inflation and unemployment. A **built-in stabilizer** is *anything which increases the government's deficit (or reduces its surplus) during a recession and increases its surplus (or reduces its deficit) during inflation without requiring explicit action by policy makers.* As Figure 12-3 reveals, this is precisely what our tax system does.

As GDP rises during prosperity, tax revenues *automatically* increase and, because they reduce spending, they restrain the economic expansion. In other words, as the economy moves toward a higher GDP, tax revenues automatically rise and move the budget from a deficit toward a surplus.

Conversely, as GDP falls during recession, tax revenues *automatically* decline, increasing spending and cushioning the economic contraction. With a falling GDP, tax receipts decline and move the public budget from a surplus toward a deficit. In Figure 12-3, the low level of income GDP_1 will automatically yield an expansionary budget deficit; the high and perhaps inflationary income level GDP_3 will automatically generate a contractionary budget surplus.

Tax Progressivity It is clear from Figure 12-3 that the size of the automatic budget deficits or surpluses and therefore built-in stability depends on the responsiveness of changes in taxes to changes in GDP. If tax revenues change sharply as GDP changes, the slope of line T in the figure will be steep and the vertical distances between T and G—the deficits or surpluses—will be large. If tax revenues change very

little when GDP changes, the slope will be gentle and built-in stability will be low.

The steepness of T in Figure 12-3 depends on the tax system in place. If it is **progressive,** meaning the average tax rate (= tax revenue/GDP) rises with GDP, the T line will be steeper than if the tax system is **proportional** or **regressive.** In a proportional tax system the average tax rate remains constant as GDP rises; in a regressive tax system the average tax rate falls as GDP rises. Tax revenues will rise with GDP under progressive and proportional tax systems and may either rise, fall, or remain the same when GDP increases under a regressive system. But what you should realize is this: *The more progressive the tax system, the greater is the economy's built-in stability.*

Changes in public policies or laws which alter the progressivity of the net tax system (taxes minus transfers and subsidies) affect the degree of built-in stability. For example, in 1993 the Clinton administration increased the highest marginal tax rate on personal income from 31 percent to 39.6 percent and boosted the corporate income tax one percentage point to 35 percent. These rises in tax rates increase the overall progressivity of the tax system, slightly bolstering the economy's built-in stability.

The built-in stability provided by our tax system has reduced the severity of business fluctuations. But built-in stabilizers can only diminish, *not* correct, major changes in equilibrium GDP. Discretionary fiscal policy—changes in tax rates and expenditures—may be needed to correct inflation or recession of any appreciable magnitude.

Full-Employment Budget

Built-in stability—the fact that tax revenues vary directly with GDP—means the **actual budget** surplus or deficit in any specific year is not a good measure of the status of fiscal policy. Here's why: Suppose the economy is at full employment at GDP$_f$ in Figure 12-4 and the government has an actual budget deficit shown by the vertical distance *ab*. Now, assume investment spending plummets, causing a recession to GDP$_r$. The government, let's assume, takes no discretionary fiscal action. Therefore, the *G* and *T* lines remain in the positions shown in the diagram. As the economy moves to GDP$_r$, tax revenues fall, and with government expenditures unaltered, the deficit rises to *ec*, expanding from *ab* (= *ed*) by the amount *dc*. This **cyclical deficit** of *dc*—so named because it relates to the business cycle—is not the result of positive countercyclical fiscal actions by government; rather it is the by-product of fiscal inaction as the economy slides into recession.

We cannot gain a meaningful picture of the government's fiscal posture—whether Congress was manipulating taxes and expenditures—by looking at the historical record of budget deficits or surpluses. The actual budget deficit or surplus reflects not only possible discretionary fiscal decisions about spending and taxes (as shown by the locations of the *G* and *T* lines in Figure 12-4), but also the level of GDP (where the economy is operating on the horizontal axis of Figure 12-4). Because tax revenues vary with GDP, the problem of comparing deficits or surpluses in any two years is that the level of GDP may be different in each year. In Figure 12-4, the actual budget deficit in year 2 (GDP$_r$) differs from that in year 1 (GDP$_f$) only because GDP is lower in year 2 than in year 1.

Resolving the Problem   Economists have resolved the problem of comparing budget deficits for different years in the business cycle by using the full-employment budget. The **full-employment budget,** also called the *structural budget, measures what the Federal budget deficit or surplus would be with existing tax and government spending structures, if the economy were at full employment throughout the year.* In Figure 12-4 the full-employment deficit or **structural deficit** is the same in year 1 and year 2 (*ab = ed*). This is the budget deficit that would have existed in year 2 even if there were no recession. It is called "structural" because it reflects the configuration of *G* and *T,* independent of the state of the economy.

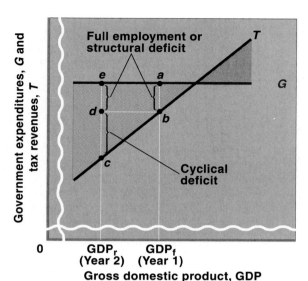

FIGURE 12-4   Full-employment (structural) deficits and cyclical deficits
The actual budget deficit for any specific year consists of the full-employment deficit (or structural deficit) and the cyclical deficit. The *full-employment* or *structural deficit* is the difference between government expenditures and tax collections which would occur if there were full-employment output (GDP$_f$). Here, this deficit is positive, since government spending exceeds tax collections at GDP$_f$. The *cyclical deficit* results from a below full-employment output (GDP$_r$). At GDP$_f$ the structural deficit is *ab*, while the cyclical budget is zero. The structural deficit at GDP$_r$ is *ed*(= *ab*); the cyclical deficit, *dc*.

In year 2 the actual budget deficit exceeds the full-employment or structural budget by *dc*. This is the amount of the cyclical budget deficit. To eliminate the *dc* cyclical deficit, government must move the economy back to full-employment output at GDP$_f$. Ironically, this may require a temporary increase in the full-employment deficit, or structural deficit, via expansionary discretionary fiscal policy. That is, government must cut taxes (shift *T* downward) or increase government spending (shift *G* upward) to move the economy from GDP$_r$ to GDP$_f$. Once prosperity is restored, government can, if it wishes, eliminate the structural deficit by increasing tax rates (shift the *T* line upward) or by reducing government spending (shift the *G* line downward).

To emphasize: Discretionary fiscal policy is reflected in deliberate *changes* in the full-employment or structural deficit, not in changes in the cyclical deficit. Since the actual budget deficit comprises both the structural and cyclical deficits, the actual budget deficit is an unreliable measure of the government's fiscal policy stance.

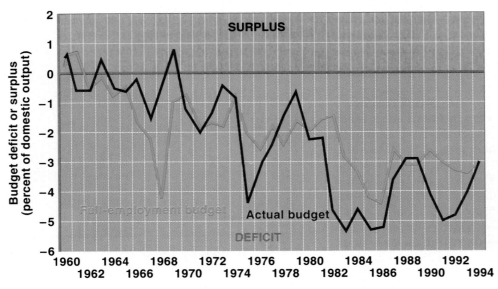

FIGURE 12-5 The full-employment budget and the actual budget Full-employment (or structural) budget deficits and surpluses often are different in size from actual budget deficits and surpluses. The full-employment budget surplus or deficit is a better indicator of the government's fiscal posture than is the actual surplus or deficit.

Historical Comparison Figure 12-5 compares the full-employment budget and the actual budget as percentages of GDP since 1959. In many years the sizes of the actual budget deficits or surpluses differ from the sizes of the deficits or surpluses of the full-employment budget. The key to assessing discretionary fiscal policy is to disregard the actual budget and instead observe the change in the *full-employment budget* in a particular year or period. For example, fiscal policy was very expansionary between 1965 and 1968 and between 1981 and 1986, reflected in the rapid increase in the full-employment deficit. Fiscal policy was contractionary in 1959, 1969, 1973, and 1987.

Also observe in Figure 12-5 that full-employment or structural deficits have been particularly large since 1981. A large part of the actual deficits during the 1980s and early 1990s were not cyclical deficits resulting from automatic deficiencies in tax revenues brought forth from below-full-employment GDP. Rather, much of the actual deficits reflected structural imbalances between government spending and tax collections caused by large cuts in tax rates in the 1980s, together with increases in government spending. The year 1989 is an example. Although the economy had achieved full employment, a sizable full-employment or structural deficit remained.

Large full-employment budget deficits have persisted into the 1990s. During the 1990s the American government has largely abandoned countercyclical fiscal policy in its attempt to reduce the large structural deficits. These deficits were so massive that financing them increased real interest rates and may have crowded out much private investment, a scenario we will discuss shortly. Thus, in the 1990s the role of stabilizing the economy has fallen nearly exclusively to the nation's central bank, the Federal Reserve. This institution and its policies are the subject of Chapters 13 to 15, while budget deficits and the public debt are the subject of Chapter 18. *(Key Question 7)*

Global Perspective 12-1 shows that budget deficits are not confined to the United States.

QUICK REVIEW 12-2

■ Tax revenues automatically increase in economic expansions and decrease in recessions; transfers automatically decrease in expansions and increase in recessions.

■ Automatic changes in taxes and transfers add a degree of built-in stability to the economy.

■ The full-employment budget compares government spending to the tax revenues that would accrue if there were full employment; it is more useful than the actual budget in revealing the status of fiscal policy.

■ Full-employment budget deficits are also called structural deficits, as distinct from cyclical deficits.

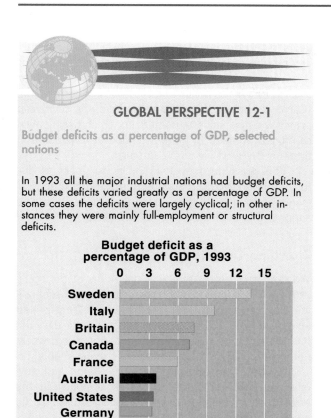

GLOBAL PERSPECTIVE 12-1

Budget deficits as a percentage of GDP, selected nations

In 1993 all the major industrial nations had budget deficits, but these deficits varied greatly as a percentage of GDP. In some cases the deficits were largely cyclical; in other instances they were mainly full-employment or structural deficits.

Budget deficit as a percentage of GDP, 1993

| | 0 | 3 | 6 | 9 | 12 | 15 |

Sweden
Italy
Britain
Canada
France
Australia
United States
Germany
Japan

Source: *Organization for Economic Cooperation and Development.*

PROBLEMS, CRITICISMS, AND COMPLICATIONS

Unfortunately, there is much difference between fiscal policy on paper and fiscal policy in practice. Let's examine specific problems government may encounter in enacting and applying fiscal policy.

Problems of Timing

Several problems of timing may arise in connection with fiscal policy.

1 Recognition Lag The recognition lag refers to the time between the beginning of a recession or inflation and the certain awareness that it is actually happening. It is difficult to predict accurately the future course of economic activity. Although forecasting tools such as the index of leading indicators (see this chapter's Last Word) provide clues to the direction of the economy, the economy may be four or six months into a recession or inflation before that fact appears in relevant statistics and is acknowledged.

2 Administrative Lag The wheels of democratic government turn slowly. There will typically be a significant lag between the time the need for fiscal action is recognized and the time action is actually taken. Congress has on occasion taken so much time in adjusting fiscal policy that the economic situation has turned around in the interim, rendering the policy action inappropriate.

3 Operational Lag There will also be a lag between the time that fiscal action is taken by Congress and the time that action affects output, employment, or the price level. Although changes in tax rates can be put into effect quickly, government spending on public works—the construction of dams, interstate highways, and so on—requires long planning periods and even longer periods of construction. Such spending is of questionable usefulness in offsetting short—for example, six- to eighteen-month—periods of recession. Because of these problems, discretionary fiscal policy has increasingly relied on tax changes.

Political Problems

Fiscal policy is created in the political arena and this greatly complicates its use in stabilizing the economy.

1 Other Goals Economic stability is *not* the sole objective of government spending and taxing policies. Government is also concerned with providing public goods and services and redistributing income (Chapter 5). A classic example occurred during World War II when massive government spending for military goods caused strong and persistent inflationary pressures in the early 1940s. The defeat of Nazi Germany and Japan was simply a higher priority goal than achieving price level stability.

2 State and Local Finance Fiscal policies of state and local governments are frequently procyclical—they do not counter recession or inflation. Unlike the Federal government, most state and local governments face constitutional or other legal requirements to balance their budgets. Like households and private businesses, state and local governments increase expenditures during prosperity and cut them during recession. During the Great Depression of the 1930s, most of the increase in Federal spending was offset by decreases in state and local spending. During the recession of 1990–1991, many state and local governments had to increase tax rates, impose new taxes, and reduce spending to offset falling tax revenues resulting from the reduced personal income and spending of their citizens.

3   Expansionary Bias?   Rhetoric to the contrary, deficits may be politically attractive and surpluses politically painful. There may well be a political bias in favor of deficits; fiscal policy may have an expansionary-inflationary bias. Tax reductions are politically popular, and so are increases in government spending, provided the constituents of the politicians promoting them share in the benefits. But higher taxes upset voters and reducing government expenditures can be politically precarious. For example, it might be political suicide for a farm-state senator to vote for tax increases and against agricultural subsidies.

4   A Political Business Cycle?   Some economists contend the goal of politicians is not to act in the interests of the national economy, but rather to get reelected. A few economists have suggested the notion of a **political business cycle.** They argue that politicians might manipulate fiscal policy to maximize voter support, even though their fiscal decisions *destabilize* the economy. In this view, fiscal policy, as we have described it, may be corrupted for political purposes and cause economic fluctuations.

The populace, it is assumed, takes economic conditions into account in voting. Incumbents are penalized at the polls if economic conditions are depressed; they are rewarded if the economy is prosperous. As an election approaches, the incumbent administration (aided by an election-minded Congress) will cut taxes and increase government spending. Not only will these actions be popular, the resulting stimulus to the economy will push all the critical economic indicators in proper directions. Output and real incomes will rise; unemployment will fall; and the price level will be relatively stable. As a result, incumbents will enjoy a very cordial economic environment for reelection.

But after the election, continued expansion of the economy is reflected increasingly in a rising price level and less in growing real incomes. Growing public concern over inflation will prompt politicians to invoke a contractionary fiscal policy. Crudely put, a "made-in-Washington" recession will be engineered by trimming government spending and increasing taxes to restrain inflation. This recession will not hurt incumbents because the next election is still two or three years away and the critical consideration for most voters is the performance of the economy in the year or so before the election. Indeed, the recession provides a new starting point from which fiscal policy can again be used to generate another expansion in time for the next election campaign.

This possible perversion of fiscal policy is disturbing but difficult to document. Although empirical evidence is inconclusive, there is some evidence to support this political theory of the business cycle.

Crowding-Out Effect

We now move from practical problems in the application of fiscal policy to a basic criticism of fiscal policy. The essence of the **crowding-out effect** is that an expansionary (deficit) fiscal policy will increase the interest rate and reduce investment spending, weakening or canceling the stimulus of the fiscal policy.

Suppose the economy is in recession and government invokes discretionary fiscal policy in the form of an increase in government spending. To do so government enters the money market to finance the deficit. The resulting increase in the demand for money raises the interest rate, the price paid for borrowing money. Because investment spending varies inversely with the interest rate, some investment will be choked off or crowded out.[2]

While few would question this logic, there is disagreement as to the size of the crowding-out effect. Some economists argue that there will be little crowding-out when there is considerable unemployment. Their rationale is that, given a recession, the stimulus provided by an increase in government spending will likely improve business profit expectations which are an important determinant of investment. Thus, investment spending need not fall—it may even increase—even though interest rates are higher.

Another consideration concerns monetary policy, which we will discuss in detail in later chapters. The monetary authorities may increase the supply of money by just enough to offset the deficit-caused increase in the demand for money. In this case the equilibrium interest rate would not change and the crowding-out effect would be zero. In the 1980s the monetary authorities restrained the growth of the

---

[2]Some interest sensitive consumption spending—for example, automobile purchases—may also be crowded out.

money supply and, consequently, the crowding-out effect of the large deficits of the 1980s may have been quite large. In comparison, in the 1960s the monetary authorities were strongly disposed to stabilize interest rates. They consequently would increase the money supply in response to higher interest rates caused by government borrowing. As a result, crowding-out was less significant.

Offsetting Saving

A few economists theorize that deficit spending is offset by an equal increase in private saving. Supposedly, people recognize that today's deficit spending will eventually require higher taxes for themselves or their heirs. People therefore increase their present saving (reduce their current consumption) in anticipation of these higher taxes. A budget deficit—*public dissaving*—produces an increase in *private saving.* This concept is termed the **Ricardian equivalence theorem,** named after British economist David Ricardo who first suggested it in the early 1800s. More formally, the theorem states that financing a deficit by borrowing has the same limited effect on GDP as financing it through a present tax increase.

In Figure 12-1, the increase in spending from the rise in government spending or decline in taxes is partially or fully offset by a decline in consumption caused by the increase in saving. Aggregate demand and real GDP therefore do not expand as predicted. Fiscal policy is either rendered totally ineffective or is severely weakened.

Although research continues on this theory, mainstream economists reject it as unrealistic and contrary to historical evidence. They point out that the large budget deficits of the 1980s were accompanied by *declines*—not increases—in the national saving rate.

Aggregate Supply and Inflation

Our discussion of complications and criticisms of fiscal policy has thus far been entirely demand-oriented. We now consider a supply-side complication. With an upsloping aggregate supply curve, some portion of the potential effect of an expansionary fiscal policy on real output and employment may be dissipated in the form of inflation. We stressed this idea in Figure 11-9.

Graphical Portrayal: Crowding Out and Inflation

Let's look at the impact of crowding out and inflation on fiscal policy through Figure 12-6. Suppose there

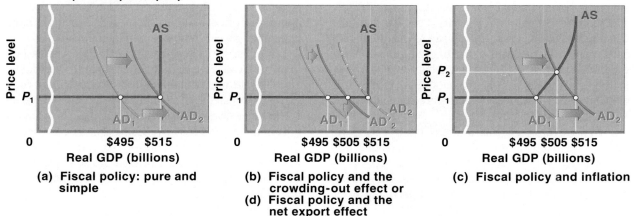

FIGURE 12-6 Fiscal policy: the effects of crowding-out, the net export effect, and inflation
With a simplified aggregate supply curve, we observe in (a) that fiscal policy is uncomplicated and works at full strength. In (b) it is assumed that some amount of private investment is crowded out by the expansionary fiscal policy so that fiscal policy is weakened. In (c) a more realistic aggregate supply curve reminds us that, when the economy is in the intermediate range of the aggregate supply curve, part of the impact of an expansionary fiscal policy will be reflected in inflation rather than in increases in real output and employment. In (d)—the same graph as (b)—we assume that fiscal policy increases the interest rate, which attracts foreign financial capital to the United States. The dollar therefore appreciates and our net exports fall, weakening the expansionary fiscal policy.

(a) Fiscal policy: pure and simple

(b) Fiscal policy and the crowding-out effect or
(d) Fiscal policy and the net export effect

(c) Fiscal policy and inflation

is a noninflationary absolute full-capacity level of real GDP at $515 billion, as shown in Figure 12-6a. For simplicity our aggregate supply curve here has no real-world intermediate range. Up to full capacity, the price level is constant. After the economy achieves full capacity the vertical range of AS prevails so that any further increase in aggregate demand would be purely inflationary.

We begin with aggregate demand at AD_1 which gives us a real output equilibrium at $495 billion. Assume now that government undertakes an expansionary fiscal policy which shifts the aggregate demand curve rightward by $20 billion to AD_2. The economy thus achieves absolute full-capacity output without inflation at $515 of GDP. We know from our previous discussion of discretionary fiscal policy (Figure 12-1) that an increase in government spending of $5 billion or a decrease in taxes of $6.67 billion would create this expansionary effect, assuming the economy's multiplier is 4. With no offsetting or complicating factors, this "pure and simple" expansionary fiscal policy moves the economy from recession to full-capacity output, greatly increasing employment.

In Figure 12-6b we complicate matters by adding the crowding-out effect. While fiscal policy is expansionary and designed to shift aggregate demand from AD_1 to AD_2, some investment may be crowded out so that aggregate demand ends up at AD_2'. Equilibrium GDP increases to only $505 billion rather than the desired $515 billion. *The crowding-out effect may weaken fiscal policy.*

In Figure 12-6c we switch to a more realistic aggregate supply curve which includes an intermediate range. We ignore the crowding-out effect so that the expansionary fiscal policy is successful in shifting aggregate demand from AD_1 to AD_2. If the aggregate supply curve was shaped as in Figure 12-6a and b, full employment would now be realized at $515 billion and the price level would remain at P_1. But we find that the upsloping intermediate range on the aggregate supply curve causes a part of the increase in aggregate demand to be dissipated in higher prices. The increase in real GDP is diminished. Specifically, the price level rises from P_1 to P_2 and real output increases to only $505 billion.

That is, the aggregate demand curve in Figure 12-6c shifts from AD_1 to AD_2, but the upsloping AS segment means we move upward along AD_2 from price level P_1 to P_2. In the real world, demand-side fiscal policy designed to achieve full employment does

not escape the realities imposed by the upsloping portion of the aggregate supply curve. *(Key Question 9)*

Fiscal Policy in the Open Economy

Additional complications arise when we recognize that our economy is a component of the world economy.

Shocks Originating from Abroad   Events and policies abroad that affect our net exports have an impact on our economy. Economies are susceptible to unforeseen international *aggregate demand shocks* which can alter domestic GDP and render domestic fiscal actions inappropriate.

Suppose we are incurring recession and have changed government expenditures and taxes to bolster aggregate demand and GDP without igniting inflation (as from AD_1 to AD_2 in Figure 12-6a). Now suppose the economies of our major trading partners unexpectedly and abruptly expand rapidly. Greater employment and rising incomes in those nations translate into more purchases of American goods. Our net exports rise, aggregate demand increases too rapidly, and we experience demand-pull inflation. Had we known in advance that our net exports would rise significantly, we would have enacted a less expansionary fiscal policy. The point is that our growing participation in the world economy brings with it the *complications* of mutual interdependence along with the *gains* from specialization and trade.

Net Export Effect   The **net export effect** may also work through international trade to reduce the effectiveness of fiscal policy. We concluded in our discussion of the crowding-out effect that an expansionary fiscal policy might boost interest rates, reducing *investment* and weakening fiscal policy. Now we want to know what effect an interest rate increase might have on our *net exports* (exports minus imports).

Suppose we undertake an expansionary fiscal policy which causes a higher interest rate. The higher interest rate will attract financial capital from abroad where interest rates are unchanged. But foreign financial investors must acquire U.S. dollars to invest in American securities. We know that an increase in the demand for a commodity—in this case dollars—will raise its price. So the price of dollars will rise in terms of foreign currencies; that is, the dollar will appreciate.

TABLE 12-1   Fiscal policy and the net export effect

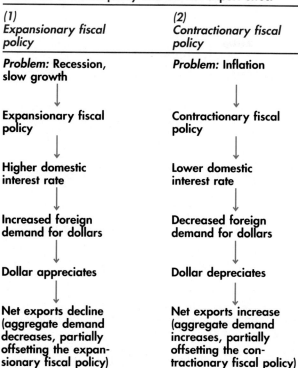

(1) Expansionary fiscal policy	(2) Contractionary fiscal policy
Problem: Recession, slow growth	**Problem: Inflation**
↓	↓
Expansionary fiscal policy	Contractionary fiscal policy
↓	↓
Higher domestic interest rate	Lower domestic interest rate
↓	↓
Increased foreign demand for dollars	Decreased foreign demand for dollars
↓	↓
Dollar appreciates	Dollar depreciates
↓	↓
Net exports decline (aggregate demand decreases, partially offsetting the expansionary fiscal policy)	Net exports increase (aggregate demand increases, partially offsetting the contractionary fiscal policy)

The decline in the net export component of aggregate demand will partially offset the expansionary fiscal policy. The aggregate demand curve will shift rightward from AD_1 to AD'_2, *not* to AD_2, and equilibrium GDP will increase from \$495 to \$505, *not* to \$515. Thus, the net export effect of fiscal policy joins the problems of timing, politics, crowding out, Ricardian effects, and inflation in complicating the "management" of aggregate demand.

Table 12-1 summarizes the net export effect resulting from fiscal policy. Column 1 reviews the analysis just discussed (Figure 12-6d). But note the net export effect works in both directions. By reducing the domestic interest rate, a *contractionary* fiscal policy *increases* net exports. In this regard, you should follow through the analysis in column 2 of Table 12-1 and relate it to the aggregate demand–aggregate supply model.

QUICK REVIEW 12-3

■ Time lags and political problems complicate fiscal policy.

■ The crowding-out effect indicates that an expansionary fiscal policy may increase the interest rate and reduce investment spending.

■ A few economists believe in the Ricardian equivalence theorem which says deficit spending creates expectations of future tax increases and therefore people privately save a dollar for each dollar of taxes they anticipate.

■ The upsloping range of the aggregate supply curve means that part of an expansionary fiscal policy may be dissipated in inflation.

■ Fiscal policy may be weakened by a net export effect which works through changes in **a** the interest rate, **b** the international value of the dollar, and **c** exports and imports.

What will be the impact of this dollar appreciation on our net exports? Because more units of foreign currencies are needed to buy our goods, the rest of the world will see our exports as being more expensive. Hence, our exports will decline. Conversely, Americans, who can now exchange their dollars for more units of foreign currencies, will buy more imports. Consequently, with American exports falling and imports rising, net export expenditures in the United States will diminish and our expansionary fiscal policy will be partially negated.[3]

A return to our aggregate demand and supply analysis in Figure 12-6b, now labeled d, will clarify this point. An expansionary fiscal policy aimed at increasing aggregate demand from AD_1 to AD_2 may hike the domestic interest rate and ultimately reduce our net exports through the process just described.

Supply-Side Fiscal Policy

We have seen how movements along the aggregate supply curve can complicate the operation of fiscal policy. Let's now turn to the possibility of a more direct link between fiscal policy and aggregate supply. Economists recognize that fiscal policy—especially tax changes—*may* alter aggregate supply and affect the price level–real output outcomes of a change in fiscal policy.

---

[3]The appreciation of the dollar will also reduce the dollar price of foreign resources such as oil imported to the United States. As a result, aggregate supply will increase and part of the contractionary net export effect described here may be offset.

LAST WORD

THE LEADING INDICATORS

One tool policy makers use to forecast the future direction of real GDP is a monthly index of a group of variables which in the past has provided advance notice of changes in GDP.

"Index of Leading Indicators Falls for Third Month—Recession Feared"; "Index of Leading Indicators Surges Again"; "Decline in Stock Market Drags Down Index of Leading Indicators." Headlines such as these appear regularly in newspapers. The focus of these articles is the Commerce Department's weighted average—or composite index—of eleven economic variables which has historically reached its peak or trough in advance of the corresponding turns in the business cycle. Changes in the index of leading indicators thus provide a clue to the future direction of the economy and may therefore shorten the length of the "recognition lag" associated with the implementation of macroeconomic policy.

Let's examine the eleven components of the index of leading indicators in terms of a predicted *decline* in GDP, keeping in mind that the opposite changes forecast a *rise* in GDP.

1 Average Workweek Decreases in the length of the average workweek of production workers in manufacturing foretell declines in future manufacturing output and GDP.

2 Initial Claims for Unemployment Insurance Higher first-time claims for unemployment insurance are as-

sociated with falling employment and subsequently sagging production.

3 New Orders for Consumer Goods A slump in the number of orders received by manufacturers for consumer goods portends reduced future production—a decline in GDP.

4 Stock Market Prices Declines in stock prices often are reflections of expected declines in corporate sales and profits. Furthermore, lower stock prices diminish consumer wealth, leading consumers to cut back on their spending. Lower stock market values also make it less attractive for firms to issue new shares of stock as a way to raise funds for investment. Hence, declines in stock prices can bring forth declines in aggregate demand and GDP.

Suppose in Figure 12-7 that aggregate demand and aggregate supply are AD_1 and AS_1 so that the equilibrium level of real GDP is Q_1 and the price level is P_1. Assume further that government concludes the level of unemployment associated with Q_1 is too high and thus invokes an expansionary fiscal policy in the form of a tax cut. The demand-side effect is to increase aggregate demand from AD_1 to, say, AD_2. This shift increases real GDP to Q_2, but also boosts the price level to P_2.

How might tax cuts affect aggregate supply? Some economists—labeled "supply-side" economists—feel that tax reductions will shift the aggregate supply curve to the right.

1 Saving and Investment Lower taxes will increase disposable incomes, increasing household saving. Similarly, tax reductions on businesses will increase the profitability of investment. In brief, lower taxes will increase saving and investment, increasing the rate of capital accumulation. The size of our "national factory"—our productive capacity—will grow more rapidly.

2 Work Incentives Lower personal income tax rates also increase after-tax wages—the price paid for work—and stimulate work incentives. Many people not already in the labor force will offer their services because after-tax wages are higher. Those already in

25

5 Contracts and Orders for New Plant and Equipment
A drop in orders for capital equipment and other investment goods implies reduced future aggregate demand and domestic output.

6 Building Permits for Houses Decreases in the number of building permits taken out for new homes augur future declines in investment and therefore the distinct possibility that GDP will fall.

7 Vendor Performance Somewhat ironically, better performance by sellers of inputs in supplying buyers in a timely fashion indicates slackening business demand and potentially falling GDP.

8 Change in Unfilled Orders of Durable Goods Decreases in the dollar amounts of unfilled orders of durable manufactured goods imply falling aggregate demand and therefore ensuing declines in GDP.

9 Change in Sensitive Raw Material Prices Declines in certain sensitive raw material prices often precede declines in domestic output.

10 The Money Supply Decreases in the money supply are associated with falling GDP. (The components of the money supply and its role in the macro economy are the subjects of Chapters 13 through 16.)

11 Index of Consumer Expectations Declines in consumer confidence indicated by this index compiled by the University of Michigan's Survey Research Center foreshadow curtailed consumption expenditures and eventual declines in domestic output.

None of these factors *alone* consistently predicts the future course of the economy. It is not unusual in any month, for example, for one or two of the indicators to be decreasing while the other indicators are increasing. Rather, changes in the *weighted average*—or composite index—of the eleven components are what in the past have provided advance notice of a change in the direction of GDP. The rule of thumb is that three successive monthly declines or increases in the index indicate the economy will soon turn in that same direction.

Although the composite index has correctly signaled business fluctuations on numerous occasions, it has not been infallible. At times the index has provided false warnings of recessions which never happened. In other instances, recessions have so closely followed the downturn in the index that policy makers have not had sufficient time to make use of the "early" warning. Moreover, changing structural features of the economy on occasion have rendered the existing index obsolete and have necessitated its revision.

Given these caveats, the index of leading indicators can best be thought of as a useful but not totally reliable signaling device which authorities must employ with considerable caution in formulating macroeconomic policy.

---

the labor force will want to work more hours and take fewer vacations.

3 Risk Taking Lower tax rates prod risk takers. Individuals and businesses will be more willing to risk their energies and financial capital on new production

FIGURE 12-7 **Supply-side effects of fiscal policy**
The traditional view is that tax cuts will increase aggregate demand as from AD_1 to AD_2, increasing both real domestic output (Q_1 to Q_2) and the price level (P_1 to P_2). If the tax reductions induce favorable supply-side effects, aggregate supply will shift rightward as from AS_1 to AS_2. This allows the economy to realize an even larger output (Q_3 compared to Q_2) and a smaller price level increase (P_3 compared to P_2).

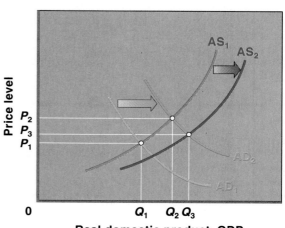

methods and new products when lower tax rates promise a larger potential after-tax reward.

Through all these avenues, lower taxes will shift aggregate supply to the right as from AS_1 to AS_2 in Figure 12-7, reducing inflation and further increasing real GDP.

Supply-siders also contend that lower tax *rates* need not result in lower tax *revenues*. In fact, lower tax rates that cause a substantial expansion of output and income may generate increases in tax revenues. This enlarged tax base may enhance total tax revenues even though tax rates are lower. While the mainstream view is that a reduction in tax rates will reduce tax revenues and increase budget deficits, the supply-side view is that tax rate reductions can be structured to increase tax revenues and reduce deficits.

Mainstream Skepticism Most economists are skeptical concerning the supply-side effects of tax cuts, particularly in view of the evidence from the supply-side tax cuts of the 1980s. First, these critics feel the hoped-for positive effects of a tax reduction on incentives to work, save and invest, and bear risks are not nearly as strong as supply-siders believe. Second, any rightward shifts of the aggregate supply curve will occur over an extended period of time, while the demand-side impact will be more immediate.

CHAPTER SUMMARY

1   Government responsibility for achieving and maintaining full employment is specified in the Employment Act of 1946. The Council of Economic Advisers (CEA) was established to advise the President on policies to fulfill the goals of the act.

2   Increases in government spending expand, and decreases contract, aggregate demand and equilibrium GDP. Increases in taxes reduce, and decreases expand, aggregate demand and equilibrium GDP. Fiscal policy therefore calls for increases in government spending and decreases in taxes—a budget deficit—to correct for recession. Decreases in government spending and increases in taxes—a budget surplus—are appropriate fiscal policy for correcting demand-pull inflation.

3   Built-in stability refers to net tax revenues that vary directly with the level of GDP. During a recession, the public budget automatically moves toward a stabilizing deficit; during expansion, the budget automatically moves toward an anti-inflationary surplus. Built-in stability lessens, but does not correct, undesired changes in the GDP.

4   The full-employment budget or structural budget measures what the Federal budgetary surplus or deficit would

be *if* the economy operated at full employment throughout the year. The full-employment budget is a meaningful indicator of the government's fiscal posture, while its actual budgetary surplus or deficit is not.

5   The enactment and application of appropriate fiscal policy are subject to certain problems and questions. The important ones are: **a** Can the enactment and application of fiscal policy be better timed to maximize its effectiveness in heading off economic fluctuations?   **b** Can the economy rely on Congress to enact appropriate fiscal policy?   **c** An expansionary fiscal policy may be weakened if it crowds out some private investment spending.   **d** Do people increase their saving in anticipation of the future higher taxes they think deficit spending will entail?   **e** Some of the effect of an expansionary fiscal policy may be dissipated in inflation. **f** Fiscal policy may be rendered ineffective or inappropriate by unforeseen events occurring within the world economy. Also, fiscal policy may precipitate changes in exchange rates which weaken its effects.   **g** Supply-side economists contend that traditional fiscal policy fails to consider the effects of tax changes on aggregate supply.

TERMS AND CONCEPTS

Employment Act of 1946	**budget deficit**	**budget surplus**	**political business cycle**
Council of Economic Advisers	**contractionary fiscal policy**	**built-in stabilizer**	**crowding-out effect**
discretionary fiscal policy	**progressive, proportional, and regressive tax systems**	**actual budget**	**Ricardian equivalence theorem**
expansionary fiscal policy		**cyclical deficit**	**net export effect**
		full-employment budget	
		structural deficit	

QUESTIONS AND STUDY SUGGESTIONS

1 What is the central thrust of the Employment Act of 1946? What is the role of the Council of Economic Advisers (CEA) in responding to this law? Class assignment: Determine the names and educational backgrounds of the present members of the CEA.

2 *Key Question* *Assume that a hypothetical economy with an MPC of .8 is experiencing severe recession. By how much would government spending have to increase to shift the aggregate demand curve rightward by $25 billion? How large a tax cut would be needed to achieve this same increase in aggregate demand? Why the difference? Determine one possible combination of government spending increases and tax decreases which would accomplish this same goal.*

3 *Key Question* *What are government's fiscal policy options for ending severe demand-pull inflation? Use the aggregate demand–aggregate supply model to show the impact of these policies on the price level. Which of these fiscal policy options do you think a "conservative" economist might favor? A "liberal" economist?*

4 (For students assigned Chapters 9 and 10) Use the aggregate expenditures model to show how government fiscal policy could eliminate either a recessionary gap or an inflationary gap (Figure 10-8). Use the concept of the balanced budget multiplier to explain how equal increases in *G* and *T* could eliminate a recessionary gap and how equal decreases in *G* and *T* could eliminate an inflationary gap.

5 Designate each statement *true* or *false* and justify your answer.

   a Expansionary fiscal policy during a depression will have a greater positive effect on real GDP if government borrows the money to finance the budget deficit than if it creates new money to finance the deficit.

   b Contractionary fiscal policy during severe demand-pull inflation will be more effective if government impounds the budget surplus rather than using the surplus to pay off some of its past debt.

6 Explain how built-in (or automatic) stabilizers work. What are the differences between a proportional, progressive, and regressive tax system as they relate to an economy's built-in stability?

7 *Key Question* *Define the "full-employment budget" and explain its significance. How does it differ from the "actual budget"? What is the difference between a structural deficit and a cyclical deficit? Suppose the economy depicted in Figure 12-4 is operating at its full-employment, noninflationary level of real output, GDP_f. What is the size of its structural deficit? Its cyclical deficit? Should government raise taxes or reduce government spending to eliminate this structural deficit? What are the risks of so doing?*

8 The actual budget deficit increased significantly in 1990 and 1991, but the full-employment budget deficit remained relatively constant. Can you think of a logical explanation?

9 *Key Question* *Briefly state and evaluate the problem of time lags in enacting and applying fiscal policy. Explain the notion of a political business cycle. What is the crowding-out effect and why is it relevant to fiscal policy? In what respect is the net export effect similar to the crowding-out effect? Do you think people increase their saving in anticipation of the future higher taxes they believe will follow government's use of expansionary fiscal policy?*

10 In view of your answers to question 9, explain the following statement: "While fiscal policy clearly is useful in combating the extremes of severe recession and demand-pull inflation, it is impossible to use fiscal policy to 'fine-tune' the economy to the full-employment, noninflationary level of real GDP and keep the economy there indefinitely."

11 Discuss: "Mainstream economists tend to focus on the aggregate demand effects of tax-rate reductions; supply-side economists emphasize the aggregate supply effects." What are the routes through which a tax cut might increase aggregate supply? If tax cuts are so good for the economy, why don't we cut taxes to zero?

12 Using Figure 12-3 as a basis for your response, explain the stabilizing or destabilizing impacts of fiscal policy if a constitutional amendment requiring an annually balanced budget were passed.

13 Use Figure 12-4 to explain why a deliberate increase in the full-employment or structural deficit which causes the economy to expand from GDP_r to GDP_f might reduce the size of the actual deficit. In requesting a tax cut in the early 1960s, President Kennedy said, "It is a paradoxical truth that tax rates are too high today and tax revenues are too low and the soundest way to raise tax revenues in the long run is to cut tax rates now." Relate this quotation to your previous answer.

14 **Advanced analysis:** (For students assigned Chapters 9 and 10) Assume that, without taxes, the consumption schedule for an economy is as shown below:

GDP, billions	Consumption, billions
$100	$120
200	200
300	280
400	360
500	440
600	520
700	600

a Graph this consumption schedule and determine the size of the MPC.

b Assume a lump-sum (regressive) tax is imposed such that the government collects $10 billion in taxes at all levels of GDP. Calculate the tax rate at each level of GDP. Graph the resulting consumption schedule and compare the MPC and the multiplier with that of the pretax consumption schedule.

c Now suppose a proportional tax system with a 10 percent tax rate is imposed instead of the regressive system. Calculate the new consumption schedule, graph it, and note the MPC and the multiplier.

d Finally, impose a progressive tax system such that the tax rate is zero percent when GDP is $100, 5 percent at $200, 10 percent at $300, 15 percent at $400, and so forth. Determine and graph the new consumption schedule, noting the effect of this tax system on the MPC and the multiplier.

e Explain why the proportional and progressive tax systems contribute to greater economic stability, while the regressive system does not. Demonstrate using a graph similar to Figure 12-3.

15 (Last Word) What is the composite index of leading economic indicators and how does it relate to discretionary fiscal policy?

PART THREE

Money, Banking, and Monetary Policy

13

MONEY AND BANKING

"**M**oney bewitches people. They fret for it, and they sweat for it. They devise most ingenious ways to get it, and most ingenuous ways to get rid of it. Money is the only commodity that is good for nothing but to be gotten rid of. It will not feed you, clothe you, shelter you, or amuse you unless you spend it or invest it. It imparts value only in parting. People will do almost anything for money, and money will do almost anything for people. Money is a captivating, circulating, masquerading puzzle."[1]

Money. A fascinating aspect of the economy. And a crucial element of economics. Money is more than a tool for facilitating the economy's operation. Operating properly, the monetary system is the lifeblood of the circular flows of income and expenditure which typify all economies. A well-operating money system is conducive to both full employment and efficient resource use. A malfunctioning monetary system can contribute to severe fluctuations in the economy's levels of output, employment, and prices, *and* can distort the allocation of resources.

In this chapter we are concerned with the nature and functions of money and the basic institutions of the American banking system. Chapter 14 examines the ways individual commercial banks and the banking system as a whole can vary the money supply. In Chapter 15 we discuss how the central banks of the economy regulate the supply of money to promote full employment and price level stability.

We begin with a review of the functions of money. Next, we shift to the supply of money and pose the question: What constitutes money in our economy? Third, we consider what "backs" the supply of money in the United States. Fourth, the demand for money is explained. Fifth, we combine the supply of money and the demand for money to portray and explain the market for money. Finally, the institutional structure and recent difficulties of the American financial system will be discussed.

THE FUNCTIONS OF MONEY

What is money? Money is what money does. Anything that performs the functions of money is money. There are three functions of money:

1 Medium of Exchange First and foremost, money is a **medium of exchange;** it is usable in buy-

---

[1]Federal Reserve Bank of Philadelphia, "Creeping Inflation," *Business Review,* August 1957, p. 3.

ing and selling goods and services. A worker in a bagel bakery does not want to be paid 200 bagels per week. Nor does the bagel bakery wish to receive, say, fresh fish for its bagels. However, money is readily acceptable as payment. It is a social invention allowing resource suppliers and producers to be paid with a "good" (money) which can be used to buy any one of the full range of items available in the marketplace. As a medium of exchange, money allows society to escape the complications of barter. And because it provides a convenient way of exchanging goods, money allows society to gain the advantages of geographic and human specialization (Figure 4-1).

2 Measure of Value Money is also a **measure of value.** Society uses the monetary unit as a yardstick for measuring the relative worth of heterogeneous goods and resources. Just as we measure distance in miles or kilometers, we gauge the value of goods and services in dollars. With a money system, we need not state the price of each product in terms of all other products for which it can be exchanged; we need not specify the price of cows in terms of corn, crayons, cigars, Chevrolets, and croissants.

This use of money as a common denominator means that the price of each product need be stated *only* in terms of the monetary unit. It permits buyers and sellers to readily compare the worth of various

commodities and resources. Such comparisons facilitate rational decision making. In Chapter 7 we used money as a measure of value in calculating the size of the GDP. Money is also used as a measure of value for transactions involving future payments. Debt obligations of all kinds are measured in the monetary unit.

3 Store of Value Finally, money serves as a **store of value.** Because money is the most liquid—the most spendable—of all assets, it is a very convenient way to store wealth. The money you place in a safe or checking account will still be available to you months or years later when you wish to use it. Most methods of holding money do not yield monetary returns such as one gets by storing wealth in the form of real assets (property) or paper assets (stocks, bonds, and so forth). However, money does have the advantage of being immediately usable by a firm or a household in meeting all financial obligations.

THE SUPPLY OF MONEY

Conceptually, anything generally acceptable as a medium of exchange *is* money. Historically, whales' teeth, elephant tail bristles, circular stones, nails, slaves (yes, human beings), cattle, beer, cigarettes,

TABLE 13-1 Alternative money definitions for the United States: M1, M2, and M3

Money definition or concept	Absolute amount (in billions)	Percentage of concept		
		M1	M2	M3
Currency (coins and paper money)	$ 347	30%	10%	8%
plus **Checkable deposits**	805*	70%	22	19
equals **M1**	$1152	100%		
plus **Noncheckable savings deposits, including MMDAs**	1186		33	28
plus **Small time deposits**	895*		25	21
plus **Money market mutual fund balances (MMMFs)**	362		10	9
equals **M2**	$3595		100%	
plus **Large time deposits**	652*			15
equals **M3**	$4247			100%

*These figures include other quantitatively smaller components.

Source: Federal Reserve Bulletin, December 1994, p. A14. Data are for September 1994.

and pieces of metal have functioned as media of exchange. In our economy the debts of governments and of commercial banks and other financial institutions are used as money, as we will see.

Defining Money: M1

Neither economists nor public officials agree on what specific items constitute the economy's money supply. Narrowly defined—and designated *M*1—the money supply is composed of two items:

1 Currency, that is, coins and paper money in the hands of the nonbank public

2 All checkable deposits, meaning deposits in commercial banks and "thrift" or savings institutions on which checks can be drawn[2]

Coins and paper money are debts of government and governmental agencies. Checking accounts represent debts of the commercial bank or savings institution. Let's comment briefly on the components of the *M*1 money supply (Table 13-1).

Currency: Coins + Paper Money

From copper pennies to silver dollars, coins are the "small change" of our money supply. Coins are a very small portion of the total money supply; they constitute only 2 or 3 percent of the total $1152 billion *M*1 money supply. Coins are "convenience money" which permit us to make very small purchases.

All coins in circulation in the United States are **token money.** This means the **intrinsic value**—the value of the bullion (metal) contained in the coin itself—is less than the face value of the coin. This is to avoid the melting down of token money for profitable sale as bullion. If our 50-cent pieces each contained 75 cents' worth of silver bullion, it would be profitable to melt them and sell the metal. Although it is illegal to do this, 50-cent pieces would disappear from circulation. This is one of the potential defects of commodity money: Its worth as a commodity may come to exceed its worth as money, ending its function as a medium of exchange.

Paper money constitutes about 28 percent of the economy's *M*1 money supply. All this $323 billion of

---

[2]In the ensuing discussion of the definitions of money several of the quantitatively less significant components are not explicitly discussed to sidestep a maze of details. For example, travelers' checks are included in the *M*1 money supply. Reference to the statistical appendix of any recent *Federal Reserve Bulletin* will provide you with more comprehensive definitions.

paper currency is in the form of **Federal Reserve Notes,** issued by the Federal Reserve Banks with the authorization of Congress. A glance at any currency in your wallet will reveal "Federal Reserve Note" at the top of the face of the bill and the Reserve Bank that issued it in the circle to the left.

Checkable Deposits

The safety and convenience of using checks have made checking accounts the most important money in the United States. You would not think of stuffing $4896.47 in bills and coins in an envelope and dropping it in a mailbox to pay a debt. But to write and mail a check for a large sum is commonplace. A check must be endorsed (signed on the reverse side) by the person cashing it; the drawer of the check subsequently receives the canceled check as an endorsed receipt attesting to the fulfillment of the obligation. Similarly, because the writing of a check requires endorsement by the drawer, the theft or loss of your checkbook is not nearly as calamitous as losing an identical amount of currency. Furthermore, it is more convenient to write a check than to transport and count out a large sum of currency. For all these reasons, *checkbook money* is the dominant form of money in our economy. In dollar volume, about 90 percent of all transactions are carried out by checks.

It might seem strange that checking accounts are part of the money supply. But it's clear why: Checks, which are nothing more than a way to transfer the ownership of deposits in banks and other financial institutions, are generally acceptable as a medium of exchange. True, as a stop at most gas stations will verify, checks are less generally accepted than currency for small purchases. But, for major purchases, sellers willingly accept checks as payment. Moreover, people can convert these deposits immediately into paper money and coins on demand; checks drawn on these deposits are thus the equivalent of currency.

To summarize:

Money, *M*1 = currency + checkable deposits

Institutions Offering Checkable Deposits

Table 13-1 shows that **checkable deposits** are the largest component of the *M*1 money supply. By glancing ahead at Figure 13-4 we see many financial institutions offer checkable deposits in the United States.

1   Commercial Banks   These banks are the mainstays of the system. They accept the deposits of households and businesses and use these financial resources to make available a wide variety of loans. Commercial bank loans provide short-term working capital to businesses and farmers, finance consumer purchases of automobiles and other durable goods, and so on.

2   Thrift Institutions   The commercial banks are supplemented by other financial institutions—savings and loan associations (S&Ls), mutual savings banks, and credit unions—collectively designated as **thrift** or **savings institutions** or simply, "thrifts." **Savings and loan associations** and **mutual savings banks** marshal the savings of households and businesses which are then used, among other things, to finance housing mortgages. **Credit unions** accept the deposits of "members"—usually a group of individuals who work for the same company—and lend these funds to finance installment purchases.

The checkable deposits of banks and thrifts are known by various names—demand deposits, NOW (negotiable order of withdrawal) accounts, ATS (automatic transfer service) accounts, and share draft accounts. Nevertheless, they are all similar in that depositors can write checks on them whenever, and in whatever amount, they choose.

Qualification   We must qualify our definition of money: Currency and checkable deposits owned by government (the Treasury) and by the Federal Reserve Banks, commercial banks, or other financial institutions are excluded from $M1$ and other money measures.

A paper dollar in the hands of Sally Sorenson obviously constitutes just $1 of the money supply. But, if we counted dollars held by banks as part of the money supply, the same $1 would count for $2 when deposited in a bank. It would count for a $1 demand deposit owned by Sorenson and also for $1 of currency resting in the bank's vault. This problem of double counting is avoided by excluding currency resting in banks (and currency redeposited in the Federal Reserve Banks or other commercial banks) in determining the total money supply.

Excluding currency held by, and demand deposits owned by, government is somewhat more arbitrary. This exclusion permits us better to gauge the money supply and rate of spending in the private sector of the economy apart from spending initiated by government policy.

Near-Monies: M2 and M3

Near-monies are certain highly liquid financial assets such as noncheckable savings accounts, time deposits, and short-term government securities. Although they do not directly function as a medium of exchange, they can be readily and without risk of financial loss converted into currency or checkable deposits. Thus, on demand you may withdraw currency from a **noncheckable savings account** at a commercial bank or thrift institution. Or, you may request that funds be transferred from a noncheckable savings account to a checkable account.

You can withdraw funds quickly from a **money market deposit account (MMDA).** These are interest-bearing accounts offered by banks and thrifts, which pool individual deposits to buy a variety of short-term securities. MMDAs have minimum balance requirements and limit how often money can be withdrawn.

As the term implies, **time deposits** only become available to a depositor at maturity. For example, a 90-day or 6-month time deposit is only available without penalty when the designated period expires. Although time deposits are somewhat less liquid than noncheckable savings accounts, they can be taken as currency or shifted into checkable accounts when they mature.

Or, through a telephone call, you can redeem shares in a **money market mutual fund (MMMF)** offered through a financial investment company. These companies use the combined funds of individual shareholders to buy short-term credit instruments such as certificates of deposit and U.S. government securities.

Money Definition M2   Thus our monetary authorities offer a second and broader definition of money:

$$\text{Money, } M2 = \begin{array}{l} M1 + \text{noncheckable savings} \\ \text{deposits} + \text{MMDAs} + \text{small} \\ \text{(less than \$100,000) time deposits} \\ + \text{MMMFs} \end{array}$$

In other words, **$M2$** includes (1) the medium of exchange items (currency and checkable deposits) comprising $M1$ *plus* (2) other items such as noncheckable savings deposits, money market deposit accounts, small time deposits, and individual money market mutual fund balances. These other items can be quickly and without loss converted into currency and checkable deposits. Table 13-1 shows that the addition of noncheckable savings deposits, MMDAs, small time deposits, and MMMFs yields an $M2$ money supply of $3595 billion compared to the narrower $M1$ money supply of $1152 billion.

Money Definition M3   A third "official" definition, **M3,** recognizes that large ($100,000 or more) time deposits—usually owned by businesses as certificates of deposit—are also easily convertible into checkable deposits. There is a market for these certificates and they can be sold (liquidated) at any time, although perhaps at the risk of a loss. Adding these large time deposits to $M2$ yields a still broader definition of money:

$$\text{Money, } M3 = \frac{M2 + \text{large (\$100,000 or}}{\text{more) time deposits}}$$

Consulting Table 13-1 again, we find the $M3$ money supply is $4247 billion.

There are still other slightly less liquid assets such as certain government securities (for example, Treasury bills and U.S. savings bonds) which can be easily converted into $M1$ money. A whole spectrum of assets exists which vary slightly from one another in terms of their liquidity or "moneyness."

Which definition of money shall we use? The simple $M1$ definition includes only items *directly* and *immediately* usable as a medium of exchange. For this reason it is an often-cited statistic in discussions of the money supply. However, for some purposes economists prefer the broader $M2$ definition. For example, $M2$ is used as one of the eleven trend variables in the index of leading indicators (Last Word, Chapter 12). And what of $M3$ and still broader definitions of money? These definitions are so inclusive that many economists question their usefulness.

We will use the narrow $M1$ definition of money in our discussion and analysis, unless stated otherwise. The important principles applying to $M1$ are also applicable to $M2$ and $M3$ because $M1$ is a base component in these broader measures.

Near Monies: Implications

Near-monies are important for several related reasons.

1   Spending Habits   These highly liquid assets affect people's consuming-saving habits. Usually, the

greater the amount of financial wealth people hold as near-monies, the greater is their willingness to spend out of their money incomes.

2   Stability   Conversion of near-monies into money or vice versa can affect the economy's stability. For example, during the prosperity-inflationary phase of the business cycle, converting noncheckable deposits into checkable deposits or currency adds to the money supply which could increase inflation. Such conversions can complicate the task of the monetary authorities in controlling the money supply and the level of economic activity.

3   Policy   The specific definition of money used is important for monetary policy. For example, the money supply as measured by $M1$ might be constant, while money defined as $M2$ might be increasing. If the monetary authorities feel it is appropriate to have an expanding supply of money, the narrow $M1$ definition would call for specific actions to increase currency and checkable deposits. But the broader $M2$ definition would suggest that the desired expansion of the money supply is already taking place and that no specific policy action is required. *(Key Question 5)*

Credit Cards

You may wonder why we have ignored credit cards —Visa, MasterCard, American Express, Discover, and so forth—in our discussion of how money is defined. After all, credit cards are a convenient means of making purchases. The answer is that credit cards are *not* really money, but rather a means of obtaining a short-term loan from the commercial bank or other financial institution which has issued the card.

When you purchase a sweatshirt with a credit card, the issuing bank will reimburse the store. Later, you reimburse the bank. You pay an annual fee for the services provided and, if you repay the bank in installments, you pay a sizable interest charge. Credit cards are merely a means of deferring or postponing payment for a short period. Your purchase of the sweatshirt is not complete until you have paid your credit-card bill.

However, credit cards—and all other forms of credit—allow individuals and businesses to "economize" in the use of money. Credit cards permit you to have less currency and checkable deposits on hand for transactions. Credit cards help you synchronize your expenditures and your receipt of income, reducing the cash and checkable deposits you must hold.

WHAT "BACKS" THE MONEY SUPPLY?

This is a slippery question. Any complete answer is likely to be at odds with preconceptions about money.

Money as Debt

The major components of the money supply—paper money and checkable deposits—are debts, or promises to pay. *Paper money is the circulating debt of the Federal Reserve Banks. Checkable deposits are the debts of commercial banks and thrift institutions.*

Paper currency and checkable deposits have no intrinsic value. A $5 bill is just a piece of paper. A checkable deposit is merely a bookkeeping entry. And coins, we know, have less intrinsic value than their face value. Nor will government redeem the paper money you hold for anything tangible, such as gold. In effect, we have chosen to "manage" our money supply. The monetary authorities attempt to provide the amount of money needed for that particular volume of business activity which will foster full employment, price level stability, and a healthy rate of economic growth.

Most economists feel that managing the money supply is more sensible than linking it to gold or any other commodity whose supply might arbitrarily and capriciously change. A large increase in the nation's gold stock as the result of new gold discovery might increase the money supply far beyond the amount needed to transact a full-employment level of business activity. Therefore rapid inflation might occur. Or, the historical decline in domestic gold production could reduce the domestic money supply to the point where economic activity was choked off and unemployment and a retarded growth rate resulted.

The point is that paper money cannot be converted into a fixed amount of gold or some other precious metal but is exchangeable only for other pieces of paper money. The government will swap one paper $5 bill for another bearing a different serial number. That is all you can get if you ask the government to redeem some of your paper money. Similarly, check money cannot be exchanged for gold but only for paper money, which, as we have just seen, will not be redeemed by the government for anything tangible.

Value of Money

If currency and checkable deposits have no intrinsic characteristics giving them value *and* if they are not backed by gold or other precious metals, then why are they money? What gives a $20 bill or a $100 checking account entry its value? A reasonably complete answer to these questions involves three points.

1 Acceptability Currency and checkable deposits are money because they are accepted as money. By virtue of long-standing business practice, currency and checkable deposits perform the basic function of money; they are acceptable as a medium of exchange. Suppose you swap a $20 bill for a shirt or blouse at a clothing store. Why does the merchant accept this piece of paper in exchange for that product? The merchant accepts paper money because he or she is confident that others will also accept it in exchange for goods and services. The merchant knows that paper money can purchase the services of clerks, acquire products from wholesalers, and pay the rent on the store. We accept paper money in exchange because we are confident it will be exchangeable for real goods and services when we spend it.

2 Legal Tender Our confidence in the acceptability of paper money is partly a matter of law; currency has been designated as **legal tender** by government. This means paper currency must be accepted in the payment of a debt or the creditor forfeits both the privilege of charging interest and the right to sue the debtor for nonpayment. Put bluntly, paper dollars are accepted as money because government says they are money. The paper money in our economy is **fiat money;** it is money because the government says it is, not because it can be redeemed for precious metal. The general acceptability of currency is also enhanced by the willingness of government to accept it in the payment of taxes and other obligations due the government.

Don't be overimpressed by the power of government. Paper currency's general acceptance in exchange is more important than government's legal tender decree in making these pieces of paper work as money. The government has *not* decreed checks to be legal tender, but they successfully perform the vast bulk of the economy's exchanges of goods, services, and resources. It's true, though, that a governmental agency—the Federal Deposit Insurance Corporation (FDIC)—insures the deposits of commercial banks and S&Ls, undoubtedly contributing to the willingness of individuals and businesses to use checkable deposits as a medium of exchange.

3   Relative Scarcity   The value of money, like the economic value of anything else, is a supply and demand phenomenon. Money derives its value from its scarcity relative to its utility (want-satisfying power). The utility of money lies in its unique capacity to be exchanged for goods and services, now or in the future. The economy's demand for money thus depends on its total dollar volume of transactions in any period plus the amount of money individuals and businesses want to hold for possible future transactions. With a reasonable constant demand for money, the supply of money will determine the value or "purchasing power" of the monetary unit.

Money and Prices

The real value or purchasing power of money is the amount of goods and services a unit of money will buy. When money rapidly loses its purchasing power, it rapidly loses its role as money.

Value of the Dollar   The amount a dollar will buy varies inversely with the price level; *a reciprocal relationship exists between the general price level and the value of the dollar.* Figure 13-1 shows this inverse relationship. When the consumer price index or "cost-of-living" index goes up, the purchasing power of the dollar goes down, and vice versa. Higher prices lower the value of the dollar because more dollars will be needed to buy a particular amount of goods and services.

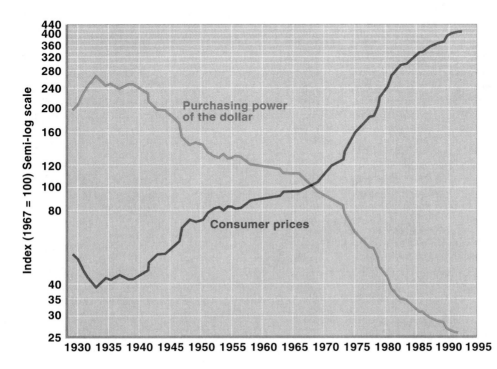

FIGURE 13-1 The price level and the value of money
A reciprocal or inverse relationship exists between the general price level and the purchasing power of the dollar. (This figure is called a "ratio" or "semilog chart" because equal vertical distances measure equal percentage changes rather than equal absolute changes.)

Lower prices increase the purchasing power of the dollar because you will need fewer dollars to obtain a specific quantity of goods and services. If the price level doubles, the value of the dollar will decline by one-half, or 50 percent. If the price level falls by one-half, or 50 percent, the purchasing power of the dollar will double.

If we let P equal the price level expressed as an index number (in hundredths) and D equal the value of the dollar, then the reciprocal relationship between them is

$$D = \frac{1}{P}$$

If the price level P equals 1.00, then the value of the dollar D is 1.00. But, if P rises from 1.00 to 1.20, D will be 0.833, meaning a 20 percent increase in the price level will reduce the value of the dollar by 16.67 percent. Check your understanding of this reciprocal relationship by determining the value of D and its percentage rise when P falls by 20 percent to 0.80. *(Key Question 7)*

Inflation and Acceptability We saw in Chapter 8 situations in which a nation's currency became worthless and unacceptable in exchange. These were circumstances where government issued so many pieces of paper currency that the value of each of these units of money was almost totally undermined. The infamous post-World War I inflation in Germany is an example. In December of 1919 there were about 50 billion marks in circulation. Four years later this figure had expanded to 496,585,345,900 billion marks! The result? The German mark in 1923 was worth an infinitesimal fraction of its 1919 value.[3]

How might inflation and the accompanying decreases in the value of a nation's currency affect the acceptability of paper currency as money? Households and businesses will accept paper currency as a medium of exchange so long as they know they can spend it without any noticeable loss in its purchasing power. But, with spiraling inflation, this is not the case. Runaway inflation, such as in Germany in the early 1920s and in several Latin-American nations in the 1980s, may significantly depreciate the value of money between the time of its receipt and its expenditure. Money will be "hot" money. It is as if the government

were constantly taxing away the purchasing power of its currency. Rapid depreciation of the value of a currency may cause it to cease functioning as a medium of exchange. Businesses and households may refuse to accept paper money in exchange because they do not want to bear the loss in its value which will occur while it is in their possession. (All this despite the fact that government says the paper currency is legal tender!) Without an acceptable domestically provided medium of exchange, the economy may try to substitute a more stable currency from another nation. Example: Many transactions in Russia and South America now occur in dollars rather than highly unstable rubles or pesos (see Last Word). At the extreme, the economy may simply revert to inefficient barter.

Similarly, people will use money as a store of value so long as there is no sizable deterioration in the value of those stored dollars because of inflation. And the economy can effectively employ the monetary unit as a measure of value only when its purchasing power is relatively stable. A yardstick of value subject to drastic shrinkage no longer permits buyers and sellers to establish the terms of trade clearly. When the value of the dollar is declining rapidly, sellers will not know what to charge and buyers will not know what to pay for goods and services.

Maintaining Money's Value

What "backs" paper money is the government's ability to keep the value of money reasonably stable. Stability entails (1) appropriate fiscal policy, as explained in Chapter 12 and (2) intelligent management or regulation of the money supply, as just explained. Businesses and households accept paper money in exchange for goods and services so long as they expect it to command a roughly equivalent amount of goods and services when they spend it. In our economy a blending of legislation, government policy, and social practice inhibit imprudent expansion of the money supply which might seriously jeopardize money's value in exchange.

What we have said with respect to paper currency also applies to checking account money—the debt of commercial banks and thrift institutions. Your checking account of $200 means your bank or thrift is indebted to you for that number of dollars. You can collect this debt in one of two ways. You can go to the bank or thrift and demand paper currency for your checkable deposit; this amounts to changing the debts

---

[3]Frank G. Graham, *Exchange, Prices and Production in Hyperinflation Germany, 1920–1923* (Princeton, N.J.: Princeton University Press, 1930), p. 13.

you hold from the debts of a bank or thrift to government-issued debts. Or, and this is more likely, you can "collect" the debt which the bank or savings institution owes you by transferring this claim by check to someone else.

For example, if you buy a $200 coat from a store, you can pay for it by writing a check, which transfers your bank's indebtedness from you to the store. Your bank now owes the store the $200 it previously owed to you. The store accepts this transfer of indebtedness (the check) as a medium of exchange because it can convert it into currency on demand or can transfer the debt to others in making purchases of its choice. Thus, checks, as means of transferring the debts of banks and thrifts, are acceptable as money because we know banks and thrifts will honor these claims.

The ability of banks and thrifts to honor claims against them depends on their not creating too many of these claims. We will see that a decentralized system of private, profit-seeking banks does not contain sufficient safeguards against the creation of too much check money. Thus, the American banking and financial system has substantial centralization and governmental control to guard against the imprudent creation of checkable deposits.

Caution: This does not mean that in practice the monetary authorities have always judiciously controlled the supplies of currency and checkable-deposit money to achieve economic stability. Indeed, many economists allege that most of the inflationary woes we have encountered historically are the consequence of imprudent increases in the money supply.

QUICK REVIEW 13-2

■ In the United States and other advanced economies, all money is essentially the debts of government, commercial banks, and thrift institutions.

■ These debts efficiently perform the functions of money so long as their value, or purchasing power, is relatively stable.

■ The value of money is not rooted in carefully defined quantities of precious metals (as in the past), but rather, in the amount of goods and services money will purchase in the marketplace.

■ Government's responsibility in stabilizing the value of the monetary unit involves (1) the application of appropriate fiscal policies, and (2) effective control over the supply of money.

THE DEMAND FOR MONEY

Now that we know what constitutes the supply of money and how the money supply is "backed," let's turn to the demand for money. There are two reasons why the public wants to hold money.

Transactions Demand, D_t

People want money as a medium of exchange to conveniently negotiate the purchase of goods and services. Households must have enough money on hand to buy groceries and pay mortgage and utility bills until the next paycheck. Businesses need money to pay for labor, materials, power, and so on. Money demanded for all such purposes is called the **transactions demand** for money.

The basic determinant of the amount of money demanded for transaction purposes is the level of nominal GDP. The larger the total money value of all goods and services exchanged in the economy, the larger will be the amount of money needed to negotiate these transactions. *The transactions demand for money varies directly with nominal GDP.* We specify *nominal* GDP because households and firms will want more money for transactions purposes if *either* prices rise *or* real output increases. In both instances there will be a larger dollar volume of transactions to accomplish.

In Figure 13-2a (Key Graph) we show the relationship between the transactions demand for money, D_t, and the interest rate. Because the transactions demand for money depends on the level of nominal GDP and is independent of the interest rate, we draw the transactions demand as a vertical line. For simplicity we assume the amount of money demanded for transactions is unrelated to changes in the interest rate. That is, higher interest rates will not reduce the amount of money demanded for transactions.[4]

The transactions demand is at $100 billion arbitrarily, but a rationale can be provided. For example, if each dollar held for transactions purposes is spent on the average three times per year *and* nominal GDP is assumed to be $300 billion, then the public would need $100 billion of money to purchase that GDP.

---

[4]This is a simplification. We would also expect the amount of money held by businesses and households to negotiate transactions to vary inversely with the interest rate. When interest rates are high, consumers and businesses will try to reduce the amount of money held for transactions purposes to have more funds to put into interest-earning assets.

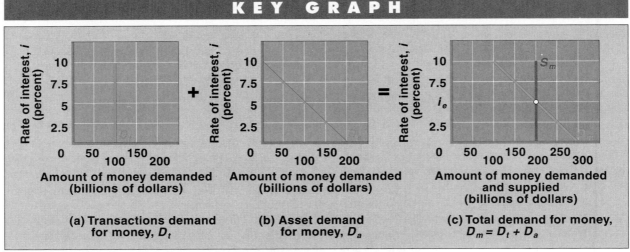

KEY GRAPH

(a) Transactions demand for money, D_t

(b) Asset demand for money, D_a

(c) Total demand for money, $D_m = D_t + D_a$

FIGURE 13-2 The demand for money and the money market
The total demand for money, D_m, is determined by horizontally adding the asset demand for money, D_a, to the transactions demand, D_t. The transactions demand is vertical because it is assumed to depend on nominal GDP rather than the interest rate. The asset demand varies inversely with the interest rate because of the opportunity cost involved in holding currency and checkable deposits which do not pay interest. Combining the money supply (stock), S_m, with total money demand, D_m, portrays the money market and determines the equilibrium interest rate, i_e.

Asset Demand, D_a

The second reason for holding money is rooted in money's function as a store of value. People may hold their financial assets in many forms—as corporate stocks, private or government bonds, or as $M1$ money. Thus, there is an **asset demand** for money.

What determines the asset demand for money? First, we must recognize that each of the various forms of holding our financial assets has advantages and disadvantages. To simplify, let's compare holding bonds with holding money as an asset. The advantages of holding money are its liquidity and lack of risk. Money is the most liquid of all assets; it is immediately usable in making purchases. Money is an attractive asset to be holding when the prices of goods, services, and other financial assets are expected to decline. When the price of a bond falls, the bondholder will suffer a loss if the bond must be sold before maturity. There is no such risk with holding money.

The disadvantage of holding money as an asset is that, compared to holding bonds, it does *not* earn interest income or, in the case of an interest-bearing

checking account, earn as much interest income as on bonds or noncheckable deposits. And idle currency earns no interest at all. Some banks and thrifts require minimum-sized checkable deposits for the depositor to be paid interest; hence, many depositors do not achieve these minimum deposit balances and therefore earn no interest. The interest paid on checkable deposits which exceed the required minimums is less than that paid on bonds and the various noncheckable deposits.

Knowing this, the problem is deciding how much of your financial assets to hold as, say, bonds and how much as money. The solution depends primarily on the rate of interest. A household or business incurs an opportunity cost when holding money (Chapter 2); interest income is forgone or sacrificed. If a bond pays 10 percent interest, then it costs $10 per year of forgone income to hold $100 as cash or in a noninterest checkable account.

It is no surprise that *the asset demand for money varies inversely with the rate of interest.* When the interest rate or opportunity cost of holding money as an asset is low, the public will choose to hold a large amount of money as assets. When the interest rate is high, it is costly to "be liquid" and the amount of assets held in the form of money will be small. When it is expensive to hold money as an asset, people will hold less of it; when money can be held cheaply, people will hold more of it. This inverse relationship between the interest rate and the amount of money people will want to hold as an asset is shown by D_a in Figure 13-2b.

Total Money Demand, D_m

As shown in Figure 13-2c, the **total demand** for money, D_m, is found by adding the asset demand horizontally to the transactions demand. (The vertical line in Figure 13-2a represents the transactions demand to which Figure 13-2b's asset demand has been added.) The resulting downsloping line in Figure 13-2c represents the total amount of money the public will want to hold for transactions and as an asset at each possible interest rate.

Also note that a change in the nominal GDP— working through the transactions demand for money —will shift the total money demand curve. Specifically, an increase in nominal GDP will mean that the public will want to hold a larger amount of money for transactions purposes and this will shift the total money demand curve to the right. For example, if nominal GDP increases from $300 to $450 billion and we continue to suppose that the average dollar held for transactions is spent three times per year, then the transactions demand line will shift from $100 to $150 billion. Thus the total money demand curve will lie $50 billion further to the right at each possible interest rate. A decline in nominal GDP will shift the total money demand curve to the left.

THE MONEY MARKET

We can combine the demand for money with the supply of money to portray the **money market** and determine the equilibrium rate of interest. In Figure 13-2c we have drawn a vertical line, S_m, to represent the money supply. The money supply is shown as a vertical line because we assume our monetary authorities and financial institutions have provided the economy with some particular *stock* of money, such as the $M1$ total shown in Table 13-1. Just as in a product or resource market (Chapter 3), the intersection of money demand and money supply determines equilibrium price. The "price" in this case is the equilib-

rium interest rate, that is, the price paid for the use of money.

If disequilibrium existed in the money market, how would the money market achieve equilibrium? Consider Figure 13-3, which replicates Figure 13-2c and adds two alternative supply-of-money curves.

1   Shortage   Suppose the supply of money is reduced from $200 billion, S_m, to $150 billion, S_{m1}. Note the quantity of money demanded exceeds the quantity supplied by $50 billion at the previous equilibrium interest rate of 5 percent. People will attempt to make up for this shortage of money by selling some of the financial assets they own (we assume for simplicity that these assets are bonds). But one person's receipt of money through the sale of a bond is another person's loss of money through the purchase of that bond. Overall, there is only $150 billion of money available. The collective attempt to get more money by selling bonds will increase the supply of bonds relative to demand in the bond market and drive down bond prices.

FIGURE 13-3   Restoring equilibrium in the money market
A decrease in the supply of money creates a temporary shortage of money in the money market. People and institutions attempt to gain more money by selling bonds. The supply of bonds therefore increases, which reduces bond prices and raises interest rates. At higher interest rates, people reduce the amount of money they wish to hold. Thus, the amount of money supplied and demanded once again is equal at the higher interest rate. An increase in the supply of money creates a temporary surplus of money, resulting in an increase in the demand for bonds and higher bond prices. Interest rates fall and equilibrium is reestablished in the money market.

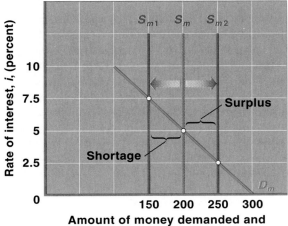

Generalization: *Lower bond prices are associated with higher interest rates* (Last Word, Chapter 5). To clarify this, suppose a bond with no expiration date pays a fixed $50 annual interest and is selling for its face value of $1000. The interest yield on this bond is 5 percent.

$$\frac{\$50}{\$1000} = 5\%$$

Now suppose the price of this bond falls to $667 because of the increased supply of bonds. The $50 fixed annual interest payment will now yield $7\frac{1}{2}$ percent to whomever buys the bond:

$$\frac{\$50}{\$667} = 7\frac{1}{2}\%$$

Because all borrowers must compete by offering to pay lenders interest yields similar to those available on bonds, a higher general interest rate emerges. In Figure 13-3 the interest rate rises from 5 percent at the money supply of $200 billion to $7\frac{1}{2}$ percent when the money supply is $150 billion. This higher interest rate raises the opportunity cost of holding money and reduces the amount of money firms and households want to hold. Specifically, the amount of money demanded declines from $200 billion at the 5 percent interest rate to $150 billion at the $7\frac{1}{2}$ percent interest rate. The money market is back into equilibrium: The quantity of money demanded and supplied are each $150 billion at the $7\frac{1}{2}$ percent interest rate.

2 Surplus An increase in the supply of money from $200 billion, S_m, to $250 billion, S_{m2}, will result in a surplus of $50 billion at the initial 5 percent interest rate. People will try to rid themselves of money by purchasing more bonds. But one person's expenditure of money is another person's receipt of money. The collective attempt to buy more bonds will increase the demand for bonds and pull bond prices upward.

Corollary: *Higher bond prices are associated with lower interest rates.* In terms of our example, the $50 interest payment on a bond now priced at, say, $2000, will yield a bond buyer only $2\frac{1}{2}$ percent:

$$\frac{\$50}{\$2000} = 2\frac{1}{2}\%$$

The point is that interest rates in general will fall as people unsuccessfully attempt to reduce their money holdings below $250 billion by buying bonds. In this case, the interest rate will fall to a new equilibrium at $2\frac{1}{2}$ percent. Because the opportunity cost of holding money now is lower—being liquid is less expensive—consumers and businesses will increase the amount of currency and checkable deposits they are willing to hold from $200 billion to $250 billion. Once again equilibrium in the money market is restored: The quantities of money demanded and supplied are each $250 billion at an interest rate of $2\frac{1}{2}$ percent.

In Chapter 15 we will discover how monetary policy attempts to change the money supply to alter the equilibrium real interest rate. A higher interest rate will reduce investment and consumption spending, decreasing aggregate demand. A lower rate will increase investment and consumption spending, increasing aggregate demand. Either situation ultimately affects the levels of real output, employment, and prices. *(Key Question 8)*

QUICK REVIEW 13-3

■ People hold money for transaction and asset purposes.

■ The total demand for money is the sum of the transaction and asset demands; it graphs as an inverse relationship between the interest rate and the quantity of money demanded.

■ The equilibrium interest rate is determined by money demand and supply; it occurs where people are willing to hold the exact amount of money being supplied by the monetary authorities.

■ Bond prices and interest rates are inversely related.

THE UNITED STATES FINANCIAL SYSTEM

In the past twenty-five years the American financial system has undergone sweeping changes and today the system remains in a state of flux. Early regulatory legislation rigidly defined the kind of business various financial institutions could conduct. For example, commercial banks provided checking accounts and made business and consumer loans. Savings and loan associations accepted savings deposits and provided these savings for mortgage lending. But a combination of competitive pressures, innovation, and deregulation in the recent past has expanded the functions of the various financial institutions and blurred the traditional distinctions between them.

The **Depository Institutions Deregulation and Monetary Control Act** (DIDMCA) of 1980 reduced or eliminated many of the historical distinctions between commercial banks and various thrift institutions. DIDMCA permitted all depository institutions to offer checkable deposits. But in extending the privilege of offering checkable deposits to the thrifts, DIDMCA requires in turn that the thrifts be subject to the same limitations on the creation of checkable deposits that apply to commercial banks. With these observations as an introduction, let's examine the framework of our financial system.

Centralization and Regulation

Although the trend has been toward deregulation of the financial system, considerable centralization and governmental control remain. This centralization and regulation has historical roots. It became painfully apparent rather early in American history that, like it or not, centralization and public control were essential for an efficient banking system.

Congress became increasingly aware of this about the turn of the twentieth century. Decentralized banking fostered the inconvenience and confusion of a heterogeneous currency, monetary mismanagement, and a money supply inappropriate to the needs of the economy. "Too much" money can precipitate dangerous inflationary problems; "too little" money can stunt the economy's growth by hindering the production and exchange of goods and services.

The United States and many foreign countries have learned through bitter experience that a decentralized, unregulated banking system is not likely to provide that particular money supply which is most conducive to the welfare of the economy as a whole.

An unusually acute money panic in 1907 was the straw that broke Congress's back. A National Monetary Commission was established to study the monetary and banking problems of the economy and to outline a course of action for Congress. The result was the Federal Reserve Act of 1913.

The Federal Reserve System

The monetary control system which has developed under the frequently amended Federal Reserve Act and DIDMCA is sketched in Figure 13-4. We must understand the nature and roles of the various segments which compose the banking system and the relationships the parts bear to one another.

Board of Governors   The kingpin of our money and banking system is the **Board of Governors** of the Federal Reserve System ("the Fed"). The seven members of this Board are appointed by the President with the confirmation of the Senate. Terms are long—fourteen years—and staggered so one member is replaced every two years. The intention is to provide the Board with continuity, experienced membership, and autonomy or independence. The Board is staffed by long-term appointment rather than elections as a way to divorce monetary policy from partisan politics.

The Board of Governors supervises and controls the operation of the money and banking system of the nation. The Board chairman is the most powerful central banker in the world. The Board's actions, which are to be in the public interest and designed to promote the general economic welfare, are made effective through certain monetary control techniques which alter the money supply.

Assistance and Advice   Several entities assist the Board of Governors in determining banking and monetary policy. The first is clearly the most important.
1   The **Federal Open Market Committee (FOMC),** made up of the Board plus five of the presidents of the Federal Reserve Banks, sets the System's policy on the purchase and sale of government securities (bills, notes, and bonds) in the open market. The open-market operations are the most significant technique available to the monetary authorities for affecting the money supply (Chapter 15).
2   Three **Advisory Councils** composed of private citizens meet periodically with the Board of Governors to voice their views on banking and monetary policy. The Federal Advisory Council comprises twelve commercial bankers, one selected annually by each of the twelve Federal Reserve Banks. The Thrift Institutions Advisory Council consists of representatives from S&Ls, savings banks, and credit unions. The third advisory group is the thirty-member Consumer Advisory Council, which includes representatives of consumers of financial services and academic and legal specialists in consumer matters. But, as their names indicate, the Councils are purely advisory. They have no policy-making powers and the Board has no obligation to heed their advice.

The Twelve Federal Reserve Banks   The twelve **Federal Reserve Banks** are (1) central banks, (2) quasi-public banks, and (3) bankers' banks.

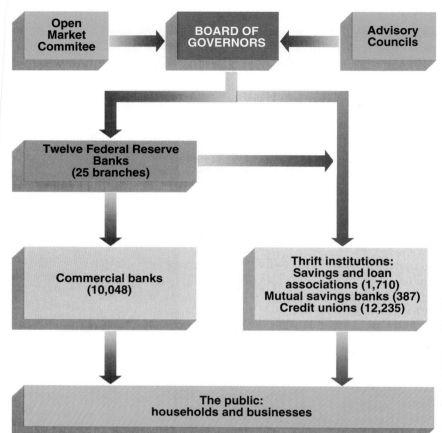

FIGURE 13-4 Framework of the Federal Reserve System and its relationship to the public
With the advice and counsel of the Open Market Committee and three Advisory Councils, the Board of Governors makes the basic policy decisions providing monetary control of our money and banking systems. These decisions are made effective through the twelve Federal Reserve Banks.

1 Central Banks Most nations have one central bank, for example, Britain's Bank of England or Germany's Bundesbank. The United States has twelve separate "central" banks, although their policies are coordinated by the Board of Governors. The twelve Federal Reserve Banks partly reflect our geographic size and economic diversity and the fact that we have a large number of commercial banks. They also are the result of a political compromise between proponents of centralization and advocates of decentralization.

Figure 13-5 locates the twelve Federal Reserve Banks and indicates the district each serves. Through these central banks the basic policy directives of the Board of Governors are made effective. The Federal Reserve Bank of New York City is the most important of these central banks; it's where Open Market Operations are centered (Chapter 15). The development of modern communication and transportation facilities has undoubtedly lessened the geographic need for a system of regional banks.

2 Quasi-Public Banks The twelve Federal Reserve Banks are quasi-governmental banks. They reflect a blend of private ownership and public control. The Federal Reserve Banks are owned by the member banks in their districts. Upon joining the Federal Reserve System, commercial banks are required to purchase shares of stock in the Federal Reserve Bank in their district. But the basic policies which the Federal Reserve Banks pursue are set by a governmental body—the Board of Governors. The central banks of American capitalism are privately owned but governmentally controlled. And the owners control neither the officials of the central banks nor their policies.

To understand Federal Reserve Banks you need to realize they are essentially public institutions. In particular, the Federal Reserve Banks are *not* motivated by profits, as are private enterprises. The policies followed by the central banks are perceived by the Board of Governors to promote the well-being of the economy as a whole. Thus, the activities of the

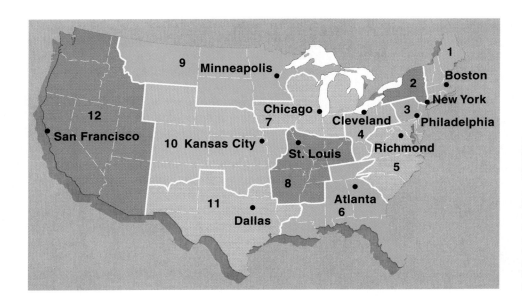

FIGURE 13-5 The twelve Federal Reserve Districts
The Federal Reserve System divides the United States into twelve districts, each of which has one central bank and in some instances one or more branches of the central bank. Hawaii and Alaska are included in the twelfth district. *(Federal Reserve Bulletin.)*

Federal Reserve Banks will frequently be at odds with the profit motive.[5] Also, the Federal Reserve Banks do not compete with commercial banks. With rare exceptions, the Federal Reserve Banks do not deal with the public, but rather, with the government and the commercial banks.

3   Bankers' Banks The Federal Reserve Banks are "bankers' banks." They perform essentially the same functions for depository institutions as depository institutions perform for the public. Just as banks and thrifts accept the deposits of and make loans to the public, so the central banks accept the deposits of and make loans to banks and thrifts. But the Federal Reserve Banks have a third function which banks and thrifts do not perform—they issue currency. Congress has authorized the Federal Reserve Banks to put into circulation Federal Reserve Notes, which constitute the economy's paper money supply.

Commercial Banks The workhorses of the American financial system are its 10,048 **commercial banks.** Roughly two-thirds of these are **state banks,** private banks operating under state charters. One-third received their charters from the Federal government; they are **national banks.** Only two of these national banks rank among the world's largest (see Global Perspective 13-1).

Thrift Institutions Thrift institutions are regulated by agencies which are separate and apart from the Board of Governors and the Federal Reserve Banks. For example, the operation of savings and loan associations is regulated and monitored by the Treasury Department's Office of Thrift Supervision. But, as we have noted, the Depository Institutions Deregulation and Monetary Control Act (DIDMCA) expanded the lending authority of all thrifts, so that S&Ls and mutual saving banks can now make consumer and business loans.

DIDMCA also has subjected S&Ls and other depository institutions to monetary control by the Federal Reserve System. In particular, thrifts now must meet the same reserve requirements as commercial banks, *and* they now can borrow from the Fed. We will find in Chapter 15 that the changing of reserve requirements and the terms under which depository institutions can borrow from the Federal Reserve Banks are two basic ways the Fed's Board of Governors controls the supply of money. In Figure 13-4 we have noted with arrows that the thrift institutions are partially subject to the control of the Board of Governors and the central banks. Decisions concerning monetary policy affect the thrifts along with the commercial banks.

[5]Though it is not their basic goal, the Federal Reserve Banks have actually operated profitably, largely as the result of Treasury debts held by them. Part of the profits has been used to pay dividends to member banks on their holdings of stock; the bulk of the remaining profits has been turned over to the United States Treasury.

GLOBAL PERSPECTIVE 13-1

The world's largest commercial banks (billions of dollars of financial capital)

Japanese firms dominate the list of the world's largest banks, as measured by their financial capital.

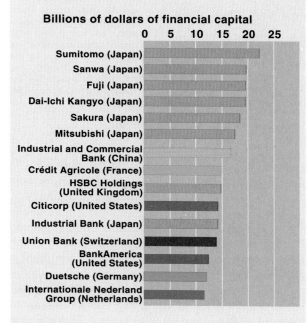

Billions of dollars of financial capital

Source: *The Banker,* as reported in the *Economist,* July 23, 1994, p. 103.

Fed Functions and the Money Supply

The Fed performs a number of functions.[6]

1   Reserves   The Federal Reserve Banks hold deposits, called *reserves,* which are made by banks and thrifts. We will find in Chapter 15 that these deposits are of strategic importance in managing the economy's money supply.

---

[6]For a detailed look at the service functions of the Federal Reserve Banks, see Board of Governors of the Federal Reserve System, *The Federal Reserve System: Purposes and Functions.* 7th ed. (1984), chaps. 1, 2, 7.

2   Check Collection   Another important function of the Fed is to provide the mechanism for the collection of checks. If Sarah writes a check on her Salem bank or thrift to Sam who deposits it in his San Diego bank or thrift, how does the San Diego bank collect the check against the Salem bank? Answer: The Fed handles it in two or three days by adjusting the aforementioned reserves of the two banks.

3   Fiscal Agents   The Federal Reserve Banks act as fiscal agents for the Federal government. The government collects huge sums through taxation, spends equally astronomical amounts, and sells and redeems bonds. The government avails itself of the Fed's facilities in carrying out these activities.

4   Supervision   The Fed supervises the operations of member banks. Periodic bank examinations assess member bank profitability; ascertain that banks perform in accordance with the myriad regulations to which they are subject; and uncover questionable practices or fraud.[7]

5   Control of Money Supply   Finally—and most important of all—the Federal Reserve System has ultimate responsibility for regulating the supply of money. *The major task of the Federal Reserve authorities is to manage the money supply in accordance with the needs of the economy as a whole.* This involves making that amount of money available which is consistent with high and rising levels of output and employment and a relatively constant price level. While all the other functions are of a more-or-less routine or service nature, the goal of correctly managing the money supply entails making basic but unique policy decisions. Chapter 15 discusses Federal Reserve monetary policy and its effectiveness. But before we turn to that subject we must explore how banks create money (Chapter 14).

Federal Reserve Independence

The Fed is essentially an independent institution. It cannot be abolished or rendered ineffective by presi-

---

[7]The Federal Reserve is not alone in the task of supervision. The individual states supervise all banks which they charter. The Comptroller of the Currency supervises all national banks and the Office of Thrift Supervision oversees all thrifts. Finally, the Federal Deposit Insurance Corporation has the power to supervise all banks and thrifts whose deposits it insures.

dential whim, nor can its role and functions be altered by Congress except by specific legislative action. As noted, the long terms of the Board's members are designed to provide them with security and isolate them from political pressures.

The independence of the Fed has been a matter of ongoing controversy.

Opponents of an independent Fed argue it is undemocratic to have a powerful agency whose members are not directly subject to the will of the people. Also, because the legislative and executive branches of government bear ultimate responsibility for the economic well-being of the nation, they should be able to manipulate *all* the policy tools essential to the economy's health. Why should Congress and the administration be responsible for the consequences of policies they do not fully control? Critics cite instances of the Fed using monetary policy to counter the effects of fiscal policy.

Proponents of independence contend that the Fed must be protected from political pressures so that it can effectively control the money supply and maintain price stability (Global Perspective 13-2). They argue it is politically expedient for Congress and the executive branch to invoke expansionary fiscal policies —tax cuts and special-interest spending win votes— and there is thus a need for an independent monetary authority to guard against consequent inflation. Without an acceptable domestically provided medium of exchange, the economy may try to substitute a more stable currency from another nation. Example: Many transactions in Russia and South America now occur in dollars rather than highly unstable rubles or pesos (Last Word). At the extreme, the economy may simply revert to inefficient barter. You will be able to clarify your own position on Federal Reserve independence after we have analyzed the working of monetary policy in Chapter 15.

BANK AND THRIFT FAILURES

Financial innovation and deregulation have enhanced competition among financial institutions and undoubtedly increased economic efficiency. Deregulation and competition, however, have also produced an unpleasant and costly side effect: a rising tide of bank and thrift failures. As we see in Table 13-2, more than 2000 banks and thrifts have failed since 1980. Saving and loan associations (S&Ls) accounted for most of

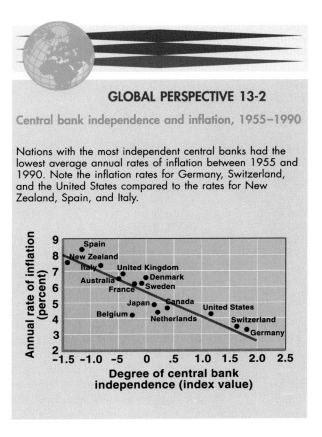

GLOBAL PERSPECTIVE 13-2

Central bank independence and inflation, 1955–1990

Nations with the most independent central banks had the lowest average annual rates of inflation between 1955 and 1990. Note the inflation rates for Germany, Switzerland, and the United States compared to the rates for New Zealand, Spain, and Italy.

the approximately 1000 insolvent thrifts.

We know business failures occur everyday in competitive market economies; they are a means of eliminating persistent and significant economic inefficiencies. Many observers believe there are too many banks and thrifts and that a major consolidation of the financial industry is required. So why are bank and thrift failures of special concern? There are two reasons.

1 Crucial Institutions Banks and thrifts are collectively and in some cases individually instrumental to the monetary system underlying the financial health of the entire economy. These financial institutions hold the money deposits of businesses and households, and as we will discover in Chapter 14, create the major portion of the nation's money supply by making loans to the public. Several of the banks and thrifts which failed in the late 1980s and early 1990s were large financial institutions. Without timely governmental action their collapse might have threatened the regional or even the national economy.

TABLE 13-2 Bank and thrift failures, 1980–1994

Year	Banks	Thrifts
1980	10	3
1981	10	11
1982	10	28
1983	42	71
1984	79	27
1985	124	34
1986	145	49
1987	206	48
1988	221	220
1989	207	327
1990	169	215
1991	124	142
1992	120	59
1993	42	9
1994	13	2

Source: Federal Deposit Insurance Corporation and Resolution Trust Corporation.

2 Bailouts by Taxpayers Bank and thrift failures present a special problem for taxpayers. The Federal government has in effect pledged its full credit to back checking and savings deposits in insured banks and thrifts. For this reason it has agreed to pay a large portion of the losses resulting from bank and thrift failures. The final bill to taxpayers for bailing out the S&L industry may approach $250 billion!

Commercial Bank Difficulties

Although a handful of large commercial banks failed in the early 1980s, bank failures throughout the rest of the 1980s consisted mainly of small institutions operating in agricultural and energy-producing regions. Poor crop prices and declines in oil and natural gas prices resulted in loan defaults and consequent bank failures in regions where the economy depends on these products. Regional recessions and falling local real estate prices in the late 1980s added to the problems facing banks and forced several to close.

The 1990–1991 recession struck a more general blow, producing significant losses in some major banks and causing several financially troubled banks to fail. One was the relatively large Bank of New England. In 1991 the Federal government moved to shore up the bank deposit insurance fund by granting the Federal Deposit Insurance Corporation (FDIC) authority to borrow from the government. Nevertheless, the banking industry remains generally sound, and most large banks have again prospered in recent years.

Savings and Loan Collapse

Of greater concern and magnitude, however, is the collapse of the savings and loan industry. More than one-third of 3000 S&Ls existing in 1987 are no longer in business! The reasons for S&L failures are somewhat complex.

Deregulation and Competition Deregulation of the banking and thrift industry in the early 1980s contributed to the S&L crisis by removing the S&Ls' previously protected role. Before the 1980s, banking laws had carved out a near monopoly for the S&Ls on home mortgage loans. When the government lifted interest-rate ceilings on deposits in banks and thrifts, competition drove up the interest on deposits. Many S&Ls were caught holding fixed-rate, long-term mortgages issued at interest rates far below rates needed to maintain and attract deposits. S&Ls responded to the resulting losses by using the provisions of new thrift legislation to shift their lending toward riskier commercial, consumer, and real estate loans which earned higher interest rates.

Deposit Insurance Banks and thrifts pay premiums to the FDIC to insure the deposits they hold. In 1980 the Federal government increased deposit insurance from $40,000 to $100,000 per account. The main purpose of deposit insurance is to prevent "bank panics" —sudden and massive deposit withdrawals by worried customers. Such bank panics destabilized the economy in the early 1930s and contributed to the Great Depression (Last Word, Chapter 14).

Somewhat ironically, deposit insurance—designed to *add* stability to the financial system—inadvertently contributed to the S&L problem. As with all insurance, deposit insurance creates a **moral hazard problem.** *This problem is that insuring an individual against risk of loss reduces the insured's incentive to prevent the loss from occurring.* In last-chance attempts to salvage their enterprises, financially troubled S&Ls offered extraordinarily high interest rates to attract deposits away from competing institutions. Knowing that accounts of $100,000 or less were fully insured, savers directed their funds to these financially shaky S&Ls. These S&Ls began making risky high-interest loans to attempt to earn interest returns above returns being paid on their expensive, newly acquired funds.

In brief, deposit insurance enabled shaky S&Ls to attract funds by removing the incentive for depositors to direct funds toward healthy financial institutions. It also encouraged S&Ls to gamble with insured deposits, or to incur more risk than otherwise was prudent for their stockholders. If the risky ventures paid off, shareholders would win. If the loans defaulted and caused the S&Ls to collapse, the government insurance fund, not S&L shareholders, would pay for depositors' losses.

Loan Defaults and Fraud Major defaults on many of these risky loans forced several large S&Ls into bankruptcy. Particularly hard hit were savings and loans in Texas and other "oil patch" states. Loan defaults in these areas increased rapidly as oil prices fell and economic conditions worsened. Speculative loans on office buildings and other real estate went into default. Furthermore, the looser banking regulations provided a convenient opportunity for some S&L officers to defraud their failing institutions. As indicated in Table 13-2, more than 1000 S&Ls failed in the late 1980s and early 1990s. Federal investigators have now detected criminal conduct in 40 percent of these failed S&Ls.

The Thrift Bailout

The losses at S&Ls eventually plunged the S&L deposit insurance fund severely into the red, forcing government to face the crisis. In August 1989 the Financial Institutions Reform, Recovery, and Enforcement Act (FIRREA) became law. The new law established the **Resolution Trust Corporation** and directed it to oversee the closing or sale of all failed S&Ls. The total cost to date has been about $200 billion, most of it paid by taxpayers.

The FIRREA also placed deposit insurance for the thrifts and banks under FDIC control. It increased premiums paid by banks and thrifts for deposit insurance and raised the thrift's capital requirements—the percentage of their assets financed by owners—to match requirements of banks. The law also for the first time permitted S&Ls to accept deposits from commercial businesses. Finally, FIRREA directs the Federal Reserve to allow bank holding companies to acquire healthy S&Ls.

Recent Developments and Reform

Sweeping changes continue to transform the financial services industry.

Declining Shares Although banks and thrifts remain the main institutions offering checkable deposits, their share of total financial assets (things of monetary value owned) has significantly fallen. In the 1980s commercial banks saw their market share fall from 37 percent to 27 percent, while the thrifts experienced a decline from 23 percent to 16 percent. Meanwhile, the market share of financial assets held by insurance companies, pension and trust funds, investment companies (mutual funds), and finance companies jumped from 39 to 57 percent. Clearly, American households and businesses are channeling more of their saving and borrowing away from banks and thrifts and toward these other financial institutions.

Globalization The world's financial markets have become increasingly integrated. Major American financial institutions have off-shore operations and foreign financial institutions have operations in the United States. Moreover, investment companies now offer a variety of international stock and bond funds. Financial capital increasingly flows globally in search of the highest risk-adjusted returns.

We must take care not to overstate this extent of international financial integration, however. Studies show that the bulk of investment in the major nations still is financed via domestic saving in those countries. But there is no doubt that money and banking has increasingly become a global activity.

Reform The fast and vast changes in the financial services industry aroused calls for regulatory reform. Legislation has been introduced to strengthen banks and thrifts, promote further competition among financial institutions, and hasten a perceived need for consolidation. Several proposed reforms would remove regulatory restrictions on banks and thrifts, increasing their competitiveness with other financial institutions. For example, in 1994 Congress enacted legislation removing Federal restrictions on interstate banking. Other proposed legislation would allow

LAST WORD

THE GLOBAL GREENBACK

Two-thirds of the $350 billion of American currency is circulating abroad.

Russians use them. So do Argentineans, Brazilians, Poles, Vietnamese, Chinese, and even Cubans. They are American dollars. Like blue jeans, computer software, and movie videos, the dollar has become a major American "export." About $235 billion of American currency is circulating overseas. Russians hold more than $20 billion in American cash, while another $5 billion to $7 billion is circulating freely in Argentina. The Polish government estimates that $5 billion of American dollars is circulating in Poland.

American currency leaves the United States when Americans buy imports, travel in other countries, or send dollars to relatives living abroad. The United States profits when American dollars stay in other countries. It costs the government about 4 cents to print a dollar. For someone abroad to obtain this new dollar, $1 worth of resources, goods, or services must be sold to Americans. These items are Ameri-

can gains. The dollar goes abroad, and assuming it stays there, it presents no claim on American resources or goods or services. Americans in effect make 96 cents on the dollar (= $1 gain in resources, goods, or services *minus* the 4-cent printing cost). It's like American Express selling travelers checks which never get cashed.

banks to own brokerage houses and insurance companies (and vice versa).

There is also a current move to streamline the regulation of banking. In 1994 the Clinton administration proposed creating a single new Federal Banking Commission to assume the regulatory duties currently exercised by the Federal Deposit Insurance Corporation, the Comptroller of the Currency, and the Office of Thrift Supervision.

Apparently the revolution in banking begun a decade or two ago has yet to run its full course. (In Chapter 15 we will examine the implications of these changes for monetary policy.)

CHAPTER SUMMARY

1   Anything that functions as   **a** a medium of exchange, **b** a measure of value, and   **c** a store of value is money.
2   The Federal Reserve System recognizes three "official" definitions of the money supply. $M1$ is currency and checkable deposits; $M2$ is $M1$ plus noncheckable savings

deposits, money market deposit accounts, small (less than $100,000) time deposits, and money market mutual fund balances; and $M3$ is $M2$ plus large ($100,000 or more) time deposits. In our analysis we concentrate on $M1$ since its components are immediately spendable.

Black markets and other illegal activity undoubtedly fuel some of the demand for American cash abroad. The dollar is king in covert trading in diamonds, weapons, and pirated software. Billions of cash dollars are involved in the narcotics trade. But the illegal use of dollars is only a small part of the story. The massive volume of dollars in other nations reflects a global search for monetary stability. Based on past experience, foreign citizens are confident the dollar's purchasing power will remain relatively steady.

Argentina has pegged its peso directly to the dollar, with the central bank issuing new pesos only when it has more dollars, gold, or other convertible reserves on hand. The result has been a remarkable decline in inflation. In Russia and the newly independent countries of eastern Europe, the dollar has retained its buying power while that of domestic currencies has plummeted. As a result, many Russian workers demand to be paid at least partially in dollars. In Brazil, where the inflation rate is more than 1000 percent annually, people have long sought the stability of dollars. In the shopping districts of Beijing and Shanghai, Chinese consumers trade their domestic renminda for dollars. In Bolivia half of all bank accounts are denominated in dollars. There is a thriving "dollar economy" in Vietnam, and even Cuba has partially legalized the use of the American currency. The dollar is the official currency in Panama and Liberia.

There is little risk to the United States in satisfying the world's demand for dollars. If all the dollars came rushing back to the United States at once, the nation's money supply would surge, possibly causing demand-pull inflation. But there is not much chance of that happening. Overall, the global greenback is a positive economic force. It is a reliable medium of exchange, measure of value, and store of value facilitating transactions which might not otherwise occur. Dollar holdings have helped buyers and sellers abroad overcome special monetary problems. The result has been increased output in those countries and thus greater output and income globally.

Source: Based partly on "The Global Greenback," *Business Week,* August 9, 1993, pp. 40–44; and "Dollar Drain: Most U.S. Greenbacks Are Overseas," *Lincoln-Star,* March 15, 1994, p. 3.

3   Money—the debts of government and depository institutions (commercial banks and thrift institutions)—has value because of the goods and services it will command in the market. Maintaining the purchasing power of money depends largely on the government's effectiveness in managing the money supply.

4   The total demand for money consists of the transactions and asset demands for money. The transactions demand varies directly with nominal GDP; the asset demand varies inversely with the interest rate. The money market combines the total demand for money with the money supply to determine the equilibrium interest rate.

5   Disequilibria in the money market are corrected through changes in bond prices. As bond prices change, interest rates move in the opposite direction. At the equilibrium interest rate, bond prices are stable and the amounts of money demanded and supplied are equal.

6   The American banking system is composed of a the Board of Governors of the Federal Reserve System, b the twelve Federal Reserve Banks, and c some 10,048 commercial banks and 14,332 thrift institutions. The Board of Governors is the basic policy-making body for the entire banking system. The directives of the Board are made effective through the twelve Federal Reserve Banks, which are simultaneously a central banks, b quasi-public banks, and c bankers' banks.

7   The major functions of the Federal Reserve System are a to hold the deposits or reserves of commercial banks and other depository institutions, b to provide facilities for the rapid collection of checks, c to act as fiscal agent for the Federal government, d to supervise the operations of member banks, and e to regulate the supply of money in terms of the best interests of the economy as a whole.

8   There were a rising number of bank and thrift failures in the 1980s and early 1990s. The collapse of major S&Ls resulted from deregulation and competition, the moral hazard problem associated with deposit insurance, loan defaults by borrowers, and criminal conduct. Thus far, the government bailout of the failed S&Ls has cost taxpayers about $200 billion.

9   Banks and thrifts recently have lost considerable market share to insurance companies, pension and trust funds, investment companies (mutual funds), and finance companies. Financial markets have increasingly become globalized. Major reform legislation has been proposed and passed relating to banks and thrifts.

TERMS AND CONCEPTS

medium of exchange	savings and loan	legal tender	Federal Open Market
measure of value	associations	fiat money	Committee
store of value	credit unions	transactions, asset,	Advisory Councils
*M*1, *M*2, *M*3	near-monies	and total demand for	Federal Reserve
token money	noncheckable savings	money	Banks
intrinsic value	accounts	money market	commercial banks
Federal Reserve Notes	MMDA (money market	Depository Institutions	state banks
checkable deposits	deposit account)	Deregulation and	national banks
thrift or savings	time deposits	Monetary Control	moral hazard problem
institutions	MMMF (money market	Act	Resolution Trust
mutual savings banks	mutual fund)	Board of Governors	Corporation

QUESTIONS AND STUDY SUGGESTIONS

1 Describe how rapid inflation can undermine money's ability to perform its three basic functions.

2 What are the disadvantages of commodity money? What are the advantages of **a** paper money and **b** check money compared with commodity money?

3 "Money is only a bit of paper or a bit of metal that gives its owner a lawful claim to so much bread or beer or diamonds or motorcars or what not. We cannot eat money, nor drink money, nor wear money. It is the goods that money can buy that are being divided up when money is divided up."[8] Evaluate and explain.

4 Fully evaluate and explain the following statements:
   a "The invention of money is one of the great achievements of the human race, for without it the enrichment that comes from broadening trade would have been impossible."

   b "Money is whatever society says it is."

   c "When prices of everything are going up, it is not because everything is worth more, but because the dollar is worth less."

   d "The difficult questions concerning paper [money] are . . . not about its economy, convenience or ready circulation but about the amount of the paper which can be wisely issued or created, and the possibilities of violent convulsions when it gets beyond bounds."[9]

   e "In most modern industrial economies of the world the debts of government and of commercial banks are used as money."

[8]George Bernard Shaw, *The Intelligent Woman's Guide to Socialism and Capitalism* (New York: Brentano's, Inc., 1982), p. 9. Used by permission of the Public Trustee and the Society of Authors.

[9]F. W. Taussig, *Principles of Economics,* 4th ed. (New York: The Macmillan Company, 1946), pp. 247–248.

5 *Key Question* *What items constitute the M1 money supply? What is the most important component of the M1 money supply? Why is the face value of a coin greater than its intrinsic value? Distinguish between M2 and M3. What are near-monies? Of what significance are they? What arguments can you make for including savings deposits in a definition of money?*

6 What "backs" the money supply in the United States? What determines the value of money? Who is responsible for maintaining the value of money? Why is it important to be able to alter the money supply? What is meant by **a** "sound money" and **b** a "52-cent dollar"?

7 *Key Question* *Suppose the price level and value of the dollar in year 1 are 1.0 and $1.00, respectively. If the price level rises to 1.25 in year 2, what is the new value of the dollar? If instead the price level had fallen to .50, what would have been the value of the dollar? What generalization can you draw from your answers.*

8 *Key Question* *What is the basic determinant of **a** the transactions demand and **b** the asset demand for money? Explain how these two demands might be combined graphically to determine total money demand. How is the equilibrium interest rate determined in the money market? How might **a** the expanded use of credit cards, **b** a shortening of worker pay periods, and **c** an increase in nominal GDP affect the transactions demand for money and the equilibrium interest rate?*

9 Suppose that a bond having no expiration date has a face value of $10,000 and annually pays a fixed amount of interest of $800. Compute and enter in the space provided either the interest rate which a bond buyer could secure at each of the bond prices listed or the bond price at each of the interest rates shown. What generalization can be drawn from the completed table?

Bond price	Interest rate %
$ 8,000	
	8.9
$10,000	
$11,000	
	6.2

10 Assume the money market is initially in equilibrium and that the money supply is now increased. Explain the adjustments toward a new equilibrium interest rate. Will bond prices be higher at the new equilibrium rate of interest? What effects would you expect that interest-rate change to have on the levels of output, employment, and prices? Answer the same questions for a decrease in the money supply.

11 How did the Depository Institutions Deregulation and Monetary Control Act of 1980 change the American banking system?

12 What is the major responsibility of the Board of Governors? Discuss the major characteristics of the Federal Reserve Banks. Of what significance is the fact that the Federal Reserve Banks are quasi-public? Do you think the Fed should be an independent institution?

13 What are the two basic functions of commercial banks and thrift institutions? State and briefly discuss the major functions of the Federal Reserve System.

14 Explain the "moral hazard problem" associated with insurance and relate this problem to the collapse of major savings and loan associations during the late 1980s and early 1990s.

15 (Last Word)   Over the years the Federal Reserve Banks have printed about $235 billion more in currency than American households, businesses, and financial institutions now hold. Where is this "missing" money? Why is it there?

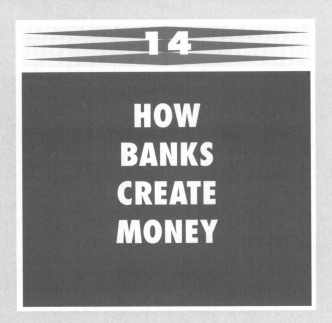

14

HOW BANKS CREATE MONEY

If you visit Washington, D.C., you might enjoy touring the United States Bureau of Engraving and Printing. There, each day more than $25 million of Federal Reserve Notes roll off the printing presses in large sheets. After machines cut the sheets into individual bills, employees ship them to twelve Federal Reserve Banks for distribution.

We are all fascinated by large amounts of money. Nevertheless, we use checkable deposits of commercial banks and thrift institutions, not currency, for most of our transactions. The amount of these deposits far exceeds the amount of currency banks hold. Who creates these checkable deposits? Loan officers at commercial banks. Their tools? Computers and computer printers. Sounds like something *60 Minutes* and a congressional committee should investigate. But in truth, banking authorities are well aware banks and thrifts create checking deposit money. In fact, the Federal Reserve *relies* on these institutions to create a large part of the nation's money supply.

Because the bulk of all checkable deposits are the demand deposits of commercial banks, this chapter will explain how they can *create* demand-deposit money. Specifically, we explain and compare how money can be created by (1) a *single* commercial bank which is part of a multibank system, and by (2) the commercial bank *system* as a whole. Keep in mind throughout our discussion that thrift institutions also provide checkable deposits. Therefore, when we say "commercial bank" we also mean "depository institution." And "checkable deposit" can be substituted for "demand deposit."

THE BALANCE SHEET OF A COMMERCIAL BANK

An understanding of the basic items on a bank's balance sheet, and how various transactions change these items, will give us the tools for analyzing the workings of our monetary and banking systems.

A **balance sheet** is a statement of assets and claims summarizing the financial position of a firm—in this case a commercial bank—at some point in time. Every balance sheet must balance, because each and every known *asset,* being something of economic value, will be claimed by someone. Can you think of an asset—something of monetary value—which no one claims? A balance sheet balances because the value of assets equals the amount of claims against those assets. The claims shown on a balance sheet are divided into two groups: the claims of the owners of a firm against the firm's assets, called *net worth,* and the claims of nonowners, called *liabilities.* Thus, a balance sheet balances because

Assets = liabilities + net worth

A balance-sheet approach to our study of the money-creating ability of commercial banks is valuable in two respects.
1 A bank's balance sheet provides a convenient point of reference from which we can introduce new terms and concepts in an orderly manner.
2 The use of balance sheets allows us to quantify certain concepts and relationships which would defy comprehension if discussed in verbal terms alone.

PROLOGUE: THE GOLDSMITHS

Using balance sheets, let's see how a **fractional reserve system of banking** operates. The characteristics and working of such a system can be better understood by considering a bit of economic history.

When the ancients began to use gold in making transactions, it became apparent that it was both unsafe and inconvenient for consumers and merchants to carry gold and have it weighed and assessed for purity every time a transaction was negotiated. It therefore became commonplace to deposit one's gold with goldsmiths whose vaults or strongrooms could be used for a fee. Upon receiving a gold deposit, the goldsmith issued a receipt to the depositor. Soon goods were traded for the goldsmiths' receipts and the receipts became the first kind of paper money.

At this point the goldsmiths—embryonic bankers—used a 100 percent reserve system; their circulating paper money receipts were fully backed by gold. But, given the public's acceptance of the goldsmiths' receipts as paper money, the goldsmiths became aware that the gold they stored was rarely redeemed. In fact, they found themselves in charge of "going concerns" where the amount of gold deposited with them in any week or month was likely to exceed the amount withdrawn.

Then some adroit goldsmith hit on the idea that paper money could be issued *in excess of* the amount of gold held. Goldsmiths would put these additional "receipts" redeemable in gold—paper money—into circulation by making interest-earning loans to merchants, producers, and consumers. Borrowers were willing to accept loans in the form of gold receipts because they were accepted as a medium of exchange.

This was the beginning of the *fractional reserve system* of banking. If, for example, our ingenious goldsmith made loans equal to the amount of gold stored, then the total value of paper money in circulation would be twice the value of the gold. Reserves would be 50 percent of outstanding paper money.

Fractional reserve banking—the system we have today—has two significant characteristics.

1 Money Creation and Reserves Banks in such a system can *create money.* When our goldsmith made loans by giving borrowers paper money which was not fully backed by gold reserves, money was being created. The quantity of such money the goldsmith could create would depend on the amount of reserves deemed prudent to keep on hand. The smaller the amount of reserves deemed necessary, the larger the amount of paper money the goldsmith could create. Although gold is no longer used to "back" our money supply (Chapter 13), bank lending (money creation) today is constrained by the amount of reserves banks feel obligated, or are required, to keep.

2 Bank Panics and Regulation Banks which operate on the basis of fractional reserves are vulnerable to bank "panics" or "runs." Our goldsmith who issued paper money equal to twice the value of gold reserves could not convert all that paper money into gold in the event all holders of that paper money appeared simultaneously demanding gold. In fact, many Europeans and American banks were once ruined by this unfortunate circumstance. However, a bank panic is highly unlikely *if* the banker's reserve and lending policies are prudent. Indeed, a basic reason why banking systems are highly regulated industries is to prevent bank runs. This is also the reason why the United States has in place a system of deposit insurance (Chapter 13).

A SINGLE COMMERCIAL BANK

We now will explore how money can be created by a single bank which is part of a multibank banking system. What accounts make up a commercial bank's balance sheet? How does a single commercial bank create money? If it can create money, can it destroy it? What factors govern how a bank creates money?

Formation of a Commercial Bank

To answer these questions we must understand what's on a commercial bank's balance sheet and how certain transactions affect it. We start with the organization of a local commercial bank.

Transaction 1: The Birth of a Bank   Suppose farsighted citizens of the metropolis of Wahoo, Nebraska (yes, there is such a place), decide their town needs a new commercial bank to provide banking services for that growing community. Assuming these enterprising individuals can secure a state or national charter for their bank, they then turn to the task of selling, say, $250,000 worth of capital stock (equity shares) to buyers, both in and out of the community. These financing efforts meet with success and the Merchants and Farmers Bank of Wahoo now exists —at least on paper. How does the Wahoo bank's balance statement appear at its birth?

The new owners of the bank have sold $250,000 worth of shares of stock in the bank—some to themselves, some to other people. As a result, the bank now has $250,000 in cash on hand and $250,000 worth of capital stock outstanding. The cash is an asset to the bank. Cash held by a bank is sometimes called **vault cash** or *till money*. The outstanding shares of stock constitute an equal amount of claims which the owners have against the bank's assets. The shares of stock are the net worth of the bank, though they are assets from the viewpoint of those who possess these shares. The bank's balance sheet reads:

BIRTH OF A BANK
BALANCE SHEET 1: WAHOO BANK

Assets		Liabilities and net worth	
Cash	$250,000	Capital stock	$250,000

Transaction 2: Becoming a Going Concern   The board of directors must now get their newborn bank off the drawing board and make it a reality. First, property and equipment must be acquired. Suppose the directors, confident of the success of their venture, purchase a building for $220,000 and $20,000 worth of office equipment. This simple transaction changes

the composition of the bank's assets. The bank now has $240,000 less in cash and $240,000 of new property assets. Using blue to denote those accounts affected by each transaction, we find that the bank's balance sheet at the end of transaction 2 appears as follows:

ACQUIRING PROPERTY AND EQUIPMENT
BALANCE SHEET 2: WAHOO BANK

Assets		Liabilities and net worth	
Cash	$ 10,000	Capital stock	$250,000
Property	240,000		

Note the balance sheet still balances, as it must.

Transaction 3: Accepting Deposits   Commercial banks have two basic functions: to accept deposits of money and to make loans. Now that our bank is operating, suppose that the citizens and businesses of Wahoo decide to deposit $100,000 in the Merchants and Farmers Bank. What happens to the bank's balance sheet?

The bank receives cash, which we know is an asset to the bank. Suppose this money is placed in the bank as demand deposits (checking accounts), rather than time deposits or savings accounts. These newly created demand deposits constitute claims which depositors have against the assets of the Wahoo bank. Thus the depositing of money in the bank creates a new liability account—demand deposits. The bank's balance sheet now looks like this:

ACCEPTING DEPOSITS
BALANCE SHEET 3: WAHOO BANK

Assets		Liabilities and net worth	
Cash	$110,000	Demand deposits	$100,000
Property	240,000	Capital stock	250,000

Although there is no direct change in the total supply of money, a change in the composition of the economy's money supply has occurred as a result of transaction 3. Bank money, or demand deposits, have *increased* by $100,000 and currency held by the nonbank public has *decreased* by $100,000. Currency held by a bank, you will recall, is *not* part of the economy's money supply.

It is apparent that a withdrawal of cash will reduce the bank's demand-deposit liabilities and its holdings of cash by the amount of the withdrawal. This, too, changes the composition, but not the total supply, of money.

Transaction 4: Depositing Reserves in a Federal Reserve Bank

All commercial banks and thrift institutions which provide checkable deposits must keep a **legal reserve** or, **required reserve.** This legal or required reserve is *an amount of funds equal to a specified percentage of its own deposit liabilities which a member bank must keep on deposit with the Federal Reserve Bank in its district or as vault cash.* To simplify we suppose our bank keeps its legal reserve *entirely* as deposits in the Federal Reserve Bank of its district. But remember that vault cash is counted as reserves and real-world banks keep a significant portion of their reserves in their vaults.

The "specified percentage" of its deposit liabilities which the commercial bank must keep as reserves is known as the **reserve ratio**—a ratio between the size of the required reserves the commercial bank must keep and the commercial bank's own outstanding deposit liabilities.

$$\text{Reserve ratio} = \frac{\text{commercial bank's required reserves}}{\text{commercial bank's demand-deposit liabilities}}$$

If the reserve ratio were $\frac{1}{10}$, or 10 percent, our bank, having accepted $100,000 in deposits from the public, would have to keep $10,000 as reserves. If the ratio were $\frac{1}{5}$, or 20 percent, $20,000 of reserves would be required. If $\frac{1}{2}$, or 50 percent, $50,000 would be required.

The Board of Governors has the authority to establish and vary the reserve ratio within limits legislated by Congress. The reserve ratio limits which now prevail are shown in Table 14-1. A 3 percent reserve is required on the first $54.0 million of demand or other checkable deposits held by an institution. The reserve requirement on an institution's checkable deposits over $54.0 million is currently 10 percent, although the Board of Governors can vary this between 8 and 14 percent. Currently, no reserves are required against noncheckable nonpersonal (business) savings and time deposits. This ratio can be varied between 0 and 9 percent. Also, after consultation with appropriate congressional committees, the Federal Reserve may impose reserve requirements for 180 days in excess of those specified in Table 14-1.

TABLE 14-1   Reserve requirements of depository institutions

Type of deposit	Current requirement	Statutory limits
Checkable deposits		
$0–54.0 million	3%	3%
Over $54.0 million	10	8–14
Noncheckable nonpersonal savings and time deposits	0	0–9

Source: Federal Reserve. Data are for 1995.

To simplify our discussion suppose the reserve ratio for commercial banks is $\frac{1}{5}$, or 20 percent, and that this requirement applies only to demand deposits. Although it's really too high, 20 percent is convenient to use in computations. And, because we are concerned with checkable (spendable) demand deposits, we ignore reserves on noncheckable savings and time deposits. The point is that reserve requirements are *fractional,* meaning they are less than 100 percent. This consideration is vital in our analysis of the lending ability of the banking system.

The Wahoo bank will just be meeting the required 20 percent ratio between its deposit in the Federal Reserve Bank and its own deposit liabilities by depositing $20,000 in the Federal Reserve Bank. We will use *reserves* in referring to those funds commercial banks deposit in the Federal Reserve Banks to distinguish them from the public's *deposits* in commercial banks.

But suppose the Wahoo bank anticipates that its holdings of the public's demand deposits will grow in the future. Thus, instead of sending just the minimum amount, $20,000, they send an extra $90,000, for a total of $110,000. In so doing, the bank will avoid the inconvenience of sending additional reserves to the Federal Reserve Bank each time its own demand-deposit liabilities increase. And, as we will see, it is on the basis of extra reserves that banks can lend and thereby earn interest income.

Actually, the bank would not deposit *all* its cash in the Federal Reserve Bank. However, because (1) banks as a rule hold vault cash only in the amount of $1\frac{1}{2}$ or 2 percent of their total assets, and (2) vault cash can be counted as reserves, we assume all the bank's cash is deposited in the Federal Reserve Bank and therefore constitutes the commercial bank's total reserves. We don't need to bother adding two assets— "cash" and "deposits in the Federal Reserve Bank"— to determine "reserves."

After depositing $110,000 of reserves at the Fed, the balance sheet of Merchants and Farmers Bank becomes:

DEPOSITS AT THE FED

BALANCE SHEET 4: WAHOO BANK

Assets		Liabilities and net worth	
Cash	$ 0	Demand	
Reserves	110,000	deposits	$100,000
Property	240,000	Capital stock	250,000

There are three things about this latest transaction you must understand.

1 Excess Reserves Some terminology: The amount by which the bank's **actual reserves** exceed its **required reserves** is the bank's **excess reserves.**

$$\frac{\text{Actual}}{\text{reserves}} - \frac{\text{required}}{\text{reserves}} = \frac{\text{excess}}{\text{reserves}}$$

In this case,

Actual reserves	$110,000
Required reserves	−20,000
Excess reserves	$90,000

The only reliable way of computing excess reserves is to multiply the bank's demand-deposit liabilities by the reserve ratio to obtain required reserves ($100,000 times 20 percent equals $20,000), then to subtract required reserves from the actual reserves listed on the asset side of the bank's balance sheet.

To understand this, you should compute excess reserves for the bank's balance sheet as it stands at the end of transaction 4, assuming that the reserve ratio is (1) 10 percent, (2) $33\frac{1}{3}$ percent, and (3) 50 percent.

Because the ability of a commercial bank to make loans depends on the existence of excess reserves, this concept is crucial in seeing how money is created by the banking system.

2 Control What is the rationale underlying the requirement that member banks deposit a reserve in the Federal Reserve Bank of their district? You might think the basic purpose of reserves is to enhance the liquidity of a bank and protect commercial bank depositors from losses. Reserves would constitute a ready source of funds from which commercial banks can meet large and unexpected cash withdrawals by depositors.

But this reasoning breaks down under scrutiny. Although historically reserves were seen as a source of liquidity and therefore protection for depositors, a bank's *legal,* or required, reserves are not great enough to meet sudden, massive cash withdrawals. If the banker's nightmare should materialize—everyone with demand deposits appearing at once to demand these deposits in cash—the legal reserves held as vault cash or at the Federal Reserve bank would be insufficient. The banker simply could not meet this "bank panic." Because reserves are fractional, demand deposits may be ten to twenty times greater than a bank's required reserves.

Commercial bank deposits must be protected by other means. We saw in Chapter 13 that periodic bank examinations are one way for promoting prudent commercial banking practices. And banking laws restrict banks as to the kinds of assets they may acquire; for example, banks are generally prohibited from buying common stocks. Furthermore, insurance funds administered by the Federal Deposit Insurance Corporation (FDIC) exist to insure individual deposits in banks and thrifts up to $100,000.

If the purpose of reserves is not to provide for commercial bank liquidity, what is their function? *Control* is the basic answer. Legal reserves permit the Board of Governors to influence the lending ability of commercial banks. Chapter 15 will examine how the Board of Governors can invoke certain policies which either increase or decrease commercial bank reserves and affect the ability of banks to grant credit. The objective is to prevent banks from *over*extending or *under*extending bank credit. To the degree that these policies are successful in influencing the volume of commercial bank credit, the Board of Governors can help the economy avoid the business fluctuations which lead to bank runs, bank failures, and collapse of the monetary system. In this indirect way—controlling commercial bank credit and thereby stabilizing the economy—reserves function to protect depositors, not as a source of liquidity. Another function of reserves is to facilitate the collection or "clearing" of checks. *(Key Question 2)*

3 Asset and Liability Note there is an apparent accounting matter which transaction 4 entails. Specifically, *the reserve created in transaction 4 is an asset to the depositing commercial bank but a liability to the Federal Reserve Bank receiving it.* To the Wahoo bank

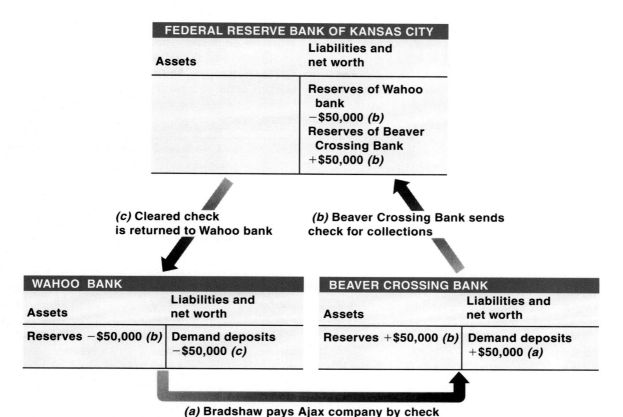

FIGURE 14-1   The collection of a check through a Federal Reserve Bank
The bank against which a check is drawn and cleared loses both reserves and deposits; the bank in which the check is deposited acquires reserves and deposits.

the reserve is an asset; it is a claim this bank has against assets of another institution—the Federal Reserve Bank. To the Federal Reserve Bank this reserve is a liability, a claim which another institution—the Wahoo bank—has against it. Just as the demand deposit you get by depositing money in a commercial bank is an asset to you and a liability to that bank, so the deposit or reserve which a commercial bank establishes by depositing money in a bankers' bank is an asset to that bank and a liability to the Federal Reserve Bank. Understand this clearly before proceeding to transaction 5.

Transaction 5: A Check is Drawn Against the Bank
Suppose Clem Bradshaw, a Wahoo farmer who deposited a substantial portion of the $100,000 in demand deposits which the Wahoo bank received in transaction 3, buys $50,000 worth of farm machinery from the Ajax Farm Implement Company of Beaver

Crossing, Nebraska. Bradshaw pays for this machinery by writing a $50,000 check, against his deposit in the Wahoo bank, to the Ajax company. We need to know (1) how this check is collected or cleared, and (2) the effect the collection of the check has on the balance sheets of the banks involved in the transaction.

To learn this, we must consider the Wahoo bank (Bradshaw's bank), the Beaver Crossing bank (the Ajax Company's bank), and the Federal Reserve Bank of Kansas City.[1] For simplicity, we deal only with changes which occur in those specific accounts affected by this transaction.

We trace this transaction in three steps, keying the steps by letters to Figure 14-1.

---

[1]Actually, the Omaha branch of the Federal Reserve Bank of Kansas City would handle the process of collecting this check.

a Bradshaw gives his $50,000 check, drawn against the Wahoo bank, to the Ajax company. Ajax deposits the check in its account with the Beaver Crossing bank. The Beaver Crossing bank increases Ajax's demand deposit by $50,000 when it deposits the check. Ajax is now paid off. Bradshaw is pleased with his new machinery.

b Now the Beaver Crossing bank has Bradshaw's check. This check is simply a claim against the assets of the Wahoo bank. The Beaver Crossing bank will collect this claim by sending this check (along with checks drawn on other banks) to the Federal Reserve Bank of Kansas City. Here a clerk will clear, or collect, this check for the Beaver Crossing bank by *increasing* Beaver's reserve in the Federal Reserve Bank by $50,000 and by *decreasing* Wahoo's reserve by a like amount. The check is collected merely by making bookkeeping notations that the Wahoo's claim against the Federal Reserve Bank has been reduced by $50,000 and Beaver's claim increased accordingly. Note these changes on the balance sheets in Figure 14-1.

c Finally, the Federal Reserve Bank sends the cleared check back to the Wahoo bank, and for the first time the Wahoo bank discovers that one of its depositors has drawn a check for $50,000 against his demand deposit. Accordingly, the Wahoo bank reduces Bradshaw's demand deposit by $50,000 and recognizes that the collection of this check has entailed a $50,000 decline in its reserves at the Federal Reserve Bank. Note that the balance statements of all three banks will balance. The Wahoo bank will have reduced both its assets and liabilities by $50,000. The Beaver Crossing bank will have $50,000 more in reserves and in demand deposits. Ownership of reserves at the Federal Reserve Bank will have changed—Wahoo owning $50,000 less, Beaver owning $50,000 more—but total reserves will stay the same.

Whenever a check is drawn against a bank and deposited in another bank, collection of that check will reduce both reserves and demand (checkable) deposits of the bank on which the check is drawn. Conversely, if a bank receives a check drawn on another bank, the bank receiving the check will, in the process of collecting it, have its reserves and deposits *increased* by the amount of the check. In our example, the Wahoo bank loses $50,000 in both reserves and deposits to the Beaver Crossing bank. But there is no loss of reserves or deposits for the banking system as a whole. What one bank loses another bank gains.

Bringing all the other assets and liabilities back into the picture, the Wahoo bank's balance sheet looks like this at the end of transaction 5:

CLEARING A CHECK

BALANCE SHEET 5: WAHOO BANK

Assets		Liabilities and net worth	
Reserves	$ 60,000	Demand deposits	$ 50,000
Property	240,000	Capital stock	250,000

You should verify that with a 20 percent reserve requirement, the bank's *excess* reserves now stand at $50,000.

Transaction 5 is reversible. If a check drawn against another bank is deposited in the Wahoo bank, the Wahoo bank will receive both reserves and deposits equal to the amount of the check as it is collected.

QUICK REVIEW 14-1

■ When a bank accepts deposits of cash, the composition of the money supply is changed, but the total supply of money is not directly altered.

■ Commercial banks and other depository institutions are required to keep legal reserve deposits, or required reserves, equal to a specified percentage of their own deposit liabilities as cash or on deposit with the Federal Reserve Bank of their district.

■ The amount by which a bank's actual reserves exceed its required reserves is called "excess reserves."

■ A bank which has a check drawn and collected against it will lose to the recipient bank both reserves and deposits equal to the value of the check.

Money-Creating Transactions of a Commercial Bank

The next three transactions are crucial because they explain (1) how a commercial bank can literally create money by making loans, (2) how money is destroyed when loans are repaid, and (3) how banks create money by purchasing government bonds from the public.

Transaction 6: Granting a Loan   In addition to accepting deposits, commercial banks grant loans to borrowers. What effect does lending by a commercial bank have on its balance sheet?

Suppose Grisley Meat Packing Company of Wahoo decides it's time to expand its facilities. Suppose, too, the company needs exactly $50,000—which just happens to be equal to the Wahoo bank's excess reserves—to finance this project.

Grisley approaches the Wahoo bank and requests a loan for this amount. The Wahoo bank knows the Grisley company's fine reputation and financial soundness and is convinced of its ability to repay the loan. So the loan is granted. The president of Grisley hands a promissory note—a high-class IOU—to the Wahoo bank. Grisley wants the convenience and safety of paying its obligations by checks. So, instead of receiving a bushelbasket full of currency from the bank, Grisley will get a $50,000 increase in its demand deposit in the Wahoo bank. From the Wahoo bank's standpoint it has acquired an interest-earning asset (the promissory note) and has created demand deposits (a liability) to "pay" for this asset.

Grisley has swapped an IOU for the right to draw an additional $50,000 worth of checks against its demand deposit in the Wahoo bank. Both parties are pleased. The Wahoo bank now possesses a new asset —an interest-bearing promissory note which it files under the general heading of "Loans." Grisley, sporting a fattened demand deposit, can now expand operations.

At the moment the loan is negotiated, the Wahoo bank's position is shown by balance sheet 6a.

WHEN A LOAN IS NEGOTIATED			
BALANCE SHEET 6a: WAHOO BANK			
Assets		**Liabilities and net worth**	
Reserves	$ 60,000	Demand	
Loans	50,000	deposits	$100,000
Property	240,000	Capital stock	250,000

All this looks simple enough. But a close examination of the Wahoo bank's balance statement will reveal a startling fact: *When a bank makes loans, it cre-*

ates money. The president of the Grisley company went to the bank with something which is *not* money —her IOU—and walked out with something that *is* money—a demand deposit.

Contrast transaction 6a with transaction 3 where demand deposits were created, but only by currency going out of circulation. There was a change in the *composition* of the money supply in that situation but no change in the total *supply* of money. But when banks lend, they create demand (checkable) deposits which *are* money. By extending credit the Wahoo bank has "monetized" an IOU. Grisley and the Wahoo bank have created and then swapped claims. The claim created by Grisley and given to the bank is not money; an individual's IOU is not generally acceptable as a medium of exchange. But the claim created by the bank and given to Grisley is money; checks drawn against a demand deposit are acceptable as a medium of exchange.

The bulk of the money we use in our economy is created through the extension of credit by commercial banks. This checking account money may be thought of as "debts" of commercial banks and thrift institutions. Checks are bank "debts" in the sense that they are claims banks and thrifts promise to pay "on demand."

But there are forces limiting the ability of a commercial bank to create demand deposits—"bank money"—by lending. The Wahoo bank can expect the newly created demand deposit of $50,000 to be a very active account. Grisley would not borrow $50,000 at, say, 7, 10, or 12 percent interest for the sheer joy of knowing funds were available if needed.

Assume that Grisley awards a $50,000 contract to the Quickbuck Construction Company of Omaha. Quickbuck, true to its name, completes the expansion job and is paid with a check for $50,000 drawn by Grisley against its demand deposit in the Wahoo bank. Quickbuck, with headquarters in Omaha, does *not* deposit this check in the Wahoo bank but instead deposits it in the Fourth National Bank of Omaha. Fourth National now has a $50,000 claim against the Wahoo bank. This check is collected in the manner described in transaction 5. As a result, the Wahoo bank *loses* both reserves and deposits equal to the amount of the check; Fourth National *acquires* $50,000 of reserves and deposits.

In summary, assuming a check is drawn by the borrower for the entire amount of the loan ($50,000) and given to a firm which deposits it in another bank, the Wahoo bank's balance sheet will read as follows *after the check has been cleared against it.*

AFTER A CHECK IS DRAWN ON THE LOAN

BALANCE SHEET 6b: WAHOO BANK

Assets		Liabilities and net worth	
Reserves	$ 10,000	Demand	
Loans	50,000	deposits	$ 50,000
Property	240,000	Capital stock	250,000

After the check has been collected, the Wahoo bank barely meets the legal reserve ratio of 20 percent (= $50,000 ÷ $10,000). The bank has *no excess reserves.* This poses a question: Could the Wahoo bank have lent more than $50,000—an amount greater than its excess reserves—and still have met the 20 percent reserve requirement if a check for the full amount of the loan were cleared against it? The answer is "No."

Here's why. Suppose the Wahoo bank had loaned $55,000 to the Grisley company. Collection of the check against the Wahoo bank would have lowered its reserves to $5,000 (= $60,000 − $55,000) and deposits would once again stand at $50,000 (= $105,000 − $55,000). The ratio of actual reserves to deposits would now be $5,000/$50,000, or only 10 percent. The Wahoo bank could thus *not* have lent $55,000.

By experimenting with other amounts over $50,000, you will find that the maximum amount the Wahoo bank could lend at the outset of transaction 6 is $50,000. This amount is identical with the amount of excess reserves the bank had available when the loan was negotiated. *A single commercial bank in a multibank banking system can lend only an amount equal to its initial preloan excess reserves.* When it lends, it faces the likelihood that checks for the entire amount of the loan will be drawn and cleared against the lending bank. A lending bank can anticipate the loss of reserves to other banks equal to the amount it lends.[2]

Transaction 7: Repaying a Loan If commercial banks create demand deposits—money—when they

make loans, is money destroyed when loans are repaid? Yes. Using balance sheets 6b and 7, we see what happens when Grisley repays the $50,000 it borrowed.

To simplify, we (1) suppose the loan is repaid not in installments but in one lump sum two years after the date of negotiation, and (2) ignore interest charges on the loan. Grisley will write a check for $50,000 against its demand deposit, which we assume was $50,000 before the Grisley loan was negotiated. As a result, the Wahoo bank's demand-deposit liabilities decline by $50,000; Grisley has given up $50,000 worth of its claim against the bank's assets. In turn, the bank will surrender Grisley's IOU which it has been holding these many months. The bank and the company have reswapped claims. But the claim given up by Grisley is money; the claim it is repurchasing —its IOU—is not. The supply of money has therefore been reduced by $50,000; that amount of demand deposits has been destroyed, unaccompanied by an increase in the money supply elsewhere in the economy.

The Grisley company's IOU has been "demonetized" as shown in balance sheet 7. The Wahoo bank's demand deposits and loans have each returned to zero. The decline in demand deposits increases the bank's holdings of excess reserves (= $10,000); this provides the basis for new loans to be made. *(Key Questions 4 and 8)*

REPAYING A LOAN

BALANCE SHEET 7: WAHOO BANK

Assets		Liabilities and net worth	
Reserves	$ 10,000	Demand	
Loans	0	deposits	$ 0
Property	240,000	Capital stock	250,000

In the unlikely event Grisley repays the loan with cash, the money supply will still decline by $50,000. In this case, Grisley would repurchase its IOU by handing over $50,000 in cash to the bank. Loan balances decline in the asset column by $50,000 and cash increases by $50,000. Remember, we exclude currency held by banks from the money supply because to include such cash would be double counting; it is apparent that this constitutes a $50,000 reduction in the supply of money.

Transaction 8: Buying Government Securities When a commercial bank buys government bonds

---

[2]Qualification: If some of the checks written on a loan are redeposited back in the lending bank by their recipients, then that bank will be able to lend an amount somewhat greater than its initial excess reserves.

from the public, the effect is substantially the same as lending. New money is created.

Assume that the Wahoo bank's balance sheet initially stands as it did at the end of transaction 5. Now suppose that, instead of making a $50,000 loan, the bank buys $50,000 of government securities from a securities dealer. The bank receives the interest-bearing bonds which appear on its balance statement as the asset "Securities" and gives the dealer an increase in its demand-deposit account. The Wahoo bank's balance sheet would appear as follows:

BUYING GOVERNMENT SECURITIES			
BALANCE SHEET 8: WAHOO BANK			
Assets		Liabilities and net worth	
Reserves	$ 60,000	Demand	
Securities	50,000	deposits	$100,000
Property	240,000	Capital stock	250,000

Demand deposits, that is, the supply of money, have been increased by $50,000, as in transaction 6. *Commercial bank bond purchases from the public increase the supply of money in the same way as does lending to the public.* The bank accepts government bonds (which are not money) and gives the securities dealer an increase in its demand deposits (which is money).

Of course, when the securities dealer draws and clears a check for $50,000 against the Wahoo bank, the bank will lose both reserves and deposits in that amount and therefore will just be meeting the legal reserve requirement. Its balance sheet will now read precisely as in 6b except that "Securities" is substituted for "Loans" on the asset side.

Finally, the selling of government bonds to the public by a commercial bank—like the repayment of a loan—will reduce the supply of money. The securities buyer will pay by check and both "Securities" and "Demand deposits" (the latter being money) will decline by the amount of the sale.

Profits, Liquidity, and the Federal Funds Market

The asset items on a commercial bank's balance sheet reflect the banker's pursuit of two conflicting goals.

1 Profits One goal is profits. Commercial banks, like any other business, seek profits. This is why the

bank makes loans and buys securities—the two major earning assets of commercial banks.

2 Liquidity The other goal is safety. For a bank, safety lies in liquidity—specifically such liquid assets as cash and excess reserves. Banks must be on guard for depositors' transforming their demand deposits into cash. Similarly, more checks may be cleared against a bank than are cleared in its favor, causing a net outflow of reserves. Bankers thus seek a balance between prudence and profits. The compromise is between earning assets and highly liquid assets.

An interesting way banks can partly reconcile the goals of profits and liquidity is to lend temporary excess reserves held at the Federal Reserve banks to other commercial banks. Normal day-to-day flows of funds to banks rarely leave all banks with their exact levels of legally required reserves. Furthermore, funds held at the Federal Reserve banks are highly liquid, but they do not draw interest. Banks therefore lend these excess reserves to other banks on an overnight basis as a way to earn additional interest without sacrificing long-term liquidity. Banks which borrow in this *Federal funds market*—the market for immediately available reserve balances at the Federal Reserve—do so because they are temporarily short of required reserves. The interest rate paid on these overnight loans is called the **Federal funds rate.**

In Figure 14-1, we would show an overnight loan of reserves from the Beaver Crossing bank to the Wahoo bank as a decrease in reserves at the Beaver Crossing bank and an increase in reserves at the Wahoo bank. Ownership of reserves at the Federal Reserve Bank of Kansas City will have changed, but total reserves there are not affected.

QUICK REVIEW 14-2

■ Banks create money when they make loans; money vanishes when bank loans are repaid.

■ New money is created when banks buy government bonds from the public; money disappears when banks sell government bonds to the public.

■ Banks balance profitability and safety in determining their mix of earning assets and highly liquid assets.

■ Banks borrow and lend temporary excess reserves on an overnight basis in the Federal funds market; the interest rate on these loans is the Federal funds rate.

THE BANKING SYSTEM: MULTIPLE-DEPOSIT EXPANSION

Thus far we have seen that a single bank in a banking system can lend one dollar for each dollar of excess reserves. The situation is different for all commercial banks taken as a group. We will find that *the commercial banking system can lend, that is, can create money, by a multiple of its excess reserves. This multiple lending is accomplished even though each bank in the system can only lend "dollar for dollar" with its excess reserves.*

The immediate task is to uncover how these seemingly paradoxical conclusions come about. To do this, we must keep our analysis uncluttered. Therefore, we will rely on three simplifying assumptions.

1 The reserve ratio for all commercial banks is 20 percent.

2 Initially all banks are exactly meeting this 20 percent reserve requirement. No excess reserves exist; all banks are "loaned up" (or "loaned out").

3 If any bank can increase its loans as a result of acquiring excess reserves, an amount equal to these excess reserves will be loaned to one borrower, who will write a check for the entire amount of the loan and give it to someone else, who deposits the check in another bank. This third assumption means the worse thing possible happens to any lending bank—a check for the entire amount of the loan is drawn and cleared against it in favor of another bank.

The Banking System's Lending Potential

Suppose a junkyard owner finds a $100 bill while dismantling a car which has been on the lot for years. He deposits the $100 in bank A, which adds the $100 to its reserves. Since we are recording only *changes* in the balance sheets of the various commercial banks, bank A's balance sheet will now appear as shown by the entries designated as (a_1):

MULTIPLE DEPOSIT EXPANSION PROCESS

BALANCE SHEET: COMMERCIAL BANK A

Assets		Liabilities and net worth	
Reserves	$+100 (a_1) $- 80$ (a_3)	Demand deposits	$+100 (a_1) $+ 80$ (a_2) $- 80$ (a_3)
Loans	$+ 80$ (a_2)		

Recall from earlier transaction 3 that this $100 deposit of currency does *not* alter the money supply. While $100 of demand-deposit money comes into being, it is offset by the $100 of currency no longer in the hands of the public (the junkyard owner). What *has* happened is that bank A has acquired *excess reserves* of $80. Of the newly acquired $100 in reserves, 20 percent, or $20, must be earmarked to offset the new $100 deposit and the remaining $80 is excess reserves. Remembering that a single commercial bank can lend only an amount equal to its excess reserves, we conclude that bank A can lend a maximum of $80. When a loan for this amount is negotiated, bank A's loans will increase by $80, and the borrower will get an $80 demand deposit. We add these figures—designated as (a_2)—to bank A's balance sheet.

But now we use our third assumption: The borrower draws a check for $80—the entire amount of the loan—and gives it to someone who deposits it in another bank, bank B. As we saw in transaction 6, bank A *loses* both reserves and deposits equal to the amount of the loan (a_3). The net result of these transactions is that bank A's reserves now stand at $20 (= $100 − $80), loans at $80, and demand deposits are at $100 (= $100 + $80 − $80). When the dust has settled, bank A is just meeting the 20 percent reserve ratio.

Recalling transaction 5, bank B *acquires* both the reserves and the deposits which bank A has lost. Bank B's balance sheet looks like this (b_1):

MULTIPLE DEPOSIT EXPANSION PROCESS

BALANCE SHEET: COMMERCIAL BANK B

Assets		Liabilities and net worth	
Reserves	$+80 (b_1) -64 (b_3)	Demand deposits	$+80 (b_1) $+64$ (b_2) -64 (b_3)
Loans	$+64$ (b_2)		

When the check is drawn and cleared, bank A *loses* $80 in reserves and deposits and bank B *gains* $80 in reserves and deposits. But 20 percent, or $16, of bank B's new reserves must be kept as required reserves against the new $80 in demand deposits. This means that bank B has $64 (= $80 − $16) in excess reserves. It can therefore lend $64 (b_2). When the borrower draws a check for the entire amount and deposits it in bank C, the reserves and deposits of bank B both fall by the $64 (b_3). As a result of these transactions, bank B's reserves now stand at $16 (= $80 − $64), loans at $64, and demand deposits at $80 (= $80 + $64 − $64). After all this, bank B is just meeting the 20 percent reserve requirement.

We are off and running again. Bank C has acquired the $64 in reserves and deposits lost by bank B. Its balance statement appears as follows (c_1):

MULTIPLE DEPOSIT EXPANSION PROCESS		
BALANCE SHEET: COMMERCIAL BANK C		
Assets	Liabilities and net worth	
Reserves $+64.00 ($c_1$) −51.20 ($c_3$) Loans +51.20 ($c_2$)	Demand deposits	$+64.00 ($c_1$) +51.20 ($c_2$) −51.20 ($c_3$)

Exactly 20 percent, or $12.80, of this new reserve will be required, the remaining $51.20 being excess reserves. Hence, bank C can safely lend a maximum of $51.20. Suppose it does ($c_2$). And suppose the borrower draws a check for the entire amount and gives it to someone who deposits it in another bank (c_3).

Bank D—the bank receiving the $51.20 in reserves and deposits—now notes these changes on its balance sheet (d_1):

MULTIPLE DEPOSIT EXPANSION PROCESS		
BALANCE SHEET: COMMERCIAL BANK D		
Assets	Liabilities and net worth	
Reserves $+51.20 ($d_1$) −40.96 ($d_3$) Loans +40.96 ($d_2$)	Demand deposits	$+51.20 ($d_1$) +40.96 ($d_2$) −40.96 ($d_3$)

It can now lend $40.96 ($d_2$). The borrower draws a check for the full amount and deposits it in another bank (d_3).

Now, if we wanted to be particularly obnoxious, we could go ahead with this procedure by bringing banks E, F, G, H, . . . , N into the picture. We merely suggest that you check through computations for banks E, F, and G, to ensure you understand the procedure.

This analysis is summarized in Table 14-2. Data for banks E through N are supplied so you may check

TABLE 14-2   Expansion of the money supply by the commercial banking system

Bank	(1) Acquired reserves and deposits	(2) Required reserves	(3) Excess reserves, or (1) − (2)	(4) Amount which the bank can lend; new money created = (3)
Bank A	$100.00 ($a_1$)	$20.00	$80.00	$ 80.00 (a_2)
Bank B	80.00 (a_3, b_1)	16.00	64.00	64.00 (b_2)
Bank C	64.00 (b_3, c_1)	12.80	51.20	51.20 (c_2)
Bank D	51.20 (c_3, d_1)	10.24	40.96	40.96 (d_2)
Bank E	40.96	8.19	32.77	32.77
Bank F	32.77	6.55	26.22	26.22
Bank G	26.22	5.24	20.98	20.98
Bank H	20.98	4.20	16.78	16.78
Bank I	16.78	3.36	13.42	13.42
Bank J	13.42	2.68	10.74	10.74
Bank K	10.74	2.15	8.59	8.59
Bank L	8.59	1.72	6.87	6.87
Bank M	6.87	1.37	5.50	5.50
Bank N	5.50	1.10	4.40	4.40
Other banks	21.97	4.40	17.57	17.57
Total amount of money created (sum of the amounts in column 4)				$400.00

your computations. Our conclusion is startling: On the basis of the $80 in excess reserves (acquired by the banking system when someone deposited $100 of currency in bank A), the *entire commercial banking system* is able to lend $400, the sum of the amounts in column 4. The banking system can lend by a multiple of 5 when the reserve ratio is 20 percent. Yet each single bank in the banking system is lending only an amount equal to its excess reserves. How do we explain this? Why can the *banking system* lend by a multiple of its excess reserves, but *each individual bank* can only lend "dollar for dollar" with its excess reserves?

The answer is that reserves lost by a single bank are not lost to the banking system as a whole. The reserves lost by bank A are acquired by bank B. Those lost by B are gained by C. C loses to D, D to E, E to F, and so forth. Although reserves can be, and are, lost by *individual* banks in the banking system, there can be no loss of reserves for the banking *system* as a whole.

An individual bank can only safely lend an amount equal to its excess reserves, but the commercial banking system can lend by a multiple of its excess reserves. This contrast, incidentally, is an illustration of why it is imperative that we keep the fallacy of composition (Chapter 1) firmly in mind. Commercial banks *as a group* can create money by lending in a manner much different from that of the *individual banks* in that system.

The Monetary Multiplier

This *demand-deposit multiplier,* or **monetary multiplier,** is similar to the income multiplier of Chapter 10. The income multiplier occurs because the expenditures of one household are received as income by another; the deposit multiplier occurs because the reserves and deposits lost by one bank are received by another bank. And, just as the size of the income multiplier is determined by the reciprocal of the MPS (the leakage into saving which occurs at each round of spending), so the deposit multiplier m is the reciprocal of the required reserve ratio R (the leakage into required reserves which occurs at each step in the lending process). In short,

$$\text{Monetary multiplier} = \frac{1}{\text{required reserve ratio}}$$

or, using symbols,

$$m = \frac{1}{R}$$

In this formula, m is the maximum amount of new demand-deposit money which can be created by a *single dollar* of excess reserves, given the value of R. By multiplying the excess reserves by the monetary multiplier, we determine the maximum amount of new demand-deposit money, D, which can be created by the banking system on the basis of any amount of excess reserves, E.

$$\begin{matrix}\text{Maximum} \\ \text{demand-deposit} \\ \text{expansion}\end{matrix} = \begin{matrix}\text{excess} \\ \text{reserves}\end{matrix} \times \begin{matrix}\text{monetary} \\ \text{multiplier}\end{matrix}$$

or, more simply,

$$D = E \times m$$

In our example of Table 14-2:

$$\$400 = \$80 \times 5$$

But keep in mind that, despite the similar rationale underlying the income and deposit multipliers, the former has to do with changes in income and the latter with changes in the supply of money.

Diagrammatic Summary Figure 14-2 depicts the final outcome from our example of a multiple-deposit expansion of the money supply. The initial deposit of $100 of currency into the bank (lower right box) creates new reserves of an equal amount (upper box). Given our assumption of a 20 percent reserve ratio, however, only $20 of currency reserves are needed to "back up" this $100 demand deposit. The excess reserves of $80 permit the creation of $400 of new demand deposits via the making of loans, indicating a monetary multiplier of 5. The $100 of new reserves supports a total supply of money of $500, comprised of the $100 of initial demand deposit plus $400 of demand deposits created through lending.

You might experiment with the following two teasers to test your understanding of multiple credit expansion by the banking system:

1 Rework the analysis in Table 14-2 (at least three or four steps of it) assuming the reserve ratio is 10 percent. What is the maximum amount of money the banking system could create upon acquiring $100 in new reserves and deposits? (No, the answer is not $800!)
2 Explain how a banking system which is "loaned up" and faced with a 20 percent reserve ratio might

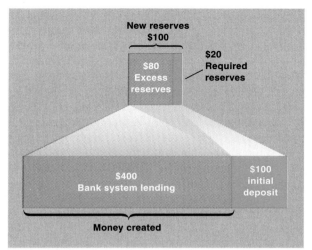

FIGURE 14-2   The outcome of the money expansion process
A deposit of $100 of currency into a checking account creates an initial demand deposit of $100. If the reserve ratio is 20 percent, only $20 of reserves are legally required to support the $100 demand deposit. The $80 of excess reserves allows the banking system to create $400 of demand deposits through making loans. The $100 of reserves supports a total of $500 of money ($100 + $400).

be forced to *reduce* its outstanding loans by $400 as a result of a $100 cash withdrawal from a demand deposit which forces the bank to draw down its reserves by $100. *(Key Question 13)*

Some Modifications

There are complications which might modify the preciseness of our analysis.

Other Leakages   Aside from the **leakage** of required reserves at each step of the lending process, two other leakages of money from commercial banks might occur, dampening the money-creating potential of the banking system.

1   Currency Drains   A borrower may request that part of his or her loan be paid in cash. Or the recipient of a check drawn by a borrower may present it at the bank to be redeemed partially or wholly in currency rather than added to the borrower's account. If the person who borrowed the $80 from bank A in our illustration asked for $16 of it in cash and the remaining $64 as a demand deposit, bank B would receive only $64 in new reserves (of which only $51.20

would be excess) rather than $80 (of which $64 was excess). This decline in excess reserves reduces the lending potential of the banking system accordingly. In fact, if the first borrower had taken the entire $80 in cash and if this currency remained in circulation, the multiple expansion process would have stopped then and there. But the convenience and safety of demand deposits make this unlikely.

2   Excess Reserves   Our analysis of the commercial banking system's ability to expand the money supply by lending is based on the supposition that commercial banks are willing to meet precisely the legal reserve requirement. To the extent that bankers hold excess reserves, the overall credit expansion potential of the banking system will be reduced. For example, suppose bank A, upon receiving $100 in new cash, decided to add $25, rather than the legal minimum of $20, to its reserves. Then it would lend only $75, rather than $80, and the monetary multiplier would be diminished accordingly.[3] In fact, the amount of excess reserves which banks have held in recent years has been very minimal. The explanation is very simple: Excess reserves earn no interest income for a bank; loans and investments do. Hence, our assumption that a bank will lend an amount equal to its excess reserves is reasonable and generally accurate.

QUICK REVIEW 14-3

■ Whereas a single bank in a multibank system can safely lend (create money) by an amount equal to its excess reserves, the banking system can lend (create money) by a multiple of its excess reserves.

■ The monetary multiplier is the reciprocal of the required reserve ratio and indicates the multiple by which the banking system can expand the money supply for each dollar of excess reserves.

■ Currency drains and a desire by banks to hold excess reserves may reduce the size of the monetary multiplier.

---

[3]Specifically, in our $m = 1/R$ monetary multiplier, we now add to R, the required reserve ratio, the additional excess reserves which bankers choose to keep. For example, if banks want to hold additional excess reserves equal to 5 percent of any newly acquired demand deposits, then the denominator becomes .25 (equal to the .20 reserve ratio plus the .05 addition to excess reserves). The monetary multiplier is reduced from 5 to 1/.25, or 4.

Need for Monetary Control

Our illustration of the banking system's ability to create money rests on the assumption that commercial banks are willing to create money by lending and that households and businesses are willing to borrow. In reality the willingness of banks to lend on the basis of excess reserves varies cyclically, and therein lies the rationale for governmental control of the money supply to promote economic stability.

When prosperity reigns banks will expand credit to the maximum of their ability. Loans are interest-earning assets and in good economic times there is little fear of borrowers' defaulting. But, as we will find in Chapters 15 and 16, the money supply has an effect on aggregate demand. By lending and thereby creating money to the maximum of their ability during prosperity, commercial banks may contribute to excessive aggregate demand and to inflation.

If recession appears on the economic horizon, bankers may hastily withdraw their invitations to borrow, seeking the safety of liquidity (excess reserves) even if it means sacrificing potential interest income. Bankers may fear large-scale withdrawal of deposits by a panicky public and simultaneously doubt the ability of borrowers to repay. It is not too surprising that some years in the Great Depression of the 1930s, banks had considerable excess reserves but lending was at a low ebb. The point is that during recession banks may decrease the money supply by cutting back on lending. This contraction of the money supply will restrain aggregate demand and intensify the recession. A rapid shrinkage of the money supply contributed to the Great Depression of the 1930s, as this chapter's Last Word indicates.

We can conclude that profit-motivated bankers can be expected to vary the money supply to reinforce cyclical fluctuations. For this reason the Federal Reserve System has at its disposal certain policy instruments to control the money supply in an anticyclical, rather than procyclical, fashion. We turn to an analysis of these policy tools in Chapter 15.

CHAPTER SUMMARY

1 The operation of a commercial bank can be understood through its balance sheet, where assets are equal to liabilities plus net worth.

2 Modern banking systems are based on fractional reserves.

3 Commercial banks are required to keep a legal reserve deposit in a Federal Reserve Bank or as vault cash. This reserve is equal to a specified percentage of the commercial bank's demand-deposit liabilities. Excess reserves are equal to actual reserves minus required reserves.

4 Banks lose both reserves and demand deposits when checks are drawn against them.

5 Commercial banks create money—create demand deposits, or bank money—when they make loans. The creation of checkable deposits by bank lending is the most important source of money in our economy. Money is destroyed when loans are repaid.

6 The ability of a single commercial bank to create money by lending depends on the size of its *excess* reserves. Generally speaking, a commercial bank can lend only an amount equal to the amount of its excess reserves. Money creation is thus limited because, in all likelihood, checks drawn by borrowers will be deposited in other banks, causing a loss of reserves and deposits to the lending bank equal to the amount it has loaned.

7 Rather than making loans, banks may decide to use excess reserves to buy bonds from the public. In doing so, banks merely credit the demand-deposit accounts of the bond sellers, thus creating demand-deposit money. Money vanishes when banks sell bonds to the public because bond buyers must draw down their demand-deposit balances to pay for the bonds.

8 Banks earn interest by making loans and purchasing bonds while they maintain liquidity by holding cash and excess reserves. Banks having temporary excess reserves often lend them overnight to banks which are short of required reserves. The interest rate paid on loans in this Federal funds market is called the Federal funds rate.

9 The commercial banking system as a whole can lend by a multiple of its excess reserves because the banking *system* cannot lose reserves, although individual banks can lose reserves to other banks in the system.

10 The multiple by which the banking system can lend on the basis of each dollar of excess reserves is the reciprocal of the reserve ratio. This multiple credit expansion process is reversible.

11 The fact that profit-seeking banks would alter the money supply in a procyclical fashion underlies the need for the Federal Reserve System to control the money supply.

LAST WORD

THE BANK PANICS OF 1930–1933

A series of bank panics in 1930–1933 resulted in a multiple contraction of the money supply.

In the early months of the Great Depression several financially weak banks became insolvent. As word spread that customers of these banks had lost their uninsured deposits, a general concern arose that something similar could happen at other banks. Depositors therefore began to withdraw funds—"cash out" their accounts—at local banks, most of which had been financially healthy. In economic terminology, the initial failures of weak banks created negative externalities or spillover costs (Chapter 5) affecting healthy banks. More than 9000 banks failed within three years.

The massive conversion of checkable deposits to currency during 1930–1933 reduced the nation's money supply. The outflow of currency from banks meant the loss of bank reserves and a multiple decline of loans and checkable deposits. Also, banks "scrambled for liquidity" to meet anticipated further withdrawals by calling in loans and selling government securities to the public. Both actions enabled banks to increase their excess reserves—reserves *not* lent out. The lost deposits (reserves) and the scramble for liquidity collapsed the money supply through a reversal of the money expansion process shown in Table 14-2.

In 1933 President Franklin Roosevelt ended the bank panics by declaring a "national bank holiday,"

which closed all banks for a week and resulted in the federally insured deposit program. Meanwhile, the nation's money supply had plummeted by 25 percent, the largest such drop in American history. This decline in the money supply contributed to the nation's worst and longest depression.

Today, a multiple contraction of the money supply of the 1930–1933 magnitude is unthinkable. FDIC insurance has kept individual bank failures from becoming general bank panics. Also, while the Federal Reserve stood idly by during the bank panics of 1930–1933, today it would take immediate actions to maintain the banking system's reserves and the nation's money supply. These actions are the subject matter of Chapter 15.

TERMS AND CONCEPTS

balance sheet	vault cash	reserve ratio	Federal funds rate
fractional reserve system of banking	legal or required reserves	actual, required, and excess reserves	monetary multiplier leakage

QUESTIONS AND STUDY SUGGESTIONS

1   Why must a balance sheet always balance? What are the major assets and claims on a commercial bank's balance sheet?

2   *Key Question   Why are commercial banks required to have reserves? Explain why reserves are assets to commercial banks but liabilities to the Federal Reserve Banks. What are excess reserves? How do you calculate the amount of excess reserves held by a bank? What is their significance?*

3 "Whenever currency is deposited in a commercial bank, cash goes out of circulation and, as a result, the supply of money is reduced." Do you agree? Explain.

4 *Key Question* *"When a commercial bank makes loans, it creates money; when loans are repaid, money is destroyed." Explain.*

5 Explain why a single commercial bank can safely lend only an amount equal to its excess reserves but the commercial banking system can lend by a multiple of its excess reserves. Why is the multiple by which the banking system can lend equal to the reciprocal of its reserve ratio?

6 Assume that Jones deposits $500 in currency into her demand deposit in the First National Bank. A half-hour later Smith negotiates a loan for $750 at this bank. By how much and in what direction has the money supply changed? Explain.

7 Suppose the National Bank of Commerce has excess reserves of $8,000 and outstanding demand deposits of $150,000. If the reserve ratio is 20 percent, what is the size of the bank's actual reserves?

8 *Key Question* *Suppose the Continental Bank has the following simplified balance sheet. The reserve ratio is 20 percent.*

Assets		(1)	(2)	Liabilities and net worth		(1)	(2)
Reserves	$22,000	___	___	Demand			
Securities	38,000	___	___	deposits	$100,000	___	___
Loans	40,000	___	___				

a *What is the maximum amount of new loans which this bank can make? Show in column 1 how the bank's balance sheet will appear after the bank has loaned this additional amount.*

b *By how much has the supply of money changed? Explain.*

c *How will the bank's balance sheet appear after checks drawn for the entire amount of the new loans have been cleared against this bank? Show this new balance sheet in column 2.*

d *Answer questions a, b, and c on the assumption that the reserve ration is 15 percent.*

9 The Third National Bank has reserves of $20,000 and demand deposits of $100,000. The reserve ratio is 20 percent. Households deposit $5,000 in currency into the bank which is added to reserves. How much excess reserves does the bank now have?

10 Suppose again that the Third National Bank has reserves of $20,000 and demand deposits of $100,000. The re-serve ratio is 20 percent. The bank now sells $5,000 in securities to the Federal Reserve Bank in its district, receiving a $5,000 increase in reserves in return. How much excess reserves does the bank now have? Why does your answer differ (yes, it does!) from the answer to question 9?

11 Suppose a bank discovers its reserves will temporarily fall slightly short of those legally required. How might it remedy this situation through the Federal funds market? Next, assume the bank finds that its reserves will be substantially and permanently deficient. What remedy is available to this bank? Hint: Recall your answer to question 4.

12 Suppose that Bob withdraws $100 of cash from his checking account at Security Bank and uses it to buy a camera from Joe, who deposits the $100 in his checking account in Serenity Bank. Assuming a reserve ratio of 10 percent and no initial excess reserves, determine the extent to which   **a** Security Bank must reduce its loans and demand deposits because of the cash withdrawal and   **b** Serenity Bank can safely increase its loans and demand deposits because of the cash deposit. Have the cash withdrawal and deposit changed the money supply?

13 *Key Question* *Suppose the simplified consolidated balance sheet shown below is for the commercial banking system. All figures are in billions. The reserve ratio is 25 percent.*

Assets		(1)	Liabilities and net worth		(1)
Reserves	$ 52	___	Demand		
Securities	48	___	deposits	$200	___
Loans	100	___			

a *How much excess reserves does the commercial banking system have? What is the maximum amount the banking system might lend? Show in column 1 how the consolidated balance sheet would look after this amount has been lent. What is the monetary multiplier?*

b *Answer question 13a assuming that the reserve ratio is 20 percent. Explain the resulting difference in the lending ability of the commercial banking system. What is the new monetary multiplier?*

14 What are banking "leakages"? How might they affect the money-creating potential of the banking system? Be specific.

15 Explain why there is a need for the Federal Reserve System to control the money supply.

16 (Last Word)   Explain how the bank panics of 1930–1933 produced a decline in the nation's money supply. Why are such panics highly unlikely today?

15

THE FEDERAL RESERVE BANKS AND MONETARY POLICY

We focused on the money-creating ability of individual banks and the commercial banking system in Chapter 14. Our discussion ended on a disturbing note: Unregulated commercial banking might contribute to cyclical fluctuations in business activity. Commercial banks will find it profitable to expand the supply of money during periods of demand-pull inflation and to restrict the money supply in seeking liquidity during depression.

In this chapter we will see how monetary authorities try to reverse the procyclical tendencies of the commercial banking system through a variety of control techniques. Their attempts are reflected in headlines such as: "Bank Reserve Requirement Eased—First Change Since 1983," "Fed Aggressively Selling Bonds," "Fed Increases Discount Rate to 3 Percent." What stories are these and similar headlines telling?

As in Chapter 14, our discussion is in terms of commercial banks because of their role in creating demand-deposit money. However, throughout our discussion the term "depository institution" can be substituted for "commercial bank" and "checkable deposits" for "demand deposits."

In this chapter, we first discuss the objectives of monetary policy and the roles of participating institutions. Next, we survey the balance sheet of the Federal Reserve Banks; through these central banks monetary policy is implemented. Third, techniques of monetary control are analyzed in detail. What are the key instruments of monetary control and how do they work? Fourth, the cause-effect chain of monetary policy is detailed and the effectiveness of monetary policy is evaluated. Finally, we present a brief recapitulation of mainstream macroeconomic theory and policy.

GOALS OF MONETARY POLICY

Before analyzing the techniques of monetary policy, we must first understand the objectives of monetary policy and identify the institutions responsible for formulating and implementing it.

Certain key points made in Chapter 13 need reemphasis here. The Board of Governors of the Federal Reserve System (the "Fed") is responsible for supervising and controlling the operation of our monetary and banking systems. This Board formulates basic policies which the banking system follows. Because it is a public body, the decisions of the Board of Governors are made in what it perceives to be the public interest. The twelve Federal Reserve Banks—our central banks—implement the policy decisions of the Board. As quasi-public banks, the Federal Reserve Banks are not guided by the profit motive, but rather pursue measures the Board of Governors recommend.

However, to say that the Board follows policies which "promote the public interest" is not enough. We must pinpoint the goal of monetary policy. *The fundamental objective of* **monetary policy** *is to assist the economy in achieving a full-employment, noninflationary level of total output.* Monetary policy consists of altering the economy's money supply to stabilize aggregate output, employment, and the price level. It entails increasing the money supply during a recession to stimulate spending and restricting it during inflation to constrain spending.

The Federal Reserve Board alters the size of the nation's money supply by manipulating the size of excess reserves held by commercial banks. Excess reserves, you will recall, are critical to the money-creating ability of the banking system. Once we see how the Federal Reserve controls excess reserves and the money supply, we will explain how changes in the stock of money affect interest rates and aggregate demand.

CONSOLIDATED BALANCE SHEET OF THE FEDERAL RESERVE BANKS

Because monetary policy is implemented by the Federal Reserve Banks, we need to consider the nature of the balance sheet of these banks. Some of their assets and liabilities differ from those found on the balance sheet of a commercial bank. Table 15-1 is a simplified consolidated balance sheet showing the pertinent assets and liabilities of the twelve Federal Reserve Banks as of September 30, 1994.

Assets

The two Fed assets we need to consider are:

1   Securities   Securities shown are government bonds which Federal Reserve Banks have purchased. These bonds consist largely of debt instruments such as Treasury bills (short-term securities) and Trea-

sury bonds (long-term securities) issued by the Federal government to finance past and present budget deficits. These securities are part of the public or national debt (Chapter 18). Some of these bonds may have been purchased directly from the Treasury, but most are bought in the open market from commercial banks or the public. Although these bonds are an important source of income to the Federal Reserve Banks, they are not bought and sold purposely for income. Rather, they are bought and sold primarily to influence the size of commercial bank reserves and therefore their ability to create money by lending.

2   Loans to Commercial Banks   For reasons we will discuss soon, commercial banks occasionally borrow from Federal Reserve Banks. The IOUs which commercial banks give to these "bankers' banks" in negotiating loans are listed as loans to commercial banks. From the Federal Reserve Banks' point of view, these IOUs are assets—they are claims against commercial banks which have borrowed from them. To commercial banks, these IOUs are liabilities. By borrowing in this way, commercial banks obtain increases in their reserves in exchange for IOUs.

Liabilities

On the liability side we find three items.

1   Reserves of Commercial Banks   We are familiar with this account. It is an asset from the viewpoint of member banks but a liability to Federal Reserve Banks.

2   Treasury Deposits   Just as businesses and private individuals find it convenient and desirable to pay their obligations by check, so does the United States Treasury. It keeps deposits in the Federal Reserve Banks and draws checks on them to pay its obligations. To the Treasury such deposits are assets; to the Federal Reserve Banks they are liabilities. The Treasury creates and replenishes these deposits by depositing tax receipts and money borrowed from the public or the banks through the sale of bonds.

3   Federal Reserve Notes   Our paper money supply consists of Federal Reserve Notes issued by the Federal Reserve Banks. In circulation, this paper money constitutes claims against assets of Federal

TABLE 15-1   Twelve Federal Reserve Banks' consolidated balance sheet, September 30, 1994 *(in millions)*

Assets		Liabilities and net worth	
Securities	$355,150	Reserves of commercial banks	$ 30,054
Loans to commercial banks	504	Treasury deposits	6,848
All other assets	61,194	Federal Reserve Notes (outstanding)	363,509
		All other liabilities and net worth	16,437
Total	$416,848	Total	$416,848

Source: *Federal Reserve Bulletin,* December 1994.

Reserve Banks and are therefore treated by them as liabilities. Just as your own IOU is neither an asset nor a liability to you when it is in your own possession, so Federal Reserve Notes resting in the vaults of Federal Reserve Banks are neither an asset nor a liability. Only notes in circulation are liabilities to the bankers' banks. These notes, which come into circulation through commercial banks, are not part of the money supply until they are in the hands of the public.

TOOLS OF MONETARY POLICY

With this cursory look at the Federal Reserve Banks' balance sheet, we can now explore how the Board of Governors of the Federal Reserve System can influence the money-creating abilities of the commercial banking system. There are three instruments of monetary control which the Board uses to influence commercial bank reserves:

1   Open-market operations
2   Changing the reserve ratio
3   Changing the discount rate

Open-Market Operations

Open-market operations are the most important way the Fed controls the money supply. **Open-market operations** refers to the *buying and selling of government bonds by the Federal Reserve Banks in the open market*—that is, the buying and selling of bonds from or to commercial banks and the general public. How do these purchases and sales of government securities affect the excess reserves of commercial banks?

Buying Securities   Suppose the Board of Governors orders the Federal Reserve Banks to buy government bonds in the open market. These securities can be purchased from commercial banks and the public. In either case the overall effect is the same—commercial bank reserves are increased.

From Commercial Banks   Let's trace the process Federal Reserve Banks use when buying government bonds *from commercial banks.*

a   Commercial banks give up part of their holdings of securities to the Federal Reserve Banks.

b   The Federal Reserve Banks pay for these securities by increasing the reserves of commercial banks by the amount of the purchase.

Just as the commercial bank may pay for a bond bought from a private individual by increasing the seller's demand deposit, so the bankers' bank may pay for bonds bought from commercial banks by increasing the banks' reserves. The consolidated balance sheets of the commercial banks and the Federal Reserve Banks will change as shown on page 296.

The upward arrow shows that securities have moved from the commercial banks to the Federal Reserve Banks. Therefore, we place a minus sign in front of "Securities" in the asset column of the balance sheet of the commercial banks. For the same reason, we place a plus sign in front of "Securities" in the asset column of the balance sheet of the Federal Reserve Banks.

The downward arrow indicates that the Federal Reserve Banks have provided reserves to the commercial banks. We therefore place a plus sign in front of "Reserves" in the balance sheet for the commercial banks. The plus sign in the liability column of the balance sheet of the Federal Reserve Banks indicates

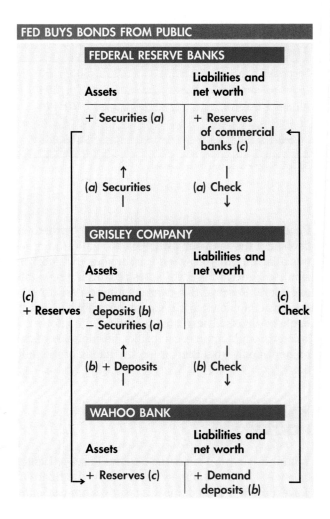

FED BUYS BONDS FROM COMMERCIAL BANKS

FEDERAL RESERVE BANKS

Assets	Liabilities and net worth
+ Securities (a)	+ Reserves of commercial banks (b)
↑ (a) Securities |	| (b) Reserves ↓

COMMERCIAL BANKS

Assets	Liabilities and net worth
− Securities (a) + Reserves (b)	

FED BUYS BONDS FROM PUBLIC

FEDERAL RESERVE BANKS

Assets	Liabilities and net worth
+ Securities (a)	+ Reserves of commercial banks (c)
↑ (a) Securities |	| (a) Check ↓

GRISLEY COMPANY

Assets	Liabilities and net worth
(c) + Reserves + Demand deposits (b) − Securities (a)	(c) Check
↑ (b) + Deposits |	| (b) Check ↓

WAHOO BANK

Assets	Liabilities and net worth
+ Reserves (c)	+ Demand deposits (b)

that commercial bank reserves have increased; they are a liability to the Federal Reserve Banks.

The important aspect of this transaction is that, when Federal Reserve Banks purchase securities from commercial banks, the reserves—and therefore the lending ability—of the commercial banks are increased.

From the Public   If Federal Reserve Banks purchase securities *from the general public,* the effect on commercial bank reserves is much the same. Suppose the Grisley Meat Packing Company has negotiable government bonds which it sells in the open market to the Federal Reserve Banks. The transaction goes like this:

a Grisley gives up securities to the Federal Reserve Banks and gets in payment a check drawn by the Federal Reserve Banks on themselves.

b Grisley promptly deposits this check in its account with its Wahoo bank.

c The Wahoo bank collects this check against the Federal Reserve Banks by sending it to the Federal Reserve Banks for collection. As a result the Wahoo bank receives an increase in its reserves.

Balance sheet changes are as follows.

We need to understand two aspects of this transaction.

1   As with Federal Reserve purchases of securities directly from commercial banks, the reserves and lending ability of the commercial banking system have been increased. This is indicated by the plus sign in front of "Reserves," showing an increase in assets of the Wahoo bank.

2   The supply of money is directly increased by the central banks' purchase of government bonds (aside from any expansion of the money supply which may occur from the increase in commercial bank reserves). This direct increase in the money supply has taken the form of an increased amount of checking account money in the economy; thus the plus sign in front of demand deposits in the Wahoo bank. Because these demand deposits are an asset as viewed by Grisley, demand deposits have increased (plus sign) on Grisley's balance sheet.

There is a slight difference between the Federal Reserve Banks' purchases of securities from the commercial banking system and from the public. Assuming all commercial banks are "loaned up" initially, Federal Reserve bond purchases *from commercial banks* will increase actual reserves and excess reserves of commercial banks by the entire amount of the bond purchases. As shown in the left side of Figure 15-1, a $1000 bond purchase from a commercial bank would increase both the actual and excess reserves of the commercial bank by $1000.

On the other hand, Federal Reserve Bank purchases of bonds *from the public* increase actual reserves but also increase demand deposits. Thus, a $1000 bond purchase from the public would increase actual reserves of the "loaned up" banking system by $1000. But with a 20 percent reserve ratio, the excess reserves of the banking system would only amount to $800. In the case of bond purchases from the pub-

lic, it is *as if* the commercial banking system had already used 20 percent of its new reserves to support $1000 worth of new demand-deposit money.

However, in each transaction the basic conclusion is the same: *When Federal Reserve Banks buy securities in the open market, commercial banks' reserves will be increased.* Assuming that the banks lend out their excess reserves, the nation's money supply will rise. Observe in Figure 15-1 that a $1000 purchase of bonds by the Federal Reserve will result in $5000 of additional money, regardless of whether the purchase was made from commercial banks or from the general public.

Selling Securities You should now suspect that Federal Reserve Bank sales of government bonds reduce commercial bank reserves. Let's see why.

To Commercial Banks Suppose the Federal Reserve Banks sell securities in the open market to *commercial banks:*

a Federal Reserve Banks give up securities which the commercial banks acquire.

FIGURE 15-1 **The Federal Reserve's purchase of bonds and the expansion of the money supply**
Assuming all banks are "loaned up" initially, a Federal Reserve purchase of a $1000 bond from either a commercial bank or the public can increase the money supply by $5000 when the reserve ratio is 20 percent. In the left portion of the diagram, the purchase of a $1000 bond from a commercial bank creates $1000 of excess reserves which support an expansion of demand deposits of $5000 through making loans. In the right portion, the purchase of a $1000 bond from the public creates only $800 of excess reserves, because $200 of reserves are required to "back up" the $1000 new demand deposit in the banking system. The commercial banks can therefore expand the money supply by $4000 by making loans. This $4000 of checking account money *plus* the initial new demand deposit of $1000 together equal $5000 of new money.

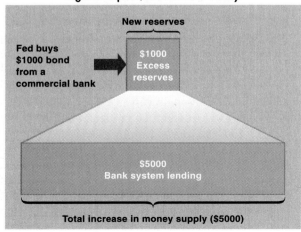
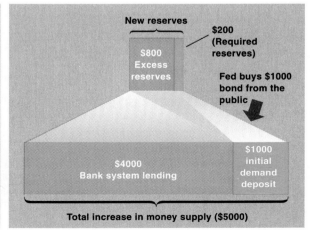

b Commercial banks pay for these securities by drawing checks against their deposits—that is, against their reserves—in Federal Reserve Banks. The banks collect these checks by reducing the commercial banks' reserves accordingly.

The balance sheet changes appear as follows:

FED SELLS BONDS TO COMMERCIAL BANKS

FEDERAL RESERVE BANKS

Assets	Liabilities and net worth
− Securities (a)	− Reserves of commercial banks (b)
(a) Securities ↓	(b) Reserves ↑

COMMERCIAL BANKS

Assets	Liabilities and net worth
− Reserves (b) + Securities (a)	

The reduction in commercial bank reserves is indicated by the minus signs before these entries.

To the Public   If Federal Reserve Banks sell securities *to the public,* the final outcome will be the same. Let's put the Grisley company on the buying end of government bonds which the Federal Reserve Banks are selling.

a The Federal Reserve Bank sells government bonds to Grisley, which pays with a check drawn on the Wahoo bank.

b The Federal Reserve Banks clear this check against the Wahoo bank by reducing its reserves.

c The Wahoo bank returns the check to Grisley, reducing Grisley's demand deposit accordingly.

The balance sheets change as shown in the right column.

Federal Reserve bond sales of $1000 to the commercial banking system reduce the system's actual and excess reserves by $1000. But a $1000 bond sale to the public reduces excess reserves by $800 because demand-deposit money is also reduced by $1000 by the sale. Since the commercial banking system has reduced its outstanding demand deposits by $1000, banks need keep $200 less in reserves.

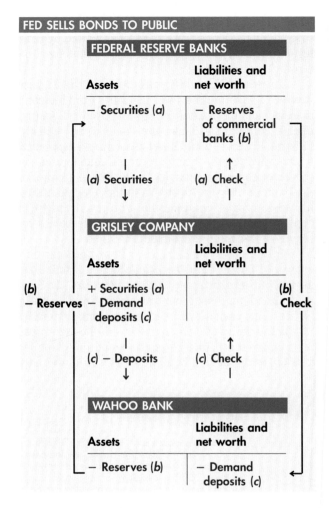

FED SELLS BONDS TO PUBLIC

Whether the Fed sells bonds to the public or to commercial banks, the conclusion is identical: *When Federal Reserve Banks sell securities in the open market, commercial bank reserves are reduced.* If all excess reserves are already lent out, this decline in commercial bank reserves will translate into a decline in the nation's money supply. In our example, a $1000 sale of government securities will result in a $5000 decline in the money supply irrespective of whether the sale was made to commercial banks or the general public. You can verify this by reexamining Figure 15-1 and tracing the effects of a *sale* of a $1000 bond by the Federal Reserve Banks either to commercial banks or the public.

What makes commercial banks and the public willing to sell government securities to, or buy them from, Federal Reserve Banks? The answer lies in the price of bonds and their interest rates. We know from

Chapter 13 that bond prices and interest rates are inversely related. When the Federal Reserve buys government bonds, the demand for them will increase. Government bond prices will rise and their interest rates will decline. The higher bond prices and their lower interest rates will prompt bank and public holders of government bonds to sell them to the Federal Reserve Banks.

When the Federal Reserve sells government bonds, the additional supply of bonds in the bond market will lower bond prices and raise their interest rates, making government bonds attractive purchases for banks and the public.

The Reserve Ratio

How can the Board of Governors manipulate the legal **reserve ratio** to influence the ability of commercial banks to lend? The following example shows how. Starting with row 2 of Table 15-2, suppose a commercial bank's balance sheet shows that reserves are $5000 and demand deposits $20,000. If the legal reserve ratio is 20 percent, the bank's *required* reserves are $4000. Since *actual* reserves are $5000, the *excess* reserves of this bank are $1000. On the basis of this $1000 of excess reserves, we saw that this single bank can lend $1000, but the banking system as a whole could create a maximum of $5000 in new checking account money by lending.

Raising the Reserve Ratio Now, what if the Board of Governors raised the legal reserve ratio from 20 to 25 percent? (See row 3.) Required reserves would jump from $4000 to $5000, shrinking excess reserves from $1000 to zero. *Raising the reserve ratio increases the amount of required reserves banks must keep. Either banks lose excess reserves, diminishing their ability*

to create money by lending, or else they find their reserves deficient and are forced to contract checkable deposits and therefore the money supply. In the case just cited, excess reserves are transformed into required reserves, and the money-creating potential of our *single bank* is reduced from $1000 to zero (column 6). The *banking system's* money-creating capacity declines from $5000 to zero (column 7).

What if the Board of Governors announced an increase in the legal reserve requirement to 30 percent? (See row 4.) The commercial bank would face the prospect of failing to meet this requirement. To protect itself against such an eventuality, the bank would be forced to lower its outstanding demand deposits and at the same time increase its reserves. To reduce its demand deposits, the bank could let outstanding loans mature and be repaid without extending new credit. To increase reserves, the bank might sell some of its bonds, adding the proceeds to its reserves. Both actions will reduce the supply of money (see Chapter 14, transactions 6 and 8).

Lowering the Reserve Ratio What would happen if the Board of Governors lowered the reserve ratio from the original 20 to 10 percent? (See row 1.) In this case, required reserves would decline from $4000 to $2000, and excess reserves would jump from $1000 to $3000. The single bank's lending or money-creating ability increases from $1000 to $3000 (column 6) and the banking system's money-creating potential expands from $5000 to $30,000 (column 7). *Lowering the reserve ratio changes required reserves to excess reserves and enhances the ability of banks to create new money by lending.*

From these examples in Table 15-2 we can see that a change in the reserve ratio affects the money-creating ability of the *banking system* in two ways:

TABLE 15-2 The effects of changes in the reserve ratio on the lending ability of commercial banks

(1) Legal reserve ratio, percent	(2) Demand deposits	(3) Actual reserves	(4) Required reserves	(5) Excess reserves, or (3) − (4)	(6) Money- creating potential of single bank, = (5)	(7) Money- creating potential of banking system
(1) 10	$20,000	$5000	$2000	$ 3000	$ 3000	$30,000
(2) 20	20,000	5000	4000	1000	1000	5,000
(3) 25	20,000	5000	5000	0	0	0
(4) 30	20,000	5000	6000	−1000	−1000	−3,333

1   It affects the size of excess reserves.
2   It changes the size of the monetary multiplier.

For example, in raising the legal reserve ratio from 10 to 20 percent, excess reserves are reduced from $3000 to $1000 and the demand-deposit multiplier is reduced from 10 to 5. The money-creating potential of the banking system declines from $30,000 (= $3000 × 10) to $5000 (= $1000 × 5).

Changing the reserve ratio is a powerful technique of monetary control, but it is used infrequently. Nevertheless, in 1992 the Federal Reserve reduced the reserve ratio from 12 to 10 percent.

The Discount Rate

One of the functions of a central bank is to be a "lender of last resort." Central banks lend to commercial banks which are financially sound but have unexpected and immediate needs for additional funds. Thus, each Federal Reserve Bank will make short-term loans to commercial banks in its district.

When a commercial bank borrows, it gives the Federal Reserve Bank a promissory note or IOU drawn against itself and secured by acceptable collateral—typically United States government securities. Just as commercial banks charge interest on their loans, so do Federal Reserve Banks charge interest on loans they grant to commercial banks. This interest rate is called the **discount rate.**

As a claim against the commercial bank, the borrowing bank's promissory note (IOU) is an asset to the lending Federal Reserve Bank and appears on its balance sheet as "Loans to commercial banks." To the commercial bank the IOU is a liability, appearing as "Loans from the Federal Reserve Banks" on the commercial bank's balance sheet.

In providing the loan the Federal Reserve Bank will *increase* the reserves of the borrowing commercial bank. Since no required reserves need be kept against loans from Federal Reserve Banks, *all* new reserves acquired by borrowing from Federal Reserve Banks would be excess reserves. These changes are reflected in the balance sheets as shown in the right column.

Note that this transaction is analogous to a private person's borrowing from a commercial bank (see Chapter 14, transaction 6).

The point is that *commercial bank borrowing from the Federal Reserve Banks increases the reserves of commercial banks, enhancing their ability to extend credit.*

COMMERCIAL BANK BORROWING FROM THE FED	
FEDERAL RESERVE BANKS	
Assets	**Liabilities and net worth**
+ Loans to commercial banks	+ Reserves of commercial banks
↑	|
IOUs	+ Reserves
|	↓
COMMERCIAL BANKS	
Assets	**Liabilities and net worth**
+ Reserves	+ Loans from the Federal Reserve Banks

The Fed's Board of Governors has the power to establish and manipulate the discount rate at which commercial banks can borrow from Federal Reserve Banks. From the commercial banks' point of view, the discount rate is a cost entailed in acquiring reserves. When the discount rate is decreased, commercial banks are encouraged to obtain additional reserves by borrowing from Federal Reserve Banks. Commercial bank lending based on these new reserves will constitute an increase in the money supply.

An increase in the discount rate discourages commercial banks from obtaining additional reserves through borrowing from the central banks. An increase in the discount rate therefore is consistent with the monetary authorities' desire to restrict the supply of money. *(Key Question 2)*

Easy Money and Tight Money

Suppose the economy is faced with recession and unemployment. The monetary authorities decide an increase in the supply of money is needed to stimulate aggregate demand to help absorb idle resources. To increase the supply of money, the Board of Governors must expand the excess reserves of commercial banks. What policies will bring this about?

1   Buy Securities   The Board of Governors should order Federal Reserve Banks to buy securities in the open market. These bond purchases will be paid for by increases in commercial bank reserves.

2 Reduce Reserve Ratio The reserve ratio should be reduced, automatically changing required reserves into excess reserves and increasing the size of the monetary multiplier.

3 Lower Discount Rate The discount rate should be lowered to induce commercial banks to add to their reserves by borrowing from Federal Reserve Banks.

This set of policy decisions is called an **easy money policy.** Its purpose is to make credit cheaply and easily available, to increase aggregate demand and employment.

Suppose, on the other hand, excessive spending is pushing the economy into an inflationary spiral. The Board of Governors should attempt to reduce aggregate demand by limiting or contracting the supply of money. The key to this goal lies in reducing the reserves of commercial banks. How is this done?

1 Sell Securities Federal Reserve Banks should sell government bonds in the open market to tear down commercial bank reserves.

2 Increase Reserve Ratio Increasing the reserve ratio will automatically strip commercial banks of excess reserves and decrease the monetary multiplier.

3 Raise Discount Rate A boost in the discount rate will discourage commercial banks from building up their reserves by borrowing at Federal Reserve Banks.

This group of directives is labeled a **tight money policy.** The objective is to tighten the supply of money to reduce spending and control inflation.

Relative Importance

Of the three monetary controls, open-market operations clearly are the most important control mechanism.

The discount rate is less important for two interrelated reasons.

1 The amount of commercial bank reserves obtained by borrowing from the central banks is typically very small. On the average only 2 or 3 percent of bank reserves are acquired in this way. Indeed, open-market operations often induce commercial banks to borrow from Federal Reserve Banks. That is, to the extent that central bank bond sales leave commercial banks temporarily short of reserves, commercial banks will be prompted to borrow from Federal Reserve Banks. Rather than being a primary tool of monetary policy, commercial bank borrowing from the Fed occurs largely in response to monetary policy as carried out by open-market operations.

2 While the manipulation of commercial bank reserves through open-market operations and the changing of reserve requirements are initiated by the Federal Reserve System, the discount rate depends on the initiative of commercial banks to be effective. For example, if the discount rate is lowered at a time when very few banks are inclined to borrow from Federal Reserve Banks, the lower rate will have little or no impact on bank reserves or the money supply.

Nevertheless, a change in the discount rate may have an "announcement effect"; it may be a clear and explicit way of communicating to the financial community and the economy as a whole the intended direction of monetary policy. Other economists doubt this, arguing that changes in the discount rate are often "passive"; it is changed to keep it in line with other short-term interest rates, rather than to invoke a policy change.

What about changes in reserve requirements? The Fed has used this instrument of monetary control only sparingly. Normally, it can accomplish its monetary goals through open-market operations, without resorting to changes in reserve requirements. The limited use of changes in the reserve ratio undoubtedly is related to the fact that reserve balances earn no interest. Higher or lower reserve requirements can have substantial effects on bank profits.

But there are more positive reasons why open-market operations have evolved as the primary technique of monetary policy. This mechanism of monetary control has the advantage of flexibility—government securities can be purchased or sold in large or small amounts—and the impact on bank reserves is prompt. Yet, compared with reserve-requirement changes, open-market operations work subtly and less directly. Furthermore, quantitatively there is no question about the potential of the Federal Reserve Banks to affect commercial bank reserves through bond sales and purchases. A glance at the consolidated balance sheet for the Federal Reserve Banks (Table 15-1) reveals very large holdings of government bonds ($355 billion), the sales of which could theoretically reduce commercial bank reserves from $30 billion to zero.

MONETARY POLICY, REAL GDP, AND THE PRICE LEVEL

Although there is no disagreement as to the tools available to the Federal Reserve to change the money supply, there is some disagreement on how changes in the money supply affect the economy. We will look at the conventional view here, waiting until Chapter 16 to present an alternative perspective.

Cause-Effect Chain

We can explain how monetary policy works toward the goal of full employment and price stability by using the three diagrams comprising Figure 15-2 (Key Graph).

Money Market   Figure 15-2a shows the money market, where the demand for money curve and the supply of money curve are brought together. Recall from Chapter 13 that the total demand for money comprises the transactions and asset demands. The transactions demand is directly related to the level of economic transactions as reflected in the size of the nominal GDP. The asset demand is inversely related to the in-terest rate. The interest rate is the opportunity cost of holding money as an asset; the higher the cost, the smaller the amount of money the public wants to hold. In Figure 15-2a the total demand for money is inversely related to the interest rate. Also, recall that an increase in nominal GDP would shift D_m to the right and a decline in nominal GDP would shift D_m to the left.

We complete our graphical portrayal of the money market by showing three potential money supply curves, S_{m1}, S_{m2}, and S_{m3}. In each case the money supply is shown as a vertical line representing some fixed amount of money determined by the Fed's Board of Governors. While monetary policy (the supply of money) helps determine the interest rate, the interest rate does not determine the location of the money supply curve.

Figure 15-2a shows the equilibrium interest rate—the interest rate equating the amount of money demanded and supplied. With money demand of D_m, if the supply of money is $125 billion ($S_{m1}$), the equilibrium interest rate will be 10 percent. At a money supply of $150 billion ($S_{m2}$), the interest rate will be 8 percent; at $175 billion ($S_{m3}$), 6 percent.

We know from Chapter 10 that the real, not the nominal, rate of interest is critical for investment decisions. So here we assume Figure 15-2a portrays real interest rates.

Investment   These 10, 8, and 6 percent interest rates are carried rightward to the investment demand curve of Figure 15-2b. This curve shows the inverse relationship between the interest rate—the cost of borrowing to invest—and amount of the nation's investment spending. At the 10 percent interest rate it will be profitable for businesses to invest $15 billion; at 8 percent, $20 billion; and at 6 percent, $25 billion.

The investment component of total spending is more likely to be affected by changes in the interest rate than is consumer spending. Of course, consumer purchases of automobiles—which depend heavily on installment credit—are sensitive to interest rates. But overall the interest rate is *not* a very crucial factor in determining how households divide their disposable income between consumption and saving.

The impact of changing interest rates on investment spending is great because of the large cost and long-term nature of such purchases. Capital equipment, factory buildings, and warehouses are tremendously expensive. In absolute terms, interest charges on funds borrowed for these purchases are considerable.

KEY GRAPH

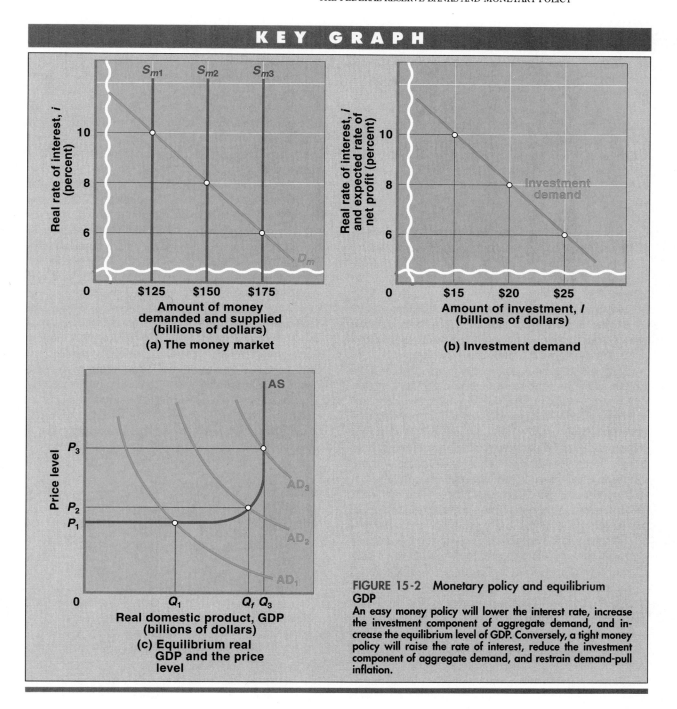

(a) The money market

Real rate of interest, i (percent)

S_{m1} S_{m2} S_{m3}

D_m

Amount of money
demanded and supplied
(billions of dollars)

(b) Investment demand

Real rate of interest, i and expected rate of net profit (percent)

Investment demand

Amount of investment, I
(billions of dollars)

(c) Equilibrium real GDP and the price level

Price level

AS

AD_3

AD_2

AD_1

Real domestic product, GDP
(billions of dollars)

FIGURE 15-2 Monetary policy and equilibrium GDP
An easy money policy will lower the interest rate, increase the investment component of aggregate demand, and increase the equilibrium level of GDP. Conversely, a tight money policy will raise the rate of interest, reduce the investment component of aggregate demand, and restrain demand-pull inflation.

Similarly, the interest cost on a house purchased on a long-term contract will be very large: A one-half percentage point change in the interest rate could amount to thousands of dollars on the total cost of a home.

Also, changes in the interest rate may affect investment spending by changing the attractiveness of capital equipment purchases versus bond purchases. If the interest rate rises on bonds, then, given the profit expectations on capital goods purchases, businesses will be more inclined to use business savings to purchase securities than to buy capital equipment. Conversely, given profit expectations on investment spending, a fall in the interest rate makes capital goods purchases more attractive than bond ownership.

In brief, the impact of changing interest rates will be primarily on investment spending and, through this channel, on aggregate demand, output, employment, and the level of prices. More specifically, as Figure 15-2b indicates, investment spending varies inversely with the interest rate.

Equilibrium GDP

Figure 15-2c shows the impact of our three interest rates and corresponding levels of investment spending on aggregate demand. Aggregate demand curve AD_1 is associated with the $15 billion level of investment, AD_2 with investment of $20 billion, and AD_3 with investment of $25 billion. That is, investment spending is one of the determinants of aggregate demand (Chapter 11). All else equal, the greater this investment spending, the further to the right lies the aggregate demand curve.

Suppose the money supply in Figure 15-2a is $125 billion (Sm_1), producing an equilibrium interest rate of 10 percent. In Figure 15-2b we see this 10 percent interest rate will bring forth $15 billion of investment spending. This $15 billion of investment spending joins with consumption spending, net exports, and government spending to yield aggregate demand curve AD_1 in Figure 15-2c. The equilibrium levels of real output and prices are Q_1 and P_1, as determined by the intersection of AD_1 and the aggregate supply curve AS.

To test your understanding of these relationships, you should explain why each of the other two levels of money supply shown in Figure 15-2a results in a different interest rate, level of investment, aggregate demand curve, and real output-price level combination.

Effects of an Easy Money Policy

We have assumed the money supply is $125 billion (Sm_1) in Figure 15-2a. Because the resulting real output Q_1 in Figure 15-2c is far below the full employment output, Q_f, the economy must be experiencing substantial unemployment. The Federal Reserve therefore should institute an *easy money policy.*

To increase the money supply the Federal Reserve Banks will take some combination of the following actions: (1) buy government securities from banks and the public in the open market, (2) lower the legal reserve ratio, or (3) lower the discount rate. The result will be an increase in excess reserves in the commercial banking system. Because excess reserves are the basis on which commercial banks and thrifts can expand the money supply by lending, the nation's money supply likely will rise. An increase in the money supply will lower the interest rate, increasing investment, aggregate demand, and equilibrium GDP.

For example, an increase in the money supply from $125 to $150 billion will reduce the interest rate from 10 to 8 percent, as indicated in Figure 15-2a, and increase investment from $15 billion to $20 billion, as shown in Figure 15-2b. This $5 billion increase in investment spending will shift the aggregate demand curve rightward by more than the increase in investment because of the multiplier effect. Assuming the economy's MPC is .75, the multiplier will be 4, meaning that the $5 billion increase in investment will shift the AD curve rightward by $20 billion (= $4 \times \$5$) at each price level. Specifically, aggregate demand will shift from AD_1 to AD_2, as shown in Figure 15-2c. This rightward shift in aggregate demand moves the economy from Q_1 to the desired full-employment output at Q_f.

Column 1 in Table 15-3 summarizes the chain of events associated with an easy money policy.

TABLE 15-3 Monetary policy: Mainstream interpretation

(1) Easy money policy	(2) Tight money policy
Problem: unemployment and recession	**Problem:** inflation
Federal Reserve buys bonds, lowers reserve ratio, or lowers the discount rate ↓	**Federal Reserve sells bonds, increases reserve ratio, or increases the discount rate** ↓
Money supply rises ↓	**Money supply falls** ↓
Interest rate falls ↓	**Interest rate rises** ↓
Investment spending increases ↓	**Investment spending decreases** ↓
Aggregate demand increases ↓	**Aggregate demand decreases** ↓
Real GDP rises by a multiple of the increase in investment	**Inflation declines**

Effects of a Tight Money Policy

Now let's assume the money supply and interest rate are $175 billion ($S_{m3}$) in Figure 15-2a. This results in an interest rate of 6 percent, investment spending of $25 billion, and aggregate demand of AD_3. As observed in Figure 15-2c, we have depicted severe demand-pull inflation. Aggregate demand AD_3 is excessive relative to the economy's full-employment level of real output Q_f. To reign in spending, the Fed will institute a *tight money policy* (column 2 of Table 15-3).

The Federal Reserve Board will direct Federal Reserve Banks to undertake some combination of the following actions: (1) sell government securities to depository institutions and to the public in the open market, (2) increase the legal reserve ratio, or (3) increase the discount rate. Banks then will discover their reserves are too low to meet the legal reserve ratio. They therefore will need to reduce their demand deposits by refraining from issuing new loans as old loans are paid back. This will shrink the money supply and increase the interest rate. The higher interest rate will reduce investment, decreasing aggregate demand and restraining demand-pull inflation.

If the Fed reduces the money supply from $175 billion ($S_{m3}$) to $150 billion ($S_{m2}$), as shown in Figure 15-2a, the interest rate will increase from 6 to 8 percent and reduce investment from $25 to $20 billion (Figure 15-2b). The consequent $5 billion decrease in investment, bolstered by the multiplier process, will shift the aggregate demand curve leftward from AD_3 to AD_2. For example, if the MPC is .75, the multiplier will be 4 and the aggregate demand curve will shift leftward by $20 billion (= 4 × $5 billion of investment) at each price level. This leftward shift of the aggregate demand curve will eliminate the excessive spending and thus the demand-pull inflation. In the real world, of course, the goal will be to stop inflation—halt further increases in the price level—rather than actually driving down the price level.

Column 2 of Table 15-3 summarizes the cause-effect chain of tight money policy on demand-pull inflation. *(Key Question 3)*

Refinements and Feedbacks

The components of Figure 15-2 allow us to (1) appreciate some of the factors determining the effectiveness of monetary policy and (2) note the existence of a "feedback" or "circularity" problem complicating monetary policy.

Policy Effectiveness   Figure 15-2 reveals the magnitudes by which an easy or tight money policy will change the interest rate, investment, and aggregate demand. These magnitudes are determined by the particular shapes of the demand for money and investment-demand curves. Pencil in other curves to see that *the steeper the D_m curve, the larger will be the effect of any given change in the money supply on the equilibrium rate of interest. Furthermore, any given change in the interest rate will have a larger impact on investment—and hence on aggregate demand and GDP—the flatter the investment-demand curve.* A specific change in quantity of money will be most effective when the demand for money curve is relatively steep and the investment-demand curve is relatively flat.

A particular change in the quantity of money will be relatively ineffective when the money-demand curve is flat and the investment-demand curve is steep. As we will find in Chapter 16, there is controversy as to the precise shapes of these curves and therefore the effectiveness of monetary policy.

Feedback Effects   You may have sensed in Figure 15-2 a feedback or circularity problem which complicates monetary policy. The problem is this: By reading from Figure 15-2a to 15-2c we discover that the interest rate, working through the investment-demand curve, is a determinant of the equilibrium GDP. Now we must recognize that causation also runs the other way. The level of GDP is a determinant of the equilibrium interest rate. This link comes about because the transactions component of the money-demand curve depends directly on the level of nominal GDP.

How does this feedback from Figure 15-2c to 15-2a affect monetary policy? It means that the increase in the GDP which an easy money policy brings about will *increase* the demand for money, partially offsetting the interest-reducing effect of the easy money policy. A tight money policy will reduce the nominal GDP. But this will *decrease* the demand for money and dampen the initial interest-increasing effect of the tight money policy. This feedback is also at the core of a policy dilemma, as we will see later. *(Key Question 4)*

Monetary Policy and Aggregate Supply

As with fiscal policy (Chapter 12), monetary policy is subject to the constraints implicit in the aggregate supply curve. The cause-effect chain represented in Figure 15-2 and Table 15-3 indicates that monetary policy primarily affects investment spending and, therefore, aggregate demand, real output, and the price level. The aggregate supply curve explains how the change in investment and aggregate demand *is divided* between changes in real output and changes in the price level.

We can see in Figure 15-2c that, if the economy is initially in the horizontal or recessionary range of the aggregate supply curve, an easy money policy will shift the aggregate demand curve rightward from AD_1 to AD_2 and have a large impact on real GDP and employment and little or no effect on the price level.

But if the economy was already near, at, or beyond full employment, an increase in aggregate demand would have little or no effect on real output and employment. It would, however, substantially increase the price level. Observe in Figure 15-2c that an increase in the aggregate demand curve from AD_2 to AD_3 would occur mainly in the vertical range of the aggregate supply curve. Needless to say, an easy money policy would be inappropriate when the economy was already achieving full employment. Figure 15-2c makes clear the reason why: It would be highly inflationary.

Similarly, a tight money policy, appropriate when the economy is fully employed and suffering demand-pull inflation, would be inappropriate when the economy is suffering substantial cyclical unemployment. The main impact of such a policy would be to reduce real output and worsen unemployment.

EFFECTIVENESS OF MONETARY POLICY

Let's evaluate how well monetary policy works.

Strengths of Monetary Policy

Most economists regard monetary policy as an essential component of our national stabilization policy, especially in the following respects:

1   Speed and Flexibility   Compared with fiscal policy, monetary policy can be quickly altered. We have seen (Chapter 12) that the application of fiscal policy may be delayed by congressional deliberations. In contrast, the Open Market Committee of the Fed-

eral Reserve Board can buy or sell securities on a daily basis and affect the money supply and interest rates.

2   Isolation from Political Pressure   Since members of the Federal Reserve Board are appointed for fourteen-year terms, they are not often subject to lobbying and pressure to remain elected. Thus the Board, more easily than Congress, can engage in politically unpopular policies which might be necessary for the long-term health of the economy. And, monetary policy itself is a more subtle and more politically conservative measure than fiscal policy. Changes in government spending directly affect the allocation of resources and, of course, tax changes can have extensive political ramifications. By contrast, monetary policy works more subtlely and therefore is more politically palatable.

3   Recent Successes   The case for monetary policy has been greatly bolstered by its successful use during the 1980s and 1990s. A tight money policy helped bring down the inflation rate from 13.5 percent in 1980 to 3.2 percent three years later.

Recently, monetary policy was successfully used to help move the economy—at first very slowly, then briskly—from the 1990–1991 recession. This success is noteworthy because the huge budget deficits of the 1980s and early 1990s had put fiscal policy on the shelf. Congressional budgeting was mainly aimed at reducing the budget deficit, not at stimulating the economy. From a fiscal policy perspective, the tax hikes and government spending reductions during this period were mildly contractionary. But the Fed's easy money policy dropped interest rates on commercial loans from 10 percent in 1990 to 6 percent in 1993. Eventually, these low interest rates had their intended effects: Investment spending and interest-sensitive consumer spending rose rapidly, increasing the economy's real GDP.

In view of America's budget deficits and these successes, monetary policy—at least for now—appears to be America's primary stabilization tool.

Shortcomings and Problems

However, monetary policy has certain limitations and encounters real-world complications.

1   Less Control?   Some economists fear that changes in banking practices (Chapter 13) may reduce—or make less predictable—the Federal Reserve's control of the money supply. Financial innovations have allowed people to move near-monies quickly from mutual funds and other investment accounts to checking accounts, and vice versa. A particular monetary policy aimed at changing bank reserves therefore might be rendered less effective by movements of funds within the financial system. For example, people might respond to a tight money policy by quickly converting near-monies in their mutual funds accounts or other liquid financial investments to money in their checking accounts. Thus, bank reserves may not fall as intended, the interest rate may not rise, and aggregate demand may not change. Also, banking and finance are increasingly global. Flows of funds to or from the United States might undermine or render inappropriate a particular domestic monetary policy.

How legitimate are these concerns? These financial developments make the Federal Reserve Board's task of monetary policy more difficult. But recent studies and Fed experience confirm that the traditional central bank tools of monetary policy remain effective in changing the money supply and interest rates.

2   Cyclical Asymmetry If pursued vigorously, tight money can destroy commercial banking reserves to the point where banks are forced to contract the volume of loans. This means a contraction of the money supply. But an easy money policy suffers from a "You can lead a horse to water, but you can't make him drink" problem. An easy money policy can only see to it that commercial banks have the excess reserves needed to make loans. It cannot guarantee that the banks will provide the loans and thus that the supply of money will increase. If commercial banks, seeking liquidity, are unwilling to lend, the efforts of the Board of Governors will be to little avail. Similarly, the public can frustrate the intentions of the Federal Reserve by deciding not to borrow excess reserves. Additionally, the money the Federal Reserve Banks interject into the system through buying bonds from the public could be used by the public to pay off existing loans.

This cyclical asymmetry has not created a major difficulty for monetary policy except during depression. During normal times, higher excess reserves translate into added lending and therefore to an increase in the money supply.

3   Changes in Velocity Total expenditures may be regarded as the money supply *multiplied* by the **velocity of money**—the number of times per year the average dollar is spent on goods and services. If the money supply is $150 billion, total spending will be $600 billion if velocity is 4, but only $450 billion if velocity is 3.

Some economists feel that velocity changes in the opposite direction from the money supply, offsetting or frustrating policy-instigated changes in the money supply. During inflation, when the money supply is restrained by policy, velocity may increase. Conversely, when policy measures are taken to increase the money supply during recession, velocity may fall.

Velocity might behave this way because of the asset demand for money. An easy money policy, for example, means an increase in the supply of money relative to the demand for it and therefore a reduction in the interest rate (Figure 15-2a). But when the interest rate—the opportunity cost of holding money as an asset—is lower, the public will hold larger money balances. This means dollars move from hand to hand—from households to businesses and back again—less rapidly. That is, the velocity of money has declined. A reverse sequence of events may cause a tight money policy to induce an increase in velocity.

4   The Investment Impact Some economists doubt that monetary policy has as much impact on investment as Figure 15-2 implies. A combination of a relatively flat money-demand curve and a relatively steep investment-demand curve will mean that a particular change in the money supply will not elicit a very large change in investment and, thus, not a large change in the equilibrium GDP (Figure 15-2).

Furthermore, the operation of monetary policy as portrayed may be complicated, or temporarily offset, by unfavorable changes in the location of the investment-demand curve. For example, a tight money policy designed to drive up interest rates may have little impact on investment spending if the investment demand curve in Figure 15-2b at the same time shifts to the right because of business optimism, technological progress, or expectations of higher future prices of capital. Monetary policy will have to raise interest rates extraordinarily high under these circumstances to be effective in reducing aggregate demand. Conversely, a severe recession may undermine business confidence, collapse the investment-demand curve to the left, and frustrate an easy money policy.

5 Interest as Income We have seen that monetary policy is predicated on the idea that interest rates and expenditures on capital goods and interest-sensitive consumer goods are *inversely* related. We must now acknowledge that businesses and households are also recipients of interest income and that the size of such income and the spending which flows from it vary *directly* with the level of interest rates.

Suppose inflation is intensifying and the Fed raises interest rates to increase the cost of capital goods, housing, and automobiles. The complication is that higher interest rates on a wide range of financial instruments (for example, bonds, certificates of deposits, checking accounts) will increase the incomes and spending of the households and businesses who own them. Such added spending is obviously at odds with the Fed's effort to restrict aggregate demand. Example: In 1991 and 1992 the Fed repeatedly lowered interest rates to stimulate a sluggish economy. One possible reason this strategy took so long to become effective was that households who were receiving 8 or 10 percent on their bonds and CDs in the late 1980s received only 4 or 5 percent in the early 1990s. This diminished interest income undoubtedly lowered their spending.

The point is this: Interest-rate changes viewed as an *expense* change spending in the *opposite* direction as the interest-rate changes. But these rate changes when viewed as *income* change spending in the *same* direction as the interest-rate changes. The change in spending by interest-income receivers partly offsets and weakens the change in spending by purchasers of capital goods, homes, and autos.

The Target Dilemma

This brings us to one of the most difficult problems of monetary policy. Should the Fed attempt to control the money supply *or* the interest rate? This **target dilemma** arises because monetary authorities cannot simultaneously stabilize both.

The Policy Dilemma To understand this dilemma, review the money market diagram of Figure 15-2a.

Interest Rate Assume the Fed's policy target is to stabilize the interest rate because interest-rate fluctuations destabilize investment spending and, working through the income multiplier, destabilize aggregate demand and the economy. Now suppose expansion of the economy increases nominal GDP and increases the transactions demand, and therefore the total demand, for money. As a result, the equilibrium interest rate will rise. To stabilize the interest rate—to bring it down to its original level—the Board of Governors would have to increase the supply of money. But this may turn a healthy recovery into an inflationary boom —exactly what the Federal Reserve wants to prevent.

A similar scenario can be applied to recession. As GDP falls, so will money demand and interest rates, provided the money supply is unchanged. But to prevent interest rates from declining, the Board would have to reduce the money supply. This decline in the supply of money would contribute to a further contraction of aggregate expenditures and intensify the recession.

Money Supply What if the Fed's policy target is the money supply, not the interest rate? Then the Fed must tolerate interest-rate fluctuations which will contribute to instability in the economy. Explanation: Assume in Figure 15-2a that the Fed achieves its desired money supply target of $150 billion. Any expansion of GDP will increase the demand for money and raise the interest rate. This higher interest rate may lower investment spending and choke off an otherwise healthy expansion. The point again is that the monetary authorities cannot simultaneously stabilize both the money supply and the interest rate.

Recent Focus: The Federal Funds Rate

Because an interest-rate target and a money-supply target cannot be realized simultaneously, which target, if either, is preferable? In the early to mid-1980s the Fed focused its policy mainly on controlling the rate of growth of the money supply, letting markets determine interest rates accordingly. But innovations in the financial industry made reliance on the $M1$ or $M2$ money supply targets unreliable. The expansion of highly liquid nonchecking accounts such as money market deposit accounts, money market mutual funds, and mutual fund investment accounts distorted the $M1$ and $M2$ data. People switched some of their money holdings from $M1$ accounts to $M2$ and $M3$ accounts. Also, velocity—historically rising at a stable rate—began to decline. The Fed therefore could no longer depend on the traditional relationships among $M1$, $M2$, and nominal GDP.

In view of these developments the Fed has turned to targeting the interest rate rather than the money supply. The goal is to peg the interest rate at the level appropriate for the state of the economy. In 1991, aiming to increase aggregate demand to lift the economy from recession, the Fed sharply reduced the Federal funds rate. (Recall from Chapter 14 that the **Federal funds rate** is the interest rate banks charge one another on overnight loans.) The Fed reduced this interest rate by aggressively buying government securities in the open market, lowering the discount rate, and reducing the reserve ratio.

Interest rates in general, including the **prime interest rate**—the rate banks charge their most creditworthy loan customers—rise and fall with the Federal funds rate. When the Fed buys bonds from banks and the public, total reserves and excess reserves in the banking system rise, making it cheaper for banks to borrow reserves from one another. That is, the Federal funds rate falls because of the greater supply of reserves in the banking system. We know that increases in reserves also increase bank lending to the public and therefore raise the money supply. As the money supply rises, the prime interest rate falls, increasing investment spending, aggregate demand, and GDP.

At first the economy only slowly expanded from the recession of 1990–1991, but in late 1993 real GDP began to surge upward. Fearing the easy money policy and low interest rates might eventually fuel renewed inflation, the Fed began to tighten monetary policy in 1994. It used open-market operations to increase the Federal funds rate, and thereby boost the prime interest rate. It also increased the discount rate.

In summary: The Fed's recent policies have been both activist and consistent with Figure 15-2. It has

TABLE 15-4 Monetary policy and the net export effect

(1) Easy money policy	(2) Tight money policy
Problem: recession, slow growth	**Problem:** inflation
Easy money policy (lower interest rate) ↓	Tight money policy (higher interest rate) ↓
Decreased foreign demand for dollars ↓	Increased foreign demand for dollars ↓
Dollar depreciates ↓	Dollar appreciates ↓
Net exports increase (increase in aggregate demand)	Net exports decrease (decrease in aggregate demand)

determined what it thinks to be the desirable interest rate for the state of the economy and then changed the money supply to achieve these interest-rate targets. The Federal Reserve Board and Federal Open Market Committee have recently focused less attention on the money aggregates themselves—$M1$ and $M2$—and more on the Federal funds and prime interest rates. *(Key Question 7)*

QUICK REVIEW 15-2

■ The Federal Reserve is engaging in an easy money policy when it increases the money supply to reduce interest rates and increase investment spending and real GDP; it is engaging in a tight money policy when it reduces the money supply to increase interest rates and reduce investment spending and inflation.

■ The steeper the money demand curve and the flatter the investment demand curve, the larger is the impact of a change in the money supply on the economy.

■ The main strengths of monetary policy are (1) speed and flexibility and (2) political acceptability; its main weaknesses are (1) potential inadequacy during recession and (2) offsetting changes in velocity.

■ The Fed faces a target dilemma because it cannot simultaneously stabilize both the money supply and interest rates over the course of a business cycle.

Monetary Policy and the International Economy

In Chapter 12 we established that linkages among economies of the world complicate domestic fiscal policy. These linkages also relate to monetary policy.

Net Export Effect We saw in Chapter 12 that an expansionary fiscal (deficit) policy will increase the demand for money and boost the domestic interest rate. The higher interest rate will increase foreign financial investment in the United States, strengthening the demand for dollars in the foreign exchange market and boosting the international price of the dollar. This dollar *appreciation* will produce lower net exports and thus weaken the stimulus of the fiscal policy (Figure 12-6d).

Will an easy money policy have a similar effect? No, as outlined in column 1 of Table 15-4, an easy or

LAST WORD

FOR THE FED, LIFE IS A METAPHOR

The popular press often depicts the Federal Reserve Board and its chair (Alan Greenspan in 1995) as Captains Courageous.

The Federal Reserve Board leads a very dramatic life, or so it seems when one reads journalistic accounts of its activities. It loosens or tightens reins while riding herd on a rambunctious economy, goes to the rescue of an embattled dollar, tightens spigots on credit . . . you get the picture. For the Fed, life is a metaphor:

The Fed as Mechanic   The Fed sometimes must roll up its sleeves and adjust the economic machinery. The Fed spends a lot of time either tightening things, loosening things, or debating about whether to tighten or loosen.

    Imagine a customer taking his car into Greenspan's Garage.

> Normally calm, Skeezix Greenspan took one look at the car and started to sweat. This would be hard to fix—it was an economy car:
>   "What's the problem?" asked Greenspan.
>   "It's been running beautifully for over six years now," said the customer. "But recently it's been acting sluggish."
>   "These cars are tricky," said Greenspan. "We can always loosen a few screws, as long as you don't mind the side effects."
>   "What side effects?" asked the customer.

>   "Nothing at first," said Greenspan. "We won't even know if the repairs have worked for at least a year. After that, either everything will be fine, or your car will accelerate wildly and go totally out of control."
>   "Just as long as it doesn't stall," said the customer. "I hate that."

The Fed as Warrior   The Fed must fight inflation. But can it wage a protracted war? There are only seven Fed governors, including Greenspan—not a big army:

> Gen. Greenspan sat in the war room plotting strategy. You never knew where the enemy

---

expansionary money policy will indeed produce a **net export effect,** but its direction will be opposite that of an expansionary fiscal policy. An easy money policy will reduce the domestic interest rate. The lower interest rate will discourage the inflow of financial capital to the United States. The demand for dollars in foreign exchange markets will fall, causing the dollar to *depreciate* in value. It will take more dollars to buy, say, a Japanese yen or a French franc. All foreign goods become more expensive to Americans and American goods become cheaper to foreigners. Our imports will thus fall and our exports will rise, or, in short, our net exports will increase. As a result, ag-

gregate expenditures and equilibrium GDP will expand in the United States.[1]

    Conclusion: Unlike an expansionary fiscal policy which *reduces* net exports, an easy money policy *increases* net exports. *Exchange rate changes in response to interest rate changes in the United States strengthen domestic monetary policy.* This conclusion holds equally for a tight money policy which we know in-

---

[1]The depreciation of the dollar will also increase the price of foreign resources imported to the United States. Aggregate supply in the United States therefore will decline and part of the expansionary effect described here may be offset.

would strike next—producer prices, retail sales, factory payrolls, manufacturing inventories.

Suddenly, one of his staff officers burst into the room: "Straight from the Western European front, sir—the dollar is under attack by the major industrial nations."

Greenspan whirled around toward the big campaign map. "We've got to turn back this assault!" he said.

"Yes sir." The officer turned to go.

"Hold it!" Greenspan shouted. Suddenly, his mind reeled with conflicting data. A strong dollar was good for inflation, right? Yes, but it was bad for the trade deficit. Or was it the other way around? Attack? Retreat? Macroeconomic forces were closing in.

"Call out the Reserve!" he told the officer.

"Uh . . . we are the Reserve," the man answered.

The Fed as the Fall Guy Inflation isn't the only tough customer out there. The Fed must also withstand pressure from administration officials who are regularly described as "leaning heavily" on the Fed to ease up and relax. This always sounds vaguely threatening:

Alan Greenspan was walking down a deserted street late one night. Suddenly a couple of thugs wearing pin-stripes and wingtips cornered him in a dark alley.

"What do you want?" Greenspan asked.

"Just relax," said one.

"How can I relax?" asked Greenspan. "I'm in a dark alley talking to thugs."

"You know what we mean," said the other. "Ease up on the federal funds rate—or else."

"Or else what?" asked Greenspan.

"Don't make us spell it out. Let's just say that if anything unfortunate happens to the gross [domestic] product, I'm holding you personally responsible."

"Yeah," added the other. "A recession could get real painful."

The Fed as Cosmic Force The Fed may be a cosmic force. After all, it does satisfy the three major criteria—power, mystery, and a New York office. Some observers even believe the Fed can control the stock market, either by action, symbolic action, anticipated action, or non-action. But saner heads realize this is ridiculous—the market has always been controlled by sunspots.

I wish we could get rid of all these romantic ideas about the Federal Reserve. If you want to talk about the Fed, keep it simple. Just say the Fed is worried about the money. This is something we all can relate to.

Source: Paul Hellman, "Greenspan and the Feds: Captains Courageous," *Wall Street Journal,* January 31, 1991, p. 18. Reprinted with permission of *The Wall Street Journal* © 1990 Dow Jones & Company, Inc. All rights reserved.

creases the domestic interest rate. To see how this happens, follow through the analysis in column 2 of Table 15-4.

Macro Stability and the Trade Balance

Assume in Table 15-4 that, in addition to domestic macroeconomic stability, a widely held economic goal is that the United States should balance its exports and imports. That is, we should achieve a balance in our international trade. In simple terms, we want to "pay our way" in international trade by earning from our exports an amount of money sufficient to finance our imports.

Consider column 1 of Table 15-4 once again, but now suppose that initially the United States has a very large balance of international trade *deficit,* which means our imports substantially exceed our exports so we are *not* paying our way in world trade. By following through our cause-effect chain in column 1 we find that an easy money policy lowers the international value of the dollar so that our exports increase and our imports decline. This increase in net exports works to correct the assumed initial balance of trade deficit.

Conclusion: *The easy money policy which is appropriate for the alleviation of unemployment and slug-*

KEY GRAPH

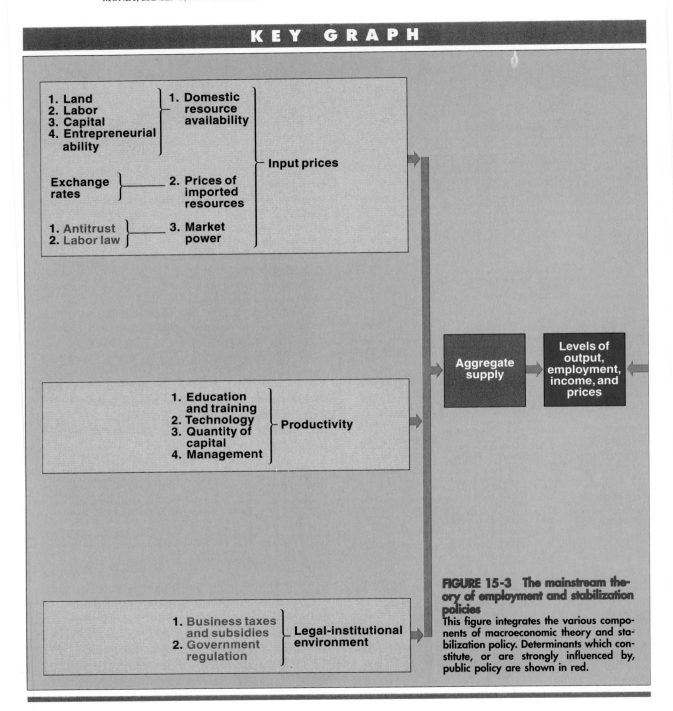

1. Land
2. Labor
3. Capital
4. Entrepreneurial ability

1. Domestic resource availability

Exchange rates

2. Prices of imported resources

Input prices

1. Antitrust
2. Labor law

3. Market power

1. Education and training
2. Technology
3. Quantity of capital
4. Management

Productivity

1. Business taxes and subsidies
2. Government regulation

Legal-institutional environment

Aggregate supply

Levels of output, employment, income, and prices

FIGURE 15-3 The mainstream theory of employment and stabilization policies
This figure integrates the various components of macroeconomic theory and stabilization policy. Determinants which constitute, or are strongly influenced by, public policy are shown in red.

gish growth is compatible with the goal of correcting a balance of trade deficit. If initially our exports were greatly in *excess* of our imports—that is, the United States had a large balance of trade *surplus*—an easy money policy would aggravate the surplus.

Now consider column 2 of Table 15-4 and assume again that at the outset the United States has a large balance of trade deficit. In invoking a tight money policy to restrain inflation we would find that net exports would decrease—our exports would fall and imports

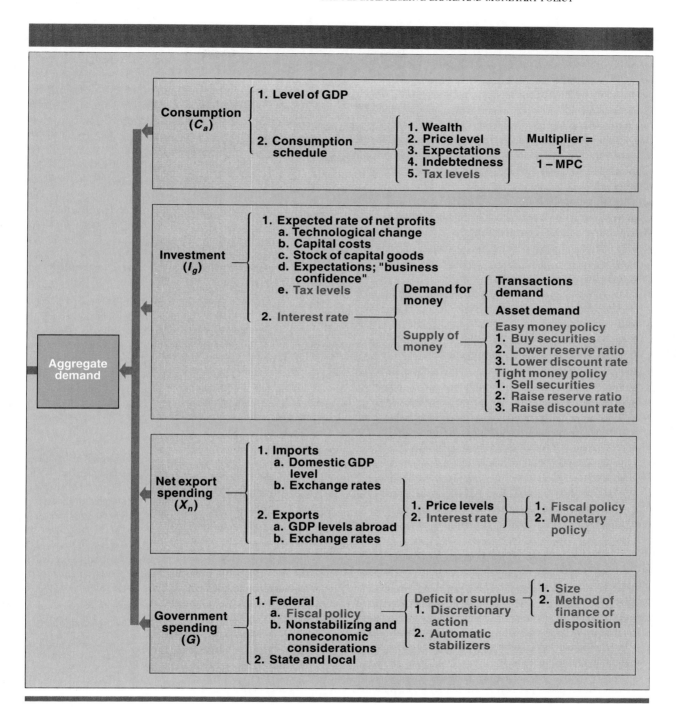

would rise. This means the trade deficit would be enlarged.

Conclusion: *A tight money policy invoked to alleviate inflation conflicts with the goal of correcting a balance of trade deficit.* If our initial problem was a trade surplus, a tight money policy would tend to resolve that surplus.

Overall we find that an easy money policy alleviates a trade deficit and aggravates a trade surplus. Similarly, a tight money policy alleviates a trade surplus and aggravates a trade deficit. The point is that certain combinations of circumstances create conflicts or tradeoffs between the use of monetary policy to achieve domestic stability and the realization of balance in the nation's international trade. *(Key Question 8)*

THE "BIG PICTURE"

Figure 15-3 (Key Graph) brings together the many analytical and policy aspects of macroeconomics discussed in this and the eight preceding chapters. This "big picture" shows how the many concepts and principles discussed relate to one another and how they constitute a coherent theory of what determines the level of resource use in a market economy.

Study this diagram and you will see that the levels of output, employment, income, and prices all result from the interaction of aggregate supply and aggregate demand. In particular, note those items—shown in red—which constitute, or are strongly influenced by, public policy.

Self-test: Suppose the economy represented by this diagram was experiencing a severe, long-lasting recession. What specific stabilization policies would you recommend? Use the linkages in this diagram to explain how your policies would work.

CHAPTER SUMMARY

1 Like fiscal policy, the goal of monetary policy is to assist the economy in achieving a full-employment, noninflationary level of total output.

2 For a consideration of monetary policy, the most important assets of the Federal Reserve Banks are securities and loans to commercial banks. The basic liabilities are the reserves of member banks, Treasury deposits, and Federal Reserve Notes.

3 The three instruments of monetary policy are **a** open-market operations, **b** changing the reserve ratio, and **c** changing the discount rate.

4 Monetary policy operates through a complex cause-effect chain: **a** Policy decisions affect commercial bank reserves; **b** changes in reserves affect the money supply; **c** changes in the money supply alter the interest rate; and **d** changes in the interest rate affect investment; **e** changes in investment affect aggregate demand; **f** changes in aggregate demand affect the equilibrium real GDP and the price level. Table 15-3 draws together all the basic notions relevant to applying easy and tight money policies.

5 The advantages of monetary policy include its flexibility and political acceptability. In the past fifteen years monetary policy has been used successfully both to reduce rapid inflation and push the economy from recession. Today, almost all economists view monetary policy as a significant stabilization tool.

6 Monetary policy has some limitations and problems. **a** Financial innovations and global considerations have made this policy more difficult to administer and its impact less certain. **b** Policy-instigated changes in the supply of money may be partially offset by changes in the velocity of money. **c** The impact of monetary policy will be lessened if the money-demand curve is flat and the investment-demand curve is steep. The investment-demand curve may also shift, negating monetary policy. **d** Changes in interest rates resulting from monetary policy change the amount of interest income received by lenders, altering some people's spending in a way counter to the intent of the monetary policy.

7 Monetary authorities face a policy dilemma in that they can stabilize interest rates *or* the money supply, but not both. Recent monetary policy has been pragmatic, focusing on the health of the economy and not on stabilizing either interest rates or the money supply exclusively. In particular, the Fed has recently focused on the Federal funds rate in setting its policy.

8 The impact of an easy money policy on domestic GDP is strengthened by an accompanying increase in net exports precipitated by a lower domestic interest rate. Likewise, a tight money policy is strengthened by a decline in net exports. In some situations, there may be a tradeoff between the use of monetary policy to affect the international value of the dollar and thus to correct a trade imbalance and the use of monetary policy to achieve domestic stability.

9 Figure 15-3 summarizes mainstream macroeconomic theory and policy and deserves your careful study.

TERMS AND CONCEPTS

monetary policy	discount rate	velocity of money	prime interest rate
open-market operations	easy and tight money	target dilemma	net export effect
reserve ratio	policies	Federal funds rate	

QUESTIONS AND STUDY SUGGESTIONS

1 Use commercial bank and Federal Reserve Bank balance sheets to demonstrate the impact of each of the following transactions on commercial bank reserves:

a Federal Reserve Banks purchase securities from private businesses and consumers.

b Commercial banks borrow from Federal Reserve Banks.

c The Board of Governors reduces the reserve ratio.

2 *Key Question   In the table below you will find simplified consolidated balance sheets for the commercial banking system and the twelve Federal Reserve Banks. In columns 1 through 3, indicate how the balance sheets would read after each of the three ensuing transactions is completed. Do not cumulate your answers; that is, analyze each transaction separately, starting in each case from the given figures. All accounts are in billions of dollars.*

ties from commercial banks. Show the new balance-sheet figures in column 3.

d *Now review each of the above three transactions, asking yourself these three questions: (1) What change, if any, took place in the money supply as a direct and immediate result of each transaction? (2) What increase or decrease in commercial banks' reserves took place in each transaction? (3) Assuming a reserve ratio of 20 percent, what change in the money-creating potential of the commercial banking system occurred as a result of each transaction?*

3 *Key Question   Suppose you are a member of the Board of Governors of the Federal Reserve System. The economy is experiencing a sharp and prolonged inflationary trend. What changes in **a** the reserve ratio, **b** the discount rate, and **c** open-market operations would you recommend? Explain in*

Consolidated balance sheet: all commercial banks

	(1)	(2)	(3)
Assets:			
Reserves . . . .$ 33	_____	_____	_____
Securities 60	_____	_____	_____
Loans 60	_____	_____	_____
Liabilities and net worth:			
Demand deposits $150	_____	_____	_____
Loans from the Federal Reserve Banks 3	_____	_____	_____

Consolidated balance sheet: twelve Federal Reserve Banks

	(1)	(2)	(3)
Assets:			
Securities $60	_____	_____	_____
Loans to commercial banks 3	_____	_____	_____
Liabilities and net worth:			
Reserves of commercial banks $33	_____	_____	_____
Treasury deposits 3	_____	_____	_____
Federal Reserve Notes 27	_____	_____	_____

a *Suppose a decline in the discount rate prompts commercial banks to borrow an additional $1 billion from the Federal Reserve Banks. Show the new balance-sheet figures in column 1.*

b *The Federal Reserve Banks sell $3 billion in securities to the public, who pay for the bonds with checks. Show the new balance-sheet figures in column 2.*

c *The Federal Reserve Banks buy $2 billion of securi-*

each case how the change you advocate would affect commercial bank reserves, the money supply, interest rates, and aggregate demand.

4 *Key Question   What is the basic objective of monetary policy? Describe the cause-effect chain through which monetary policy is made effective. Using Figure 15-2 as a point of reference, discuss how **a** the shapes of the demand for money and investment-demand curves and **b** the size of the MPC* *influence the effectiveness of monetary policy. How do feedback effects influence the effectiveness of monetary policy?*

5 Evaluate the overall effectiveness of monetary policy. Why have open-market operations evolved as the primary means of controlling commercial bank reserves? Discuss the specific limitations of monetary policy.

6 Explain the observation that the Fed cannot simultaneously stabilize interest rates and the money supply. Explain why the target of a stable interest rate might contribute to ongoing inflation.

7 *Key Question   Distinguish between the Federal funds rate and the prime interest rate. In what way is the Federal funds rate a measure of the tightness or looseness of monetary policy? In 1994 the Fed used open-market operations to increase the Federal funds rate. What was the logic? What was the effect on the prime interest rate?*

8 *Key Question   Suppose the Federal Reserve decides to engage in a tight money policy as a way to reduce demand-pull inflation. Use the aggregate demand–aggregate supply model to show the intent of this policy for a closed economy. Next, introduce the open economy and explain how changes in the international value of the dollar might affect the location of your aggregate demand curve.*

9 Design an antirecession stabilization policy, involving both fiscal and monetary policies, which is consistent with **a** a relative decline in the public sector, **b** greater income equality, and **c** a high rate of economic growth. Explain: "Truly effective stabilization policy presumes the coordination of fiscal and monetary policy."

10 (Last Word) How do each of the following metaphors apply to the Federal Reserve's role in the economy: Fed as a mechanic; Fed as a warrior; Fed as a fall guy?

Problems and Controversies in Macro-economics

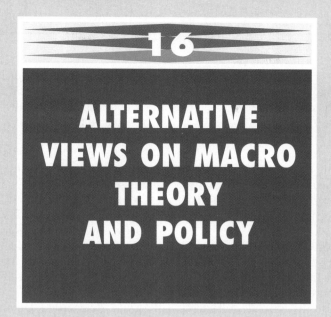

ALTERNATIVE VIEWS ON MACRO THEORY AND POLICY

Macroeconomic theory and stabilization policy as represented in Figure 15-3 has dominated the thinking of most economists in all market-oriented industrial economies since World War II. In the United States, Democratic and Republican administrations alike have accepted these precepts, at least as evidenced by policy actions. Presently, the stabilization policies of nearly all the major industrial nations can be understood through Figure 15-3.

But it would be misleading to suggest there is agreement on all aspects of macroeconomic theory and stabilization policy. Both historically and presently, macroeconomics is the subject of much dispute. In this chapter we explore points of disagreement among "camps" of macroeconomists, vividly contrasting alternative views. Keep in mind that differences in perspectives of individual economists rarely are as extreme as suggested by these polar comparisons.

First, we contrast the crude, simplified forms of classical and Keynesian macroeconomic theories, then examine the *monetarist school,* whose leader is Milton Friedman, winner of the 1976 Nobel Prize in economics. Friedman asserted that the role of money in determining the level of economic activity and the price level was much greater than suggested by early Keynesian theory. Next, we turn to the *rational expectations theory* (RET) which asserts that expectations created by traditional stabilization policies will largely render these policies ineffective. Finally, we point out that some aspects of monetarism and RET have been absorbed into mainstream macroeconomic thinking.

Chapter 17 continues the debate over stabilization policy and analyzes the problem of simultaneous inflation and unemployment. In Chapter 18, issues involving the troublesome budget deficits and public debt are discussed. Part 4 concludes with Chapter 19, which examines the process, problems, and policies of economic growth.

CLASSICS AND KEYNES: AD-AS INTERPRETATION

Recall from Chapter 9 that **classical economics** suggests that full employment is the norm in a market economy and that a *laissez faire* ("let it be") policy by government is best. Yet Keynes contended that recurring recessions or depressions with widespread unemployment are characteristic of laissez faire capitalism, and activist government policies are required to avoid wastes of idle resources.

These two views of the macroeconomic world

—classical and Keynesian—can be restated and compared in their simple forms through aggregate demand and aggregate supply curves.

Classical View

The classical view is that the aggregate supply curve is vertical and exclusively determines the level of real output. The downsloping aggregate demand curve is stable and solely establishes the price level.

Vertical Aggregate Supply Curve

In the classical perspective, the aggregate supply curve is a vertical line as shown in Figure 16-1a. This line is located at the full-employment level of real output, which in this particular designation is also the absolute full-capacity level of real output. According to the classical economists, the economy will operate at its full-employment level of output, Q_f, because of (1) Say's law (Chapter 9) and (2) responsive, flexible prices and wages.

We stress that classical economists believed that Q_f does *not* change in response to changes in the price level. Observe that as the price level falls from P_1 to P_2 in Figure 16-1a, real output remains anchored at Q_f.

But this stability of output might seem at odds with Chapter 3's upsloping supply curves for individual products. There we found that lower prices would make production less profitable and cause producers to offer *less* output and employ *fewer* workers. The classical response to this view is that input costs would fall along with product prices to leave *real* profits and output unchanged.

Consider a one-firm economy in which the firm's owner must receive a *real* profit of $20 to produce the full-employment output of 100 units. Recall from Chapter 8 that what ultimately counts is the *real* reward one receives and not the level of prices. Assume the owner's only input (aside from personal entrepreneurial talent) is 10 units of labor hired at $8 per worker for a total wage cost of $80 (= $10 \times \$8$). Also suppose the 100 units of output sell for $1 per unit so that total revenue is $100 (= $100 \times \$1$). This firm's *nominal* profit is $20 (= $\$100 - \$80$) and, using the $1 price to designate the base price index of 100 percent, its *real* profit is also $20 (= $\$20 \div 1.00$). Well and good; full employment is achieved. But suppose the price level declines by one-half. Would our producer still earn the $20 of real profits needed to induce production of a 100-unit full-employment output?

The classical answer is "Yes." Now that product price is only $.50, total revenue will only be $50 (= $100 \times \$.50$). But the cost of 10 units of labor will be reduced to $40 (= $10 \times \$4$) because the wage rate will be halved. Although *nominal* profits fall to $10 (= $\$50 - \$40$), *real* profits remain at $20. By dividing money profits of $10 by the new price index (expressed as a decimal) we obtain *real* profits of $20 (= $\$10 \div .50$).

With perfectly flexible wages there would be no change in the real rewards and therefore the production behavior of businesses. With perfect wage flexibility, a change in the price level will not cause the economy to stray from full employment.

Stable Aggregate Demand

The classical economists theorized that money underlies aggregate demand. The amount of real output which can be purchased depends on (1) the quantity of money households and businesses possess and (2) the purchasing power or real value of that money as determined by the price level. The purchasing power of the dollar refers to the real quantity of goods and services a dollar will buy. Thus, as we move down the vertical axis of Figure 16-1a, the price level is falling. This means the purchasing power of each dollar increases and therefore the specific quantity of money can buy a larger quantity of real output. If the price level declined by one-half, a particular quantity of money would now purchase a real output twice as large. With a fixed money supply, the price level and real output are inversely related.

And what of the *location* of the aggregate demand curve? According to the classical economists, aggregate demand will be stable if the nation's monetary authorities maintain a constant supply of money. With a fixed aggregate supply, increases in the supply of money will shift the aggregate demand curve rightward and spark demand-pull inflation. Reductions in the supply of money will shift the curve leftward and trigger deflation. The key to price-level stability, then, said the classical economists, is to control the nation's money supply to prevent unwarranted shifts in aggregate demand.

A final observation: Even if there are declines in the money supply and therefore in aggregate demand, the economy depicted in Figure 16-1a will *not* experience unemployment. Admittedly, the immediate effect of a decline in aggregate demand from AD_1 to AD_2 is an excess supply of output since the aggregate output of goods and services exceeds aggregate

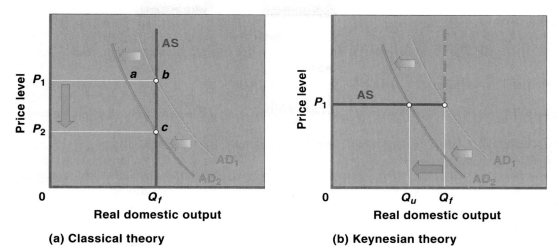

(a) Classical theory   **(b) Keynesian theory**

FIGURE 16-1   **Classical and Keynesian views of the macroeconomy**
According to classical theory (a), aggregate supply will determine the full-employment level of real domestic output while aggregate demand will establish the price level. Aggregate demand normally is stable, but if it should decline, say, as shown from AD_1 to AD_2, the price level will quickly fall from P_1 to
P_2 to eliminate the temporary excess supply of ab and to restore full employment at c. The Keynesian
view (b) is that aggregate demand is unstable and that price and wages are downwardly inflexible. An
AD_1 to AD_2 decline in aggregate demand has no effect on the price level. Rather, real output falls from
Q_f to Q_u and can remain at this equilibrium indefinitely.

spending by the amount ab. But, with the presumed
downward flexibility of product and resource prices,
this excess supply will reduce product prices along
with workers' wages and the prices of other inputs.
As a result, the price level will quickly decline from
P_1 to P_2 until the amounts of output demanded and
supplied are brought once again into equilibrium, this
time at c. While the price level has fallen from P_1 to
P_2, real output remains at the full-employment level.

Keynesian View

The core of crude, or extreme, **Keynesianism** is that
product prices and wages are downwardly inflexible,
resulting in what is graphically represented as a horizontal aggregate supply curve. Also, aggregate demand is subject to periodic changes caused by
changes in the determinants of aggregate demand
(Table 11-1).

**Horizontal Aggregate Supply Curve (to Full-Em-
ployment Output)**   The downward inflexibility of
prices and wages discussed in Chapter 11 translates
to a horizontal aggregate supply curve as shown in
Figure 16-1b. Here, a decline in real output from Q_f
to Q_u will have no impact on the price level. Con-

versely, an increase in real output from Q_u to Q_f will
also leave the price level unchanged. The aggregate
supply curve therefore extends from zero real output
rightward to the full-employment output Q_f. Once full
employment is reached, the aggregate supply curve
becomes vertical in this simplified view. This is shown
by the vertical (dashed) line extending upward from
the horizontal aggregate supply curve at Q_f.

Unstable Aggregate Demand   Keynesian economists view aggregate demand as unstable from one
period to the next, even without changes in the money
supply. In particular, the investment component of aggregate demand fluctuates, altering the location of the
aggregate demand curve. Suppose aggregate demand
in Figure 11-1b declines from AD_1 to AD_2. The sole
impact of this decline in aggregate demand will be on
output and employment because real output falls from
Q_f to Q_u while the price level remains constant at P_1.
Moreover, Keynesians believe that unless there is a
fortuitous offsetting increase in aggregate demand,
real output may remain at Q_u, which is below the full-
employment level Q_f. Active macroeconomic policies
of aggregate demand management by government
are essential to avoid the wastes of recession and depression. *(Key Question 1)*

KEYNESIANS AND MONETARISM

Classical economics has emerged in modern forms. One is **monetarism,** which holds that markets are highly competitive and that a competitive market system gives the economy a high degree of macroeconomic stability. Like classical economics, monetarism argues that the price and wage flexibility provided by competitive markets would cause fluctuations in aggregate demand to alter product and resource prices rather than output and employment. Thus the market system would provide substantial macroeconomic stability *were it not for governmental interference in the economy.*

The problem, as the monetarists see it, is that government has fostered and promoted downward wage-price inflexibility through the minimum-wage law, pro-union legislation, farm price supports, pro-business monopoly legislation, and so forth. The free-market system could provide macroeconomic stability, but, despite good intentions, government interference has undermined this capability. Furthermore, monetarists argue that government has contributed to the instability of the system—to the business cycle—through its clumsy and mistaken attempts to achieve greater stability through *discretionary* fiscal and monetary policies.

In view of the preceding comments, it is no surprise that monetarists have a strong *laissez faire* or free-market orientation. Governmental decision making is held to be bureaucratic, inefficient, harmful to individual incentives, and frequently characterized by policy mistakes which destabilize the economy. Furthermore, as emphasized by Friedman, centralized decision making by government inevitably erodes in-dividual freedoms.[1] The public sector should be kept to the smallest possible size.

Keynesians and monetarists therefore are opposed in their conceptions of the private and public sectors.

To the Keynesian, the instability of private investment causes the economy to be unstable. Government plays a positive role by applying appropriate stabilization medicine.

To the monetarist, government has harmful effects on the economy. Government creates rigidities which weaken the capacity of the market system to provide stability. It also embarks on monetary and fiscal measures which, although well intentioned, aggravate the instability they are designed to cure.

The Basic Equations

Keynesian economics and monetarism each build their analysis on specific equations.

Aggregate Expenditures Equation As indicated in Chapters 9 and 10, Keynesian economics focuses on aggregate spending and its components. The basic Keynesian equation is:

$$C_a + I_g + X_n + G = \text{GDP} \qquad (1)$$

This theory says that the aggregate amount of after-tax consumption, gross investment, net exports, and government spending determines the total value of the goods and services sold. In equilibrium, $C_a + I_g + X_n + G$ (aggregate expenditures) is equal to GDP (real output).

Equation of Exchange Monetarism focuses on money. The fundamental equation of monetarism is the **equation of exchange:**

$$MV = PQ \qquad (2)$$

where M is the supply of money; V is the **velocity of money,** that is, *the number of times per year the average dollar is spent on final goods and services; P* is the price level or, more specifically, *the average price at which each unit of physical output is sold;* and Q is the physical volume of all goods and services produced.

The label "equation of exchange" is easily understood. The left side, MV, represents the total

[1]Friedman's philosophy is effectively expounded in two of his books: *Capitalism and Freedom* (Chicago: The University of Chicago Press, 1962); and, with Rose Friedman, *Free to Choose* (New York: Harcourt Brace Jovanovich, 1980).

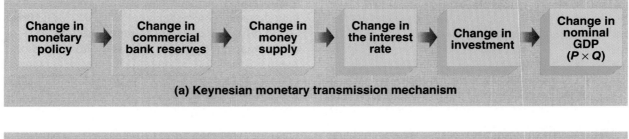

(a) Keynesian monetary transmission mechanism

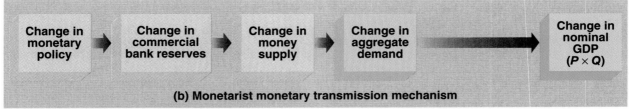

(b) Monetarist monetary transmission mechanism

FIGURE 16-2 Alternative views of the monetary transmission mechanism
Keynesians (a) emphasize the roles of interest rates and investment spending in explaining how changes in the money supply affect nominal GDP. On the other hand, monetarists (b) contend that changes in the money supply cause direct changes in aggregate demand and thereby changes in nominal GDP.

amount *spent* by purchasers of output, while the right side, PQ, represents the total amount *received* by sellers of that output.

> The difference between the two approaches can be compared with two ways of looking at the flow of water through a sewer pipe—say, at the rate of 6000 gallons per hour. A neo-Keynesian investigator might say that the flow of 6000 gallons an hour consisted of 3000 gallons an hour from a paper mill, 2000 gallons an hour from an auto plant, and 1000 gallons an hour from a shopping center. A monetarist investigator might say that the sewer flow of 6000 gallons an hour consisted of an average of 200 gallons in the sewer at any one time with a complete turnover of the water 30 times every hour.[2]

Both the Keynesian and monetarist approaches are helpful in understanding macroeconomics. In fact, the Keynesian equation can be readily "translated" into monetarist terms. In the monetarist approach, total spending is the supply of money multiplied by its velocity. In short, MV is the monetarist counterpart of equilibrium $C_a + I_g + X_n + G$. Because MV is the total amount spent on final goods in one year, it is equal to nominal GDP. Furthermore, nominal GDP is the sum of the physical outputs of various goods and services (Q) multiplied by their respective prices (P).

That is, $GDP = PQ$. We can therefore restate the Keynesian $C_a + I_g + X_n + G = GDP$ equation in nominal terms as the monetarist equation of exchange, $MV = PQ$.[3]

The two approaches are two ways of looking at much the same thing. But the critical question remains: Which theory more accurately portrays macroeconomics and therefore is the better basis for economic policy?

Spotlight on Money The Keynesian equation puts money in a secondary role. Indeed, the Keynesian conception of monetary policy (Chapter 15) entails a rather lengthy transmission mechanism, as shown in Figure 16-2a. A change in monetary policy alters the nation's supply of money. The change in the money supply affects the interest rate, which changes the level of investment. When the economy is operating at less than capacity, changes in investment affect nominal GDP ($= PQ$) by changing real output (Q) through the income multiplier effect. Alternatively, when the economy is achieving full employment, changes in investment affect nominal GDP by altering the price level (P).

---

[2]Werner Sichel and Peter Eckstein, *Basic Economic Concepts* (Chicago: Rand McNally College Publishing Company, 1974), p. 344.

[3]Technical footnote: There is an important conceptual difference between the Keynesian $C_a + I_g + X_n + G$ and the MV component of the equation of exchange. The former indicates planned or *intended* expenditures, which equal actual expenditures only in equilibrium, while MV reflects *actual* spending.

Keynesians contend there are many loose links in this cause-effect chain with the result that monetary policy is an uncertain and weak stabilization tool compared with fiscal policy. For example, recall from Figure 15-2 that monetary policy will be relatively ineffective if the demand for money curve is flat and the investment-demand curve is steep. Also, the investment-demand curve may shift adversely so that the impact of a change in the interest rate on investment spending is muted or offset. Nor will an easy money policy be very effective if banks and other depository institutions are not anxious to lend or the public eager to borrow.

Monetarists believe that money and monetary policy are more important in determining the level of economic activity than do the Keynesians. *Monetarists hold that changes in the money supply are the single most important factor in determining the levels of output, employment, and prices.* They see a different cause-effect chain between the supply of money and the level of economic activity than the Keynesian model suggests. Rather than limiting the effect of an increase in money to bond purchases and consequent declines in the interest rate, monetarists theorize that an increase in the money supply drives up the demand for all assets—real or financial—as well as for current output. Under conditions of full employment, the prices of all these items will rise. Monetarists also say the velocity of money is stable—meaning it does not fluctuate wildly and does not change in response to a change in the money supply itself. Thus, changes in the money supply will have a predictable effect on the level of nominal GDP $(= PQ)$. More precisely, an increase in M will increase P or Q, or some combination of both P and Q; a decrease in M will do the opposite.

Monetarists believe that, although a change in M may cause short-run changes in real output and employment as market adjustments occur, the long-run impact of a change in M will be on the price level. Monetarists think the private economy is inherently stable and usually operates at the full-employment level of output. The exact level of that full-employment output depends on such "real" factors as the quantity and quality of labor, capital, and land and upon technology (Chapter 19). The point is that, if Q is constant at the economy's capacity output, then changes in M will lead to changes in P.

Monetarism implies a more direct transmission mechanism than does the Keynesian model. Observe in Figure 16-2b that monetarists view changes in the money supply as producing direct changes in aggregate demand which alter nominal GDP. Monetarists contend that changes in the money supply affect all components of aggregate demand, not just investment. Furthermore, changes in aggregate demand allegedly affect nominal GDP in the long run primarily through changes in the price level, not through changes in real output.

Velocity: Stable or Unstable?

A critical theoretical issue in the Keynesian–monetarist debate centers on whether the velocity of money, V, is stable. As used here, "stable" is *not* synonymous with "constant." Monetarists are aware that velocity is higher today than in 1945. Shorter pay periods, greater use of credit cards, and faster means of making payments have increased velocity since 1945. These factors have enabled people to reduce their cash and checkbook holdings relative to the size of the nominal GDP.

What monetarists mean when they say velocity is stable is that the factors altering velocity change gradually and predictably. Changes in velocity from one year to the next can be easily anticipated. Moreover, velocity does *not* change in response to changes in the supply of money itself.

If velocity is stable, the equation of exchange tells us that monetarists are correct in claiming that a direct, predictable relationship exists between the money supply and nominal GDP $(= PQ)$.

Suppose M is 100, V is 1, and nominal GDP is 100. Also assume velocity increases annually at a stable rate of 2 percent. Using the equation of exchange, we can predict that a 5 percent annual growth rate of the money supply will result in about a 7 percent increase in nominal GDP. M will increase from 100 to 105, V will rise from 1 to 1.02, and nominal GDP will increase from 100 to about 107 $(= 105 \times 1.02)$.

But if V is not stable, then the Keynesian contention that money plays a secondary role in macroeconomics is quite plausible. If V is variable and unpredictable from one period to another, the link between M and PQ will be loose and uncertain. A steady growth of M will not necessarily translate into a steady growth of nominal GDP.

Monetarists: V Is Stable What rationale do monetarists offer for their contention that V is stable? They argue that people have a stable desire to hold money relative to holding other financial and real assets and buying current output. The factors determining the amount of money people and businesses wish to hold at any specific time are independent of the supply of money. Most importantly, the amount of money the public will want to hold will depend on the level of nominal GDP.

Example: Suppose that, when the level of nominal GDP is $400 billion, the amount of money the public wants or *desires* to hold to buy this output is $100 billion ($V$ is 4). If we further assume that the *actual* supply of money is $100 billion, we can say that the economy is in equilibrium with respect to money; the *actual* amount of money supplied equals the amount the public *desires* to hold.

In the monetarist view an increase in the money supply of, say, $10 billion will upset this equilibrium since the public will find itself holding more money or liquidity than it wants; the actual amount of money held exceeds the amount of holdings desired. The reaction of the public (households and businesses) is to restore its desired balance of money relative to other items such as stocks and bonds, factories and equipment, houses and automobiles, and clothing and toys. The public has more money than it wants; the way to get rid of it is to buy things. But one person's spending of money leaves more cash in someone else's checkable deposit or billfold. That person, too, tries to "spend down" excess cash balances.

The collective attempt to reduce cash balances will increase aggregate demand, boosting the nominal GDP. Because velocity is 4—the typical dollar is spent four times per year—nominal GDP must rise by $40 billion. When nominal GDP reaches $440 billion, the *actual* money supply of $110 billion again will be the amount which the public *desires* to hold, and equilibrium will be reestablished. Spending on goods and services will increase until nominal GDP has increased enough to restore the original equilibrium relationship between nominal GDP and the money supply.

The relationship GDP/M defines V. A stable relationship between GDP and M means a stable V.

Keynesians: V Is Unstable   In the Keynesian view the velocity of money is variable and unpredictable. This position can be understood through the Keynesian conception of the demand for money (Chapter 13). Money is demanded, not only to use in negotiating transactions, but also to hold as an asset. Money demanded for *transactions* purposes will be "active" money—money changing hands and circulating through the income-expenditures stream. Transactions dollars have some positive velocity; the average transactions dollar may be spent, say, six times per year and buy $6 of output. In this case V is 6 for each transactions dollar.

But money demanded and held as an *asset* is "idle" money. These dollars do *not* flow through the income-expenditures stream, so their velocity is zero. Therefore, the overall velocity of the entire money supply will depend on how it is divided between transactions and asset balances. The greater the relative importance of "active" transactions balances, the larger will be V. The greater the relative significance of "idle" asset balances, the smaller will be V.

Using this framework, Keynesians discredit the monetarist transmission mechanism—the allegedly dependable relationship between changes in M and changes in GDP—arguing that a significant portion of any increase in the money supply may go into asset balances, *causing V to fall*. In the extreme, assume *all* the increase in the money supply is held by the public as additional asset balances. The public simply hoards the additional money and uses none of it for transactions. The money supply will have increased, but velocity will decline by an offsetting amount so that there will be no effect on the amount of aggregate demand and the size of nominal GDP.

We can consider the Keynesian position on a more advanced level by referring to Figure 13-2. There, the relative importance of the asset demand for money varies inversely with the rate of interest. An *increase* in the money supply will *lower* the interest rate. That will make it less expensive to hold money as an asset, so the public will hold larger zero-velocity asset balances. Therefore, the overall velocity of the money supply will fall. A *reduction* in the money supply will *raise* the interest rate, increasing the cost of holding money as an asset. The resulting decline in asset balances will increase the overall velocity of money.

In the Keynesian view velocity varies (1) directly with the rate of interest and (2) inversely with the supply of money. If this is correct, the stable relationship between M and nominal GDP in the monetarist's transmission mechanism does *not* exist because V will vary whenever M changes.

We can now better appreciate a point made at the end of Chapter 15 in discussing possible shortcomings of monetary policy. We indicated that V tends to change in the opposite direction from M. Our present

PROBLEMS AND CONTROVERSIES IN MACROECONOMICS

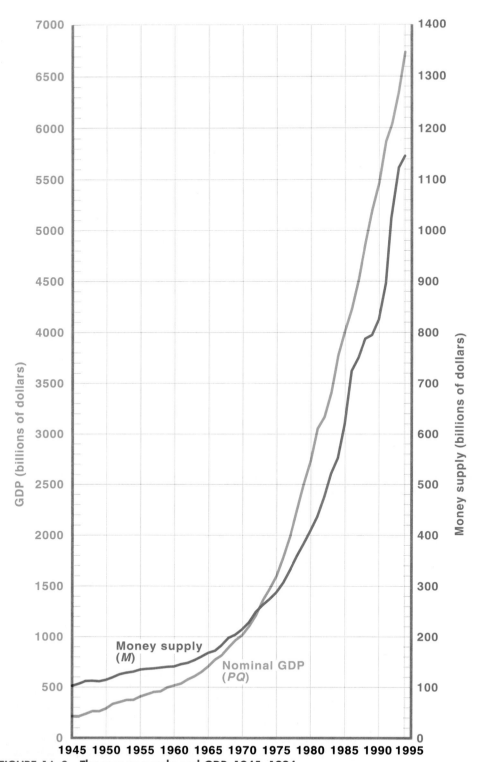

FIGURE 16-3 The money supply and GDP, 1945–1994
Monetarists cite the close positive correlation between the money supply and nominal GDP as evidence
in support of their position that money is the critical determinant of economic activity and the price level.
They assume that the money supply is the "cause" and the GDP is the "effect," an assumption which
Keynesians question. Monetarists also feel that the close correlation between *M* and nominal GDP indi-
cates that the velocity of money is stable. *(Economic Report of the President.)*

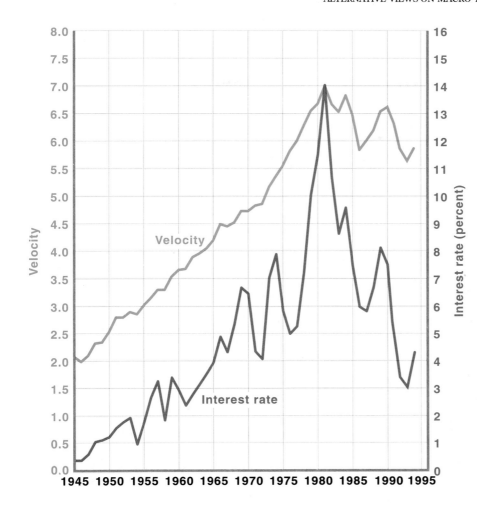

FIGURE 16-4 The velocity of money and the interest rate, 1945–1994
Keynesians argue that the velocity of money varies both cyclically and secularly. Hence, they conclude that any link between a change in the money supply and the subsequent change in nominal GDP is tenuous and uncertain. More specifically, Keynesians contend that velocity varies directly with the rate of interest because a lower interest rate will increase the size of zero-velocity asset balances and therefore lower the overall velocity of money. *(Economic Report of the President.)*

discussion reveals the cause-effect chain through which this might occur.

Empirical Evidence The stability of V is an empirical question and an appeal to "the facts" would seem to settle the issue. But the facts are not easy to discern or interpret.

Monetarists think the empirical evidence supports their position. In Figure 16-3 the money supply and the nominal domestic output (PQ) are both plotted. Since $MV = PQ$, the close correlation between M and PQ suggests that V is stable. Monetarists reason that the money supply is the causal force in determining nominal GDP; causation runs from M to nominal GDP.

But Keynesians offer two rebuttals.

1 By simple manipulation of $MV = PQ$, we find that $V = PQ/M = \text{GDP}/M$. That is, we can empirically calculate the value of V by dividing each year's nominal output (GDP) by the money supply. Keynesians contend that the resulting data, shown in Figure 16-4, repudiate the monetarist contention that V is stable. There was considerable year-to-year variation in velocity even during the so-called "steady" upward trend of velocity between 1945 and 1982. Also, note that the behavior of velocity has changed markedly since 1982. In some of these years velocity has declined.

Keynesians also point out that the close correlation between the velocity of money and the interest rate shown in Figure 16-4 supports their analysis that velocity varies directly with the rate of interest. (The short-term interest rate used here is the rate on three-month Treasury bills.) Velocity, in the Keynesian view, is variable both cyclically and secularly and these variations downgrade the role of money as a determinant of output, employment, and the price level.

Keynesians add this reminder: Given the large size of the money supply, a small variation in velocity can have a substantial impact on nominal GDP. Assume M is $300 billion and V is 5. A modest 10 percent increase in V will increase nominal GDP by $150 billion. That is, MV—and therefore PQ—are initially $1500 billion (= 300×5). Now, if V increases by 10 percent to 5.5, PQ will be $1650 billion (= MV = 300×5.5). *A very small variation in V can offset a large absolute change in M.*

2   Keynesians respond to Figure 16-3 by noting that *correlation* and *causation* are different. Changes in nominal GDP in Figure 16-3 may have been caused by changes in aggregate expenditures ($C_a + I_g + X_n + G$), as suggested by the Keynesian model. Perhaps a favorable change in business expectations increased investment. Also, the indicated growth in the nominal output may have prompted—indeed, necessitated—that businesses and consumers borrow more money from commercial banks to finance this rising volume of economic activity.

Keynesians claim that causation may run from aggregate expenditures *to* output *to* the money supply, rather than from the money supply *to* aggregate demand *to* output as monetarists content. The point, argue Keynesians, is that the data of Figure 16-3 are as consistent with the Keynesian view as they are with the monetarist position.

The question of the stability of V remains a crucial point of conflict between Keynesians and monetarists. For example, the great instability of M1 velocity (the velocity shown in Figure 16-4) in the 1980s led many monetarists to change their focus to the seemingly more stable M2. But in the past few years, the relationship between M2 and nominal GDP and the price level has also become unpredictable. Acknowledging these difficulties, some monetarists have looked to still broader measures of the money supply; others have narrowed their focus to the *monetary base*—currency in circulation plus bank reserves.

However, the experience of the last decade has been unkind to the strict monetarist view that M1 or M2 velocity is stable and predictable. Keynesians are quick to point out that a theory without a clearly defined key variable—the money supply—does not offer solid ground for establishing macroeconomic policy.

QUICK REVIEW 16-2

■ Keynesians view the economy as inherently unstable and therefore requiring stabilization through active fiscal and monetary policies; monetarists see the economy as relatively stable in the absence of government interference.

■ Keynesians focus on the aggregate expenditures equation ($C_a + I_g + X_n + G = \text{GDP}$) while monetarists base their analysis on the equation of exchange ($MV = PQ$).

■ Keynesians see changes in the money supply as working through changes in interest rates, investment, and aggregate expenditures; monetarists envision a direct link between the money supply, aggregate demand, and nominal GDP.

■ Keynesians contend velocity ($V = PQ/M$) varies directly with the interest rate and inversely with the money supply, whereas monetarists think velocity is relatively stable.

Policy Debates

Differences in Keynesian and monetarist theories spill over into the area of stabilization policy.

The Fiscal Policy Debate   Keynesians acknowledge the importance of monetary policy, but they believe fiscal policy is a more powerful and reliable stabilization tool. This is implied by the basic equation of Keynesianism. Government spending is a direct component of aggregate expenditures and thus aggregate demand. And taxes are only one short step removed, since tax changes allegedly affect consumption and investment in dependable and predictable ways.

Monetarists downgrade or reject fiscal policy as a stabilization tool. They believe that fiscal policy is weak and ineffectual because of the **crowding-out effect** (Chapter 12). Suppose government runs a budgetary deficit by selling bonds, which means borrowing from the public. By borrowing, government competes with private businesses for funds. Government borrowing will increase the demand for money, raise the interest rate, and crowd out a substantial amount of private investment which otherwise would have been profitable. Thus, the net effect of a budget deficit on aggregate expenditures is unpredictable and, at best, modest.

The workings of the crowding-out effect can be seen from a more analytical perspective by referring back to Figure 15-2. Financing the government's deficit will increase the demand for money, shifting the D_m curve of Figure 15-2a to the right. With a fixed money supply, S_m, the equilibrium interest rate will rise. This interest rate increase will be large, according to the monetarists, because the D_m curve is relatively steep.

Furthermore, monetarists believe that the investment-demand curve of Figure 15-2b is relatively flat, meaning investment spending is very sensitive to changes in the interest rate. The initial increase in the demand for money causes a relatively large rise in the interest rate which, projected off an interest-sensitive investment-demand curve, causes a large decline in the investment component of aggregate expenditures. The resulting large contractionary effect offsets the expansionary impact of the fiscal deficit and, on balance, the equilibrium GDP is unaffected. So sayeth Friedman: ". . . in my opinion, the state of the budget by itself has no significant effect on the course of nominal [money] income, on inflation, on deflation, or on cyclical fluctuations."[4]

If a deficit was financed by issuing new money, the crowding-out effect could be avoided and the deficit would be followed by economic expansion. *But,* the monetarists point out, the expansion would be due *not* to the fiscal deficit per se, but rather to the creation of additional money.

Keynesians, for the most part, do not deny that some investment may be crowded out. But they perceive the amount as small, and conclude that the net impact of an expansionary fiscal policy on equilibrium GDP will be substantial. In Figure 15-2, the extreme Keynesian view is that the demand for money curve is relatively flat and the investment demand curve is steep. (You may recall that this combination makes monetary policy relatively weak and ineffective.) An increase in D_m will cause a very modest increase in the interest rate which, when projected off a steep investment-demand curve, will result in a very small decrease in the investment component of aggregate expenditures. Little investment will be crowded out.

Keynesians *do* acknowledge that a deficit financed by creating new money will have a greater

stimulus than one financed by borrowing. In Figure 15-2a, for any given increase in D_m there is some increase in S_m which will leave the interest rate, and therefore the volume of investment, unchanged.

Monetary Policy: Discretion or Rules? We portray the Keynesian conception of monetary policy in Figure 15-2. Keynesians believe that the demand for money curve is relatively flat and the investment-demand curve relatively steep, weakening monetary policy as a stabilization tool. We have also seen that, in contrast, monetarists contend that the money demand curve is very steep and the investment-demand curve quite flat, a combination meaning a change in the money supply has a powerful effect on the equilibrium level of nominal GDP. This is monetarism's fundamental contention—the money supply is the critical determinant of the level of economic activity and the price level.

However, strict monetarists do *not* advise use of easy and tight money policies to modify "downs" and "ups" of the business cycle. Friedman contends that, historically, *discretionary* changes in the money supply made by monetary authorities have *destabilized* the economy.

Examining the monetary history of the United States from the Civil War up to the establishment of the Federal Reserve System in 1913 and comparing this with the post-1913 record, Friedman concludes that, even if the economically disruptive World War II period is ignored, the latter (post-1913) period was clearly more unstable. Much of this decline in economic stability after the Federal Reserve System became effective is attributed to faulty decisions by the monetary authorities. *In the monetarist view economic instability is more a product of monetary mismanagement than it is of any inherent destabilizers in the economy.* There are two sources of monetary mismanagement.

1 Irregular Time Lags Although the monetary transmission mechanism is direct, changes in the money supply affect nominal GDP only after a long and variable time period. Friedman's empirical work suggests that a change in the money supply may significantly change GDP in as short a period as six to eight months or in as long a period as two years. Because it is virtually impossible to predict the time lag of a policy action, there is little chance of determining accurately when specific policies should be in-

[4]Statement by Friedman in Milton Friedman and Walter Heller, *Monetary vs. Fiscal Policy* (New York: W. W. Norton & Company, Inc., 1969), p. 51.

voked or which policy—easy or tight money—is appropriate.

In view of the uncertain duration of this time lag, the use of discretionary monetary policy to "fine-tune" the economy for cyclical "ups" and "downs" may backfire and intensify these cyclical changes. Suppose an easy money policy is invoked because the economic indicators suggest a mild recession. But assume now that within the following six months the economy, for reasons unrelated to public policy actions, reverses itself and moves into the prosperity-inflationary phase of the cycle. At this point the easy money policy becomes effective and reinforces the inflation.

2 Interest Rate: Wrong Target Monetarists argue that monetary authorities have typically tried to control interest rates to stabilize investment and therefore the economy. Recalling Chapter 15's discussion of the targeting dilemma, the problem is that the Fed cannot simultaneously stabilize both the money supply and interest rates. In trying to stabilize interest rates, the Fed might *destabilize* the economy.

Suppose the economy is coming out of a recession and is currently approaching full employment, with aggregate demand, output, employment, and the price level all increasing. This expanding volume of economic activity will increase the demand for money and therefore raise the interest rate. Now, if monetary authorities want to stabilize interest rates, they will embark on an easy money policy. But this expansionary monetary policy will add to aggregate expenditures when the economy is already on the verge of an inflationary boom. The attempt to stabilize interest rates will fan existing inflationary fires and make the economy less stable. A similar scenario plays out for an economy moving into recession.

The Monetary Rule Monetarist moral: Monetary authorities should stabilize, not the interest rate, but the rate of growth of the money supply. Specifically, Friedman advocates legislating the **monetary rule** that the money supply be expanded each year at the same annual rate as the potential growth of our real GDP, meaning the supply of money should be increased steadily at 3 to 5 percent per year.

> Such a rule . . . would eliminate . . . the major cause of instability in the economy—the capricious and unpredictable impact of countercyclical monetary policy. As long as the money supply grows at a constant rate each year, be it 3, 4, or 5 percent, any decline into recession will be temporary. The liquidity pro-

vided by a constantly growing money supply will cause aggregate demand to expand. Similarly, if the supply of money does not rise at a more than average rate, any inflationary increase in spending will burn itself out for lack of fuel.[5]

Keynesian response: Despite a somewhat spotty record, it would be foolish to replace discretionary monetary policy with a monetary rule. Arguing that *V* is variable both cyclically and secularly, Keynesians contend that a constant annual rate of increase in the money supply could contribute to substantial fluctuations in aggregate expenditures and promote economic instability. We concluded in Chapter 15 that wide fluctuations in interest rates and investment spending would accompany any shift from the interest rate target. As one Keynesian had quipped, the trouble with monetary rule is that it tells the policy maker: "Don't do something, just stand there." *(Key Question 5)*

AD-AS Analysis

Let's now contrast monetarist and Keynesian views in terms of the aggregate demand–aggregate supply model. By bringing aggregate supply into the picture we can see more clearly the implications of each model for real output and the price level. We can also further our understanding of policy differences.

Contrasting Portrayals Figure 16-5a portrays the monetarist perspective and Figure 16-5b, the crude Keynesian conception. The difference on the demand side concerns the factors which will shift the aggregate demand curve. To monetarists the aggregate demand curve will shift rightward or leftward because of an increase or decrease, respectively, in the money supply. Keynesians are more general, recognizing that in addition to changes in private spending both fiscal and monetary policy can shift the aggregate demand curve.

On the supply side we find that monetarists view the aggregate supply curve as very steep or, in the long run, vertical, while Keynesians see it as quite flat, or in the extreme case, horizontal. This is not new to us as a glance back at Figure 11-5 will confirm. The aggregate supply curve presented there has a horizontal or near-horizontal range and a vertical or near-vertical range. The flat range reflects the belief that

---

[5]Lawrence S. Ritter and William L. Silber, *Money,* 5th ed. (New York: Basic Books, Inc., Publishers, 1984), pp. 141–142.

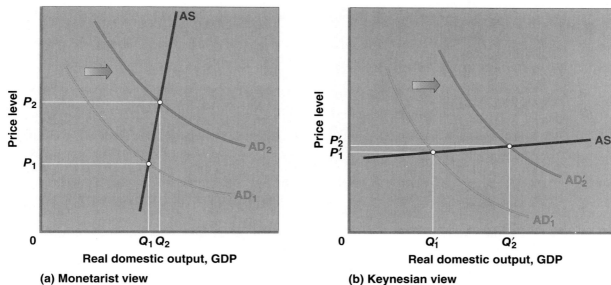

FIGURE 16-5 Monetarism, Keynesianism, and the aggregate demand–aggregate supply model
The monetarist view (a) is that the aggregate supply curve is relatively steep, which means that a change in aggregate demand will have a large effect on the price level but only cause a small change in real output and employment. The Keynesian conception (b) envisions a relatively flat aggregate supply curve which implies that a change in aggregate demand will cause large changes in real output and employment and small changes in the price level.

the economy can operate short of the full-employment or capacity level, while a vertical range reflects the classical heritage of monetarism and the belief that flexible prices and wages continuously move the economy toward full employment.

Policy Implications   These different conceptions of the aggregate supply curve relate to stabilization policy. In the monetarist view a change in aggregate demand affects primarily the price level and has little impact on real GDP. This conclusion derives from the assumption that, if the Federal Reserve adheres to a monetary rule, the economy will be operating near or at its full-employment output at all times. If policy makers try to use stabilization policy to increase real output and employment, their efforts will be largely in vain. As aggregate demand shifts from AD_1 to AD_2 in Figure 16-5a, we get a very modest increase in real output (Q_1 to Q_2) but a large increase in the price level (P_1 to P_2). The economy will pay a high "price" in terms of inflation to realize very modest increases in output and employment.

In comparison, the Keynesian conception indicates that an expansionary policy will have large effects on production and employment and little impact

on the price level. This conclusion derives from the assumption that, because of its inherent instability, the private economy may be operating far below its production potential. Thus in Figure 16-5b we find that the AD_1' to AD_2' increase in aggregate demand will entail a large increase in real output (Q_1' to Q_2') while eliciting only a small price level increase (P_1' to P_2'). To Keynesians, when the economy operates at less than its capacity, large gains in real output and employment can be obtained at a small inflationary cost.

Once the economy has reached full-employment output, the debate between Keynesians and monetarists ends. Both agree that expansionary stabilization policies will produce demand-pull inflation in the vertical range of aggregate supply.

Debate over the Monetary Rule   The aggregate demand–aggregate supply model also can help clarify the debate over the monetarists' call for a monetary rule. In Figure 16-6 suppose for simplicity that the aggregate supply curve is vertical, rather than near-vertical as in Figure 16-5a. Also assume the economy is operating at the Q_1 full-employment level of GDP. The aggregate supply curve shifts rightward from AS to AS', depicting a typical or average annual

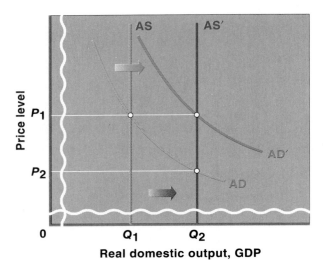

FIGURE 16-6   The monetary rule and the aggregate demand–aggregate supply model
Monetarists favor a monetary rule which would fix the increase in the money supply over time to the average increase in real output. An increase in aggregate demand (AD to AD') thus would match an increase in aggregate supply (AS to AS') and the price level would remain constant. Keynesians counter that the monetary rule will not guarantee that aggregate demand will shift from AD to AD'. Because of instability within the private economy, aggregate demand may either shift to the right of AD', creating demand-pull inflation, or fail to shift all the way to AD', resulting in deflation.

increase in full-employment real output. Such increases in aggregate supply result from real factors such as added resources and improved technology.

Monetarists argue that a monetary rule tying increases in the money supply to the typical rightward shift of the aggregate supply curve will ensure the aggregate demand curve shifts rightward from AD to AD'. As a result, real GDP will rise from Q_1 to Q_2 and the price level will remain constant at P_1. A monetary rule will allegedly promote price stability.

Keynesians dispute the close predictable link between changes in the money supply and changes in aggregate demand. They see two different scenarios.

1   During the period in question, the investment-demand curve (Figure 15-2b) may shift rapidly to the right because of optimistic business expectations. If so, the aggregate demand curve in Figure 16-6 will move to some point rightward of AD' and demand-pull inflation will occur. The monetary rule will not accomplish its goal of maintaining price stability. According to Keynesians, a contractionary fiscal policy accompanied by a tight money policy can hold the

rightward shift of aggregate demand to AD', thereby avoiding the inflation.

2   Suppose the investment-demand curve collapses leftward because of pessimistic business expectations. Aggregate demand will *not* increase from AD to AD' in Figure 16-6 and again the monetary rule flunks the price stability test: The price level falls from P_1 to P_2. By increasing the aggregate demand to AD', argue Keynesians, an expansionary fiscal policy accompanied by an easy money policy can avoid the deflation. Or, if the price level is inflexible downward at P_1, expansionary stabilization policies can prevent the loss of potential output otherwise occurring (Q_1Q_2).

QUICK REVIEW 16-3

■ In contrast to Keynesians, monetarists believe fiscal policy is weak and ineffectual because of a severe crowding-out effect.

■ Monetarists see the money demand curve as relatively steep and the investment-demand curve as relatively flat, implying that monetary policy has strong impacts on nominal GDP.

■ Strict monetarists advocate that the Federal Reserve adhere to a monetary rule whereby it expands the money supply at a fixed annual rate approximating the growth of potential output.

RATIONAL EXPECTATIONS THEORY

Keynesian economics and monetarism are not alone in the battle for the minds of economists, policy makers, and students. Developed largely since the mid-1970s, **rational expectations theory** (RET) has entered the fray. Although several variants of RET have emerged, including Keynesian ones, we will discuss the version associated with the *new classical economics*. (Other aspects of the new classical economics will be discussed in Chapter 17.) Our goal in introducing RET is to relate it to the debate over whether stabilization policy should be discretionary, as Keynesians argue, or based on rules, as monetarists contend. First, some relevant background on RET.

Rational expectations theory follows the thrust of economic theory in suggesting that people behave rationally. Market participants gather information and process it intelligently to form expectations about things in which they have a monetary stake. If financial investors, for instance, expect stock market prices to fall, they sell their shares in anticipation of that decline. The increased availability of stock in the market results in an immediate drop in prices offered per share. When consumers learn that a drought is expected to boost food prices, some of them purchase storable food products in advance of the price hike. These expectations cause an increase in market demand which in turn produces an increase in food prices before the food crop is even harvested.

But RET contains a second basic element which gives it its "new classical" flavor. Like classical economics, rational expectations theory assumes that all markets—both product and resource—are highly competitive. Therefore, wages and prices are flexible both upward and downward. RET goes further, assuming that new information is quickly (in some cases instantaneously) taken into account in the demand and supply curves of such markets. So equilibrium prices and quantities quickly adjust to new events (technological change), market shocks (a drought or collapse of the OPEC oil cartel), or changes in public policies (a shift from tight to easy money). Both product and resource prices are highly flexible and change quickly as consumers, businesses, and resource suppliers change their economic behavior as they get new information.

Policy Frustration

RET adherents contend that *the aggregate responses of the public to its expectations will render anticipated discretionary stabilization policies ineffective.* Consider monetary policy. Suppose monetary authorities announce an easy money policy is in the offing. Purpose: To increase real output and employment. But based on past experience, the public anticipates that this expansionary policy will be inflationary and take self-protective actions. Workers will press for higher nominal wages. Businesses will increase the prices of products. Lenders will raise interest rates.

All these responses are designed to prevent inflation from having anticipated adverse effects on the *real* incomes of workers, businesses, and lenders. But collectively this behavior raises wage and price levels and the increase in aggregate demand brought about by the easy money policy is completed dissipated in higher prices and wages. Real output and employment do *not* expand.

In Keynesian terms, the increase in real investment spending which the easy money policy was designed to generate (Figure 15-2) never materializes.

The expected rate of net profit on investment remains unchanged since the price of capital rises in lockstep with the prices of the extra production which the capital allows. Also, the nominal interest rate rises proportionately to the price level, leaving the real interest rate unchanged. No increase in real investment spending happens and no expansion of real GDP occurs.

In the monetarists' equation of exchange, the easy money policy increases M and thus aggregate expenditures, MV. But the public's expectation of inflation elicits an increase in P by a percentage equal to the increase in MV. Despite the increased MV, real output, Q, and employment are therefore unchanged.

Note carefully what has occurred here. The decision to increase M was made to increase output and employment. But the public, acting on the expected effects of easy money, has taken actions which have frustrated the policy's goal. Easy money has been translated into inflation, rather than into desired increases in real output and employment.

AD-AS Interpretation

We can better understand the RET view of policy ineffectiveness by examining Figure 16-7. This diagram restates the classical model from Figure 16-1a. Here we show the aggregate supply curve as being *vertical.*

Once again, assume an expansionary monetary policy shifts the aggregate demand curve rightward from AD_1 to AD_2. Why doesn't this increase in aggregate demand increase real output significantly (as in the Keynesian model of Figure 16-5b) or at least slightly (as in the monetarist model of Figure 16-5a)? According to RET, the answer is that consumers, businesses, and workers will anticipate that an expansionary policy means rising prices and will have built the expected effects into their market decisions concerning product prices, nominal wage rates, nominal interest rates, and so forth. Markets will instantaneously adjust, bringing the price level upward from P_1 to P_2. The economy does not move beyond output Q_1 because the price level rises by precisely the amount required to cancel any impact the expansionary policy might have had on real output and employment. *The combination of rational expectations and instantaneous market adjustments*—in this case upward wage, price, and interest rate flexibility—dooms the policy change to ineffectiveness. As aggregate demand expands from AD_1 to AD_2, the economy moves

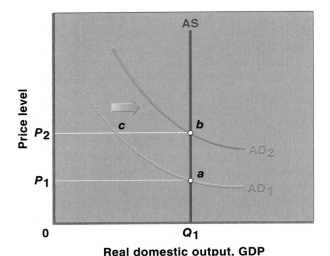

FIGURE 16-7 Rational expectations and the aggregate demand–aggregate supply model
Rational expectations theory implies that the aggregate supply curve is vertical. Strictly interpreted, the theory suggests that an increase in aggregate demand from, say, AD_1 to AD_2 will immediately result in an offsetting increase in the price level (P_1 to P_2) so that real domestic output will remain unchanged at Q_1. Conversely, a decline in aggregate demand from AD_2 to AD_1 will instantaneously reduce the price level from P_2 to P_1, leaving real domestic output and employment unchanged.

upward along the vertical aggregate supply curve directly from point a to point b. The only result is a higher price level; the *real* incomes of workers, businesses, lenders, and others are all unchanged because they have rationally anticipated the effects of public policy and have incorporated their expectations into market decisions to cause the resulting upshift of nominal wages, nominal profits, and nominal interest rates.

Presumably a decline in aggregate demand from AD_2 to AD_1 would do precisely the opposite. Instead of causing unemployment, the economy would move directly along the aggregate supply curve from b to a.

In the "old" classical theory there would be a period when a decline in aggregate demand would cause a temporary "lapse" from full employment until market adjustments were completed. The economy would first move from b to c in Figure 16-7, but then in time falling prices and wages would move the economy down AD_1 to full employment at point a. But in the RET version of the "new" classical economics, prices would adjust instantaneously to the anticipated policy so that the real output and employment would not deviate from Q_1.

In the "old" classical economics changes in aggregate demand could cause short-run changes in output and employment. But the decision-making process and instantaneous market adjustments of the strict RET form of "new" classical economics preclude this.

Postscript: While RET supports monetarism in arguing for policy rules rather than discretion, their rationales are quite different. In the rational expectations theory, policy is ineffective, not because of policy errors or inability to time decisions properly, but because of public reaction to the expected effects of these policies. Monetarists are saying that discretionary policy doesn't work because monetary authorities do not have enough information about time lags and such. RET supporters claim that discretionary policy is ineffective because the public has considerable knowledge concerning policy decisions and their impacts.

Evaluation

RET has stirred up macroeconomics in the past two decades. Anyone exposed to RET thinking looks at the macroeconomy from a somewhat different perspective. The appeal of RET stems from at least two considerations.

1 As with monetarism, RET is an option which might fill the void left by Keynesian economics' alleged inability to explain and correct by policy the simultaneous inflation and unemployment of the 1970s and early 1980s.

2 RET is strongly rooted in the theory of markets or, in other words, in microeconomics (defined in Chapter 1). Therefore, RET purports to provide linkages between macro- and microeconomics which economists have long sought.

But criticisms of RET are manifold and persuasive enough so that at this point most economists do *not* subscribe to strict interpretations of RET. Here are three basic criticisms.

1 Behavior Many economists question whether people are, or can be, as well-informed as RET assumes. Can households, businesses, and workers understand how the economy works and what the impact will be of, say, the Fed's announced decision to increase its annual *M2* money target growth rate from $3\frac{1}{2}$ to 5 percent? After all, economists who specialize in forecasting frequently mispredict the *direction* of changes in output, employment, and prices, much less correctly indicate the *amounts* by which such variables will change.

RET proponents argue they are not suggesting that people always make *perfect* forecasts, but rather that they do not make consistent forecasting errors which can be exploited by policy makers. Furthermore, RET theorists point out that key decision-making institutions—large corporations, major financial institutions, and labor organizations—employ full-time economists to help anticipate impacts of newly implemented public policies. It allegedly is impossible to fool important decision-making institutions in the economy on a consistent basis. But the issue of whether people and institutions behave as RET suggests is highly controversial.

2 Sticky Prices A second criticism of RET is that most markets are *not* sufficiently competitive to adjust instantaneously (or even rapidly) to changing market conditions. While the stock market and certain commodity markets experience day-to-day or minute-to-minute price changes, many sellers can control within limits the prices they charge. When demand falls, for example, these sellers resist price cuts so that the impact is on output and employment (see Figure 11-10). This is particularly true of labor markets where union and individual contracts keep wages unresponsive to changing market conditions for extended periods. If markets adjust quickly and completely as RET suggests, how do we explain the decade of severe unemployment of the 1930s or the high $7\frac{1}{2}$ to $9\frac{1}{2}$ percent unemployment rates which persisted over the 1981–1984 period?

3 Policy and Stability There is substantial domestic and international evidence to indicate that, contrary to RET predictions, economic policy has affected real GDP and employment. Thus, in the post-World War II period, when government has more actively invoked stabilization policies, fluctuations in real output have been less than in earlier periods. *(Key Question 12)*

ABSORPTION INTO THE MAINSTREAM

George Stigler, a Nobel Prize winning economist and historian of economic theory, once stated: "New ideas [in economics] do not lead to the abandonment of the previous heritage; the new ideas are swallowed up by

the existing corpus, which is thereafter a little different. And sometimes a little better."[6] As revolutionary as they were, Keynesian ideas themselves did not supplant the existing, micro-based economic heritage. Instead, economics simply incorporated the new macroeconomics within its expanded domain.

The controversies discussed in this chapter have forced economists to rethink some of the fundamental aspects of macroeconomics. And as is true of many debates, much compromise and revision of positions have occurred. Although considerable disagreement remains—for example, the "rules" versus "discretion" debate—contemporary macroeconomics has absorbed several of the fundamental ideas of monetarism and RET. Three examples:

1 Money Matters There are few economists today who embrace the extreme Keynesian view that "money isn't important." Mainstream economics now incorporates the monetarist view that "money matters" in the economy. This is demonstrated by the emphasis we have given monetary policy in this book (Chapters 13–15). Changes in the money supply and interest rates are mainstream tools for pushing the economy toward full employment or pulling it back from expansionary booms and attendant inflation.

In the last half of the 1980s and thus far in the 1990s, government has largely abandoned discretionary fiscal policy because of large full-employment, or structural, deficits (Figure 12-5). Elected officials have deemed tax cuts or increases in government expenditure to be economically undesirable under these conditions. Tax increases and reductions in government expenditures have been aimed at reducing the deficit, largely independently of the state of the economy. Thus, Federal Reserve monetary policy, not countercyclical fiscal policy, has recently been the tool for stabilizing the economy.

Also, macroeconomics has incorporated the monetarist precept that excessive growth of the money supply over long periods is a source of rapid inflation (see Global Perspective 16-1). This consensus view is reflected in our previous discussions of demand-pull inflation (Chapter 8) and maintaining the domestic value of the dollar (Chapter 13).

In summary, mainstream macroeconomics has accepted one part of monetarism—the importance of the money supply and monetary policy—while rejecting an-

---

[6]George J. Stigler, *Five Lectures on Economic Problems* (London: Longmans, Green, 1949), p. 24.

GLOBAL PERSPECTIVE 16-1

Money supply growth and inflation in selected high-inflation economies

Nations with high average annual rates of inflation typically have high average annual rates of money growth.

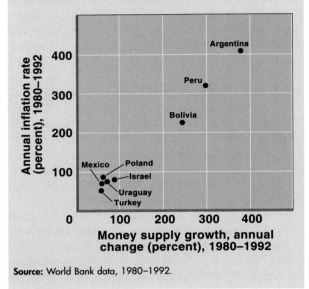

Source: World Bank data, 1980–1992.

other—the monetary rule expounded by strict monetarism.

2 Crowding Out and Coordination Thanks to the monetarists' emphasis on the crowding-out effect, mainstream economists now incorporate this idea within their analysis and are more fully aware of the wisdom of coordinating fiscal and monetary policy. If fiscal policy generates a sizable crowding-out effect which diminishes the effectiveness of fiscal policy, then it is imperative that an appropriate monetary policy be applied simultaneously to negate any potential crowding out of private investment.

3 Expectations and Markets Mainstream economists and policy makers are now more aware of expectations and how they might affect the economy and the outcome of a policy change. We have seen in previous chapters that expectations can shift the aggregate expenditures schedule in the Keynesian model (Chapters 9 and 10) and the aggregate demand curve in the AD-AS model. In Chapter 17 we emphasize the effects of expectations on aggregate supply.

Thanks to RET, mainstream economics increasingly searches for the links between microeconomics and macroeconomics. We are increasingly aware that what happens to the aggregate levels of output, employment, and prices depends on how individual product and resource markets work. Some Keynesians incorporate rational expectation assumptions directly into their macro analysis. Unlike the new classical-based RET, however, this analysis also assumes imperfect product and resource markets. Even with rational expectations, downward price and wage inflexibility lead to Keynesian conclusions: Instability *can* occur in the economy and fiscal and monetary policies *can* work.

Thus, monetarism and RET have both had a discernible impact on macro theory and policy. Disagreements in this case have led to new insights. An expanded and altered body of widely accepted macroeconomic principles has emerged and is a new base of agreement among professionals and policy makers. The modern macroeconomics studied in previous chapters descends from Keynesian macroeconomics, but it is different and better than it was before the monetarist and rational expectations critiques. *(Key Question 13)*

CHAPTER SUMMARY

1 Classical economists see **a** a vertical aggregate supply curve which establishes the level of real output, and **b** a stable aggregate demand curve which establishes the price level.

Keynesians envision **a** a horizontal aggregate supply curve at less-than-full-employment levels of real output, and **b** an inherently unstable aggregate demand curve.

The following four statements contrast the polar Keynesian and monetarist positions on a number of critical points.

2 Basic differences: The *Keynesian* view is that the market system is not sufficiently competitive and flexible to ensure macroeconomic stability. An activist stabilization policy, centered on fiscal policy, is required to remedy this shortcoming.

LAST WORD

"REAL" BUSINESS CYCLE THEORY

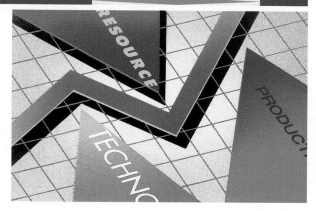

A handful of proponents of rational expectations theory (RET) stand traditional economic theory on its head by arguing that business cycles are caused by real factors affecting aggregate supply rather than by fluctuations in aggregate demand.

Keynesians and monetarists conclude that business cycles largely result from changes in aggregate demand. But RET (new classical) theorists rule out aggregate demand changes as likely causes of long-lasting changes in real output. They contend the economy adjusts quickly—if not instantaneously—to changes in aggregate demand through rapid changes in nominal wages and other input prices (Figure 16-7).

But history shows that long-lasting business recessions and expansions *have* occurred. If changes in aggregate demand are not the reason, what are the causes?

A small group of new classical economists has hypothesized that business cycles are caused by factors which disturb the long-run growth trend of aggregate supply. In this view, recessions begin on the supply side of the economy, not on the demand side as traditionally assumed. In other words, "real" factors—technology, resource availability, and productivity—all affecting aggregate supply are the alleged causes of business cycles. In contrast, traditional theory sees "monetary" factors that alter aggregate demand as the usual source of cyclical instability.

An example focusing on a recession will clarify this new classical thinking. Suppose productivity—output per worker—declines because an increase in the world price of oil makes it prohibitively expensive to operate certain types of machinery. This decline in productivity implies a reduction in the economy's ability to produce real output and therefore a leftward shift of its (vertical) aggregate supply curve. As real output falls in response to the decline in aggregate supply, people need less money to buy the reduced volume of goods and services. That is, the decline in output reduces the demand for money. Moreover, the slowdown in business activity lessens business borrowing from banks, reducing the supply of money.

In this scenario, changes in the supply of money respond passively to changes in the demand for money. The decline in the money supply in turn reduces aggregate demand (shifts the AD curve leftward) to the same extent as the initial decline in aggregate supply. The result is that real equilibrium output is lower, while the price level remains unchanged. Like the simple Keynesian model (Figure 16-1b), the real business cycle theory allows for a decline in real output in the presence of a constant price level. (You should test your comprehension of the real business cycle theory by using the AD-AS model in Figure 16-7 to diagram it.)

The policy implications of the real business cycle theory are as unusual and controversial as the theory itself.

1   Demand-management policies are inappropriate and doomed to fail. Expansionary stabilization policy in this situation will not increase real output; instead, it will cause inflation.

2   Deviations of aggregate supply from its long-term growth trend should not be the source of social concern. In the real business cycle theory, gains from "real" business booms roughly match the output losses arising from "real" downturns. The *net* long-run costs of business cycles therefore are allegedly modest. The emphasis of public policy should be on stimulating long-term economic growth rather than on trying to stabilize the economy.

Conventional economists reject the real business cycle theory, claiming it does not square with the facts of past business cycles. But, at a minimum, the theory shows that conventional macroeconomic theory is not the only analytical game in town.

The *monetarist* view is that markets are highly competitive and conducive to macroeconomic stability. Monetarists favor a *laissez faire* policy.

3   Analytical framework: To *Keynesians* the basic determinant of real output, employment, and the price level is the level of aggregate expenditures. Their basic equation is $C_a + I_g + X_n + G = $ GDP. Components of aggregate expenditures are determined by a wide variety of factors which, for the most part, are unrelated to the supply of money.

Monetarism focuses on the equation of exchange: $MV = PQ$. Because velocity V is basically stable, the critical determinant of the price level (P) is the supply of money (M).

4   Fiscal policy: The *Keynesian* position is that because **a** government spending is a component of aggregate expenditures and **b** tax changes have dependable effects on consumption and investment, fiscal policy is a powerful stabilization tool.

Monetarists argue that fiscal policy is weak and uncertain in its effects. Unless financed by an increase in the money supply, deficit spending will raise the interest rate and crowd out private investment spending.

5   Monetary policy: *Keynesians* argue that monetary policy entails a lengthy transmission mechanism, involving monetary policy decisions, bank reserves, the interest rate, investment, and finally the nominal GDP. Uncertainties at each step in the mechanism limit the effectiveness and dependability of monetary policy. Money matters, but its manipulation through monetary policy is not as powerful a stabilization device as fiscal policy. Specifically, the combination of a relatively flat demand for money curve and a relatively steep investment-demand curve makes monetary policy relatively ineffective.

Monetarists believe that the relative stability of V indicates a rather dependable link between the money supply and nominal GDP. However, monetarists think that because of **a** variable time lags in becoming effective and **b** the incorrect use of the interest rate as a guide to policy, the application of discretionary monetary policy to "fine-tune" the economy is likely to fail. In practice, monetary policy has tended to destabilize the economy. Monetarists therefore recommended a monetary rule whereby the money supply is increased in accordance with the long-term growth of real GDP.

Statements 6 and 7 contain the essence of rational expectations theory (RET).

6   RET is based on two assumptions: **a** consumers, businesses, and workers understand how the economy works; are able to assess the future effects of policy and other changes; and adjust their decisions to further their own self-interests; **b** markets are highly competitive and prices and wages adjust quickly to changes in demand and supply.

7   RET holds that, when the public reacts to the expected effects of stabilization policy, the effectiveness of such policy will be negated. This theory therefore supports policy rules as opposed to discretionary policy.

8   Several aspects of monetarism and rational expectations have been incorporated into mainstream macroeconomic analysis, including the ideas that **a** "money matters," in the macroeconomy; **b** excessive growth of money over long periods is inflationary; **c** fiscal policy may crowd out some private investment; and **d** expectations play an important role in the economy.

TERMS AND CONCEPTS

classical economics	equation of exchange	crowding-out effect	rational expectations
Keynesianism	velocity of money	monetary rule	theory
monetarism			

QUESTIONS AND STUDY SUGGESTIONS

1 *Key Question   Use the aggregate demand–aggregate supply model to compare classical and Keynesian interpretations of* **a** *the aggregate supply curve, and* **b** *the stability of the aggregate demand curve. Which model do you think is more realistic?*

2 Explain: "The debate between Keynesians and monetarists is an important facet of the larger controversy over the role of government in our lives."

3 State and explain the basic equations of Keynesianism and monetarism. "Translate" the Keynesian equation into the monetarist equation.

4 In 1994 the money supply (*M*1) was approximately $1150 billion and the nominal GDP was about $6737 billion. What was the velocity of money in 1994? Figure 16-4 indicates that velocity increased steadily between the mid-1940s and 1982 and then leveled off and declined. Can you think of reasons to explain these trends?

5 *Key Question   What is the transmission mechanism for monetary policy according to* **a** *Keynesians and* **b** *monetarists? What significance do the two schools of thought apply to money and monetary policy as a determinant of economic activity? According to monetarism, what happens when* *the actual supply of money exceeds the amount of money which the public wants to hold?*

6 Why do monetarists recommend that a "monetary rule" be substituted for discretionary monetary policy? Explain: "One cannot assess what monetary policy is doing by just looking at interest rates." Indicate how an attempt to stabilize interest rates can be destabilizing to the economy.

7 Answer the ensuing questions on the basis of the following information for a hypothetical economy in year 1: money supply = $400 billion; long-term annual growth of real GDP = 3 percent; velocity = 4. Assume that the banking system initially has no excess reserves and that the reserve requirement is 10 percent. Also, suppose that velocity is constant and that the economy initially is operating at its full employment level of output.

    a What is the level of nominal GDP in year 1 in this economy?

    b Suppose that the Federal Reserve adheres to the monetarist's rule through open-market operations. What amount of bonds will it have to sell to, or buy from, commercial depository institutions or the public between years 1 and 2 to meet its monetary rule?

8 Explain why monetarists assert fiscal policy is weak and ineffective. What specific assumptions do **a** monetarists and **b** strict Keynesians make with respect to the shapes of the demand for money and investment-demand curves? Why are the differences significant?

9 Indicate the precise relationship between the demand for money and the velocity of money. Discuss in detail: "The crucial issue separating Keynesians from monetarists is whether or not the demand for money is sensitive to changes in the rate of interest." Explain the Keynesian contention that a change in *M* is likely to be accompanied by a change in *V* in the opposite direction.

10 Explain and evaluate these statements in terms of Keynesian, monetarist, and RET views:

    a "If the national goal is to raise income, it can be achieved only by raising the money supply."

    b "The size of a Federal budget deficit is not impor-

tant. What is important is how the deficit is financed."

    c "There is no reason in the world why, in an equation like $MV = PQ$, the *V* should be thought to be independent of the rate of interest. There is every plausible reason for the velocity of circulation to be a systematic and increasing function of the rate of interest."

    d "Monetarists assume that the *PQ* side of the equation of exchange is 'passive'; Keynesians assume it is 'active.'"

    e "If expectations are rational, then monetary policy cannot be used to stabilize production and employment. It only determines the price level."

11 Explain how rational expectations might impede discretionary stabilization policies. Relate Chapter 12's Ricardian equivalence theorem to the idea of RET. Do you favor discretionary policies or rules? Justify your position.

12 *Key Question* *Use the aggregate demand–aggregate supply model to sketch graphically the* **a** *monetarist,* **b** *Keynesian, and* **c** *rational expectations theories of the macroeconomy. Carefully compare the implications of each for public policy. In what respect, if any, does your RET portrayal differ from the "old" classical model of Figure 16-1a?*

13 *Key Question* *Which of the following tenets of monetarism and RET have been absorbed into mainstream macroeconomics?*

    a *The Fed should increase the money supply at a fixed annual rate.*

    b *Money matters; it is an important factor in determining real GDP and the price level.*

    c *Excessive growth of the money supply over long periods will cause inflation.*

    d *Fiscal policy may cause a crowding-out effect.*

    e *Expectations are important; they can influence the locations of the aggregate demand and supply curves.*

    f *Changes in expectations created by traditional fiscal and monetary policy will render these policies completely ineffective.*

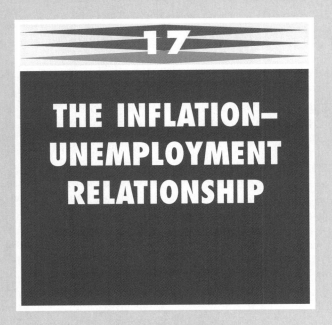

17

THE INFLATION–UNEMPLOYMENT RELATIONSHIP

In Chapter 16 we presented the basic ideas of monetarism and the rational expectations theory (RET) and contrasted them with the Keynesian perspective. There we saw that, although mainstream economics has incorporated several of the insights of monetarism and RET, disputes remain on such matters as the degree of inherent instability in the economy and the effectiveness of active stabilization policy. This chapter continues our discussion of modern developments and controversies in macroeconomics. In particular we will examine various explanations of the *simultaneous* occurrence of inflation and rising unemployment. By focusing on expectations, this chapter deepens our understanding of how the economy works. Our discussion also becomes more inclusive; in particular, we examine supply-side economics.

In this chapter we first derive and examine the *Phillips Curve,* used to explain the apparent tradeoff between unemployment and inflation. Next, we introduce another theory—the *natural rate hypothesis*—to analyze the economy's encounters with stagflation. Then, we advance our understanding by exploring the distinction between short-run and long-run aggregate supply. This permits us to extend our earlier analysis of demand-pull and cost-push inflation. Finally, policies designed to deal with stagflation are discussed.

THE PHILLIPS CURVE

We begin with some background to help us better understand the Phillips Curve.

Analytical and Historical Background

The Keynesian analysis of Chapters 9 and 10 focused on aggregate expenditures as the main determinant of real output and employment. The simplest Keynesian model implies that the economy may realize *either* unemployment (a recessionary gap) *or* inflation (an inflationary gap), but *not both simultaneously.*

In the aggregate demand and supply model, the strict Keynesian analysis assumes a "reverse L"-shaped aggregate supply curve (Figure 16-1b). Over the horizontal range of the curve, increases in aggregate demand expand real output and employment at a constant price level until full employment is achieved. Further increases in aggregate demand place the economy in the vertical range of aggregate supply, over which real output will remain constant, but inflation will occur. Presumably some "right" level of aggregate demand which intersects the aggregate supply curve precisely at the full-employment level of output would give us the best of all possible macroeconomic worlds: full employment *and* a stable price level (Q_f in Figure 16-1b).

This simple Keynesian model provided a satisfactory explanation of the economy's macro behavior over the four decades before the 1970s. The Great Depression, the World War II inflationary boom, and most of the macroeconomic ups and downs in the 1950s and 1960s can be interpreted and understood reasonably well within the context of this analysis.

But this situation changed in the 1970s. The coexistence of inflation and unemployment—indeed, simultaneously *increasing* unemployment and a *rising* price level—became common and was the central macroeconomic problem of the 1970s and early 1980s. There were two serious stagflationary episodes—1973–1975 and 1978–1980—which were not explainable through the aggregate expenditures model. These unusual periods can be better understood by (1) explicitly recognizing the more realistic *upsloping*, or intermediate range, of aggregate supply; and (2) allowing for leftward shifts of the aggregate supply curve.

The Phillips Curve: Concept and Data

The more realistic model is shown in Figure 17-1. Recall that the aggregate demand curve slopes downward due to the wealth, interest rate, and foreign purchases effects. With respect to aggregate supply, we know that the three ranges of the curve—the horizontal, upsloping, and vertical ranges—depend on what happens to production costs as real GDP expands. Real output and the price level are determined by the intersection of AD and AS.

In Figure 17-1 we perform a simple mental experiment. Suppose in a specific period aggregate demand expands from AD_0 to AD_2. This shift might result from a change in any one of the determinants of aggregate demand discussed in Chapter 11. Businesses may decide to buy more investment goods or government may decide to increase its expenditures. Whatever the cause of the aggregate demand increase, the price level rises from P_0 to P_2 and real output expands from Q_0 to Q_2.

Now let's compare what would have happened if the increase in aggregate demand had been larger, say, from AD_0 to AD_3. The new equilibrium tells us the amount of inflation and the growth of real output would have been greater (and the unemployment rate smaller). Similarly, suppose aggregate demand in our specific year had only increased modestly from AD_0

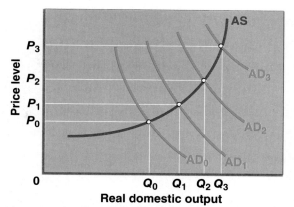

FIGURE 17-1   The effect of changes in aggregate demand on real output and the price level
Comparing the effects of various possible increases in aggregate demand yields the conclusion that the larger the increase in aggregate demand, the greater will be the resulting inflation and the greater the increase in real output. Because real output and the unemployment rate are inversely related, we can generalize that, given aggregate supply, high rates of inflation should be accompanied by low rates of unemployment.

to AD_1. Compared with our shift from AD_0 to AD_2, the amount of inflation and growth of real output would have been smaller (and the unemployment rate larger).

The generalization from this mental experiment is this: *The greater the rate of growth of aggregate demand, the higher will be the resulting inflation rate and the larger the growth of real output (and the lower the unemployment rate).* If aggregate demand grows more slowly, the smaller will be the resulting inflation and the slower the growth of real output (and the higher the unemployment rate). More simply, *high rates of inflation are accompanied by low rates of unemployment and vice versa.* Figure 17-2a generalizes how the expected relationship should look.

Do the facts fit the theory? Empirical work by economists in the late 1950s and 1960s verified this inverse relationship. It came to be known as the **Phillips Curve,** named after A. W. Phillips, who developed this concept in Great Britain. Figure 17-2b shows the relationship between the unemployment rate and the rate of inflation in the United States for 1961–1969. The line generalizing on the data portrays the inverse relationship. Based on this kind of empirical evidence economists believed a stable, predictable tradeoff existed between unemployment and inflation. Furthermore, national economic policy was built on this supposed tradeoff.

PROBLEMS AND CONTROVERSIES IN MACROECONOMICS

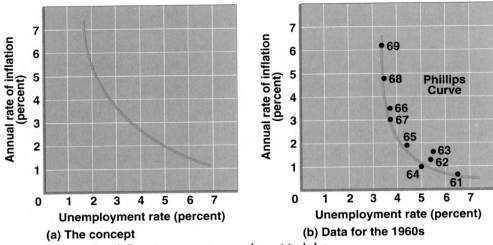

FIGURE 17-2 The Phillips Curve: concept and empirical data
The Phillips Curve purported to show a stable relationship between the unemployment rate and the rate of inflation. Because this relationship is inverse, there would presumably be a tradeoff between unemployment and inflation. Data points for the 1960s seemed to confirm the Phillips Curve concept. (Note: Inflation rates are on a December-to-December basis and unemployment rates are for all workers, including resident members of the armed forces.)

Logic of the Phillips Curve

How can the Phillips Curve be explained? What causes the apparent tradeoff between full employment and price level stability?

The factors underlying the Phillips Curve are the same as those previously used to explain the intermediate range of the aggregate supply curve. Certain imbalances—"bottlenecks" and structural problems—arise in labor markets as the economy expands toward full employment. "The" labor market in the United States comprises an extremely large number of individual labor markets which are stratified and distinct both occupationally and geographically. This labor market diversity suggests that, as the economy expands, full employment will *not* be realized simultaneously in each labor market. While full employment and labor shortages may exist for some occupations and regions, unemployment will persist for others. This disparity means that in an expanding economy, even though the overall unemployment rate may be, say $6\frac{1}{2}$ or 7 percent, scarcities will develop for specific labor and for labor in certain geographic areas. Wage rates of such workers will rise. Rising wage rates mean higher costs and necessitate higher prices. The net result is rising prices even though the economy as a whole is still operating short of full employment.

Why won't labor market adjustments eliminate these bottlenecks? Why, for example, do not unemployed laborers become craftworkers? The answer is that such shifts cannot be made quickly enough to eliminate the bottlenecks. The training for a new occupation is costly in time and money. Also, even if an unemployed laborer has the ability, time, and money to acquire new skills and relocate, an unemployed laborer in Kalamazoo may not be aware of the shortage of skilled craftworkers in Kenosha.

Then, too, artificial restrictions on the shiftability of workers sustain structural imbalances. For example, discrimination based on race, ethnic background, or gender can keep qualified workers from available positions. Similarly, licensing requirements and union restrictions on the number of available apprenticeships inhibit the leveling out of imbalances between specific labor markets.

In brief, labor market adjustments are neither sufficiently rapid nor complete enough to prevent production costs and product prices from rising *before* overall full employment is achieved.

Stabilization Policy Dilemma

If the Phillips Curve remains fixed as in Figure 17-2, policy makers are faced with a dilemma. Traditional fiscal and monetary policies merely alter aggregate

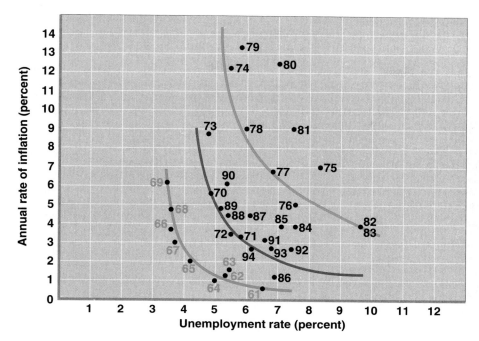

FIGURE 17-3 Inflation rates and unemployment rates, 1961–1994
Data points for 1961–1994 suggest no clear relationship between unemployment rates and rates of inflation. This raises questions as to the stability or existence of the Phillips Curve. Some economists think the curve shifted to the right in the 1970s and early 1980s as shown, and then collapsed back inward during the later 1980s. (Note: Inflation rates are on a December-to-December basis and unemployment rates are for all workers, including resident members of the armed forces.)

demand. They do nothing to correct the labor market imbalances and monopoly power fueling premature inflation. Specifically, the manipulation of aggregate demand through fiscal and monetary measures simply moves the economy *along* the Phillips Curve. An expansionary fiscal policy and easy money policy which boost aggregate demand and achieve a lower rate of unemployment will simultaneously produce a higher rate of inflation. A restrictive fiscal policy and a tight money policy can be used to reduce the rate of inflation, but only at the cost of a higher unemployment rate and more forgone production.

Policies to manage aggregate demand can be used to choose a point on the Phillips Curve, but such policies do not improve the "unemployment rate–inflation rate" tradeoff embodied in the curve. According to the Phillips Curve, it is impossible to achieve "full employment without inflation."

STAGFLATION: A SHIFTING PHILLIPS CURVE?

The concept of a stable Phillips Curve broke down in the 1970s and 1980s. Events during those years were clearly at odds with the inflation rate–unemployment rate tradeoff theorized in the Phillips Curve. Figure 17-3 enlarges Figure 17-2b by adding data for 1970 to

1994. The clear inverse relationship of 1961–1969 now becomes obscure and highly questionable.

Note in Figure 17-3 that in many years of the 1970s the economy experienced inflation *and* rising unemployment—in a word, **stagflation.** Trace, for example, the data points for 1972–1974 and 1977–1980. At best, these data suggest the Phillips Curve shifted to less desirable positions where each level of unemployment is accompanied by more inflation or where each level of inflation is accompanied by more unemployment. The downsloping lines to the northeast of the original Phillips Curve suggest such rightward shifts. At worst, the data imply no dependable tradeoff between unemployment and inflation.

Aggregate Supply Shocks

What caused the stagflation of the 1970s and early 1980s? One answer is that a series of cost shocks or **aggregate supply shocks** occurred. These disturbances on the cost or supply side make a difference. Remember that we derived the inverse relationship between the rate of inflation and the unemployment rate shown in Figure 17-2a by changing the level of *aggregate demand* in the intermediate range of the aggregate supply curve in Figure 17-1.

Now look at our cost-push inflation model graphed as Figure 17-4. Here a decrease (leftward

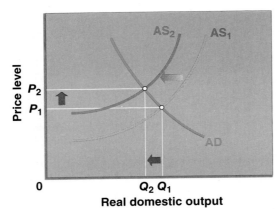

FIGURE 17-4 Adverse aggregate supply shocks and stagflation

In the mainstream interpretation, in 1973–1975 a series of supply shocks, including sharply increased energy costs, higher agricultural commodity prices, higher import prices, diminishing productivity growth, and inflationary expectations, shifted the aggregate supply curve leftward. The result was stagflation—a higher price level accompanied by a decline in real output. A similar scenario occurred in 1978–1980.

shift) of *aggregate supply* causes the unemployment rate and the price level to vary *directly*. Both increase to cause stagflation. This, say mainstream economists, is what happened in 1973–1975 and again in 1978–1980.

Let's consider the series of more-or-less random adverse shocks which raised unit production costs and shifted the aggregate supply curve leftward, as from AS$_1$ to AS$_2$ in Figure 17-4, to generate the Great Stagflation of 1973–1975. More technically, we want to examine how changes in several of the determinants of aggregate supply (Chapter 11) contributed to stagflation.

1 OPEC and Energy Prices   First and foremost, the Organization of Petroleum Exporting Countries (OPEC) oil cartel quadrupled oil prices. The cost of producing and distributing virtually every product and service rose sharply.

2 Agricultural Shortfalls   Severe global agricultural shortfalls occurred in 1972 and 1973, particularly in Asia and the Soviet Union. In response, American agricultural exports expanded sharply, reducing domestic supplies of agricultural commodities. The resulting higher prices for raw agricultural products in the United States meant higher costs to industries producing food and fiber products. These higher costs were passed on to consumers as higher prices.

3 Depreciated Dollar   In 1971–1973, the dollar was reduced in value to achieve greater balance between national exports and imports. Depreciation of the dollar meant that it took more dollars to buy a unit of foreign money, which increased prices of all American imports. Because many American imports are production inputs, unit production costs increased and the aggregate supply curve shifted leftward.

4 Demise of Wage-Price Controls   In 1971–1974 the Nixon administration imposed wage and price controls which suppressed inflationary pressures. When these were abandoned in 1974, both businesses and input suppliers pushed up their prices rapidly to recoup the price increases they had to forgo during the control period. This upsurge increased unit costs and product prices.

5 Productivity Decline   The stagflation episodes of the 1970s and early 1980s were not due solely to the four supply shocks just discussed. More subtle considerations involving productivity and expectations were also at work. The rate of growth of labor productivity—the efficiency of labor—began to decline in the mid-1960s and continued to fall throughout the 1970s (Chapter 19). This decline in the growth rate of output per worker-hour increased unit production costs. An increase in unit labor costs (that is, labor cost per unit of output) approximates the difference between the increase in nominal-wage rates and the increase in labor productivity. More precisely:

| Percentage change in unit labor costs | $\approx$ | percentage change in nominal-wage rates | $-$ | percentage change in labor productivity | (1) |

If hourly nominal wages are currently $5.00 and a worker produces 10 units per hour, unit labor costs will be $.50.

If nominal wages increase by 10 percent to $5.50 per hour and productivity also increases by 10 percent to 11 units per hour, then unit labor costs will be unchanged. That is, $5.00/10 = $5.50/11 = $.50. In equation (1), 10 percent (change in nominal wages) *minus* 10 percent (change in productivity) *equals* no increase in unit labor costs.

Similarly, if nominal wages were to rise by 10 percent and labor productivity does not increase at all, unit labor costs would go up by 10 percent. If the wage rate was $5.00 initially and output per hour was 10 units, labor costs would be $.50. But with wages $5.50

and output still at 10 units per hour, unit labor costs would be $.55, a 10 percent increase. In equation (1), 10 percent *minus* zero percent *equals* a 10 percent increase in unit labor costs. Since labor costs are 70 to 80 percent of production costs, product prices rise roughly with increases in unit labor costs.

What should we conclude from our simple equation when we think about stagflation? Answer: For any specific size of nominal wage increase, a decline in productivity will boost unit production costs and shift the aggregate supply curve leftward.

6   Inflationary Expectations and Wages   The inflation of the 1970s had its genesis in the inflation of the late 1960s which was caused by expanded military spending on the Vietnam war. By the early 1970s workers had been exposed to a period of accelerating inflation. As a result, nominal-wage demands of labor began to include the expectation of an increasing rate of inflation. Most employers, expecting to pass on higher wage costs in this context of mounting inflation, did not resist labor's demands for larger and larger increases in nominal wages. These nominal-wage increases raised unit production costs and reduced aggregate supply, as from AS₁ to AS₂ in Figure 17-4.

We can incorporate both **inflationary expectations** *and* declining labor productivity in equation (1) as causes of stagflation. If nominal wage increases are accelerating and the growth rate of labor productivity is falling, there will be a double impetus for unit labor costs—and ultimately product prices—to rise.

Synopsis   All these factors combined in the 1970s to adversely shift the aggregate supply curve to yield the worst possible macroeconomic world—falling output and rising unemployment combined with a rising price level (Figure 17-4). The unemployment rate shot up from 4.8 percent in 1973 to 8.3 percent in 1975, contributing to a $47 billion *decline* in real GDP. In the same period the price level increased by 21 percent.

Like a bad dream, the 1973–1975 stagflation scenario recurred in 1978–1980. In this instance OPEC imposed an enormous $21 per barrel increase in oil prices. Coupled with rising prices of agricultural commodities, the price level rose by 26 percent over the 1978–1980 period, while unemployment jumped from 6.0 to 7.5 percent. Real GDP grew by a very modest 2 percent annual rate over the three-year period.

Regardless of the causes of stagflation, it was clear in the 1970s that the Phillips Curve did not represent a stable relationship. Adverse (leftward) shifts in aggregate supply were at work, which explained those unhappy occasions when the inflation rate and the unemployment rate increased simultaneously. To many economists the experience in the 1970s and early 1980s suggested the Phillips Curve was shifting to the right and confronting the economy with higher rates of inflation *and* unemployment. *(Key Question 1)*

Stagflation's Demise: 1982–1989

A return look at Figure 17-3 reveals a clear inward movement of the inflation-unemployment points between 1982 and 1989. By 1989 the stagflation of the 1970s and early 1980s had subsided. One precursor to this favorable trend was the deep recession of 1981–1982, largely caused by a purposely tight money policy. The recession propelled the unemployment rate to 9.5 percent in 1982. With so many workers unemployed, those who were working accepted smaller increases in their nominal wages—or in some cases wage reductions—to preserve their jobs. Firms, in turn, had to restrain price hikes to maintain their relative shares of a greatly diminished market.

Other factors were at work. Foreign competition throughout 1982–1989 suppressed wage and price hikes in several basic industries such as automobiles and steel. Deregulation of the airline and trucking industries also resulted in wage reductions or so-called "wage-givebacks." A decline in OPEC's monopoly power produced a stunning fall in the price of oil and its derivative products.

All these factors combined to reduce unit production costs and to shift the aggregate supply curve rightward (as from AS₂ to AS₁ in Figure 17-4). Meanwhile, a record-long peacetime economic expansion created 17 million new jobs between 1982 and 1989. The previously high unemployment rate fell from 9.5 percent in 1983 to 6.1 percent in 1987 and to 5.2 percent in 1989. Figure 17-3 reveals that the inflation unemployment points for 1987–1989 are closer to the points associated with the Phillips Curve for the 1960s than to the points in the late 1970s and early 1980s.

During the Great Stagflation of the mid-1970s, inflation and unemployment simultaneously *increased;* during some of the years of the economic expansion of 1983–1989 inflation and unemployment simultaneously *declined.* Global Perspective 17-1 is relevant to this latter period.

GLOBAL PERSPECTIVE 17-1

The misery index, selected nations, 1984–1994

The so-called "misery index" adds together a nation's unemployment rate and its inflation rate to get a measure of national economic discomfort. For example, a nation with a 5 percent rate of unemployment and 5 percent inflation rate would have a misery index number of 10, as would a nation with an 8 percent unemployment rate and 2 percent inflation.

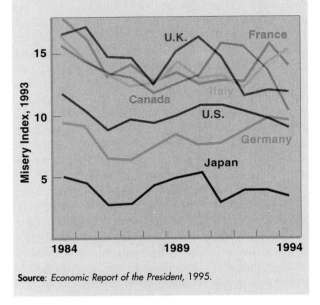

Source: *Economic Report of the President*, 1995.

NATURAL RATE HYPOTHESIS

The standard explanation for the scattering of inflation rate–unemployment points to the right of the 1960s Phillips Curve is that a series of supply shocks shifted the aggregate supply curve *leftward,* moving the Phillips Curve rightward and upward as in Figure 17-3. The inward collapse of inflation rate–unemployment points in the 1980s occurred because of *rightward* shifts of the aggregate supply curve. This Keynesian-based view holds that a tradeoff between the inflation rate and the unemployment rate still exists, but that changes in aggregate supply may alter the menu of inflation and unemployment choices—shift the Phillips Curve itself—during abnormal periods.

A second explanation of simultaneously higher rates of unemployment and inflation, the **natural rate**

hypothesis, is associated with new classical thinking. It questions the existence of the downsloping Phillips Curve as in Figure 17-2. This view says the economy is stable in the long run at the natural rate of unemployment. We know from Chapter 8 that the natural rate of unemployment is the rate of unemployment existing when cyclical unemployment is zero; it is the full-employment rate of unemployment.

According to the natural rate hypothesis, misguided full-employment policies, based on the incorrect assumption of a stable Phillips Curve, will result in an increasing rate of inflation. The natural rate hypothesis has its empirical roots in Figure 17-3, where you can argue that a vertical line located at a presumed 6 percent natural rate of unemployment represents the inflation-unemployment "relationship" better than the traditional downsloping Phillips Curve. In the natural rate hypothesis, any rate of inflation is compatible with the economy's natural rate of unemployment.

There are two variants of the natural rate interpretation of the inflation-unemployment data points shown in Figure 17-3: the adaptive expectations and rational expectations theories.

Adaptive Expectations Theory

The **theory of adaptive expectations** assumes people form their expectations of future inflation on the basis of previous and present rates of inflation and only gradually change their expectations as experience unfolds. The adaptive expectations theory was popularized by Milton Friedman and is consistent with both the traditional monetarist and new classical perspectives.

Adaptive expectations suggest there may be a tradeoff between inflation and unemployment in the short run, but not in the long run. Any attempt to reduce the unemployment rate below the natural rate sets in motion forces which destabilize the Phillips Curve and shift it rightward. Thus, the adaptive expectations view distinguishes between a "short-run" and "long-run" Phillips Curve.

Short-Run Phillips Curve   Consider Phillips Curve PC_1 in Figure 17-5. Suppose the economy initially is experiencing a 3 percent rate of inflation and a 6 percent natural rate of unemployment. In the adaptive expectations theory, such short-run curves as PC_1 (drawn as straight lines for simplicity) exist because

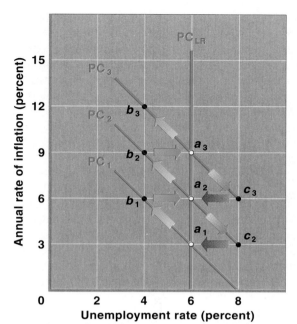

FIGURE 17-5 The adaptive expectations theory
The expansion of aggregate demand may temporarily increase profits and therefore output and employment (a_1 to b_1). But nominal wages will soon rise, reducing profits and thereby negating the short-run stimulus to production and employment (b_1 to a_2). Consequently, in the long run there is no tradeoff between the rates of inflation and unemployment; the long-run Phillips Curve is vertical. This suggests expansionary policies will generate increasing inflation rather than a lower rate of unemployment. On a more positive note, it also implies restrictive stabilization policies can reduce inflation without creating long-lived increases in unemployment.

the actual rate of inflation is not always the same as the expected rate.

Establishing an additional point on Phillips Curve PC_1 will clarify this. We begin at a_1, where we assume nominal wages are set on the expectation that the 3 percent rate of inflation will continue. But now suppose that government mistakenly judges the full-employment unemployment rate to be 4 percent instead of 6 percent. This misjudgment might occur because the economy temporarily achieved a 4 percent rate of unemployment in an earlier period. To achieve the targeted 4 percent rate of unemployment, suppose government invokes expansionary fiscal and monetary policy.

The resulting increase in aggregate demand boosts the rate of inflation to 6 percent. With a specific level of nominal wages, *set on the expectation that the rate of inflation would continue to be 3 percent,* the higher product prices raise business profits. Firms re-

spond to expanded profits by increasing output and therefore hiring more workers. In the short run, the economy moves to b_1, which, in contrast with a_1, entails a lower rate of unemployment (4 percent) and a higher rate of inflation (6 percent). This movement from a_1 to b_1 is consistent with our earlier interpretation of the Phillips Curve. Presumably, the economy has accepted some inflation as the "cost" of achieving a reduced level of unemployment. But the natural rate theorists interpret the movement from a_1 to b_1 differently. They see it as only a manifestation of the following principle: *When the actual rate of inflation is higher than expected, profits temporarily rise and the unemployment rate temporarily falls.*

Long-Run Vertical Phillips Curve Point b_1 is *not* a stable equilibrium position in this theory. Workers will recognize their nominal wages have not been rising as fast as inflation and will therefore obtain nominal wage increases to restore their lost purchasing power. But, as nominal wages rise to restore the previous level of real wages existing at a_1, business profits fall to their earlier level. This profit reduction means that the original motivation of businesses to increase output and employ more workers disappears.

Unemployment then returns to its natural level at point a_2. Note, however, that the economy now faces a higher actual *and* expected rate of inflation—6 percent rather than 3 percent. Because the higher level of aggregate demand which originally moved the economy from a_1 to b_1 still exists, the inflation it engendered persists.

In view of the higher 6 percent expected rate of inflation, the short-run Phillips Curve shifts upward from PC_1 to PC_2. An "along-the-Phillips Curve" kind of movement from a_1 to b_1 on PC_1 is merely a short-run or transient phenomenon. In the long run—after nominal wages catch up with price level increases—unemployment will return to the natural rate at a_2 and a new short-run Phillips Curve PC_2 exists at the higher expected rate of inflation.

This process may now be repeated. Government may reason that certain extraneous, chance events have frustrated its expansionist policies, and will try again. Policy measures are used to increase aggregate demand and the scenario repeats. Prices rise momentarily ahead of nominal wages, profits expand, and output and employment increase (a_2 to b_2). But, in time, workers press for, and are granted, higher nominal wages to restore their level of real wages. Profits thus fall to their original level, pushing employment back to the normal rate at a_3. Government's "reward" for forcing the actual rate of unemployment below the natural rate is the perverse one of a still higher (9 percent) rate of inflation.

If we conceive of a_1b_1, a_2b_2, and a_3b_3 as a series of short-run Phillips Curves, the adaptive expectations theory says that governmental attempts through policy to move along the short-run Phillips Curve (a_1 to b_1 on PC_1) *cause* the curve to shift to a *less* favorable position (PC_2, then PC_3, and so on). A stable Phillips Curve with the dependable series of unemployment rate–inflation rate tradeoffs does not exist.

There is, in fact, no higher rate of inflation (such as 6 percent at b_1) which can be accepted as the "cost" of reduced unemployment in the *long run*. The *long-run relationship* between unemployment and inflation is shown by the vertical line through a_1, a_2, and a_3. Any rate of inflation is consistent with the 6 percent natural rate of unemployment. The Phillips Curve tradeoff portrayed earlier in Figure 17-2 does not exist.

Disinflation   We can also employ the adaptive expectations theory to explain **disinflation**—reductions in the rate of inflation. Suppose in Figure 17-5 the economy is at a_3 where the inflation rate is 9 percent and the unemployment rate is 6 percent. A significant decline in aggregate demand such as that occurring in the 1981–1982 recession will reduce inflation below the 9 percent expected rate, say, to 6 percent. Business profits will fall because product prices are rising less rapidly than wages. The nominal wage increases, remember, were set on the assumption that the 9 percent rate of inflation would continue. In response to the profit decline, firms will reduce their employment and consequently the unemployment rate will rise. The economy will temporarily slide downward from point a_3 to c_3 along the short-run Phillips Curve PC_3. In the natural rate theory, *when the actual rate of inflation is lower than the expected rate, profits temporarily fall and the unemployment rate temporarily rises.*

Firms and workers will eventually adjust their expectations to the new 6 percent rate of inflation and thus newly negotiated wage increases will decline. Profits will be restored, employment will rise, and the unemployment rate will return to its natural rate of 6 percent at point a_2. Because the expected rate of inflation is now 6 percent, the short-run Phillips Curve PC_3 will shift leftward to PC_2.

If aggregate demand falls further, the scenario will continue. Inflation will decline from 6 percent to,

say, 3 percent, moving the economy from a_2 to c_2 along PC_2. The lower-than-expected rate of inflation (lower prices) has squeezed profits and reduced employment. But, in the long run, firms will respond to the lower profits by reducing their nominal wage increases. Profits will be restored and unemployment will return to its natural rate at a_1 as the short-run Phillips Curve moves from PC_2 to PC_1. Once again, the long-run Phillips Curve is vertical at the natural rate of unemployment. *(Key Question 2)*

Rational Expectations Theory

The adaptive expectations theory assumes increases in nominal wages lag behind increases in the price level. This lag gives rise to *temporary* increases in profits which *temporarily* stimulate employment.

The **rational expectations theory** (Chapter 16) is the second variant of the natural rate hypothesis. This theory contends that businesses, consumers, and workers understand how the economy functions and they use available information to protect or further their own self-interests. In particular, people understand how government policies will affect the economy and anticipate these impacts in their own decision making.

Suppose that, when government invokes expansionary policies, workers anticipate inflation and a subsequent decline in real wages. They therefore immediately incorporate this expected inflation into their nominal wage demands. If workers correctly and fully anticipate the amount of price inflation and adjust their current nominal wage demands accordingly to maintain their real wages, then even the temporary increases in profits, output, and employment will *not* occur. Instead of the temporary increase in employment from a_1 to b_1 in Figure 17-5, the movement will be directly from a_1 to a_2. Fully anticipated inflation by labor means there will be no short-run decline in unemployment. Price inflation, fully anticipated in the nominal-wage demands of workers, will generate a vertical line through a_1, a_2 and a_3.

The policy implication is this: Fiscal and monetary policy designed to achieve a misspecified full-employment rate of unemployment will increase inflation, not lower unemployment. Note that the adaptive and rational expectations theories are consistent with the conservative philosophy that government's attempts to do good deeds typically fail and at considerable cost to society. In this instance the "cost" is accelerating inflation.

Changing Interpretations

Interpretations of the Phillips Curve have changed dramatically over the past three decades. The original idea of a stable tradeoff between unemployment and inflation gave way to the adaptive expectations view that, while a short-run tradeoff existed, no such tradeoff occurred in the long run. The more controversial rational expectations theory stresses that macroeconomic policy is completely ineffective because it is anticipated by workers. Not even a short-run tradeoff between unemployment and inflation exists. Taken together, the natural rate hypotheses (adaptive and rational expectations theories) conclude that demand-management policies cannot influence real output and employment in the long run, but only the price level. This conclusion is clearly contrary to predictions of the original Phillips Curve (Figure 17-2b).

Which perspective is correct? Does an inverse relationship exist between the unemployment rate and the inflation rate as the original Phillips Curve implied? Or is there no long-run tradeoff as the natural rate theory contends? Perhaps the safest answer is that most economists accept the notion of a short-run tradeoff while recognizing that in the long run such a tradeoff is much less likely. They also believe aggregate supply shocks can cause stagflation. The episodes of rising unemployment and inflation during the 1970s and early 1980s were *not* exclusively the results of misguided stabilization policies.

QUICK REVIEW 17-1

■ The original Phillips Curve showed an apparently stable, inverse relationship between annual unemployment rates and inflation rates over a period of years.

■ Stagflation occurred in 1973–1975 and 1978–1980 and produced Phillips Curve data points above and to the right of the Phillips Curve for the 1960s.

■ The following aggregate supply shocks caused stagflation during the 1970s and early 1980s: *a* OPEC oil price hikes, *b* poor agricultural harvests, *c* rapid dollar depreciation, *d* the demise of wage-price controls, *e* a productivity decline, and *f* inflationary expectations.

■ According to the natural rate hypothesis, the economy automatically gravitates to its natural rate of unemployment; therefore the Phillips Curve is vertical in the long run.

AGGREGATE SUPPLY REVISITED

The distinction between short-run Phillips Curves and the long-run vertical Phillips Curve has stimulated new thinking about aggregate supply.

In Figures 17-1 and 17-2a we derived the Phillips Curve by shifting aggregate demand rightward along a *stable* aggregate supply curve. Firms responded to the increasing price level by producing more output and increasing their employment. Thus, the unemployment rate fell as the price level rose.

The natural rate theory suggests, however, that the aggregate supply curve in Figure 17-1 is stable only so long as nominal wages do not increase in response to the rise in the price level. Once workers fully recognize the price level has risen, they will demand and receive higher nominal wages to restore their real wages. An increase in nominal wages, other things equal, will shift the aggregate supply curve leftward. That is, a change in nominal wages is one of the determinants of aggregate supply (Table 11-2).

The simplified aggregate supply curve—with its horizontal, intermediate, and vertical ranges—therefore needs to be refined to account for changes in nominal wages *induced* by changes in the price level. That means we must distinguish between short-run and long-run aggregate supply.

Definitions: Short Run and Long Run

Here *the short run is a period in which input prices—particularly nominal wages—remain fixed as the price level changes.* There are two reasons why input prices may remain constant for a time even though the price level has changed.

1 Workers may not immediately be aware of the existence of a higher or lower price level. If so, they will not know their real wages have changed and will not adjust their wage demands accordingly.

2 Many employees are hired under fixed-wage contracts. Unionized employees, for example, receive nominal wages based on their collective bargaining agreements. Also, most managers and many professionals receive set salaries established in annual contracts.

The upshot of both—the lack of information about the price level and the existence of labor contracts—is that changes in the price level do not immediately change nominal wages.

The long run is a period in which input prices (wages) are fully responsive to changes in the price level.

PROBLEMS AND CONTROVERSIES IN MACROECONOMICS

With sufficient time, workers gain full information about price level changes and thus ascertain the effects on their real wage. Workers will be aware that a price level increase has reduced their real wage and that a price level decline has increased their real wage. More importantly, in the long run workers and employers are freed from their existing labor contracts and can negotiate changes in nominal wages and salaries.

With these definitions in mind, let's reexamine Chapter 11's discussion of aggregate supply.

Short-Run Aggregate Supply

Consider the **short-run aggregate supply curve** AS_1 in Figure 17-6a. This curve is constructed on two assumptions: (1) the initial price level is P_1, and (2) nominal wages have been established on the expectation that the price level P_1 will persist. Observe from point a_1 that the economy is operating at its full-employment level of real output Q_f at price level P_1. This real output is the real production forthcoming when the economy is operating at its natural rate of unemployment.

Now let's determine the consequence of changes in the price level by examining an *increase* in the price level from P_1 to P_2. Because nominal wages are fixed in the short run, the higher product prices associated with P_2 will enhance profits. In response to the higher

profits, producers will increase their output from Q_f to Q_2 as indicated by the move from a_1 to a_2 on AS_1. Observe that at Q_2 the economy is operating beyond its full-employment output. This is made possible by extending work-hours of part-time and full-time workers, enticing new workers such as homemakers and retirees into the labor force, and hiring and training the structurally unemployed. Thus, the nation's unemployment rate will decline below its natural rate.

How will producers respond when there is a *decrease* in the price level from P_1 to P_3 in Figure 17-6a? Firms will discover their profits have diminished or disappeared. After all, product prices have dropped while nominal wages have not. Producers therefore will reduce employment and production and, as revealed by point a_3, real output will fall to Q_3. This decline in real output will be accompanied by an unemployment rate greater than the natural rate.

Long-Run Aggregate Supply

By definition, nominal wages are fully responsive in the long run to changes in the price level. What are the implications of this for aggregate supply?

In Figure 17-6b again suppose the economy initially is at point a_1 (P_1 and Q_f). Our previous discussion indicated that an *increase* in the price level from P_1 to P_2 will move the economy from point a_1 to a_2 along the short-run aggregate supply curve AS_1. In

FIGURE 17-6   Short-run and long-run aggregate supply
In the short run (a), input prices such as nominal wages are assumed to be fixed based on price level P_1. An increase in the price level will bolster profits and entice firms to expand real output. Alternatively, a decrease in the price level will reduce profits and real output. The short-run AS curve therefore slopes upward. In the long run (b), a price level rise will increase nominal wages and thus shift the short-run AS curve leftward. Conversely, a decrease in the price level will reduce nominal wages and shift the short-run AS curve rightward. The long-run AS curve therefore is vertical.

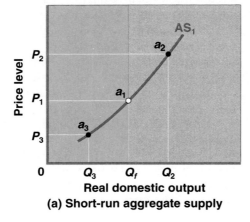

(a) Short-run aggregate supply

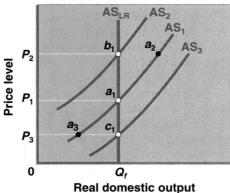

(b) Long-run aggregate supply

the long run, workers will discover their real wages have fallen as a result of this increase in the price level. They will therefore demand and presumably receive higher nominal wages to restore their previous level of real wages. The short-run aggregate supply curve will shift leftward from AS_1 to AS_2, where it will reflect the *higher* price level P_2 and the expectation that P_2 will continue. The leftward shift in the short-run aggregate supply to curve AS_2 will move the economy from a_2 to b_1. Real output will fall to its full-employment level and the unemployment rate will return to its natural rate.

A *decrease* in the price level from P_1 to P_3 in Figure 17-6b will work in the opposite way. The economy will initially move from point a_1 to point a_3, where profits will be squeezed or eliminated because prices have fallen and nominal wages have not. But this is the short-run response. With enough time, the lower price level P_3, which has increased the real wage, together with the higher unemployment associated with the reduction in real output, will diminish nominal wages. Sufficiently lower nominal wages will shift the short-run aggregate supply curve rightward from AS_1 to AS_3 and real output will return to Q_f at point c_1.

By tracing a line between the long-run equilibrium points b_1, a_1, and c_1, a **long-run aggregate supply curve** appears. It is vertical at the full-employment level of real output, Q_f.

Keynesian versus New Classical Policy Implications

The conception of aggregate supply represented in Figure 17-6b implies that wage and price flexibility will drive the economy toward full employment. For this reason this model is identified with the natural rate hypothesis, or **new classical economics.**

In new classical thinking, fully *anticipated* price level changes do *not* change the level of real output because nominal wages immediately change in the same direction and by the same percentage as the price level change. Only the long-run aggregate supply curve is relevant when price level changes are anticipated. This is why government stabilization policies allegedly fail to affect real output. This is simply the rational expectations view.

Unanticipated changes in the price level—so called **price-level surprises**—*do* produce short-term fluctuations in real output. These temporary changes in real output, say the new classical econo-

mists, result from unanticipated changes—or shocks—in aggregate demand and supply.

Suppose an unanticipated increase in foreign demand for American goods increases our price level. This moves the economy along its short-run aggregate supply curve to a higher level of real output. But in the long run, nominal wages and other input prices will increase in response to the higher price level and the economy will return to its full-employment real output.

New classical generalization: *Although price level surprises arising from aggregate demand and aggregate supply shocks may create short-run macroeconomic instability, the economy is stable in the long run at the full-employment level of output.*

Modern Keynesians dismiss the assumption of highly competitive markets and instantaneously adjusting prices and wages which underlie the RET aspect of new classical economics. But they no longer quarrel with the distinction between short- and long-run aggregate supply. Instead, they contend that experience has shown the adjustment of nominal wages critical to the vertical long-run aggregate supply curve is painfully slow, particularly in a downward direction. Because nominal wages are quite inflexible downward, years may go by before the economy moves from a point such as a_3 to c_1 in Figure 17-6b. Therefore, the assumption of a fixed aggregate supply curve underlying the analysis in previous chapters is not only useful for simplifying complex theory, but realistic for all but long periods of time. Moreover, mainstream macroeconomists continue to call for active use of stabilization policies to reduce the high costs of severe unemployment or inflation. But new classical economists view the long run as either instantaneous or relatively short; they therefore favor a hands-off policy by government to permit the economy to adjust *itself* to the full-employment level of real output.

DEMAND-PULL AND COST-PUSH INFLATION

Let's apply our new tools of short-run and long-run aggregate supply to inflation.

Demand-Pull Inflation

Demand-pull inflation occurs when an increase in aggregate demand pulls up the price level. We earlier depicted this inflation by shifting an aggregate de-

KEY GRAPH

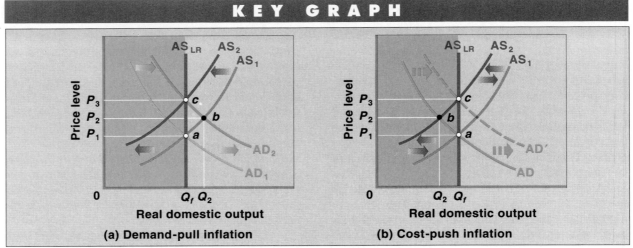

FIGURE 17-7 Demand-pull and cost-push inflation revisited
In (a) an increase in AD will drive up the price level and increase real output in the short run. But, in the long run, nominal wages will rise and AS will shift leftward. Real output will return to its previous level and the price level will rise still further. In (b) cost-push inflation occurs when AS shifts leftward. If government counters the decline in real output by increasing AD to the broken line, the price level will rise even further. On the other hand, if government allows a recession to occur, nominal wages eventually will fall and the AS curve will shift back rightward to its original location. Observe that the long-run AS curves are vertical in both (a) and (b).

mand curve rightward along a stable aggregate supply curve (Figure 11-8b and 11-8c).

In our more detailed version of aggregate supply, however, an increase in the price level will eventually produce an increase in nominal wages and thus a leftward shift of the short-run aggregate supply curve itself. This is shown in Figure 17-7a (Key Graph). Suppose the price level is P_1, at the intersection of aggregate demand curve AD_1 and aggregate supply curve AS_1. The aggregate supply curve AS_1 is a short-run curve based on the nominal wages associated with the price level P_1. These nominal wages were set on the expectation that P_1 would persist. Observe that at a the economy is achieving its full-employment real output Q_f.

Now consider the effects of an increase in aggregate demand as shown by the rightward shift from AD_1 to AD_2 in Figure 17-7a. This shift can result from any one of a number of factors, including an increase in the money supply, an increase in investment spending, and so on (Table 11-1). Whatever its cause, the increase in aggregate demand boosts the price level from P_1 to P_2 and expands output to Q_2 at point b.

So far, nothing new. But what will happen to the short-run aggregate supply curve once workers realize their real wages have fallen and once their existing contracts have expired? Nominal wages will rise, and as they do, the short-run aggregate supply curve will shift leftward, eventually from AS_1 to AS_2. Consequently, the price level will further increase to P_3 at point c and the equilibrium level of output will return to its full-employment level Q_f.

In the short run, demand-pull inflation will drive up the price level and increase real output; in the long run, only the price level will rise. In the long run, the increase in aggregate demand has only moved the economy along its vertical aggregate supply curve AS_{LR}.

Cost-Push Inflation

Cost-push inflation arises from factors which increase the cost of production at each price level—factors that shift the aggregate supply curve leftward—and therefore increase the price level (Figure 11-11).

But our previous analysis has considered only short-run aggregate supply. Let's now examine the cost-push theory in its long-run context.

Analysis Look at Figure 17-7b where the economy is initially assumed to be operating at the P_1 and Q_f levels of price and output at point a. Suppose that, by exerting monopoly power, labor unions secure nominal wage gains exceeding advances in labor productivity. Moreover, suppose many nonunion employers, wishing to deter unionism in their own enterprises, respond by increasing the nominal wages they pay to keep them proportionate to union wage scales. As wages and unit production costs rise, the short-run aggregate supply curve shifts leftward, as depicted by the move from AS_1 to AS_2. The price level jumps from P_1 to P_2, as shown by point b. In this case, aggregate supply curve AS_2 has resulted from a wage rate hike and therefore is the *cause* of the price level rising from P_1 to P_2. The shift of the aggregate supply curve from AS_1 to AS_2 is not a *response* to a price level increase as it was in our previous discussions of short versus long-run aggregate supply.

Policy Dilemma Cost-push inflation creates a dilemma for policy makers. If aggregate demand in Figure 17-7b remains at AD—the curve does not shift—real output will decline from Q_f to Q_2. Government can counter this recession and its attendant unemployment by using stabilization policies to increase aggregate demand to AD'. But there is a potential policy trap here. An increase in aggregate demand to AD' will further aggravate inflation by increasing the price level from P_2 to P_3 at point c.

And the P_2 to P_3 increase in the price level is not likely to be a one-time boost because wage earners will respond to their decline in real wages by seeking and receiving increases in nominal wages. If successful, the higher nominal wages will cause a further increase in per unit production costs. This would shift the short-run aggregate supply curve to a position to the left of AS_2. This (unshown) leftward shift of the short-run aggregate supply curve is in *response* to the higher price level P_3 which was caused by the rightward shift of aggregate demand to AD'. You may wish to draw in this leftward shift of AS to convince yourself that it will regenerate the stagflation problem.

In brief, government will have to increase aggregate demand once again to restore the Q_f level of real output. But if government does so, the scenario may simply repeat itself.

The point is that leftward shifts in the short-run aggregate supply curve may be induced when government applies expansionary demand management policy to alleviate output reductions resulting from cost-push inflation. These shifts in short-run aggregate supply frustrate attainment of full employment and increase the price level.

Suppose government recognizes this policy trap and decides *not* to increase aggregate demand from AD to AD'. Instead, it implicitly decides to allow a cost-push induced recession to run its course. Widespread layoffs, plant shutdowns, and business failures eventually will occur. At some point there will be sufficient slack in labor markets to reduce nominal wages and thus undo the initial leftward shift of short-run aggregate supply. In time a severe recession will shift the short-run aggregate supply from AS_2 back to AS_1. The price level will return to P_1 at a and the full-employment level of output will be restored along long-run aggregate supply AS_{LR}.

Two generalizations emerge:

1 *If government attempts to maintain full employment under conditions of cost-push inflation, an inflationary spiral is likely.*

2 *If government takes a hands-off approach to cost-push inflation, a recession will occur.* Although the recession eventually will undo the initial rise in production costs, the economy in the meanwhile will experience high unemployment and a loss of real output. *(Key Question 7)*

QUICK REVIEW 17-2

■ The short-run aggregate supply curve has a positive slope because nominal wages are assumed to be fixed as the price level changes.

■ The long-run aggregate supply curve is vertical because wages and other input prices eventually respond fully to changes in the price level.

■ In the short run, demand-pull inflation will increase both the price level and domestic output; in the long run, only the price level will rise.

■ Cost-push inflation creates a policy dilemma for government: If it engages in an expansionary stabilization policy to increase output, an inflationary spiral may ensue; if it does nothing, a recession will occur.

Other Options   Experiences with cost-push inflation and the difficulties in using demand-management policies to deal with it (Figure 17-7b) have led government to seek out additional policy options. In Figure 17-7b these policies are designed to prevent the aggregate supply curve from shifting leftward as from AS_1 to AS_2. Or, if the economy already is experiencing stagflation at the intersection of AD and AS_2, the goal would be to shift the aggregate supply curve rightward toward AS_1. Similarly, in terms of the Phillips Curve (whether conceived of as a downsloping curve or a vertical line) the policy goal is to shift the curve leftward to provide a better inflation rate–unemployment rate tradeoff for society. In particular, economists who interpreted the data points for the 1970s and 1980s in Figure 17-3 as reflecting rightward shifts of the Phillips Curve sought means of shifting the curve back to the more desirable position which seemed relevant for the 1960s.

Generally speaking, three categories of policies have been used: (1) employment and training policy; (2) wage-price, or incomes, policy; and (3) the set of policies known as "supply-side economics."

EMPLOYMENT AND TRAINING POLICY

The goal of **employment and training policy** is to improve the efficiency of labor markets so that any specific level of aggregate demand will be associated with a lower level of unemployment. The purpose of employment and training policy is to achieve a better matching of workers to jobs, thereby reducing labor market imbalances or bottlenecks. Several different kinds of programs will provide a better matching of workers to jobs.

Vocational Training

Programs of vocationally oriented education and training permit marginal and displaced workers to be more quickly reemployed. Various government programs provide for institutional and on-the-job training for the unemployed, for disadvantaged youth, and for older workers whose skills are meager or obsolete. New government programs emphasize apprenticeship training to ease the transition from high school to work, thus reducing the high unemployment rates for youth who do not attend college.

Job Information

A second employment and training policy aims at improving the flow of job information between unemployed workers and potential employers and with enhancing the geographic mobility of workers. For example, a number of attempts have been made recently to modernize the United States Employment Service to increase its effectiveness in bringing job seekers and employers together.

Nondiscrimination

Another facet of employment and training policy tries to reduce or eliminate artificial obstacles to employment. Discrimination has been a roadblock in matching workers and jobs; it is a factor in explaining why unemployment rates for blacks are roughly twice as high as for whites. The Civil Rights Act of 1964 attempts to improve the use of labor resources by removing discrimination because of race, religion, gender, or ethnic background as an obstacle to employment or union membership.

WAGE-PRICE (INCOMES) POLICIES

A second approach to stagflation sees monopoly power and labor market imbalances as inevitable facts of economic life. This approach seeks to alter the behavior of labor and product-market monopolists to make their wage and price decisions more compatible with the goals of full employment and price level stability. As we distinguish between **wage-price guideposts** and **wage-price controls,** we'll see they differ primarily in degree. Both guideposts and controls establish standards of noninflationary wage and price increases. But guideposts rely on voluntary compliance by labor and business, whereas under controls the standards are enforced by law.

Wage-price guideposts and wage-price controls are also referred to as **incomes policies.** That's because they are designed to constrain excessive rises in nominal income payments (wages, rents, interest, profits) which presumably are contributing to inflation. By limiting the increases in nominal income and prices, incomes policies affect real income—the amount of goods and services you can obtain with your nominal income. Real income depends on the two targets of wage-price guideposts or controls: the size of the nominal income and the prices of the goods and services bought.

There have been five periods in recent American history when incomes policies have been applied:

1   Comprehensive controls during World War II
2   Selective controls during the Korean war in the early 1950s
3   Guideposts during the early 1960s under the Kennedy-Johnson administrations
4   The Nixon administration's wage-price controls of 1971–1974
5   The Carter administration's guideposts of 1978

The Wage-Price Policy Debate

Incomes policy has evoked heated and prolonged debate in the United States. The debate centers on two points.

1   Workability and Compliance   Critics argue that voluntary *guideposts* fail because they ask business and labor leaders to forgo the goals of maximum profits and higher wages. A union leader will not gain favor with members by reducing wage demands; nor does a corporate official become endeared to stockholders by bypassing profitable price increases. For these reasons little voluntary cooperation can be expected from labor and management.

Wage and price *controls* have the force of law and, therefore, government can force labor and management to obey. Nevertheless, problems of enforcement and compliance can be severe, particularly if wage and price controls are comprehensive and maintained for an extended time. *Black markets*—illegal markets where prices exceed legal maximums—become common. Furthermore, firms can circumvent price controls by lowering the quality or size of their product. If the price of a candy bar is frozen at 40 cents, its price can be effectively doubled by reducing its size by one-half!

Proponents of incomes policies say inflation is frequently fueled by *inflationary expectations*. Workers demand unusually large nominal wage increases because they expect future inflation to diminish their real incomes. Employers give in to these demands because they, too, anticipate an inflationary environment where higher costs can be easily passed along to consumers. A strong wage-price control program can quell inflationary expectations by convincing labor and management that the government does not in-

tend to allow inflation to continue. Therefore, workers do not need anticipatory wage increases. And firms are put on notice that they may not be able to shift higher costs to consumers via price increases. Expectations of inflation can generate inflation; wage-price controls can undermine those expectations.

2   Allocative Efficiency and Rationing   Opponents of incomes policies say effective guideposts or controls interfere with the allocative function of the market system. Effective price controls prohibit the market system from making necessary price adjustments. If the demand for some product should increase, its price could *not* rise to signal society's wish for more output and therefore more resources to produce it.

Also, controls strip the market mechanism of its rationing function—its ability to equate quantity demanded and quantity supplied. Product shortages thus result. Which buyers are to obtain the product and which are to do without? The product can be rationed on a first-come-first-served basis or by favoritism. But both are highly arbitrary and inequitable; those first in line or those able to cultivate a friendship with the seller get as much of the product as they want while others get none at all. Government may therefore have to impartially ration the product to all consumers by issuing ration coupons to prospective buyers on an equitable basis. But governmental rationing contributes to the problem of compliance noted earlier.

Defenders of incomes policies respond as follows: If effective guideposts or controls are imposed on a competitive economy, then in time the resulting rigidities will impair allocative efficiency. But it is *not* correct to assume that resource allocation will be efficient in the absence of a wage-price policy. Cost-push inflation allegedly arises *because* big labor and big businesses possess monopoly power and consequently have the capacity to distort the allocation of resources.

Effectiveness

How effective have incomes policies been? The direct wage-price controls during World War II did contain —or at least defer—the serious inflation which otherwise would have occurred. In contrast, the 1962 wage and price guideposts did little to arrest the growing demand-pull inflation of the mid-1960s. The wage and price controls of 1971–1974 not only failed to achieve their purposes, but worsened stagflation by causing inefficiencies in the allocation of resources. The Carter administration guideposts of 1979 also failed dismally.

In view of this historical record, there remains little support for incomes policies among American macroeconomists. Nevertheless, wage and price controls are still occasionally tried in other nations, particularly those facing hyperinflation. Normally, these controls are a part of a larger set of policies—including a tight money policy—designed to break the price-wage inflationary spiral. *(Key Question 8)*

SUPPLY-SIDE ECONOMICS

In the past two decades, some economists have stressed low growth of productivity and real output as causes of stagflation and the relatively weak performance of our economy. These **supply-side economists** assert that mainstream economics does not come to grips with stagflation because its focal point is aggregate demand.

Supply-side economists contend that changes in aggregate supply—shifts in the short-run and long-run aggregate supply curve—must be recognized as an "active" force in determining both the levels of inflation *and* unemployment. Economic disturbances can be generated on the supply side, as well as on the demand side. By emphasizing the demand side, mainstream economists have neglected certain supply-side policies which might alleviate stagflation.

Tax-Transfer Disincentives

Supply-side economists argue that the spectacular growth of our tax-transfer system has negatively affected incentives to work, invest, innovate, and assume entrepreneurial risks. The tax-transfer system allegedly has eroded the economy's productivity and this decline in efficiency has meant higher production costs and stagflation. The argument is that higher taxes reduce the after-tax rewards of workers and producers, making work, innovations, investing, and risk bearing less financially attractive. According to supply-side economists, *marginal tax rates* are most relevant to decisions to undertake *additional* work and *additional* saving and investing.

Incentives to Work   Supply-siders believe that how long and how hard individuals work depends on how

much additional *after-tax* earnings they derive from this extra work. To induce more work—to increase aggregate inputs of labor—marginal tax rates on earned incomes should be reduced. Lower marginal tax rates increase the attractiveness of work and increase the opportunity cost of leisure. Thus, individuals will choose to substitute work for leisure. This increase in productive effort can occur in many ways: by increasing the number of hours worked per day or week; by encouraging workers to postpone retirement; by inducing more people to enter the labor force; by making people willing to work harder; and by discouraging long periods of unemployment.

Transfer Disincentives   Supply-side economists also believe the existence of a wide variety of public transfer programs has eroded incentives to work. Unemployment compensation and welfare programs have made the job loss less of an economic crisis for some people. The fear of being unemployed and therefore the need to be a disciplined, productive worker is simply less acute than previously. Most transfer programs are structured to discourage work! Our social security and aid to families with dependent children programs are such that transfers are reduced sharply if recipients earn income. These programs encourage recipients *not* to be productive by imposing a "tax" in the form of a loss of transfer benefits on those who work.

Incentives to Save and Invest   The rewards to saving and investing have also been reduced by high marginal tax rates. Assume you save $1000 at 10 percent, so that you earn $100 interest per year. If your marginal tax rate is 40 percent, your after-tax interest earnings will be $60 and the after-tax interest rate you receive is only 6 percent. While you might be willing to save (forgo current consumption) for a 10 percent return on your saving, you might prefer to consume when the return is only 6 percent.

Saving, remember, is the prerequisite of investment. Thus supply-side economists recommend lower marginal tax rates on saving. They also call for lower taxes on investment income to ensure there are ready investment outlets for the economy's enhanced pool of saving. One of the determinants of investment spending is the *after-tax* net profitability of that spending.

To summarize: Lower marginal tax rates encourage saving and investing. Workers will therefore find themselves equipped with more and technologically superior machinery and equipment. Labor productivity will rise, and this will hold down increases in unit labor costs and the price level.

Laffer Curve

In the supply-side view, reductions of marginal tax rates will shift Figure 17-4's aggregate supply curve from AS_2 toward AS_1, alleviating inflation, increasing real output, and reducing the unemployment rate. Moreover, according to supply-side economist Arthur Laffer, lower tax *rates* are compatible with constant or even enlarged tax *revenues*. Supply-side tax cuts need not cause Federal budget deficits.

This idea is based on the **Laffer Curve.** As shown in Figure 17-8, this curve depicts the relationship between tax rates and tax revenues. As tax rates increase from zero to 100 percent, tax revenues increase from zero to some maximum level (at *m*) and then decline to zero. Tax revenues decline beyond some point because higher tax rates discourage economic activity, diminishing the tax base (domestic output and national income). This is easiest to see at the extreme where tax rates are 100 percent. Tax revenues here are reduced to zero because the 100 percent confiscatory tax rate has halted production. A 100 percent tax rate applied to a tax base of zero yields no revenue.

In the early 1980s Laffer suggested we were at some point such as *n* where tax rates were so high that production had been discouraged to the extent that tax revenues were below the maximum at *m*. If the economy is at *n*, then lower tax *rates* are quite compatible with constant total tax *revenues*. In Figure 17-8 we simply lower tax rates, moving from point *n* to point *l*, and government will collect the same amount of tax revenue. Laffer's reasoning is that lower tax rates will stimulate incentives to work, save and invest, innovate, and accept business risks, thus triggering an expansion of domestic output and national income. This enlarged tax base will sustain tax revenues even though tax rates are lower. Indeed, between *n* and *m* lower tax rates will result in increased tax revenues.

Supply-side economists think tax rates can be lowered without incurring budget deficits for two additional reasons.

1 Less Tax Evasion Tax avoidance and evasion will decline. High marginal tax rates prompt taxpayers to avoid taxes through various tax shelters (for example, buying municipal bonds on which interest earned is tax free) or to conceal income from the In-

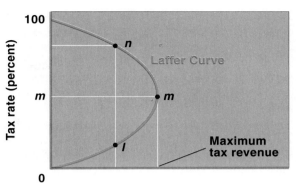

FIGURE 17-8   The Laffer Curve
The Laffer Curve suggests that up to point *m* higher tax rates will result in larger tax revenues. But still higher rates will adversely affect incentives to produce, reducing the size of the national income tax base to the extent that tax revenues decline. It follows that, if tax rates are above 0*m*, tax reductions will produce increases in tax revenues. The controversial empirical question is to determine at what actual tax rates will tax revenues begin to fall.

ternal Revenue Service. Lower tax rates reduce the inclination to engage in such activities.

2 Reduced Transfers The stimulus to production and employment which a tax cut provides reduces government transfer payments. For example, more job opportunities reduce unemployment compensation payments and decrease a budget deficit.

Criticisms of the Laffer Curve

The Laffer Curve and its supply-side policy implications have been subject to severe criticism.

1 Taxes: Incentives and Time A fundamental criticism has to do with the sensitivity of economic incentives to changes in tax rates. Skeptics say there is ample empirical evidence that the impact of a tax reduction on incentives is small, of uncertain direction, and relatively slow to emerge. For example, with respect to work incentives, studies indicate that decreases in tax rates lead some people to work more, but others to work less. Those who work more are enticed by the higher after-tax pay; they substitute work for leisure because the opportunity cost of leisure has increased. Those who work less do so because the higher after-tax pay increases their ability to "buy leisure." They can meet their after-tax income goals while working fewer hours.

2   Reinforcing Inflation   Most economists think demand-side effects of a tax cut exceed supply-side effects. Thus, tax cuts undertaken when the economy is expanding or at its full-employment output will produce large increases in aggregate demand which will overwhelm any increase in aggregate supply. Large budget deficits and inflation will result.

3   Position on Curve   Skeptics feel the Laffer Curve is merely a logical proposition asserting there must be some level of tax rates between zero and 100 percent where tax revenues will be maximized. Economists of all persuasions can agree with this. But the issue of where a particular economy is located on the Laffer Curve is an empirical question. If we assume —as Laffer did in the early 1980s—that we are at n in Figure 17-8, then tax rate cuts will increase tax revenues. But critics say the economy's location on the Laffer Curve is undocumented and unknown. If the economy is at any point southwest of m, then tax reductions will reduce tax revenues and create budget deficits.

Other Supply-Side Tenets

Although removing tax-transfer disincentives is the main idea of supply-side economics, there are two other tenets.

1   The Tax "Wedge"   Supply-side economists note that the historical growth of the public sector has increased the nation's tax bill both absolutely and as a percentage of the national income. In the mainstream view, higher taxes represent a withdrawal of purchasing power from the economy and therefore have a contractionary or anti-inflationary effect (Chapter 12). Supply-siders argue to the contrary: They contend that sooner or later most taxes are incorporated into business costs and shifted forward to consumers as higher prices. Taxes entail a cost-push effect.

Supply-side economists point out that in the 1970s and 1980s state and local governments substantially increased sales and excise taxes and the Federal government has sharply boosted payroll (social security) taxes. These are precisely the taxes incorporated in business costs and reflected in higher prices. Such taxes drive a "wedge" between the costs of resources and the price of a product. As government has grown, this **tax wedge** has increased, shifting the aggregate supply curve leftward.

2   Overregulation   Supply-siders also claim that government's regulatory involvement in the economy has adversely affected productivity and costs. Two points should be noted here.

1   "Industrial" regulation—government regulation of specific industries such as transportation or communications—frequently provides firms in the regulated industry with a legal monopoly or cartel. Governmental regulation protects such firms from competition, the result being that these firms are less efficient and incur higher costs of production.

2   The "social" regulation of industry has increased substantially in the past two decades. New government regulations have been imposed on industry in response to the problems of pollution, product safety, worker health and safety, and equal access to job opportunities. Supply-side economists point out that social regulation has greatly increased costs of doing business. The overall impact of both varieties of regulation is that costs and prices are higher and there is a tendency toward stagflation. *(Key Question 10)*

Reaganomics: The Program

The elements of supply-side economics that have just been outlined provided the intellectual underpinnings for the economic policies of the Reagan administration (1981–1988). **Reaganomics** consisted of these four policies:

1   The growth of the Federal government was restrained by freezes and cuts in spending on social and welfare programs. Defense spending, however, was increased significantly.

2   Government regulation of private businesses was substantially reduced.

3   The administration encouraged the Federal Reserve System to hold the growth rate of the money supply to a rate considered noninflationary, yet sufficiently expansive to allow for economic growth.

4   Personal and corporate income tax rates were reduced sharply beginning in 1981. The tax system was reformed in 1986 reducing the marginal tax rate on wealthy taxpayers from 50 percent to 28 percent.

Reaganomics: Did It Work?

The real world is an imperfect laboratory for judging the success of a vast socioeconomic experiment such as Reaganomics. Also, Congress did not accept all the expenditure reductions which the Reagan administration requested in its program. Finally, the Reagan years witnessed significant declines in inflation and interest rates, a record-long peacetime economic expansion, and attainment of full employment. Having acknowledged these points, it is nevertheless fair to say that, *as such,* supply-side economics largely failed to accomplish its goals.

The facts are these:

1 Any immediate output effects of the Reagan tax cuts were overwhelmed by the tight money policy being undertaken by the Federal Reserve to reduce the then-existing rapid inflation. The economy fell into severe back-to-back recessions in 1980–1982.

2 The inflation rate fell sharply from annual rates of 13.5 percent in 1980 to 3.2 percent in 1983. Since 1983 the inflation rate has remained relatively low. But most economists attribute the decline in inflation to the 1980–1982 recessions, caused by the Federal Reserve's tight money policy, and to declines in oil prices. Rightward shifts in aggregate supply resulting from tax cuts and deregulation were *not* major factors in reducing inflation.

3 The Reagan tax cuts contributed to burgeoning Federal budget deficits (Chapter 18). The prediction of the Laffer Curve that tax cuts would enhance tax revenues beyond those associated with normal economic expansions simply did not bear fruit. These large deficits may have increased interest rates, crowding out some unknown amount of private investment and depressing both export-dependent and import-competing industries. A record high U.S. balance of payments deficit resulted. In 1990, the Bush administration and Congress were forced to enact a tax-spending package designed to reduce the deficit by $500 billion over a five-year period. The top marginal tax rate increased from 28 percent to 31 percent. But large deficits persisted, and in 1993 the Clinton administration again raised taxes, pushing the top marginal tax rate to 39.6 percent.

4 There is little evidence that Reaganomics had any significant positive impacts on saving and investment rates or incentives to work. The savings rate trended downward throughout the 1980s. Productivity growth surged in 1983 and 1984, as is usual during recovery, but was disappointingly low in the rest of the 1980s and early 1990s.

5 Most economists attribute the post-1982 economic recovery to the demand-side expansionary effects of the Reagan tax cuts and not to the use of tax cuts as an antistagflation, supply-side measure.

In summary, the evidence casts considerable doubt on the central supply-side proposition that tax cuts can directly and significantly shift the nation's production possibilities curve and aggregate supply curve rightward more rapidly than their historical pace.

QUICK REVIEW 17-3

■ Policy options for stagflation include: employment and training policies; incomes policies (wage-price guideposts and controls); and supply-side economics (tax cuts, deregulation).

■ The Laffer Curve contends that, when tax rates are higher than optimal, tax reductions can expand real output and simultaneously increase tax revenue.

■ The supply-side policies of Reaganomics did not increase aggregate supply more rapidly than otherwise would have been expected.

RECAP: ALTERNATIVE MACROECONOMIC PERSPECTIVES

Here and in Chapter 16 we have seen that a number of theories purport to explain how the national economy operates. We have presented the central ideas and policy implications of Keynesianism, monetarism, rational expectations theory, and supply-side economics.

Table 17-1 summarizes major aspects of these theories and policy perspectives. In reviewing the table, you will see there is no direct reference to "new classical economics." This viewpoint is simply that associated with the natural rate hypothesis which asserts that the economy tends automatically to achieve equilibrium at its full potential level of output—at its natural rate of unemployment. The natural rate hypothesis is supported by economists of the monetarist and rational expectations persuasions.

CHAPTER SUMMARY

1 Using the AD-AS model to compare the impacts of different size increases in aggregate demand on the price level and real output yields the generalization that high rates of inflation are associated with low rates of unemployment and

TABLE 17-1   Alternative macroeconomic theories and policies

| Issue | Keynesianism | Natural rate hypothesis | | Supply-side economics |
		Monetarism	Rational expectations	
View of the private economy	Inherently unstable	Stable in long run at natural rate of unemployment	Stable in long run at natural rate of unemployment	May stagnate without proper work, saving, and investment incentives
Cause of the observed instability of the private economy	Investment plans unequal to saving plans (changes in AD); AS shocks	Inappropriate monetary policy	Unanticipated AD and AS shocks in the short run	Changes in AS
Appropriate macro policies	Active fiscal and monetary policy; occasional use of incomes policies	Monetary rule	Monetary rule	Policies to increase AS
How changes in the money supply affect the economy	By changing the interest rate, which changes investment, and real GDP	By directly changing AD which changes GDP.	No effect on output because price-level changes are anticipated	By influencing investment and thus AS
View of the velocity of money	Unstable	Stable	No consensus	No consensus
How fiscal policy affects the economy	Changes AD and GDP via the multiplier process	No effect unless money supply changes	No effect on output because price-level changes are anticipated	Affects GDP and price level via changes in AS
View of cost-push inflation	Possible (wage-push, AS shock)	Impossible in the long run in the absence of excessive money supply growth	Impossible in the long run in the absence of excessive money supply growth	Possible (productivity decline, higher costs due to regulation, etc.)

vice versa. This inverse relationship is known as the Phillips Curve and empirical data for the 1960s were generally consistent with it. Labor market imbalances explain the Phillips Curve tradeoff.

2   In the 1970s the Phillips Curve apparently shifted rightward, reflecting stagflation. A series of supply shocks in the form of higher energy and food prices, a depreciated dollar, and the demise of the Nixon wage-price freeze were involved in the 1973–1975 stagflation. More subtle factors such as inflationary expectations and a decline in productivity growth also contributed to stagflationary tendencies. Following the recession of 1981–1982, the Phillips Curve shifted inward toward its original position. By 1989 stagflation had subsided.

3   The adaptive expectations variant of the natural rate hypothesis argues that in the long run the traditional Phillips Curve tradeoff does not exist. Expansionary demand-management policies will shift the short-run Phillips Curve upward, resulting in increasing inflation with no permanent decline in unemployment.

4   The rational expectations variant of the natural rate hypothesis contends that the inflationary effects of expansionary policies will be anticipated and reflected in nominal wage demands. As a result, there will be no short-run increase in employment and thus no short-run Phillips Curve.

5   In the short run—where nominal wages are fixed—an increase in the price level increases profits and real output. Conversely, a decrease in the price level reduces profits and real output. Thus, the short-run aggregate supply curve is upward-sloping. In the long run—where nominal wages are variable—price level increases raise nominal wages and shift the short-run aggregate supply curve leftward. Conversely, price level declines shift the short-run aggregate supply curve rightward. The long-run aggregate supply curve therefore is vertical at the full-employment level of output.

6   In the short run, demand-pull inflation increases the price level *and* real output. Once nominal wages have increased, the temporary increase in real output dissipates.

7   In the short run, cost-push inflation increases the price level and reduces real output. Unless government expands aggregate demand, nominal wages eventually will decline

LAST WORD

PROFIT SHARING: MAKING WAGES FLEXIBLE

One of the problems of reducing inflation is that un-employment may result. Can greater downward wage flexibility be achieved to soften the impact of a decline in aggregate demand on employment?

Our comparisons of Keynesian and new classical views of the macroeconomy suggest that if wages are stable, employment will decline when aggregate demand falls. Most economists recognize that labor contracts, among other considerations, make wages downwardly inflexible, at least in the short run. The declines in labor demand accompanying recessions therefore primarily affect employment. This problem has led some economists to propose profit sharing as a way to increase the downward flexibility of wage rates. The idea is to make labor markets operate more like the new classical model, with its vertical aggregate supply curve, by creating greater employment stability.*

The essence of these profit-sharing proposals is to tie some portion of wages directly to the firm's profitability, making profit-sharing payments a part of workers' pay. Instead of paying workers a guaranteed wage rate of, say, $10 per hour, workers might be guaranteed $5 per hour (the base wage) and additional compensation equal to some predetermined percentage of the firm's profits (the profit-share wage). Total compensation (base wage + profit-share wage) may exceed or fall short of $10 per hour, depending on the firm's economic fortunes.

How would such a plan affect employment? Initially assume workers are receiving $10 per hour— $5 as a guaranteed wage and another $5 as profit-sharing compensation. Now suppose a recession occurs and the employer's sales and profits plummet. The $5 of profit-sharing income will fall and might decline to zero so that the actual wages paid by the firm fall from $10 to $5 an hour. With the new depressed demand for labor, the firm would clearly

choose to employ more workers under this wage system than the standard system. Hourly wages will have automatically fallen from $10 to $5.

There are a number of criticisms of these profit-sharing wage plans. The plans might jeopardize the wage uniformity and wage gains achieved by organized labor. A further criticism is that employers might respond to the low base wage by adopting production techniques which use relatively more labor and less capital. Because the amount of capital equipment per worker is critical to productivity and economic growth, this pay scheme might impair the long-run expansion of real GDP. At the pragmatic level, critics point out that wage plans linked to profits eliminate the present certainty which workers have as to whether their employers have properly fulfilled the labor contract. With profit sharing, employers might use accounting and other techniques to hide profits and therefore evade paying share wages.

Finally, there is the fundamental question as to whether workers will accept more jobs and greater employment stability in exchange for a reduced hourly wage guarantee and higher variability of earnings. But it should be noted that in the past decade a growing number of union and nonunion contracts have contained profit-sharing arrangements. Although a full-blown profit-sharing economy seems improbable, limited profit-sharing appears to be spreading.

*This idea is developed in detail in Martin L. Weitzman, *The Share Economy* (Cambridge, Mass.: Harvard University Press, 1984).

---

under conditions of recession and the short-run aggregate supply curve will shift back to its initial location. Prices and real output will eventually return to their original levels.

8 Employment and training policies, wage-price (incomes) policies, and supply-side policies have been used as antistagflation measures.

9 Employment and training programs are designed to reduce labor market imbalances; they include vocational training, job information, and nondiscrimination programs.

10 Incomes policies comprise wage-price guideposts or controls. Economists debate the desirability of these policies in terms of their workability and their impact on re-

source allocation. Presently, there is little support among economists for these policies.

11 Supply-side economists trace stagflation to the growth of the public sector and, specifically, to the adverse effects of the tax-transfer system on incentives. Other factors are the growing tax "wedge" between production costs and product prices and government overregulation of businesses. Based on the Laffer Curve, supply-side economists advocated sizable tax cuts such as undertaken by the Reagan administration as a remedy for stagflation. Evidence has cast doubt on the validity of the supply-side view.

TERMS AND CONCEPTS

Phillips Curve	disinflation	new classical	wage-price guideposts
stagflation	rational expectations	economics	wage-price controls
aggregate supply	theory	price-level surprises	incomes policies
shocks	short-run aggregate	demand-pull inflation	supply-side economics
inflationary	supply curve	cost-push inflation	Laffer Curve
expectations	long-run aggregate	employment and	tax wedge
natural rate hypothesis	supply curve	training policy	Reaganomics
theory of adaptive			
expectations			

QUESTIONS AND STUDY SUGGESTIONS

1 *Key Question Employ the aggregate demand–aggregate supply model to derive the Phillips Curve. What events occurred in the 1970s to cast doubt on the stability and existence of the Phillips Curve?*

2 *Key Question Use an appropriate diagram to explain the adaptive expectations rationale for concluding that in the long run the Phillips Curve is a vertical line.*

3 Explain rational expectations theory and its relevance to analysis of the Phillips Curve.

4 Assume the following information is relevant for an industrially advanced economy in 1996–1998:

Year	Price level Index	Rate of Increase in labor productivity	Index of Industrial production	Unemployment rate	Average hourly wage rates
1996	167	4%	212	4.5%	$8.00
1997	174	3	208	5.2	8.67
1998	181	2.5	205	5.8	9.50

Describe in detail the macroeconomic situation faced by this society. Is cost-push inflation evident? What policy proposals would you recommend?

5 Evaluate or explain the following statements:

a "Taken together, the adaptive expectations and rational expectations theories imply that demand-management policies cannot influence the real level of economic activity in the long run."

b "The essential difference between the adaptive expectations theory and rational expectations theory is that inflation is unanticipated in the former and anticipated in the latter."

6 Suppose the full-employment level of real output (*Q*) for a hypothetical economy is $250 and the price level (*P*) initially is 100. Use the short-run aggregate supply schedules below to answer the questions which follow.

AS(P_{100})		AS(P_{125})		AS(P_{75})	
P	Q	P	Q	P	Q
125	280	125	250	125	310
100	250	100	220	100	280
75	220	75	190	75	250

a What will be the level of real output in the *short run* if the price level unexpectedly rises from 100 to 125 because of an increase in aggregate demand? Falls unexpectedly from 100 to 75 because of a decrease in aggregate demand? Explain each situation.

b What will be the level of real output in the *long run* when the price level rises from 100 to 125? Falls from 100 to 75? Explain each situation.

c Show the circumstances described in questions 6a and 6b on graph paper and derive the long-run aggregate supply curve.

The national or **public debt** is the total accumulation of the Federal government's total deficits and surpluses which have occurred through time. At the end of 1994 the public debt was about $4.6 trillion.

The term "public debt" as ordinarily used does *not* include the entire public sector; in particular, state and local finance is omitted. While the Federal government has been incurring large deficits, state and local governments in the aggregate have been realizing surpluses. For example, in 1994 all state and local governments combined had a budgetary surplus in excess of $25 billion.[2]

BUDGET PHILOSOPHIES

Is it good or bad to incur deficits and let the public debt grow? Should the budget be balanced annually, if necessary by legislation or constitutional amendment? We saw in Chapter 12 that countercyclical fiscal policy should move the Federal budget toward a deficit during recession and toward a surplus during inflation. This means an activist fiscal policy is unlikely to result in a balanced budget in any particular year. Is this a matter of concern?

Let's approach this question by examining the economic implications of several contrasting budget philosophies.

Annually Balanced Budget

Until the Great Depression of the 1930s, the **annually balanced budget** was accepted as a desirable goal of public finance. On examination, however, it becomes clear that an annually balanced budget is not compatible with government fiscal activity as a countercyclical, stabilizing force. Worse yet, an annually balanced budget intensifies the business cycle.

Illustration: Suppose the economy encounters a siege of unemployment and falling incomes. As Figure 12-3 shows, in such circumstances tax receipts will automatically decline. To balance its budget, government must either (1) increase tax rates, (2) reduce government expenditures, or (3) do both. All these policies are contractionary; each further dampens, rather than stimulates, aggregate demand.

Similarly, an annually balanced budget will intensify inflation. Again, Figure 12-3 tells us that, as nom-

inal incomes rise during the course of inflation, tax collections will automatically increase. To avoid the impending surplus, government must either (1) cut tax rates, (2) increase government expenditures, or (3) do both. But any of these policies will add to inflationary pressures.

An annually balanced budget is not economically neutral; the pursuit of such a policy is procyclical, not countercyclical. Despite this problem, there is considerable support for a constitutional amendment requiring an annually balanced budget.

More recently, some economists have advocated an annually balanced budget, not because of a fear of deficits and a mounting public debt, but because they feel an annually balanced budget is essential in constraining an undesirable and uneconomic expansion of the public sector. Budget deficits, they argue, are a manifestation of political irresponsibility. Deficits allow politicians to give the public the benefits of government programs while *currently* avoiding raising taxes to pay for them.

These economists believe government has a tendency to grow larger than it should because there is less popular opposition to this growth when it is financed by deficits rather than taxes. Wasteful governmental expenditures are likely to creep into the Federal budget when deficit financing is readily available. Conservative economists and politicians want legislation or a constitutional amendment to force a balanced budget to slow government growth. They view deficits as a symptom of a more fundamental problem—government encroachment on the private sector.

Cyclically Balanced Budget

The idea of a **cyclically balanced budget** is that government exerts a countercyclical influence and at the same time balances its budget. However, this budget would not be balanced annually—there is nothing sacred about twelve months as an accounting period—but rather, over the course of the business cycle.

The rationale is simple, plausible, and appealing. To offset recession, government should lower taxes and increase spending, purposely incurring a deficit. During the ensuing inflationary upswing, taxes would be raised and government spending slashed. The resulting surplus could be used to retire the Federal debt incurred in financing the recession. Government fiscal operations would therefore exert a positive countercyclical force, and the government could still

---

[2]This figure includes the states' pension funds. If these funds are excluded, the states collectively suffered a budgetary deficit in 1994.

balance its budget—not annually, but over a period of years.

The problem with this budget philosophy is that the upswings and downswings of the business cycle may not be of equal magnitude and duration. The goal of stabilization may therefore conflict with balancing the budget over the cycle. A long and severe slump, followed by a modest and short period of prosperity, would mean a large deficit during the slump, little or no surplus during prosperity, and a cyclical deficit in the budget.

Functional Finance

With **functional finance,** a balanced budget—annually or cyclically—is secondary. The primary purpose of Federal finance is to provide for noninflationary full employment—to balance the economy, not the budget. If this objective causes either persistent surpluses or a large and growing public debt, so be it. In this philosophy, the problems of government deficits or surpluses are minor compared with the undesirable alternatives of prolonged recession or persistent inflation. The Federal budget is first and foremost an instrument for achieving and maintaining macroeconomic stability. How best to finance government spending—through taxation or borrowing—depends on existing economic conditions. Government should not hesitate to incur any deficits and surpluses required to achieve macroeconomic stability and growth.

To those who express concern about the large Federal debt which the pursuit of functional finance might entail, proponents of this budget philosophy offer three arguments.

1 Our tax system is such that tax revenues automatically increase as the economy expands. Assuming constant government expenditures, a deficit successful in stimulating equilibrium GDP will be partially self-liquidating (Figure 12-3).

2 Because of its taxing powers and the ability to create money, the government's capacity to finance deficits is virtually unlimited.

3 Those who support functional finance contend that a large Federal debt is less burdensome than most people think. *(Key Question 1)*

TABLE 18-1 **Quantitative significance of the public debt: the public debt and interest payments in relation to GDP, selected years, 1929–1994***

(1) Year	(2) Public debt, billions	(3) Gross domestic product, billions	(4) Interest payments, billions	(5) Public debt as percentage of GDP, (2) ÷ (3)	(6) Interest payments as percentage of GDP, (4) ÷ (3)	(7) Per capita public debt
1929	$ 16.9	$ 103.2	$ 0.7	16%	0.7%	$ 134
1940	50.7	100.1	1.1	51	1.1	384
1946	271.0	211.6	4.2	128	2.0	1917
1950	256.9	286.7	4.5	90	1.6	1667
1955	274.4	403.3	5.1	68	1.3	1654
1960	290.5	513.4	6.8	57	1.3	1610
1965	322.3	702.7	8.4	46	1.2	1659
1970	380.9	1010.7	14.1	38	1.4	1858
1975	541.9	1585.9	23.0	34	1.5	2507
1980	909.1	2708.0	52.7	34	1.9	3992
1982	1137.3	3149.6	84.4	36	2.7	4898
1984	1564.7	3777.2	113.1	41	3.0	6620
1986	2120.6	4268.6	131.0	50	3.1	8812
1988	2601.3	4900.4	146.0	53	3.0	10,616
1990	3206.6	5546.1	176.5	58	3.2	12,831
1992	4002.1	6020.2	186.8	66	3.1	15,670
1994	4643.7	6736.9	191.6	69	2.8	17,816

*In current dollars.

Source: Economic Report of the President, 1994; U.S. Department of Commerce.

THE PUBLIC DEBT: FACTS AND FIGURES

Because modern fiscal policy endorses unbalanced budgets to stabilize the economy, its application may lead to a growing public debt. Let's consider the public debt—its causes, characteristics, and size; and its burdens and benefits.

The public debt, as column 2 of Table 18-1 shows, has grown considerably since 1929. As noted, the public debt is the accumulation of all past deficits, minus surpluses, of the Federal budget.

Causes

Why has our public debt increased historically? What has caused us to incur these large and persistent deficits? The answer is fourfold: wars, recessions, tax cuts, and lack of political will.

Wars Some of the public debt has resulted from the deficit financing of wars. The public debt increased substantially during World War I and grew more than fivefold during World War II.

Consider World War II and the options it posed. The task was to reallocate a substantial portion of the economy's resources from civilian to war goods production. Government expenditures for armaments and military personnel soared. There were three financing options: increase taxes, print the needed money, or use deficit financing. Government feared that tax financing would require tax rates so high they would diminish incentives to work. The national interest required attracting more people into the labor force and encouraging those already participating to work longer hours. Very high tax rates were felt to interfere with these goals. Printing and spending additional money would be inflationary. Thus, much of World War II was financed by selling bonds to the public, thereby draining off spendable income and freeing resources from civilian production so they would be available for defense industries.

Recessions Another cause of the public debt is recessions and, more specifically, the built-in stability characterizing our fiscal system. In periods when the national income declines, tax collections automatically fall and deficits arise. Thus the public debt rose during the Great Depression of the 1930s and, more recently, during the recessions of 1974–1975, 1980–1982, and 1990–1991.

Tax Cuts A third consideration has accounted for much of the large deficits since 1981. The Economic Recovery Tax Act of 1981 provided for substantial cuts in both individual and corporate income taxes. The Reagan administration and Congress did *not* make offsetting reductions in government outlays, thereby building a *structural deficit* into the Federal budget in the sense that the budget would not balance even if the economy were operating at full-employment. Unfortunately, the economy was not at full employment during most of the early 1980s. The 1981 tax cuts combined with the severe 1980–1982 recessions to generate rapidly rising annual deficits which were $128 billion in 1982, accelerating to $221 billion by 1986. Although annual budget deficits declined between 1986 and 1989, they remained historically high even though the economy reached full employment. Due partly to the earlier tax rate cuts, tax revenues were not high enough to cover rising Federal spending. Annual deficits, and thus the public debt, rose again in 1991–1993 as the economy experienced recession and the Federal government incurred massive expenses in bailing out failed savings and loan associations.

Lack of Political Will Without being too cynical we might also assert that deficits and a growing public debt are the result of lack of political will and determination. Spending often gains votes; tax increases precipitate political disfavor. While opposition to deficits is expressed by politicians and their constituencies, *specific* proposals to cut spending programs or raise taxes typically encounter more opposition than support.

Particularly difficult to cut are **entitlement programs,** the subject of this chapter's Last Word. These programs, such as social security, Medicaid (health care for the poor), Medicare (health care for those on social security), and veterans' benefits, "entitle" or guarantee particular levels of transfer payments (Chapter 5) to all who fit the programs' criteria. Total spending on these programs automatically rises along with the number of qualifying individuals and has rocketed in recent years, contributing to budget deficits and the rising public debt. Cutting these benefits produces severe political opposition. For example, older Americans may favor smaller budget deficits so long as funds for social security and Medicare are not reduced.

Similarly, new taxes or tax increases to reduce budget deficits may be acceptable in the abstract, but far less popular when specific tax changes are proposed. The popular view of taxation seems to be "Don't tax me, don't tax thee, tax the person behind the tree." But there are not enough taxpayers "behind the tree" to raise the amounts of new revenue needed to close the budget deficit.

The Clinton administration's struggle to pass a deficit-reduction package in 1993 is an example of the political difficulties of reducing spending and increasing taxes. The specific package of spending cuts and tax increases passed the Senate by only a single vote, even though nearly all senators agreed that deficit reduction was a worthy goal.

Quantitative Aspects

In 1994 the public debt reached $4600 billion—that's $4.6 trillion. That's more than twice what it was a mere eight years ago. If every sesame seed on every Big Mac ever sold was worth one dollar, the total wouldn't be sufficient to pay off the public debt. As of 1993, McDonald's had used 2.49 trillion seeds (178 on each of 14 billion Big Macs) in 25 years, compared to the $4.6 trillion debt.[3]

But we must not fear large, seemingly incomprehensible numbers. You will see why when we put the size of the public debt into better perspective.

Debt and GDP   A bald statement of the absolute size of the debt ignores that the wealth and productive ability of our economy have also increased tremendously. A wealthy nation can more easily incur and carry a large public debt than a poor nation. That's why it is more meaningful to measure changes in the public debt *in relation to* changes in the economy's GDP, as shown in column 5 in Table 18-1. Instead of the seventeenfold increase in the debt between 1950 and 1994 shown in column 2, we find that the relative size of the debt was less in 1994 than in 1950. However, our data show that the relative size of the debt has doubled since the early 1980s. Also, column 7 indicates that on a per capita basis the nominal debt has increased more or less steadily through time.

International Comparisons   As shown in Global Perspective 18-1, other industrial nations have public debts similar to, or greater than, those in the United States. As a percentage of GDP, public debt in 1994 was larger in Belgium, Italy, Canada, the Netherlands,

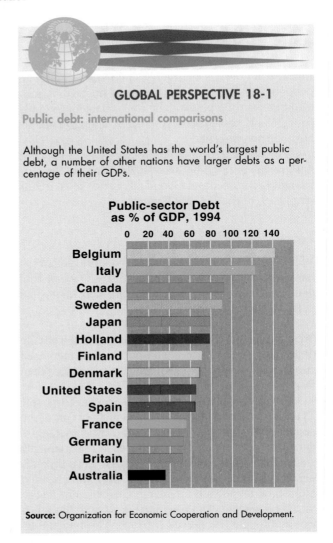

GLOBAL PERSPECTIVE 18-1

Public debt: international comparisons

Although the United States has the world's largest public debt, a number of other nations have larger debts as a percentage of their GDPs.

Public-sector Debt as % of GDP, 1994

Belgium
Italy
Canada
Sweden
Japan
Holland
Finland
Denmark
United States
Spain
France
Germany
Britain
Australia

Source: Organization for Economic Cooperation and Development.

Sweden, Japan, and Denmark than in the United States.

Interest Charges   Many economists think the primary burden of the debt is the annual interest charge accruing as a result. The absolute size of these interest payments is shown in column 4 of Table 18-1. Interest payments have increased sharply beginning in the 1970s. This reflects not only increases in the debt, but also periods of very high interest rates. Interest on the debt is now the fourth largest item of expenditures in the Federal budget (Figure 5-7). Interest charges as a percentage of the GDP are shown in column 6 of Table 18-1. Interest payments as a proportion of GDP have increased significantly in recent years. This ratio reflects the level of taxation (the av-

---

[3]Sam Ward, "How Big Is Our Debt?" *USA Today,* May 6, 1993, p. 1.

erage tax rate) required to service the public debt. In 1994 government had to collect taxes equal to 2.8 percent of GDP to pay interest on its debt.

Ownership   Figure 18-1 indicates that about two-thirds of the total public debt is held outside the Federal government by state and local governments, banks and other financial institutions, and private parties. The remaining one-third is held by Federal agencies and the Federal Reserve. Foreign individuals and institutions hold only about 14 percent of the total debt, a percentage which has not changed much in the past few years. This statistic is significant because, as we will see shortly, the implications of internally and externally held debt are different.

Accounting and Inflation   The data on budget deficits and public debt may not be as straightforward as they appear. Governmental accounting procedures may not reflect government's actual financial position. Private firms have a separate capital budget because, in contrast to current expenses on labor and raw materials, expenditures for capital equipment represent tangible money-making assets. The Federal government treats expenditures for highways, harbors, and

public buildings the same as it does welfare payments, while in fact the former outlays are investments in physical assets. Federal budget deficits in the 1980s and 1990s would have been smaller had the Federal government employed a capital budget which included depreciation costs.

Also, inflation works to benefit debtors. A rising price level reduces the real value or purchasing power of the dollars paid back by borrowers. Taking this "inflationary tax" into account further reduces the sizes of budget deficits and public debt.

All of this is quite controversial. But the point is there are different ways of measuring the public debt and government's overall financial position. Some of these alternative measures differ greatly from the data presented in Table 18-1.

QUICK REVIEW 18-1

■ A budget deficit is an excess of government expenditures above tax revenues in a particular year; the public debt is the total accumulation of budget deficits and surpluses through time.

■ The three major budget philosophies are *a* an annually balanced budget; *b* a budget balanced over the business cycle; and *c* functional finance.

■ The $4.6 trillion public debt has resulted mainly from wartime financing, recessions, tax cuts, and lack of political will.

■ United States public debt as a percentage of GDP is less than it was in 1950 and is in the midrange of such debt among major industrial nations.

FIGURE 18-1   Ownership of the public debt
Two-thirds of the public debt is held outside the Federal government; one-third is held internally by Federal agencies and the Federal Reserve. Only 14 percent of the public debit is foreign owned.

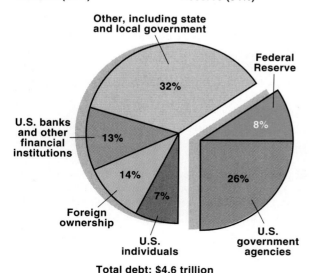

Debt held outside the Federal government and Federal Reserve (66%)

Debt held by the Federal government and Federal Reserve (34%)

Other, including state and local government

Federal Reserve

32%

8%

U.S. banks and other financial institutions

13%

14%

7%

26%

Foreign ownership

U.S. individuals

U.S. government agencies

Total debt: $4.6 trillion

ECONOMIC IMPLICATIONS: FALSE ISSUES

How does the public debt and its growth affect the economy? Can a mounting public debt bankrupt the nation? Does the debt place a burden on our children and grandchildren?

These are false or bogus issues. The debt is not about to bankrupt the government or the nation. Nor, except under certain specific circumstances, does the debt place a burden on future generations.

Going Bankrupt?

Can a large public debt bankrupt the government, making it unable to meet its financial obligations? No, for the following three reasons.

1 Refinancing There is no reason why the public debt need be reduced, much less eliminated. As portions of the debt fall due each month, government does not cut expenditures or raise taxes to provide funds to *retire* the maturing bonds. (We know that with depressed economic conditions, this would be unwise fiscal policy.) Rather, the government *refinances* the debt; it sells new bonds and uses the proceeds to pay off holders of the maturing bonds.

2 Taxation Government has the constitutional authority to levy and collect taxes. A tax increase is a government option for gaining sufficient revenue to pay interest and principal on the public debt. Financially distressed private households and corporations *cannot* raise revenue via taxes; government *can*. Private households and corporations *can* go bankrupt; the Federal government *cannot*.

3 Creating Money Bankruptcy is also difficult to imagine because the Federal government can print money to pay both principal and interest on the debt. A government bond obligates the government to redeem that bond for some specific amount of money on its maturity date. Government can use the proceeds from the sale of other bonds *or* it can create the needed money to retire the maturing bonds. The creation of new money to pay interest on debt or to retire debt *may* be inflationary. But it is difficult to conceive of governmental bankruptcy when government has the power to create new money by running the printing presses.

Shifting Burdens

Does the public debt impose a burden on future generations? Recall that per capita debt in 1994 was $17,816. Does each newborn child in 1994 enter the world to be handed a $17,816 bill from Uncle Sam? Not really!

We first must ask to whom we owe the public debt. The answer is that, for the most part, we owe it to ourselves. About 86 percent of our government bonds are owned and held by citizens and institutions —banks, businesses, insurance companies, governmental agencies, and trust funds—within the United States. Thus *the public debt is also a public credit.* While the public debt is a liability to the American people (as taxpayers), most of the same debt is simultaneously an asset to the American people (as holders of

Treasury bills, Treasury notes, Treasury bonds, and U.S. Saving Bonds).

To retire the public debt would call for a gigantic transfer payment where Americans would pay higher taxes and government would pay out most of those tax revenues to those same taxpaying individuals and institutions in the aggregate in redeeming the U.S. securities they hold. Although a redistribution of income would result from this huge financial transfer, it need not entail any immediate decline in the economy's aggregate wealth or standard of living. Repayment of an internally held public debt entails no leakage of purchasing power from the economy as a whole. New babies who on the average inherit the $17,816 per person public debt obligation will also be bequeathed that same amount of government securities.

We noted earlier that the public debt increased sharply during World War II. Was some of the economic burden of World War II shifted to future generations by the decision to finance military purchases through the sale of government bonds? No. Recalling the production possibilities curve, we realize that the economic cost of World War II was the civilian goods society had to forgo in shifting scarce resources to war goods production. Regardless of whether society financed this reallocation through higher taxes or borrowing, the real economic burden of the war would have been the same. The burden of the war was borne almost entirely by those who lived during the war; they were the ones who did without a multitude of consumer goods to permit the United States to arm itself and its allies.

Also, wartime production may slow the growth of a nation's stock of capital as resources are shifted from production of capital goods to production of war goods. As a result, future generations inherit a smaller stock of capital goods. This occurred in the United States during World War II. But, again, this shifting of costs is independent of how a war is financed.

QUICK REVIEW 18-2

■ There is no danger of the Federal government going bankrupt because it need only refinance (not retire) the public debt and can raise revenues, if needed, through higher taxes or printing money.

■ Usually, the public debt is not a means of shifting economic burdens to future generations.

IMPLICATIONS AND ISSUES

We must be careful not to leave the impression that the public debt is of no concern among economists. The large debt *does* pose some real potential problems, although economists attach varying importance to them.

Income Distribution

The distribution of government security ownership is uneven. Some people own much more than their $17,816 per capita share; others less or none at all. Although our knowledge of the ownership of the public debt by income class is limited, we presume that ownership is concentrated among wealthier groups. Because the tax system is mildly progressive, payment of interest on the public debt probably increases income inequality. If greater income equality is one of our social goals, then this redistributive effect is clearly undesirable.

Incentives

Table 18-1 indicates that the present public debt necessitates annual interest payments of $192 billion. With no increase in the size of the debt, this annual interest charge must be paid out of tax revenues. These added taxes may dampen incentives to bear risk, to innovate, to invest, and to work. In this indirect way, a large public debt can impair economic growth. As noted earlier, the ratio of interest payments to GDP indicates the level of taxation needed to pay interest on the debt. Thus, many economists are concerned that this ratio is roughly twice as high as it was two decades earlier (column 6 of Table 18-1).

External Debt

External debt—U.S. debt held by citizens and institutions of foreign countries—*is* a burden. This part of the public debt is *not* "owed to ourselves," and in real terms the payment of interest and principal requires transferring some of our real output to other nations. Foreign ownership of the public debt is higher today than in earlier periods. In 1960 only 5 percent of the debt was foreign-owned; today foreign ownership is 14 percent. The assertion that "we owe the debt to ourselves" and the implication that the debt should thus be of little concern is less accurate

than it was four decades ago. But, we must also note that an increased foreign share of the public debt is not a continuing trend; it has remained relatively constant since 1988. *(Key Question 3)*

Curb on Fiscal Policy

A large and growing public debt makes it politically difficult to use fiscal policy during a recession. For example, in 1991 and 1992 the Fed substantially reduced interest rates to stimulate a sluggish economy. But this easy money policy was slow to expand output and reduce unemployment. Had the public debt not been at an historic high and increasing due to the aforementioned structural deficit, it would have been politically feasible to reduce taxes or increase government spending to generate the stimulus of a deficit. But the growing "debt problem" ruled out this stimulus on political grounds. In general, a large and growing public debt creates political impediments to the use of antirecessionary fiscal policy.

Crowding Out and the Stock of Capital

There is a potentially more serious problem. One way the public debt can transfer a real economic burden to future generations is by causing future generations to inherit a smaller stock of capital goods—a smaller "national factory." This possibility involves Chapter 12's **crowding-out effect,** the notion that deficit financing will increase interest rates and reduce private investment spending. If this happens, future generations would inherit an economy with a smaller production capacity and, other things equal, the standard of living would be lower than otherwise.

Suppose the economy is operating at its full-employment level of output and the Federal budget is initially in balance. Now for some reason government increases its level of spending. The impact of this increase in government spending will fall on those living when it occurs. Think of Chapter 2's production possibilities curve with "government goods" on one axis and "private goods" on the other. In a full-employment economy an increase in government spending will move the economy *along* the curve toward the government-goods axis, meaning fewer private goods.

But private goods may be consumer or investment goods. If the increased government goods are provided at the expense of *consumer goods,* then the present generation bears the entire burden as a lower current standard of living. The current investment level is *not* affected and therefore neither is the size of the national factory inherited by future generations. But if the increase in government goods means a reduction in production of *capital goods,* then the present generation's level of consumption (standard of living) will be unimpaired. But in the future our children and grandchildren will inherit a smaller stock of capital goods and will have lower income levels.

Two Scenarios Let's sketch the two scenarios yielding these different results.

First Scenario Suppose the presumed increase in government spending is financed by an increase in taxation, say, personal income taxes. We know most income is consumed. Therefore, consumer spending will fall by almost as much as the increase in taxes. Here, the burden of the increase in government spending falls primarily on today's generation; it has fewer consumer goods.

Second Scenario Assume the increase in government spending is financed by increasing the public debt, meaning government enters the money market and competes with private borrowers for funds. With the supply of money fixed, this increase in money demand will increase the interest rate—the "price" paid for the use of money.

In Figure 18-2 the curve I_{d1} reproduces the investment-demand curve of Figure 9-5. (Ignore curve I_{d2} for now.) The investment-demand curve is downsloping, indicating investment spending varies inversely with the interest rate. Here, government deficit financing drives up the interest rate, reducing private investment. If government borrowing increases the interest rate from 6 to 10 percent, investment spending would fall from $25 to $15 billion. That is, $10 billion of private investment would be crowded out.

Conclusion: An assumed increase in public goods production is more likely to come at the expense of private investment goods when financed by deficits. In comparison with tax financing, the future generation inherits a smaller national factory and therefore has a lower standard of living with deficit financing.

Two Qualifications But there are two loose ends to our discussion which might mitigate or even elimi-

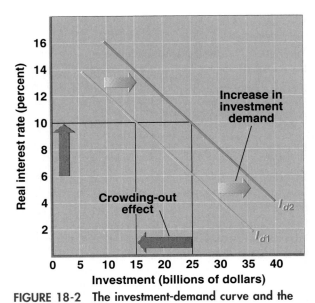

FIGURE 18-2 The investment-demand curve and the crowding-out effect
The crowding-outing effect suggests that, with a fixed investment-demand curve (I_{d1}), an increase in the interest rate caused by a government deficit will reduce private investment spending and decrease the size of the "national factory" inherited by future generations. In this case an increase in the interest rate from 6 to 10 percent crowds out $10 billion of private investment. However, if the economy is initially in a recession, the government deficit may improve profit expectations of businesses and shift the investment-demand curve rightward as from I_{d1} to I_{d2}. This shift may offset the crowding-out effect wholly or in part.

nate the size of the economic burden shifted to future generations.

1 Public Investment Our discussion has neglected the character of the increase in government spending. Just as private goods may involve consumption or investment, so it is with public goods. If the increase in government spending consists of consumption-type outlays—subsidies for school lunches or provision of limousines for government officials—then our second scenario's conclusion that the debt increase has shifted a burden to future generations is correct. But what if the government spending is investment-type outlays, for example, for construction of highways, harbors, and flood-control projects? Similarly, what if they are "human capital" investments in education, job training, and health?

Like private expenditures on machinery and equipment, **public investments** increase the economy's future production capacity. The capital stock of future generations need not be diminished, but rather its composition is changed so there is more public capital and less private capital.

2 Unemployment The other qualification relates to our assumption that the initial increase in government expenditures occurs when the economy is at full employment. Again the production possibilities curve reminds us that, *if* the economy is at less than full employment or, graphically, at a point inside the production possibilities curve, then an increase in government expenditures can move the economy *to* the curve without any sacrifice of either current consumption or private capital accumulation. If unemployment exists initially, deficit spending by government need *not* mean a burden for future generations in the form of a smaller national factory.

Look at Figure 18-2 again. If deficit financing increases the interest rate from 6 to 10 percent, a crowding-out effect of $10 billion will occur. But the increase in government spending will stimulate a recession economy via the multiplier effect, improving profit expectations and shifting private investment demand rightward to I_{d2}. In the case shown, investment spending remains at $25 billion despite the higher 10 percent interest rate. Of course, the increase in investment demand might be smaller or larger than that in Figure 18-2. In the former case the crowding-out effect would not be fully offset; in the latter, it would be more than offset. The point? An increase in investment demand counters the crowding-out effect. *(Key Question 7)*

RECENT FEDERAL DEFICITS

Federal deficits and the growing public debt have been in the economic spotlight in the last decade.

Enormous Size

As Figure 18-3 makes clear, the absolute size of annual Federal deficits increased enormously in the 1980s and 1990s. The average annual deficit for the 1970s was approximately $35 billion. In the 1980s annual deficits averaged five times that amount. Consequently, the public debt tripled during the same time (Table 18-1).

The Federal deficit jumped to $269 billion in 1991 and $290 billion in 1992, mainly because of the 1990–1991 recession and a weak recovery, which

slowed the inflow of tax revenues. Government's expensive bailout of the savings and loan associations also contributed to the huge deficits in these years. The deficits then began to fall in 1993 and 1994 as the economy's expansion quickened and the Clinton administration's efforts to reduce the deficit took hold.

Understatement? The most recent annual budget deficits shown in Figure 18-3 may be understated. Over the past few years government has raised more money from social security taxes than it has paid out as benefits to current retirees. The purpose of this surplus is to prepare for the future time when "baby boomers" retire. Some economists argue that these revenues should be excluded when calculating present deficits because they represent future government obligations on a dollar-for-dollar basis. In this view the social security surplus should not be considered as an offset to *current* government spending. When we exclude the social security surplus from the deficit figures, budget deficits rise by as much as $60 billion annually.

Rising Interest Costs Column 4 of Table 18-1 indicates that interest payments on the public debt have increased more than thirteenfold since 1970. Interest payments were $192 billion in 1994, an amount greater than the entire deficit in many previous years! Because interest payments are part of government expenditures, the debt feeds on itself through interest charges. Interest payments on the debt are the only component of government spending which Congress cannot cut. The spiraling of such payments therefore complicates the problem of controlling government spending and the size of future deficits.

Inappropriate Policy Some of our large annual deficits have occurred in an economy operating at or close to full employment. Historically, deficits—particularly sizable ones—have been associated with wartime finance and recessions. While the 1980–1982 and 1990–1991 recessions contributed to huge deficits, it is clear that the large continuing deficits reflects the 1981 tax cuts and rising government spending. In terms of Figure 12-3, the 1981 tax cuts shifted the tax line downward. Meanwhile, mainly due to increased entitlement spending, the government spending line shifted upward. Thus, even at a full-employment level of output (GDP$_2$) sizable structural deficits remained.

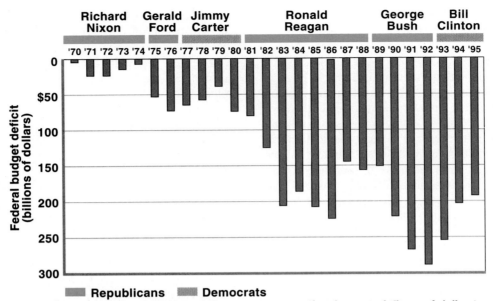

FIGURE 18-3   Annual Federal budget deficits, 1970–1995 (fiscal year in billions of dollars)
Compared to the 1970s, annual budget deficits in the 1980s and first-half of the 1990s are strikingly high.
(Economic Report of the President, 1995. Fiscal years are twelve-month periods ending September 30 of each
year, rather than December 31 as for calendar years. The number for 1995 is an estimate.)

Large deficits during times of economic prosperity raise the concern of fueling demand-pull inflation. To counteract potentially rising prices, the Federal Reserve is forced to employ a tighter monetary policy. Along with the strong demand for money in the private sector, the tight money policy raises real interest rates and reduces investment spending. The greatest potential for budget deficits to produce a crowding-out effect occurs when the economy is near or at full employment.

Balance of Trade Problems   Large budget deficits make it difficult for the nation to achieve a balance in its international trade. As we will see, large annual budget deficits promote imports and stifle exports. Also, budget deficits are thought to be a main cause of two related phenomena: (1) our status as the "world's leading debtor nation" and (2) the so-called "selling of America" to foreign investors.

BUDGET DEFICITS AND TRADE DEFICITS

Many economists see cause-effect between Federal budget deficits and balance of trade deficits. Figure 18-4 is a guide to understanding their thinking.

Higher Interest Rates

Beginning with boxes 1 and 2, we note again that in financing its deficits government must enter the money market to compete with the private sector for funds. We know this drives up real interest rates. High real interest rates have two important effects. First, as shown in box 3, they discourage private investment spending; this is the crowding-out effect. When the economy is close to full employment, the crowding-out effect is likely to be large. Therefore, although willing to admit that the short-run impact of deficits is expansionary, some economists express concern that the long-run effect of structural deficits will retard the economy's growth rate. They envision deficits being used to finance entitlement programs and consumption-type government goods at the expense of investment in modernized factories and equipment. Deficits, it is contended, are forcing the economy onto a slower long-run growth path.

Dollar Appreciation

The second effect, shown by box 4, is that high real interest rates on both American government and private securities make financial investment in the

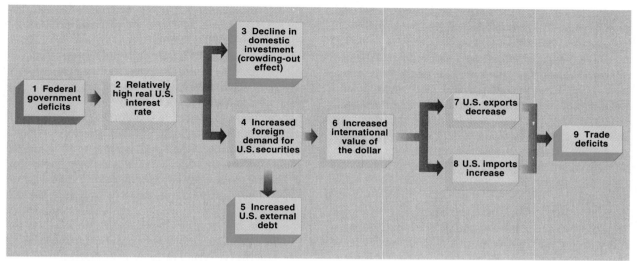

FIGURE 18-4   Budget deficits and trade deficits
Economists contend that large deficits may have a variety of effects. Deficits increase domestic interest rates, resulting in both crowding out of private investment and an increase in the demand for American securities. The latter increases our externally held debt and the demand for dollars. The strong demand for dollars raises the international value of the dollar, making our exports more expensive to foreigners and imports cheaper to Americans. As our exports fall and our imports rise, a contractionary trade deficit arises.

United States more attractive for foreigners. While the resulting inflow of foreign funds helps finance both the deficit and private investment, box 5 reminds us that this inflow represents an increase in our external debt. Paying interest on and retiring debts to the rest of the world means a reduction in future real output available to our domestic economy.

Box 6 indicates that, to purchase high-yielding American securities, foreigners must first buy American dollars with their own currencies. This increases the worldwide demand for dollars and increases the international price or exchange value of the dollar. To illustrate: Suppose that prior to our incurring large deficits, the dollar ($) and the French franc (F) exchanged in the market at a rate of $1 = F10. But now the financing of our large deficits increases real interest rates in the United States, increasing the demand for dollars with which to buy American securities. Suppose this raises the price of the dollar to, say, $1 = F11.

Trade Deficits

This appreciation of the dollar will eventually depress our exports (box 7) and increase our imports (box 8), leading to an "unfavorable" balance of trade. Let's see

how this comes about. We know that exchange rates link the price levels of the world's nations. When the value of the dollar increases—when dollars become more expensive to foreigners—all American goods become more expensive to foreign buyers.

In our example the increase in the value of the dollar from $1 = F10 to $1 = F11 increases prices of all American goods by 10 percent to the French. The American product that formerly cost 10 francs now costs 11 francs. The French will react to this by buying fewer American goods; American exports will fall. Conversely, at the higher exchange rate Americans get 11 rather than 10 francs for a dollar, so French goods are cheaper to Americans. We therefore buy more French goods; our imports rise. Bringing these together, American net exports (exports *minus* imports) fall and a trade deficit emerges (box 9).

Net exports are a component of aggregate demand. A trade deficit implies negative net exports and has a contractionary effect on the economy. As our exports fall, unemployment will rise in American exporting industries such as agriculture, aircraft, and computers. American import-competing industries such as automobiles and basic steel will also be adversely affected. The increase in the value of the dollar makes Japanese and German imports of these products cheaper and American auto and steel industries and find themselves with excess production capacity and redundant labor.

The foregoing comments reiterate our earlier analysis (Chapter 12) that an expansionary fiscal policy may be less stimulating to the economy than simple analysis suggests. The expansionary impact of a deficit might be weakened by both the resulting *crowding-out effect* (box 3) and the negative *net export effect* (box 9).

Related Effects

There are three complications here.

1   The inflow of foreign funds does augment domestic funds and helps keep American real interest rates lower than otherwise. The inflow of foreign funds to the United States diminishes the size of the crowding-out effect. From the standpoint of foreign nations transferring funds to the United States, their domestic investment and long-term economic growth will be smaller.

2   Deficit-caused high real interest rates in America impose an increased burden on heavily indebted developing countries such as Mexico and Brazil. Their dollar-denominated debts to American banks and the banks of other industrial nations become more costly to service when our real interest rates rise.

Our large budget deficits—particularly through the upward pressure they exert on domestic real interest rates—pose something of a threat to the international credit system and to American banks.

3   A trade deficit means we are not exporting enough to pay for our imports. The difference can be paid for in two ways. One, we can borrow from people and institutions in foreign lands. In the late 1980s when the American trade deficit was severe, the United States became the world's leading debtor nation. Two, U.S. assets such as factories, shopping centers, and farms can be sold to foreign investors. This, too, happened in the late 1980s and early 1990s. To pay our debts and repurchase these assets, we must in the future export more than we import. In the future we will need to consume and invest less than we produce.

Contrary View: Ricardian Equivalence Theorem

A few economists disagree with the analysis just outlined. They adhere to the **Ricardian equivalence**

theorem (Chapter 12) which says financing a deficit by borrowing has the same effect on GDP as financing it through a present tax increase. People are supposedly aware that deficits today will require higher future taxes to pay the added interest expense resulting from the increase in the public debt. Households therefore spend less today—saving more—in anticipation of having less future after-tax income available for consumption. Because the increase in private saving perfectly offsets the increase in government borrowing, the real interest rate does not change. Thus neither a crowding-out effect nor a trade deficit necessarily emerges from a budget deficit. In Figure 18-4 the Ricardian equivalence theorem breaks the chain between box 1 and box 2, negating all the effects purportedly following (boxes 3 through 9).

But most economists reject this unusual perspective. They claim instead that the 1980s and early 1990s provide ample evidence of negative foreign-sector effects of large budget deficits. A glance at line 4 on the inside back cover of this text shows that high trade deficits (negative net exports) accompanied the large budget deficits of the late 1980s and early 1990s (Figure 18-3). *(Key Question 8)*

> ## QUICK REVIEW 18-3
>
> ■ The borrowing and interest payments associated with the public debt may *a* increase income inequality, *b* require higher taxes which dampen incentives, *c* curb the use of antirecessionary fiscal policy, and *d* impede the growth of the nation's capital stock *if* public borrowing significantly crowds out private investment.
>
> ■ Recent Federal deficits are of concern because of *a* their enormous size, *b* the possibility they may be understated, *c* rising total interest costs, and *d* their inappropriateness when the economy is near, or at, full-employment output.
>
> ■ Budget deficits can be linked to trade deficits as follows: Budget deficits increase domestic real interest rates; the dollar appreciates; American exports fall, and American imports rise.

Policy Responses

Concern with large budget deficits and an expanding public debt has spawned several policy responses.

Budget Legislation of 1990   In November 1990 Congress attacked the deficit problem by passing the **Budget Reconciliation Act of 1990,** a package of tax increases and spending cuts designed to reduce budget deficits by $500 billion between 1991 and 1996.

This act sought to enhance tax revenue through (1) an increase in the marginal tax rate for wealthy Americans from 28 to 31 percent; (2) lower allowable deductions and personal exemptions for wealthy individuals; (3) higher payroll taxes for medical care; (4) increased excise taxes on gasoline, tobacco, alcoholic beverages, and airline tickets; and (5) a new luxury tax on expensive jewelry, furs, cars, boats, and personal aircraft. This law also set a goal of lopping $260 billion from government spending between 1991 and 1996, the brunt of cuts being borne by national defense, farm programs, and Federal pensions.

Tax increases and expenditure cuts in the midst of recession are counter to conventional fiscal policy. But Congress and the Bush administration reasoned that deficit reduction was essential to lower real interest rates and increase investment—to achieve a reverse crowding-out effect. They also recognized that without these actions deficits would climb to unprecedented, politically costly heights.

The **Budget Enforcement Act of 1990** accompanied the Budget Reconciliation Act and established a "pay-as-you-go" test for new spending or tax decreases. Between 1991 and 1996 new legislation that increased government spending had to be offset by a corresponding decrease in existing spending or an increase in taxes. Likewise, new tax reductions had to be accompanied by offsetting tax increases or spending cuts. Also, this law placed legally binding caps (with exceptions for emergencies) on Federal spending for each of these five years.

Deficit Reduction Act of 1993   By 1992 it became clear that the budget legislation of 1990—although helpful in slowing government spending—would still leave budget deficits of $175 to $225 billion annually. Spurred by the Clinton administration, Congress passed the **Deficit Reduction Act of 1993.** This law is designed to increase tax revenues by $250 billion over five years and to reduce Federal spending by a similar amount.

The tax increases fall mainly, but not exclusively, on high-income households. The three major tax hikes are: (1) an increase in the top marginal tax rate of the personal income tax from 31 percent to 39.6 percent; (2) an increase in the corporate income tax rate from 34 percent to 35 percent; (3) and a boost in the Federal excise tax on gasoline from 14.1 cents per gallon to 18.4 cents per gallon.

The largest spending "cut" will result from holding all discretionary spending—spending not mandated by law—to 1993 nominal levels. Normally, this spending would rise at least as fast as inflation. Also, the law achieves major spending cuts via reductions in government health care payments to doctors and hospitals, delays in the cost-of-living adjustment for government retirees, and reform of the student-loan program.

The budget legislation of 1990 and the Deficit Reduction Act of 1993 will clearly reduce Federal deficits, barring a new recession. But economists agree that these laws will not soon reduce budget deficits to zero.

Other Proposals   Concern with balancing the budget has prompted a variety of other deficit-reduction proposals. One calls for a constitutional amendment requiring a balanced budget. Another calls for reform enabling the President to veto spending measures on a line-item basis.

Constitutional Amendment   The most extreme proposal is that a constitutional amendment should be passed which mandates that Congress balance the budget each year. This proposed **balanced budget amendment** assumes Congress will continue to act "irresponsibly" because government spending enhances and tax increases diminish a politician's popular support. Political rhetoric notwithstanding, Federal deficits allegedly will continue until a constitutional amendment forces a balanced budget. Critics of this proposal remind us that an annually balanced budget has a procyclical or destabilizing effect on the economy.

Line-Item Veto   The **line-item veto** would permit the President to veto individual spending items in appropriation bills. A typical appropriations bill merges hundreds of programs and projects into a single piece of legislation. Governors in the majority of states currently possess line-item veto authority for their state budgets, but the President does not have this veto power for the Federal budget. Proponents of this reform argue it would allow the President to cull from appropriation bills "pork-barrel" projects for which local or regional benefits are less than the costs to the nation's taxpayers. The line-item veto might reduce government spending and help the Federal government balance its budget. Opponents argue that the line-item veto would give far too much power to the

LAST WORD

CUT ENTITLEMENTS TO REDUCE THE DEFICIT?

Spending on programs which "entitle" people to specified transfer payments is rising rapidly, contributing to budget deficits.

The accompanying figure divides Federal spending into three components and shows spending trends as a percentage of GDP.

1 *Interest spending* consists of Federal interest payments on the public debt. Since 1980 interest payments have increased from 1.2 percent to 2.8 percent of GDP, mainly because of the quadrupling of the public debt.

2 *Discretionary spending* involves programs controlled by annual appropriation bills. Congress can decide how much it wants to spend on these programs each year; it has full "discretion" over the amounts spent. This component of Federal expenditures includes spending on defense, transportation, law enforcement, and government operations. Observe that discretionary spending shrunk from 13.5 percent of GDP in 1962 to about 8 percent in 1994.

3 *Mandatory spending*—or "entitlement spending"—comprises benefits paid out in programs such as social security, Medicare, Medicaid, veterans' compensation and pensions, agricultural subsidies, aid to families with dependent children, Supplementary Security Income, and food stamps. This

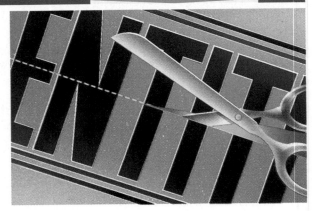

spending is mandated by past legislation which directs Congress to pay out specified benefits to all eligible recipients. Entitlement spending grows when Congress adds new transfer programs or raises benefit levels in existing programs. It also expands when more people become eligible for the benefits. Entitlement spending doubled between 1962 and 1994, rising from 6 percent to 12 percent of GDP.

It is clear from the diagram that rapidly rising Federal entitlements and interest payments are squeezing discretionary spending. Entitlements and

President—power, they say, which might easily be abused for political purposes.

Positive Role of Debt

Having completed this survey of imagined and real problems of deficits and the public debt, we conclude our discussion on a more positive note. Debt—both public and private—plays a positive role in a prosperous and growing economy. As income expands, so does saving. Macroeconomic theory and fiscal policy tell us that if aggregate demand is to be sustained at the full-employment level, this expanding volume of

saving or its equivalent must be obtained and spent by consumers, businesses, or government. The process by which saving is transferred to spenders is *debt creation*. Consumers and businesses *do* borrow and spend a great amount of saving. The total private debt in the United States is about $9 trillion.

But if households and businesses are not willing to borrow and thereby increase private debt sufficiently fast to absorb the growing volume of saving, an increase in public debt must absorb the remainder. If this doesn't happen the economy will falter from full employment and not realize its growth potential.

CHAPTER SUMMARY

1   A budget deficit is the excess of government expenditures over its receipts; the public debt is the total accumulation of its deficits and surpluses over time.

2   Budget philosophies include the annually balanced budget, the cyclically balanced budget, and functional finance. The basic problem with an annually balanced bud-

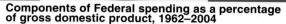

Components of Federal spending as a percentage of gross domestic product, 1962–2004

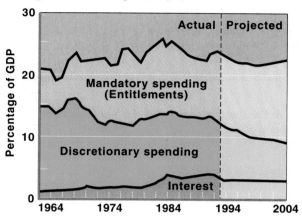

interest are projected to consume *all* Federal tax revenues by 2015, leaving the Federal government with no money for education, children's programs, highways, national defense, or anything else.

Solutions proposed to avoid this startling scenario include:

1   Tax rate increases
2   Eliminating some entitlement programs
3   Reducing benefit levels in some or all entitlement programs

4   Denying wealthier citizens social security and Medicare benefits
5   Reducing health care benefits under Medicare
6   Fully taxing entitlement benefits as if they were ordinary income

None of these possibilities is politically popular. *About half of all American families receive benefits from one or more of the eleven largest entitlement programs.* A recent poll found that 61 percent of the public favored cutting government entitlement programs to curb the deficit. But when asked if they favored cuts in programs such as social security, Medicare, and farm subsidies, 66 percent said "no."

Social security and Medicare are the largest Federal entitlement programs. Social security is currently sound, collecting more revenues from 110 million workers than it pays to 41 million beneficiaries. But this self-financing will end in 2029 because of growing social security payments to the massive baby-boom generation. Spending for Medicare—the fastest growing entitlement program—will rise even more when the baby boomers retire.

Led by the Bipartisan Congressional Commission on Entitlements and Tax Reform, policy makers have begun to confront this issue. There is little doubt the question of what to do about entitlements will be the subject of intense discussion for some time to come.

Source: The Bipartisan Commission on Entitlements and Tax Reform, the Congressional Budget Office, and news sources.

get is that it is procyclical rather than countercyclical. Similarly, it may be difficult to balance the budget over the course of the business cycle if upswings and downswings are not of roughly comparable magnitude. Functional finance is the view that the primary purpose of Federal finance is to stabilize the economy, and problems associated with consequent deficits or surpluses are of secondary importance.

3   Historically, growth of the public debt has been caused by the deficit financing of wars and by recessions. The large structural deficits in recent years are primarily the result of earlier tax reductions, accompanied by increases in entitlement spending.

4   The public debt was $4.6 trillion in 1994, two-thirds of which was held by the public and one-third by government agencies and the Federal Reserve. Since the 1970s the debt and associated interest charges have increased as a percentage of the GDP. The debt has also been rising on a per capita basis.

5   The argument that a large public debt may bankrupt the government is false because   a the debt need only be

refinanced rather than refunded and   b the Federal government has the power to levy taxes and create money.

6   The crowding-out effect aside, the public debt is not a vehicle for shifting economic burdens to future generations.

7   More substantive problems associated with public debt include the following: a Payment of interest on the debt probably increases income inequality.   b Interest payments on the debt require higher taxes which may impair incentives.   c A large and growing public debt creates political impediments to the use of antirecessionary fiscal policy. d Paying interest or principal on the portion of the debt held by foreigners entails a transfer of real output abroad. e Government borrowing to refinance or pay interest on the debt may increase interest rates and crowd out private investment spending.

8   Federal budget deficits have been much larger in the 1980s and 1990s than earlier. Many economists think these large deficits have increased real interest rates in the United States which have then   a crowded out private investment and   b increased foreign demand for American securities. Increased demand for American securities has increased

the international value of the dollar, causing American exports to fall and American imports to rise. The resulting trade deficits exert a contractionary effect on our domestic economy.

9   Proposed or enacted remedies for large deficits and public debt include   a budget legislation of 1990 which raised taxes, cut expenditures, and forced Congress to off-set new spending or tax cuts with either reductions in existing spending or tax increases;   b the Deficit Reduction Act of 1993 which cut expenditures and raised personal income tax rates, the corporate income tax rate, and the Federal tax on gasoline;   c a proposed constitutional amendment mandating an annually balanced budget; and   d giving the President line-item veto authority.

TERMS AND CONCEPTS

budget deficit
public debt
annually balanced
  budget
cyclically balanced
  budget

functional finance
entitlement programs
external debt
crowding-out effect
public investments

Ricardian equivalence
  theorem
Budget Reconciliation
  Act of 1990
Budget Enforcement
  Act of 1990

Deficit Reduction Act
  of 1993
balanced budget
  amendment
line-item veto

QUESTIONS AND STUDY SUGGESTIONS

1   *Key Question   Assess the potential for using fiscal policy as a stabilization tool under   a an annually balanced budget,   b a cyclically balanced budget, and   c functional finance.*

2   What have been the major sources of the public debt historically? Why were deficits so large in the 1980s? Why did the deficit rise in 1991 and 1992?

3   *Key Question   Discuss the two ways of measuring the size of the public debt. How does an internally held public debt differ from an externally held public debt? What would be the effects of retiring an internally held public debt? An externally held public debt? Distinguish between refinancing and retiring the debt.*

4   Explain or evaluate each of the following statements:
    a   "A national debt is like a debt of the left hand to the right hand."

    b   "The least likely problem arising from a large public debt is that the Federal government will go bankrupt."

    c   "The basic cause of our growing public debt is a lack of political courage."

    d   "The social security reserves are not being reserved. They are being spent, masking the real deficit."

5   Is the crowding-out effect likely to be larger during recession or when the economy is near full employment? Explain.

6   Some economists argue that the quantitative importance of the public debt can best be measured by interest payments on the debt as a percentage of the GDP. Can you explain why?

7   *Key Question   Is our $4.6 trillion public debt a burden to future generations? If so, in what sense? Why might deficit financing be more likely to reduce the future size of our "national factory" than tax financing of government expenditures?*

8   *Key Question   Trace the cause-and-effect chain through which large deficits might affect domestic real interest rates, domestic investment, the international value of the dollar, and our international trade. Comment: "There is too little recognition that the deterioration of America's position in world trade is more the result of our own policies than the harm wrought by foreigners." Provide a critique of this position, using the idea of Ricardian equivalence.*

9   Explain how a significant decline in the nation's budget deficit would be expected to affect   a the size of our trade deficit,   b the total debt Americans owe to foreigners, and   c foreign purchases of U.S. assets such as factories and farms.

10   What was the essence of the 1990 Budget Reconciliation and Budget Enforcement Acts? What taxes were raised in the Deficit Reduction Act of 1993? Explain: "The success of the Deficit Reduction Act of 1993 in reducing the budget deficit is predicated on the expectation that there won't be a recession between 1993 and 1998."

11   Would you favor a constitutional amendment requiring the Federal budget to be balanced annually? Why or why not? Do you favor giving the president the authority to veto line-items of appropriation bills? Why or why not?

12   (Last Word) What is meant by the term "entitlement programs"? Cite several examples of these programs. Why have entitlement programs grown so rapidly? What are the implications for future generations if this growth continues?

ECONOMIC GROWTH

Despite periods of cyclical instability, economic growth in the United States has been impressive during this century. Real output has increased fifteenfold while population has only tripled, making five times more goods and services available to the average American than in 1900—and the quality of today's output is far superior. Economic growth has created material abundance, lifted the standard of living, and eased the unlimited wants–scarce resource dilemma.

But the American growth story is not all upbeat. Since 1970 economic growth in America has slowed considerably relative to earlier periods. Of twenty-four advanced industrial nations, only three grew more slowly than the United States over the past three decades.

We begin by defining economic growth. Next, we develop an analytical perspective on economic growth. How can we depict growth within our graphical models? Then, the long-term growth record of the United States and the various factors contributing to it are explored. This enables us to examine the causes of the slowdown in American productivity which began in the 1970s. So-called "doomsday" models of economic collapse are presented and critiqued. Finally, government policies designed to boost the rate of growth are briefly considered.

GROWTH ECONOMICS

Growth economics examines why production capacity increases over time. It also deals with the policy question of how to increase the economy's full employment level of real GDP.

Two Definitions

Economic growth can be defined and measured in two ways:
1 An increase in real GDP occurring over a period of time.

2 An increase in real GDP *per capita* occurring over time

In measuring military potential or political preeminence, the first definition is more relevant. But per capita output is superior for comparing living standards. While India's GDP is $215 billion compared to Denmark's $124 billion, per capita GDP is $26,000 in Denmark and only $310 in India.

Economic growth by either definition is usually calculated as annual percentage *rates* of growth. If real GDP was $200 billion last year and $210 billion this year, we can calculate the rate of growth by subtracting last year's real GDP from this year's real GDP and comparing the difference to last year's real GDP. The growth rate in this example is ($210 − $200)/$200, or 5 percent.

Growth as a Goal

Growth is a widely held economic goal. The growth of total output relative to population means a higher standard of living. An expanding real output means greater material abundance and implies a more satisfactory answer to the economizing problem. *A growing economy is in a better position to meet people's wants and resolve socioeconomic problems both domestically and internationally.* A growing economy enjoys an increment in its annual real output which it can use to satisfy new or existing wants more effectively.

An expanding real wage or salary income makes new opportunities available to individuals and families —a vacation trip, a home computer, a college education for each child—without sacrificing other opportunities and enjoyments. A growing economy can take on new programs to alleviate poverty and clean up the environment *without* impairing existing levels of consumption, investment, and public goods production. *Growth lessens the burden of scarcity.* A growing economy, unlike a static one, can consume more while increasing its capacity to produce more in the future. By easing the burden of scarcity—by relaxing society's production constraints—economic growth allows a nation to attain economic goals more fully and to undertake new endeavors which require output.

Arithmetic of Growth

Why do economists get excited about small changes in the rate of growth? Because it really matters whether an economy grows at 4 percent or 3 percent. For the United States, with a current real GDP of about $5342 billion, the difference between a 3 and a 4 percent growth rate is about $53 billion of output per year. For a very poor country, a 0.5 percent change in the growth rate may mean the difference between starvation and mere hunger.

When viewed over a period of years, an apparently small difference in the rate of growth becomes highly significant because of compounding. Suppose Alphania and Betania have identical GDPs, but Alphania grows at a 4 percent annual rate, while Betania grows at 2 percent. Based on the "rule of 70" (Chapter 8), Alphania's GDP would double in about

eighteen years (= 70 ÷ 4); Betania's would take thirty-five years (= 70 ÷ 2) to double.

Some argue that growth is more important than achieving economic stability. Eliminating a gap between actual GDP and potential GDP might increase the national income by, say, 6 percent on a one-time basis. But a 3 percent annual growth rate will increase the national income by 6 percent in two years and will provide that 6 percent biannual increment indefinitely.

INGREDIENTS OF GROWTH

There are six ingredients in the growth of any economy.

Supply Factors

Four factors relate to the physical ability of an economy to grow. They are (1) the quantity and quality of its natural resources, (2) the quantity and quality of its human resources, (3) the supply or stock of capital goods, and (4) technology. These are the **supply factors** in economic growth—the physical agents of greater production. The availability of more and better resources, including the stock of technological knowledge, is what permits an economy to produce a greater real output.

Demand and Efficiency Factors

Two other considerations contribute to growth. First, there is a **demand factor.** To realize its growing production potential, a nation must achieve full employment of its expanding supplies of resources. This requires a growing level of aggregate demand.

The supply and demand factors in growth are related. Unemployment can retard the rate of capital accumulation and slow expenditures for research. Conversely, a low rate of innovation and investment can cause unemployment.

Second, there is the **efficiency factor.** To achieve its production potential, a nation must obtain not only full employment of its resources, but also full production from them. We must use additional resources in the least-costly way ("productive efficiency") in producing those goods and services most valued by society ("allocative efficiency"). The ability to expand production is not sufficient for the maximum expansion of total output. Also required are the actual employment of expanded resource supplies *and* the efficient use of those resources to get the maximum amount of useful goods produced.

GRAPHICAL ANALYSIS

The six factors underlying economic growth are placed in proper perspective through Chapter 2's production possibilities curves and Chapter 17's aggregate demand and aggregate supply analysis.

Growth and Production Possibilities

Recall that a curve such as *AB* in Figure 19-1 is a best-performance curve. It indicates the various *maximum* combinations of products the economy can produce with its fixed quantity and quality of natural, human, and capital resources, and its stock of technological knowledge. An improvement in any of the supply factors will push the production possibilities curve outward, as shown by the shift from *AB* to *CD* in Figure 19-1. Increases in the quantity or quality of resources and technological progress will accomplish this.

But the demand and efficiency factors remind us the economy need not attain its maximum production potential. The curve may shift outward but leave the economy behind at some level of operation such as *a* on *AB*. Because *a* is inside the new curve *CD*, the economy has not achieved its growth potential. This enhanced production potential will not be realized unless (1) aggregate demand increases sufficiently to sustain full employment, and (2) the additional resources are employed efficiently so they make the maximum possible dollar contribution to output.

An increase in aggregate demand must move the economy from *a* to a point on *CD*. And, to realize the greatest increase in the monetary value of its output —its greatest real GDP growth—this location on *CD* must be optimal. We know from Chapter 2 that this "best allocation" is determined by expanding production of each good until its marginal benefit equals its marginal cost (Figure 2-2). Here, we assume this optimal combination of capital and consumer goods is *b*.

Example: The net increase in the labor force of the United States is roughly 2 million workers per year. This increment raises the production capacity of the economy. But obtaining the extra output these added workers can produce presumes they can find jobs and that these jobs are in firms and industries

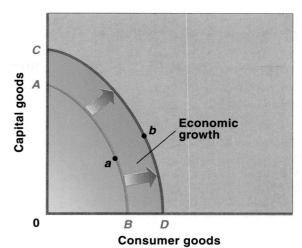

FIGURE 19-1 Economic growth and the production possibilities curve
Economic growth is indicated by an outward shift of the production possibilities curve, as from *AB* to *CD*. Increases in the quantity and quality of resources and technological advance permit this shift; full employment and economic efficiency are essential to its realization, that is, to the movement from point *a* to *b*.

where their talents are fully and optimally used. Society doesn't want new labor force entrants to be unemployed. Nor does it want pediatricians working as plumbers, or workers producing goods which have higher marginal costs than marginal benefits. *(Key Question 2)*

Labor and Productivity Although demand and efficiency considerations are important, discussions of growth focus primarily on the supply side. Figure 19-2 provides a framework for discussing the supply factors in growth. It indicates two fundamental ways society can increase its real output and income: (1) by increasing its inputs of resources, and (2) by increasing the productivity of those inputs. Let's focus on inputs of labor. We can say *our real GDP in any year depends on the input of labor (measured in worker-hours) multiplied by* **labor productivity** *(measured as real output per worker per hour)*.

Total output = worker-hours × labor productivity

Illustration: Assume an economy has 10 workers, each working 2000 hours per year (50 weeks at 40 hours per week). The total input of worker-hours therefore is 20,000 hours. If productivity—average

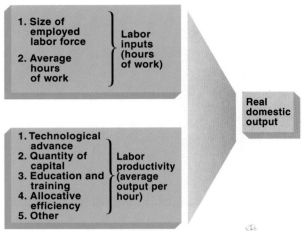

FIGURE 19-2 The determinants of real output
Real GDP can be usefully viewed as the product of the quantity of labor inputs multiplied by labor productivity.

real output per worker-hour—is $5, then total output or real GDP will be $100,000 (= 20,000 × $5).

What determines the number of hours worked each year? And what determines labor productivity? Figure 19-2 provides some answers. The hours of labor input depend on the size of the employed labor force and the length of the average workweek. Labor force size depends on the size of the working age population and the **labor force participation rate**—*the percentage of the working age population actually in the labor force.* The average workweek is governed by legal and institutional considerations and by collective bargaining.

Productivity is determined by technological progress, the quantity of capital goods available to workers, the quality of labor itself, and the efficiency with which inputs are allocated, combined, and managed. Productivity increases when the health, training, education, and motivation of workers are improved; when workers have more and better machinery and natural resources with which to work; when production is better organized and managed; and when labor is reallocated from less efficient industries to more efficient industries.

AD–AS Framework

We can also view economic growth through the long-run aggregate supply and aggregate demand analysis developed in Figures 17-6 and 17-7. Suppose aggre-

gate demand is AD_1 and long-run and short-run aggregate supply curves are AS_1 and AS_1' as shown in Figure 19-3. The initial equilibrium price level is P_1 and the level of real output is Q_1.

Recall that the upward slope of short-run aggregate supply curve AS_1' shows that a change in the price level will alter the level of real output. In the long run, however, wages and other input prices will fully adjust to the new price level, making the aggregate supply curve vertical at the economy's full-employment or potential level of real output. As with the location of the production possibilities curve, real supply factors—the quantity and quality of resources and technology—determine the long-run level of full-employment real output. Price level changes do not alter the location of the production possibilities curve; neither do they change the location of the long-run aggregate supply curve.

Aggregate Supply Shifts Now assume changes in the supply factors listed in Figure 19-2 shift the long-run aggregate supply curve rightward from AS_1 to AS_2. This means the production possibilities curve in Figure 19-1 has been pushed outward.

Aggregate Demand Shifts If aggregate demand remains at AD_1, the increase in long-run aggregate supply from AS_1 to AS_2 eventually will overcome downward price and wage rigidity and reduce the price level. But in recent decades a rising, not a falling, price level has accompanied economic growth. This suggests that aggregate demand has increased more rapidly than long-run aggregate supply. We show this in Figure 19-3 by shifting aggregate demand from AD_1 to AD_2, which results from changes in one or more of the determinants of aggregate demand (Table 11-1).

The combined increases in aggregate supply and aggregate demand in Figure 19-3 have produced economic growth of Q_1Q_2 and a rise in the price level from P_1 to P_2. At price level P_2, the economy confronts a new short-run aggregate supply curve AS_2'. (If not clear why, review Figure 17-6.)

Also, nominal GDP (= $P \times Q$) has increased more rapidly than real GDP (= Q) because of inflation. This diagram describes the secular trend of nominal GDP, real GDP, and the price level in the United States, a fact you can confirm by examining rows 5, 18, and 21 on the inside covers of this book. (*Key Question 3*)

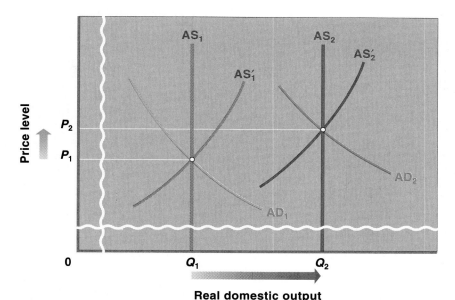

FIGURE 19-3 Economic growth and aggregate demand–aggregate supply analysis
Long-run and short-run aggregate supply curves have shifted rightward over time, as from AS_1 and AS'_1 to AS_2 and AS'_2. Meanwhile, aggregate demand has shifted rightward even more rapidly. The outcome of these combined shifts has been economic growth, shown as the increase in real output from Q_1 to Q_2, accompanied by inflation, shown as the rise in the price level from P_1 to P_2.

UNITED STATES GROWTH

Table 19-1 provides an overview of economic growth in the United States over past decades as viewed through our two definitions of growth. Column 2 shows the economy's growth as measured by increases in real GDP. Although not steady, the growth of real GDP has been strong. *Real GDP has increased nearly sixfold since 1940.* But our population has also grown significantly. Using our second definition of growth, we find in column 4 that *real per capita GDP was almost three times larger in 1994 than in 1940.*

What about our *rate* of growth? Global Perspective 19-1 shows that the post-1948 growth rate of the United States' real GDP has been 3.1 percent per year. Not shown, real GDP per capita has grown at almost 2 percent per year.

These bare numbers must be modified.

1 Improved Products and Services The figures of Table 19-1 and Global Perspective 19-1 do *not* fully take into account improvements in the quality of products and services, and thus understate the growth of economic well-being. Purely quantitative data do not accurately compare an era of ice-boxes and LPs and one of refrigerators and CDs.

2 Added Leisure The increases in real GDP and per capita GDP shown in Table 19-1 were accomplished despite large increases in leisure. The standard workweek, once seventy hours, is now about

TABLE 19-1 Real GDP and per capita GDP, 1929–1994

(1) Year	(2) GDP, billions of 1987 dollars	(3) Population millions	(4) Per capita GDP, 1987 dollars (2) ÷ (3)
1929	$ 841	122	$ 6,893
1933	592	126	4,698
1940	919	132	6,962
1945	1615	140	11,536
1950	1428	152	9,395
1955	1773	166	10,681
1960	1973	181	10,902
1965	2474	194	12,753
1970	2876	205	14,029
1975	3222	214	15,056
1980	3776	228	16,561
1985	4280	239	17,908
1990	4897	250	19,588
1994	5342	261	20,467

Source: Economic Report of the President, 1995.

GLOBAL PERSPECTIVE 19-1

Average annual growth rates since 1948, selected nations

Real GDP has grown less rapidly in the United States than in several other advanced industrial countries since 1948. Japan and Germany have had the highest average annual growth rates in this period.

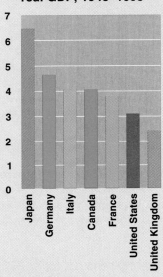

Average annual growth of real GDP, 1948–1993

Japan · Germany · Italy · Canada · France · United States · United Kingdom

Source: Organization for Economic Cooperation and Development.

concern in the United States that Japan will overtake America as the world's leading economic power.

QUICK REVIEW 19-1

■ Economic growth can be viewed as either the increase in real GDP or real GDP per capita over time.

■ Graphically, growth is shown as outward shifts of the production possibilities curve or as combined rightward shifts of aggregate supply and aggregate demand curves.

■ Annual growth of real GDP in the United States has averaged more than 3 percent since World War II.

ACCOUNTING FOR GROWTH

Economist Edward F. Denison spent most of his professional career quantifying the relative importance of the factors contributing to economic growth. His conceptual framework corresponds closely to the factors in Figure 19-2. Denison's most recent estimates are shown in Table 19-2. Over the 1929–1982 period, he calculated that real national income grew by 2.9 percent per year. He then estimated what percentage of this annual growth was due to each factor shown in the table.

Inputs versus Productivity

The most evident conclusion from Denison's data is that *productivity growth has been the most important force underlying the growth of our real output and national income.* Increases in the quantity of labor (item 1) account for only about one-third of the increase in real national income in this period; two-thirds is attributable to rising labor productivity (item 2).

Quantity of Labor

Our population and labor force have both expanded significantly. Over the 1929–1982 period considered by Denison, total population grew from 122 to 232 million and the labor force increased from 49 to 110 million workers. Reductions in the length of the workweek reduced the growth of labor inputs before World War II, but the workweek has declined little since then. Declining birthrates in the past twenty-five years

forty hours. The result again is an understatement of economic well-being.

3   Environmental Effects   But these measures of growth do *not* take into account adverse effects which growth may have on the environment and the quality of life. If growth debases the physical environment and creates a stressful work environment our data will overstate the benefits of growth.

4   International Comparisons   The growth record of the United States is less impressive than the growth of several other industrially advanced nations. As seen in Global Perspective 19-1, Japan's growth rate has averaged more than twice the United States' growth over the past several decades. And there is

TABLE 19-2   The sources of growth in U.S. real national income, 1929–1982

Sources of growth	Percent of total growth
(1) Increase in quantity of labor	32
(2) Increase in labor productivity	68
(3) Technological advance	28
(4) Quantity of capital	19
(5) Education and training	14
(6) Economies of scale	9
(7) Improved resource allocation	8
(8) Legal-human environment and other	−9
	100

Source: Edward F. Denison. *Trends in American Economic Growth, 1929–1982* (Washington: The Brookings Institution, 1985), p. 30. Details may not add to totals because of rounding.

have slowed the growth of the native population, but this slowdown has been partly offset by increased immigration. Of most significance, however, has been a surge of participation of women in labor markets. Largely fueled by this trend, our labor force has grown by about 2 million workers per year during the past twenty-five years.

Technological Advance

Technological advance (item 3 in Table 19-2) is a critical engine of growth, accounting for 28 percent of the increase in real national income between 1929 and 1982.

Technological advance includes not merely new production techniques but also new managerial methods and new forms of business organization. Generally, it is linked with the discovery of new knowledge, which permits combining a specific amount of resources in new ways to achieve a larger output.

Technological advance and capital formation (investment) are closely related; technological advance often requires investment in new machinery and equipment. The purchase of new computers not only means more of these computers, but quicker, more powerful computers embodying new technology. And it is necessary to construct new nuclear power plants to apply improved nuclear power technology. However, modern crop-rotation practices and contour plowing are ideas which contribute to output, al-

though they do not necessarily use new kinds or increased amounts of capital equipment.

Technological advance has been both rapid and profound. Gas and diesel engines, conveyor belts, and assembly lines are significant developments of the past. More recently, technology has produced automation and the push-button factory. Bigger, faster, and more fuel-efficient commercial aircraft, integrated microcircuits, computers, xerography, containerized shipping, and nuclear power—not to mention biotechnology, lasers, and superconductivity—are technological achievements which were in the realm of fantasy only a generation or two ago.

Quantity of Capital

Some 19 percent—almost one-fifth—of the annual growth of real national income between 1929 and 1982 was attributable to increases in the quantity of capital (item 4). A worker will be more productive when equipped with more capital goods. And a nation acquires more capital through saving and the investment in plant and equipment which these savings make possible. A recent estimate suggests that total output will increase by about one-fourth of a percentage point for each extra percentage of GDP invested in machinery and equipment.

The critical consideration for labor productivity is the amount of capital goods *per worker*. The aggregate stock of capital might expand in a specific period, but if the labor force also increases rapidly, labor productivity need not rise because each worker will not necessarily be better-equipped. This happened in the 1970s and 1980s when the labor force surged, contributing to a slowing of American productivity growth.

The quantity of capital per worker has increased in the United States. The amount of capital equipment (machinery and buildings) per worker is currently about $52,000.

Two addenda:

1   The United States has been saving and investing a smaller percentage of its GDP in recent years than most other industrial advanced nations. This helps explain our less impressive growth. Levels of investment as a percentage of GDP and rates of increases in real GDP per capita are positively related (Global Perspective 2-1).

2   Investment is not only private, but also public. Our infrastructure—the highways and bridges, the public transit systems, the wastewater treatment

facilities, the municipal water systems, the airports —faces growing problems of deterioration, technological obsolescence, and insufficient capacity to serve future growth.

Also, public capital (infrastructure) and private capital are complementary. Investments in new highways promote private investment in new factories and retail establishments along their routes. Industrial parks which are developed by local governments in turn attract manufacturing firms. Some economists view the slowdown in the development of our infrastructure as a significant source of reduced private investment.

Education and Training

Ben Franklin once said: "He that hath a trade hath an estate." He meant that education and training improve a worker's productivity and result in higher earnings. Like investment in physical capital, investment in human capital is an important means of increasing labor productivity. Denison's estimates in Table 19-2 indicate that 14 percent of the growth in our real national income is attributable to such improvements in the quality of labor (item 5).

Perhaps the simplest measure of labor quality is the level of educational attainment. Figure 19-4 reflects educational gains in the past several decades. Currently 80 percent of the population, aged 25 or more, has at least a high school education. Twenty-two percent has acquired a college education or more.

FIGURE 19-4 Changes in the educational attainment of the adult population
The percentage of the population, aged 25 or more, completing high school and college has been rising in recent decades. (*Statistical Abstract of the United States, 1994,* p. 157.)

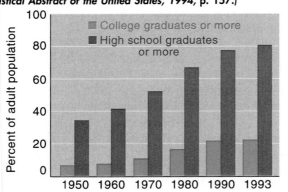

It is clear from Figure 19-4 that education has become accessible to more and more people.

But there are concerns about the quality of American education. Scores on standardized college admissions tests have declined relative to scores of a few decades ago. Furthermore, American students in science and mathematics do not do as well as students in many other industrialized nations. Japanese children have a longer school day and attend school 240 days per year compared to 180 in the United States. Also, we have been producing fewer engineers and scientists, a problem which may trace back to inadequate training in math and science in elementary and high schools. And it is argued that on-the-job training (apprenticeship programs) in Japan and Germany—nations with fast rates of productivity growth—are more available and far superior to those in the United States.

Resource Allocation and Scale Economies

Table 19-2 also tells us that labor productivity has increased because of economies of scale (item 6) and improved resource allocation (item 7).

Improved Resource Allocation Improved resource allocation means that workers over time have reallocated themselves from low-productivity employment to high-productivity employment. Historically, much labor has shifted from agriculture, where labor productivity is low, to manufacturing, where it is quite high. More recently, labor has shifted away from some manufacturing industries to even higher-productivity industries such as legal, health, consulting, and financial services. As a result of such shifts, the average productivity of American workers in the aggregate has increased.

Also, labor market discrimination has historically denied women and minorities access to high-productivity jobs. The decline of such discrimination over time has shifted these groups from low-productivity jobs to higher-productivity jobs, increasing overall labor productivity and raising real GDP.

Tariffs, import quotas, and other barriers to international trade (Chapter 6) often keep resources in relatively unproductive employments. The long-run movement toward freer international trade has therefore improved the allocation of resources and expanded real output.

Economies of Scale Economies of scale are production advantages deriving from increased market and firm size. A large corporation often can select more efficient production techniques than can a small-scale firm. A large manufacturer of autos can use elaborate assembly lines with computerization and robotics, while smaller producers must settle for less advanced technologies. Markets have increased in scope over time and firms have increased in size, allowing more efficient production methods to be used. Accordingly, labor productivity has increased and economic growth has occurred.

Detriments to Growth

Some developments detract from the growth of real output and income. The entry for the legal and human environment (item 8) in Table 19-2 aggregates these detriments to productivity growth. Since 1929 there have been several changes in the regulation of industry, environmental pollution, and worker health and safety, which have negatively affected growth. The expansion of government regulation in such areas as pollution control, worker health and safety, and access for the disabled has diverted investment spending away from growth-increasing capital goods and toward expenditures for cleaner air and water, greater worker protection, and improved access for disabled workers and consumers. A firm required to spend $1 million on a new scrubber to meet government standards for air pollution or to make its stores accessible to the disabled will not have that $1 million to spend on machinery and equipment which would expand real output. The diversion of resources to deal with dishonesty and crime, the effects of work stoppages because of labor disputes, and the impact of bad weather on agricultural output are also factors which impede economic growth.

It should be noted that, while worker safety, clean air and water, equal access for the disabled, and the overall quality of life may come at the expense of economic growth, the reverse is also true. Economic growth does not automatically enhance society's welfare. Growth of real output may involve opportunity costs of other things (a clean environment, a fair society) we value more highly. Productivity measures output per hour of work, *not* overall well-being per hour of work. Increases in real GDP are not necessarily matched with equal increases in well-being. Thus, society may rationally decide to "trade off"

some economic growth to achieve other desirable ends. *(Key Question 5)*

Other Factors

There are other difficult-to-quantify considerations which affect an economy's growth rate. For example, America's generous and varied supplies of natural resources have been an important contributor to our economic growth. We enjoy an abundance of fertile soil, desirable climatic and weather conditions, large quantities of most mineral resources, and generous sources of power. With the possible exceptions of Russia and Canada, the United States has a larger variety and greater quantity of natural resources than any other nation.

While an abundant natural resource base is helpful to growth, a meager resource base does not doom a nation to slow growth. Although Japan's natural resources are severely constrained, its post-World War II growth has been remarkable (Global Perspective 19-1). In contrast, some of the impoverished countries of Africa and South America have substantial amounts of natural resources.

There are additional unmeasurable factors affecting a nation's growth rate. In particular, the overall social-cultural-political environment of the United States generally has promoted economic growth. Several factors contribute to this favorable environment.

1 Unlike many other nations, there are virtually no social or moral taboos on production and material progress. American social philosophy has embraced material advance as an attainable and desirable economic goal. The inventor, the innovator, and the business executive are accorded high degrees of prestige and respect in American society.

2 Americans have traditionally possessed healthy attitudes toward work and risk taking; our society has benefited from a willing labor force and an ample supply of entrepreneurs.

3 Our market system has many personal and corporate incentives encouraging growth; our economy rewards actions which increase output.

4 Our economy is founded on a stable political system characterized by democratic principles, internal order, the right of property ownership, the legal status of enterprise, and the enforcement of contracts. One recent study has shown that politically open societies grow much more rapidly on average than those where freedom is limited.

Though difficult to quantify, these characteristics have provided an excellent foundation for American economic growth.

Aggregate Demand, Instability, and Growth

As seen in Table 19-2, Denison's analysis is designed to explain the growth of actual, not potential or full-employment, real national income. The 2.9 percent annual growth rate the table attempts to explain includes changes in real GDP caused by fluctuations in aggregate demand. Our annual growth rate would have been approximately 0.2 to 0.3 percentage points higher over this period if the economy's full-employment output had been obtained year after year. Deviations from full employment arising from deficiencies of aggregate demand cause the actual rate of growth to fall short of the potential rate.

A glance back at Figure 8-5 reminds us that the actual performance of our economy occasionally falls short of its potential output. The Great Depression of the 1930s in particular was a serious blow to the United States' long-run growth record. Between 1929 and 1933 our real GDP (measured in 1987 prices) actually *declined* from $823 to $587 billion. In 1939 the real GDP was about at the same level as in 1929 (see line 18 on table inside front cover). More recently, the severe 1980–1982 recessions cost the United States more than $600 billion in lost output and income.

But this is only part of the picture. Cyclical unemployment can have harmful "carry-over" effects on the growth rate in subsequent years of full employment through the adverse effects it may have on other growth factors. Unemployment depresses investment and capital accumulation. Furthermore, the expansion of research budgets may be slowed by recession

so that technological progress diminishes; union resistance to technological change may stiffen; and so forth. Though it is difficult to quantify the impact of these considerations on the growth rate, they undoubtedly have had an effect.

QUICK REVIEW 19-2

■ Increases in labor productivity account for about two-thirds of increases in real output; the use of more labor inputs accounts for one-third.

■ Improved technology, more capital, more education and training, economies of scale, and improved resource allocation are the main contributors to growth.

■ Growth rates in the United States have been erratic, particularly because of fluctuations in aggregate demand.

THE PRODUCTIVITY SLOWDOWN

In the 1970s—and to a lesser degree in the 1980s and early 1990s—the United States experienced a much-publicized productivity slowdown. This has led to concern that America is in relative economic decline. Table 19-3 portrays the course of United States labor productivity in the post-World War II period. Observe in column 2 that for about two decades following World War II (1948–1966) labor productivity increased at a vigorous average annual rate of 3.2 percent, only to decline sharply in the 1966–1973 period. This was followed by a dismal performance in the years 1973–1981, and a modest resurgence of productivity growth since 1981. Although labor productivity growth has been slowing worldwide, American productivity growth has been slower than in most other major industrialized nations. The United States still enjoys the highest absolute level of output per worker, but its productivity advantage is diminishing.

Significance

Our productivity slowdown has many implications.

1 Standard of Living Productivity growth is the basic source of improvements in real wage rates and the standard of living. Real income per worker-hour can only increase at the same rate as real output per worker-hour. More output per hour means more real income to distribute for each hour worked. The sim-

TABLE 19-3 Growth of labor productivity and real per capita GDP, 1948–1994

(1) Period	(2) Annual productivity growth rate	(3) Annual real per capita GDP, growth rate
1948–1966	3.2	2.2%
1966–1973	2.0	2.0
1973–1981	0.7	1.1
1981–1990	1.3	1.8
1990–1994	2.0	1.2

Source: Economic Report of the President, 1988, p. 67. End points of calculations are cyclical peaks, except for 1994. Updated.

plest case is of Robinson Crusoe on his deserted island. The number of fish he can catch or coconuts he can pick per hour *is* his real income or wage per hour.

We observe in column 3 of Table 19-3 that the broadest measure of living standards—the growth of real per capita GDP—followed the path of labor productivity. Living levels thus measured grew by only 1.1 percent per year during the severe 1973–1981 productivity stagnation compared to 2.2 percent in the 1948–1966 postwar decades.

The slowdown in productivity is also reflected in Figure 19-5 which tracks the median real income of American families since 1947. Median family income increased substantially in real terms from 1947 to 1973. But it fell during the 1980s and is not much higher today than in 1973.

2   Inflation   We saw in Chapter 17 that productivity increases offset increases in nominal wage rates, partly or fully lessening cost-push inflationary pressures. Other things equal, a decline in the rate of productivity growth contributes to rising unit labor costs and a higher rate of inflation. Many economists believe that productivity stagnation contributed to the unusually high inflation rates of the 1970s.

3   World Markets   Other things equal, our slow rate of productivity growth compared to our major international trading partners increases relative prices of American goods in world markets. The result is a decline in our competitiveness and a loss of international markets for American producers.

Causes of the Slowdown

There is no consensus among experts as to why American productivity growth has slowed and fallen behind the rates of Japan and western Europe. Because so many factors affect productivity, there may be no simple explanation. However, let's survey some of the possible causes.

Labor Quality   One possibility is that slower improvements in labor quality may have dampened productivity growth. Three factors may have been at work.

1   Decline in Experience Level   The experience level of the labor force may have declined. The large number of baby-boom workers who entered the labor force had little experience and training and were therefore less productive. The labor force participation of women increased significantly over the past two decades. Many were married women with little or no prior labor force experience who therefore had low productivity.

2   Less Able Workers   The declining test scores of students on standardized examinations during the past few decades perhaps indicates a decline in worker capabilities. If so, this decline may have contributed to the productivity slowdown.

3   Slowing of Rise in Educational Attainment   The historical rise in the average level of educational at-

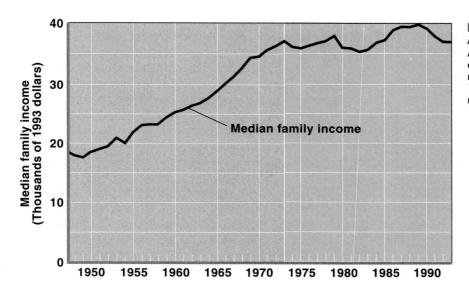

FIGURE 19-5 Median income of American families, 1947–1993 After World War II the median real income of American families grew rapidly until the early 1970s. Since 1973 real family income has stagnated. (Bureau of the Census.)

tainment of the labor force has been slowing in recent years. The median number of years of school completed by the adult population was 12.1 in 1970 and increased to only 12.7 by 1993.

Technological Progress Technological advance—usually reflected in improvements in the quality of capital goods and the efficiency with which inputs are combined—may also have faltered. Technological progress is fueled by expenditures for formal research and development (R&D) programs. In the United States, R&D spending declined as a percentage of GDP from a peak of 3 percent in the mid-1960s to about 1 percent by the late 1970s, before rising again in the 1980s.

However, some economists discount the R&D decline in explaining the productivity slowdown. They say R&D *spending* alone tells us little about R&D *accomplishments*. There is clear evidence of continuing technological advance during the past two decades.

Investment A high positive correlation exists between the percentage of a nation's GDP devoted to investment goods and the productivity increases it achieves. A worker using a bulldozer can move more earth per hour than the same worker using a hand shovel. An engineer using a computer can complete a design task more rapidly than with pencil and paper.

The United States has been investing a smaller percentage of its GDP than in earlier periods. Several factors may have contributed to the weak growth of investment.

1   Low Saving Rate The United States has had a low saving rate which, coupled with strong private and public demands for credit, has resulted in high real interest rates relative to historical standards. High interest rates discourage investment spending.

2   Import Competition Growing import competition may have made some American producers reluctant to invest in new capital equipment. They may have shifted more investment overseas toward nations with low-wage workers.

3   Regulation The expansion of government regulations in the areas of pollution control, worker health and safety, and access for the disabled diverted some investment spending away from output-increasing capital goods. This investment spending may

have increased total utility to society, but did not directly increase output itself. The composition of investment may have shifted toward uses which do not increase productivity.

4   Reduced Infrastructure Spending Reduced spending on the economy's infrastructure may have slowed productivity growth. We have noted that these public capital goods are complementary to private capital goods. Data show that between 1950 and 1970 the public capital stock of infrastructure grew at a 4.1 percent annual rate, and labor productivity growth was 2.0 percent per year. During 1971–1985, however, the yearly increase in the infrastructure fell to 1.6 percent and the annual productivity increase dropped to 0.8 percent. A slowing of spending on public investment goods may have contributed to diminishing private investments and to declines in productivity growth.

Energy Prices Perhaps the prime suspect in the productivity slowdown was the large increases in oil prices occurring in 1973–1975 and in 1978–1980. Productivity growth diminished sharply after the quadrupling of oil prices in 1973–1975. Also, the impact of rocketing energy prices was worldwide, as was the productivity slowdown.

The direct impact of higher oil prices was to increase the cost of operating capital equipment, in effect raising the "price" of capital relative to labor. Producers were therefore more inclined to use less productive labor-intensive techniques.

The indirect macroeconomic effects of leaping energy prices may have had even more to do with reducing productivity growth. The two episodes of soaring energy prices produced stagflation—inflationary recessions. Government's restrictive macroeconomic policies to control inflation worsened and prolonged the periods of recession and slow economic growth. Recessions diminish productivity—output per worker—since output normally declines more rapidly than employment. The long periods of underuse of productive capacity in many industries probably contributed to the productivity slowdown.

Industrial Relations A different view of the productivity slowdown stresses institutional forces. The way work is organized, the attitudes and behavior of workers and managers, communication between labor and management, and the division of authority among managers and workers allegedly account for much of our poor productivity performance compared to Japan and western Europe. The argument is that American industrial relations reflect an adversarial relationship between managers and their employees. Feeling alienated from their employers, workers do not participate in the decisions governing their daily work lives; they do not identify with the objectives of their firms, and therefore are not motivated to work hard and productively. Managers are judged, rewarded, and motivated by short-term profits and thus, it is argued, give little attention to long-term plans and strategies critical to attaining high rates of productivity growth.

Japanese industries, in contrast, provide lifetime employment security for most of their work force, allow for worker participation in decision making, and use profit-sharing or bonuses to provide a direct link between the economic success of a firm and worker incomes. Furthermore, the direct interest workers have in the competitiveness and profitability of their enterprise reduces the need for supervisory personnel. The result is a commonality of interest and cooperation between management and labor, greater flexibility in job assignment, and more willingness of workers to accept technological change. Lifetime employment provides an incentive for heavy investment by employers in training and retraining their workers.

A Resurgence?

Since 1981 there has been a modest improvement in productivity growth. In Table 19-3 the 0.7 percent annual productivity growth for 1973–1981 improved to a 1.3 percent annual increase between 1981–1990. The recession of 1990–1991 halted this upward trend; productivity growth fell back to 0.7 percent in 1990 and was only 1.0 percent in 1991. But productivity surged to 3.0 percent in 1992 and averaged 2.0 percent over the 1990–1994 period.

Many of the factors depressing productivity growth have dissipated or been reversed. Energy prices are stable and the stagflation problem overcome. Since 1977 research and development spending has been increasing as a percentage of GDP. Innovations in computers, telecommunications, robotics, genetic engineering, and superconductors are providing a big stimulus to productivity. Although higher than a few years earlier, interest rates are still low, promoting purchases of new plant and equipment. Wages of college graduates have risen relative to wages of high school graduates and this wage pre-

mium should soon attract more students to universities.

The inexperienced baby-boomers who flooded labor markets in the 1960s and 1970s are now moving into the 25- to 54-year-old prime labor force as more mature, more productive workers. While American industrial relations remain distinctly different from the cooperative "shared vision" of Japanese managers and workers, the problems imposed by recession and increasing foreign competition are pushing American workers and managers in that direction. Worker involvement and profit-sharing plans are becoming more common in American industry.

Nevertheless, it is unclear at this point whether the recent revival of productivity is transitory or permanent. *(Key Question 8)*

DOOMSDAY MODELS

Annual 2 to 7 percent rates of economic growth in the industrial nations—compounded year after year—raise these questions: Can economic growth in industrially advanced nations continue over the next few decades? Can it continue over the next century?

Computer modelers[1] have developed complex simulation models called **doomsday models,** indicating that the world economy is using resources and dumping wastes at rates which the planet cannot sustain. Population and industrial production, it is argued, are expanding at exponential (2, 4, 16, 256, . . .) rates. Modern industrial production depends heavily on exhaustible natural resources which allegedly are fixed in supply. Industrial economies also employ the environment—which has a limited absorptive capacity—for waste disposal. In this view, we must ultimately run out of certain natural resources—oil, coal, copper, arable land—critical to the production process. Also, the increased waste inevitably resulting from economic growth will overwhelm the absorptive capacity of the world's ecological system. Air, water, and solid waste pollution will worsen.

The "Standard Run" Model

Figure 19-6 shows one computer simulation. This scenario assumes the world proceeds along its historical

---

[1]Donella H. Meadows, Dennis L. Meadows, and Jorgen Randers, *Beyond the Limits* (Post Mills, Vt.: Chelsea Green Publishers, 1992). Also see Dennis L. Meadows, et al., *The Limits to Growth* (Washington: Potomac Associates, 1972).

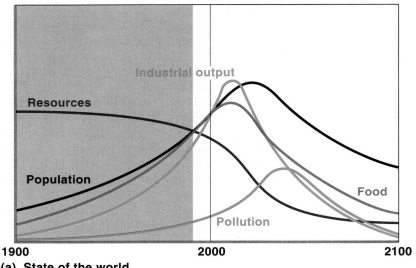

(a) State of the world

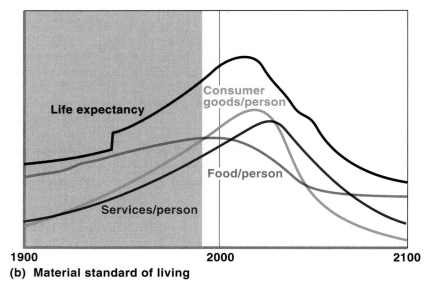

(b) Material standard of living

FIGURE 19-6 Growth and collapse: a doomsday model
This computer model assumes that "The world society proceeds along its historical path as long as possible without major policy change. Population and industry output grow until a combination of environmental and natural resource constraints eliminate the capacity of the capital sector to sustain investment. Industrial capital begins to depreciate faster than the new investment can rebuild it. As it falls, food and health services also fall, decreasing life expectancy and raising the death rate." (Meadows, Meadows, and Randers, op. cit., pp. 132–133.)

paths of production and population growth with no policy changes and that technological advances occur "according to established patterns." In Figure 19-6a, population, industrial output, and food production all grow significantly in the 1900–1990 period. But then in the early twenty-first century the economy stops growing and, in effect, collapses. Why?

After 2000, pollution reaches a level at which the fertility of land is seriously reduced and food production begins to fall. Nonrenewable resources become increasingly scarce and more costly to obtain. As a result, the world economy must shift more investment to the agricultural sector and to the discovery, ex-

traction, and refining of raw materials. In time this reallocation of investment means that industrial capital declines as depreciation exceeds new industrial investment spending. As the stock of industrial capital declines, the agricultural and service (including health) sectors also falter because they have become dependent on industrial outputs such as hospital laboratories and equipment, fertilizers, and pesticides. We find in Figure 19-6 that, as food and health services per capita decline, life expectancy falls and population declines.

Other computer simulations use more optimistic assumptions on industrial and population growth and the rate of technological progress. But, although the timing and magnitude of the changes are different, the basic conclusion is the same—population and production growth will tip the world's economic and life-support systems into collapse.

Doomsday Evidence

The "doomsday" modelers see evidence of economic and environmental collapse. Desperate people in the poorest nations chop down forests for firewood, altering local and perhaps global weather patterns. Land is overcultivated and overgrazed, reverting to desert, and the planet's ability to feed its population is diminished. In the last half of the 1980s, food production per capita declined in more than ninety nations. Fisheries have been exploited beyond sustainable rates; fish are being taken from the world's oceans at rates beyond which they are being regenerated.

Toward a Sustainable Society

The world must make hard decisions to achieve a sustainable society—"one that can persist over generations, one that is far-seeing enough, flexible enough, and wise enough not to undermine either its physical or its social systems of support."[2] Specific recommendations include: (1) slowing and eventually stopping the exponential growth of population and industrial output; (2) minimizing the use of nonrenewable resources such as fossil fuels and minerals; (3) limiting the rates of use of renewable resources such as forests and fisheries to their rates of regeneration; and (4) restricting pollution emissions to amounts which can be assimilated by the environment.

Criticisms

Doomsday modeling is controversial and it has prompted a number of rebuttals.

1 Fun and Games with Numbers The doomsdayers have *assumed* continuing exponential growth of population and output growth, while *assuming* absolute limits on natural resources and technological capabilities. The outcome of resulting computer simulations is merely the inevitable consequence of these

assumptions. But are these assumptions realistic? To paraphrase an old joke, one can project the reproduction rate of alligators and conclude that in fifty years we will be up to our eyeballs in alligators. The point is that a different—and equally or more plausible—set of assumptions would yield a more positive portrayal of humanity's future.

2 Technology and Expanding Resources Another rebuttal to doomsday models is that technological advance expands supplies of existing resources and creates new resources. Technological progress permits us to use existing resources more efficiently, effectively increasing their supplies. In 1900 the lowest-grade copper ore that was economically mineable was about 3 percent; technological advance now makes 0.35 ore mineable. Similarly, thanks to improvements in search and extraction techniques, the world's known oil reserves are several times larger than they were a few decades ago.

Technology also allows us to discover or develop substitutes for existing resources and therefore to expand our resource base. The development of fiber optics, for example, has meant that a single ultrathin fiber can replace over 600 copper wires, making it less likely (and perhaps irrelevant) if we "run out" of copper. Similarly, future developments in solar, geothermal, or hydrogen power may add to our resource base, making it unnecessary to worry over our supplies of oil, coal, and natural gas.

In general, technological progress makes it erroneous to assume natural resource supplies are fixed. Rather, such supplies depend on our technological knowledge and because that knowledge has been expanding, so also have our stocks of resources. Resource supplies, it is argued, are limited only by human ingenuity. Doomsday critics point out that the relative prices of practically all mineral resources have in fact been *declining,* indicating they are *less* scarce.

3 Market Signals Changes in market prices generate signals which work to offset the economic collapse indicated by the doomsday models. If reserves of copper, aluminum, or oil become increasingly scarce, their prices will rise and two responses automatically occur. First, users of the resource will be more strongly motivated to conserve such resources either by employing substitutes (for example, plastic for copper pipes in new housing) or by developing new resource-saving techniques (more fuel-efficient autos and machinery in the case of oil). Second,

---

[2]Meadows, Meadows, and Randers, op. cit.

higher resource prices also spur resource producers to expand output by mining lower-grade ores or by recycling, both of which may have been economically unfeasible at lower prices. The point is the price mechanism automatically induces responses which alleviate resource shortages.

Recap

Whether you agree with the doomsday pessimists or with the critics of the doomsday models, certain messages and questions emerge from the limits-to-growth debate. For example, the fundamental question of scarcity has a time dimension. Absolutely exhaustible resources which are used today will not be available tomorrow. What is the optimal way to allocate such resources through time?

The debate also emphasizes that growth is not an unmitigated good. The impact of an ever-expanding output on the environment and on lifestyles must be taken into account in any evaluation of future growth.

Finally, the debate points out that factors which fall partially outside the realm of economics—in particular, population growth—have a critical bearing on our economic well-being. *(Key Question 12)*

QUICK REVIEW 19-3

■ Economists have cited the following reasons for America's slowdown in productivity in the past twenty-five years: *a* declines in labor quality, *b* a slowing of technological progress, *c* decreasing investment spending as a percentage of GDP, *d* higher energy prices, and *e* growth-impeding labor relations.

■ Computer modelers have developed simulation models indicating the world is using resources and dumping wastes at unsustainable rates.

■ To prevent complete economic collapse, "doomsday" modelers recommend slowing and eventually stopping the exponential growth of population and industrial output.

■ Critics of the "doomsday" models argue that *a* technological advance expands the supplies of existing resources and creates new resources, making it erroneous to assume that natural resource supplies are fixed; and *b* the price mechanism automatically reduces the use of increasingly scarce resources and encourages the development and use of new resources.

GROWTH POLICIES

If we accept the view that economic growth is desirable and sustainable, then the question arises as to what public policies might best stimulate growth. Several policies are either in use or have been suggested.

Demand-Side Policies

Low growth is often the consequence of inadequate aggregate demand and resulting GDP gaps. The purpose of demand-side policies is to eliminate or reduce the severity of recessions through active fiscal and monetary policy. The idea is to use government tools to increase aggregate demand at an appropriate, noninflationary pace. Adequate aggregate demand not only keeps present resources fully employed, it also creates an incentive for firms to expand their operations. In particular, low real interest rates (easy money policy) promote high levels of investment spending. This spending leads to capital accumulation, which expands the economy's capacity to produce.

Supply-Side Policies

These policies emphasize factors which will directly increase the potential or full-capacity output of the economy over time. The goal is to shift Figure 19-3's long-run and short-run aggregate supply curves rightward. Policies fitting this category include tax policies designed to stimulate saving, investment, and entrepreneurship. For example, by lowering or eliminating the tax on interest earned from savings accounts, the return on saving will increase and so will the amount of saving. Likewise, by lowering or eliminating the deduction of interest expenses on your personal income tax, consumption will be discouraged and saving encouraged. Some economists favor a national consumption tax as a full or partial replacement for the personal income tax. The idea is to penalize consumption and thereby encourage saving.

On the investment side, some economists propose eliminating the corporate income tax or allowing generous tax credits for business investment spending. If effective, this proposal would increase both aggregate demand and aggregate supply.

Industrial and Other Policies

There are other potential growth-stimulating policies which economists of various persuasions recommend. Some advocate an **industrial policy** whereby government would take a direct, active role in shaping the structure and composition of industry to promote growth. Thus government might take steps to hasten expansion of high-productivity industries and speed the movement of resources out of low-productivity industries. Government might also increase its expenditures on basic research and development to stimulate technological progress. Also, increased expenditures on basic education and apprenticeship skill training may help increase the quality and productivity of labor.

While the litany of potential growth-enhancing policies is long and involved, most economists agree it is not easy to increase a nation's growth rate.

CHAPTER SUMMARY

1   Economic growth may be defined either as   **a** an expanding real output (income) or   **b** an expanding per capita real output (income). Growth lessens the burden of scarcity and provides increases in real output which can be used to resolve domestic and international socioeconomic problems.

2   The supply factors in economic growth are   **a** the quantity and quality of a nation's natural resources,   **b** the quantity and quality of its human resources,   **c** its stock of capital facilities, and   **d** its technology. Two other factors —a sufficient level of aggregate demand and economic efficiency—are essential for the economy to realize its growth potential.

3   Economic growth can be shown graphically as an outward shift of a nation's production possibilities curve or as a rightward shift of its aggregate supply curve.

4   The post-World War II growth rate of real GDP for the United States has been more than 3 percent; real GDP per capita has grown at about 2 percent.

5   Real GDP in the United States has grown, partly because of increased inputs of labor, and primarily because of increases in the productivity of labor. Technological progress, increases in the quantity of capital per worker, improvements in the quality of labor, economies of scale, and improved allocation of labor are among the more important factors which increase labor productivity.

6   The rate of productivity growth declined sharply in the 1970s, causing a slowdown in the rise of our living standards and contributing to inflation. Although productivity growth has increased in the 1980s and early 1990s, it remains substantially below the rates attained in the two decades after World War II.

7   Suspected causes of the decline in productivity growth include decreases in labor quality, slowing of technological progress, declining investment spending as a percentage of GDP, higher energy prices, and adversarial labor relations.

8   Computer simulations called "doomsday models" indicate the world is using resources and dumping waste at rates which will result in the collapse of industrial output and food production somewhere near the year 2025. To stop this collapse, say the "doomsdayers," the world must quickly slow and eventually stop the exponential growth of population and industrial output.

9   Critics challenge the assumption of absolute limits on the supply of natural resources in the doomsday models, pointing out that technological advance expands the supplies of existing resources and creates new resources. Critics also argue these models overlook the role of the price mechanism in offsetting the predicted economic collapse. Declining resource supplies result in higher resource prices which automatically reduce the use of the higher-price inputs while expanding the development and use of new resources.

10   Growth-promoting policies include both demand-side and supply-side policies, along with efforts to shape the composition of industry.

TERMS AND CONCEPTS

supply, demand, and efficiency factors in growth	economic growth labor productivity	labor force participation rate infrastructure	doomsday models industrial policy

QUESTIONS AND STUDY SUGGESTIONS

1   Why is economic growth important? Explain why the difference between a 2.5 percent and a 3.0 percent annual growth rate might be of great significance.

2   *Key Question   What are the major causes of economic growth? "There are both a demand and a supply side to economic growth." Explain. Illustrate the operation of both sets*

PROBLEMS AND CONTROVERSIES IN MACROECONOMICS

LAST WORD

IS GROWTH DESIRABLE?

Economists usually take for granted that growth is desirable. Is it?

The Antigrowth View Critics of growth say industrialization and growth result in pollution, global warming, ozone depletion, and other environmental problems. These adverse spillover costs occur because inputs in the production process reenter the environment as some form of waste. The more rapid our growth and the higher our standard of living, the more waste the environment must absorb—or attempt to absorb. In an already wealthy society, further growth usually means satisfying increasingly trivial wants at the cost of mounting threats to our ecological system.

Critics of growth also argue there is little compelling evidence that economic growth has solved sociological problems such as poverty, homelessness, and discrimination. Consider poverty. In the antigrowth view, American poverty is a problem of distribution, not production. The requisite for solving the problem is commitment and political courage to redistribute wealth and income, not further increases in output.

Antigrowth sentiment also says that while growth may permit us to "make a better living," it does not give us "the good life." We may be producing more and enjoying it less. Growth means assembly-line jobs, worker burnout, and alienated employees who

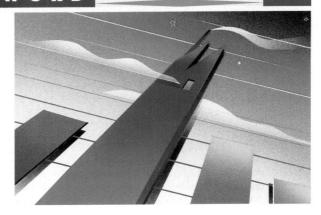

have little or no control over decisions affecting their lives. The changing technology at the core of growth poses new anxieties and new sources of insecurity for workers. Both high-level and low-level workers face the prospect of having their hard-earned skills and experience rendered obsolete by an onrushing technology. High-growth economies are high-stress economies, which may impair our physical and mental health.

In Defense of Growth The primary defense of growth is that it is the path to greater material abundance and rising living standards. Rising output and incomes allow us to buy:

---

of factors in terms of the production possibilities curve.

3 *Key Question* *Suppose an economy's real GDP is $30,000 in year 1 and $31,200 in year 2. What is the growth rate of its real GDP? Assume that population was 100 in year 1 and 102 in year 2. What is the growth rate of GDP per capita? Between 1959 and 1993 the nation's price level rose by over 285 percent while its real output increased by almost 66 percent. Use the aggregate demand–aggregate supply model to show these outcomes graphically.*

4 Briefly describe the growth record of the United States. Compare the rates of growth in real GDP and real GDP per capita, explaining any differences. How does the American growth rate compare to the rates of Japan and Germany since World War II? To what extent might growth rates understate or overstate economic well-being?

5 *Key Question* *To what extent have increases in our real GDP been the result of more labor inputs? Of increasing*

labor productivity? Discuss the factors which contribute to productivity growth in order of their quantitative importance.

6 Using examples, explain how changes in the allocation of labor can affect labor productivity.

7 How do you explain the close correlation between changes in the rate of productivity growth and changes in real wage rates? Discuss the relationship between productivity growth and inflation.

8 *Key Question* *Account for the recent slowdown in the United States' rate of productivity growth. What are the consequences of this slowdown? "Most of the factors which contributed to poor productivity growth in the 1970s are now behind us and are unlikely to recur in the near future." Do you agree?*

9 "If we want economic growth in a free society, we may

more education, recreation, and travel, more medical care, closer communications, more skilled personal and professional services, and better-designed as well as more numerous products. It also means more art, music, and poetry, theater, and drama. It can even mean more time and resources devoted to spiritual growth and human development.*

Growth also enables us to improve the nation's infrastructure, enhance the care of the sick and elderly, provide greater access for the disabled, and provide more police and fire protection. Economic growth may be the only realistic way to reduce poverty, since there is little political support for greater redistribution of income. The way to improve the economic position of the poor is to increase household incomes through higher productivity and economic growth. Also, a no-growth policy among industrial nations might severely limit growth in poor nations. Foreign investment and development assistance in these nations would fall, keeping the world's poor in poverty longer.

Economic growth has not made labor more unpleasant or hazardous, as critics suggest. New machinery is usually less taxing and less dangerous than the machinery it replaces. Air-conditioned work-

places are more pleasant than steamy workshops. Furthermore, why would an end to economic growth reduce materialism or alienation? The loudest protests against materialism are heard in those nations and groups who now enjoy the highest levels of material abundance! The high standard of living which growth provides has increased our leisure and given us more time for reflection and self-fulfillment.

Does growth threaten the environment? The connection between growth and environment is tenuous, say growth proponents. Increases in economic growth need not mean increases in pollution. Pollution is not so much a by-product of growth as it is a "problem of the commons." Much of the environment—streams, lakes, oceans, and the air—are treated as "common property," with no restrictions on their use. The commons have become our dumping grounds; we have overused and debased them. Environmental pollution is a case of spillover or external costs, and correcting this problem involves regulatory legislation or specific taxes ("effluent charges") to remedy misuse of the environment.

There *are* serious pollution problems. But limiting growth is the wrong solution. Growth has allowed economies to reduce pollution, be more sensitive to environmental considerations, set aside wilderness, and clean up hazardous waste, while still enabling rising household incomes.

---

*Alice M. Rivlin, *Reviving the American Dream* (Washington: Brookings Institution, 1992), p. 36.

---

have to accept a measure of instability." Evaluate. The philosopher Alfred North Whitehead once remarked that "the art of progress is to preserve order amid change and to preserve change amid order." What did he mean? Is this contention relevant for economic growth? What implications might this have for public policy? Explain.

10 Comment on the following statements:

   a "Technological advance is destined to play a more important role in economic growth in the future than it has in the past."

   b "Nations headed by dictators on average have faster growth rates than democratic nations."

   c "Many public capital goods are complementary to private capital goods."

   d "Racial and gender discrimination are impediments to productivity growth."

11 What is the world's economic future as predicted by

recent computer simulation models? What is the basis for this outcome, according to the models?

12 *Key Question Explain the following, and cite examples to illustrate: "Some of the our present economic resources were not viewed as resources a century ago. Likewise, many things not now thought of as resources may become resources in the future." What role does the price mechanism play in this matter? How does this relate to the doomsday models?*

13 Suppose you are the chair of the Council of Economic Advisers and have been asked to prepare a set of proposals for increasing the productivity of American workers as a way to raise our rate of economic growth. What would you put on your list? What impediments would you envision in accomplishing your policies?

14 (Last Word) Do you think economic growth is desirable? Explain your position on this issue.

PART FIVE

Micro-economics of Product Markets

20

DEMAND AND SUPPLY: ELASTICITIES AND APPLICATIONS

Scarce resources. Unlimited wants. That's what economics is all about. It's because of unlimited wants we must manage efficiently how we use our scarce resources. Our economic system tries to do that in two ways. One is the full employment of all available resources—the subject matter of macroeconomics. The other is to use efficiently those employed resources. This is the focus of microeconomics to which we now turn.

Capitalistic economies rely on the market system to allocate resources. So we'll begin by looking at individual prices and the market system, specifically how the market operates and how efficient it is in utilizing resources within the framework of capitalism. To examine that efficiency, we will analyze individual prices under a variety of contrasting market arrangements.

In Chapter 3 we examined demand and supply analysis. If your recollection of that material is hazy, you might review Chapter 3's Quick Reviews, Key Graph, and Chapter Summary. In this chapter we will extend our understanding of demand and supply as follows:

1   We will explain the concept of price elasticity as it applies to both demand and supply and present a number of applications.

2   We will generalize the elasticity concept by introducing both cross and income elasticity of demand.

3   Finally, as an application of demand and supply analysis, we will examine the potential effects of legally fixed prices on individual markets.

PRICE ELASTICITY OF DEMAND

The law of demand means consumers will respond to a price decline by buying more of a product. But the degree of consumer responsiveness to a price change may vary considerably from product to product and between different price ranges for the same product.

The responsiveness, or sensitivity, of consumers to a change in the price of a product is measured by the **price elasticity of demand.** Demand for some products is such that consumers are highly responsive to price changes; modest price changes lead to very large changes in the quantity purchased. The demand for such products is said to be *relatively elastic* or simply *elastic.* For other products, consumers are quite unresponsive to price changes; substantial price changes result only in modest changes in the amount purchased. In such cases demand is *relatively inelastic* or simply *inelastic.*

The Price Elasticity Formula

Economists measure the degree of elasticity or inelasticity of demand by the coefficient E_d in this price elasticity formula:

$$E_d = \frac{\text{percentage change in quantity demanded of product X}}{\text{percentage change in price of product X}}$$

These *percentage* changes are calculated by dividing the change in price by the original price and the consequent change in quantity demanded by the original quantity demanded. Thus, our formula restated:

$$E_d = \frac{\text{change in quantity demanded of X}}{\text{original quantity demanded of X}} \div \frac{\text{change in price of X}}{\text{original price of X}}$$

Use of Percentages   Why use percentages rather than absolute amounts in measuring consumer responsiveness? The answer is twofold.

1   Choice of Units   If we use absolute changes, our impression of buyer responsiveness will be arbitrarily affected by the choice of units. To illustrate: If the price of product X falls from $3 to $2 and consumers increase their purchases from 60 to 100 pounds, it may appear that consumers are quite sensitive to price changes and therefore that demand is elastic. After all, a price change of "one" has caused a change in the amount demanded of "forty." But by changing the monetary unit from dollars to pennies (why not?), we find a price change of "one hundred" causes a quantity change of "forty," giving the impression of inelasticity. Using percentage changes avoids this problem. This particular price decline is 33 percent whether measured in terms of dollars ($1/$3) or pennies (100¢/300¢).

2   Comparing Products   By using percentages we can more meaningfully compare consumer responsiveness to changes in the prices of different products. It makes little sense to compare the effects on quantity demanded of a $1 increase in the price of a $10,000 auto with a $1 increase in the price of a $1 can of Coors. Here the price of the auto is rising by .01 percent while the beer price is up by 100 percent! If we increased the price of both products by 1 percent—$100 for the car and 1¢ for the can—we would

obtain a more sensible comparison of consumer sensitivity to the price changes.

Ignore Minus Sign   We know from the downsloping demand curve that price and quantity demanded are inversely related. This means that the price elasticity coefficient of demand will always be a *negative* number. For example, if price declines, then quantity demanded will increase. This means that the numerator in our formula will be positive and the denominator negative, yielding a negative E_d. For an increase in price, the numerator will be negative but the denominator positive, again yielding a negative E_d.

Economists usually ignore the minus sign and simply present the *absolute value* of the elasticity coefficient to avoid an ambiguity which might otherwise arise. It can be confusing to say that an E_d of -4 is greater than one of -2. This possible confusion is avoided when we say an E_d of 4 reveals greater elasticity than one of 2. In what follows we therefore ignore the minus sign in the coefficient of price elasticity of demand and merely show the absolute value. Incidentally, the ambiguity does not arise with supply because price and quantity are positively related.

Interpretations   Now let's interpret our formula.

1   Elastic   Demand is **elastic** if a given percentage change in price results in a *larger* percentage change in quantity demanded. Example: If a 2 percent decline in price results in a 4 percent increase in quantity demanded, demand is elastic. In such cases where demand is elastic, E_d will be greater than 1; in this case it will be 2.

2   Inelastic   If a given percentage change in price is accompanied by a relatively smaller change in quantity demanded, demand is **inelastic.** Illustration: If a 3 percent decline in price leads to only a 1 percent increase in amount demanded, demand is inelastic. Specifically, E_d is .33 in this instance. It is apparent that the E_d will always be less than 1 when demand is inelastic.

3   Other Cases   The borderline case separating elastic and inelastic demands occurs where a percentage change in price and the accompanying percentage change in quantity demanded are equal. For example, a 1 percent drop in price causes a 1 percent increase in amount sold. This special case is termed **unit elasticity,** because E_d is exactly 1, or unity.

When economists say demand is "inelastic," they do not mean consumers are completely unresponsive to a price change. The term **perfectly inelastic** demand refers to the extreme situation where a price change results in no change whatsoever in the quantity demanded. Approximate examples: an acute diabetic's demand for insulin or an addict's demand for heroin. A demand curve parallel to the vertical axis —such as D_1 in Figure 20-1—shows this graphically.

Conversely, when economists say demand is "elastic," they do not mean consumers are completely responsive to a price change. In the extreme situation, where a small price reduction would cause buyers to increase their purchases from zero to all they could obtain, we say that demand is **perfectly elastic.** A perfectly elastic demand curve is a line parallel to the horizontal axis such as D_2 in Figure 20-1. We will see in Chapter 23 that such a demand curve applies to a firm selling in a purely competitive market.

Refinement: Midpoints Formula

The hypothetical demand data shown in Table 20-1 are useful in explaining an annoying problem which arises in applying the price elasticity formula. In calculating E_d for the \$5–\$4 price range, should we use the \$5–4 units price–quantity combination or the \$4–5 units combination as a point of reference in calculating percentage changes in price and quantity which the elasticity formula requires? Our choice will influence the outcome.

Using the \$5–4 unit reference point, the price change is from \$5 to \$4, so the percentage decrease

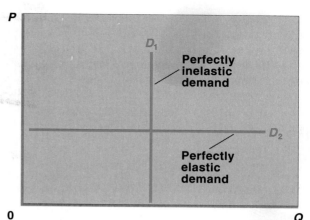

FIGURE 20-1   Perfectly inelastic and elastic demand
A perfectly inelastic demand curve, D_1, graphs as a line parallel to the vertical axis; a perfectly elastic demand curve, D_2, is drawn parallel to the horizontal axis.

in price is 20 percent and the quantity change is from 4 to 5 units, so the percentage increase in quantity, is 25 percent. Substituting in the formula, the elasticity coefficient is 25/20, or 1.25, indicating that demand is somewhat elastic.

But, using the \$4–5 unit reference point, the price change is from \$4 to \$5, making the percentage increase in price 25 percent, and the quantity change is from 5 to 4 units, or a 20 percent decline in quantity. The elasticity coefficient is therefore 20/25, or 0.80, meaning demand is slightly inelastic. Which is it? Is demand elastic or inelastic?

A solution to this problem is to use *averages* of the two prices and two quantities under consideration

TABLE 20-1   Price elasticity of demand as measured by the elasticity coefficient and the total revenue test

(1) Total quantity demanded per week	(2) Price per unit	(3) Elasticity coefficient, E_d	(4) Total revenue (1) × (2)	(5) Total revenue test
1	\$8		\$ 8	
		5.00		Elastic
2	7		14	
		2.60		Elastic
3	6		18	
		1.57		Elastic
4	5		20	
		1.00		Unit elastic
5	4		20	
		0.64		Inelastic
6	3		18	
		0.38		Inelastic
7	2		14	
		0.20		Inelastic
8	1		8	

for reference points. In the $5–$4 price-range case, the price reference is $4.50, and the quantity reference 4.5 units. The percentage change in price is now about 22 percent and the percentage change in quantity also about 22 percent, giving us an E_d of 1. This solution estimates elasticity at the midpoint of the $5–$4 price range. We now can refine our earlier statement of the elasticity formula to read:

$$E_d = \frac{\text{change in quantity}}{\text{sum of quantities}/2} \div \frac{\text{change in price}}{\text{sum of prices}/2}$$

Substituting data for the $5–$4 price range, we get

$$E_d = \frac{1}{9/2} \div \frac{1}{9/2} = 1$$

This indicates that *at* the $4.50–4.5 price–quantity midpoints the price elasticity of demand is unity. Here a 1 percent price change would result in a 1 percent change in quantity demanded.

In column 3 you should verify the elasticity calculations for the $1–$2 and $7–$8 price ranges. The interpretation of E_d for the $1–$2 range is that a 1 percent change in price will change quantity demanded by 0.20 percent. For the $7–$8 range a 1 percent change in price will change quantity demanded by 5 percent.

Graphical Analysis

In Figure 20-2a we have plotted our demand curve from Table 20-1. This portrayal brings two points into focus.

1 Elasticity and Price Range Elasticity typically varies over the different price ranges of the same demand schedule or curve. For all straight-line and most other demand curves, demand is more elastic in the upper left segment ($5–$8 price range) than in the lower right portion ($4–$1 price range).

This reality is a consequence of the arithmetic properties of the elasticity measure. Specifically, in the upper left segment the percentage change in quantity is large because the original quantity from which the percentage quantity change is derived is small. Similarly, this is where the percentage change in price is small because the original price from which the percentage price change is calculated is large. The relatively large percentage change in quantity divided by the relatively small change in price yields an elastic demand—a large E_d.

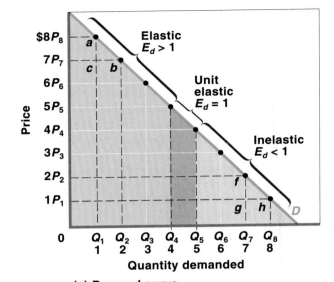

(a) Demand curve

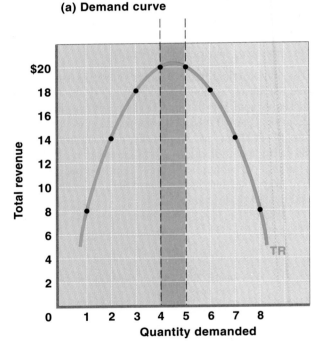

(b) Total revenue curve

FIGURE 20-2 Price elasticity of demand and its relation to total revenue
As shown in (a), the typical demand curve is elastic in high price ranges and inelastic in low price ranges. In (b) total revenue rises in the elastic range as price is reduced. Where demand elasticity is unity, a change in price will not change total revenue. In this range total revenue is maximized. Price reductions in the inelastic range of the demand curve cause total revenue to fall.

The reverse holds true for the lower right segment of the demand curve. Here the percentage change in quantity is small because the original quantity from which the percentage change is determined is large. Similarly, the percentage change in price is large because the original price from which the relative price change is calculated is small. The small percentage change in quantity divided by the relatively large percentage change in price results in an inelastic demand—a low E_d.

Assignment: Draw two linear demand curves parallel to one another. Demonstrate that for any specific price change demand is more elastic on the curve closer to the origin.

2 Elasticity versus Slope

The graphical appearance—the slope—of a demand curve is *not* a sound basis for judging its elasticity. The catch is that the slope—the flatness or steepness—of a demand curve is based on *absolute* changes in price and quantity, while elasticity involves *relative* or *percentage* changes in price and quantity.

Observe in Figure 20-2a that our demand curve is linear, which by definition means the slope is constant throughout. But we have demonstrated that such a curve is elastic in its high-price ($8–$5) range and inelastic in its low-price ($4–$1) range. *(Key Question 2)*

QUICK REVIEW 20-1

■ Price elasticity of demand measures the extent to which consumers change the quantity of a product they purchase when its price changes.

■ Price elasticity of demand is the ratio of the percentage change in quantity demanded to the percentage change in price. The average of the prices and quantities are used in calculating the percentage changes.

■ When price elasticity is greater than 1, demand is elastic; when less than 1, it is inelastic. When equal to 1, demand is of unit elasticity.

■ Demand is typically elastic in the high-price (low-quantity) range and inelastic in the low-price (high-quantity) range of the demand curve.

The Total-Revenue Test

Total revenue is determined by multiplying price by quantity demanded. Price elasticity of demand compares the relative sizes of changes in price and quantity demanded. Therefore, it must tell us what happens to total revenue. Indeed, perhaps the easiest way to infer whether demand is elastic or inelastic is to employ the **total-revenue test,** that is, to observe what happens to total revenue—total expenditures from the buyer's viewpoint—when product price changes.

1 Elastic Demand If demand is *elastic,* a *decrease* in price will *increase* total revenue. Even though a lesser price is received per unit, enough additional units are sold to more than make up for the lower price. This is shown in Figure 20-2a for the $8–$7 price range of our demand curve from Table 20-1. (Ignore Figure 20-2b for the moment.) Total revenue, of course, is price times quantity. Thus, the area shown by the rectangle $0P_8aQ_1$ is total revenue ($8) when price is P_8 ($8) and quantity demanded is Q_1 (1 unit). When price declines to P_7 ($7), increasing the quantity demanded to Q_2 (2 units), total revenue changes to $0P_7bQ_2$ ($14), which is obviously larger than $0P_8aQ_1$. It is larger because the *loss* in revenue from the lower price per unit (area P_7P_8ac) is *less* than the *gain* in revenue due to the larger sales (area Q_1cbQ_2) accompanying the lower price. Specifically, the $1 price reduction applies to the original 1 unit (Q_1) for a loss of $1. But the lower price increases sales by 1 unit (Q_1 to Q_2) with a resulting gain in revenue of $7. Thus, the *net increase* in total revenue is $6 (= $7 − $1).

This reasoning is reversible: If demand is elastic, a price *increase* will *reduce* total revenue. The *gain* in total revenue caused by the higher unit price (area P_7P_8ac) is *less* than the *loss* in revenue associated with the accompanying fall in sales (Q_1cbQ_2). *If demand is elastic, a price change will change total revenue in the opposite direction.*

2 Inelastic Demand If demand is *inelastic,* a price *decrease* will *reduce* total revenue. The modest increase in sales will not offset the decline in revenue per unit, and the net result is that total revenue declines. This is true for the $2–$1 price range of our demand curve, as shown in Figure 20-2a. Initially, total revenue is $0P_2fQ_7$ ($14) when price is P_2 ($2) and quantity demanded is Q_7 (7 units). If we reduce price to P_1 ($1), quantity demanded will increase to Q_8 (8 units). Total revenue will change to $0P_1hQ_8$ ($8), which is clearly less than $0P_2fQ_7$. It is smaller because the loss in revenue from the lower unit price (area P_1P_2fg) *is larger* than the *gain* in revenue from the accompanying increase in sales (area Q_7ghQ_8). The $1 decline in price applies to 7 units (Q_7) with a consequent revenue loss of $7. The sales increase accompanying this lower price is 1 unit (Q_7 to Q_8) which results in a revenue gain of $1. The overall result is a *net decrease* in total revenue of $6 (= $1 − $7).

Again, our analysis is reversible: If demand is inelastic, a price increase will increase total revenue. *If demand is inelastic, a price change will change total revenue in the same direction.*

3 Unit Elasticity In the special case of *unit elasticity,* an increase or decrease in price will leave total revenue unchanged. Loss in revenue from a lower unit price will be exactly offset by the gain in revenue from the accompanying increase in sales. Conversely, the gain in revenue from a higher unit price will be exactly offset by the revenue loss associated with the accompanying decline in the amount demanded.

In Figure 20-2a we find that at the $5 price 4 units will be sold to yield total revenue of $20. At $4 a total of 5 units will be sold, again resulting in $20 of total revenue. The $1 price reduction causes the loss of $4 in revenue on the 4 units that could have been sold for $5 each. This is exactly offset by a $4 revenue gain which results from the sale of 1 more unit at the lower $4 price.

Graphical Portrayal The relationship between price elasticity of demand and total revenue can be demonstrated graphically by comparing Figures 20-2a and 20-2b. In Figure 20-2b we have graphed the eight total revenue–quantity demanded points from columns 1 and 4 of Table 20-1.

Lowering price over the $8–$5 price range increases total revenue. We know from the elasticity coefficient calculations in Table 20-1 that demand is *elastic* in this range so any given percentage decline in price results in a larger percentage increase in the quantity demanded. The lower price per unit is more than offset by the increase in sales and, consequently, total revenue rises.

The $5–$4 price range is characterized by *unit* elasticity. Here the percentage decline in price produces an equal percentage increase in the quantity demanded. The price cut is exactly offset by increased purchases so total revenue is unchanged.

Finally, our calculations of E_d tell us that in the $4–$1 price range demand is *inelastic,* meaning that

any given percentage decline in price will be accompanied by a smaller percentage increase in sales, causing total revenue to diminish.

Our logic is reversible. A price *increase* in the elastic $8–$5 price range will reduce total revenue. Similarly, a price *increase* in the inelastic $4–$1 range raises total revenue. *(Key Questions 4 and 5)*

Reprise Table 20-2 summarizes the characteristics of price elasticity of demand and merits careful study.

Determinants of Price Elasticity of Demand

There are no ironclad generalizations concerning determinants of the elasticity of demand. The following points, however, are valid and helpful.

1 Substitutability Generally, the larger the number of good substitute products available, the greater the elasticity of demand. We will find later that in a purely competitive market, where by definition there are many perfect substitutes for the product of any given seller, the demand curve to that single seller will be perfectly elastic. If one competitive seller of carrots or potatoes raises its price, buyers will turn to the readily available perfect substitutes of its many rivals. Similarly, we would expect the lowering of world trade barriers to increase the elasticity of demand for most products by making more substitutes available. With unimpeded trade Hondas, Toyotas, Nissans, Mazdas, Volkswagens, and other foreign cars become effective substitutes for domestic autos. At the other extreme, the diabetic's demand for insulin or an addict's demand for heroin is highly inelastic—there are no close substitutes.

The elasticity of demand for a product depends on how narrowly the product is defined. Demand for Quaker State motor oil is more elastic than is the overall demand for motor oil. Many other brands are readily substitutable for Quaker State's oil, but there is no good substitute for motor oil.

2 Proportion of Income Other things equal, the higher the price of a good relative to your budget, the greater will be your elasticity of demand for it. A 10 percent increase in the price of pencils or chewing gum will amount to only a few pennies, with little response in the amount you demand. A 10 percent increase in the price of automobiles or housing means price increases of perhaps $1500 and $10,000, respectively. These increases are significant fractions of

TABLE 20-2   Price elasticity of demand: a summary

Absolute value of elasticity coefficient	Terminology	Description	Impact on total revenue (expenditures) of a price:	
			Increase	Decrease
Greater than 1 $(E_d > 1)$	"Elastic" or "relatively elastic"	Quantity demanded changes by a larger percentage than does price	Total revenue decreases	Total revenue increases
Equal to 1 $(E_d = 1)$	"Unit" or "unitary elastic"	Quantity demanded changes by the same percentage as does price	Total revenue is unchanged	Total revenue is unchanged
Less than 1 $(E_d < 1)$	"Inelastic" or "relatively inelastic"	Quantity demanded changes by a smaller percentage than does price	Total revenue increases	Total revenue decreases

the annual incomes of many families, and quantities purchased could be expected to diminish significantly.

3   Luxuries versus Necessities   The demand for "necessities" tends to be inelastic; for "luxuries," elastic. Bread and electricity are generally regarded as necessities; it is difficult to get along without them. A price increase will not reduce significantly the amount of bread consumed or the amounts of lighting and

power used in a household. Note the very low price elasticities of these goods in Table 20-3. An extreme case: You will not decline an operation for acute appendicitis because the physician's fee has just gone up!

On the other hand, Caribbean cruises and emeralds are luxuries which, by definition, can be forgone. If the price of cruises or emeralds rises, you need not buy and will encounter no great hardship.

TABLE 20-3   Selected price elasticities of demand

Product or service	Price elasticity of demand	Product or service	Price elasticity of demand
Housing	.01	Milk	.63
Electricity (household)	.13	Household appliances	.63
Bread	.15	Movies	.87
Telephone service	.26	Beer	.90
Medical care	.31	Shoes	.91
Eggs	.32	Motor vehicles	1.14
Legal services	.37	China, glassware, tableware	1.54
Automobile repair	.40	Restaurant meals	2.27
Clothing	.49	Lamb and mutton	2.65

Main sources: H. S. Houthakker and Lester D. Taylor, *Consumer Demand in the United States: Analyses and Projections,* 2d ed. (Cambridge, Mass.: Harvard University Press, 1970); P. S. George and G. A. King, *Consumer Demand for Food Commodities in the United States with Projections for 1980* (Berkeley: University of California Press, 1971); and Ahsan Mansur and John Whalley, "Numerical Specification of Applied General Equilibrium Models: Estimation, Calibration, and Data," in Herbert E. Scarf and John B. Shoven, *Applied General Equilibrium Analysis* (New York: Cambridge University Press, 1984).

The demand for salt is highly inelastic on several counts. It is a "necessity"; there are few good substitutes available; and finally, salt is a negligible item in the family budget.

4 Time Generally, product demand is more elastic the longer the time period under consideration because many consumers are creatures of habit. When the price of a product rises, it takes time to find and experiment with other products to see if they are acceptable. Consumers may not immediately reduce their purchases very much when the price of beef rises by 10 percent, but in time they may shift to chicken or fish, for which they will "develop a taste." Another consideration is product durability. Studies show that "short-run" demand for gasoline is more inelastic at 0.2 than is "long-run" demand at 0.7. In the long run, large, gas-guzzling automobiles wear out and, with rising gasoline prices, are replaced by smaller, higher-mileage cars.

An empirical study of commuter rail transportation in the Philadelphia area estimates that "long-run" elasticity of demand is almost three times as great as "short-run" elasticity. Short-run commuter responses (defined as those occurring immediately at the time of a fare change) are inelastic at 0.68. In contrast, the long-run response (defined as those occurring over a four-year period) is elastic at 1.84. The greater long-run elasticity occurs because over time potential rail commuters can make choices concerning automobile purchases, car pooling, and the locations of residences and employment. These different elasticities led to the prediction that the commuter system, with about 100,000 riders, could immediately *increase* daily revenues by $8000 by increasing the price of a one-way ticket by $.25 or about 9 percent. Why? Because short-run demand is inelastic. But in the long run the same 9 percent fare increase is estimated to *reduce* total revenue per day by over $19,000 because demand is elastic. This implies that a fare increase which is profitable in the short run may lead to financial difficulties in the long run.[1]

Table 20-3 shows estimated price elasticities of demand for a number of products. You should use the elasticity determinants just discussed to attempt to explain each of these elasticity coefficients. *(Key Question 9)*

---

[1]Richard Voith, "Commuter Rail Ridership: The Long and the Short Haul," *Business Review* (Federal Reserve Bank of Philadelphia), November–December 1987, pp. 13–23.

QUICK REVIEW 20-2

■ A price change will cause total revenue to vary in the opposite direction when demand is elastic and in the same direction when demand is inelastic.

■ Price elasticity of demand is greater *a* the larger the number of substitutes available; *b* the higher the price of a product relative to one's budget; *c* the greater the extent to which the product is a luxury; and *d* the longer the time period involved.

Some Practical Applications

The concept of price elasticity of demand has great practical significance, as seen in the following examples.

1 Bumper Crops The demand for most farm products is highly inelastic, perhaps 0.20 or 0.25. As a result, increases in the output of farm products arising from a good growing season or from productivity increases depress both the prices of farm products and total revenues (incomes) of farmers. For farmers as a group, the inelastic nature of demand for their products means a bumper crop may be undesirable. For policy makers it means higher total farm income depends on the restriction of farm output.

2 Automation The impact of rapid technological advance on the level of employment depends in part on the elasticity of demand for the product being manufactured. Suppose a firm installs new laborsaving machinery, resulting in technological unemployment of 500 workers. Assume too that part of the cost reduction resulting from this technological advance is passed on to consumers as reduced product prices. The effect of this price reduction on the firm's sales and therefore the quantity of labor it requires will depend on the elasticity of product demand. An elastic demand might increase sales to the extent that some of, all, or even more than the 500 displaced workers are reabsorbed by the firm. An inelastic demand will mean that few, if any, displaced workers will be reemployed, because the increase in the volume of the firm's sales and output will be small.

3 Airline Deregulation Deregulating the airlines in the late 1970s initially increased the profits of many carriers. The reason was that deregulation increased competition among the airlines, lowering air fares. Lower fares, coupled with an elastic demand for air travel, increased revenues. Because additional costs associated with flying full, as opposed to partially empty, aircraft are minimal, revenues increased ahead of costs and profits were enhanced. This profitability was not to last, for three reasons: The competitive scramble for new routes competed profits away; rising fuel prices increased operating costs; and persistent "fare wars" cut into profits.

4 Excise Taxes Government pays attention to elasticity of demand when selecting goods and services on which to levy excise taxes. If a $1 tax is levied on a product and 10,000 units are sold, tax revenue will be $10,000. If government now raises the tax to $1.50, and the consequent higher price reduces sales to 5,000 because of an elastic demand, tax revenue will *decline* to $7,500. A higher tax on a product with an elastic demand will bring in less tax revenue. Therefore, legislatures will seek out products having inelastic demands—liquor, gasoline, and cigarettes—when levying excises. In fact, the Federal government increased taxes on these three categories of goods in 1991 in trying to reduce the budget deficit.

But government's record is not impeccable in this regard. In 1991 Congress imposed a 10 percent excise tax on yachts costing more than $100,000. Believing the demand for yachts to be inelastic, Congress felt the impact on sales would be small and therefore anticipated the tax would raise $1.5 billion over five years. But demand turned out to be more elastic than thought. Many boat owners responded by deciding to keep their old boats longer and some prospective first-time buyers abandoned their plans to buy pleasure boats. In south Florida sales dropped by nearly 90 percent, since many prospective buyers avoided the tax by buying their crafts in the Bahamas. Government revenue from the tax was also reduced by the 1990–1991 recession which shifted the demand for most durable goods—yachts included—to the left. In 1991 the 10 percent excise raised a meager $30 million in revenue.

The tax, coupled with the recession, had a devastating impact on boat manufacturers. In the first year of the tax a third of all United States yacht-building companies halted production and more than 20,000 workers lost their jobs. In 1993 Congress repealed the tax.

5 Cocaine and Street Crime The belief that the demand for crack-cocaine by addicts is highly inelastic poses some awkward tradeoffs in law enforcement.

The approach typically used in attempting to reduce cocaine addiction is restricting supply, that is, making the drug less readily available by cracking down on its shipment into the United States.

But what will happen if this policy is successful? Given the highly inelastic demand, the street price to addicts will rise sharply while the amount purchased will decrease only slightly. From the drug dealers' viewpoint this means greatly increased revenues and profits. From the addicts' viewpoint it means greater total expenditures on cocaine. Because much of the income which addicts spend on cocaine comes from crime—shoplifting, burglary, prostitution, muggings—these crimes will increase as addicts increase their total expenditures for cocaine. Here, the effort of law-enforcement authorities to control the spread of drug addiction may increase the amount of crime committed by addicts.

In recent years proposals to legalize drugs have been widely debated. Proponents contend drugs should be treated like alcohol; they should be made legal for adults and regulated for purity and potency. The current war on drugs, it is argued, has been unsuccessful and the associated costs—including enlarged police forces, the construction of more prisons, an overburdened court system, and untold human costs—have increased markedly. Legalization would allegedly reduce drug trafficking greatly by taking the profit out of it. Crack-cocaine, for example, is cheap to produce and could be sold at a low price in a legal market. Because the demand of addicts is highly inelastic, the amount consumed at the lower price will only increase modestly. Total expenditures for cocaine by addicts will decline and so will the street crime which finances these expenditures.

Opponents of legalization say that, in addition to the addict's inelastic demand, there is another segment to the market where demand may be more elastic. These are the occasional users or "dabblers." Dabblers will use cocaine when its price is low, but abstain or substitute, say, alcohol when cocaine's price is high. For this group the lower price of cocaine associated with legalization will increase consumption by dabblers and in time turn many of them into addicts. This will increase street crime and enlarge all the social costs associated with drug use.

6 Minimum Wage The Federal minimum wage prohibits employers from paying covered workers less than $4.25 per hour. Critics contend that an above-equilibrium minimum wage moves employers back up their downsloping labor demand curves and causes unemployment, particularly among teenage workers. On the other hand, workers who remain employed at the minimum wage will receive higher incomes than otherwise. The amount of income lost by the unemployed and the income gained by those who keep their jobs will depend on the elasticity of demand for teenage labor. Research suggests demand for teenage labor is quite inelastic, possibly as low as 0.15 or 0.25. If correct, it means income gains associated with the minimum wage exceed income losses. The case made by critics of the minimum wage would be stronger if the demand for teenage workers were elastic.

PRICE ELASTICITY OF SUPPLY

The concept of price elasticity also applies to supply. If producers are responsive to price changes, supply is elastic. If they are relatively insensitive to price changes, supply is inelastic.

We calculate the degree of price elasticity or inelasticity of supply in the same way as for demand, except we substitute "percentage change in quantity *supplied*" for "percentage change in quantity *demanded*."

$$E_s = \frac{\text{percentage change in quantity supplied of product X}}{\text{percentage change in price of product X}}$$

For reasons explained earlier, the midpoints of the changes in quantity supplied and price are used in calculations. Suppose price were to increase from \$4 to \$6, causing quantity supplied to rise from 10 to 14. The percentage change in quantity supplied would be $\frac{4}{12}$, or 33 percent, and the percentage change in price would be $\frac{2}{5}$, or 40 percent. Substituting in our formula, we determine elasticity of supply to be 40 ÷ 33 or +1.21. Because price and quantity supplied are directly related, E_s will always be positive.

The main determinant of the **price elasticity of supply** is the amount of *time* a producer has to respond to a specific change in product price. We can expect a greater output response—and therefore greater elasticity of supply—the longer the time a firm has to adjust to a given price change. A firm's response to an increase in the price of product X depends on its ability to shift resources from the production of other products (whose prices we assume remain constant) to the production of X. And shifting

resources takes time: the greater the time, the greater the resource "shiftability." Thus, the greater will be the output response and the elasticity of supply.

In analyzing the impact of time on elasticity of supply, economists distinguish between the immediate market period, the short run, and the long run.

1 The Market Period The immediate **market period** is so short a time that producers cannot respond to a change in demand and price. Suppose a small truck farmer brings an entire season's output of tomatoes—one truckload—to market. The supply curve will be perfectly inelastic (vertical); the farmer will sell the truckload whether the price is high or low. Why? Because he cannot offer more tomatoes than his one truckload if the price of tomatoes should be higher than he had anticipated. Though he might like to offer more, tomatoes cannot be produced overnight. Another full growing season is needed to respond to a higher-than-expected price by producing more than one truckload. Similarly, because the product is perishable, the farmer cannot withhold it from the market. If the price is lower than anticipated, he will still sell the entire truckload. Costs of production, incidentally, will not be important in this decision. Though the price of tomatoes may fall far short of production costs, the farmer will nevertheless sell out to avoid a total loss through spoilage. During a very short time, our farmer's supply of tomatoes is fixed; only one truckload can be offered no matter how high the price. The perishability of the product forces the farmer to sell all, no matter how low the price.

Figure 20-3a illustrates the truck farmer's perfectly inelastic supply curve in the market period. Note that this and other truck farmers cannot respond to an assumed increase in demand; they do not have time to increase the amount supplied. The price increase from P_o to P_m simply rations a fixed supply to buyers, but elicits no increase in output.[2]

2 The Short Run In the **short run,** the plant capacity of individual producers and the industry is presumed fixed. But firms *do* have time to use their fixed plants more or less intensively. Thus, in the short run, our truck farmer's plant—comprised of land and farm machinery—is fixed. But he does have time in the

---

[2]The supply curve need not be perfectly inelastic (vertical) in the market period. If the product is not perishable, producers may choose, at low current prices, to store some of their product for future sale. This will cause the market supply curve to have some positive slope.

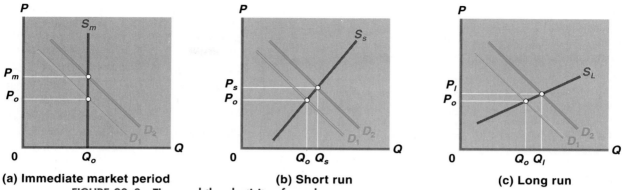

(a) Immediate market period   **(b) Short run**   **(c) Long run**

FIGURE 20-3   Time and the elasticity of supply
The greater the amount of time producers have to adjust to a change in demand, the greater will be their output response. In the immediate market period (a) there is insufficient time to change output, and so supply is perfectly inelastic. In the short run (b) plant capacity is fixed, but output can be altered by changing the intensity of its use; supply is therefore more elastic. In the long run (c) all desired adjustments—including changes in plant capacity—can be made, and supply becomes still more elastic.

short run to cultivate tomatoes more intensively by applying more labor and more fertilizer and pesticides to the crop. The result is a greater output response to the presumed increase in demand; this greater output response is reflected in a more elastic supply of tomatoes, as shown by S_s in Figure 20-3b. Note that the increase in demand is met by a larger quantity adjustment (Q_o to Q_s) and a smaller price adjustment (P_o to P_s) than in the market period; price is therefore lower than in the market period.

3   The Long Run   The **long run** is a time period sufficiently long so that firms can make all desired resource adjustments; individual firms can expand (or contract) their plant capacities, and new firms can enter (or existing firms can leave) the industry. In the "tomato industry" our truck farmer can acquire additional land and buy more machinery and equipment. Furthermore, more farmers may be attracted to tomato production by increased demand and higher price. These adjustments mean an even greater supply response, that is, an even more elastic supply curve S_L. The result, shown in Figure 20-3c, is a small price effect (P_o to P_l) and a large output effect (Q_o to Q_l) in response to the increase in demand. *(Key Question 14)*

There is no total-revenue test for elasticity of supply. Supply shows a positive or direct relationship between price and amount supplied; the supply curve is upsloping. Regardless of the degree of elasticity or in-

elasticity, price and total revenue will always move together.

CROSS AND INCOME ELASTICITY OF DEMAND

While price elasticities measure the responsiveness of the quantity of a product demanded or supplied to a change in its price, it is also useful to know how the consumption of a good is affected by a change in the price of a related product or by a change in income.

Cross Elasticity of Demand

Suppose Coca-Cola is considering a reduction in the price of its Sprite brand. Not only will it want to know something about the price elasticity of demand for Sprite (will the price cut increase or decrease total revenue?), but it will also be interested in knowing if the increased sales of Sprite will come at the expense of Coke itself. How sensitive is the quantity demanded of one product (Coke) to a change in the price of a second product (Sprite)? To what extent will the lower price and increased sales of Sprite reduce the sales of Coke?

The concept of **cross elasticity of demand** sheds light on such questions by measuring how sensitive consumer purchases of *one* product (say X) are to a change in the price of some *other* product (say

Y). We calculate cross elasticity of demand like simple price elasticity except we relate the percentage change in the consumption of X to a percentage change in the price of Y:

$$E_{xy} = \frac{\text{percentage change in quantity demanded of X}}{\text{percentage change in price of Y}}$$

This elasticity concept allows us to quantify and more fully understand substitute and complementary goods as introduced in Chapter 3.

Substitute Goods If cross elasticity of demand is *positive*—that is, the quantity demanded of X varies directly with a change in the price of Y—then X and Y are *substitute goods*. For example, an increase in the price of butter (Y) will cause consumers to buy more margarine (X). The larger the positive coefficient, the greater the substitutability between the two products.

Complementary Goods When cross elasticity is *negative,* then we know that X and Y "go together" and are *complementary goods*. Thus an increase in the price of cameras will decrease the amount of film purchased. The larger the negative coefficient, the greater the complementarity between the two goods.

Independent Goods A zero or near-zero cross elasticity suggests that the two products are unrelated or *independent goods*. For example, we would not expect a change in the price of butter to have any impact on the purchases of film.

Income Elasticity of Demand

Income elasticity of demand measures the percentage change in the quantity of a product demanded which results from some percentage change in consumer incomes:

$$E_i = \frac{\text{percentage change in quantity demanded}}{\text{percentage change in income}}$$

Normal Goods For most goods the income elasticity coefficient will be *positive*. Again recalling Chapter 3, those products of which more is purchased as incomes increase are called *normal* or *superior* goods. But the positive income elasticity coefficient varies greatly among products. For example, the income elasticity of demand for automobiles has been estimated to be about +3.00, while for most farm products it is only about +0.20.

Inferior Goods A *negative* income elasticity coefficient designates an *inferior good*. Retreaded tires, cabbage, bus tickets, used clothing, and muscatel wine are likely candidates. Consumers *decrease* their purchases of such products as incomes *increase.*

Applications Estimates of income elasticity can be useful for individuals and policy makers. If you are investing in the stock market, you may be seeking out "growth industries" whose stock values are forecast to rise substantially over time. Other things equal, a high income elasticity for industry X's product provides a clue that it will be such an industry, while a low income elasticity for Y suggests it will not. For example, the indicated high positive income elasticity of demand for automobiles suggests a greater likelihood of long-run prosperity in comparison to agriculture's low income elasticity which implies chronic problems.

A local government would find the income elasticity of demand for new real estate invaluable in estimating future receipts from property taxes. If local incomes are rising by, say, 3 percent per year, will that result in a proportionately larger or smaller increase in the purchases of new housing and therefore in the property tax base?

Finally, some estimates of the income elasticity of demand for health care are about +1.0, indicating that spending on health care rises proportionately with incomes. This tells reformers that the inordinate rise in health care spending experienced in the past two or three decades is caused by factors other than income growth. *(Key Questions 16 and 17)*

Table 20-4 provides a convenient synopsis of the cross and income elasticity concepts.

APPLICATIONS: LEGAL PRICES

Supply and demand analysis and the elasticity concept will be applied repeatedly in the remainder of this book. Let's strengthen our understanding of these analytical tools and their significance by examining some of the implications of legal prices.

On occasion the general public and government feel that supply and demand result in prices either unfairly high to buyers or unfairly low to sellers. In such

TABLE 20-4   Cross and income elasticity of demand: a summary

Value of coefficient	Description	Type of good(s)
Cross elasticity:		
Positive $(E_{wz} > 0)$	Quantity demanded of W changes in same direction as change in price of Z	Substitutes
Negative $(E_{xy} < 0)$	Quantity demanded of X changes in opposite direction as change in price of Y	Complements
Income elasticity:		
Positive $(E_i > 0)$	Quantity demanded of the product changes in same direction as change in income	Normal or superior
Negative $(E_i < 0)$	Quantity demanded of the product changes in opposite direction as change in income	Inferior

instances government may intervene by legally limiting how high or low the price may go.

Price Ceilings and Shortages

A **price ceiling** *is the maximum legal price a seller may charge for a product or service.* A price at or below the ceiling is legal; a price above it is not. The rationale for ceiling prices on specific products is that they purportedly enable consumers to obtain some "essential" good or service they could not afford at the equilibrium price. Rent controls and usury laws (which specify maximum interest rates which may be charged to borrowers) are examples. Ceiling prices or general price controls have been used in attempting to restrain the overall rate of inflation in the economy. Price controls were invoked during World War II and to a lesser extent during the Korean conflict.

World War II Price Controls   Let's turn back the clock to World War II and analyze the effects of a ceiling price on butter. The booming wartime prosperity of the early 1940s was shifting demand for butter to the right so that, as in Figure 20-4, the equilibrium or market price *P* was, say, $1.20 per pound. The rapidly rising price of butter was contributing to inflation and rationing out of the butter market those families whose money incomes were not keeping up with the soaring cost of living. To help stop inflation and to keep butter on the tables of the poor, govern-

ment imposed a ceiling price P_c of, say, $.90 per pound. To be effective a ceiling price must be *below* the equilibrium price. A ceiling price of $1.50 would have no immediate impact on the butter market.

What will be the effects of this $.90 ceiling price? The rationing ability of the free market will be rendered ineffective. At the ceiling price there will be a persistent shortage of butter. The quantity of butter demanded at P_c is Q_d and the quantity supplied is only Q_s; a persistent excess demand or shortage in the amount Q_sQ_d occurs. The size of this shortage varies

FIGURE 20-4   **Price ceilings result in persistent shortages**
Because a price ceiling—a maximum legal price—such as P_c results in a persistent product shortage, indicated by the distance Q_sQ_d, government must ration the product to achieve an equitable distribution.

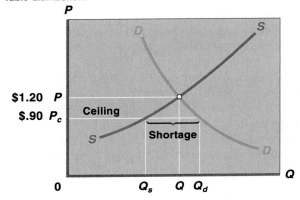

directly with the price elasticities of supply and demand. The greater the elasticities, the greater the shortage.

The important point is that the legal price P_c prevents the usual market adjustment where competition among buyers would bid up price, inducing more production and rationing some buyers out of the market until the shortage disappears at the equilibrium price and quantity, P and Q.

By preventing these market-clearing adjustments from occurring, the ceiling price poses problems born of the market disequilibrium.

1 **Rationing Problem** How is the available supply Q_s to be apportioned among buyers who want amount Q_d? Should supply be distributed on a first-come, first-served basis, that is, to those willing and able to stand in line the longest? Or should the grocer distribute butter on the basis of favoritism? An unregulated shortage is hardly conducive to the equitable distribution of butter. To avoid catch-as-catch-can distribution, government must establish some formal system of rationing the product to consumers. This was done during World War II by issuing ration coupons to individuals on an equitable basis. An effective rationing system entails the printing of ration coupons equal to Q_s pounds of butter and their equitable distribution among consumers so that the rich family of four and the poor family of four will both get the same number of coupons.

2 **Black Markets** But ration coupons do not prevent a second problem from arising. Specifically, the demand curve in Figure 20-4 tells us there are many buyers willing to pay more than the ceiling price. And, of course, it is more profitable for grocers to sell above the ceiling price. Thus, despite the sizable enforcement bureaucracy which accompanied World War II price controls, illegal *black markets*—markets where products were bought and sold at prices above the legal limits—flourished for many goods. Counterfeiting of ration coupons was also a problem.

Rent Controls Some 200 American cities—including New York City, Boston, and San Francisco—have rent controls. Such legislation is well-intended. Its goals are to protect low-income families from escalating rents caused by perceived housing shortages and to make housing more affordable to the poor.

What are the actual economic effects? On the demand side, it is true that below-equilibrium rents will mean that more families are willing to consume rental housing; the quantity of rental housing demanded will increase at the lower price. The problem occurs on the supply side. Price controls make it less attractive for landlords to offer housing on the rental market. In the short run they may sell their apartments or convert them to condominiums. In the long run low rents make it unprofitable for owners to repair or renovate their rental units. Rent controls are one cause of abandoned apartment buildings found in larger cities. Also, potential new investors in housing such as insurance companies and pension funds will find it more profitable to invest in office buildings, shopping malls, or motels where rents are not controlled.

In brief, rent controls distort market signals so that resources are misallocated: Too few resources are allocated to rental housing, too many to alternative uses. Ironically, although rent controls are often legislated to lessen the effects of perceived housing shortages, in fact, controls are a primary cause of such shortages.

Credit Card Interest Ceilings In recent years several bills have been introduced in Congress to impose a nationwide interest-rate ceiling on credit card accounts. Several states now have such laws and others have legislation under consideration. The usual rationale for interest-rate ceilings is that the banks and retail stores issuing such cards are presumably "gouging" users and, in particular, lower-income users by charging interest rates that average about 16 or 17 percent.

What might be the responses to the legal imposition of below-equilibrium interest rates on credit cards?[3] Lower interest income associated with a legal interest ceiling would require issuers to reduce costs or enhance revenues.

1 Card issuers might tighten credit standards to reduce nonpayment losses and collection costs. In particular, low-income people and young people who have not yet established their creditworthiness would find it more difficult to obtain credit cards.

2 The annual fee charged card holders might be increased as might the fee charged merchants for processing credit card sales. Similarly, card users might be charged a fee for every transaction.

---

[3]Glenn B. Canner and James T. Fergus, "The Economic Effects of Proposed Ceilings on Credit Card Interest Rates," *Federal Reserve Bulletin,* January 1987, pp. 1–13.

3 Card users now have a "grace period" when the credit provided is interest-free. This period might be shortened or eliminated.

4 Certain "enhancements" which accompany some cards—for example, extended warranties on products bought with a card—might be eliminated.

5 Finally, retail stores which issue cards might increase their merchandise prices to help offset the decline of interest income. This would mean that customers who pay cash would in effect be subsidizing customers who use credit cards.

Rock Concerts Below-equilibrium pricing should not be associated solely with government policies. Rock superstars sometimes price their concert tickets below the market-clearing price. Tickets are usually rationed on a first-come, first-served basis and ticket "scalping" is common. Why should rock stars want to subsidize their fans—at least those fortunate enough to obtain tickets—with below-equilibrium prices? Why not set ticket prices at a higher, market-clearing level and realize more income from a tour?

The answer is that long lines of fans waiting hours or days for bargain-priced tickets catch the attention of the press, as does an occasional attempt by ticketless fans to "crash" a sold-out concert. The millions of dollars worth of free publicity undoubtedly stimulates cassette and CD sales from which much of any rock group's income is derived. Thus, the "gift" of below-equilibrium ticket prices a rock star gives to fans also benefits the star. And the gift imposes costs upon fans—the opportunity cost of time spent waiting in line to buy tickets.

Incidentally, many people regard the ticket scalping often associated with musical or athletic events as a form of extortion, where the extortionist's (seller's) gain is the victim's (buyer's) loss. But to most economists, the fact that scalping is a voluntary transaction suggests that both seller and buyer gain or the exchange would not occur. Such exchanges redistribute assets (tickets) from those who value them less to those who value them more. The concert or game also benefits from having an audience which most wants to be there (Last Word, Chapter 3).

Price Floors and Surpluses

Price floors *are minimum prices fixed by government.* A price at or above the price floor is legal; a price below it is not. Price floors above equilibrium prices have generally been invoked when society has felt that the free functioning of the market system has not provided a sufficient income for certain groups of resource suppliers or producers. Minimum-wage legislation and the support of agricultural prices are two examples of government price floors. Let's examine price floors as applied to a specific farm commodity.

Suppose the going market price for corn is $2 per bushel, and as a result of this price, many farmers realize extremely low incomes. Government decides to help out by establishing a legal price floor or "price support" of $3 per bushel.

What will be the effects? At any price above the equilibrium price, quantity supplied will exceed quantity demanded, that is, there will be a persistent excess supply or surplus of the product. Farmers will be willing to produce and offer for sale more than private buyers are willing to purchase at the price floor. The size of this surplus will vary directly with the elasticity of demand and supply. The greater the elasticity of demand and supply, the greater the resulting surplus. As with a ceiling price, the rationing ability of the free market has been disrupted by imposing a legal price.

Figure 20-5 illustrates the effect of a price floor. Let *SS* and *DD* be the supply and demand curves for corn. Equilibrium price and quantity are *P* and *Q*, respectively. If government imposes a price floor of P_f, farmers will produce Q_s, but private buyers will only

FIGURE 20-5 Price floors result in persistent surpluses
A price floor—a minimum legal price—such as P_f gives rise to a persistent product surplus, indicated by the distance Q_dQ_s. Government must either purchase these surpluses or take measures to eliminate them by restricting product supply or increasing product demand.

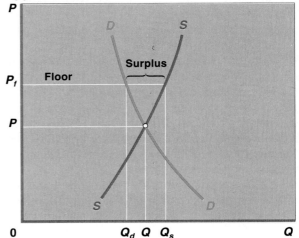

LAST WORD

MARKET FORCES AND THE VALUE OF EDUCATION

Recent growth in the earnings of college-educated workers relative to less-educated workers reflects the fact that the supply of highly educated workers has not kept pace with a rapidly growing demand for their skills.

Comparisons of the real average (median) incomes of college and high-school graduates show that the gap between the two—called the "college premium"—has risen sharply since 1980. In other words, the value of education has been increasing. This widening income disparity can be understood in terms of the changing demand and supply for the services of college- and high-school-educated workers.

On the vertical axis of the graph we measure the ratio of the median income of college graduates to the median income of high-school graduates. A ratio of 1.5 would indicate that college graduates earn 50 percent more than high-school graduates. The horizontal axis indicates the percentage of young people (aged 25–34) with four years or more of college. The vertical (perfectly inelastic) supply curves reflect the fact that the quantity of college graduates does not respond quickly to a change in the income ratio. For example, if the ratio rises, it will take four or five years for the additional college enrollees to earn their degrees and enter the labor market. The downsloping demand curves indicate that the smaller the college premium, the more college-trained workers employers will choose to hire.

In 1967 we observe an earnings ratio of about 1.5, indicating that in that year college graduates earned almost 50 percent more than high-school graduates. But by 1987 this gap had risen to over 70 percent. Explanation: Despite the increase in the supply of college graduates (from about $16\frac{1}{2}$ to over 24 percent of the 25–34 age group), demand increased by a relatively greater amount.

Why? On the demand side, it appears that technological advance since about 1980 has been increasingly "skill-biased." Innovation has raised the productivity and therefore the demand for more-educated workers more than the productivity of less-skilled workers. Computerization of the workplace alone may explain one-third to two-thirds of the in-

---

take Q_d off the market at that price. The surplus is the excess of Q_s over Q_d.

Government may cope with the surplus a price floor entails in two basic ways.

1   It might restrict supply (for example, acreage allotments by which farmers agree to take a certain amount of land out of production) or increase demand (for example, researching new uses for agricultural products). In these ways the difference between the equilibrium price and the price floor and thereby the size of the resulting surplus might be reduced.

2   If these efforts are not wholly successful, then government must purchase the surplus output (thereby subsidizing farmers) and store or otherwise dispose of it (Chapter 33).

Recapitulation

Price ceilings and floors rob the free-market forces of supply and demand of their ability to bring the supply decisions of producers and the demand decisions of buyers into accord with one another. Freely determined prices automatically ration products to buyers; legal prices do not. Therefore, government must accept the administrative problem of rationing which stems from price ceilings and the problem of buying or eliminating surpluses which price floors create. Legal prices entail controversial tradeoffs. Alleged benefits of price ceilings and floors to consumers and producers, respectively, must be set against costs associated with consequent shortages and surpluses.

creased returns to education. Greater use of high-tech capital goods in manufacturing is also relevant.

The demand side of the market has also been affected by the lowering of world trade barriers. Lower barriers have increased the demand for the high-tech products we export and for the more-educated workers producing them. Conversely, freer trade has expanded our domestic demand for low-cost imports made by less-skilled workers abroad. Such imports have effectively increased the competition faced by less-educated workers in the United States, stifling their earnings growth. A rise in the number of low-skilled immigrants to the United States in the 1980s has also slowed the earnings growth of less-educated workers.

Why didn't the supply of college graduates increase more than shown in the graph and thereby keep the college premium from rising? After all, as the earnings gap began to rise in the early 1980s, wouldn't this induce more people to enter and eventually graduate from college? Other factors—in particular, the rising real costs of a college education—have restricted growth in the supply of college graduates. In the 1980s the cost of college rose by two times the rate of inflation in public colleges and by three times the inflation rate in private schools. At the same time, government grants and loans to students fell behind the inflation rate.

Conclusions: The increasing economic value of a college education is explained in terms of a rising relative demand for college-educated labor which in turn is based on skill-biased technological change and the

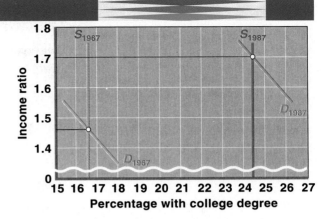

impacts of freer world trade. The lagging supply of college-trained workers is the result of rapidly rising real costs of a college education and cuts in education subsidies.

Some implications: First, an individual's economic well-being is more closely tied to her or his educational attainment than in the past. Second, wage disparities between more- and less-educated workers have been growing and contribute to greater income inequality in the economy as a whole. Third, the prosperity of any city, state, or region depends increasingly upon its commitment to education.

Source: Based on Erica L. Groshen and Colin Drozdowski, "The Recent Rise in the Value of Education: Market Forces at Work," *Economic Commentary* (Federal Reserve Bank of Cleveland, August 15, 1992).

Furthermore, our discussions of World War II price controls, rent controls, and interest rate ceilings on credit cards show that governmental interference with the market can have unintended, undesirable side effects. Rent controls may discourage housing construction and repair. Instead of protecting low-income families from high interest charges, interest rate ceilings may simply make credit unavailable to them.

QUICK REVIEW 20-3

■ Price elasticity of supply is the ratio of the percentage change in quantity supplied to the percentage change in price. The elasticity of supply varies

directly with the amount of time producers have to respond to the price change.

■ Cross elasticity of demand is the percentage change in the quantity demanded of one product divided by the percentage change in the price of another product. If the cross elasticity coefficient is positive, the two products are substitutes; if negative, they are complements.

■ Income elasticity is the percentage change in quantity demanded divided by the percentage change in income. A positive coefficient indicates a normal or superior good. The coefficient is negative for an inferior good.

■ Legal prices—ceilings and floors—negate the rationing function of prices and cause unintended side effects.

CHAPTER SUMMARY

1 Price elasticity of demand measures consumer response to price changes. If consumers are relatively sensitive to price changes, demand is elastic. If they are relatively unresponsive to price changes, demand is inelastic.

2 The price elasticity formula measures the degree of elasticity or inelasticity of demand. The formula is

$$E_d = \frac{\text{percentage change in quantity demanded of X}}{\text{percentage change in price of X}}$$

The averages of prices and quantities under consideration are used as reference points in determining percentage changes in price and quantity. If E_d is greater than 1, demand is elastic. If E_d is less than 1, demand is inelastic. Unit elasticity is the special case in which E_d equals 1.

3 A perfectly inelastic demand curve is portrayed by a line parallel to the vertical axis; a perfectly elastic demand curve is shown by a line above and parallel to the horizontal axis.

4 Elasticity varies at different price ranges on a demand curve, tending to be elastic in the northwest segment and inelastic in the southeast segment. Elasticity cannot be judged by the steepness or flatness of a demand curve on a graph.

5 If price and total revenue move in opposite directions, demand is elastic. If price and total revenue move in the same direction, demand is inelastic. Where demand is of unit elasticity, a change in price will leave total revenue unchanged.

6 The number of available substitutes, the size of an item in one's budget, whether the product is a luxury or necessity, and time are all determinants of elasticity of demand.

7 The elasticity concept also applies to supply. Elasticity of supply depends on the shiftability of resources between alternative employments. This shiftability in turn varies directly with the time producers have to adjust to a given price change.

8 Cross elasticity gauges how sensitive the purchases of one product are to changes in the price of another product. It is measured by the percentage change in the quantity demanded of product X divided by the percentage change in the price of product Y. Positive cross elasticity identifies substitute goods; negative cross elasticity indicates complementary goods.

9 Income elasticity indicates the responsiveness of consumer purchases to a change in income. It is measured by the percentage change in the quantity demanded of the product divided by the percentage change in income. It is positive for normal goods and negative for inferior goods.

10 Legally fixed prices upset the rationing function of equilibrium prices. Effective price ceilings result in persistent product shortages and, if an equitable distribution of the product is sought, government will have to ration the product to consumers. Price floors lead to product surpluses; government must purchase these surpluses *or* eliminate them by imposing restrictions on production or by increasing private demand.

TERMS AND CONCEPTS

price elasticity of
    demand
elastic versus inelastic
    demand
unit elasticity
perfectly inelastic
    demand

perfectly elastic
    demand
total-revenue test
price elasticity of
    supply

market period
short run and long
    run
cross elasticity of
    demand

income elasticity of
    demand
price ceiling
price floor

QUESTIONS AND STUDY SUGGESTIONS

1 Review questions 1, 4, and 8 at the end of Chapter 3.

2 *Key Question   Graph the accompanying demand data and then use the midpoints formula to determine price elasticity of demand for each of the four price changes. What can you conclude about the relationship between the slope of a curve and its elasticity? Explain in a nontechnical way why demand is elastic in the northwest segment of the demand curve and inelastic in the southeast segment.*

Product price	Quantity demanded
$5	1
4	2
3	3
2	4
1	5

3 In 1987 the average price of a home rose from $97,000

in April to $106,800 in May. During the same period home sales fell from 724,000 to 616,000 units. If we assume that mortgage interest rates and all other factors affecting home sales are constant, what do these figures suggest about the elasticity of demand for housing?

4 *Key Question* *Calculate total revenue data from the demand schedule in question 2. Graph total revenue below your demand curve. Generalize on the relationship between price elasticity and total revenue.*

5 *Key Question* *How will the following changes in price affect total revenue (expenditures) —that is, will total revenue increase, decline, or remain unchanged?*

    a *Price falls and demand is inelastic.*

    b *Price rises and demand is elastic.*

    c *Price rises and supply is elastic.*

    d *Price rises and supply is inelastic.*

    e *Price rises and demand is inelastic.*

    f *Price falls and demand is elastic.*

    g *Price falls and demand is of unit elasticity.*

6 In some industries, for example, the petroleum industry, producers justify their reluctance to lower prices by arguing that demand for their products is inelastic. Explain.

7 You are sponsoring an outdoor rock concert. Your major costs—for the band, land rent, and security—are largely independent of attendance. Use the concept of price elasticity of demand to explain how you might establish ticket prices to maximize profits.

8 In the 1970s the Organization of Petroleum Exporting Countries (OPEC) became operational as a cartel which reduced the world supply of oil, greatly increasing OPEC's revenues and profits. What can you infer regarding the elasticity of demand for oil? Would you expect countries exporting bananas or pineapples to be able to emulate OPEC? Explain.

9 *Key Question* *What are the major determinants of price elasticity of demand? Use these determinants in judging whether demand for each of the following products is elastic or inelastic:* **a** *oranges;* **b** *cigarettes;* **c** *Winston cigarettes;* **d** *gasoline;* **e** *butter;* **f** *salt;* **g** *automobiles;* **h** *football games;* **i** *diamond bracelets; and* **j** *this textbook.*

10 Empirical estimates suggest the following price elasticities of demand: 0.6 for physicians' services; 4.0 for foreign travel; and 1.2 for radio and television receivers. Use the generalizations for the determinants of elasticity developed in this chapter to explain each of these figures.

11 What effect would a rule stating that university students must live in university dormitories have on the price elasticity of demand for dormitory space? What impact might this in turn have on room rates?

12 "If the demand for farm products is highly price in-elastic, a bumper crop may reduce farm incomes." Evaluate and illustrate graphically.

13 You are chairperson of a state tax commission responsible for establishing a program to raise new revenue through excise taxes. Would elasticity of demand be important to you in determining those products on which excises should be levied? Explain.

14 *Key Question* *In May 1990 Vincent van Gogh's painting "Portrait of Dr. Gachet" sold at auction for $82.5 million. Portray this sale in a demand and supply diagram and comment on the elasticity of supply.*

15 In the 1950s the local Boy Scout troop in Jackson, Wyoming, decided to gather and sell at auction elk antlers shed by thousands of elk wintering in the area. Buyers were mainly local artisans who used the antlers to make belt buckles, buttons, and tie clasps. Price per pound was 6¢ and the troop took in $500 annually. In the 1970s a fad developed in Asia which involved grinding antlers into powder to sprinkle on food for purported aphrodisiac benefits. In 1979 the price per pound of elk antlers in the Jackson auction was $6 per pound and the Boy Scouts earned $51,000! Show graphically and explain these dramatic increases in price and total revenue. Assuming no shift in the supply curve of elk antlers, use the midpoints formula to calculate the coefficient for the elasticity of supply.

16 *Key Question* *Suppose the cross elasticity of demand for products A and B is +3.6 and for products C and D it is −5.4. What can you conclude about how products A and B and products C and D are related?*

17 *Key Question* *The income elasticities of demand for movies, dental services, and clothing have been estimated to be +3.4, +1.0, and +0.5, respectively. Interpret these coefficients. What does it mean if the income elasticity coefficient is negative?*

18 Why is it desirable for ceiling prices to be accompanied by government rationing? And for price floors to be accompanied by surplus-purchasing or output-restricting or demand-increasing programs? Show graphically why price ceilings entail shortages and price floors result in surpluses. What effect, if any, does elasticity of demand and supply have on the size of these shortages and surpluses? Explain.

19 "Rent controls are a kind of self-fulfilling prophecy. They are designed to cope with housing shortages, but instead create such shortages." Do you agree?

20 To contain rapidly rising health care costs, some reformers have proposed price ceilings on doctors, for example, a maximum fee for an office visit. What would be the likely consequences?

21 (Last Word) What has happened to the earnings gap between college-educated and high-school educated workers in recent years? Use demand and supply-side factors to explain this change.

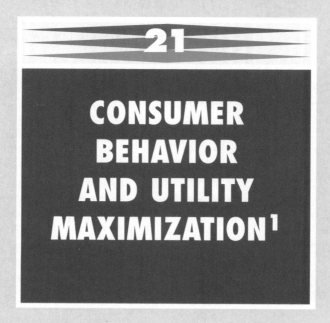

21

CONSUMER BEHAVIOR AND UTILITY MAXIMIZATION[1]

You have probably seen the T-shirts which say: "I'd rather be shopping," or "Shop 'till you drop." We do seem to be a nation of shoppers. In 1994 Americans spent about $4.6 trillion on goods and services. This spending amounted to about 93 percent of U.S. after-tax income. Consumption per person was $17,752 in that year.

One concern of microeconomics is explaining consumer spending. If you were to compare the shopping carts of two consumers, you would observe striking differences. Why does Paula have potatoes, parsnips, pomegranates, and Pepsi in her cart, while Sam has sugar, saltines, soap, Spam, and 7-Up in his? Why didn't Paula also buy pork and pimentos? Why didn't Sam have soup and spaghetti on his grocery list? In this chapter, we will learn how individual consumers allocate their money incomes among the various goods and services available to them. Why does a consumer buy some specific bundle of goods rather than any one of a number of other collections of goods available? As we examine these issues we will also strengthen our understanding of the law of demand.

TWO EXPLANATIONS OF THE LAW OF DEMAND

The law of demand is based on common sense. A high price discourages consumers from buying; a low price encourages them to buy. We now explore two complementary explanations of the downsloping nature of the demand curve which will back up our everyday observations. (A third explanation, based on indifference curves, is more advanced and is summarized in the appendix to this chapter.)

Income and Substitution Effects

In Chapter 3 the downsloping demand curve was explained in terms of income and substitution effects.

Whenever a product's price decreases, two things happen to cause the amount demanded to increase.

1 Income Effect The **income effect** is the impact a change in the price of a product has on a consumer's real income and consequently on the quantity of that product demanded. If the price of a product—say, steak—declines, the real income or purchasing power of anyone buying that product will increase. This increase in real income will be reflected in increased purchases of many products, including steak. With a constant money income of $20 per week you

---

[1]Some instructors may choose to omit this chapter. This can be done without impairing the continuity and meaning of ensuing chapters.

can buy 10 pounds of steak at $2 per pound. But if the price of steak falls to $1 per pound and you buy 10 pounds, $10 per week is freed to buy more of both steak and other commodities. A decline in the price of steak increases the consumer's real income, enabling him or her to purchase more steak.[2] This is called the *income effect.*

2 Substitution Effect

The **substitution effect** is the impact a change in a product's price has on its relative expensiveness, and consequently on the quantity demanded. When the price of a product falls it becomes cheaper relative to all other products. Consumers will substitute the cheaper product for other products which are now relatively more expensive. In our example, as the price of steak falls—prices of other products being unchanged—steak will become more attractive to the buyer. At $1 per pound it is a "better buy" than at $2. The lower price will induce the consumer to substitute steak for some of the now relatively less attractive items in the budget. Steak may be substituted for pork, chicken, veal, fish, and other foods. A lower price increases the relative attractiveness of a product and the consumer will buy more of it. This is the *substitution effect.*

The income and substitution effects combine to make a consumer able and willing to buy more of a specific good at a low price than at a high price.

Law of Diminishing Marginal Utility

A second explanation of the downsloping demand curve is that, although consumer wants in general may be insatiable, wants for specific commodities can be fulfilled. In a given span of time, where buyers' tastes are unchanged, consumers can get as much of specific goods and services as they want. The more of a specific product consumers obtain, the less they will want more units of the same product.

This can be readily seen for durable goods. A consumer's want for an automobile, when he or she has none, may be very strong; the desire for a second car is less intense; for a third or fourth, very weak. Even the wealthiest families rarely have more than a half-dozen cars, although their incomes would allow them to purchase a whole fleet of them.

Terminology Economists theorize that specific consumer wants can be fulfilled with succeeding units of

---

[2]We assume here that steak is a *normal* or *superior* good.

a commodity in the law of diminishing marginal utility. Recall that a product has utility if it can satisfy a want. **Utility** is want-satisfying power. The utility of a good or service is the satisfaction or pleasure one gets from consuming it. Three characteristics of this concept must be emphasized.

1 "Utility" and "usefulness" are not synonymous. Paintings by Picasso may be useless functionally and yet offer great utility to art connoisseurs.

2 Implied in the first point is the fact that utility is a subjective notion. The utility of a specific product will vary widely from person to person. A bottle of muscatel wine may yield substantial utility to the Skid Row alcoholic, but zero or negative utility to the local MADD president. Eyeglasses have great utility to someone who is extremely far- or near-sighted, but no utility to a person having 20-20 vision.

3 Because utility is subjective, it is difficult to quantify. But for purposes of illustration, assume we can measure satisfaction with units we will call "utils." This mythical unit of satisfaction is a convenient pedagogical device allowing us to quantify consumer behavior.

Total Utility and Marginal Utility We must carefully distinguish between total utility and marginal utility. **Total utility** is the total amount of satisfaction or pleasure a person derives from consuming some specific quantity—say, 10 units—of a good or service. **Marginal utility** is the *extra* satisfaction a consumer realizes from an additional unit of that product—say, from the eleventh unit. Alternatively, we can say marginal utility is the *change* in total utility resulting from the consumption of one more unit of a product.

Figure 21-1a and b and the accompanying table reveal the total utility–marginal utility relationship for fast-food hamburgers. Starting at the origin in Figure 21-1a, we observe that through the first five units total utility increases but at a diminishing rate. Total utility reaches a maximum at the sixth unit and then declines (column 2 of the table). The change in total utility accompanying each additional hamburger, by definition, measures marginal utility (column 3 of the table). Hence, in Figure 21-1b we find marginal utility is positive but diminishing through the fifth unit (because total utility increases at a declining rate). Marginal utility is zero for the sixth unit (because total utility is at a maximum). Marginal utility then becomes negative with the seventh unit and beyond (because total utility is falling). Figure 21-1b and the table tell us that each successive hamburger yields less and

FIGURE 21-1   Total and marginal utility
In (a) we observe that, as more of a product is consumed, total utility increases at a diminishing rate, reaches a maximum, and then declines. Marginal utility, by definition, reflects the changes in total utility. Thus, in (b) we find marginal utility diminishes with increased consumption, becomes zero where total utility is at a maximum, and is negative when total utility declines.

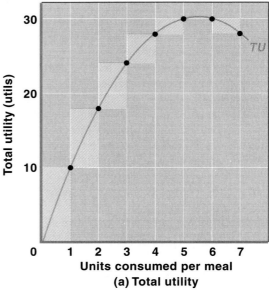

(a) Total utility

(1) Hamburgers consumed per meal	(2) Total utility	(3) Marginal utility, D(2)
0	0	
1	10	10
2	18	8
3	24	6
4	28	4
5	30	2
6	30	0
7	28	-2

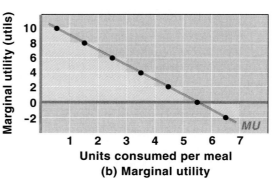

(b) Marginal utility

less extra utility than the previous one as the consumer's want for hamburgers comes closer and closer to fulfillment.[3] The notion that marginal utility will decline as the consumer acquires additional units of a specific product is known as the **law of diminishing marginal utility.** *(Key Question 2)*

Relation to Demand and Elasticity   How does the law of diminishing marginal utility explain why the demand curve for a specific product is downsloping? If successive units of a good yield smaller and smaller amounts of marginal, or extra, utility, then the consumer will buy additional units of a product only if its price falls. The consumer for whom these utility data are relevant may buy two hamburgers at a price of $1. But, owing to diminishing marginal utility from additional hamburgers, a consumer will choose *not* to buy more at this price. After all, giving up money really means giving up other goods, that is, alternative ways of getting utility. Therefore, additional hamburgers are "not worth it" unless the price (sacrifice of other goods) declines. (When marginal utility becomes negative, McDonald's or Burger King would have to pay *you* to consume another hamburger!) From the seller's viewpoint, diminishing marginal utility forces the seller to lower the price so buyers will take more of the product. This rationale supports the notion of a downsloping demand curve.

---

[3]Technical footnote: For a time the marginal utility of successive units of a product may increase. A second glass of lemonade on a hot day may yield more extra satisfaction than the first. But beyond some point we can expect the marginal utility of additional glasses to decline. Also, note in Figure 21-1b that marginal utility is graphed at the halfway points. For example, we graph marginal utility of 4 utils at $3\frac{1}{2}$ units because the 4 utils refers neither to the third nor the fourth unit per se, but to the *addition* of the fourth unit.

The amount by which marginal utility declines as more units of a product are consumed will determine its price elasticity of demand. Other things equal, if marginal utility falls sharply as successive units are consumed, we would expect demand to be inelastic. Conversely, modest declines in marginal utility as consumption increases imply an elastic demand.

QUICK REVIEW 21-1

■ The law of demand can be explained in terms of the income effect (a decline in price increases the consumer's purchasing power) and the substitution effect (a product whose price falls is substituted for other products).

■ Utility is the benefit or satisfaction a person receives from consuming a good or service.

■ The law of diminishing marginal utility indicates that the gains in satisfaction will decline as successive units of a given product are consumed.

■ Diminishing marginal utility provides a rationale for *a* the law of demand and *b* differing price elasticities.

THEORY OF CONSUMER BEHAVIOR

As well as explaining the law of demand, the idea of diminishing marginal utility explains how consumers should allocate their money income among the many goods and services available for purchase.

Consumer Choice and Budget Restraint

The typical consumer's situation is like this:

1 Rational Behavior The consumer is a rational person, trying to dispose of his or her money income to derive the greatest amount of satisfaction, or utility, from it. Consumers want to get "the most for their money" or, technically, to maximize total utility.

2 Preferences The consumer has clear-cut preferences for various goods and services available in the market. We assume buyers have a good idea of how much marginal utility they will get from successive units of the various products they might purchase.

3 Budget Restraint At any point in time, the consumer's money income is limited. Because the consumer supplies limited amounts of human and property resources to businesses, the income payments to him or her are also limited. Thought of this way, all consumers face a *budget restraint,* even those who earn millions of dollars annually. Of course, this income limitation is more severe for typical consumers with average incomes than for those with extraordinarily high incomes.

4 Prices Goods and services have price tags on them. They are scarce in relation to the demand for them, or, stated differently, producing them uses scarce and therefore valuable resources. In our examples we will suppose that product prices are not affected by the amounts of specific goods which the individual consumer buys; pure competition exists on the buying or demand side of the market.

If a consumer has limited dollars and the products he or she wants have price tags on them, the consumer can purchase only a limited amount of goods. The consumer cannot buy everything wanted when each purchase exhausts a portion of a limited money income. It is precisely this point which brings the economic fact of scarcity home to the individual consumer.

> In making his choices, our typical consumer is in the same position as the Western prospector . . . who is restocking for his next trip into the back country and who is forced by the nature of the terrain to restrict his luggage to whatever he can carry on the back of one burro. If he takes a great deal of one item, say baked beans, he must necessarily take much less of something else, say bacon. His job is to find that collection of products which, in view of the limitations imposed on the total, will best suit his needs and tastes.[4]

The consumer must compromise; he or she must choose among alternative goods to obtain with limited money income the most satisfying mix of goods and services. Different individuals will choose different mixes of goods. And, as shown in Global Perspective 21-1, mixes of goods will vary among nations.

Utility-Maximizing Rule

Of all the different sets of goods and services a consumer can obtain within his or her budget, which specific set will yield the maximum utility or satisfaction?

---

[4]E. T. Weiler, *The Economic System* (New York: The Macmillan Company, 1952), p. 89.

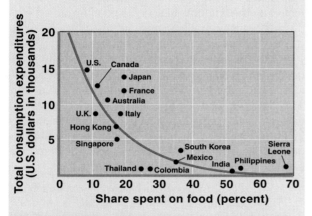

GLOBAL PERSPECTIVE 21-1

Shares of household budgets spent on food, selected nations

Consumer spending patterns differ not only among individuals, but among nations. One striking feature is that, although households in rich countries spend larger absolute amounts on food than do poor countries, households in poor nations spend a much larger proportion of their budgets on food.

Source: Judith Jones Putnam and Jane E. Allhouse, *Food Consumption, Prices, and Expenditures, 1970–92* (U.S. Department of Agriculture, 1993, Economic Research Service Statistical Bulletin 867).

$10. Holly's preferences for these two products and their prices will be basic data determining the combinations of A and B which will maximize her satisfaction. Table 21-1 summarizes Holly's preferences for products A and B. Column 2a shows the amount of extra or marginal utility she will derive from each successive unit of A. Column 3a reflects her preferences for product B. In each case the relationship between the number of units of the product consumed and the corresponding marginal utility reflects the law of diminishing marginal utility. Diminishing marginal utility is assumed to begin with the first unit of each product purchased.

Marginal Utility per Dollar   Before we apply the utility-maximizing rule to these data, we must put the marginal-utility information of columns 2a and 3a on a per-dollar-spent basis. A consumer's choices will be influenced not only by the extra utility which successive units of A will yield, but also by how many dollars (and therefore how many units of alternative good B) she must give up to obtain those added units of A.

The rational consumer must compare the extra utility from each product with its added cost (that is, its price). Suppose you prefer a pizza whose marginal utility is, say, 36 utils to a movie whose marginal utility is 24 utils. But if the pizza's price is $12 and the movie only $6, you would choose the movie rather than the pizza! Why? Because the marginal utility per dollar spent would be 4 utils for the movie (4 = 24 ÷ $6) compared to only 3 utils for the pizza (3 = 36 ÷

To maximize satisfaction *the consumer's money income should be allocated so that the last dollar spent on each product purchased yields the same amount of extra (marginal) utility.* We call this the **utility-maximizing rule.** When the consumer is "balancing his margins" in accordance with this rule, there will be no incentive to alter his or her expenditure pattern. The consumer will be in *equilibrium* and, barring a change in tastes, income, or the prices of the various goods, will be worse off—total utility will decline—by any alteration in the set of goods purchased.

Numerical Example   An illustration will help explain this rule. For simplicity we limit our discussion to two products, but the analysis applies to any number of goods. Suppose consumer Holly is trying to decide which combination of two products—A and B—she should purchase with her limited daily income of

TABLE 21-1   The utility-maximizing combination of products A and B obtainable with an income of $10*

(1) Unit of product	(2) Product A: price = $1		(3) Product B: price = $2	
	(a) Marginal utility, utils	(b) Marginal utility per dollar (MU/price)	(a) Marginal utility, utils	(b) Marginal utility per dollar (MU/price)
First	10 ✓	10	24 ✓	12
Second	8 ✓	8	20 ✓	10
Third	7	7	18 ✓	9
Fourth	6	6	16 ✓	8
Fifth	5	5	12	6
Sixth	4	4	6	3
Seventh	3	3	4	2

*It is assumed in this table the amount of marginal utility received from additional units of each of the two products is independent of the quantity of the other product. For example, the marginal utility schedule for product A is independent of the amount of B obtained by the consumer.

TABLE 21-2 Sequence of purchases in achieving consumer equilibrium

Potential choice	Marginal utility per dollar	Purchase decision	Income remaining
1 { First unit of A	10	First unit of B for $2	$8 = $10 − $2
{ First unit of B	12		
2 { First unit of A	10	First unit of A for $1	$5 = $8 − $3
{ Second unit of B	10	and second unit of B for $2	
3 { Second unit of A	8	Third unit of B for $2	$3 = $5 − $2
{ Third unit of B	9		
4 { Second unit of A	8	Second unit of A for $1	$0 = $3 − $3
{ Fourth unit of B	8	and fourth unit of B for $2	

$12). You could buy two movies for $12 and, assuming the marginal utility of the second movie is, say, 16 utils, total utility would be 40 utils. Forty units of satisfaction from two movies is clearly superior to 36 utils from the same $12 expenditure on one pizza. *To make the amounts of extra utility derived from differently priced goods comparable, marginal utility must be put on a per-dollar-spent basis.* This is done in columns 2b and 3b. These figures are obtained by dividing the marginal-utility data of columns 2a and 3a by the assumed prices of A and B—$1 and $2, respectively.

Decision-Making Process Now we have Holly's preferences—on unit and per dollar bases—and the price tags of A and B before us. With $10 to spend, in what order should Holly allocate her dollars on units of A and B to achieve the highest degree of utility within the $10 limit imposed by her money income? What specific combination of A and B will she have obtained at the time that she exhausts her $10?

Concentrating on columns 2b and 3b of Table 21-1, we find that Holly should first spend $2 on the first unit of B, because its marginal utility per dollar of 12 utils is higher than A's 10 utils. But now Holly finds herself indifferent about whether she should buy a second unit of B or the first unit of A, because the marginal utility per dollar of both is 10 utils. So she buys both of them. Holly now has 1 unit of A and 2 of B. With this combination of goods the last dollar spent on each yields the same amount of extra utility. Does this combination of A and B therefore represent the maximum amount of utility which Holly can obtain? The answer is "No." This collection of goods only costs $5 [= (1 × $1) + (2 × $2)]; Holly has $5 remaining, which she can spend to achieve a still higher level of total utility.

Examining columns 2b and 3b again, we find Holly should spend the next $2 on a third unit of B because marginal utility per dollar for the third unit of B is 9 compared to 8 for the second unit of A. But now, with 1 unit of A and 3 of B, we find she is again indifferent to a second unit of A and a fourth unit of B. So Holly purchases one more unit of each. Marginal utility per dollar is now the same at 8 utils for the last dollar spent on each product, *and* Holly's money income of $10 is exhausted [(2 × $1) + (4 × $2)]. *The utility-maximizing combination of goods attainable by Holly is 2 units of A and 4 of B.*[5] By summing the marginal utility information of columns 2a and 3a we find that Holly is realizing 18 (= 10 + 8) utils of satisfaction from the 2 units of A and 78 (= 24 + 20 + 18 + 16) utils of satisfaction from the 4 units of B. Her $10, optimally spent, yields 96 (= 18 + 78) utils of satisfaction. Table 21-2 summarizes this step-by-step process for maximizing consumer utility and merits your careful study.

Inferior Options There are other combinations of A and B obtainable with $10. But none will yield a level of total utility as high as 2 units of A and 4 of B. For example, 4 units of A and 3 of B can be obtained for $10. However, this combination violates the utility-maximizing rule; total utility here is only 93 utils, clearly inferior to the 96 utils yielded by 2 of A and 4 of B. Furthermore, there are other combinations of A and B (such as 4 of A and 5 of B *or* 1 of A and 2 of B) where the marginal utility of the last dollar spent is

---

[5]To simplify, we assume that Holly spends her entire income; she neither borrows nor saves. Saving can be regarded as a utility-yielding commodity and incorporated in our analysis. It is treated thus in question 4 at the end of the chapter.

the same for both A and B. But all such combinations are either unobtainable with Holly's limited money income (as 4 of A and 5 of B) or fail to exhaust her money income (as 1 of A and 2 of B) and therefore do not yield her the maximum utility attainable.

Problem: Suppose Holly's money income was $14 rather than $10. What now would be the utility-maximizing combination of A and B? Are A and B normal or inferior goods? *(Key Question 4)*

Algebraic Restatement

Our rule merely says that a consumer will maximize her satisfaction when she allocates her money income so that the last dollar spent on product A, the last on product B, and so forth, yield equal amounts of additional, or marginal, utility. Now the marginal utility per dollar spent on A is indicated by MU of product A divided by the price of A (column 2b of Table 21-1) and the marginal utility per dollar spent on B by MU of product B divided by the price of B (column 3b of Table 21-1). Our utility-maximizing rule merely requires that these ratios be equal. That is,

$$\frac{\text{MU of product A}}{\text{price of A}} = \frac{\text{MU of product B}}{\text{price of B}}$$

and, of course, the consumer must exhaust her available income. Our illustration in Table 21-1 shows us that the combination of 2 units of A and 4 of B fulfills these conditions in that

$$\frac{8}{1} = \frac{16}{2}$$

and the consumer's $10 income is spent.

If the equation is not fulfilled, there will be some reallocation of the consumer's expenditures between A and B, from the low to the high marginal-utility-per-dollar product, which will increase the consumer's total utility. For example, if the consumer spent $10 on 4 of A and 3 of B, we would find that

$$\frac{\text{MU of A: 6 utils}}{\text{price of A: \$1}} < \frac{\text{MU of B: 18 utils}}{\text{price of B: \$2}}$$

The last dollar spent on A provides only 6 utils of satisfaction, and the last dollar spent on B provides 9 (= 18 ÷ $2). On a per dollar basis, units of B provide more extra satisfaction than units of A. Hence, the consumer will increase total satisfaction by purchasing more of B and less of A. As dollars are reallocated from A to B, the marginal utility from additional units

of B will decline as the result of moving *down* the diminishing marginal-utility schedule for B, and the marginal utility of A will rise as the consumer moves *up* the diminishing marginal-utility schedule for A. At some new combination of A and B—specifically, 2 of A and 4 of B—the equality of the two ratios and therefore consumer equilibrium will be achieved. As we already know, the net gain in utility is 3 utils (= 96 − 93).

MARGINAL UTILITY AND THE DEMAND CURVE

Once you understand the idea of the utility-maximizing rule it's easy to see why the demand curve is downsloping. Recall that the basic determinants of an individual's demand curve for a specific product are (1) preferences or tastes, (2) money income, and (3) prices of other goods. The utility data of Table 21-1 reflect our consumer's preferences. We continue to suppose that Holly's money income is $10. And, concentrating on the construction of a simple demand curve for product B, we assume that the price of A—representing "other goods"—is $1.

Deriving the Demand Curve   We can now derive a simple demand schedule for B by considering alternative prices at which B might be sold and determining the quantity our consumer will purchase. We have already determined one such price-quantity combination in explaining the utility-maximizing rule: Given tastes, income, and prices of other goods, our rational consumer will purchase 4 units of B at $2. Now assume the price of B falls to $1. The marginal-utility-per-dollar data of column 3b of Table 21-1 will double, because the price of B has been halved; the new data for column 3b are in fact identical to those in column 3a. The purchase of 2 units of A and 4 of B is no longer an equilibrium combination. By applying the same reasoning used to develop the utility-maximizing rule, we now find Holly's utility-maximizing position is 4 units of A and 6 of B. We sketch Holly's demand curve for B as in Table 21-3, confirming a downsloping demand curve.

Income and Substitution Effects Revisited   At the beginning of this chapter we indicated that increased purchases of a good whose price had fallen could be understood in terms of the substitution and income effects. Although our analysis does not let us sort out

TABLE 21-3 The demand schedule for product B

Price per unit of B	Quantity demanded
$2	4
1	6

these two effects quantitatively, we can see intuitively how each is involved in the increased purchase of product B.

The *substitution effect* can be understood by referring back to our utility-maximizing rule. Before the price of B declined, Holly was in equilibrium in that $MU_A(8)/P_A(\$1) = MU_B(16)/P_B(\$2)$, when purchasing 2 units of A and 4 units of B. But after B's price falls from $2 to $1, $MU_A(8)/P_A(\$1) < MU_B(16)/P_B(\$1)$ or, more simply stated, the last dollar spent on B now yields more utility (16 utils) than does the last dollar spent on A (8 utils). This indicates that a switching of expenditures from A to B is needed to restore equilibrium; that is, a *substitution* of now cheaper B for A will occur in the bundle of goods which Holly purchases.

What about the *income effect?* The assumed decline in the price of B from $2 to $1 increases Holly's real income. Before the price decline, Holly was in equilibrium when buying 2 of A and 4 of B. But at the lower $1 price for B, Holly would have to spend only $6 rather than $10 on this same combination of goods. She has $4 left over to spend on more of A, more of B, or more of both. In short, the price decline of B has caused Holly's *real* income to increase so that she can now obtain larger amounts of A and B with the same $10 nominal or *money* income. The portion of the 2-unit increase in her purchase of B due to this increase in real income is the income effect. *(Key Question 5)*

QUICK REVIEW 21-2

■ The theory of consumer behavior assumes that, with limited money incomes and given product prices, consumers make rational choices on the basis of well-defined preferences.

■ A consumer maximizes utility by allocating money income so that the marginal utility per dollar spent is the same for every good purchased.

■ A downsloping demand curve can be derived by changing the price of one product in the consumer-behavior model.

APPLICATIONS AND EXTENSIONS

Many real-world phenomena can be explained by applying the theory of consumer behavior.

The Compact Disc Takeover

It is difficult to realize that compact discs made their American debut as recently as 1983. The CD revolutionized the retail music industry, pushing the vinyl long-playing record to virtual extinction. In 1983 less than 1 million CDs were sold in the United States as compared to almost 210 million LP discs. But by 1992 over 407 million CDs were sold, while the sales of LPs plummeted to less than 3 million. What caused this swift turnabout?

1 Preference Changes The quality of CDs prompted a massive shift of consumer preferences from LPs to CDs. CDs are played with a laser beam, not a phonograph needle, and therefore are virtually impervious to the scratches and wear which plague LPs. CDs also provide a wider range of sound and greater brilliance of tone. They can also hold more than 70 minutes of music. All of these features make CDs preferable to LPs for most consumers.

2 CD Player Prices While prices of CDs themselves have not fallen significantly, prices of CD players have. Costing $1000 or more a decade ago, most players currently sell for under $200. While CDs and LPs are substitute goods, CD players and CDs are clearly complementary goods. The lower prices for players has increased the demand for CDs.

In short, a technologically based change in consumer tastes coupled with a sharp price fall in CD players have revolutionized the retail music market.

The Diamond–Water Paradox

Before economists understood the distinction between total and marginal utility, they were puzzled by the fact that some "essential" goods had much lower prices than other "unimportant" goods. Why would water, essential to life, be priced far below diamonds, whose usefulness is much less?

The paradox is resolved when we first acknowledge that in most places water is in great supply relative to demand—thus, a low price. Diamonds, in contrast, are rare and costly to mine, cut, and polish. Their supply is small relative to demand so their price is high.

Second, our utility-maximizing rule tells us that consumers should purchase any good until the ratio of its marginal utility to price is the same as that ratio for all other goods. Although the *marginal* utility of water may be low because it is plentiful and its price is low, the *total* utility derived from its consumption is exceedingly large because of the great quantity consumed. Conversely, the total utility derived from diamonds is low because the very high price which reflects the scarcity of diamonds causes consumers to purchase relatively few of them. In short, the total utility derived from water is relatively great and the total utility derived from diamonds is relatively small, but it is *marginal* utility which is relevant to the price people are willing to pay for a good. Water yields much more total utility to us than do diamonds, even though the utility of an additional gallon of water is much less than the utility of an additional diamond. Society would gladly give up *all* of the diamonds in the world if that were necessary to obtain *all* of the water in the world. But society would rather have an *additional* diamond than an *additional* gallon of water, given the abundant stock of water available.

The Value of Time

The theory of consumer behavior has been generalized to take the economic value of *time* into account. Both consumption and production activities have a common characteristic—they take time. Time is a valuable economic resource; by working—by using an hour in productive activity—one may earn $6, $10, $50, or more, depending on one's education and skills. By using that hour for leisure or in consumption activities, one incurs the opportunity cost of forgone income; you sacrifice the $6, $10, or $50 you could have earned by working.

Imagine a consumer who is considering the purchase of a round of golf, on the one hand, and a concert, on the other. The market price of the golf game is $15 and the concert is $20. But the golf game is more time-intensive than the concert. Suppose you will spend four hours on the golf course, but only two hours at the concert. If your time is worth $7 per hour —as evidenced by the $7 wage rate you can obtain by working—then the "full price" of the golf game is $43 (the $15 market price *plus* $28 worth of time). Similarly, the "full price" of the concert is $34 (the $20 market price *plus* $14 worth of time). We find that,

contrary to what market prices alone indicate, the "full price" of the concert is really *less* than the "full price" of the golf game.

If we now assume that the marginal utilities derived from successive golf games and concerts are identical, traditional theory would indicate that one should consume more golf games than concerts because the market price of the former is lower ($15) than the latter ($20). But when time is taken into account, the situation is reversed and golf games are more expensive ($43) than concerts ($34). Hence, it is rational in this case to consume more concerts than golf games.

By taking time into account, we can explain certain observable phenomena which traditional theory does not. It may be rational for the unskilled worker or retiree whose time has little or no market value to ride a bus from Peoria to Pittsburgh. But the corporate executive, whose time is very valuable, will find it cheaper to fly, even though bus fare is only a fraction of plane fare. It is sensible for the retiree, living on a modest social security check and having ample time, to spend many hours shopping for bargains. It is equally intelligent for the highly paid physician, working 55 hours per week, to patronize the hospital cafeteria and to buy a new television set over the phone.

People in other nations feel affluent Americans are "wasteful" of food and other material goods, but "overly economical" in the use of time. Americans who visit less developed countries find that time is used casually or "squandered," while material goods are very highly prized and carefully used. These differences are not a paradox or a case of radically different temperaments. The differences are primarily a rational reflection that the high labor productivity characteristic of an advanced society gives time a high market value, whereas the opposite is true in a less developed country.

Buying Medical Care

The way we pay for certain goods and services affects their prices at the time we buy them and significantly alters the amount purchased. Let's go back to Table 21-1. Suppose the $1 price for A is its "true" price or opportunity cost. But now, for some reason, its price is only, say, $.20. How would you respond? Clearly you would buy more than at the $1 price.

Consider medical care. Americans who have health insurance pay a fixed premium once a month

LAST WORD

THE INEFFICIENCY OF CHRISTMAS GIFT-GIVING

The theory of consumer behavior assumes that individual consumers know their preferences better than anyone else. This raises the question as to whether gift-giving—consumer choices rendered by someone other than the ultimate consumer—is inefficient.

A recent study by Yale's Joel Waldfogel[*] suggests that Christmas gift-giving is inefficient to the extent that between a tenth and one-third of the value of those gifts is lost because they do not match their recipients' tastes. Professor Waldfogel surveyed two groups of his students, asking them to compare the estimated price of each Christmas gift with what they would be willing to pay for it. For example, Aunt Flo may have paid $13 for the Barry Manilow CD she gave you, but you would only pay $6.50 for it. Hence, a $6.50 or 50 percent loss of value.

In one of the surveys students estimated that, while family and friends paid an average of $438 for the recipient's total gifts, the recipient students would only be willing to pay $313 for the same gifts, reflecting a value loss of $125. Conclusion: Christmas gift-giving destroyed about one-third of the gift value.

Two other questions were explored. First, does the value loss vary with the social distance between giver and receiver? Second, which givers are most likely to give cash?

On the first question it was found that noncash gifts from more distant relatives such as grandparents, aunts, and uncles entail greater value loss than gifts received from friends, siblings, parents, and "significant others." Furthermore, gifts from grandparents, aunts, and uncles were much more likely to be

*Joel Waldfogel, "The Deadweight Loss of Christmas," *American Economic Review,* December 1993, pp. 1328–1336.

exchanged. The point is that more distant relatives are less likely to be aware of the recipient's consumption preferences.

The answer to the second question entails an off-setting consideration. Many grandparents, aunts, and uncles apparently realize they are uninformed about the receiver's tastes and therefore are more likely to give cash. For example, about 42 percent of grandparents give cash, while only about 10 percent of parents and no "significant others" did so. Cash gifts, of course, can be spent by the recipient as he or she wishes and therefore entail no efficiency loss.

Noting that holiday gift-giving nationwide was estimated to be $38 billion in 1992, Professor Waldfogel calculates an aggregate efficiency loss between $4 and $13 billion.

Conclusions: There is a value loss or inefficiency in noncash gift-giving. Noncash gifts from more distant relatives entail greater value losses than do gifts from those "close" to the recipient. Those more socially distant are more likely to give cash which avoids any value loss.

---

which covers, say, 80 percent of all incurred health care costs. This means that, if you actually need to purchase health care, its price to you will be only 20 percent of the actual market price. What will you do? When ill, you will purchase a great deal more of medical services than if confronted with the full price. Financing health care through insurance is an important factor in explaining soaring absolute expenditures on health care and the growth of such spending as a percent of domestic output (Chapter 35).

The purchase of meals follows similar reasoning.

If you buy a meal at an all-you-can-eat buffet, you will tend to eat more than if you purchased it item by item. Why not eat that second dessert—it's already paid for!

Transfers and Gifts

Government provides eligible households with both *cash transfers* (social security and public assistance) and in-kind or *noncash transfers* which specify particular purchases (food stamps and subsidies for housing and medical care). Most economists believe noncash transfers are less efficient than cash transfers because the specified uses (food, housing, medical care) may not match the recipient's preferences. Stated differently, consumers know their own preferences better than the government.

Look back to Table 21-1. Suppose Holly has zero earned income, but is given the choice of a $2 cash transfer or a noncash transfer of 2 units of A. Because 2 units of A can be bought with $2, these two transfers are of equal monetary value. But by spending the $2 *cash* transfer on the first unit of B, Holly could obtain 24 utils. The *noncash* transfer of the first 2 units of A would only yield 18 (= 10 + 8) units of utility. Conclusion: The noncash transfer is less efficient—it yields less utility—than the cash transfer.

As this chapter's Last Word demonstrates, the same reasoning applies to private gifts. Research suggests that noncash gifts to others entail a substantial efficiency or utility loss.

CHAPTER SUMMARY

1   The law of demand can be explained in terms of the income and substitution effects or the law of diminishing marginal utility.

2   The income effect says that a decline in the price of a product will enable the consumer to buy more of it with a fixed money income. The substitution effect points out that a lower price will make a product relatively more attractive and therefore increase the consumer's willingness to substitute it for other products

3   The law of diminishing marginal utility states that beyond some point, additional units of a specific good will yield declining amounts of extra satisfaction to a consumer.

4   We may assume the typical consumer is rational and acts on the basis of well-defined preferences. Because income is limited and goods have prices, the consumer can-

not purchase all the goods and services he or she might like to have. The consumer should therefore select that attainable combination of goods which will maximize his or her utility or satisfaction.

5   The consumer's utility will be maximized when income is allocated so that the last dollar spent on each product purchased yields the same amount of extra satisfaction. Algebraically, the utility-maximizing rule is fulfilled when

$$\frac{\text{MU of product A}}{\text{price of A}} = \frac{\text{MU of product B}}{\text{price of B}}$$

and the consumer's total income is spent.

6   The utility-maximizing rule and the demand curve are logically consistent. Because marginal utility declines, a lower price is needed to induce the consumer to buy more.

TERMS AND CONCEPTS

income effect	total utility	law of diminishing	utility-maximizing rule
substitution effect	marginal utility	marginal utility	
utility			

QUESTIONS AND STUDY SUGGESTIONS

1   Explain the law of demand through the income and substitution effects, using a price increase as a point of departure for your discussion. Explain the law of demand in terms of diminishing marginal utility.

2   *Key Question*   *Complete the following table.*

Units consumed	Total utility	Marginal utility
0	0	—
1	8	8
2		10
3	25	
4	30	
5		3
6	34	

3   Mrs. Peterson buys loaves of bread and quarts of milk each week at prices of $1 and 80 cents, respectively. At present she is buying these two products in amounts such that the marginal utilities from the last units purchased of the two products are 80 and 70 utils, respectively. Is she buying the utility-maximizing combination of bread and milk? If not, how should she reallocate her expenditures between the two goods?

4   *Key Question*   *Columns 1 through 4 of the accompanying table show the marginal utility, measured in terms of utils, which Ricardo would get by purchasing various amounts of products A, B, C, and D. Column 5 shows the marginal utility Ricardo gets from saving. Assume that the prices of A, B, C, and D are $18, $6, $4, and $24, respectively, and that Ricardo has a money income of $106.*

Column 1		Column 2		Column 3		Column 4		Column 5	
Units of A 18	MU	Units of B 6	MU	Units of C 4	MU	Units of D 24	MU	No. of dollars saved	MU
1	72	1	24	1	15	1	36	1	5
2	54	2	15	2	12	2	30	2	4
3	45	3	12	3	8	3	24	3	3
4	36	4	9	4	7	4	18	4	2
5	27	5	7	5	5	5	13	5	1
6	18	6	5	6	4	6	7	6	$\frac{1}{2}$
7	15	7	2	7	$3\frac{1}{2}$	7	4	7	$\frac{1}{4}$
8	12	8	1	8	3	8	2	8	$\frac{1}{8}$

MONIQUE

a What quantities of A, B, C, and D will ~~Ricardo~~ MONIQUE purchase in maximizing his utility?

b How many dollars will ~~Ricardo~~ MONIQUE choose to save?

c Check your answers by substituting them into the algebraic statement of the utility-maximizing rule.

5 *Key Question* You are choosing between two goods, X and Y, and your marginal utility from each is as shown below. If your income is $9 and the prices of X and Y are $2 and $1, respectively, what quantities of each will you purchase in maximizing utility? Specify the amount of total utility you will realize. Assume that, other things remaining unchanged, the price of X falls to $1. What quantities of X and Y will you now purchase? Using the two prices and quantities for X, derive a demand schedule for X.

Units of X	MU_x	Units of Y	MU_y
1	10	1	8
2	8	2	7
3	6	3	6
4	4	4	5
5	3	5	4
6	2	6	3

6 How can time be incorporated into the theory of consumer behavior? Foreigners frequently point out that Americans are very wasteful of food and other material goods and very conscious of, and overly economical in, their use of time. Can you explain this observation?

7 Explain:

a "Before economic growth, there were too few goods; after growth, there is too little time."

b "It is irrational for an individual to take the time to be completely rational in economic decision making."

8 In the last decade or so there has been a dramatic expansion of small retail convenience stores—such as Kwik Shops, 7-Elevens, Gas 'N Shops—although their prices are generally much higher than those in the large supermarkets. Can you explain their success?

9 "Nothing is more useful than water: but it will purchase scarce any thing; scarce any thing can be had in exchange for it. A diamond, on the contrary, has scarce any value in use; but a very great quantity of goods may frequently be had in exchange for it."[6] Explain.

10 Use the theory of consumer behavior to explain how the purchase of health care through insurance can lead to its overconsumption.

11 **Advanced analysis:** Let $MU_a = z = 10 - x$ and $MU_b = z = 21 - 2y$, where z is marginal utility measured in utils, x is the amount spent on product A, and y is the amount spent on B. Assume the consumer has $10 to spend on A and B; that is, $x + y = 10$. How is the $10 best allocated between A and B? How much utility will the marginal dollar yield?

12 (Last Word) Explain why private and public gift-giving might entail economic inefficiency. Distinguish between cash and noncash gifts in your answer.

[6]Adam Smith, *The Wealth of Nations* (New York: Modern Library, Inc., originally published in 1776), p. 28.

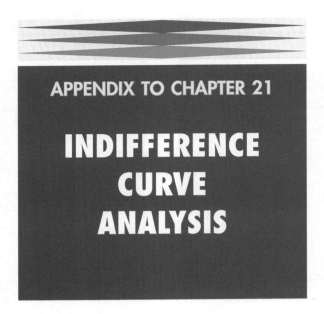

APPENDIX TO CHAPTER 21

INDIFFERENCE CURVE ANALYSIS

A more advanced explanation of consumer behavior and equilibrium is based upon (1) budget lines and (2) indifference curves.

The Budget Line: What Is Attainable

A **budget line** *shows various combinations of two products which can be purchased with a given money income.* If the price of product A is $1.50 and the price of B is $1.00, then the consumer could purchase all the combinations of A and B shown in Table 1 with $12 of money income. At one extreme the consumer might spend all of his or her income on 8 units of A and have nothing left to spend on B. Or, by giving up 2 units of A and thereby "freeing" $3, the consumer could have 6 units of A and 3 of B. And so on to the other extreme, at which the consumer could buy 12 units of B at $1.00 each, spending his or her entire money income on B with nothing left to spend on A.

Figure 1 shows the budget line graphically. The slope of the budget line measures the ratio of the price of B to the price of A; more precisely, the absolute value of the slope is $P_B/P_A = \$1.00/\$1.50 = 2/3$. This is the mathematical way of saying that the consumer must forgo 2 units of A (measured on the vertical axis) at $1.50 each to have $3 to spend on 3 units of B (measured on the horizontal axis). In moving down the budget or price line, 2 of A (at $1.50 each) must be given up to obtain 3 of B (at $1.00 each). This yields a slope of $\frac{2}{3}$.

There are two other characteristics of the budget line you should know about.

1 Income Changes The location of the budget line varies with money income. An *increase* in money income will shift the budget line to the *right;* a *decrease* in money income will move it to the *left.* To verify this, recalculate Table 1 assuming money income is (*a*) $24 and (*b*) $6 and plot the new budget lines in Figure 1.

2 Price Changes A change in product prices will also shift the budget line. A decline in the prices of both products—the equivalent of a real income increase—will shift the curve to the right. You can verify this by recalculating Table 1 and replotting Figure 1 assuming that $P_A = \$.75$ and $P_B = \$.50$. Conversely, an increase in the prices of A and B will shift the curve to the left. Now assume $P_A = \$3$ and $P_B = \$2$ and rework Table 1 and Figure 1 to substantiate this statement.

Note in particular what happens if we change P_B while holding P_A (and money income) constant. You should verify that, if we lower P_B from $1.00 to $.50,

TABLE 1 The budget line: combinations of A and B attainable with an income of $12

Units of A (price = $1.50)	Units of B (price = $1.00)	Total expenditures
8	0	$12 (= $12 + $0)
6	3	$12 (= $9 + $3)
4	6	$12 (= $6 + $6)
2	9	$12 (= $3 + $9)
0	12	$12 (= $0 + $12)

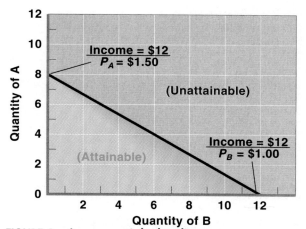

FIGURE 1   A consumer's budget line
The budget line shows all the various combinations of any two products which can be purchased, given the prices of the products and the consumer's money income.

the budget line will fan outward to the right. Conversely, by increasing P_B from \$1.00 to \$1.50, the line will fan inward to the left. In both instances the line remains "anchored" at 8 units on the vertical axis because P_A has not changed.

Indifference Curves: What Is Preferred

Budget lines reflect "objective" market data involving income and prices. The budget line reveals combinations of A and B which are attainable, given money income and prices.

Indifference curves, on the other hand, embody "subjective" information about consumer preferences for A and B. An **indifference curve** *shows all combinations of products A and B which will yield the same total level of satisfaction or utility to the consumer.* Table 2 and Figure 2 present a hypothetical indifference curve for products A and B. The consumer's subjective preferences are such that he or she will realize the same total utility from each combination of A and

TABLE 2   An indifference schedule

Combination	Units of A	Units of B
j	12	2
k	6	4
l	4	6
m	3	8

B shown in the table or curve; hence, the consumer will be indifferent as to which combination is actually obtained.

It is essential to understand several characteristics of indifference curves.

1   Downsloping   Indifference curves are downsloping because both product A and product B yield utility to the consumer. In moving from combination *j* to combination *k,* the consumer obtains more of B, increasing his or her total utility. But because total utility anywhere on the curve is the same, some of A must be taken away to decrease total utility by a precisely offsetting amount. "More of B" necessitates "less of A" so that the quantities of A and B are inversely related. Any curve which reflects inversely related variables is downsloping.

2   Convex to Origin   But, as viewed from the origin, a downsloping curve can be concave (bowed outward) or convex (bowed inward). A concave curve has an increasing (steeper) slope as one moves down the curve, while a convex curve has a diminishing (flatter) slope as one moves down it. (Recall that the production possibilities curve of Figure 2-1 is concave, reflecting the law of increasing opportunity costs.) Note in Figure 2 that *the indifference curve is convex as viewed from the origin.* That is, the slope diminishes or becomes flatter as we move from *j* to *k,* to *l,* to *m,*

FIGURE 2   A consumer's indifference curve
Every point on an indifference curve represents some combination of products A and B which is equally satisfactory to the consumer; that is, each combination of A and B embodies the same level of total utility.

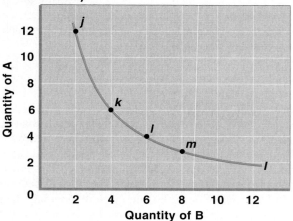

and so on down the curve. Technically, the slope of the indifference curve measures the **marginal rate of substitution** (MRS) because it shows the rate, at the margin, at which the consumer will substitute one good for the other (B for A) to remain equally satisfied. The diminishing slope of the indifference curve means the willingness to substitute B for A *diminishes* as one moves down the curve.

The rationale for this convexity, that is, for a diminishing MRS, is that a consumer's subjective willingness to substitute B for A (or vice versa) will depend on the amounts of B and A he or she has to begin with. Consider Table 2 and Figure 2 again, beginning at point *j*. Here, in relative terms, the consumer has a substantial amount of A and very little of B. This means that "at the margin" B is very valuable (that is, its marginal utility is high), while A is less valuable at the margin (its marginal utility is low). The consumer will then be willing to give up a substantial amount of A to get, say, 2 more units of B. In this case, the consumer is willing to forgo 6 units of A to get 2 more units of B; the MRS is $\frac{6}{2}$, or 3.

But at point *k* the consumer has less A and more B. Here A will be somewhat more valuable, and B less valuable, at the margin. Considering the move from point *k* to point *l*, the consumer is only willing to give up 2 units of A to get 2 more units of B so the MRS is only $\frac{2}{2}$, or 1. Having still less of A and more of B at point *l*, the consumer is only willing to give up 1 unit of A in return for 2 more of B and the MRS falls to $\frac{1}{2}$.

In general, as the amount of B *increases,* the marginal utility of additional units of B *decreases.* Similarly, as the quantity of A *decreases,* its marginal utility *increases.* In Figure 2 we see that in moving down the curve the consumer will be willing to give up smaller and smaller amounts of A to offset acquiring each additional unit of B. The result is a curve with a diminishing slope, a curve which is convex viewed from the origin. The MRS declines as one moves southeast along the indifference curve.

3 Indifference Map The single indifference curve of Figure 2 reflects some constant (but unspecified) level of total utility or satisfaction. It is possible—and useful or our analysis—to sketch a whole series of indifference curves or an **indifference map** as shown in Figure 3. Each curve reflects a different level of total utility. Specifically, each curve to the *right* of our original curve (labeled I_3 in Figure 3) reflects combinations of A and B which yield *more* utility than I_3. Each curve to the *left* of I_3 reflects *less* total util-

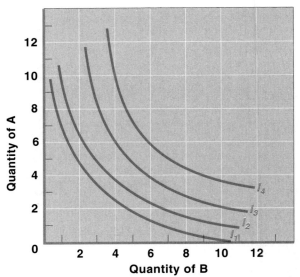

FIGURE 3   An indifference map
An indifference map is comprised of a set of indifference curves. Each successive curve further from the origin indicates a higher level of total utility. That is, any combination of products A and B shown by a point on I_4 is superior to any combination of A and B shown by a point on I_3, I_2, or I_1.

ity than I_3. *As we move out from the origin each successive indifference curve represents a higher level of utility.* This can be demonstrated by drawing a line in a north-easterly direction from the origin and noting that its points of intersection with each successive curve entail larger amounts of *both* A and B and therefore a higher level of total utility.

Equilibrium at Tangency

Noting that the axes of Figures 1 and 3 are identical, we can determine the consumer's **equilibrium position** by combining the budget line and the indifference map as shown in Figure 4. By definition, the budget line indicates all combinations of A and B the consumer can attain, given his or her money income and the prices of A and B. Of these attainable combinations, the consumer will most prefer that combination which yields the greatest satisfaction or utility. Specifically, *the utility-maximizing combination will be the one lying on the highest attainable indifference curve.*

In terms of Figure 4 the consumer's utility-maximizing or equilibrium combination of A and B is at point *X* where the budget line is *tangent* to I_3. Why

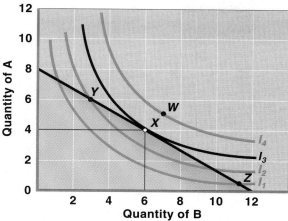

FIGURE 4   **The consumer's equilibrium position**
The consumer's equilibrium position is at point X, where the budget line is tangent to the highest attainable indifference curve, I_3. In this case the consumer will buy 4 units of A at $1.50 per unit and 6 of B at $1 per unit with a $12 money income. Points Z and Y also represent attainable combinations of A and B, but yield less total utility as is evidenced by the fact they are on lower indifference curves. While W would entail more utility than

not point Y? Because Y is on a lower indifference curve, I_2. By trading "down" the budget line—by shifting dollars from purchases of A to purchases of B— the consumer can get on an indifference curve further from the origin and thereby increase total utility from the same income. Why not Z? Same reason: Point Z is on a lower indifference curve, I_1. By trading "up" the budget line—by reallocating dollars from B to A—the consumer can get on higher indifference curve I_3 and increase total utility.

How about point W on indifference curve I_4? While it is true that W would yield a higher level of total utility than X, point W is beyond (outside) the budget line and hence *not* attainable to the consumer. Point X is the best or optimal *attainable* combination of products A and B. At this point we note that, by definition of tangency, the slope of the highest attainable indifference curve equals the slope of the budget line. Because the slope of the indifference curve reflects the MRS and the slope of the budget line is P_B/P_A, the optimal or equilibrium position is where

$$\text{MRS} = \frac{P_B}{P_A}$$

Appendix Key Question 3 is recommended at this point.

The Measurement of Utility

There is an important difference between the marginal-utility theory and the indifference curve theory of consumer demand. The marginal-utility theory assumes that utility is *numerically* measurable. The consumer is assumed to be able to say *how much* extra utility he or she derives from an extra unit of A or B. Given the prices of A and B, the consumer must be able to measure the marginal utility derived from successive units of A and B to realize the utility-maximizing (equilibrium) position as indicated by

$$\frac{\text{Marginal utility of A}}{\text{price of A}} = \frac{\text{marginal utility of B}}{\text{price of B}}$$

The indifference curve approach poses a less stringent requirement for the consumer: He or she need only specify whether a given combination of A and B yields more, less, or the same amount of utility than some other combination of A and B. The consumer need only say, for example, that 6 of A and 7 of B yield more (or less) satisfaction than 4 of A and 9 of B; indifference curve analysis does *not* require the consumer to specify *how much* more (or less) satisfaction will be realized.

When the equilibrium situations in the two approaches are compared we find that (1) in the indifference curve analysis the MRS equals P_B/P_A; however, (2) in the marginal-utility approach the ratio of marginal utilities equals P_B/P_A. We therefore deduce that the MRS is equivalent in the marginal-utility approach to the ratio of marginal utilities of the two goods.[7]

Deriving the Demand Curve

We noted earlier that, given the price of A, an increase in the price of B will cause the budget line to fan inward to the left. This fact can be used to derive a demand curve for product B. In Figure 5a we reproduce Figure 4 as showing our initial consumer equilibrium at point X. The budget line in determining this equilibrium position assumes a money income of $12 and that $P_A = \$1.50$ and $P_B = \$1.00$. Let's examine what happens to the equilibrium position if we increase P_B

---

[7]Technical footnote: If we begin with the utility-maximizing rule, $MU_A/P_A = MU_B/P_B$, then multiply through by P_B and divide through by MU_A, we obtain $P_B/P_A = MU_B/MU_A$. In indifference curve analysis we know that the optimal or equilibrium position is where $\text{MRS} = P_B/P_A$. Hence, MRS also equals MU_B/MU_A.

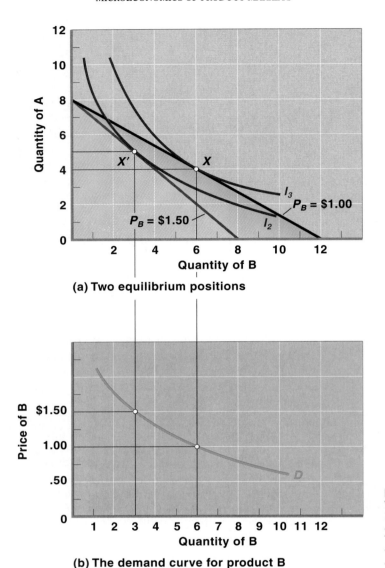

(a) Two equilibrium positions

(b) The demand curve for product B

FIGURE 5 **Deriving the demand curve**
When the price of B is increased from $1.00 to $1.50 in (a) the equilibrium position moves from *X* to *X'*, decreasing the quantity of B demanded from 6 to 3 units. The demand curve for B is determined in (b) by plotting the $1.00–6 units and the $1.50–3 units price-quantity combinations for B.

to $1.50, holding money income and the price of A constant.

The result is shown in Figure 5a. The budget line fans to the left, yielding a new equilibrium point of tangency with lower indifference curve I_2 at point X'. At X' the consumer is buying 3 units of B and 5 of A compared to 4 of A and 6 of B at X. Our interest is in B and we note that we have sufficient information to locate the demand curve for product B. We know that at equilibrium point X the price of B is $1.00 and 6 units are purchased; at equilibrium point X' the price of B is $1.50 and 3 units are purchased.

These data are shown graphically as a demand curve for B in Figure 5b. Note that the horizontal axes of Figure 5a and b are identical; both measure the quantity demanded of B. We can therefore drop perpendiculars from Figure 5a down to the horizontal axis of Figure 5b. On the vertical axis of Figure 5b we locate the two chosen prices of B. Connecting these prices with the relevant quantities demanded, we locate two points on the demand curve for B. By simple manipulation of the price of B in an indifference curve–budget line context, a downsloping demand curve for B can be derived. We have derived the law of demand assuming "other things equal" since *only* the price of B has been changed. The price of A as well as the consumer's income and tastes have re-

mained constant when deriving the consumer's demand curve for product B.

APPENDIX SUMMARY

1   The indifference curve approach to consumer behavior is based on the consumer's budget line and indifference curves.
2   The budget line shows all combinations of two products which the consumer can purchase, given money income and product prices.
3   A change in product prices or money income will shift the budget line.
4   An indifference curve shows all combinations of two products which will yield the same level of total utility to the consumer. Indifference curves are downsloping and convex to the origin.

5   An indifference map consists of a number of indifference curves; the further from the origin, the higher the level of total utility associated with each curve.
6   The consumer will select that point on the budget line which puts him or her on the highest attainable indifference curve.
7   Changing the price of one product shifts the budget line and determines a new equilibrium position. A downsloping demand curve can be determined by plotting the price-quantity combinations associated with old and new equilibrium positions.

APPENDIX TERMS AND CONCEPTS

budget line
indifference curve

marginal rate of
substitution

indifference map
equilibrium position

APPENDIX QUESTIONS AND STUDY SUGGESTIONS

1   What information is embodied in a budget line? What shifts will occur in the budget line when money income   a increases and   b decreases? What shifts will occur in the budget line as the price of the product shown on the horizontal axis   a increases and   b decreases?

2   What information is contained in an indifference curve? Why are such curves   a downsloping and   b convex to the origin? Why does total utility increase as the consumer moves to indifference curves further from the origin? Why can't indifference curves intersect?

3   *Appendix Key Question   Using Figure 4, explain why the point of tangency of the budget line with an indifference curve is the consumer's equilibrium position. Explain why any point where the budget line intersects an indifference curve will not be equilibrium. Explain: "The consumer is in equilibrium where MRS = P_B/P_A."*

4   Assume that the data in the accompanying table indi-

cate an indifference curve for Mr. Chen. Graph this curve, putting A on the vertical and B on the horizontal axis. Assuming the prices of A and B are $1.50 and $1.00, respectively, and that Chen has $24 to spend, add the resulting budget line to your graph. What combination of A and B will Chen purchase? Does your answer meet the MRS = P_B/P_A rule for equilibrium?

Units of A	Units of B
16	6
12	8
8	12
4	24

5   Explain graphically how indifference analysis can be used to derive a demand curve.

6   **Advanced analysis:** Demonstrate that the equilibrium condition MRS = P_B/P_A is the equivalent of the utility-maximizing rule $MU_A/P_A = MU_B/P_B$.

THE COSTS OF PRODUCTION

Product prices are determined by the interaction of demand and supply. In preceding chapters we examined factors underlying demand. As observed in Chapter 3, the basic factor underlying the ability and willingness of firms to supply a product is the cost of production. Production of any good requires economic resources which, because of their relative scarcity, bear price tags. The amount of any product a firm is willing to supply depends on the prices (costs) and the productivity of the resources essential to its production, on the one hand, and the price the product will bring in the market, on the other.

This chapter considers the general nature of production costs. Product prices are introduced in the following chapters, and supply decisions of producers are then explained.

ECONOMIC COSTS

Costs exist because resources are scarce and have alternative uses. To use a bundle of resources in producing some particular good means that certain alternative production opportunities have been forgone. *Costs in economics deal with forgoing the opportunity to produce alternative goods and services.* The **economic cost,** or **opportunity cost,** of any resource in producing a good is its value or worth in its best alternative use.

This concept of costs can be seen in the production possibilities curve of Chapter 2. At point *C* in Table 2-1 the opportunity cost in real terms of producing 100,000 *more* pizzas is the 3,000 industrial robots which must be forgone. The steel used for armaments is not available for manufacturing automobiles or constructing apartment buildings. And if an assembly-line worker can produce automo-

biles or washing machines, then the cost to society in employing this worker in an automobile plant is the contribution the worker would otherwise have made in producing washing machines. The cost to you in reading this chapter is the alternative uses of your time—studying for a biology exam or going to a movie—which you must forgo while you read it.

Explicit and Implicit Costs

Let's now consider costs from the firm's viewpoint. Keeping in mind the notion of opportunity costs, we can say that *economic costs are those payments a firm must make, or incomes it must provide, to resource suppliers to attract these resources away from alternative production opportunities.* These payments or incomes may be either explicit or implicit.

The monetary payments—the "out-of-pocket" or cash expenditures a firm makes to "outsiders" who supply labor services, materials, fuel, transportation services, and power—are called **explicit costs.** Explicit costs are payments to nonowners of the firm for the resources they supply.

But, in addition, a firm may use certain resources the firm itself owns. Our concept of opportunity costs tells us that, regardless of whether a resource is owned or hired by an enterprise, there is a cost involved in using that resource in a specific employment. The costs of such self-owned, self-employed resources are nonexpenditure or **implicit costs.** To the firm, those implicit costs are the money payments the self-employed resources could have earned in their best alternative employments.

Example: Suppose you are earning $20,000 a year as a sales representative for a compact disc manufacturer. You decide to open a store to sell CDs at the retail level. You invest $20,000 in savings which has been earning you $1000 per year. Also, you decide your new firm will occupy a small store which you own and have been renting out for $5000 per year. One clerk is hired to help you in the store.

After a year's operations you total up your accounts and find the following:

Total sales revenue		$120,000
Cost of CDs......................	$40,000	
Clerk's salary..................	20,000	
Utilities	5,000	
Total (explicit) costs...		65,000
Accounting profit...		55,000

But this accounting profit does not accurately reveal the economic status of your venture because it ignores implicit costs. What is economically significant is the total amount of resources used (as opposed to dollars expended) in your enterprise. By providing your own financial capital, building, and labor, you are entailing implicit costs or forgone incomes of $1000 in interest, $5000 in rent, and $20,000 in wages. Also, suppose that your entrepreneurial talent is worth $5000 annually in other business endeavors of similar scope. Thus:

Accounting profit...		$55,000
Forgone interest	$ 1,000	
Forgone rent	5,000	
Forgone wages	20,000	
Forgone entrepreneurial income ..	5,000	
Total implicit costs...		31,000
Economic profit...		24,000

Normal Profits as a Cost

The $5000 minimum payment required to keep your entrepreneurial talents engaged in this enterprise is called a **normal profit.** As is true of implicit rent or implicit wages, your normal return for performing entrepreneur functions is an implicit cost. If this minimum, or normal, return is not realized, you will withdraw your efforts from this line of production and reallocate them to a more attractive line of production. Or you may cease being an entrepreneur, collect your $1000 interest per year, rent your store for $5000, and become a $20,000 wage or salary earner.

The economist includes as costs all payments—explicit and implicit, the latter including a normal profit—required to attract and retain resources in a specific line of production.

Economic, or Pure, Profits

Economists and accountants use the term "profits" differently. *Accounting profits are the firm's total revenue less its explicit costs.* But economists define profits in another way. **Economic profits** *are total revenue less all costs (explicit and implicit, the latter including a normal profit to the entrepreneur).* Therefore, when an economist says a firm is just covering its costs, it means all explicit and implicit costs are being met and the entrepreneur is receiving a return just large enough to retain his or her talents in the present line of production.

If a firm's total revenue exceeds all its economic costs, any residual goes to the entrepreneur. This residual is called an *economic,* or *pure, profit.* In short:

$$\text{Economic profit} = \text{total revenue} - \text{opportunity cost of all inputs}$$

In our example, this economic profit is $24,000 (= $120,000 − $96,000). An economic profit is not a cost, because by definition it is a return in excess of the normal profit required to retain the entrepreneur in this particular line of production. Even if the economic profit is zero, the entrepreneur is still covering all explicit and implicit costs, including a normal profit. In our example, so long as accounting profits are $31,000 or more (economic profits zero or more), you will be earning the $5000 normal profit and will continue to operate your CD store.

Figure 22-1 shows the relationship among various cost and profit concepts. From our example, pen-

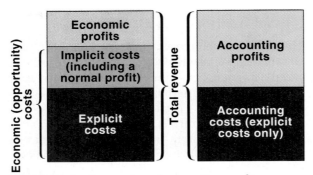

FIGURE 22-1   Economic and accounting profits
Economic profits are equal to total revenue less opportunity costs. Opportunity costs are the sum of explicit and implicit costs and include a normal profit to the entrepreneur. Accounting profits are equal to total revenue less accounting (explicit) costs.

cil in the various cost data in the appropriate blocks. (*Key Question 2*)

Short Run and Long Run

The costs a firm or industry incurs in producing any specific output will depend on the adjustments it can make in the amounts of the various resources it employs. The quantities employed of many resources—most labor, raw materials, fuel, and power—can be varied easily and quickly. Other resources require more time for adjustment. The capacity of a manufacturing plant, that is, the size of the factory building and the amount of machinery and equipment therein, can only be varied over a considerable period of time. In some heavy industries it may take several years to alter plant capacity.

Short Run: Fixed Plant   Because of these differences in time necessary to vary quantities of various resources used in production, we need to distinguish between the short run and the long run. The **short run** is a period of time too brief for an enterprise to alter its plant capacity, yet long enough to permit a change in the level at which the fixed plant is used. The firm's plant capacity is fixed in the short run, but output can be varied by applying larger or smaller amounts of labor, materials, and other resources to that plant. Existing plant capacity can be used more or less intensively in the short run.

Long Run: Variable Plant   From the viewpoint of existing firms, the **long run** is a period extensive enough for these firms to change the quantities of *all*

resources employed, including plant capacity. From the industry's viewpoint, the long run also encompasses enough time for existing firms to dissolve and leave the industry or for new firms to be created and enter the industry. *While the short run is a "fixed-plant" period, the long run is a "variable-plant" period.*

Illustrations   If a General Motors plant hired 100 extra workers or added an entire shift of workers, this would be a short-run adjustment. If the same GM plant added a new wing to its building and installed more equipment, this would be a long-run adjustment.

Note that the short run and the long run are *conceptual* rather than specific calendar time periods. In light manufacturing industries, changes in plant capacity may be negotiated almost overnight. A small T-shirt firm can increase its plant capacity in a few days or less by ordering and installing a couple of new cutting tables and several extra sewing machines. But heavy industry is a different story. It may take Exxon several years to construct a new oil refinery.

QUICK REVIEW 22-1

■ Explicit costs are money payments a firm makes to outside suppliers of resources; implicit costs are the opportunity costs associated with a firm's use of resources it owns.

■ Economic profits are total revenue less all explicit and implicit costs, including a normal profit.

■ In the short run a firm's plant capacity is fixed; in the long run a firm can vary its plant size.

SHORT-RUN PRODUCTION COSTS

A firm's costs of producing any output will depend not only on prices of needed resources, but also on technology—the quantity of resources it takes to produce that output. It is the technological aspect of costs which we now consider. In the short run a firm can change its output by adding variable resources to a fixed plant. But how does output change as more and more variable resources are added to the firm's fixed resources?

Law of Diminishing Returns

The answer is provided in general terms by the **law of diminishing returns,** also called the "law of diminishing marginal product" and the "law of variable proportions." This law states that *as successive units of a variable resource (say, labor) are added to a fixed resource (say, capital or land), beyond some point the extra, or marginal, product attributable to each additional unit of the variable resource will decline.* If additional workers are applied to a constant amount of capital equipment, as is the case in the short run, output will eventually rise by smaller and smaller amounts as more workers are employed.

Rationale   Suppose a farmer has a fixed amount of land—80 acres—planted in corn. If the farmer does not cultivate the cornfields (clear the weeds) at all, the yield will be 40 bushels per acre. If the land is cultivated once, output may rise to 50 bushels per acre. A second cultivation may increase output to 57 bushels per acre, a third to 61, and a fourth to 63. Further cultivations will add little or nothing to total output. Successive cultivations add less and less to the land's yield. If this were not so, the world's needs for corn could be fulfilled by extremely intense cultivation of this single 80-acre plot of land. Indeed, if diminishing returns did not occur, the world could be fed out of a flowerpot.

The law of diminishing returns also holds true in nonagricultural industries. Assume a small planing mill is manufacturing wood furniture frames. It has a specific amount of equipment—lathes, planers, saws, sanders. If this firm hired just one or two workers, total output and productivity (output per worker) would be very low. These workers would perform many different jobs, and the advantages of specialization would be lost. Time would also be lost in switching from one job to another, and machines would stand idle much of the time. In short, the plant would be understaffed, and production inefficient because there is too much capital relative to labor.

These difficulties would disappear as more workers were added. Equipment would be more fully used, and workers could now specialize on a single job. Time would no longer be lost from job switching. Thus, as more workers are added to the initially understaffed plant, the extra or marginal product of each will rise due to more efficient production.

But this cannot go on indefinitely. As still more workers are added, problems of overcrowding will arise. Workers must wait in line to use the machinery, so now *workers* will be underused. Total output increases at a diminishing rate because, with the fixed plant size, each worker will have less capital equipment to work with as more and more labor is hired.

The extra, or marginal, product of additional workers declines because the plant is more intensively staffed. There will be more labor in proportion to the fixed amount of capital goods. In the extreme case, the continuous addition of labor to the plant would use up all standing room, and production would be brought to a standstill.

Note that the law of diminishing returns assumes all units of variable inputs—workers in this case—are of equal quality. Each successive worker is presumed to have the same innate ability, motor coordination, education, training, and work experience. Marginal product ultimately diminishes, not because successive workers are qualitatively inferior, but because more workers are being used relative to the amount of plant and equipment available.

Numerical Example   Table 22-1 presents a numerical illustration of the law of diminishing returns. Column 2 indicates the **total product** resulting from combining each level of labor input in column 1 with a fixed amount of capital goods.

Marginal product, column 3, shows the *change* in total output associated with each additional input of labor. Note that with no labor inputs, total product is zero; a plant with no workers in it will yield no output. The first two workers reflect increasing returns, their marginal products being 10 and 15 units, respectively. But then, beginning with the third worker, marginal product—the increase in total product—diminishes continuously and actually becomes zero with the eighth worker and negative with the ninth.

Average product or output per worker (also called "labor productivity") is shown in column 4. It is calculated by dividing total product (column 2) by the number of workers that produced it (column 1).

Graphical Portrayal   Figure 22-2a and b (Key Graph) shows the law of diminishing returns graphically and will help you understand the relationships between total, marginal, and average product. Note first that total product goes through three phases: It rises initially at an increasing rate; then it increases but at a decreasing rate; finally it reaches a maximum and declines.

Geometrically, marginal product is the slope of the total product curve. Marginal product measures the changes in total product associated with each successive worker. Thus, the three phases of total product are also reflected in marginal product. Where total product is increasing at an increasing rate,

KEY GRAPH

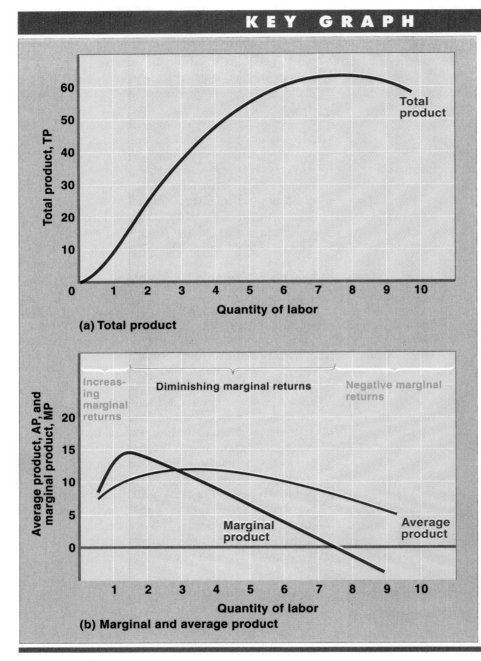

(a) Total product

(b) Marginal and average product

FIGURE 22-2 The law of diminishing returns
As a variable resource (labor) is added to fixed amounts of other resources (land or capital), the resulting total product will eventually increase by diminishing amounts, reach a maximum, and then decline as in (a). Marginal product in (b) reflects the changes in total product associated with each input of labor. Average product is simply output per worker. Note that marginal product intersects average product at the maximum average product.

marginal product is necessarily rising. Here extra workers are adding larger and larger amounts to total product. Similarly, where total product is increasing but at a decreasing rate, marginal product is positive but falling. Each additional worker adds less to total product than did preceding workers. When total product is at a maximum, marginal product is zero. When total product declines, marginal product becomes negative.

Average product also reflects the same general "increasing-maximum-diminishing" relationship between variable inputs of labor and output as does mar-

TABLE 22-1   **The law of diminishing returns**

(1) Inputs of the variable resource (labor)	(2) Total product	(3) Marginal product $\Delta 2/\Delta 1$	(4) Average product (2)/(1)
0	0		—
1	10	10 ⎫ Increasing	10
2	25	15 ⎭ marginal returns	$12\frac{1}{2}$
3	37	12	$12\frac{1}{3}$
4	47	10	$11\frac{3}{4}$
5	55	8 ⎬ Diminishing marginal returns	11
6	60	5	10
7	63	3	9
8	63	0 ⎫ Negative	$7\frac{7}{8}$
9	62	−1 ⎭ marginal returns	$6\frac{8}{9}$

ginal product. But note the relationship between marginal product and average product: Where marginal product exceeds average product, average product will rise. And wherever marginal product is less than average product, average product must be declining. It follows that marginal product intersects average product where average product is at a maximum.

This relationship is a mathematical necessity. If you add a number to a total which is greater than the current average of that total, the average must rise. And if you add a number to a total which is less than the current average of that total, the average falls. You raise your average course grade only when your score on an additional (marginal) examination is greater than the average of all your past scores. If your grade on an additional exam is below your current average, your average will be pulled down. In our production example, so long as the amount an additional worker adds to total product exceeds the average product or "productivity" of all workers already employed, average product will rise. Conversely, when an extra worker adds an amount to the total product which is less than the present average product, then that worker will lower average product or "productivity."

The law of diminishing returns is embodied in the shapes of all three curves. But, as our earlier definition of the law of diminishing returns indicates, economists are most concerned with marginal product. The stages of increasing, diminishing, and negative marginal product (returns) are shown in Figure 22-2b. Glancing up at columns 1 and 3 of Table 22-1, we observe increasing returns for the first two workers, decreasing returns for workers 3 through 8, and negative returns for the ninth worker. *(Key Question 4)*

Fixed, Variable, and Total Costs

The production data described by the law of diminishing returns must be coupled with resource prices to determine the total and per unit costs of producing various levels of output. We know that in the short run some resources—those associated with the firm's plant—are fixed. Others are variable. This means that in the short run costs can be classified as either fixed or variable.

Fixed Costs   **Fixed costs** *are those costs which in total do not vary with changes in output.* Fixed costs are associated with the very existence of a firm's plant and therefore must be paid even if its output is zero. Such costs as interest on a firm's bonded indebtedness, rental payments, a portion of depreciation on equipment and buildings, insurance premiums, and the salaries of top management and key personnel are generally fixed costs. In column 2 of Table 22-2 we assume that the firm's total fixed costs are $100. By definition, this fixed-cost prevails at all levels of output, including zero. Fixed costs cannot be avoided in the short run.

Variable Costs   **Variable costs** *are those costs which change with the level of output.* They include payments for materials, fuel, power, transportation services,

MICROECONOMICS OF PRODUCT MARKETS

TABLE 22-2 Total-, average-, and marginal-cost schedules for an individual firm in the short run

Total-cost data				Average-cost data			
(1) Total product (Q)	(2) Total fixed cost (TFC)	(3) Total variable cost (TVC)	(4) Total cost (TC) $TC = TFC + TVC$	(5) Average fixed cost (AFC) $AFC = \dfrac{TFC}{Q}$	(6) Average variable cost (AVC) $AVC = \dfrac{TVC}{Q}$	(7) Average total cost (ATC) $ATC = \dfrac{TC}{Q}$	(8) Marginal cost (MC) $MC = \dfrac{\text{change in } TC}{\text{change in } Q}$
0	$100	$ 0	$ 100				
1	100	90	190	$100.00	$90.00	$190.00	$ 90
2	100	170	270	50.00	85.00	135.00	80
3	100	240	340	33.33	80.00	113.33	70
4	100	300	400	25.00	75.00	100.00	60
5	100	370	470	20.00	74.00	94.00	70
6	100	450	550	16.67	75.00	91.67	80
7	100	540	640	14.29	77.14	91.43	90
8	100	650	750	12.50	81.25	93.75	110
9	100	780	880	11.11	86.67	97.78	130
10	100	930	1030	10.00	93.00	103.00	150

most labor, and similar variable resources. In column 3 of Table 22-2 we find that the total of variable costs changes directly with output. But note that *the increases in variable costs associated with each one-unit increase in output are not constant.* As production begins, variable costs will for a time increase by a *decreasing* amount; this is true through the fourth unit of output. Beyond the fourth unit, however, variable costs rise by *increasing* amounts for each successive unit of output.

The reason for this lies in the law of diminishing returns. Because of increasing marginal product, smaller and smaller increases in the amounts of variable resources will be needed for a time to get each successive unit of output produced. Because all units of the variable resources are priced the same, total variable costs will increase by decreasing amounts. But when marginal product begins to decline as diminishing returns are encountered, larger and larger additional amounts of variable resources are needed to produce each successive unit of output. Total variable costs will therefore increase by increasing amounts.

Total Cost **Total cost** is the *sum of fixed and variable costs at each level of output.* It is shown in column

4 of Table 22-2. At zero units of output, total cost is equal to the firm's fixed costs. Then for each unit of production—1 through 10—total cost varies by the same amounts as does variable cost.

Figure 22-3 shows graphically the fixed-, variable-, and total-cost data of Table 22-2. Note that total variable cost is measured vertically from the horizontal axis and total fixed cost is added vertically to total variable cost in locating the total-cost curve.

The distinction between fixed and variable costs is significant to the business manager. Variable costs can be controlled or altered in the short run by changing production levels. Fixed costs are beyond the business executive's present control; they are incurred in the short run and must be paid regardless of output level.

Per Unit, or Average, Costs

Producers are certainly interested in their total costs, but they are equally concerned with *per unit,* or *average, costs.* In particular, average-cost data are more meaningful for making comparisons with product price, which is always stated on a per unit basis. Average fixed cost, average variable cost, and average total cost are shown in columns 5 to 7 of Table 22-2.

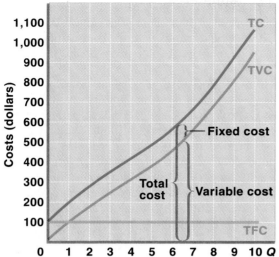

FIGURE 22-3 Total cost is the sum of fixed and variable costs
Total variable costs (TVC) change with output. Fixed costs are independent of the level of output. The total cost (TC) of any output is the vertical sum of the fixed and variable costs of that output.

Let's see how these unit-cost figures are derived and how they vary as output changes.

1 AFC **Average fixed cost** (AFC) for any output is found by dividing total fixed cost (TFC) by that output (Q). That is,

$$AFC = \frac{TFC}{Q}$$

While total fixed costs are, by definition, independent of output, AFC will decline so long as output increases. As output increases, a given total fixed cost of $100 is being spread over a larger and larger output. When output is just 1 unit, total fixed costs and AFC are equal at $100. But at 2 units of output, total fixed costs of $100 become $50 worth of fixed costs per unit; then $33.33, as $100 is spread over 3 units; and $25, when spread over 4 units. This is commonly referred to as "spreading the overhead." We find in Figure 22-4 that AFC graphs as a continually declining curve as total output is increased.

2 AVC **Average variable cost** (AVC) for any output is calculated by dividing total variable cost (TVC) by that output (Q):

$$AVC = \frac{TVC}{Q}$$

AVC declines initially, reaches a minimum, and then increases again. Graphically, this is a U-shaped or saucer-shaped AVC curve, as shown in Figure 22-4.

Because total variable cost reflects the law of diminishing returns, so must the AVC figures, which are derived from total variable cost. Due to increasing returns, it takes fewer and fewer additional variable resources to produce each of the first 4 units of output. As a result, variable cost per unit will decline. AVC hits a minimum with the fifth unit of output, and beyond this point AVC rises as diminishing returns require more and more variable resources to produce each additional unit of output.

In simpler terms, at low levels of output production will be relatively inefficient and costly, because the firm's fixed plant is understaffed. Not enough variable resources are being combined with the firm's plant; production is inefficient, and per unit variable costs are therefore relatively high. As output expands, however, greater specialization and better utilization of the firm's capital equipment will yield more efficiency, and variable cost per unit of output will decline. As more variable resources are added, a point will be reached where diminishing returns are incurred. The firm's capital equipment will now be staffed more intensively, and therefore each added input will not increase output by as much as preceding inputs. This means AVC will eventually increase.

You can verify the U or saucer shape of the AVC curve by returning to Table 22-1. Assume the price

FIGURE 22-4 **The average-cost curves**
AFC falls as a given amount of fixed costs is apportioned over a larger and larger output. AVC initially falls because of increasing marginal returns but then rises because of diminishing marginal returns. Average total cost (ATC) is the vertical sum of average variable cost (AVC) and average fixed cost (AFC).

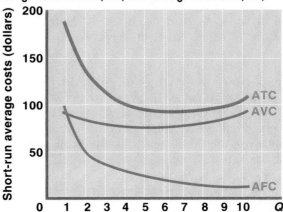

of labor is $10 per unit. By dividing average product (output per worker) into $10 (price per worker), you will determine labor cost per unit of output. Because we have assumed labor to be the only variable input, labor cost per unit of output is variable cost per unit of output or AVC. When average product is initially low, AVC will be high. As workers are added, average product rises and AVC falls. When average product is at its maximum, AVC will be at its minimum. Then, as still more workers are added and average product declines, AVC will rise. The "hump" of the average-product curve is reflected in the saucer or U shape of the AVC curve. A glance ahead at Figure 22-6 will confirm this graphically.

3 ATC Average total cost (ATC) for any output is found by dividing total cost (TC) by that output (Q) or by adding AFC and AVC at that level of output:

$$ATC = \frac{TC}{Q} = AFC + AVC$$

These data are shown in column 7 of Table 22-2. Graphically ATC is found by adding vertically the AFC and AVC curves, as in Figure 22-4. Thus the vertical distance between the ATC and AVC curves measures AFC at any level of output.

Marginal Cost

One final and very crucial cost concept remains—marginal cost. **Marginal cost** (MC) *is the extra, or additional, cost of producing one more unit of output.* MC can be determined for each additional unit of output by noting the *change* in total cost which that unit's production entails.

$$MC = \frac{\text{change in TC}}{\text{change in } Q}$$

Our data are structured so that the "change in Q" is always "1," so we have defined MC as the cost of *one* more unit of output.

Calculations In column 4 of Table 22-2, production of the first unit of output increases total cost from $100 to $190. Therefore, the additional, or marginal, cost of that first unit is $90 (column 8). The marginal cost of the second unit is $80 (= $270 − $190); the MC of the third is $70 (= $340 − $270); and so forth. MC for each of the 10 units of output is shown in column 8.

MC can also be calculated from the total-variable-cost column because the only difference between to-

tal cost and total variable cost is the constant amount of fixed costs ($100). Thus, the *change* in total cost and the *change* in total variable cost associated with each additional unit of output are always the same.

Marginal Decisions Marginal cost designates those costs which the firm can directly and immediately control. Specifically, MC indicates those costs incurred in producing the last unit of output and, simultaneously, the cost which can be "saved" by reducing total output by the last unit. Average-cost figures do *not* provide this information. For example, suppose the firm is undecided whether to produce 3 or 4 units of output. At 4 units Table 22-2 indicates that ATC is $100. But the firm does not increase its total costs by $100 by producing, nor does it "save" $100 by not producing, the fourth unit. Rather, the change in costs involved here is only $60, as the MC column of Table 22-2 reveals.

A firm's decisions regarding what output level to produce are typically marginal decisions, that is, decisions to produce a few more or a few less units. Marginal cost is the change in costs to produce one more or one less unit of output. When coupled with marginal revenue (which we will find in Chapter 23 indicates the change in revenue from one more or one less unit of output) marginal cost allows a firm to determine if it is profitable to expand or contract its production level. The analysis in the next four chapters centers on these marginal calculations.

Graphical Portrayal Marginal cost is shown graphically in Figure 22-5 (Key Graph). Marginal cost declines sharply, reaches a minimum, and then rises rather abruptly. This mirrors the fact that variable cost, and therefore total cost, increases first by decreasing amounts and then by increasing amounts (see Figure 22-3 and columns 3 and 4 of Table 22-2).

MC and Marginal Product The marginal-cost curve's shape is a reflection of, and the consequence of, the law of diminishing returns. The relationship between marginal product and marginal cost can be seen by looking back to Table 22-1. If each successive unit of a variable resource (labor) is hired at a constant price, the marginal cost of each extra unit of output will *fall* so long as the marginal product of each additional worker is *rising*. This is so because marginal cost is the (constant) price or cost of an extra worker divided by his or her marginal product. Hence, in Table 22-1, suppose each worker can be hired for

KEY GRAPH

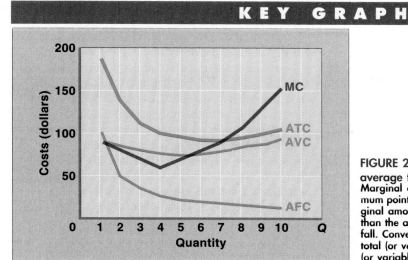

FIGURE 22-5 The relationship of marginal cost to average total cost and average variable cost Marginal cost (MC) cuts both ATC and AVC at their minimum points. This is so because whenever the extra or marginal amount added to total cost (or variable cost) is less than the average of that cost, the average will necessarily fall. Conversely, whenever the marginal amount added to total (or variable) cost is greater than the average of total (or variable) cost, the average must rise.

$10. Because the first worker's marginal product is 10 and hiring this worker increases the firm's costs by $10, the marginal cost of each of these 10 extra units of output will be $1 (= $10 ÷ 10). The second worker also increases costs by $10, but the marginal product is 15, so that the marginal cost of each of these 15 extra units of output is $.67 (= $10 ÷ 15). In general, so long as marginal product is rising, marginal cost will be falling.

But as diminishing returns set in—in this case, with the third worker—marginal cost will begin to rise. Thus, for the third worker, marginal cost is $.83 (= $10 ÷ 12); $1.00 for the fourth worker; $1.25 for the fifth; and so on. *Assuming a constant price (cost) of the variable resource, increasing returns will be reflected in a declining marginal cost and diminishing returns in a rising marginal cost.* The MC curve is a mirror reflection of the marginal product curve. As seen in Figure 22-6, when marginal product is rising, marginal cost is necessarily falling. When marginal product is at its maximum, marginal cost is at its minimum. And when marginal product is falling, marginal cost is rising.

Relation of MC to AVC and ATC

The marginal cost curve intersects both the AVC and ATC curves at their minimum points. As noted earlier, this marginal-average relationship is a mathematical necessity, which a simple illustration will reveal. Suppose a professional baseball pitcher has allowed his opponents an aver-

age of 3 runs per game in the first three games he has pitched. Now, whether his average falls or rises as a result of pitching a fourth (marginal) game will depend on whether the additional runs he allows in that extra game are fewer or more than his current 3-run average. If he allows fewer than 3 runs—for example, 1—in the fourth game, his total runs will rise from 9 to 10, and his average will fall from 3 to $2\frac{1}{2}$ (= 10 ÷ 4). Conversely, if he allows more than 3 runs—say, 7—in the fourth game, his total will increase from 9 to 16 and his average will rise from 3 to 4 (= 16 ÷ 4).

So it is with costs. When the amount added to total cost (marginal cost) is less than the average of total cost, ATC will fall. Conversely, when marginal cost exceeds ATC, ATC will rise. This means in Figure 22-5 that so long as MC lies below ATC, ATC will fall, and where MC is above ATC, ATC will rise. Therefore, at the point of intersection where MC equals ATC, ATC has just ceased to fall but has not yet begun to rise. This, by definition, is the minimum point on the ATC curve. *The marginal-cost curve intersects the average-total-cost curve at the ATC curve's minimum point.*

Because MC can be defined as the addition either to total cost *or* to total variable cost resulting from one more unit of output, this same rationale explains why the MC curve also crosses the AVC curve at the latter's minimum point. No such relationship exists for the MC curve and the average-fixed-cost curve,

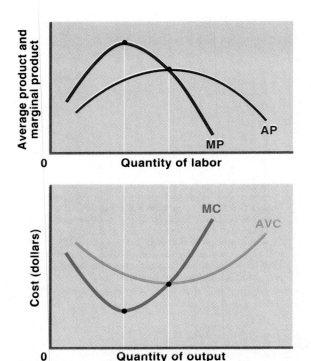

FIGURE 22-6   The relationship between productivity curves and cost curves
The marginal cost (MC) and average-variable-cost (AVC) curves are mirror images of the marginal product (MP) and average-product (AP) curves, respectively. Assuming labor is the only variable input and that its price (the wage rate) is constant, MC is found by dividing the wage rate by MP. Thus, when MP is rising, MC is falling; when MP reaches its maximum, MC is at its minimum; and when MP is diminishing, MC is rising. A similar relationship holds between AP and AVC.

because the two are not related; marginal cost includes only those costs which change with output, and fixed costs by definition are independent of output. *(Key Question 7)*

Shifting the Cost Curves

Changes in either resource prices or technology will cause cost curves to shift. If fixed costs had been higher—say, $200 rather than the $100 we assumed in Table 22-2—then the AFC curve in Figure 22-5 would be shifted upward. The ATC curve would also be at a higher position because AFC is a component of ATC. But the positions of the AVC and MC curves would be unaltered because their locations are based on the prices of variable rather than fixed resources. Thus, if the price (wage) of labor or some other variable input rose, the AVC, ATC, and MC curves would

all shift upward, but the position of AFC would remain unchanged. Reductions in the prices of fixed or variable resources will entail cost curve shifts exactly opposite to those just described.

If a more efficient technology were discovered, then the productivity of all inputs would increase. The cost figures in Table 22-2 would all be lower. To illustrate, if labor is the only variable input and wages are $10 per hour and average product is 10 units, then AVC would be $1. But if a technological improvement increases the average product of labor to 20 units, then AVC will decline to $.50. More generally, an upward shift in the productivity curves shown in the top portion of Figure 22-6 will mean a downward shift in the cost curves portrayed in the bottom portion of that diagram. (See Global Perspective 22-1.)

QUICK REVIEW 22-2

◼ The law of diminishing returns indicates that, beyond some point, output will increase by diminishing amounts as a variable resource (labor) is added to a fixed resource (capital).

◼ In the short run the total cost of any level of output is the sum of fixed and variable costs (TC = TFC + TVC).

◼ Average fixed, average variable, and average total costs are fixed, variable and total cost per unit of output; marginal cost is the cost of producing one more unit of output.

◼ Average fixed cost declines continuously as output increases; average variable cost and average total cost are U-shaped, reflecting increasing and then diminishing returns; marginal cost falls but then rises, intersecting both average variable and average total cost at their minimum points.

PRODUCTION COSTS IN THE LONG RUN

In the long run an industry and the individual firms it comprises can undertake all desired resource adjustments. The firm can alter its plant capacity; it can build a larger plant or revert to a smaller plant than assumed in Table 22-2. The industry can also change its plant size; the long run allows sufficient time for new firms to enter or existing firms to leave an industry. The impact of the entry and exodus of firms into and from an industry will be discussed in the next chapter; here we are concerned only with changes in plant capacity made by a single firm. We will couch our analysis in terms of ATC, making no distinction between fixed and variable costs because all resources, and therefore all costs, are variable in the long run.

Firm Size and Costs

Suppose a single-plant manufacturer begins on a small scale and, as the result of successful operations, expands to successively larger plant sizes. What happens to average total costs as this occurs? For a time successively larger plants will lower average total costs. However, eventually the building of a still larger plant may cause ATC to rise.

Figure 22-7 illustrates this situation for five possible plant sizes. ATC-1 is the average-total-cost curve for the smallest of the five plants, and ATC-5 for the largest. Constructing larger plants will lower minimum per unit costs through plant size 3. But beyond this point a larger plant will mean a higher level of minimum average total costs.

The Long-Run Cost Curve

The vertical lines perpendicular to the output axis in Figure 22-7 indicate those outputs at which the firm should change plant size to realize the lowest attainable per unit costs of production. For all outputs up to 20 units, the lowest per unit costs are attainable

GLOBAL PERSPECTIVE 22-1

Unit labor costs in manufacturing, selected nations

Labor costs—wages to workers—are a large percentage of ATC for most firms. Average labor costs in manufacturing have risen in the United States, shifting many ATC curves upward. But labor costs have risen even faster in many other countries.

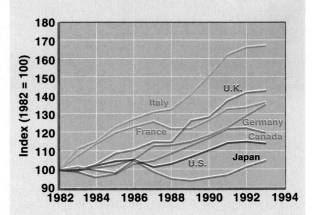

Source: Federal Reserve Bank of Cleveland, *Economic Trends*, November 1994, p. 19.

FIGURE 22-7 The long-run average-total-cost curve: five possible plant sizes
The long-run average-total-cost curve is made up of segments of the short-run cost curves (ATC-1, ATC-2, etc.) of the various-sized plants from which the firm might choose. Each point on the bumpy planning curve shows the least unit cost attainable for any output when the firm has had time to make all desired changes in its plant size.

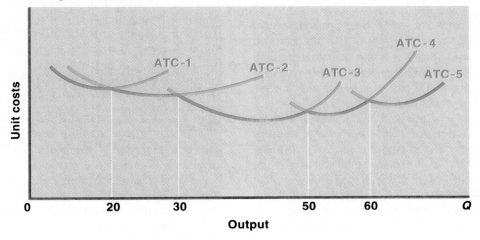

KEY GRAPH

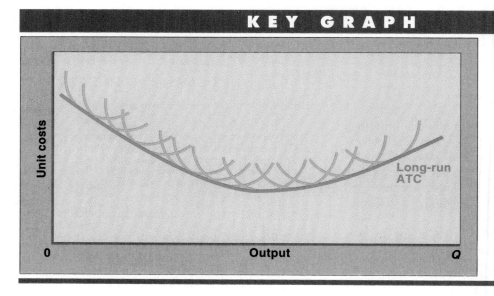

FIGURE 22-8 The long-run average-total-cost curve: unlimited number of plant sizes
If the number of possible plant sizes is very large, the long-run average-total-cost curve approximates a smooth curve. Economies of scale, followed by diseconomies of scale, cause the curve to be U-shaped.

with plant size 1. However, if the firm's volume of sales expands to some level greater than 20 but less than 30 units, it can achieve lower per unit costs by constructing a larger plant—plant size 2. Although *total* cost will be higher at the greater levels of production, the cost *per unit* of output will be less. For any output between 30 and 50 units, plant size 3 will yield the lowest per unit costs. For the 50- to 60-unit range of output, plant size 4 must be built to achieve the lowest unit costs. Lowest per unit costs for any output over 60 units demand construction of the still larger plant size 5.

Tracing these adjustments, we can conclude that the long-run ATC curve for the enterprise will comprise segments of the short-run ATC curves for the various plant sizes which can be constructed. *The long-run ATC curve shows the least per unit cost at which any output can be produced after the firm has had time to make all appropriate adjustments in its plant size.* In Figure 22-7 the heavy, bumpy curve is the firm's long-run ATC curve or, as it is often called, the firm's planning curve.

In most lines of production the choice of plant sizes is much wider than in our illustration. In many industries the number of possible plant sizes is virtually unlimited, and in time quite small changes in the volume of output (sales) will lead to changes in plant size. Graphically, this implies an unlimited number of short-run ATC curves, as suggested by Figure 22-8 (Key Graph). The minimum ATC of producing each

possible level of output is shown by the long-run ATC curve. Rather than being comprised of *segments* of short-run ATC curves as in Figure 22-7, the long-run ATC curve is made up of all the *points of tangency* of the theoretically unlimited number of short-run ATC curves from which the long-run ATC curve is derived. Hence, the planning curve is smooth rather than bumpy.

Economies and Diseconomies of Scale

We have accepted the contention that for a time larger and larger plant size will involve lower unit costs but that beyond some point successively larger plants will mean higher average total costs. Exactly why is the long-run ATC curve U-shaped? Note, first, that the law of diminishing returns does *not* apply in the long run. That's because diminishing returns presumes one resource is fixed in supply while the long run assumes all resources are variable. Also, our discussion assumes resource prices are constant. We can explain the U-shaped long-run average-cost curve in terms of economies and diseconomies of large-scale production.

Economies of Scale **Economies of scale** or, more commonly, economies of mass production, explain the downsloping part of the long-run ATC curve, as indicated in Figure 22-9a. As plant size increases, a number of factors will for a time lead to lower average costs of production.

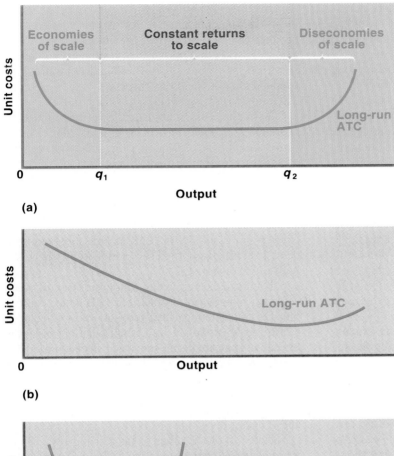

(a)

(b)

(c)

FIGURE 22-9 **Various possible long-run average-total-cost curves**
(a) Where economies of scale are rather rapidly exhausted and diseconomies not encountered until a considerably large scale of output has been achieved, long-run average total costs will be constant over a wide range of output. (b) When economies of scale are extensive and diseconomies remote, the ATC will fall over a wide range of production. (c) If economies of scale are exhausted quickly, followed immediately by diseconomies, minimum unit costs will be encountered at a relatively low output.

1 Labor Specialization Increased specialization in the use of labor is feasible as a plant increases in size. Hiring more workers means jobs can be divided and subdivided. Each worker may now have just one task to perform instead of five or six distinct operations in the productive process. Workers can work full time on those particular operations at which they have special skills. In a small plant skilled machinists may spend half their time performing unskilled tasks, leading to higher production costs.

Further, large scale allows dividing of work operations, which helps workers become proficient at the specific tasks assigned them. The jack-of-all-trades doing five or six jobs will not likely be efficient in any of them. Concentrating on one task, the same worker may become highly efficient.

Finally, greater specialization eliminates the loss of time which accompanies the shifting of workers from one job to another.

2 Managerial Specialization Large-scale production also means better use of, and greater specialization in, management. A supervisor who can handle twenty workers will be under-used in a small plant hiring only ten people. The production staff can be doubled with no increase in administrative costs.

Nor will small firms be able to use management specialists to best advantage. In a small plant a sales specialist may have to divide his or her time between several executive functions—for example, marketing, personnel, and finance. A larger scale of operations will mean that the marketing expert can supervise sales and product distribution full time, while appropriate specialists perform other managerial functions. Greater efficiency and lower unit costs are the net result.

3 Efficient Capital Small firms often cannot employ the most technologically efficient equipment. In many lines of production this machinery is available only in very large and extremely expensive units. Furthermore, effective utilization of this equipment demands a high volume of production, so only large-scale producers can afford and operate the best available equipment.

In the automobile industry the most efficient fabrication method employs robotics and elaborate assembly-line equipment. Effective use of this equipment demands an annual output of an estimated 200,000 to 400,000 automobiles (Chapter 26). Only very large-scale producers can afford to purchase and use this equipment efficiently. The small-scale producer is faced with a dilemma. To fabricate automobiles using other equipment is inefficient and therefore more costly per unit. The alternative of purchasing the most efficient equipment and underusing it with a small level of output is also inefficient and costly.

4 By-Products The large-scale producer can better use by-products than a small firm. The large meatpacking plant makes glue, fertilizer, pharmaceuticals, and a host of other products from animal remnants which would be discarded by smaller producers.

5 Other Factors Many products entail design, development, and certain other "start-up" costs which must be incurred irrespective of projected sales. These costs decline per unit as output is increased. Similarly, advertising costs decline per auto, per computer, per stereo system, and per case of beer as more units are produced.

All these technological considerations—greater specialization in labor and management, the ability to use the most efficient equipment, and effective use of by-products—contribute to lower unit costs for the producer able to expand its scale of operations. From a slightly different perspective, an increase in *all* resources of, say, 10 percent will cause a more-than-proportionate increase in output of, say, 20 percent. The necessary result will be a decline in ATC.

In many American manufacturing industries economies of scale have been of great significance. Firms which have expanded their scale of operations to realize economies of mass production have survived and flourished. Those unable to expand are high-cost producers, doomed to a marginal existence or ultimate insolvency.

Diseconomies of Scale But in time the expansion of a firm *may* lead to diseconomies and therefore higher per unit costs.

The main factor causing **diseconomies of scale** lies with managerial problems in efficiently controlling and coordinating a firm's operations as it becomes a large-scale producer. In a small plant a single key executive may make all the basic decisions for the plant's operation. Because of the firm's smallness, the executive is close to the production line and can readily comprehend the firm's operations, easily digest information gained from subordinates, and make clear and efficient decisions.

This neat picture changes as a firm grows. There are now many management levels between the executive suite and the assembly line; top management is far removed from the actual production operations of the plant. One person cannot assemble, understand, and digest all the information essential to rational decision making in a large-scale enterprise. Authority must be delegated to many vice-presidents, second vice-presidents, and so forth. This expansion in depth and width of the management hierarchy leads to problems of communication, coordination, and bureaucratic red tape, and the possibility that decisions of various subordinates will fail to mesh. Similarly, decisions may be sluggish in that they fail to quickly reflect changes in consumer tastes or technology. The result is impaired efficiency and rising average total costs.

Also, in massive production facilities workers may feel alienated from their jobs and have little commitment to productive efficiency. Opportunities to shirk—to avoid work in favor of on-the-job leisure—may be greater in large plants than in small ones. Large plants susceptible to worker alienation and shirking may require additional worker supervision, which increases costs.

Again, thought of differently, an increase in *all* resources of 10 percent will cause a less-than-proportionate increase in output of, say, 5 percent. As a consequence, ATC will increase. Diseconomies of scale are illustrated by the rising portion of the long-run cost curve in Figure 22-9a.

Constant Returns to Scale   In some instances there may exist a rather wide range of output between the output level at which economies of scale are exhausted and the point at which diseconomies of scale are encountered. That is, there will be a range of **constant returns to scale** over which long-run average cost is constant. The q_1q_2 output range of Figure 22-9a is relevant. Here a given percentage increase in *all* inputs of 10 percent will cause a proportionate 10 percent increase in output. Thus, ATC does not change.

Applications and Illustrations   There are many examples and applications of economies and diseconomies of scale.

Textbooks   Next semester when you buy texts at your bookstore compare the prices of introductory or basic texts with prices of more specialized, advanced books. You may be surprised that the price of a two-semester principles of economics text is not much more—and sometimes less—than that of a one-semester advanced text. This is true even though the principles text may be 200 pages longer and has a multicolor format, while the advanced book is in mundane black and white. Economies of scale are at work here. Both introductory and advanced texts entail design, editing, and typesetting costs which are more or less the same per page whether 5000 copies (of the advanced text) or 100,000 copies (of the basic text) are printed. With basic books these costs are spread over many more units of output, meaning lower unit costs and a comparatively low price per book.

Stealth Bombers   The notion of economies of scale has been invoked in debate over the national defense budget. When the Pentagon was proposing a fleet of 132 B-2 Stealth bombers, the estimated cost per plane was $580 million. But a proposed cut to 75 bombers by the Secretary of Defense caused the cost per plane to surge to over $800 million. The per plane cost increase was due to the loss of scale economies asso-

ciated with the smaller order. Many of the substantial costs involved in the design and experimental work in developing the plane are the same regardless of the number of units produced. These costs are clearly significantly less per plane as more are manufactured.

General Motors   Executives of large corporations attest to the realities of diseconomies of scale. A former General Motors president commented thus on GM's Chevrolet division:

> Chevrolet is such a big monster that you twist its tail and nothing happens at the other end for months and months. It is so gigantic that there isn't any way to really run it. You just sort of try to keep track of it.

Similarly, a former GM vice-president provided this insider's view of Chevrolet:

> One of the biggest . . . problems was in the manufacturing staff. It was overburdened with layer upon layer of management. . . . A plant manager reported to a city manager who reported to a regional manager who reported to a manager of plants who reported to me, the general manager. Consequently, the manager of the Chevrolet Gear and Axle plant on Detroit's near east side who was only a few miles away from my office, was almost light years away in terms of management reporting channels.

Adams and Brock's[1] study of the auto industry concluded that the hierarchical and bureaucratic management which accompanies size inhibits its efficiency. They noted that in the 1980s many large and diversified corporations divested themselves of various divisions and subsidiaries to enhance managerial efficiency, that is, to offset diseconomies of scale.

In recent years GM—the world's largest corporation—has found itself with both a declining market share and a substantial cost disadvantage. GM's labor costs per car are nearly $800 more than Ford's and $500 more than Chrysler's. To offset scale diseconomies GM has given each of its five automotive divisions (Chevrolet, Buick, Pontiac, Oldsmobile, and Cadillac) greater autonomy with respect to styling, engineering, and marketing decisions. The goal is to reduce the layers of managerial approval required in decision making so each division can respond more rapidly and with greater precision to changes

---

[1]Walter Adams and James W. Brock, *The Bigness Complex* (New York: Pantheon Books, 1986), chap. 3. The above two quotations are cited in Adams and Brock.

ECONOMIES OF SCALE AND INDUSTRIAL CONCENTRATION

Is market concentration explainable in terms of economies of scale?

It is sometimes argued that industrial concentration —the dominance of a market by a small number of firms—is justified on the basis of economies of scale. If a firm's long-run average-cost curve declines over an extended range of output, total consumption of the product may only support a few efficient (minimum unit cost) producers (Figure 22-9b).

Research studies suggest that industrial concentration is generally *not* warranted on the basis of economies of scale. The minimum efficient scale (MES) —the smallest plant size at which minimum unit cost would be attained—has been determined for a number of industries, twelve of which are listed in the accompanying table. Column 2 compares the MES output with domestic consumption of each product to determine the percentage of total consumption which a single MES plant could produce. For example, a cigarette manufacturer of minimum efficient scale can produce about 6.6 percent of the domestic consumption of cigarettes.

By dividing the percentage of domestic consumption which an MES plant could produce into 100 percent (total domestic consumption), you can calculate the number of efficient plants which consumption will support. Thus we observe in column 3 that 15 MES plants (= 100 percent ÷ 6.6 percent) are compatible with domestic cigarette consumption.

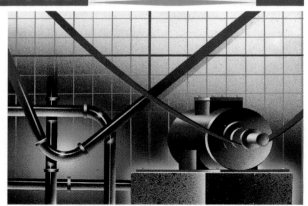

In a few industries—small diesel engines, turbo generators, electric motors, and refrigerators—some level of concentration is required to realize scale economies. But for most of the industries shown, the minimum efficient plant sizes are small compared to the domestic market for each product. This suggests that economies of scale do *not* provide a rationale or justification for a high degree of concentration in most of the industries studied. The fact that the four largest firms in the beer industry actually provide 87 percent of domestic beer output and the four largest cigarette manufacturers control 92 percent of the domestic cigarette market (Table 26-1) is not explainable solely in terms of economies of scale.

There are qualifications. The data cited in the table refer only to *production* economies. Multiplant firms

in technology and consumer tastes. For its Saturn automobile GM created a separate company. In late 1994 GM announced it would reorganize into a small car group and a midsize and luxury group in the hope of cutting costs and bringing new cars to the market faster.

Bank Mergers Sometimes expected economies of scale fail to materialize. This has generally been the case for the large number of commercial bank mergers which occurred in the 1980s. The conventional wisdom is that the consolidation of banks, particularly those with overlapping markets, would yield significant cost economies. Some branches can be closed and cost savings might be realized by combining support services such as computer processing, advertising, auditing, and legal work. But several recent studies of bank mergers conclude that, in general, they have not significantly reduced costs thus far. One possible explanation is that long-run costs in the banking industry may resemble Figure 22-9a which means that, after banks reach a modest size, there are no significant cost economies associated with further expansion. Bigger in banking may not necessarily mean better in terms of costs.

MES and Industry Structure

Economies and diseconomies of scale are an important determinant of an industry's structure. Here it is

Minimum efficient plant sizes as a percentage of domestic consumption

(1) Industry	(2) Minimum efficient scale as a percentage of domestic consumption	(3) Number of efficient plants compatible with domestic consumption
Diesel engines (small)	25.5%	4
Turbogenerators	23.0	4
Electric motors	15.0	7
Refrigerators	14.1	7
Cellulosic synthetic fiber	11.1	9
Passenger automobile production	11.0	9
Commercial aircraft	10.0	10
Cigarettes	6.6	15
Printing paper	4.4	23
Beer brewing	3.4	29
Bicycles	2.1	48
Petroleum refining	1.9	53

Source: F. M. Scherer, *Industrial Market Structure and Economic Performance*, 2d ed. (Boston: Houghton Mifflin Company, 1980), pp. 96–97.

—and therefore higher levels of industrial concentration than those suggested by column 3 of the table —may be justified on the basis of other nonproduction advantages. For example, a large multiplant firm may be able to economize on management services by drawing on a common pool of accountants, lawyers, and financial planners to serve all of its plants. Similarly, a multiplant firm may realize economies in advertising, raising money capital, or in product distribution. On the other hand, it is conceivable that diseconomies could be associated with some aspects of multiplant operation. In any event, even when adjustments are made for such factors, the general conclusion remains that economic concentration in many industries cannot be justified on the basis of economies of scale.

helpful to introduce the concept of **minimum efficient scale** (MES) which is the smallest level of output at which a firm can minimize long-run average costs. In Figure 22-9a this occurs at O_{q1} units of output. Because of the extended range of constant returns to scale, firms producing substantially larger outputs could also realize the minimum attainable average costs. Specifically, firms would be equally efficient within the q_1q_2 range. We would therefore not be surprised to find an industry with such cost conditions to be populated by firms of quite different sizes. The apparel, food processing, furniture, wood products, and small appliance industries provide approximate examples. With an extended range of constant returns to scale, relatively large and relatively small firms could coexist in an industry and be equally viable.

Compare this with Figure 22-9b where economies of scale are extensive and diseconomies are remote. Here the long-run average-cost curve will decline over an extended range of output, the case in the automobile, aluminum, steel, and other heavy industries. Given consumer demand, efficient production will be achieved only with a small number of industrial giants. Small firms cannot realize the minimum efficient scale and will not be viable. In the extreme, economies of scale might extend beyond the market's size, resulting in what is termed a natural monopoly (Chapter 24). A **natural monopoly** is a market situation where unit costs are minimized by having one firm produce the particular good or service.

Where economies of scale are few and diseconomies quickly encountered, minimum efficient size occurs at a small level of output as shown in Figure 22-9c. In such industries a particular level of consumer demand will support a large number of relatively small producers. Many retail trades and some types of farming fall into this category. So do certain types of light manufacturing, such as the baking, clothing, and shoe industries. Fairly small firms are as efficient as, or more efficient than, large-scale producers in such industries.

The point is that the shape of the long-run average-cost curve, as determined by economies and diseconomies of scale, can be significant in determining the structure and competitiveness of an industry. Whether an industry is "competitive"—populated by a relatively large number of small firms—or "concentrated"—dominated by a few large producers—is sometimes a reflection of an industry's technology and the resulting shape of its long-run average-cost curve.

But we must be cautious because industry structure does not depend on cost conditions alone. Government policies, geographic size of a market, managerial ability, and other factors must be considered in explaining the structure of a given industry. Indeed, this chapter's Last Word presents empirical evidence suggesting that many industries are much more concentrated than can be justified on the basis of economies of scale. *(Key Question 10)*

QUICK REVIEW 22-3

■ Most firms have U-shaped long-run average-cost curves, reflecting economies and then diseconomies of scale.

■ Economies of scale are the consequence of greater specialization of labor and management, more efficient capital equipment, and the use of by-products.

■ Diseconomies of scale are caused by problems of coordination and communication which arise in large firms.

■ Minimum efficient scale is the smallest level of output at which a firm's long-run average total costs are at a minimum.

CHAPTER SUMMARY

1   Economic costs include all payments which must be received by resource owners to ensure continued supply of these resources in a particular line of production. This definition includes explicit costs, which flow to resource suppliers separate from a given enterprise, and also implicit costs, the remuneration of self-owned and self-employed resources. One of the implicit cost payments is a normal profit to the entrepreneur.

2   In the short run a firm's plant capacity is fixed. The firm can use its plant more or less intensively by adding or subtracting units of variable resources, but the firm does not have sufficient time to alter plant size.

3   The law of diminishing returns describes what happens to output as a fixed plant is used more intensively. As successive units of a variable resource such as labor are added to a fixed plant, beyond some point the resulting marginal product associated with each additional worker declines.

4   Because some resources are variable and others fixed, costs can be classified as variable or fixed in the short run. Fixed costs are independent of the level of output; variable costs vary with output. The total cost of any output is the sum of fixed and variable costs at that output.

5   Average fixed, average variable, and average total costs

are fixed, variable, and total costs per unit of output. Average fixed costs decline continuously as output increases, because a fixed sum is being spread over a larger and larger number of units of production. Average variable costs are U-shaped, reflecting the law of diminishing returns. Average total cost is the sum of average fixed and average variable costs; it too is U-shaped.

6   Marginal cost is the extra, or additional, cost of producing one more unit of output. Graphically, the marginal cost curve intersects the ATC and AVC curves at their minimum points.

7   Lower resource prices shift cost curves downward as does technological progress. Higher input prices shift cost curves upward.

8   The long run is a period of time sufficiently long for a firm to vary the amounts of all resources used, including plant size. In the long run all costs are variable. The long-run ATC, or planning, curve is composed of segments of the short-run ATC curves, representing the various plant sizes a firm can construct in the long run.

9   The long-run ATC curve is generally U-shaped. Economies of scale are first encountered as a small firm expands. Greater specialization in the use of labor and management, ability to use the most efficient equipment, and more com-

plete utilization of by-products—all contribute to economies of scale. Diseconomies of scale stem from the managerial complexities which accompany large-scale production. The relative importance of economies and diseconomies of scale in an industry is often an important determinant of the structure of that industry.

TERMS AND CONCEPTS

economic (opportunity) cost	law of diminishing returns	average fixed cost	constant returns to scale
explicit and implicit costs	total, marginal, and average product	average variable cost	minimum efficient scale
normal and economic profits	fixed costs	average total cost	natural monopoly
short run and long run	variable costs	marginal cost	
	total costs	economies and diseconomies of scale	

QUESTIONS AND STUDY SUGGESTIONS

1 Distinguish between explicit and implicit costs, giving examples of each. What are the explicit and implicit costs of attending college? Why does the economist classify normal profits as a cost? Are economic profits a cost of production?

2 *Key Question   Gomez runs a small pottery firm. He hires one helper at $12,000 per year, pays annual rent of $5,000 for his shop, and materials cost $20,000 per year. Gomez has $40,000 of his own funds invested in equipment (pottery wheels, kilns, and so forth) which could earn him $4,000 per year if alternatively invested. Gomez has been offered $15,000 per year to work as a potter for a competitor. He estimates his entrepreneurial talents are worth $3,000 per year. Total annual revenue from pottery sales is $72,000. Calculate accounting profits and economic profits for Gomez's pottery.*

3 Which of the following are short-run and which are long-run adjustments?   a Wendy's builds a new restaurant; b Acme Steel Corporation hires 200 more workers;   c A farmer increases the amount of fertilizer used on his corn crop; and   d An Alcoa plant adds a third shift of workers.

4 *Key Question   Use the following data to calculate marginal product and average product.*

Inputs of labor	Total product	Marginal product	Average product
0	0	15	
1	15	17	15
2	34	19	17
3	51	14	17
4	65	9	16.25
5	74	6	14.8
6	80	3	13.33
7	83	1	11.86
8	82		10.25

Plot total, marginal, and average product and explain in detail the relationship between each pair of curves. Explain why marginal product first rises, then declines, and ultimately becomes negative. What bearing does the law of diminishing returns have on short-run costs? Be specific. "When marginal product is rising, marginal cost is falling. And when marginal product is diminishing, marginal cost is rising." Illustrate and explain graphically.

5 Why can the distinction between fixed and variable costs be made in the short run? Classify the following as fixed or variable costs: advertising expenditures, fuel, interest on company-issued bonds, shipping charges, payments for raw materials, real estate taxes, executive salaries, insurance premiums, wage payments, depreciation and obsolescence charges, sales taxes, and rental payments on leased office machinery. "There are no fixed costs in the long run; all costs are variable." Explain.

6 List the fixed and variable costs associated with owning and operating an automobile. Suppose you are considering whether to drive your car or fly 1000 miles to Florida for spring break. Which costs—fixed, variable, or both—would you take into account in making your decision? Would any implicit costs be relevant? Explain.

7 *Key Question A firm has fixed costs of $60 and variable costs as indicated in the table below. Complete the table. When finished, check your calculations by referring to question 4 at the end of Chapter 23.*

Total product	Total fixed cost	Total variable cost	Total cost	Average fixed cost	Average variable cost	Average total cost	Marginal cost
0	$_____	$ 0	$_____	$_____	$_____	$_____	$_____
1	_____	45	_____	_____	_____	_____	_____
2	_____	85	_____	_____	_____	_____	_____
3	_____	120	_____	_____	_____	_____	_____
4	_____	150	_____	_____	_____	_____	_____
5	_____	185	_____	_____	_____	_____	_____
6	_____	225	_____	_____	_____	_____	_____
7	_____	270	_____	_____	_____	_____	_____
8	_____	325	_____	_____	_____	_____	_____
9	_____	390	_____	_____	_____	_____	_____
10	_____	465	_____	_____	_____	_____	_____

a *Graph fixed cost, variable cost, and total cost. Explain how the law of diminishing returns influences the shapes of the variable-cost and total-cost curves.*

b *Graph AFC, AVC, ATC, and MC. Explain the derivation and shape of each of these four curves and their relationships to one another. Specifically, explain in nontechnical terms why the MC curve intersects both the AVC and ATC curves at their minimum points.*

c *Explain how the locations of each curve graphed in question 7b would be altered if (1) total fixed cost had been $100 rather than $60, and (2) total variable cost had been $10 less at each level of output.*

8 Indicate how each of the following would shift the a marginal cost curve, b average variable cost curve, c average fixed cost curve, and d average total cost curve of a manufacturing firm. In each case specify the direction of the shift.

a A reduction in business property taxes

b An increase in the nominal wages of production workers

c A decrease in the price of electricity

d An increase in insurance rates on plant and equipment

e An increase in transportation costs

9 Suppose a firm has only three possible plant size options as shown in the accompanying figure. What plant size will the firm choose in producing a 50, b 130, c 160, and d 250 units of output? Draw the firm's long-run average-cost curve on the diagram and define this curve.

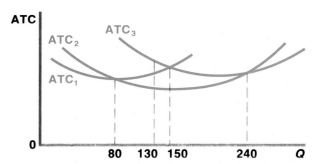

10 *Key Question Use the concepts of economies and diseconomies of scale to explain the shape of a firm's long-run ATC curve. What is the concept of minimum efficient scale? What bearing may the exact shape of the long-run ATC curve have on the structure of an industry?*

11 (Last Word) Use the concept of minimum efficient scale to explain the number of efficient firms an industry can support. Is market concentration—the presence of only a few firms in an industry—explainable in terms of economies of scale?

23

PRICE AND OUTPUT DETERMINATION: PURE COMPETITION

Chapters 20 to 22 have given us the basic tools of analysis for understanding how product price and output are determined. But a firm's decisions concerning price and production will vary depending on the character of the industry in which it is operating. There is no "average" or "typical" industry. The business sector of our economy comprises an almost infinite number of different market situations; no two industries are alike. At one extreme we find a single producer dominating a market; at the other thousands of firms, each supplying a minute fraction of market output. Between these extremes lies an unlimited variety of market structures.

FOUR MARKET MODELS

Any attempt to examine each specific industry would be an impossible task. We seek a more realistic objective—to define and discuss several basic market structures, or models. In so doing, we will acquaint ourselves with the *general* way in which price and output are determined in most of the market types characterizing our economy.

Economists envision four distinct market situations: (1) pure competition, (2) pure monopoly, (3) monopolistic competition, and (4) oligopoly. They will be considered in this order here and in the next three chapters. These four market models differ in the number of firms in the industry; whether the product is standardized or differentiated; and how easy or difficult it is for new firms to enter the industry.

The main characteristics of these four models are outlined below and in Table 23-1 with more detailed definitions to follow.

1 In **pure competition** there are a very large number of firms producing a standardized product (wheat or peanuts). New firms can enter the industry very easily.

2 At the other extreme, **pure monopoly** (Chapter 24) is a market in which one firm is the sole seller of a product or service (a local electric company). Entry of additional firms is blocked so that the firm *is* the industry. Because there is only one product, there is no product differentiation.

3 **Monopolistic competition** (Chapter 25) is characterized by a relatively large number of sellers producing differentiated products (women's clothing, furniture, books). Differentiation is the basis for product promotion and development. Entry to a monopolistically competitive industry is quite easy.

4 In **oligopoly** (Chapter 26) there are a few sellers; this "fewness" means that pricing and output decisions are interdependent. Each firm is affected by the decisions of rivals and must take these decisions into account in determining its own price-output behavior. Products may be standardized (steel or aluminum) or differentiated (automobiles and computers). Generally, entry to oligopolistic industries is very difficult.

TABLE 23-1 Characteristics of the four basic market models

| Characteristic | Market Model | | | |
	Pure competition	Monopolistic competition	Oligopoly	Pure monopoly
Number of firms	A very large number	Many	Few	One
Type of product	Standardized	Differentiated	Standardized or differentiated	Unique; no close substitutes
Control over Price	None	Some, but within rather narrow limits	Circumscribed by mutual interdependence; considerable with collusion	Considerable
Conditions of entry	Very easy, no obstacles	Relatively easy	Significant obstacles present	Blocked
Nonprice competition	None	Considerable emphasis on advertising, brand names trademarks, etc.	Typically a great deal, particularly with product differentiation	Mostly public relations advertising
Examples	Agriculture	Retail trade, dresses, shoes	Steel, automobiles, farm implements, many household appliances	Local utilities

These definitions and the characteristics outlined in Table 23-1 will come into sharper focus as we examine each model in detail.

We will find it convenient occasionally to distinguish between the characteristics of a purely competitive market and those of all other basic market structures—pure monopoly, monopolistic competition, and oligopoly. To facilitate such comparisons we will employ **imperfect competition** as a generic term to designate all those market structures deviating from the purely competitive market model.

PURE COMPETITION: CONCEPT AND OCCURRENCE

Let's focus on pure competition, beginning with an elaboration of our definition.

1   Very Large Numbers   A basic feature of a purely competitive market is the presence of a large number of independently acting sellers, usually offering their products in a highly organized market. Markets for farm commodities, the stock market, and the foreign exchange market are illustrative.

2   Standardized Product   Competitive firms produce a standardized or homogeneous product. Given price, the consumer is indifferent as to the seller from which the product is purchased. In a competitive market the products of firms, B, C, D, and E, are viewed by the buyer as perfect substitutes for firm A's product. Because of standardization, there is no reason for *nonprice competition,* that is, competition based on differences in product quality, advertising, or sales promotion.

3   "Price Taker"   In a purely competitive market *individual firms* exert no significant control over product price. This characteristic follows from the preceding two. Under pure competition each firm produces such a small fraction of total output that increasing or decreasing its output will not perceptibly influence total supply or, therefore, product price.

Assume there are 10,000 competing firms, each currently producing 100 units of output. Total supply is therefore 1,000,000. Now suppose one of these firms cuts its output to 50 units. This will not affect price, because this restriction of output by a single firm has almost no impact on total supply. The total quantity supplied declines from 1,000,000 to 999,950

—not enough of a change in total supply to affect product price noticeably. In short, the individual competitive producer is a **price taker;** the competitive firm cannot adjust market price, but can only adjust to it.

That means the individual competitive producer is at the mercy of the market; product price is a given datum over which the producer exerts no influence. The firm gets the same price per unit for a large output as it does for a small output. To ask a price higher than the going market price would be futile. Consumers will not buy from firm A at $2.05 when its 9999 competitors are selling an identical, and therefore perfect substitute, product at $2 per unit. Conversely, because firm A can sell as much as it chooses at $2 per unit, there is no reason for it to charge a lower price, say, $1.95, for to do so would shrink its profits.

4   Free Entry and Exit   New firms can freely enter and existing firms can freely leave purely competitive industries. No significant obstacles—legal, technological, financial, or other—prohibit new firms from forming and selling their outputs in competitive markets.

Relevance   Pure competition is rare in practice. But this does not mean that an analysis of how competitive markets work is irrelevant:
1   A few industries more closely approximate the competitive model than any other market structure. For example, much can be learned about American agriculture by understanding competitive markets.
2   Pure competition provides the simplest context in which to apply the revenue and cost concepts developed in previous chapters. Pure competition is a clear and meaningful starting point for any discussion of price and output determination.
3   The operation of a purely competitive economy gives us a standard, or norm, against which the efficiency of the real-world economy can be compared and evaluated.

Pure competition is a market model which helps us observe and evaluate what goes on in the real world.

Our analysis of pure competition has four objectives. First, we will examine demand from the competitive seller's viewpoint. Second, we consider how a competitive producer adjusts to market price in the short run. Next, we explore the nature of long-run adjustments in a competitive industry. Finally, we eval-

uate the efficiency of competitive industries from the standpoint of society.

DEMAND TO A COMPETITIVE SELLER

Because each competitive firm offers a negligible fraction of total supply, the individual firm cannot perceptibly influence the market price which the forces of total demand and supply have established. The competitive firm does *not* have a price policy—it is not able to adjust price. Rather, the firm can merely *adjust to* the market price, which it must regard as determined by the market. The competitive seller is a *price taker,* not a *price maker.*

Perfectly Elastic Demand

Stated technically, the demand curve of the individual competitive firm is *perfectly elastic.* Columns 1 and 2 of Table 23-2 show a perfectly elastic demand curve where market price is assumed to be $131. The firm cannot obtain a higher price by restricting output; nor need it lower price to increase its sales volume.

We are *not* saying that the *market* demand curve is perfectly elastic in a competitive market. Instead, it

TABLE 23-2   The demand and revenue schedules for a purely competitive firm

Firm's demand or average-revenue schedule		Revenue data	
(1) Product price (average revenue)	(2) Quantity demanded (sold)	(3) Total revenue	(4) Marginal revenue
$131	0	$ 0	
131	1	131	$131
131	2	262	131
131	3	393	131
131	4	524	131
131	5	655	131
131	6	786	131
131	7	917	131
131	8	1048	131
131	9	1179	131
131	10	1310	131

is a downsloping curve as a glance ahead at Figure 23-7b reveals. In fact, the total-demand curves for most agricultural products are quite *in*elastic, even though agriculture is the most competitive industry in our economy. However, the demand schedule faced by the *individual firm* in a purely competitive industry is perfectly elastic.

The distinction comes about in this way. For the industry—all firms producing a particular product—a larger sales volume can be realized only by accepting a lower product price. All firms, acting independently but simultaneously, can and do affect total supply and therefore market price. But not so for the individual firm. If a *single* producer increases or decreases output, the outputs of all other competing firms being constant, the effect on total supply and market price is negligible. The single firm's demand or sales schedule is therefore perfectly elastic, as shown in Figures 23-1 and 23-7a. This is the fallacy of composition at work. What is true for the industry or group of firms (a downsloping, less than perfectly elastic, demand curve) is *not* true for the individual, purely competitive firm (a perfectly elastic demand curve).

Average, Total, and Marginal Revenue

The firm's demand schedule is simultaneously a revenue schedule. What appears in column 1 of Table 23-2 as price per unit to the purchaser is revenue per unit, or **average revenue,** to the seller. To say that a buyer must pay $131 per unit is to say that the revenue per unit, or average revenue, received by the seller is $131. Price and average revenue are the same thing seen from different points of view.

Total revenue for each sales level can be determined by multiplying price by the corresponding quantity the firm can sell. Multiply column 1 by column 2, and the result is column 3. In this case, total revenue increases by a constant amount, $131, for each additional unit of sales. Each unit sold adds exactly its constant price to total revenue.

When a firm is pondering a change in its output, it will consider how its revenue will *change* as a result of that shift in output. What will be the additional revenue from selling another unit of output? **Marginal revenue** is the change in total revenue, that is, the extra revenue, which results from selling one more unit of output. In column 3 of Table 23-2 total revenue is zero when zero units are sold. The first unit of output sold increases total revenue from zero to $131. Marginal revenue—the increase in total revenue from the sale of the first unit of output—is therefore $131. The second unit sold increases total revenue from $131 to $262, so marginal revenue is again $131. Note in column 4 that marginal revenue is a constant $131, because total revenue increases by a constant amount with every extra unit sold.

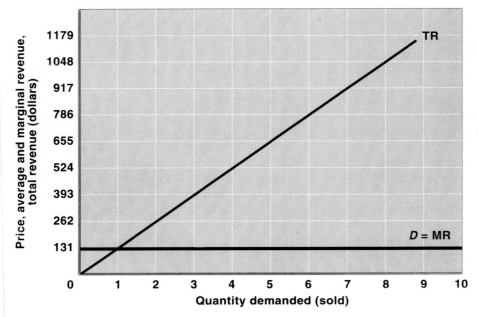

FIGURE 23-1 Demand, marginal revenue, and total revenue of a purely competitive firm
Because it can sell additional units of output at a constant price, the marginal-revenue curve (MR) of a purely competitive firm coincides with its perfectly elastic demand curve (D). The firm's total-revenue curve (TR) is a straight upsloping line.

Under purely competitive conditions, product price is constant to the individual firm; added units therefore can be sold without lowering product price. Each additional unit of sales adds exactly its price—$131 in this case—to total revenue, and marginal revenue *is* this increase in total revenue. Marginal revenue is constant under pure competition because additional units can be sold at a constant price. *(Key Question 3)*

Graphical Portrayal

The competitive firm's demand curve and total- and marginal-revenue curves are shown graphically in Figure 23-1. The demand or average-revenue curve is perfectly elastic. The marginal-revenue curve coincides with the demand curve because product price is constant to the competitive firm. Each extra unit of sales increases total revenue by $131. Total revenue is a straight line up to the right. Its slope is constant —it is a straight line—because marginal revenue is constant.

QUICK REVIEW 23-1

■ **In a purely competitive industry there are a large number of firms producing a homogeneous product and no significant entry barriers.**

■ **The competitive firm's demand curve is perfectly elastic at the market price.**

■ **Marginal and average revenue coincide with the firm's demand curve; total revenue rises by the amount of product price for each additional unit sold.**

PROFIT MAXIMIZATION IN THE SHORT RUN: TWO APPROACHES

In the short run the competitive firm has a fixed plant and maximizes its profits or minimizes its losses by adjusting its output through changes in the amounts of variable resources (materials, labor, and so forth) it employs. The economic profits it seeks are defined as the difference between total revenue and total costs. Indeed, this is the direction of our analysis. The revenue data of the previous section and the cost data of Chapter 22 must be brought together so the profit-maximizing output for the firm can be determined.

There are two ways to determining the level of output at which a competitive firm will realize maxi-

mum profits or minimum losses. One compares total revenue and total costs; the other compares marginal revenue and marginal costs. Both approaches apply not only to a purely competitive firm but also to firms operating in any of the other three basic market structures. To understand output determination under pure competition, we will use both approaches, emphasizing the marginal approach. Also, hypothetical data in both tabular and graphical form will be employed to clarify the two approaches.

Total-Revenue–Total-Cost Approach

Confronted with the market price of its product, the competitive producer is faced with three related questions: (1) Should we produce? (2) If so, what amount? (3) What profit (or loss) will be realized?

At first, the answer to question 1 seems obvious: "You should produce if it is profitable to do so." But the situation is more complex than this. In the short run part of the firm's total costs is variable costs, and the remainder is fixed costs. Fixed costs have to be paid "out of pocket" even when the firm is closed down. In the short run a firm takes a loss equal to its fixed costs when it produces zero units of output. This means that, although there may be no level of output at which the firm can realize a profit, the firm might still produce if it can realize a loss less than the fixed-cost loss it will face in closing down. Thus, the correct answer to "Should we produce?" is: *The firm should produce in the short run if it can realize either (1) a profit or (2) a loss less than its fixed costs.*

Assuming the firm *will* produce, the second question becomes relevant: "How much should be produced?" The answer: *In the short run the firm should produce that output at which it maximizes profits or minimizes losses.*

We now examine three cases demonstrating the validity of these two generalizations and answer our third query by indicating how profits and losses can be calculated. In the first case the firm will maximize its profits by producing. In the second case it will minimize its losses by producing. In the third case the firm will minimize its losses by closing down. We will assume the same short-run cost data for all three cases and explore the firm's production decisions when faced with three different product prices.

Profit-Maximizing Case   In all three cases we employ cost data with which we are already familiar. Columns 2 through 4 of Table 23-3 repeat the fixed-,

TABLE 23-3 The profit-maximizing output for a purely competitive firm: total-revenue–total-cost approach (prices: $131, $81, $71)

(1) Total product	(2) Total fixed cost	(3) Total variable cost	(4) Total cost	Price: $131		Price: $81		Price: $71	
				(5) Total revenue	(6) Profit	(7) Total revenue	(8) Profit	(9) Total revenue	(10) Profit
0	$100	$ 0	$ 100	$ 0	$−100	$ 0	$−100	$ 0	$−100
1	100	90	190	131	− 59	81	−109	71	−119
2	100	170	270	262	− 8	162	−108	142	−128
3	100	240	340	393	+ 53	243	− 97	213	−127
4	100	300	400	524	+124	324	− 76	284	−116
5	100	370	470	655	+185	405	− 65	355	−115
6	100	450	550	786	+236	486	− 64	426	−124
7	100	540	640	917	+277	567	− 73	497	−143
8	100	650	750	1048	+298	648	−102	568	−182
9	100	780	880	1179	+299	729	−151	639	−241
10	100	930	1030	1310	+280	810	−220	710	−320

variable-, and total-cost data developed in Table 22-2. Assuming that market price is $131, we derive total revenue for each output level by multiplying output by price, as we did in Table 23-2. These data are presented in column 5. Then in column 6 the profit or loss at each output level is found by subtracting total cost (column 4) from the total revenue (column 5). Now we have all the data needed to answer the three questions.

Should the firm produce? Yes, because it can realize a profit by doing so. How much? Nine units, because column 6 tells us this is the output at which total economic profits will be at a maximum. The size of that profit in this **profit-maximizing case?** $299.

Figure 23-2a compares total revenue and total cost graphically. Total revenue is a straight line, because under pure competition each additional unit adds the same amount—its price—to total revenue (Table 23-2).

Total costs increase with output; more production requires more resources. But the rate of increase in total costs varies with the relative efficiency of the firm. Specifically, the cost data reflect Chapter 22's law of diminishing returns. For a time the rate of increase in total cost is less and less as the firm uses its fixed resources more efficiently. Then, after a time, total cost begins to rise by ever-increasing amounts because of the inefficiencies accompanying more intensive use of the firm's plant.

Comparing total cost with total revenue in Figure 23-2a, note that a **break-even point** (normal-profit

position) occurs at about 2 units of output. If our data were extended beyond 10 units of output, another such point would occur where total cost would catch up with total revenue, as shown in Figure 23-2a. Any output outside these break-even points will entail losses. Any output within these points will produce an economic profit. Maximum profit is achieved where the vertical difference between total revenue and total cost is greatest. For our particular data this is at 9 units of output where maximum profit is $299.

Loss-Minimizing Case Assuming no change in costs, the firm may not realize economic profits if the market yields a price considerably below $131. Suppose the market price is only $81. As column 8 of Table 23-3 indicates, at this price all levels of output will lead to losses. But the firm will *not* close down because, by producing, it realizes a loss considerably less than the $100 fixed-cost loss it would incur by closing down, that is, producing zero units of output. Specifically, in this **loss-minimizing case,** the firm will minimize its losses by producing 6 units of output. The resulting $64 loss is clearly preferable to the $100 loss from producing zero units—closing down. By producing 6 units the firm earns a total revenue of $486, sufficient to pay all the firm's variable costs ($450) and also a substantial portion—$36 worth—of the firm's $100 of fixed costs.

In general, whenever total revenue exceeds total *variable* costs, the firm will produce because all the variable costs as well as some portion of total fixed

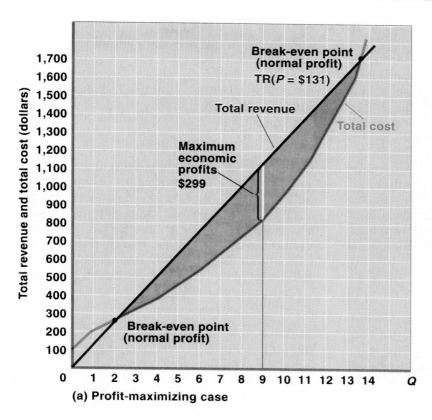

(a) Profit-maximizing case

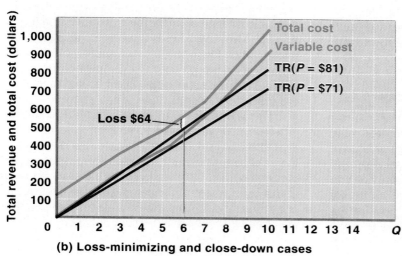

(b) Loss-minimizing and close-down cases

FIGURE 23-2   The profit-maximizing (a), loss-minimizing, and close-down cases (b), as shown by the total-revenue–total-cost approach
A firm's profits are maximized in (a) at that output where total revenue exceeds total cost by the maximum amount. A firm will minimize its losses in (b) by producing at that output at which total cost exceeds total revenue by the smallest amount. However, if there is no output where total revenue exceeds total variable costs, the firm will minimize losses in the short run by closing down.

costs can be paid out of revenue. If the firm closed down, all of its total fixed costs would have to be paid out of the entrepreneur's pocket. By producing some output, the firm's loss will be less than its total fixed cost. Note that there are several other outputs which entail a loss less than the firm's $100 fixed costs; but at 6 units of output the loss is minimized.

Close-Down Case   Assume finally that the market price is a mere $71. Given short-run costs, column 10 of Table 23-3 indicates that at all levels of output, losses will exceed the $100 fixed-cost loss that firm will incur by closing down. Thus, in this **close-down case,** the firm will minimize its losses by halting production, that is, by producing zero units of output.

Figure 23-2b demonstrates the loss-minimizing and close-down cases graphically. In the loss-minimizing case, the total revenue line TR ($P = \$81$) exceeds total variable cost by the maximum amount at 6 units of output. Here total revenue is $486, and the firm recovers all its $450 of variable costs and also $36 worth of its fixed costs. The firm's minimum loss is $64, better than the $100 fixed-cost loss involved in closing down.

In the close-down case, the total-revenue line TR ($P = \$71$) lies below the total-variable-cost curve at all points; there is no output at which variable costs can be recovered. By producing, the firm would incur losses exceeding its fixed costs. The firm's best choice is to close down and pay it's $100 fixed-cost loss out of pocket

QUICK REVIEW 23-2

■ **In the short run a firm should produce if it can achieve a profit or attain a loss which is smaller than its total fixed costs.**

■ **Profits are maximized where the excess of total revenue over total cost is greatest.**

■ **Losses are minimized where the excess of total cost over total revenue is smallest and is some amount less than total fixed costs.**

■ **If losses at all levels of output exceed total fixed costs, the firm should close down in the short run.**

Marginal-Revenue–Marginal-Cost Approach

Another way a competitive firm decides the amounts it would offer at each possible price is to determine and compare the amounts that each *additional* unit of output will add to total revenue and to total cost. The firm should compare the *marginal revenue* (MR) and the *marginal cost* (MC) of each successive unit of output. Any unit of output whose marginal revenue exceeds its marginal cost should be produced, because on each such unit the firm gains more in revenue from its sale that it adds to costs in producing that unit. Hence, the unit of output is adding to total profits or, as the case may be, subtracting from losses. Similarly, if the marginal cost of a unit of output exceeds its marginal revenue, the firm should avoid producing that unit because it reduces profits (or increases losses). It will add more to costs than to revenue; such a unit will not "pay its way."

MR = MC Rule In the initial stages of production, where output is relatively low, marginal revenue will usually (but not always) exceed marginal cost. It is therefore profitable to produce through this range of output. But at later stages of production, where output is relatively high, rising marginal costs will exceed marginal revenue. Obviously, to maximize profits, producing units of output in this range is to be avoided.

Separating these two production ranges will be a unique point at which marginal revenue equals marginal cost. This point is the key to the output-determining rule: *The firm will maximize profits or minimize losses by producing at that point where marginal revenue equals marginal cost.* We call this profit-maximizing guide the **MR = MC rule.** For most sets of MR and MC data, there will be no nonfractional level of output at which MR and MC are precisely equal. In such instances the firm should produce the last complete unit of output whose MR exceeds its MC.

Three Characteristics There are three features of this MR = MC rule you should know.

1 The rule assumes the firm will choose to produce rather than close down. Shortly, we will note that marginal revenue must be equal to, or must exceed, average variable cost, or the firm will prefer to close down rather than produce the MR = MC output.

2 The MR = MC rule is an accurate guide to profit maximization for all firms, be they purely competitive, monopolistic, monopolistically competitive, or oligopolistic. The rule's application is *not* limited to the special case of pure competition.

3 The MR = MC rule can be restated in a slightly different form when applied to a purely competitive firm. Product price is determined by the market forces of supply and demand, and although the competitive firm can sell as much or as little as it chooses at that price, the firm cannot manipulate the price itself. In technical terms the demand, or sales, schedule faced by a competitive seller is perfectly elastic at the going market price. The result is that product price and marginal revenue are equal; that is, each extra unit sold adds precisely its price to total revenue as shown in Table 23-2 and Figure 23-1. Thus, under pure competition—and *only* under pure competition—we may substitute price for marginal revenue in the rule, so that it reads as follows: *To maximize profits or minimize losses the competitive firm should produce at that point where price equals marginal cost ($P = $ MC).*

marginal cost unusually high. The price–
al-cost relationship improves with increased
tion. On the next 5 units—2 through 6—price
ls marginal cost. Each of these 5 units adds
to revenue than to cost, more than compensat-
or the "loss" taken on the first unit. Beyond 6
, however, MC exceeds MR (= P). The firm
ld therefore produce at 6 units. In general, the
it-seeking producer should always compare mar-
al revenue (or price under pure competition) with
 rising portion of the marginal-cost schedule or
rve.

oss Determination Will production be profitable?
No, because at 6 units of output average total costs of
$91.67 exceed price of $81 by $10.67 per unit. Multi-
ply by the 6 units of output, and we find the firm's total loss is $64. Alternatively, comparing total revenue
of $486 (= 6 × $81) with total cost of $550 (= 6 ×
$91.67), the firm's loss is $64.

Then why produce? Because this loss is less than
the firm's $100 of fixed costs—the $100 loss the firm
would incur in the short run by closing down. The
firm receives enough revenue per unit ($81) to cover
its average variable costs of $75 and also provide $6
per unit, or a total of $36, to apply against fixed costs.
Therefore, the firm's loss is only $64 (= $100 – $36),
rather than $100.

Graphical Portrayal This case is shown graphically
in Figure 23-4. Whenever price exceeds the minimum
average variable cost but falls short of average total
cost, the firm can pay part, but not all, of its fixed costs

by producing. In this instance total variable costs are
shown by the area 0VGF. Total revenue, however, is
0PEF, greater than total variable costs by VPEG. This
excess of revenue over variable costs can be applied
against total fixed costs, represented by area VACG.
If it produces 6 units, the firm's loss is only area PACE;
if it closes down, its loss would be its fixed costs shown
by the larger area VACG.

Close-Down Case Suppose now that the market
yields a price of only $71. It will now pay the firm to
close down, to produce nothing, because there is no
output at which the firm can cover its average variable costs, much less its average total cost. In other
words, the smallest loss it can realize by producing is
greater than the $100 worth of fixed costs it will lose
by closing down. The best action is to close down.

This can be verified by comparing columns 3 and
8 of Table 23-5 and can be seen in Figure 23-5. Price
comes closest to covering average variable costs at
the MR (= P) = MC output of 5 units. But even here,
price or revenue per unit would fall short of average
variable cost by $3 (= $74 – $71). By producing at
the MR (= P) = MC output, the firm would lose its
$100 worth of fixed costs plus $15 ($3 on each of the
5 units) worth of variable costs, for a total loss of $115.
This compares unfavorably with the $100 fixed-cost
loss the firm would incur by closing down and thereby
producing no output. It will pay the firm to close down
rather than operate at a $71 price or at any price less
than the minimum average variable cost of $74.

The close-down case obligates us to modify our
MR (= P) = MC rule. A competitive firm will maxi-

FIGURE 23-4 The short-run
loss-minimizing position of a
purely competitive firm
If price exceeds the minimum AVC
but is less than ATC, the P = MC
... 6 units will permit the
... In this

TABLE 23-4 The profit-maximizing output for a purely competitive firm: marginal-revenue-equals-marginal-cost approach (price = $131)

(1) Total product	(2) Average fixed cost	(3) Average variable cost	(4) Average total cost	(5) Marginal cost	(6) Price = marginal revenue	(7) Total economic profit (+) or loss (−)
0				$ 90	$131	$–100
1	$100.00	$90.00	$190.00	80	131	– 59
2	50.00	85.00	135.00	70	131	– 8
3	33.33	80.00	113.33	60	131	– 53
4	25.00	75.00	100.00	70	131	+124
5	20.00	74.00	94.00	80	131	+185
6	16.67	75.00	91.67	90	131	+236
7	14.29	77.14	91.43	110	131	+277
8	12.50	81.25	93.75	130	131	+298
9	11.11	86.67	97.78	150	131	+299
10	10.00	93.00	103.00			+280

This **P = MC rule** is simply a special case of the MR = MC rule.

Now let's apply the MR = MC or, because we are considering pure competition, the P = MC rule, using the same three prices as in our total-revenue–total-cost approach to profit maximization.

Profit-Maximizing Case Table 23-4 reproduces the unit- and marginal-cost data derived in Table 22-2. It is, of course, the marginal-cost data of column 5 in Table 23-4 which we will compare with price (equal to marginal revenue) for each unit of output. Suppose first that market price, and therefore marginal revenue, is $131, as shown in column 6.

What is the profit-maximizing output? We see that every unit of output up to and including the ninth adds more to total revenue than to cost. Price, or marginal revenue, exceeds marginal cost on all the first 9 units of output. Each unit therefore adds to the firm's profits and should be produced. The tenth unit, however, will not be produced, because it would add more to costs ($150) than to revenue ($131).

Profit Calculations The level of economic profits realized by the firm can be calculated from the unit-cost data. Multiplying price ($131) by output (9), we find total revenue is $1179. Total cost of $880 is found by

multiplying average total cost ($97.78) by output (9).[1] The difference of $299 (= $1179 – $880) is economic profits.

Another means of calculating economic profits is to determine profit *per unit* by subtracting average total cost ($97.78) from product price ($131) and multiplying the difference (per unit profits of $33.22) by the level of output (9). By verifying the figures in column 7 of Table 23-4 you will find that any output other than that indicated to be most profitable by the MR (= P) = MC rule will mean either losses or profits less than $299.

Graphical Portrayal Figure 23-3 (Key Graph) compares price and marginal cost graphically. Here per unit economic profit is indicated by the distance AP. When multiplied by 9 units, the profit-maximizing output, the resulting total economic profit is shown by the rectangular area labeled "economic profit."

Note that the firm is seeking to maximize its *total* profit, not its *per unit* profits. Per unit profits are largest at 7 units of output, where price exceeds average total cost by $39.57 (= $131 – $91.43). But by

[1]In most instances the unit-cost data are rounded figures. Therefore, economic profits calculated from them will typically vary by a few cents from the profits determined in the total-revenue–total-cost approach. We here ignore the few-cents differentials and make our answers consistent with the results of the total-revenue–total-cost approach.

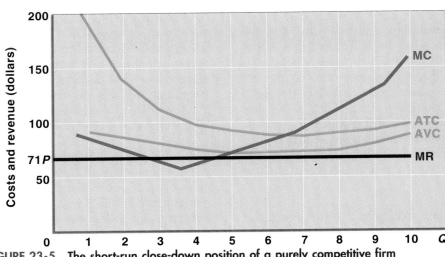

FIGURE 23-5   The short-run close-down position of a purely competitive firm
If price falls short of minimum AVC, the competitive firm will minimize its losses in the short run by closing down. There is no level of output at which the firm can produce and realize a loss smaller than its total fixed costs.

mize profits or minimize losses in the short run by producing that output at which MR $(= P) = MC$, *provided that price exceeds minimum average variable cost.*

Marginal Cost and the Short-Run Supply Curve

You will recognize that we have simply selected three different prices and asked how much the profit-seeking competitive firm, faced with certain costs, would choose to offer or supply in the market at each of these prices. This information—product price and corresponding quantity supplied—constitutes the supply schedule for the competitive firm.

Table 23-6 summarizes the supply schedule data for the three prices chosen—$131, $81, and $71. You should apply the MR $(= P) = MC$ rule (modified by the close-down case) to verify the quantity-supplied data for the $151, $111, $91, and $61 prices and calculate the corresponding profits or losses.

We confirm that the supply schedule is upsloping. Here price must be $74 (equal to minimum average variable cost) or greater before any output is supplied. And because the marginal cost of successive units of output is increasing, the firm must get successively higher prices for it to be profitable to produce these additional units of output.

Generalized Depiction   Figure 23-6 (Key Graph) generalizes on our application of the MR $(= P) = MC$ rule. We have drawn the relevant cost curves and from the vertical axis have extended a series of marginal-revenue lines from some possible prices the market might set for the firm. The crucial prices are P_2 and P_4.

Our close-down case reminds us that at any price *below* P_2—that price equal to the minimum average variable cost—the firm should close down and supply nothing. Actually, by producing Q_2 units of output *at* a price of P_2, the firm will just cover its variable costs, and its loss will be equal to its fixed costs. The firm therefore would be indifferent as to closing down *or* producing Q_2 units of output. But at any price be-

TABLE 23-6   The supply schedule of a competitive firm confronted with the cost data of Table 23-4

Price	Quantity supplied	Maximum profit (+) or minimum loss (−)
$151	10	$___
131	9	+299
111	8	___
91	7	___
81	6	− 64
71	0	−100
61	0	___

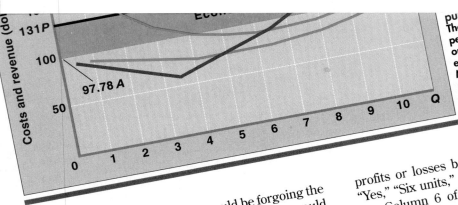

97.78 A

131P

100

50

producing only 7 units, the firm would be forgoing the production of 2 additional units of output which would clearly contribute to total profits. The firm is happy to accept lower per unit profits if the additional profits associated with the extra units of sales more than compensate for the lower per unit profits.

Loss-Minimizing Case   Now let's assume that market price is $81 rather than $131. Should the firm produce? If so, how much? And what will the resulting

The P = MC output . . . petitive producer to maximize pro . . . or minimize losses. In this case price exceeds average total cost at the P = MC output of 9 units. Economic profits per unit of AP are realized; total economic profits are indicated by the rectangle so labeled.

profits or losses be? The answers, respectively, are "Yes," "Six units," and "A loss of $64."

Column 6 of Table 23-5 shows the new price (equal to marginal revenue) beside the same unit- and marginal-cost data presented in Table 23-4. Comparing columns 5 and 6, we find that the first unit of output adds $90 to total cost but only $81 to total revenue. One might conclude: "Don't produce—close down!" But this would be hasty. Remember that in the very early stages of production, marginal product is low,

TABLE 23-5   The loss-minimizing outputs for a purely competitive firm: marginal-revenue-equals-marginal-cost approach (prices = $81 and $71)

(1) Total product	(2) Average fixed cost	(3) Average variable cost	(4) Average total cost	(5) Marginal cost	(6) $81 price = marginal revenue	(7) Profit (+) or loss (−), $81 price	(8) $71 price = marginal revenue	(9) Profit (+) or loss (−), $71 price
0								
1	$100.00	$90.00	$190.00	$ 90	$81	$−100	$71	$−100
2	50.00	85.00	135.00	80	81	−109	71	−119
3	33.33	80.00	113.33	70	81	−108	71	−128
4	25.00	75.00	100.00	60	81	− 97	71	−127
5	20.00	74.00	94.00	70	81	− 76	71	−116
6	16.67	75.00	91.67	80	81	− 65	71	−115
7	14.29	77.14	91.43	90	81	− 64	71	−124
8	12.50	81.25	93.75	110	81	− 73	71	−143
9	11.11	86.67	97.78	130	81	−102	71	−182
10	10.00	93.00	103.00	150	81	−151	71	−241
						−220		−320

KEY GRAPH

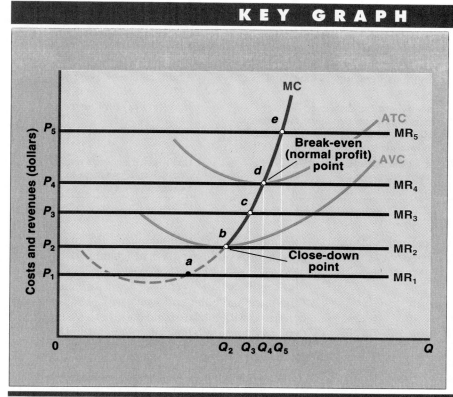

FIGURE 23-6 The $P = MC$ rule and the competitive firm's short-run supply curve
Application of the $P = MC$ rule, as modified by the close-down case, reveals that the (solid) segment of the firm's MC curve which lies above AVC is the firm's short-run supply curve. More specifically, at price P_1, $P = MC$ at point a, but the firm will produce no output because P_1 is less than minimum AVC. At price P_2 the firm is in equilibrium at point b where it produces Q_2 units and incurs a loss equal to its fixed costs. At P_3 equilibrium is at point c where output is Q_3 and losses are less than fixed costs. Equilibrium is at point d if price is P_4; in this case the firm earns a normal profit because at output Q_4 price equals ATC. At price P_5 the firm reaches an equilibrium at point e and maximizes its economic profit by producing Q_5 units.

low P_2, such as P_1, the firm will close down and supply zero units of output.

P_4 is strategic because it is the price at which the firm will just break even—earn a normal profit—by producing Q_4 units of output, as indicated by the MR $(= P) = MC$ rule. Here total revenue will just cover total costs (including a normal profit).

At P_3 the firm supplies Q_3 units of output and minimizes its losses. At any other price between P_2 and P_4 the firm will minimize its losses by producing to the point where MR $(= P) = MC$.

At any price above P_4 the firm will maximize its economic profits by producing to the point where MR $(= P) = MC$. Thus at P_5 the firm will realize the greatest profits by supplying Q_5 units of output.

The basic point is that each of the various MR $(= P) = MC$ intersection points shown as b, c, d, and e in Figure 23-6 indicates a possible product price (on the vertical axis) and the corresponding quantity which the profit-seeking firm would supply at that price (on the horizontal axis). These points locate the supply curve of the competitive firm. Because noth-

ing would be produced at any price below the minimum average variable cost, we can conclude that *the portion of the firm's marginal-cost curve lying above its average-variable-cost curve is its* **short-run supply curve.** The solid segment of the marginal-cost curve is the short-run supply curve in Figure 23-6. This is the link between production costs and supply in the short run.

Supply Curve Shifts In Chapter 22 we saw that changes in such factors as the prices of variable inputs or in technology will shift the marginal-cost or short-run supply curve to a new location. For example, a wage increase would shift the supply curve in Figure 23-6 upward as viewed from the horizontal axis (leftward as viewed from the vertical axis), constituting a decrease in supply. Similarly, technological progress which increases the productivity of labor would shift the marginal-cost or supply curve downward as viewed from the horizontal axis (rightward as viewed from the vertical axis). This represents an increase in supply. You should determine how (1) a

TABLE 23-7   Summary of competitive output determination in the short run

Question	Total-revenue–total-cost approach	Marginal-revenue–marginal-cost approach
Should this firm produce?	Yes, if TR exceeds TC or if TC exceeds TR by some amount less than total fixed cost.	Yes, if price is equal to, or greater than, minimum average variable cost.
What quantity should be produced to maximize profits?	Produce where the excess of TR over TC is a maximum or where the excess of TC over TR is a minimum (and less than total fixed costs).	Produce where MR or price equals MC.
Will production result in economic profit?	Yes, if TR exceeds TC. No, if TC exceeds TR.	Yes, if price exceeds average total cost. No, if average total cost exceeds price.

specific tax on the product and (2) a per unit subsidy on this product would shift the supply curve.

QUICK REVIEW 23-3

■ Profits are maximized or losses minimized at that output at which marginal revenue (or price in pure competition) equals marginal cost.

■ At any price below minimum average variable cost the firm will minimize losses by closing down.

■ The segment of the firm's marginal-cost curve which lies above average variable cost is its short-run supply curve.

■ Table 23-7 is a convenient check sheet on the total-revenue–total-cost and MR = MC approaches to determining the competitive firm's profit-maximizing output.

Firm and Industry: Equilibrium Price

Having developed the competitive firm's short-run supply curve by applying the MR (= P) = MC rule, we now determine which of the various price possibilities will actually be the equilibrium price.

From Chapter 3 we know that in a purely competitive market, equilibrium price is determined by *total,* or market, supply, and total demand. To derive total supply, the supply schedules or curves of the individual competitive sellers must be summed. Thus in Table 23-8, columns 1 and 3 repeat the individual competitive firm's supply schedule derived in Table 23-6. We now assume that there are 1000 competitive firms in this industry, each having the same total and unit costs as the single firm we discussed. This lets us calculate the total- or market-supply schedule

(columns 2 and 3) by multiplying the quantity-supplied figures of the single firm (column 1) by 1000.

Market Price and Profits   To determine equilibrium price and output, this total-supply data must be compared with total-demand data. Let's assume total-demand data are as shown in columns 3 and 4 of Table 23-8. Comparing the total quantity supplied and total quantity demanded at the seven possible prices, we determine that the equilibrium price is $111, and the equilibrium quantity 8000 units for the industry—8 units for each of the 1000 identical firms.

Will these conditions of market supply and demand make this a prosperous or an unprosperous industry? Multiplying product price ($111) by output (8 units), we find the total revenue of each firm is $888. Total cost is $750, found by multiplying average total cost of $93.75 by 8, or simply by looking at column 4 of Table 23-3. The $138 difference is the economic profit of each firm.

TABLE 23-8   Firm and market supply and market demand

(1) Quantity supplied, single firm	(2) Total quantity supplied, 1000 firms	(3) Product price	(4) Total quantity demanded
10	10,000	$151	4,000
9	9,000	131	6,000
8	8,000	111	8,000
7	7,000	91	9,000
6	6,000	81	11,000
0	0	71	13,000
0	0	61	16,000

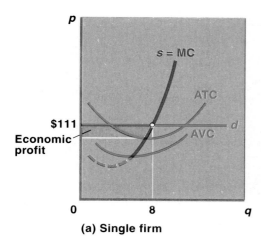

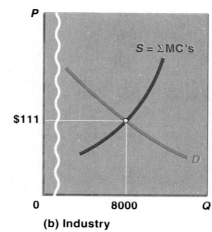

FIGURE 23-7 Short-run competitive equilibrium for a firm (a) and the industry (b) The horizontal sum of the 1000 firms' supply curves (s) determines the industry supply curve (S). Given industry demand (D), the short-run equilibrium price and output for the industry are $111 and 8000 units. Taking the equilibrium price as given datum, the representative firm establishes its profit-maximizing output at 8 units and, in this case, realizes the economic profit shown by the area labeled as such.

(a) Single firm   (b) Industry

Another way of calculating economic profits is to determine *per unit* profit by subtracting average total cost ($93.75) from product price ($111) and multiplying the difference (per unit profits of $17.25) by the firm's equilibrium level of output (8). For the industry, total economic profit is $138,000. This, then, is a prosperous industry.

Graphical Portrayal Figure 23-7a and b shows this analysis graphically. The individual supply curves of each of the 1000 identical firms—one of which is shown as *s* in Figure 23-7a—are summed horizontally to get the total supply curve *S* of Figure 23-7b. Given total demand *D,* equilibrium price is $111, and equilibrium quantity for the industry is 8000 units. This equilibrium price is given and unalterable to the individual firm; that is, each firm's demand curve is perfectly elastic at the equilibrium price, indicated by *d.* Because price is given and constant to the individual firm, the marginal-revenue curve coincides with the demand curve. This $111 price exceeds average total cost at the firm's equilibrium MR (= P) = MC output, resulting in a situation of economic profits similar to that already portrayed in Figure 23-3.

Assuming no changes in cost or market demands, these diagrams reveal a genuine *short-run* equilibrium situation. There are no shortages or surpluses in the market to cause price or total quantity to change. Nor can any of the firms in the industry improve their profits by altering their output. Note, too, that higher unit and marginal costs, on the one hand, or a weaker market demand situation, on the other, could pose a loss situation similar to Figure 23-4. You are urged to

sketch, in Figure 23-7a and b, how higher costs and a less favorable demand could cause a short-run equilibrium situation entailing losses.

Firm versus Industry Figure 23-7a and b underscores a point made earlier. Product price is a given datum to the *individual* competitive firm, but at the same time, the supply plans of all competitive producers *as a group* are a basic determinant of product price. If we recall the fallacy of composition, we find there is no inconsistency here. Though each firm, supplying a negligible fraction of total supply, cannot affect price, the sum of the supply curves of all the firms in the industry constitutes the industry supply curve, and this curve does have an important bearing on price. *Under competition, equilibrium price is a given datum to the individual firm and simultaneously is the result of the production (supply) decisions of all firms taken as a group. (Key Question 4)*

PROFIT MAXIMIZATION IN THE LONG RUN

In the long run firms can make adjustments which there isn't time to make in the short run. In the short run there are a specific number of firms in an industry, each with a fixed, unalterable plant. True, firms may close down in the sense that they produce zero units of output in the short run; but they do not have sufficient time to liquidate their assets and go out of business. By contrast, in the long run firms already in an industry have sufficient time either to expand

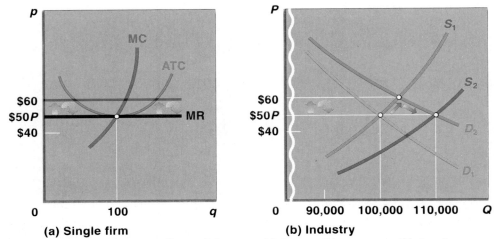

FIGURE 23-8   Temporary profits and the reestablishment of long-run equilibrium in a representative firm (a) and the industry (b)
A favorable shift in demand (D_1 to D_2) will upset the original equilibrium and produce economic profits. But profits will cause new firms to enter the industry, increasing supply (S_1 to S_2) and lowering product price until economic profits are once again zero.

or contract their plant capacities. More importantly, the number of firms in the industry may either increase or decrease as new firms enter or existing firms leave. We now examine how these long-run adjustments modify our conclusions concerning short-run output and price determination.

Assumptions

We will make three simplifying assumptions, none of which will impair the validity of our conclusions.

1   Entry and Exodus   The only long-run adjustment is the entry and exodus of firms. Furthermore, we ignore the short-run adjustments already analyzed, in order to grasp the nature of long-run competitive adjustments.

2   Identical Costs   All firms in the industry have identical cost curves. This assumption lets us discuss an "average," or "representative," firm knowing that all other firms in the industry are similarly affected by any long-run adjustments which occur.

3   Constant-Cost Industry   The industry under discussion is a constant-cost industry. This means that the entry and exodus of firms will *not* affect resource prices or, therefore, the locations of the unit-cost schedules of individuals firms.

Goal

We will describe long-run competitive adjustments verbally and graphically. The basic conclusion we seek to explain is: *After all long-run adjustments are completed, product price will be exactly equal to, and production will occur at, each firm's point of minimum average total cost.*

This conclusion follows from two basic facts: (1) Firms seek profits and shun losses, and (2) under competition, firms are free to enter and leave industries. If price initially exceeds average total costs, the resulting economic profits will attract new firms to the industry. But this industry expansion will increase product supply until price is brought back down to equality with minimum average total cost. Conversely, if price is initially less than average total cost, resulting losses will cause firms to leave the industry. As they leave, total product supply will decline, bringing price back up to equality with minimum average total cost.

Zero Economic Profit Model

Suppose the average or representative firm in a purely competitive industry is initially in long-run equilibrium. This is shown in Figure 23-8a, where price and minimum average total cost are equal at, say, $50. Economic profits here are zero; the industry is in equi-

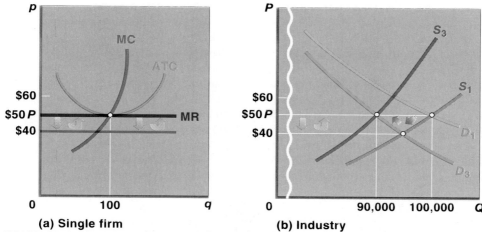

(a) Single firm   **(b) Industry**

FIGURE 23-9 Temporary losses and the reestablishment of long-run equilibrium in a representative firm (a) and the industry (b)
An unfavorable shift in demand (D_1 to D_3) will upset the original equilibrium and produce losses. But losses will cause firms to leave the industry, decreasing supply (S_1 to S_3) and increasing product price until all losses have disappeared.

librium or "at rest," because there is no tendency for firms to enter or leave the industry. The existing firms are earning only normal profits which are incorporated in their cost curves. The market price in Figure 23-8b is determined by total, or industry, demand and supply, as shown by D_1 and S_1. (The market supply schedule, incidentally, is a *short-run* schedule; the industry's long-run supply schedule will be developed in our discussion.) By examining the quantity axes of the two graphs, we note that if all firms are identical, there must be 1000 firms in the industry, each producing 100 units, to achieve the industry's equilibrium output of 100,000 units.

Entry Eliminates Economic Profits

Let's upset the long-run equilibrium of Figure 23-8 and trace subsequent adjustments. Suppose a change in consumer tastes increases product demand from D_1 to D_2. This favorable shift in demand will create economic profits; the new price of $60 exceeds average total cost of $50, creating an economic profit of $10 per unit. *These economic profits will lure new firms into the industry.* Some entrants will be newly created firms; others will shift from less prosperous industries.

As firms enter, the market supply of the product will increase, pushing product price below $60. Economic profits will persist, and entry will continue un-

til short-run market supply has increased to S_2. At this point, price (= $50) is again equal to minimum average total cost at $50. The economic profits caused by the boost in demand have been competed away to zero, and as a result, the previous incentive for more firms to enter the industry has disappeared. Long-run equilibrium is restored at this point.

Figure 23-8 tells us that upon reestablishment of long-run equilibrium, industry output is 110,000 units and that each firm in the now expanded industry is producing 100 units. We can conclude that the industry is now composed of 1100 firms; that is, 100 new firms have entered the industry.

Exodus Eliminates Losses

To strengthen our understanding of long-run competitive equilibrium, let's reverse our analysis. In Figure 23-9a and b, the $50 price and curves S_1 and D_1 show the initial long-run equilibrium situation used as a point of departure in our previous analysis.

Now suppose that consumer demand falls from D_1 to D_3. This forces price down to $40, making production unprofitable. *In time resulting losses will induce firms to leave the industry.* The reason is that owners can realize a normal profit elsewhere rather than the below-normal profit (losses) now confronting them. As capital equipment wears out and contractual obligations expire, some firms will simply fold. As this exodus of firms proceeds, however, industry supply will decrease, moving from S_1 toward S_3. As this occurs, price will begin to rise from $40 back toward $50. Losses will force firms to leave the industry until supply has declined to S_3, at which point price is again exactly $50, barely consistent with minimum average total cost. The exodus continues until losses are eliminated and long-run equilibrium is again restored.

Observe in Figure 23-9a and b that total quantity supplied is now 90,000 units and each firm is producing 100 units. The industry is populated by only 900 firms rather than the original 1000 since losses have forced 100 firms out of business.

You may have noted that we have sidestepped the question of which firms will leave the industry when losses occur by assuming all firms have identical cost curves. In the "real world" entrepreneurial talents differ so that, even if resource prices and technology are the same for all firms, inferior entrepreneurs would incur higher costs and therefore be the first to leave the industry when product demand declined. Similarly, other resources may be heterogeneous and also give rise to cost differences. For example, firms with less productive labor forces will be high-cost producers and likely candidates to quit the industry when product demand decreases.

Our prestated conclusion has now been verified. Competition, reflected in the entry and exodus of firms, forces price into equality with the minimum long-run average total cost of production, and each firm produces at the point of minimum long-run average total cost. Note, too, that these cases of expanding- and declining-industries explain the functioning of consumer sovereignty, a concept discussed in Chapter 4.

Long-Run Supply for a Constant-Cost Industry

What is the character of the **long-run supply curve** which evolves from this analysis of the expansion or contraction of a competitive industry? Although our discussion deals with the long run, we have noted that the market supply curves of Figures 23-8b and 23-9b are short-run industry supply curves. However, the analysis permits us to sketch the nature of the long-run supply curve for this competitive industry. The crucial factor in determining the shape of the industry's long-run supply curve is the effect, if any, which changes in the number of firms in the industry will have on the costs of the individual firms in the industry.

Constant-Cost Industry In the foregoing analysis of long-run competitive equilibrium we assumed the industry under discussion was a **constant-cost industry.** This means that industry expansion or contraction through the entry or exodus of firms will not affect resource prices or, therefore, production costs. Graphically, the entry or exodus of firms does *not* change the position of the long-run average-total-cost curves of individual firms in the industry. When will this be the case? For the most part, when the industry's demand for resources is small in relation to the total demand for those resources. This is most likely to occur when the industry employs unspecialized resources which are being demanded by many other industries. In short, when the particular industry's demand for resources is a negligible component of total demand, the industry can expand or contract without significantly affecting resource prices and costs.

Perfectly Elastic Supply What will the long-run supply curve for a constant-cost industry look like? The answer is contained in our previous discussion of the long-run adjustments toward equilibrium which profits or losses will initiate. There we assumed that entrance or departure of firms would not affect costs. The result was that entry or exodus of firms would alter industry output but always bring product price back to the original $50 level, where it is just consistent with the unchanging minimum average total cost of production. Specifically, we discovered that the industry would supply 90,000, 100,000, or 110,000 units of output, all at a price of $50 per unit. *The long-run supply curve of a constant-cost industry is perfectly elastic.*

This is demonstrated graphically in Figure 23-10, where the data from Figures 23-8 and 23-9 are retained. Suppose industry demand is originally D_1, industry output is Q_1 (100,000), and product price is Q_1P_1 ($50). This situation, referring to Figure 23-8, is one of long-run equilibrium. Now assume that demand increases to D_2, upsetting this equilibrium. The resulting economic profits will attract new firms. Because this is a constant-cost industry, entry will continue and industry output will expand until price is driven back down to the unchanged minimum average-total-cost level. This will be at price Q_2P_2 ($50) and output Q_2 (110,000).

This analysis, now referring to Figure 23-9, is reversible. A decline in short-run industry demand from D_1 to D_3 will cause an exodus of firms and ultimately restore equilibrium at price Q_3P_3 ($50) and output Q_3

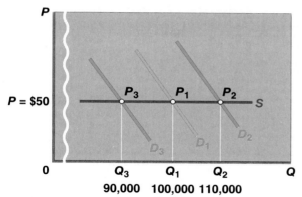

FIGURE 23-10 The long-run supply curve for a constant-cost industry is perfectly elastic
Because the entry or exodus of firms does not affect resource prices or, therefore, unit costs, an increase in demand (D_1 to D_2) will cause an expansion in industry output (Q_1 to Q_2) but no alteration in price ($Q_1P_1 = Q_2P_2$). Similarly, a decrease in demand (D_1 to D_3) will cause a contraction of output (Q_1 to Q_3) but no change in price ($Q_1P_1 = Q_3P_3$). This means that the long-run industry supply curve (S) will be perfectly elastic.

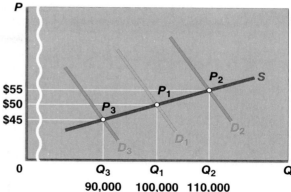

FIGURE 23-11 The long-run supply curve for an increasing-cost industry is upsloping
In an increasing-cost industry the entry of new firms in response to an increase in demand (D_3 to D_1 to D_2) will bid up resource prices and thereby increase unit costs. As a result, an increased industry output (Q_3 to Q_1 to Q_2) will be forthcoming only at higher prices ($Q_2P_2 > Q_1P_1 > Q_3P_3$). The long-run industry supply curve (S) is therefore upsloping.

(90,000). A line connecting all points, such as these three, shows the various price–quantity supplied combinations most profitable when firms have had enough time to make *all* desired adjustments to assumed changes in industry demand. By definition, this line is the industry's long-run supply curve. In a constant-cost industry this line—*S* in Figure 23-10—is perfectly elastic.

Long-Run Supply for an Increasing-Cost Industry

But constant-cost industries are a special case. Most industries are **increasing-cost industries,** meaning their average-total-cost curves shift upward as the industry expands and downward as the industry contracts. Usually, the entry of new firms will bid up resource prices and therefore raise unit costs for individual firms in the industry. When an industry is using a significant portion of some resource whose total supply is not readily increased, the entry of new firms will increase resource demand in relation to supply and boost resource prices. This is particularly so in industries using specialized resources whose initial supply is not readily augmented. Higher resource prices will result in higher long-run average total costs for firms in the industry. The higher costs take the form of an upward shift in the firm's long-run average-total-cost curve.

The net result is that when an increase in product demand causes economic profits and attracts new firms to the industry, a two-way squeeze on profits will eliminate those profits. The entry of new firms will increase market supply and lower product price; the entire average-total-cost curve will shift upward. The equilibrium price will now be higher than it was originally. The industry will produce a larger output at a higher price because industry expansion has increased average total costs, and in the long run product price must cover these costs. Greater output will be forthcoming at a higher price, or, more technically, the industry supply curve for an increasing-cost industry will be upsloping. Instead of getting either 90,000, 100,000, or 110,000 units at the same price of $50, in an increasing-cost industry 90,000 units might be forthcoming at $45; 100,000 at $50; and 110,000 at $55. The higher price is required to induce more production because costs per unit of output increase as the industry expands.

We show this in Figure 23-11. Original market demand, industry output, and price are D_1, Q_1 (100,000), and Q_1P_1 (50), respectively. An increase in demand to D_2 will upset this equilibrium and lead to economic profits. As new firms enter, (1) industry supply will increase, driving product price down to minimum average total cost, and (2) resource prices will rise, causing average total costs of production to rise. Because of these average-total-cost increases, the new long-run

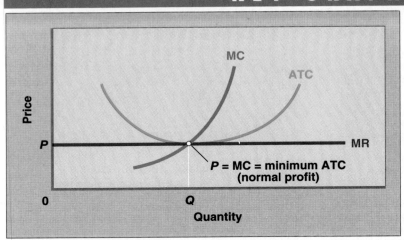

KEY GRAPH

FIGURE 23-12 The long-run equilibrium position of a competitive firm, $P = MC =$ minimum ATC
The equality of price and minimum average total cost indicates that the firm is using the most efficient known technology and is charging the lowest price P and producing the greatest output Q consistent with its costs. The equality of price and marginal cost indicates that resources are being allocated in accordance with consumer preferences.

equilibrium price will be established at some level *above* the original price, such as Q_2P_2 ($55).

Conversely, a decline in demand from D_1 to D_3 will make production unprofitable and cause firms to leave the industry. The resulting decline in the demand for resources relative to their supply will lower resource prices and reduce average total costs of production. The new equilibrium price will be established at some level *below* the original price, such as Q_3P_3 ($45). Connecting these three equilibrium positions, we derive an upsloping long-run supply curve shown by S in Figure 23-11.

Long-Run Supply for a Decreasing-Cost Industry

In industries known as **decreasing-cost industries** firms may experience lower costs as the industry expands. Classic example: As more mines are established in a given locality, each firm's costs in pumping out water seepage may decline. With more mines pumping, seepage into each is less, and pumping costs are therefore reduced. Furthermore, with only a few mines in an area, industry output might be so small that only relatively primitive and therefore costly transportation facilities are available. But as the number of firms and industry output expand, a railroad might build a spur into the area and thereby significantly reduce transportation costs.

You are urged to replicate the analysis underlying Figure 23-11 to show that the long-run supply

curve of a decreasing-cost industry will be *downsloping*. (Key Question 8)

PURE COMPETITION AND EFFICIENCY

Whether a purely competitive industry is one of constant or increasing costs, the final long-run equilibrium position for each firm will have the same basic characteristics. As shown in Figure 23-12 (Key Graph) price (and marginal revenue) will settle where they are equal to minimum average total cost. However, we discovered in Chapter 22 that the marginal-cost curve intersects, and is therefore equal to, average total cost at the point of minimum average total cost. In the long-run equilibrium position, "everything is equal." MR $(= P) = MC =$ minimum ATC.

This triple equality tells us that, although a competitive firm may realize economic profits or losses in the short run, it will earn only a normal profit by producing in accordance with the MR $(= P) = MC$ rule in the long run. Also, this triple equality suggests certain conclusions of great social significance concerning the efficiency of a purely competitive economy.

Economists agree that, subject to certain qualifications we will discuss shortly, a purely competitive economy will lead to a most efficient use of society's scarce resources. *A competitive price economy will use the limited amounts of resources available to society in a way which maximizes the satisfactions of consumers.*

Efficient use of limited resources requires that two conditions—allocative efficiency and productive efficiency—are fulfilled.

First, to achieve **allocative efficiency,** resources must be apportioned among firms and industries to obtain the particular mix of products which is most wanted by society (consumers). Allocative efficiency is realized when it is impossible to alter the composition of total output to achieve a net gain for society.

Second, **productive efficiency** requires that each good in this optimum product mix be produced in the least costly way. To facilitate our discussion of how these conditions would be achieved under purely competitive conditions, let's examine the second point first.

1   Productive Efficiency: *P* = Minimum ATC   In the long run, competition forces firms to produce at the point of minimum average total cost of production and to charge that price which is just consistent with these costs. This is a most desirable situation from the consumer's point of view. It means that firms must use the best available (least-cost) technology or they will not survive. Stated differently, the minimum amount of resources will be used to produce any particular output.

For example, glance back at the final equilibrium position shown in Figure 23-9a. Each firm in the industry is producing 100 units of output by using $5000 (equal to average total cost of $50 *times* 100 units) worth of resources. If that same output had been produced at a total cost of, say, $7000, resources would be used inefficiently. Society would be faced with the net loss of $2000 worth of alternative products. Note, too, that consumers benefit from the lowest product price possible under the cost conditions currently prevailing. Finally, the costs involved in each instance are only those costs essential in producing a product. Because products are standardized in competitive industries, there will be no selling or promotional costs added to production costs in determining product price.

2   Allocative Efficiency: *P* = MC   But the competitive production of *any* collection of goods does not necessarily make for an efficient allocation of resources. Production must not only be technologically efficient, but must also be the "right goods," goods consumers want most. The competitive market system works so that resources are allocated to produce a total output whose composition best fits consumer preferences.

We must first grasp the social meaning of competitive product and resource prices. *The money price of any product—product X— is society's measure, or index, of the relative worth of that product at the margin.* In other words, price reflects the marginal benefit derived from the good. Similarly, recalling the notion of opportunity costs, *the marginal cost of producing X measures the value, or relative worth, of the other goods which the resources used in producing an extra unit of X could otherwise have produced.* In short, product price measures the marginal benefit, or satisfaction, which society gets from additional units of X, and the marginal cost of an additional unit of X measures the sacrifice, or cost to society, of other goods in using resources to produce more of X.

Underallocation: P > *MC*   Under competition, the production of each product will occur up to that precise point at which price is equal to marginal cost (Figure 23-12). The profit-seeking competitor will realize the maximum possible profit only by equating price and marginal cost. To produce short of the MR (= *P*) = MC point will mean less than maximum profits to the individual firm and an *under*allocation of resources to this product from society's standpoint. The fact that price exceeds marginal cost indicates that society values additional units of X more highly than the alternative products the appropriate resources could otherwise produce.

To illustrate, if the price or marginal benefit of a shirt is $20 and its marginal cost is $16, producing an additional shirt will cause a net increase in total output of $4. Society will gain a shirt valued at $20, while the alterative products sacrificed by allocating more resources of shirts would only be valued at $16. Whenever society can gain something valued at $20 by giving up something valued at $16, the initial allocation of resources must have been inefficient.

Overallocation: P < *MC*   For similar reasons, the production of X should not go beyond the output at which price equals marginal cost. To do so would entail less than maximum profits for producers and an *over*allocation of resources to X from the standpoint of society. To produce X at some point at which marginal cost exceeds price or marginal benefit means resources are being used in the production of X by sacrificing alternative goods society values more highly than the added units of X.

For example, if the price of a shirt is $20 and its marginal cost is $26, then the production of one less shirt would result in a net increase in society's total output of $6. Society would lose a shirt valued at $20, but reallocating the freed resources to their best alternative uses would increase the output of some other good valued at $26. Again, whenever society is able to give up something valued at $20 in return for something valued at $26, the original allocation of resources must have been inefficient.

Efficient Allocation Our conclusion is that *under pure competition, profit-motivated producers will produce each commodity up to that precise point where price (marginal benefit) and marginal cost are equal. This means that resources are efficiently allocated under competition.* Each good is produced to the point at which the value of the last unit is equal to the value of the alternative goods sacrificed by its production. To alter the production of X would reduce consumer satisfactions. To produce X beyond the $P = MC$ point would sacrifice alternative goods whose value to society exceeds that of the extra units of X. To produce X short of the $P = MC$ point would sacrifice units of X which society values more than the alternative goods resources can produce.

Dynamic Adjustments A further attribute of purely competitive markets is their ability to restore efficiency in the use of resources when disrupted by dynamic changes in the economy. In a competitive economy, any changes in consumer tastes, resource supplies, or technology will automatically set in motion appropriate realignments of resources. As we have already explained, an increase in consumer demand for product X will increase its price. Disequilibrium will occur in that, at its present output, the price of X will now exceed its marginal cost. This will create economic profits in industry X and stimulate its expansion. Its profitability will permit the industry to bid resources away from now less pressing uses. Expansion in this industry will end only when the price of X again equals its marginal cost, that is, when the value of the last unit produced once again equals the value of the alternative goods society forgoes in producing that last unit of X.

Similarly, changes in supplies of particular resources or in production techniques will upset existing price–marginal-cost equalities by either raising or lowering marginal cost. These inequalities will cause business executives, in either pursuing profits or shunning losses, to reallocate resources until price once again equals marginal cost in each line of production. In so doing, they correct any inefficiencies in the allocation of resources which changing economic data may temporarily impose on the economy.

"Invisible Hand" Revisited A final point: The highly efficient allocation of resources which a purely competitive economy fosters comes about because businesses and resource suppliers freely seek to further their own self-interests. The "invisible hand" (Chapter 4) is at work in a competitive market system. In a competitive economy, businesses employ resources until the extra, or marginal, costs of production equal the product price. This not only maximizes profits for individual producers but simultaneously results in a pattern of resource allocation which maximizes consumer satisfaction. The competitive market system organizes the private interests of producers along lines which are fully in accord with society's interest in using scarce resources efficiently. *(Key Question 10)*

QUICK REVIEW 23-4

■ In the long run the entry of firms will compete away profits and the exodus of firms will eliminate losses so that price equals minimum average total cost.

■ The long-run supply curves of constant-, increasing-, and decreasing-cost industries are perfectly elastic, upsloping, and downsloping, respectively.

■ In purely competitive markets both productive efficiency (price equals minimum average total cost) and allocative efficiency (price equals marginal cost) are achieved in the long run.

Qualifications

Our conclusion that a purely competitive market system results in both productive and allocative efficiency must be qualified in several respects.

The Income Distribution Problem The contention that pure competition will allocate resources efficiently is predicated on some particular distribution of money income. Money income is distributed among households in some specific way, and this distribution results in a certain structure of demand. The competitive market system then brings about an efficient allocation of resources or, stated differently, an output of goods and services whose composition maximizes fulfillment of these particular consumer demands.

But if the distribution of money income is altered so that the structure of demand changes, would the competitive market system negotiate a new allocation of resources? "Yes," the market system would reallocate resources and therefore change the composition of output to maximize the fulfillment of this new pattern of consumer wants. The question, then, is which of these two "efficient" allocations of resources is the "most efficient"? Which allocation of resources yields the greatest level of satisfaction to society?

There is no *scientific* answer to this question. If all people were alike in their capacities to obtain satisfaction from income and in their contributions to output, economists could recommend that income be distributed equally and that the allocation of resources appropriate to *that* distribution would be the "best" or "most efficient" of all. But, people differ in their education, productivity, experiences, and environment, not to mention their mental and physical characteristics. Such differences can be used to argue for an unequal distribution of income.

The distribution of income associated with the workings of a purely competitive market system is in fact quite unequal (Chapter 34) and therefore may lead to the production of trifles for the rich while denying basic needs of the poor. Many economists believe that the distribution of income which pure competition provides should be modified by public action. They maintain that allocative efficiency is hardly a virtue if it is a response to an income distribution which offends prevailing standards of equity.

Market Failure: Spillovers and Public Goods   Under competition each producer will assume only those costs which it *must* pay. This correctly implies that in some lines of production there are significant costs producers can and do avoid, usually by polluting the environment. Recall from Chapter 5 that these avoided costs accrue to society and are aptly called *spillover* or *external costs*. On the other hand, consumption of certain goods and services, such as education and measles vaccinations, yields widespread satisfactions, or benefits, to society as a whole. These satisfactions are called *external* or *spillover benefits*.

The profit-seeking activities of producers will bring about an allocation of resources which is efficient from society's point of view only if marginal cost embodies *all* the costs which production entails and product price accurately reflects *all* the benefits which society gets from a good's production. Only in this case will competitive production at the MR (= *P*) =

MC point balance the *total* sacrifices and satisfactions of society and result in an efficient allocation of resources. If price and marginal cost are not accurate indexes of sacrifices and satisfactions—if sizable spillover costs and benefits exist—production at the MR (= *P*) = MC point will *not* signify an efficient allocation of resources.

Remember, too, the point of the lighthouse example in Chapter 5: The market system does not provide for social or public goods, that is, for goods to which the exclusion principle does *not* apply. Despite its other virtues, the competitive price system ignores an important class of goods and services—national defense, flood-control programs, and so forth—which can and do yield satisfaction to consumers but which cannot be priced and sold through the market system.

Production Techniques   Purely competitive markets may not always entail the use of the most efficient production techniques or encourage development of improved techniques. There are both a static (or "right now") aspect and a dynamic (or "over time") aspect of this criticism.

Natural Monopolies   The static aspect involves the *natural monopoly* problem introduced in Chapter 22. In certain lines of production, existing technology may be such that a firm must be a large-scale producer to realize the lowest unit costs of production. Given consumer demand, this suggests that a relatively small number of large-scale producers is needed if production is to be carried on efficiently. Existing mass-production economies might be lost if such an industry were populated by the large number of small-scale producers pure competition requires.

Technological Progress   The dynamic aspect of this criticism concerns the willingness and ability of purely competitive firms to undertake technological advance. The progressiveness of pure competition is debated by economists. Some authorities believe that a purely competitive economy would *not* foster a very rapid rate of technological progress. They argue, first, that the incentive for technological advance may be weak under pure competition because the profit rewards accruing to an innovating firm from a cost-reducing technological improvement will be quickly competed away by rival firms adopting the new technique. Second, the small size of the typical competitive firm and the fact that it tends to "break even" in

LAST WORD

"CREATIVE DESTRUCTION" AS A COMPETITIVE FORCE

The famous Austrian—later American—economist, Joseph Schumpeter (1883–1950), held that models such as pure competition are inadequate because they view markets in a static or point-in-time framework. Schumpeter argued that technological progress is a much more important, dynamic form of competition which occurs over extended periods of time.

Schumpeter viewed competition as a dynamic process involving development of new products and markets, new production and transportation techniques, and even new forms of business organization. Such innovations were viewed by Schumpeter as a process of "creative destruction" because creation of new products and production methods simultaneously destroyed the market (often monopoly) positions of firms committed to existing products and old ways of doing business. In Schumpeter's words:

In capitalist reality . . . it is . . . competition from

the new commodity, the new technology, the new source of supply, the new type of organization (the largest-scale unit of control for instance)—competition which commands a decisive cost or quality advantage and which strikes not at the margins of the profits and the outputs of the existing firms but at their foundations and their very lives. This kind of competi-

the long run raise serious questions whether such producers could finance substantial programs of organized research.

Range of Consumer Choice A purely competitive economy might not provide a sufficient range of consumer choice or foster development of new products. This criticism, like the previous one, has both a static and a dynamic aspect. Pure competition means product standardization, whereas other market structures—for example, monopolistic competition and, frequently, oligopoly—encompass a wide range of types, styles, and quality gradations of any product.

This product differentiation widens the consumer's range of free choice and simultaneously allows buyers to more completely fulfill their preferences. Similarly, critics of pure competition point out that, just as pure competition is not likely to be progressive in developing new production techniques, nor is this market structure conducive to improving existing products or creating completely new ones.

The question of progressiveness of various market structures in terms of both production techniques and product development will recur in the following three chapters.[2]

CHAPTER SUMMARY

1 The market models of **a** pure competition, **b** pure monopoly, **c** monopolistic competition, and **d** oligopoly are classifications into which most industries can be fitted with reasonable accuracy.

2 A purely competitive industry comprises a large number of independent firms producing a standardized product. Pure competition assumes that firms and resources are mobile among different industries.

3 No single firm can influence market price in a competitive industry; the firm's demand curve is perfectly elastic and price therefore equals marginal revenue.

---

[2]Instructors who want to consider agriculture as a case study in pure competition should insert Chapter 33 at this point.

tion is . . . so . . . important that it becomes a matter of comparative indifference whether competition in the ordinary sense functions more or less promptly; the powerful lever that in the long run expands output and brings down prices is in any case made of other stuff.*

Historical examples of creative destruction as a competitive force are abundant. In the 1800s railroads began to compete with wagons, ships, and barges in transporting freight, only to have their dominant market position undermined by trucks and, still after, by airplanes. Similarly, the rapid development of the dehydrated and quick-frozen food industries during World War II intensified the competition which paper and plastic containers provide for the can industry. Movies competed with live theater, only to be challenged in turn by television. Typewriter manufacturers face severe competition because of the development of word processors and personal comput-

*Joseph A. Schumpeter, *Capitalism, Socialism, and Democracy*, 3d ed. (New York: Harper & Row, Publishers, Incorporated, 1950), pp. 84–85.

ers. Cable television assaults the networks; fax machines replace mail; mass discounters such as Wal-Mart attack Sears and Montgomery Ward; and personal computers challenge mainframe computers. Eye surgery (radial kerototomy) competes with glasses and contacts in correcting nearsightedness and astigmatism.

Acetate 78-rpm phonograph records were supplanted by vinyl long-playing records after World War II. Cassettes then challenged LP records, and now development of compact discs has doomed them. In 1983, when CDs were introduced, record companies shipped over 295 million LPs and only 800,000 CDs. In 1992 less than 3 million LPs were produced, compared to 407 million CDs. CDs have also put a competitive squeeze on cassettes, whose shipments fell from 450 million in 1988 to 360 million in 1991.

The point is that competition must be defined more broadly than a simple entry of firms into existing profitable industries. Technological progress is a fundamental competitive force which over time can undermine existing industries—even monopolies—and eliminate any economic profits they enjoy.

4 Short-run profit maximization by a competitive firm can be analyzed by a comparison of total revenue and total cost or through marginal analysis. A firm will maximize profits by producing that output at which total revenue exceeds total cost by the greatest amount. Losses will be minimized by producing where the excess of total cost over total revenue is at a minimum and less than total fixed costs.

5 Provided price exceeds minimum average variable cost, a competitive firm will maximize profits or minimize losses in the short run by producing that output at which price or marginal revenue equals marginal cost. If price is less than average variable cost, the firm will minimize its losses by closing down. If price is greater than average variable cost but less than average total cost, the firm will minimize its losses by producing the $P = MC$ output. If price exceeds average total cost, the $P = MC$ output will provide maximum economic profits for the firm.

6 Applying the MR ($= P$) $=$ MC rule at various possible market prices leads to the conclusion that the segment of the firm's short-run marginal-cost curve lying above average variable cost in its short-run supply curve.

7 In the long run, competitive price will equal the minimum average total cost of production because economic profits will cause firms to enter a competitive industry until those profits have been competed away. Conversely,

losses will force the exodus of firms from the industry until product price once again barely covers unit costs.

8 The long-run supply curve is perfectly elastic for a constant-cost industry, upsloping for an increasing-cost industry, and downsloping for a decreasing-cost industry.

9 The long-run equality of price and minimum average total cost means that competitive firms will use the most efficient known technology and charge the lowest price consistent with their production costs.

10 The equality of price and marginal cost implies that resources will be allocated in accordance with consumer tastes. The competitive price system will reallocate resources in response to a change in consumer tastes, technology, or resource supplies to maintain allocative efficiency over time.

11 Economists recognize four possible deterrents to allocative efficiency in a competitive economy. a There is no reason why the competitive market system will result in an optimal distribution of income. b In allocating resources, the competitive model does not allow for spillover costs and benefits or for the production of public goods. c A purely competitive industry may preclude the use of the best-known production techniques and foster a slow rate of technological advance. d A competitive system provides neither a wide range of product choice nor an environment conducive to the development of new products.

TERMS AND CONCEPTS

pure competition	price taker	close-down case	increasing-cost
pure monopoly	average, total, and	MR (= P) = MC rule	industry
monopolistic	marginal revenue	short-run supply curve	decreasing-cost
competition	profit-maximizing case	long-run supply curve	industry
oligopoly	break-even point	constant-cost industry	allocative efficiency
imperfect competition	loss-minimizing case		productive efficiency

QUESTIONS AND STUDY SUGGESTIONS

1 Briefly indicate the basic characteristics of pure competition, pure monopoly, monopolistic competition, and oligopoly. Under which of these market classifications does each of the following most accurately fit? **a** a supermarket in your home town; **b** the steel industry; **c** a Kansas wheat farm; **d** the commercial bank in which you or your family has an account; **e** the automobile industry. In each case justify your classification.

2 Strictly speaking, pure competition never has existed and probably never will. Then why study it?

3 *Key Question* *Use the following demand schedule to determine total and marginal revenue for each possible level of sales.*

Product price	Quantity demanded	Total revenue	Marginal revenue
$2	0	$___	$___
2	1	___	___
2	2	___	___
2	3	___	___
2	4	___	___
2	5	___	___

a *What can you conclude about the structure of the industry in which this firm is operating? Explain.*

b *Graph the demand, total-revenue, and marginal-revenue curves for this firm.*

c *Why do the demand and marginal-revenue curves coincide?*

d *"Marginal revenue is the change in total revenue." Do you agree? Explain verbally and graphically, using the data in the table.*

4 *Key Question* *Assume the following unit-cost data are for a purely competitive producer:*

Total product	Average fixed cost	Average variable cost	Average total cost	Marginal cost
0				$45
1	$60.00	$45.00	$105.00	40
2	30.00	42.50	72.50	35
3	20.00	40.00	60.00	30
4	15.00	37.50	52.50	35
5	12.00	37.00	49.00	40
6	10.00	37.50	47.50	45
7	8.57	38.57	47.14	55
8	7.50	40.63	48.13	65
9	6.67	43.33	50.00	75
10	6.00	46.50	52.50	

a *At a product price of $32, will this firm produce in the short run? Why or why not? If it does produce, what will be the profit-maximizing or loss-minimizing output? Explain. Specify the amount of economic profit or loss per unit of output.*

b *Answer the questions of 4a assuming product price is $41.*

c *Answer the questions of 4a assuming produce price is $56.*

d *Complete the short-run supply schedule for the firm, and indicate the profit or loss incurred at each output (columns 1 to 3).*

(1) Price	(2) Quantity supplied, single firm	(3) Profit (+) or loss (−)	(4) Quantity supplied, 1500 firms
$26	___	$___	___
32	___	___	___
38	___	___	___
41	___	___	___
46	___	___	___
56	___	___	___
66	___	___	___

e *Explain: "That segment of a competitive firm's marginal-cost curve which lies above its average-variable-cost curve constitutes the short-run supply curve for the firm." Illustrate graphically.*

f *Now assume there are 1500 identical firms in this competitive industry; that is, there are 1500 firms, each of which has the same cost data shown here. Calculate the industry supply schedule (column 4).*

g *Suppose the market demand data for the product are as follows:*

Price	Total quantity demanded
$26	17,000
32	15,000
38	13,500
41	12,000
46	10,500
56	9,500
66	8,000

What will equilibrium price be? What will equilibrium output be for the industry? For each firm? What will profit or loss be per unit? Per firm? Will this industry expand or contract in the long run?

5 Why is the equality of marginal revenue and marginal cost essential for profit maximization in all market structures? Explain why price can be substituted for marginal revenue in the MR = MC rule when an industry is purely competitive.

6 Explain "A competitive producer must look to average variable cost in determining whether or not to produce in the short run, to marginal cost in deciding on the best vol-ume of production, and to average total cost to calculate profits or losses." Why might a firm produce at a loss in the short run rather than close down?

7 Many grocery stores in urban areas now stay open 24 hours a day even though they have relatively few customers at night. Distinguishing between fixed and marginal costs, explain how this strategy might maximize a firm's profits.

8 *Key Question* Using diagrams for both the industry and a representative firm, illustrate competitive long-run equilibrium. Assuming constant costs, employ these diagrams to show how **a** an increase, and **b** a decrease, in market demand will upset this long-run equilibrium. Trace graphically and describe verbally the adjustment processes by which long-run equilibrium is restored. Now rework your analysis for increasing- and decreasing-cost industries and compare the three long-run supply curves.

9 Suppose a decrease in demand occurs in a competitive increasing-cost industry. Contrast the product price and industry output existing after all long-run adjustments are completed with those which originally prevailed.

10 *Key Question* In long-run equilibrium, P = minimum ATC = MC. Of what significance for economic efficiency is the quality of P and minimum ATC? The equality of P and MC? Distinguish between productive efficiency and allocative efficiency in your answer.

11 Explain why some economists believe that an unequal distribution of income might impair the allocative efficiency of a competitive market system. What other criticisms can be made of a purely competitive economy?

12 (Last Word) What is Schumpeter's process of "creative destruction"? How does it function as a competitive force?

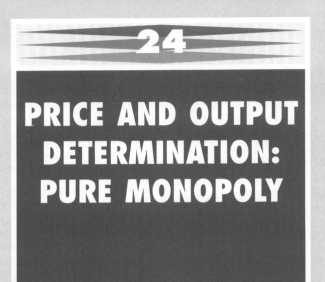

24

PRICE AND OUTPUT DETERMINATION: PURE MONOPOLY

You deal with monopolies—sole sellers of products and services—daily. When you mail a letter, you are using the services of the United States Postal Service, a governmentally sponsored monopoly. Similarly, when you make a local telephone call, turn on your lights, or subscribe to cable TV, you are patronizing monopolies.

We now jump from pure competition to the opposite end of the industry spectrum (Table 23-1) and examine the characteristics, bases, price-output behavior, and social desirability of monopoly. How is a pure monopoly defined? What conditions underlie its existence? How does a monopolist's price-output behavior compare with that of a purely competitive industry? Do monopolists achieve the productive and allocative efficiency associated with pure competition? If not, can government policies improve the price-output behavior of a pure monopolist?

PURE MONOPOLY: INTRODUCTION

Absolute or **pure monopoly** exists when *a single firm is the sole producer of a product for which there are no close substitutes.* Let's first examine the characteristics of pure monopoly and then provide examples.

Characteristics

1 Single Seller A pure, or absolute, monopolist is a one-firm industry. A single firm is the only producer of a specific product or the sole supplier of a service; the firm and the industry are synonymous.

2 No Close Substitutes The monopolist's product is unique in that there are no good, or close, sub-

stitutes. From the buyer's viewpoint, there are no reasonable alternatives. The buyer who does not buy the product from the monopolist has no alternative but to do without.

3 "Price Maker" The individual firm operating under pure competition exercises no influence over product price; it is a "price taker." This is so because it contributes only a negligible portion of total supply. In contrast, the pure monopolist is a *price maker;* the firm exercises considerable control over price because it is responsible for, and therefore controls, the total quantity supplied. Confronted with a downsloping demand curve for its product, the monopolist can change product price by manipulating the quantity of the product supplied. If it is advantageous, the monopolist will use this power.

4   Blocked Entry   A pure monopolist has no immediate competitors because there are barriers to entry. Economic, technological, legal, or other obstacles must exist to keep new competitors from coming into the industry if monopoly is to persist. Entry under conditions of pure monopoly is totally blocked.

5   Advertising   Since there are no close substitutes for the monopolist's product, what does this imply for advertising it? Depending on the type of product or service offered, a monopolist may or may not advertise. For example, a pure monopolist selling a luxury good such as diamonds might advertise heavily to increase demand for the product. The result might be that more people will buy diamonds rather than take vacations. Local public utilities, on the other hand, normally see no point in large expenditures for advertising: People wanting water, gas, electric power, and local telephone service already know from whom they must buy these necessities.

Examples

In most cities governmentally owned or regulated public utilities—gas and electric companies, the water company, the cable TV company, and the telephone company—are all monopolies or virtually so. There are no close substitutes for services provided by these public utilities. Of course, there is almost always *some* competition. Candles or kerosene lights are imperfect substitutes for electricity; telegrams, letters, and courier services can be substituted for the telephone. But such substitutes are typically either costly, less convenient, or unappealing.

The classic example of a private, unregulated monopoly is the De Beers diamond syndicate which effectively controls 80 to 90 percent of the world's diamond supply (Last Word). But in the United States major manufacturing monopolies are rare and frequently transient in that in time new competitors emerge to erode their single-producer status.

> . . . monopoly in the sense of a single seller is virtually nonexistent in nationwide U.S. manufacturing industries of appreciable size. The rate at which near-monopolies have faded appears to have exceeded the rate of new appearance by a substantial margin. In 1962 Gillette made 70 percent of domestic razor blade sales, but its position was eroded, first by the appearance of Wilkinson's stainless steel blades and then by Bic's aggressive marketing of disposable razors. Eastman Kodak's 90 percent share of amateur

film sales and 65 percent share of all film sales, including instant photo packs, was sharply challenged in the 1980s by import competition from Fuji. General Motors' share of diesel locomotive sales probably remains near 75 percent. For decades Western Electric supplied roughly 85 percent of U.S. telephone equipment, but its position faded rapidly owing to technological changes of the 1970s and the antitrust-induced divestiture in 1984 of affiliated Bell Telephone local operating companies, ending a captive market situation. IBM's 72 to 82 percent share of the digital computer market during the 1960s fell as new rivals captured mini- and microcomputer applications. Xerox's 75 to 80 percent share of electrostatic copier revenues declined with the erosion of its patent position during the 1970s. . . . During much of the 1960s and 1970s, Boeing controlled roughly two-thirds of noncommunist world jet airliner placements. With the rise of Europe's Airbus Consortium, Boeing's share declined to 50 percent in the late 1980s.[1]

Professional sports leagues embody monopoly power by granting member clubs franchises to be the sole suppliers of their services in designated geographic areas. Aside from Chicago, New York, and one or two other extremely large metropolitan areas, American cities are served by a single professional baseball, football, hockey, or basketball team. If you want to see a live major-league professional basketball game in Phoenix or Seattle, you must patronize the Suns and the Sonics, respectively.

Monopoly may also be geographic. A small town may have only one airline or railroad. The local bank, movie, or bookstore may approximate a monopoly in a small, isolated community.

Importance

We should understand the workings of pure monopoly for two reasons.

1   A not insignificant amount of economic activity—perhaps 5 or 6 percent of domestic output—is carried out under conditions approaching pure monopoly.

2   A study of pure monopoly yields valuable insights concerning the more common market structures of monopolistic competition and oligopoly, discussed in Chapters 25 and 26. These two market situations combine in differing degrees characteristics of pure competition and pure monopoly.

---

[1]F. M. Scherer and David Ross, *Industrial Market Structure and Economic Performance*, 3d ed. (Chicago: Rand McNally College Publishing Company, 1990), p. 82.

BARRIERS TO ENTRY

The absence of competitors characterizing pure monopoly is largely explainable in terms of factors which prohibit additional firms from entering an industry. These **barriers to entry** also explain the existence of oligopoly and monopolistic competition between the market extremes of pure competition and pure monopoly.

In pure monopoly, entry barriers effectively block all potential competition. Less formidable barriers permit the existence of oligopoly, a market dominated by a few firms. Still weaker barriers result in the fairly large number of firms which characterizes monopolistic competition. The absence of entry barriers helps explain the very large number of competing firms which is the basis of pure competition. The point is that barriers to entry are pertinent not only to the extreme case of pure monopoly but also to the "partial monopolies" so characteristic of our economy.

Economies of Scale

Modern technology in some industries is such that efficient, low-cost production can be achieved only if producers are extremely large both absolutely and in relation to the market. Where economies of scale are very significant, a firm's long-run average-cost schedule will decline over a wide range of output (Figure 22-9b). Given market demand, the achieving of low unit costs and therefore low unit prices for consumers depends on the existence of a small number of firms or, in the extreme case, only one firm.

Figure 24-1 is helpful. Here we observe economies of scale—that is, declining average total costs—throughout the relevant range of production. As a result, any particular level of output can be produced at the least cost when there is a single producer—a monopoly. Note that the monopoly could produce 200 units at a per unit cost of $10 for a total cost of $2000. If two firms comprised the industry and each produced 100 units, unit cost would be $15 and total cost would rise to $3000 (200 × $15). A still more competitive situation with four firms each producing 50 units would boost unit and total costs to $20 and $4000 (200 × $20) respectively. Conclusion: To produce any output with minimum total cost—with the fewest resources—the industry must be a pure monopoly.

If a pure monopoly initially exists, it is easy to see why economies of scale will function as an entry bar-

rier to protect that firm from competition. New firms attempting to enter the industry as small-scale producers will have little or no chance to survive and expand. Small-scale entrants cannot realize the cost economies of the monopolist and therefore cannot realize the profits necessary for survival and growth.

The other option is to start out big, that is, to enter the industry as a large-scale producer. But it is extremely difficult for a new and untried enterprise to secure the money capital needed to obtain the massive capital facilities needed to realize all economies of scale. The financial obstacles to "starting big" are so great in most cases as to be prohibitive. Economies of scale explain why efforts to enter such industries as automobiles, aluminum, and basic steel are extremely rare.

The circumstances we have just described define a natural monopoly. A *natural monopoly* exists when economies of scale are so great that a good or service can be produced by one firm at an average total cost lower than if produced by more than one firm.

Our discussion implies that the monopoly's lower unit costs allow it to charge a lower price than if the industry were more competitive. But this may not happen. As we will see, a pure monopolist may set its price far above unit costs and realize substantial economic profits. The cost advantage of a natural monopoly may accrue to the monopolist as profits and not to consumers in the form of lower prices. For this reason government typically regulates natural monopolies, specifying the price they may charge.

Most of the so-called public utilities—electric and gas companies, bus firms, local water and telephone companies—are regulated natural monopolies. It would be wasteful if a community had several firms supplying water or electricity. Technology is such in these industries that large-scale and extensive capital expenditures on generators, pumping and purification equipment, water mains, and transmission lines are required. This problem is aggravated because capital equipment must be sufficient to meet peak demands on hot summer days when lawns are being watered and air conditioners operated.

So single producers are given exclusive franchises by government. But in return for this sole right to supply electricity, water, or bus service to a particular geographic area, government reserves the right to regulate their prices and services to prevent abuses of the monopoly power it has granted. Some of the problems associated with regulation are considered later in this chapter and in Chapter 32.

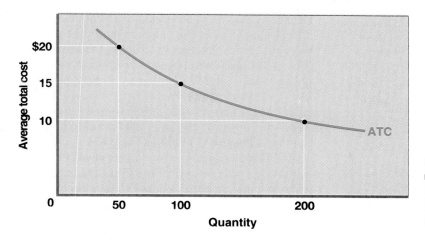

FIGURE 24-1   Economies of scale: the natural monopoly case
If average total costs decline over an extended range of output, least cost production may be realized only if there is a single producer. This is what defines a natural monopoly.

Legal Barriers: Patents and Licenses

We have just noted that government frequently gives exclusive franchises to natural monopolies. Government also creates legal entry barriers in awarding patents and licenses.

Patents   By granting an inventor the exclusive right to produce or license a product for seventeen years, American patent laws aim to protect the inventor from having the product or process usurped by rivals who have not shared in the time, effort, and money outlays which have gone into its development. At the same time patents provide the inventor with a monopoly position for the life of the patent.

Patent control figured prominently in the growth of modern-day industrial giants such as National Cash Register, General Motors, Xerox, Polaroid, General Electric, and du Pont. The United Shoe Machinery Company is a notable example of patent control being abused to achieve monopoly power. United Shoe became the exclusive supplier of certain essential shoemaking machines through patent control. It extended its monopoly power to other types of shoemaking machinery by requiring all lessees of its patented machines to sign a "tying agreement" in which shoe manufacturers agreed also to lease all other shoemaking machinery from United Shoe. This allowed United Shoe to monopolize the market until partially effective antitrust action was taken by the government in 1955.

Research underlies the development of patentable products. Firms which gain monopoly power by their own research or by purchasing the patents of others can consolidate and strengthen their market position. The profits from one patent can finance the research required to develop new patentable products. In the pharmaceutical industry, patents on prescription drugs have produced large monopoly profits which have helped finance the discovery of new patentable medicines. Monopoly power achieved through patents may well be self-sustaining.

Licenses   Entry into an industry or occupation may be limited by government licensing. At the national level the Federal Communications Commission licenses radio and television stations. In many large cities you need a municipal license to drive a taxicab. The consequent restriction of the supply of cabs creates monopolistic earnings for cab owners and drivers. In a few instances government might license itself to provide some product and thereby create a public monopoly. For example, the sale of liquor in some states is exclusively through state-owned retail outlets. Similarly, many states have in effect "licensed" themselves to run lotteries.

Ownership of Essential Resources

Private property can be used by a monopoly as an obstacle to potential rivals. A firm owning or controlling a resource essential to the production process can prohibit the creation of rival firms. The Aluminum Company of America retained its monopoly position in the aluminum industry for many years through its control of all basic sources of bauxite, the ore used in producing aluminum ingots. At one time the International Nickel Company of Canada (now called Inco) controlled 90 percent of the world's known nickel reserves. As this chapter's Last Word details, most of

GLOBAL PERSPECTIVE 24-1

Competition from foreign multinational corporations

The market power of American firms is diminished by competition from foreign corporations operating within the United States. The table shows the top ten multinational manufacturing corporations ranked by sales from United States operations. Foreign multinationals produced an estimated 20 percent of American manufacturing output in 1993, up from 4 percent in 1977. They employ over 12 percent of our industrial labor force.

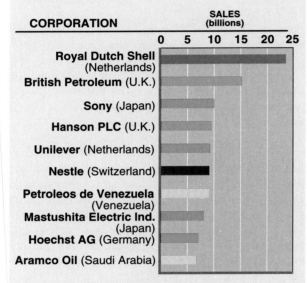

Source: *Wall Street Journal,* December 2, 1994. Data from the Wharton School, University of Pennsylvania.

the world's known diamond mines are owned or effectively controlled by the De Beers Company of South Africa. Similarly, it is very difficult for new professional sports leagues to evolve when existing leagues have contracts with the best players and leases on the major stadiums and arenas.

Two Implications

Our discussion of barriers to entry suggests two noteworthy points about monopoly.

1 Relatively Rare Barriers to entry are rarely complete—meaning pure monopoly is relatively rare. Although research and technological advance may

strengthen the market position of a firm, technology may also undermine existing monopoly power. Recall the concept of "creative destruction" from Chapter 23's Last Word. Over time the creation of new technologies can destroy existing monopoly positions. The development of courier delivery systems, fax machines, and electronic mail has eroded the monopoly power of the postal service. Cable television monopolies are challenged by new technologies which enable telephone companies to transmit audio and visual signals and thereby provide TV programs to consumers at any time they choose to view them.

Similarly, existing patent advantages may be circumvented by the development of new and distinct, yet substitutable, products. New sources of strategic resources may be found. It is probably only a modest overstatement to say that monopoly in the sense of a one-firm industry persists over time only with the sanction or aid of government, as with the postal service's monopoly on the delivery of first-class mail.

2 Desirability We have implied that monopolies may be desirable or undesirable from the standpoint of economic efficiency. The public utilities and economies-of-scale arguments suggest that market demand and technology may be such that efficient low-cost production presupposes the existence of monopoly. On the other hand, our comments on resource ownership, patents, and licensing as sources of monopoly imply more undesirable connotations of monopoly.

MONOPOLY DEMAND

Let's begin our analysis of the price-output behavior of a pure monopolist by making three assumptions.
1 Our monopolist's status is secured by patents, economies of scale, or resource ownership.
2 The firm is *not* governmentally regulated.
3 The firm is a single-price monopolist; it charges the same price for all units of output.

The crucial difference between a pure monopolist and a purely competitive seller lies on the demand side of the market. Recall from Chapter 23 that the purely competitive seller faces a perfectly elastic demand schedule at the market price determined by industry supply and demand. The competitive firm is a "price taker" which can sell as much or as little as it wants at the going market price. Each additional unit sold will add a constant amount—its price—to the

TABLE 24-1   Revenue and cost data of a pure monopolist

Revenue data				Cost data			
(1) Quantity of output	(2) Price (average revenue)	(3) Total revenue	(4) Marginal revenue	(5) Average total cost	(6) Total cost	(7) Marginal cost	(8) Profit (+) or loss (−)
0	$172	$ 0			$ 100		$−100
			$162			$ 90	
1	162	162		$190.00	190		− 28
			142			80	
2	152	304		135.00	270		+ 34
			122			70	
3	142	426		113.33	340		+ 86
			102			60	
4	132	528		100.00	400		+128
			82			70	
5	122	610		94.00	470		+140
			62			80	
6	112	672		91.67	550		+122
			42			90	
7	102	714		91.43	640		+ 74
			22			110	
8	92	736		93.73	750		− 14
			2			130	
9	82	738		97.78	880		−142
			− 18			150	
10	72	720		103.00	1030		−310

firm's total revenue. That means marginal revenue for the competitive seller is constant and equal to product price. Therefore, total revenue increases by a constant amount, that is, by the constant price of each unit sold. (Refer to Table 23-2 and Figure 23-1 for price, marginal-revenue, and total-revenue relationships for the purely competitive firm.)

The monopolist's demand curve—indeed, the demand curve of *any* imperfectly competitive seller —is much different. Because the pure monopolist *is* the industry, its demand, or sales, curve is the industry demand curve.[2] And the industry demand curve is not perfectly elastic, but rather is downsloping, as illustrated by columns 1 and 2 of Table 24-1.

There are three implications of a downsloping demand curve which you must understand.

Price Exceeds Marginal Revenue

A downsloping demand curve means that a pure monopoly can increase its sales only by charging a lower unit price for its product. *Because the monopolist must lower price to boost sales, marginal revenue is less than price (average revenue) for every level of output except the first.* The reason? Price cuts will apply not only to the extra output sold but also to *all* other units of output

put which otherwise could have been sold at a higher price. Each additional unit sold will add to total revenue its price *less* the sum of the price cuts which must be taken on all prior units of output.

In Figure 24-2 we have extracted two price-quantity combinations—$142-3 units and $132-4 units— from the monopolist's demand curve. By lowering price from $142 to $132, the monopolist can sell one more unit and gain as revenue the fourth unit's price of $132 as indicated. But to sell this fourth unit for $132, the monopolist must lower price on the first 3 units from $142 to $132. This $10 reduction on 3 units results in a $30 revenue loss. The *net* change in total revenue, or marginal revenue, from selling the fourth unit is $102, the $132 gain minus the $30 loss.

This same idea is evident in Table 24-1, where we observe that the marginal revenue of the second unit of output is $142 rather than its $152 price, because a $10 price cut must be taken on the first unit to increase sales from 1 to 2 units. Similarly, to sell 3 units the firm must lower price from $152 to $142. The resulting marginal revenue will be $122—the $142 addition to total revenue which the third unit of sales provides less $10 price cuts on the first 2 units of output. This rationale explains why the marginal-revenue data of column 4 of Table 24-1 fall short of product price in column 2 for all levels of output except the first. Because marginal revenue is, by definition, the increase in total revenue associated with each additional unit of output, the declining marginal-revenue

[2]Recall in Chapter 23 that we presented separate diagrams for the purely competitive industry *and* for a single firm in that industry. Because with pure monopoly the firm and the industry are one and the same, we need only a single diagram.

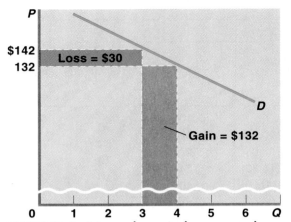

FIGURE 24-2 **Price and marginal revenue under pure monopoly**

A pure monopolist—or any imperfect competitor with a downsloping demand curve—must reduce price to sell more output. As a consequence, marginal revenue will be less than price. In our example, by reducing price from $142 to $132 the monopolist gains $132 from the sale of the fourth unit. But from this gain must be subtracted $30 which reflects the $10 price cut which has been made on each of the first three units. Hence, the fourth unit's marginal revenue is $102 (= $132 − $30), considerably less than its $132 price.

figures in column 4 mean total revenue will increase at a diminishing rate as shown in column 3 of Table 24-1.

The relationships between the demand, marginal-revenue, and total-revenue curves, introduced in Chapter 20, are portrayed graphically in Figure 24-3a and b. In this diagram we have extended the demand and revenue data of columns 1 through 4 of Table 24-1 by continuing to assume that successive $10 price cuts will each elicit one additional unit of sales. That is, 11 units can be sold at $62, 12 at $52, and so forth.

In addition to the fact that the marginal-revenue curve lies *below* the demand curve, note the special relationship between total revenue and marginal revenue. Because marginal revenue is, by definition, the change in total revenue, we observe that so long as total revenue is increasing, marginal revenue is positive. When total revenue reaches its maximum, marginal revenue is zero. When total revenue is diminishing, marginal revenue is negative.

Price Maker

In all imperfectly competitive markets in which downsloping demand curves are relevant—that is,

purely monopolistic, oligopolistic, and monopolistically competitive markets—firms have a price policy. By virtue of their ability to influence total supply, the output decisions of these firms necessarily affect product price.

This is most evident in pure monopoly, where one firm controls total output. Faced with a downsloping demand curve, in which each output is associated with some unique price, the monopolist unavoidably determines price in deciding what volume of output to produce. The monopolist simultaneously chooses both price and output. In columns 1 and 2 of Table 24-1 we find that the monopolist can sell only an output of 1 unit at a price of $162, only an output of 2 units at a price of $152 per unit, and so forth.

This does not mean that the monopolist is "free" of market forces in establishing price and output or that the consumer is completely at the monopolist's mercy. In particular, the monopolist's downsloping demand curve means that it cannot raise price without losing sales, or gain sales without charging a lower price.

Price Elasticity

The total-revenue test for price elasticity of demand is the basis for our third conclusion. Recall from Chapter 20 that the total-revenue test tells us that, when demand is elastic, a decline in price will increase total revenue. Similarly, when demand is inelastic, a decline in price will reduce total revenue. Beginning at the top of the demand curve in Figure 24-3, observe that for all price reductions from $172 down to approximately $82, total revenue increases (and marginal revenue therefore is positive). This means that demand is elastic in this price range. Conversely, for price reductions below $82, total revenue decreases (marginal revenue is negative), which indicates that demand is inelastic.

Our generalization is that a monopolist will never choose a price-quantity combination where price declines cause total revenue to decrease (marginal revenue to be negative). *The profit-maximizing monopolist will always want to avoid the inelastic segment of its demand curve in favor of some price-quantity combination in the elastic segment.* By lowering price into the inelastic range, total revenue will decline. But the lower price is associated with a larger output and therefore increased total costs. Lower revenue and higher costs mean diminished profits. *(Key Question 4)*

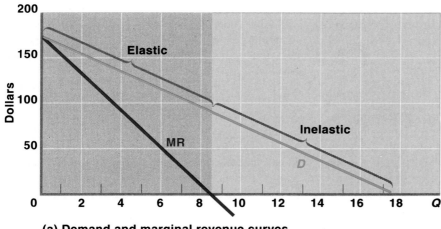

(a) Demand and marginal revenue curves

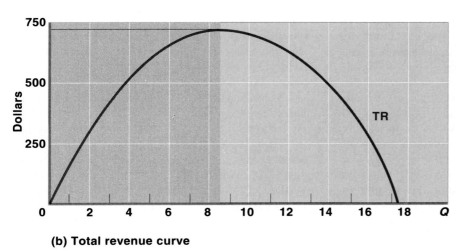

(b) Total revenue curve

FIGURE 24-3 Demand, marginal revenue, and total revenue of an imperfectly competitive firm

Because it must lower price to increase its sales, an imperfectly competitive firm's marginal-revenue curve (MR) lies below its downsloping demand curve (D). Total revenue (TR) increases at a decreasing rate, reaches a maximum, and then declines. Note that, because MR is the change in TR, a unique relationship exists between MR and TR. In moving down the elastic segment of the demand curve, TR is increasing and, hence, MR is positive. When TR reaches its maximum, MR is zero. And in moving down the inelastic segment of the demand curve, TR is declining, so MR is negative. A monopolist or other imperfectly competitive seller will never choose to lower price into the inelastic segment of its demand curve because by doing so it will simultaneously reduce total revenue and increase production costs, thereby lowering profits.

QUICK REVIEW 24-1

■ A pure monopolist is the sole supplier of a product or service for which there are no close substitutes.

■ Monopolies exist because of entry barriers such as economies of scale, patents and licenses, and the ownership of essential resources.

■ The monopolist's demand curve is downsloping, causing the marginal revenue curve to lie below it.

■ The downsloping demand curve means that the monopolist is a "price maker."

■ As long as a firm is on the inelastic segment of its demand curve, it can increase total revenue and reduce total costs—thereby increasing profits—by raising price.

OUTPUT AND PRICE DETERMINATION

What specific price-quantity combination on its demand curve will a profit-maximizing monopolist choose? To answer this we must add production costs to our understanding of monopoly demand.

Cost Data

On the cost side, we will assume that, although the firm is a monopolist in the product market, it hires resources competitively and employs the same technology as our competitive firm in the preceding chapter. This lets us use the cost data developed in Chapter 22 and applied in Chapter 23 so we can compare the price-output decisions of a pure monopoly with those of a pure competitor. Columns 5 through 7 of Table 24-1 restate the pertinent cost concepts of Table 22-2.

MR = MC Rule

A profit-seeking monopolist will employ the same rationale as a profit-seeking firm in a competitive industry. It will produce each successive unit of output so long as it adds more to total revenue than it does to total cost. The firm will produce up to that output at which marginal revenue equals marginal cost (MR = MC).

A comparison of columns 4 and 7 in Table 24-1 indicates that the profit-maximizing output is 5 units; the fifth unit is the last unit of output whose marginal revenue exceeds its marginal cost. What price will the monopolist charge? The downsloping demand curve of columns 1 and 2 in Table 24-1 indicates that there is only one price at which 5 units can be sold: $122.

This analysis is presented graphically in Figure 24-4 (Key Graph), where the demand, marginal-revenue, average-total-cost, and marginal-cost data of Table 24-1 have been drawn. Comparing marginal revenue and marginal cost confirms that the profit-maximizing output is 5 units or, more generally, Q_m. The unique price at which Q_m can be sold is found by extending a perpendicular line up from the profit-maximizing point on the output axis and then at right angles from the point at which it hits the demand curve to the vertical axis. The indicated price is $122 or, more generally, P_m. To charge a price higher than P_m, the monopolist must move up the demand curve, meaning that sales will fall short of the profit-maximizing level Q_m. Specifically, the firm will fail to produce units of output whose marginal revenue exceeds their marginal cost. If the monopolist charges less than P_m, it would involve a sales volume in excess of the profit-maximizing output.

Columns 2 and 5 of Table 24-1 indicate that, at 5 units of output, product price of $122 exceeds average total cost of $94. Economic profits are therefore $28 per unit; total economic profits are then $140 (= 5 × $28). In Figure 24-4, per unit profit is indicated by the distance AP_m, and total economic profits are found by multiplying this unit profit by the profit-maximizing output Q_m.

The same profit-maximizing combination of output and price can also be determined by comparing the total revenue and total costs incurred at each pos-sible level of production. You should employ columns 3 and 6 of Table 24-1 to verify the conclusions reached through our graphical marginal-revenue–marginal-cost analysis. Similarly, an accurate graphing of total revenue and total cost against output will also show the greatest differential (the maximum profit) at 5 units of output. *(Key Question 5)*

No Monopoly Supply Curve

Recall that the supply curve of a purely competitive firm is that portion of its marginal-cost curve lying above average variable costs (Figure 23-6). The supply curve is determined by applying the P = MC profit-maximization rule. At any given market-determined price the purely competitive seller will maximize profits by equating that price (which is equal to marginal revenue) with marginal cost. When market price increases or decreases, the competitive firm will move up or down its marginal-cost curve because it is profitable to produce more or less output. We find each price to be uniquely associated with a specific output, thus defining the supply curve.

At first glance we would suspect that the pure monopolist's marginal-cost curve would also be its supply curve. But this is *not* the case. *The pure monopolist has no supply curve.* The reason is that there is no unique relationship between price and quantity supplied. The price and amount supplied depend on the location of the demand (and therefore marginal-revenue) curves. Like the competitive firm, the monopolist equates marginal revenue and marginal cost, but for the monopolist marginal revenue is less than price. Because the monopolist does *not* equate marginal cost to price, it is possible for different demand conditions to bring about different profit-maximizing prices for the same output. To convince yourself of this, refer to Figure 24-4 and pencil in a steeper (less elastic) demand curve, drawing its corresponding marginal-revenue curve so that it intersects marginal cost at the same point as does the present marginal-revenue curve. With the steeper demand curve, this new MR = MC output will yield a higher price. Conclusion: There is no single, unique price associated with output level Q_m, and therefore no supply curve for the pure monopolist.

Misconceptions Concerning Monopoly Pricing

Our analysis explodes some popular fallacies concerning monopoly behavior.

KEY GRAPH

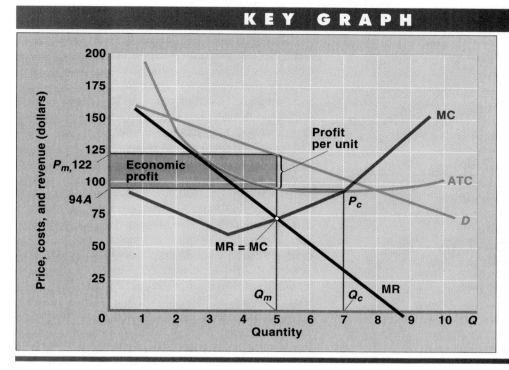

FIGURE 24-4 The profit-maximizing position of a pure monopolist
The pure monopolist maximizes profits by producing the MR = MC output. In this instance profit is AP_m per unit, and total economic profits are measured by the shaded rectangle.

1   Not Highest Price   Because a monopolist can manipulate output and price, people often believe it "will charge the highest price it can get." This is a misguided assertion. There are many prices above P_m in Figure 24-4, but the monopolist shuns them because they entail a smaller-than-maximum profit. These higher prices move the monopolist back into output ranges where MR exceeds MC, indicating that larger outputs are profitable. *Total* profits are the difference between *total* revenue and *total* costs, and each of these two determinants of profits depends on quantity sold as much as on price and unit cost.

2   Total, Not Unit, Profits   The monopolist seeks maximum *total* profits, not maximum *unit* profits. In Figure 24-4 a careful comparison of the vertical distance between average total cost and price at various possible outputs indicates that per unit profits are greater at a point slightly to the left of the profit-maximizing output Q_m. This is seen in Table 24-1, where unit profits at 4 units of output are $32 (= $132 − $100) compared with $28 (= $122 − $94) at the profit-maximizing output of 5 units. Here the monopolist accepts a lower-than-maximum per unit profit because additional sales more than compensate for lower unit

profits. A profit-seeking monopolist would rather sell 5 units at a profit of $28 per unit (for a total profit of $140) than 4 units at a profit of $32 per unit (for a total profit of only $128).

3   Losses   Pure monopoly does *not* guarantee economic profits. True, the likelihood of economic profits is greater for a pure monopolist than for a purely competitive producer. In the long run the latter is doomed by the free and easy entry of new firms to a normal profit; barriers to entry permit the monopolist to perpetuate economic profits in the long run.[3] Unlike the competitive situation, entry barriers keep out potential entrants who would increase supply, drive price down, and eliminate economic profits.

Like the pure competitor, the monopolist will not persistently operate at a loss. Faced with losses, the firm's owners will move their resources to alternative industries offering higher returns. Thus we can ex-

---

[3]A related point is that the distinction between the short run and the long run is less important under monopoly than it is under pure competition. With pure competition the entry or exit of firms guarantees that economic profits will be zero in the long run. But with pure monopoly barriers to entry prevent the competing away of economic profits by new firms.

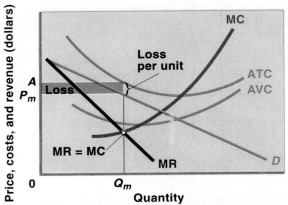

FIGURE 24-5   The loss-minimizing position of a pure monopolist
If demand D is weak and costs are high, the pure monopolist may be unable to make a profit. Because P_m exceeds AVC at Q_m, it will minimize losses in the short run by producing at that output where MR = MC. Loss per unit is AP_m and total losses are indicated by the shaded rectangle.

pect the monopolist to realize a normal profit or better in the long run. However, if the demand and cost situation faced by the monopolist is less favorable than shown in Figure 24-4, short-run losses will be realized. Despite its dominance in the market, the monopolist shown in Figure 24-5 suffers a loss, as shown, because of weak demand and relatively high costs. Yet it continues to operate for the time being since its total loss is less than its fixed costs. More precisely, observe that at Q_m the monopolist's price P_m exceeds its average variable cost. Although the government's rail corporation AMTRAK has a virtual monopoly in long-distance passenger train service, it frequently operates at a loss. The same is true of the postal service.

ECONOMIC EFFECTS OF MONOPOLY

Let's now evaluate pure monopoly from the standpoint of society as a whole. We will examine (1) price, output, and efficiency; (2) income distribution; (3) some uncertainties caused by difficulties in making cost comparisons between competitive and monopolistic firms; and (4) technological progress.

Price, Output, and Efficiency

In Chapter 23 we concluded that pure competition would result in both "productive efficiency" and "al-

locative efficiency." Productive efficiency is realized because free entry and exodus of firms would force firms to operate at the optimal rate of output where unit costs of production would be at a minimum. Product price would be at the lowest level consistent with average total costs. In Figure 24-4 the competitive firm would sell Q_c units of output at a price of P_c.

Allocative efficiency is reflected in the fact that production under competition would occur up to that point at which price (the measure of a product's value or marginal benefit to society) would equal marginal cost (the measure of the alternative products forgone by society in producing any given commodity).

Figure 24-4 indicates that, *given the same costs,* a purely monopolistic firm will produce much less desirable results. The pure monopolist will maximize profits by producing an output of Q_m and charging a price of P_m. *The monopolist will find it profitable to sell a smaller output and to charge a higher price than would a competitive producer.*[4] Output Q_m is short of the Q_c point where average total costs are minimized (the intersection of MC and ATC). In column 5 of Table 24-1, ATC at the monopolist's 5 units of output is $94.00 compared to the $91.43 which would result under pure competition. Also, at Q_m units of output, product price is considerably greater than marginal cost. This means that society values additional units of this monopolized product more highly than it does the alternative products these resources could otherwise produce. The monopolist's profit-maximizing output results in an underallocation of resources; the monopolist finds it profitable to restrict output and

[4]In Figure 24-4 the price-quantity comparison of monopoly and pure competition is from the vantage point of the single purely competitive *firm* of Figure 23-7a. An equally illuminating approach is to start with the purely competitive *industry* of Figure 23-7b, reproduced below. Recall that the competitive industry's supply curve

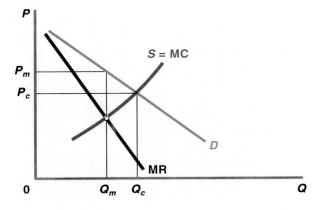

therefore employ fewer resources than are justified from society's standpoint. Neither productive nor allocative efficiency is achieved in monopolized markets.

Income Distribution

In general, business monopoly contributes to inequality in income distribution. By virtue of their market power, monopolists charge a higher price than would a purely competitive firm with the same costs; monopolists in effect can levy a "private tax" on consumers and obtain substantial economic profits. These monopolistic profits are not widely distributed because corporate stock ownership is largely concentrated in the hands of upper income groups. The owners of monopolistic enterprises tend to be enriched at the expense of the rest of society.

Exception: If the buyers of a monopoly product are wealthier than the owners of the monopoly, the monopoly may *reduce* income inequality. Undoubtedly, some international commodity monopolies such as those involving metals, bananas, and coffee redistribute the world's income from wealthy consuming nations to poorer developing nations. But, in general, we conclude that monopoly contributes to income inequality.

Cost Complications

Our evaluation of pure monopoly has led us to conclude that, *given identical costs,* a purely monopolistic firm will find it profitable to charge a higher price, pro-

---

S is the horizontal sum of the marginal-cost curves of all the firms in the industry. Comparing this with industry demand *D*, we get the purely competitive price and output of P_c and Q_c. Now suppose that this industry becomes a pure monopoly as a result of a wholesale merger or one firm's somehow buying out all its competitors. Assume, too, that no changes in costs or market demand result from this dramatic change in the industry's structure. What were formerly, say, 100 competing firms are now a pure monopolist consisting of 100 branch plants.

The industry supply curve is now the marginal-cost curve of the monopolist, the summation of the MC curves of its many branch plants. The important change, however, is on the market demand side. From the viewpoint of each individual competitive firm, demand was perfectly elastic, and marginal revenue was therefore equal to price. Each firm equated MC to MR (and therefore to *P*) in maximizing profits (Chapter 23). But industry demand and individual demand are the same to the pure monopolist; the firm *is* the industry, and thus the monopolist correctly envisions a downsloping demand curve *D*. This means that marginal revenue MR will be less than price; graphically the MR curve lies below the demand curve. In choosing the profit-maximizing MC = MR position, the monopolist selects an output Q_m which is smaller, and a price P_m which is greater, than if the industry were organized competitively.

duce a smaller output, and foster an allocation of economic resources inferior to that of a purely competitive industry. These contrasting results are rooted in the entry barriers characterizing monopoly.

Now we must recognize that costs may *not* be the same for purely competitive and monopolistic producers. Unit costs incurred by a monopolist may be either larger or smaller than those facing a purely competitive firm. There are four reasons why costs may differ: (1) economies of scale, (2) the notion of "X-inefficiency," (3) monopoly-preserving expenditures, and (4) the "very long-run" perspective which allows for technological progress. We examine the first three issues in this section and technological progress in the ensuing section.

Economies of Scale Revisited   The assumption that unit costs available to the purely competitive and the purely monopolistic firm are the same may not hold in practice. Given production techniques and therefore production costs, consumer demand may not be sufficient to support a large number of competing firms producing at an output which permits each firm to realize all *existing* economies of scale. In such instances a firm must be large in relation to the market —it must be monopolistic—to produce efficiently (at low unit cost). This is the natural monopoly case discussed earlier.

Most economists conclude that the natural monopoly or public utilities case is not significant enough to undermine our general conclusions concerning the restrictive nature of monopoly. Evidence suggests that the large corporations in many manufacturing industries now have more monopoly power than can be justified on the grounds that they are merely availing themselves of existing economies of scale. Again, Chapter 22's Last Word provides relevant evidence suggesting that most industries could be quite competitive at smaller firm sizes without sacrificing economies of scale.

X-Inefficiency   While economies of scale *might* argue for monopoly in a few cases, the notion of X-inefficiency suggests that monopoly costs might be *higher* than costs associated with more competitive industries. What is X-inefficiency? Why might it plague monopolists more than competitors?

All the average-total-cost curves used in this and other chapters are based on the assumption that the firm chooses from *existing* technologies the most efficient one or, in other words, that technology which

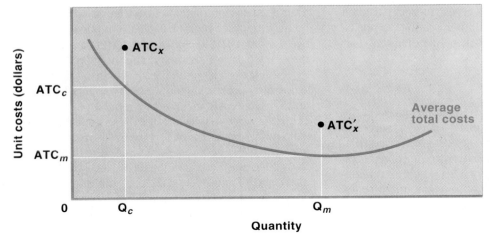

FIGURE 24-6 X-ineffi-ciency
This diagram demonstrates that X-inefficiency—the inefficient internal operation of a firm—results in higher-than-necessary costs. For example, unit costs might be ATC_x rather than ATC_c for Q_c units of output and ATC'_x rather than ATC_m for the Q_m level of output.

permits the firm to achieve the minimum average total cost for each level of output. **X-inefficiency** occurs when a firm's actual costs of producing any output are greater than the minimum possible costs. In Figure 24-6 X-inefficiency is represented by unit costs of ATC_x (as opposed to ATC_c) for output Q_c and average total costs of ATC'_x (rather than ATC_m) for output Q_m. Any point above the average-total-cost curve in Figure 24-6 is attainable but reflects internal inefficiency or "bad management" by the firm.

Why does X-inefficiency occur if it reduces profits? The answer is managers may often have goals—firm growth, an easier work life, avoidance of business risk, providing jobs for incompetent friends and relatives—which conflict with cost minimization. Or X-inefficiency may arise because a firm's workers are poorly motivated or ineffectively supervised. Or a firm may simply become lethargic and inert, relying on rules-of-thumb in decision making as opposed to relevant calculations of costs and revenues.

For our purposes the relevant question is whether monopolistic firms are more susceptible to X-inefficiency than are competitive producers. Presumably they are. Theoretically, firms in competitive industries are continually under pressures from rivals which force them to be internally efficient to survive. But monopolists and oligopolists are sheltered from competitive forces by entry barriers, and such an environment leads to X-inefficiency.

Empirical evidence on X-inefficiency is largely anecdotal and sketchy, but it does suggest that X-inefficiency is greater the smaller the amount of competition. A reasonable estimate is that X-inefficiency may be 5 percent or more of costs for monopolists, but only 3 percent for an "average" oligopolistic industry in which the four largest firms produce 60 percent of total output.[5] In the words of one authority: "The evidence is fragmentary, but it points in the same direction. X-inefficiency exists, and it is more apt to be reduced when competitive pressures are strong than when firms enjoy insulated market positions."[6]

Rent-Seeking Expenditures Economists use the term **rent-seeking behavior** in referring to activities designed to transfer income or wealth to a particular firm or resource supplier at someone else's or society's expense. We have seen that a monopolist can earn economic profits even in the long run. Therefore, it is no surprise a firm may go to considerable expense to acquire or maintain monopoly privileges granted by government. A monopolist's barrier to entry may depend on legislation or an exclusive license provided by government as in radio and television broadcasting. To sustain or enhance the consequent economic profits, the monopolist may spend large amounts on legal fees, lobbying, and public relations advertising to persuade government to grant or sustain its privileged position. These expenditures add nothing to the firm's output, but clearly increase its costs. Rent-seeking expenditures mean that monopoly might entail higher costs and a greater efficiency loss than suggested by Figure 24-4.

[5]William G. Shepherd, *The Economics of Industrial Organization,* 3d ed. (Englewood Cliffs, N.J.: Prentice-Hall, Inc. 1990), p. 129. For a rather extensive review of case study evidence of X-inefficiency, see Scherer and Ross, op. cit., pp. 668–672.

[6]Scherer and Ross, op. cit., p. 672.

Technological Progress: Dynamic Efficiency

We have noted that our condemnation of monopoly must be qualified where *existing* mass-production economies might be lost if an industry comprises a large number of small, competing firms. Now we must consider the issue of **dynamic efficiency,** or whether monopolists are more likely to develop more efficient production techniques over time than competitive firms. Are monopolists more likely to improve productive technology, thereby lowering (shifting downward) their average-total-cost curves, than are competitive producers? Although we will concentrate on changes in productive techniques, the same question applies to product improvement. Do monopolists have greater means and incentives to improve their products and thus enhance consumer satisfaction? This is fertile ground for honest differences of opinion.

The Competitive Model

Competitive firms certainly have the incentive—indeed, a market mandate—to employ the most efficient *known* productive techniques. Their survival depends on being efficient. But competition deprives firms of economic profit—an important means and a major incentive to develop *new* and improved productive techniques or *new* products. The profits of technological advance may be short-lived to the innovating competitor. An innovating firm in a competitive industry will find that its rivals will soon duplicate or imitate any technological advance it may achieve; rivals will share the rewards but not the costs of successful technological research.

The Monopoly Model

In contrast—thanks to entry barriers—a monopolist may persistently realize substantial economic profits. Hence, the pure monopolist will have greater financial resources for technological advance than competitive firms. But what about the monopolist's incentives for technological advance? Here the picture is clouded.

There is one imposing argument suggesting that the monopolist's incentives to develop new techniques or products will be weak: The absence of competitors means there is no automatic stimulus to technological advance in a monopolized market. Because of its sheltered market position, the pure monopolist can afford to be inefficient and lethargic. The keen rivalry of a competitive market penalizes the inefficient; an inefficient monopolist does not face this penalty simply because it has no rivals. The monopolist has every reason to be satisfied with the status quo, to become complacent. It might well pay the monopolist to withhold or "file" technological improvements in both productive techniques and products to exploit existing capital equipment fully. New and improved techniques and products may be suppressed by monopolists to avoid losses caused by the sudden obsolescence of existing machinery and equipment. And, even when improved techniques are belatedly introduced by monopolists, the accompanying cost reductions will accrue to the monopolist as increases in profits and only partially, if at all, to consumers in the form of lower prices and increased output.

Proponents of this view point out that in a number of industries which approximate monopoly—for example, steel and aluminum—interest in research has been minimal. Such advances as have occurred have come largely from outside the industry or from smaller firms making up the "competitive fringe" of the industry.

There are at least two counterarguments:

1 Technological advance lowers unit costs and expands profits. As our analysis of Figure 24-4 implies, lower costs will give rise to a profit-maximizing position which involves a larger output and a lower price. Any expansion of profits will not be transitory; barriers to entry protect the monopolist from profit encroachment by rivals. In short, technological progress is profitable to the monopolist and therefore will be undertaken.

2 Research and technological advance may be one of the monopolist's barriers to entry; hence, the monopolist must persist and succeed in technological advance or fall prey to new competitors, including those located abroad. Technological progress, it is argued, is essential to the maintenance of monopoly.

A Mixed Picture

What can be said as a summarizing generalization on the economic efficiency of pure monopoly? In a static economy, where economies of scale are equally accessible to purely competitive and monopolist firms, pure competition will be superior to pure monopoly because pure competition forces use of the best-known technology and allocates resources according to the wants of society. However, when economies of scale available to the monopolist are not attainable by small competitive producers, or in a dynamic context in which changes in the rate of technological advance must be considered, the inefficiencies of pure monopoly are somewhat less evident.

Two Policy Options   There are two policy options when pure monopoly creates substantial economic inefficiency and appears to be long-lasting.

1   *Antitrust*   As we will detail in Chapter 32, government can file charges against the monopoly under the antitrust laws, seeking to break up the monopoly into competing firms.

2   *Public Utility Regulation*   Society can allow the monopoly to continue, but directly regulate its prices and operations. We will explore this option—public utility regulation—later in this chapter and also in Chapter 32.

QUICK REVIEW 24-2

■ The monopolist maximizes profits (or minimizes losses) at the output where MR = MC and charges the price on its demand curve which corresponds to this output.

■ Assuming identical costs, a monopolist will be less efficient than a purely competitive firm because the monopolist produces less output and charges a higher price.

■ The inefficiencies of monopoly may be offset or lessened by economies of scale and technological progress, but intensified by the presence of X-inefficiency and rent-seeking expenditures.

PRICE DISCRIMINATION

Before turning to regulated monopoly, let's extend our analysis to consider price discrimination. We have assumed the monopolist charges a uniform price to all buyers. But under certain conditions the monopolist can exploit its market position more fully and increase profits by charging different prices to different buyers. In so doing the seller is engaging in price discrimination. **Price discrimination** *occurs when a given product is sold at more than one price and these price differences are not justified by cost differences.*

Conditions

The opportunity to engage in price discrimination is not readily available to all sellers. Price discrimination is workable when three conditions are realized.

1   Monopoly Power   The seller must be a monopolist or, at least, possess some degree of monopoly power, that is, some ability to control output and price.

2   Market Segregation   The seller must be able to segregate buyers into separate classes where each group has a different willingness or ability to pay for the product. This separation of buyers is usually based on different elasticities of demand as later illustrations will make clear.

3   No Resale   The original purchaser cannot resell the product or service. If buyers in the low-price segment of the market can easily resell in the high-price segment, the monopolist's price discrimination strategy creates competitive sellers with the monopolist in the high-price segment of the market. This competition will reduce price in the high-price segment and undermine the monopolist's price discrimination policy. This suggests that service industries such as the transportation industry or legal and medical services, where resale is impossible, are especially susceptible to price discrimination.

Illustrations

Price discrimination is widely practiced in our economy. The sales representative who must communicate important information to corporate headquarters has a highly inelastic demand for long-distance telephone service and pays the high daytime rate. The college student "reporting in" to the folks at home has an elastic demand and defers the call to take advantage of lower evening or weekend rates. Electric utilities frequently segment their markets by end uses, such as lighting and heating. The absence of reasonable substitutes means the demand for electricity for illumination is inelastic and the price per kilowatt hour for this use is high. But the availability of natural gas and petroleum as alternatives to electrical heating makes the demand for electricity less inelastic for this purpose and the price charged is lower. Similarly, industrial users of electricity are typically charged lower rates than residential users because the former can construct their own generating equipment while the individual household cannot.

Movie theaters and golf courses vary their charges on the basis of time (higher rates in the evening and on weekends when demand is strong) and age (ability to pay). Railroads vary the rate charged per ton mile of freight according to the market value of the product being shipped. The shipper of 10 tons of television sets or costume jewelry will be charged more than the shipper of 10 tons of gravel or coal. Airlines charge high fares to traveling executives, whose demand for travel is inelastic, and offer lower fares in the guise of "family rates" and "standby fares" to attract vacationers and others whose demands are more elastic. Hotels, restaurants, theaters, and pharmacies give discounts to retired people. In international trade, price discrimination is called "dumping." A South Korean electronics manufacturer, for example, might sell TV sets for $100 less in the United States than it charges domestically.

Consequences

There are two economic consequences of price discrimination.

1 It is not surprising that a monopolist will be able to increase its profits by practicing price discrimination.
2 Other things being equal, a discriminating monopolist will produce a larger output than a nondiscrimination monopolist.

1 More Profits The simplest way to understand why price discrimination can yield additional profits is to look again at our monopolist's downsloping demand curve in Figure 24-4. Although the profit-maximizing uniform price is $122, the segment of the demand curve lying above the profit area in Figure 24-4 tells us there are buyers willing to pay *more than* P_m ($122) rather than forgo the product.

If the monopolist can identify and segregate each of these buyers and charge the maximum price each would pay, the sale of any given level of output will be more profitable. In columns 1 and 2 of Table 24-1 we note that buyers of the first 4 units of output would be willing to pay more than the equilibrium price of $122. If the seller could practice perfect price discrimination by extracting the maximum price each buyer would pay, total revenue would increase from $610 (= $122 × 5) to $710 (= $122 + $132 + $142 + $152 + $162) and profits would increase from $140 (= $610 − $470) to $240 (= $710 − $470).

2 More Production Other things being the same, the discriminating monopolist will choose to produce a larger output than the nondiscriminating monopolist. Recall that when the nondiscriminating monopolist lowers price to sell additional output, the lower price will apply not only to the additional sales but also to *all* prior units of output. As a result, marginal revenue is less than price and, graphically, the marginal-revenue curve lies below the demand curve. The fact

that marginal revenue is less than price is a disincentive to increased production.

But when a perfectly discriminating monopolist lowers price, the reduced price applies *only* to the additional unit sold and *not* to prior units. Hence, price and marginal revenue are equal for any unit of output. Graphically, the perfectly discriminating monopolist's marginal-revenue curve will coincide with its demand curve and the disincentive to increased production is removed.

As indicated in Table 24-1, because marginal revenue now equals price, the discriminating monopolist will find that it is profitable to produce 7, rather than 5, units of output. The additional revenue from the sixth and seventh units is $214 (= $112 + $102). Thus total revenue for 7 units is $924 (= $710 + $214). Total costs for 7 units are $640, so profits are $284.

Ironically, although price discrimination increases the monopolist's profit compared to a nondiscriminating monopolist, it also results in greater output and thus less allocative inefficiency. In our example, the output level of 7 units matches the output which would occur in pure competition. That is, allocative efficiency ($P = $MC) is achieved.

Graphical Summary Figure 24-7 summarizes the effects of price discrimination. Figure 24-7a merely restates Figure 24-4 in a generalized form to show the position of a nondiscriminating monopolist as a benchmark. The nondiscriminating monopolist produces output Q_1 (where MR = MC) and charges a price of Q_1c (= 0b). Total revenue is area $0bcQ_1$ and economic profit is area *abcd*.

In Figure 24-7b the monopolist engages in perfect price discrimination, charging each buyer the highest price he or she is willing to pay. Starting at zero, each successive unit is sold for the price indicated by the corresponding point on the demand curve. This means that the demand and marginal-revenue curves coincide because the monopolist need *not* cut price on preceding units to sell more output. Thus, the most profitable output is at Q_2 (where MR = MC) which is greater than Q_1. Total revenue is area $0fgQ_2$ and total cost is area $0hjQ_2$. The discriminating monopolist's economic profit of *hfgj* is clearly larger than the single-price monopolist's profit of *abcd*.

The impact of discrimination on consumers is mixed. Those buying each unit out to Q_1 will pay more than the nondiscriminatory price of Q_1c. But those additional consumers brought into the market by discrimination will pay less than Q_1c. Specifically, they

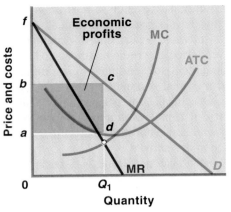

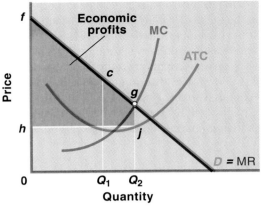

(a) Single-price monopolist **(b) Perfectly discriminating monopolist**

FIGURE 24-7 A single-price versus a perfectly discriminating monopolist
The perfectly discriminating monopolist (graph b) realizes a larger profit (*hfgj* as compared to *abcd*) and produces a larger output (Q_2 rather than Q_1) than would a single-price monopolist (graph a). Consumers on the *fc* range of the demand curve (in graph b) will pay higher prices with discrimination, while those on the *cg* segment will pay less.

will pay the various prices shown on the *cg* segment of the $D = MR$ curve.

To summarize: As compared to a one-price monopoly, price discrimination results in more profits, a greater output, and higher prices for many consumers but lower prices for those purchasing the extra output. *(Key Question 6)*

REGULATED MONOPOLY

Most purely monopolistic industries are natural monopolies and subject to regulation. The prices or rates public utilities—local telephone companies, natural gas and electricity suppliers—charge are determined by a Federal, state, or local regulatory commission or board.

Figure 24-8 shows the demand and long-run cost conditions of a natural monopoly. Because of the advantages of larger firm size, demand cuts the long-run average-total-cost curve at a point where it is still falling. It would be inefficient to have many firms in such an industry because, by dividing the market, each firm would move further to the left on its average-total-cost curve so unit costs would be substantially higher. The relationship between market demand and costs is such that the attainment of low unit costs presumes only one producer.

We know by application of the $MR = MC$ rule that P_m and Q_m are the profit-maximizing price and output which the unregulated monopolist would choose. Because price exceeds average total cost at Q_m, the monopolist enjoys a substantial economic profit. Furthermore, price exceeds marginal cost, indicating an underallocation of resources to this product or service. Can government regulation bring about better results from society's point of view?

Socially Optimal Price: $P = MC$

If the objective of our regulatory commission is to achieve allocative efficiency, it should attempt to establish a legal (ceiling) price for the monopolist equal to *marginal cost*. Remembering that each point on the market demand curve designates a price-quantity combination, and noting that marginal cost cuts the demand curve only at point r, it is clear that P_r is the only price equal to marginal cost. The imposition of this maximum or ceiling price causes the monopolist's effective demand curve to become $P_r r D$; the demand curve becomes perfectly elastic, and therefore $P_r = MR$, out to point r, where the regulated price ceases to be effective.

Confronted with the legal price P_r, the monopolist will maximize profits or minimize losses by producing Q_r units of output, because it is at this output

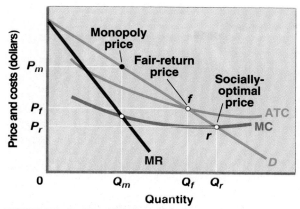

FIGURE 24-8 Regulated monopoly
Price regulation can improve the social consequences of a natural monopoly. The socially optimal price P_r will result in an efficient allocation of resources but is likely to entail losses and therefore call for permanent public subsidies. The "fair-return" price P_f will allow the monopolist to break even, but will not fully correct the underallocation of resources.

that MR (= P_r) = MC. By making it illegal to charge more than P_r per unit, the regulatory agency has eliminated the monopolist's incentive to restrict output to benefit from a higher price.

In short, by imposing the legal price P_r and letting the monopolist choose its profit-maximizing or loss-minimizing output, the allocative results of pure competition can be simulated. Production takes place where P_r = MC, and this equality indicates an efficient allocation of resources to this product or service. This price which achieves allocative efficiency is called the **socially optimal price.**

"Fair-Return" Price: P = ATC

But the socially optimal price P_r may pose a problem of losses for the regulated firm. The price which equals marginal cost may be so low that average total costs are not covered, as is shown in Figure 24-8. The result is losses. The reason lies in the basic character of public utilities. Because they are required to meet "peak" demands (both daily and seasonally) for their product or service, they have substantial excess production capacity when demand is relatively "normal." This high level of investment in capital facilities means that unit costs of production are likely to decline over a wide range of output. In technical terms, the market demand curve in Figure 24-8 cuts marginal cost at a point to the left of the marginal-cost–average-total-cost intersection, so the socially optimal price is below ATC. Therefore, to enforce a socially

optimal price on the regulated monopolist would mean short-run losses, and in the long run bankruptcy for the utility.

What to do? One option would be a public subsidy to cover the loss which marginal-cost pricing would entail. Another possibility is condoning price discrimination and hoping that the additional revenue gained will permit the firm to cover costs.

In practice, regulatory commissions have pursued a third option; they tend to back away somewhat from the objective of allocative efficiency and marginal-cost pricing. Most regulatory agencies in the United States are concerned with establishing a **"fair-return" price.** This is so because, as the courts have seen it, a socially optimal price would lead to losses and eventual bankruptcy and thereby deprive the monopoly's owners of their private property without "due process of law." The Supreme Court has held that regulatory agencies must permit a "fair return" to owners.

Remembering that total costs include a normal or "fair" profit, we see that the "fair" or "fair-return" price in Figure 24-8 would be P_f, where price equals *average* total cost. Because the demand curve cuts average total cost only at point *f*, clearly P_f is the only price which permits a fair return. The corresponding output at regulated price P_f will be Q_f. Total revenue of $0P_f f Q_f$ will equal total costs of the same amount and the firm will realize a normal profit.

Dilemma of Regulation

Comparing results of the socially optimal price (P = MC) and the fair-return price (P = ATC) suggests a policy dilemma, sometimes termed the **dilemma of regulation.** When price is set to achieve the most efficient allocation of resources (P = MC), the regulated utility is likely to suffer losses. Survival of the firm would presumably depend on permanent public subsidies out of tax revenues. On the other hand, although a fair-return price (P = ATC) allows the monopolist to cover costs, it only partially resolves the underallocation of resources which the unregulated monopoly would foster. That is, the fair-return price would only increase output from Q_m to Q_f, while the socially optimal output is Q_r. Despite this problem, regulation can improve on the results of monopoly from the social point of view. Price regulation can simultaneously reduce price, increase output, and reduce the economic profits of monopolies. *(Key Question 14)*

DE BEERS' DIAMONDS: ARE MONOPOLIES FOREVER?

De Beers Consolidated Mines of South Africa is one of the world's strongest and most enduring monopolies, having dominated the diamond market for over sixty years.

De Beers produces about 50 percent of all rough-cut diamonds in the world and buys for resale a large portion of the diamonds produced by other mines worldwide. As a result, it markets over 80 percent of the world's diamonds to a select group of diamond manufacturers and dealers.

Monopoly Behavior DeBeers' behavior and results are closely portrayed by the unregulated monopoly model of Figure 24-4. It sells only that quantity of diamonds which will yield an "appropriate" (monopoly) price. This price bears little relationship to production costs, and profits have been enormous. In "good" years profits are 60 percent of total revenues

and rates of return on equity capital are 30 percent or more.

When demand falls, De Beers will restrict sales to maintain price. The excess of production over sales is reflected in growing diamond stockpiles held by De Beers. It also attempts to bolster demand through ad-

---

QUICK REVIEW 24-3

■ Price discrimination occurs when a seller charges different prices which are not based on cost differentials.

■ The conditions necessary for price discrimination are: *a* monopoly power; *b* the segregation of buyers on the basis of different demand elasticities;

and *c* the inability of buyers to resell the product.

■ Monopoly price can be reduced and output increased through government regulation.

■ The socially optimal price ($P = MC$) achieves allocative efficiency but may result in losses; the fair-return price ($P = ATC$) yields a normal profit but falls short of allocative efficiency.

CHAPTER SUMMARY

1 A pure monopolist is the sole producer of a commodity for which there are no close substitutes.

2 Barriers to entry, in the form of **a** economies of scale, **b** patent ownership and research, and **c** ownership or control of essential resources, help explain the existence of pure monopoly and other imperfectly competitive market structures.

3 The pure monopolist's market situation differs from a competitive firm's in that the monopolist's demand curve is downsloping, causing the marginal-revenue curve to lie below the demand curve. Like the competitive seller, the pure monopolist will maximize profits by equating marginal revenue and marginal cost. Barriers to entry may permit a monopolist to acquire economic profits even in the long run. Note, however, that **a** the monopolist does not charge "the highest price it can get"; **b** the maximum total profit

sought by the monopolist rarely coincides with maximum unit profits; **c** high costs and a weak demand may prevent the monopolist from realizing any profit at all; and **d** the monopolist will want to avoid the inelastic range of its demand curve.

4 With the same costs, the pure monopolist will find it profitable to restrict output and charge a higher price than would a competitive seller. This restriction of output causes resources to be misallocated, as is evidenced by the fact that price exceeds marginal cost in monopolized markets.

5 In general, monopoly increases income inequality.

6 The costs of monopolists and competitive producers may not be the same. On the one hand, economies of scale may make lower unit costs accessible to monopolists but not to competitors. On the other hand, X-inefficiency—the failure to produce with the least-costly combination of in-

vertising ("diamonds are forever"). When demand is strong, it increases sales by reducing its diamond inventories.

De Beers controls the production of mines it does not own in several ways. First, it tries to convince independent producers that "single-channel" or monopoly marketing through De Beers is in their best interests in that it maximizes profits. Second, mines which circumvent De Beers are likely to find that the market is suddenly flooded from De Beers' stockpiles with the particular kind of diamonds that the "rogue" mine produces. The resulting price decline and loss of profits are likely to bring the mine into the De Beers fold. Finally, De Beers will simply purchase and stockpile diamonds produced by independent mines so their added supply will not "spoil" the market.

Threats and Problems   But even such an enduring monopoly as De Beers faces threats and problems. First, new diamond discoveries have resulted in a growing leakage of diamonds into world markets outside De Beers' control. For example, wildcat prospecting and trading in Angola has forced De Beers to spend $300 million or more per year to keep such diamonds off the market. The recent discovery of potentially great diamond supplies in Canada's Northwest Territories poses a future threat. Similarly, although Russia has been a part of the De Beers monopoly, this cash-strapped country has been selling as much as $500 million in diamonds per year (about one-fourth of its annual output) directly onto world markets. When new Siberian mines are brought into production, the additional output will pose a further threat to De Beers. Russia's estimated $4 to $8 billion stockpile of diamonds constitutes another potential future source of uncontrolled supply.

De Beers' diamond inventories are now an estimated $5 billion, an amount exceeding its annual sales. Observers wonder whether De Beers' capacity to absorb future unregulated production will reach a breaking point, at which time the monopoly will unravel. Although diamonds may be forever, De Beers may not.

puts—is more common to monopolists than to competitive firms and monopolists may make sizable expenditures to maintain monopoly privileges conferred by government.

7   Economists disagree as to how conducive pure monopoly is to technological advance. Some feel pure monopoly is more progressive than pure competition because its ability to realize economic profits helps finance technological research. Others, however, argue that absence of rival firms and the monopolist's desire to exploit fully its existing capital facilities weaken the monopolist's incentive to innovate.

8   A monopolist can increase its profits by practicing price discrimination, provided it can segregate buyers on the basis of different elasticities of demand and the product or service cannot be readily transferred between the segregated markets. Other things equal, the discriminating monopolist will produce a larger output than will the nondiscriminating monopolist.

9   Price regulation can be invoked to eliminate wholly or partially the tendency of monopolists to underallocate resources and to earn economic profits. The "socially optimal" price is determined where the demand and marginal-cost curves intersect; the "fair-return" price is determined where the demand and the average-total-cost curves intersect.

TERMS AND CONCEPTS

pure monopoly	rent-seeking behavior	socially optimal price	the dilemma of
barriers to entry	dynamic efficiency	fair-return price	regulation
X-inefficiency	price discrimination		

QUESTIONS AND STUDY SUGGESTIONS

1   "No firm is completely sheltered from rivals; all firms compete for consumer dollars. Pure monopoly, therefore, does not exist." Do you agree? Explain. How might you use Chapter 20's concept of cross elasticity of demand to judge whether monopoly exists?

2   Discuss the major barriers to entry. Explain how each barrier can foster monopoly or oligopoly. Which barriers, if any, do you feel give rise to monopoly that is socially justifiable?

3 How does the demand curve faced by a purely monopolistic seller differ from that confronting a purely competitive firm? Why does it differ? Of what significance is the difference? Why is the pure monopolist's demand curve not perfectly inelastic?

4 *Key Question* *Use the demand schedule below to calculate total revenue and marginal revenue. Plot the demand, total-revenue, and marginal-revenue curves and carefully explain the relationships between them. Explain why the marginal revenue of the fourth unit of output is $3.50, even though its price is $5.00. Use Chapter 20's total-revenue test for price elasticity to designate the elastic and inelastic segments of your graphed demand curve. What generalization can you make regarding the relationship between marginal revenue and elasticity of demand? Suppose that somehow the marginal cost of successive units of output were zero. What output would the profit-seeking firm produce? Finally, use your analysis to explain why a monopolist would never produce in that range of its demand curve which is inelastic.*

Price	Quantity demanded	Price	Quantity demanded
$7.00	0	$4.50	5
6.50	1	4.00	6
6.00	2	3.50	7
5.50	3	3.00	8
5.00	4	2.50	9

5 *Key Question* *Suppose a pure monopolist is faced with the demand schedule shown below and the same cost data as the competitive producer discussed in question 4 at the end of Chapter 23. Calculate total and marginal revenue and determine the profit-maximizing price and output for this monopolist. What is the level of profits? Verify your answer graphically and by comparing total revenue and total cost.*

Price	Quantity demanded	Total revenue	Marginal revenue
$115	0	$_____	
100	1	_____	$_____
83	2	_____	_____
71	3	_____	_____
63	4	_____	_____
55	5	_____	_____
48	6	_____	_____
42	7	_____	_____
37	8	_____	_____
33	9	_____	_____
29	10	_____	_____

6 *Key Question* *If the firm described in question 5 could engage in perfect price discrimination, what would be the level of output? Of profits? Draw a diagram showing the relevant demand, marginal-revenue, average-total-cost, and marginal-cost curves and the equilibrium price and output for a nondiscriminating monopolist. Use the same diagram to show the equilibrium position of a monopolist able to practice perfect price discrimination. Compare equilibrium outputs, total revenues, economic profits, and consumer prices in the two cases. Comment on the economic desirability of price discrimination.*

7 Assume a pure monopolist and a purely competitive firm have the same unit costs. Contrast the two with respect to **a** price, **b** output, **c** profits, **d** allocation of resources, and **e** impact upon the distribution of income. Since both monopolists and competitive firms follow the MC = MR rule in maximizing profits, how do you account for the different results? Why might the costs of a purely competitive firm and a monopolist *not* be the same? What are the implications of such cost differences?

8 Critically evaluate and explain:

a "Because they can control product price, monopolists are always assured of profitable production by simply charging the highest price consumers will pay."

b "The pure monopolist seeks that output which will yield the greatest per unit profit."

c "An excess of price over marginal cost is the market's way of signaling the need for more production of a good."

d "The more profitable a firm, the greater its monopoly power."

e "The monopolist has a price policy; the competitive producer does not."

f "With respect to resource allocation, the interests of the seller and of society coincide in a purely competitive market but conflict in a monopolized market."

g "In a sense the monopolist makes a profit for not producing; the monopolist produces profits more than it does goods."

9 Carefully evaluate the following widely held viewpoint. Can you offer any arguments to the contrary?

A monopoly is usually not under pressure to *invent* new products or methods. Nor does it have strong incentives to *innovate:* to apply those new inventions in practice and bring new products to the market. *The monopoly may choose to invent and innovate, but it will do so only at its own pace.* Because the new product cuts the value of the existing products, the monopoly will tend to hold back on innovation. Typically it innovates only when a smaller competitor forces its hand. Even if its capital is outdated or its products mediocre, a monopolist may prefer to protect and continue them rather than to replace them with better ones.[7]

[7]William G. Shepherd, *Public Policies Toward Business,* 8th ed. (Homewood, Ill.: Richard D. Irwin, Inc., 1991), p. 36.

10 Assume a monopolistic publisher has agreed to pay an author 15 percent of the total revenue from the sales of a text. Will the author and the publisher want to charge the same price for the text? Explain.

11 Suppose a firm's demand curve lies below its average-total-cost curve at all levels of output. Can you conceive of any circumstance in which production might be profitable?

12 Are colleges and universities engaging in price discrimination when they charge full tuition to some students and provide financial aid to others? What are the advantages and disadvantages of this practice?

13 Explain verbally and graphically how price (rate) regulation may improve the performance of monopolies. In your answer distinguish between **a** socially optimal (marginal-cost) pricing and **b** fair-return (average-total-cost) pricing. What is the "dilemma of regulation"?

14 *Key Question* *It has been proposed that natural monopolists should be allowed to determine their profit-maximizing outputs and prices and then government should tax their profits away and distribute them to consumers in proportion to their purchases from the monopoly. Is this proposal as socially desirable as requiring monopolists to equate price with marginal cost or average total cost?*

15 (Last Word) Explain how De Beers has an almost complete monopoly of the world diamond market, although it only produces one-half of world output. What are the threats to its market power?

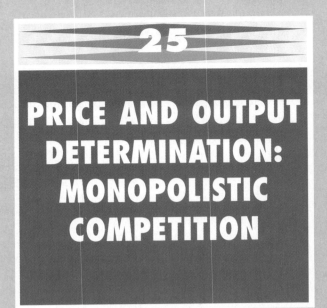

PRICE AND OUTPUT DETERMINATION: MONOPOLISTIC COMPETITION

In a town of any reasonable size, you have a wide array of choices in buying many products. Suppose you want to purchase a sweater. You might patronize a discount store whose newspaper flier advertises an imported acrylic for $15. Or you might select a fleece pullover with your college's logo and colors advertised in your campus newspaper for $25 on sale at your bookstore. You might buy a cotton knit for $45 from a mail-order catalog. Or you could shop at an upscale clothier and pay $80 or $90 or more for a wool sweater. These product choices reflect the world of monopolistic competition where competition is not only based on price, but also on product quality, services, and advertising.

Pure competition and pure monopoly are the exceptions, not the rule, in our economy. Most market structures fall somewhere between these two extremes. In this chapter we examine monopolistic competition, which suggests a blending of monopoly and competition. More specifically, monopolistic competition involves a considerable amount of competition mixed with a small dose of monopoly power.

Our objectives are to (1) define and discuss the nature and prevalence of monopolistic competition, (2) analyze and evaluate the price-output behavior of monopolistically competitive firms, and (3) explain and assess the role of nonprice competition, that is, competition based on product quality and advertising, in monopolistically competitive industries.

MONOPOLISTIC COMPETITION: CONCEPT AND OCCURRENCE

The defining characteristics of **monopolistic competition** are: (1) a relatively large number of sellers; (2) product differentiation; and (3) easy entry to, and exit from, the industry. The first and third characteristics provide the "competitive" aspect of monopolis-

tic competition; the second characteristic contributes the "monopolistic" aspect.

Relatively Large Numbers

Monopolistic competition does not require hundreds or thousands of firms as does pure competition but only a fairly large number—say 25, 35, 60, or 70.

Several characteristics of monopolistic competition follow from the presence of relatively large numbers.

1   Small Market Share   Each firm has a comparatively small percentage of the total market, so each has limited control over market price.

2   No Collusion   A relatively large number of firms ensures that collusion—concerted action by firms to restrict output and rig price—is all but impossible.

3   Independent Actions   With numerous firms in the industry, there is no feeling of mutual interdependence among them; each firm determines its policies without considering possible reactions of rival firms. This is a very reasonable way to act in a market in which there are numerous rivals. The 10 or 15 percent increase in sales which firm X may realize by cutting prices will be spread so thinly over its 20, 40, or 60 rivals that, for all practical purposes, the impact on their sales will be imperceptible. Rivals' reactions can be ignored because the impact of one firm's actions on each of its many rivals is so small that these rivals will have no reason to react.

Product Differentiation

Also in contrast to pure competition, monopolistic competition has the fundamental feature of **product differentiation.** Purely competitive firms produce a standardized or homogeneous product; monopolistically competitive producers turn out variations of a particular product.

Because of product differentiation, economic rivalry typically takes the form of **nonprice competition**—competition in terms of product quality, services to consumers, location and accessibility, and advertising.

Let's examine these aspects of nonprice competition.

1   Product Quality   Product differentiation may take the form of physical or qualitative differences in products themselves. "Real" differences in functional features, materials, design, and workmanship are vital aspects of product differentiation. Personal computers, for example, differ in terms of hardware capacity, software, graphics, and how "user-friendly"

they are. There are scores of competing principles of economics texts which differ in content, organization, presentation and readability, pedagogical aids, and graphics and design. Most cities will have a variety of retail stores selling men's and women's clothing varying greatly in styling, materials, and quality of workmanship. Similarly, one fast-food hamburger chain may feature lean beef, while a competitor stresses the juiciness of its hamburgers.

Credit cards may seem like homogeneous "products," differing only in annual fees and interest-rate charges. Not so. Some provide rebates on purchases; others offer free airline travel miles; and still others offer extended warranties on products purchased on credit.

2   Services   Services and conditions surrounding the sale of a product are forms of product differentiation. One grocery store may stress the helpfulness of its clerks who bag your groceries and carry them to your car. A "warehouse" competitor may leave bagging and carrying to its customers, but feature lower prices. "One-day" clothes cleaning may be preferred to cleaning of equal quality which takes three days. The "snob appeal" of a store, the courteousness and helpfulness of clerks, the firm's reputation for servicing or exchanging its products, and credit availability are all service aspects of product differentiation. Pizza restaurants compete on the basis of whether they offer delivery services.

3   Location   Products may also be differentiated as to location and accessibility. Small minigroceries or convenience stores successfully compete with large supermarkets, even though they have a more limited range of products and charge higher prices. They compete on the basis of location—being close to customers and on busy streets—and by staying open 24 hours a day. A gas station's proximity to the interstate highway gives it a locational advantage which may allow it to sell gasoline at a higher price than could a gas station in a city 2 or 3 miles from the interstate.

4   Advertising and Packaging   Product differentiation may also arise from perceived differences created through advertising, the use of brand names and trademarks, and packaging. While there are many aspirin-type products, promotion and advertising may convince headache sufferers that Bayer or Anacin is superior and worth a higher price than a generic substitute. A celebrity's name associated with jeans or perfume may enhance those products in the minds of buyers. Many consumers regard toothpaste in a "pump" container preferable to the same toothpaste in a conventional tube. Environment-friendly "green" packaging or "clear" beverages and liquid soaps are used to attract additional customers.

One implication of product differentiation is that, despite the relatively large number of firms, monopolistically competitive producers do have limited control over the prices of their products. Consumers prefer the products of specific sellers and *within limits* will pay more to satisfy those preferences. Sellers and buyers are not linked at random, as in a purely competitive market.

Easy Entry

Entry into monopolistically competitive industries is relatively easy. The fact that monopolistically competitive producers are typically small-sized firms, both absolutely and relatively, suggests that economies of scale and capital requirements are few. On the other hand, compared with pure competition, added financial barriers may result from the need to develop a product different from one's rivals and the obligation to advertise it. Some existing firms may hold patents

on their products and copyrights on their brand names and trademarks, enhancing the difficulty and cost of successfully imitating them.

Illustrations

Table 25-1 lists manufacturing industries approximating monopolistic competition. In addition, retail stores in metropolitan areas are generally monopolistically competitive; grocery stores, gasoline stations, barber shops, dry cleaners, clothing stores, and restaurants operate under conditions similar to those we have described.

PRICE AND OUTPUT DETERMINATION

Let's analyze the price-output behavior of a monopolistically competitive firm. Assume initially that the firms in the industry are producing *specific* products and engaging in a *specific* amount of promotional activity. Later we'll see how product variation and advertising modify our discussion.

The Firm's Demand Curve

Our explanation is couched in terms of Figure 25-1 (Key Graph). The basic features of this diagram, which distinguishes it from our analyses of pure competition and pure monopoly, is the elasticity of the firm's individual demand, or sales, curve. *The demand curve faced by a monopolistically competitive seller is highly, but not perfectly, elastic.* It is much more elastic than the demand curve of the pure monopolist, because the monopolistically competitive seller faces many rivals producing close-substitute goods. The pure monopolist has no rivals at all. Yet, for two reasons, the monopolistically competitive seller's sales curve is not perfectly elastic as is the purely competitive producer's: First, the monopolistically competitive firm has fewer rivals, and, second, the products of these rivals are close but not perfect substitutes.

The precise degree of elasticity of the monopolistically competitive firm's demand curve will depend on the exact number of rivals and the degree of product differentiation. The larger the number of rivals and the weaker the product differentiation, the greater will be the elasticity of each seller's demand curve, that

TABLE 25-1   Percentage of output* produced by firms in selected low-concentration manufacturing industries

Industry	Four largest firms	Eight largest firms	Twenty largest firms
Men's and boys' suits and coats	34%	47%	64%
Mattresses and bedsprings	33	38	47
Prefab metal buildings	27	40	58
Book publishing	24	38	62
Upholstered furniture	24	35	51
Wood furniture	20	29	43
Metal house furniture	18	29	50
Paperboard boxes	16	26	44
Bolts, nuts, and rivets	16	24	40
Fur goods	16	24	39
Women's and misses' suits and coats	13	23	39
Metal doors	13	19	33
Women's and misses' dresses	6	10	18

*As measured by value of industry shipments. Data are for 1987
Source: Bureau of the Census, 1987 Census of Manufacturers.

KEY GRAPH

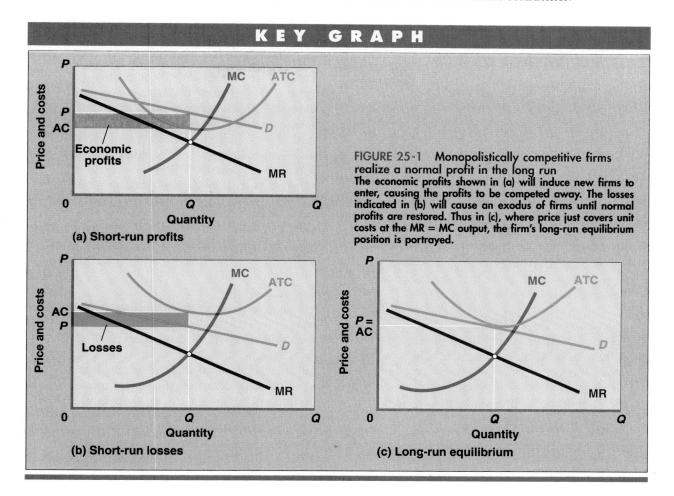

FIGURE 25-1 Monopolistically competitive firms realize a normal profit in the long run

The economic profits shown in (a) will induce new firms to enter, causing the profits to be competed away. The losses indicated in (b) will cause an exodus of firms until normal profits are restored. Thus in (c), where price just covers unit costs at the MR = MC output, the firm's long-run equilibrium position is portrayed.

(a) Short-run profits

(b) Short-run losses

(c) Long-run equilibrium

is, the closer monopolistic competition will be to pure competition.

The Short Run: Profits or Losses

The firm will maximize its profits or minimize its losses in the short run by producing that output designated by the equality of marginal cost and marginal revenue. Our firm of Figure 25-1a produces an output *Q*, charges a price *P,* and realizes an economic profit. But a less favorable cost and demand situation may exist, putting the monopolistically competitive firm in the position of incurring losses in the short run. This is illustrated in Figure 25-1b. In the short run the monopolistically competitive firm may either realize an economic profit or face losses.

The Long Run: Break Even

In the long run a monopolistically competitive firm will earn only a normal profit or, in other words, break even.

Profits: Firms Enter   In the short-run profits case, Figure 25-1a, economic profits will attract new rivals, because its easy to enter the industry. As new firms enter, the demand curve faced by the typical firm will fall (shift to the left) and become more elastic. Why? Because each firm has a smaller share of the total demand and now faces a larger number of close-substitute products. This causes the economic profits to disappear. When the demand curve is tangent to the average-total-cost curve at the profit-maximizing output, as shown in Figure 25-1c, the firm is just breaking even (making a normal profit). Output Q is the equilibrium output for the firm. As Figure 25-1c clearly indicates, any deviation from that output will entail average total costs which exceed product price and, therefore, losses for the firm. Furthermore, economic profits have been competed away, and there is no incentive for more firms to enter.

Losses: Firms Leave When the industry suffers short-run losses—as shown in Figure 25-1b—some firms will exit in the long run. Faced with fewer substitute products and blessed with an expanded share of total demand, surviving firms will see their losses disappear and gradually give way to normal profits. (For simplicity we have assumed constant costs; shifts in the cost curves as firms enter or leave would complicate our discussion slightly, but would not alter the conclusions.)

Complications The representative firm in the monopolistic competition model breaks even, or earns only a normal profit, in the long run. This outcome may not always occur, however, in the real world of small firms which have some monopoly power but also face competition. Three real-world complications are noteworthy.
1   Some firms may achieve product differentiation to an extent which cannot be duplicated by rivals even over a long time. A gasoline station may have the only available location at the busiest intersection in town. Or a firm may hold a patent giving it a slight and more-or-less permanent advantage over imitators. Such firms are, in effect, monopolists and may realize a sliver of economic profits even in the long run.
2   Remember that entry is not completely unrestricted. Because of product differentiation, there are likely to be greater financial barriers to entry than otherwise. This suggests monopoly power, with some economic profits persisting even in the long run.
3   A final consideration may work in the opposite direction, causing losses—below-normal profits—to remain in the long run. The proprietors of a corner delicatessen persistently accept a return less than they could earn elsewhere because their business is a "way of life" to them. The suburban barber ekes out a meager existence, because cutting hair is "all he wants to do." With all things considered, however, the long-run normal profit equilibrium of Figure 25-1c is a reasonable portrayal of reality.

MONOPOLISTIC COMPETITION AND ECONOMIC INEFFICIENCY

Recalling our evaluation of competitive pricing in Chapter 23, we know that economic efficiency requires the triple equality of price, marginal cost, and average total cost. When price and marginal cost are equal, there will be the realization of *allocative efficiency*—the allocation of the right amount of resources to the product. When price equals minimum average total cost *productive efficiency* or the use of the most efficient (least-cost) technology will result. Productive efficiency means consumers will enjoy the largest volume of the product and the lowest price which least-cost conditions allow.

Excess Capacity

In monopolistically competitive markets excess capacity occurs and neither allocative nor productive efficiency is realized. An examination of Figure 25-2, which enlarges the relevant portion of Figure 25-1c and adds detail, shows that the monopolistic element in monopolistic competition causes a modest underallocation of resources. Price (p) exceeds marginal cost (m) in long-run equilibrium, indicating that society values additional units of this commodity more than the alternative products the needed resources can otherwise produce.

Furthermore, in contrast to purely competitive firms, we observe in Figure 25-2 that monopolistically competitive firms are characterized by **excess capacity,** meaning they produce somewhat short of the most efficient (least unit cost) output. Production entails higher unit costs (p) than the minimum attainable at (a). This means a somewhat higher price (p) than would result under competition (a). Consumers do *not* benefit from the largest output and lowest price which cost conditions permit. Indeed, monopolistically competitive firms must charge a higher than competitive price in the long run to achieve a normal profit.

Viewed differently, if each firm could produce at the most efficient output, fewer firms could produce the same total output, and the product could be sold at a lower price. Monopolistically competitive industries are overcrowded with firms, each of which is underutilized, that is, operating short of optimal capacity. This is typified by many kinds of retail establishments, for example, the thirty or forty gasoline stations, all operating with excess capacity, that pop-

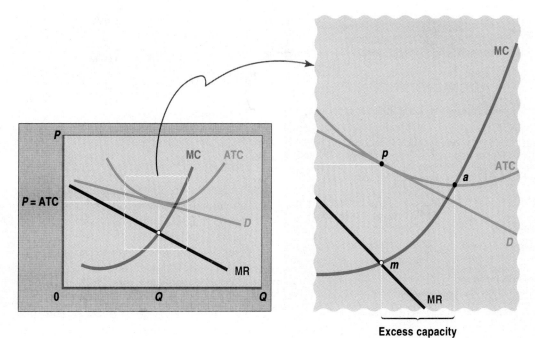

FIGURE 25-2 The inefficiency aspects of monopolistic competition
In long-run equilibrium a monopolistically competitive firm achieves neither allocative nor productive efficiency. An underallocation of resources occurs because the product price of *p* exceeds marginal cost of *m*. Productive efficiency is not realized because production occurs where the average total cost of *p* exceeds the minimum attainable average total cost of *a*.

ulate a medium-sized city. Monopolistic competition results in the underutilized plants, and consumers who are penalized through higher than competitive prices for this underutilization. *(Key Question 2)*

QUICK REVIEW 25-1

■ Monopolistic competition refers to industries which comprise a relatively large number of firms, operating noncollusively, in the production of differentiated products.

■ In the short run a monopolistically competitive firm will maximize profits or minimize losses by producing that output at which marginal revenue equals marginal cost.

■ In the long run easy entry and exodus of firms causes monopolistically competitive firms to earn only a normal profit.

■ A monopolistically competitive firm's equilibrium output is such that price exceeds marginal cost (indicating that resources are underallocated to the product) and price exceeds minimum average total cost (implying that consumers do not get the product at the lowest unit cost and price attainable).

NONPRICE COMPETITION

The situation portrayed in Figure 25-1c and Figure 25-2 is not very satisfying to the monopolistically competitive producer which captures only a normal profit. Therefore, monopolistically competitive producers will try to improve on the long-run equilibrium position.

How do they do this? Through nonprice competition in the form of product differentiation and advertising. Each firm has a product distinguishable in some more-or-less tangible way from those of its rivals. The product is presumably subject to further variation, that is, to product development. The emphasis on real product differences and the creation of perceived differences may be achieved through advertising and related sales promotion. The profit-realizing firm of Figure 25-1a will not stand by and watch new competitors encroach on its profits by duplicating or imitating its product, copying its advertising, and matching its services to consumers. Rather, the firm will attempt to sustain its profits and stay ahead of competitors through further product development and by enhancing the quantity and qual-

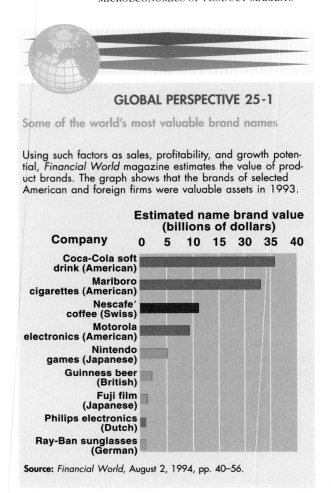

GLOBAL PERSPECTIVE 25-1

Some of the world's most valuable brand names

Using such factors as sales, profitability, and growth potential, *Financial World* magazine estimates the value of product brands. The graph shows that the brands of selected American and foreign firms were valuable assets in 1993.

Estimated name brand value
(billions of dollars)

Source: *Financial World,* August 2, 1994, pp. 40–56.

left of the minimum average total costs will production take place (Figure 25-2). But the greater the product differentiation, the more likely diverse tastes will be fully satisfied. The greater the excess capacity problem, the wider the range of consumer choice.

There are two considerations here: (1) product differentiation at a point in time, and (2) product improvement over a period of time.

Product Differentiation

Product differentiation means that at any point in time the consumer will be offered a wide range of types, styles, brands, and quality gradations of any given product. Compared with pure competition, this suggests possible advantages to the consumer. The range of choice is widened, and variations and shadings of consumer tastes are more fully met by producers.

But skeptics warn that product differentiation may reach the point where the consumer becomes confused and rational choice becomes time-consuming and difficult. Variety may add spice to the consumer's life, but only up to a point. A woman shopping for lipstick may be bewildered by the vast array of products available. Revlon alone offers more than 150 shades of lipstick, of which over 40 are "pink"! Worse, some observers fear that the consumer, faced with a myriad of similar products, may judge product quality by price; the consumer may irrationally assume that price is an index of product quality.

Product Development

Product competition is vital to technological innovation and product betterment over a period of time. Such product development may be cumulative in two different ways. First, a successful product improvement by one firm obligates rivals to imitate or, if they can, improve on this firm's temporary market advantage or suffer losses. Second, profits realized from a successful product improvement can finance further improvements.

Again, there are critics. They say many product alterations are more apparent than real, consisting of frivolous and superficial changes which do *not* improve the product's durability, efficiency, or usefulness. A more exotic container or bright packaging is frequently the extent of product development. It is argued, too, that particularly with durable and semidurable consumer goods, development may follow a pattern of "planned obsolescence," where firms im-

ity of its advertising. In this way it might prevent the long-run outcome of Figure 25-1c from becoming a reality. True, product development and advertising will add to the firm's costs, but they can also increase the demand for its product. If demand increases by more than enough to compensate for development and promotional costs, the firm will have improved its profit position. As Figure 25-1c suggests, the firm may have little or no prospect of increasing profits by price cutting. So why not practice nonprice competition?

The likelihood that easy entry will promote product variety and product improvement is possibly a redeeming feature of monopolistic competition which may offset, wholly or in part, its inefficiencies. In fact, there is a tradeoff between product differentiation and the production of a given product at the minimum average cost. The stronger the product differentiation (the less elastic the demand curve), the further to the

prove a product only by that amount necessary to make the average consumer dissatisfied with last year's model.

Do the advantages of product differentiation, properly discounted, outweigh the inefficiencies of monopolistic competition? It is difficult to say, short of examining specific cases; and even then, concrete conclusions are hard to come by.

THE ECONOMICS OF ADVERTISING

A monopolistically competitive producer may gain at least a temporary edge on rivals by altering its product. It may also seek the same result by attempting to influence consumer preferences through advertising and sales promotion. Advertising *may* be a mechanism through which a firm can increase its share of the market and enhance consumer loyalty to its particular product.

Controversy and Scope

There is considerable disagreement as to the economic and social desirability of advertising. Since advertising and promotional expenditures in the United States were estimated to be almost $150 billion in 1993, the issues involved are significant. This amount was roughly equal to the amount all state and local governments spent on public welfare. Hence, if advertising is wasteful, any potential virtues of monopolistically competitive markets are thereby dimmed, and the need for corrective public policies is indicated.

Two Views

The controversy has generated two opposite views of advertising.[1] In outlining these two views, bear in mind that advertising is not confined to monopolistic competition. Product differentiation and heavy advertising are also characteristic of many oligopolistic industries (Chapter 26). Thus, our comments are equally germane to these industries.

The **traditional view** envisions advertising as a redundant and economically wasteful expenditure which generates economic concentration and mo-

nopoly power. The **new perspective** on advertising sees it as an efficient means for both providing information to consumers and enhancing competition. Let's contrast these two views in three critical areas.

1 Persuasion or Information? The traditional view holds that the main purpose of advertising is to manipulate or persuade consumers, that is, to alter their preferences in favor of the advertiser's product. A television beer commercial or a newspaper cigarette ad conveys little or no useful information to consumers. Advertising is often based on misleading and extravagant claims which confuse and frequently insult the intelligence of consumers, not enlighten them. Indeed, advertising may well persuade consumers in some cases to pay high prices for much-acclaimed but inferior products, forgoing better but unadvertised products selling at lower prices.

The new perspective contends that consumers need information about product characteristics and prices to make rational (efficient) decisions. Advertising is alleged to be a low-cost means of providing that information. Suppose you are in the market for a CD player and there was no newspaper or magazine advertising of this product. To make a rational choice you might have to spend several days visiting electronics stores to determine the prices and features of various brands. This entails both direct costs (gasoline, parking fees) and indirect costs (the value of your time). Advertising, it is argued, reduces your "search time" and minimizes these costs.

2 Concentration or Competition? Does advertising generate monopoly or stimulate competition? The traditional view envisions some firms as being more successful than others in establishing "brand loyalty" through advertising, that is, in persuading consumers to buy their products. As a consequence, such firms are able to increase their sales, expand their market share, and enjoy enlarged profits. Larger profits permit still more advertising and further enlargement of the firm's market shares and profits. In short, successful advertising leads to the expansion of some firms at the expense of others and therefore to increased industrial concentration. Consumers in time lose the advantages of competitive markets and face the disadvantages of monopolized markets. Furthermore, potential new entrants to the industry will need to incur large advertising costs to establish their product in the marketplace; thus, advertising costs may be a barrier to entry.

[1]The ensuing discussion draws upon Robert B. Eklund, Jr., and David S. Saurman, *Advertising and the Market Process* (San Francisco: Pacific Research Institute for Public Policy, 1988).

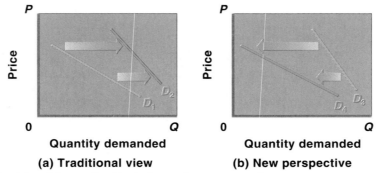

FIGURE 25-3 Advertising and a firm's demand curve: two views

The traditional view of advertising sees advertising as a device which increases the successful advertiser's market share and enhances brand loyalty. The result is greater market concentration as the demand curve of the successful advertiser shifts rightward and becomes more inelastic as shown by the D_1 to D_2 movement in panel (a). The new perspective regards advertising as a means of increasing consumer awareness of substitute products, thereby enhancing competition. Consequently, advertising in an industry will cause each firm's demand curve to shift leftward and become more elastic, as portrayed by the movement from D_3 to D_4 in panel (b).

The traditional view is portrayed graphically in Figure 25-3a. By successfully generating brand loyalty through advertising, the firm's demand curve shifts rightward from D_1 to D_2, implying a larger market share. The fact that curve D_2 is less elastic than D_1 indicates a lessening of competition; successful advertising has convinced consumers that there exist fewer good substitutes for this firm's product. The less elastic demand curve also means that the producer can charge higher prices with less loss of sales.

The new perspective says advertising enhances competition. By providing information about the variety of substitute products available, advertising diminishes monopoly power. In fact, advertising is frequently associated with the introduction of new products designed to compete with existing brands. Could the Hyundai and Isuzu automobiles have gained a foothold in the American market without advertising? How about Act II microwave popcorn and Softsoap?

In terms of Figure 25-3b, advertising, in a world of costly and imperfect knowledge, makes consumers more aware of the range of substitutable products available to them and provides them with valuable information on the prices and characteristics of these goods. With no advertising, consumers may only be aware that products B and C were good substitutes for A. But advertising provides them with the knowledge that D, E, and F are also substitutable for A. As a consequence of the advertising of all firms in the industry, the demand curve of firm A shifts leftward, as from D_3 to D_4 in Figure 25-3b, and becomes more

elastic. Both of these changes reflect enhanced competition.

3 Wasteful or Efficient? The traditional view says advertising is economically wasteful. First, it makes markets less competitive and therefore obstructs the realization of either allocative or productive efficiency. Second, advertising allegedly diverts human and property resources from higher-valued uses. For example, timber, which is needed in the production of housing, is squandered on unsightly billboards and on producing the paper used for advertising supplements in local newspapers. Advertising allegedly constitutes an inefficient use of scarce resources. Finally, advertising expenditures contribute to higher costs which are ultimately reflected in higher prices to consumers.

The new perspective views advertising as an efficiency-enhancing activity. It is an inexpensive means of providing useful information to consumers and thus lowers search costs. By enhancing competition, advertising is conducive to both greater allocative and productive efficiency. Finally, by facilitating the successful introduction of new products, advertising is conducive to technological progress.

A narrower perspective on the efficiency aspects of advertising is shown in Figure 25-4. It focuses on the notion that advertising has two effects: (1) It is designed to increase demand and (2) it increases costs.

Scenario one: Through successful advertising a firm increases its demand, permitting it to expand production and sales from, say, Q_1 to Q_2. Despite the fact

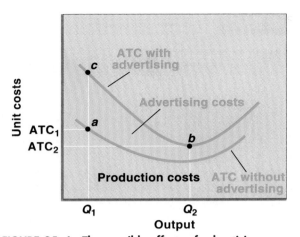

FIGURE 25-4 The possible effects of advertising on a firm's output and average costs
Proponents of advertising contend that advertising will expand the firm's production from, say, *a* to *b* and lower unit costs as economies of scale are realized. Some critics argue that advertising is more likely to increase average total costs and leave output largely unchanged, as is suggested by the movement from *a* to *c*.

that advertising outlays will shift the firm's average-total-cost curve upward, unit costs decline from ATC_1 to ATC_2 as the firm moves from point *a* to point *b*. Greater productive efficiency resulting from economies of scale more than offsets the increase in unit costs due to advertising. Consumers will therefore get the product at a lower price with advertising than they would without.

Scenario two: What if the advertising efforts of all firms are essentially self-canceling? The advertising campaign of one clothing manufacturer is offset by equally costly campaigns waged by rivals so that each firm's demand curve is unchanged. Little or no additional clothing is actually purchased and each firm's market share stays the same. But, because of the advertising, the cost and therefore the price of clothing is higher. Instead of moving from *a* to *b*, self-canceling advertising moves the firm from *a* to *c*. The consumer faces a higher product price because of advertising.

These conflicting scenarios suggest that the impact of advertising on output, unit costs, and prices is unclear and ambiguous. *(Key Questions 6 and 9)*

Empirical Evidence

There are important empirical studies which lend credence to both of these views. For example, a study of the role of advertising in forty-one industries manufacturing consumer goods concluded that advertising is generally anticompetitive. Specifically, the report said that "the heavy volume of advertising expenditures in some industries serves as a barrier to new competition in the markets served by these industries."[2] Prices of heavily advertised goods exceed their marginal costs, reflecting a misallocation of resources. Furthermore, for many of the studied industries expenditures for advertising were found to be "excessive" and wasteful of scarce resources.

In contrast, another study concluded that advertising is a procompetitive force, reasoning that, if advertising promotes monopoly power, then industries which advertise most heavily should be the ones which increase their prices the most and their outputs the least over time (recall Figure 24-4). Examining price and output changes of some 150 major industries over the 1963–1977 period, this study found that generally those industries with higher-than-average levels of advertising had *lower*-than-average rates of price increases and *higher*-than-average rates of output increase. Conclusion: Rather than contributing to monopoly power, advertising generally enhances competition.[3]

There are other industry studies which suggest that advertising enhances competition and has economically desirable results. A study of the eyeglasses industry compared prices in states where professional codes of ethics permitted optometrists to advertise with those where codes prohibited or restricted advertising. The conclusion was that prices of eyeglasses were 25 to 40 percent higher in states where advertising was restricted.[4] A study of retail drug prices, comparing states where advertising was permitted with those in which it was not, found that prescription drug prices were about 5 percent lower in states which permitted advertising.[5] Finally, a study of the toy industry concluded that television advertising affected substantial price reductions:

[2]William S. Comanor and Thomas A. Wilson, *Advertising and Market Power* (Cambridge, Mass.: Harvard University Press, 1974), p. 239.

[3]E. Woodrow Eckard, Jr., "Advertising, Concentration, and Consumer Welfare," *Review of Economics and Statistics,* May 1988, pp. 340–343.

[4]Lee and Alexandra Benham, "Regulating the Professions: A Perspective on Information Control," *Journal of Law and Economics,* October 1975, pp. 421–447.

[5]John F. Cady, *Restricted Advertising and Competition: The Case of Retail Drugs* (Washington: American Enterprise Institute, 1976).

LAST WORD

THE MARKET FOR PRINCIPLES OF ECONOMICS TEXTBOOKS

The market for principles texts embraces a number of the characteristics of monopolistic competition.

Currently there are fifty or more economics texts which could be used in the principles course. If you compared a number of them, you would find considerable differences. While there is some variation in subject matter, most cover the same core topics. Books do vary considerably as to the rigor and detail with which material is presented. They also vary as to reading level. Some books have a one-color format, others use multicolor diagrams and tables. Books vary greatly in the use of such pedagogical devices as photos, "boxed features," cartoons, learning objectives, intrachapter summaries, and glossaries. Publishers seek the mix of these features which they hope will be most appealing to instructors and students.

Texts are also differentiated by their accompanying "packages" of ancillary materials. These include study guides, videos, and computer tutorial and simulation programs to aid student understanding. Instructor manuals, test banks, and overhead transparencies are designed to save instructor time and enhance teacher productivity. Were you to trace the

introduction and development of these various pedagogical aids and instructional materials, you would find that when any one of them was introduced and proved attractive to adopters, that feature would be quickly incorporated into future editions of most other old and new books.

Product differentiation is accompanied by considerable nonprice competition. Texts are advertised by direct mail and in widely read economics journals. Publishers provide potential adopters with free copies and use "trade fair" booths at economics conventions

Advertising cuts distribution margins on advertised brands for two reasons: *first*, advertising causes goods to turn over rapidly so they can be sold profitably with smaller markups, and *second*, advertising creates product identity—which, in differentiated products, permits the public to compare prices between stores, thus setting a limit on the retailer's freedom to mark up. Products which are both heavily advertised and are fast sellers will be pulled through the distribution channels with the lowest markups of all.[6]

Evidence on the economic effects of advertising is mixed because studies are usually plagued by data problems and difficulties in determining cause and effect. Suppose it is found that firms which do a great deal of advertising seem to have considerable monopoly power and large profits. Does this mean advertising creates barriers to entry which generate monopoly power and profits? Or do entry barriers

associated with factors remote from advertising cause monopoly profits which allow firms to spend lavishly in advertising their products? In any event, at this time there is no consensus on the economic implications of advertising.

QUICK REVIEW 25-2

■ Monopolistically competitive firms may seek economic profits through product differentiation, product development, and advertising.

■ The traditional view of advertising alleges that it is a persuasive rather than informative activity; it promotes economic concentration and monopoly power; and it is a source of economic waste and inefficiency.

■ According to the new perspective, advertising is a low-cost source of information for consumers; a means of increasing competition by making consumers aware of substitutable products; and a source of greater efficiency in the use of resources.

[6]Robert L. Steiner, "Does Advertising Lower Consumer Prices?" *Journal of Marketing*, October 1973, p. 21.

to publicize their wares. Sales representatives of the various publishers—who receive bonuses for exceeding sales quotas—prowl the halls of academia to make professors aware of the distinguishing features and alleged advantages of their particular text. Over 1 million students take principles courses each year so the battle for market shares is vigorous.

Price competition plays a secondary role in the textbook market. First, unlike most markets, the product is chosen for the consumer by a second party. Your instructor—who gets a free text (and teacher's aids) from the publisher and may not even be aware of its retail price—decides the text you must read for the course. Second, instructors usually put textbook quality above price. It would prove very costly to students to use an inaccurate, poorly written text which might impair the teaching-learning process. The significant exception is that over the years more and more instructors have opted for lower-priced paperbacks which split micro and macro components of the course. Thus, a student taking only one semester of economics can avoid the higher cost of a two-semester hardback.

Competition for any given text arises not only from rival books, but also from the used-book market. While new copies of a text dominate its first-year sales, used books often dominate the second and third years of its revision cycle. That means that publishers and authors (who receive no income from used-book sales) "compete with themselves" shortly after a revision is published. Many students prefer a used book selling at, say, $38 or $40 to a new copy at $50 or $55. Furthermore, bookstores typically make a larger profit on used books and therefore "push" them over new ones. Used copies of a given text are obviously very good substitutes for new copies and they undoubtedly increase the price elasticity of demand for new copies.

While there are no artificial barriers to entering the market, the widespread use of multicolor formats and the obligation to provide an array of student-instructor ancillary items poses a significant financial barrier. It may take an investment of $1 million or more for a publisher to enter the market with a text and ancillaries comparable to those already on the market. Even so, it is not uncommon to find two or three new entries in the market every year.

In summary, the economics textbook market is characterized by product differentiation and nonprice competition. Price competition is muted and the only entry barrier is financial.

Source: Based on Timothy Tregarthen, "The Market for Principles of Economics Texts," *The Margin,* March 1987, pp. 14–15; and Joseph E. Stiglitz, "On the Market for Principles of Economics Textbooks: Innovation and Product Differentiation," *Journal of Economic Education,* Spring 1988, pp. 171–177.

Monopolistic Competition and Economic Analysis

Our discussion of nonprice competition implies that the equilibrium situation of a monopolistically competitive firm is more complex than the previous graphical analysis indicates. Figure 25-1 *assumes* a given product and a given level of advertising expenditures. But we now know these are not given in practice. The monopolistically competitive firm must juggle three factors—price, product, and promotion—in seeking maximum profits. What specific variety of product, selling at what price, and supplemented by what level of promotional activity, will result in the greatest level of profits attainable? This complex situation is not easily expressed in a simple, meaningful economic model. At best we can note that each possible combination of price, product, and promotion poses a different demand and cost (production plus promotion) situation for the firm, some one of which will allow it maximum profits. In practice, this optimal combination cannot be readily forecast but must be sought by trial and error. Even here, certain limitations may be imposed by the actions of rivals. A firm may not eliminate its advertising expenditures for fear its share of the market will decline sharply, benefiting its rivals who do advertise. Similarly, patents held by rivals will rule out certain desirable product variations.

CHAPTER SUMMARY

1 The distinguishing features of monopolistic competition are: **a** There are enough firms so that each has little control over price, mutual interdependence is absent, and collusion is virtually impossible; **b** products are characterized by real and perceived differences and by varying conditions surrounding their sale so that economic rivalry entails both price and nonprice competition; and **c** entry to the industry is relatively easy. Many aspects of retailing, and some industries where economies of scale are few, approximate monopolistic competition.

2   Monopolistically competitive firms may earn economic profits or incur losses in the short run. The easy entry and exodus of firms result in a normal profit in the long run.

3   The long-run equilibrium position of the monopolistically competitive producer is less socially desirable than that of a purely competitive firm. Under monopolistic competition, price exceeds marginal cost, suggesting an underallocation of resources to the product, and price exceeds minimum average total cost, indicating that consumers do not get the product at the lowest price which cost conditions would allow.

4   Product differentiation provides a means by which monopolistically competitive firms can offset the long-run tendency for economic profits to approximate zero. Through product development and advertising, a firm may strive to increase the demand for its product more than nonprice competition increases its cost.

5   Product differentiation affords the consumer a greater variety of products at any point in time and improved products over time. Whether these features fully compensate for the inefficiencies of monopolistic competition is a complex and unresolved question.

6   The traditional and new perspective views of advertising differ as to whether advertising **a** is persuasive or informative, **b** promotes monopoly or competition, and **c** impairs or improves efficiency in resource use. Empirical evidence reveals no consensus as to whether advertising is an anti- or procompetitive force.

7   In practice the monopolistic competitor seeks that specific combination of price, product, and promotion which will maximize its profits.

TERMS AND CONCEPTS

monopolistic competition
product differentiation

nonprice competition
excess capacity

traditional and new perspective views of advertising

QUESTIONS AND STUDY SUGGESTIONS

1   How does monopolistic competition differ from pure competition? From pure monopoly? Explain fully what product differentiation entails.

2   *Key Question   Compare the elasticity of the monopolistically competitive producer's demand curve with that of* **a** *a pure competitor, and* **b** *a pure monopolist. Assuming identical long-run costs, compare graphically the prices and outputs which would result under pure competition and monopolistic competition. Contrast the two market structures in terms of allocative and productive efficiency. Explain: "Monopolistically competitive industries are characterized by too many firms, each of which produces too little."*

3   "Monopolistic competition is monopoly up to the point at which consumers become willing to buy close-substitute products and competitive beyond that point." Explain.

4   "Competition in quality and in service may be quite as effective in giving the buyer more for her money as is price competition." Do you agree? Explain why monopolistically competitive firms frequently prefer nonprice to price competition.

5   Critically evaluate and explain:
    a "In monopolistically competitive industries economic profits are competed away in the long run;

hence, there is no valid reason to criticize the performance and efficiency of such industries."

    b "In the long run monopolistic competition leads to a monopolistic price but not to monopolistic profits."

6   *Key Question   Compare the traditional and new perspective view of advertising. Which do you feel is more accurate?*

7   Do you agree with the following statements?
    a "The amount of advertising which a firm does is likely to vary inversely with the real differences in its product."

    b "If each firm's advertising expenditures merely tend to cancel the effects of its rivals' advertising, it is clearly irrational for these firms to maintain large advertising budgets."

8   Carefully evaluate the two views expressed in the following statements:
    a "It happens every day. Advertising builds mass demand. Production goes up—costs comes down. More people can buy—more jobs are created. Each stimulates the next in a cycle of productivity and plenty, which constantly creates a better life for you."

b "Advertising constitutes 'inverted education'—a costly effort to induce people to buy without sufficient thought and deliberation and therefore to buy things they don't need. Furthermore, advertising outlays vary directly with the level of consumer spending." Which view do you feel is the more accurate? Justify your position.

9 *Key Question* *Advertising can have two effects: It increases a firm's output and it increases unit costs. Explain how the relative size of these two effects may impact consumers.*

10 (Last Word) Describe the price and nonprice competition which is present in the market for economics textbooks. What is the effect of the used-book market?

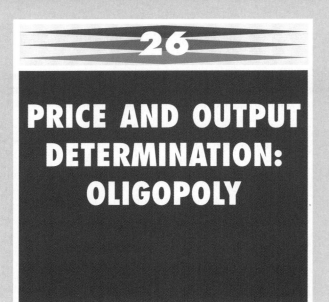

26

PRICE AND OUTPUT DETERMINATION: OLIGOPOLY

In many of our manufacturing, mining, and wholesaling industries, a few firms are dominant. Such industries are called oligopolies, the subject of this chapter. We have five objectives. (1) We first define oligopoly, assess its occurrence, and note the reasons for its existence. (2) Our major goal is to survey the possible courses of price-output behavior which oligopolistic industries might follow. (3) The role of nonprice competition, that is, competition based on product development and advertising, in oligopolistic industries is briefly discussed. (4) Next, we comment on the economic efficiency and social desirability of oligopoly. (5) Finally, many of the salient aspects of oligopoly are underscored in a brief case study of the automobile industry.

OLIGOPOLY: CONCEPT AND OCCURRENCE

What are the characteristics of oligopoly? How frequently is it encountered in our economy? Why has this industry structure developed?

Oligopoly Defined

Oligopoly exists when a few large firms, producing a homogeneous or differentiated product, dominate a market. "Fewness" means that the firms are mutually interdependent in that each must consider the possible reactions of its rivals to its price, advertising, and product development decisions.

But what is meant by "a few" firms? This is necessarily vague, because the market model of oligopoly covers much ground, ranging between pure monopoly, on the one hand, and monopolistic competition,

on the other. Thus oligopoly encompasses the aluminum industry, in which three firms dominate an entire national market, and the situation in which ten or fifteen gasoline stations may enjoy roughly equal shares of the petroleum products market in a medium-sized town. Generally, when we hear of the "Big Three," "Big Four" or "Big Six," we can be sure they refer to an oligopolistic industry.

Homogeneous or Differentiated Products Oligopolies may be **homogeneous** or **differentiated;** that is, the firms in an oligopolistic industry may produce standardized or differentiated products. Many industrial products—steel, zinc, copper, aluminum, lead, cement, industrial alcohol—are virtually standardized products in the physical sense and are produced under oligopolistic conditions. On the other hand, many consumer goods industries—automobiles, tires, detergents, greeting cards, breakfast ce-

TABLE 26-1   Concentration ratios and Herfindahl indices in selected high-concentration manufacturing industries

(1) Industry	(2) Percentage of industry output* produced by four largest firms	(3) Herfindahl index	(1) Industry	(2) Percentage of industry output* produced by four largest firms	(3) Herfindahl index
Chewing gum	96	ND	Flat glass	82	1968
Household laundry equipment	93	2855	Turbines and generators	80	2162
Cigarettes	92	ND	Gypsum products	75	1887
Electric lamps (bulbs)	91	ND	Primary aluminum	74	1934
Motor vehicles	90	ND	Aircraft	72	1686
Small arms ammunition	88	ND	Tires and innertubes	69	1897
Primary copper	87	ND	Household vacuum cleaners	69	1508
Breakfast cereals	87	2207	Motorcycles and bicycles	66	1453
Beer and malt beverages	87	ND	Soap and detergents	65	1698
Household refrigerators and freezers	85	2256	Prerecorded records and tapes	63	1505
Greeting card publishing	85	2830	Telephones	63	1933

*As measured by value of shipments. Data are for 1987, except primary copper which is for 1977.
ND means not disclosed.
Source: Bureau of the Census, 1987; Census of Manufacturers (1992).

reals, cigarettes, and many household appliances—are differentiated oligopolies.

Concentration Ratios   Economists use **concentration ratios** as an approximate measure of the structure of an industry. The data in column 2 of Table 26-1 show the four-firm concentration ratios—the percentage of total industry sales accounted for by the four largest firms—for a number of oligopolistic industries. For example, 92 percent of the cigarettes and 87 percent of all breakfast cereals produced in the United States are manufactured by the four largest firms in each industry.

When the largest four firms control 40 percent or more of the total market, that industry is considered oligopolistic. Using this benchmark, roughly one-half of all United States manufacturing industries are oligopolies.

While concentration ratios provide useful insights on the competitiveness or monopolization of various industries, they are subject to several shortcomings.

1   Localized Markets   Concentration ratios pertain to the nation as a whole, while relevant markets for some products are actually highly localized because

of high transportation costs. For example, the four-firm concentration ratio for ready-mix concrete is only 8 percent, suggesting a highly competitive industry. But the sheer bulk of this product limits the relevant market to a given town or metropolitan area and in such localized markets we typically find oligopolistic suppliers. At the local level, some aspects of the retail trade—particularly in small- and medium-sized towns—are characterized by oligopoly.

2   Interindustry Competition   Definitions of industries are somewhat arbitrary and we must be aware of **interindustry competition,** that is, competition between two products associated with different industries. Table 26-1's high concentration ratios for the aluminum and copper industries understate the degree of competition because aluminum and copper compete in many applications—for example, in the market for electrical transmission lines.

3   World Trade   The data are for American products and therefore often overstate monopoly power because they do not take into account the **import competition** of foreign suppliers. The automobile industry is a highly relevant illustration. While Table

26-1 tells us that four American firms account for 90 percent of the domestic production of motor vehicles, it ignores the fact that about one-third of the automobiles purchased in the United States are imports.

4   Herfindahl Index   Another problem with concentration ratios is that they fail to measure accurately the distribution of market power among the several dominant firms. Suppose in the long-distance telephone industry one firm controlled all service. In a second industry—say, the automobile industry—assume four firms exist and each has 25 percent of the market. For both industries the four-firm concentration ratio would be 100 percent. But the telecommunications industry would be a pure monopoly, while the auto industry would be an oligopoly characterized perhaps by significant economic rivalry. Most economists would agree that market power would be substantially greater in the telecommunications than in the auto industry, a fact not reflected in the identical 100 percent concentration ratios.

The **Herfindahl index** deals with this problem. This index is *the sum of the squared market shares of all firms in the industry.* By squaring the market shares, much greater weight is given to larger firms than smaller ones. In the hypothetical case of the single-firm telecommunications industry, the index would be 100^2 or 10,000. For the supposed four-firm auto industry the index would be $25^2 + 25^2 + 25^2 + 25^2$ or 2500. To generalize, the larger the Herfindahl index, the greater the degree of market power within an industry. Note in Table 26-1 that the four-firm concentration ratios for the prerecorded records and tapes industry and the telephone manufacturing industry are the same at 63 percent. But the telephone makers' Herfindahl index of 1933 suggests greater market power than the recording industry's 1505 index. *(Key Questions 3 and 4)*

As we will find in Chapter 32, antitrust officials sometimes use the Herfindahl index in deciding whether to approve or reject proposed corporate mergers.

5   Performance   Concentration ratios tell us little about the actual market performance of various industries. Industries X and Y may have identical four-firm concentration ratios of 85 percent. Industry X may be characterized by vigorous price competition and technological progress, evidenced by improved product and production techniques. In contrast, firms of industry Y may price their products collusively and be technologically stagnant. From society's viewpoint the "competitive" performance of industry X is clearly superior to the "monopolistic" performance of Y, a fact concealed by the identical concentration ratios.

Causes: Entry Barriers

The same barriers to entry which give rise to pure monopoly are relevant in explaining the existence of oligopoly. Historically, in many industries technological progress has made more and more economies of scale attainable over time. Many industries started out with a primitive technology, few economies of scale, and many competitors. But as technology improved and economies of scale became increasingly pronounced, the less alert or less aggressive firms fell by the wayside and a few producers emerged. Economies of scale are important in a number of industries such as the aircraft, rubber, and cement industries. While three or four firms can achieve minimum efficient scale (MES), new firms would have such a small market share as to not realize MES. Therefore, they could not survive as high-cost producers.

A closely related barrier is that the capital investment required to enter certain industries—the cost of obtaining necessary plant and equipment—is so great as to discourage entry. The cigarette, automobile, steel, and petroleum-refining industries, for example, are all characterized by very high capital requirements. Prodigious advertising outlays may provide a financial barrier to entry, as some economists have argued is the case in the cigarette industry.

The ownership or control of basic raw materials explains the historical dominance of the Aluminum Company of America in the production of aluminum ingots. In the electronics, chemicals, photographic equipment, office machine, and pharmaceutical industries patents have served as entry barriers.

Firm mergers may also give rise to oligopoly. Combining two or more formerly competing firms by merger may increase their market share substantially, enabling the new and larger production unit to achieve greater economies of scale.

Another motive underlying the "urge to merge" is market power. A firm that is larger both absolutely and relative to the market may have greater ability to control the market for, and the price of, its product than does a smaller, more competitive producer. Also, the large size which merger entails may give the firm the advantage of being a "big buyer" and permit it to demand and obtain lower prices (costs) from input suppliers.

OLIGOPOLY BEHAVIOR: A GAME THEORY OVERVIEW

Oligopoly pricing behavior has the characteristics of a game of strategy such as poker, chess, or bridge. The best way to play your hand in a poker game depends on the way rivals play theirs. Players must pattern their actions according to the actions and expected reactions of rivals. Let's use a simple **game theory model** to grasp the basics of oligopolistic pricing behavior. Specifically, let's assume a **duopoly**—a two-firm oligopoly—exists.

Consider Figure 26-1 which shows the price-profit or profit-payoffs matrix for two firms producing athletic shoes. Pricing policies or strategies for the firms—say, Leapers and Jumpers—are shown along the top and left margins, respectively. Entries in the matrix show the profit payoffs to the two firms associated with any given combination of pricing strategies. Leapers' profit (in millions) is shown in the northeast gold portion of each cell and Jumpers' profit is in the southwest green portion. For example, if both firms adopt a high-price strategy (cell A), each will realize a $12 million profit. Alternatively, if Jumpers follows a high-price policy and Leapers a low-price policy (cell B), Jumpers profit will be only $6 million and Leapers' will be $15 million.

Although the data of Figure 26-1 are hypothetical, the profit figures are not arbitrarily chosen. In reality, if Jumpers committed itself to a high price and did not vary from it, Leapers could increase its profits by choosing a low price and gaining market share at Jumpers' expense. The same rationale applies if Leapers commits to a high price and Jumpers opts for a low price.

Mutual Interdependence

The most evident point demonstrated by Figure 26-1 is the **mutual interdependence** of oligopolists. Each firm's profits will depend not only on its own pricing strategy, but also on that of its rivals. As we have just observed, if Jumpers adopts a high-price policy, its profit will be $12 million *provided* Leapers also employs a high-price strategy (cell A). But if Leapers uses a low-price strategy against Jumpers' high-price strategy (cell B), Leapers will increase its market share and thereby its profits from $12 to $15 million. Leapers' higher profits come at the expense of Jumpers, whose profits fall from $12 to $6 million. Jumpers' high-price strategy is only a "good" strategy *if* Leapers employs the same strategy. Indeed, a good, workable definition of oligopoly is that *oligopoly exists when the number of firms in an industry is so small that each must consider the reactions of rivals in formulating its price policy.*

Collusive Tendencies

A second point is that oligopoly often leads to **collusion,** meaning some sort of formal or informal arrangement to coordinate pricing strategies or fix prices. To illustrate in terms of Figure 26-1, suppose that initially both firms are *independently* following high-price strategies. Each realizes a $12 million profit (cell A).

FIGURE 26-1   Profit payoffs for a two-firm oligopoly
Both firms would realize the largest profit of $12 million if each adhered to a high-price policy (cell A). But if they are acting independently or competitively, either might achieve a higher profit of $15 million by adopting a low-price policy against its rival's high-price policy (cells B and C). Such independent pricing causes the outcome to gravitate to cell D, where profits are only $8 million. Collusion can be used to establish mutual high prices and increase each firm's profits from $8 million (cell D) to $12 million (cell A). But cells B and C remind us of the temptation to cheat on a collusive agreement.

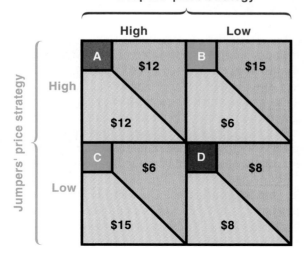

Leapers' price strategy

	High	Low
High	A $12 / $12	B $15 / $6
Low	C $6 / $15	D $8 / $8

Jumpers' price strategy

Observe that *either* Leapers or Jumpers could increase its profits by switching to a low-price strategy (cell B or C). If Leapers uses a low-price strategy against Jumpers' high-price strategy, its profits will increase to $15 million and Jumpers' will fall to $6 million. But by comparing cells B and D, we note that when Leapers shifts to a low-price policy, Jumpers would be better off if it also adopted a low-price policy. By doing so its profit would increase from $6 million (cell B) to $8 million (cell D).

Similarly, starting again at cell A, if Jumpers switched to a low-price policy against Leapers' high-price strategy, Jumpers' profit would increase to $15 million and Leapers' would fall to $6 million (cell C). And, again, Leapers could increase its profit from $6 (cell C) to $8 million (cell D) by also switching to a low-price policy.

What we find is that independent action by oligopolists will likely lead to mutual "competitive" low-price strategies. Independent oligopolists compete with respect to price and this leads to lower prices and lower profits. This is clearly beneficial to consumers, but not to the oligopolists who experience lower profits than if both had used high-price strategies (cell A).

How can oligopolists avoid the low-profit outcome of cell D? The answer is *not* to establish prices competitively or independently, but rather to collude. Specifically, the two firms must agree to establish and maintain a high-price policy. Each firm thus will increase its profits from $8 million (cell D) to $12 million (cell A). We will discuss a variety of specific collusive practices later in this chapter.

Incentive to Cheat

The payoff matrix also explains why an oligopolist might be strongly tempted to cheat on a collusive agreement. Suppose as a result of collusion Jumpers and Leapers both agree to high-price policies with each earning $12 million in profits (cell A). The temptation to cheat on this pricing agreement arises because either firm can increase its profits to $15 million by lowering its price (cell B or C). If Jumpers agrees to a high-price policy but secretly "cheats" on that agreement by actually charging low prices, the outcome moves from cell A to cell C. Result? Jumpers' profit rises to $15 million and Leapers' falls to $6 million. The same reasoning applies to Leapers, which could move the outcome from cell A to cell B by cheating. *(Key Question 5)*

QUICK REVIEW 26-1

■ Oligopolistic industries comprise a "few" firms producing either homogeneous or differentiated products.

■ The four-firm concentration ratio shows the percentage of an industry's sales accounted for by the four largest firms; the Herfindahl index measures the degree of market power in an industry by summing the squares of the market shares held by each firm.

■ Oligopolies result from scale economies, control of patents or strategic resources, or mergers.

■ Game theory reveals that *a* oligopolies are mutually interdependent in their pricing policies; *b* collusion will enhance oligopoly profits; and *c* there is a temptation for oligopolists to cheat on a collusive agreement.

FOUR OLIGOPOLY MODELS

To gain further insights on oligopolistic price-output behavior, we will examine four distinct models: (1) the kinked demand curve, (2) collusive pricing, (3) price leadership, and (4) cost-plus pricing.

Why not a single model as in our discussions of the other market structures? There is no standard portrait of oligopoly for two reasons.

1 Diversity Oligopoly encompasses a greater range and diversity of market situations than other market structures. It includes "tight oligopoly" in which two or three firms dominate an entire market, as well as the "loose oligopoly" in which six or seven firms share, say, 70 or 80 percent of a market while a "competitive fringe" of firms share the remainder. It includes both product differentiation and standardization. It includes cases where firms act in collusion and those where they act independently. It embodies situations in which barriers to entry are very strong and those in which they are not quite so strong. In short, the diversity of oligopoly precludes development of a simple market model which provides a general explanation of oligopolistic behavior.

2 Interdependence The fact of mutual interdependence is a significant complication. The inability of a firm to predict with certainty the reactions of its rivals makes it virtually impossible to estimate the demand and marginal-revenue data faced by an oligopolist. Without such data, firms cannot determine their profit-maximizing price and output even in theory, as we will presently see.

Despite these analytical difficulties, two interrelated characteristics of oligopolistic pricing have been observed. First, if the macroeconomy is generally stable, oligopolistic prices are typically inflexible or "sticky." Prices change less frequently in oligopoly than under pure competition, monopolistic competition, and in some instances, pure monopoly. Second, when oligopolistic prices do change, firms are likely to change their prices together; oligopolistic price behavior suggests there are incentives to act in concert or collusively in setting and changing prices.

Kinked Demand: Noncollusive Oligopoly

Imagine an oligopolistic industry comprising just three firms, A, B, and C, each having about one-third of the total market for a differentiated product. Assume the firms are "independent," meaning they do not engage in collusive practices in setting prices. Suppose, too, that the going price for firm A's product is PQ and its current sales are Q, as shown in Figure 26-2a.

Now the question is, "What does the firm's demand, or sales, curve look like?" Mutual interdependence, and the uncertainty of rivals' reactions which interdependence entails, make this question difficult to answer. The location and shape of an oligopolist's demand curve depend on how the firm's rivals will react to a price change introduced by A. There are two plausible assumptions about the reactions of A's rivals.

Match Price Changes One possibility is that firms B and C will exactly match any price change initiated by A. In this case, A's demand and marginal-revenue curves will look like D_1D_1 and MR_1MR_1 in Figure 26-2a. If A cuts price, its sales will increase very modestly, because its two rivals will do likewise to prevent A from gaining any price advantage over them. The small increase in sales which A (and its two rivals) will realize is at the expense of other industries; A will gain no sales from B and C. If A raises the going price, its sales will fall only modestly, because B and C match

FIGURE 26-2 The kinked demand curve
The nature of a noncollusive oligopolist's demand and marginal-revenue curves as shown in (a) will depend on whether its rivals will match (D_1D_1 and MR_1MR_1) or ignore (D_2D_2 and MR_2MR_2) any price changes which it may initiate from the current price PQ. In all likelihood an oligopolist's rivals will ignore a price increase but follow a price cut. This causes the oligopolist's demand curve to be kinked (D_2PD_1) and the marginal-revenue curve to have a vertical break, or gap (fg) as shown in (b). Furthermore, because any shift in marginal costs between MC_1 and MC_2 will cut the vertical (dashed) segment of the marginal-revenue curve, no change in either price PQ or output Q will occur.

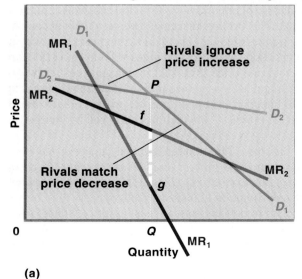

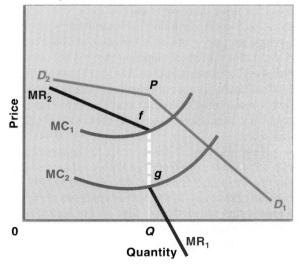

(a)   (b)

its price increase, so A does not price itself out of the market. The industry loses some sales to other industries, but A loses no customers to B and C.

Ignore Price Changes The other possibility is that firms B and C will ignore any price change by A. In this case, the demand and marginal-revenue curves faced by A will resemble D_2D_2 and MR_2MR_2 in Figure 26-2a. The demand curve in this case is considerably more elastic than under the assumption that B and C will match A's price changes. The reasons are clear. If A lowers its price and its rivals do not, A will gain sales significantly at the expense of its two rivals because it will be underselling them. Conversely, if A raises its price and its rivals do not, A will lose many customers to B and C, which will be underselling it. Because of product differentiation, however, A's sales do not fall to zero when it raises its price; some of A's customers will pay the higher price because they have strong preferences for A's product.

A Mixed Strategy Now, which is the most logical assumption for A to make on how its rivals will react to any price change it might initiate? The answer is "some of each"! Common sense and observation of oligopolistic industries suggest that price declines will be matched as a firm's competitors act to prevent the price cutter from taking their customers. But price increases will be ignored, because rivals of the price-increasing firm stand to gain the business lost by the price booster. In other words, the dark blue D_2P segment of the "rivals ignore" demand curve seems relevant for price increases, and the dark blue PD_1 segment of the "rivals follow" demand curve is more realistic for price cuts. It is logical, or at least a good guess, that a noncollusive oligopolist faces a **"kinked" demand curve** like D_2PD_1 as shown in Figure 26-2b. (Ignore the MC_1 and MC_2 curves for now.) The curve is highly elastic above the going price, but much less elastic or even inelastic below that price.

Note also that if it is correct to suppose that rivals will follow a price cut but ignore an increase, the marginal-revenue curve of the oligopolist will also have an odd shape. It, too, will be made up of two segments—the brown MR_2f part of the marginal-revenue curve appropriate to D_2D_2 and the brown gMR_1 chunk of the marginal-revenue curve appropriate to D_1D_1 in Figure 26-2a. Because of the sharp differences in elasticity of demand above and below the going price, there is a gap, or what we can treat as a ver-

tical segment, in the marginal-revenue curve. In Figure 26-2b the marginal-revenue curve is shown by the two brown lines connected by the dashed vertical segment, or gap.

Price Inflexibility This analysis goes far to explain why price changes may be infrequent in noncollusive oligopolistic industries.

1 The kinked-demand schedule gives each oligopolist reason to believe that any change in price will be for the worse. Many of a firm's customers will desert it if it raises its price. If it lowers its price, its sales at best will increase very modestly. Even if a price cut increases its total revenue somewhat, the oligopolist's costs may well increase by a more-than-offsetting amount. If the blue PD_1 segment of its sales schedule is *inelastic* in that E_d is less than 1, the firm's profits will surely fall. A price decrease will lower the firm's total revenue, and the production of a somewhat larger output will increase total costs.

Worse yet, a price cut by A may be *more* than met by B and C; A's initial price cut may start a **price war;** so A's sales may actually decline as its rivals charge still lower prices. These are all good reasons on the demand side of the picture why noncollusive oligopolies might follow live-and-let-live or don't-upset-the-applecart price policies. If the resulting profits are satisfactory to the several firms at the existing price, it may seem prudent to them not to alter that price.

2 The other reason for price inflexibility under noncollusive oligopoly works from the cost side of the picture. The broken marginal-revenue curve accompanying the kinked demand curve suggests that, within limits, substantial cost changes will have no effect on output and price. Any shift in marginal cost between MC_1 and MC_2 as shown in Figure 26-2b will result in no change in price or output; MR will continue to equal MC at output Q at which price PQ will be charged.

Criticisms The kinked-demand analysis has two shortcomings. First, *it does not explain how the going price gets to be at PQ (Figure 26-2) in the first place.* It only helps to explain why oligopolists may be reluctant to deviate from an existing price which yields them a "satisfactory" or "reasonable" profit. The kinked demand curve explains price inflexibility but not price itself.

Second, when the macro environment is unstable, oligopoly prices are not as rigid—particularly in an upward direction—as the kinked-demand theory implies. During inflationary periods such as the 1970s and the early 1980s, oligopolistic producers raised their prices frequently and substantially. Such price increases might be better explained in terms of collusive oligopoly. *(Key Question 6)*

Collusion and Cartels

Our game theory model suggests that oligopoly is conducive to collusion. *Collusion* occurs when firms in an industry reach an overt ("open" or "observable") or covert ("secret" or "concealed") agreement to fix prices, divide or share the market, or otherwise restrict competition among themselves. The disadvantages and uncertainties of the noncollusive, kinked-demand model to producers are obvious. There is always the danger of a price war breaking out. In particular, in a general business recession each firm will find itself with excess capacity, and can reduce per unit costs by increasing its market share. Then, too, a new firm may surmount entry barriers and initiate aggressive price cutting to gain a foothold in the market. In addition, the kinked demand curve's tendency toward rigid prices may adversely affect profits if general inflationary pressures increase costs. Stated differently, collusive control over price may permit oligopolists to reduce uncertainty, increase profits, and perhaps even prohibit entry of new rivals.

Price and Output   Where will price and output be established under **collusive oligopoly?** Assume once again there are three firms—A, B, and C—producing in this instance homogeneous products. Each firm has identical cost curves. Each firm's demand curve is indeterminate unless we know how its rivals will react to any price change. Therefore, suppose each firm assumes its two rivals will match either a price cut or a price increase. In other words, each firm's demand curve is of the D_1D_1 type in Figure 26-2a. Assume further that the demand curve for each firm is identical. Given identical cost and identical demand and marginal revenue data, we can say that Figure 26-3 represents the position of each of our three oligopolistic firms.

What price and output combination should each firm choose? If firm A were a pure monopolist, the answer would be clear: Establish output at Q, where marginal revenue equals marginal cost, charge the corresponding price PQ, and enjoy the maximum profit attainable. However, firm A *does* have two rivals sell-

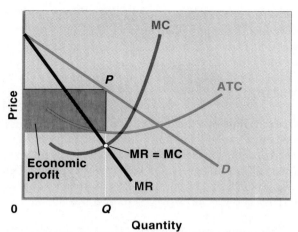

FIGURE 26-3   Collusion and the tendency toward joint-profit maximization
If oligopolistic firms face identical or highly similar demand and cost conditions, they may choose to behave collusively and maximize joint profits. The price and output results are essentially the same as those of pure (unregulated) monopoly; each oligopolist charges price *PQ* and produces output *Q*.

ing identical products, and if A's assumption that its rivals will match its price proves to be incorrect, the consequences could be disastrous for A. Specifically, if B and C actually charge prices below PQ, then firm A's demand curve will shift sharply to the left as its potential customers turn to its rivals, which are now selling the same product at a lower price. Of course, A can retaliate by cutting its price too; but this will move all three firms down their demand curves, lowering their profits, and perhaps even driving them to some point where average total cost exceeds price and losses are incurred.

So the question becomes, "Will B and C want to charge a price below PQ?" Under our assumptions, and recognizing that A will have little choice except to match any price they may set below PQ, the answer is "No." Faced with the same demand and cost circumstances, B and C will find it in their interest to produce Q and charge PQ. This is a curious situation; each firm finds it most profitable to charge the same price PQ, but only if its rivals will actually do so! How can the three firms realize the PQ-price and Q-quantity solution in which each is keenly interested? How can this be made a reality so that all three can avoid the less profitable outcomes associated with either higher or lower prices?

The answer is evident: The firms will all be motivated to collude—to "get together and talk it over"

—and agree to charge the same price *PQ*. In addition to reducing the possibility of price warring, each firm will obtain the maximum profit. And for society, the result is the same as if the industry were a pure monopoly composed of three identical plants (see Chapter 24).

Overt Collusion: the OPEC Cartel

Collusion may assume a variety of forms. The most comprehensive form of collusion is the cartel which typically involves a formal written agreement with respect to both price and production. Output must be controlled—that is, the market must be shared—to maintain the agreed-upon price.

The most spectacularly successful international cartel of recent decades has been OPEC (the Organization of Petroleum Exporting Countries). Comprising thirteen nations, OPEC was extremely effective in the 1970s in restricting oil supply and raising prices. The cartel was able to raise world oil prices from $2.50 to $11.00 per barrel within a six-month period in 1973–1974. By early 1980 price hikes had brought the per barrel price into the $32 to $34 range. The result was enormous profits for cartel members, a substantial stimulus to worldwide inflation, and serious international trade deficits for oil importers.

OPEC was highly effective in the 1970s for several reasons. First, it dominated the world market for oil. If a nation imported oil, it was almost obligated to do business with OPEC. Second, world demand for oil was strong and expanding in the 1970s. Finally, the "short-run" demand for oil was highly inelastic because the economies of oil-importing nations such as the United States were locked into gas-guzzling automobiles and energy-intensive housing and capital equipment. This inelasticity meant that a small restriction of output by OPEC would result in a relatively large price increase. As shown in Figure 26-4, in 1973–1974 and again in 1979–1980 OPEC was able to achieve enormous increases in oil prices and only incur a very modest decline in sales. With this inelastic demand, higher prices meant greatly increased total revenues to OPEC members. The accompanying smaller output meant lower total costs. The combination of more total revenue and lower total costs resulted in greatly expanded profits. (We discuss the serious weakening of the OPEC cartel later in this chapter.)

Covert Collusion: The Electrical Equipment Conspiracy

Cartels are illegal in the United States and hence collusion has been covert or secret. In 1960 an extensive price-fixing and market-sharing scheme involving heavy electrical equipment such as transformers, turbines, circuit breakers, and switchgear was uncovered. Elaborate covert schemes were developed by such participants as General Electric, Westinghouse, and Allis-Chalmers to rig prices and divide the market. Consider switch gear equipment:

> At . . . periodic meetings, a scheme or formula for quoting nearly identical prices to electric utility companies, private industrial corporations and contractors was used by defendant corporations, designated by their representatives as a "phase of the moon" or "light of the moon" formula. Through cyclic rotating positioning inherent in the formula one defendant corporation would quote the low price, others would quote intermediate prices and another would quote the high price; these positions would be periodically rotated among the defendant corporations. . . . This formula was designed to permit each defendant corporation to know the exact price it and every other defendant corporation would quote on each prospective sale.
>
> At these periodic meetings, a cumulative list of sealed bid business secured by all of the defendant corporations was also circulated and the representatives present would compare the relative standing of

FIGURE 26-4   The OPEC cartel and the world oil market

Because of the inelasticity of the demand for oil, in 1973–1974 and again in 1979–1980 the OPEC cartel was able to obtain a dramatic increase in the price of oil (P_1 to P_2) accompanied by only a very modest decline in production and sales (Q_1 to Q_2). Total revenue thus rose.

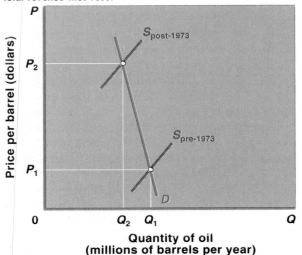

Quantity of oil
(millions of barrels per year)

each corporation according to its agreed upon percentage of the total sales pursuant to sealed bids. The representatives present would then discuss particular future bid invitations and designate which defendant corporation should submit the lowest bid therefore, the amount of such bid, and the amount of the bid to be submitted by others.[1]

Twenty-nine manufacturers and forty-six company officials were indicted in this "great electrical conspiracy" which violated our antitrust laws. Substantial fines, jail penalties, and lawsuits by victimized buyers were the final outcome.

In innumerable other instances collusion is even more subtle. **Gentlemen's agreements** frequently are struck at cocktail parties, on the golf course, by phone calls, or at trade association meetings where competing firms reach a verbal agreement on product price, leaving market shares to the ingenuity of each seller as reflected in nonprice competition. Although they too collide with the antitrust laws, the elusive character of gentlemen's agreements makes them more difficult to detect and prosecute successfully.

Other Examples Additional illustrations of covert collusion are not difficult to find. In 1993 Borden, Pet, and Dean food companies, among others, either pleaded guilty or were convicted of rigging bids on the prices of milk products sold to schools and military bases. By phone or at luncheons, company executives agreed in advance who would submit the low bid for each school district or military base. In 1992 the government accused eight major airlines of fixing fares during the 1988–1992 period. Agreements to increase fares or eliminate discounts were accomplished by communicating fare proposals through their computerized ticket information system. The makers of SOS and Brillo steel wool scouring pads were recently indicted for coordinating by telephone their price increases and discounts.

Obstacles to Collusion In practice cartels and similar collusive arrangements are difficult to establish and maintain. Let's briefly consider several important barriers to collusion.

---

[1]Jules Backman, *The Economics of the Electrical Machinery Industry* (New York: New York University Press, 1962), pp. 135–138, abridged. Reprinted by permission.

1 Demand and Cost Differences When oligopolists' costs and product demands differ, it is more difficult to agree on price. Where products are differentiated and changing frequently over time, this would be the case. Indeed, even with highly standardized products, we would expect that firms might have somewhat different market shares and would operate with differing degrees of productive efficiency. Thus it is likely that even homogeneous oligopolists would have different demand and cost curves.

In either event, unlike the cartel of Figure 26-3, differences in costs and demand will mean that the profit-maximizing price for each firm will differ; there will be no single price readily acceptable to all. Price collusion therefore depends on compromises and concessions—to arrive at a degree of "understanding" which in practice is often difficult to attain.

For example, the MR = MC positions of firms A, B, and C may call for them to charge $12, $11, and $10 respectively, but this price cluster or range may be unsatisfactory to one or more of the firms. Firm A may feel that differences in product quality justify only a $1.50, rather than a $2, price differential between its product and that of firm C. In short, cost and demand differences make it difficult for oligopolists to agree on a single price or a "proper" cluster of prices; these differentials are therefore an obstacle to collusion.

2 Number of Firms Other things equal, the larger the number of firms, the more difficult it is to achieve a cartel or other form of price collusion. Agreement on price by three or four producers that control an entire market is much more readily accomplished than it is when ten firms each have roughly 10 percent of the market, or where the Big Three have, say, 70 percent of the market, while a "competitive fringe" of eight or ten smaller firms battles for the remainder.

3 Cheating As our game theory model made clear, there is a temptation for collusive oligopolists to engage in clandestine price cutting, that is, to make secret price concessions to get additional business.

The difficulty with cheating is that buyers paying a high price may become aware of the lower-priced sales and demand similar treatment. Or buyers receiving price concessions from one oligopolist may use this concession as a wedge to get even larger price concessions from the firm's rivals. The attempt of buyers to play sellers against one another may precipitate price warring among the firms. Although it is potentially profitable, secret price concessions threaten the maintenance of collusive oligopoly over time. Collusion is more likely to persist when cheating is deterred because it is easy to detect and punish.

4 Recession Recession is usually an enemy of collusion because slumping markets increase average costs. In technical terms, as the oligopolists' demand and marginal-revenue curves shift to the left (Figure 26-3), each firm moves back to a higher point on its average-total-cost curve. Firms find they have substantial excess productive capacity, sales are down, unit costs are up, and profits are being squeezed. Under these conditions, businesses may feel they can better avoid serious profit reductions by price cutting in the hope of gaining sales at the expense of rivals.

5 Potential Entry The enhanced prices and profits which result from collusion may attract new entrants, including foreign firms. Such entry would increase market supply and reduce prices and profits. Therefore, successful collusion requires that colluding oligopolists can block entry of new producers.

6 Legal Obstacles: Antitrust Our antitrust laws (Chapter 32) prohibit cartels and the kind of price-fixing collusion we have been discussing. Therefore, less obvious means of price rigging—such as price leadership—have evolved in the United States.

OPEC in Disarray The highly successful OPEC oil cartel of the 1970s fell into disarray in the 1980s. The reasons for OPEC's decline relate closely to the obstacles to collusion we have just explained.

1 New Suppliers The dramatic runup of oil prices in the 1970s stimulated the search for new oil reserves, and soon non-OPEC nations, which OPEC could not block from entering world markets, became part of the world oil industry. Great Britain, Norway, Mexico, and the former Soviet Union have all become major world oil suppliers. As a result, OPEC's share of world oil production fell sharply.

2 Conservation On the demand side, oil conservation, worldwide recession in the early 1980s, and expanded use of alternative energy sources (such as coal, natural gas, and nuclear power) all reduced the demand for oil. The combination of greater production by non-OPEC nations and a decline in world demand generated an "oil glut" and seriously impaired OPEC's ability to control world oil prices.

3 Cheating OPEC has had a serious cheating problem stemming from the relatively large number of members (thirteen) and the diversity of their economic circumstances. Saudi Arabia is the dominant cartel member; it has the largest oil reserves and is probably the lowest-cost producer. Saudi Arabia has favored a "moderate" pricing policy because it has feared that very high oil prices would hasten development of alternative energy sources (such as solar power and synthetic fuels) and increase the attractiveness of existing substitutes such as coal and natural gas. These developments would greatly reduce the value of its vast oil reserves. Saudi Arabia also has a small population and a very high per capita domestic output. But other members—for example, Nigeria and Venezuela—are very poor, have large populations, and are burdened with large external debts. Still others—Iran, Iraq, and Libya—have had large military commitments. All of these members have had immediate needs for cash. Thus, there has been substantial cheating whereby some members have exceeded assigned production quotas and have sold oil at prices below those agreed to by the cartel. Thus, although OPEC's official oil price reached $34 per barrel in 1979, it is currently about $17 per barrel.

Price Leadership

Price Leadership is a type of gentlemen's agreement by which oligopolists can coordinate their price behavior without engaging in outright collusion. Formal agreements and clandestine meetings are *not* involved. Rather, a practice evolves whereby the "dominant" firm—usually the largest or the most efficient in the industry—initiates price changes, and all other firms more-or-less automatically follow that price change. Such industries as farm machinery, anthracite coal, cement, copper, gasoline, newsprint, tin cans, lead, sulfur, rayon, fertilizer, glass containers, steel, automobiles, and nonferrous metals are practicing, or have in the recent past practiced, price leadership.

Cigarette Pricing The cigarette industry is a classic example of tight price leadership. The Big Three, producing from 68 to 90 percent of total output, evolved a highly profitable practice of price leadership which resulted in virtually identical prices over the entire 1923 to 1941 period.

Between 1923 and 1941, virtual price identity prevailed continuously among the Big Three's standard brands, although certain other cigarettes of similar size and quality sold in smaller quantities at premium prices, and premium-priced Philip Morris grew through heavy advertising to a 6 percent market share. During this period there were eight standard brand list price changes. Reynolds led six of them, five upward and one downward, and was followed each time, in most cases within twenty-four hours of its announcement. The other two changes were downward revisions during 1933 led by American and followed by the other standard brand vendors. . . . Throughout this period, the return on invested capital realized by Reynolds, American, and Ligget & Myers averaged 18 percent after taxes— roughly double the rate earned by American manufacturing industry as a whole.[2]

Since the mid-1940s cigarette pricing has been less rigid. In early 1993 Philip Morris, faced with strong price competition from discount brands and a declining market share, cut the price of its Marlboro brand. Reynolds responded by cutting prices on its Winston and Camel brands. Then Philip Morris lowered the price of its Merit, Virginia Slims, and others of its brands. Price rigidity, punctuated by periods of price warring, is characteristic of oligopoly.

Leadership Tactics   The examination of price leadership in a variety of industries suggests that the price leader is likely to observe the following tactics.

1   Infrequent Changes   Because price changes always carry some risk that rivals will not follow, price adjustments will be made infrequently. The price leader will *not* respond pricewise to minuscule day-to-day changes in cost and demand conditions. Price will be changed only when cost and demand conditions have been altered significantly and on an industry-wide basis by, for example, industrywide wage increases, an increase in taxes, or an increase in the price of some basic input such as energy. In the automobile industry price adjustments traditionally have been made when new models are introduced each fall.

2   Communication   Impending price adjustments are often communicated by the price leader to the industry through speeches by major executives, trade publication interviews, and so forth. By publicizing

"the need to raise prices" the price leader can elicit a consensus among its competitors for the actual increase.

3   Limit Pricing   The price leader does not necessarily choose the price which maximizes short-run profits for the industry. The reason for this is that the industry may want to discourage new firms from entering. If barriers to entry are based on cost advantages (economies of scale) of existing firms, these cost barriers may be surmounted by new entrants *if* product price is set high enough. New firms which are relatively inefficient because of their small size may survive and grow if the industry's price is very high. To discourage new competitors and maintain the current oligopolistic structure of the industry, price may be established below the short-run profit-maximizing level. This strategy of establishing a price which prevents the entry of new firms is called *limit pricing*.

Cost-Plus Pricing

A fourth view of oligopolistic price behavior centers on what is variously known as *markup, rule-of-thumb,* or **cost-plus pricing.** In this case the oligopolist uses a formula to estimate cost per unit of output and a markup is applied to cost to determine price. Unit costs, however, vary with output and therefore the firm must assume some typical or target level of output. For example, the firm's average-cost figure may be that which is realized when the firm is operating at, say, 75 or 80 percent of capacity. A markup, usually in the form of a percentage, is applied to average total cost in determining price. An appliance manufacturer may estimate unit costs of dishwashers to be $250, to which a 50 percent markup is applied. This yields a $375 price to retailers.

The markup is 50 percent rather than 25 or 100 percent because the firm is seeking some target profit or rate of return on its investment. Consider the pricing technique used by General Motors for over four decades prior to the advent of aggressive foreign competition in the mid-1970s.

> GM started with the goal of earning, on the average over the years, a return of approximately 15 percent after taxes on total invested capital. Not knowing how many autos would be sold and hence unit costs (including prorated fixed costs), it calculated costs on the assumption of operation at 80 percent of conservatively rated capacity. A standard price was calculated by adding to unit cost a sufficient profit margin to

[2]F. M. Scherer and David Ross, *Industrial Market Structure and Economic Performance,* 3d ed. (Boston: Houghton Mifflin Company, 1990), p. 250.

yield the desired 15 percent after-tax return. The rule would be adjusted across the product line to take account of actual and potential competition, business conditions, long-run strategic goals and other factors. Actual profit then depended on the number of vehicles sold. Between 1960 and 1979, GM's actual return on stockholders' equity fell below 15 percent in only four years, all marked by recession and/or OPEC-induced gasoline price shocks. The average return was 17.6 percent. After 1979, however, recession and intensifying import competition caused GM frequently to fall short of its target.[3]

Two final points. First, this cost-plus method of pricing is consistent with collusion or price leadership. If producers in an industry have roughly similar costs, adherence to a common pricing formula will result in highly similar prices and price changes. As we will find in the case study which concludes this chapter, General Motors used cost-plus pricing *and* was until recently the price leader in the automobile industry.

Second, cost-plus pricing has special advantages for multiproduct firms which would otherwise be faced with the difficult and costly process of estimating demand and cost conditions for perhaps hundreds of different products. In practice, it is virtually impossible to allocate correctly certain common overhead costs such as power, lighting, insurance, and taxes to specific products.

NONPRICE COMPETITION

We have explained why oligopolists are averse to price competition. This aversion may lead to informal collusion on price. In the United States, however, price collusion is usually accompanied by nonprice competition. It is typically through nonprice competition that each firm's share of the total market is determined. This emphasis on nonprice competition has its roots in two facts.

1 Less Easily Duplicated Price cuts can be quickly and easily met by a firm's rivals. Because of this the possibility of a firm significantly increasing its share of the market through price competition is small; rivals will promptly cancel any potential gain in sales by matching price cuts. And, of course, the risk is always present that price competition will precipitate disastrous price warring. Nonprice competition is

less likely to get out of hand. Oligopolists seem to feel that more permanent advantages can be gained over rivals through nonprice competition because product variations, improvements in productive techniques, and successful advertising gimmicks cannot be duplicated so quickly and completely as price reductions.

2 Greater Financial Resources There is a more evident reason for the tremendous emphasis which oligopolists put on nonprice competition: Manufacturing oligopolists are typically blessed with substantial financial resources with which to support advertising and product development. Although nonprice competition is a basic characteristic of both monopolistically competitive and oligopolistic industries, oligopolists are typically in a financial position to indulge in nonprice competition more fully.

OLIGOPOLY AND ECONOMIC EFFICIENCY

Is oligopoly an "efficient" market structure from society's standpoint? How does the price-output behavior of the oligopolist compare with a purely competitive firm?

Allocative and Productive Efficiency

Many economists believe that the outcome of oligopolistic markets is approximately that shown in Figure 26-3. As compared to the benchmark of pure competition (Figure 23-12), the oligopolist's production occurs where price exceeds marginal cost and short of that output where average total cost is minimized. In the terminology of Chapters 23 and 24, neither allocative efficiency ($P = MC$) nor productive efficiency ($P = $ minimum ATC) is likely to occur under oligopoly.

One may even argue that oligopoly is actually less desirable than pure monopoly because pure monopoly in the United States is frequently subject to government regulation to mitigate abuses of market power. Informal collusion among oligopolists may yield price and output results similar to pure monopoly, yet at the same time maintain the outward appearance of several independent and "competing" firms.

Two qualifications are relevant. First, in recent years foreign competition has generated more rivalry in a number of oligopolistic markets—autos and steel,

---

[3]Ibid., p. 262.

for example—and has tended to undermine such cozy arrangements as price leadership and cost-plus pricing and stimulate more competitive pricing. Second, recall that oligopolistic firms may purposely keep prices below the short-run, profit-maximizing level to deter entry where entry barriers are less formidable.

Dynamic Efficiency

What about the "very long run" perspective where we allow for innovation in terms of improvements in product quality and more efficient production methods?

Competitive View   One view is that competition provides a compelling incentive to be technologically progressive. If a competitive firm does not seize the initiative, one or more rivals will introduce an improved product or a cost-reducing production technique which may drive it from the market. As a matter of short-term profits and long-term survival, competitive firms are under persistent pressure to improve products and lower costs through innovation.

Some adherents of this **competitive view** allege that oligopolists may have an incentive to impede innovation and restrain technological progress. The large corporation wants to maximize profits by exploiting fully all its capital assets. Why rush to develop and introduce a new product (for example, fluorescent lights) when that product's success will render obsolete all equipment designed to produce an existing product (incandescent bulbs)? It is not difficult to cite oligopolistic industries in which interest in research and development has been modest at best. Examples: the steel, cigarette, and aluminum industries.

Schumpeter-Galbraith View   In contrast, the **Schumpeter-Galbraith view** holds that technological advance is a competitive force (see Chapter 23's Last Word) and large oligopolistic firms with market power are necessary for rapid technological progress. Many such firms are located in the United States and Japan. (Global Perspective 26–1)

High R&D Costs   It is argued, first, that modern research to develop new products and new productive techniques is incredibly expensive. Therefore, only large oligopolistic firms can finance extensive research and development (R&D) activities.

Barriers and Profits   Second, the existence of barriers to entry gives the oligopolist some assurance that

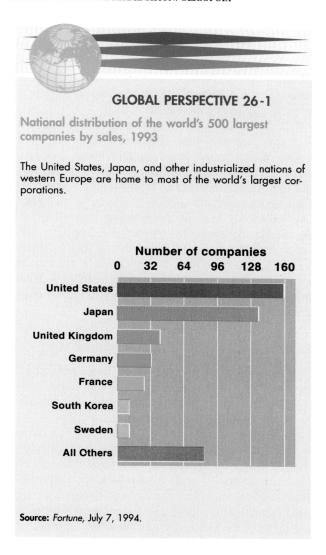

GLOBAL PERSPECTIVE 26-1

National distribution of the world's 500 largest companies by sales, 1993

The United States, Japan, and other industrialized nations of western Europe are home to most of the world's largest corporations.

Source: *Fortune*, July 7, 1994.

it will realize any profit rewards from successful R&D endeavors. In Galbraith's words:

> The modern industry of a few large firms [is] an excellent instrument for inducing technical change. It is admirably equipped for financing technical development. Its organization provides strong incentives for undertaking development and for putting it into use. . . . In the modern industry shared by a few large firms, size and the rewards accruing to market power combine to insure that resources for research and technical development will be available. The power that enables the firm to have some influence on prices insures that the resulting gains will not be passed on to the public by imitators (who have stood none of the costs of development) before the outlay for development can be recouped. In this way market

power protects the incentive to technical development.[4]

Bluntly put, small competitive firms have neither the *means* nor the *incentives* to be technologically progressive; large oligopolists do.

If the Schumpeter-Galbraith view is correct, it suggests that over time oligopolistic industries will foster rapid product improvement, lower unit production costs, lower prices, and perhaps a greater output and more employment than would the same industry organized competitively. There is anecdotal and case-study evidence suggesting that many oligopolistic manufacturing industries—television and other electronics products, home appliances, automobile tires—have been characterized by substantial improvements in product quality, falling relative prices, and expanding levels of output and employment.

Technological Progress: The Evidence

Which view is more nearly correct? Empirical studies have yielded ambiguous results. The consensus, however, seems to be that giant oligopolies are probably *not* a fountainhead of technological progress. A pioneering study[5] of sixty-one important inventions made from 1880 to 1965 indicates that over half were the work of independent inventors disassociated from corporate industrial research laboratories. Such substantial advances as air conditioning, power steering, the ballpoint pen, cellophane, the jet engine, insulin, xerography, the helicopter, and the catalytic cracking of petroleum have this individualistic heritage. Other equally important advances have come from small- and medium-sized firms.

According to this study, about two-thirds—forty out of sixty-one—of the basic inventions of this century have been initiated by independent inventors or the research activities of relatively small firms. This is not to deny that in a number of oligopolistic industries—for example, the aircraft, chemical, petroleum, and electronics industries—research activity has been pursued vigorously and fruitfully. But even here the picture is clouded by the fact that a very substantial portion of the research carried on in the aircraft-missile, electronics, and communications industries is heavily subsidized with public funds.

Some leading researchers in this field have tentatively concluded that technological progress in an industry may be determined more by the industry's scientific character and "technological opportunities" than by its market structure. There may simply be more ways to progress in the electronics and computer industries than in the brickmaking and cigarette industries, whether they are organized competitively or oligopolistically.

QUICK REVIEW 26-2

■ The kinked demand curve model is based on the assumption that an oligopolist's rivals will match a price cut but ignore a price increase. This model is consistent with observed price rigidity found in some oligopolistic industries.

■ A cartel is a collusive association of firms which establishes a formal agreement to determine price and to divide the market among participants.

■ Price leadership occurs when one firm—usually the largest or most efficient—determines price, and rival firms establish identical or similar prices.

■ Cost-plus pricing means that a firm establishes price by adding a percentage markup to the average total cost of its product.

■ Oligopoly is conducive to neither allocative nor productive efficiency. There is disagreement as to whether oligopoly fosters technological progress.

AUTOMOBILES: A CASE STUDY[6]

The automobile industry provides an informative case study of oligopoly, illustrating many of the points made in this chapter. It also indicates that market structure is not permanent and, in particular, that foreign competition can upset the oligopolists' "quiet life."

Market Structure Although there were over eighty auto manufacturers in the early 1920s, several mergers (most notably the combining of Chevrolet, Pon-

---

[4]John Kenneth Galbraith, *American Capitalism,* rev. ed. (Boston: Houghton Mifflin Company, 1956), pp. 86–88. Also see Joseph Schumpeter, *Capitalism, Socialism, and Democracy* (New York: Harper & Row Publishers, Inc., 1942).

[5]John Jewkes, David Sawers, and Richard Stillerman, *The Sources of Invention,* rev. ed. (New York: St. Martin's Press, Inc., 1968).

[6]This section draws heavily on Walter Adams and James W. Brock, "Automobiles," in Walter Adams and James Brock (eds.), *The Structure of American Industry,* 9th ed. (Englewood Cliffs, N.J.: Prentice-Hall, Inc., 1995), pp. 65–92; and John E. Kwoka, Jr., "Automobiles: Overtaking an Oligopoly," in Larry Duetsch (ed.), *Industry Studies* (Englewood Cliffs, N.J.: Prentice-Hall, Inc., 1993).

tiac, Oldsmobile, Buick, and Cadillac into General Motors), many failures during the Great Depression of the 1930s, and the increasing role of entry barriers—all reduced numbers in the industry. Currently, three large firms—General Motors (GM), Ford, and Chrysler—dominate the market for domestically produced automobiles.

These firms are gigantic: According to *Fortune* magazine, GM, Ford, and Chrysler were the first, second, and eighth largest manufacturing companies in the United States in 1993 as measured by sales. All three are leading truck manufacturers, produce household appliances, are involved in defense contracting and finance and banking, and have extensive overseas interests. GM has a virtual monopoly in producing buses and diesel locomotives in the United States.

Entry Barriers   Entry barriers are substantial, as evidenced by the fact that it has been about six decades since an American firm successfully entered the automobile industry. The primary barrier is economies of scale. It is estimated that the minimum efficient scale for a producer is about 300,000 autos per year. However, given the uncertainties of consumer tastes, experts feel a truly viable firm must produce at least two different models. Hence, to have a reasonable prospect of success a new firm would have to produce about 600,000 autos per year.

The estimated cost of an integrated plant (involving the production of engines, transmissions, other components, and product assembly) might be as much as $1.2 to $1.4 billion. Other entry barriers include the need for extensive advertising and far-flung dealer networks (GM has over 15,500 dealers and Chrysler has 10,500) which provide spare parts and repair service. A newcomer also would face the expensive task of overcoming existing brand loyalties. Because the domestic automobile industry spent $2.9 billion on advertising in 1992, this is no small matter.

Price Leadership and Profits   The indicated industry structure—a few firms with high entry barriers—has been fertile ground for collusive or coordinated pricing. GM traditionally was the price leader. Each fall, with the introduction of new models, GM would establish prices for its basic models and Ford and Chrysler would set the prices of their comparable models accordingly. (Details of how GM established its prices were outlined in the earlier section on cost-plus pricing.)

In the past several decades automobile prices have moved up steadily and often at a rate in excess of the overall rate of inflation. And despite large periodic declines in demand and sales, automobile prices have displayed considerable downward rigidity, although import competition and recession have caused rebates and financing subsidies to become common in recent years.

Over the years price leadership has proved to be very profitable. In the 1947–1977 period the Big Three earned an average profit rate significantly greater than that of all United States manufacturing corporations taken as a whole.

Styling and Technology   In addition to advertising, nonprice competition has centered historically on styling changes and the introduction of new models. In practice styling changes have been stressed over technological advance. As early as the 1920s GM recognized that the replacement market was becoming increasingly important compared to the market for first-time purchasers. Therefore, its strategy—later adopted by other manufacturers—became one of annual styling changes accompanied by model proliferation. The purpose is to achieve higher sales and profits by encouraging consumers to replace their autos with greater frequency and to encourage buyers to shift their purchase from basic to "upscale" models.

But competition did *not* focus on product quality.

> Autos were being built in ways that had changed very little in decades. Each company had large and expensive engine, transmission, stamping, and other production plants located all around the country, each of which shipped components to assembly facilities. The latter still resembled Henry Ford's original assembly line, with paramount importance given to maintaining continuous operation of the line. To ensure that the line never stopped, large numbers of all necessary components were held in inventory, extra workers were available to replace those absent or on break at any time, and repair stations were located at the end of each line to fix defective vehicles that came off the line.
>
> This approach provided very little incentive for quality production, since ill-fitting parts could still be installed and poorly assembled vehicles would be attended to elsewhere. The results were both poor quality and high cost.[7]

---

[7]Kwoka, ibid., p. 68.

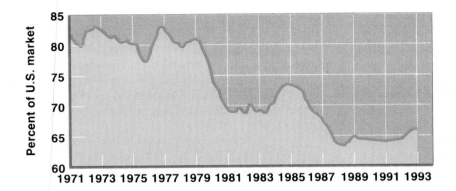

FIGURE 26-5 Big Three sales as a share of the United States automobile market.
Although GM, Ford, and Chrysler commanded about 80 percent of domestic car sales in the 1970s, that share fell sharply in the late 1970s and 1980s. There has been a modest resurgence of market share for the Big Three in the mid-1990s.

Wages and Work Rules High costs were also due to high wages and restrictive work rules. The high profits of the Big Three were shared with their union, the United Automobile Workers. Wage increases were persistently greater than productivity increases, so that labor costs per auto rose. By 1980 wages in the auto industry were 50 percent greater than wages for manufacturing as a whole. The companies also accepted union-imposed work rules which restricted management's flexibility in assigning tasks to workers. The effect of such rules was to diminish worker productivity.

To summarize: The post-World War II auto industry was a "complacent oligopoly," characterized by (1) no price competition; (2) substantial profits; (3) emphasis on styling changes, model proliferation, and advertising; (4) neglect of product quality; and (5) high labor costs.

Foreign Competition This state of affairs changed abruptly in the early 1970s with the advent of more vigorous competition by foreign—particularly Japanese—producers. As Figure 26-5 shows, the Big Three's share of the American market declined through most of the 1970s and 1980s.

There were several reasons for the growth of foreign competition. First, OPEC-inspired increases in gasoline prices in the early 1970s prompted a shift in American consumer demand toward smaller, fuel-efficient imports from Japan and Germany. Second, many consumers perceived the imports as having quality advantages. A 1990 consumer survey of auto quality found seven Japanese, two German, and only one American car ranked in the top ten. Third, lower overseas wages and higher labor productivity gave the

Japanese and South Koreans a substantial cost advantage in producing compact cars.

Responses American producers initially responded to this new competition in two ways. First, the industry—with the support of organized labor—successfully lobbied government for protection. The result, beginning in 1981, was "voluntary" import quotas on Japanese cars which effectively restrained competition. But, rather than take their advantage in the form of increased sales and market share, American producers boosted auto prices. One study suggests that the import quotas increased the profits of the Big Three by $2.8 billion in 1983 alone.

The second response of domestic producers was to co-opt and mitigate foreign competition by initiating an elaborate network of joint ownership arrangements and joint ventures with foreign producers. Chrysler owns about one-fourth of Mitsubishi and imports both compact cars and parts from the latter. Mitsubishi in turn is a part owner of Korea's Hyundai Motor Company. General Motors has a joint production arrangement with Toyota in California and has significant ownership shares in other lesser-known Japanese auto manufacturers. Ford owns about one-fourth of Mazda. These arrangements cast a cloud of doubt on the contention that foreign competition has had an important "disciplining" effect on American auto manufacturers. Indeed, this interlocking system of joint ventures may be establishing "the groundwork for cartelizing the world automobile industry."[8]

[8]Walter Adams and James W. Brock, "Joint Ventures, Antitrust, and Transnational Cartelization," *Northwestern Journal of International Law & Business,* Winter 1991, p. 465.

But the Japanese have responded to import quotas and the uncertainties inherent in the changing dollar-yen exchange rate by building automobile plants in the United States. These "transplants" produce about 10 percent of the cars sold in the United States. The success of Japanese production in America is reflected in the fact that they built eight new factories in the United States in the 1980s, precisely the number closed by the Big Three in the 1987–1989 period.

Restructuring and Resurgence? Despite record losses in the early 1990s, there are signs in the mid-1990s that the American Big Three have gone through a difficult period of restructuring and may be meeting the import challenge.

There are several reasons for this potential revival. First, American producers have upgraded product quality. While the perceived quality gap between Japanese and American cars remains, it has narrowed substantially. Second, the Big Three—especially Chrysler and Ford—have increased productivity and reduced costs by imitating Japanese "lean" production methods. These methods entail the use of fewer parts suppliers, carrying smaller inventories, a more flexible work force, and greater attention to quality. Third, the yen has appreciated substantially compared to the dollar, meaning each dollar spent on a Japanese car generates a smaller yen profit for Japanese producers. This has necessitated increases in the dollar prices of Japanese autos to preserve profitability. Thus Japanese cars may now cost $2000 to $3000 more than their American counterparts, shifting demand to the Big Three. Note in Figure 26-5 that the Big Three's share of the domestic market has stabilized in recent years.

While the future of the automobile industry is uncertain, it is clear that enhanced competition has greatly altered the Big Three's "complacent oligopoly" of the 1950s and 1960s. GM's price leadership is a thing of the past. Current pricing is more competitive with ten companies producing and about thirty selling in the United States market. And, as Global

GLOBAL PERSPECTIVE 26-2

American producers and the global auto market

Big Three automobile sales are heavily concentrated in the North American and western European markets, where currently some 63 percent of global vehicle sales occur. However, sales growth is accelerating in Asia, Latin America, and central and eastern Europe, where America's Big Three are generally much less active than European and Japanese producers. In comparison, sales growth is declining in North America and western Europe where the Big Three's presence is strongest. Will American firms again have to play "catch-up" with their global rivals?

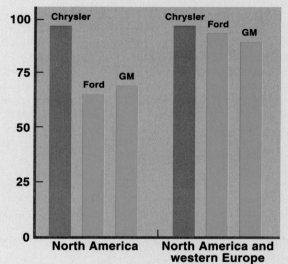

Source: U.S. Department of Commerce and Federal Reserve Bank of Chicago.

Perspective 26-2 suggests, rising incomes are expected to stimulate auto sales in many of the less developed areas of the world, presenting new competitive challenges.

CHAPTER SUMMARY

1 Oligopolistic industries are characterized by the presence of a few firms, each having a significant fraction of the market. Firms thus situated are mutually interdependent; the behavior of any one firm directly affects, and is affected by, the actions of rivals. Products may be virtually uniform or significantly differentiated. Various barriers to entry underlie and maintain oligopoly.

2 Concentration ratios can be used as a measure of oli-

LAST WORD

THE BEER INDUSTRY: OLIGOPOLY BREWING?

The beer industry was once populated by hundreds of firms and an even larger number of brands. But this industry has increasingly become concentrated and is now an oligopoly.

The brewing industry has undergone profound changes since World War II which have increased the degree of concentration in the industry. In 1947 slightly over 400 independent brewing companies existed in the United States. By 1967 there were 124 and by 1980 only 33 survived. While the five largest brewers sold only 19 percent of the nation's beer in 1947, the Big Five brewers currently sell 93 percent of the nation's domestically produced beer. The Big Two—Anheuser-Busch (at 45 percent) and Miller (at 23 percent)—produce 68 percent. Why the change?

Changes on the demand side of the market have contributed to the "shake-out" of small brewers from the industry. First, there is evidence that in the 1970s consumer tastes shifted from the stronger-flavored beers of the small brewers to the light, dry products of the larger brewers. Second, there has been a relative shift from the consumption of beer in taverns to consumption in the home. The significance of this change is that taverns were usually supplied with kegs from local brewers to avoid the relatively high cost of shipping kegs. But the acceptance of aluminum cans for home consumption made it possible for large, distant brewers to compete with the local brewers because the former could now ship their products by truck or rail without breakage.

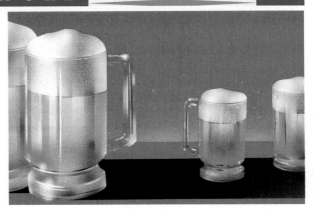

Developments on the supply side of the market have been even more profound. Technological advances have speeded up the bottling or closing lines so that, for example, the number of cans of beer which could be filled and closed per minute increased from 900 to 1500 between 1965 and the late 1970s. Currently the most modern canning lines can close 2000 cans per minute. Large plants are also able to reduce labor costs through the automating of brewing and warehousing. Furthermore, plant construction costs per barrel are about one-third less for a 4.5-million-barrel plant than for a 1.5-million-barrel plant. As a consequence of these and other economies, it is estimated that unit production costs decline sharply up to the point at which a plant produces 1.25 million

---

gopoly and market power. By giving more weight to larger firms, the Herfindahl index is designed to measure market dominance in an industry.

3 Game theory **a** shows the mutual interdependence of oligopolists' price policies; **b** reveals the tendency to act collusively; and **c** explains the temptation to cheat on collusive agreements.

4 Important models of oligopoly include: **a** the kinked-demand model, **b** collusive oligopoly, **c** price leadership, and **d** cost-plus pricing.

5 Noncollusive oligopolists may face a kinked demand curve. This curve and the accompanying marginal-revenue curve help explain the price rigidity which often characterizes such markets; they do not, however, explain the level of price.

6 The uncertainties inherent in noncollusive pricing promote collusion. Collusive oligopolists maximize joint profits—that is, behave like pure monopolists. Demand and cost differences, a "large" number of firms, "cheating" through secret price concessions, recessions, and the antitrust laws are all obstacles to collusive oligopoly.

7 Price leadership is an informal means of collusion where the largest or most efficient firm in the industry initiates price changes and the other firms follow.

8 With cost-plus or markup pricing, oligopolists estimate their unit costs at some target level of output and add a percentage "markup" to determine price.

9 Market shares in oligopolistic industries are usually determined on the basis of nonprice competition. Oligopolists emphasize nonprice competition because **a** advertising

barrels per year. Average costs continue to decline, but less significantly, up to the 4.5-million-barrel capacity at which all scale economies seem to be exhausted. Evidence of the importance of scale economies is reflected in statistics which show that over time there has been a steady decline in breweries producing less than 2 million barrels per year. Because the construction of a modern 4-million-barrel capacity brewery costs about $250 million, economies of scale may now constitute a significant barrier to entry.

"Blindfold" taste tests confirm that most mass-produced American beers taste alike. Thus great emphasis has been placed on advertising. And here the large firms which sell nationally (Anheuser-Busch, Miller) enjoy cost advantages over regional producers (Grain Belt, Pearl) because national television advertising is less costly per viewer than local spot TV advertising.

Although mergers have occurred, they have not been a fundamental cause of increased concentration in the brewing industry. Rather, mergers have been largely the result of failing small breweries selling out. Dominant firms have expanded by creating new brands—Lite, Keystone, Milwaukee's Best, and Genuine Draft, for example—rather than acquiring them. This has sustained product differentiation, despite the declining number of major brewers.

The ascendancy of the Miller Brewing Company from the seventh to the second largest producer in the 1970s was due in large measure to advertising and product differentiation. When Miller was acquired by the Philip Morris Company in 1970, the new management made two big changes. First, Miller High Life beer was "repositioned" into that segment of the market where potential sales were the greatest. Sold previously as the "champagne of beers," High Life had appealed heavily to upper-income consumers and women who only drank beer occasionally. Miller's new television ads featured young blue-collar workers who were inclined to be greater beer consumers. Second, Miller then developed its low-calorie Lite beer which was extensively promoted with the infusion of Philip Morris advertising dollars. Lite proved to be the most popular new product in the history of the beer industry and contributed significantly to Miller's dramatic rise in the industry.

Currently, the beer industry does not appear to have engaged in economically undesirable behavior. There has been no evidence of collusion and current excess productive capacity prompts the large brewers to compete for market shares. The fact that historically there has been considerable turnover in the ranking of the largest firms is further evidence of competition. Miller, ranked eighth in 1968, rose to number two in 1977 and has maintained that position. In comparison, Schlitz and Pabst were the second and third largest brewers in the mid-1970s, but now are only "also rans."

Source: Based on Kenneth G. Elzinga, "Beer," in Walter Adams and James Brock (eds.), *The Structure of American Industry,* 9th ed. (Englewood Cliffs, N.J.: Prentice-Hall, Inc., 1995), pp. 119–151; and Douglas F. Greer, "Beer: Causes of Structural Change," in Larry Duetsch (ed.), *Industry Studies* (Englewood Cliffs, N.J.: Prentice-Hall, Inc., 1993).

and product variations are less easy for rivals to match, and b oligopolists frequently have ample resources to finance nonprice competition.

10 Neither allocative nor productive efficiency is realized in oligopolistic markets. The competitive view envisions oligopoly as being inferior to more competitive market structures in promoting product improvement and cost-decreasing innovations. The Schumpeter-Galbraith view is that oligopolists have both the incentive and financial resources to be technologically progressive.

TERMS AND CONCEPTS

oligopoly	import competition	collusion	cartel
homogeneous and	Herfindahl index	kinked demand curve	price leadership
differentiated	game theory model	price war	cost-plus pricing
oligopoly	duopoly	collusive oligopoly	competitive and
concentration ratios	mutual	gentlemen's	Schumpeter-
interindustry competition	interdependence	agreements	Galbraith views

QUESTIONS AND STUDY SUGGESTIONS

1 Why do oligopolies exist? List five or six oligopolists whose products you own or regularly purchase. What distinguishes oligopoly from monopolistic competition?

2 "Fewness of rivals means mutual interdependence, and mutual interdependence means uncertainty as to how those few rivals will react to a price change by any one firm." Explain. Of what significance is this for determining demand and marginal revenue? Other things equal, would you expect mutual interdependence to vary directly or inversely with the degree of product differentiation? With the number of firms? Explain.

3 *Key Question* *What is the meaning of a four-firm concentration ratio of 60 percent? 90 percent? What are the shortcomings of concentration ratios as measures of market power?*

4 *Key Question* *Suppose that in industry A five firms have annual sales of 30, 30, 20, 10, and 10 percent of total industry sales. For the five firms in industry B the figures are 60, 25, 5, 5, and 5 percent. Calculate the Herfindahl index for each industry and compare their likely competitiveness.*

5 *Key Question* *Explain the general character of the data in the following profits-payoff matrix for oligopolists C and D. All profit figures are in thousands.*

	C's price →	
D's price ↓	$40	$35
$40	$57 / $60	$59 / $55
$35	$50 / $69	$55 / $58

a *Use the table to explain the mutual interdependence which characterizes oligopolistic industries.*

b *Assuming no collusion, what is the likely outcome?*

c *Given your answer to question **b**, explain why price collusion is mutually profitable. Why might there be a temptation to cheat on the collusive agreement?*

6 *Key Question* *What assumptions about a rival's responses to price changes underlie the kinked demand curve? Why is there a gap in the marginal-revenue curve? How does*
the kinked demand curve explain oligopolistic price rigidity? What are the shortcomings of the kinked-demand model?

7 Why might price collusion occur in oligopolistic industries? Assess the economic desirability of collusive pricing. Explain: "If each firm knows that the price of each of its few rivals depends on its own price, how can the prices be determined?" What are the main obstacles to collusion? Apply these obstacles to the weakening of OPEC in the 1980s.

8 Assume the demand curve shown in question 4 in Chapter 24 applies to a pure monopolist which has a constant marginal cost of $4. What price and output will be most profitable for the monopolist? Now assume the demand curve applies to a two-firm industry (a "duopoly") and that each firm has a constant marginal cost of $4. If the firms collude, what price and quantity will maximize their joint profits? Demonstrate why it might be profitable for one of the firms to cheat. If the other firm becomes aware of this cheating, what will happen?

9 Explain how price leadership might evolve and function in an oligopolistic industry. Is cost-plus pricing compatible with collusion?

10 "Oligopolistic industries have both the means and the inclination for technological progress." Do you agree? Explain.

11 "If oligopolists really want to compete, they should do so by cutting their prices rather than by squandering millions of dollars on advertising and other forms of sales promotion." Do you agree? Why don't oligopolists usually compete by cutting prices?

12 Using Figure 26-3, explain how a collusive oligopolist might increase its profits by offering secret price concessions to buyers. On the diagram, indicate the amount of additional profits which the firm may realize. What are the risks involved in such a policy?

13 Identify aspects of the structure and behavior of the automobile industry which are oligopolistic. Why did the Big Three lose domestic market share to foreign producers in the 1970s and 1980s? What have been the responses of domestic producers to increased foreign competition?

14 (Last Word) What demand and supply factors have altered the beer industry from monopolistic competition to oligopoly?

Micro-
economics
of Resource
Markets

PRODUCTION AND THE DEMAND FOR RESOURCES

We explored the pricing and output of goods and services under a variety of product market structures in the preceding four chapters. The purely competitive cucumber farmer considers the market price and decides how many acres to plant. The monopolistically competitive local restaurant decides on the best combination of price, quality, and advertising to maximize its profits. The automobile manufacturer pays close attention to the business strategies of rivals and sets its price and production plans accordingly. The local telephone monopoly files requests for rate increases before the state utility board, and then provides service to all customers.

Although firms and market structures differ greatly, firms in general have something in common. In producing their product—be it cucumbers, sandwiches, automobiles, or telephone service—they must hire productive resources. Among other resources, the cucumber farmer needs land, tractors, fertilizer, and pickers. The restaurant buys kitchen equipment and hires cooks and waiters. The auto manufacturer purchases production materials and hires executives, accountants, engineers, and assembly-line workers. The telephone company leases land, buys telephone poles and wires, and hires operators and billing clerks.

In this chapter we turn from the pricing and production of goods to the pricing and employment of resources needed in production. Land, labor, capital, and entrepreneurial resources directly or indirectly are owned and supplied by households. In terms of our circular flow model of the economy (Chapters 2, 5, and 6), we shift attention from the bottom loop of the diagram, where firms supply and households demand products, to the top loop, where households supply and businesses demand resources.

SIGNIFICANCE OF RESOURCE PRICING

There are several reasons to study resource pricing.

1 Money Incomes The most basic fact about resource prices is that they are a major determinant of

money or nominal incomes. The expenditures businesses make in acquiring economic resources flow as wage, rent, interest, and profit incomes to those households which supply the human and property resources at their disposal.

2 Resource Allocation Just as product prices ration finished goods and services to consumers, so resource prices allocate scarce resources among industries and firms. An understanding of how resource prices affect resource allocation is particularly significant since, in a dynamic economy, the efficient allocation of resources over time calls for continuing shifts in resources among alternative uses.

3 Cost Minimization To the firm, resource prices are costs, and to realize maximum profits a firm must produce the profit-maximizing output with the most efficient (least costly) combination of resources. Given technology, resource prices play the major role in determining the quantities of land, labor, capital, and entrepreneurial ability that will be combined in the productive process (Table 4-1).

4 Policy Issues Finally, there are a myriad of ethical questions and public policy issues surrounding the resource market. What degree of income inequality is acceptable? Should a special tax be levied on "excess" profits? Is it desirable for government to establish a wage floor in the form of a legal minimum wage? What about legal ceilings on interest rates? Are current government subsidies to farmers justifiable? Chapter 34 will explore the facts and ethics of income distribution.

COMPLEXITIES OF RESOURCE PRICING

Economists generally agree on the basic principles of resource pricing. Yet they disagree as to the variations in these principles which are made when they are applied to specific resources and particular markets. While economists agree that the pricing and employment of economic resources, or factors of production, are a supply and demand phenomenon, they also recognize that in particular markets resource supply and demand may assume unique and often complex dimensions. This is further complicated when supply and demand forces are altered or even supplanted by the policies and practices of government, business firms, or labor unions, among other institutional considerations.

Our objective in this chapter is to explain the factors underlying the demand for economic resources. We will couch our discussion in terms of labor, recognizing that the principles outlined also apply to land, capital, and entrepreneurial ability. In Chapter 28 our understanding of resource demand will be combined

with a discussion of labor supply in analyzing wage rates. Then in Chapter 29 the supply side of the markets for property resources will be incorporated to analyze the prices of, and returns to, land, capital, and entrepreneurial talent.

MARGINAL PRODUCTIVITY THEORY OF RESOURCE DEMAND

The least complicated approach to resource demand assumes a firm hires a specific resource in a competitive market and sells its product in a competitive market. The simplicity of this situation lies in the fact that under competition the firm as a "price taker" can dispose of as little or as much output as it chooses at the going market price. The firm is selling such a negligible fraction of total output that it exerts no influence whatsoever on product price. Similarly, in the resource market, competition means that the firm is hiring such a small fraction of the total supply of the resource that its price is unaffected by the quantity the firm purchases.

Resource Demand as a Derived Demand

The demand for resources is a **derived demand;** it is derived from the products or services which resources help produce. Resources usually do not directly satisfy consumer wants, but do so indirectly by producing goods and services. No one wants to consume an acre of land, a John Deere tractor, or the labor services of a farmer, but households do want to consume the food and fiber products these resources help produce. Similarly, the demand for automobiles generates a demand for automobile workers and the demands for such services as income tax preparation, haircuts, and child care create derived demands for accountants, barbers, and child-care workers.

Marginal Revenue Product (MRP)

The derived nature of resource demand implies that the strength of the demand for any resource will depend on (1) the productivity of the resource in helping to create a good, and (2) the market value or price of the good it is producing. A resource which is highly productive in turning out a commodity highly valued by society will be in great demand. On the other hand, demand will be very weak for a relatively unproductive resource which is only capable of producing some good not in great demand by households. There will be no demand for a resource which is phenomenally efficient in producing something no one wants to purchase!

Productivity   The roles of productivity and product price in determining resource demand can be clearly seen in Table 27-1. Here we assume a firm adds one variable resource—labor—to its fixed plant. Columns 1 through 3 remind us that the law of diminishing returns will apply here, causing the **marginal product** (MP) of labor to fall beyond some point. (It might be helpful to review the section, "Law of Diminishing Returns," in Chapter 22 at this point.) For simplicity, we assume diminishing marginal productivity sets in with the first worker hired.

Product Price   But the derived demand for a resource also depends on the price of the commodity it produces. Column 4 adds this price information. Product price is constant, in this case at $2, because we are supposing a competitive product market. The firm is a "price-taker" and can sell as few or as many units of output as it wants to at this price.

Multiplying column 2 by column 4, we get the total-revenue data of column 5. From these total-revenue data we can compute **marginal revenue product** (MRP)—*the increase in total revenue resulting from the use of each additional variable input (labor, in this case)*. MRP is indicated in column 6.

Rule for Employing Resources: MRP = MRC

The MRP schedule—columns 1 and 6—is the firm's demand schedule for labor. To explain why, we must first discuss the rule which guides a profit-seeking firm in hiring any resource. *To maximize profits, a firm should hire additional units of any given resource so long as each successive unit adds more to the firm's total revenue than it does to its total costs.*

Economists have special terms designating what each additional unit of labor or other variable resource adds to total cost and what it adds to total revenue. We already know MRP measures how much each successive worker adds to total revenue. The amount which each additional unit of a resource adds to the firm's total (resource) cost is called **marginal resource cost** (MRC). Thus we can restate our rule for hiring resources as follows: *It will be profitable for a firm to hire additional units of a resource up to the point at which that resource's MRP is equal to its MRC.* If

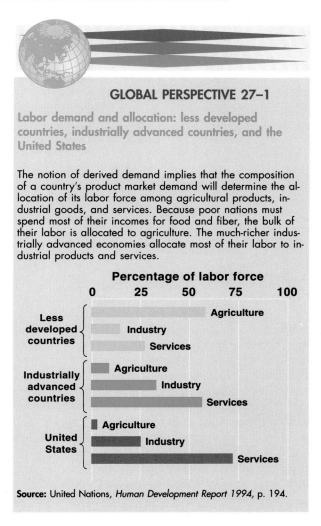

GLOBAL PERSPECTIVE 27–1

Labor demand and allocation: less developed countries, industrially advanced countries, and the United States

The notion of derived demand implies that the composition of a country's product market demand will determine the allocation of its labor force among agricultural products, industrial goods, and services. Because poor nations must spend most of their incomes for food and fiber, the bulk of their labor is allocated to agriculture. The much-richer industrially advanced economies allocate most of their labor to industrial products and services.

Source: United Nations, *Human Development Report 1994*, p. 194.

the number of workers a firm is currently hiring is such that the MRP of the last worker exceeds his or her MRC, the firm can clearly profit by hiring more workers. But if the number being hired is such that the MRC of the last worker exceeds the MRP, the firm is hiring workers who are not "paying their way," and it can thereby increase its profits by laying off some workers. You may have recognized that this **MRP = MRC rule** is very similar to the MR = MC profit-maximizing rule employed throughout our discussion of price and output determination. The rationale of the two rules is the same, but the point of reference is now *inputs* of resources, rather than *outputs* of product.

MRP Is a Demand Schedule

Just as product price and marginal revenue are equal in a purely competitive product market, so *resource*

TABLE 27-1 The demand for a resource: pure competition in the sale of the product

(1) Units of resource	(2) Total product	(3) Marginal product (MP), or Δ(2)*	(4) Product price	(5) Total revenue, or (2) × (4)	(6) Marginal revenue product (MRP), or Δ(5)*
0	0		$2	$ 0	
		7			$14
1	7		2	14	
		6			12
2	13		2	26	
		5			10
3	18		2	36	
		4			8
4	22		2	44	
		3			6
5	25		2	50	
		2			4
6	27		2	54	
		1			2
7	28		2	56	

*Δ indicates a "change in."

price and marginal resource cost are equal when a firm is hiring a resource competitively. In a purely competitive labor market the wage rate is set by the total, or market, supply of, and the market demand for, labor. Because it hires such a small fraction of the total supply of labor, a single firm cannot influence this wage rate. This means that total resource cost increases by exactly the amount of the going wage rate for each additional worker hired; the wage rate and MRC are equal. It follows that so long as it is hiring labor competitively, *the firm will hire workers to the point at which their wage rate (or MRC) is equal to their MRP.*[1]

In terms of the data in column 6 of Table 27-1, if the wage rate is $13.95, the firm will hire only one worker. This is so because the first worker adds $14 to total revenue and slightly less—$13.95—to total costs. In other words, MRP exceeds MRC for the first worker so it is profitable to hire that worker. For each successive worker, however, MRC exceeds MRP, indicating that it will not be profitable to hire any of those workers. If the wage rate is $11.95, by the same reasoning we discover that it will pay the firm to hire both the first and second workers. Similarly, if the wage rate is $9.95, three will be hired. If $7.95, four. If $5.95, then five. And so forth. It is evident that *the MRP schedule constitutes the firm's demand for labor, because each point on this schedule (curve) indicates the number of workers which the firm would hire at*

each possible wage rate which might exist. This is shown graphically in Figure 27-1.

The rationale employed here is familiar to us. Recall in Chapter 23 that we applied the price-equals-marginal-cost or *P* = MC rule for the profit-maximizing *output* to discover that the portion of the competitive firm's short-run marginal-cost curve lying about average variable cost is the short-run *product supply* curve (Figure 23-6). Presently we are applying the MRP = MRC rule for the profit-maximizing *input* to the firm's MRP curve and determining that this curve is the input or *resource demand* curve.

FIGURE 27-1 The purely competitive seller's demand for a resource
The MRP curve is the resource demand curve. The location of the curve depends on the marginal productivity of the resource and the price of the product. Under pure competition product price is constant; therefore, diminishing marginal productivity is the sole reason why the resource demand curve is downsloping.

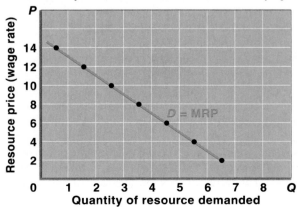

---

[1]The logic here is the same as that which allowed us to change the MR = MC profit-maximization rule to *P* = MC for the purely competitive seller of Chapter 23.

TABLE 27-2 The demand for a resource: imperfect competition in the sale of the product

(1) Units of resource	(2) Total product	(3) Marginal product (MP), or Δ(2)	(4) Product price	(5) Total revenue, or (2) × (4)	(6) Marginal revenue product (MRP), or Δ(5)
0	0		$2.80	$ 0	
		7			$18.20
1	7		2.60	18.20	
		6			13.00
2	13		2.40	31.20	
		5			8.40
3	18		2.20	39.60	
		4			4.40
4	22		2.00	44.00	
		3			2.25
5	25		1.85	46.25	
		2			1.00
6	27		1.75	47.25	
		1			−1.05
7	28		1.65	46.20	

Resource Demand under Imperfect Competition

Our analysis of labor demand becomes slightly more complex when we assume the firm is selling its product in an imperfectly competitive market. Pure monopoly, oligopoly, and monopolistic competition in the product market all mean that the firm's product demand curve is downsloping; the firm must accept a lower price to increase its sales.

The productivity data of Table 27-1 are retained in columns 1–3 of Table 27-2. But here we assume in column 4 that product price must be lowered to sell the marginal product of each successive worker. The MRP of the purely competitive seller of Table 27-1 falls for one reason: Marginal product diminishes. But the MRP of the imperfectly competitive seller falls for two reasons: Marginal product diminishes *and* product price falls as output increases.

It must be emphasized that the lower price accompanying every increase in output applies in each case not only to the marginal product of each successive worker but also to all prior units which otherwise could have sold at a higher price. To illustrate: The second worker's marginal product is 6 units. These 6 units can be sold for $2.40 each or, as a group, for $14.40. But this is *not* the MRP of the second worker. To sell these 6 units, the firm must take a 20-cent price cut on the 7 units produced by the first worker—units which could have been sold for $2.60 each. Thus, the MRP of the second worker is only $13.00 [= $14.40 − (7 × 20 cents)]. Similarly, the third worker's MRP is $8.40. Although the 5 units this

worker produces are worth $2.20 each in the market, the third worker does not add $11.00 to the firm's total revenue when account is taken of the 20-cent price cut which must be taken on the 13 units produced by the first two workers. In this case the third worker's MRP is only $8.40 [= $11.00 − (13 × 20 cents)]. The other figures in column 6 are similarly explained.

The result is that the MRP curve—the resource demand curve—of the imperfectly competitive producer is less elastic than that of a purely competitive producer. At a wage rate or MRC of $11.95, both the purely competitive and the imperfectly competitive seller will hire two workers. But at $9.95, the competitive firm will hire three and the imperfectly competitive firm only two. And at $7.95, the purely competitive firm will take on four employees and the imperfect competitor only three. This difference in elasticity can be seen by graphing the MRP data of Table 27-2 as in Figure 27-2 and comparing them with Figure 27-1.[2]

It is not surprising that the imperfectly competitive producer is less responsive to wage cuts in terms of workers employed than is the purely competitive producer. The imperfect competitor's relative reluctance to employ more resources and produce more output when resource prices fall is the resource mar-

---

[2]Note that the points in Figures 27-1 and 27-2 are plotted halfway between each number of workers because MRP is associated with the *addition* of one more worker. Thus, in Figure 27-2, for example, the MRP of the second worker ($13.00) is plotted not at 1 or 2, but rather at $1\frac{1}{2}$. This "smoothing" technique also allows us to present a continuously downsloping curve rather than one which moves downward in discrete steps as each worker is hired.

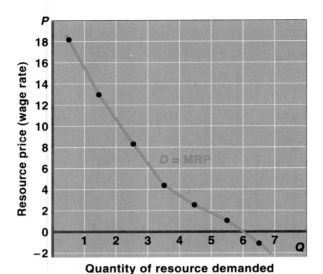

FIGURE 27-2 The imperfectly competitive seller's demand for a resource
An imperfectly competitive seller's resource demand curve slopes downward because marginal product diminishes and product price falls as output increases.

ket reflection of the imperfect competitor's tendency to restrict output in the product market. Other things equal, the imperfectly competitive seller will produce less of a product than would a purely competitive seller. In producing this smaller output, it will demand fewer resources.

But one important qualification exists. We noted in Chapters 24 and 26 that the market structures of pure monopoly and oligopoly *might* lead to technological progress and a higher level of production, more employment, and lower prices in the long run than would a purely competitive market. The resource demand curve in these cases would not be restricted. (*Key Question 2*)

Market Demand for a Resource

We can now derive the market demand curve for a resource. Recall that the total, or market, demand curve for a product is developed by summing horizontally the demand curves of all individual buyers in the market. Similarly, the market demand curve for a particular resource can be derived in essentially the same way—that is, by summing the individual demand or MRP curves for all firms hiring that resource.

DETERMINANTS OF RESOURCE DEMAND

What will alter the demand for a resource, that is, shift the demand curve? What are the determinants of labor demand? The derivation of resource demand suggests two related factors—the resource's productivity and the market price of the product it is producing. And our previous analysis of changes in product demand (Chapter 3) suggests another factor—changes in the prices of other resources.

Changes in Product Demand

Because resource demand is a derived demand, any change in the demand for the product will affect product price and therefore the MRP of the resource. Other things equal, *a change in the demand for the product that a particular type of labor is producing will shift labor demand in the same direction.*

In Table 27-1, assume an increase in product demand which boosts product price from $2 to $3. You should calculate the new labor demand curve and plot it in Figure 27-1 to verify that it lies to the right of the old curve. Similarly, a drop in product demand and price will shift the labor demand curve to the left.

Productivity Changes

Other things unchanged, *a change in the productivity of labor will shift the labor demand curve in the same direction.* If we were to double the MP data of column 3 in Table 27-1 we would find that the MRP data would also double, indicating an increase in labor demand.

The productivity of any resource can be altered in several ways.

1 Nonlabor Inputs The marginal productivity data for, say, labor will depend on the quantities of other resources with which it is combined. The greater the amount of capital and land resources with which labor is combined, the greater will be the marginal productivity and the demand for labor.

2 Technological Progress Technological improvements will have the same effect. The better the quality of the capital, the greater the productivity of labor. Steelworkers employed with a given amount of real capital in the form of modern oxygen furnaces are more productive than when employed with the same amount of real capital embodied in old open-hearth furnaces.

3 Labor Quality Improvements in the quality of the variable resource itself—labor—will increase marginal productivity and therefore the demand for labor. In effect, we have a new demand curve for a different, more skilled, kind of labor.

All these considerations help explain why the average level of (real) wages is higher in the United States than in many other nations. American workers are generally healthier and better trained than those of these other nations, and in most industries they work with a larger and more efficient stock of capital goods and more abundant natural resources. This spells a strong demand for labor. On the supply side of the market, labor is *relatively* scarce compared with some other nations. A strong demand and a relatively scarce supply result in high wage rates. This will be discussed further in Chapter 28.

Prices of Other Resources

Just as changes in the prices of other products will change the demand for a specific commodity, so changes in the prices of other resources can be expected to alter the demand for a particular resource. Just as the effect of a change in the price of product X on the demand for product Y depends on whether X and Y are substitute or complementary goods (Chapter 3), so the effect of a change in the price of resource A on the demand for resource B will depend on their substitutability or their degree of complementarity.

Substitute Resources Suppose in a certain production process that technology is such that labor and capital are substitutable for one another. A firm can produce some given output with a relatively small amount of labor and a relatively large amount of capital or vice versa. Now assume the price of machinery falls. The resulting impact on the demand for labor will be the net result of two opposed effects: the substitution effect and the output effect.

1 Substitution Effect The decline in the price of machinery will prompt the firm to substitute machinery for labor. This is the obvious adjustment to make if the firm seeks to produce any given output in the least costly fashion. At given wage rates, smaller quantities of labor will now be employed. This **substitution effect** will decrease the demand for labor.

2 Output Effect Because the price of machinery has fallen, the costs of producing various outputs will also have declined. With lower costs, the firm will find it profitable to produce and sell a larger output. This greater output will increase the demand for all resources, including labor. For a reduction in the price of machinery, this **output effect** will increase the demand for labor.

To repeat: The *substitution effect* indicates a firm will purchase more of an input whose relative price has fallen and, conversely, use less of an input whose relative price has risen. Thus a decline in the price of capital will increase the relative price of labor and therefore decrease the demand for labor. The *output effect* occurs because a change in an input price will alter production costs and therefore the profit-maximizing output in the same direction. A decrease in the price of capital will lower production costs, increase the profit-maximizing output, and therefore increase the demand for labor.

The substitution and output effects work in opposite directions. For a decline in the price of machinery, the substitution effect decreases and the output effect increases the demand for labor. The net impact on labor demand will depend on the relative sizes of the two opposed effects. If the substitution effect outweighs the output effect, the reduction in the price of capital reduces the demand for labor. If the reverse holds true, the demand for labor will increase. *If the substitution effect outweighs the output effect, a change in the price of a substitute resource will change the demand for labor in the same direction. If the out-*

put effect exceeds the substitution effect, a change in the price of a substitute resource will change the demand for labor in the opposite direction.

Complementary Resources   Recall from Chapter 3 that certain products, such as cameras and film or computers and software, are complementary goods in that they "go together" and are jointly demanded. Resources may also be complementary; an increase in the quantity of one of them used in the production process will require an increase in the amount used of the other as well, and vice versa. Suppose a small manufacturer of metal products uses punch presses as its basic piece of capital equipment. Each press is designed to be operated by one worker; the machine is not automated—it won't run itself—and a second worker would be wholly redundant.

Assume technological advance in the production of these presses substantially reduces their costs. Now there can be no negative substitution effect because labor and capital must be used in *fixed proportions,* one person for one machine. Capital cannot be substituted for labor. But there is a positive output effect for labor. Other things equal, the reduction in the price of capital goods means lower production costs. It will therefore be profitable to produce a larger output. In doing so the firm will use both more capital and more labor. When labor and capital are complementary, a decline in the price of machinery will increase the demand for labor through the output effect. Conversely, in the case of an increase in the price of capital, the output effect will reduce the demand for labor. *A change in the price of a complementary resource will cause the demand for labor to change in the opposite direction.*

Recap: The demand curve for labor will *increase* (shift rightward) when:
1   The demand for (and therefore the price of) the product produced by that labor increases
2   The productivity (MP) of labor increases
3   The price of a substitute input decreases, provided the output effect is greater than the substitution effect
4   The price of a substitute input increases, provided the substitution effect exceeds the output effect
5   The price of a complementary input decreases
Be sure that you can "reverse" these generalizations to explain a *decrease* in labor demand.

Real-World Applications

The determinants of labor demand have great practical significance, as seen in the following examples.

1   American Auto Workers   In 1995 there were 400,000 fewer workers in the American automobile industry than in 1979. Two factors help explain this dramatic decline in jobs. First, foreign competition, particularly from Japanese producers, has reduced the demand for American cars. The shares of the United States market accounted for by American firms has fallen from about 80 percent in 1979 to about 66 percent today. This decline in demand for American cars has sharply reduced the derived demand for American auto workers. A second factor has been the spread of robotic technology in auto manufacturing. Industrial robots have been substituted for assembly-line labor, further reducing the demand for auto workers.

2   Fast-Food Workers   In the past several years, McDonald's and other fast-food establishments have advertised to attract housewives and older people to work in their restaurants. A major reason for this is that more and more women are working outside the home, causing families to substitute restaurant meals for home-prepared meals. This increase in the demand for restaurant meals has increased the demand for fast-food workers. Because the labor supply of traditional fast-food workers—teenagers—has not kept pace, many restaurants are now recruiting housewives and retired workers.

3   Personal Computers   During the last decade there has been a remarkable drop in the average price of personal computers and an equally impressive rise in the computing power of the typical machine. The effects of these developments on labor demand have been both positive and negative. Between 1975 and 1990, employment in the computer services industry (programming and software) grew at an annual 12 percent rate. And in some offices, computers and labor (keyboard personnel) have been complementary inputs. Thus, the decline in computer prices has reduced production costs to the extent that product or service prices have dropped, sales have increased, and the derived demand for computer operators has increased. In contrast, in other offices computers have been substituted for labor, reducing the demand for labor and allowing these firms to use fewer workers to produce their goods and services. Example: In late 1993 the IRS announced that an upgrade of its computer system would reduce by one-third the number of people needed to process tax returns and do other manual chores.

4 Defense Cutbacks The end of the Cold War and the resulting reductions in American defense spending has slashed labor demand by the military. An estimated 800,000 to 1 million *military* jobs will be lost between 1993 and 1998. Also, the Federal spending cuts on defense will significantly reduce the demand for labor in industries producing aircraft, missiles, tanks, and other military hardware. Estimates suggest the loss of 1 million defense-related *civilian* jobs between 1993 and 1998.

5 Contingent Workers One of the biggest labor market changes of recent years has been that many employers have reduced the size of their full-time "core" work forces and simultaneously increased their use of contingent workers (part-time, temporary, and subcontracted). Why has the demand for contingent workers increased? First, increasingly expensive fringe benefits such as health insurance, pension plans, paid vacations, and sick leave are typically not

TABLE 27-3 Determinants of labor demand: factors that shift the labor demand curve

1 Changes in product demand Examples: Computer software increases in popularity, increasing the demand for workers at software firms; consumers increase their demand for leather coats, increasing the demand for tanners.

2 Productivity changes Examples: An increase in the skill levels of glass blowers increases the demand for their services; computer-assisted graphic design increases the productivity of, and demand for, graphic artists.

3 Changes in the prices of other resources Examples: An increase in the price of electricity increases the costs of producing aluminum and reduces the demand for aluminum workers; the price of security equipment used by businesses to protect against illegal entry falls, decreasing the demand for night guards; the price of telephone switching equipment decreases, greatly reducing the cost of telephone service, which in turn increases the demand for telemarketers.

provided for contingent workers, making their employment less costly. Second, contingent workers give firms more flexibility in responding to changing economic conditions. As product demand shifts, firms can readily increase or decrease the sizes of their work forces through altering their employment of contingent workers. This flexibility enhances the competitive positions of firms and often improves their ability to succeed in international markets.

Table 27-3 provides additional illustrations to reinforce your understanding of the determinants of labor demand.

ELASTICITY OF RESOURCE DEMAND

The factors just discussed are responsible for shifts in the location of resource demand curves. Such changes in demand must be distinguished from a change in the quantity of a resource demanded. The latter does not entail a shift in the resource demand curve. Rather it reflects a movement from one point to another on a stable resource demand curve, because of a change in the price of the specific resource under consideration. In Table 27-1 and Figure 27-1 we note that an increase in the wage rate from $5.95 to $7.95 will reduce the quantity of labor demanded from five to four workers.

What determines the sensitivity of producers to changes in resource prices? Or, more technically, what determines the elasticity of resource demand—the percentage change in the quantity demanded of a resource divided by the percentage change in its price? Several generalizations provide insights needed to answer this question.

1 Rate of MP Decline A purely technical consideration—the rate at which the marginal product of the variable resource declines—is crucial. *If the marginal product of labor declines slowly as it is added to a fixed amount of capital, the MRP, or demand curve for labor, will decline slowly and tend to be highly elastic.* A small decline in the price of such a resource will yield a relatively large increase in the amount demanded. Conversely, if the marginal productivity of labor declines sharply, the MRP, or labor demand curve, will decline rapidly. This means that a relatively large decline in the wage rate will be accompanied by a modest increase in the amount of labor hired; resource demand will be inelastic.

2 Ease of Resource Substitutability

The degree to which resources are substitutable is also a determinant of elasticity. *The larger the number of good substitute resources available, the greater will be the elasticity of demand for a particular resource.* If a furniture manufacturer finds that five or six different types of wood are equally satisfactory in making coffee tables, a rise in the price of any one type of wood may cause a sharp drop in the amount demanded as the producer substitutes other woods. At the other extreme, it may be impossible to substitute; bauxite is absolutely essential in the production of aluminum ingots. Thus, the demand for it by aluminum producers is inelastic.

Time can play a role in the input substitution process. For example, a firm's truck drivers may obtain a substantial wage increase with little or no immediate decline in employment. But over time, as the firm's trucks wear out and are replaced, the company may purchase larger trucks and thereby be able to deliver the same total output with fewer drivers. Alternatively, as the firm's trucks depreciate, it might turn to entirely different means of transportation. As a second example, recently developed commercial aircraft have been specifically designed to require only two pilots rather than the customary three.

3 Elasticity of Product Demand

The elasticity of demand for any resource will depend on the elasticity of demand for the product it helps produce. *The greater the elasticity of product demand, the greater the elasticity of resource demand.* The derived nature of resource demand would lead us to expect this relationship. A small rise in the price of a product with great elasticity of demand will sharply reduce output and therefore bring about a relatively large decline in the amounts of various resources demanded. This correctly implies that the demand for the resource is elastic.

Remember that the resource demand curve of Figure 27-1 is more elastic than the resource demand curve shown in Figure 27-2. The difference arises because in Figure 27-1 we assume a perfectly elastic product demand curve, while Figure 27-2 is based on a downsloping or less than perfectly elastic product demand curve.

4 Labor-Cost–Total-Cost Ratio

The larger the proportion of total production costs accounted for by a

resource, the greater will be the elasticity of demand for that resource. In the extreme, if labor costs were the only production cost, then a 20 percent increase in wage rates would shift the firm's cost curves upward by 20 percent. Given the elasticity of product demand, this substantial increase in costs would cause a relatively large decline in sales and a sharp decline in the amount of labor demanded. Labor demand would be elastic. But if labor costs were only 50 percent of production costs, then a 20 percent increase in wage rates would only increase costs by 10 percent. With the same elasticity of product demand, a relatively small decline in sales and therefore in the amount of labor demanded would result. The demand for labor would be inelastic. *(Key Question 4)*

QUICK REVIEW 27-2

■ A resource demand curve will shift because of changes in product demand, changes in the productivity of the resource, and changes in the prices of other inputs.

■ If resources A and B are substitutable, a decline in the price of A will decrease the demand for B provided the substitution effect exceeds the output effect. But if the output effect exceeds the substitution effect, the demand for B will increase.

■ If resources C and D are complements, a decline in the price of C will increase the demand for D.

■ The elasticity of demand for a resource will be less the more rapid the decline in marginal product; the smaller the number of substitutes; the smaller the elasticity of product demand; and the smaller the proportion of total cost accounted for by the resource.

OPTIMAL COMBINATION OF RESOURCES

So far we have considered one variable input, labor. But in the long run firms can vary the amounts of *all* the resources they use. That's why we need to consider what combination of resources a firm will choose when all are variable. While our analysis will be based on two resources, it can be extended to any number.

We will consider two interrelated questions:

1   What is the least-cost combination of resources to use in producing *any* particular level of output?
2   What combination of resources will maximize a firm's profits?

TABLE 27-4 The least-cost and profit-maximizing combination of labor and capital*

Labor (price = $8)					Capital (price = $12)				
(1) Quantity	(2) Total product	(3) Marginal product	(4) Total revenue	(5) Marginal revenue product	(1') Quantity	(2') Total product	(3') Marginal product	(4') Total revenue	(5') Marginal revenue product
0	0	0	$ 0	$ 0	0	0	0	$ 0	$ 0
1	12	12	24	24	1	13	13	26	26
2	22	10	44	20	2	22	9	44	18
3	28	6	56	12	3	28	6	56	12
4	33	5	66	10	4	32	4	64	8
5	37	4	74	8	5	35	3	70	6
6	40	3	80	6	6	37	2	74	4
7	42	2	84	4	7	38	1	76	2

*To simplify, it is assumed in this table that the productivity of each resource is independent of the quantity of the other. For example, the total and marginal product of labor is assumed not to vary with the quantity of capital employed.

Observe that there are other combinations of labor and capital which will yield 50 units of output. For example, 5 units of labor and 1 unit of capital will produce 50 (= 37 + 13) units, but we find that total cost is now higher at $52 [= (5 × $8) + (1 × $12)], meaning average unit cost has risen to $1.04 (= $52/50). By employing 5 units of labor and 1 of capital the least-cost rule would be violated in that $MP_L/P_L = 4/8$ is less than $MP_C/P_C = 13/12$, indicating more capital and less labor should be employed to produce this output.

Similarly, 50 units of output also could be produced with 2 units of labor and 3 of capital. The total cost of the 50 units of output would again be $52 [= (2 × $8) + (3 × $12)], or $1.04 per unit. Here equation (1) is not fulfilled in that $MP_L/P_L = 10/8$ which exceeds $MP_C/P_C = 6/12$. This inequality suggests that the firm should use more labor and less capital.

Recap: While there may be several combinations of labor and capital capable of producing a specific output—in this case 50 units—only that combination which fulfills equation (1) will minimize costs.

Maximizing Profits

Will 50 units of output maximize the firm's profits? No, because the profit-maximizing rule stated in equation (2) is *not* fulfilled when employing 3 units of labor and 2 of capital. We know that to maximize profits any given input should be employed until its price equals its marginal revenue product ($P_L = MRP_L$ and $P_C = MRP_C$). But for 3 units of labor we find in column 5 that labor's MRP is $12 while its price is only $8. This means it is prof-

itable to hire more labor. Similarly, for 2 units of capital we observe in column 5' that MRP is $18 and capital's price is only $12, indicating that more capital should also be employed. When hiring 3 units of labor and 2 of capital to produce 50 units of output, the firm is underemploying both inputs. Labor and capital are both being used in less than profit-maximizing amounts.

The marginal revenue products of labor and capital are equal to their prices and equation (2) is fulfilled when the firm is employing 5 units of labor and 3 units of capital. This is therefore the profit-maximizing combination of inputs.[5] The firm's total cost will be $76, which is made up of $40 (= 5 × $8) worth of labor and $36 (= 3 × $12) worth of capital. Total revenue of $130 is determined by multiplying total output of 65 (= 37 + 28) by the $2 product price or, alternatively, by simply summing the total revenue attributable to labor ($74) and to capital ($56). The difference between total revenue and total cost is, of course, the firm's economic profit which in this instance is $54 (= $130 − $76). Equation (2) is fulfilled when 5 units of labor and 3 of capital are employed: $MRP_L/P_L = 8/8 = MRP_C/P_C = 12/12 = 1$. You should experiment with other combinations of labor and capital to demonstrate that they will yield an economic profit less than $54.

[5]Because we are dealing with discrete (nonfractional) increases in the two outputs, you should also be aware that in fact the employment of 4 units of labor and 2 of capital is equally profitable. The fifth unit of labor's MRP and its price are equal (at $8), so that the fifth unit neither adds to, nor subtracts from, the firm's profits. The same reasoning applies to the third unit of capital.

Our example also verifies our earlier assertion that a firm using the profit-maximizing combination of inputs is also necessarily producing the resulting output with the least cost. In fulfilling equation (2) the firm is automatically fulfilling equation (1). In this case for 5 units of labor and 3 of capital we observe that $MP_L/P_L = 4/8 = MP_C/P_C = 6/12$.[6] *(Key Questions 5 and 7)*

MARGINAL PRODUCTIVITY THEORY OF INCOME DISTRIBUTION

Our discussion of resource pricing is the cornerstone of the controversial view that economic justice is one of the outcomes of a competitive capitalist economy. Table 27-1 tells us, in effect, that labor receives an income payment equal to the marginal contribution it makes to the firm's revenue. Bluntly stated, labor is paid what it is economically worth. Therefore, if you are willing to accept the ethical proposition "To each according to what he or she creates," the marginal productivity theory seems to provide a fair and equitable distribution of income. Because the marginal productivity theory equally applies to capital and land, the distribution of all incomes can be regarded as equitable.

An income distribution whereby workers and owners of property resources are paid in accordance with their contribution to output sounds fair. But there are serious criticisms of the **marginal productivity theory of income distribution.**

1 Inequality Critics argue that the distribution of income resulting from payment according to marginal productivity may be highly unequal because productive resources are very unequally distributed in the first place. Aside from differences in genetic endowments, individuals encounter substantially different opportunities to enhance their productivity through education and training. Some may not be able to participate in production at all because of mental or physical handicaps and would obtain no income under a system of distribution based solely on marginal productivity. Ownership of property resources is also highly unequal. Many landlords and capitalists obtain their property by inheritance rather than through their own productive effort. Hence, income from inherited property resources conflicts with the "To each according to what one creates" proposition. This reasoning can lead us to advocate government policies to modify the income distribution resulting from payments made strictly according to marginal productivity.

2 Monopsony and Monopoly The marginal productivity theory rests on the assumption of competitive markets. We will find in Chapter 28 that labor markets, for example, are riddled with imperfections. Some employers exert monopsony power in hiring workers. And some workers, through labor unions, professional associations, and occupational licensing laws, brandish monopoly power in selling their services. Indeed, the process of collective bargaining over wages suggests a power struggle over the division of income. In this struggle market forces—and income shares based on marginal productivity—are pushed into the background. In short, we will find that, because of real-world market imperfections, wage rates and other resource prices frequently do *not* measure contributions to domestic output.

CHAPTER SUMMARY

1 Resource prices are a determinant of money incomes, and simultaneously ration resources to various industries and firms.

2 The demand for any resource is derived from the product it helps produce. That means the demand for a resource will depend on its productivity and the market value (price) of the good it is producing.

3 The marginal revenue product schedule of any resource is the demand schedule for that resource. This follows from the rule that a firm hiring under competitive conditions will find it most profitable to hire a resource up to the point where the price of the resource equals its marginal revenue product.

4 The demand curve for a resource is downsloping, because the marginal product of additional inputs of any resource declines in accordance with the law of diminishing

---

[6]Footnote 1 in Chapter 28 modifies our least-cost and profit-maximizing rules for the situation in which a firm is hiring resources under imperfectly competitive conditions. Where there is imperfect competition in the resource market, the marginal resource cost (MRC)—the cost of an extra input—exceeds the resource price (P). Hence, we must substitute MRC for P in the denominators of equations (1) and (2).

LAST WORD

INPUT SUBSTITUTION: THE CASE OF CABOOSES

Substituting among inputs—particularly when jobs are at stake—can be quite controversial.

A firm will achieve the least-cost combination of inputs when the last dollar spent on each makes the same contribution to total output. This rule also implies that a firm is unimpeded in changing its input mix in response to technological changes or changes in input prices. Unfortunately, in the real world the substitution of new capital for old capital and the substitution of capital for labor may be controversial and difficult to achieve.

Consider railroad cabooses. The railroads claim that technological advance has made the caboose obsolete. In particular, railroads want to substitute a "trainlink" which can be attached to the coupler of the last car of a train. This small black box contains a revolving strobe light and instruments which monitor train speed, airbrake pressure, and other relevant data which it transmits to the locomotive engineer. The trainlink costs only $4000 in comparison to $80,000 for a new caboose. And, of course, the trainlink replaces one member of the train crew.

The railroads cite substantial cost economies—perhaps as much as $400 million per year—from this rearrangement of capital and labor inputs. But the United Transportation Union (UTU) which represents railroad conductors and brakemen fears that the recent trend toward the demise of the caboose portends a decline in the demand for its members. The union therefore has made a concerted, but largely unsuccessful, effort to halt the elimination of cabooses on trains.

The UTU's basic argument is that the elimination of cabooses will reduce railroad safety. The union contends that, unlike humans, trainlink cannot detect broken wheels or axles nor overheated bearings. From the vantage point of the railroads this looks like featherbedding—the protection of unnecessary jobs. The railroads contend that available data show no safety differences between trains using and those not using cabooses. Indeed, safety may be enhanced without cabooses because many injuries are incurred by crew who are riding in cabooses.

While cabooses are virtually extinct in Europe, they are the rule in Canada. In the United States the railway unions have lobbied successfully for legislation in several states which makes cabooses mandatory. But in the vast majority of states the use of cabooses remains a matter of collective bargaining negotiations. In any event, the case of cabooses indicates clearly that input substitution is not always as simple as economic analysis would suggest.

---

returns. When a firm is selling in an imperfectly competitive market, the resource demand curve will fall for a second reason: Product price must be reduced to permit the firm to sell a larger output. The market demand for a resource can be derived by summing horizontally the demand curves of all firms hiring that resource.

5 The demand for a resource will shift as the result of **a** a change in the demand for, and therefore the price of, the product the resource is producing; **b** changes in the productivity of the resource; and **c** changes in prices of other resources.

6 If resources A and B are substitutable, a decline in the price of A will decrease the demand for B provided the sub-

stitution effect is greater than the output effect. But if the output effect exceeds the substitution effect, a decline in the price of A will increase the demand for B.

7 If resources C and D are complementary or jointly demanded, there is only an output effect and a change in the price of C will change the demand for D in the opposite direction.

8 The elasticity of resource demand will be greater **a** the slower the rate at which the marginal product of the resource declines, **b** the larger the number of good substitute resources available, **c** the greater the elasticity of demand for the product, and **d** the larger the proportion of total production costs attributable to the resource.

9 Any level of output will be produced with the least costly combination of resources when the marginal product per dollar's worth of each input is the same, that is, when

$$\frac{\text{MP of labor}}{\text{price of labor}} = \frac{\text{MP of capital}}{\text{price of capital}}$$

10 A firm will employ the profit-maximizing combination of resources when the price of each resource is equal to its marginal *revenue* product, or algebraically, when

$$\frac{\text{MRP of labor}}{\text{price of labor}} = \frac{\text{MRP of capital}}{\text{price of capital}} = 1$$

TERMS AND CONCEPTS

* derived demand
* marginal product
* marginal revenue product   *moneyvalue*

* marginal resource cost
* MRP = MRC rule substitution and output effects

* least-cost combination of resources
* profit-maximizing combination of resources

* marginal productivity theory of income distribution

QUESTIONS AND STUDY SUGGESTIONS

1 What is the significance of resource pricing? Explain in detail how the factors determining resource demand differ from those underlying product demand. Explain the meaning and significance of the notion that the demand for a resource is a *derived* demand. Why do resource demand curves slope downward?

2 *Key Question* Complete the following labor demand table for a firm which is hiring labor competitively and selling its product in a competitive market.

Units of labor	Total product	(Additional) Marginal product	Product price	Total revenue	Marginal revenue product
1	17	14	$2	$ 34	$ 28
2	31	12	2	62	24
3	43	10	2	86	20
4	53	7	2	106	14
5	60	5	2	120	10
6	65		2	130	

TP×P=TR *additional*

a How many workers will the firm hire if the going wage rate is $27.95? $19.95? Explain why the firm will not hire a larger or smaller number of workers at each of these wage rates.

b Show in schedule form and graphically the labor demand curve of this firm.

c Now redetermine the firm's demand curve for labor, assuming that it is selling in an imperfectly competitive market and that, although it can sell 17 units at $2.20 per unit, it must lower product price by 5 cents to sell the marginal product of each successive worker. Compare this demand curve with that derived in question 2b. Which curve is more elastic? Explain.

3 Distinguish between a change in resource demand and a change in the quantity of a resource demanded. What spe-

cific factors might lead to a change in resource demand? A change in the quantity of a resource demanded?

4 *Key Question* What factors determine the elasticity of resource demand? What effect will each of the following have on the elasticity or the location of the demand for resource C, which is being used in the production of commodity X? Where there is any uncertainty as to the outcome, specify the causes of that uncertainty.

a An increase in the demand for product X.

b An increase in the price of substitute resource D.

c An increase in the number of resources substitutable for C in producing X.

d A technological improvement in the capital equipment with which resource C is combined.

e A decline in the price of complementary resource E.

f A decline in the elasticity of demand for product X due to a decline in the competitiveness of the product market.

5 *Key Question* Suppose the productivity of labor and capital are as shown below. The output of these resources sells in a purely competitive market for $1 per unit. Both labor and capital are hired under purely competitive conditions at $1 and $3 respectively.

Units of capital	MP of capital	Units of labor	MP of labor
1	24	1	11
2	21	2	9
3	18	3	8
4	15	4	7
5	9	5	6
6	6	6	4
7	3	7	1
8	1	8	½

MRP *3* *MRP* *1*

MRP=MRC   *total production=96 + = 46*

profit maximizing output 142

a What is the least-cost combination of labor and capital to employ in producing 80 units of output? Explain.

b What is the profit-maximizing combination of labor and capital for the firm to employ? Explain. What is the resulting level of output? What is the economic profit?

c When the firm employs the profit-maximizing combination of labor and capital determined in 5b, is this combination also the least costly way of producing the profit-maximizing output? Explain.

6 Using the substitution and output effects, explain how a decline in the price of resource A *might* cause an increase in the demand for substitute resource B. If resources C and D are complementary and used in fixed proportions, what will be the impact of an increase in the price of C on the demand for D?

7 *Key Question* In each of the following four cases MRP_L and MRP_C refer to the marginal revenue products of labor and capital, respectively, and P_L and P_C refer to their prices. Indicate in each case whether the conditions are consistent with maximum profits for the firm. If not, state which resource(s) should be used in larger amounts and which resource(s) should be used in smaller amounts.

   a $MRP_L = \$8$; $P_L = \$4$; $MRP_C = \$8$; $P_C = \$4$.

   b $MRP_L = \$10$; $P_L = \$12$; $MRP_C = \$14$; $P_C = \$9$.

   c $MRP_L = \$6$; $P_L = \$6$; $MRP_C = \$12$; $P_C = \$12$.

   d $MRP_L = \$22$; $P_L = \$26$; $MRP_C = \$16$; $P_C = \$19$.

8 **Advanced analysis:** Demonstrate algebraically that the condition for the profit-maximizing level of output is the equivalent of the condition for the profit-maximizing combination of inputs.

9 If each input is paid in accordance with its marginal revenue product, will the resulting distribution of income be ethically just?

10 (Last Word) Use the example of railroad cabooses to explain why firms do not always employ the least-cost combination of resources.

28

THE PRICING AND EMPLOYMENT OF RESOURCES: WAGE DETERMINATION

The most important price you will encounter in your lifetime will likely be your wage rate. It will be critical in determining your economic well-being. The following facts and questions may be of more than casual interest.

Fact: Real wages and therefore living standards have increased historically in the United States. Question: What forces account for these increases?

Fact: Union workers generally receive higher wages than nonunion workers in the same occupation. Question: How do unions obtain this wage advantage?

Fact: The average salary for major league baseball players in 1994 was $1,188,679 compared to about $36,000 for teachers. Question: What causes differences in wages and incomes?

Fact: Most people are paid a certain hourly wage rate. But some workers are paid by the number of units produced or receive commissions and royalties. Question: What is the rationale for various compensation schemes?

Having explored the major factors underlying resource demand, we now introduce supply as it characterizes the markets for labor, land, capital, and entrepreneurial ability, to understand how wages, rents, interest, and profits are determined. We discuss wages before other resource prices because to the majority of households the wage rate is the most important price in the economy; it is the sole or basic source of income. About three-fourths of the national income is in the form of wages and salaries.

Our objectives in discussing wage determination are to (1) understand the forces underlying the general level of wage rates in the United States; (2) see how wage rates are determined in particular labor markets by presenting several representative labor market models; (3) analyze the impact of unions on the structure and level of wages; (4) discuss the economic effects of the minimum wage; (5) explain wage differentials; and (6) survey a number of compensation schemes which link pay to worker performance.

Throughout this chapter we will rely on the marginal productivity theory of Chapter 27 as an explanation of labor demand.

MEANING OF WAGES

Wages, or wage rates, are the price paid for the use of labor. Economists use the term "labor" broadly to apply to payments received by (1) workers in the pop-ular sense of the term, that is, blue- and white-collar workers of almost infinite variety; (2) professional people—lawyers, physicians, dentists, teachers; and (3) owners of small businesses—barbers, plumbers, television repairers, and a host of retailers—for the labor services they provide in operating their own businesses.

Wages may take the form of bonuses, royalties, commissions, and monthly salaries, but unless otherwise noted, we will use "wages" to mean wage rates per unit of time—per hour, per day, and so forth. This will remind us that the wage rate is a price paid for units of labor service. It also lets us distinguish clearly between "wages" and "earnings," the latter depending on wage rates *and* the number of hours or weeks of labor service supplied in the market.

We also distinguish between nominal wages and real wages. **Nominal wages** are the amount of money received per hour, per day, per week, and so on. **Real wages** are the quantity of goods and services you can obtain with nominal wages; real wages are the "purchasing power" of nominal wages.

Your real wages depend on your nominal wages and the prices of the goods and services you purchase. The percentage change in real wages can be determined by subtracting the percentage change in the price level from the percentage change in nominal wages. Thus an 8 percent increase in nominal wages during a year when the price level increases by 5 percent yields a 3 percent increase in real wages. Unless otherwise indicated, our discussion will be in terms of real wage rates by assuming the level of product prices is constant.

GENERAL LEVEL OF WAGES

Wages differ among nations, regions, occupations, and individuals. Wage rates are vastly higher in the United States than in China or India; they are generally higher in the north and east of the United States than in the south; plumbers are paid less than NFL punters; physician Adams may earn twice as much as physician Bennett for the same number of hours of work. Wage rates also differ by gender, race, and ethnic background.

The general level of wages, like the general level of prices, is a composite concept encompassing a wide range of different specific wage rates. It includes the wages of bakers, barbers, baseball players, and brain surgeons. Nevertheless, the average wage is a useful point of departure in making and explaining international and interregional wage comparisons.

International wage comparisons are admittedly complex and suspect. But data such as in Global Perspective 28-1 suggest that the general level of real

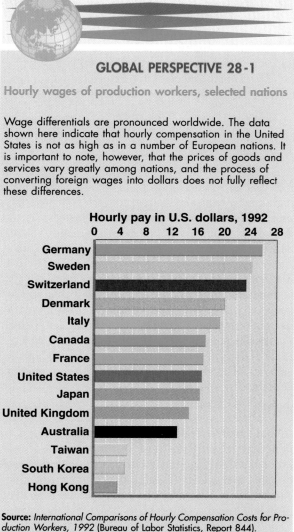

GLOBAL PERSPECTIVE 28-1

Hourly wages of production workers, selected nations

Wage differentials are pronounced worldwide. The data shown here indicate that hourly compensation in the United States is not as high as in a number of European nations. It is important to note, however, that the prices of goods and services vary greatly among nations, and the process of converting foreign wages into dollars does not fully reflect these differences.

Hourly pay in U.S. dollars, 1992

	0	4	8	12	16	20	24	28
Germany								
Sweden								
Switzerland								
Denmark								
Italy								
Canada								
France								
United States								
Japan								
United Kingdom								
Australia								
Taiwan								
South Korea								
Hong Kong								

Source: *International Comparisons of Hourly Compensation Costs for Production Workers, 1992* (Bureau of Labor Statistics, Report 844).

wages in the United States is relatively high—although not the highest—globally.

The simplest explanation for our high real wages is that the demand for labor has been great relative to the supply.

Role of Productivity

We know the demand for labor—or any other resource—depends on its productivity. In general, the greater the productivity of labor, the greater the demand for it. And, given the total supply of labor, the stronger the demand, the higher the average level of real wages. The demand for American labor has been strong because it is highly productive. There are several reasons for this high productivity.

1   Capital   American workers are used in conjunction with large amounts of capital equipment. A recent estimate indicates total physical capital (machinery and buildings) per worker is about $52,000.

2   Natural Resources   Natural resources are abundant in relation to the size of the labor force. The United States is richly endowed with arable land, mineral resources, and sources of industrial power. The fact that American workers have large amounts of high-quality natural resources to work with is perhaps most evident in agriculture where, historically, the growth of productivity has been dramatic (Chapter 33).

3   Technology   The level of technological advance is generally higher in the United States than in most foreign nations. American workers in many industries use not only more capital equipment but better (technologically superior) equipment than do the vast majority of foreign workers. Similarly, work methods are steadily being improved through detailed scientific study and research.

4   Labor Quality   The health, vigor, education and training, and work attitudes of American workers are generally superior to those of the workers of most other nations. This means that, even with the same quantity and quality of natural and capital resources, American workers would be more efficient than many of their foreign counterparts.

5   Other Factors   Less tangible items underlying the high productivity of American labor are (a) the efficiency and flexibility of American management; (b) a business, social, and political environment which puts great emphasis on production and productivity; and (c) the vast size of the domestic market, which provides the opportunity for firms to realize mass-production economies.

Real Wages and Productivity

The dependence of real hourly wages on the productivity level is indicated in Figure 28-1. Note the close relationship in the long run between real hourly wages and output per labor-hour. When you recall that real income and real output are two ways of viewing the same thing, it is no surprise that *real income (earnings) per worker can increase only at about the same rate as output per worker.* More real output per hour means more real income to distribute for each hour worked. We cannot divide up what isn't produced. The simplest case is Robinson Crusoe on the deserted island. The number of coconuts he can pick or fish he can catch per hour *is* his real wage per hour.

Secular Growth and Stagnation

But simple supply and demand analysis suggests that, even if the demand for labor is strong in the United States, increases in the supply of labor will reduce the general level of wages over time. It is certainly true that the American population and the labor force have grown significantly over the decades. Historically, these increases in the supply of labor have been more

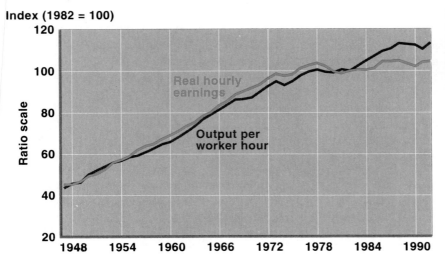

Index (1982 = 100)

FIGURE 28-1   Output per hour and real average hourly earnings   Over a long period of years there has been a close relationship between real hourly earnings and output per worker-hour. (*Department of Labor, Monthly Labor Review.*)

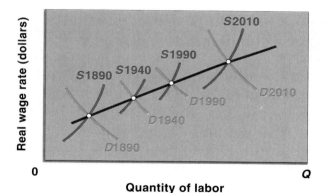

FIGURE 28-2 The secular trend of real wages in the United States
The productivity of American labor has increased substantially in the long run, causing the demand for labor to increase in relation to the supply. The result has been increases in real wages.

than offset by increases in the demand for labor arising from the productivity-increasing factors discussed above. The result historically has been a long-run, or secular, increase in wage rates and employment, as suggested by Figure 28-2.

But a glance at Figure 28-1 suggests a more disturbing point. Real hourly wages and weekly earnings have been stagnant since 1979. In 1994 the average real hourly wage in all private nonmanufacturing industries was $7.40, down from $8.17 in 1979. Average weekly real earnings were $256 in 1994, compared to $292 in 1979. There is no consensus as to the causes of these slowdowns, but the following are frequently cited: diminished rates of capital accumulation and the reallocation of labor from high-productivity manufacturing industries to low-productivity service industries. Also mentioned are the deterioration of labor force skills due to the declining quality of education; the surge of labor force supply associated with large numbers of "baby boomers," immigrants, and married women entering the labor force; and management strategies that stress short-term profitability at the expense of research and development and innovative labor relations programs which might increase productivity.

The globalization of production may also be a factor. When production can be effectively outsourced to less developed countries, the effective supply of unskilled workers is greatly expanded. This global market for unskilled labor pulls down the real wages of such workers in the United States and other industrialized nations. Stated differently, with the global-

ization of the market for unskilled labor and increased mobility of capital, unskilled American workers must work for wages roughly equal to those of the unskilled in lower-wage nations or lose their jobs because production will be relocated to those countries. In fact, the real wages of less skilled American workers have declined significantly pulling down the average level of real wages.

WAGES IN PARTICULAR LABOR MARKETS

We now turn from the general level of wages to specific wage rates. What determines the wage rate received by some specific type of worker? Demand and supply analysis again is revealing. Our analysis covers some half-dozen basic market models.

Competitive Model

In a purely **competitive labor market:**
1 Many firms are competing with one another in hiring a specific type of labor.
2 Numerous qualified workers with identical skills are independently supplying this type of labor service.
3 "Wage taker" behavior pertains to both firms and workers; neither can exert control over the market wage rate.

Market Demand Suppose there are many—say, 200—firms demanding a particular type of semiskilled or skilled labor. These firms need not be in the same industry; industries are defined in terms of the products they produce and not of the resources they employ. Thus, firms producing wood-frame furniture, window and door frames, and cabinets will all demand carpenters. The total, or market, demand for the labor in question can be determined by summing horizontally the labor demand curves (the MRP curves) of the individual firms, as suggested in Figure 28-3a and b (Key Graph).

Market Supply On the supply side of the picture, we assume there is no union; workers compete individually for available jobs. The supply curve for a particular type of labor will be upsloping, reflecting that, in the absence of unemployment, employers as a group will have to pay higher wage rates to obtain more workers. This is so because firms must bid these workers away from other industries, occupations, and

KEY GRAPH

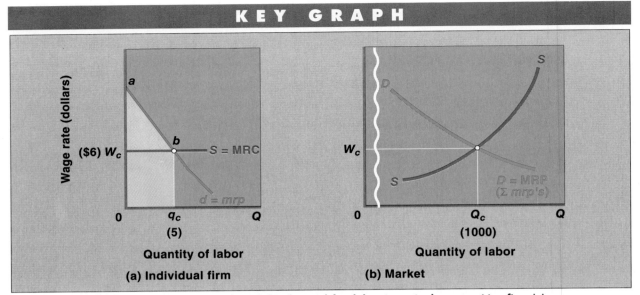

FIGURE 28-3   The supply of, and the demand for, labor in a single competitive firm (a) and in a competitive market (b)
In a competitive labor market the equilibrium wage rate W_c and number of workers employed Q_c are determined by supply SS and demand DD, as shown in (b). Because this wage rate is given to the individual firm hiring in the market, its labor supply curve, $S = MRC$, is perfectly elastic, as in (a). The firm finds it most profitable to hire workers up to the MRP = MRC point. The area $0abq_c$ represents the firm's total revenue of which the area $0W_cbq_c$ is its total wage cost; the remaining area W_cab is available for paying nonlabor resources.

localities. Within limits, workers have alternative job opportunities; that is, they may work in other industries in the same locality, or they may work in their present occupations in different cities or states. In a full-employment economy the group of firms in this particular labor market must pay higher and higher wage rates to attract this type of labor away from these alternative job opportunities. Similarly, higher wages are necessary to induce individuals not currently in the labor force to seek employment.

More technically, the market supply curve rises because it is an *opportunity cost* curve. To attract workers to this particular employment the wage rate paid must cover the opportunity costs of alternative uses of time spent, either in other labor markets, in household activities, or in leisure. Higher wages attract more people to this employment—people who were not attracted by lower wages because their opportunity costs were too high.

Market Equilibrium   The equilibrium wage rate and the equilibrium level of employment for this type of

labor are determined at the intersection of the labor demand and labor supply curves. In Figure 28-3b the equilibrium wage rate is W_c ($6), and the number of workers hired is Q_c (1000). To the individual firm the wage rate W_c is given. Each of the many hiring firms employs such a small fraction of the total available supply of this type of labor that none can influence the wage rate. The supply of labor is perfectly elastic to the individual firm, as shown by S in Figure 28-3a.

Each individual firm will find it profitable to hire workers up to the point at which the going wage rate is equal to labor's MRP. This is merely an application of the MRP = MRC rule developed in Chapter 27. (Indeed, the demand curve in Figure 28-3a is based on Table 27-1.)

As Table 28-1 indicates, *because resource price is given to the individual competitive firm, the marginal cost of that resource (MRC) will be constant and equal to resource price (the wage rate).* In this case the wage rate and hence the marginal cost of labor are constant to the individual firm. Each additional worker hired adds precisely his or her wage rate ($6 in this case)

TABLE 28-1 The supply of labor: pure competition in the hire of labor

(1) Units of labor	(2) Wage rate	(3) Total labor cost (wage bill)	(4) Marginal resource (labor) cost
0	$6	$ 0	
1	6	6	$6
2	6	12	6
3	6	18	6
4	6	24	6
5	6	30	6
6	6	36	6

to the firm's total resource cost. The firm then will maximize its profits by hiring workers to the point at which their wage rate, and therefore marginal resource cost, equals their marginal revenue product. In Figure 28-3a the "typical" firm will hire q_c (5) workers.

Note that the firm's total revenue from hiring q_c workers can be found by summing their MRPs. In this case the total revenue from the five workers is indicated by the area $0abq_c$ in Figure 28-3a. Of this total revenue, the area $0W_cbq_c$ is the firm's total wage cost and the triangular area W_cab represents additional revenue available to reward other inputs such as capital, land, and entrepreneurship. *(Key Questions 3 and 4)*

Monopsony Model

In a purely competitive labor market each employer hires too small an amount of labor to influence the wage rate. Each firm is a "wage taker"; it can hire as little or as much labor as it needs at the market wage, as reflected in its perfectly elastic labor supply curve.

Characteristics Let's now consider the case of **monopsony,** which describes an employer with monopolistic buying (hiring) power. Monopsony has the following characteristics:

1 The firm's employment is a large portion of the total employment of a particular kind of labor.

2 This type of labor is relatively immobile, either geographically or in the sense that, if workers sought alternative employment, they would have to acquire new skills.

3 The firm is a "wage maker" in that the wage rate it must pay varies directly with the number of workers it employs.

In some instances the monopsonistic power of employers is virtually complete because there is only one major employer in a labor market. For example, the economies of some towns and cities depend almost entirely on one major firm. A silver-mining concern may be the basic source of employment in a remote Idaho or Colorado town. A New England textile mill, a Wisconsin paper mill, or a farm-belt food processor may provide most of the employment in its locality. Anaconda Mining is the dominant employer in Butte, Montana.

In other cases *oligopsony* may prevail; three or four firms may each hire a large portion of the supply of labor in a particular market. Our study of oligopoly correctly suggests there is a strong tendency for oligopsonists to act in concert—much like a monopsonist—in hiring labor.

Upsloping Supply to Firm When a firm hires a considerable portion of the total available supply of a particular type of labor, its decision to employ more or fewer workers will affect the wage rate paid to that labor. Specifically, *if a firm is large in relation to the labor market, it will have to pay a higher wage rate to obtain more labor.* For simplicity's sake suppose there is only one employer of a particular type of labor in a specified geographic area. In this extreme case, the labor supply curve to that firm and the total supply curve for the labor market are identical. This supply curve, for reasons already made clear, is upsloping, indicating that the firm must pay a higher wage rate to attract more workers. This is shown by *SS* in Figure 28-4. The supply curve is in effect the average-cost-of-labor curve from the firm's perspective; each point on it indicates the wage rate (cost) per worker which must be paid to attract the corresponding number of workers.

MRC Exceeds Wage Rate But the higher wages needed to attract *additional* workers will also have to be paid to *all* workers currently employed at lower wage rates. If not, labor morale will deteriorate, and the employer will be plagued with labor unrest because of wage-rate differentials existing for the same job. As for cost, payment of a uniform wage to all workers will mean that the cost of an extra worker—the marginal resource (labor) cost (MRC)—will exceed the wage rate by the amount necessary to bring the

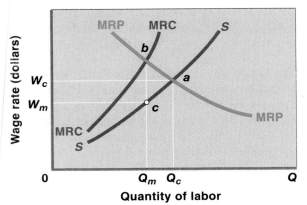

FIGURE 28-4   **The wage rate and level of employment in a monopsonistic labor market**
In a monopsonistic labor market the employer's marginal resource (labor) cost curve (MRC) lies above the labor supply curve (S). Equating MRC with labor demand MRP at point *b*, the monopsonist will hire Q_m workers (compared with Q_c under competition) and pay the wage rate W_m (compared with the competitive wage W_c).

wage rate of all workers currently employed up to the new wage level.

Table 28-2 illustrates this point. One worker can be hired at a wage rate of $6. But hiring a second worker forces the firm to pay a higher wage of $7. Marginal resource (labor) cost is $8—the $7 paid the second worker plus a $1 raise for the first worker. That is, total labor cost is $14 (= 2 × $7) rather than $13, which would be the case if the first worker was paid $6 and the second paid $7. Thus, the MRC of the second worker is $8 (= $14 − $6), not the $7 wage rate paid the second worker. Similarly, the marginal labor cost of the third worker is $10—the $8 which must

be paid to attract this worker from alternative employments plus $1 raises—from $7 to $8—for the first two workers.

The important point is that *to the monopsonist, marginal resource (labor) cost will exceed the wage rate.* Graphically, the MRC curve (columns 1 and 4 in Table 28-2) will lie above the average-cost, or supply, curve of labor (columns 1 and 2 in Table 28-2). This is shown graphically in Figure 28-4.

Equilibrium   How much labor will the firm hire, and what wage rate will it pay? To maximize profits the firm will equate marginal resource (labor) cost with the MRP.[1] The number of workers hired by the monopsonist is indicated by Q_m, and the wage rate paid, W_m, is indicated by the corresponding point on the labor supply, or average-cost-of-labor, curve. The firm need not pay a wage equal to MRP. As we see from the labor supply curve, it need pay only W_m to attract the Q_m desired number of workers.

Contrast these results with those which a competitive labor market would have yielded. With competition in the hire of labor, the level of employment would have been greater (Q_c), and the wage rate would have been higher (W_c). It simply does not pay the monopsonist to hire workers up to the point at which the wage rate and labor's MRP are equal. *Other things equal, the monopsonist maximizes its profits by hiring a smaller number of workers and thereby paying a less-than-competitive wage rate.* Society gets a smaller output,[2] and workers get a wage rate less by

TABLE 28-2   **The supply of labor: monopsony in the hire of labor**

(1) Units of labor	(2) Wage rate	(3) Total labor cost (wage bill)	(4) Marginal resource (labor) cost
0	$ 5	$ 0	
1	6	6	$ 6
2	7	14	8
3	8	24	10
4	9	36	12
5	10	50	14
6	11	66	16

---

[1]The fact that MRC exceeds resource price when resources are hired or purchased under imperfectly competitive (monopsonistic) conditions calls for adjustments in Chapter 27's least-cost and profit-maximizing rules for hiring resources. [See equations (1) and (2) in the "Optimal Combination of Resources" section of Chapter 27.] Specifically, we must substitute MRC for resource price in the denominators of our two equations. That is, with imperfect competition in the hiring of both labor and capital, equation (1) becomes

$$\frac{MP_L}{MRC_L} = \frac{MP_C}{MRC_C} \tag{1'}$$

and equation (2) is restated as

$$\frac{MRP_L}{MRC_L} = \frac{MRP_C}{MRC_C} = 1 \tag{2'}$$

In fact, equations (1) and (2) can be regarded as special cases of (1') and (2') in which firms happen to be hiring under purely competitive conditions and resource price is therefore equal to, and can be substituted for, marginal resource cost.

[2]This is analogous to the monopolist's restricting output as it sets product price and output on the basis of marginal revenue, not product demand. In this instance, resource price is set on the basis of marginal labor (resource) cost, not resource supply.

bc than their marginal revenue product. Just as a monopolistic seller finds it profitable to restrict product output to realize an above-competitive price for its goods, so the monopsonistic employer of resources finds it profitable to restrict employment to depress wage rates and therefore costs, that is, to realize below-competitive wage rates.[3]

Examples Monopsonistic labor market outcomes are not common in our economy. There are typically many potential employers for most workers, particularly when these workers are occupationally and geographically mobile. Also, as we will see momentarily, unions often counteract monopsony power in labor markets. Nevertheless, economists have found evidence of monopsony in such diverse labor markets as those for nurses, professional athletes, public school teachers, newspaper employees, and some building trades workers.

In the case of nurses the major employers in most localities are a relatively small number of hospitals. Furthermore, the highly specialized skills of nurses are not readily transferable to other occupations. It has been found in accordance with the monopsony model that, other things equal, the smaller the number of hospitals in a town or city (that is, the greater the degree of monopsony), the lower the beginning salaries of nurses.

Although *potential* employers for professional athletes are quite numerous, the market historically has been characterized by ingenious collusive devices which employers have used with success to limit competition in the hire of labor. The National Football League, the National Basketball Association, and the American and National Baseball Leagues have established rules which tie a player to one team and prevent him from selling his talents to the highest bidder on the open (competitive) market. In particular, through the new player draft, the team which selects or "drafts" a player has the exclusive right to bargain a contract with that player. Furthermore, the so-called reserve clause in each player's contract gives his team the exclusive right to purchase his services for the next season. Though recent court cases and collective bargaining agreements stipulating "free agency"

for experienced players have made the labor markets for professional athletes more competitive, collusive monopsony persists.

As detailed in this chapter's Last Word, empirical studies have shown that prior to 1976 baseball players (despite very high salaries) were paid substantially less than their estimated MRPs, which is, of course, consistent with Figure 28-4. However, beginning in 1976 players were allowed to become "free agents"—they became free to sell their services to any interested team—after their sixth season of play. A comparison of the salaries of the first group of free agents with their estimated MRPs indicates that the competitive bidding of teams for free agents brought their salaries and MRPs into close accord as our competitive model suggests. *(Key Question 6)*

> **QUICK REVIEW 28-1**
>
> ■ Real wages have increased historically in the United States because labor demand has increased relative to labor supply.
>
> ■ Real wages per worker have increased at approximately the same rate as worker productivity.
>
> ■ The competitive employer is a "wage taker" and employs workers at the point where the wage rate or MRC equals MRP.
>
> ■ The labor supply curve to a monopsonist is upsloping, causing MRC to exceed the wage rate for each worker. Other things equal, the monopsonist will hire fewer workers and pay a lower wage rate than would a purely competitive employer.

Three Union Models

Thus far, we have assumed that workers actively compete in the sale of their labor services. In some markets workers "sell" their labor services collectively through unions. To view the economic impact of unions in the simplest context, let's first suppose a union is formed in an otherwise competitive labor market. That is, a union is now bargaining with a relatively large number of employers.

Unions seek many goals. The basic one is to raise wage rates. The union can pursue this objective in several ways.

Increasing the Demand for Labor From the union's viewpoint, the most desirable technique for raising wage rates is to increase the demand for labor. As shown in Figure 28-5, an increase in the de-

---

[3]Will a monopsonistic employer also be a monopolistic seller in the product market? Not necessarily. The New England textile mill may be a monopsonistic employer, yet face severe domestic and foreign competition in selling its product. In other cases—for example, the automobile and steel industries—firms have both monopsonistic and monopolistic (oligopolistic) power.

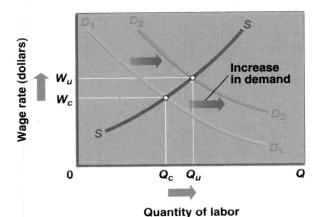

FIGURE 28-5   Unions and the demand for labor
When unions can increase the demand for labor (D_1D_1 to D_2D_2), higher wage rates (W_c to W_u) and more jobs (Q_c to Q_u) can be realized.

mand for labor will result in *both* higher wage rates and more jobs. The relative sizes of these increases will depend on the elasticity of labor supply.

A union might increase labor demand by altering one or more of the determinants of labor demand (Chapter 27). Specifically, a union can attempt to (1) increase the demand for the product or service it is producing, (2) enhance labor productivity, or (3) alter the prices of other inputs.

1   Increase Product Demand   Unions may attempt to increase the demand for the products they help produce—and hence increase the derived demand for their own labor services—by advertising, political lobbying, or featherbedding.

Union television ads urging consumers to "buy the union label" are relevant. Historically, the International Ladies Garment Workers Union (ILGWU) has joined with its employers to finance advertising campaigns to bolster demand for their products. Also, the Communications Workers of America (CWA) helped finance a $2 million "Call or Buy Union" campaign to convince telephone users to choose the long-distance services and equipment of AT&T and Western Union Corporation, which together provided almost 100,000 CWA jobs.

On the political front we see construction unions lobbying for new highway or urban renewal projects. Teachers' unions and associations push for increased public spending on education. Unions connected with the aerospace industry lobby to increase military

spending. And some unions have vigorously supported their employers in seeking protective tariffs or import quotas designed to exclude competing foreign products. The steelworkers and automobile workers both have sought such forms of protection. Thus, a decline in the supply of imported cars through tariffs or negotiated agreements between nations will increase import prices, increasing the demand for highly substitutable American-made autos and boosting the derived demand for American auto workers.

Some unions have sought to expand the demand for labor by forcing make-work, or featherbedding, rules on employers. Before contrary court rulings, the Railway Brotherhoods forced railroads to hire train crews of a certain minimum size; diesel engines had to have a fireman even though there was no fire.

2   Increase Productivity   While many decisions affecting labor productivity—for example, decisions concerning quantity and quality of real capital—are made unilaterally by management, there is a growing interest in establishing joint labor-management committees designed to increase labor productivity.

3   Increase Prices of Substitutes   Unions might enhance the demand for their labor by increasing the prices of substitute resources. An example is that unions—whose workers are generally paid significantly more than the minimum wage—strongly support increases in the minimum wage. An alleged reason for this backing is that unions want to increase the price of substitutable low-wage, nonunion labor. A higher minimum wage for nonunion workers will deter employers from substituting them for union workers, thereby bolstering the demand for union workers.

Similarly, unions can also increase the demand for their labor by supporting public actions which *reduce* the price of a complementary resource. Unions in industries using large amounts of energy might actively oppose rate increases proposed by electric or natural gas utilities. Where labor and energy are complementary, an energy price increase might reduce the demand for labor through Chapter 27's output effect.

Unions recognize that their capacity to influence the demand for labor is tenuous and uncertain. As many of our illustrations imply, unions are frequently trying to forestall *declines* in labor demand rather than actually increase it. In view of these considerations, it is not surprising that union efforts to increase wage rates have concentrated on the supply side of the market.

Exclusive or Craft Unionism   Unions may boost wage rates by reducing the supply of labor. Historically, organized labor has favored policies restricting the supply of labor to the economy as a whole to bolster the general level of wages. Labor unions have supported legislation which has (1) restricted immigration, (2) reduced child labor, (3) encouraged compulsory retirement, and (4) enforced a shorter workweek.

More relevant for present purposes, specific types of workers have adopted, through unions, techniques designed to restrict their numbers. This is especially true of *craft unions*—unions which comprise workers of a given skill, such as carpenters, bricklayers, and plumbers. These unions have frequently forced employers to agree to hire only union workers, giving the union virtually complete control of the supply of labor. Then, by following restrictive membership policies—long apprenticeships, very high initiation fees, the limitation or prohibition of new members—the union causes an artificial restriction of the labor supply. As indicated in Figure 28-6, this results in higher wage rates. This approach to achieving wage increases is called **exclusive unionism.** Higher wages result from excluding workers from the union and therefore from the supply of labor.

Occupational licensing is another means of restricting the supplies of specific kinds of labor. Here a group of workers in an occupation will pressure state or municipal governments to pass a law which provides that, say, barbers (physicians, plumbers, beauticians, egg graders, pest controllers) can practice their trade only if they meet certain specified requirements. These requirements might specify the level of education, amount of work experience, the passing of an examination, and personal characteristics ("the practitioner must be of good moral character"). The licensing board administering the law is typically dominated by members of the licensed occupation. The result is self-regulation, conducive to polices that reflect self-interest. In short, imposing arbitrary and irrelevant entrance requirements or constructing an unnecessarily stringent examination can restrict entrants to the occupation.

Ostensibly, the purpose of licensing is to protect consumers from incompetent practitioners. But licensing laws are frequently abused in that the number of qualified workers is artificially restricted, re-

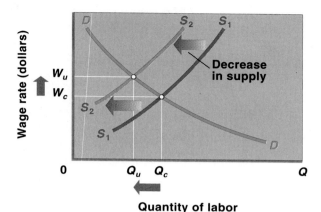

FIGURE 28-6   Exclusive or craft unionism
By reducing the supply of labor (S_1S_1 to S_2S_2) through the use of restrictive membership policies, exclusive unions achieve higher wage rates (W_c to W_u). However, the restriction of labor supply also reduces the number of workers employed (Q_c to Q_u).

sulting in above-competitive wages and earnings for those in the occupation (Figure 28-6). Furthermore, licensing requirements often specify a residency requirement which inhibits the interstate movement of qualified workers. Some 600 occupations are now licensed in the United States.

Inclusive or Industrial Unionism   Most unions, however, do not attempt to limit their membership. On the contrary, they seek to organize all available or potential workers. This is characteristic of the so-called *industrial unions*—unions, such as the automobile workers and steelworkers, which seek all unskilled, semiskilled, and skilled workers in an industry as members. A union can afford to be exclusive when its members are skilled craftsmen for whom substitute workers are not readily available in quantity. But a union that comprises unskilled and semiskilled workers will undermine its own existence by limiting its membership, causing numerous highly substitutable nonunion workers to be available for employment.

If an industrial union includes virtually all workers in its membership, firms will be under great pressure to agree to the wage rate demanded by the union. By going on strike the union can deprive the firm of its entire labor supply.

Inclusive unionism is illustrated in Figure 28-7. Initially, the competitive equilibrium wage rate is W_c, and the level of employment is Q_c. Now suppose an industrial union is formed, and it imposes a

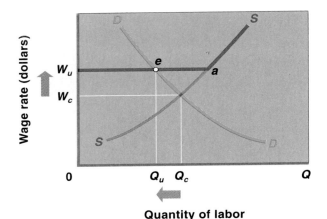

FIGURE 28-7   Inclusive or industrial unionism
By organizing virtually all available workers and thereby controlling the supply of labor, inclusive industrial unions may impose a wage rate, such as W_u, which is above the competitive wage rate W_c. The effect is to change the labor supply curve from SS to $W_u aS$. At the W_u wage rate, employers will cut employment from Q_c to Q_u.

higher, above-equilibrium wage rate of, say, W_u. This wage rate changes the supply curve of labor to the firm from the preunion SS curve to the postunion $W_u aS$ curve.[4] No workers will be forthcoming at a wage rate less than that demanded by the union. If employers decide it is better to pay this higher wage rate than to suffer a strike, they will cut back on employment from Q_c to Q_u.

By agreeing to the union's W_u wage demand, individual employers become "wage takers" at this wage and therefore face a perfectly elastic labor supply curve over the $W_u a$ range. Because labor supply is perfectly elastic, MRC is equal to the W_u wage over this range. The Q_u level of employment results from employers equating MRC (= W_u) with MRP as embodied in the labor demand curve.

Note that at W_u there is an excess supply or surplus of labor in the amount ea. Without the union—that is, in a purely competitive labor market—these unemployed workers might accept lower wages and the wage rate would fall to the W_c competitive equi-

librium level where quantity demanded equals quantity supplied. But this doesn't happen because workers are acting collectively through their union. Workers cannot individually offer to work for less than W_u; nor can employers contractually pay less.

Wage Increases and Unemployment

Have unions been successful in raising the wages of their members? Evidence suggests that union members on the average achieve a 10 to 15 percent wage advantage over nonunion workers.

As Figures 28-6 and 28-7 suggest, the wage-raising actions of both exclusive and inclusive unionism reduce employment. A union's success in achieving above-equilibrium wage rates is tempered by the consequent decline in the number of workers employed. This unemployment effect acts as a restraining influence on union wage demands. A union cannot expect to maintain solidarity within its ranks if it seeks a wage rate so high that joblessness will result for, say, 20 or 30 percent of its members.

The unemployment impact of wage increases might be mitigated in two ways.

1   Growth   The normal growth of the economy increases the demand for most kinds of labor through time. Thus a rightward shift of the labor demand curves in Figures 28-6 and 28-7 could offset, or more than offset, any unemployment effects associated with the indicated wage increases. There would still be an employment restricting aspect to the union wage increases but it would be a decline in the rate of growth of job opportunities, not of an absolute decline in the number of jobs.

2   Elasticity   The size of the unemployment effect will depend on the elasticity of demand for labor. The more inelastic the demand, the smaller will be the amount of unemployment accompanying a given wage-rate increase. If unions have sufficient bargaining strength, they *may* obtain provisions in their collective bargaining agreements which reduce the substitutability of other inputs for labor and thereby reduce the elasticity of demand for union labor. For example, a union may force employers to accept rules blocking the introduction of new machinery and equipment. Or the union may bargain successfully for severance or layoff pay, which increases the cost to the firm of substituting capital for labor when wage rates are increased. Similarly, the union might gain a

---

[4]Technically, the wage rate W_u makes the labor supply curve perfectly elastic over the $W_u a$ range in Figure 28-7. If employers hire any number of workers in this range, the union-imposed wage rate is effective and must be paid, or the union will supply no labor at all—the employers will be faced with a strike. If employers want more workers than $W_u a$, they will have to bid up wages above the union's minimum. This will only occur if the market demand curve for labor shifts rightward so that it intersects the aS range of the labor supply curve.

contract provision prohibiting the firm from subcontracting production to nonunion (lower-wage) firms or relocating work to low-wage workers overseas, effectively restricting the substitution of cheaper labor for union workers.

For these and other reasons the unemployment restraint on union wage demands may be less pressing than our exclusive and inclusive union models suggest.

Bilateral Monopoly Model

Suppose a strong industrial union is formed in a labor market which is monopsonistic rather than competitive. In other words, we combine the monopsony model with the inclusive unionism model. The result is **bilateral monopoly.** The union is a monopolistic "seller" of labor which controls labor supply and can influence wage rates, but it faces a monopsonistic employer (or combination of oligopsonistic employers) of labor who can also affect wages by altering its employment. This is not an extreme or special case. In such industries as steel, automobiles, meatpacking, and farm machinery, "big labor"—one huge industrial union—bargains with "big business"—a few huge industrial giants.

Indeterminate Outcome   This situation is shown in Figure 28-8, which superimposes Figure 28-7 on 28-4. The monopsonistic employer will seek the below-competitive-equilibrium wage rate W_m and the union presumably will press for some above-competitive-equilibrium wage rate such as W_u. Which will result? We cannot say with certainty. The outcome is logically indeterminate since economic theory does not explain what the resulting wage rate will be. We should expect the wage outcome to lie somewhere between W_m and W_u. Beyond that, about all we can say is that the party with the most bargaining power and the most effective bargaining strategy will be able to get its opponent to agree to a wage close to the one it seeks.

Desirability   It is possible that the wage and employment outcomes might be more socially desirable than the term bilateral monopoly would imply. Monopoly on one side of the market *might* in effect cancel out the monopoly on the other side of the market, yielding competitive or near-competitive results. If either the union or management prevailed in this market—that is, if the actual wage rate were determined

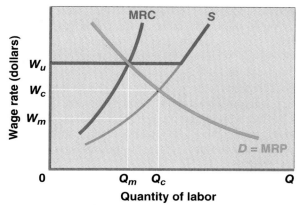

FIGURE 28-8   Bilateral monopoly in the labor market
When a monopsonistic employer seeks the wage rate W_m and the inclusive union it faces seeks an above-equilibrium wage rate such as W_u, the actual outcome is logically indeterminate.

at either W_u or W_m—employment would be restricted to Q_m (where MRP = MRC), which is below the competitive level.

But now suppose the monopoly power of the union roughly offsets the monopsony power of management, and a bargained wage rate of about W_c, which is the competitive wage, is agreed upon. Once management agrees to this wage rate, its incentive to restrict employment disappears; no longer can the employer depress wage rates by restricting employment. Thus management equates the bargained wage rate W_c (=MRC) with MRP and finds it most profitable to hire Q_c workers. With monopoly on both sides of the labor market, it may be possible that the resulting wage rate and level of employment will be closer to competitive levels than if monopoly existed on only one side of the market. *(Key Question 8)*

The Minimum-Wage Controversy

Since the passage of the Fair Labor Standards Act in 1938, the United States has had a Federal **minimum wage.** The minimum wage has ranged from about 40 to 50 percent of the average wage paid to manufacturing workers and is currently $4.25 per hour. Roughly 90 percent of all nonsupervisory workers are covered. Our analysis of the effects of union wage-fixing raises the question of how effective minimum-wage legislation is as an antipoverty device.

Case against the Minimum Wage   Critics, reasoning in terms of Figure 28-7, contend that an effective (above-equilibrium) minimum wage will simply push employers back up their MRP or labor demand curves since it is now profitable to hire fewer workers. The higher wage costs may even force some firms out of business. Some of the poor, low-wage workers whom the minimum wage was designed to help will now find themselves out of work! Critics say a worker who is unemployed at a minimum wage of $4.25 per hour is clearly worse off than if he or she were employed at a market wage rate of, say, $3.50 per hour.

A second criticism is that the minimum wage is poorly targeted as an antipoverty device. It is designed to provide a "living wage" which will allow less-skilled workers to earn enough so that they and their families can escape poverty. However, critics argue that the primary impact of the minimum wage is on teenage workers, many of whom belong to relatively affluent families.

Case for the Minimum Wage Advocates say critics analyze the impact of the minimum wage in an unrealistic context. Figure 28-7, advocates claim, assumes a competitive and static market. But a minimum wage in a monopsonistic labor market (Figure 28-8) suggests that the minimum wage can increase wage rates without causing unemployment. Indeed, a higher minimum wage may even produce more jobs by eliminating the monopsonistic employer's motive to restrict employment.

Furthermore, an effective minimum wage may increase labor productivity, shifting the labor demand curve to the right and offsetting any unemployment effects which the minimum wage might induce.

But how might a minimum wage increase productivity? First, a minimum wage may have a *shock effect* on employers. Firms using low-wage workers may be inefficient in the use of labor; the higher wage rates imposed by the minimum wage will presumably shock these firms into using labor more efficiently, and so the productivity of labor rises. Second, some argue that higher wages will increase the real incomes and therefore the health, vigor, and motivation of workers, making them more productive.

Evidence Which view is correct? The consensus of the many research studies of the minimum wage is that it does cause some unemployment, particularly among teenage (16 to 19 years) workers. It is estimated that a 10 percent increase in the minimum wage will reduce teenage employment by 1 to 3 per-

cent. Young adults (age 20 to 24) are also adversely affected; a 10 percent increase in the minimum wage would reduce employment for this group by 1 percent or less. Blacks and women, who are disproportionately represented in low-wage occupations, tend to suffer larger declines in employment than white males. The other side of the coin is that those who remain employed receive higher incomes and may escape poverty. The overall antipoverty effect of the minimum wage is thus a mixed, ambivalent one. Those who lose their jobs are plunged deeper into poverty; those who remain employed may escape poverty.

WAGE DIFFERENTIALS

Why do corporate executives and professional athletes receive $1,000,000 or more per year while laundry workers and retail clerks get a paltry $14,000 or $15,000 per year? Why does an entertainer from San Diego dressed as a chicken earn $250,000 a year while someone frying chickens at KFC earns $12,000? Table 28-3 indicates the substantial **wage differentials** among certain occupations. Our objective now is to gain some insight as to why these differentials exist.

Once again the forces of supply and demand provide a general answer. If the supply of a particular type of labor is great in relation to the demand for it, the resulting wage rate will be low. But if demand is great

TABLE 28-3 Average hourly and weekly earnings in selected industries, August 1994

Industry	Average hourly gross earnings	Average weekly gross earnings
Bituminous coal	$17.72	$804
Motor vehicles	16.86	769
Chemicals	15.15	650
Construction	14.77	588
Printing and publishing	12.12	469
Fabricated metals	11.88	508
Food products	10.60	444
Hotels and motels	7.51	240
Retail trade	7.43	221
Laundries and dry cleaning	7.35	249
Apparel and textiles	7.35	278

Source: U.S. Department of Labor, *Employment and Earnings,* October 1994.

and the supply relatively small, wages will be high. Though it is a good starting point, this supply and demand explanation is not particularly revealing. To discover *why* supply and demand conditions differ in various labor markets, we must probe those factors underlying the supply and demand of particular types of labor.

If (1) all workers were homogeneous, (2) all jobs were equally attractive to workers, and (3) labor markets were perfectly competitive, all workers would receive precisely the same wage rate. This is not a startling statement. It suggests that in an economy having one type of labor and in effect one type of job, competition would result in a single wage rate for all workers. The statement is important only because it suggests reasons why wage rates do differ in practice. (1) Workers are not homogeneous. They differ in abilities and in education and training and, as a result, fall into noncompeting occupational groups. (2) Jobs vary in attractiveness; the nonmonetary aspects of various jobs are not the same. (3) Labor markets are characterized by imperfections.

Noncompeting Groups

Workers are not homogeneous; they differ in their mental and physical capacities *and* in their education and training. At any point in time the labor force can be thought of as falling into many **noncompeting groups,** each composed of one or several occupations for which the members of this group qualify.

Ability Few workers have the abilities to be brain surgeons, concert violinists, research chemists, entertainers, or professional athletes. The result is that supplies of these particular types of labor are very small in relation to the demand for them and consequently wages and salaries are high. These and similar groups do not compete with one another nor with other skilled or semiskilled workers. The violinist does not compete with the surgeon, nor does the garbage collector or retail clerk compete with either the violinist or the surgeon.

The concept of noncompeting groups is a flexible one; it can be applied to various subgroups and even to specific individuals in a given group. Some especially skilled surgeons can command higher fees than their run-of-the-mill colleagues performing the same operations. Shaquille O'Neal, Hakeem Olajuwon, Patrick Ewing, and a few others demand and get salaries many times more than the average profes-

sional basketball player. Their less-talented colleagues are only imperfect substitutes.

Investing in Human Capital: Education Noncompeting groups—and therefore wage differentials—also exist because of differing amounts of investment in human capital. A **human capital investment** refers to expenditures on education and training which improve the skills and therefore, the productivity of workers. Like business purchases of machinery and equipment, expenditures which increase a worker's productivity can be regarded as investments because *current* expenditures or costs are incurred with the intention that these costs will be more than compensated for by an enhanced *future* flow of earnings.

Figure 28-9 indicates, first, that individuals with larger investments in education do achieve higher incomes during their careers than those who have made smaller education investments. A second point is that the earnings of more-educated workers rise more rapidly than those of less-educated workers. The pri-

FIGURE 28-9 **Education levels and individual income**
Investment in education yields a return in the form of an income differential enjoyed throughout one's work-life. (*U.S. Bureau of the Census. Data are for males in 1991.*)

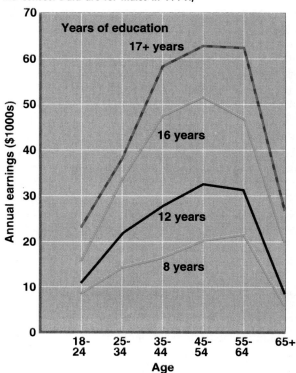

mary reason for this is that more-educated workers usually get more on-the-job training.

Although education yields higher incomes, it also entails costs. A college education involves not only direct costs (tuition, fees, books) but also indirect or opportunity costs (forgone earnings). Does the higher pay received by more-educated workers compensate for these costs? The answer is "Yes." Rates of return are estimated to be 10 to 13 percent for investing in a secondary education and 8 to 10 percent for higher education. One generally accepted estimate is that each year of schooling raises a worker's wage by about 8 percent. Also, in recent years the pay gap between college graduates and high school graduates has increased sharply. Since 1980 the college–high school pay gap has risen from 37 to 66 percent for women and from 34 to 60 percent for men.

Compensating Differences

If a group of workers in a particular noncompeting group is equally capable of performing several different jobs, you might expect the wage rate would be identical for each of these jobs. Not so. A group of high school graduates may be equally capable of becoming bank clerks or unskilled construction workers. But these jobs pay different wages. In virtually all localities, construction laborers receive higher wages than bank clerks.

These differences can be explained on the basis of the *nonmonetary aspects* of the two jobs. The construction job involves dirty hands, a sore back, the hazard of accidents, and irregular employment, both seasonally and cyclically. The banking job means a white shirt, pleasant air-conditioned surroundings, and little fear of injury or layoff. Other things equal, it is easy to see why workers would rather pick up a deposit slip than a shovel. That's why contractors must pay higher wages than banks pay to compensate for the unattractive nonmonetary aspects of construction jobs. These wage differentials are called **compensating differences** because they must be paid to compensate for nonmonetary differences in various jobs.

Market Imperfections

The notion of noncompeting groups helps explain wage differentials between various jobs for which limited numbers of workers are qualified. Compensating differences aid in understanding wage differentials on certain jobs for which workers in the same noncompeting group are equally qualified. Market imperfections in the form of various immobilities help explain wage differences paid on identical jobs.

1   Geographic Immobilities   Workers take root geographically. They are reluctant to leave friends, relatives, and associates, to force their children to change schools, to sell their houses, and to incur the costs and inconveniences of adjusting to a new job and a new community. Geographic mobility is likely to be low for older workers with seniority rights and substantial claims to pension payments upon retirement. Similarly, an optometrist or dental hygienist qualified to practice in one state may not meet licensing requirements of other states, so his or her ability to move geographically is impeded. Also, workers who may be willing to move may be ignorant of job opportunities and wage rates in other areas. As Adam Smith noted over two centuries ago, "A man is of all sorts of luggage the most difficult to be transported." The reluctance or inability of workers to move enables geographic wage differentials for the same occupation to persist.

2   Institutional Immobilities   Geographic immobilities may be reinforced by artificial restrictions on mobility imposed by institutions. We have noted that craft unions find it to their advantage to restrict membership. After all, if carpenters and bricklayers become plentiful, the wages they can command will decline. Thus the low-paid nonunion carpenter of Brush, Colorado, may be willing to move to Chicago in the pursuit of higher wages. But his chances of successfully doing so are slim. He may be unable to get a union card; and no card, no job. The professions impose similar artificial restraints. For example, at most universities individuals lacking advanced degrees are automatically not considered for employment as teachers. Apart from competence as a teacher and command of the subject matter, a "union card"—an M.A. or preferably a Ph.D.—is the first requisite for employment.

3   Sociological Immobilities: Discrimination   We must acknowledge sociological immobilities in the form of discrimination. Despite legislation to the contrary, women workers frequently receive less pay than men on the same job. The consequence of racial and ethnic discrimination is that blacks, Hispanics, and other minorities historically have been forced to accept lower wages on given jobs than fellow workers receive.

A final point: It is typical that all three considerations—noncompeting groups, compensating differences, and market imperfections—help explain actual wage differentials. For example, the differential between the wages of a physician and a construction worker is largely explainable on the basis of noncompeting groups. Physicians fall into a noncompeting group where, because of mental and financial requisites to entry, the supply of labor is small in relation to demand, and wages are therefore high. In construction work, where mental and financial prerequisites are much less significant, the supply of labor is great in relation to demand and wages are low when compared with those of physicians. However, were it not for the unpleasantness of the construction worker's job and the fact that his craft union pursues restrictive membership policies, the differential would probably be even greater than it is.

QUICK REVIEW 28-2

■ Unions may achieve above-competitive wage rates by increasing labor demand, restricting supply (exclusive unionism) or by bargaining (inclusive unionism).

■ Bilateral monopoly occurs where a monopsonist bargains with an inclusive union. Wages and employment are indeterminant in this situation.

■ Proponents of the minimum wage argue that it is an effective means of assisting the working poor; critics contend that it is poorly targeted and causes unemployment.

■ Wage differentials are attributable to differences in worker abilities and education, nonmonetary differences in jobs, and market imperfections.

PAY AND PERFORMANCE

The models of wage determination presented in this chapter presume that worker compensation is always a standard hourly wage rate, for example, $5, $10, or $25 per hour. In fact, pay schemes are often more complex in composition and purpose. For example, many workers receive annual salaries rather than hourly pay. Also, pay plans are frequently designed by employers to elicit some desired level of performance by workers.

The Principal–Agent Problem

Firms hire workers because workers help produce goods or services which firms can sell for a profit. Workers may be thought of as the firm's *agents*—parties who are hired to advance the interests of the firm. Firms may be regarded as *principals* or parties who hire others (agents) to help them achieve their goals. Principals and their agents have a common interest. The principal's (firm's) objective is profits, and agents (workers) are willing to help firms earn profits in return for payments of wage income.

But the interests of firms and workers are not identical and when these interests diverge a so-called **principal–agent problem** arises. Agents might increase their utility by **shirking** on the job, that is, by providing less than agreed-upon worker effort or by taking unauthorized work breaks. Workers may improve their well-being by increasing their leisure—through reduced work effort and work time—without forfeiting income. The night watchman in a warehouse may leave work early or spend time reading a novel as opposed to making the assigned rounds. A salaried manager may spend much time out of the office, visiting about personal interests with friends, rather than attending to company business.

Firms (principals) have a profit incentive to reduce or eliminate shirking. One option is to monitor workers; but monitoring is often difficult and costly. Hiring another worker to supervise or monitor our night watchman might double the costs of having a secure warehouse. Another way of resolving a principal–agent problem is through some sort of **incentive pay plan** which ties worker compensation more closely to worker output or performance. Such incentive pay schemes include piece rates, commissions and royalties, bonuses and profit sharing, seniority pay, and efficiency wages.

Piece Rates   *Piece rates* are compensation paid in proportion to the number of units of output a worker produces. By paying fruit pickers by the bushel and typists by the page, the principal need not be concerned with shirking or monitoring costs.

Commissions and Royalties   Unlike piece rates, which link pay to units of output, commissions and royalties tie pay to the *value* of sales. Realtors, insurance agents, stockbrokers and retail salespersons commonly receive *commissions* based on the monetary value of their sales. *Royalties* are paid to record-

LAST WORD

PAY AND PERFORMANCE IN PROFESSIONAL BASEBALL

Professional baseball has provided an interesting "laboratory" in which the predictions of wage theory have been empirically tested.

Until 1976 professional baseball players were bound to a single team through the so-called "reserve clause" which prevented players from selling their talents on the open (competitive) market. Stated differently, the reserve clause conferred monopsony power on the team which originally drafted a player. As we saw in this chapter, labor market theory would lead us to predict that this monopsony power would permit teams to pay wages less than a player's marginal revenue product (MRP). However, since 1976 major league players have been able to become "free agents" at the end of their sixth season of play and at that time can sell their services to any team. Orthodox theory suggests that free agents should be able to increase their salaries and bring them more closely into accord with their MRPs. Research confirms both predictions.

Scully* found that before baseball players were legally able to become free agents their salaries were substantially below their MRPs. Scully estimated a player's MRP as follows. First, he determined the relationship between a team's winning percentage and its revenue. Then he estimated the relationship between various possible measures of player productivity and a team's winning percentage. He found the ratio of strikeouts to walks for pitchers and the slugging averages for hitters (all nonpitchers) to be the best indicators of a player's contribution to the win-

*Gerald W. Scully, "Pay and Performance in Major League Baseball," *American Economic Review,* December 1974, pp. 915–930.

ning percentage. These two estimates were combined to calculate the contribution of a player to a team's total revenue.

Scully calculated that prior to free agency the estimated MRPs of both pitchers and hitters were substantially greater than player salaries. Table 1 shows the relevant data for pitchers. Column 1 indicates pitcher performance as measured by lifetime strikeout-to-walk ratio. A higher ratio indicates a better pitcher. Column 2 indicates MRP after player training costs are taken into account and column 3 shows actual average salary for pitchers in each quality class. As expected, salaries were far less than MRPs. Even the lowest quality pitchers (those with a 1.60 strikeout-to-walk ratio) received on the average salaries amounting to only about 54 percent of their MRPs. Observe, too, that the gap between MRP and average salary widens as player quality improves. "Star" players were exploited more than other players. The best pitchers received salaries which were only about 21 percent of their MRPs, according to Scully. The same general results apply to hitters. For example,

---

ing artists and authors based on a certain percentage of sales revenue.

Bonuses and Profit Sharing *Bonuses* are payments beyond one's annual salary based on some factor such as performance of the individual worker or the firm. A professional baseball player may receive bonuses for a high batting average, the number of home runs, or the number of runs batted in. A manager may receive bonuses based on the profit performance of his or her unit. *Profit sharing* allo-

cates a specified percentage of a firm's profits to its employees.

Seniority Pay Wages and earnings generally increase with job tenure. One recent explanation of this is that it is advantageous to both workers and employers to pay junior workers less than their MRPs and senior workers more than their MRPs. Such *seniority pay* may be an inexpensive way of reducing shirking when monitoring costs are high. If shirkers are discovered and dismissed, they will forgo the high

TABLE 1   Marginal revenue products and salaries of professional baseball pitchers, pre-free agency 1968–1969

(1) Performance*	(2) Marginal revenue product	(3) Salary
1.60	$ 57,600	$31,100
1.80	80,900	34,200
2.00	104,100	37,200
2.20	127,400	40,200
2.40	150,600	43,100
2.60	173,900	46,000
2.80	197,100	48,800
3.00	220,300	51,600
3.20	243,600	54,400
3.40	266,800	57,100
3.60	290,100	59,800

*Strikeout-to-walk ratio.
Source: Scully, op. cit., p. 923.

the least productive hitters on the average received a salary equal to about 37 percent of their MRPs.

Sommers and Quinton† have assessed the economic fortunes of fourteen players who constituted the "first family" of free agents. In accordance with the predictions of labor market theory, their research indicates that the competitive bidding of free agency brought the salaries of free agents more closely into accord with their estimated MRPs. The data for the five free-agent pitchers are shown in Table 2 where we find a surprisingly close correspondence between estimated MRPs and salaries. Although MRP and salary differences are larger for hitters, Sommers and

†Paul M. Sommers and Noel Quinton, "Pay and Performance in Major League Baseball: The Case of the First Family of Free Agents," *Journal of Human Resources,* Summer 1982, pp. 426–435.

TABLE 2   Estimated marginal revenue products and player costs, first class of free agents 1977

(1) Pitcher	(2) Marginal revenue product	(3) Annual contract cost*
Garland	$282,091	$230,000
Gullett	340,846	349,333
Fingers	303,511	332,000
Campbell	205,639	210,000
Alexander	166,203	166,667

*Includes annual salary, bonuses, the value of insurance policies and deferred payments, etc.
Source: Sommers and Quinton, op. cit., p. 432.

Quinton conclude that the overturn of the monopsonistic reserve clause "has forced owners into a situation where there is a greater tendency to pay players in relation to their contribution to team revenues."

How have baseball team owners reacted to the escalating salaries under free agency? In early 1986 the players' union filed a grievance charging that the twenty-six professional baseball clubs had acted in concert against signing any of the players who became free agents in 1985. In fact, of the sixty-two players who became free agents in 1985, only two had signed contracts with a different team before the season began. In effect, the players charged that owners had attempted to restore some of the monopsony power which they previously had possessed. Such collusive action is illegal because it violates the basic collective bargaining agreement which exists between players and owners. In the fall of 1987 an arbitrator ruled that baseball owners had conspired to "destroy" the free-agent market and in 1990 the courts ordered club owners to pay $102.5 million in lost salaries to players.

seniority pay accruing in later years of employment. From the firm's standpoint, turnover is reduced because workers who quit will forfeit the high seniority pay. Less turnover means a more experienced and therefore more productive work force. The increased productivity of workers is the source of extra sales revenue from which the firm and the workers, respectively, enhance their profits and lifetime pay. Young workers may accept wages which are initially less than their MRPs for the opportunity to participate in a labor market where in time the reverse will

be true. The increased work effort and higher average productivity may be appealing to workers because these factors are the source of higher lifetime earnings.

Efficiency Wages   The notion of *efficiency wages* suggests employers might get greater effort from their workers by paying them relatively high, above-equilibrium wage rates. Glance back at Figure 28-3 which shows a competitive labor market where the equilibrium wage rate is $6. What if an employer decided to pay an above-equilibrium wage of $7 per hour? Rather than put the firm at a cost disadvantage compared to rival firms paying only $6, the higher wage *might* improve worker effort and productivity so that unit labor costs actually fall. For example, if each worker produces 10 units of output per hour at the $7 wage rate compared to only 6 units at the $6 wage rate, unit labor costs will be only $.70 (= $7 ÷ 10) for the high-wage firm as opposed to $1.00 (= $6 ÷ 6) for firms paying the equilibrium wage.

An above-equilibrium wage might enhance worker efficiency in several ways. The higher wage permits the firm to attract higher-quality workers. Worker morale should be higher. Turnover will be reduced, resulting in a more experienced work force, greater worker productivity, and also lower recruitment and training costs. Because the opportunity cost of losing a high-wage job is greater, workers are likely to put forth their best efforts with less supervision and monitoring.

Two Addenda

Our discussion of pay-for-performance schemes requires two additional comments.

Solutions as Problems "Solutions" to principal–agent problems sometimes yield undesirable results. First example: In the early 1990s Sears offered its service advisors at its auto-repair shops sales commissions based on the dollar amounts of parts and services recommended and bought. The idea was to align the interest of these service advisors with the profit interest of the corporation. By aggressively identifying and fixing needed repairs, the service managers could enhance Sears' profit while adding to their own total pay.

But the plan backfired! In 1992 government officials detected widespread fraud in Sears' auto shops in California. They found that many Sears service representatives were recommending unneeded repairs, such as new springs and shock absorbers, to increase sales and commissions. This fraud in California resulted in nationwide negative publicity, government legal action, and a large loss of automotive business at Sears.

Second example: In 1987 workers at General Motor's factory in Flint, Michigan stamped out body panels for GM cars. As a cooperative gesture and to promote teamwork, GM managers decided to allow 500 workers to leave the factory each day without punching out their timecards. Workers were free to leave when they finished producing the day's quota of parts. To GM's surprise, the new incentive caused productivity to skyrocket. Collectively, workers—some of whom had worked at GM for twenty years—found new ways to meet their joint quota by noon!

The problem arose when GM management, perceiving itself as paying a full-day's pay for what it now considered to be a half-day's work, upped the daily production quota. Demoralized workers felt betrayed by management and threatened a strike.

Equilibrium Revisited Pay-for-performance plans also tell us that labor-market equilibrium is often more complex than the simple determination of wage rates and employment (Figures 28-3 through 28-8). When principal–agent problems involving shirking and monitoring costs arise, decisions must also be made with respect to the most effective compensation scheme. When we recognize that work effort and productivity are related to the form of worker compensation, the choice of pay plan is not a matter of indifference to the employer, the employee, or society.

CHAPTER SUMMARY

1 Wages are the price paid per unit of time for the services of labor.

2 The long-run growth of real wages is closely correlated with labor productivity.

3 Global comparisons suggest that real wages in the United States are relatively high, but not the highest, internationally.

4 Real wages and earnings have been stagnant for the past fifteen years.

5 Specific wage rates depend on the structure of the particular labor market. In a competitive market the equilibrium wage rate and level of employment are determined at the intersection of labor supply and demand.

6 Under monopsony the marginal resource cost curve will lie above the resource supply curve, because the monopsonist must bid up wage rates in hiring extra workers and pay that higher wage to *all* workers. The monopsonist will hire fewer workers than under competitive conditions to achieve less-than-competitive wage rates (costs) and thereby greater profits.

7 A union may raise competitive wage rates by **a** increasing the derived demand for labor **b** restricting the supply of labor through exclusive unionism, and **c** directly enforcing an above-equilibrium wage rate through inclusive unionism.

8 In many industries the labor market takes the form of bilateral monopoly, in which a strong union "sells" labor to a monopsonistic employer. The wage rate outcome of this labor market model is logically indeterminate.

9 On the average, unionized workers realize wage rates 10 to 15 percent higher than comparable nonunion workers.

10 Economists disagree about the desirability of the minimum wage as an antipoverty mechanism. While it causes unemployment for some low-income workers, it raises the incomes of others who retain their jobs.

11 Wage differentials are largely explainable in terms of **a** noncompeting groups arising from differences in the capacities and education of different groups of workers; **b** compensating wage differences, that is, wage differences which must be paid to offset nonmonetary differences in jobs; and **c** market imperfections in the form of geographic, artificial, and sociological immobilities.

12 The principal–agent problem arises when workers shirk—provide less-than-expected effort. Firms may combat this by monitoring workers or by creating incentive pay schemes which link worker compensation to effort.

TERMS AND CONCEPTS

nominal and real
  wages
competitive labor
  market
exclusive and inclusive
  unionism

monopsony
occupational licensing
bilateral monopoly
minimum wage
wage differentials

noncompeting groups
human capital
  investment
compensating
  differences

principal–agent
  problem
shirking
incentive pay plan

QUESTIONS AND STUDY SUGGESTIONS

1 Explain why the general level of wages is higher in the United States than in most foreign nations. What is the most important single factor underlying the long-run increase in average real wage rates in the United States?

2 What factors might explain the stagnation of real wages in the past fifteen years?

3 *Key Question* *Describe wage determination in a labor market in which workers are unorganized and many firms actively compete for the services of labor. Show this situation graphically, using W_1 to indicate the equilibrium wage rate and Q_1 to show the number of workers hired by the firms as a group. Compare the labor supply curve of the individual firm with that of the total market and explain any differences. In the firm's diagram identify total revenue, total wage cost, and revenue available for the payment of nonlabor resources.*

4 *Key Question* *Complete the accompanying labor supply table for a firm hiring labor competitively.*

Units of labor	Wage rate	Total labor cost (wage bill)	Marginal resource (labor) cost
0	$14	$___ 0	$___ 0
1	14	___ 14	___ 14
2	14	___ 28	___ 14
3	14	___ 42	___ 14
4	14	___ 56	___ 14
5	14	___ 70	___ 14
6	14	___ 84	___ 14

a *Show graphically the labor supply and marginal resource (labor) cost curves for this firm. Explain the relationships of these curves to one another.*

b *Compare these data with the labor demand data of question 2 in Chapter 27. What will the equilibrium wage rate and level of employment be? Explain.*

5 Using the diagram you have drawn in answering question 3, suppose that the formerly competing firms form an employers' association which hires labor as a monopsonist would. Describe verbally the impact upon wage rates and employment. Adjust the graph, showing the monopsonistic wage rate and employment level as W_2 and Q_2, respectively. Using this monopsony model, explain why hospital administrators sometimes complain about a "shortage" of nurses. Do you have suggestions for correcting any such shortage?

6 *Key Question* *Assume a firm is a monopsonist which can hire its first worker for $6, but must increase the wage rate by $3 to attract each successive worker. Show the labor supply and marginal labor cost curves graphically and explain their relationships to one another. Compare these data with the labor demand data of question 2 for Chapter 27. What will be the equilibrium wage rate and the level of employment? Why do these differ from your answer to question 4?*

7 Describe the techniques which unions might employ to raise wages. Evaluate the desirability of each from the viewpoint of **a** the union, and **b** society as a whole. Explain: "Craft unionism directly restricts the supply of labor; industrial unionism relies upon the market to restrict the number of jobs."

8 *Key Question* *Assume a monopsonistic employer is paying a wage rate of W_m and hiring Q_m workers, as indicated in Figure 28-8. Now suppose that an industrial union is formed and that it forces the employer to accept a wage rate of W_c. Explain verbally and graphically why in this instance the higher wage rate will be accompanied by an increase in the number of workers hired.*

9 A critic of the minimum wage has contended, "The effects of minimum wage legislation are precisely the opposite of those predicted by those who support them. Government can legislate a minimum wage, but cannot force employers to hire unprofitable workers. In fact, minimum wages cause unemployment among low-wage workers who can least afford to give up their small incomes." Do you agree? What bearing does the elasticity of labor demand have on this assessment? What factors might possibly offset the potential unemployment effects of a minimum wage?

10 On the average do union workers receive higher wages than comparable nonunion workers?

11 What are the basic considerations which help explain wage differentials? What long-run effect would a substantial increase in safety for underground coal miners have on their wage rates in comparison to other workers?

12 "Many of the lowest-paid people in society—for example, short-order cooks—also have relatively poor working conditions. Hence, the notion of compensating wage differentials is disproved." Do you agree? Explain.

13 What is meant by investment in human capital? Use this concept to explain **a** wage differentials, and **b** the long-run rise of real wage rates in the United States.

14 What is the principal–agent problem? Have you ever worked in a setting where this problem has arisen? If so, do you think increased monitoring would have eliminated the problem? Why don't firms simply hire more supervisors to eliminate shirking?

15 Professional baseball players are paid for only the first four games of the potential seven games of the World Series. Explain.

16 The notion of efficiency wages suggests that an above-equilibrium wage rate will elicit a more-than-offsetting increase in worker productivity. By what specific means might the higher wage cause worker productivity to rise? Why might young workers accept a seniority pay plan under which they are initially paid less than their MRPs?

17 (Last Word) Use your understanding of competitive and monopsonistic labor markets to explain the changes in professional baseball players' salaries caused by free agency.

THE PRICING AND EMPLOYMENT OF RESOURCES: RENT, INTEREST, AND PROFITS

In urban areas such as Tokyo, an acre of land may sell for more than $85 million. An acre of desert may cost $650,000 along the Las Vegas casino strip, while an acre of land in the middle of the Nevada desert can be bought for almost $60. *How do land prices and rents get established?*

If you put money in a three-month certificate of deposit in early 1991, you probably received an interest rate of about 7 percent. One year later that CD paid only about 3.7 percent. *What factors determine interest rates and explain why they change?*

The news media continually document the profit and loss performance of firms and industries. The makers of Nintendo and Sega video games have reaped large profits. And the firm which produces AZT, a drug which prolongs the life of AIDs patients, doubled its profits over a three-year period. Meanwhile, automakers have experienced wide swings in their earnings and airlines have recently suffered record losses. *What are the sources of profits and losses? What functions do they serve?*

Emphasis in the previous two chapters was on labor markets because wages and salaries account for about three-fourths of our national income. In this chapter we focus on three other sources of income—rent, interest, and profits—which compose the remaining one-fourth of national income.

ECONOMIC RENT

To most people "rent" means the money one must pay for a two-bedroom apartment or a dormitory room. To the business executive, "rent" is a payment made for use of a factory building, machinery, or warehouse facilities. These commonsense definitions of rent can be confusing and ambiguous. Dormitory room rent, for example, includes interest on the money capital the university has borrowed to finance the dormitory's construction, wages for custodial service, utility payments, and so forth.

Economists use "rent" in a narrower, less ambiguous sense: **Economic rent** *is the price paid for use of land and other natural resources which are completely fixed in total supply.* The unique supply conditions of land and other natural resources—their fixed supply—make rental payments distinguishable from wage, interest, and profit payments.

Let's examine this feature and some of its implications through supply and demand analysis. We'll assume, first, that all land is the same grade or quality —each available acre of land is equally productive. Suppose, too, that all land has just one use, being capable of producing just one product—say, corn. And assume that land is being rented in a competitive market—many corn farmers are demanding and many landowners are offering land in the market.

In Figure 29-1, SS indicates the supply of arable farmland available in the economy as a whole, and D_2 the demand of farmers for use of that land. As with all economic resources, demand is derived demand. It is downsloping because of the law of diminishing returns and because, for farmers as a group, product price must be reduced to sell additional units of output.

Perfectly Inelastic Supply

The unique feature of our analysis is on the supply side: For all practical purposes the supply of land is perfectly inelastic, as reflected in SS. Land has no production cost; it is a "free and nonreproducible gift of nature." The economy has so much land, and that's that. Of course, within limits any parcel of land can be made more usable by clearing, drainage, and irrigation. But these are capital improvements and not changes in the amount of land as such. Furthermore, such variations in the usability of land are a very small fraction of the total amount of land and do not undermine the basic argument that land and other natural resources are in virtually fixed supply.

Changes in Demand

The fixed nature of the supply of land means demand is the only active determinant of land rent; supply is passive. And what determines the demand for land? Those factors discussed in Chapter 27—the price of the product grown on the land, the productivity of land (which depends in part on the quantity and quality of the resources with which land is combined), and the prices of those other resources which are combined with land.

If in Figure 29-1, the demand for land should increase from D_2 to D_1 or decline from D_2 to D_3, land rent would change from R_2 to R_1 or R_3. But the amount of land supplied would remain unchanged at $0S$. Changes in economic rent will have no impact on the amount of land available; the supply of land is simply not augmentable. In technical terms, there is a large price effect and no quantity effect when the demand for land changes. If demand for land is only D_4, land rent will be zero; land will be a "free good" because it is not scarce enough in relation to demand for it to

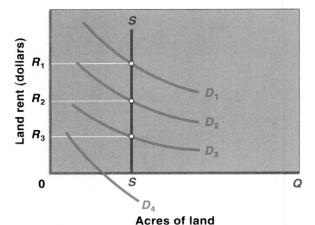

FIGURE 29-1   The determination of land rent
Because the supply of land and other natural resources is perfectly inelastic (SS), demand is the sole active determinant of land rent. An increase (D_2 to D_1) or decrease (D_2 to D_3) in demand will cause considerable changes in rent (R_2 to R_1 and R_2 to R_3). If demand is very small (D_4) relative to supply, land will be a "free good."

command a price. This situation was approximated in the free-land era of American history.

Figure 29-1 helps explain the astronomical Japanese land prices noted at the outset of this chapter. Japan's population is 120 million, roughly one-half that of the United States. Japan's land, however, is only about 4 percent of the United States'. Furthermore, habitable land in Japan is roughly 1/60th that of the United States. With these numbers in mind, it is easier to comprehend why a square meter of land in central Toyko was priced at about $279,000 in 1990.[1]

Land Rent Is a Surplus

The perfect inelasticity of the supply of land must be contrasted with the relative elasticity of such property resources as apartment buildings, machinery, and warehouses. These resources are *not* fixed in total supply. A higher price will give entrepreneurs the incentive to construct and offer larger quantities of these property resources. Conversely, a decline in their prices will induce suppliers to allow existing facilities to depreciate and not be replaced. The same reasoning applies to the total supply of labor. Within

---

[1]This paragraph is based on Douglas Stone and William T. Ziemba, "Land and Stock Prices in Japan," *Journal of Economic Perspectives,* Summer 1993, p. 150.

limits, a higher average level of wages will induce more workers to enter the labor force, and lower wages will cause them to drop out. The supplies of nonland resources are upsloping which means the prices paid to such resources perform an **incentive function.** A high price provides an incentive to offer more; a low price, to offer less.

Not so with land. Rent serves no incentive function, because the total supply of land is fixed. If rent is $10,000, $500, $1, or $0 per acre, the same amount of land will be available to society for production. Rent could be eliminated without affecting the productive potential of the economy. For this reason economists consider rent to be a *surplus*—a payment which is not necessary to ensure that land will be available to the economy as a whole.[2]

A Single Tax on Land

If land is a free gift of nature, costs nothing to produce, and would be available even without rental payments, why should rent be paid to those who by historical accident, by inheritance, or by crook happen to be landowners? Socialists have long argued that all land rents are unearned incomes. They argue land should be nationalized—owned by the state—so that any payments for its use can be used by the government to further the well-being of the entire population rather than being used by a landowning minority.

Henry George's Proposal   In the United States, criticism of rental payments has taken the form of a **single-tax movement** which gained much support in the late nineteenth century. Spearheaded by Henry George's provocative book *Progress and Poverty* (1879), this reform movement maintained that economic rent could be taxed away completely without impairing the available supply of land or, therefore, the productive potential of the economy as a whole.

George observed that as population grew and the geographic frontier closed, landowners enjoyed larger and larger rents from their landholdings. These in-

crements in rent were the result of a growing demand for a resource whose supply was perfectly inelastic; some landlords were receiving fabulously high incomes, not through rendering any productive effort, but solely from holding advantageously located land. Henry George stated that these increases in land rent belonged to the economy as a whole; he held that land rents should be taxed away and spent for public uses.

Indeed, George held that there was no reason to tax away only 50 percent of the landowner's unearned rental income. Why not take 70 or 90 or 99 percent? In seeking popular support for his ideas on land taxation, Henry George proposed that taxes on rental income be the *only* tax levied by government.

George's case for taxing land was based not only on equity or fairness, but also on efficiency grounds. In particular, unlike virtually every other tax, a tax on land does *not* alter or distort the use or allocation of land. For example, a tax on wages may reduce after-tax wages and weaken incentives to work. An individual who decides to participate in the labor force at a $6 before-tax wage rate may decide to drop from the labor force and go on welfare when an income tax reduces the after-tax wage rate to $4.50. Similarly, a property tax on buildings lowers returns to investors in such property, causing them in time to reallocate their money capital toward other investments. But no such reallocations of resources occur when land is taxed. The most profitable use for land before it is taxed remains the most profitable use after the tax is imposed. Of course, a landlord could withdraw land from production when a tax is imposed, but this would mean no rental income at all.

Criticisms   Critics of the single tax on land say:
1   Current levels of government spending are such that a land tax alone would not bring in enough revenue; it cannot be considered realistically as a *single* tax.
2   Most income payments comprise elements of interest, rent, wages, and profits. Land is typically improved in some manner by productive effort, and economic rent cannot be readily disentangled from payments for capital improvements. As a practical matter, it would be difficult to determine how much of any given income payment is actually rent.
3   The question of unearned income goes beyond land and land ownership. Many people other than landowners benefit from receipt of "unearned" income associated with a growing economy. For example, consider the capital gains income received by

---

[2]A portion—in some instances a major portion—of wage and salary incomes may be a surplus in that these incomes exceed the minimum amount necessary to keep an individual in his or her current line of work. For example, in 1994 the *average* salary paid to major league baseball players was about $1,189,000 per year. In the next best occupational option as, say, a college coach, a player might earn only $40,000 or $50,000 per year. Most of his current income is therefore a surplus. In the twilight of their careers, professional athletes sometimes accept sizable salary reductions rather than seek employment in alternative occupations.

someone who, some twenty or twenty-five years ago, chanced to purchase (or inherit) stock in a firm which has experienced rapid growth. How is this income different from the rental income of the landowner?

4 Historically a piece of land is likely to have changed ownership many times. *Former* owners may have been the beneficiaries of past increases in land rent. It is hardly fair to tax *current* owners who paid the competitive market price for land.

Productivity Differences

Thus far we have assumed all units of land are of the same grade. This is plainly not so. Different acres vary greatly in productivity. These productivity differences stem primarily from differences in soil fertility and such climatic factors as rainfall and temperature. These factors explain why Iowa soil is excellently suited to corn production, the plains of eastern Colorado are much less so, and desert wasteland of New Mexico is incapable of corn production. These productivity differences will be reflected in resource demand. Competitive bidding by farmers will establish a high rent for the very productive Iowa land. Less productive Colorado land will command a much lower rent, and New Mexico land no rent at all.

Location may be equally important in explaining differences in land rent. Other things equal, renters will pay more for a unit of land which is strategically located with respect to materials, labor, and customers than for a unit of land whose location is remote from these markets. Witness the extremely high land rents in large metropolitan areas.

The rent differentials arising from quality differences in land can be seen by viewing Figure 29-1 from a slightly different perspective. Suppose, as before, that only corn can be produced on four grades of land, *each* of which is available in the fixed amount $0S$. When combined with identical amounts of capital, labor, and other cooperating resources, the productivity—or, more specifically, the marginal revenue productivity—of each grade of land is reflect in demand curves D_1, D_2, D_3, and D_4. Grade 1 land is the most productive, as reflected in D_1, whereas grade 4 is the least productive, as is shown by D_4. The resulting economic rents for grades 1, 2, and 3 land will be R_1, R_2, and R_3 respectively, the rent differentials mirroring differences in productivity of the three grades of land. Grade 4 land is so poor in quality that it would not pay farmers to bring it fully into production; it would be a "free" and only partially used resource.

Alternative Uses and Costs

We have also supposed that land has only one use. Actually, we know land normally has alternative uses. An acre of Iowa farm land may be useful in raising not only corn, but also wheat, oats, barley, and cattle; or it may be useful as a house or factory site.

This indicates that, although land is a free gift of nature and has no production cost from the viewpoint of society as a whole, the rental payments of individual producers are *costs*. The total supply of land will be available to society even if no rent is paid for its use. But, from the standpoint of individual firms and industries, land has alternative uses, and therefore payments must be made by firms and industries to attract that land from those other uses. Such payments by definition are costs. Again, the fallacy of composition (Chapter 1) has entered our discussion. From society's standpoint, there is no alternative but for land to be used by society. Therefore, to society, rents are a surplus, not a cost. But because land has alternative uses, the rental payments of corn farmers or any other individual user are a cost; such payments are required to attract land from alternative uses. *(Key Question 2)*

> ## QUICK REVIEW 29-1
>
> ■ Economic rent is the price paid for resources such as land, the supply of which is perfectly inelastic.
>
> ■ Land rent is a surplus in that land would be available to society even if rent were not paid.
>
> ■ The surplus nature of land rent was the basis for Henry George's single-tax movement.
>
> ■ Differential rents allocate land among alternative uses.

INTEREST

The interest rate is the price paid for the use of money. It is the amount of money that must be paid for the use of one dollar for a year.

1 Stated as Percentage Because it is paid in kind, interest is typically stated as a percentage of the amount of money borrowed rather than as an absolute amount. It is less clumsy to say that interest is 12 percent annually than that interest is "$120 per year per $1000." Furthermore, stating interest as a percentage makes it easy to compare interest paid on loans of different absolute amounts. By expressing interest as a

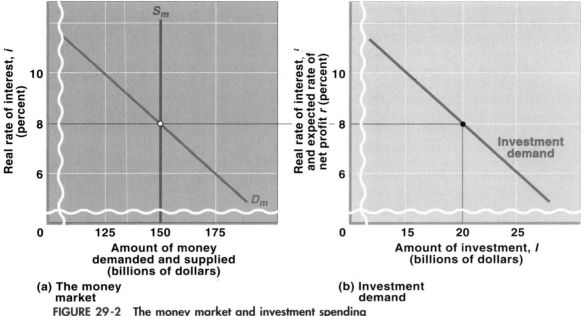

FIGURE 29-2   The money market and investment spending
The demand for and the supply of money determine the equilibrium interest rate. Projecting this rate off the investment curve determines aggregate investment expenditures. In this case an 8 percent interest rate results in $20 billion of investment.

percentage, we can immediately compare an interest payment of, say, $432 per year per $2880 and one of $1800 per year per $12,000. Both interest payments are 15 percent—which is not obvious from the absolute figures.

2   Money Not a Resource

Money is *not* an economic resource. As coins, paper currency, or checking accounts, money is not productive; it cannot produce goods and services. However, businesses "buy" the use of money, because money can be used to acquire capital goods—factory buildings, machinery, warehouses, and so forth. These facilities clearly do contribute to production. Thus, in hiring the use of money capital, business executives are ultimately buying the use of real capital goods.

Determining the Interest Rate

The theory of interest rate determination and its relationship to aggregate investment have been presented in Part 3 and need only be summarized here.[3]

---

[3]You should review the following sections: "The Demand for Money" in Chapter 13; "Monetary Policy, Real GDP, and the Price Level," in Chapter 15; and "Investment" in Chapter 9.

In Figure 29-2a we portray the money market which you first saw in Figure 15-2a. Recall that the total demand for money comprises **transactions** and **asset demands.** The transaction demand is directly related to the level of nominal GDP, while the asset demand is inversely related to the interest rate. Graphed against the interest rate, the total demand for money curve, D_m, is downsloping.

The money supply, S_m, is a vertical line on the assumption that the monetary authorities determine some stock of money (money supply) independent of the rate of interest. The intersection of the demand for money curve and the money supply curve determines the equilibrium rate of interest, which is 8 percent in this case.

The Investment Decision   Now consider Figure 29-2b which shows how the interest rate relates to the purchase of real capital. The investment-demand curve is constructed by aggregating all possible investment projects and ranking them from highest to lowest in terms of their expected rates of net profits. By projecting the equilibrium interest rate of Figure 29-2a off the investment-demand curve of Figure 29-2b, we determine the amount of investment the business sector will find profitable to undertake. All in-

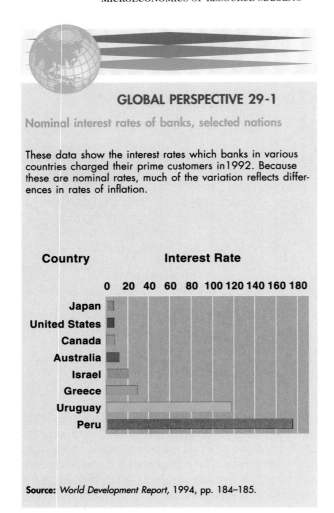

GLOBAL PERSPECTIVE 29-1

Nominal interest rates of banks, selected nations

These data show the interest rates which banks in various countries charged their prime customers in 1992. Because these are nominal rates, much of the variation reflects differences in rates of inflation.

Source: *World Development Report,* 1994, pp. 184–185.

vestment projects whose expected rate of net profits exceeds the equilibrium interest rate will be undertaken. In this case $20 billion is profitable.

Nominal and Real Interest Rates This discussion of the role of the interest rate in the investment decision assumes no inflation. If inflation occurs, we must distinguish between money or nominal interest rates and real interest rates. The **nominal interest rate** is the rate of interest expressed in dollars of current value. The **real interest rate** is the rate of interest expressed in dollars of constant or inflation-adjusted value. The real interest rate is the nominal rate less the rate of inflation.

An example will clarify this distinction. Suppose that the nominal interest rate and the rate of inflation are both 10 percent. If you borrow $100, you must pay back $110 a year from now. However, because of 10 percent inflation each of these 110 dollars will be worth 10 percent less. Hence, the real value or purchasing power of your $110 repayment at the end of the year is only $100. In inflation-adjusted dollars you are borrowing $100 and at year's end paying back $100. While the nominal interest rate is 10 percent, the real interest rate is zero. By subtracting the 10 percent inflation rate from the 10 percent nominal interest rate, we determine that the real interest rate is zero.

It's the real interest rate, not the nominal rate, that affects investment decision. Thus in the late 1970s and early 1980s nominal interest rates were unusually high; 12, 15, and 18 percent rates were common. You might think these high nominal rates would choke off investment; after all, there are relatively few investment opportunities promising an expected rate of return over 15 or 18 percent. But this didn't occur; investment spending was strong during this period. Anticipating continuing inflation, prospective investors planned to repay their borrowings in dollars of depreciated real value. While nominal interest rates were very high, inflation made real interest rates much lower and investment continued unabated. *The real interest rate, not the nominal rate, is critical to the investment decision. (Key Questions 4 and 6)*

Range of Rates

Although economists often speak in terms of a single interest rate, there is a cluster or range of interest rates. Table 29-1 lists many interest rates referred to in the media. These rates range from 5 to 16 percent. Why the differences?

1   Risk Varying degrees of risk on loans are important. The greater the chance the borrower will not repay the loan, the more interest the lender will charge to compensate for this risk.

2   Maturity The length or maturity of a loan also affects the interest rate. Other things equal, long-term loans usually command higher rates of interest than do short-term loans. The long-term lender suffers the inconvenience and possible financial sacrifice of forgoing alternative uses for his or her money for a greater period of time.

TABLE 29-1 Selected interest rates, August 1994

Type of interest rate	Annual percentage
30-year Treasury bond rate (Federal government security used to finance the public debt)	7.52%
90-day Treasury bill rate (Federal government security used to finance the public debt)	4.62
Prime interest rate (Interest rate charge by banks to their best corporate customers)	7.75
30-year mortgage rate (Fixed-interest rate on loans for houses)	7.67
4-year automobile loan rate (Interest rate for new autos by automobile finance companies)	9.92
Tax-exempt state and municipal bond rate (Interest rate paid on a low-risk bond issued by a state or local government)	5.85
Federal funds rate (Interest rate on overnight loans between banks)	4.66
Consumer credit card rate (Interest rate charged for credit card purchases)	16.15

Source: Federal Reserve Bulletin.

3 Loan Size Given two loans of equal length and risk, the interest rate usually will be somewhat higher on the smaller of the two loans because administrative costs of a large and a small loan are about the same absolutely.

4 Taxability Interest on certain state and municipal bonds is exempt from Federal income taxation. Because lenders are interested in their after-tax rate of interest, states and local governments can attract lenders even though they pay lower interest rates. Thus, a high-income lender may prefer a 6 percent interest rate on a tax-exempt municipal bond compared to an 8 percent taxable interest rate on a corporate bond.

5 Market Imperfections Market imperfections also explain some interest rate differentials. The small-town bank which monopolizes the local money market may charge high interest rates on consumer loans because households find it inconvenient and costly to "shop around" at banks in somewhat distant cities. The large corporation, on the other hand, can survey a number of rival investment houses in floating a new bond issue, and can secure the lowest obtainable rate.

Pure Rate of Interest

To circumvent the difficulties in discussing the whole structure of interest rates, economists talk of "the" interest rate or the **pure rate of interest.** This pure rate is best approximated by the interest paid on long-term, virtually riskless bonds such as the long-term bonds of the United States government (thirty-year Treasury bonds). This interest payment can be thought of as being made solely for the use of money over an extended time period, because risk and administrative costs are negligible and the interest on such securities is not distorted by market imperfections. In the fall of 1994 the pure interest rate was about $7\frac{1}{2}$ percent.

Role of the Interest Rate

The interest rate is an extremely important price as it simultaneously affects both the *level* and *composition* of investment goods production.

Interest and Domestic Output Figure 29-2b reminds us that, other things equal, a change in the equilibrium rate of interest will move businesses along the aggregate investment-demand curve, changing the level of investment and the equilibrium level of GDP. Indeed, the big message of Chapter 15 was that the interest rate is an "administered price." This means the monetary authorities purposely manipulate the money supply to influence the interest rate and thereby the levels of output, employment, and prices. Recall that an easy (low interest rate) monetary policy increases investment and expands the economy; a tight (high interest rate) monetary policy chokes off investment and constrains the economy.

Interest and the Allocation of Capital Prices are rationing devices. The interest rate is no exception; it allocates money capital and therefore physical capital to various firms and investment projects. It rations the available supply of money or liquidity to investment projects whose rate of return or expected profitability is sufficiently high to warrant payment of the going interest rate.

If the expected rate of net profits of additional physical capital in the computer industry is 12 percent and the required funds can be secured at an interest rate of 8 percent, the computer industry will be able, in terms of profit, to borrow and expand its capital facilities. If the expected rate of net profits of additional capital in the steel industry is expected to be only 6 percent, it will be unprofitable for this industry to accumulate more capital goods at the 8 percent interest rate. *The interest rate allocates money, and ultimately physical capital, to those industries in which it will be most productive and therefore most profitable. Such an allocation of capital goods is in the interest of society as a whole.*

But the interest rate does not ration capital to its most productive uses perfectly. Large oligopolistic borrowers are in a better position than competitive borrowers to pass interest costs on to consumers by virtue of their ability to control output and thereby manipulate their prices. Also, the size and prestige of large industrial concerns may help them obtain money capital on favorable terms, whereas the market for money capital screens out less-well-known firms whose profit expectations might be superior.

Application: Usury Laws

A number of states have passed *usury laws* which specify the maximum interest rate at which loans can be made. The purpose is to make credit more widely available to borrowers, particularly those with low incomes.

We can assess the impact of such legislation with the help of Figure 29-2a. The equilibrium interest rate is 8 percent, but now a usury law specifies that lenders cannot charge more than, say, 6 percent. The effects are as follows:

1 Nonmarket Rationing At 6 percent the quantity of money demanded exceeds the quantity supplied—there is a shortage of money. The market interest rate no longer rations money to borrowers, so lenders (banks) will do the rationing.. We can expect them to make loans to the most credit-worthy borrowers (wealthy, high-income people), which defeats the goal of usury laws. Low-income people excluded from the market may be forced to turn to unscrupulous loan sharks who charge interest rates several times above the market rate.

2 Gainers and Losers Credit-worthy borrowers will gain from usury laws because they will pay below-market interest rates. Lenders (ultimately bank stockholders) will be losers, receiving 6 rather than 8 percent on each dollar loaned.

3 Inefficiency We have just discussed how the equilibrium interest rate allocates money to those investments where the expected rate of return (productivity) is greatest. The rationing of credit under usury laws is less likely to provide financing for the most productive projects. Suppose Holly has a project so promising she would pay 8 percent for funds to finance it. Ben has a less promising investment and would only be willing to pay 6 percent for financing. If the market rationed funds, Holly's highly productive project would receive funds and Ben's would not. This allocation of funds is in the interest of both Holly and society. But with a 6 percent usury rate, there is a fifty-fifty chance Ben will be funded and Holly will not. Legal maximum interest rates may ration funds to less-productive uses.

> ## QUICK REVIEW 29-2
>
> ■ Interest is the price paid for the use of money.
>
> ■ The total demand for money comprises the transaction and asset demands; the money supply is determined by monetary policy.
>
> ■ There exists a range of interest rates which is influenced by risk, maturity, loan size, taxability, and market imperfections.
>
> ■ The equilibrium real interest rate affects the aggregate level of investment and therefore the level of domestic output; it also allocates money and real capital to specific industries and firms.
>
> ■ Usury laws which establish an interest rate ceiling below the market rate *a* deny credit to low-income people; *b* subsidize high-income borrowers and penalize lenders; and *c* diminish the efficiency with which investment funds are allocated.

ECONOMIC PROFITS

As with rent, economists define profits more narrowly than accountants do. To accountants, "profit" is what remains of a firm's total revenue after it has paid individuals and other firms for materials, capital, and labor supplied to the firm. To the economist, this conception is too broad and therefore is ambiguous. The difficulty is that the accountant's view of profits considers only **explicit costs:** the payments made by the firm to outsiders. It ignores **implicit costs:** the payments to similar resources owned and self-employed by a firm. In other words, this concept of profits fails to allow for implicit wage, rent, and interest costs. **Economic,** or **pure, profits** are what remain after *all* opportunity costs—both explicit and implicit wage, rent, and interest costs and a normal profit—have been subtracted from a firm's total revenue (Figure 22-1). Economic profits may be either positive or negative (losses).

For example, as the economist sees it, farmers who own their land and equipment and provide all their own labor grossly overstate their economic profits if they merely subtract their payments to outsiders for seed, insecticides, fertilizer, and gasoline from their total revenues. Actually, much or possibly all of what remain are the implicit rent, interest, and wage costs the farmers forgo in deciding to self-employ the resources they own rather than make them available in alternative employments. Interest on capital or wages for labor contributed by farmers are no more profits than are payments which would be made if outsiders had supplied these resources. Economic profits are a residual—the total revenue remaining after *all* costs are taken into account.

Role of the Entrepreneur

The economist views profits as the return to a very special type of human resource—entrepreneurial ability. The entrepreneur (Chapter 2) (1) takes the initiative to combine other resources in producing a good or service; (2) makes basic, nonroutine policy decisions for the firm; (3) introduces innovations in the form of new products or production processes; and (4) bears the economic risks associated with all these functions.

Part of the entrepreneur's return is called a **normal profit.** This is the minimum return or payment necessary to retain the entrepreneur in some specific line of production. This normal profit payment is a cost (Chapter 22). However, we know that a firm's total revenue may exceed its total costs (explicit, implicit, the latter inclusive of a normal profit). This extra or excess revenue above all costs is an economic, or pure, profit. This residual—which is *not* a cost because it is in excess of the normal profit required to

retain the entrepreneur in the industry—accrues to the entrepreneur. The entrepreneur is the residual claimant.

Economists offer several theories to explain why this residual or economic profit might occur. These explanations relate to:
1   The *risks* which the entrepreneur bears by functioning in a dynamic and therefore uncertain environment or by being innovative.
2   The possibility of attaining *monopoly power.*

Sources of Economic Profit

To understand economic profits and the entrepreneur's functions let's examine an artificial economic environment where pure profits would be zero. Then, by noting real-world deviations from this environment, we can find the sources of economic profit.

In a purely competitive static economy, pure profits would be zero. By a **static economy** we mean one in which basic data—resource supplies, technological knowledge, and consumer tastes—are constant and unchanging. A static economy is a changeless one in which all determinants of cost and supply data, on the one hand, and demand and revenue data, on the other, are constant.

Given the static nature of these data, the economic future is perfectly foreseeable; economic uncertainty is nonexistent. The outcome of price and production policies is accurately predictable. Furthermore, the static nature of such a society precludes innovational change. Under pure competition any pure profits (positive or negative) which might have existed initially in various industries will disappear with the entry or exodus of firms in the long run. All costs—explicit and implicit—will therefore be covered in the long run, leaving no residual in the form of pure profits (Figure 23-12).

The notion of zero economic profits in a static, competitive economy enhances our understanding of profits by suggesting that profits are linked to the dynamic nature of real-world capitalism and its accompanying uncertainty. Furthermore, it indicates that economic profits may arise from a source apart from the directing, innovating, risk-bearing functions of the entrepreneur. And that source is the presence of some degree of monopoly power.

Uncertainty, Risk, and Profits   In a dynamic economy the future is always uncertain. This means the entrepreneur must assume risks. Profits can be thought of in part as a reward for assuming these risks.

In linking pure profits with uncertainty and risk bearing, we must distinguish between risks which are insurable and those which are not. Some types of risks —fires, floods, theft, and accidents to employees— are measurable in that actuaries can accurately estimate their average occurrence. As a result, these risks are insurable. Firms can avoid, or at least provide for, them by incurring a known cost in the form of an insurance premium. It is the bearing of **uninsurable risks** which is a potential source of economic profits.

Basically, such uninsurable risks are uncontrollable and unpredictable changes in demand (revenue) and supply (cost) conditions facing the firm. Some of these uninsurable risks stem from unpredictable changes in the general economic environment or, more specifically, from the business cycle. Prosperity brings substantial windfall profits to most firms; depression means widespread losses. In addition, changes are constantly taking place in the structure of the domestic and world economies. Even in a full-employment, noninflationary economy, changes are always occurring in consumer tastes, technology, and resource supplies. Example: Technological change has been such that vinyl long-playing records have given way to cassettes and cassettes have partially lost their market to compact discs.

Such changes continually alter the revenue and cost data faced by individual firms and industries, leading to changes in the structure of the business population as favorably affected industries expand and adversely affected industries contract. Changes in government policies are pertinent at both levels. Appropriate fiscal and monetary policies of government may reverse a recession, whereas the establishment or elimination of a tariff may alter significantly the demand and revenue data of the affected industry.

The point is that profits and losses can be associated with the bearing of uninsurable risks stemming from cyclical, structural, and policy changes in the economy.

Uncertainty, Innovations, and Profits The uncertainties just discussed are external to the firm; they are beyond the control of the individual firm or industry. One other dynamic feature of capitalism—innovation—occurs at the initiative of the entrepreneur. Business firms deliberately introduce new methods of production and distribution to affect their costs fa-

vorably and new products to influence their revenue favorably. The entrepreneur purposely undertakes to upset existing cost and revenue data in a way which hopefully will be profitable.

But again, uncertainty enters the picture. Despite exhaustive market surveys, new products or modifications of existing products may be economic failures. Three-dimensional movies, the Yugo and Fiero automobiles, and disk cameras come readily to mind. Similarly, of the many new novels, textbooks, and tapes which appear every year, only a handful garner large profits. Nor is it known with certainty whether a new machine will actually provide the cost economies predicted for it while it is still in the blueprint stage. Innovations purposely undertaken by entrepreneurs entail uncertainty, just as do those changes in the economic environment over which an individual enterprise has no control. In a sense, innovation as a source of profits is merely a special case of risk bearing.

Under competition and in the absence of patent laws, profits from innovations will be temporary. Rival firms will imitate successful (profitable) innovations, competing away all economic profits. Nevertheless, innovational profits may always exist in a progressive economy as new, successful innovations replace older ones whose associated profits have been eroded or competed away.

Monopoly Profits Thus far, we have emphasized that profits are related to the uncertainties and uninsurable risks surrounding dynamic events which enterprises are exposed to or initiate themselves. The existence of monopoly in some form is a final source of economic profits. Because of its ability to restrict output and deter entry, a monopolist may persistently enjoy above-competitive prices and economic profits, if demand is strong relative to costs (Figure 24-4).

There are both a causal relationship and a distinction between uncertainty, on the one hand, and monopoly, on the other, as sources of profits. The causal relationship involves the fact that an entrepreneur can reduce uncertainty, or at least manipulate its effects, by achieving monopoly power. The competitive firm is unalterably exposed to the vagaries of the market; the monopolist, however, can control the market to a degree and offset or minimize potentially adverse effects of uncertainty. Furthermore, innovation is a source of monopoly power; the short-run uncertainty associated with the introduction of new techniques or new products may be borne for the purpose of achieving a measure of monopoly power.

The distinction between profits stemming from uncertainty and from monopoly has to do with the social desirability of these two sources of profits. Bearing the risks inherent in a dynamic and uncertain economic environment and the undertaking of innovations are socially desirable functions. The social desirability of monopoly profits is very doubtful. Monopoly profits typically are founded on output restriction, above competitive prices, and a contrived misallocation of resources. *(Key Question 8)*

Functions of Profits

Profit is the prime mover, or energizer, of the capitalistic economy. As such, profits influence both the level of resource utilization and the allocation of resources among alternative uses.

Investment and Domestic Output It is profits—or better, the *expectation* of profits—which induce firms to innovate. Innovation stimulates investment, total output, and employment. Innovation is a fundamental aspect of economic growth, and it is the pursuit of profit which underlies most innovation. However, profit expectations are volatile, with the result that investment, employment, and the rate of growth have been unstable. Profits have functioned imperfectly as a spur to innovation and investment.

Profits and Resource Allocation Perhaps profits perform more effectively the task of allocating resources among alternative lines of production. Entrepreneurs seek profits and shun losses. The occurrence of economic profits is a signal that society wants that particular industry to expand. Profit rewards are more than an inducement for an industry to expand; they also are the financial means by which firms in such industries can add to their productive capacities.

Losses signal society's desire for the afflicted industries to contract; losses penalize businesses which fail to adjust their productive efforts to those goods and services most preferred by consumers. This is not to say that profits and losses result in an allocation of resources now and forever attuned to consumer preferences. In particular, the presence of monopoly in both product and resource markets impedes the shiftability of firms and resources, as do the various geographic, artificial, and sociological immobilities discussed in Chapter 28.

> ## QUICK REVIEW 29-3
>
> ■ Pure or economic profits are determined by subtracting all explicit and implicit costs (including a normal profit) from a firm's total revenue.
>
> ■ Economic profits result from *a* the bearing of uninsurable risks, *b* innovation, and *c* monopoly power.
>
> ■ Profits and profit expectations affect the levels of investment and domestic output and also allocate resources among alternative uses.

INCOME SHARES

The discussions of Chapter 28 and 29 would be incomplete without a brief empirical summary on the importance of wages, rent, interest, and profits as proportions or relative shares of the national income. Table 29-2 provides an historical look at income shares in terms of the income categories used in our national income accounts. Although these accounting conceptions of income do not neatly fit the economist's definition of wages, rent, interest, and profits, they do yield some usable insights about the relative size and trends of income shares.

Current Shares

The most recent 1982–1993 figures in the table reveal the dominant role of labor income. Defining labor income narrowly as "wages and salaries," labor currently receives almost 75 percent of the national income. But some economists argue that since proprietors' income is largely composed of wages and salaries, it should be added to the official "wages and salaries" category to determine labor income. When we use this broad definition, labor's share rises to about 80 percent of national income. Although we label our system a "capitalist economy," the capitalist share of national income—the sum "corporate profits," "interest," and "rent"—is only about 20 percent of the national income.

Historical Trends

What can be deduced from Table 29-2 about historical trends? Let's concentrate on the dominant wage share. Using the narrow definition of labor's share as simply "wages and salaries," we see an increase from about 55 to almost 75 percent in this century.

TABLE 29-2 Relative shares of national income, 1900–1993 (decade or period averages of shares for individual years)

| (1) Decade | (2) Wages and salaries | (3) Pro- prietors' income | Property (capital) income | | | |
			(4) Cor- porate profits	(5) Interest	(6) Rent	(7) Total
1900–1909	55.0%	23.7%	6.8%	5.5%	9.0%	100%
1910–1919	53.6	23.8	9.1	5.4	8.1	100
1920–1929	60.0	17.5	7.8	6.2	7.7	100
1930–1939	67.5	14.8	4.0	8.7	5.0	100
1939–1948	64.6	17.2	11.9	3.1	3.3	100
1949–1958	67.3	13.9	12.5	2.9	3.4	100
1954–1963	69.9	11.9	11.2	4.0	3.0	100
1963–1970	71.7	9.6	12.1	3.5	3.2	100
1971–1981	75.9	7.1	8.4	6.4	2.2	100
1982–1993	73.6	7.6	8.4	10.5	0.7	100

Source: Irving Kravis, "Income Distribution: Functional Share," *International Encyclopedia of Social Sciences,* vol. 7 (New York: The Macmillan Company and Free Press, 1968), p. 134, updated. Details may not add to totals because of rounding.

Structural Challenges Although there are several tentative explanations of these data, one prominent theory is based on the structural changes which have occurred in our economy.

1 Corporate Growth Noting the relative constancy of the capitalist share (the sum of columns 4, 5, and 6)—roughly 20 percent in both the 1900–1909 and the 1982–1993 periods—we find that the expansion of labor's share has come primarily at the expense of the share going to proprietors. This suggests that the evolution of the corporation as the dominant form of business enterprise is an important explanatory factor. Individuals who would have operated their own corner groceries in the 1920s are the hired managers of corporate supermarkets in the 1980s or 1990s.

2 Changing Industry-Mix The changing output-mix and therefore the industry-mix which have occurred historically have increased labor's share. Overall, there has been a long-term change in the composition of output and industry away from land- and capital-intensive production and toward labor-intensive production. Again, crudely stated, there has been an historical reallocation of labor from agriculture (where labor's share is quite low) to manufacturing (where labor's share is rather high) and, finally, to private and public services (where labor's share is very high). These shifts account for much of the growth of labor's share reflected in column 2 of Table 29-2.

Unions? It is tempting to explain an expanding wage share in terms of the growth of labor unions. But there are difficulties with this approach.

1 The growth of the labor movements in the United States does not fit very well chronologically with the growth of labor's share of the national income. Much of the growth of "wages and salaries" occurred between 1900 and 1939; much of the growth in the labor movement came in the last few years of the 1930s and the war years of the early 1940s. Furthermore, although unions have been in relative decline since the mid-1950s, "wages and salaries" have continued to rise.

2 Wage increases for union members may come at the expense of wages of unorganized workers. That is, in obtaining higher wages, unions restrict employment opportunities (Figures 28-6 and 28-7) in organized industries. Unemployed workers and new labor-force entrants therefore seek jobs in nonunion sectors. Resulting increases in labor supply depress wage rates in nonunion jobs. If this scenario is correct, then higher wages for union workers may be achieved, not at the expense of the capitalist share, but rather at the expense of the nonunion wage share. Overall, the total labor share—union plus nonunion—could well be unaffected by unions.

3 If the national income is disaggregated into in-

LAST WORD

DETERMINING THE PRICE OF CREDIT

There are a variety of lending practices which can cause the effective interest rate to be quite different from what it appears to be.

Borrowing and lending—receiving and granting credit—are a way of life. Individuals receive credit when they negotiate a mortgage loan and when they use their credit cards. Individuals make loans when they open a savings account in a commercial bank or buy a government bond.

It is sometimes difficult to determine exactly how much interest we pay and receive in borrowing and lending. Let's suppose that you borrow $10,000 which you agree to repay plus $1,000 of interest at the end of the year. In this instance the interest rate is 10 percent per year. To determine the interest rate (i) we compare interest paid with the amount borrowed:

$$i = \frac{\$1,000}{\$10,000} = 10\%$$

But in some cases a lender, say, a bank, will *discount* the interest payment at the time the loan is made. Thus, instead of giving the borrower $10,000, the bank discounts the $1,000 interest payment in advance, giving the borrower only $9,000. This increases the interest rate:

$$i = \frac{\$1,000}{\$9,000} = 11\%$$

While the absolute amount of interest paid is the same, in this second case the borrower has only $9,000 available for the year.

An even more subtle point is that, to simplify their calculations, many financial institutions assume a 360-day year (twelve 30-day months). This means the borrower has the use of the lender's funds for five days less than the normal year. This use of a "short year" also increases the interest rate paid by the borrower.

The interest rate paid can change dramatically if a loan is repaid in installments. Suppose a bank lends you $10,000 and charges interest in the amount of $1,000 to be paid at the end of the year. But the loan contract requires you to repay the $10,000 loan in 12 equal monthly installments. The effect of this is that the average amount of the loan outstanding during the year is only $5,000. Hence:

$$i = \frac{\$1,000}{\$5,000} = 20\%$$

Here interest is paid on the total amount of the loan ($10,000) rather than the outstanding balance (which averages $5,000 for the year), making for a much higher interest rate.

Another fact which influences the effective interest rate is whether or not interest is *compounded.* Suppose you deposit $10,000 in a savings account which pays a 10 percent interest rate compounded semiannually. In other words, interest is paid on your "loan" to the bank twice a year. At the end of the first six months, $500 of interest (10% of $10,000 for one-half a year) is added to your account. At the end of the year, interest is calculated on $10,500 so that the second interest payment is $525 (10% of $10,500 for one-half a year). Hence:

$$i = \frac{\$1,025}{\$10,000} = 10.25\%$$

This means that a bank advertising a 10 percent interest rate compounded semiannually is actually paying more interest to its customers than a competitor paying a simple (noncompounded) interest rate of 10.20 percent.

Two pieces of legislation have attempted to clarify interest charges and payments. The *Truth in Lending Act* of 1968 requires lenders to state the costs and terms of consumer credit in concise and uniform language, in particular, as an annual rate. More recently, the *Truth in Savings Act* of 1991 requires all advertisements of deposit accounts by banks and savings and loans to disclose all fees connected with such accounts, their interest rate, and the annual percentage yield on the account. Nevertheless, "Let the borrower (or depositor) beware" remains a fitting motto in the world of credit.

dustry sectors and the historical trend of the wage share in each sector is examined, we reach a curious conclusion. Generally, labor's share has grown more rapidly in those sectors where unions are weak than in sectors which are highly unionized.

CHAPTER SUMMARY

1 Economic rent is the price paid for the use of land and other natural resources whose total supplies are fixed.

2 Rent is a surplus since land would be available to the economy as a whole even without rental payments. The notion of land rent as a surplus gave rise to the single-tax movement of the late 1800s.

3 Differences in land rent are explainable in terms of differences in productivity due to the fertility and climatic features of land and in its location.

4 Land rent is a surplus rather than a cost to the economy as a whole; however, because land has alternative uses from the standpoint of individual firms and industries, rental payments of firms and industries are correctly regarded as costs.

5 Interest is the price paid for the use of money. The theory of interest envisions a total demand for money comprised of transactions and asset demands. The supply of money is primarily the consequence of monetary policy.

6 The equilibrium interest rate influences the level of investment and helps ration financial and physical capital to specific firms and industries. The real interest rate, not the nominal rate, is critical to the investment decision.

7 Although designed to make funds available to low-income borrowers, usury laws allocate credit to high-income persons; subsidize high-income borrowers at the expense of lenders; and lessen the efficiency with which investable funds are allocated.

8 Economic, or pure, profits are the difference between a firm's total revenue and its total costs, the latter defined to include implicit costs, which include a normal profit. Profits accrue to entrepreneurs for assuming the uninsurable risks associated with organizing and directing economic resources and innovating. Profits also result from monopoly power.

9 Profit expectations influence innovating and investment activities and therefore the level of employment. The basic function of profits and losses, however, is to induce that allocation of resources which is in general accord with the tastes of consumers.

10 The largest share of the national income goes to labor. Narrowly defined as "wages and salaries," labor's relative share has increased through time. When more broadly defined to include "proprietors' income," labor's share has been about 80 percent and the capitalist share about 20 percent of national income since 1900.

TERMS AND CONCEPTS

economic rent	nominal versus real interest rate	explicit and implicit costs	static economy
incentive function			uninsurable risks
single-tax movement	pure rate of interest	normal profit	
transactions and asset demands for money	usury laws	economic or pure profit	

QUESTIONS AND STUDY SUGGESTIONS

1 How does the economist's usage of the term "rent" differ from everyday usage? "Though rent need not be paid by society to make land available, rental payments are very useful in guiding land into the most productive uses." Explain.

2 *Key Question   Explain why economic rent is a surplus to the economy as a whole but a cost of production from the standpoint of individual firms and industries. Explain: "Rent performs no 'incentive function' in the economy."*

3 If money capital is not an economic resource, why is interest paid and received for its use? What considerations account for the fact that interest rates differ greatly on various types of loans? Use these considerations to explain the relative size of the interest rates charged on the following:

   a A ten-year $1000 government bond

   b A $20 pawnshop loan

   c An FHA thirty-year mortgage loan on a $97,000 house

   d A 24-month $12,000 commercial bank loan to finance an automobile

e A 60-day $100 loan from a personal finance company

4 *Key Question* *What is the basic determinant of the transactions demand for money? The asset demand for money? Combine these graphically with the supply of money to determine the interest rate. Comment: "The interest rate is an administered price."*

5 What are the major economic functions of the interest rate? How might the fact that many businesses finance their investment activities internally affect the efficiency with which the interest rate performs its functions?

6 *Key Question* *Distinguish between nominal and real interest rates. Which is more relevant in making investment decisions? If the nominal interest rate is 12 percent and the inflation rate is 8 percent, what is the real rate of interest? At various times during the 1970s savers earned nominal rates of interest on their savings accounts which were less than the rate of inflation so that their savings earned negative real interest. Why, then, did they save?*

7 Historically, usury laws which put below-equilibrium ceilings on interest rates have been used by some states on the grounds that such laws will make credit available to poor people who could not otherwise afford to borrow. Critics of such laws contend that it is poor people who are most likely to be hurt by such laws. Which view is correct?

8 *Key Question* *How do the concepts of business profits and economic profits differ? Why are economic profits smaller than business profits? What are the three basic sources of economic profits? Classify each of the following in accordance with these sources:*

a *A firm's profits from developing and patenting a ballpoint pen containing a permanent ink cartridge*

b *A restaurant's profit which results from construction of a new highway past its door*

c *The profit received by a firm benefit from an unanticipated change in consumer tastes*

9 Why is the distinction between insurable and uninsurable risks significant for the theory of profits? Carefully evaluate: "All economic profits can be traced to either uncertainty or the desire to avoid it." What are the major functions of profits?

10 Explain the absence of economic profit in a purely competitive, static economy. Realizing that the major function of profits is to allocate resources in accordance with consumer preferences, evaluate the allocation of resources in such an economy.

11 What has happened to the wage, profit, interest, and rent shares of national income over time? Explain the alleged growth of labor's share in terms of structural changes in the economy. Have unions affected the size of labor's share?

12 (Last Word) Assume you borrow $5000 and pay back the $5000 plus $250 in interest at the end of the year. What is the interest rate? What would the interest rate be if the $250 of interest had been discounted at the time the loan was made? What would the interest rate be if you were required to repay the loan in twelve equal monthly installments?

PART
SEVEN

Government and Current Economic Problems

30

GOVERNMENT AND MARKET FAILURE: PUBLIC GOODS, THE ENVIRONMENT, AND INFORMATION PROBLEMS

The economic activities of government affect your well-being every day. If you attend a public college or university, taxpayers heavily subsidize your education. When you receive a check from your part-time or summer job, you see deductions for income and social security taxes. The beef in your Big Mac has been examined by government inspectors to prevent contamination and to ensure quality. Laws requiring seat belts and motorcycle helmets—and the sprinkler system government mandates in your dormitory—are all intended to enhance your safety. If you are a woman, a member of a minority group or disabled, legislation is designed to enhance your education and employment opportunities.

In this chapter and in Chapter 31 we will deepen our understanding of government's role in the economy and identify some of the problems government faces in carrying out its economic activities. We begin by returning to the topic of *market failure* introduced in Chapter 6. Our tools of marginal analysis permit us to provide a fuller discussion of public goods and externalities. Next, the pervasive externality—pollution—is discussed in some detail. Finally, we examine *information failures* in the private sector to determine their implications for government participation in the economy.

In Chapter 31 our discussion of government continues with an analysis of *government failure* and the microeconomics of taxation. The chapters which follow in Part 7 involve economic problems government has attempted to resolve—with varying degrees of success. Chapter 32 examines the problem of monopoly and anticompetitive business practices. Chapter 33 looks at the farm problem. In Chapter 34 we discuss the problems of poverty and income inequality and Chapter 35 probes the much publicized problems associated with our health care system. Chapter 36 investigates such labor market issues as unionism, discrimination, and migration. The better you understand the analysis in this and the next chapter, the clearer will be your understanding of government's involvement in these areas.

PUBLIC GOODS: EXTENDING THE ANALYSIS

A *private* good is divisible—it comes in small enough units to be afforded by individual buyers. It is also subject to the exclusion principle—those unable or unwilling to pay are excluded from the product's benefits.

A market demand curve for a private good is the *horizontal* summation of demand curves representing each buyer (review Table 3-2 and Figure 3-2). If Adams wants to buy 3 hot dogs at $1 each; Benson, 1 hot dog; and Conrad, 2 hot dogs; the market demand will reflect that 6 hot dogs (= 3 + 1 + 2) are demanded at a $1 price. The market demand resulting from the sum of the desires of each potential buyer creates a possibility for sellers to gain revenue and garner a profit. The equilibrium amount of a private good produced and purchased is dictated by product price, jointly determined by market demand and supply. This equilibrium output is optimal; it maximizes the combined well-being of the buyers and sellers, the only people affected by the transactions.

A snag develops, however, if we try to apply this same line of thinking to a public good. A *public good* is indivisible and does not fit the exclusion principle. Once the good is provided, the producer cannot exclude nonpayers from receiving its indivisible benefits. Because potential buyers will obtain the benefit from a public good whether or not they pay for it, they will *not* reveal their true preferences for it. They will become *free riders* who will *not* voluntarily pay for the public good in the marketplace. *The market demand curve for a public good will be nonexistent or significantly understated.* The demand for the product expressed in the marketplace will not generate enough revenue to cover the costs of production, even though the collective benefits of the good may exceed the economic costs.

Demand for Public Goods

How might we determine society's optimal (economically efficient) amount of a public good in view of this problem? Suppose Adams and Benson are the only people in the economy and their true demand schedules for a public good, say, national defense, are shown as columns 1 and 2 and columns 1 and 3 of Table 30-1.

These demand schedules are "phantom" demand curves since the two people will not actually reveal

TABLE 30-1   Demand for a public good, two individuals

(1) Quantity	(2) Adams' willingness to pay (price)		(3) Benson's willingness to pay (price)		(4) Collective willingness to pay (price)
1	$4	+	$5	=	$9
2	3	+	4	=	7
3	2	+	3	=	5
4	1	+	2	=	3
5	0	+	1	=	1

their preferences in the marketplace. Instead, we assume this information has been discovered through a survey indicating Adams' and Benson's willingness to pay for each added unit of the public good, rather than go without it.

Suppose government produces 1 unit of this public good. Because the exclusion principle does not apply, neither Adams nor Benson will voluntarily offer to pay for this unit because each can consume it without paying. Adams' consumption of the good does not preclude Benson from also consuming it, and vice versa. But the combined amount of money these two citizens are willing to pay, rather than each not having this one unit of the good, can be determined through Table 30-1. Columns 1 and 2 show that Adams would be willing to pay $4 for the first unit of the public good; columns 1 and 3 show that Benson would be willing to pay $5 for it. The $9 price (column 4) these two are jointly willing to pay is the sum of the amounts *each* is willing to pay. For the second unit of the public good the collective price they are willing to pay is $7 (= $3 by Adams plus $4 by Benson).

We could then do the same for the third unit, and so on. Looking at the collective willingness to pay (column 4) for each additional unit, we construct a collective demand schedule for a public good. Rather than adding the *quantities demanded* at each price as when determining the market demand for a private good, we are adding the *prices* people collectively are willing to pay for the last unit of the public good at each quantity demanded.

Figure 30-1 shows the same summing procedure graphically, using data from Table 30-1 to illustrate the adding-up process. We are summing Adams' and Benson's demand curves for the public good *vertically* to derive the collective demand curve. The height of the collective demand curve D_c at 2 units of output, for example, is $7—the sum of the amount that Adams and Benson together are willing to pay

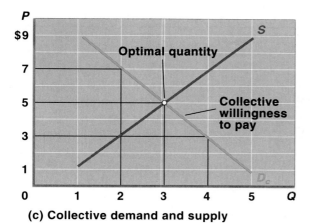

(c) Collective demand and supply

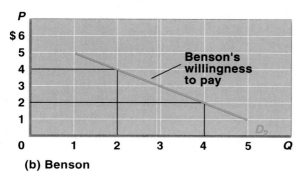

(b) Benson

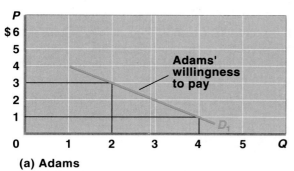

(a) Adams

FIGURE 30-1 The optimal amount of a public good
Graphically the collective demand curve D_c for the public good shown in (c) is found by summing vertically the individual demand curves D_1 and D_2 exhibited in (a) and (b). Government should provide 3 units of the public good, because at that quantity the combined marginal benefit, as measured by citizens' willingness to pay for the last unit (shown by D_c), equals the good's marginal cost (shown by S).

for the second unit (= \$3 + \$4). Likewise, the height of the collective demand curve at 4 units of the public good is \$3 (= \$1 + \$2).

Our collective demand curve D_c is based on the monetary value of the perceived benefits of the extra units that are equally available to both persons for si-

multaneous consumption. The curve slopes downward because of the law of diminishing marginal utility: Successive units of the public good will yield less added satisfaction than the previous units. *(Key Question 1)*

Optimal Quantity of a Public Good

We can now determine the optimal quantity of the specific public good alluded to in Figure 30-1. The collective demand curve D_c measures the marginal benefit of each unit of this particular good to society, whereas the supply curve S measures the marginal cost of each unit. The supply curve slopes upward because of the law of diminishing returns, which applies whether making missiles (public goods) or mufflers (private goods).

Optimal output occurs where marginal benefit equals marginal cost (MB = MC). In this case, the optimal quantity of the public good is 3 units—the intersection of the collective demand curve D_c and the supply curve S. At 3 units the combined willingness to pay for the extra unit—the marginal benefit to society—just matches that unit's marginal cost (\$5 = \$5). This "marginal benefit equals marginal cost" principle is analogous to the MR = MC output rule and the MRP = MRC input rule for maximizing profit. *(Key Question 2)*

Benefit-Cost Analysis

Economic theory thus provides guidance to efficient decision making in the public sector. This guidance can be helpful in understanding **benefit-cost analysis.**

Concept Suppose government is contemplating a flood-control project. The economizing problem tells us that any decision to use more resources in the public sector will involve both a benefit and a cost. The benefit is the extra satisfaction resulting from the output of more public goods; the cost is the loss of satisfaction associated with the accompanying decline in the production of private goods (or some alternative public good). Should the resources needed be shifted from the private to the public sector? "Yes," *if* the benefits from the extra public goods exceed the cost resulting from having fewer private goods. The answer is "No" *if* the value or cost of the forgone private goods is greater than the benefits associated with the extra public goods.

TABLE 30-2 Benefit-cost analysis for a flood-control project

(1) Plan	(2) Total annual cost of project	(3) Marginal cost	(4) Total annual benefit (reduction in damage)	(5) Marginal benefit	(6) Net benefit or (4) − (2)
Without protection	$ 0		$ 0		$ 0
		$ 3,000		$ 6,000	
A: Levees	3,000		6,000		3,000
		7,000		10,000	
B: Small reservoir	10,000		16,000		6,000
		8,000		9,000	
C: Medium reservoir	18,000		25,000		7,000
		12,000		7,000	
D: Large reservoir	30,000		32,000		2,000

Source: Adapted from Otto Eckstein, *Public Finance,* 3d ed. (Englewood Cliffs, N.J.: Prentice-Hall, Inc., 1973), p. 23. Used with permission.

But benefit-cost analysis can indicate more than whether a public program is worth doing. It can also help government decide the extent to which a project should be pursued. Economic questions are not questions to be answered simply by "Yes" or "No," but rather are matters of "how much" or "how little."

There is no doubt that a flood-control project is a public good since the exclusion principle is not readily applicable. Should government undertake a flood-control project in a particular river valley? If so, what is the proper size or scope for the project?

Illustration Table 30-2 lists a series of increasingly ambitious and increasingly costly flood-control plans. To what extent, if at all, should government undertake flood control? The answers depend on costs and benefits. Costs in this case are largely the capital costs of constructing and maintaining levees and reservoirs; benefits are reduced flood damage.

A glance at all the plans shows that for each plan total benefits (column 4) exceed total costs (column 2), indicating that a flood-control project on this river is economically justifiable. We can see this directly in column 6 where total annual costs (column 2) are subtracted from total annual benefits (column 4).

But the question of the optimal size or scope for this project remains. This answer is determined by comparing the additional, or *marginal,* cost and the additional, or *marginal,* benefit associated with each plan. The guideline is the one we just established: Pursue an activity or project as long as the marginal benefit (column 5) exceeds the marginal cost (column 3). Stop the activity or project at, or as close as pos-

sible to, that point at which the marginal benefit equals the marginal cost.

In this case Plan C—the medium-sized reservoir —is the best plan. Plans A and B are too modest; in both cases the marginal benefit exceeds the marginal cost. Plan D's marginal cost ($12,000) exceeds the marginal benefit ($7000) and therefore cannot be justified. Plan D isn't economically justifiable; it overallocates resources to this project. Plan C is closest to the optimum; it expands flood control so long as marginal benefits exceed marginal costs.

Seen slightly differently, the **marginal benefit = marginal cost rule** will determine which plan provides the maximum excess of total benefits (column 4) over total costs (column 2) or, in other words, the plan which yields the maximum *net* gain or benefit to society. We confirm directly in column 6 that the maximum net benefit (of $7000) is associated with Plan C.

Benefit-cost analysis shatters the myth that "economy in government" and "reduced government spending" are synonymous. "Economy" is concerned with using resources efficiently. If a government program yields a lower marginal benefit than the marginal benefit attainable from the best alternative private use—that is, if costs exceed benefits—then the proposed public program should *not* be undertaken. But if benefits exceed cost, then it would be uneconomical or "wasteful" *not* to spend on that government program. Economy in government does *not* mean minimization of public spending; it means allocating resources between the private and public sectors until no net benefits can be had from further reallocations. *(Key Question 3)*

EXTERNALITIES REVISITED

We can now better understand Chapter 5's discussion of government policies designed to correct the market failure we call externalities or spillovers. Recall that a spillover is a cost or benefit accruing to an individual or group—a third party—which is *external* to the market transaction. An example of a spillover cost is pollution; an example of a spillover benefit, inoculations. When there are spillover costs, an overproduction of the product occurs and there is an overallocation of resources to this use. Underproduction and underallocation of resources result from spillover benefits. Let's demonstrate both graphically.

Spillover Costs

Figure 30-2a illustrates how spillover or external costs affect the allocation of resources. When spillover costs occur—when producers shift some of their costs onto the community—their marginal costs are lower. The

supply curve does not include or "capture" all the costs legitimately associated with production of the good. Therefore, the producer's supply curve, S, understates total costs of production; it lies to the right of the supply curve which would include all costs, S_t. By polluting—creating spillover costs—the firm enjoys lower production costs and the supply curve S.

The result, shown in Figure 30-2a, is that equilibrium output Q_e is larger than optimal output Q_o. This means resources are *overallocated* to the production of this commodity; too many units of the product are produced.

Spillover Benefits

Figure 30-2b shows the impacts of spillover benefits on resource allocation. Spillover benefits mean the market demand curve, which reflects only private benefits, understates total benefits. The market demand curve does not capture all the benefits associated with the provision and consumption of goods and services entailing spillover benefits. Thus D in Figure 30-2b indicates the benefits private individuals derive from, say, inoculations against communicable diseases. Watson and Wienberg privately benefit when they get vaccinated, but so too do associates Alvarez and Anderson who are less likely to contract the disease from them. Magnified to the entire population, inoculations mean a healthier and more productive workforce, yielding widespread output and income benefits to society. D_t includes the private benefits (D) from inoculations *plus* the additional, or spillover, benefits accruing to society at large.

While market demand D and supply S_t would yield an equilibrium output of Q_e, this output would

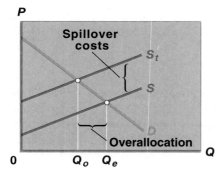

(a) The case of spillover costs

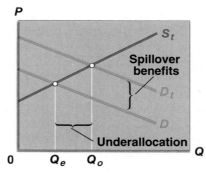

(b) The case of spillover benefits

FIGURE 30-2 Spillover costs and spillover benefits
With spillover costs in (a) we find that the lower costs borne by businesses, as reflected in S, fail to reflect all costs, as embodied in S_t. Consequently, the equilibrium output Q_e is greater than the efficient or optimal output Q_o. Spillover benefits in (b) cause society's total benefits from a product, as shown by D_t, to be understated by the market demand curve, D. As a result, the equilibrium output Q_e is less than the optimal output Q_o.

be less than the optimal output Q_o, shown by the intersection of D_t and S_t. The market would not produce enough vaccinations; resources would be underallocated to this use.

Economists have explored several approaches— many involving government—to solve the problems of spillover costs and spillover benefits. But let's first look at circumstances where government intervention is not needed.

Individual Bargaining

In some situations externalities can be solved through individual bargaining.

Coase Theorem According to the **Coase theorem,** conceived by Ronald Coase, negative or positive spillovers do *not* require government intervention where (1) property ownership is clearly defined, (2) the number of people involved is small, and (3) bargaining costs are negligible. Government should confine its role under these circumstances to encouraging bargaining between affected individuals or groups. Because the economic self-interests of the parties are at stake, bargaining with one another will enable them to find an acceptable solution to the problem. Property rights place a price tag on an externality, creating an opportunity cost for both sides. A compelling incentive emerges for the parties to find ways to solve the externality problem.

Extended Example Suppose the owner of a large parcel of forest land is considering contracting with a logging company to clear-cut (totally cut) thousands of acres of mature fir trees. The complication is that the forest surrounds a lake with a popular resort on its shore. The resort is on land owned by the resort owner. The unspoiled beauty of the general area attracts vacationers from all over the nation to the resort. Should state or local government intervene to prevent the tree cutting?

According to the Coase theorem, the forest owner and the resort owner can resolve this situation without government intervention. As long as *one* of the parties to the dispute has property rights to what is at issue, an incentive will exist for *both* parties to negotiate a solution acceptable to each. In our example, the owner of the timberland holds the property rights to the land to be logged. The owner of the resort therefore has an incentive to negotiate with the forest

owner to reduce the logging impact. Excessive logging of the forest surrounding the resort will reduce tourism and revenues to the resort owner.

But what is the economic incentive of the forest owner to explore the possibility of an agreement with the resort owner? The answer draws directly on the idea of opportunity cost. One cost incurred by the owner in logging the forest is the forgone payment which the forest owner could obtain from the resort owner for agreeing *not* to clear-cut the fir trees. The resort owner should be willing to make a lump-sum or annual payment to the owner of the forest to avoid or minimize the spillover cost. Or, perhaps the resort owner will be willing to buy the forested land at a high price to prevent the logging. As viewed by the forest owner, a payment to preclude logging or a purchase price above the value of the land as a tree farm are *opportunity costs* of logging the land.

We would predict a negotiated agreement which both parties would regard as better than clear-cutting the firs. The Coase theorem suggests government intervention would not be needed to correct this potential externality.

Limitations Unfortunately, many negative externalities involve large numbers of affected parties, high bargaining costs, and community property such as air and water. Private bargaining in these situations will not remedy the spillover costs. For example, the acid-rain problem in the United States and Canada affects millions of people spread out over two nations. The vast number of affected parties could not independently negotiate an agreement to remedy this problem. In this example, we must rely on both governments to find acceptable solutions.

Nevertheless, the Coase theorem reminds us that clearly defined property rights can be a positive factor in remedying some spillover costs and spillover benefits.

Liability Rules and Lawsuits

Although private negotiation may not be a realistic solution to most externality problems, clearly established property rights may be helpful in another way. Government has established a framework of laws which define private property and protect it from damage done by other parties. These laws—and the legal tort (wrongful act) system to which they give rise —permit those suffering spillover costs to sue for damages.

Consider the following. Suppose the Ajax Degreaser Company regularly dumps leaky barrels containing solvents into a nearby canyon owned by Bar Q ranch. Bar Q eventually discovers this dump site, and, after tracing the drums to Ajax, immediately contacts its lawyer. Ajax gets sued! Not only will Ajax have to pay for the cleanup, it may well have to pay Bar Q additional damages for despoiling its property.

Clearly defined property rights and government specified liability rules provide an avenue for remedying some externality problems. They do so directly by forcing the perpetrator of the harmful externality to pay damages to those injured. They do so indirectly by discouraging firms and individuals from generating negative externalities, for fear of being sued. It is not surprising that many externalities do *not* involve private property, but rather property held in common. It is the *public* bodies of water, the *public* lands, and the *public* air, where ownership is less clear, which often bear the brunt of negative externalities.

Caveat: Like private negotiations, private lawsuits to resolve externalities have their own limitations. Lawsuits are expensive, time-consuming, and have uncertain outcomes. Large legal fees and major time delays in the court system are commonplace. Also, the uncertainty associated with the court outcome reduces the effectiveness of this approach. Will the court accept your claim that your emphysema has resulted from the smoke emitted by the factory next door, or will it conclude that your ailment is unrelated to the plant's pollution? Can you prove that a specific firm in the area is the source of the contamination of your well? What are Bar Q's options if Ajax Degreaser goes out of business during the litigation?

Government Intervention

Other approaches to achieving economic efficiency may be needed when externalities affect large numbers of people or when community interests are at stake. Specifically, direct controls and taxes can be used to counter spillover costs; subsidies and government provision are available for dealing with spillover benefits.

Direct Controls   The most direct approach to reducing negative externalities is legislation placing limits on the amount of the activity taking place. To date, this approach has dominated public policy in the United States. Clean air legislation limits the amounts of nitrogen oxide, particulates, and other substances plants can emit into the air. Clean water legislation specifies the amount of heavy metals, detergents, and other pollutants firms can place into rivers and bays. Toxic-waste laws dictate special procedures and dump sites for disposing of contaminated soil and solvents. Violation of these laws means fines and, occasionally, imprisonment.

Direct controls force offending firms to incur costs associated with pollution control. Thus, the private marginal costs of producing these goods rise. The supply curve S of Figure 30-3a—which we know

FIGURE 30-3   Correcting for spillover costs (negative externalities)
Spillover costs (a) result in an overallocation of resources. This overallocation can be corrected by direct controls or, as shown in (b), by imposing a specific tax, T, which raises the firm's marginal costs and shifts its supply curve from S to S_t.

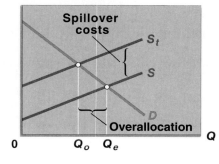

(a) The case of spillover costs

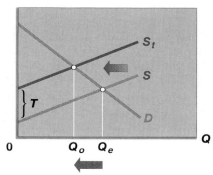

(b) Correcting the overallocation of resources via a tax

reflects only private marginal costs—shifts leftward from S to S_t, as shown in Figure 30-3b. Product price increases, equilibrium output falls from Q_e to Q_o, and the initial Q_eQ_o overallocation of resources shown in Figure 30-3a is corrected.

Specific Taxes A second policy approach to spillover costs is to levy specific taxes or emission charges on the perpetrators. For example, the Federal government has placed an excise tax on manufacturers of chlorofluorocarbons (CFCs) which deplete the stratospheric ozone layer protecting the earth from excessive solar ultraviolet radiation. This substance is used widely as a coolant in refrigeration, a blowing agent for foam, and a solvent for electronics. Facing such a tax, manufacturers must decide whether to pay it or expend additional funds to purchase or develop substitute products. In either case, the tax will increase the marginal cost of producing CFCs, shifting the private supply curve for this product leftward.

Look closely at Figure 30-3. A specific tax equal to T per unit in Figure 30-3b will increase the firm's marginal costs, shifting the supply curve from S to S_t. Equilibrium price will therefore increase and equilibrium output will decline from Q_e to the economically efficient level Q_o. The overallocation of resources shown in Figure 30-3a will be eliminated.

Subsidies and Government Provision Where spillover benefits or positive externalities are large and diffuse—as with inoculations—government has three options for correcting the underallocation of resources.

1 Subsidies to Buyers Figure 30-4a repeats the case of spillover benefits described earlier. Government could correct the underallocation of resources —in this case, to inoculations—by subsidizing consumers of the product. It could give each new mother in the United States a discount coupon to be used to obtain a series of inoculations for her child. These coupons would reduce the "price" to the mother by, say, 50 percent. In terms of Figure 30-4b, this program would increase the demand for inoculations from D to D_t. The number of vaccinations would rise from Q_e to Q_o, eliminating the underallocation of resources shown in Figure 30-4a.

2 Subsidies to Producers As it relates to supply, a subsidy is a specific tax in reverse; taxes impose an extra cost on producers, while subsidies reduce their costs. In Figure 30-4c a subsidy of U per inoculation to physicians and medical clinics will reduce marginal costs and shift the supply curve rightward from S_t to S'_t. Output will increase from Q_e to the optimal level

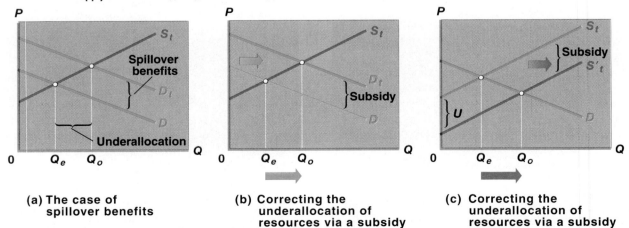

FIGURE 30-4 Correcting for spillover benefits (positive externalities)
Spillover benefits (a) result in an underallocation of resources. This underallocation can be corrected by a subsidy to consumers, as shown in (b), which increases market demand from D to D_t. Alternatively, the underallocation can be eliminated by providing producers with a subsidy of U, which increases their supply curve from S_t to S'_t, as shown in (c).

(a) The case of spillover benefits

(b) Correcting the underallocation of resources via a subsidy to consumers

(c) Correcting the underallocation of resources via a subsidy to producers

Q_o and thus the underallocation of resources shown in Figure 30-4a will be corrected.

3   Government Provision   Finally, where spillover benefits are extremely large, government may decide to provide the product as a public good. The U.S. government largely eradicated the crippling disease polio by administering free vaccines to all children. India ended smallpox by paying people in rural areas to come to public clinics to have their children vaccinated. *(Key Question 4)*

A Market for Externality Rights

One novel policy approach suggested to remedy spillover costs involves limited government action. The idea is for government to create a **market for externality rights.** We confine our discussion to pollution, although other externalities might also lend themselves to this approach.

The air, rivers, lakes, oceans, and public lands, such as parks and streets, are all objects for pollution because the *rights* to use these resources are either held "in common" by society or are unspecified by law. As a result, no specific private individual or institution has an incentive to restrict the use or maintain the purity or quality of these resources because no one has the right to realize a monetary return from doing so.

We maintain the property we own—we paint and repair our homes periodically—in part because we will gain the value of these improvements at the time of resale. But, as long as "rights" to air, water, and certain land resources are commonly held and these resources are freely available, there will be no incentive to maintain them or restrict their use. The result? These natural resources are "overconsumed" and thereby polluted. But would they be consumed to this extent if there were a cost to pollute them—a market for the right to pollute them?

Creating a Market   In this approach, an appropriate pollution-control agency would determine the amount of pollutants which can be discharged into the water or air of a specific region annually and still maintain the quality of the water or air at some acceptable standard. The agency may determine that 500 tons of pollutants can be discharged into Metropolitan Lake and "recycled" by Nature. Thus, 500 pollution rights, each entitling the owner to dump 1 ton of pollutants into the lake in the particular year, are made available

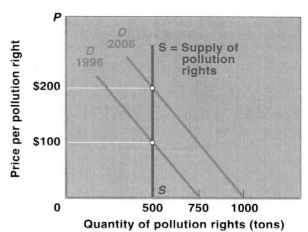

FIGURE 30-5   The market for pollution rights
Pollution can be controlled by having a public body determine the amount of pollution which the atmosphere or a body of water can safely recycle and sell these limited rights to polluters. The effect is to make the environment a scarce resource with a positive price. Economic and population growth will increase the demand for pollution rights over time, but the consequence will be an increase in the price of pollution rights rather than more pollution.

for sale each year. The resulting supply of pollution rights is fixed and therefore perfectly inelastic, as shown in Figure 30-5.

The demand for pollution rights—in this case D_{1996}—will take the same downsloping form as the demand for any other input. At high prices, polluters either will stop polluting or will pollute less by acquiring pollution-abatement equipment. An equilibrium market price for pollution rights of $100 will be determined at which an environment-preserving quantity of pollution rights will be rationed to polluters. Without this market—that is, if the use of the lake as a dump site for pollutants were free—750 tons of pollutants would be discharged into the lake and it would be "overconsumed," or polluted, in the amount of 250 tons.

Over time, as human and business populations expand, demand will increase, as from D_{1996} to D_{2006}. *Without* a market for pollution rights, pollution would occur in 2006 in the amount of 500 tons beyond that which can be assimilated by Nature. *With* the market for pollution rights, price will rise from $100 to $200 and the amount of pollutants will remain at 500 tons —the amount which the lake can recycle.

Advantages   This scheme has several advantages relative to direct controls. Most importantly, it reduces society's costs because pollution rights can be bought and sold. Suppose it costs Acme Pulp Mill $20 a year to reduce a specific noxious waterborne discharge by 1 ton while it costs Zemo Chemicals $8000 a year to accomplish this same 1-ton reduction. Also assume that Zemo wants to expand its production of chemicals, but doing so will increase its pollution discharge by 1 ton.

Without a market for pollution rights, Zemo will have to use $8000 of society's scarce resources to keep the 1 ton pollution discharge from occurring. But with a market for pollution rights, Zemo has another option: It can buy 1 ton of pollution rights for the $100 price shown in Figure 30-5. Acme would be willing to sell Zemo 1 ton of pollution rights for $100, because that amount is more than Acme's $20 costs of reducing pollution by 1 ton. Zemo increases its discharge by 1 ton; Acme reduces its discharge by 1 ton. Zemo benefits ($8000 − $100), Acme benefits ($100 − $20), and society benefits ($8000 − $20). Rather than using $8000 of its resources to hold the discharge at the specified level, society uses $20 of its resources.

Market-based plans have other advantages. Potential polluters are confronted with an explicit monetary incentive not to pollute: They must buy rights to pollute. Conservation groups can fight pollution by buying up and withholding pollution rights, reducing actual pollution below governmentally determined standards. As the demand for pollution rights increases over time, the growing revenue from the sale of the specific quantity of pollution rights could be devoted to environment improvement. Similarly, with time the rising price of pollution rights should stimulate the search for improved techniques to control pollution.

Administrative and political problems have dissuaded government from abandoning direct controls —uniform emission standards—for a full-scale market for pollution rights. But, as we will soon discuss, such markets *have* emerged for air pollution rights. Also, legislation has established a system of pollution rights, or "tradeable emission allowances," as part of a plan to reduce sulfur dioxide emitted by coal-burning public utilities. These firms are the major source of acid rain.

Table 30-3 reviews the methods for correcting externalities.

Society's Optimal Amount of Externality Reduction

Negative externalities such as pollution reduce the recipient's utility rather than increase it. They are not economic goods but "economic bads." If something is bad, shouldn't society eliminate it? Why should society allow firms or municipalities to discharge *any* impure waste into public waterways or emit *any* pollution into our air?

Reducing a negative spillover has a "price." Society must decide how much of a reduction it wants to "buy." Totally eliminating pollution may not be desirable, even if it were technologically feasible. Because of the law of diminishing returns, cleaning up the last 10 percent of effluents from an industrial smokestack normally is far more costly than cleaning up the previous 10 percent. Eliminating that 10 percent is likely more costly than cleaning up the prior 10 percent, and so on.

The marginal cost (MC) to the firm and hence to society—the opportunity cost of the extra resources used—rises as more and more pollution is reduced. At some point MC may rise so high that it exceeds society's marginal benefit (MB) of further pollution abatement (reduction). Additional actions to reduce

TABLE 30-3 Methods for dealing with externalities

Problem	Resource allocation outcome	Ways to correct
Spillover costs (negative externalities)	Overallocation of resources	1 Individual bargaining 2 Liability rules and lawsuits 3 Tax on producers 4 Direct controls 5 Market for externality rights
Spillover benefits (positive externalities)	Underallocation of resources	1 Individual bargaining 2 Subsidy to consumers 3 Subsidy to producers 4 Government provision

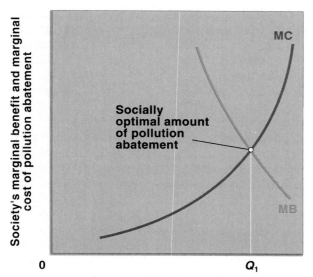

FIGURE 30-6   Society's optimal amount of pollution abatement

The optimal amount of externality reduction—in this case pollution abatement—occurs at Q_1 where society's marginal cost and marginal benefit of reducing the negative externality are equal. Reductions of pollution beyond Q_1 will reduce economic efficiency by overallocating resources to pollution control.

pollution will therefore lower society's well-being; total cost will rise by more than total benefit.

MC, MB, and Equilibrium Quantity   Observe in Figure 30-6 the rising marginal cost curve MC and the downsloping marginal benefit curve, MB. Society's marginal benefits of pollution abatement decline because of the law of diminishing marginal utility. The benefits from reducing pollution are a reflection of utility, and marginal utility (not total utility) falls as greater amounts of pollution abatement are achieved.

The **optimal reduction of an externality** occurs where society's marginal benefit and marginal cost of reducing that externality are equal (MB = MC). In Figure 30-6 this optimal amount of pollution abatement is Q_1. When MB exceeds MC, additional abatement moves society toward economic efficiency; the added benefit of cleaner air or water exceeds the benefit of any alternative use of the required resources. When MC exceeds MB, further abatement reduces economic efficiency; there would be greater benefits from using resources in some other way than using them to further reduce pollution.

In reality, it is difficult to measure the marginal costs and benefits of pollution control. Nevertheless, Figure 30-6 is useful in demonstrating that some pollution may be socially efficient. This is so, not because pollution is desirable, but because beyond some level of control, further abatement may reduce our net well-being.

Shifts in Locations of Curves   The locations of the marginal-cost and marginal-benefit curves in Figure 30-6 are not forever fixed; they can, and probably do, shift over time. For example, suppose the technology of pollution control equipment improves noticeably. We would expect the cost of pollution abatement to fall, society's MC curve to shift rightward, and the optimal level of abatement to rise. As another example, suppose society wants cleaner air and water because of new information about adverse health effects of pollution. The MB curve in Figure 30-6 would shift rightward, and the optimal level of pollution control would increase beyond Q_1. Test your understanding of these statements by drawing new MC and MB curves in Figure 30-6. *(Key Question 7)*

POLLUTION: A CLOSER LOOK

Pollution, the most acute negative externality facing industrial society, provides a relevant illustration of several of the concepts and public policies just discussed. This spillover takes several forms, including air, water, and solid-waste (garbage) pollution. How big are these problems? What are their causes? What public policies are in place to reduce them?

Dimensions of the Problem

We know some rivers, lakes, and bays have turned into municipal and industrial sewers. Almost half our population drinks water of dubious quality. There are more than 25,000 major industrial and utility sources of air pollution, which contributes to lung cancer, emphysema, pneumonia, and other respiratory diseases. Nearly 1 billion pounds of toxic chemicals—some of them carcinogens—are released into the air each year. Solid-waste disposal has become an acute problem for many cities as the most readily available dump sites have been filled and citizens resist the establishment of new dumps or incinerators near them.

The nations of eastern Europe are so polluted that it will take several decades, at best, for them to be cleaned up. Government has identified hundreds of dangerous toxic-waste disposal sites in the United States. Within the past decade, giant oil spills in Alaska and the Persian Gulf have seriously damaged those two ecosystems. Passive cigarette smoke has been found to cause cancer in nonsmokers.

Global consequences of environmental pollution are equally disturbing. Some scientists contend that the concentrations of industry, people, structures, and cement which constitute cities might create air and heat pollution sufficient to cause irreversible and potentially disastrous global warming through the so-called greenhouse effect. Headlines warn us that our continued use of CFCs has contributed to a rising rate of skin cancer by depleting the earth's stratospheric ozone layer.

Causes: The Law of Conservation of Matter and Energy

The root of the pollution problem can best be envisioned through the **law of conservation of matter and energy.** This law holds that matter can be transformed to other matter or into energy but can never vanish. All inputs (fuels, raw materials, water, and so forth) used in the economy's production processes will ultimately result in an equivalent residual of waste. For example, unless it is continuously recycled, the cotton found in a T-shirt ultimately will be abandoned in a closet, buried in a dump, or burned in an incinerator. Even if burned it will not truly vanish; instead, it will be transformed into heat and smoke.

Fortunately, the ecological system—Nature, if you are over fifty—has the self-regenerating capacity which allows it, within limits, to absorb or recycle such wastes. But the volume of such residuals has tended to outrun this absorptive capacity.

Why has this happened? Why do we have a pollution problem? There are lots of reasons, but four big ones.

1 Population Density One reason is population growth. An ecological system which may accommodate 50 or 100 million people may begin to break down under the pressures of 200 or 300 million.

2 Rising Incomes Economic growth means that each person consumes and disposes of more output. Paradoxically, a rising GDP (gross domestic product) means a rising GDG (gross domestic garbage). A high standard of living permits Americans to own over

190 million motor vehicles. But autos and trucks pollute the air and give rise to the problem of disposing of some 11 or 12 million junked vehicles annually. Additionally, about 200 million tires hit the nation's scrap heap each year.

But we must not overgeneralize. While solid waste increases with GDP, this is not the case with all pollutants. For example, concentrations of smoke (fine suspended particles), heavier suspended particles, and sulfur dioxide on average decrease when a nation's per capita GDP rises above $5000 per year. Expanded national income enables countries to "buy" cleaner air and water through enacting pollution control measures. Nevertheless, there is no doubt that industrialization itself—and the resulting increase in GDP—has brought with it serious pollution problems.

3 Technology Technological change may also contribute to pollution. For example, the addition of lead to gasoline posed a serious threat to human health, leading to the government requirement of unleaded fuel. The development and widespread use of "throw-away" containers made of virtually indestructible aluminum or plastic add to the solid-waste crisis. Some detergent soap products have been highly resistant to sanitary treatment and recycling.

4 Incentives Profit-seeking manufacturers will choose the least-cost combination of inputs and will bear only unavoidable costs. If they can dump waste chemicals into rivers and lakes rather than pay for expensive treatment and proper disposal, businesses might be inclined to do so. Manufacturers which can will discharge smoke rather than purchase expensive abatement facilities. The result is air pollution—and, in the economist's jargon—the shifting of certain costs to the community at large as external or spillover costs. Enjoying lower "internal" costs than if they had not polluted the environment, the producers can sell their products more cheaply, expand their production, and obtain larger profits.

But it is neither just nor accurate to lay the entire blame for pollution at the door of industry. A well-intentioned firm wanting to operate in a socially responsible way with respect to pollution may find itself in an untenable position. If an individual firm "internalizes" all its external or spillover costs by installing, say, water-treatment and smoke-abatement equipment, the firm will have a cost disadvantage compared to its polluting competitors. The socially responsible firm will have higher costs and will be forced to raise its product price. The "reward" for the pollution-conscious firm is a declining market for its product, diminished profits, and, in the extreme, bankruptcy. This means effective action to combat pollution must be undertaken collectively through government.

Also, even though an important function of government is to correct the misallocation of resources which accompanies spillover costs, most major cities are heavy contributors to the pollution problem. Municipal power plants are contributors to air pollution; many cities discharge inadequately treated sewage into rivers or lakes because it is cheap and convenient to do so.

Many individuals avoid the costs of proper refuse pickup and disposal by burning their garbage or illegally dumping it in the woods. We also find it easier to use throw-away containers rather than recycle "return" containers. Most families with babies opt for the convenience of disposable diapers which glut landfills rather than using reusable cloth diapers. Emissions from woodstoves, fireplaces, outdoor grills, and even lawn mowers and outboard motors become pollution problems in some towns and cities.

Antipollution Policy

American antipollution policy comprises a complex maze of laws, regulations, taxes, markets for pollution rights, and government-financed cleanup activity. Much of this complexity derives from the sheer number of pollution sources and the thousands of specific substances emitted into the air or placed into the water or garbage dumps. We have selected three components of antipollution policy for examination: the Superfund law, the Clean Air Act of 1990, and incentives to recycle.

The Superfund Law Before the **Superfund law of 1980,** companies disposed of their chemical waste by storing it next to their plants, flushing it into nearby waterways, or paying to have it hauled away for special disposal. Once the toxic waste was removed from their premises, those who produced it had no further liability. Many of the individuals and firms hauling the hazardous waste improperly stored it in leaky drums or dumped it into private and public landfills.

The Superfund law established direct controls, specific taxes, and liability rules in addressing the toxic waste problem. It asserted Federal control over

the contaminated sites and assigned liability for the improperly dumped waste to the firms producing, transporting, and dumping it. Also, the law imposed a tax on manufacturers of toxic chemicals, with revenues flowing into a "Superfund," to be used by the Environmental Protection Agency (EPA) to help finance the cleanup of the 1250 toxic waste sites. Once the decontamination work is under way, the Federal government sues the allegedly responsible parties to try to recover all or part of the expense.

How has the Superfund concept worked? On the plus side, the tax on chemical producers has raised billions of dollars. Also, some of the nation's most toxic waste sites have been cleaned up. On the negative side, the Superfund became a political "public works" project. Politicians fought among themselves to get their home state or local dump sites on the cleanup list and to establish the highest priority for cleanup efforts in their locales. Decontamination of the toxic-waste sites not only eliminates health hazards, it brings money and jobs to the cleansed area.

Numerous studies, hearings, and appeals are required to decide on the proper scope and method of cleanup for each site. This process has taken considerable time and has had the unpleasant side-effect of draining enormous sums from the Superfund. Reports indicate that millions of dollars have gone toward dubious overhead expenses charged to the government by private contractors. Lawyers' fees and other litigation expenses have ballooned. Firms are fighting government suits, suing one another to determine liability, and suing their insurance companies. The stakes are large because the total cost of cleanup is an estimated $100 billion. As of 1994, businesses and government had spent $13 billion on cleanup— $3 billion of it going to lawyers.

After fourteen years, only about 220 of the 1250 toxic-waste sites on the Superfund list have actually been decontaminated. Work now is underway on about 600 other sites. This slow start and the litigation morass have prompted Congress to reexamine the Superfund law, looking for ways to streamline the liability and cleanup rules. New legislation to reduce the litigation and modify the clean-up requirements was proposed in Congress in 1994.

Clean Air Act of 1990 Direct controls in the form of *uniform emission standards*—limits on allowable pollution—have historically dominated American air pollution policy. The **Clean Air Act of 1990** continues this tradition, but also establishes a limited market for pollution rights. The five provisions of this law are as follows.

1 Toxic Air Pollution Factories and businesses must install "maximum achievable control technology" to reduce emissions of 189 toxic chemicals by 90 percent by the year 2000.

2 Urban Smog Smog-causing pollution in about 100 cities with unhealthy air must be reduced by 15 percent within six years and 3 percent annually after that until air quality standards are met.

3 Motor Vehicles Auto tailpipe emissions, the major cause of urban smog, must be reduced 30 to 60 percent by 1998. Also, the law requires the sale of cleaner blends of gasoline in the nine cities with the worst smog problems. In Los Angeles, 300,000 cars must be powered by alternative fuels by 1999.

4 Ozone Depletion The use of CFCs which deplete the ozone layer must be curtailed by 50 percent by 1998. Although not a part of this law, the excise tax on CFCs previously discussed will help accomplish this reduction.

5 Acid Rain To stop the destruction of lakes and forests by acid rain, coal-burning electric utilities must cut their annual emissions of sulfur dioxide by about 50 percent. The law also creates a market for pollution rights similar to that shown in Figure 30-5 by allowing utilities to trade *emission credits* provided by government. Some utilities may choose to reduce sulfur dioxide emissions by more than amounts specified, selling their emission credits to other utilities that find it less costly to buy the credits than install additional pollution-control equipment.

Trading of Pollution Rights The acid-rain provisions of the Clean Air Act of 1990 complement other air pollution policies which permit exchange of pollution rights. The EPA now permits firms to exchange pollution rights internally and externally.

Polluters are allowed to transfer air pollution rights internally between individual sources within their plants. That is, as long as they meet the overall pollution standard assigned to them, firms may increase one source of pollution by offsetting it with reduced pollution from another part of their operations.

The EPA also permits external trading of pollution rights. It has set targets for reducing air pollution

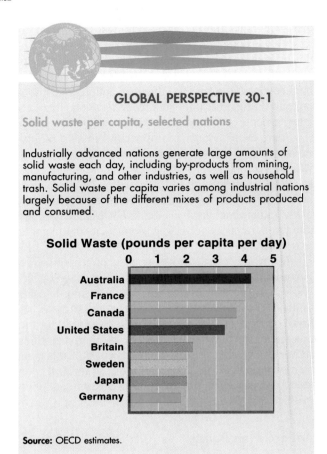

GLOBAL PERSPECTIVE 30-1

Solid waste per capita, selected nations

Industrially advanced nations generate large amounts of solid waste each day, including by-products from mining, manufacturing, and other industries, as well as household trash. Solid waste per capita varies among industrial nations largely because of the different mixes of products produced and consumed.

Solid Waste (pounds per capita per day)

	0	1	2	3	4	5
Australia						
France						
Canada						
United States						
Britain						
Sweden						
Japan						
Germany						

Source: OECD estimates.

in regions where the minimum standards are not being met. Previously, new pollution sources could not enter these regions unless existing polluters went out of business. In the last decade, the EPA has allowed firms which reduce their pollution below set standards to sell their pollution rights to other firms. A new firm desiring to locate in the Los Angeles area, for example, might be able to buy rights to emit 20 tons of nitrous oxide annually from an existing firm which has reduced its emissions below its allowable limit. The price of these emission rights will depend on their supply and demand.

A growing market for such rights has emerged. The acid-rain provisions of the Clean Air Act of 1990 have greatly expanded this market. In the first annual EPA auction of sulfur dioxide rights in 1993, utilities and others bought $21 million of such rights. These buyers, in turn, can sell these rights to others through the Chicago Board of Trade, which has established a formal market for sulfur dioxide emission rights.

Solid-Waste Disposal and Recycling

Nowhere is the law of conservation of matter and energy more apparent than in solid-waste disposal (Global Perspective 30-1). The 165 million tons of garbage which accumulate annually in our landfills have become a growing externality problem. Landfills in the northeast, in particular, are either completely full or rapidly filling up. Garbage from there and elsewhere is now being transported hundreds of miles across state lines to dumps in other states.

On the receiving end, people in rural areas near newly expanding dumps are understandably upset about the increased truck traffic on their highways and growing mounds of smelly garbage in local dumps. Also, some landfills are producing serious groundwater pollution.

The high opportunity cost of urban and suburban land, and the negative externalities created by dumps, make the landfill solution to solid waste increasingly expensive. An alternative garbage policy is to incinerate it in plants which produce electricity. But people object to having garbage incinerators—a source of truck traffic and air pollution—close to their homes. What's the solution to the growing problem of solid waste?

Although garbage dumps and incinerators remain the main ways of garbage disposal, recycling is receiving increased attention. According to the EPA, 90 percent of lead-acid batteries, 55 percent of aluminum cans, 45 percent of corrugated boxes, 30 percent of newspapers, 21 percent of plastic soft drink bottles, and 20 percent of glass beer bottles are now being recycled.

Market for Recyclable Inputs The incentives for recycling can be shown through Figure 30-7a where we have drawn a demand and supply curve for some recyclable product, say, glass.

The demand for recyclable glass derives from manufacturers of glass who use it as a resource in producing new glass. The demand curve for recyclable glass slopes downward, telling us that manufacturers will increase their purchases of recyclable glass as its price falls.

The location of the resource demand curve in Figure 30-7a depends partly on the demand for the product using the recycled glass. The greater the demand for the product, the greater is the demand for the recyclable input. The location of the curve also depends on the technology and thus the cost of using original raw materials rather than recycled glass in the production process. The more costly it is to use original materials relative to recycled glass, the further to the right will be the demand curve for recyclable glass.

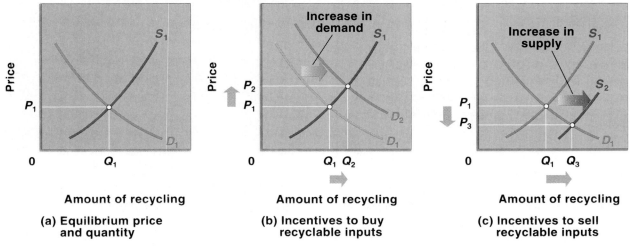

FIGURE 30-7 The economics of recycling
The equilibrium price and amount of materials recycled are determined by supply and demand, as shown in (a). In (b), policies which increase the incentives for producers to buy recyclable inputs shift the demand curve rightward and raise both equilibrium price and the amount of recycling. In (c), policies which encourage households to recycle increase supply and expand the equilibrium amount of recycling but also reduce the equilibrium price of recyclable inputs.

(a) Equilibrium price and quantity

(b) Incentives to buy recyclable inputs

(c) Incentives to sell recyclable inputs

The supply curve for recyclable glass slopes upward in the typical fashion because higher prices increase the incentive for households to recycle. The location of the supply curve depends on such factors as the attitudes of households toward recycling and the cost to them of alternative disposal.

The equilibrium price P_1 and quantity Q_1 in Figure 30-7a are determined at the intersection of the supply and demand curves. At price P_1 the market clears; there is neither a shortage nor a surplus of recyclable glass.

Policy Suppose government wants to encourage recycling as an alternative to land dumps or incineration. It could do this in one of two ways.

1 Demand Incentives Government could increase recycling by increasing the demand for recycled inputs. If the demand curve in Figure 30-7b shifts from D_1 rightward to D_2, equilibrium price and quantity will increase to P_2 and Q_2. A policy which might accomplish this goal would be to place specific taxes on the inputs which are substitutable for recycled glass in the production process. Such taxes would encourage firms to use more of the untaxed recycled glass and less of the original taxed inputs. Or government could shift its purchases toward goods produced with recycled inputs and require that its contractors do the same. Example: In 1993 the Federal government announced a new policy requiring 20 percent or more recycled content in every piece of writing and copying paper purchased by Federal agencies.

Also, environmental awareness by the public can contribute to rightward shifts of the demand curve for recycled resources. Fearing negative consumer backlashes against their products, firms such as Procter & Gamble (disposable diapers) and McDonald's (packaging of fast foods) have undertaken multimillion dollar campaigns to use recycled plastic and paper.

2 Supply Incentives As shown in Figure 30-7c, government can also increase recycling by shifting the supply curve rightward, as from S_1 to S_2. Equilibrium price would fall from P_1 to P_3 and equilibrium quantity—in this case, recyclable glass—would rise from Q_1 to Q_3. Many local governments have implemented specific policies which fit within this framework. For example, they encourage recycling by providing curbside pickup of recyclable goods such as glass, aluminum cans, and newspapers at a lower monthly fee than for pickup of normal garbage.

In a few cases, supply incentives for recyclables have been so effective that the prices of some recycled items have fallen to zero. You can envision this outcome by shifting the supply curve in Figure 30-7c further and further rightward. Some cities now are *paying* manufacturers to truck away certain recyclable products such as mixed paper (negative price) rather than charging them a price. This may or may not promote economic efficiency. The cost of paying firms to take away recyclable products may be lower than the cost of alternative disposal, particularly in view of the negative externalities of dumps and incinerators. If so, recycling will promote economic efficiency.

However, a policy of paying firms to take away recyclable items need not always be economical. In some cases it may be more costly to recycle goods than to bury or incinerate them, even when externalities are considered. If so, recycling will *reduce* efficiency rather than increase it.

Government's task is to find the optimal amount of recycling compared to alternative disposal of garbage. It can do this by estimating and comparing the marginal benefit and marginal cost of recycling. And, incidentally, consumers as a group can reduce the initial accumulation of garbage by not buying products with excessive packaging.

QUICK REVIEW 30-2

■ Policies for coping with the overallocation of resources caused by spillover costs are *a* private bargaining, *b* liability rules and lawsuits, *c* direct controls, *d* specific taxes, and *e* markets for externality rights.

■ Policies for correcting the underallocation of resources associated with spillover benefits are *a* private bargaining, *b* subsidies to producers, *c* subsidies to consumers, and *d* government provision.

■ The optimal amount of negative externality reduction occurs where society's marginal cost and marginal benefit of reducing the externality are equal.

■ The ultimate cause of pollution is the law of conservation of matter and energy, which holds that matter can be transformed into other matter or into energy, but cannot vanish.

■ Recent policies to reduce pollution include the Superfund law of 1980, the Clean Air Act of 1990, and recycling.

INFORMATION FAILURES

Thus far we have added new detail and insights concerning two types of market failure: public goods and externalities. There is another, more subtle, market failure. This inefficiency results when either buyers or sellers have incomplete or inaccurate information and their cost of obtaining better information is prohibitive. Technically stated, this form of market failure occurs because of **asymmetric information**— unequal knowledge possessed by the parties to a market transaction. Buyers and sellers do not have identical information about price, quality, or some other aspect of the good or service.

Market information normally is sufficient to ensure that goods and services are produced and purchased in economically efficient quantities. But in some cases, inadequate information makes it difficult to distinguish legitimate from illegitimate sellers, or legitimate from illegitimate buyers. In these markets, society's scarce resources will not be used efficiently, implying that government should intervene by increasing the information available to the market participants. Under rarer circumstances government may itself supply a good for which information problems have prohibited profitable production.

Inadequate Information About Sellers

We begin by asking how inadequate information about *sellers* and their products can cause market failure. Examining the market for gasoline and the services of surgeons will give us an answer.

Gasoline Market   Assume an absurd situation. Suppose there is no system of weights and measures established by law, no government inspection of gasoline pumps, and no laws against false advertising. Each gas station can use whatever measure it chooses; it can define a gallon of gas as it pleases. A station can advertise that its gas is 87 octane when in fact it is only 75. It can rig its pumps to indicate it is providing more gas than the amount being delivered.

Obviously, the consumer's cost of obtaining reliable information under these conditions is exceptionally high, if not prohibitive. Each consumer will have to buy samples of gas from various gas stations, have them tested for octane level, and pour gas into a measuring device to see how the station has calibrated the pump. Also, the consumer will need to use a hand calculator to ascertain if the machine is correctly multiplying the price per gallon by the number of gallons. And these activities will need to be repeated regularly, since the station owner can alter the product quality and the accuracy of the pump at will.

Because of the high costs of obtaining information about the seller, many customers will opt out of this chaotic market. One tankful of a 50 percent solution of gasoline and water will be enough to discourage motorists from further driving. More realistically, the conditions described in this market will encourage consumers to vote for political candidates who promise to provide a governmental solution. The oil companies and honest gasoline suppliers will not object to this government intervention. They will realize that, by enabling this market to work, accurate information will expand their total sales.

Government has intervened in the market for gasoline and other markets having similar information difficulties. It has established a system of weights and measures, employed inspectors to check the accuracy of gasoline pumps, and passed laws against fraudulent claims and misleading advertising. There can be no doubt that these government activities have produced net benefits for society.

Licensing of Surgeons   Let's look at another example of how inadequate information about sellers can create market failure. Suppose that anyone can hang out a shingle and claim to be a surgeon in much the same way that anyone can become a house painter. The market will eventually sort out the true surgeons from those who are learning by doing or are fly-by-night operators who move into and out of an area. As people die from unsuccessful surgery, lawsuits for malpractice eventually will eliminate the medical imposters. People needing surgery for themselves or their loved ones can glean information from newspaper reports and solicit information from people—or their relatives—who have undergone similar operations.

But this process of generating information for those needing surgery will take considerable time and will impose unacceptably high human and economic costs. There is a fundamental difference between an amateurish paint job on one's house and being on the receiving end of heart surgery by a bogus physician. The marginal cost of obtaining information about sellers in this market is excessively high. The risk of proceeding without good information will result in an underallocation of resources to surgery.

Government has remedied this market failure through a system of qualifying tests and licensing. This licensing enables consumers to obtain inexpensive information about a service they only infrequently buy. Government has taken a similar role in several other areas of the economy. For example, it approves new medicines, regulates the securities industry, and requires warnings on containers of potentially hazardous substances. It also requires warning labels on cigarette packages and disseminates information about communicable diseases. It issues warnings about unsafe toys and inspects restaurants for health-related violations.

Inadequate Information About Buyers

Just as inadequate information about sellers can keep markets from achieving economic efficiency, so can inadequate information about *buyers*. These buyers can be consumers buying products or firms buying resources.

Moral Hazard Problem   Private markets may underallocate resources to a particular good or service for which there is a severe **moral hazard problem.** *The moral hazard problem is the tendency of one party to a contract to alter her or his behavior in ways which are costly to the other party.*

To understand this point, suppose a firm offers an insurance policy which pays a set amount of money per month to people who suffer divorces. The attraction of this insurance is that it pools the economic risk of divorce among thousands of people and, in particular, protects spouses and children from the economic hardship which divorce often brings. Unfortunately, the moral hazard problem reduces the likelihood that insurance companies can profitably provide this type of insurance contract.

After taking out this insurance, some people will alter their behavior in ways which impose heavy costs on the insurer. Married couples will have less of an incentive to get along and to iron out marital difficulties. At the extreme, some people might be motivated to obtain a divorce, collect the insurance, and then live together. The insurance promotes *more* divorces, the very outcome it protects against. The moral hazard difficulty will force the insurer to charge such high premiums for this insurance that few policies will be bought. If the insurer could identify in advance those

people most prone to alter their behavior, the firm could exclude them from buying it. But the firm's marginal cost of getting this information is too high compared to the marginal benefit. Thus, this market fails.

Divorce insurance is not available in the marketplace. But society recognizes the benefits of insuring against the hardships of divorce. It has corrected for this underallocation of "hardship insurance" through child-support laws which dictate payments—when the economic circumstances warrant—to the spouse who retains the children. Alimony laws also play a role.

Government provides "divorce insurance" of sorts through the Aid to Families with Dependent Children (AFDC) program. If a divorce leaves a spouse with children destitute, the family is eligible for AFDC payments. Government intervention does not eliminate the moral hazard problem; instead, it offsets its adverse effects. Unlike private firms, government need not earn a profit to continue the insurance.

The moral hazard concept has numerous applications. We mention them to reinforce your understanding of the basic principle.

1   Drivers may be less cautious because they have car insurance.
2   Medical malpractice insurance may increase the amount of malpractice.
3   Guaranteed contracts for professional athletes may reduce the quality of their performance.
4   Unemployment compensation insurance may lead some workers to shirk.
5   Government insurance on bank deposits may encourage banks to make risky loans.

Adverse Selection Problem   Another information problem resulting from inadequate information about buyers is the **adverse selection problem.** *The adverse selection problem arises when information known by the first party to a contract is not known by the second, and, as a result, the second party incurs major costs.* Unlike the moral hazard problem, which arises *after* a person signs a contract, the adverse selection problem arises *at the time* a person signs the contract.

In insurance, the adverse selection problem is that people most likely to receive insurance payouts are those who will buy insurance. For example, those in poorest health will seek to buy the most generous health insurance policies. Or, at the extreme, a person planning to hire an arsonist to "torch" his failing business has an incentive to buy fire insurance.

Our hypothetical divorce insurance sheds further light on the adverse selection problem. If the insurance firm sets the premiums on the basis of the average rate of divorce, many of the married couples about to get a divorce will buy insurance. An insurance premium based on average probabilities will make for a great insurance buy for those about to get divorced. Meanwhile, those in highly stable marriages will opt against buying it.

The adverse selection problem will eliminate the pooling of risk which is the basis for profitable insurance. The insurance rates needed to cover payouts will be so high that few people will wish or be able to buy this insurance.

Where private firms underprovide insurance because of information problems, government often establishes some type of social insurance. Government can require everyone in a particular group to enter the insurance pool and therefore can overcome the adverse selection problem. Although the social security system in the United States is partly an insurance and partly a welfare program, in its broadest sense it is insurance against poverty during old age. The social security insurance program overcomes the adverse selection problem by requiring nearly universal participation. People who are most likely to need the minimum benefits that social security provides automatically are participants in the program. So, too, are those not likely to need the benefits.

Workplace Safety The labor market also provides an example of how inadequate information about buyers (employers) can produce market failures.

For several reasons employers have an economic incentive to provide safe workplaces. A safe workplace reduces the amount of disruption of the production process created by job accidents and lowers the costs of recruiting, screening, training, and retaining new workers. It also reduces a firm's worker compensation insurance premiums (legally required insurance against job injuries).

But a safe workplace has an expense. Safe equipment, protective gear, and slower paces of work all entail costs. The firm will compare its marginal cost and marginal benefit of providing a safer workplace in deciding how much safety to provide. Will this amount of job safety achieve social efficiency, as well as maximize the firm's profits?

The answer is "Yes" if the labor and product markets are competitive and workers are fully aware of job risks at various places of employment. With full information, workers will avoid employers having unsafe workplaces. The supply of labor to these establishments will be greatly restricted, forcing them to boost their wages to attract a work force. These higher wages give the employer an incentive to provide socially desirable levels of workplace safety; safer workplaces will reduce wage expenses. Only firms which find it very costly to provide safer workplaces will choose to pay high compensating wage differentials, rather than reduce workplace hazards.

But a serious problem arises when workers *do not know* that particular occupations or workplaces are unsafe. Because information about the buyer is inadequate—that is, about the employer and the workplace—the firm may *not* need to pay a wage premium to attract its work force. Its incentive to remove safety hazards therefore is diminished and its profit-maximizing level of workplace safety will be less than socially desirable. In brief, the labor market will fail because of asymmetric information—in this case, sellers (workers) having less information than buyers (employers).

Government has several options for remedying this information problem.

1 It can directly provide information to workers about the injury experience of various employers, much like it publishes the on-time performance of the various airlines.

2 It can mandate that firms provide information to workers about known workplace hazards.

3 It can establish standards of workplace safety and enforce them through inspection and penalties.

The Federal government has mainly employed the "standards and enforcement" approach to improve workplace safety, but some contend that an "information" strategy might be less costly and more effective. *(Key Question 13)*

QUICK REVIEW 30-3

■ Asymmetric information can cause markets to fail, causing society's scarce resources to be allocated inefficiently.

■ The moral hazard problem is the tendency of one party to a contract to alter its behavior in ways which are costly to the other party; for example, a person who buys insurance may incur added risk.

■ As it relates to insurance, the adverse selection problem is the tendency of people who are most likely to collect insurance benefits to buy large amounts of insurance.

L A S T   W O R D

USED CARS: THE MARKET FOR "LEMONS"

Asymmetric product information could result in markets where sellers offer only defective goods.

A new car loses much of its market value as the buyer drives it off the sales lot. Physical depreciation cannot explain this large loss of value, since the same new car can sit on the dealer's lot for weeks, or even months, and retain its value.

One explanation of this paradox rests on the idea of asymmetric information about *used* cars.* Auto owners have much more knowledge about the mechanical condition of their vehicles than do potential buyers of used cars. At the time of the purchase, individual buyers of used cars find it difficult to distinguish between so-called "lemons"—defective cars —and vehicles of the same car make and model that operate perfectly. Therefore, a single price emerges for used cars of the same year, make, and model

*The classical article on this topic is George A. Akerlof, "The Market for 'Lemons': Qualitative Uncertainty and the Market Mechanism," *Quarterly Journal of Economics,* August 1970, pp. 488–500.

whether they are lemons or high-quality vehicles. This price roughly reflects the average quality of the vehicles, influenced by the proportion of lemons to high-quality cars. The higher the proportion of lemons, the lower are prices of used cars.

An adverse selection problem now becomes evident. Owners of lemons have an incentive to sell their

Qualification

People have found many ingenious ways to overcome information difficulties short of government intervention. For example, many firms offer product warranties to overcome the lack of information about themselves and their products. Franchising also helps overcome this problem. When you visit McDonald's or Holiday Inn, you know precisely what you are going to get, as opposed to Sam's Hamburger Shop or the Bates Motel.

Also, some private firms and organizations have

specialized in providing information to buyers and sellers. *Consumer Reports* and the *Mobil Travel Guide* provide product information, labor unions collect and disseminate information about job safety, and credit bureaus provide information to insurance companies. Brokers, bonding agencies, and intermediaries also provide information to clients.

However, economists agree that the private sector cannot remedy all information problems. In some situations government intervention is desirable to promote an efficient allocation of society's scarce resources.

CHAPTER SUMMARY

1 Graphically, the collective demand curve for a particular public good can be found by summing *vertically* each of the individual demand curves for that good. The demand curve resulting from this process indicates the collective willingness to pay for the last unit of any given amount of the public good.

2 The optimal quantity of a public good occurs where the combined willingness to pay for the last unit—the marginal

benefit of the good—equals the good's marginal cost.

3 Benefit-cost analysis can provide guidance as to the economic desirability and most efficient scope of public goods output.

4 Spillovers or externalities cause the equilibrium output of certain goods to vary from the optimal output. Spillover costs result in an overallocation of resources which can be corrected by legislation or specific taxes. Spillover benefits

cars to unsuspecting buyers, while owners of high-quality autos will wish to keep their cars. Therefore, most used cars on the market will be of lower quality than the same car models which are *not* for sale. As people become aware of this, the demand for used cars will decline and prices of used cars will fall. These lower prices will further reduce the incentive of owners of high-quality used cars to offer them for sale. At the extreme, only lemons will appear on the market; *poor-quality products will drive out high-quality products.*

We thus have a solution to our paradox. Once a buyer drives a new car away from the dealership, the auto's value becomes the value set in the lemons' market. This is true even though the probability is high that the new car is of high quality.

The instantaneous loss of new car value would be even greater were it not for several factors. Because new-car warranties are transferable to used-car buyers, purchasers of low-mileage late-model cars are protected against costly repairs. Thus, the demand for these vehicles rises. Also, prospective buyers can distinguish good cars from lemons by hiring mechanics to perform inspections. Moreover, sellers can signal potential buyers that their cars are not lemons through ads such as "Must sell, transferred abroad," "Divorce forces sale." Of course, the buyer must determine the truth of these claims. Additionally, auto rental companies routinely sell high-quality, late-model cars, increasing the ratio of good cars to lemons in the used-car market.

Government also plays a role in solving the market failure evident in the lemons' market. Many states have "lemon laws" which force auto dealers to take back defective new cars. Supposedly, dealers do not offer these lemons for sale in the used-car market until completing all needed repairs. Also, some states require dealers to either offer warranties on used cars or explicitly state that a car is offered "as is." The latter designation gives the buyer a good clue that the car may be defective.

In brief, both private and governmental initiatives temper the lemons' problem. Nevertheless, this principle is applicable to a wide variety of used products such as autos, computers, and cameras, which are complex and occasionally defective. Buying any of these used products remains a somewhat risky transaction.

---

are accompanied by an underallocation of resources which can be corrected by subsidies to consumers, subsidies to producers, or government provision.

5 According to the Coase theorem, private bargaining is capable of solving potential externality problems where **a** the property rights are clearly defined, **b** the number of people involved is small, and **c** bargaining costs are negligible.

6 Clearly established property rights and liability rules permit some spillover costs to be prevented or remedied through private lawsuits. Lawsuits, however, are costly, time-consuming, and uncertain as to their results.

7 Direct controls and specific taxes can improve resource allocation in situations where externalities affect many people and community resources. Both direct controls (smokestack emission standards) and specific taxes (taxes on firms producing toxic chemicals) increase production costs and hence product price. As product price rises, the externality is reduced since less of the output is bought and sold.

8 Markets for pollution rights, where people can buy and sell the rights to a fixed amount of pollution, put a price on pollution and encourage firms to reduce or eliminate it.

9 The socially optimal amount of externality abatement occurs where society's marginal cost and marginal benefit of reducing the externality are equal. This optimal amount of pollution abatement is likely to be less than a 100 percent reduction. Changes in technology or changes in society's attitudes about pollution can affect the optimal amount of pollution abatement.

10 The law of conservation of matter and energy is at the heart of the pollution problem. Matter can be transformed into other matter or into energy, but does not disappear. If not recycled, all production will ultimately end up as waste.

11 The Superfund law of 1980 places a tax on producers of chemicals and uses the proceeds to clean up toxic-waste dumps. The Clean Air Act of 1990 seeks to **a** reduce toxic air pollution, **b** hasten smog reduction in urban areas, **c** limit the use of substances which are depleting the earth's ozone layer, and **d** reduce acid rain by cutting emissions of sulfur dioxide. Under the law, utilities are able to buy and sell emission credits for sulfur dioxide.

12 Recycling is a recent response to the growing garbage disposal problem. The equilibrium price and quantity of recyclable inputs depend on their demand and supply. Government can encourage recycling through either demand or supply incentives.

13 Asymmetric information between sellers and buyers can cause markets to fail. The moral hazard problem occurs when people alter their behavior after they sign a contract, imposing costs on the other party. As it relates to insurance, the adverse selection problem occurs when people who are of above-average risk buy large amounts of insurance.

TERMS AND CONCEPTS

benefit-cost analysis
marginal benefit =
   marginal cost rule
Coase theorem

market for externality
   rights
optimal reduction of an
   externality

law of conservation of
   matter and energy
Superfund law of 1980
Clean Air Act of 1990

asymmetric information
moral hazard problem
adverse selection
   problem

QUESTIONS AND STUDY SUGGESTIONS

1 *Key Question* *Based on following three individual de-mand schedules for a particular good, and assuming these three people are the only ones in the society, determine* **a** *the market demand schedule on the assumption that the good is a private good, and* **b** *the collective demand schedule on the assumption that the good is a public good. Explain the differences, if any, in your schedules.*

Individual 1		Individual 2		Individual 3	
P	**Q_d**	**P**	**Q_d**	**P**	**Q_d**
$8	0	$8	1	$8	0
7	0	7	2	7	0
6	0	6	3	6	1
5	1	5	4	5	2
4	2	4	5	4	3
3	3	3	6	3	4
2	4	2	7	2	5
1	5	1	8	1	6

2 *Key Question* *Use your demand schedule for a public good determined in question 1 and the following supply schedule to ascertain the optimal quantity of this public good. Why is this the optimal quantity?*

P	**Q_s**
$19	10
16	8
13	6
10	4
7	2
4	1

3 *Key Question* *The following table shows the total costs and total benefits in billions for four different antipollution programs of increasing scope. Which program should be undertaken? Why?*

Program	Total cost	Total benefit
A	$ 3	$ 7
B	7	12
C	12	16
D	18	19

4 *Key Question* *Why are spillover costs and spillover benefits also called negative and positive "externalities"? Show graphically how a tax can correct for a spillover cost and a subsidy to producers can correct for a spillover benefit. How*
does a subsidy to consumers differ from a subsidy to produc-ers in correcting for a spillover benefit?

5 An apple-grower's orchard provides nectar to a neigh-bor's bees, while a beekeeper's bees help the apple grower by pollinating the apple blossoms. Use Figure 30-2b to ex-plain why this situation might lead to an underallocation of resources to apple growing and to beekeeping. How might this underallocation get resolved via the means suggested by the Coase theorem?

6 Explain: "Without a market for pollution rights, dump-ing pollutants into the air or water is costless; in the pres-ence of the right to buy and sell pollution rights, dumping pollution creates an opportunity cost for the polluter." What is the significance of this fact to the search for better tech-nology to reduce pollution?

7 *Key Question* *Manipulate the MB curve in Figure 30-6 to explain the following statement: "The optimal amount of pollution abatement for some substances, say, water from storm drains, is very low; the optimal amount of abatement for other substances, say, cyanide poison, is close to 100 per-cent." Explain.*

8 Relate the law of conservation of matter and energy to: **a** the air pollution problem; and **b** the solid-waste disposal problem.

9 What is the Superfund? How is it financed and for what purpose is it used? Are there any Superfund sites in your area? If so, determine the current status of the cleanup ef-forts.

10 Which provisions of the Clean Air Act of 1990 reflect the direct controls approach to pollution? Which provision directly incorporates a market for pollution rights?

11 Explain why there may be insufficient recycling of products when the externalities associated with landfills and garbage incinerators are not considered. What demand and supply incentives might government provide to promote more recycling?

12 Why is it in the interest of new home buyers *and* builders of new homes to have government building codes and building inspectors?

13 *Key Question*   *Place an M beside items in the following list which describe a moral hazard problem; place an A beside those which describe an adverse selection problem.*

   a *A person with a terminal illness buys several life insurance policies through the mail.*

   b *A person drives carelessly because he or she has insurance.*

   c *A person who intends to "torch" his warehouse takes out a large fire insurance policy.*

   d *A professional athlete who has a guaranteed contract fails to stay in shape during the off-season.*

   e *A woman anticipating having a large family takes a job with a firm which offers exceptional child-care benefits.*

14 (Last Word) Relate the prices of used cars to the following two problems: **a** asymmetric information and   **b** adverse selection.

31

PUBLIC CHOICE THEORY AND TAXATION

Why does government elicit so much public disenchantment and distrust? One reason is the apparent failure of costly government programs to resolve socioeconomic ills. For example, it is argued that foreign aid programs have contributed little or nothing to the economic growth of the less developed nations. We hear reports that well-financed state and Federal school enrichment programs have had no perceptible impact on the educational attainment of students. Some programs have fostered the very problems they were designed to solve: Our farm programs were originally designed to save the family farm, but instead have subsidized large corporate farms which have driven family farms out of business.

There are charges that government agencies have become mired in paperwork. It is alleged that the public bureaucracy has developed trivial regulations and embodies great duplication of effort; that obsolete programs persist; that various agencies work at cross purpose; and so on.

Just as there are limitations or failures in the private sector's market system, it seems there are inherent deficiencies in the political processes, bureaucratic agencies, and tax systems within the public sector.

This chapter will examine some of these difficulties. Specifically, we scrutinize the problems society has in revealing its true preferences through majority voting. This is followed by a discussion of *government failure*—the contention that certain characteristics of the public sector hinder government's ability to assist the market system in achieving an efficient allocation of resources. Next, we examine taxes and tax incidence to see how taxes are apportioned in the United States and who bears the burden. After examining recent and proposed tax reforms, we briefly discuss the conservative and liberal stances on government and economic freedom.

We'll see that this is a chapter on **public choice theory**—the economic analysis of government decision making; and on selected topics and problems of **public finance**—the study of public expenditures and revenues.

REVEALING PREFERENCES THROUGH MAJORITY VOTING

Which public goods should government produce and in what amounts? In what circumstances and through what methods should government intervene to correct for externalities? How should the tax burden of financing government be apportioned?

Decisions like these concern government and are made collectively in the United States through a democratic process relying heavily on majority voting. Candidates for office offer voters alternative policy packages and we elect people who we think will make the best decisions on our collective behalf. Voters "retire" officials who do not adequately represent their collective wishes and elect persons who convince them they will better reflect the collective wants of the electorate. Also, citizens periodically have opportunities at the state and local level to vote directly on ballot issues involving public expenditures or new legislation.

Although this democratic process generally works well at revealing society's true preferences, it has shortcomings. Just as the market fails in some cases to allocate resources efficiently, our system of voting sometimes produces inefficiencies and inconsistencies.

Inefficient Voting Outcomes

Providing a public good having a total benefit greater than its total cost will add to society's well-being. Unfortunately, majority voting raises the possibility of economically inefficient outcomes. Voters may defeat a proposal to provide a public good even though it may yield total benefits exceeding its total cost. And it's possible that majority voting could result in provision of a public good costing more than the benefits it yields.

Illustration: Inefficient "No" Vote   Suppose a public good, say, national defense, can be provided at a total expense of $900. Also, assume there are only three individuals—Adams, Benson, and Conrad—in the society and they will share the $900 tax expense equally, each paying $300 of tax if the good is provided. Suppose, as illustrated in Figure 31-1a, that Adams is willing to pay $700 to have this good; Benson, $250; and Conrad, $200.

What might be the result if a majority vote is determined on whether or not this good will be provided? Although people do not always vote strictly on the basis of their own economic interest, it is likely Benson and Conrad will vote "No" because they will incur tax expenses of $300 each while gaining benefits of only $250 and $200, respectively. The majority vote in this case will defeat the proposal even though the total benefit of $1150 (= $700 for Adams + $250 for Benson + $200 for Conrad) exceeds the total cost of $900. More resources should be devoted to this good, but they are not.

Illustration: Inefficient "Yes" Vote   We can construct an example illustrating the converse—the majority favoring the provision of a public good even though its total cost exceeds its total benefit. Figure 31-1b shows the details. Again, Adams, Benson, and Conrad will equally share the $900 cost of the public

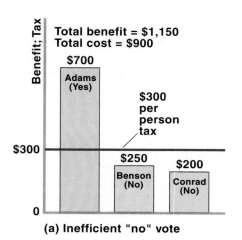

(a) Inefficient "no" vote

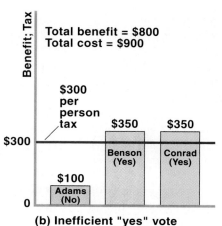

(b) Inefficient "yes" vote

FIGURE 31-1 Inefficient voting outcomes
Majority voting can produce inefficient decisions. In (a) majority voting leads to rejection of a public good which would entail a greater total benefit than total cost. In (b) majority voting results in provision of a public good having a higher total cost than total benefit.

good; they each will be taxed $300. But, now Adams is only willing to pay $100 for the public good, rather than forgo it. Meanwhile, Benson and Adams are willing to pay $350 each. They will vote for the public good; Adams will vote against it. The election will result in a public good costing $900 which produces total benefits of $800 (= $100 for Adams + $350 for Benson + $350 for Conrad). Society's resources will be inefficiently allocated to this public good.

Conclusion The point of our examples is that an inefficiency may occur as either an overproduction or underproduction of a specific public good, and therefore an overallocation or underallocation of resources for that particular use. In Chapter 30 we saw that government might improve economic efficiency by providing public goods which the market system would not make available. Now we have extended that analysis to reveal that government might fail to provide some public goods whose production is economically justifiable while providing other goods not economically warranted.

Our examples illustrate that people have only a single vote no matter how much they might gain or lose from a public good. In both examples shown in Figure 31-1, if buying votes were legal, Adams would be willing to purchase a vote from either Benson or Conrad, paying for it out of prospective personal gain. In the marketplace the consumer can decide *not* to buy a good, even though it is popular with others. Also, specific goods are normally available to people with strong preferences for them even though most consumers conclude that product prices exceed the marginal utilities of these goods. A consumer can buy beef tongues and fresh squid in some supermarkets, but it is doubtful these products would be available under a system using majority voting to stock the shelves. On the other hand, you cannot easily "buy" national defense once the majority has decided it is not worth buying.

Because it fails to incorporate the strength of the preferences of the individual voter, majority voting may produce economically inefficient outcomes.

Interest Groups and Logrolling Ways exist through which inefficiencies associated with majority voting *may* get resolved. Two examples:

1   Interest Groups Those who have a strong preference for a public good may band together into an interest group and use advertisements, mailings, and the like to try to convince others of the merits of a public good. In our first example (Figure 31-1a), Adams might try to convince Benson and Conrad it is in their interest to vote for national defense—that it is worth more than the $250 and $200 values they place on it. Such appeals are common in contemporary American politics.

2   Political Logrolling Logrolling—*the trading of votes to secure favorable outcomes on decisions which otherwise would be adverse*—can turn an inefficient outcome into an efficient one. In our first example (Figure 31-1a), perhaps Benson has a strong preference for a different public good, say, a new road, which Adams and Conrad do not think is worth the tax expense. Now, an opportunity had developed for Adams and Benson to trade votes to ensure provision of *both* national defense and the new road. The majority vote (Adams and Benson) in our three-person society will result in a positive vote for both national defense and the road. Without the logrolling, each would have been rejected. This logrolling will add to society's well-being if, as was true for national defense, the road creates a positive overall net benefit.

Logrolling need not increase economic efficiency. We could construct a scenario in which both national defense and the road individually cost more than the total benefits they each provide, and yet both would be provided because of vote trading. All that is necessary for the road and national defense to be provided is that Adams and Benson each secure net gains from their favored public good.

The tax cost imposed on Conrad by the expenditures for national defense and the road could exceed Conrad's benefits so much that it swamped the combined net benefit received by Adams and Benson from the public goods. Under majority voting and logrolling, government will provide each of the public goods and shift a large net burden to Conrad. Political scientists call this practice "pork-barrel politics" (getting public goods for constituents from the public barrel).

Logrolling can either increase or diminish economic efficiency depending on the circumstances.

The Paradox of Voting

Another difficulty with majority voting is the **paradox of voting,** *a situation where society may not be able to rank its preferences consistently through majority voting.*

TABLE 31-1 Paradox of voting

Public Good	Preferences		
	Adams	Benson	Conrad
National defense	1st choice	3d choice	2d choice
Road	2d choice	1st choice	3d choice
Weather warning system	3d choice	2d choice	1st choice

Election	Voting outcomes winner
1 National defense vs. road	National defense (preferred by Adams and Conrad)
2 Road vs. weather warning system	Road (preferred by Adams and Benson)
3 National defense vs. weather warning system	Weather warning system (preferred by Benson and Conrad)

Preferences   Consider Table 31-1 where we again assume a community of three voters: Adams, Benson, and Conrad. Suppose the community has three alternative public goods from which to choose: national defense, a road, and a weather warning system. We would expect each member of the community to arrange the order of the three alternatives according to her or his preferences and then select the one preferred. This implies that each voter will state that he or she prefers national defense to a road; a road to a weather warning system; or whatever. We can then attempt to determine the collective preference scale of the community using a majority voting procedure. Specifically, a vote can be held between any two of the public goods and the winner of the contest matched against the third public good.

The three goods and the assumed individual preferences of the three voters are listed in the top of Table 31-1. In the lower part, outcomes of various elections are listed. The upper portion indicates that Adams prefers national defense to the road and the road to the weather warning system. This implies Adams prefers national defense to the weather warning system. Benson values the road more than the weather warning system and the warning system more than national defense. Conrad's first choice is

the weather warning system, second choice is national defense, and third choice is the road.

Voting Outcomes   Consider the outcomes of three hypothetical elections decided through majority vote. First, let's match national defense against the road in an election. In Table 31-1 national defense will win this contest because a majority of voters, Adams and Conrad, prefer national defense to a road. This outcome is reported in row (1) of the lower part of the table, where election outcomes are summarized. Next we hold an election to see whether this community wants a road or a weather warning system. A majority of voters, Adams and Benson, prefer the road to the weather warning system, as shown in row (2).

We have determined that the majority in this community prefer national defense to a road *and* prefer a road to a weather warning system. It seems logical to conclude the community prefers national defense to a weather warning system. But it does not!

To demonstrate this, consider a direct election between national defense and the weather warning system. In row (3) a majority of voters, Benson and Conrad, prefer the weather warning system to national defense. As indicated in Table 31-1, majority voting falsely implies that this community is irrational: it seems to prefer national defense to a road *and* a road to a weather warning system, but would rather have a weather warning system than national defense.

The problem is not irrational preferences, but rather a flawed procedure for determining those preferences. Majority voting can yield opposing outcomes depending on how the vote on public expenditures or other public issues is ordered. Majority voting fails under some circumstances to make *consistent* choices that reflect the community's underlying preferences. As a consequence, government might find it difficult to provide the "correct" public goods by acting in accordance with majority voting. *(Key Question 2)*

Median-Voter Model

One final aspect of majority voting reveals insights into real-world phenomena. The **median-voter model** suggests that *under majority rule the median voter will in a sense determine the outcomes of elections.* The median voter is the person holding the middle position on an issue: One-half of the other voters have stronger preferences for an expenditure on a public good, amount of taxation, or the degree of government regulation, the other one-half have weaker—or negative—preferences. The extreme voters on each side of an issue prefer the median choice rather than the other extreme position, so the median voter's choice will predominate.

Example Suppose a society composed of Adams, Benson, and Conrad has reached agreement that as a society it needs a weather warning system. Each independently is to submit a total dollar amount he or she thinks should be spent on the warning system, assuming each will be taxed one-third of that amount. An election will determine the size of the system. Because each person can be expected to vote for his or her own proposal, no majority will occur if all the proposals are placed on the ballot at the same time. Thus, the group decides they will first vote between two of the proposals and then match the winner of that vote against the remaining proposal.

The three proposals are as follows: Adams desires a $400 system; Benson wants an $800 system; Conrad opts for a $300 system. Which proposal will win? The median-voter model suggests it will be the $400 proposal submitted by the median voter, Adams. One-half of the other voters favors a more costly system; one-half favors a less costly system. To understand why the $400 system will be the outcome we need to conduct two elections.

First, suppose that the $400 proposal is matched against the $800 proposal. Adams naturally will vote for her $400 proposal, but how will Benson and Conrad vote? Benson will vote for his own $800 proposal. Conrad—who proposed a $300 expenditure for the warning system—will vote for the $400 proposal rather than the one for $800. Adams' $400 proposal is selected by a 2-to-1 majority vote.

Next, we match the $400 proposal against the $300 proposal. Again the $400 proposal wins, because it gets a vote from Adams and one from Benson, who proposed the $800 expenditure and for that reason prefers a $400 expenditure to a $300 one. Adams—the median voter in this case—in a sense is the person who has decided the level of expenditure on a weather warning system for this society.

Real-World Applicability Although a simple illustration, this idea explains much. We *do* note a tendency for public choices to match up closely with the median view. We observe political candidates taking one set of positions to win the nomination of their political parties; they appeal to the median voter *within the party* to get the nomination. They then shift their views more closely to the political center when they square off against their opponent from the opposite political party. In effect, they redirect their appeal toward the median voter *within the total population.* They also try to label their opponents as being too liberal, or too conservative, and out of touch with "mainstream American." And they conduct polls and adjust their positions on issues accordingly.

Implications Two implications of the median voter model arise.
1 Many people will be dissatisfied by the extent of government involvement in the economy. The size of government will largely be determined by the median preference, leaving many people desiring a much larger, or a much smaller, public sector. In the marketplace you can buy zero zucchinis, 2 zucchinis, or 200 zucchinis, depending on how much you enjoy them. In the public sector you get the number of Stealth bombers and interstate highways the median voter prefers.
2 Some people may "vote with their feet" by moving into political jurisdictions where the median voter's preferences are closer to their own. Someone may move from the city to a suburb where the level of government services and therefore taxes are lower. Or they may move into an area known for its excellent, but expensive, school system. Demographic changes within political jurisdictions also occur which change the median preference.

For these reasons, and because our personal preferences for government activity are not static, the median preference within political jurisdictions shifts over time. Also, information about people's preferences is imperfect, leaving much room for politicians to mistake the true median position. *(Key Question 3)*

PUBLIC SECTOR FAILURE

It is clear that the economic functions of government are not always performed effectively and efficiently. Just because the economic results of the market are not entirely satisfactory, it does not necessarily follow that the political process will do better.

We might agree that government has a legitimate role in dealing with the instances of market failure; government should make adjustments for spillover costs and benefits, provide public goods and services, provide information, and so forth. We might also accept benefit-cost analysis as a guide to economically efficient decision making in the public sector. But a fundamental question remains: Are there inherent problems or shortcomings within the public sector which constrain governmental decision making as a mechanism for promoting economic efficiency?

Casual reflection suggests there may be significant divergence between "sound economics" and "good politics." Sound economics calls for the public sector to pursue various programs so long as marginal benefits exceed marginal costs. Good politics, however, suggests that politicians support those programs and policies which will maximize their chance of getting elected and retained in office.

Let's briefly consider some reasons for **public sector failure**—why the public sector may function inefficiently in an economic sense.

Special Interests and "Rent Seeking"

Ideally, public decisions promote the general welfare or, at least, the interests of the vast majority of the citizenry. But, instead, government often promotes the goals of small special-interest groups to the detriment of the larger public.

Special-Interest Effect Efficient public decision making is often impaired by a **special-interest effect.** A special-interest issue is a program or policy from which a small number of people individually will receive *large* gains at the expense of a vastly larger number of persons who individually suffers *small* losses.

The small group of potential beneficiaries will be well informed and highly vocal on this issue, pressing politicians for approval. The large numbers who face very small losses will generally be uninformed and indifferent on this issue; they have little at stake. Politicians feel they will clearly lose the support of the small special-interest group which supports the program if they vote against it. But politicians will *not* lose the support of the large group of uninformed voters who will evaluate them on other issues in which these voters have a stronger interest. Furthermore, the politicians' inclination to support special-interest legislation is enhanced by the fact that such groups are often more than willing to help finance the campaigns of "right-minded" politicians. The result is that the politician will support the special-interest program, even though it may not be economically desirable from a social point of view.

Rent-Seeking Behavior This pursuit through government of a transfer of wealth at someone else's or society's expense is called **rent-seeking behavior.** Here, "rent" means any payment to a resource supplier, business, or other organization above the amount which would occur under competitive market conditions. Corporations, trade associations, labor unions, and professional organizations employ vast resources to secure "rent" directly or indirectly dispensed by government. Government provides this "rent" through legislation and policies which increase payments to some groups, leaving others or society less well off.

There are many examples of special-interest or rent-seeking groups realizing legislation and policies unjustified on the basis of efficiency or equity: tariffs on foreign products which limit competition and raise prices to consumers; tax loopholes which benefit only the wealthy; public work projects which cost more than the benefits they yield; occupational licensing which goes beyond what's needed to protect consumers; and large subsidies to farmers by taxpayers.

Clear Benefits, Hidden Costs

Some say vote-seeking politicians will not *objectively* weigh all costs and benefits of various programs, as economic rationality demands, in deciding which to support and which to reject. Because political officeholders must seek voter support every few years, politicians favor programs with immediate and clearcut benefits, on the one hand, and vague, difficult-to-identify, or deferred costs, on the other. Conversely, politicians will look askance at programs embodying immediate and easily identifiable costs along with future benefits which are diffuse and vague.

Such biases in the area of public choice can lead politicians to reject economically justifiable programs and to accept programs which are economically irrational. Example: A proposal to construct and expand mass-transit systems in large metropolitan areas may be economically rational on the basis of objective benefit-cost analysis (Table 30-2). But if (1) the program is to be financed by immediate increases in highly visible income or sales taxes *and* (2) benefits will accrue only a decade hence when the project is completed, the vote-seeking politician may oppose the program.

Assume, on the other hand, that a proposed program of Federal aid to municipal police forces is *not* justifiable on the basis of objective benefit-cost analysis. But if costs are concealed and deferred through deficit financing, the program's modest benefits may loom so large that it gains political approval.

Limited and Bundled Choice

Public choice theorists also argue that the political process is such that citizens and their elected representatives are forced to be less selective in the choice of public goods and services than they are in the choice of private goods and services.

In the market sector, the citizen *as consumer* can reflect personal preferences precisely by buying certain goods and forgoing others. However, in the public sector the citizen *as voter* is confronted with two or more candidates for office, each of whom represents different "bundles" of programs (public goods and services). In no case is the bundle of public goods represented by any particular candidate likely to fit precisely the wants of the particular voter. Voter Smith's favored candidate for office may endorse national health insurance, the development of nuclear energy, subsidies to tobacco farmers, and tariffs on imported automobiles. Citizen Smith votes for this candidate because the bundle of programs she endorses comes closest to matching Smith's preferences, even though Smith may oppose tobacco subsidies and tariffs on foreign cars.

The voter must take the bad with the good; in the public sector, we are forced to "buy" goods and services we do not want. It is as if, in going to a sporting goods store, you were forced to buy an unwanted pool cue to get a wanted pair of running shoes. This is a situation where resources are *not* being used efficiently to best satisfy consumer wants. In this sense, the provision of public goods and services is inherently inefficient.

Similarly, the limited-choice, bundling problem confronts Congress. Appropriations legislation combines hundreds, even thousands, of spending items into a single bill. These bills may contain spending items unrelated to the main purpose of the legislation. Congressional representatives must vote the entire package—yea or nay. Unlike consumers in the marketplace, they cannot be selective. *(Key Question 6)*

Bureaucracy and Inefficiency

It is contended that private businesses are innately more efficient than public agencies. The reason is *not* that lazy and incompetent workers somehow end up in the public sector, while the ambitious and capable gravitate to the private sector. Rather, it is that the market system creates incentives and pressures for internal efficiency which are absent in the public sector. The managers of private enterprises have a strong personal incentive—increased profits—to be efficient in their operation. Whether a private firm is in a competitive or monopolistic environment, lower costs through efficient management contribute to enlarged profits. There is no tangible personal gain—a counterpart to profits—for the government bureau chief who achieves efficiency within his or her domain.

There is simply less incentive to be cost-conscious in the public sector. In a larger sense the market system imposes an explicit test of performance on private firms—the test of profits and losses. An efficient firm is profitable and therefore successful; it survives, prospers, and grows. An inefficient enterprise is unprofitable and unsuccessful; it declines and in time goes bankrupt and ceases to exist. But there is no similar, clear-cut test for us to assess efficiency or inefficiency of public agencies. How can anyone determine whether TVA, a state university, a local fire department, the Department of Agriculture, or the Bureau of Indian Affairs is operating efficiently?

Cynics argue that a public agency which uses its resources inefficiently may be in line for a budget increase! In the private sector, inefficiency and monetary losses lead to abandonment of certain activities —the discontinuing of certain products and services. But government, it is contended, is loath to abandon activities in which it has failed. Some suggest the typical response of government to failure of a program is to double its budget and staff. This means public sector inefficiency may be sustained on a larger scale.

Furthermore, returning to our earlier comments on special-interest and rent-seeking groups, public programs spawn new constituencies of bureaucrats and beneficiaries whose political clout causes programs to be sustained or expanded after they have fulfilled their goals—or even if they have failed miserably in their mission. Relevant bureaucrats, school administrators, and teachers may band together to become a highly effective special-interest group for sustaining inefficient programs of Federal aid to education or for causing these programs to be expanded beyond the point at which marginal benefits equal marginal costs.

Some government bureaucrats have a tendency to develop detailed, costly, and, in some cases, ridiculous regulations. We take up government regulation in Chapter 32.

Some specific suggestions have been offered recently to deal with the problems of bureaucratic inefficiency. Benefit-cost analysis is one approach. It has also been proposed that all legislation establishing new programs contain well-defined performance standards so the public can better judge efficiency. Further, the suggestion has been made that expiration dates—so-called "sunset laws"—be written into all new programs, forcing a thorough periodic evaluation which might indicate the need to abandon the program. Also, in 1993 the Clinton administration released a "reinventing government review," which detailed inefficiencies in government and made numerous recommendations to remove them. A commission has now been established to review those recommendations and package them into a single piece of legislation.

The Last Word at the end of this chapter highlights several recent media-reported examples of the special-interest effect, the problem of limited and bundled choices, and problems of government bureaucracy. You might want to read through these examples now, relating each point to the discussion we have just completed.

QUICK REVIEW 31-1

■ Majority voting can produce voting outcomes which are inefficient; projects having greater total benefits than total costs can be defeated and projects having greater total costs than total benefits can be approved.

■ The paradox of voting occurs where voting by majority rule fails to provide a consistent ranking of society's preferences for public goods and services.

■ The median-voter model suggests that under majority rule the voter having the middle preference will determine the outcome of an election.

■ Public sector failure allegedly occurs because of rent-seeking by special-interest groups, short-sighted political behavior, limited and bundled choices, and bureaucratic inefficiency.

Imperfect Institutions

Its possible to argue that these criticisms of public sector efficiency are overdrawn and too cynical. Perhaps. Nevertheless, they are sufficiently persuasive to shake our faith in a simplistic concept of a benevolent

government responding with precision and efficiency to the wants of its citizenry. The market system of the private sector is by no means perfectly efficient. Government's economic functions are attempts to correct the market system's shortcomings. But the public sector may also be subject to deficiencies in fulfilling its economic functions. "The relevant comparison is not between perfect markets and imperfect governments, nor between faulty markets and all-knowing, rational, benevolent governments, but between inevitably imperfect institutions."[1]

One implication of the fact that the market system and public agencies are both imperfect institutions is that, in practice, it can be difficult to determine whether some particular activity can be performed with greater success in the private or the public sector. It is easy to reach agreement on opposite extremes: National defense must lie in the public sector, whereas wheat production can best be accomplished in the private sector. But what about health insurance? The provisions of parks and recreation areas? Fire protection? Garbage collection? Housing? Education? It is very hard to assess each type of good or service and to say unequivocally that its provision should be assigned to either the public or the private sector. Evidence? All the goods and services just mentioned are provided in part by both private enterprises and public agencies.

APPORTIONING THE TAX BURDEN

We now turn from the difficulties of making collective decisions on the types and amounts of public goods to the difficulties in deciding how those goods should be financed.

The characteristics of public goods and services make it hard to measure precisely how their benefits are apportioned among individuals and institutions. It is virtually impossible to determine accurately how much John Doe benefits from military installations, a network of highways, a public school system, the national weather bureau, and local police and fire protection.

The situation is a bit different on the taxation side of the picture. Studies reveal with somewhat greater clarity the way the overall tax burden is apportioned. This is a question affecting each of us. Although the

---

[1]Otto Eckstein, *Public Finance,* 3d ed. (Englewood Cliffs, N.J.: Prentice-Hall, Inc., 1973), p. 17.

average citizen is concerned with the overall level of taxes, chances are he or she is even more interested in exactly how the tax burden is allocated among individual taxpayers.

Benefits Received versus Ability to Pay

There are two basic philosophies on how the economy's tax burden should be apportioned.

Benefits-Received Principle   The **benefits-received principle** of taxation asserts that households and businesses should purchase the goods and services of government in the same way other commodities are bought. Those who benefit most from government-supplied goods or services should pay the taxes necessary for financing them. A few public goods are financed on this basis. Gasoline taxes are typically earmarked for financing highway construction and repairs. People who benefit from good roads pay the cost of those roads. Difficulties immediately arise, however, when an accurate and widespread application of the benefits principle is considered:

1   How does government determine the benefits individual households and businesses receive from national defense, education, and police and fire protection? Recall that public goods provide widespread spillover benefits and that the exclusion principle is inapplicable. Even in the seemingly tangible case of highway finance we find it difficult to measure benefits. Individual car owners benefit in different degrees from good roads. And those who do not own cars also benefit. Businesses certainly benefit greatly from the widening of their markets which good roads encourage.

2   Government efforts to redistribute income would be self-defeating if financed on the basis of the benefits principle. It would be absurd and self-defeating to ask poor families to pay the taxes needed to finance their welfare payments! It would be ridiculous to think of taxing only unemployed workers to finance the unemployment compensation payments which they receive.

Ability-to-Pay Principle   The **ability-to-pay principle** of taxation contrasts sharply with the benefits principle. Ability-to-pay taxation rests on the idea that the tax burden should be geared directly to a taxpayer's income and wealth. In the United States the ability-to-pay principle means that individuals and businesses with larger incomes should pay more

taxes—both absolutely and relatively—than those with more modest incomes.

What is the rationale of ability-to-pay taxation? Proponents argue that each additional dollar of income received by a household will yield smaller and smaller increments of satisfaction or marginal utility. Because consumers act rationally, the first dollars of income received in any period of time will be spent on high-urgency goods which yield the greatest marginal utility. Successive dollars of income will go for less urgently needed goods and finally for trivial goods and services. This means a dollar taken through taxes from a poor person who has few dollars is a greater utility sacrifice than is a dollar taken by taxes from the rich person who has many dollars. To balance the sacrifices which taxes impose on income receivers, taxes should be apportioned according to the amount of income a taxpayer receives.

This argument is appealing, but problems of application exist here too. Although we might agree that the household earning $100,000 per year has a greater ability to pay taxes than a household receiving $10,000, exactly *how much more* ability to pay does the first family have compared with the second? Should the rich person pay the *same percentage* of his or her larger income—and hence a larger absolute amount—as taxes? Or should the rich be made to pay a *larger fraction* of this income as taxes? And how much larger should that fraction be?

The problem is there is no scientific way of measuring someone's ability to pay taxes. In practice, the answer hinges on guesswork, the tax views of the political party in power, expediency, and how urgently the government needs revenue.

Progressive, Proportional, and Regressive Taxes

Any discussion of the ability-to-pay and the benefits-received principles of taxation leads ultimately to the question of tax rates and the manner in which tax rates change as income increases.

Definitions   Taxes are classified as progressive, proportional, or regressive. These designations focus on the relationship between tax rates and *income* simply because all taxes—regardless of whether on income or on a product or building or parcel of land—are ultimately paid out of someone's income.

1   A tax is **progressive** if its average rate *increases* as income increases. Such a tax claims not only a larger absolute amount, but also a larger fraction or percentage of income as income increases.

2 A **regressive** tax has an average rate which *declines* as income increases. Such a tax takes a smaller and smaller proportion of income as income increases. A regressive tax may or may not take a larger absolute amount of income as income expands.

3 A tax is **proportional** when its average rate *remains the same,* regardless of the size of income.

We can illustrate these ideas with the personal income tax. Suppose tax rates are such that a household pays 10 percent of its income in taxes, regardless of the size of its income. This is a proportional income tax.

Now suppose the rate structure is such that the household with an annual taxable income of less than $10,000 pays 5 percent in income taxes; the household realizing an income of $10,000 to $20,000 pays 10 percent; $20,000 to $30,000 pays 15 percent; and so forth. This would be a *progressive* income tax.

Now for the case where the rates decline as taxable income rises: You pay 15 percent if you earn less than $10,000; 10 percent if you earn $10,000 to $20,000; 5 percent if you earn $20,000 to $30,000; and so forth. This is a *regressive* income tax.

In general, progressive taxes are those which bear down most heavily on the rich; regressive taxes are those which hit the poor hardest. *(Key Question 9)*

Applications What can we say about the progressivity, proportionality, or regressivity of the taxes in the United States?

1 *Personal Income Tax* We noted in Chapter 5 that the Federal *personal income tax* is progressive with marginal tax rates ranging from 15 to 39.6 percent. The deductibility of interest on home mortgages and property taxes, along with the exemption of interest income from state and local bonds, partly erodes the progressivity of the tax.

2 *Sales Taxes* At first glance a *general sales tax* with, say, a 3 percent rate would seem to be proportional. But in fact it is regressive with respect to income. A larger portion of a poor person's income is exposed to the tax than is true for a rich person; the rich avoid the tax on the part of income which is saved, whereas the poor are unable to save. Example: "Poor" Smith has an income of $15,000 and spends it all. "Rich" Jones has an income of $300,000 but spends only $200,000. Assuming a 3 percent sales tax applies

to all expenditures of each individual, we find Smith will pay $450 (3 percent of $15,000) in sales taxes, and Jones will pay $6000 (3 percent of $200,000). While *all* of Smith's $15,000 income is subject to the sales tax, only two-thirds of Jones' $300,000 income is taxed. Thus, while Smith pays $450, or 3 percent, of a $15,000 income as sales taxes, Jones pays $6000, or just 2 percent, of a $300,000 income. We conclude that the general sales tax is regressive.

3 *Corporate Income Tax* The Federal *corporate income tax* is essentially a flat-rate proportional tax with a 35 percent tax rate. But this assumes that corporation owners (shareholders) bear the tax. Some tax experts argue that at least a part of the tax is passed through to consumers in the form of higher product prices. To the extent that this occurs, the tax is regressive like a sales tax.

4 *Payroll Taxes* Payroll or social security taxes are regressive because they apply to only a fixed absolute amount of your income. For example, in 1995, payroll tax rates were 7.65 percent, but this applies only to the first $61,200 of your wage income. A person earning exactly $61,200 would pay $4681.80 or 7.65 percent of his or her wage income; someone with twice that income, or $122,400, would also pay $4681.80—only 3.825 percent of his or her wage income.

This regressivity is enhanced because the payroll tax excludes nonwage income. If our individual with the $122,400 wage income also received $77,600 in nonwage (dividend, interest, rent) income, then the payroll tax would amount to only 2.34 percent (= $4681.80 ÷ $200,000) of the total income.

5 *Property Taxes* Most economists conclude that *property taxes* on buildings are regressive for the same reasons as are sales taxes. First, property owners add the tax to the rents which tenants are charged. Second, property taxes, as a percentage of income, are higher for poor families than for rich families because the poor must spend a larger proportion of their incomes for housing.[2] The alleged regressivity of the property tax may be reinforced because property-tax rates are not likely to be uniform between various po-

---

[2]Controversy arises in part because empirical research, which compares the value of housing to lifetime (rather than a single year's) income, suggests that this ratio is approximately the same for all income groups.

litical subdivisions. If property values decline in, say, a decaying central-city area, property-tax rates must be increased in the city to bring in a specific amount of revenue. But in a wealthy suburb, where the market value of housing is rising, a particular amount of tax revenue can be maintained with lower property-tax rates.

TAX INCIDENCE AND EFFICIENCY LOSS

Determining whether a particular tax is progressive, proportional, or regressive is complicated because taxes do not always stick where they are levied. We therefore need to locate as best we can the final resting place of a tax, or, **tax incidence.** The tools of elasticity of supply and demand will help. Let's focus on a hypothetical excise tax on wine producers. Do producers pay this tax, or do they shift it to wine consumers? This analysis will provide a logical bridge to a discussion of other aspects of the economic burden of a tax.

Elasticity and Tax Incidence

Figure 31-2 shows the market for a certain domestic wine and the no-tax equilibrium price and quantity of $4 per bottle and 15 million bottles. Assume government levies a specific sales or excise tax of $1 per bottle on this wine. What is the incidence of this tax?

Division of Burden Assuming that government places the tax on sellers (suppliers), the tax can be viewed as an addition to the supply price of the product. While sellers were willing to offer, for example, 5 million bottles of untaxed wine at $2 per bottle, they must now receive $3 per bottle—$2 plus the $1 tax —to offer the same 5 million bottles. Sellers must get $1 more for each quantity supplied to receive the same per unit price they were getting before the tax. The tax shifts the supply curve upward as shown in Figure 31-2, where S is the "no-tax" supply curve and S_t is the "after-tax" supply curve.

Careful comparison of after-tax supply and demand with the pretax equilibrium reveals that with the tax the equilibrium price is $4.50 per bottle, compared with the before-tax price of $4.00. In this case, one-half of the tax is paid by consumers as a higher price and the other half by producers as a lower after-tax price. Consumers pay 50 cents more per bot-

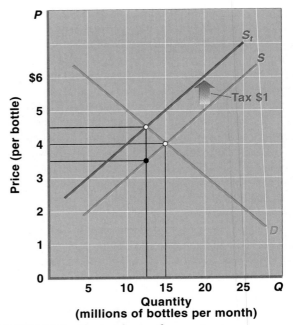

FIGURE 31-2 The incidence of an excise tax
An excise tax of a specified amount, say, $1 per unit, shifts the supply curve upward by the amount of the tax. This results in a higher price ($4.50) to the consumer and a lower after-tax price ($3.50) to the producer. In this particular case, consumers and producers equally share the burden of the tax.

tle and, after remitting the $1 tax per unit to government, producers received $3.50, or 50 cents less than the $4.00 before-tax price. In this instance, consumers and producers share the burden of the tax equally; producers shift half the tax to consumers in the form of a higher price and bear the other half themselves.

Elasticities If the elasticities of demand and supply were different from those shown in Figure 31-2, the incidence of tax would also be different. Two generalizations are relevant.

1 *With a specific supply, the more inelastic the demand for the product, the larger the portion of the tax shifted to consumers.* To verify this, sketch graphically the extreme cases where demand is perfectly elastic and perfectly inelastic. In the first case the incidence of the tax is entirely on sellers; in the second, the tax is shifted entirely to consumers.

Figure 31-3 contrasts the more likely cases where demand might be elastic (D_e) or inelastic (D_i) in the relevant price range. In the elastic demand case of Figure 31-3a, a small portion of the tax (PP_e) is shifted to consumers and most of the tax (PP_a) is borne by producers. In the inelastic demand case of Figure

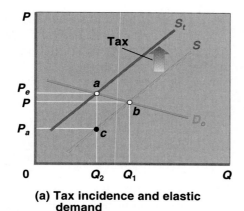

**(a) Tax incidence and elastic
demand**

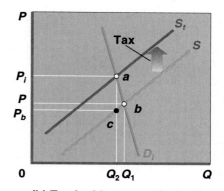

**(b) Tax incidence and inelastic
demand**

FIGURE 31-3 Demand elasticity and the incidence of an excise tax
In (a) we find that, if demand is elastic in the relevant price range, price will rise modestly (P to P_e) when an excise tax is levied. Hence, the producer bears most of the tax burden. But if demand is inelastic as in (b), the price to the buyer will increase substantially (P to P_i) and most of the tax is shifted to consumers.

31-3b, most of the tax (PP_i) is shifted to consumers and only a small amount (PP_b) is paid by producers.

The decline in equilibrium quantity is smaller, the more inelastic the demand. This recalls one of our previous applications of the elasticity concept: Revenue-seeking legislatures place heavy excise taxes on liquor, cigarettes, automobile tires, and other products whose demands are thought to be inelastic.

2 *With a specific demand, the more inelastic the supply, the larger the portion of the tax borne by producers.* While the demand curves are identical, the supply

curve is elastic in Figure 31-4a and inelastic in Figure 31-4b. For the elastic supply curve most of the tax (PP_e) is shifted to consumers and only a small portion (PP_a) is borne by producers or sellers. But where supply is inelastic, the reverse is true. The major portion of the tax (PP_b) falls on sellers and a relatively small amount (PP_i) is shifted to buyers. Quantity also declines less with an inelastic supply than it does with an elastic supply.

Gold is an example of a product with an inelastic supply and therefore one where the burden of an ex-

FIGURE 31-4 Supply elasticity and the incidence of an excise tax
Part (a) indicates that with an elastic supply an excise tax results in a large price increase (P to P_e) and the tax is therefore paid largely by consumers. But if supply is inelastic as in (b), the price rise will be small (P to P_i) and sellers will have to bear most of the tax.

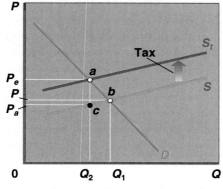

**(a) Tax incidence and elastic
supply**

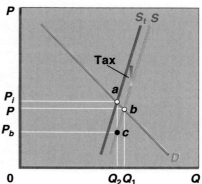

**(b) Tax incidence and inelastic
supply**

cise tax would fall mainly on producers. On the other hand, because the supply of baseballs is elastic, much of an excise tax on baseballs would get passed to consumers.

Efficiency Loss of a Tax

We have just observed that an excise tax on producers in a market characterized by typical supply and demand curves is borne partly by producers and partly by consumers. Let's look more closely at the burden of an excise tax. Figure 31-5 is identical to Figure 31-2 but contains additional detail needed for our discussion.

Tax Revenues   The $1 excise tax on wine increases the market price from $4 to $4.50 per bottle and reduces the equilibrium quantity from 15 to 12.5 million bottles. Government's tax revenue is $12.5 million (= $1 × 12.5 million bottles), an amount shown as the rectangle labeled *efac* in Figure 31-5. In this case, the elasticities of supply and demand are such that consumers and producers each pay one-half of this total

amount, or $6.25 million apiece (= $.50 × 12.5 million bottles). Government uses this $12.5 million of tax revenue to provide public goods and services. There is no loss of well-being to society as a whole from this transfer from consumers and producers to government.

Efficiency Loss   The $1 tax on wine requires consumers and producers to pay $12.5 million of taxes, but also *reduces the equilibrium amount of wine produced and consumed by 2.5 million bottles*. The fact that 2.5 million more bottles of wine were demanded and supplied prior to the tax means they provided benefits in *excess* of their costs of production. We can see this from the following simple analysis.

The *ab* segment of demand curve *D* in Figure 31-5 indicates the willingness to pay—the marginal benefit—associated with each of these 2.5 million bottles consumed before the tax. The *cb* segment of supply curve *S* reflects the marginal cost of each of the bottles of wine. For all but the very last one of these 2.5 million bottles, the marginal benefit (shown by *ab*) exceeds the marginal cost (shown by *cb*). The reduction of well-being because these 2.5 million bottles are not produced is indicated by the triangle *abc*. This triangle shows the **efficiency loss of the tax**. *This loss is the sacrifice of net benefit accruing to society because consumption and production of the taxed product are reduced below their allocatively efficient levels.*

Role of Elasticities   Most taxes create some degree of efficiency loss; how much depends on supply and demand elasticities. Glancing back to Figure 31-3, we observe that the efficiency loss triangle *abc* is greater in Figure 31-3a, where demand is relatively elastic, than in Figure 31-3b, where demand is relatively inelastic. Similarly, the area *abc* is greater in Figure 31-4a than in Figure 31-4b, indicating a larger efficiency loss where supply is more elastic.

The principle our analysis establishes is that the amount of efficiency loss of an excise tax or sales tax varies from market to market depending on the elasticities of supply and demand. *Other things equal, the greater the elasticities of supply and demand, the greater the efficiency loss of a particular tax.* Two taxes yielding equal revenues do not necessarily have equal tax burdens for society. This fact complicates government's job of determining the best way to collect its needed tax revenues. Government must consider the efficiency losses of taxes in designing an optimal tax system.

FIGURE 31-5   Efficiency loss of a tax
The levy of a $1 excise tax per bottle of wine increases the price per bottle to $4.50 and reduces the equilibrium quantity by 2.5 million bottles. Government's tax revenue is $12.5 million (area *efac*). The efficiency loss of the tax is the amount shown as triangle *abc*.

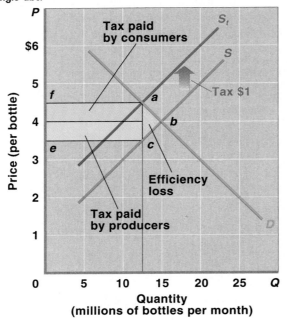

Qualifications   We must qualify our analysis. Other tax goals in many instances may be more important than the goal of minimizing efficiency losses from taxes. Two examples follow.

1   Redistributive Goals   Government may wish to impose progressive taxes as a way to redistribute income. The 10 percent excise tax the Federal government placed on selected luxuries in 1990 was an example. Because the demand for luxuries is elastic, efficiency losses from this tax were substantial. However, Congress apparently concluded that the benefits from the redistribution effects of this tax would exceed these efficiency losses.

In 1993 Congress repealed the luxury taxes on personal airplanes and yachts, mainly because the taxes had reduced quantity demanded so much that widespread layoffs of workers were occurring in these industries. But the 10 percent tax on automobiles priced above $30,000 remains.

2   Reducing Negative Externalities   Government may have intended the $1 tax on wine in Figure 31-5 to reduce consumption of wine by 2.5 million bottles. It may have concluded that consumption of alcoholic beverages produces certain negative externalities. Therefore, it might have levied this tax to adjust the market supply curve for these costs to reduce the amount of resources allocated to wine (Figure 30-3b). *(Key Question 11)*

Probable Incidence of U.S. Taxes

Now that we understand tax shifting and incidence, let's look at the probable incidence of each of the major sources of tax revenue in the United States.

Personal Income Tax   The incidence of the personal income tax generally falls on the individual because there is a little chance for shifting it. But there might be exceptions. Individuals and groups who can control the price of their labor services may be able to shift a part of the tax. Doctors, dentists, lawyers, and other professional people who can readily increase their fees may do so because of the tax. Unions might regard personal income taxes as part of the cost of living and, as a result, bargain for higher wages. If they are successful, they may shift part of the tax from workers to employers who, by increasing prices, shift the wage increase to the public. Generally, however, the individual on whom the tax is initially levied bears

the burden of the personal income tax. The same ordinarily holds true of payroll and inheritance taxes.

Corporate Income Tax   The incidence of the corporate income tax is much less certain. The traditional view is that a firm currently charging the profit-maximizing price and producing the profit-maximizing output will have no reason to change price or output when a corporate income tax is imposed. That price and output combination yielding the greatest profit before the tax will still be the most profitable after government takes a fixed percentage of the firm's profits in the form of income taxes. In this view, the company's stockholders (owners) must bear the incidence of the tax in the form of lower dividends or a smaller amount of retained earnings.

However, some economists argue that the corporate income tax is shifted in part to consumers through higher prices and to resource suppliers through lower prices. In modern industry, where a small number of firms may control a market, producers may not be in the profit-maximizing position initially. By fully exploiting their market position currently, monopolistic firms might elicit adverse public opinion and governmental censure. They may await such events as increases in tax rates or wage increases by unions to provide an "excuse" or rationale for price increases with less fear of public criticism. When this occurs, a portion of the corporate income tax may be shifted to consumers through higher prices. Both positions are plausible. The incidence of the corporate income tax may well be shared by stockholders and the firm's customers and resource suppliers.

Sales and Excise Taxes   Sales and excise taxes are the "hidden taxes" of our economy. They are hidden because they are often partly or largely shifted by sellers to consumers through higher product prices. There may be some difference in the shiftability of sales taxes and excises, however. Because a sales tax covers a much wider range of products than an excise, there is little chance for consumers to resist the price boosts which sales taxes entail. They can't reallocate their expenditures to untaxed, lower-priced products.

Excises, however, fall on a select list of goods. Therefore, the possibility of consumers turning to substitute goods and services is greater. An excise tax on theater tickets which does not apply to other types of entertainment might be difficult to pass on to consumers via price increases. Why? The answer is provided in Figure 31-3a, where demand is elastic. Price boosts on theater tickets might result in considerable substituting of alternative types of entertainment by consumers. The higher price will reduce sales so much that a seller will be better off to bear all, or a large portion of, the excise rather than the sharp decline in sales.

With other excises, modest price increases may have smaller effects on sales. Excises on gasoline, cigarettes, and alcoholic beverages are examples. Here there are few good substitute products to which consumers can turn as prices rise. For these commodities, the seller is better able to shift the tax (Figure 31-3b).

Property Taxes Many property taxes are borne by the property owner because there is no other party to whom they can be shifted. This is typically true in the case of taxes on land, personal property, and owner-occupied residences. Even when land is sold, the property tax is not likely to be shifted. The buyer will discount the value of the land to allow for the future taxes which must be paid on it, and this expected taxation will be reflected in the price a buyer is willing to offer for the land.

Taxes on rented and business property are a different story. Taxes on rented property can be, and usually are, shifted wholly or in part from the owner to the tenant by the process of boosting the rent. Business property taxes are treated as a business cost and therefore are taken into account in establishing product price; thus such taxes are ordinarily shifted to the firm's customers.

Table 31-2 summarizes this discussion of the shifting and incidence of taxes.

The American Tax Structure

Is the overall tax structure—Federal, state, and local taxes combined—progressive, proportional, or regressive? This is difficult to answer because estimates of the distribution of the total tax burden are quite sensitive to assumptions made regarding tax incidence. To what extent are the various taxes shifted and who bears the ultimate burden? For example, we have already cited the disagreement among the experts as to the incidence of the corporate income tax. Also, in 1993 the marginal tax rate on wealthy Americans was increased from 31 percent to 39.6 percent. To what extent has this tax hike increased progressivity of the American tax system?

The consensus view held by those studying this subject is as follows.

1 Federal Tax System The Federal tax system is progressive and despite many changes in the tax law this progressivity has not significantly changed since 1977. Between 1977 and 1992 the Federal tax burden of the poorest 20 percent of the population fell slightly from 9.3 percent to 8.6 percent of their incomes. Meanwhile, during these years the tax burden of the richest 20 percent fell from 27.2 to 26.8 of their incomes. The tax burdens of all other income receivers increased slightly.

The progressivity of the Federal personal income tax has increased since 1990. Partly offsetting this increase in progressivity, however, has been the growing effect of the payroll or social security tax. If all income were subject to the social security tax, the tax would be proportional. But the tax only applies to income from work and then only to a set maximum amount ($61,200 in 1995). Thus, the social security payroll tax is regressive. A person with an annual salary of $200,000 pays a smaller percentage of that income to the social security tax than a person earning $50,000. Moreover, the social security tax does not apply to nonwork income such as interest income and dividends, which tend to rise with earnings.

2 State and Local Tax System The state and local tax structures are largely regressive. As a percentage of income, property taxes and sales taxes fall as income rises. Also, state income taxes are generally less progressive than the Federal income tax.

3 Combined Tax System The overall American tax system is slightly progressive. This means the tax system—itself—only slightly redistributes income from the wealthy to the poor.

Caution one: Because wealthy Americans earn a disproportionately high amount of the total income, they also pay a disproportionately high amount of the total tax. (This would be true even for a proportional tax system, or possibly even a regressive tax system.) For example, the top 10 percent of income earners in the United States pay about 50 percent of the total personal income tax; the bottom 50 percent of income earners, less than 10 percent.

Caution two: While the American tax system does not substantially alter the distribution of income, the American system of transfer payments does reduce income inequality. Transfer payments to the poorest

TABLE 31-2 The probable incidence of taxes

Type of tax	Probable incidence
Personal income tax	The household or individual on which it is levied.
Corporate income tax	Some economists conclude the firm on which it is levied bears the incidence; others conclude the tax is shifted, wholly or in part, to consumers and resource suppliers.
Sales tax	Consumers who buy the taxed products.
Specific excise taxes	Consumers, producers, or shared by each depending on elasticities of demand and supply.
Property taxes	Owners in the case of land and owner-occupied residences; tenants in the case of rented property; consumers in the case of business property.

fifth of the income receivers almost quadruple their collective incomes. The American tax-transfer system is much more progressive than the American tax system alone.

QUICK REVIEW 31-3

■ The benefits-received principle holds that government should assess taxes on individuals according to the amount of benefits they receive, regardless of their income; the ability-to-pay tax principle holds that people should be taxed according to their income, regardless of the benefits they receive from government.

■ As income increases, the average tax rate rises for a progressive tax, remains the same for a proportional tax, and falls for a regressive tax.

■ The more inelastic product demand, the larger the portion of an excise tax borne by consumers; the more inelastic the supply, the larger the portion borne by producers.

■ The efficiency loss of a tax is the loss of output for which marginal benefits exceed marginal costs.

■ Considering the probable incidences of American taxes (Table 31-2), the American tax structure is deemed to be slightly progressive.

TAX REFORM

Large Federal budget deficits and concerns about America's low savings and investment rates have prompted actual and proposed reforms of the Federal tax code.

Deficit Reduction Act of 1993

Between 1985 and 1992 Federal budget deficits averaged over $200 billion annually. In 1993 Congress responded to these deficits by passing the **Deficit Reduction Act** (DRA), designed to reduce the deficit by about $500 billion over five years. About one-half the deficit reduction will result from cuts in expenditures; the other one-half from tax increases, most of which will fall on upper-income households. The major tax changes are:

1 An increase in the top marginal tax rate—the tax paid on additional income—from 31 percent to 39.6 percent for individuals and couples having taxable income above $250,000.
2 Inclusion of 85 percent of social security benefits as taxable income for recipients having nonsocial security income above specified levels.
3 Elimination of the $135,000 cap on the amount of annual wages and self-employment income subject to the Medicare tax which funds health care for people living on social security benefits.
4 A boost in the Federal excise tax on gasoline from 14.1 cents per gallon to 18.4 cents.
5 An increase in the 34 percent tax rate on corporate income to 35 percent for taxable corporate income above $10 million.
6 A decrease from 85 percent to 50 percent in that part of meals and entertainment costs deductible as a business expense.

Calls for a Value-Added Tax

While the Deficit Reduction Act of 1993 involved significant reform, there is still considerable pressure for further changes in our tax system. These pressures

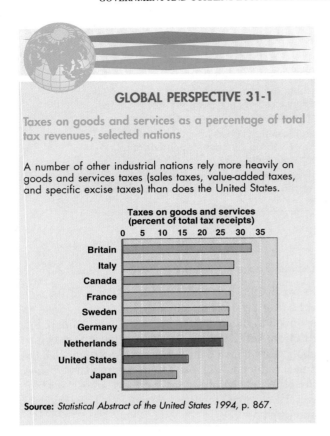

GLOBAL PERSPECTIVE 31-1

Taxes on goods and services as a percentage of total tax revenues, selected nations

A number of other industrial nations rely more heavily on goods and services taxes (sales taxes, value-added taxes, and specific excise taxes) than does the United States.

Taxes on goods and services (percent of total tax receipts)

Britain, Italy, Canada, France, Sweden, Germany, Netherlands, United States, Japan

Source: *Statistical Abstract of the United States 1994*, p. 867.

reflect a concern for America's low rates of saving, investment, and economic growth. Some observers recommend that the entire Federal tax system be recast to encourage economic expansion and improved international competitiveness.

The argument is that in the past few decades the productivity of American workers has stagnated relative to workers in Japan, Germany, and a number of other industrialized nations. One consequence is that several of our basic industries—for example, automobiles, steel, and electronics—have fallen prey to foreign competition. In the aggregate our imports have greatly exceeded our exports.

Some economists contend that we must "reindustrialize" our economy by making massive new investments in machinery and equipment to stimulate our economic growth. Retooled with large amounts of modern machinery and equipment, the productivity of American workers will once again increase. But you will recall from Chapter 2's production possibilities curve that with full employment, more investment implies offsetting cuts in consumption. Some feel that a structural overhaul of our present tax system can

bring about the required increases in investment and reductions in consumption.

One proposal is that the corporate income tax should be lowered or eliminated. This would enhance the expected profitability of investment and stimulate spending on new plants and equipment. But if the economy is at or close to full employment, how can the required resources be released from the production of consumer goods? One way to achieve this is to levy a **value-added tax (VAT)** on consumer goods. VAT is like a retail sales tax, except that the tax applies only to the difference between the value of a firm's sales and the value of its purchases from other firms. VAT would amount to a national sales tax on consumer goods. Most European countries—for example, Great Britain, Germany, and Sweden—currently use VAT as a source of revenue. This is reflected in Global Perspective 31-1.

The point to note is that VAT penalizes consumption. It's possible to avoid paying VAT by saving rather than consuming. And we know that saving (refraining from consumption) will release resources from consumer goods and make them available for investment goods. Elimination of the corporate income tax and installation of VAT will allegedly alter the composition of our domestic output away from consumption and toward investment with the result that our productivity growth and "competitive edge" will be strengthened.

THE ISSUE OF FREEDOM

We end our discussion of government decision making by considering an elusive question: What is the relationship between the role and size of the public sector and individual freedom? Although no attempt is made here to explore this issue in depth, let's outline two divergent views.

The Conservative Position

Many conservative economists feel that, in addition to the economic costs in any expansion of the public sector, there is also a cost in the form of diminished individual freedom. Here's why.

First, there is the "power corrupts" argument.[3] "Freedom is a rare and delicate plant . . . history con-

---

[3]Milton Friedman, *Capitalism and Freedom* (Chicago: The University of Chicago Press, 1962), p. 2.

LAST WORD

"PUBLIC SECTOR FAILURE" IN THE NEWS

There are recurring reports in the media of the special-interest effect; limited and bundled choices; and government bureaucracy.

Examples:

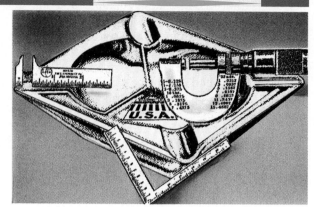

- An agricultural aid package to Russia required that 75 percent of the goods be shipped by high-cost U.S. flag vessels. The donation of $121 million of food cost American taxpayers an extra $45 million, which was in effect a subsidy to the American shipping industry. (Associated Press)
- Tacked onto the 1994 Defense Appropriations bill were many items of nondefense spending, including: *a* $20 billion for breast cancer research, *b* $6 million for the World Cup soccer tournament, *c* $3.7 million to renovate a pier in New London, Connecticut, *d* $2.5 million for an exhibit at the Queens Hall of Science in New York, *e* $2.3 million for cell-adhesion research at an unidentified nonprofit institution, *f* $2 million for the 1996 Olympic Games in Atlanta, and *g* $5 million for a redevelopment project in Waterbury, Connecticut. (*Boston Globe*)
- In 1991 Congress required the military to buy $70 million in combat boots in 1992, even though supply depots were overstocked with 2 million pairs. Four small American companies produce the boots. (*Baltimore Sun*)
- Some of the deals offered for votes for the North American Free Trade Agreement included: *a* a $10 million Trade Center in Texas named after a representative from Texas, *b* a $10 million bridge over railroad tracks in Houston, *c* a requirement that manhole covers bear the clear imprint of the countries where they were made, to satisfy lawmakers from twenty-one states where "Made in America" manhole covers are produced, and *d* a delay in a move to increase grazing fees on western range land. (*Knight-Ridder Newspapers*)
- The 1993 Appropriations bill contained: *a* $11.5 million to modernize a power plant in Philadelphia's naval yard, targeted to close; *b* $19.6 mil-

lion to create jobs in Ireland (an annual subsidy begun as a tribute to House Speaker Tip O'Neill but continued since); *c* $22 million for the Robert C. Byrd memorial dams and locks in West Virginia, named after the chairman of the Senate Appropriations Committee. (*Parade Magazine*)
- The 1994 Appropriations bill contained: *a* $1 million for the Palmer Chiropractic School in Davenport, Iowa, to conduct chiropractic demonstrations in rural areas; and *b* $2.4 million to help Burlington, Iowa, design and build a facility that will provide 200 parking spaces for eighteen Federal employees. (*Washington Post*)
- A standard, regulation Federal ashtray has ten pages of specifications. The testing procedures include putting the ashtray on a maple plank, 44.5 millimeters thick, using a hammer to hit the ashtray with a steel punch point ground to a 60 percent angle. "The specimen should break into a small number of irregularly shaped pieces, not greater in number than 35." To be counted as regulation shards, they must be "6.4 millimeters or more, on any three of its adjacent edges...." (*Newsweek*)
- It took twenty-three Federal employees to approve the purchase of laptop computers bought for $3,500 each. These computers were priced at $1500 each at the local retail computer store. (*Newsweek*)

firms that the great threat to freedom is the concentration of power . . . by concentrating power in political hands, [government] is . . . a threat to freedom."

Second, we can be selective in the market system of the private sector, using our income to buy pre-

cisely what we choose and rejecting unwanted commodities. But, as noted, in the public sector—even assuming a high level of political democracy—conformity and coercion are inherent. If the majority decides in favor of certain governmental actions—to build a reservoir, to establish a system of national health insurance, to provide a guaranteed annual income—the minority must conform. The "use of political channels, while inevitable, tends to strain the social cohesion essential for a stable society."[4] Because decisions can be rendered selectively by individuals through markets, the need for conformity and coercion is lessened and this "strain" reduced. The scope of government should be strictly limited.

Finally, the power and activities of government should be dispersed and decentralized.

> If government is to exercise power, better in the county than in the state, better in the state than in Washington. If I do not like what my local community does, be it in sewage disposal, or zoning, or schools, I can move to another local community, and though few may take this step, the mere possibility acts as a check. If I do not like what my state does, I can move to another. If I do not like what Washington imposes, I have few alternatives in this world of jealous nations.[5]

The Liberal Stance

But liberal economists are skeptical of the conservative position. They say the conservative view is based on the **fallacy of limited decisions.** That is, conservatives implicitly assume that during any particular period there is a limited, or fixed, number of decisions to be made in the operation of the economy. If government makes more of these decisions in per-

forming its stated functions, the private sector of the economy will necessarily have fewer "free" decisions or choices to make. This is considered fallacious reasoning. By sponsoring the production of public goods, government is *extending* the range of free choice by permitting society to enjoy goods and services which would not be available without governmental provision.

We can argue it is largely through the economic functions of government that we have freed ourselves in some measure from ignorance, unemployment, poverty, disease, crime, discrimination, and other ills. In providing most public goods, government does not typically undertake production itself, but rather purchases these goods through private enterprise. When government decides to build an interstate highway, private concerns are given the responsibility of making many specific decisions and choices in connection with carrying out this decision.

One of American's leading economists has summarized the liberal view in these words:

> Traffic lights coerce me and limit my freedom. Yet in the midst of a traffic jam on the unopen road, was I really "free" before there were lights? And has the algebraic total of freedom, for me or the representative motorist or the group as a whole, been increased or decreased by the introduction of well-engineered stop lights? Stop lights, you know, are also go lights . . . When we introduce the traffic light, we have, although the arch individualist may not like the new order, by cooperation and coercion created by ourselves greater freedom.[6]

CHAPTER SUMMARY

1 Majority voting creates a possibility of **a** an underallocation or overallocation of resources to a particular public good, and **b** inconsistent voting outcomes. The median-voter model predicts that, under majority rule, the person holding the middle position on an issue will determine the election outcome.

2 Public choice theorists cite reasons why government might be inefficient in providing public goods and services. **a** There are strong reasons for politicians to support special-interest legislation. **b** Public choice may be biased in favor of programs with immediate and clear-cut benefits and

difficult-to-identify costs *and* against programs with immediate and easily identified costs and vague or deferred benefits. **c** Citizens as voters and congressional representatives face limited and bundled choices as to public goods and services, whereas consumers in the private sector can be highly selective. **d** Government bureaucracies have less incentive to operate efficiently than do private businesses.

3 The benefits-received principle of taxation is that those who receive the benefits of goods and services provided by government should pay the taxes required to finance them.

---

[4]Ibid., p. 23.

[5]Ibid., p. 3.

[6]Paul A. Samuelson, "Personal Freedoms and Economic Freedoms in the Mixed Economy," in Earl F. Cheit (ed.), *The Business Establishment* (New York: John Wiley & Sons, Inc., 1964), p. 219.

The ability-to-pay principle is that those who have greater income should be taxed absolutely and relatively more than those who have less income.

4 The Federal personal income tax is progressive. The corporate income tax is essentially proportional. General sales, excise, payroll, and property taxes are regressive.

5 Excise taxes affect supply and therefore equilibrium price and quantity. The more inelastic the demand for a product, the greater the portion of the tax shifted to consumers. The greater the inelasticity of supply, the larger the portion of the tax borne by the seller.

6 Taxation involves loss of some output whose marginal benefit exceeds its marginal cost. The more elastic the supply and demand curves, the greater is the efficiency loss of a particular tax.

7 Sales taxes are likely to be shifted; personal income taxes are not. Specific excise taxes may or may not be shifted to consumers, depending on the elasticities of demand and supply. There is a disagreement as to whether corporate income taxes are shifted. Property taxes on owner-occupied property are borne by the owner; taxes on rented property are borne by tenants.

8 The Federal tax structure is progressive; the state–local tax structure, regressive; and the overall tax structure, mildly progressive.

9 The Deficit Reduction Act of 1993 increased the top personal income tax rate from 31 percent to 39.6 percent for couples earning more than $250,000 annually. DRA also boosted the Federal gasoline tax by 4.3 cents per gallon and raised the corporate income tax from 34 to 35 percent.

10 Proponents of a value-added tax—a tax similar to a national sales tax—argue that it should replace the corporate income tax. A VAT allegedly would reduce consumption, spur saving and investment, and thereby boost economic growth and American international competitiveness.

11 Conservative and liberals disagree as to the relationship between the size of government and the degree of individual freedom in a society.

TERMS AND CONCEPTS

public choice theory	special-interest effect	progressive tax	Deficit Reduction Act
public finance	rent-seeking behavior	regressive tax	of 1993
logrolling	benefits-received	proportional tax	value-added tax (VAT)
paradox of voting	principle	tax incidence	fallacy of limited
median-voter model	ability-to-pay principle	efficiency loss of a tax	decisions
public sector failure			

QUESTIONS AND STUDY SUGGESTIONS

1 Explain how affirmative and negative majority votes can sometimes lead to inefficient allocations of resources to public goods. Is this problem likely to be greater under a benefits-received or an ability-to-pay tax system? Use the information in Figure 31-1a and b to show how society might be better off if Adams were allowed to buy votes.

2 *Key Question Explain the paradox of voting through reference to the accompanying table which shows the ranking of three public goods by voters Larry, Curley, and Moe.*

Public good	Larry	Curley	Moe
Courthouse	2d choice	1st choice	3d choice
School	3d choice	2d choice	1st choice
Park	1st choice	3d choice	2d choice

3 *Key Question Suppose that there are only five people in a society and that each favors one of the five flood-control options shown in Table 30-2 (include no protection as one of the options). Explain which of these flood-control options will be selected using a majority rule. Will this option be the optimal size of the project from an economic perspective?*

4 Carefully evaluate: "The public, as a general rule gets less production in return for a dollar spent by government than from a dollar spent by private enterprise."

5 "To show that a perfectly functioning government can correct some problem in a free economy is not enough to justify governmental intervention, for government itself does not function perfectly." Discuss in detail.

6 *Key Question How does the problem of limited and bundled choice in the public sector relate to economic efficiency? Why are public bureaucracies alleged to be less efficient than public enterprises?*

7 Explain: "Politicians would make more rational economic decisions if they weren't running for reelection every few years." Do you think this statement has a bearing on the growth of our public debt?

8 Distinguish between the benefits-received and the ability-to-pay principles of taxation. Which philosophy is more evident in our present tax structure? Justify your answer. To which principle of taxation do you subscribe? Why?

9 *Key Question Suppose a tax is such that an individual with an income of $10,000 pays $2,000 of tax; a person with an income of $20,000 pays $3,000 of tax; a person with an income of $30,000 pays $4,000 of tax, and so forth. What is each person's average tax rate? Is this tax regressive, proportional, or progressive?*

10 What is meant by a progressive tax? A regressive tax? A proportional tax? Comment on the progressivity or regressivity of each of the following taxes, indicating in each case your assumption concerning tax incidence:

   a The Federal personal income tax

   b A 3 percent state general sale tax

   c A Federal excise tax on automobile tires

   d A municipal property tax on real estate

   e The Federal corporate income tax

11 *Key Question What is the incidence of an excise tax when demand is highly inelastic? Elastic? What effect does the elasticity of supply have on the incidence of an excise tax? What is the efficiency loss of a tax and how does it relate to elasticity of demand and supply?*

12 Comment on the overall progressivity or regressivity of the United States tax system.

13 Suppose you are a chairperson of a state tax commission responsible for establishing a program to raise new revenue through excise taxes. Would elasticity of demand be important to you in determining those products on which excises should be levied? Explain.

14 How did the Deficit Reduction Act of 1993 specifically affect: a the top personal income tax rate; b the corporate income tax rate; and c the Federal gasoline tax? Which one of these three tax hikes will increase the progressivity of the overall tax system? Which one will reduce the progressivity of the overall tax system?

15 Suppose you are convinced that the long-run viability of the United States as a world industrial power necessitates that investment be increased and consumption reduced as proportions of the nation's output. What specific changes in the tax structure would you recommend to achieve this alteration of output?

16 "The market economy is the only system compatible with political freedom. We therefore should greatly restrain the economic scope of government." Do you agree?

17 **Advanced analysis:** Suppose the equation for the demand curve for some product X is $P = 8 - .6Q$ and the supply curve is $P = 2 + .4Q$. What is the equilibrium price and quantity? Now suppose an excise tax is imposed on X such that the new supply equation is $P = 4 + .4Q$. How much tax revenue will this excise tax yield the government? Graph the curves and label the area of the graph which represents the tax collection TC and the area which represents the efficiency loss of the tax EL. Briefly explain why area EL is the efficiency loss of the tax but TC is not.

18 (Last Word) How do the concepts of "pork-barrel" politics and "logrolling" relate to the items listed in the Last Word?

ANTITRUST, REGULATION, AND INDUSTRIAL POLICY

What do zippers, popcorn, industrial diamonds, airline tickets, video cassette recorders, baby formula, and steel wool soap pads have in common? Answer: All have been the object of private or governmental *antitrust* suits within the past five years.

How are electricity, natural gas, local phone calls, and railroad service related? This is easier. All are "utilities" and subject to *industrial regulation*—government regulation of prices (rates) within selected industries.

What do workplace safety standards, infant seats, acid rain, affirmative action, access for the disabled, and auto fuel economy have in common? Answer: All are the objects or results of *social regulation*—government regulation of the conditions under which goods are produced, their physical characteristics, and the impact of their production on society.

And what do government subsidies to the auto industry to promote fuel efficient automobiles, to the computer industry to develop "flat glass" monitor screens, and to manufacturers who export goods have in common? All are components of *industrial policy*—government policies to promote selected industries or products.

Antitrust, industrial regulation, social regulation, and industrial policy—each are government interventions in the marketplace. To explain why and how, we first clarify some terms and summarize the debate over the desirability of industrial concentration. Next, we examine government policy toward monopoly and anticompetitive business practices. Then, we discuss the more recent and controversial social regulation of industry. Finally, we look at examples of industrial policy and the issues relating to it.

INDUSTRIAL CONCENTRATION: DEFINITIONS

In Chapter 24 we developed and applied a strict definition of monopoly. A *pure*, or *absolute*, monopoly, we said, is a one-firm industry—a situation where a unique product is being produced entirely by a single firm, and entry to the industry is blocked by insurmountable barriers.

In this chapter we will use *industrial concentration* to include pure monopoly and markets in which there is much potential monopoly power. **Industrial concentration** *exists whenever a single firm or a small number of firms controls the major portion of the output of an industry.* One, two, or three firms dominate the industry, potentially resulting in higher-than-competitive prices and sustainable economic profits. This definition, which is closer to how most people understand the "monopoly problem," includes many industries previously designated as oligopolies.

"Industrial concentration" in this chapter refers to industries in which firms are large in absolute terms *and* in relation to the total market. Examples are the electrical equipment industry, where General Electric and Westinghouse, large by an absolute standard, dominate the market; the automobile industry, where General Motors, Ford, and Chrysler are dominant; the chemical industry, led by du Pont, Dow Chemical, and Union Carbide; the aluminum industry, where three firms—Alcoa, Alumax, and Reynolds—reign supreme; and the cigarette industry, where the two large producers Philip Morris and RJR Nabisco command the lion's share of this large market.

INDUSTRIAL CONCENTRATION: BENEFICIAL OR HARMFUL?

It is unclear whether industrial concentration helps or hinders the working of our economy.

The Case Against Industrial Concentration

We stated the case against monopoly and oligopoly in previous chapters. Let's review and extend those arguments.

1 Inefficient Resource Allocation Monopolists and oligopolists find it possible and profitable to restrict output and charge higher prices than if their industry were organized competitively. With pure competition, production occurs where $P = MC$. This equality specifies an efficient allocation of resources because price measures the marginal value or benefit to society of an extra unit of output, while marginal cost reflects the cost or sacrifice of alternative goods. In maximizing profits a monopolist equates not price, but marginal revenue with marginal cost. At this $MR = MC$ point, price will exceed marginal cost, designating an underallocation of resources to the monopolized product. As a result, the economic well-being of society is less than it would be with pure competition.

2 Unprogressive Critics say industrial concentration is neither essential for achieving mass-production economies nor conducive to technological progress.

Empirical studies suggest that "fewness" is not essential for achieving economies of scale in most manufacturing industries. Normally, firms need only realize a small percentage—in many cases less than 3 or 5 percent—of the total market to achieve low-cost production; industrial concentration is *not* a prerequisite of productive efficiency.

Furthermore, the basic unit for technological efficiency is not the firm, but the individual plant. You can correctly argue that productive efficiency calls for, say, a large-scale, integrated auto-manufacturing plant. But it is perfectly consistent to argue that there is no technological justification for General Motors, which is a giant business corporation composed of a number of geographically distinct plants. In this view, many existing firms have attained a size and structure far larger than necessary for achieving full economies of scale. (See Chapter 22's Last Word.)

Nor does technological progress depend on huge corporations with substantial monopoly power. Large size and market power do *not* correlate closely with technological progress. Instead, the sheltered position of firms in highly concentrated industries may promote inefficiency and lethargy; there is no competition to spur productive efficiency. Furthermore, monopolists and oligopolists often resist or suppress technological advances which may cause sudden obsolescence of their existing machinery and equipment.

3 Income Inequality Industrial concentration is criticized as a contributor to income inequality. Because of entry barriers, monopolists and oligopolists can charge a price above average total cost and consistently realize economic profits. These profits go to corporate stockholders and executives who are generally among the upper-income groups.

4 Political Dangers Because economic power and political clout seem to go hand in hand, it is argued that giant corporations exert undue influence over government. This is reflected in legislation and government policies which are congenial, not to the public interest, but to the preservation and growth of large firms. Big businesses allegedly have exerted political power to become primary beneficiaries of defense contracts, tax loopholes, patent policy, tariff and quota protection, and other subsidies and privileges. (Recall our discussion of rent-seeking activities in Chapter 31.)

Defenses of Industrial Concentration

Industrial concentration *does* have significant defenses.

1 Superior Products   One defense is that monopolists and oligopolists have gained their market dominance by offering superior products. Large firms do not coerce consumers to buy, say, Colgate or Crest toothpaste, soft drinks from Coca-Cola and Pepsi, software from Microsoft, ketchup from Heinz, or soup from Campbell. Consumers have collectively decided that these products are more desirable than those offered by other producers. Monopoly profits and large market shares have been "earned."

2 Underestimating Competition   Another defense of industrial concentration is that economists may view competition too narrowly. While there may be only a few firms producing a specific product, those firms may face **interindustry competition.** Firms may have competition from other firms producing distinct but highly substitutable products. There may be only a handful of firms responsible for the nation's output of aluminum. But aluminum faces competition in specific markets from steel, copper, wood, plastics, and a host of other products.

Foreign competition must also be taken into account. While General Motors, Ford, and Chrysler dominate domestic automobile production, strong import competition constrains their pricing and output decisions. While there are only a handful of U.S. aluminum producers, they still face stiff competition from foreign producers.

Furthermore, the large profits resulting from full exploitation of a monopolist's market power induce potential competitors to enter the industry. **Potential competition** restrains the price and output decisions of firms now possessing market power. These firms wish to deter entry, and one way to do that is to keep prices low.

3 Economies of Scale   Where existing technology is highly advanced, only large producers—firms which are large both absolutely and in relation to the market—can obtain low unit costs and therefore sell to consumers at low prices. The traditional antimonopoly contention that industrial concentration means less output, higher prices, and an inefficient allocation of resources assumes that cost economies would be

equally available to firms whether the industry's structure was highly competitive or quite monopolistic. This is frequently not so; economies of scale may be accessible only if competition—in the sense of a large number of firms—is absent.

4 Technological Progress   Recall the *Schumpeter-Galbraith view* that monopolistic industries—in particular, three- and four-firm oligopolies—generate a high rate of technological progress. Oligopolistic firms have both the financial resources *and* the incentives to undertake technological research.

QUICK REVIEW 32-1

■ Industrial concentration exists whenever a single firm or a small number of firms controls the major portion of an industry's output.

■ The case against industrial concentration is that it entails allocative inefficiency, impedes technological progress, promotes income inequality, and poses political dangers.

■ Those who defend industrial concentration contend it arises from superior performance and economies of scale; is countered by interindustry, foreign, and potential competition; and generates both the wherewithal and incentives for technological progress.

THE ANTITRUST LAWS

The sharp conflict of opinion over the merits of industrial concentration is probably why government policy toward concentration has not been clear-cut and consistent. Although the thrust of Federal legislation and policy has been to maintain and promote competition, we will examine policies and acts which have furthered the development of monopoly and oligopoly.

Historical Background

Our economy, although steeped in the philosophy of free, competitive markets, has produced a suspicious, fearful public attitude toward industrial concentration. Dormant in the nation's early years, this distrust of big business bloomed in the decades following the Civil War. The widening of local markets into national markets as transportation facilities improved, the ever-increasing mechanization of production, and the increasingly widespread adoption of the corporate form of business enterprise contributed to the development of "trusts"—or monopolies—in the 1870s and 1880s. Trusts developed in the petroleum, meat-packing, railroad, sugar, lead, coal, whiskey, and tobacco industries, among others, during this era.

Not only were questionable tactics used in monopolizing these industries, but the resulting market power was exerted to the detriment of all who did business with them. Farmers and small businesses, being particularly vulnerable to the growth and tactics of large corporate monopolies, were among the first to oppose them. Consumers and labor unions were not far behind in their opposition.

Because of the development of industries in which market forces no longer provided adequate control to ensure socially tolerable behavior, two techniques of control have been adopted as substitutes for, or supplements to, the market.

1 Regulatory Agencies In those few markets where economic realities preclude the effective working of the market—where there is "natural monopoly"—we have established public *regulatory agencies* to control economic behavior.

2 Antitrust Laws In most other markets where economic and technological conditions have not made monopoly essential, social control has taken the form of antimonopoly or *antitrust legislation* designed to inhibit or prevent the growth of monopoly.

First, let's consider the antitrust legislation which, as refined and extended by various amendments, constitute the basic law of the land with respect to corporate size and concentration.

Sherman Act of 1890

Public resentment of the trusts which developed in the 1870s and 1880s culminated in the **Sherman Act** in 1890. This cornerstone of antitrust legislation is surprisingly brief and, at first glance, directly to the point. The core of the act is embodied in two provisions:
In Section 1:

> Every contract, combination in the form of a trust or otherwise, or conspiracy, in restraint of trade or commerce among the several states, or with foreign nations is hereby declared to be illegal. . . .

In Section 2:

> Every person who shall monopolize, or attempt to monopolize, or combine or conspire with any person or persons, to monopolize any part of the trade or commerce among the several states, or with foreign nations, shall be deemed guilty of a misdemeanor. . . .

This act made monopoly and "restraints of trade"—for example, collusive price fixing or the dividing up of markets among competitors—criminal offenses against the Federal government. Either the Department of Justice or parties injured by monopoly or anticompetitive behavior could file suits under the Sherman Act. Firms found in violation of the act could be ordered dissolved by the courts, or injunctions could be issued to prohibit practices deemed unlawful under the act. Fines and imprisonment were also possible results of successful prosecution. Further, parties injured by illegal combinations and conspiracies could sue for *treble damages*—triple the amount of monetary injury done them. The Sherman Act seemed to provide a sound foundation for positive government action against business monopolies.

However, early court interpretations raised serious questions about the effectiveness of the Sherman Act and it became clear that a more explicit statement of the government's antitrust sentiments was needed. The business community itself sought a clearer statement of what was legal and illegal.

Clayton Act of 1914

This needed elaboration of the Sherman Act came in the form of the 1914 **Clayton Act.** The following sections of the Clayton Act were designed to strengthen and make explicit the intent of the Sherman Act:

Section 2 *outlaws price discrimination* between purchasers when such discrimination is not justified on the basis of cost differences.

Section 3 *forbids exclusive,* or **"tying," contracts** whereby a producer would sell a product only on condition that the buyer acquire other products from the same seller and not from competitors.

Section 7 *prohibits acquisition of stocks* of competing corporations when the outcome is to lessen competition.

Section 8 *prohibits formation of* **interlocking directorates**—the situation where a director of one firm is also a board member of a competing firm—in large corporations where the effect would be to reduce competition.

There was little in the Clayton Act not already stated by implication in the Sherman Act. The Clayton Act merely attempted to sharpen and clarify the general provisions of the Sherman Act. Also, the Clayton Act sought to outlaw the techniques by which monopoly might develop and, in this sense, was a preventive measure. The Sherman Act, by contrast, was aimed more at punishing existing monopolies.

Federal Trade Commission Act of 1914

The **Federal Trade Commission Act** created the five-member Federal Trade Commission (FTC), responsible for enforcing the antitrust laws and the Clayton Act in particular. The FTC was given the power to investigate unfair competitive practices on its own initiative or at the request of injured firms. The Commission could hold public hearings on such complaints and, if necessary, issue **cease-and-desist orders** where "unfair methods of competition in commerce" were discovered.

The **Wheeler-Lea Act** of 1938 gave the FTC the additional responsibility of policing "deceptive acts or practices in commerce." As a result, the FTC tries to protect the public against false or misleading advertising and the misrepresentation of products.

The Federal Trade Commission Act, as modified by the Wheeler-Lea Act, thus did two things: (1) it broadened the range of illegal business behavior and (2) it established independent antitrust agency with the authority to investigate and initiate court cases. Today, the FTC and the United States Justice Department jointly enforce the antitrust laws.

Celler-Kefauver Act of 1950

This act amended Section 7 of the Clayton Act, which prohibits a firm from acquiring the *stock* of competitors when the acquisition would reduce competition. Firms could evade Section 7 by acquiring the physical *assets* (plant and equipment) of competing firms, rather than their stocks. The **Celler-Kefauver Act** plugged this loophole by prohibiting one firm from obtaining physical assets of another firm when the effect would be to lessen competition. *(Key Question 2)*

ANTITRUST: ISSUES AND IMPACT

The effectiveness of any law depends on the vigor of government enforcement and how the courts interpret the law. The Federal government has varied considerably in its willingness to apply the antitrust acts.

Administrations holding a laissez-faire philosophy about industrial concentration have sometimes emasculated the acts by ignoring them or by cutting the budgets of enforcement agencies.

Similarly, the courts have run hot and cold in interpreting antitrust laws. At times, they have applied them with vigor, adhering closely to the spirit and objectives of the laws. In other cases, the courts have interpreted the acts in ways which rendered them completely innocuous. Let's examine three issues which arise in interpreting antitrust laws.

Behavior or Structure?

A comparison of two landmark Court decisions reveals two distinct approaches in the application of antitrust.

In the 1920 **U.S. Steel case** the courts applied the **rule of reason,** saying that not every monopoly is illegal. Only monopolies which "unreasonably" restrain trade—so-called "bad trusts"—are subject to antitrust action. The Court held in this case that size was not an offense; although U.S. Steel clearly *possessed* monopoly power, it was innocent because it had not resorted to illegal acts against competitors in obtaining that power, nor had it unreasonably used its monopoly power.

In the **Alcoa case** of 1945 the courts did a turnabout. The Court held that, even though a firm's behavior might be legal, mere possession of monopoly power (Alcoa had 90 percent of the aluminum ingot market) violated the antitrust laws.

These two cases point to a controversy in antitrust policy. Should an industry be judged by its *behavior* (as in the U.S. Steel case) or by its *structure* (as in the Alcoa case)?

"Structuralists" say an industry which is highly concentrated will behave like a monopolist. The economic performance of these industries will be undesirable. Such industries are therefore legitimate targets for antitrust action.

"Behavioralists" assert the relationship between structure and performance is tenuous and unclear. They feel a concentrated industry may be technologically progressive and have a good record of providing products of increasing quality at reasonable prices. If the industry has served society well and engaged in no anticompetitive practices, it should not be accused of antitrust violation simply because it is highly concentrated. Why use antitrust to penalize efficient, well-managed firms?

Since the Alcoa decision of 1945, the courts have reverted to the rule of reason. The sentiment among antitrust economists and those responsible for enforcing the antitrust laws has also swung away from the strict structuralist view. For example, in 1982 the government dropped its 13-year-long monopolization case against IBM on the grounds that IBM had not unreasonably restrained trade.

Defining the Market

Courts often make decisions about existing market power based on the size of the market share of the dominant firm. If the market is defined broadly, then the firm's market share will appear to be small. If the market is defined narrowly, the market share will be large. It is the task of the Court to determine the relevant market for a particular product.

In the **du Pont cellophane case** of 1956 the government contended that du Pont, along with a licensee, had 100 percent of the cellophane market. But the Supreme Court defined the market broadly to include all "flexible packaging materials"—waxed paper, aluminum foil, and so forth, in addition to cellophane. Despite du Pont's total dominance of the "cellophane market," it only controlled 20 percent of the market for "flexible packaging materials." The Court ruled this did not constitute a monopoly.

Other Desirable Goals

Achieving economic efficiency through competition is only one of society's goals. Strict enforcement of antitrust law occasionally may conflict with some other worthy goal. Examples:

1 Balance of Trade Large trade deficits have recently led government to seek ways to increase American exports. Antitrust actions to, say, undo a merger of two chemical suppliers, break up a dominant aircraft manufacturer, or dissolve an emerging software monopolist might weaken the targeted firms, reducing their competitiveness and sales abroad. Our total exports might therefore decline and our trade deficit worsen. Should government strictly enforce antitrust laws, even when significant amounts of American exports are potentially at stake? Should the antitrust goal of efficiency supersede the goal of balancing exports and imports?

2 Defense Cutbacks Recent cutbacks in defense spending have reduced government purchases of military equipment, placing some major defense suppliers in financial jeopardy. Should government allow defense firms to merge, bolstering sagging profits, thus reducing the number of laid-off workers which otherwise might occur? Or should government block such mergers as violations of the Clayton Act, allowing the market to sort matters out, perhaps through bankruptcies? In 1994 the Defense Department and antitrust regulators reached an informal agreement, easing the way for consolidation of the defense industry via mergers.

3 Emerging New Technologies Occasionally, new technologies combine to create new products and services. A current example is the meshing of computers and communications technologies to create the "information superhighway," a generic name for the eventual hookups of computers, telephones, television sets, and other communications devices. This interactive "highway" will improve communications capabilities of households, businesses, and governments across the globe. It will also allow them to access unprecedented amounts of information via a click of a "mouse," and directly buy and sell goods and services. The emergence of this new technology has set off a spate of "megamergers" involving entertainment companies, telecommunication companies, computer manufacturers, and software producers. Should government strictly enforce Section 7 of the Clayton Act to block some of these mergers, specifically those which increase industrial concentration and threaten to reduce competition? Or should government temporarily suspend antitrust rules to encourage the major restructuring of industries and speed the introduction of this new technology? Hastening the development of the information superhighway may also increase our exports of these services and decrease our trade deficit.

By itself, each of these tradeoffs triggers controversy. The issue of antitrust enforcement becomes more complex when it conflicts with other desirable social goals. Some argue that gains from an antitrust policy must be weighed against the effects of the policy on these conflicting objectives. Others contend that selective enforcement of antitrust laws is a facet of government industrial policy (discussed later) which dangerously interferes with the market process. Obviously, different policy makers may well view these considerations and tradeoffs differently.

Effectiveness

Have the antitrust laws been effective? This is difficult to answer. But some insight can be gained by noting how the laws have been applied to existing market structures, mergers, and price fixing.

Existing Market Structures The application of antitrust laws to existing market structures has been lenient. Generally, a firm will be sued if it has more than 60 percent of the relevant market and there is evidence suggesting the firm used abusive conduct to achieve or maintain its market dominance. The most significant recent "victory" against existing market structure was the 1982 out-of-court settlement between the government and AT&T. AT&T was charged in 1974 with violating the Sherman Act by engaging in anticompetitive actions designed to maintain its domestic telephone communications monopoly. As part of the settlement, AT&T agreed to divest itself of its twenty-two regional telephone operating companies. Since 1982, however, the Federal government has filed no significant antitrust suits to break up existing market structure.

Mergers The treatment of mergers varies with the type of merger and its effect on industry concentration.

Merger Types There are three basic types of mergers, as shown in Figure 32-1. This diagram shows two stages of production—the input stage, and the output, or final product stage—for two distinct final-good industries: autos and beer. Each rectangle (A, B, C, ..., X, Y, Z) represents a particular firm.

A **horizontal merger** *is a merger between two competitors selling similar products in the same market.* In Figure 32-1 this type of merger is shown as a combination of glass producers T and U. Other hypothetical examples of horizontal mergers would be Ford Motor Company merging with General Motors or Anheuser-Busch merging with Coors.

A **vertical merger**—*the merging of firms at different stages of the production process in the same industry*—is shown in Figure 32-1 as a merger between firm Z, a hops producer, and firm F, a brewery. Vertical mergers involve firms having buyer–seller relationships. Actual examples of mergers of this type are PepsiCo's mergers with Pizza Hut, Taco Bell, and Kentucky Fried Chicken. PepsiCo supplies soft drinks to each of these fast-food outlets.

A **conglomerate merger** *is the merger of a firm in one industry with a firm in another unrelated industry.* In Figure 32-1 a merger between firm C, an auto manufacturer, and firm D, a brewery, is a conglomerate merger. Actual examples: the merger between Philip Morris, a cigarette company, and Miller Brewing; the merger between International Telephone and Telegraph (ITT) and Sheraton Hotel Corporation.

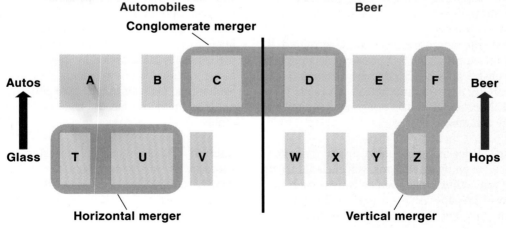

FIGURE 32-1 Types of mergers
Horizontal mergers (T + U) bring together firms selling the same products; vertical mergers (F + Z) connect firms having a buyer-seller relationship; and conglomerate mergers (C + D) join unrelated firms.

Merger Guidelines: The Herfindahl Index The Federal government has established merger guidelines based on the Herfindahl index (Chapter 26) which measures the sum of the squared values of market shares within an industry. An industry of four firms, each with a 25 percent market share, has a Herfindahl index of 2500 ($= 25^2 + 25^2 + 25^2 + 25^2$). In pure competition, where each firm's market share is minute, the index approaches 0 ($= 0^2 + 0^2 + \ldots 0^2$). In pure monopoly, the index of that one firm is 10,000 ($= 100^2$).

Government uses Section 7 of the Clayton Act to block *horizontal* mergers which will substantially lessen competition. Government is likely to challenge a horizontal merger if the post-merger Herfindahl index for the industry would be high (above 1800) and the merger has substantially increased the index (added 100 or more points). But other factors such as the impact of foreign competition and ease of entry of new firms are also considered. Also, horizontal mergers are usually allowed when one of the merging firms is on the verge of bankruptcy.

Most *vertical* mergers escape antitrust prosecution because they do not substantially lessen competition in either of the two markets. In Figure 32-1 neither the Herfindahl index in the hops industry nor the index in the beer industry changes when the vertical merger between firms Z and F occurs. However, a vertical merger between large firms in highly concentrated industries may be challenged. In a 1949 case du Pont had acquired a controlling interest in General Motors' stock. General Motors then purchased about two-thirds of the paint and almost half the fabrics used in auto manufacturing from du Pont. The impact was to effectively foreclose other paint and fabric manufacturers from selling to GM. The Court ordered du Pont to divest itself of GM stock and sever the tie between the two firms.

Conglomerate mergers are generally permitted. If an auto manufacturer acquires a brewery, no antitrust action is likely because neither firm has increased the market share of its own market as a result. The Herfindahl index would remain unchanged in each industry. *(Key Question 5)*

Price Fixing Price fixing is treated strictly. Evidence of price fixing, even by small firms, will elicit antitrust action as will other collusive activities such as schemes to divide up sales in a market. In the parlance of antitrust law, these activities are known as **per se violations;** they are "in and of themselves" illegal, and therefore *not* subject to the rule of reason. To gain a conviction, the government or other party making the charge need only show that there was a conspiracy to fix prices or divide up sales, not that the conspiracy succeeded or caused serious damage to other parties.

Price-fixing investigations and court actions are common. Recent examples:

1 Panasonic agreed to refund $16 million to buyers of consumer electronics, as part of an antitrust settlement for requiring wholesalers and retailers to charge minimum prices for its products.

2 The FTC charged the three largest makers of baby formula with rigging bids to a Federal food program for low-income women and children.

3 Several senior managers of major dairy firms pled guilty to rigging bids on school milk contracts in various states.

4 Five distributors of popcorn agreed to pay $6.8 million to Old Dutch Foods and other customers overcharged for popcorn.

5 YKK Inc., the nation's largest zipper maker, agreed to an FTC action to end its attempts to get a competitor, Talon, to stop offering free equipment to customers who buy zipper components. The FTC ruled these attempts were "invitations to collude."

6 Miles Inc. and Bayer's Dial Corporation were found to have fixed the price of S.O.S. and Brillo soap pads. Bayer pled guilty, agreeing to pay $4.5 million. Dial wasn't prosecuted because it voluntarily reported the price-fixing agreement under a Justice Department amnesty program.

7 The nation's major airlines settled a suit brought by the Justice Department, which had charged them with fixing prices of airline tickets through a computerized fare system.

The government's vigor in prosecuting price fixing has driven it deeper underground; today price fixing is usually surrounded by great secrecy. Also, collusive action is now much less formal. Price leadership and common cost-plus pricing formulas have often replaced formal price-fixing arrangements.

Caution All our statements about the application of antitrust law are generalizations. Each potential antitrust case has unique circumstances which may make it an exception. Also, the strictness with which antitrust laws are interpreted has varied greatly among various administrations. The Reagan administration adopted a lenient enforcement posture toward existing market structures and mergers, while taking a strict position on price fixing. The Bush administration continued the heavy emphasis on prosecuting price fixing, and the Clinton administration has continued the policy.

Moreover, the Clinton administration has "declared war" on *vertical price fixing,* treating it as a per se violation of the antitrust laws. This price fixing consists of a producer requiring its retail distributors to sell its product at or above a specific minimum price. An example would be a blue jeans manufacturer setting a minimum $40 retail price on its famous name blue jeans. By eliminating price discounting, minimum price requirements impede competition at the retail level.

Restricting Competition

We must not conclude that government policies are consistently procompetition. There are exemptions from antitrust laws and a number of public policies have reduced competition.

Antitrust Exemptions Labor unions and agricultural cooperatives have been exempt, subject to limitations, from antitrust laws. We will see in Chapter 33 that Federal legislation and policy have provided some measure of monopolistic power for agriculture and have kept agricultural prices above competitive levels. Similarly, in Chapter 36 we will discover that, since 1930, Federal legislation has generally promoted growth of strong labor unions. This federally sponsored growth has resulted, according to some authorities, in union monopolies whose goal is above competitive wage rates. At state and local levels many occupational groups have successfully established licensing requirements arbitrarily restricting entry to certain occupations. These requirements keep wages and earnings above their competitive levels.

Patents American **patent laws**—the first passed in 1790—provide monetary incentive for innovators by granting them exclusive rights to produce and sell a new product or machine for a period of seventeen years. Patent grants protect the innovator from competitors who would quickly imitate this product and share in their profits, though not the cost and effort, of the research.

Few contest the desirability of this particular aspect of our patent laws, because innovation can weaken and undermine existing monopoly power. However, the granting of a patent frequently amounts to the granting of monopoly power in the production of the patented item. Many economists think the length of patent protection—seventeen years—is much too long.

The role of patent laws in the growth of industrial concentration is large. Du Pont, General Electric, American Telephone and Telegraph, Eastman Kodak, Alcoa, and many other industrial firms have attained monopoly power in part through their ownership of certain patent rights.

Trade Barriers We must also recognize that tariffs and similar trade barriers shield American producers from foreign competition. Protective tariffs are discriminatory "taxes" against goods of foreign firms. These taxes make it difficult and sometimes impossible for foreign producers to compete in American markets with American firms. The result is a less competitive domestic market and an environment aiding the growth of domestic industrial concentration.

QUICK REVIEW 32-2

■ The Sherman Act of 1890 outlaws trade restraints and monopolization; the Clayton Act of 1914 as amended by the Celler-Kefauver Act of 1950 outlaws price discrimination, tying contracts, mergers lessening competition, and interlocking directorates.

■ The Federal Trade Commission Act of 1914 and the Wheeler-Lea Act of 1938 give the Federal Trade Commission (FTC) authority to investigate unfair methods of competition and deceptive acts or practices of commerce.

■ "Structuralists" say highly concentrated industries will behave like a monopolist; "behaviorists" hold that the relationship between industry structure and firm behavior is uncertain.

■ Presently, government treats existing industrial concentration leniently; blocks most horizontal mergers between large, profitable firms in concentrated industries; and vigorously prosecutes price fixing by firms of all sizes.

■ Government policies such as antitrust exemptions, patents, tariffs, and occupational licensure restrict competition.

NATURAL MONOPOLIES AND THEIR REGULATION

Antitrust assumes society will benefit by preventing monopoly from evolving or by dissolving monopoly where it already exists. We now consider a special case in which there is an economic rationale for an industry to be organized monopolistically.

Natural Monopoly

A **natural monopoly** exists when economies of scale are so extensive that a single firm can supply the entire market at lower unit cost than could a number of competing firms. Such conditions exist for the *public utilities,* such as electricity, water, gas, telephone service, and so on (Chapter 24). In these cases economies of scale in producing and distributing the product are very large and large-scale operations are necessary if low unit costs—and a low price—are to be obtained (see Figure 24-9b). In this situation competition is uneconomic. If the market were divided among many producers, economies of scale would not be achieved, unit costs would be high, and high prices would be necessary to cover those costs.

There are two possible alternatives for promoting socially acceptable behavior on the part of a natural monopoly. One is public ownership and the other is public regulation.

Public ownership or some approximation of it has been established in a few instances; the Postal Service, the Tennessee Valley Authority, and Amtrak at the national level, while mass transit, the water system, and garbage collection are public enterprises at the local level.

But *public regulation* has been the option pursued most extensively in the United States. Table 32-1 lists the major Federal regulatory commissions (industrial regulation) and their jurisdictions. All states also have such regulatory bodies for intrastate natural monopolies. Seven percent of the nation's output is produced by regulated industries.

The intent of "natural monopoly" legislation is embodied in the **public interest theory of regulation.** This theory says such industries will be regulated for the benefit of the public, so that consumers may be assured quality service at reasonable rates. The rationale? If competition is inappropriate, *regulated* monopolies should be established to avoid possible

TABLE 32-1 The main Federal regulatory commissions: industrial regulation

Commission (year established)	Jurisdiction
Interstate Commerce Commission (1887)	Railroads, trucking, buses, water, shipping, express companies, etc.
Federal Energy Regulatory Commission (1930)*	Electricity, gas, gas pipelines, oil pipelines, water power sites.
Federal Communications Commission (1934)	Telephones, television, cable television, radio, telegraph, CB radios, ham operators, etc.

*Originally called the Federal Power Commission; renamed in 1977.

abuses of uncontrolled monopoly power. Regulation should guarantee that consumers benefit from the economies of scale—the lower per unit cost—which their natural-monopoly position allows public utilities to achieve. In practice, regulators seek to establish rates which will cover production costs and yield a "fair" or "reasonable" return to the enterprise.

The goal is to set price equal to average total cost. (Review the "Regulated Monopoly" section of Chapter 24.)

Problems

There is considerable disagreement on how effective regulation is in practice. Let's examine three criticisms.

1 Costs and Inefficiency There are a number of interrelated problems associated with cost containment and efficiency in the use of resources.

A goal of regulation is to establish prices so regulated firms will receive a "normal" or "fair" return above their production costs. But this means firms are operating on the basis of cost-plus pricing and, therefore, have no incentive to contain costs. Higher costs will mean larger total profits, so why develop or accept cost-cutting innovations if your "reward" will be a reduction in price? Stated technically, regulation fosters considerable X-inefficiency (Chapter 24).

A regulated firm may resort to accounting skulduggery to overstate its costs and obtain a higher, unjustified profit. In many instances prices are set by the commission so the firm will receive a stipulated rate of return based on the value of its real capital. This poses a special problem. To increase profits the regulated firm might make an uneconomic substitution of capital for labor, contributing to an inefficient allocation of resources within the firm (X-inefficiency).

2 Commission Deficiencies Another criticism is that the regulatory commissions function inadequately because they are "captured" or controlled by the industries they are supposed to regulate. Commission members often were executives in these very industries. Therefore, regulation need *not* be in the public interest, but rather, may protect and nurture the comfortable position of the natural monopolist. It is alleged that regulation becomes a way to guarantee profits and protect the regulated industry from new competition which technological change might create.

3 Regulating Competitive Industries Perhaps the most profound criticism of industrial regulation is that it has sometimes been applied to industries which are *not* natural monopolies and which, without regulation, would be quite competitive. Specifically, regulation has been used in industries such as trucking and airlines where economies of scale are not great and entry barriers are relatively weak. In such instances regulation itself, by limiting entry, may create the monopoly rather than the conditions portrayed in Figure 24-1. The result is higher prices and less output than without regulation. Contrary to the public interest theory of regulation, the beneficiaries of regulation are the regulated firms and their employees. The losers are the public and potential competitors barred from entering the industry.

Example: Regulation of the railroads by the Interstate Commerce Commission (ICC) was justified in the late 1800s and the early decades of this century. But by the 1930s the nation had developed a network of highways and the trucking industry had seriously undermined the monopoly power of the railroads. At this time it would have been desirable to dismantle the ICC and let railroads and truckers, along with barges and airlines, compete with one another. Instead, the regulatory net of the ICC was cast wider in the 1930s to include interstate truckers. *(Key Question 10)*

Legal Cartel Theory

The regulation of potentially competitive industries has produced the **legal cartel theory of regulation.** In the place of socially minded officials *forcing* regulation on natural monopolies to protect consumers, this view sees practical politicians as supplying the "service" of regulation to firms which *want* to be regulated. Regulation is desired because it constitutes a legal cartel which can be highly profitable to regulated firms. Specifically, the regulatory commission performs such functions as dividing up the market (for example, the Civil Aeronautics Board, prior to deregulation, assigned routes to specific airlines) and restricting potential competition by enlarging the cartel (for example, adding the trucking industry to the ICC's domain). While private cartels are unstable and often break down (Chapter 26), the special attraction of a government-sponsored cartel under the guise of regulation is that it endures. The legal cartel theory of regulation suggests that regulation results from rent-seeking activities (Chapter 31).

Proponents of the legal cartel theory of regulation note the Interstate Commerce Act was supported by the railroads and that the trucking and airline industries both supported the extension of regulation to their industries, arguing that unregulated competition was severe and destructive.

Occupational licensing (Chapter 28) is a labor market manifestation of the legal cartel theory. Certain occupational groups—barbers, interior designers, or dietitians—demand licensure because it protects the public from charlatans and quacks. But the real reason may be to limit occupational entry so that practitioners may receive monopoly incomes.

DEREGULATION

The legal cartel theory, increasing evidence of inefficiency in regulated industries, and the contention that government was regulating potentially competitive industries all contributed to deregulation in the 1970s and 1980s. Congress passed legislation which deregulated in varying degrees the airline, trucking, banking, railroad, natural gas, and television broadcasting industries. Moreover, deregulation occurred in the telecommunications industry where antitrust authorities dismantled the *regulated monopoly* known as the

Bell System (AT&T). Together, the deregulation of the 1970s and 1980s comprised "one of the most important experiments in economic policy in our time."[1]

Controversy

Deregulation has been controversial and the nature of the dispute is predictable. Basing their arguments on the legal cartel theory, proponents of deregulation contended it would lower prices, increase output, and eliminate bureaucratic inefficiencies. Some critics of deregulation, embracing the public interest theory, argued deregulation would result in gradual monopolization of some of the deregulated industries by one or two firms. The result would be higher prices, diminished output, and deteriorating service. Other critics were concerned deregulation would lead to excessive competition and industry instability and that vital services (for example, transportation) would be withdrawn from smaller communities. Still others stressed that, as increased competition reduced each firm's revenues, firms would lower their safety standards to reduce costs and remain profitable.

Deregulation Outcomes

It is perhaps still too soon to declare deregulation either a success or a failure in all specific industries. For example, while deregulation of the railroads has been a clear success, *re*regulation has occurred in some industries, notably cable television. But studies show the overall effect of deregulation has been positive. Deregulation of industries formerly subjected to industrial regulation is now contributing an estimated $35.8 to $46.2 billion annually to society's well-being through lower prices, lower costs, and increased output. The majority of these efficiency gains are accruing in three industries: airlines ($13.7 to $19.7), railways ($10.4 to $12.9), and trucking ($10.6). Much smaller gains are occurring in the telecommunications, cable television, stockbrokering, and natural gas industries.[2] (In this Chapter's Last Word we examine the effects of deregulation in the airlines industry in some detail.)

---

[1]Clifford Winston, "Economic Deregulation: Days of Reckoning for Microeconomists," *Journal of Economic Literature,* September 1993, p. 1263.

[2]Ibid., p. 1284.

QUICK REVIEW 32-3

■ Natural monopoly occurs where economies of scale are so extensive that only a single firm can produce the product at minimum cost.

■ The public interest theory of regulation holds that government must regulate business to prevent allocative inefficiency arising from monopoly power.

■ The legal cartel theory of regulation suggests that firms seek government regulation to reduce price competition and ensure stable profits.

■ Deregulation initiated in the past two decades is now yielding large annual efficiency gains for society.

SOCIAL REGULATION

The "regulation" just discussed is economic or **industrial regulation.** With this regulation the government is concerned with the overall economic performance of a few specific industries, but focusing on pricing and service to the public.

Beginning in the early 1960s, government regulation of a new type evolved and grew rapidly. This **social regulation** is concerned with the conditions under which goods and services are produced, the impact of production on society, and the physical characteristics of goods themselves. For example, the Occupational Safety and Health Administration (OSHA) is concerned with protecting workers against occupational injuries and illnesses and the Consumer Products Safety Commission (CPSC) specifies minimum standards for potentially unsafe products.

The main Federal regulatory commissions dealing with social regulation are listed in Table 32-2.

Distinguishing Features

Social regulation differs from economic regulation in several ways.

1 Social regulation is often applied "across the board" to all industries and directly affects far more producers. While the Interstate Commerce Commission (ICC) focuses only on specific portions of the transport industry, OSHA's rules and regulations apply to every employer.

2 Social regulation involves government in the details of the production process. For example, rather than specifying safety standards for products, CPSC

TABLE 32-2 The main Federal regulatory commissions: social regulation

Commission (year established)	Jurisdiction
Food and Drug Administration (1906)	Safety and effectiveness of food, drugs, and cosmetics
Equal Employment Opportunity Commission (1964)	Hiring, promotion, and discharge of workers
Occupational Safety and Health Administration (1971)	Industrial health and safety
Environmental Protection Agency (1972)	Air, water, and noise pollution
Consumer Product Safety Commission (1972)	Safety of consumer products

mandates—often in detail—certain characteristics which products must have.

3 Social regulation has expanded rapidly while industrial regulation has waned. Between 1970 and 1979 government created twenty new Federal regulatory agencies. More recently, Congress has established new regulations enforced by existing regulatory agencies. Example: The Equal Employment Opportunity Commission—responsible for enforcing the nation's laws against workplace discrimination on the basis of race, gender, age, or religion—has the added duty of enforcing the Americans with Disabilities Act of 1990. Under this social regulation businesses must provide reasonable accommodations for qualified workers and job applicants with disabilities. Also, sellers must provide reasonable access for disabled customers.

The names of the better-known regulatory agencies in Table 32-2 suggest the reason for their creation and growth: Much of our society had achieved a reasonably affluent level of living by the 1960s and attention shifted to improvements in the quality of life. This improvement called for safer and better products, less pollution, better working conditions, and greater equality of opportunity.

Costs and Criticisms

The overall objectives of social regulation are laudable. But there is controversy as to whether the benefits of these regulatory efforts justify the costs.

Costs The costs of social regulation are *administrative costs,* such as salaries paid to employees of the commissions, office expenses, and the like; and *compliance costs,* the costs incurred by businesses and state and local governments in meeting the requirements of regulatory commissions. In 1994 total administrative costs of social regulation were about $12 billion.[3] Because compliance costs are approximately twenty times administrative costs, the total cost of social regulation in 1994 was about $240 billion. In 1994, 99,000 full-time employees worked for Federal regulatory agencies involved in social regulation.[4]

Cost estimates for specific types of regulations are also available. The U.S. Council on Environmental Quality has estimated that the cost of pollution control for the 1979–1988 period totaled over $700 billion. Federally required safety and antipollution equipment has increased the price of the typical automobile by as much as $2,200.[5] Business firms in the United States spend more than $5 billion annually to meet OSHA requirements.[6]

Criticisms Critics argue that our economy is now subject to overregulation, that regulatory activities have been carried to the point where the marginal costs of regulation exceed the marginal benefits (Chapters 2 and 30).

Uneconomic Goals Those concerned with overregulation contend, first, that many social regulation laws are poorly drawn so that regulatory objectives and standards are often stated in legal, political, or engineering terms which result in the pursuit of goals beyond the point at which marginal benefits equal marginal costs. Businesses complain that regulators press for small increments of improvement, unmindful of costs. A requirement to reduce pollution by an incremental 5 percent may cost as much as required to achieve the first 95 percent reduction.

Inadequate Information Decisions must often be made and rules promulgated on the basis of inade-

---

[3]Center for the Study of American Business, Washington University.

[4]Ibid.

[5]Robert W. Crandall, et al., *Regulating the Automobile* (Washington: The Brookings Institution, 1986), p. 43.

[6]Murray L. Weidenbaum, *Business, Government, and the Public,* 4th ed. (Englewood Cliffs, N.J.: Prentice-Hall, Inc., 1990), p. 144.

quate information. CPSC officials may make decisions about carcinogens in products based on limited experiments with laboratory animals.

Unintended Side Effects Critics argue that regulations produce many unintended side effects which greatly boost the full cost of regulation. For example, Federal gas mileage standards for automobiles may cause an estimated 2200 to 3900 traffic deaths a year. The reason? Manufacturers have reduced the weight of vehicles to meet the increasingly stringent standards. All else equal, drivers of lighter cars have a higher fatality rate than drivers of heavier vehicles.

Overzealous Personnel Opponents of social regulation say the regulatory agencies may attract overzealous personnel who "believe" in regulation. For example, the EPA staff allegedly is composed of "environmentalists" who are strongly inclined to punish polluters. "Treating all polluters as sinners is . . . much easier than making quantitative judgments about optimal levels of cleanliness in the air and water, but it leads to inefficient regulations, especially where government statutes imply rigid, national, uniform standards.[7]

It is further argued that the bureaucrats of the new regulatory agencies are sensitive to criticism by Congress or some special interest group such as consumerists, environmentalists, or organized labor. The result is bureaucratic inflexibility and the establishment of extreme or nonsensical regulations so that no watchdog group will question the agency's commitment to its social goal. OSHA's much-ridiculed specification of the shape of toilet seats and its proposal that farmers and ranchers provide toilet facilities within five minutes' walking distance of any point where employees are at work are examples. In the words of one critic:

> No realistic evaluation of . . . government regulation comfortably fits the notion of benign and wise officials making altogether sensible decisions in the society's greater interests. Instead we find waste, bias, stupidity, concentration on trivia, conflicts among the regulators and, worst of all, arbitrary and uncontrolled power.[8]

---

[7]William Lilley III and James C. Miller III, "The New 'Social Regulation,'" *The Public Interest,* Spring 1977, p. 58.

[8]Murray L. Weidenbaum, "The Cost of Overregulating Business," *Tax Review,* August 1975, p. 33.

Economic Implications

If overregulation does exist—and that is subject to debate—what are its consequences?

1 Higher Prices Social regulation increases product prices. It does this directly because compliance costs normally get passed on to consumers. Furthermore, social regulation indirectly contributes to higher product prices by reducing labor productivity. Resources invested in antipollution equipment are not available for investment in new machinery to increase output per worker. Where wage rates are inflexible downward, declines in labor productivity increase marginal and average total costs of production. In effect, product supply curves shift leftward, causing product prices to rise.

2 Slower Innovation Social regulation may have a negative impact on the rate of innovation. The fear that a new, technologically superior plant will not meet with EPA approval or that a new product may run into difficulties with CPSC may persuade a firm to produce the same old product in the same old way.

3 Reduced Competition Social regulation may have an anticompetitive effect since it usually is a relatively greater economic burden for small firms than for large firms. The costs of complying with social regulation are, in effect, fixed costs. Smaller firms produce less output over which to distribute these costs and, hence, their compliance costs per unit of output put them at a competitive disadvantage with their larger rivals. The burden of social regulation is more likely to put small firms out of business, contributing to the increased concentration of industry.

In Support of Social Regulation

The problems which social regulation confronts are serious and substantial. In 1992, 8500 workers died in job-related accidents in the United States. Particulate and ozone pollution still plagues our major cities, imposing large costs in terms of reduced property values and increased health-care expenses. Thousands of children and adults die each year in accidents involving poorly designed products. Discrimination against blacks, other minorities, females, the disabled, and older workers reduces their earnings and also imposes heavy costs on society.

According to proponents of social regulation, the relevant economic test of whether it is worthwhile is not whether its costs are high or low, but rather whether benefits *exceed* costs. After years of neglect, society cannot expect to cleanse the environment, enhance the safety of the workplace, improve the safety of the automobile, and enhance economic opportunity without incurring substantial costs.

Cost calculations may paint too dim a picture. Benefits are taken for granted, are more difficult to measure than costs, and may accrue to society only after an extended period.

Benefits of social regulation have been substantial. Examples: It is estimated that highway fatalities would be 40 percent greater annually without auto safety features mandated through regulation.[9] Compliance with child safety-belt laws has significantly reduced the auto fatality rate for small children.[10] The National Ambient Air Quality Standards set by law have been reached in nearly all parts of the nation for sulfur dioxide, nitrogen dioxide, and lead. Affirmative action regulations have significantly increased labor demand for blacks and females.[11] Use of childproof lids have resulted in a 90 percent decline in child deaths caused by accidental swallowing of poisonous substances.[12]

Defenders of social regulation assert these and other benefits are well worth the costs of social regulation. These costs are simply the "price" a society must pay to create a hospitable, sustainable, and just society.

Although we can expect social regulation to continue to be controversial, the policy question has moved away from whether or not social regulation should occur. Rather the questions now are: How and when should social regulation be used? Can we improve social regulation to make it more efficient? Are the decision makers aware of the marginal costs, as well as the marginal benefits? *(Key Question 12)*

---

[9]Crandall, op. cit., p. 155.

[10]*Economic Report of the President, 1987* (Washington: 1987), p. 188.

[11]Jonathon S. Leonard, "The Impact of Affirmative Action on Employment," *Journal of Labor Economics,* October 1984, pp. 439–463.

[12]U.S. Product Safety Commission estimate.

QUICK REVIEW 32-4

■ Social regulation is concerned with conditions under which goods and services are produced, the effect of production on society, and physical characteristics of goods themselves.

■ Critics of social regulation say uneconomic policy goals, inadequate information, unintended side effects, and overzealous personnel create regulatory costs which exceed regulatory benefits.

■ Defenders of social regulation point to the large benefits arising from policies which keep dangerous products from the marketplace, reduce workplace injuries and deaths, contribute to clean air and water, and reduce employment discrimination.

INDUSTRIAL POLICY

In recent years industrial policy has joined antitrust, industrial regulation, and social regulation as a distinct form of government involvement with business. **Industrial policy** *comprises governmental actions to promote the economic vitality of specific firms or industries.* Antitrust, industrial regulation, and social regulation alter the structure or restrict the conduct of private firms, generally reducing their revenues or increasing their costs. Industrial policy promotes the interests of selected firms and industries, usually adding to their profitability.

Antecedents

Governmental promotion of industries has a long, controversial history. In the 1600s and 1700s European governments subscribed to a set of policies known as mercantilism. At the heart of mercantilism was the belief that a nation's wealth consisted of its precious metals. Because merchants received inflows of gold in return for their exports, governments established elaborate policies to promote trade surpluses (exports in excess of imports). Such policies included tariffs on finished goods, free importation of resources, and granting of monopoly trading privileges to selected companies (such as the East India Company and the Hudson Bay Company). Governments also regulated production techniques to ensure the quality of exports and, in general, subsidized production in their exporting industries.

America's history is also full of examples of industrial policy. In the 1800s government granted free land to railroads to promote their westward expansion. This expansion hastened economic development, increased productivity, and raised national output and employment. Government has heavily subsidized American agriculture over the decades, boosting profits in that industry. And, government's massive spending on national defense has fostered a military armament industry.

Recent Emphasis

There has recently been a growing concern that the United States' industrial preeminence has been seriously eroded. Our domestic markets have been flooded with foreign steel, automobiles, motorcycles, cameras, watches, sporting goods, and electronic equipment. Some believe these imports imply that we have lost our global competitiveness.

Noting Japanese success, many union and business leaders and politicians—but not so many economists—feel the United States needs a strong industrial policy to reverse what appears to them to be our industrial decline. They argue that government should take a more active and direct role in determining the structure and composition of American industry. Government, they say, should use low-interest loans, loan guarantees, favorable tax treatment, research and development subsidies, antitrust immunity, and even foreign trade protection to accelerate the development of "high-tech" industries and to revitalize certain core manufacturing industries such as steel. Presumably, as a result, the American economy will enjoy a higher average level of productivity and be more competitive in world markets.

Although the Federal government has not committed to a comprehensive industrial policy, there are many examples of specific programs consistent with this concept.

1 Auto Industry The surge of Japanese auto imports during the 1970s and 1980s placed tremendous financial pressure on American auto producers. The Federal government responded with a series of actions to promote the domestic industry. In 1979 it "bailed out" the failing Chrysler Corporation by providing $1.5 billion of loan guarantees to financial institutions which were lending to Chrysler to keep it afloat. In the mid-1980s government negotiated "voluntary" export restrictions on automobiles imported from Japan. In these agreements the Japanese government and auto firms agreed to limit the number of auto exports to America. More recently, the American government has initiated a heavily subsidized research and development program with the Big Three American producers to design and produce a revolutionary fuel-efficient gasoline engine.

2 Synfuel Program In response to the "oil crisis" of the mid-1970s, government established a subsidy program to promote development of alternative fuels. Much money went into development of so-called synthetic fuels such as oil squeezed from oil shale and natural gas converted from coal. Overall, this government effort was a dismal failure. In 1991 the program was shut down after an expense of $1.3 billion. Government still heavily subsidizes the ethanol industry, which develops fuel from corn.

3 Export-Import Bank This Federal "bank" subsidizes interest rates on loans to foreign buyers of American exports. These subsidies directly benefit American exporters of goods bought on credit. In effect, the subsidies reduce the total price (product price plus interest on loan) to the foreign buyer.

4 Sematech In 1987 government and industry set up a consortium, called Sematech, allowing producers of semiconductors (microcircuits) to join together—immune from antitrust laws—to engage in research and share production techniques. The purpose was to strengthen this industry's ability to compete more effectively with Japanese firms. It is generally agreed this effort has accomplished its intended goal.

5 Flat-Glass Technology In 1994 the Clinton administration announced a $1 billion plan to help industry compete with Japan in developing flat-panel computer screens. At the time, the United States' world market share was only 3 percent; Sharp and other Japanese firms dominated the market. Because these screens have many high-tech military applications, the administration justified this massive subsidy on a national defense basis. But it was clear this subsidy had as much to do with industrial policy as with military needs.

Controversy

Opponents of industrial policy raise several issues.

1 Deindustrialization? Has the United States in fact deindustrialized? Has our manufacturing sector declined enough to justify subsidies to industries? Statistics suggest not. While the composition of manufacturing output has changed, manufacturing in the aggregate accounts for about the same percentage (20 percent) of GDP as it did in 1950. Similarly, manufacturing's share of the nation's expenditures on new plant and equipment was nearly identical in 1994 and in 1950. Employment in manufacturing has declined from 34 to 15 percent of total employment in the 1950–1994 period, but that reflects the growth of labor productivity rather than industrial demise.

2 Foreign Experience Advocates of industrial policy cite Japan and its Ministry of International Trade and Industry (MITI) as a model. In the post-World War II era, Japan has achieved rapid economic growth; it has been highly successful in penetrating world markets and has had a much-publicized industrial policy. Yet the overall role of industrial policy as a factor in Japanese industrial success is not clear. Subsidies to some of Japan industries have clearly succeeded (semiconductors, machine tools, steel, and ship building). In others, Japan's industrial policy has failed (aluminum smelting, petrochemicals, high-definition television). In still other instances, Japanese industries have developed successfully without government support (electronics, motorcycles).

Critics point out that Japan's MITI tried unsuccessfully to block Honda and Mazda from entering the Japanese auto industry. Also, while government support gave Japanese firms an early lead in research on high-definition television, American producers have implemented a better technology, placing Japan far behind in development of this new product.

Neither has European industrial policy been consistently successful. Although Europe's subsidized development of Airbus Industries, a manufacturer of commercial aircraft, has been successful, Europe's subsidization of the supersonic transport aircraft was a failure.

3 Markets and Politics While "short-circuiting" the market mechanism through promotion of selected industries sounds appealing, critics question the government's ability to identify what industries will be winners or losers. The issue here is whether private investors using capital markets have better foresight than public officials in determining where investment funds ought to be channeled. Critics argue that private investors have greater incentive in investing their *own* funds to obtain accurate information on the future prospects of various industries and technologies than might government bureaucrats in investing *taxpayers'* funds.

Furthermore, might not government use its power to allocate investment funds to buy political support of subsidized industries? Is it possible the economic goals of enhanced industrial efficiency and encouragement of exports might be subverted to the political goal of getting reelected? It is feared that the expansion of industrial policy might lead to "lemon" socialism—government support or ownership of declining industries, dying companies, and inefficient technologies.

Proponents of industrial policy counter that many leading American products were developed with direct government support, particularly through national defense spending. Commercial aircraft, the supercomputer, the PC mouse, and the Internet information system are examples. The argument is that government industrial policy targeted at key, high-technology applications in the private sector facilitates entrepreneurial forces and ultimately enhances the dynamic efficiency associated with the market system. By subsidizing research and development efforts, industrial policy reduces the risk of exploring and applying new technologies. These technologies often spur complementary products and entire new industries, boosting a nation's productivity, standard of living, and international competitiveness. *(Key Question 14)*

CHAPTER SUMMARY

1 The case against industrial concentration contends that it **a** causes a misallocation of resources; **b** retards the rate of technological advance; **c** promotes income inequality; and **d** poses a threat to political democracy.

2 The defense of industrial concentration maintains: **a** firms have obtained their large market shares by offering superior products; **b** interindustry and foreign competition, along with potential competition from new industry entrants, make American industries more competitive than generally believed; **c** some degree of monopoly may be essential to realize economies of scale; and **d** monopolies and oligopolies are technologically progressive.

LAST WORD

DEREGULATION OF THE AIRLINES

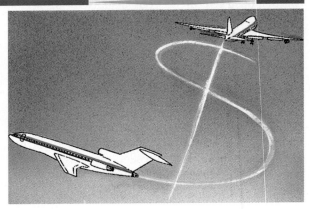

Perhaps the most publicized case of deregulation involves the Airline Deregulation Act of 1978. Previously, the Civil Aeronautics Board (CAB) controlled airline fares, allocated interstate routes, and controlled industry entry. Deregulation freed airlines to set their own rates, select their own routes, and allowed newcomers to compete. Has airline deregulation succeeded?

Although the airline industry was deregulated almost two decades ago, it is still adjusting to deregulation. Nevertheless, some of its effects have become clear.

Fares Deregulation has exerted downward pressure on fares, with overall fares rising less rapidly than the general price level. Discount air tickets, in particular, have increased in availability and declined in price.

Today, fares generally are about 20 percent lower in real terms than before deregulation. Of course, fare reductions have not been uniform in all airline markets. Passengers flying from some cities have enjoyed greater decreases in fares than from others.

Deregulation has produced lower fares for two reasons. First, competition among air carriers has driven down prices. Before regulation, ticket prices greatly exceeded the average total cost (ATC) of passenger service. Competition has reduced fares and economic profits; prices are closer to ATC. Second, competition has pressured firms to reduce costs. The industry's "hub and spoke" route system—analogous to a bicycle wheel—has reduced costs by allowing airlines to use smaller planes on the spoke routes and wide-bodied craft between the major hub air-

ports. Wide-body aircraft cost less to operate per seat mile than smaller aircraft.

Also, entry of nonunion airlines has forced the major carriers to negotiate wage reductions with their unions. Some airlines have established two-tier wage systems paying new workers less than current employees. Union work rules have been made more flexible to increase worker productivity and reduce wage costs. Airlines are increasingly leasing work such as airline maintenance to lower-cost outside companies.

Service and Safety While some major airlines have withdrawn service from a few smaller cities, commuter airlines usually fill the resulting void. The hub and spoke system has increased flight frequencies at most airports. It has also reduced the amount of airline switching required of passengers. Measures of service quality such as "complaints per 10,000 passengers" are sharply lower today than in the era of regulation.

---

3 The cornerstone of antitrust policy consists of the Sherman Act of 1890 and the Clayton Act of 1914. The Sherman Act specifies that "Every contract, combination . . . or conspiracy in the restraint of interstate trade . . . is . . . illegal," and that any person who monopolizes or attempts to monopolize interstate trade is guilty of a misdemeanor.

4 The Clayton Act was designed to bolster and make more explicit the provisions of the Sherman Act. It declared that price discrimination, tying contracts, intercorporate stockholdings, and interlocking directorates are illegal when their effect is the lessening of competition.

5 The Federal Trade Commission Act of 1914 created the Federal Trade Commission to investigate antitrust violations and to prevent the use of "unfair methods of competition." Empowered to issue cease-and-desist orders, the

Commission also serves as a watchdog agency for the false and deceptive representation of products.

6 The Celler-Kefauver Act of 1950 prohibits one firm from acquiring the assets of another firm where the result is a lessening of competition.

7 Issues in applying antitrust laws include: **a** the problem of determining whether an industry should be judged by its structure or its behavior; **b** defining the scope and size of the dominant firm's market; and **c** balancing the gains from antitrust against other desirable goals such as balancing exports and imports, consolidating the national defense industry, and encouraging new technologies.

8 Antitrust officials are more likely to challenge price fixing and horizontal mergers among large firms than they are to break up existing market structures.

On the negative side, more frequent stopovers now required in hub cities have increased average travel time between cities. Also, by increasing the volume of traffic, deregulation has contributed to greater airport congestion, resulting in more frequent and longer flight delays.

There is mixed evidence whether deregulation has reduced the safety margin of air transportation. The greater volume of air traffic has resulted in higher reported instances of near-collisions in midair. But the accident and fatal accident rates of airlines are much lower today than before deregulation. Furthermore, deregulation has prevented an estimated 800 deaths annually on the nation's highways, because lower fares have enticed people to substitute air travel for more dangerous automobile travel.

Industry Structure Airline deregulation initially induced entry of many new carriers. But in the past several years the industry has gone through a "shakeout" in which many firms have failed and others have merged with stronger competitors. In 1994, American, United, and Delta accounted for about 60 percent of domestic air service. Moreover, there still remains excess capacity and severe economic losses in some parts of the industry. Thus far, consolidation of the industry has not brought with it sustained profitability, even for the dominant firms.

Growing concentration in the airlines industry is of much concern. Some think consolidation of the industry eventually may be detrimental to the very goals of deregulation itself. Studies show that fares at airports dominated by one or two airlines are as much as 25 percent higher than at airports where competition is more brisk. Moreover, entry of new carriers into the industry is more difficult than many economists predicted. The lack of airport capacity —at least in the short term—means that airline markets are far from being perfectly competitive. A firm wishing to enter a particular market because existing carriers are earning economic profits cannot do so if long-term leases allow existing carriers to control the airline gates.

Airline tactics also make successful entry difficult. Airline reservation systems developed by the major carriers often give their own flights priority listings on the computers used by travel agents. Frequent-flyer programs—discounts based on accumulated flight mileage—encourage passengers to use dominant existing carriers rather than new entrants. Also, price matching by existing carriers makes it difficult for new entrants to lure customers through lower ticket prices.

Conclusion Although it is too soon for a definitive assessment of airline deregulation, most economists see a positive outcome to date. While airlines lost billions of dollars during and immediately following the recession of 1990–1991, the survivors are positioned to regain strong profitability. Also, although lasting entry has proved difficult, there are some success stories. In particular, Southwest Airlines has expanded its direct flight, low-fare approach far beyond its original geographical domain. The Federal government has estimated that airline deregulation produced a $100 billion net benefit to society in the 1980s. As we noted in this chapter, airline deregulation is now yielding society net benefits of $13.7 to $19.7 billion annually.

9 With respect to agriculture, labor, occupational licensing, patents, and international trade barriers, government policies have tended to restrict competition.

10 The objective of industrial regulation is to protect the public from the market power of natural monopolies by regulating prices and quality of service. Critics contend that industrial regulation is conducive to inefficiency and rising costs and that in many instances it constitutes a legal cartel for the regulated firms. Legislation passed in the late 1970s and the 1980s has brought about varying degrees of deregulation in the airline, trucking, banking, railroad, and television broadcasting industries. Studies indicate that deregulation is producing sizable annual gains to society through lower prices, lower costs, and increased output.

11 Social regulation is concerned with product safety, safer working conditions, less pollution, and greater economic opportunity. Critics contend that businesses are over-regulated in that marginal costs exceed marginal benefits, while defenders dispute that contention.

12 Industrial policy consists of government actions promoting the economic vitality of specific industries or firms. Proponents of industrial policy see it as a way to strengthen the industrial sector, speed development of new technologies, increase productivity, and increase international competitiveness. Critics charge that industrial policy substitutes the whims of politicians and bureaucrats for the hard scrutiny of entrepreneurs and business executives in allocating society's resources.

TERMS AND CONCEPTS

industrial
  concentration
interindustry
  competition
foreign competition
potential competition
Sherman Act
Clayton Act
tying contracts

interlocking
  directorates
cease-and-desist order
Wheeler-Lea Act
Federal Trade
  Commission Act
Celler-Kefauver Act
U.S. Steel case
rule of reason

Alcoa case
du Pont cellophane
  case
horizontal, vertical,
  and conglomerate
  mergers
per se violations
patent laws
natural monopoly

public interest theory
  of regulation
legal cartel theory of
  regulation
industrial regulation
social regulation
industrial policy

QUESTIONS AND STUDY SUGGESTIONS

1 You are president of General Motors or Ford. Discuss critically the case against industrial concentration. Now suppose you are a representative for a consumer organization, attempting to convince a congressional committee that industrial concentration is a significant factor contributing to high prices. Critically evaluate the case for industrial concentration.

2 *Key Question* *Describe the major provisions of the Sherman and Clayton acts. Who is responsible for enforcing these laws?*

3 Briefly indicate the basic issue involved in the U.S. Steel, Alcoa, and du Pont cellophane cases. What issues in antitrust enforcement are implicit in these cases?

4 Explain how strict enforcement of the antitrust laws might conflict with **a** promoting exports to achieve a balance of trade; **b** easing burdens in the defense industry; and **c** encouraging new technologies. Do you see any dangers of using selective antitrust enforcement as part of an industrial policy?

5 *Key Question* *How would you expect antitrust authorities to react to **a** a proposed merger of Ford and Chrysler; **b** evidence of secret meetings by contractors to rig bids for highway construction projects; **c** a proposed merger of a large shoe manufacturer and a chain of retail shoe stores; and **d** a proposed merger of a small life insurance company and a regional candy manufacturer.*

6 Suppose a proposed merger of firms will simultaneously lessen competition and reduce unit costs through economies of scale. Do you think such a merger should be allowed?

7 In 1986 PepsiCo Inc., which then had 28 percent of the soft drink market, proposed to acquire the Seven-Up Co. Shortly thereafter the Coca-Cola Company, with 39 percent of the market, indicated it wished to acquire the Dr. Pepper

Company. Seven-Up and Dr. Pepper each controlled about 7 percent of the market. In your judgment, was the government's decision to block these mergers appropriate?

8 "The antitrust laws serve to penalize efficiently managed firms." Do you agree?

9 "The social desirability of any given business enterprise should be judged not on the basis of the structure of the industry in which it finds itself, but rather on the basis of the market performance and behavior of that firm." Analyze critically.

10 *Key Question* *What types of industries should be subjected to industrial regulation? What specific problems does industrial regulation entail? Why might an inefficient combination of capital and labor be employed by a regulated natural monopoly?*

11 In view of the problems in regulating natural monopolies, compare socially optimal (marginal-cost) pricing and fair-return pricing by referring again to Figure 24-8. Assuming a government subsidy might be used to cover any loss entailed by marginal-cost pricing, which pricing policy would you favor? What problems might this subsidy entail?

12 *Key Question* *How does social regulation differ from industrial regulation? What types of costs and benefits are associated with social regulation?*

13 The following are research estimates of the average cost per life saved of three specific social regulations: 1967 automobile steering column protection rule costs $100,000 per life saved; 1979 FDA ban on DES (a suspected carcinogen) in cattle feed costs $132 million per life saved; the EPA's proposed restrictions on disposal of dioxins and solvents on land costs $3.5 billion per life saved.[13] Based on

---

[13]*Economic Report of the President, 1987* (Washington: 1987), p. 183.

this information, do you favor each of these social regulations? If not, why not? Discuss: "Implicit within the setting of safety standards for products is the valuation of human life."

14 *Key Question   What is industrial policy and how does it differ from antitrust, industrial regulation, and social regulation? Why might businesses look more favorably on industrial* *policy than these other policies? Cite an example of industrial policy. What are the pros and cons of industrial policy?*

15   (Last Word) What does it mean when we say that the airline industry has been deregulated? What have been the impacts of deregulation on fares, service and safety, and industry structure? Some say "the jury is still out on airline deregulation." Speculate on what they may mean.

33

AGRICULTURE: ECONOMICS AND POLICY

$\blacksquare$n economic analysis of American agriculture can be justified on a number of grounds:

1 Agriculture is one of the nation's largest industries. Consumers spend about 15 percent of their after-tax incomes on food and other farm products (Table 5-1). Gross farm income was about $220 billion in 1994 and approximately 2 percent of the labor force is employed in agriculture. American farmers produce 50 percent of the world's soybeans, 40 percent of all corn, and 25 percent of the world's beef.

2 Agriculture is an industry which—in the absence of government farm programs—is a real-world example of Chapter 23's purely competitive model. The industry comprises many firms selling virtually standardized products. Agriculture is an industry which can be understood by applying the demand and supply tools of competitive markets.

3 Farm markets provide evidence of the intended and unintended effects of government policies which interfere with the forces of supply and demand.

4 Agriculture reflects the increasing globalization of markets. In recent decades the economic ups and downs of American agriculture have been closely tied to its ability to gain access to world markets. Also, agriculture was a major focal point of the recently completed Uruguay Round negotiations of the General Agreement on Tariffs and Trade.

5 Farm policies provide excellent illustrations of Chapter 31's special-interest effect and rent-seeking behavior.

ECONOMICS OF AGRICULTURE

Historically, farmers have frequently faced severe problems of fluctuating prices and relatively low incomes. We distinguish between (1) the **short-run farm problem** of year-to-year fluctuations in farm prices and incomes, and (2) the **long-run farm problem** relating to forces causing agriculture to be a declining industry.

Short-Run Problem: Price and Income Instability

The short-run farm problem is the result of: (1) an inelastic demand for agricultural products; (2) fluctuations in farm output; and (3) shifts in the demand curve.

Inelastic Demand for Agricultural Products In most developed societies, the price elasticity of demand for agricultural products is low. For farm products in the aggregate, the elasticity coefficient is estimated to be from .20 to .25. These figures suggest the prices of agricultural products would have to fall by 40 to 50 percent for consumers to increase their purchases by a mere 10 percent. Consumers apparently put a low value on additional agricultural output compared with alternative goods.

Why is this so? Recall that the basic determinant of elasticity of demand is substitutability. When the price of a product falls, the consumer will tend to substitute *that* product for other products whose prices presumably have not fallen. But in wealthy societies this "substitution effect" is very modest for food. People simply do not switch from three to five or six meals each day in response to declines in the relative prices of agricultural products. An individual's capacity to substitute food for other products is subject to very real biological constraints.

The inelasticity of agricultural demand can also be explained in terms of diminishing marginal utility. In a wealthy society, the population by and large is well fed and well clothed; it is relatively saturated with the food and fiber of agriculture. Therefore, additional agricultural output involves rapidly diminishing marginal utility. Thus it takes very large price cuts to induce small increases in consumption. Curve D in Figure 33-1 portrays the inelastic demand for agricultural products.

Fluctuations in Output   The inelastic demand for farm products magnifies small changes in agricultural production into relatively larger changes in farm prices and incomes. Farmers have limited control over their production. First, floods, droughts, unexpected frost, insect damage, and similar disasters can mean poor crops, while an excellent growing season may mean bumper crops. Weather factors are beyond the control of farmers, yet they exert an important influence on production.

Second, the highly competitive nature of agriculture makes it impossible for farmers to form a huge combination to control production. If the millions of widely scattered and independent producers should by chance plant an unusually large or abnormally small portion of their land, extra large or small outputs would result even if the growing season were normal.

Combining the instability of farm production with the inelastic demand for farm products in Figure

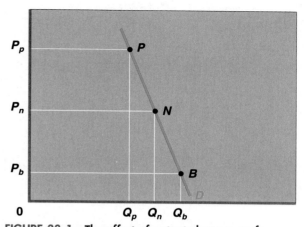

FIGURE 33-1   The effect of output changes on farm prices and incomes
Because of the inelasticity of demand for farm products, a relatively small change in output (Q_n to Q_p or Q_b) will cause relatively large changes in farm prices (P_n to P_p or P_b) and incomes ($0P_nNQ_n$ to $0P_pPQ_p$ or $0P_bBQ_b$).

33-1, we can see why farm prices and incomes are unstable. Even if we assume that market demand for agriculture products is stable at D, its price inelasticity will magnify small changes in output into relatively large changes in farm prices and income. For example, assume that a "normal" crop of Q_n results in a "normal" price of P_n and a "normal" farm income of $0P_nNQ_n$. But a bumper crop or a poor crop will cause large deviations from these normal prices and incomes; these results stem from the inelasticity of demand for farm products.

If a good growing season occurs, the resulting bumper crop of Q_b will reduce farm incomes from $0P_nNQ_n$ to $0P_bBQ_b$. When demand is inelastic, an increase in the quantity sold will be accompanied by a *more than* proportionate decline in price. The net result is that total revenue, that is, total farm income, will decline.

Similarly, for farmers as a group, a poor crop caused by, say, drought may boost farm incomes. A poor crop of Q_p will raise total farm income from $0P_nNQ_n$ to $0P_pPQ_p$. A decline in output will cause a *more than* proportionate increase in price when demand is inelastic. Ironically, for farmers as a group, a poor crop may be a blessing and a bumper crop a hardship. Conclusion: *Given a stable market demand for farm products, the inelasticity of that demand will turn relatively small changes in output into relatively larger changes in farm prices and incomes.*

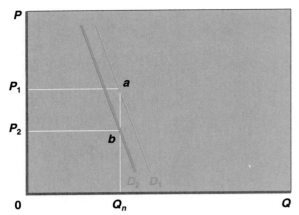

FIGURE 33-2 The effect of demand changes on farm prices and incomes
Because of the highly inelastic demand for agricultural products, a small shift in demand (D_1 to D_2) will cause drastically different levels of farm prices (P_1 to P_2) and farm incomes ($0P_1aQ_n$ to $0P_2bQ_n$) to be associated with a given level of production Q_n.

Fluctuations in Domestic Demand The other aspect of the short-run instability of farm incomes has to do with shifts in the demand curve for agricultural products. Suppose that somehow agricultural output is stabilized at the "normal" level of Q_n in Figure 33-2. Now, because of the inelasticity of the demand for farm products, short-run fluctuations in the demand for these products—prompted perhaps by cyclical changes in the economy—will cause markedly different prices and incomes to be associated with this level of production that we assume to be constant.

A slight drop in demand from D_1 to D_2 will reduce farm income from $0P_1aQ_n$ to $0P_2bQ_n$. A relatively small decline in demand gives farmers a drastically reduced money reward for the same amount of production. Conversely, a slight increase in demand—as from D_2 to D_1—will bring an equally sharp increase in farm income for the same volume of output. These large price-income changes occur because demand is inelastic.

It is tempting to argue that the sharp declines in farm prices which accompany a decrease in demand will cause many farmers to close down in the short run, reducing total output and alleviating these price-income declines. But farm production is relatively insensitive to price changes, because farmers' fixed costs are high compared with their variable costs. Interest, rental, tax, and mortgage payments on land, buildings, and equipment are the major costs faced by the farmer. These are fixed charges. Furthermore,

the labor supply of farmers and their families can also be regarded as a fixed cost. So long as they stay on their farms, farmers cannot reduce their costs by firing themselves! This means their variable costs are for the small amounts of hired help they may employ, plus expenditures for seed, fertilizer, and fuel. As a result of this high volume of fixed costs, farmers are almost invariably better off when working their land than when sitting idle and attempting to pay their fixed costs out of pocket.

Unstable Foreign Demand American agriculture's dependence on world markets is also a source of demand volatility. The incomes of American farmers are sensitive to changes in weather and crop production *in other countries.* Similarly, cyclical fluctuations in incomes in Europe or Japan, for example, can shift the demand for American farm products. So can changes in foreign economic policies. If the nations of western Europe decide to provide their farmers with greater protection from foreign (American) competition, American farmers will have less access to those markets and export demand will fall. International politics can also add to demand instability. Changing political relations between the United States and the Soviet Union boosted American grain sales in the early 1970s, but reduced them at the end of that decade. Changes in the international value of the dollar can be critical. Depreciation of the dollar in the 1970s increased the demand for American farm products, while appreciation of the dollar decreased foreign demand in the early 1980s.

To summarize: The increasing relative importance of exports has increased the instability of the demand for American farm products. Farm exports are affected, not only by weather, income fluctuations, and economic policies abroad, but also by international politics and fluctuations in the international value of the dollar. *(Key Question 1)*

Figure 33-3 shows the Department of Agriculture's index of inflation-adjusted prices received by farmers for crops and livestock during most of this century. The short-run problem of price volatility is clearly evident. So also is the long-run problem of declining farm prices which we examine next.

Long-Run Problem: A Declining Industry

Two more characteristics of agricultural markets must be added to price inelasticity of demand to ex-

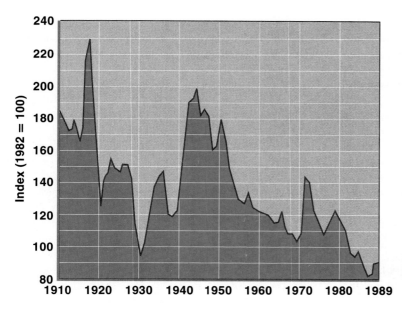

FIGURE 33-3 Index of real prices received by farmers
The course of farm prices during this century reflects both volatility and decline. All of the individual crop and livestock prices which comprise this index show a similar downward trend and most reflect even greater short-run volatility.

plain why agriculture has been a declining industry:
1 Over time the supply of agricultural products has increased rapidly because of technological progress.
2 Demand for agricultural products has increased slowly over time because demand for them is inelastic with respect to income.

Technology and Supply Increases When a price-inelastic and slowly increasing demand for farm products is accompanied by a rapidly increasing supply, there is persistent pressure for farm prices and incomes to fall.

A rapid rate of technological advance, particularly since World War I, has caused significant increases in the supply of agricultural products. This technological progress has many roots: the electrification and mechanization of farms; improved techniques of land management and soil conservation; irrigation; development of hybrid crops; availability of improved fertilizers and insecticides; and improvements in breeding and care of livestock.

These technological advances have been very significant. The amount of capital used per worker increased fifteen times over the 1930–1980 period, permitting a fivefold increase in the amount of land cultivated per farmer. The simplest general index is the increasing number of people which a single farmer's output will support. In 1820 each farm worker produced enough food and fiber to support four persons; by 1947, about fourteen. By 1994 each farmer produced enough to support 125 people! Unques-

tionably, productivity in agriculture has risen significantly. Since World War II, physical productivity in agriculture has advanced at a rate *twice* as fast as in the nonfarm economy.

It is worth noting that most technological advances have *not* been initiated by farmers but rather are the result of government-sponsored programs of research and education and the work of farm machinery producers. Land-grant colleges, experiment stations, county agents of the Agricultural Extension Service, educational pamphlets issued by the U.S. Department of Agriculture, and the research departments of farm machinery, pesticide, and fertilizer producers are the primary sources of technological advance in American agriculture.

Lagging Demand Increases in demand for agricultural commodities have failed to keep pace with technologically inspired increases in their supply. The reason lies in the two major determinants of agricultural demand—incomes and population.

Income Inelastic Demand In less developed countries, consumers must devote the bulk of their meager incomes to agricultural products—food and clothing—to sustain themselves. But as income expands beyond subsistence and the problem of hunger eventually gives way to one of obesity, consumers will increase their outlays on food at ever-declining rates. Once consumers' stomachs are filled, their thoughts turn to the amenities of life which industry, not agriculture, provides. Economic growth in the United States has boosted average per capita income far beyond the level of subsistence. As a result, *increases in the incomes of American consumers lead to less than proportionate increases in expenditures on farm products.*

In technical terms, the demand for farm products is *income-inelastic;* it is quite insensitive to increases in income. Estimates indicate that a 10 percent increase in real per capita after-tax income means at most an increase in consumption of farm products of only 2 percent. Certain farm products—for example, cabbages and lard—may be inferior goods. As incomes increase, purchases of these products may actually *decrease* (Chapter 3).

Population Growth   Population is a different proposition. Despite the fact that, after a minimum income level is reached, each individual consumer's intake of food and fiber will become relatively fixed, more consumers increase the demand for farm products. In most advanced nations demand for farm products increases at a rate roughly corresponding to the rate of population growth. But population increases, added to the relatively small increase in the purchase of farm products which occurs as incomes rise, have not been great enough to match accompanying increases in

FIGURE 33-4   A graphical summary of the long-run farm problem
In the long run, increases in the demand for agricultural products (D to D₁) have not kept pace with the increases in supply (S to S₁) which technological advances have permitted. Coupled with the fact that agricultural demand is inelastic, these shifts have tended to depress farm prices (as from P to P₁) and income (as from 0PAQ to 0P₁BQ₁).

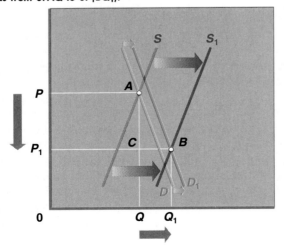

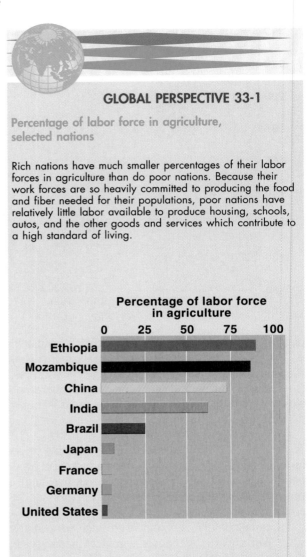

GLOBAL PERSPECTIVE 33-1

Percentage of labor force in agriculture, selected nations

Rich nations have much smaller percentages of their labor forces in agriculture than do poor nations. Because their work forces are so heavily committed to producing the food and fiber needed for their populations, poor nations have relatively little labor available to produce housing, schools, autos, and the other goods and services which contribute to a high standard of living.

Source: United Nations, *Human Development Report, 1994,* pp. 162–163, 194. Data are for 1990–1992..

farm output. Indeed, it is pertinent to note that birthrates are down and United States population growth has slowed in recent decades.

Graphical Portrayal   Coupled with the inelastic demand for agricultural products, these shifts in supply and demand have tended to reduce farm incomes. This is illustrated in Figure 33-4, where a large increase in supply is shown against a very modest increase in demand. Because of the inelastic demand for farm products, these shifts have resulted in a sharp decline in farm prices accompanied by relatively small increases in sales. Farm incomes therefore tend to decline. Graphically, income before the increase in supply occurs (measured by rectangle $0PAQ$) will exceed farm income after supply increases ($0P_1BQ_1$). The income "loss" of P_1PAC is not fully offset by the income "gain" of $QCBQ_1$. *Given an inelastic demand for farm products, an increase in the supply of farm products relative to the demand for them has created persistent tendencies for farm incomes to be low in comparison to nonfarm incomes.*

Consequences   The consequences have been those predicted by the purely competitive model. Because of the demand and supply conditions just outlined, farm incomes were substantially less than nonfarm incomes during most of the post-World War II period. But this income differential triggered a massive exodus of labor from agriculture to other sectors of the economy as shown by Table 33-1. Consequently, farm incomes have risen relative to nonfarm incomes so that rough equality was realized by the mid-1980s. In the late 1980s and early 1990s average incomes of farm households were higher than those of nonfarm households. But we must be cautious of such comparisons because many farm families earn a sizable portion of their incomes from nonfarm activities. A farmer may devote half time to farming and the other half as a mechanic in town. Or the husband may farm while his wife works as a nurse or teacher in a nearby city. *(Key Question 3)*

As Global Perspective 33-1 indicates, poor nations have much higher percentages of their labor forces in agriculture than do the United States and other industrialized nations.

QUICK REVIEW 33-1

■ Agricultural prices and incomes are volatile in the short run because an inelastic demand translates small changes in farm output and demand into relatively larger changes in prices and incomes.

■ Technological progress has generated large increases in supplies of farm products over time.

■ Increases in demand for farm products have been modest because demand is inelastic with respect to income and population growth has been slow.

■ The combination of large increases in supply and small increases in demand has made agriculture a declining industry.

TABLE 33-1   The declining farm population, selected years, 1910–1993

| Year | Farm population | | Number of farms (thousands) |
	Millions	Percentage of total population	
1910	32.1	35	6,366
1920	31.9	30	6,454
1930	30.5	25	6,295
1940	30.5	23	6,102
1950	23.0	15	5,388
1960	15.6	9	3,962
1970	9.7	5	2,954
1980	7.2	3	2,440
1985	5.4	2	2,293
1993	4.6*	2	2,068

Source: Statistical Abstract of the United States; Economic Report of the President.
*Authors' estimate.

ECONOMICS OF FARM POLICY

American agriculture has received massive subsidies which began in the 1930s. The "farm program" involves (1) farm prices, incomes, and output; (2) soil and water conservation; (3) agricultural research; (4) farm credit; (5) crop insurance; (6) subsidized sale of farm product in world markets; and other factors. It came into being and has persisted since the 1930s. However, the typical American farmer and the average politician have both viewed "the farm problem" as a price-income problem and it is this aspect of farm policy which we will explore. We examine the economics of policy at this point, deferring political aspects until later.

Size and Rationale

Farm subsidies are massive. In aggregate terms the 1985 farm bill cost taxpayers about $80 billion during its five-year life. The farm bill passed in 1990 is expected to cost $40 to $55 billion over five years. In 1992 one-third of farm income was from government subsidies, down from two-fifths in 1987.

A variety of arguments have been made to justify farm subsidies.

1   Farmers are comparatively poor and should therefore receive higher prices and incomes through public help.

2   Farming—and particularly the "family farm"—is a fundamental American institution and should be nurtured as a "way of life."

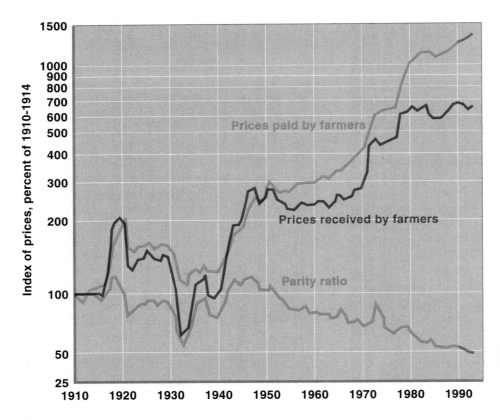

FIGURE 33-5 Prices paid and received by farmers, 1910–1994
In the past five decades the prices paid by farmers have increased ahead of prices received. As a result, the parity ratio—the ratio of prices received to prices paid—has been less than 100 percent.

3 Farmers are subject to certain extraordinary hazards—floods, droughts, and invasion by hordes of insects—to which other industries are not exposed and which cannot be fully insured.

4 While farmers are faced with highly competitive markets for their outputs, they buy inputs from industries which have considerable market power. Most firms from which farmers buy fertilizer, farm machinery, and gasoline have some capacity to control their prices. Farmers, in contrast, are at the "mercy of the market" in selling their outputs. Agriculture is the last stronghold of pure competition in an otherwise imperfectly competitive economy; it warrants public aid to offset the disadvantageous terms of trade which result (see Figure 33-5).

Background: The Parity Concept

The *Agricultural Adjustment Act of 1933* established the **parity concept** as a cornerstone of agricultural policy. The simple rationale of the parity concept can be readily grasped in both real and nominal terms. In real terms, parity says that year after year for a given output of farm products, a farmer should be able to

acquire a specific total amount of goods and services. A given real output should always result in the same real income. "If a farmer could take a bushel of corn to town in 1912 and sell it and buy himself a shirt, he should be able to take a bushel of corn to town today and buy a shirt." In nominal terms, *the parity concept suggests that the relationship between the prices received by farmers for their output and the prices they must pay for goods and services should remain constant.* The parity concept implies that, if the price of shirts tripled over some time period, then the price of corn should triple too. This is considered 100 percent of parity.

Figure 33-5 indicates why farmers would benefit from having the prices of their products based on 100 percent of parity. This graph shows prices paid and received by farmers from 1910 to 1994 as percentages of the 1910–1914 base period. By 1994 prices paid had increased almost fourteenfold and prices received had increased almost seven times compared to the base period.

The **parity ratio** shown in Figure 33-5 is the ratio of prices received relative to prices paid. That is:

$$\frac{\text{Parity}}{\text{ratio}} = \frac{\text{prices received by farmers}}{\text{prices paid by farmers}}$$

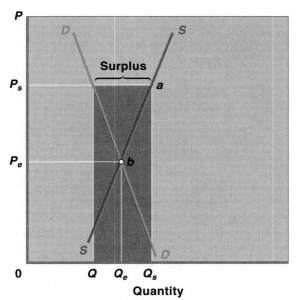

FIGURE 33-6 Effective price supports result in farm surpluses
Application of the parity concept obligates government to support farm prices at above-equilibrium levels. These supported prices result in persistent surpluses of farm products.

In April of 1994 the parity ratio was about 50 percent (= 7 ÷ 14), indicating that prices received in 1994 were one-half as high relative to prices paid as they were in the 1910–1914 period. A farm policy calling for 100 percent of parity would require substantially higher prices for farm products to bring the parity ratio up to 100. *(Key Question 8)*

Economics of Price Supports

The concept of parity prices provides the rationale for government *price floors* on farm products. In agriculture these minimum prices are called **price supports.** The fact that, in the long run, the market prices received by farmers have not generally kept abreast of prices paid by them means that to achieve parity or some percentage thereof, the government may be required to establish above-equilibrium, or "support," prices on farm products. Although specific price support programs have been many and varied, the following discussion captures the essence of government's attempts to use price floors to stabilize and enhance farmers' incomes.

Price supports have a number of effects, many of which are subtle and negative. Suppose, in Figure 33-6, that the support price is P_s compared with equilibrium price P_e.

1 Surplus Output The most obvious result is product surpluses. Private consumers will be willing to purchase only $0Q$ units at the supported price, while farmers will supply $0Q_s$ units. What happens to the QQ_s surplus which results? The government must buy it to make the above-equilibrium support price effective. Huge surpluses of farm commodities accumulated in the 1950s and 1960s and stocks of many farm products remain large. For example, the government holds stocks of wheat and other grains which represent about one year's domestic consumption. As we will see, this surplus production is symptomatic of an overallocation of resources to agriculture.

2 Farmers Gain Farmers gain from price supports. In Figure 33-6, gross revenues rise from the free-market level of $0P_ebQ_e$ to the supported level of $0P_saQ_s$.

3 Consumer Loss Consumers lose; they will pay a higher price (P_s rather than P_e) and consume less (Q rather than Q_e) of the product. In some instances differences between the market price and the supported price can be substantial. For example, the price of a pound of sugar is double the world market price; a quart of fluid milk is estimated to be twice as high as it would be without government programs. It is worth noting that the burden of higher food prices falls disproportionately on the poor because they spend a larger proportion of their incomes on food.

4 Resource Overallocation Society also loses because price supports contribute to economic inefficiency by encouraging an overallocation of resources to agriculture. A price floor or support (P_s) gives rise to a greater commitment of resources to the agricultural sector than would be generated by the free market (P_e). In terms of Chapter 23's purely competitive model, the market supply curve in Figure 33-6 represents the aggregated marginal costs of all farmers producing this product. An efficient allocation of resources occurs where market price, P_e, is equal to marginal cost at point b. The resulting output of Q_e reflects an efficient allocation of resources. In contrast, the Q_s output associated with the P_s price support represents an overallocation of resources; for all units of output in the Q_eQ_s range, marginal costs exceed the prices people would be willing to pay for these units. Simply stated, the cost of the extra production exceeds its benefit to society. Society incurs an "efficiency loss."

5 Other Social Losses Society at large loses in three other ways.

First, taxpayers will pay higher taxes to finance the government's purchase of the surplus. In Figure 33-6, this added tax burden will amount to the surplus output QQ_s, multiplied by its price P_s—as shown by the shaded area. Recall, too, that the mere collection of taxes imposes an efficiency loss (Figure 31-5). Storage costs add to this tax burden.

Second, government's intervention in agriculture entails administrative costs. Well over 100,000 bureaucrats are needed to administer price supports and other farm programs. Overall the agricultural bureaucracy costs about $600 million per year.

Third, "rent-seeking" activity—the pursuit of political support for legislation to secure or maintain a transfer of income or wealth—is costly and socially wasteful. Farm groups spend considerable sums to sustain political support for price supports and other programs which enhance farm incomes. Illustration: In the United States the third largest contributor to campaign funds—after doctors and lawyers—is the sugar industry which contributes more than all labor unions combined.

6 Environmental Costs We know from Figure 33-6 that price supports stimulate additional production. Although some of this extra output may require additional land, much of the added production comes from greater use of fertilizer and pesticides. Unfortunately, pesticides and fertilizers are also poisons which may pollute the environment (for example, groundwater) and pose health risks to farmworkers and to consumers as residues in food. Research shows a positive relationship between the level of price-support subsidies and the use of agrichemicals.

Farm policy may cause environmental problems in less obvious ways. First, farmers receive price supports only on land which is consistently used for a specific product such as corn or wheat. This creates a disincentive to practice crop rotation, which is a non-chemical technique for controlling pests. Farm policy thus encourages the substitution of chemical for non-chemical pest control.

Second, we know from the concept of derived demand (Chapter 27) that an increase in the price of a product will increase the demand for relevant inputs. In this instance the imposition of price supports increases the demand for land. They tend to bring more land into farm production, which is often lower-quality "marginal" land such as steeply sloped, highly

erodable land or wetlands which provide wildlife habitat. Similarly, price supports induce the use of more water for irrigation and the resulting runoff may contribute to soil erosion.

7 International Costs The costs of farm price supports go beyond those implicit in Figure 33-6. Price supports generate economic distortions which transcend national boundaries. For example, above-equilibrium price supports make the American market attractive to foreign producers. But inflows of foreign agricultural products would increase supplies in the United States, aggravating our problem of agricultural surpluses. To prevent this from happening the United States is likely to impose import barriers in the form of tariffs or quotas. These barriers often restrict the production of more efficient foreign producers, while simultaneously encouraging more production from less efficient American producers. The result is a less efficient use of world agricultural resources. This chapter's Last Word suggests this is the case for sugar.

Similarly, as the United States and other industrially advanced countries with similar agricultural programs dump surplus farm products on world markets, the prices of such products are depressed. Less developed countries—heavily dependent on world commodity markets—are hurt because their export earnings are reduced. Thus, United States subsidies for rice production have imposed significant costs on Thailand, a major rice exporter. Similarly, our cotton programs have adversely affected Egypt, Mexico, and other cotton-exporting nations. *(Key Question 9)*

Coping with Surpluses

Knowledge of the tools of supply and demand suggests that programs designed to *reduce* market supply or *increase* market demand would help bring the market price up to the desired supported price, thereby reducing or eliminating farm surpluses (Figure 33-6).

Restricting Supply On the supply side, public policy has long been aimed at restricting farm output. In particular, "set aside" or **acreage allotment programs** have accompanied price supports. In return for price supports on their crops, farmers must agree to limit the number of acres planted. Attempting to bring quantity supplied and quantity demanded into balance, the Department of Agriculture estimates the amount of each product which private buyers will take at the supported price. This amount is then translated into the number of acres of planting which will produce this amount. The total acreage figure is apportioned among states, counties, and ultimately individual farmers.

Similarly, various programs have been employed whereby the Department of Agriculture makes direct payments to farmers for removing land entirely from crop production. For example, under the *soil bank* program, the government in effect rented land from farmers. Such idle land was to be planted in cover crops or timber, not in cash crops.

Have these supply-restricting programs been successful? It is difficult to give an unqualified answer. Certainly they have not eliminated surplus farm production. The reason is that acreage reduction results in less than proportionate declines in production. Farmers retire their worst land and keep their best in production. The tilled acres are cultivated more intensively. Better seed, more and better fertilizer and insecticides, and more labor will enhance output per acre. Nonparticipating farmers may expand their acreage in anticipation of higher prices. However, without these output controls, accumulated farm surpluses and their associated costs would have been much greater than has actually been the case.

Bolstering Demand Government has followed several paths to augment the demand for agricultural products.

1 New Uses Both government and private industry have spent considerable sums on research to uncover new uses for agricultural commodities. The production of "gasohol"—a blend of gasoline and alcohol made from grain—is a current and controversial attempt to create a new demand for agricultural output. Most experts conclude that we have been only modestly successful in such endeavors.

2 Domestic and Foreign Demand Government has initiated a variety of programs to argument domestic consumption of farm products. For example, the *food stamp program* is designed to bolster low-income families' demand for food. Similarly, our **Food for Peace program** under Public Law 480 has permitted less developed countries to buy our surplus farm products with their own currencies, rather than with dollars. Some $200 million is spent per year to advertise and promote global sales of American farm products. Furthermore, in international trade bargaining, our negotiators have pressed hard to persuade foreign nations to reduce protective tariffs and other barriers against our farm products.

Although the government's supply-restricting and demand-increasing efforts undoubtedly helped reduce the amount of surplus production, they have not been successful in eliminating surpluses.

CRITICISMS OF FARM POLICY

After more than a half century of experience with government policies designed to stabilize and enhance farm incomes, there is considerable evidence to suggest these programs are not working well. There is growing feeling among economists and political leaders that the goals and techniques of farm policy must be reexamined and revised. Some of the more important criticisms of agricultural policy follow.

Symptoms and Causes

Our farm programs have failed to get at the causes of the farm problem. Public policy toward agriculture is designed to treat symptoms, not causes. The root *cause* of the farm problem has been a misallocation of resources between agriculture and the rest of the economy. Historically, the problem has been one of too many farmers. The effect or symptom of this misallocation of resources was relatively low farm incomes. *For the most part, public policy in agriculture has been oriented toward supporting farm prices and incomes rather than toward alleviating the resource allocation problem, which is the fundamental cause of relatively low farm incomes.*

Some critics argue further that price-income supports have encouraged people to stay in agriculture when they otherwise would have migrated to some nonfarm occupation. That is, the price-income orientation of the farm program has deterred the reallocation of resources necessary to resolve the long-run farm problem.

Misguided Subsidies

Price-income support programs have most benefited those farmers who least need government assistance. Assuming the goal of our farm program is bolstering of low farm incomes, it follows that any program of government aid should be aimed at farmers at the bottom of the farm income distribution. But the poor, small-output farmer does not produce and sell enough in the market to get much aid from price supports. It is the large corporate farm which reaps the benefits by virtue of its large output.

In 1992, for example, the 7 percent of all farms with sales of $250,000 or more received almost 32 percent of all direct government subsidies. The poorest 54 percent of all farmers—those who earned less than $20,000 from farming in 1992—received about 4 percent of all direct subsidy payments. If public policy must be designed to supplement farm incomes, a strong case can certainly be made for making those benefits vary inversely, rather than directly, with one's position in the income distribution. An income-support program should be geared to *people,* not *commodities.* Many economists contend that, on equity grounds, direct income subsidies to poor farmers are highly preferable to indirect price support subsidies which go primarily to large and prosperous farmers.

A related point concerns land values. The price and income benefits which various farm programs provide are eventually capitalized into higher farmland values. By making crops more valuable, price supports have made the land itself more valuable. Sometimes this is helpful to farmers, but often it is not. Farmers rent about 40 percent of their farmland, mostly from well-to-do nonfarm landlords. Thus, price supports become a subsidy to people *not* actively engaged in farming.

Policy Contradictions

The complexity and multiple objectives embedded in farm policy yield conflicts and contradictions. Subsidized research is aimed at increasing farm productivity and increasing the supply of farm products, while acreage reserve and "set aside" programs pay farmers to take land out of production to reduce supply. Price supports for crops mean increased feed costs for ranchers and high prices for animal products to consumers. Tobacco farmers have been subsidized at a time when serious health problems are associated with tobacco consumption. Our sugar program raises sugar prices for domestic growers by imposing import quotas which conflict with our free trade policies. Conservation programs call for the retirement of vulnerable land, while price supports provide incentives to bring such acreage into production.

Declining Effectiveness

There is also reason to believe that farm policy has become less effective in accomplishing its goals. In the 1930s most farms were small, semi-isolated units which employed modest amounts of machinery and equipment and provided most of their own inputs. Now farms are larger, highly capital-intensive, and closely integrated with both domestic and international economies.

Farmers now depend on others for seed, fertilizers, insecticides, and so forth. American agriculture uses more than twice as much physical capital (machinery and buildings) per worker as does the economy as a whole. This means farmers now need to borrow large amounts of money to finance purchases of capital equipment and land *and* for operating capital. Despite an elaborate farm policy designed to enhance farm incomes, high interest rates can easily precipitate losses or bankruptcy for many farmers. Dependence on export markets can also undermine farm policy. A fall in foreign incomes or an increase in the international value of the dollar (which makes American farm products more expensive to foreigners) can unexpectedly reduce American farm exports and easily wipe out any positive effects of agricultural programs on farm incomes. In short, a much wider range of variables may now alter farm incomes and diminish the effectiveness of farm programs.

THE POLITICS OF FARM POLICY

In view of these criticisms, we may ask why we have an extensive and costly farm program. Why not abandon price supports and return to free markets? Why do farm programs persist although the farm population—and the farm vote—has declined historically (Table 33-1)?

Public Choice Theory Revisited

We can respond to these questions largely in terms of Chapter 31's public choice theory. Recall that *rent-seeking behavior* involves a group—a labor union, firms in a particular industry, or farmers producing a particular product—pursuing political means to transfer income or wealth to themselves at the expense of another group or society as a whole. The *special-interest effect* refers to a program or policy from which a small group receives *large* benefits at the expense of a much larger group who *individually* suffer *small* losses.

Suppose a specific group of farmers—peanut or sugar growers or dairy farmers—organize themselves and establish a well-financed political action committee (PAC). The PAC's job is to promote the establishment and perpetuation of government programs which will transfer income to the group (rent-seeking behavior). The PAC vigorously lobbies senators and representatives to enact or perpetuate price supports and establish import quotas for peanuts, sugar, or milk. They do this by making political contributions to sympathetic legislators. Although peanut production is heavily concentrated in a few states such as Georgia, Alabama, and Texas, the PAC will make contributions to nonpeanut state legislators to gain support.

However, if an interest group—peanut or sugar growers—is small, how can it successfully line its own pockets at the expense of society as a whole? The answer: Although the aggregate costs of the group's program might be considerable, the cost imposed on *each individual* taxpayer is small (the special-interest effect). Citizen-taxpayers are likely uninformed about and indifferent to issues like these because they have little at stake. Unless you grow sugar beets or peanuts, you have probably no idea how much those programs cost you as an individual taxpayer and consumer, and you do not raise cain, so to speak, if your legislator votes for a sugar program. Civil rights, educational reform, and peace in the Middle East may seem to be much more urgent political issues to you than a program for a handful of peanut or sugar farmers.

There is also political *logrolling* (Chapter 31), the trading of votes on policies and programs to change a negative outcome into a positive outcome. Senator Foghorn votes for a program which benefits Senator Moribund's constituents and Moribund returns the favor. For example: Many members of Congress who represent low-income urban areas vote in favor of farm subsidies. In return, representatives of agricultural areas support such programs as food stamps which provide subsidized food for the poor. Thus we have a rural-urban coalition through which representatives from both areas provide benefits for their constituents and enhance their reelection chances. Such coalitions help explain why farm subsidies persist and why the food stamp program has been greatly expanded over the years. The so-called agribusiness industry also lends political support to farm subsidies because they increase the amounts of agrichemicals and farm machinery that farmers are able to buy. And, needless to say, the 100,000 or so government employees whose jobs depend on farm programs are highly supportive.

Public choice theory also tells us that politicians are more likely to favor programs having hidden costs. As we have seen, this is often true of farm programs. In discussing Figure 33-6 we found that price supports involve, not simply an explicit transfer from taxpayer to farmer, but also the costs hidden in higher food prices, storage costs for surplus output, bureaucratic costs of administering farm programs, and costs associated with both domestic and international misallocations of resources. While the explicit or direct cost of the peanut program to taxpayers is only about $4 million a year, the price increase provided by the program carries a hidden subsidy (cost) of $190 million per year. Because the cost of the peanut program is largely indirect and hidden, the program is much more acceptable to politicians and the public than if all costs were explicit.

Other Factors

One or two less obvious considerations may be at work to explain the persistence of expensive farm programs.

Political Demography One contention is that our government is biased toward farmers because rural seats in the Senate embody fewer voters than do urban seats. For example, Nebraska, an agricultural state with a population of 1.5 million, has two senators, the same as urban New Jersey with a population of about 7.5 million.

Rising Incomes Curiously, historically rising incomes of consumers may have sustained the general population's toleration of farm subsidies. People are less sensitive to the price of food as they grow richer because they spend a diminishing proportion of their income on food.

New Directions?

Farm subsidies may decline in the future.

1 Declining Farm Population As farm population has declined, its political clout has also diminished. The farm population was about 25 percent of the total in the 1930s when many of our farm programs were established. That population now is less than 2 percent of the total. Urban lawmakers have a 9-to-1 advantage over their rural colleagues. More and more legislators are critically examining farm programs from the vantage point of their effect on consumers' grocery bills rather than farm incomes.

2 Budget Deficits Continued pressures to balance the Federal budget have brought farm subsidies under increased political scrutiny.

3 Program Excesses Program excesses have been increasingly publicized, perhaps weakening the special-interest effect. Examples: In one year in the late 1980s a large California cotton grower received $12 million in subsidy payments; the crown prince of Liechtenstein received a subsidy in excess of $2 million as a partner in a Texas rice farm; and 112 dairy farmers received $1 million each under a program designed to reduce the size of dairy herds. Water subsidies to farmers in California's Westland Water District average $500,000 per farm. The Gallo Winery received $5 million in 1991 to promote its products in world markets. McDonald's was awarded $465,000 to advertise its Chicken McNuggets overseas while Sunkist Growers got almost $10 million to promote citrus.

Also, the nonfarm population has become increasingly aware and critical of farm programs. Programs created in the 1930s to help smaller farms are being reevaluated now that agriculture is dominated by large farms increasingly like any other business.

4 Policy Conflicts It is increasingly apparent that domestic farm programs are seriously at odds with the objective of free world trade. This conflict merits more detailed consideration.

WORLD TRADE AND FARM POLICY

A more critical attitude toward farm subsidies is reflected in American negotiations designed to reduce world trade barriers to agricultural products.

Policy Impacts

Consider the impacts of current farm programs on world trade. Virtually every industrialized country—the United States, Canada, Japan, among others—intervenes in agriculture by subsidizing and providing protective trade barriers. For example, the European Union (EU)—made up of fifteen western European nations—has established high prices for its domestic agricultural products. These price supports have a number of consequences.

1 To maintain high domestic prices the EU must restrict imports (supplies) of foreign farm products. It does this by imposing import tariffs (excise taxes) and quotas (specific quantitative limits on foreign goods).

2 Although the EU was once an importer of food, high price supports have induced European farmers to produce much more output than European consumers want to purchase.

3 To rid itself of these agricultural surpluses the EU has heavily subsidized their export into world markets.

The effects on the United States are that: (1) our farmers have great difficulty in selling to EU nations because of their trade barriers; and (2) subsidized exports from the EU depress world prices for agricultural products, making these markets less attractive to our farmers.

Perhaps most importantly, from an international perspective farm programs such as those of the EU and the United States distort world agricultural trade and thereby the international allocation of agricultural resources. Encouraged by artificially high prices, farmers in industrially advanced nations produce more agricultural output than they would otherwise. The resulting surpluses flow into world markets where they depress prices. This means farmers in countries with no farm programs—often less developed countries—face artificially low prices for their exports, which signals them to produce less. In this way farm price distortions alter production away from that based on productive efficiency or comparative advantage (Chapter 6). For example, price supports cause American agricultural resources to be allocated to sugar production, although sugar can be produced at perhaps half the cost in the Caribbean and Australia.

One estimate suggests that the benefits of free, undistorted agricultural trade to the industrially advanced economies alone would be about $35 billion per year, with the United States, the EU, and Japan as the major beneficiaries. Accompanying benefits are (1) increased American farm exports, which would reduce our international balance of payments deficit; and (2) reduced expenditures on our domestic farm programs, which would help reduce the Federal budget deficit. Thus the United States has compelling economic reasons to favor the liberalization of international agricultural trade.

QUICK REVIEW 33-2

■ The parity ratio, which is the basis for price supports, shows the ratio of prices received to prices paid by farmers.

■ Price supports cause surplus production which government must buy and store; raise both farmer incomes and food prices to consumers; and generate an overallocation of resources to agriculture.

■ Farm policy has been criticized for: delaying the exodus of resources from farming; allocating most subsidies to wealthier farmers; conflicting with other policies such as freer world trade; not effectively resolving farm problems; and being very costly.

■ The persistence of farm programs is largely explainable in terms of rent-seeking behavior, the special-interest effect, political logrolling, and other aspects of public choice theory.

■ The farm programs of the United States, the European Union, and other industrialized nations have contributed to a misallocation of the world's agricultural resources.

GATT: The Uruguay Round

Under the sponsorship of the General Agreement on Tariffs and Trade (GATT), a new world trade agreement was reached in 1994. Called the Uruguay Round of negotiations, the agreement went into effect in 1995 with its provisions to be phased in over a ten-year period. It embodies significantly freer trade for American and world agriculture. Major provisions include the following. Export subsidies—most importantly by the European Union—will be significantly reduced, increasing the competitiveness of American farmers in world markets. Industrially advanced nations agree to reduce their price support programs by 20 percent by the year 2000. Nations agree to cut their tariffs on agricultural products—by 15 percent for the industrially advanced countries and by 10 percent for the less developed countries. Furthermore, nontariff trade barriers such as import quotas have been replaced by less-restrictive tariffs. For example, the United States has agreed to phase out import quotas on sugar, dairy products, and peanuts in favor of tariffs. Japan and South Korea have agreed to open their markets to limited rice imports. In short, the new agreement reduces farm subsidies and trade barriers which contribute to the misallocation of resources both domestically and worldwide.

More generally, studies suggest that world income could increase by as much as $6 trillion over

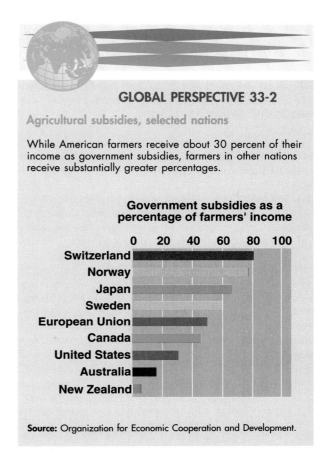

GLOBAL PERSPECTIVE 33-2

Agricultural subsidies, selected nations

While American farmers receive about 30 percent of their income as government subsidies, farmers in other nations receive substantially greater percentages.

Government subsidies as a percentage of farmers' income

Source: Organization for Economic Cooperation and Development.

the next ten years as a result of the Uruguay Round. This will increase the demand for such income-sensitive farm products as meat, fruit, and vegetables. United States farm exports might increase by an estimated $4.7 to $8.7 billion by the year 2005, boosting agricultural export-related employment by some 1,900,000 jobs. Our government's farm program outlays could fall by as much as $2.6 billion in 2005, although American farmers could expect to have higher net incomes by $2.5 billion in 2005 because of the overall impact of the new agreement.

Farm Act of 1990

In addition to the GATT provisions, recent farm legislation reflects efforts to (1) cut the cost of farm subsidies and (2) increase the role of market (as opposed to supported) prices in agricultural decision making. Specifically, the **Farm Act of 1990** reduces by 15 percent the acreage covered by price guarantees, thereby reducing the cost of subsidy programs. The potential blow to farmers is softened by allowing them

LAST WORD

THE SUGAR PROGRAM: A SWEET DEAL

The sugar program is a sweet deal for domestic sugar producers, but it imposes heavy costs on domestic consumers and foreign producers.

The United States' program of price supports for sugar has entailed significant effects both domestically and internationally.

1 Domestic Costs Recent price supports for some 15,000 American sugar producers have maintained domestic sugar prices at about double the world price. The estimated aggregate cost to domestic consumers is about $1 billion per year. Furthermore, the effect of artificially high sugar prices is "regressive" because poor households spend a larger percentage of their income on food than do high-income households. On the other hand, each sugar grower receives from subsidies alone an amount estimated to be twice the nation's average family income. One farm in 1991 received an estimated $30 million in benefits! Thirty-three farms obtained more than $1 million each in benefits.

2 Import Quotas As a consequence of our high domestic price supports, foreign sugar producers have a very strong incentive to sell their outputs in the United States. But an influx of lower priced foreign

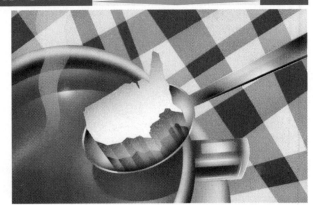

sugar into our domestic market would undermine domestic price supports. Hence, our government has imposed import quotas on foreign sugar. As the difference between United States-supported prices and world prices has increased, import quotas have become more restrictive, with the result that imported sugar has become a declining proportion of our consumption of sweeteners. About 30 percent of our sugar was imported in 1975; currently only 3 or 4 percent is imported. Our agricultural policy in the domestic sugar industry largely dictates our international trade policy with respect to that product.

---

to plant the affected acres in alternative crops. Farmers' decisions on these alternative crops will be based on market price signals. For example, many corn and wheat farmers may put the 15 percent reduction in price-supported land into soybeans or sunflowers, based on growing conditions and anticipated prices. In short, the new farm act simultaneously reduces farm subsidies and increases the role of market forces.

Market-Oriented Income Stabilization

From a long-term perspective it seems increasingly likely that farm policy will shift from the goal of enhancing to that of stabilizing farm incomes. The goal of *stabilization* is to reduce the sharp year-to-year fluctuations in farm incomes and prices, but to accept the long-run average of farm prices and incomes which

free markets would provide. This contrasts with income *enhancement*, which seeks to provide farmers with commodity prices and incomes higher than free markets would yield. Government might moderate the boom and bust character of agricultural markets by supporting prices and accumulating surplus stocks when prices fall significantly below the long-run trend of prices. Conversely, government would augment supply by selling from these stocks when prices rise significantly above the long-run trend.

Proponents feel that the **market-oriented income stabilization policy** has a number of advantages. First, government involvement in agriculture would be diminished in that programs of supply management through acreage reduction would be abandoned. Second, prices would reflect long-run equilibrium levels and therefore lead to an efficient allocation of resources between agriculture and the rest of the

3 *Less Developed Countries* The loss of the American market has had a number of very harmful effects on many of the less developed sugar-exporting countries such as the Philippines, Brazil, and a number of Central American countries.

First, exclusion from the American market has significantly reduced their export earnings—estimated to be as much as $7 billion per year—and national incomes. The decline in export revenues is important because many of the sugar-producing countries are highly dependent on such revenues to pay interest and principal on massive external debts owed to the United States and other industrially advanced nations.

Second, barred by quotas from sale in the United States market, the sugar produced by the less developed countries has been added to world markets, where the increased supply has depressed the world price of sugar.

Third, under the impetus of domestic price supports, American sugar production has increased to the extent that the United States may soon change from a sugar-importing to a sugar-exporting nation. That is, our sugar program may soon be a source of new competition for the sugar producers of the less developed countries. Sugar price supports in the European Community have already turned that group of nations into sugar exporters.

4 *Global Resource Misallocation* From both a domestic and a global perspective, the sugar price support programs of the United States and other industrially advanced economies have distorted the worldwide allocation of agricultural resources. Price supports have signaled an overallocation of resources to sugar production by less efficient American producers. American import quotas and consequent low world sugar prices have signaled more efficient foreign producers to restrict their production. High-cost producers are producing more and low-cost producers are producing less sugar, resulting in an inefficient allocation of the world's agricultural resources.

5 *Substitutes and Jobs* The artificially high price of sugar, coupled with nutritional concerns, has caused a shift of demand toward corn-based and artificial sweeteners. Sugar's share of the American market for sweeteners has declined by one-half since 1970. One estimate suggests that the artificial sweetener industry makes almost as much from the sugar program ($1 billion per year) as do sugar growers themselves.

Also, in the past decade an estimated 7000 jobs have been lost because of refinery closings due to the decline of sugar imports. American candy manufacturers ponder the relocation of plants and jobs abroad where sugar prices are lower.

Source: Based primarily on *Economic Report of the President, 1987* (Washington: 1987), pp. 165–169. Updated.

economy. By providing farmers with incomes consistent with market-clearing prices, the market system would provide the needed signals to accelerate movement of farmers to nonfarm jobs. Third, taxpayer costs would be significantly reduced. And, fourth, the lower average level of farm prices would help to stimulate agricultural exports.

GLOBAL VIEW: FEAST OR FAMINE?

The American farm problem—supply outrunning demand and farm policies which foster surplus production—is not common to most other nations. Many less developed nations, not to mention the former Soviet Union, must persistently import food. We frequently read of malnutrition, chronic food shortages, and famine in Africa and elsewhere. In the future—say, four or five decades from now—will the world be unable to feed itself?

Pessimism

While there is no simple response to this question, it is of interest to summarize some of the pros and cons pertinent to the issue. Pessimists, envisioning impending famine as demand increases ahead of supply, make these arguments:

1 The quantity of arable land is finite and its quality is being seriously impaired by wind and water erosion.

2 Urban sprawl and industrial expansion continue to convert agricultural land to nonagricultural uses.

3 Our underground water system upon which farmers depend for irrigation is being mined so fast that farmlands in some areas will have to be abandoned.

4 World population continues to grow; every day there are thousands of new mouths to feed.

5 Some environmentalists suggest that unfavorable long-run climatic changes will undermine future agricultural production.

Optimism

Optimists offer these counterarguments.

1 The number of acres planted to crops has been increasing and the world is far from bringing all its arable land into production.

2 Agricultural productivity continues to rise and the possibility of dramatic productivity breakthroughs lies ahead as we enter the age of genetic engineering. There is also room for substantial productivity increases in the agricultural sectors of less developed countries. For example, improved economic incentives for farm workers in China helped expand agricultural output by about one-third between 1980 and 1985. Food production could be greatly increased in many poor nations by removing existing government price controls which establish below-equilibrium prices.

3 The rate of growth of world population has been diminishing.

4 We must reckon with the adjustment processes elicited by the market system. If food shortages were to develop, food prices would rise. Higher prices would simultaneously induce more production, constrain the amount demanded, and head off the shortages.

5 The real-world price for food has been falling for many decades, suggesting that food supply has increased more rapidly than food demand.

The "feast or famine" debate is highly speculative; a clear picture of the world's future production capabilities and consumption needs is not easily discerned. The main point is that American agricultural policies should take global considerations into account.

CHAPTER SUMMARY

1 In the short run, the highly inelastic nature of agricultural demand translates small changes in output and small shifts in domestic or foreign demand into large fluctuations in prices and incomes.

2 Rapid technological advance, coupled with a highly inelastic and relatively constant demand for agricultural output, has caused agriculture to be a declining industry.

3 Historically, agricultural policy has been price-centered and based on the parity concept which suggests that the relationship between prices received and paid by farmers should be constant.

4 The use of price floors or supports has a number of economic effects: **a** surplus production occurs; **b** the incomes of farmers are increased; **c** consumers pay higher prices for farm products; **d** an overallocation of resources to agriculture occurs; **e** society pays higher taxes to finance the purchase and storage of surplus output; **f** pollution increases because of the greater use of agrichemicals and vulnerable land; and **g** other nations bear the costs associated with import barriers and depressed world farm commodity prices.

5 Government has pursued with limited success programs to reduce the supply of, and increase the demand for, agricultural products to reduce the surpluses associated with price supports.

6 Farm policy has been criticized for **a** confusing symptoms (low farm incomes) with causes (excess capacity); **b** providing the largest subsidies to high-income farmers; **c** contradictions among specific farm programs; and **d** declining effectiveness.

7 The persistence of agricultural subsidies can be explained in terms of public choice theory and, in particular, in terms of rent-seeking behavior, the special-interest effect, and political logrolling.

8 Recent GATT provisions call for reduced export subsidies for agricultural products; the limited opening of Japanese and South Korean markets to rice imports; and a lessening of American barriers on sugar, dairy products, and peanuts.

9 The Farm Act of 1990 reduces the amount of land to which price supports apply and enhances the use of market prices in agricultural decision making.

10 The United States may be moving toward a policy of stabilizing, but not enhancing, farm incomes.

TERMS AND CONCEPTS

short-run farm problem
long-run farm problem
parity concept
parity ratio

price supports
acreage allotment
    programs

Food for Peace program
Farm Act of 1990

market-oriented income
    stabilization policy

QUESTIONS AND STUDY SUGGESTIONS

1 *Key Question* *"The supply and demand for agricultural products are such that small changes in agricultural supply will result in drastic changes in prices. However, large changes in farm prices have modest effects on agricultural output." Carefully evaluate. (Hint: A brief review of the distinction between supply and quantity supplied may be of assistance.) Do exports increase or reduce the instability of demand for farm products?*

2 What relationship, if any, can you detect between the fact that the farmer's fixed costs of production are large and the fact that the supply of most agricultural products is generally inelastic? Be specific in your answer.

3 *Key Question* *Explain how each of the following contributes to the farm problem:* a *the inelasticity of demand for farm products,* b *rapid technological progress in farming,* c *the modest long-run growth in demand for farm commodities, and* d *the competitiveness of agriculture.*

4 The key to efficient resource allocation is shifting resources from low-productivity to high-productivity uses. Given the high and expanding physical productivity of agricultural resources, explain why many economists want to divert resources from farming in the interest of greater allocative efficiency.

5 "Industry complains of the higher taxes it must pay to finance subsidies to agriculture. Yet the trend of agricultural prices has been downward while industrial prices have been moving upward, suggesting that on balance agriculture is actually subsidizing industry." Explain and evaluate.

6 "Because consumers as a whole must ultimately pay the total incomes received by farmers, it makes no real difference whether this income is paid through free farm markets or through supported prices supplemented by subsidies financed out of tax revenue." Do you agree?

7 Suppose you are president of a local chapter of one of the major farm organizations. You are directed by the chapter's membership to formulate policy statements for the chapter covering the following topics: a antitrust policy, b monetary policy, c fiscal policy, and d tariff policy. Briefly outline the policy statements which will best serve the interests of farmers. What is the rationale underlying each statement? Do you see any conflicts or inconsistencies in your policy statements?

8 *Key Question* *If in a given year the indexes of prices received and paid by farmers were 120 and 165 respectively, what would the parity ratio be? Explain the meaning of this ratio.*

9 *Key Question* *Carefully demonstrate the economic effects of price supports. Explicitly include environmental and global impacts in your answer. On what grounds do economists contend that price supports cause a misallocation of resources?*

10 Reconcile these two statements: "The farm problem is one of overproduction." "Despite the tremendous productive capacity of American agriculture, plenty of Americans are going hungry." What assumptions about the market system are implied in your answer?

11 Use public choice theory to explain the size and persistence of subsidies to agriculture.

12 What are the effects of farm programs such as those of the United States and the European Union on a domestic agricultural prices; b world agricultural prices; c the international allocation of agricultural resources?

13 What are the major criticisms of farm policy? Do you feel government should attempt to enhance farm incomes, stabilize farm incomes, or allow farm incomes to be determined by free markets? Justify your position.

14 (Last Word) Indicate the gains and losses associated with the United States' sugar program.

34

INCOME INEQUALITY AND POVERTY

It is not difficult to muster casual evidence which suggests substantial economic disparity in the United States. NBA superstar Michael Jordan earned an estimated $36 billion in 1992, about $4 million for playing basketball and the remainder from product endorsements. Seventy-one major league baseball players made $3 million or more in 1992. San Francisco outfielder Barry Bonds earns over $7 million per year, estimated to be $11,253 every time he faces a pitcher. In contrast, the President of the United States is paid $200,000 per year and the typical schoolteacher receives $36,000. A full-time minimum-wage employee at a fast-food restaurant will make $8,700 per year.

A recent study concludes that 5.5 million American children—one in eight—go hungry and that another 6 million are nutritionally "at risk." In certain rural counties of the Deep South infant mortality rates exceed those of some less developed countries of Asia and Latin America.

The Census Bureau reports that over 39 million Americans—over 15 percent of the population—live in poverty. Estimates indicate that 500,000 to 600,000 Americans are homeless. At the same time, Bill Gates (age 40 and a college dropout) has amassed a fortune estimated at $9.2 billion from his Microsoft Computer Corporation.

Government data indicate that income disparity is increasing in the United States; at present the richest fifth of the population receive 47 percent of the total income while the poorest fifth receives only about 4 percent.

The question of how income should be distributed has a long and controversial history in both economics and philosophy. Should our national income and wealth be more or less equally distributed than is now the case? Or, in terms of Chapter 4, is society making the proper response to the "For whom" question?

We begin by surveying some basic facts concerning the distribution of income in the United States. Next, the major causes of income inequality are considered. Third, we examine the debate over income inequality and the tradeoff between equality and efficiency implied by this debate. Fourth, we will look at the poverty problem. Finally, we consider public policy; existing income-security programs are outlined and alternative approaches to welfare reform are discussed.

TABLE 34-1 The distribution of personal income by families, 1993

(1) Personal income class	(2) Percentage of all families in this class
Under $10,000	10
$10,000–$14,999	7
$15,000–$24,999	16
$25,000–$34,999	15
$35,000–$49,999	18
$50,000–$74,999	19
$75,000–$99,999	8
$100,000 and over	7
	100

Source: Bureau of the Census, press release.

INCOME INEQUALITY: SOME FACTS

How equally—or unequally—is income distributed in the United States? How wide is the gulf between rich and poor? Has the degree of income inequality increased or lessened over time?

Personal Income Distribution

Average income in the United States is among the highest in the world. The average income for all families was $36,959 in 1993. But now we must examine how income is distributed around the average. In Table 34-1 we see that 7 percent of all families have annual incomes of $100,000 or more, while one family in ten has an annual income of less than $10,000.

These figures suggest *considerable* **income inequality** *in the United States.*

Trends in Income Inequality

Over a period of years economic growth has raised incomes: *Absolutely,* the entire distribution of income has been moving upward over time. Has this changed the *relative* distribution of income? Incomes can move up absolutely, and the degree of inequality may or may not be affected. Table 34-2 indicates the relative distribution of income. We divide the total number of income receivers into five numerically equal groups, or *quintiles,* and show the percentage of total personal (before-tax) income obtained by each in selected years. Let's examine the data in Table 34-2 over three periods: 1929–1947, 1947–1969, and 1969–1993.

1929–1947 Period Comparison of the income distribution data for 1929 and 1947 suggests a significant reduction in income inequality between these years. Note in Table 34-2 the declining percentage of personal income going to the top quintile and the increasing percentage received by the other four quintiles. Many of the forces at work during World War II undoubtedly contributed to this decline in inequality. Warborn prosperity eliminated the many low incomes caused by the severe unemployment of the 1930s, reduced wage and salary differentials, boosted depressed farm incomes through sharp increases in farm prices, temporarily diminished discrimination in employment, and was accompanied by a decline in property incomes as a share of the national income.

1947–1969 Period Many of the forces making for greater equality during World War II became less ef-

TABLE 34-2 Percentage of total before-tax income received by each one-fifth, and by the top 5 percent, of families, selected years

Quintile	1929	1935–1936	1947	1955	1969	1979	1993
Lowest 20 percent	12.5	4.1	5.0	4.8	5.6	5.3	4.1
Second 20 percent		9.2	11.8	12.2	12.4	11.6	9.9
Third 20 percent	13.8	14.1	17.0	17.7	17.7	17.5	15.7
Fourth 20 percent	19.3	20.9	23.1	23.7	23.7	24.1	23.3
Highest 20 percent	54.4	51.7	43.0	41.6	40.6	41.6	47.0
Total	100.0	100.0	100.0	100.0	100.0	100.0	100.0
Top 5 percent	30.0	25.6	17.2	16.8	15.6	15.7	20.0

Source: Bureau of the Census.

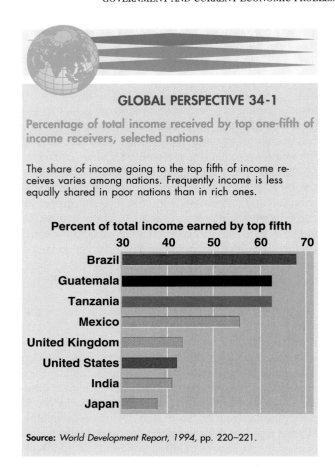

GLOBAL PERSPECTIVE 34-1

Percentage of total income received by top one-fifth of income receivers, selected nations

The share of income going to the top fifth of income receives varies among nations. Frequently income is less equally shared in poor nations than in rich ones.

Percent of total income earned by top fifth

	30	40	50	60	70
Brazil					
Guatemala					
Tanzania					
Mexico					
United Kingdom					
United States					
India					
Japan					

Source: *World Development Report, 1994*, pp. 220–221.

fective after the war. Between 1947 and 1969, the quintile distribution continued its previous trend toward less inequality, but at a far slower pace. The income share of the lowest income group rose by .6 of a percentage point between 1947 and 1969, while that of the wealthiest quintile fell by 2.4 percentage points.

1969–1993 Period The distribution of income by quintiles has become more unequal since 1969. In 1993 the lowest 20 percent of families received only 4.1 percent of total before-tax income, compared to 5.6 percent in 1969. Meanwhile, the income share received by the highest 20 percent rose from 40.6 percent to 47 percent.

Causes of Growing Inequality

Growing income inequality in the last decade has attracted the attention of many scholars. A number of interrelated hypotheses have been suggested.

1 Taxes and Transfers Legislation in the 1980s reduced Federal marginal tax rates such that high-income people are being taxed at rates below the levels of the 1960s and 1970s. Conversely, welfare benefits for the poor have been cut or have not kept pace with inflation.

2 Demographic Changes The entrance of large numbers of less experienced and less skilled "baby boomers" into the labor force in the 1970s and 1980s may have contributed to greater income inequality. As large numbers of younger people entered the labor force, the median age of the average worker fell. Since younger workers typically earn less than older workers, overall income inequality rose. In addition, the labor-force participation of the wives of high-income husbands increased at a faster rate than for low-income husbands, adding to family income disparity. Finally, the number of unmarried or divorced women with children—who are very likely to have low incomes—has increased greatly.

3 Import Competition More competition from imports in the 1970s and 1980s severely reduced the demand for and employment of less skilled but highly paid workers in such industries as automobiles and steel. The decline in such jobs reduced the average wage for less skilled workers. It also swelled the ranks of workers in already low-paying industries, placing further downward pressure on wages in such industries. Similarly, the farming out of jobs of unskilled workers to lower-wage workers in less developed countries has exerted downward wage pressure in the United States.

4 Demand for Highly Skilled Workers Perhaps the most significant contributor to growing income inequality has been an increasing demand for workers with high levels of education and skills. Many companies have restructured their production techniques in ways which require more highly skilled, better-educated workers. Also, several industries requiring high-skilled workers have newly emerged or expanded greatly. Examples include computer software development, business consulting, biotechnology, health care, and advanced communications systems. Because skilled workers remain relatively scarce, their wages have been bid up so that the wage gap between them and less-educated workers has increased. Since 1980 the college–high school pay gap has risen from 37 to 66 percent for women and from

34 to 60 percent for men. One study estimates that workers who use computers earn 10 to 15 percent more than otherwise similar workers who do not.

Caution: When we note growing income inequality, we are *not* saying that "the rich are getting richer and the poor are getting poorer" in an absolute sense. Rather what has happened is that, while incomes grew absolutely in all quintiles, growth was fastest in the top quintile.

The Lorenz Curve

The degree of income inequality can be seen through a **Lorenz curve** as shown in Figure 34-1. Here we *cumulate* the "percentage of families" on the horizontal axis and the "percentage of income" on the vertical axis. The theoretical possibility of a completely equal distribution of income is represented by the diagonal line because such a line indicates that any given percentage of families receives that same percentage of income. That is, if 20 percent of all families receive 20 percent of total income, 40 percent receive 40 percent, 60 percent receive 60 percent, and so on, all these points will fall on the diagonal line.

By plotting the 1993 data from Table 34-2 we locate the Lorenz curve to visualize the actual distribution of income. Observe that the bottom 20 percent of all families received about 4.1 percent of the income as shown by point *a;* the bottom 40 percent received 14 percent (= 4.1 + 9.9) as shown by point *b;* and so forth. The area between the diagonal line and the Lorenz curve, determined by the extent to which the Lorenz curve sags away from the line of perfect equality, indicates the degree of income inequality. The larger this area or gap, the greater the degree of income inequality. If the actual income distribution were perfectly equal, the Lorenz curve and the diagonal would coincide and the gap would disappear.

At the opposite extreme is the situation of complete inequality where 1 percent of families have 100 percent of the income and the rest have none. In this case the Lorenz curve would coincide with the horizontal and right vertical axes of the graph, forming a right angle at point *f* as indicated by the heavy reverse-"L" line. This extreme degree of inequality would be indicated by the entire area southeast of the diagonal (area 0*ef*).

The Lorenz curve can be used to contrast the distribution of income at different points in time, among different groups (for example, blacks and whites), be-

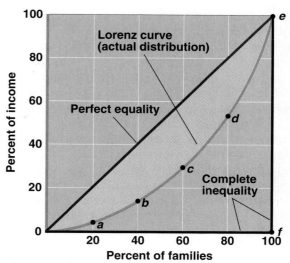

FIGURE 34-1   The Lorenz curve
The Lorenz curve is a convenient means of visualizing the degree of income inequality. Specifically, the area between the line of perfect equality and the Lorenz curve reflects the degree of income inequality.

fore and after taxes and transfer payments are taken into account, or among different countries. As previously observed, the data in Table 34-2 tell us that the Lorenz curve shifted slightly toward the diagonal between 1947 and 1969 and then back away from the diagonal between 1969 and 1993. Comparisons with other nations suggest that the recent trend toward greater inequality in the distribution of income in the United States is quite similar to that in most other industrially advanced countries. *(Key Question 2)*

TWO ADJUSTMENTS

There are two major criticisms of the census data presented thus far. First, the income concept is too narrow. Second, the income accounting period of one year is too short.

Broadened Income Concept

The census figures of Tables 34-1 and 34-2 show the distribution of *nominal* income and include not only wages, salaries, dividends, and interest, but also all *cash transfer payments* such as social security, unemployment compensation benefits, and welfare payments to families with dependent children. The data are *before taxes* and therefore do not account for the effects of personal income and payroll (social security) taxes which are levied directly on income receivers. Nor do they include in-kind or **noncash transfers** which provide specified goods or services rather than cash. Noncash transfers include such things as Medicare, Medicaid, housing subsidies, and food stamps.

What impact would the use of a broader income concept—one that included both taxes and noncash transfers—have on income distribution data? Because our overall tax system is only modestly progressive, after-tax data would reveal only slightly less inequality. Noncash transfers, however, are extremely important for the poorest quintile and their inclusion would clearly diminish the degree of inequality. A glance ahead at column 2 in the table accompanying Figure 34-2 shows income distribution by quintiles with both taxes and transfers (including noncash transfers) taken into account. We observe greater income equality when taxes and in-kind transfers are included.

Income Mobility: The Time Dimension

Another objection to the census data is that they portray the distribution of income in a single year and conceal the possibility that over a period of time—a few years, a decade, or even a lifetime—earnings might be more equal. If Ben earns $1000 in year 1 and $100,000 in year 2, while Holly earns $100,000 in year 1 and only $1000 in year 2, do we have income inequality? The answer depends on the period of measurement. Annual data would reveal great income inequality; but for the two-year period we have complete equality.

This is important because there is evidence to suggest that there is considerable "churning around" in the distribution of income over time. In fact, most income receivers follow an age-earnings profile where their income starts at relatively low levels, reaches a peak during middle age, and then declines. A glance back at Figure 28-9 reveals this general pattern. It follows that, even if people received the same stream of income over their lifetimes, considerable income inequality would still exist in any given year because of age differences. In any year the young and old would receive low incomes while the middle-aged received high incomes. This would occur despite complete equality of lifetime incomes.

What happens if we move from a "snapshot" view of income distribution in a single year to a "time exposure" view portraying the mobility of people between income classes over time? The answer is that we find considerable mobility both up and down, suggesting that income is more equally distributed over a five-, ten-, or twenty-year period than in a single year.

A recent Treasury Department study measures income mobility by tracing the movement of people from their quintile location in 1979 to their quintile status in 1988. It was found that slightly over two-thirds of those in the poorest quintile in 1979 had moved somewhere into the top three quintiles by 1988. Almost 18 percent of the lowest quintile jumped to the richest quintile during this decade. Undoubtedly this group included many who were in college in 1979, but who graduated and became high-income doctors, lawyers, and accountants by 1988. Two-thirds of the people in the middle quintile changed to another quintile in the ten-year period, approximately 20 percent becoming poorer and 47 percent becoming richer. For the richest quintile in 1979, one-third fell to a lower quintile by 1988.

The point of the Treasury study is that (1) there exists "significant household income mobility over time" and (2) the longer the time period considered, the more equal the distribution of income.

GOVERNMENT AND REDISTRIBUTION

One of the basic functions of government is to redistribute income. As Figure 34-2 and its table reveal, the distribution of household income *before* taxes and transfers are taken into account is substantially less equal than the distribution *after* taxes and transfers are included.[1] *Government's tax system and transfer programs do reduce significantly the degree of inequality in the distribution of income.* Most of the reduction in income inequality—roughly 80 percent of it—is attributable to transfer payments. As noted a moment ago, the before-tax and after-tax distributions of income do not differ greatly. But transfers are vital in

---

[1]The "before" data in this table differ from the data of Table 34-2 because the latter includes cash transfers. Also, the data in Table 34-2 are for families (a group of two persons or more related by birth, marriage, or adoption and residing together), whereas the data in Figure 34-2 are for all households (one or more persons occupying a housing unit). Finally, the data in Figure 34-2 are based on a broader concept of income than the data in Table 34-2.

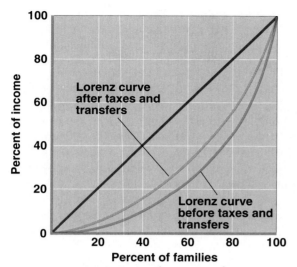

Percent of income received, 1992

Quintile	(1) Before taxes and transfers	(2) After taxes and transfers
Lowest 20 percent	1.0	5.1
Second 20 percent	7.8	11.0
Third 20 percent	15.6	16.7
Fourth 20 percent	25.3	23.9
Highest 20 percent	50.4	43.3

Source: Bureau of the Census, *Measuring the Effect of Benefits and Taxes on Income and Poverty: 1992,* Current Population Report, Series P-60, No. 186-RD, 1993, p. xii. The data include all money income from private sources, including realized capital gains and employer-provided health insurance. The "after taxes and transfers" data include the value of noncash transfers as well as cash transfers.

FIGURE 34-2 **The impact of government taxes and transfers on income inequality**
The distribution of personal income is significantly more equal after taxes and transfer payments are taken into account. Transfers account for most of the lessening of inequality and provide most of the income received by the lowest quintile of families.

contributing to greater income equality. Government transfer payments account for over 75 percent of the income of the lowest quintile and have been the most important means of alleviating poverty in the United States.

CAUSES OF INCOME INEQUALITY

Why does the United States have the degree of income inequality evidenced in Tables 34-1 and 34-2? In general, we note that the market system is an impersonal mechanism. It has no conscience, and does not cater to ethical standards concerning what is an "equitable," or "just," distribution of income. In fact, the basically individualistic environment of the capitalist economy is very permissive of a high degree of income inequality. Factors contributing to income inequality include the following.

1 Ability Differences People have different mental, physical, and aesthetic talents. Some have inherited the exceptional mental qualities essential to entering the high-paying fields of medicine, dentistry, and law. Others, rated as "dull normals" or "mentally retarded," are assigned to the most menial and low-paying occupations or are incapable of earning income at all. Some are blessed with the physical ca-

pacity and coordination to become highly paid professional athletes. A few have the talent to become great artists or musicians. In brief, native talents enable some individuals to make contributions to total output which command very high incomes. Others are in much less fortunate circumstances.

2 Education and Training Individuals differ significantly in the amounts of education and training they have obtained and, hence, in their capacities to earn income. In part, these differences are a matter of voluntary choice. Smith chooses to enter the labor force upon high school graduation, while Jones decides to attend college. On the other hand, such differences may be involuntary: Smith's family may simply be unable to finance a college education. Also, firms provide much on-the-job training. They tend to select workers with the most formal education for advanced and extensive on-the-job training.

3 Discrimination Simple supply and demand analysis suggests how discrimination—in this case labor market discrimination—generates income inequality. Suppose gender discrimination restricts women to such occupations as secretaries and teachers—once considered strictly "female" jobs. This means that the supplies of female workers will be great relative to demand in these few occupations so that wages and incomes will be low. Conversely, discrimination means males do not have to compete with women in "male" occupations (carpenters, pilots, accountants). This means supply is artificially limited relative to demand in these occupations, with the result that wages and incomes are high.

4 Tastes and Risks Incomes differ because of differences in "job tastes." Those willing to take arduous, unpleasant jobs—for example, underground mining and automobile assembly—and to work long hours with great intensity will tend to earn more. Some people boost their incomes by "moonlighting" —by holding two jobs. Individuals also differ in their willingness to assume risk. We refer here not only to the auto race driver and professional boxer but to the entrepreneur who assumes risk. Though most fail, the fortunate few who gamble successfully on the introduction of a new product or service may realize very substantial incomes.

5 Distribution of Wealth How do income and wealth differ? Income is a *flow* concept; it represents a stream of wage and salary earnings, along with rents, interest, and profits, as portrayed in Chapter 2's circular flow. Wealth is a *stock* concept, reflecting at a particular moment the financial and real assets an individual has accumulated over time. A retired person may have very little income, but a home, savings accounts, and a pension plan can add up to considerable wealth. A new college graduate may be earning a substantial income as an accountant, middle manager, or engineer, but has yet to accumulate significant wealth.

In fact, the ownership of wealth is very unequal and therefore the earnings from that wealth contribute to income inequality. Those who own more machinery, real estate, farmland, stocks and bonds, and savings accounts receive more income from that greater ownership. A recent Federal Reserve study shows that in 1989 the richest 1 percent of all families had net assets of $5.7 trillion, compared to $4.8 trillion for the bottom 90 percent of all families. The richest 10 percent of all families held 68 percent of all net assets, while the remaining 90 percent owned 32 percent. The top 1 percent of income receivers owned 49 percent of all stocks, 62 percent of business assets, 78 percent of bonds and trusts, and 45 percent of nonresidential real estate. Comparisons for 1983 and 1989 indicate that the distribution of wealth has become increasingly unequal or concentrated, contributing to the trend toward greater income inequality.

6 Market Power Ability to "rig the market" on your own behalf is undoubtedly a factor in accounting for income inequality. Certain unions and professional groups have adopted policies limiting the supplies of their productive services, thereby boosting the incomes of those "on the inside." Legislation which provides for occupational licensing for barbers, beauticians, taxi drivers, and so forth, can exert market power favoring the licensed group. Likewise in the product market; profit receivers in particular stand to benefit when their firm develops some degree of monopoly power.

7 Luck, Connections, and Misfortune There are other forces which play a part in explaining income inequality. Luck, chance, and "being in the right place at the right time" have all caused individuals to stumble into fortunes. Discovering oil on a run-down farm or meeting the right press agent have accounted for some high incomes. Nor can personal contacts and political influence be discounted as means of attaining the higher income brackets. On the other hand, economic misfortunes such as prolonged illness, serious accident, death of the family breadwinner, and unemployment may plunge a family into poverty. The burden of such misfortunes is borne very unevenly by the population and contributes to the degree of income inequality. *(Key Question 5)*

QUICK REVIEW 34-1

■ Income inequality has increased in the last decade; currently the top fifth of all families receive 47 percent of before-tax income and the bottom fifth receive 4 percent.

■ The Lorenz curve portrays income inequality graphically.

■ Broadening the income concept and recognition of "churning" within the income distribution over time both lessen perceived income inequality.

■ Government taxes and transfer payments significantly reduce income inequality.

■ Differences in ability, education, job tastes, property ownership, and market power—along with discrimination and luck—help explain income inequality.

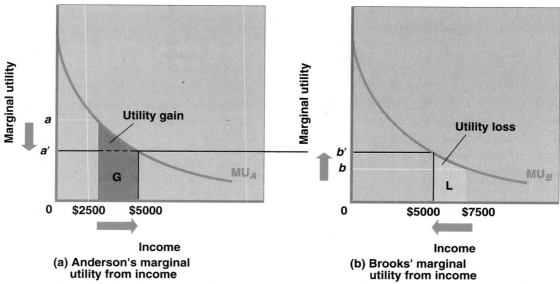

FIGURE 34-3   The utility-maximizing distribution of a specific income
Proponents of income equality argue that, given identical "marginal utility from income" curves, Anderson and Brooks will maximize their combined utility when any given income (say, $10,000) is equally distributed. If income is unequally distributed ($2500 to Anderson and $7500 to Brooks), the marginal utility derived from the last dollar will be greater for Anderson (0a) than for Brooks (0b) and, hence, a redistribution toward equality will result in a net increase in total utility. The utility gain shown by area G in panel (a) exceeds the utility loss indicated by area L in panel (b). When equality is achieved, the marginal utility derived from the last dollar of income will be equal for both consumers (0a' = 0b') and, therefore, there is no further redistribution of income which will increase total utility.

EQUALITY VERSUS EFFICIENCY

The critical policy issue concerning income inequality is: What is the optimal amount? While there is no generally accepted answer, we can learn much by exploring the cases for and against greater equality.

The Case for Equality: Maximizing Utility

The basic argument for an equal distribution of income is that income equality is necessary if consumer satisfaction or utility is to be maximized. The rationale for this argument is shown in Figure 34-3 where it is assumed that the money incomes of two individuals, Anderson and Brooks, are subject to diminishing marginal utility (Chapter 21). In any time period income receivers spend the first dollars received on products they value most—on products whose marginal utility is high. As their most pressing wants become satisfied, consumers then will spend additional dollars of

income on less important, lower marginal utility, goods. The identical diminishing "marginal utility from income" curves reflect the assumption that Anderson and Brooks have the same capacity to derive utility from income.

Now suppose there is $10,000 worth of income (output) to be distributed between Anderson and Brooks. The best or optimal distribution would be an equal distribution which causes the marginal utility of the last dollar spent to be the same for both persons. We can prove this by demonstrating that, for an initially unequal distribution of income, the combined total utility of two individuals can be increased by distributing income more equally.

For example, suppose initially the $10,000 of income is distributed unequally so Anderson gets $2500 and Brooks receives $7500. The marginal utility from the last dollar received by Anderson is high (0a) and the marginal utility from Brooks' last dollar of income is low (0b). Clearly, redistribution of a dollar's worth of income from Brooks to Anderson—that is, toward greater equality—would increase (by 0a − 0b) the combined total utility of the two consumers. This will continue until income is equally distributed with each person receiving $5000. Anderson's utility gain (area G in Figure 34-3a) exceeds Brooks' loss (area L in Figure 34-3b). At this point the marginal utility of the last dollar is identical for Anderson and Brooks ($0a' = 0b'$) and further redistribution cannot increase total utility.

The Case for Inequality: Incentives and Efficiency

Although the logic of the argument for equality is sound, critics attack its fundamental assumption that there exists some fixed amount of income to be distributed. Critics of income equality argue that *the way in which income is distributed is an important determinant of the amount of income produced and available for distribution.*

Suppose once again in Figure 34-3 that Anderson earns $2500 and Brooks earns $7500. In moving toward equality, society (government) must *tax* away some of Brooks' income and *transfer* it to Anderson. This tax-transfer process will diminish the income rewards of high-income Brooks and raise the income rewards of low-income Anderson and in so doing reduce the incentives of both to *earn* high incomes. Why should high-income Brooks work hard, save and invest, or undertake entrepreneurial risks, when the rewards from such activities will be reduced by taxation? And why should low-income Anderson be motivated to increase his income through market activities when government stands ready to transfer income to him? Taxes are a reduction in the rewards from increased productive effort; redistribution through transfers is a reward for diminished effort.

In the extreme, imagine a situation in which government levies a 100 percent tax on income and distributes the tax revenue equally to its citizenry. Why work hard? Why work at all? Why assume business risks? Why save—forgo current consumption—to invest? The economic incentives to "get ahead" will have been removed and the productive efficiency of the economy—and the amount of income to be distributed—will diminish. The way the income pie is distributed affects the size of that pie! *The basic argument for income inequality is that inequality is essential to maintain incentives to produce output and income.*

The Equality–Efficiency Tradeoff[2]

The essence of the income (in)equality debate is that there exists a fundamental **tradeoff between equality and efficiency.**

> The contrasts among American families in living standards and in material wealth reflect a system of rewards and penalties that is intended to encourage effort and channel it into socially productive activity. To the extent that the system succeeds, it generates an efficient economy. But that pursuit of efficiency necessarily creates inequalities. And hence society faces a tradeoff between equality and efficiency.[3]

The problem for a society inclined toward egalitarianism is how to achieve a given redistribution of income so as to minimize the adverse effects on economic efficiency. Consider this *leaky-bucket analogy.* Assume society agrees to shift income from the rich to the poor. But the money must be transferred from affluent to indigent in a leaky bucket. The leak represents an efficiency loss—the loss of output and income—due to the harmful effects of the tax-transfer process on incentives to work, to save and invest, and to accept entrepreneurial risk. It also reflects the fact that resources must be diverted to the bureaucracies which administer the tax-transfer system.

How muck leakage will society accept and continue to endorse the redistribution? If cutting the income pie in more equal slices tends to shrink the pie, what amount of shrinkage will society tolerate? Is a loss of one cent on each redistributed dollar acceptable? Five cents? Twenty-five cents? Fifty cents? This basic question permeates political debates over extensions and contractions of our income-maintenance programs.

Fueling this debate over the equality–efficiency tradeoff are studies which suggest that the loss from the redistribution bucket may be quite high.

> Edgar Browning and William Johnson . . . concluded that the upper-income groups bearing the costs of the taxes would sacrifice $350 for every $100 that the poor gained—a net efficiency loss of $250. In Arthur Okun's terms, the leaks in the redistribution bucket are enormous—starting out with a bucket of $350

---

[2]This section is based on Arthur M. Okun, *Equality and Efficiency: The Big Tradeoff* (Washington: The Brookings Institution, 1975).
[3]Ibid., p. 1.

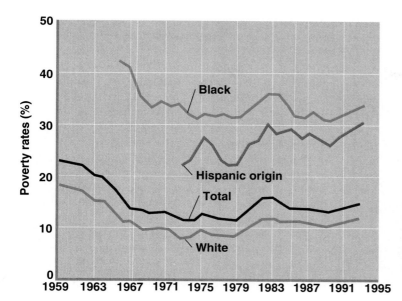

FIGURE 34-4 Poverty rates: total population and by race, 1959–1993
Over the 1959–1993 period poverty rates for blacks and Hispanics have been much higher than the national average, while the rate for whites has been below average. Although the total poverty rate declined sharply in the 1959–1969 period, it stabilized in the 1970s only to increase significantly in the early 1980s.

raised from the nonpoor, $250 is lost on the way to delivering it to the poor. For several reasons, critics of this study have found the estimate to be substantially too high. However, even if cut in half, this loss would be troublesome. Would our society be willing to accept a loss of economic efficiency of $125—or even $100—in order to equalize the distribution of income by transferring $100 to the poor? The answer is by no means clear.[4]

THE DISMAL ECONOMICS OF POVERTY

Many people are less concerned with the larger question of income distribution than they are with the more specific issue of income inadequacy. Armed with some background information on income inequality, we now turn to the poverty problem. How extensive is poverty in the United States? What are the characteristics of the poor? And what is the best strategy to lessen poverty?

Defining Poverty

Poverty does not lend itself to precise definition. But we might say that a family lives in poverty when its

[4]Robert H. Haveman, "New Policy for the New Poverty," *Challenge,* September-October 1988, p. 32.

basic needs exceed its available means of satisfying them. A family's needs have many determinants: its size, its health, the ages of its members, and so forth. Its means include currently earned income, transfer payments, past savings, property owned, and so on.

The definitions of poverty developed by concerned government agencies are based on family size. In 1993 an unattached individual receiving less than $7,363 per year was living in poverty. For a family of four the poverty line was $14,763. For a family of six, it was $19,718. Applying these definitions to income data for the United States, it is found that *15.1 percent of the nation—some 39.3 million people—lives in poverty.*

Who Are the Poor?

Unfortunately for purposes of public policy, the poor are heterogeneous; they can be found in all geographic regions, they are whites and nonwhites, they include large numbers of both rural and urban people, they are both old and young. But, as Figure 34-4 indicates, poverty is far from randomly distributed. Poverty rates for blacks and Hispanics are above the national average; the rate for whites is slightly below average.

Figure 34-5 provides additional detail. While the total **poverty rate**—the percentage of the total population living in poverty—was 15.1 percent in 1993,

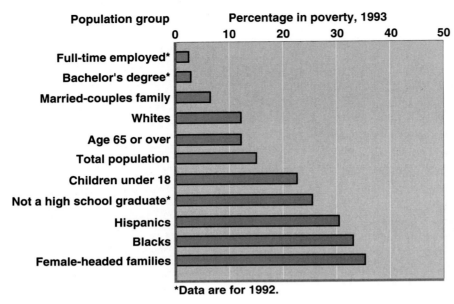

FIGURE 34-5 The distribution of poverty, 1993
Poverty is disproportionately borne by minorities, children, the less-educated, and families headed by women. People who are employed full time, have a college degree, and are married are highly unlikely to live in poverty.

the rates for blacks, Hispanics, and whites were 33.1, 30.6, and 12.2 percent, respectively.

The incidence of poverty is extremely high among female-headed families and over one-fifth of all children under 18 years of age live in poverty. Figure 34-5 also tells us that full-time employment, education, and marriage are all associated with low poverty rates. And, thanks to a generous social security system, the incidence of poverty among the elderly is less than for the population as a whole.

The high poverty rates for children are especially disturbing because in a very real sense poverty breeds poverty. Poor children are at greater risk for a range of long-term problems, including poor health and inadequate education, crime, drugs, and teenage pregnancy. Many of today's impoverished children will reach adulthood unhealthy, illiterate, and unemployable. The increased concentration of poverty among children bodes poorly for reducing poverty in the future. It also implies problems for increasing the future productivity of the labor force because poor children receive less and generally inferior education.

Recalling our previous comments on movement or "churning" within the income distribution, we know that there is considerable movement in and out of poverty. Just over half of those who are in poverty one year will remain below the poverty line the next year. On the other hand, poverty is much more persistent for some groups, in particular black and Hispanic families, families headed by women, those with

little education and few labor market skills, and those who are dysfunctional because of drugs, alcoholism, or mental illness.

Poverty Trends

In Figure 34-4, we see the total poverty rate fell significantly between 1959 and 1969, stabilized between 11 and 13 percent over the next decade, and then increased during the early 1980s. In 1993 the rate was 15.1 percent, the highest since 1983.

A "Black Underclass"?

Some say the city ghettos are spawning a "black underclass" which is trapped in a permanent cycle of poverty, broken homes, welfare, and, frequently, drugs and crime. Relevant statistics are alarming: 1 out of 2 black youths live in poverty; 1 out of 2 black youths grows up without a father; nearly 40 percent of black teenagers are unemployed; 1 out of 4 births is to a black teenager; more than 80 percent of children born to black teenagers are illegitimate; the infant-mortality rate for blacks is twice as high as it is for whites; homicide is the leading cause of death for black males ages 15 to 34; and one-fifth of all black males between 15 and 34 have criminal records.

It is argued that in the social and economic isolation of the urban ghetto a new culture—a culture of poverty and dependency—has evolved where attitudes, values, and morality are substantially different from those of mainstream America. Welfare programs —Aid to Families with Dependent Children (AFDC), food stamps, housing subsidies, and the rest—have allegedly undermined incentives to work and have created welfare-dependent families. Furthermore, the historical exodus from the central city of middle-class blacks has left drug dealers, prostitutes, hustlers, and small-time criminals as role models for poor black youngsters who remain. Low-quality schools grossly underprepare minority youth for the job market, while a lenient and overburdened legal system increases the attractiveness of crime as an alternative to work.

At the level of policy, the black underclass view asserts that, although there has been a significant lessening in discrimination over the past several decades and although hundreds of billions have been expended on antipoverty programs, the poverty problem persists. The implication is that the responsibility for poverty rests largely on the poor themselves and that self-help is essential to the alleviation of poverty.

Critics of the black underclass view contend that it is a simplistic and callous position which incorrectly implies that the blame for poverty rests with its victims and not with larger social and economic considerations. Critics also point out that central-city poverty is heterogeneous and has a multitude of causes. What is needed is a far-reaching effort to eliminate racial segregation in housing and schooling, compensatory training and education, more accessible job opportunities, and an income maintenance program which does not discourage work. Black poverty, it is argued, is primarily the result of societal neglect that is inherently racist.

The "Invisible" Poor

These facts and figures on the extent and character of poverty may be difficult to accept. After all, ours is an affluent society. How do we square the depressing statistics on poverty with everyday observations of abundance? The answer lies mainly in the fact that much American poverty is hidden; it is largely invisible.

There are three reasons for this invisibility. First, a sizable proportion of the people in the poverty pool change from year to year. Research has shown that as many as one-half of those in poverty are poor for only one or two years before successfully climbing out of poverty. Many of these people are not visible as permanently downtrodden and needy. Second, the

"permanently poor" are increasingly isolated. Poverty persists in slums and ghettos of large cities and is not readily visible from the freeway or commuter train. Similarly, rural poverty and the chronically depressed areas of Appalachia, the South, and the Southwest are also off the beaten path. Third, and perhaps most important,

> The poor are politically invisible. . . . [They] do not, by far and large, belong to unions, to fraternal organizations, or to political parties. They are without lobbies of their own; they put forward no legislative program. As a group they are atomized. They have no face; they have no voice.[5]

The American poor have been labeled "the world's least revolutionary proletariat."

THE INCOME MAINTENANCE SYSTEM

The existence of a wide variety of income-maintenance programs (Table 34-3) is evidence that alleviation of poverty has been accepted as a legitimate goal of public policy. Despite cutbacks in many programs in recent years, income-maintenance programs still involve substantial monetary outlays and large numbers of beneficiaries. Total spending for income maintenance has expanded from about 4 percent of domestic production in 1940 to over 14 percent currently.

Our income-maintenance system consists of two kinds of programs: (1) social insurance programs and (2) public assistance or "welfare" programs.

Social Insurance Programs

Social insurance programs partially replace earnings lost due to retirement, disability, and temporary unemployment and provide health insurance for the elderly. "Social security" (technically Old Age, Survivors, and Disability Health Insurance or OASDHI), unemployment compensation, and Medicare are the main social insurance programs. Benefits are viewed as earned rights and do not carry the stigma of public charity. These programs are financed primarily out of Federal payroll taxes. In these programs the population pools the risk of income loss due to retirement, unemployment, disability, or illness. Workers (and

---

[5]Michael Harrington, *The Other America: Poverty in the United States,* rev. ed. (New York: The Macmillan Company, 1970), p. 14.

TABLE 34-3   Characteristics of major income-maintenance programs

Program	Basis of eligibility	Source of funds	Form of aid	Expenditures* (billions)	Beneficiaries (millions)
Social Insurance Programs					
Old Age, Survivors, and Disability Health Insurance (OASDHI)	Age, disability, or death of parent or spouse; individual earnings	Federal payroll taxes on employers and employees	Cash	$302	42
Medicare	Age or disability	Federal payroll tax on employers and employees	Subsidized health insurance	143	36
Unemployment compensation	Unemployment	State and Federal payroll taxes on employers	Cash	35	9
Public Assistance Programs					
Supplemental Security Income (SSI)	Age or disability; income	Federal revenues	Cash	21	6
Aid to Families with Dependent Children (AFDC)	Certain families with children; income	Federal-state-local revenues	Cash and services	16	14
Food Stamps	Income	Federal revenues	Vouchers	25	27
Medicaid	Persons eligible for AFDC or SSI and medically indigent	Federal-state-local revenues	Subsidized medical services	76	31

*Expenditures by Federal, state, and local governments; excludes administrative expenses.

Source: Congressional Budget Office and *Statistical Abstract of the United States, 1994.* Expenditures data are for 1993; beneficiaries data for 1992.

employers) pay a part of wages into a government fund while they are working and then they are *entitled* to benefits when they retire or when the specified misfortunes occur.

OASDHI and Medicare

OASDHI is a gigantic social insurance program financed by compulsory payroll taxes levied on both employers and employees. Generically known as "social security," the program replaces earnings lost because of a worker's retirement, disability, or death. A payroll tax of 7.65 percent is levied on both worker and employer and applies to the first $61,200 of wage income. Workers may retire at 65 with full benefits or at 62 with reduced benefits. When the worker dies, benefits accrue to the survivors. Special provisions provide benefits for disabled workers. Currently, social insurance covers over 90 percent of the work force and some 42 million people received OASDHI checks averaging about $675 per month.

Medicare was appended to OASDHI in 1965. The hospital insurance it provides for the elderly and disabled is financed out of a payroll tax. Medicare also makes available a low-cost voluntary insurance program which helps pay doctor fees.

Unemployment Compensation

All fifty states sponsor unemployment insurance programs. **Unemployment compensation** is financed by a modest payroll tax which varies by state and the size of each firm's payroll. Any insured worker who becomes unemployed can, after a short waiting period (usually a week), become eligible for benefit payments. Almost all wage and salary workers are covered by the program. Size of payments and the number of weeks they may be received vary considerably from state to state. Generally speaking, benefits approximate 35 percent of a worker's wages up to a certain maximum payment. Benefits averaged $175 weekly in 1992. The number of beneficiaries and the level of total disbursements vary greatly over the business cycle.

Public Assistance Programs

Public assistance, or *welfare, programs* provide benefits for those who are unable to earn income because of permanent handicaps or dependent children. These programs are financed out of general tax revenues and are regarded as public charity. These programs are "means tested" in that individuals and families must demonstrate low incomes to qualify for aid. The Federal government finances about two-thirds of the welfare program expenditures.

Many needy persons who do not qualify for social insurance programs are assisted through the Federal government's **Supplemental Security Income (SSI) program.** The purpose of SSI is to establish a uniform, nationwide minimum income for the aged, blind, and disabled who are unable to work and do not qualify for OASDHI aid. Over half the states provide additional income supplements to the aged, blind, and disabled.

The **Aid to Families with Dependent Children (AFDC)** program is state-administered, but partly financed with Federal grants. The program provides aid to families in which dependent children do not have the financial suport of a parent, usually the father, because of death, disability, divorce, or desertion.

The **food stamp program** is designed to provide all low-income Americans with a "nutritionally adequate diet." Under the program eligible households receive monthly allotments of coupons which are redeemable for food. The amount of food stamps received varies inversely with a family's earned income.

Medicaid helps finance medical expenses of individuals participating in both the SSI and the AFDC programs.

There also exists a variety of other welfare programs (largely in the form of noncash transfers) not listed in Table 34-3. Head Start provides education, nutrition, and social services to economically disadvantaged 3- and 4-year olds. Housing assistance in the form of rent subsidies and funds for construction are available to low-income families. The Job Training Partnership Act finances education and training for the poor and Pell Grants provides assistance to needy undergraduate students. Of special mention is the **Earned Income Tax Credit (EITC)** which is a refundable tax credit for low-income working families with children. Established in 1975, the credit reduces the income taxes owed by such families or provides them with a cash payment if the credit exceeds their tax liability.

QUICK REVIEW 34-2

■ The fundamental argument for income equality is that it maximizes consumer utility; the basic argument for income inequality is that it is necessary to stimulate economic incentives.

■ By government standards over 39 million people or 15 percent of the population live in poverty.

■ Our income maintenance system comprises both social insurance programs and public assistance ("welfare") programs.

"The Welfare Mess"

There is no doubt that the income maintenance system—as well as local relief, housing subsidies, minimum-wage legislation, veterans' benefits, private transfers through charities, pensions, and supplementary unemployment benefits—provides important means of alleviating poverty. Nevertheless, the system has been subject to many criticisms in recent years.

1 Administrative Inefficiencies Critics charge that the haphazard growth of our welfare programs has created a clumsy and inefficient system, characterized by red tape and dependence on a huge bureaucracy for its administration. Administrative costs account for large portions of the total budget for many programs.

> The amount necessary to lift every man, woman, and child in America above the poverty line has been calculated, and it is *one-third* of what is in fact spent on poverty programs. Clearly, much of the transfer ends up in the pockets of highly paid administrators, consultants, and staff as well as higher income recipients of benefits from programs advertised as anti-poverty efforts.[6]

2 Inequities Serious inequities arise in welfare programs in that people with similar needs may be treated very differently.

> Benefit levels vary widely among States and among different demographic and family groups. Geo-

---

[6] Thomas Sowell, *Markets and Minorities* (New York: Basic Books, Inc., Publishers, 1981), p. 122.

TABLE 34-4 The negative income tax: three plans for a family of four

Plan One ($8000 guaranteed income and 50% benefit-reduction rate)			Plan Two ($8000 guaranteed income and 25% benefit-reduction rate)			Plan Three ($12,000 guaranteed income and 50% benefit-reduction rate)		
Earned income	NIT subsidy	Total income	Earned income	NIT subsidy	Total income	Earned income	NIT subsidy	Total income
$ 0	$8,000	$ 8,000	$ 0	$8,000	$ 8,000	$ 0	$12,000	$12,000
4,000	6,000	10,000	8,000	6,000	14,000	8,000	8,000	16,000
8,000	4,000	12,000	16,000	4,000	20,000	16,000	4,000	20,000
12,000	2,000	14,000	24,000	2,000	26,000	24,000*	0	24,000
16,000*	0	16,000	32,000*	0	32,000			

*Indicates break-even income. Determined by dividing the guaranteed income by the benefit-reduction rate.

graphic differentials arise primarily because benefits under the two major public assistance programs—AFDC and Medicaid—are essentially controlled by the States. As a result, sharp disparities in benefit levels exist between the poorer, rural States and the wealthier, more urban areas....[7]

A family in New York City might receive welfare benefits two times as great as the same family in Mississippi. Control of the system is fragmented and some low-income families "fall between the cracks" while other families collect benefits to which they are not entitled.

3 Work Incentives A major criticism is that most of our income-maintenance programs impair incentives to work. This is because all welfare programs are constructed so that a dollar's worth of earned income yields less than a dollar of net income. As earned income increases, program benefits are reduced, constituting a "tax" on earnings. An individual or family participating in several welfare programs may find that, when the loss of program benefits and the effect of income and payroll taxes on earnings are taken into account, the individual or family is absolutely worse off by working. In effect, the marginal tax rate on earned income exceeds 100 percent! Small wonder that a minimum-wage job is unattractive to a welfare mother who will lose both AFDC payments and (after a year) Medicaid health coverage in addition to paying for child care.

There are other criticisms. Noncash transfers interfere with freedom of consumer choice. Public assistance programs sap initiative and encourage de-

pendence. AFDC regulations in most states promote family breakup by encouraging unemployed fathers to abandon their families so the spouse and children can qualify for benefits. AFDC benefits subsidize birth outside of marriage; nearly one-half of the mothers in the AFDC program have illegitimate children. Welfare programs foster social divisiveness between workers and welfare recipients. For example, working mothers with small children may wonder why poor mothers receiving AFDC should not also work for their money.

REFORM PROPOSALS

These criticisms have led to calls to reform the public assistance system. Although reform proposals have taken many forms, two approaches have dominated: negative income tax schemes and "workfare" plans.

Negative Income Tax

One contention is that the entire patchwork of existing welfare programs should be replaced by a **negative income tax** (NIT). The term NIT suggests that, just as the present (positive) income tax calls for families to "subsidize" the government through taxes when their incomes rise *above* a certain level, the government should subsidize households with NIT payments when household incomes fall *below* a certain level.

Comparing Plans Let's examine the two critical elements of any NIT plan. First, a NIT plan specifies a **guaranteed annual income** below which family in-

---

[7]*Economic Report of the President, 1978,* pp. 225–226.

comes would not be allowed to fall. Second, the plan embodies a **benefit-reduction rate** which indicates the rate at which subsidy benefits are reduced or "lost" as a consequence of earned income.

Consider Plan One of the three plans shown in Table 34-4. In Plan One guaranteed annual income is assumed to be $8000 and the benefit-reduction rate is 50 percent. If the family earns no income, it will receive a NIT subsidy of $8000. If it earns $4000, it will lose $2000 ($4000 of earnings *times* the 50 percent benefit-reduction rate) of subsidy benefits and total income will be $10,000 (= $4000 of earnings *plus* $6000 of subsidy). If $8000 is earned, the subsidy will fall to $4000, and so on. Note that at $16,000 the NIT subsidy becomes zero. The level of earned income at which the subsidy disappears and at which normal (positive) income taxes apply to further increases in earned income is called the **break-even income.**

We might criticize Plan One on the grounds that a 50 percent benefit-reduction rate is too high and therefore does not provide sufficient incentives to work. Thus, in Plan Two the $8000 guaranteed income is retained, but the benefit-reduction rate is reduced to 25 percent. But note that the break-even level of income increases to $32,000 and many more families would now qualify for NIT subsidies. Furthermore, a family with any given earned income will now receive a larger NIT subsidy. For both of these reasons, a reduction of the benefit-reduction rate to enhance work incentives will raise the cost of a NIT plan.

Examining Plans One and Two, still another critic might argue that the guaranteed annual income is too low—it does not get families out of poverty. Plan Three raises the guaranteed annual income to $12,000 and retains the 50 percent benefit-reduction rate of Plan One. While Plan Three does a better job of raising the incomes of the poor, it too yields a higher break-even income than Plan One and would therefore be more costly. Furthermore, if the $12,000 income guarantee of Plan Three were coupled with Plan Two's 25 percent benefit-reduction rate to strengthen work incentives, the break-even income level would shoot up to $48,000 and add even more to NIT costs.[8]

---

[8]You may have sensed the generalization that, given the guaranteed income, the break-even level of income varies *inversely* with the benefit-reduction rate. Specifically, the break-even income can be found by dividing the guaranteed income by the benefit-reduction rate. Thus, for Plan One, $8000/.50 = $16,000. Can you also demonstrate that, given the benefit-reduction rate, the break-even level of income varies *directly* with the guaranteed income?

Goals and Conflicts By comparing these three plans we find conflicts or tradeoffs among the goals of an "ideal" income-maintenance plan. First, a plan should be effective in getting families out of poverty. Second, it should provide adequate incentives to work. Third, the plan's costs should be "reasonable." Table 34-4 tells us that these three objectives conflict with one another and that compromises or tradeoffs are necessary.

Plan One, with a low guaranteed income and a high benefit-reduction rate, keeps costs down. But the low-income guarantee means it is not very effective in eliminating poverty and the high benefit-reduction rate weakens work incentives. In comparison, Plan Two has a lower benefit-reduction rate and therefore stronger work incentives. But it is more costly because it involves a higher break-even income and therefore pays benefits to more families.

Compared to Plan One, Plan Three entails a higher guaranteed income and is more effective in eliminating poverty. While work incentives are the same as with Plan One, the higher guaranteed income makes the plan more costly. The problem is to find the magic numbers which will provide a "decent" guaranteed income, maintain "reasonable" incentives to work, and entail "acceptable" costs. While abolishing most of our current public assistance programs in favor of the NIT might be an improvement, the NIT is fraught with internal tradeoffs and should not be regarded as a panacea. In fact, reform efforts have moved away from the NIT in recent years. *(Key Question 11)*

Workfare Plans

However desirable a NIT might be, political realities are such that piecemeal changes in the income maintenance system are more likely. Most critical attention has focused on AFDC, for several reasons. First, AFDC may encourage family dissolution. Second, it is contended that the program encourages—or at least subsidizes—illegitimate births. Third, some critics contend that AFDC is conducive to a "culture of poverty" where poverty becomes a way of life and is passed from generation to generation. Fourth, according to government studies, many recipients of AFDC receive benefits fraudulently. Fifth, as more middle-class mothers with children join the labor force, a consensus is emerging that poor mothers receiving AFDC should also work for incomes they receive.

These criticisms have led to **workfare proposals**—also called "welfare-to-work" plans—which would alter the AFDC program by providing work, training, and education activities to help, and eventually require, welfare recipients to move from public assistance to employment. People on welfare who undertake training or enter the labor force would also receive child care and transportation subsidies. As an additional aspect of this approach, earnings of absentee parents—whether married or unmarried—would be taken directly from workers' paychecks to pay child support.

Family Support Act   Several states have had some success in their experiments with the "welfare-to-work" approach to poverty. The success of these state programs helped generate support for an overhaul of the AFDC program nationally. In late 1988 Congress passed and the President signed into law the **Family Support Act of 1988 (FSA),** more commonly called the *Welfare Reform Act of 1988*. This act embraces the workfare approach and includes the following provisions:

1   Each state must establish a Job Opportunities and Basic Skills program (JOBS) through which AFDC parents will be offered basic and remedial education, literacy classes, job skills training, job readiness activities, and job placement.

2   States must provide child care and Medicaid coverage for 12 months to welfare families switching from welfare rolls to employment. The purpose is to reduce the costs of moving from welfare to work and to lessen the incentives to stay on welfare.

3   All states must begin offering welfare benefits to qualified two-parent families when the main wage earner is unemployed. The purpose of this provision is to reduce the incidence of family break-up associated with the AFDC program.

Supporters of the law believe it can play a role in helping end a "culture of welfare" in which dropping out of school, having a child, and going on welfare have allegedly become a normal way of life for part of the welfare population.

Recent Proposals   The Clinton administration is pledged to "end welfare as we know it" by building on the provisions of FSA. Components of its emerging program include:

1   Expansion of the Earned Income Tax Credit which effectively increases wage rates and makes work more attractive. The provision of universal health care and expanded access to child care—perhaps through an enlarged Head Start program—would also reduce the costs of moving from welfare to work.

2   Child support would be improved by using the IRS to withhold child support payments from the wages of fathers who refuse to pay.

3   Strengthening the education and training provisions of FSA which prepare AFDC recipients to enter the work force.

4   The period a welfare recipient can receive AFDC payments would be limited to, say, two years. In late 1993 the administration approved a Wisconsin plan to experiment in several counties with a two-year limit to assess the impacts of time limits.

The Republican "Contract with America" seeks to discourage illegitimacy and teen pregnancies by prohibiting welfare to minor mothers and denying increased AFDC payments to anyone who has additional children while on welfare. The contract endorses the two-years-and-out concept and calls for work requirements for those receiving AFDC. It also recommends that legal immigrants be denied welfare.

CHAPTER SUMMARY

1   The distribution of personal income in the United States reflects considerable inequality. The Lorenz curve shows the degree of income inequality graphically.

2   Income inequality lessened significantly between 1929 and the end of World War II, but inequality has increased since 1969.

3   The use of a broadened concept of income which includes noncash transfers and taxes *and* recognition that the positions of individual families in the distribution of income change over time would reveal less income inequality than do standard census data.

4   Government taxes and transfers—particularly transfers—lessen the degree of income inequality significantly.

5   Causes of income inequality include discrimination and differences in abilities, education and training, job tastes, the unequal distribution of wealth, and market power.

6   The basic argument for income equality is that it maximizes consumer satisfaction from a given income. The main argument against income equality is that equality undermines incentives to work, invest, and assume risks, thereby reducing the amount of income available for distribution.

7   Current statistics reveal that 15 percent of the nation

LAST WORD

WELFARE FOR THE RICH

The conventional wisdom is that redistribution policies overwhelmingly shift income from rich to poor. But in many instances the reverse is true.

Various government programs and policies reallocate income from taxpayers at large to rich families and prosperous corporations. These subsidies take many forms, including direct cash transfers, tax breaks, and the underpricing of government resources or services. Let's consider a few illustrations.

1   *Tax Code*   The modest progressivity of the Federal personal income tax is diminished by certain allowable deductions which reduce the taxable incomes of the well-to-do. Examples: Mortgage interest payments are deductible, as are real estate property taxes. Interest income on municipal bonds is tax-free. Affluent people also can defer taxes by putting part of their earnings into government-sanctioned pension plans.

2   *Agricultural Subsidies*   Farmers currently receive $11 billion per year in direct cash subsidies. These accrue largely to the wealthiest farmers because subsidies vary directly with the volume of production. The richest 7 percent of all farms with sales of $250,000 or more in 1992 received 32 percent of these payments.

Government also subsidizes certain farmers by the use of import quotas or prohibitions, allowing them to charge domestic prices which are much higher than world prices. This is the case for sugar where some thirty-three sugar farms received benefits of $1 million or more in 1991; one profited to the tune of $30 million.

Under a market promotion program, large and prosperous corporations receive direct cash subsidies to promote their products globally. Some of the largest beneficiaries in 1991 were Sunkist Growers ($10 million), Gallo Wines ($5 million), Dole Pineapple ($3 million), Pillsbury ($2.9 million), and McDonald's ($65,000).

3   *Land and Water Policy*   Government-owned resources are often leased or sold at prices below their market value. These include timber, grazing land, and water. Example: Under the archaic Mining Law of 1872, mining companies can buy Federal land for $2.50–$5.00 per

acre and resell at market prices. In an extreme case 17,000 acres were bought for $42,500 and resold to major oil companies a few weeks later for $37 million. Example: Water subsidies to farmers from underpricing in California's Westland Water District average $500,000 per farm.

4   *Rural Doctors*   Medicine is one of the highest-paid professions with average incomes of $177,000 in 1993. Yet under a Federal program designed to attract doctors to rural areas, physicians can get up to $50,000 of their educational loans repaid by locating in a rural area for two years; a four-year commitment will repay up to $120,000.

5   *Wooing Industry*   States often compete vigorously with subsidy packages to lure large corporations. South Carolina offered some $130 million in subsidies to attract a BMW auto plant in 1992. In 1993 Alabama paid the same amount (calculated to be a subsidy of $90,000 per-job) to land a Mercedes-Benz factory.

6   *Medicare*   Medicare–Part B, which pays for physicians and medical supplies, is heavily subsidized. For a 65-year-old in 1991, premiums only covered about 17 percent of total costs, the remainder being paid out of general tax revenues. The lifetime Medicare subsidy for men who were 65 in 1991 is estimated at over $25,000; for women (who generally live longer than men) the lifetime subsidy is $39,000.

lives in poverty. Poverty is concentrated among blacks, Hispanics, female-headed families, and young children.

8   Our present income-maintenance system is composed of social insurance programs (OASDHI, Medicare, and un-employment compensation) and public assistance programs (SSI, AFDC, food stamps, and Medicaid).

9   Present welfare programs have been criticized as administratively inefficient, fraught with inequities, and detri-

mental to work incentives. Reform proposals have been of two basic types: negative income tax proposals and "workfare" plans.

10   The Clinton administration's welfare proposals include: a expansion of the Earned Income Tax Credit;   b more aggressive pursuit of child support payments;   c expanded education and training for AFDC recipients; and   d limiting AFDC payments to two years.

TERMS AND CONCEPTS

income inequality	OASDHI	Aid to Families with	benefit-reduction rate
Lorenz curve	Medicare	Dependent Children	guaranteed annual
noncash transfers	unemployment	(AFDC)	income
tradeoff between	compensation	Medicaid	break-even income
equality and	Supplemental Security	Earned Income Tax	workfare proposals
efficiency	Income (SSI)	Credit (EITC)	Family Support Act of
poverty rate	food stamp program	negative income tax	1988 (FSA)

QUESTIONS AND STUDY SUGGESTIONS

1   Using quintiles, briefly summarize the degree of income inequality in the United States. What criticisms have been made of standard Census Bureau data on income inequality? How and to what extent does government contribute to income equality?

2   *Key Question Assume Al, Beth, Carol, David, and Ed receive incomes of $500, $250, $125, $75, and $50 respectively. Construct and interpret a Lorenz curve for this five-person economy. What percentage of total income is received by the richest and by the poorest quintiles?*

3   What factors have contributed to increased income inequality in the past decade or so?

4   Why is the lifetime distribution of income more equal than the distribution in any given year?

5   *Key Question Briefly discuss the major causes of income inequality. With respect to income inequality, is there any difference between inheriting property and inheriting a high IQ? Explain.*

6   Use the "leaky-bucket analogy" to discuss the equality–efficiency tradeoff. Compared to our present income-maintenance system, do you feel that a negative income tax would reduce the leak?

7   Should a nation's income be distributed to its members according to their contributions to the production of that total income or to the members' needs? Should society attempt to equalize income *or* economic opportunities? Are the issues of "equity" and "equality" in the distribution of income synonymous? To what degree, if any, is income inequality equitable?

8   Analyze in detail: "There need be no tradeoff between equality and efficiency. An 'efficient' economy which yields an income distribution which many regard as unfair may cause those with meager income rewards to become discouraged and stop trying. Hence, efficiency is undermined. A fairer distribution of rewards may generate a higher average productive effort on the part of the population, thereby enhancing efficiency. If people think they are playing a fair economic game and this belief causes them to try harder, an economy with an equitable income distribution may be efficient as well."[9]

9   Comment on or explain:
a   "To endow everyone with equal income will make for very unequal enjoyment and satisfaction."
b   "Equality is a 'superior good'; the richer we become, the more of it we can afford."
c   "The mob goes in search of bread, and the means it employs is generally to wreck the bakeries."
d   "Under our welfare system we have foolishly clung to the notion that employment and receipt of assistance must be mutually exclusive."
e   "Some freedoms may be more important in the long run than freedom from want on the part of every individual."
f   "Capitalism and democracy are really a most improbable mixture. Maybe that is why they need each other—to put some rationality into equality and some humanity into efficiency."
g   "The incentives created by the attempt to bring about a more equal distribution of income are in conflict with the incentives needed to generate increased income."

---

[9]Paraphrased from Andrew Schotter, *Free Market Economics* (New York: St. Martin's Press, 1985), pp. 30–31.

10 What are the essential differences between social insurance and public assistance programs? What are the criticisms of our present income-maintenance system?

11 *Key Question* *The table shown below contains three illustrative negative income tax (NIT) plans.*

Plan One			Plan Two			Plan Three		
Earned income	NIT subsidy	Total income	Earned income	NIT subsidy	Total income	Earned income	NIT subsidy	Total income
$ 0	$4,000	$4,000	$ 0	$4,000	$ 4,000	$ 0	$ 8,000	$ 8,000
2,000	3,000	5,000	4,000	3,000	7,000	4,000	6,000	10,000
4,000	2,000	6,000	8,000	2,000	10,000	8,000	4,000	12,000
6,000	1,000	7,000	12,000	1,000	13,000	12,000	2,000	14,000

a *Determine the basic benefit, the benefit-reduction rate, and the break-even income for each plan.*

b *Which plan is the most costly? The least costly? Which plan is most effective in reducing poverty? The least effective? Which plan contains the strongest disincentive to work? The weakest disincentive to work?*

c *Use your answers in part 11b to explain the following statement: "The dilemma of the negative income tax is that you cannot bring families up to the poverty level and simultaneously preserve work incentives and minimize program costs."*

12 "The father of a child has a responsibility to help support that child, irrespective of whether or not he is married to the mother. In addition, the able-bodied single mother has a responsibility to help support her child by working." Do you agree? How might these "principles" be incorporated into a welfare program? What problems might arise in implementing this program in the real world?

13 (Last Word) What various means does government use to subsidize high-income people? Provide a specific illustration of each.

35

THE ECONOMICS OF HEALTH CARE

Rarely can you look at a newspaper or television news without seeing a story about America's soaring health care costs, seriously ailing or injured people with no health insurance, or government insurance programs draining Federal and state budgets. Stories also document disputes between employers and workers over sharing the costs of health insurance. Indeed, the major cause of strikes in recent years has been health care benefits and who pays for them. We even learn of companies breaking promises to provide health insurance to retirees. Moreover, difficult ethical questions concerning "extreme care" for the acutely or terminally ill have arisen. The desirability of some form of national health insurance has become a central focus of congressional debate.

In this chapter we (1) examine the economic aspects of our health care problems, (2) use a demand and supply framework to explain the rapid increases in health care costs, and (3) discuss some ways of reforming the health care system.

THE HEALTH CARE INDUSTRY

The boundaries of the health care industry are not easily discerned, making it difficult to define. Nevertheless, according to government economists, it includes:

> . . . services provided in hospitals, nursing homes, laboratories, and physicians' and dentists' offices. It also includes prescription and nonprescription drugs, artificial limbs, and eyeglasses, as well as the services of nontraditional practitioners. But many goods and services that may strongly affect health, such as fitness club services and food, are not included in the usual definition.

The U.S. health care industry employs 9 million people, including over 600,000 physicians; by com-

parison, the automobile manufacturing industry employs about 800,000 people. Inpatient services are provided by approximately 6,500 hospitals containing over 1 million hospital beds. One-half of these hospitals are private, non-profit institutions, some 30 percent are operated by Federal, State, and municipal governments, and the remainder are operated privately on a for-profit basis.[1]

TWIN PROBLEMS: COSTS AND ACCESS

There are two highly publicized problems with our health care system. First, expenditures on—and costs

---

[1] *Economic Report of the President, 1993,* p. 121.

of—health care are high and growing rapidly. Second, many Americans do not have access—or have only limited access—to health care. To improve our health care system we need to control costs and make it more accessible.

These two problems are interrelated in that sharply rising health care costs make health care unaffordable to a significant portion of our population. Indeed, there is evidence that a dual system of health care is evolving in the United States. Those with insurance or other financial resources receive the best medical treatment available in the world. But an increasing number of people do not seek out even the most basic treatment because of their inability to pay.

RISING HEALTH CARE COSTS

What we see and hear most about our health care "crisis" is the steep increase in costs.

Dimensions of Cost Increases

Health care expenditures and costs in the United States have been rising (1) absolutely, (2) as a percentage of gross domestic product, and (3) on a per capita basis.

1 Aggregate Spending Recently, total health care spending has been increasing by $70 to $80 billion per year. In absolute terms aggregate health care spending will balloon from $666 billion in 1990 to over $800 billion in 1992 and almost $1.7 trillion in the year 2000. These increases average 9.6 percent per year.

Figure 35-1 provides us with an overview of the major types of health care spending in panel a and the sources of funds for these expenditures in panel b. In a we find that hospitals account for 37 cents of each health care dollar spent, while physicians and other health care services (dental, vision, and home care) account for 19 and 24 cents, respectively.

The big message in panel b is that three-fourths of health care expenditures are financed by insurance. Public insurance (Medicaid, Medicare, and insurance government provides for veterans and current military and civilian employees) is the source of 43 cents of each dollar spent. Private insurance accounts for 33 cents, meaning that public and private insurance combined provide 76 cents of each dollar expended. The remaining 24 cents comes directly out of the health care consumer's pocket, usually as insurance deductibles (where the insured pays the first $250 or $500 of each year's health care costs before insurance becomes effective) or copayments (where the insured pays, say, 20 percent of all health care costs and the insurance company pays the other 80 percent).

FIGURE 35-1 **Health care expenditures and finance**
Most health care expenditures are for hospitals and physicians' services. Public and private insurance pays for about three-fourths of health care. Source: *Health Care Financing Review*, Fall 1994. Data are for 1993.

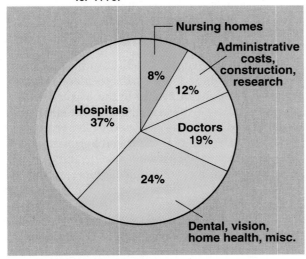

(a) Health care expenditures

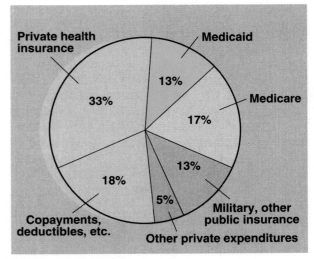

(b) Sources of funds

Recall that *Medicare* is a nationwide Federal health care program available to social security beneficiaries and the disabled. It consists of a *hospital insurance* program which, after a deductible of $696 (in 1994), covers all reasonable costs for the first sixty days of inpatient care per "benefit period" and lesser amounts (on a cost-sharing basis) for a number of additional days. Coverage is also provided for posthospital nursing services, home health care, and hospice care for the terminally ill. Participation in the *medical insurance* portion of Medicare (physician services, laboratory and other diagnostic tests, and outpatient hospital services) is voluntary, but heavily subsidized by government. The $41.10 monthly premiums (1994) charged participants only cover about one-fourth of the costs of the benefits provided.

Medicaid provides payment for medical benefits to certain low-income people, including the elderly, blind, disabled, children, and adults with dependent children. Those who qualify for Aid to Families with Dependent Children (AFDC) or the Supplementary Security Income (SSI) program (Chapter 34) are automatically eligible for Medicaid. Nevertheless, Medicaid covers less than one-half of those in poverty. The costs of Medicaid are shared by the Federal government and the states. On an average the states fund 43 percent and the Federal government 57 percent of each Medicaid dollar.

Only about 25 percent of each dollar spent on health care is financed by direct out-of-pocket payments by individuals. The fact that most of our health care is paid for by third-parties—private insurance companies or government—is an important contributor to rising health care costs.

2 Percentage of GDP Figure 35-2 reveals how much health care spending has been increasing as a percentage of gross product. Health care spending absorbed 6 percent of GDP in 1965 but rose to 12 percent of GDP by 1990. Congressional Budget Office (CBO) projections indicate that, if current trends and government policies continue, health care spending will amount to 18 percent of GDP by the year 2000.

3 Per Capita Spending: International Comparisons Figure (a) in Global Perspective 35-1 reveals that among twenty-four of the most industrialized nations, per capita health care spending is clearly the highest in the United States. It is no surprise that

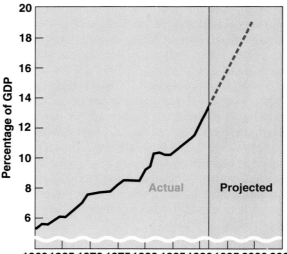

FIGURE 35-2 National health care expenditures as a percentage of gross domestic product
Aggregate health care spending rose from 6 percent of GDP in 1965 to 12 percent by 1990 and is projected to increase to 18 percent of GDP by the year 2000. (Congressional Budget Office.)

health care spending varies directly with incomes. In fact, health care expenditures per person rise approximately in proportion with per capita income. But the United States is clearly "off the trend." Our high per capita GDP does not fully explain our very high level of spending per capita. The message of Figure (b) is that, while per capita health care expenditures have been rising in most countries, the highest level and fastest rate of growth is in the United States.

Quality of Care: Are We Healthier?

It is difficult to compare health care quality among countries. Yet there is general agreement that medical care (though not health) in the United States is probably *the* best in the world. Average life expectancy in the United States has increased by five years since 1960, and American physicians and hospitals employ the most advanced medical equipment and technologies available in the world. Furthermore, more than half of the world's medical research funding is done in the United States. As a result, the incidence of disease has been declining and the quality of treatment improving. Polio has been virtually eliminated, ulcers are now successfully treated without surgery, angioplasty and coronary bypass surgery have greatly benefited those with heart disease, sophisticated body scanners are increasingly available as diagnostic tools, and organ transplants and replacement of knees and hips with prostheses are more and more common.

That's the good news. Alas, there is other news. Despite new screening and treatment technologies, the mortality rate for breast cancer patients has shown little change. Tuberculosis—a virtually forgotten disease—has reappeared. The AIDS epidemic has claimed over 160,000 American lives. More generally, some experts contend that high levels of health care spending do *not* result in significantly better health and well-being. Although United States health care expenditures are the highest in the world—absolutely, as a proportion of GDP, and on a per capita basis— we rank eighth in world life expectancy, eleventh in maternal mortality, and twenty-second in infant mortality. The U.S. Office of Technology Assessment concludes that "the U.S. ranks low internationally on most health indicators."

Economic Implications of Rising Costs

There are many implications of rising health care expenditures and costs. Briefly, here are some of the more obvious effects.

1   Reduced Access   Because of rising health care costs, fewer employers offer health insurance to their workers. The number of uninsured is large and growing. We will consider this issue in detail momentarily.

2   Labor Market Effects   Soaring health care costs have had several adverse effects on labor markets.

Slower Wage Growth   Workers' total compensation (wages plus benefits, including health insurance paid by employers) must be in accord with their productivity (Figure 28-1). This means that with no productivity gains, compensation won't increase. It also means that rising health care costs squeeze some part of wages and nonhealth benefits out of the unchanged total compensation package. In the long run, workers bear the burden of rising health care costs (and therefore health insurance costs) in the form of slower growing wages. Although slow productivity growth has been the fundamental cause of stagnating real wages in the past decade or so, rising health insurance costs have been a contributing factor.

GLOBAL PERSPECTIVE 35-1

International comparisons of health care spending

While per capita spending on health care increases with per capita GDP, the high level of American health care expenditures does not seem justified by our income level. Furthermore, per capita health care spending in the United States is growing faster than in other nations.

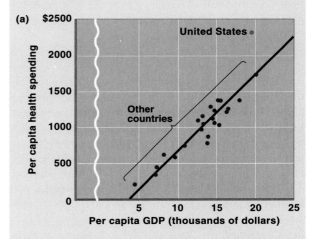

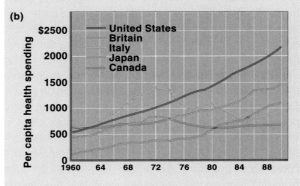

Source: George Schieber and others, "Heath Care Systems in Twenty-Four Countries," *Health Affairs*, Fall 1991, pp. 7–21; and OECD.

Reduced Mobility   If workers can move freely from lower-productivity, lower-wage jobs to higher productivity, higher-wage jobs, they benefit and so does the economy. A worker may stay in an undesirable job because a job change will mean full or partial loss of health insurance. Someone with a history of illness—

for example, prior treatment of cancer—might find it difficult or impossible to qualify for insurance on a new job. Hence, some workers suffer "job lock"— they are locked into their present jobs because health insurance is not transferable.

The shiftability of workers into and out of the labor force is also constrained by high insurance costs. To illustrate, a young parent might want to drop out of the labor force or work part-time for a few years to attend college or spend more time with preschool children. But to do so might mean loss of company-paid insurance benefits and the need to either buy a very expensive individual policy or run the risk of being uninsured.

Part-Time and Temporary Workers The high cost of employer-provided health insurance has caused some employers to restructure their work forces. Full-time workers with health insurance benefits are employed in smaller numbers in favor of uninsured part-time or temporary workers. Similarly, a large, prosperous employer with a generous health care plan might reduce its health insurance costs by discharging its lower-wage workers—janitors, gardeners, and cafeteria staff—and have these tasks performed by independent contractors.

3 Government Budgets The budgetary problems of Federal, state, and local governments are worsened by spiraling health care expenditures. Spending for health care through Medicare and Medicaid is by far the fastest-growing component of the Federal budget. Assuming constant taxes, accommodation of these expenditure increases means that the Federal government must reduce other budget components such as national defense, education, and environmental programs, or, alternatively, it must sacrifice efforts to contain budget deficits and accept the consequent growth of the public debt. States are also finding it increasingly difficult to maintain the rapidly rising costs of their share of the Medicaid bill. Because most states are required by law to balance their budgets each year, growing Medicaid expenditures have spawned higher state tax rates and searches for new sources of tax revenue. Many states have been forced to reduce spending on nonhealth programs such as infrastructure, welfare, and education. The financial problems currently faced by many state universities and colleges are partly a reflection of burgeoning state Medicaid costs. Local governments face similar budget strains in trying to finance public health services, hospitals, and clinics.

The Basic Problem

Growing expenditures in the automobile or computer industries would be a sign of prosperity, not a cause for alarm. But to most informed observers rising health care expenditures tell a different story.

The production of health care requires scarce resources such as capital in the form of hospitals and diagnostic equipment and highly skilled labor such as physicians, technicians, and nurses. Spiraling health care costs have led most experts to the conclusion that *our aggregate consumption of health care is so great that at the margin it is worth less than the alternative goods and services these resources could otherwise have produced.* In other words, we are consuming health care beyond the point where the marginal utility or benefits we get from it equal the marginal costs of producing it. This *overallocation* of resources to health care imposes a real economic loss upon society. Resources wasted on the overuse of the health care system could be used more productively to support education, improve the environment, construct new housing and roads, or for the "reindustrialization" of various sectors of the economy. The overallocation of resources to health care is the result of a number of factors, including the way health care is financed, the asymmetry of information between consumer and provider, and the interaction of health care insurance with technological progress in the industry.

LIMITED ACCESS: THE UNINSURED

Even though there is a societal overallocation of resources to health care, not all Americans have access to it. In 1993 almost 40 million Americans—about 15 percent of the total population—had no health insurance for the entire year. As health care costs and therefore health insurance premiums continue to rise, we can expect the number of uninsured to also grow.

Who are the medically uninsured? As incomes rise, so does the probability of being insured. Thus it is no surprise that the uninsured are concentrated among the poor. Medicaid is designed to provide health care for the poor who are on welfare. But many poor people work at low- or minimum-wage jobs, earning "too much" to qualify for Medicaid yet not enough to afford private health insurance. Interestingly, 52 percent of the uninsured have a family head who works full time. We also find many single-parent families and black Americans to be uninsured simply because they are more likely to be poor.

Curiously, those with excellent health and those with the poorest health also tend to be uninsured. Many young people with excellent health simply choose not to buy health insurance. The chronically ill find it very difficult and too costly to obtain insurance because of the likelihood they will incur substantial future health care costs. Because private health insurance is frequently obtained through your employer, the unemployed are likely to lack insurance. When you lose your job you lose your insurance.

Workers for small firms are also less likely to enjoy health insurance. One reason is that administrative costs are high. Administrative costs for a small firm may absorb 30 to 40 percent of insurance premiums, as opposed to only 10 percent for a large firm. Furthermore, corporations can deduct their payments to health insurance, realizing substantial tax savings. Small unincorporated firms do not receive this tax break.

Low-wage workers are also less likely to be insured. Earlier we explained that in the long run the costs of health care insurance are passed on by employers to workers as lower wages. This option isn't available to employers paying the minimum wage. As health care insurance costs increase, employers cut this benefit out of the compensation package they pay their minimum and low-wage workers. As a result, these workers are typically uninsured.

Although many of the uninsured forgo health care, some do not. A few are able to pay directly or out-of-pocket. Others may wait until their illness reaches a critical stage and then go to the hospital for admittance or be treated in the emergency room. These methods of treatment are inappropriate and unnecessarily costly. It is estimated that hospitals provide over $10 billion of uncompensated health care per year. Hospitals then attempt to shift these costs to those who have insurance or who can pay out-of-pocket. *(Key Question 2)*

QUICK REVIEW 35-1

■ Health care costs in the United States have been increasing absolutely, as a percentage of domestic output, and per capita.

■ Rising health care costs have caused *a* more people to find health insurance unaffordable; *b* adverse labor market effects, including slower real wage growth, diminished worker mobility, and increased use of part-time and temporary workers; and *c* restriction of nonhealth spending by governments.

■ The basic problem with rising health care spending is that it reflects an overallocation of resources to the health care industry.

■ Approximately one-seventh of all Americans— some 40 million people—do not have health insurance.

WHY THE RAPID RISE IN COSTS?

At some risk of oversimplification, the rising prices and costs of health care services can be explained by a simple market model in which demand has been increasing relative to supply. But first let's note certain characteristics of this market.

Peculiarities of the Health Care Market

We know that purely competitive markets achieve both allocative and productive efficiency—the most desired products are produced in the least costly way. We also have found that many imperfectly competitive markets—perhaps aided in some cases by regulation or potential antitrust actions—provide outcomes generally accepted as efficient. What then are the special features of the health care market which have contributed to escalating costs?

Ethical and Equity Considerations When buying and selling decisions involve quality of human life— indeed, life or death—ethical questions inevitably intervene. While we might not consider it immoral or inequitable if a person can't buy a Buick Park Avenue or a personal computer, society does regard it to be unfair and inequitable for people to be denied access to basic health care. In general, society regards health care as an "entitlement" or a "right" and is reluctant to ration it solely by price and income.

Asymmetric Information Health care buyers typically have little or no understanding of complex diagnostic and treatment procedures, while health care sellers of those procedures—the physicians—possess detailed information. This creates the unusual situation where the doctor (supplier) as the agent of the patient (consumer) tells the patient what health care services he or she should consume.

Spillover Benefits The medical care market often generates external or spillover benefits—benefits to third parties. For example, immunization against polio, smallpox, or measles benefits the immediate purchasers. But it also benefits society because it reduces the risk that members of society will be infected by a highly contagious disease. Similarly, a healthy labor force is more productive, contributing to the general prosperity and well-being of society.

Third-Party Payments: Insurance Because about three-fourths of all health care expenses are paid through public or private insurance, health care consumers directly pay much lower out-of-pocket "prices" than otherwise. These lower prices are a distortion that results in "excess" consumption of health care services.

Increasing Demand for Health Care

With these four features in mind, let's consider some factors which have increased the demand for health care over time.

1 Rising Incomes: Role of Elasticities Health care is a normal good and therefore increases in national income have resulted in increases in the demand for health care. While there is some disagreement as to the exact *income* elasticity of demand for health care, several studies for industrially advanced countries suggest that the income elasticity coefficient is about + 1.0. This means that per capita health care spending rises approximately in proportion to increases in per capita income (Global Perspective 35-1). For example, a 3 percent increase in incomes will generate a 3 percent increase in health care expenditures.

Estimates of the *price* elasticity of demand for health care suggest it is quite inelastic, with this coefficient being as low as 0.2. This means that the quantity of health care consumed declines relatively little as price increases. For example, a 10 percent increase in price would reduce quantity demanded by only 2

percent. An important consequence is that total health care spending will increase as the price of health care rises.

The relative insensitivity of health care spending to price changes is due to four factors. First, people consider health care to be a "necessity," not a "luxury." There are few, if any, good substitutes for medical care in treating injuries, infections, and alleviating various ailments. Second, medical treatment is often provided in an emergency situation where price considerations are secondary or irrelevant. Third, most consumers prefer a long-term relationship with their doctors and therefore do not "shop around" when health care prices rise. Fourth, most patients have insurance and are therefore insulated and largely unaffected by the price of health care. If insured patients pay only, say, 20 percent of their health care expenses, they are less concerned with price increases or price differences between hospitals and between doctors than if they paid 100 percent themselves. *(Key Question 7)*

2 An Aging Population The United States population is aging. People 65 years of age and older comprised approximately 9 percent of the population in 1960 but almost 13 percent by 1994. Projections for the year 2030 indicate almost 21 percent of the population will be 65 or over.

This aging of the population affects the demand for health care because older people encounter more frequent and more prolonged spells of illness. Specifically, those 65 and older consume about three and one-half times as much health care as those between 19 and 64. In turn, people over 84 consume almost two and one-half times as much health care as those in the 65 to 69 age group. Health care expenditures are often extraordinarily high in the last year of one's life.

Looking ahead, in the early part of the next century the "baby boomers"—the 76 million people born between 1946 and 1964—will be reaching old age. We can expect this to generate a substantial boost in the demand for health care.

3 Unhealthy Lifestyles[2] Substance abuse—specifically, the problematic use of alcohol, tobacco,

---

[2]This section is based on *Substance Abuse: The Nation's Number One Health Problem,* prepared by the Institute for Health Policy, Brandeis University, for the Robert Wood Johnson Foundation, Princeton, N.J., 1993.

and illicit drugs—does great damage to health and is therefore an important component of the demand for health care services. Alcohol is a major cause of traffic accidents and liver disease. Between 25 and 40 percent of all general hospital patients are there because of complications related to alcoholism. Tobacco use markedly increases the probability of cancer, heart disease, bronchitis, and emphysema. Illicit drugs are a major contributor to violent crime and the spread of AIDS. In addition, illicit drug users make over 370,000 costly visits to hospital emergency rooms each year. Nearly 500,000 Americans die each year from alcohol, tobacco, and illicit drug use. It is estimated that the direct cost of substance abuse is $34 billion of "unnecessary" health care annually.

The good news is that in recent years cigarette smoking has declined substantially, although it has increased among young women. Also, the number of heavy drinkers has diminished somewhat, and cocaine use among casual users is down. Nevertheless, substance abuse remains an important contributor to the demand for health care. Healthier lifestyles would undoubtedly help curtail rising health care costs.

4   The Role of Doctors   Physicians may increase the demand for health care in a variety of ways.

Asymmetric Information   Because health care services are so technically complex and are infrequently purchased, the consumer is generally uninformed about purchase decisions. While you might be well informed about hamburgers or even more complex products such as personal computers, you are likely to be poorly or completely uninformed about the purpose or effectiveness of magnetic resonance imaging or endoscopy. Thus the health care market is unusual. The seller has information that is not totally understood by the buyer. This **asymmetric information** (Chapter 30)—that is, imbalance of information—results in the supplier, not the demander, deciding on the types and amounts of health care to be consumed. Health care consumers in effect delegate most of their decisions to their physicians, resulting in "supplier-induced demand."

Because (1) the prices of medical treatments or procedures are rarely discussed or publicized, and (2) doctors are paid on a **fee-for-service** basis, there is again a strong incentive to overconsume health care services. The uncomfortable fact is that health care suppliers have an economic interest in higher health care spending. More surgery is performed in the United States, where doctors are paid a fee for each operation, than in foreign countries, where doctors are paid annual salaries unrelated to the number of operations they perform. Furthermore, a recent study concludes that doctors who own x-ray or ultrasound machines do four to four and one half times as many tests as doctors who refer their patients to radiologists. More generally, studies suggest that up to one-third of common medical tests and procedures are either inappropriate or of questionable value.

This shift of consumption decisions to the seller effectively eliminates much of the power buyers might have in controlling the level and growth of health care spending.

Defensive Medicine   "Become a doctor and support a lawyer," says a bumper sticker. The number of medical malpractice lawsuits increases every year. Today, every patient represents not only a need for medical care but also a possible malpractice suit. As a result, physicians tend to practice **defensive medicine,** recommending more tests and procedures than might be warranted medically or economically, to reduce the chance of incurring a malpractice suit or as a basis for successfully defending against one.

Medical Ethics   Medical ethics may drive up the demand for health care in two ways:
1   Doctors are ethically committed to use "best practice" techniques in serving their patients. This often entails intensive use of costly medical procedures of only marginal benefit to patients.
2   Public values seem to support the medical ethic that human life should be sustained as long as possible. This makes it difficult to confront the notion that health care is provided with scarce resources and therefore must be rationed like any other good. Can society continue to provide $5000 per day intensive care to a comatose patient unlikely to be restored to reasonable health? Prevailing public priorities seem to indicate that such care should be provided and this preference bolsters demand for health care.

Role of Insurance

We noted in Figure 35-1 that three-fourths of health care costs are not direct out-of-pocket payments by health care consumers, but are paid by private health insurance companies or government through Medicare and Medicaid.

A Positive Role Individuals and families are faced with potentially devastating monetary losses from a variety of hazards. Your house might burn down; you may be in an auto accident; or you may suffer a serious illness. An insurance program is a system of protection against the huge monetary losses which result from such hazards. A number of people agree to pay certain amounts (premiums) periodically in return for the guarantee that they will be compensated if they should incur a particular hazard or misfortune. Insurance is a means by which one pays a relatively small known cost for protection against an uncertain and much larger cost. While this is the essence of the beneficial role of health insurance, we must also recognize that it contributes to rising costs and overconsumption of health care.

Moral Hazard Revisited The *moral hazard problem* (Chapter 30) is the tendency of one party to an agreement to alter her or his behavior in a way that is costly to the other party. Health care insurance can change behavior in two ways. First, some insured people might be less careful about their health, taking fewer steps to prevent accident or illness. Second, insured individuals have greater incentives to use health care more intensively than if they didn't have insurance. Let's consider both aspects of moral hazard.

1   Less Prevention Health insurance might generate increases in the demand for health care by encouraging behaviors which require more health care. Although we might expect most people with health care insurance to be as careful about their health as those without insurance, some might be more inclined to smoke, avoid exercise, and eat unhealthy foods, knowing they have insurance. Similarly, some individuals may take up skiing or rodeo bull-riding if they have insurance covering the costs of orthopedic surgeons. And, if insurance covers rehabilitation programs, some people might be more inclined to experiment with alcohol or drugs.

2   Overconsumption Insured people go to doctors more often and request more diagnostic tests and more complex treatments than if they were uninsured. This is so because, with insurance, the price or opportunity cost of consuming health care is grossly understated to the consumer. For example, many individuals with private insurance pay a fixed premium for coverage and then, aside from a modest "deductible," their health care is "free." This differs from most markets where the buyer or demander faces a price that reflects the full opportunity cost of the good or service. In most markets, price provides a direct economic incentive to restrict the products' use. But through insurance one's health care is prepaid, creating an incentive to overuse the health care system. We purchase medical services and procedures which we might forgo if we had to pay the full price out of our own pockets. Of course, the penalty for overconsuming will ultimately show up in higher insurance premiums, but these are shared by all policyholders, which reduces the cost increase for the individual health care consumer.

Also, the availability of insurance removes the consumer's *budget restraint* when he or she decides to consume health care. Recall from Chapter 21 that budget constraints limit the purchases of most products. Patients face minimal or no costs at the time they receive health care—they have little or no budget constraint when they purchase health care because insurance pays the bills. The result? Health care is "overconsumed."

Tax Subsidy Federal tax policy toward employer-financed health insurance constitutes a **tax subsidy** which strengthens the demand for health care services. The underlying rationale for this policy is that positive spillover benefits (Chapters 5 and 30) are associated with having a healthy, productive work force. Therefore, it is appropriate to make health care more widely available to workers and their families. Government does this by exempting employer-paid private health insurance from both Federal income and payroll (social security) taxation. This tax exemption makes private health care insurance more accessible to more of the population but it also contributes to greater consumption of health care. Combined with other factors, the result is an overconsumption of health care.

To illustrate: If the marginal tax rate is 28 percent, a worker can receive $1 worth of health care instead of 72 cents worth of after-tax pay. The 28-cent difference is a tax subsidy to health care. Because workers will buy more health insurance at 72 cents than at $1, the exclusion of health insurance from taxation increases expenditures on health insurance, increasing the demand for health care. One recent estimate suggests this tax subsidy costs the Federal government $65 billion per year in forgone revenue and boosts private health *insurance* spending by about one-third. Actual health *care* spending may be 10 to 20 percent higher than otherwise because of the tax subsidy.

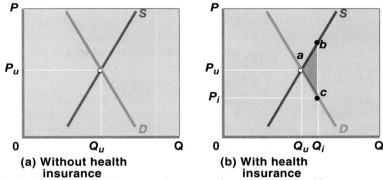

FIGURE 35-3 Insurance and the overallocation of resources to health care
Without health insurance in (a) the optimal amount of health care consumed would be Q_u. But the availability of private and public insurance in (b) reduces the direct price of health care from P_u to P_i, resulting in its overconsumption (Q_i rather than Q_u) and an overallocation of resources to the health care
industry. The efficiency loss is indicated by area abc.

Graphic Portrayal A simple demand and supply
model shows how insurance affects the health care
market. Figure 35-3a depicts a competitive market for
health care services where demand curve D shows
demand for health care services if all consumers were
uninsured and S represents the supply of health care.
At market price P_u the equilibrium quantity of health
care would be Q_u.

Recall from our theory of competitive markets
that output Q_u results in allocative efficiency which
means there is no better alternative use for the resources allocated to producing health care at that level
of output. To see what we mean by "no better use,"
we must realize that:

1 The price of each successive unit (shown by each
price along demand curve D) indicates the marginal
utility or benefit which consumers receive from that
unit.
2 The supply curve is simultaneously the marginal
cost curve (Figure 23-6). As we move up along the
supply curve, each point indicates the marginal cost
of each successive unit of health care.
3 It follows that each unit produced up to the equilibrium Q_u units entails marginal benefits which exceed marginal costs. At Q_u marginal benefits equal
marginal costs, designating allocative efficiency. No
matter what else those resources could have produced, the greatest net benefit to society is realized
by using those resources to produce Q_u units of health
care.

But allocative efficiency only occurs when we pay
in full for a product, as in our analysis of Figure

35-3a. What happens when we introduce health insurance that covers, say, one-half of all health care
costs? In Figure 35-3b, with health insurance paying
half the price, the consumer in effect is confronted
with price P_i (= $1/2\ P_u$). The health care consumer
reacts by purchasing Q_i units rather than just Q_u. This
is economically inefficient because between Q_u and
Q_i each unit's marginal cost to society exceeds its marginal benefit. Each unit of health care between Q_u and
Q_i reflects an overallocation of resources to health
care. The total efficiency or welfare loss is shown by
the area abc. Because health insurance typically covers 80, not just 50, percent of health care costs, the
welfare loss suggested by Figure 35-3b is understated. On the other hand, this loss may not be as
large as the 80 percent figure would imply because of
the positive spillovers associated with health care.[3]

Note that Figure 35-3b embodies a dilemma or
tradeoff between efficiency and equity. Our standards
of fairness or equity in the United States lead us to
believe all citizens should have access to basic health
care. That's why government created social insurance
in the form of Medicare and Medicaid. Also, the Federal government provides a "tax subsidy" to private
health insurance by exempting employer-paid plans
from income and payroll taxes. Again, this makes
health care more accessible. The problem, as Figure

[3]Technical footnote: The supply curve S is not a shortage-causing
constraint at price P_i in Figure 35-3b. Insurance reduces the direct
cost of health care to the insured so that the supply curve in effect
shifts rightward (not shown) so that it intersects demand at
point c.

35-3b shows, is that the greater the availability of insurance (and the greater the implied "subsidy" to health care providers, and the greater access to health care on equity grounds), the greater will be the over-allocation of resources to the health care industry. This overallocation would be even greater if health care were provided completely "free" under a program of national health insurance. Consumers would purchase health care so long as the marginal utility or benefit to them as individuals was positive, irrespective of the true cost to society. *(Key Question 10)*

Supply Factors in Rising Costs

The costs underlying the supply of health care have greatly increased, slowing the growth of supply.

Physician Supply Conventional wisdom has been that physician groups—for example, the American Medical Association—have purposely kept admissions to medical schools, and therefore the supply of doctors, artificially low. The alleged result is high fees to patients and exorbitant incomes for physicians. In fact, the average income of physicians was almost $177,000 in 1993, highest of all the major professions.

While there is some historical evidence supporting this view, it is now largely discredited. First, in recent decades the number of physicians per 100,000 of population has been increasing. In 1975 there were 169 physicians per 100,000 people; by 1992 there were 224.

Second, physicians' incomes may be high for reasons that have nothing to do with supply restriction. Physicians typically are highly able, highly motivated people, most of whom would have earned high incomes had they chosen other professions. Also, medical training entails four years of college, four years of medical school, an internship, and perhaps three or four years of postgraduate training for a specialty. It is not uncommon for new medical practitioners to be $50,000 or $100,000 in debt for their education, facing substantial costs in equipping an office, and working 60 or more hours per week.

Third, in comparing the economic status of professionals, it is more meaningful to compare rates of return on their educational investments than simply incomes. Recent data show that primary care physicians earn an annual rate of return on their educational investments of 16 percent over their working lives. This compares unfavorably to returns of 25 and 29 percent for lawyers and business school graduates,

respectively. The difference is largely that lawyers and business people have significantly lower school costs and spend fewer years in school, entering the labor force sooner. (Admittedly, some medical specialists experience far higher rates of return than primary-care physicians.)

Finally, some economists question whether further increases in the supply of doctors would reduce physician fees and costs. The "target income hypothesis" contends that physicians seek a certain target income and that, if the number of patients per doctor declined due to an increase in physician supply, doctors would respond by increasing fees per patient. It is relevant that hospital costs have been rising even though one-third of the nation's hospital beds are empty on any given day. It would not seem logical to advocate an increase in hospital beds to bring down these rising costs!

Slow Productivity Growth Although difficult to measure, productivity growth—which tends to reduce costs and increase supply—has allegedly been slow in the health care industry. One possible reason for this is that health care is a service and it is generally more difficult to increase productivity for services than for goods. How do you significantly increase the productivity of nursing-home employees?

Also, health care providers—physicians and hospitals—have traditionally been paid by public and private insurers on a fee-for-service basis. Because such payments guarantee providers they will always cover costs, there has been no strong incentive to reduce costs by increasing productivity.

Changes in Medical Technology Some technological advances in medicine have decreased costs. For example, the development of vaccines for polio, smallpox, and measles have greatly reduced health care expenditures for the treatment of such communicable diseases.

But a number of authorities contend that most new medical technologies—new health care "product lines"—developed since World War II have greatly increased the cost of medical care. Increasingly sophisticated body scanners have partly usurped x-ray machines. A $20 or $40 x-ray has given way to a scan costing as much as $1000 or $2500. Fearful of becoming technologically obsolete, hospitals want to offer the latest equipment and procedures. Doctors and hospital administrators both realize that to pay for such equipment it must be used extensively. Organ transplant technology has been extremely costly. Prior to the development of this technology, a person with a serious liver malfunction died. Now a liver transplant can cost $200,000 or more with subsequent medical attention and medication to prevent organ rejection costing $10,000 to $20,000 per year for the patient's life. It is estimated that the total cost for the 4000 to 4700 persons who could benefit from liver transplants would be $1 billion per year. Similarly, some 600,000 AIDS patients might benefit from the drug AZT, but the total cost would be almost $2 billion annually.[4]

One hypothesis is that the historical willingness of private and public insurance to pay for new treatments without regard to costs has provided the incentive to develop and use new technologies. Insurers in effect have encouraged the research and development (R&D) sector of the health care industry to create new technologies regardless of costs.

Furthermore, there may be a "dynamic interplay" between incentives to develop new medical technologies and the character of the health care insurance system:

> . . . it is clear that much of the growth in health care expenditures during the post-World War II period has resulted not from increased prices for existing technologies, but from the price for new technologies. Newly developed technologies have driven up both costs of care and the demand for insurance, while also expanding the range of services for which consumers demand insurance. At the same time, expanding insurance coverage, which includes more people as well as a growing array of health care inputs, has provided an increased incentive to the R&D sector to develop new technologies, and a growing incentive for . . . consumers who could benefit from particular new technologies to seek a wider definition of what would be covered by insurance.[5]

Illustration: After Medicare in 1985 agreed to pay for magnetic resonance imaging scans, sales of MRI machines rose dramatically.

Relative Importance

According to most analysts, these demand and supply factors vary significantly in the way they affect ris-

ing health care costs. In general, rising incomes, an aging population, and defensive medicine may impact costs in a relatively minor way. The Congressional Budget Office estimates that demographic changes have accounted for only about 5 percent of the increase in per capita health care spending over 1965–1990. And since the income elasticity of demand is only +1.0, the growth of personal income cannot explain much of the cost increase over the past forty years. Defensive medicine is also discounted as a major factor in rising health care costs in part because malpractice insurance premiums account for less than 1 percent of national health care spending.

Many experts feel that advances in medical technology, interacting with traditional fee-for-service health insurance (as described in the previous quotation), are the major causes of spiraling health care costs. Through technological progress, great strides have been made in the diagnosis, treatment, and prevention of illness. But the third-party (insurance) payment system provides little or no incentive to limit the development or use of these new technologies because it has no mechanism to force a balancing of costs and benefits.

One recent study suggests that an aging population, rising incomes, increased insurance coverage, and low productivity growth in the health care industry account for between one-third and one-half of the growth of health care expenditures. The rest of the increase appears to be the result of advances in medical technology.

[4]The transplant and AIDS data are cited in Burton A. Weisbrod, "The Health Care Quadrilemma: An Essay on Technological Change, Insurance, Quality of Care, and Cost Containment," *Journal of Economic Literature,* June 1991, pp. 532, 540.

[5]Ibid., pp. 546–547.

QUICK REVIEW 35-2

■ Characteristics of the health care market are **a** the widespread view of health care as a "right"; **b** asymmetric information between consumers and suppliers; **c** the presence of spillover benefits; and **d** payment by insurance.

■ The demand for health care has increased for many reasons, including rising incomes, an aging population, unhealthy lifestyles, asymmetric information between patients and doctors, defensive medicine, and a fee-for-service payment system based on health insurance.

■ The costs of health care have increased (that is, supply has grown slowly) primarily because of **a** relatively slow productivity growth in the health care industry, and **b** improvements in health care technologies.

REFORMING THE HEALTH CARE SYSTEM

What, if anything, can be done to increase access to the health care system? And how might health care costs be contained? Reforming our health care system to achieve these two goals will be difficult. First, there is an inherent tradeoff between the two objectives: Greater access to the system will mean rising costs. Second, health care reform is complex because expectations (for example, access to the "best" medical care), tradition (the "right" to choose one's doctor), and the goals of self-interest groups (private insurers, drug companies, physicians, and hospitals) all come into play.

This latter point may be especially significant. The rearrangement of costs and benefits in an industry which accounts for almost one-seventh of the total economy will not be accepted passively by the numerous affected interest groups. Physicians, hospitals, health insurers, and drug companies seek to prevent price controls on their services and products. Older people—represented by the American Association of Retired Persons—want government to pay a larger portion of long-term (nursing home) health care. Health insurance companies hope their business will not be curtailed by reforms. Labor unions are advocating a generous basic-benefits package, while opposing taxation of employer-financed health insurance. Psychiatrists, physical therapists, and chiropractors want their services included in any new proposal. Trial lawyers want existing malpractice laws left alone. Small businesses strongly oppose any mandate that all companies must provide health insurance for their employees. The liquor and tobacco industries are fearful that additional "sin" taxes will be levied upon them to help finance any reform proposal.

Achieving Universal Access

How can health care—or, more specifically, health care insurance—be made available to all American citizens? Let's briefly consider three proposals.

"Play or Pay" Because much of the nation's health insurance is paid by employers, one way is to expand that coverage using a **play or pay** approach. *All* employers would be required to either provide a basic health insurance program for their workers and their dependents ("play") or pay a special payroll tax to finance health insurance for uninsured workers

("pay"). People not insured because they are not in the labor force would be covered by some form of publicly sponsored health care plan.

Such proposals are likely to affect the labor market, leading to lower real wages, on the one hand, but greater mobility on the other, because workers would not lose health benefits by changing jobs. Also, unemployment might increase in firms currently paying wages at or near the minimum wage.

Tax Credits and Vouchers Another approach, using **tax credits and vouchers,** would provide health insurance to the poor. A tax credit would be provided for low-income individuals and families—for example, $1500 for a single person and $4000 for a family of four—for purchasing health insurance. The size of the tax credit would diminish as the recipient's income rises. Those whose incomes are so low as to be exempt from the income tax would be issued a voucher to purchase health insurance. This proposal is essentially a tax subsidy designed to make insurance more affordable to low-income people.

National Health Insurance (NHI) The most far-reaching and controversial proposal is to establish a system of **national health insurance** along the lines of the present Canadian system. The Federal government would provide a basic package of health care to every citizen at no direct charge or at a low-cost-sharing level. The system would be financed out of tax revenues rather than premiums.

NHI is *not* the same as socialized medicine. Under NHI the government would not own health care facilities such as hospitals, clinics, and nursing homes. Nor would health care practitioners—doctors, nurses, and technicians—be government employees. Under NHI government would simply sponsor and finance basic health care for all citizens. Although the role of private health insurers would be constrained under NHI, they could provide health insurance for any medical procedures not covered in the basic NHI health care package.

Arguments for NHI

1   It is the simplest and most direct way of providing universal access to health care.
2   It allows patients to choose their own physicians.
3   It would reduce administrative costs. The present system, it is argued, is administratively chaotic and expensive because 1500 private health care insurers are involved, each with its own procedures and claim

forms. Administration costs in the Canadian system are less than 5 percent of total health care costs compared with almost 17 percent in the United States.

4 It separates health care availability from employment and therefore would increase labor mobility and would abate the trend to part-time and temporary workers.

5 It would make it possible for government to use its single-insurer market power to contain costs. Government can apply its bargaining power to negotiate or establish fees for various medical procedures and thus control physician and hospital costs. Hospitals would operate on budgets negotiated with the government.

Arguments Against NHI

1 Government-determined price ceilings on physicians' services are not likely to control costs. Doctors can protect their incomes from fixed fees by manipulating the quantity of care they provide a patient. Suppose the maximum fee for an office visit is $25. Doctors could spread a given number of diagnostic tests over three or four office visits, although the tests could be done in one visit. Or a doctor might require an office visit to explain test results instead of phoning the patient. Similar arguments apply to government regulation of hospital charges.

2 In the Canadian system patients may have long waits for certain diagnostic procedures and surgeries. This is the result of the Canadian government's efforts to control expenditures by restricting hospital budgets for capital spending. To illustrate, while the United States has some 2000 hospitals with magnetic resonance imaging machines, Canada has only fifteen and a waiting list to use them. NHI might strongly conflict with American expectations of medical care "on demand."

3 The Federal government does not have a very good record of containing costs. Despite its potential bargaining power, the Department of Defense, for example, has a long history of cost overruns and mismanagement. And we have seen that costs have spiraled upward under the government's Medicare and Medicaid programs. Also recall (Figure 35-3b) that insurance is a critical factor in the overconsumption of health care. Under NHI a completely "free" basic health care package would prompt consumers to "purchase" health care so long as marginal benefits were positive, regardless of the true cost to society.

4 Subtle and perhaps undesirable redistributional effects would result under NHI. Under private health insurance, a given health care insurance package costs the same regardless of the insured's income. This makes the insurance cost resemble a regressive tax, since low-income workers pay a larger percentage of their income for the insurance than do high-income insurees. If NHI were financed out of personal income tax revenues, this financing would be progressive. Under NHI those with low incomes would receive health insurance and pay little or none of the cost. While some might view this as desirable, others feel that income redistribution in the United States has been overdone and that further redistribution through NHI would be unfair. Depending on the type of tax and its size, employers and workers in industries such as automobiles and steel might receive windfalls in the form of higher profits and wages when their health insurance programs would be replaced by NHI. Employers and workers in small retail establishments and fast-food restaurants, where health insurance is typically absent, might not realize such gains.

Cost Containment: Altering Incentives

Can we control the growth of health care costs by reducing incentives to overconsume health care?

Deductibles, Copayments, and PPOs Insurance companies have reacted to rising health care costs by imposing sizable **deductibles** and **copayments** on those they insure. Instead of covering all of an insuree's medical costs, a policy might now specify that the insuree pay the first $250 or $500 of each year's health care costs (the deductible) and 15 or 20 percent of all additional costs (the copayment). The deductible and copayment are intended to alleviate the overuse problem by generating a direct opportunity cost to the user of health care. The deductible has the added advantage of reducing the administrative costs of insurance companies in processing many small claims.

Some insurance companies have teamed with hospitals and doctors to provide discounts on their services. Policy holders receive a list of cooperating hospitals and doctors—collectively called a **preferred provider organization** (PPO)—and are given, say, 80 to 100 percent reimbursement of health care costs when treated by PPO physicians and hospitals. The insurance company reimburses only 60 to 70 percent if a patient chooses a doctor or hospital outside the PPO.

LAST WORD

HEALTH CARE REFORM: PHYSICIANS VERSUS ECONOMISTS

Economists protest "blank-check medicine"; physicians argue that economists know prices but not values.

Tensions are surfacing between doctors and economists, two groups of expert witnesses who will be providing advice to Congress in coming months as the battle over health care reform heats up.

The advice from both groups: Beware what the other side is saying.

"Physicians sometimes talk as if money grew on trees," complains Uwe Reinhardt, a health economist at Princeton University.

"Economists can't have the last word," said Dr. Arnold Relman, a professor of Medicine at Harvard and former editor of the *New England Journal of Medicine.* "They have a benighted and constricted view. They know the price of most things but they don't know the value of most things," said Relman.

To the doctors, it comes down to a simple question: Whom do you trust when you need your appendix out? The man in the surgeon's mask or the man with the green eyeshade?

To the economists, there are no simple questions when billions of dollars of other people's money are involved, and certainly no right of doctors to practice blank-check medicine.

Doctors see economists as bloodless, unfeeling number crunchers meddling in medicine without a license and oblivious to the best interests of individual patients.

Economists believe many doctors worry more

about protecting their own incomes and their clinical autonomy—the freedom to use whatever tests and procedures they deem fit—and ignore the legitimate interests of the taxpaying public.

Each group believes the other has had too much influence in the debate over health care reform.

To Henry Aaron, an economist at the Brookings Institution who specializes in health issues, the reasons for the conflict between doctors and economists are obvious.

"Doctors think they know what is going on inside hospitals and physicians offices—and they do," Aaron said. They think economists don't—and most do not. Economists think doctors can't think analytically and most don't. When doctors pronounce sagely on matters of economics they sound foolish, just as economists sound foolish when they speak on what doctors should do.

Health Maintenance Organizations (HMOs)

About 40 million Americans now receive their medical care from some 600 **health maintenance organizations.** HMOs are organizations which contract with employers, insurance companies, labor unions, or governmental units to provide medical care for the workers in their organizations.

HMOs alter the traditional fee-for-service payment system, offering prepaid health plans financed by fixed monthly premiums from their members. Because HMOs can lose money if they provide "too much" care, they have an incentive to hold down costs by controlling the use of tests and treatments whose costs might exceed their benefits. HMOs are considered "managed care" systems because utilization and spending are "managed" or controlled by close monitoring of physician and provider behavior to eliminate unnecessary diagnostic tests and remedial treatments. HMO doctors might not order a CAT scan because they are monitored and often part of an organization with a fixed budget, while a fee-for-service physician would face little or no control and have a monetary incentive to do it. The meeting of cost-control goals often results in an "incentive pool" of funds which is shared by doctors and hospitals participating in the HMO.

The advantage to consumers is that HMOs provide health care at lower costs than traditional private

Aaron said, "This should all be motivation for collaboration rather than backbiting."

But when economist Reinhardt suggested that smokers are probably lowering heath costs because they die so much earlier than other people, his point was brushed aside by Dr. J. Michael McGinnis, assistant secretary for health promotion and disease prevention in the Department of Health and Human Services.

"Economists argue the wrong way," sniffed McGinnis. "To an economist the only cheap person is a dead person."

Reinhardt believes there is a major cultural clash between economists and doctors that is most apparent when they discuss costs and benefits.

"Every economist worth the name would argue that an efficient health system is one that would ration health care pervasively—and systematically withhold from patients procedures that are marginally beneficial, like mammograms for 40-year-old women," Reinhardt said.

"Doctors consider that outrageous," he said. Doctors believe they must practice "top-of-the-curve medicine, applying any procedure that in a statistical sense has any benefit at all, no matter how small," Reinhardt said.

Doctors working in their own environment may argue that their patients are the most important consideration, while the economist looks at the bigger environment and asks how society as a whole is using its limited resources, said Jeffrey Rubin, a professor of economics at Rutgers University.

"If you are spending 'X' amount of dollars on medical care, you are spending fewer dollars on some-thing else which could also have a social good of equal or greater value, such as programs like better housing, pollution control and nutrition, that also effect public health," Rubin said.

Dr. Edmund Pellegrino, an expert on medical ethics and chief of general internal medicine at the Georgetown University Medical Center, is the kind of doctor who believes a physician "owes primary fidelity to the patient and not to others even if those others have some legitimate interests in the use of resources."

Pellegrino fears that doctors have been "discredited" in the debate over reform, partly because they have failed to emphasize the "primacy" of the needs of the patient.

"We have unfortunately argued about the limitation on the physician's autonomy as if it was the first order," Pellegrino said. "Physician autonomy ought not to be limited. Why? Because to limit that autonomy is to limit discretionary space—discretionary space which is necessary in the care of the multiple variations and nuances that go into the individual human predicament of illness."

While economists may not always agree with doctors about the priority of medical care, Pellegrino said, their viewpoint tends to change when they themselves are sick or injured.

"It's a very different thing to be in the horizontal position than in the vertical position," Pellegrino said. "The horizontal economist has a very different order of priorities than the vertical economist."

Source: Miles Benson, "Doctors, Economists, Tangle over Health Care Reform," *Seattle Times,* January 11, 1994, p. 13. Reprinted by permission of Newhouse News Service.

insurance. The disadvantages are that patients usually forgo the "right" to choose their doctor and sometimes have to wait to have certain tests and procedures performed.

Medicare and DRG   In 1983 the Federal government altered the way it made payments for hospital services received by Medicare patients. Rather than simply pay for all the costs of what a physician or hospital decided should be a patient's treatment and length of hospital stay, Medicare substituted payments based on a **diagnosis-related-group system** (DRG). Under DRG a hospital will receive a *fixed* payment based on one of 468 diagnostic categories (for example, an appendicitis) best characterizing a patient's condition and needs.

DRG payments obviously provide hospitals with incentives to restrict the amounts of resources used in treating each patient. Under DRG it is no surprise that the length of hospital stays has fallen sharply and more patients are treated on an outpatient basis. Critics, however, argue that this is evidence of diminished quality of medical care.

Status Report on Reform

In October 1993 the Clinton administration submitted its proposed *Health Security Act* (HSA) to Congress.

Running over 1300 pages, it was a very complex and controversial proposal. It was rejected by Congress after extended and rancorous debate.

A major feature of HSA was universal insurance coverage for a standard package of health care benefits. This was to be realized through an *employer mandate* which would have obligated all employers to provide health insurance for their workers. The unemployed and those not in the labor force were to obtain insurance through regional *health alliances* established by each state as either government agencies or nonprofit organizations.

But HSA was criticized for its complexity and costliness, because it created new bureaucracies, and on the grounds that employer mandates imposed an unwarranted intrusion on the private sector.

The importance of health care issues assures their continued attention, but the more conservative makeup of the current Congress suggests that future reform efforts are likely to be piecemeal.

CHAPTER SUMMARY

1   The health care industry comprises 9 million workers, including over 600,000 physicians, and 6500 hospitals.

2   Health care costs have been rising absolutely, as a percentage of GDP, and on a per capita basis.

3   Rising health care costs have **a** reduced access to the health care system; **b** contributed to slower real wage growth, reduced worker mobility, and expanded the employment of part-time and temporary workers; and **c** caused governments to restrict spending on nonhealth programs and to raise taxes.

4   The core of the health care problem is an overallocation of resources to the health care industry.

5   About 40 million Americans—about one-seventh of the population—do not have health insurance. The uninsured are concentrated among the poor, the chronically ill, the unemployed, the young, those employed by small firms, and low-wage workers.

6   Special characteristics of the health care market include: **a** the belief that health care is a "right"; **b** an imbalance of information between consumers and suppliers; **c** the presence of spillover benefits; and **d** the payment of most health care expenses by private or public insurance.

7   While rising incomes, an aging population, and substance abuse have all contributed to an increasing demand for health care, the role of doctors is also significant. Because of asymmetric information, physicians essentially determine the demand for their own services. The fee-for-service payment system, combined with defensive medicine to protect against malpractice suits, also increases demand for health care.

8   The moral hazard problem arising from health insurance takes two forms: **a** people may be less careful of their health, and **b** there is an incentive to overconsume health care.

9   The exemption of employer-paid health insurance from the Federal income tax subsidizes health care demand.

10   Slow productivity growth in the health care industry and, more importantly, cost-increasing advances in health care technology have restricted the supply of medical care and boosted prices.

11   Reforms designed to increase access to the health care system include: **a** "play or pay" proposals designed to increase employer-sponsored health insurance; **b** tax credits and vouchers to provide care for low-income families; and **c** national health insurance.

12   Insurance companies have introduced deductibles, copayments, and preferred provider organizations in attempting to contain health care costs.

13   Health maintenance organizations provide prepaid health services financed by monthly premiums, circumventing the traditional fee-for-service payment system.

TERMS AND CONCEPTS

asymmetric information	"play or pay"	copayments	health maintenance
fee-for-service payments	tax credits and vouchers	preferred provider	organizations (HMO)
defensive medicine	national health insurance	organization (PPO)	diagnosis-related-group
tax subsidy	deductibles		system (DRG)

QUESTIONS AND STUDY SUGGESTIONS

1 Why would increased spending on, say, automobiles or computers be regarded as economically desirable? Why, then, is there so much concern about rising expenditures in the health care industry?

2 *Key Question* *What are the "twin problems" of the health care industry? How are they related?*

3 Briefly describe the main features of Medicare and Medicaid, indicating how each is financed.

4 What are the implications of rapidly rising health care costs for **a** the growth of real wage rates, and **b** government budgets? Explain.

5 Who are the main groups without health insurance?

6 Indicate the special characteristics of the health care market and specify how each affects our health care problems.

7 *Key Question* *What are the estimates of the income and price elasticities of demand for health care? How does each relate to rising health care costs?*

8 Briefly discuss the demand and supply factors which contribute to rising health costs. Specify how **a** asymmetric information, **b** fee-for-service payments, **c** defensive medicine, and **d** medical ethics, might cause health care costs to rise.

9 "Health care expenditures have been rising principally because of the technological transformation of medical care." Do you agree?

10 *Key Question* *Using the concepts in Chapter 21's discussion of consumer behavior, explain how health care insurance results in an overallocation of resources to the health care industry. Use a demand and supply diagram to specify the resulting efficiency loss.*

11 If public school expenditures had been financed the same way as health care, what do you think would have happened to public school expenditures? To technological advance in public education?

12 How is the moral hazard problem relevant to the health care market?

13 What is the rationale for exempting a firm's contribution to its workers' health insurance from income taxation? What is the impact of this exemption on allocative efficiency in the health care industry?

14 Comment on or explain:

a "To contain health care costs, it is essential to change the way doctors and hospitals are paid."

b "Providing health insurance to achieve equity goals creates a tradeoff with the efficient allocation of resources to the health care industry."

c "Improved health habits are desirable, but would not necessarily reduce health care costs. For example, the deaths of many smokers are from sudden and lethal heart attacks and are therefore medically inexpensive."

d "Our problem is simply that the opportunity cost of health care is too low."

e "A fundamental dilemma is that, if insurance deductibles are high enough to blunt the incentive to overconsume health care, most families will face unacceptable financial loss from illness."

f "If government were to require employer-sponsored health insurance for all workers, the likely result would be an increase in the unemployment of low-wage workers."

g "While American medicine is the best in the world, our health care delivery system is perhaps the least efficient among industrially advanced nations."

15 Briefly describe **a** "play or pay"; **b** tax credits and vouchers; and **c** national health insurance as means of increasing access to health care. What are the major criticisms of national health insurance?

16 What are **a** preferred provider organizations and **b** health maintenance organizations? Explain how each is designed to alleviate the overconsumption of health care.

17 (Last Word) What is the basic source of disagreement between economists and physicians regarding health care provision?

LABOR-MARKET ISSUES: UNIONISM, DISCRIMINATION, AND IMMIGRATION[1]

In this chapter we examine three labor market issues: unionism, discrimination, and immigration.

1 The first section consists of a detailed look at organized labor, collective bargaining, and the economic effects of unionism. What are the reasons for the historical growth and the recent decline of unionism? What impact do unions have on wages, efficiency and productivity, and the distribution of earnings?

2 We next discuss labor market discrimination, its dimensions, and its costs.

3 Finally, we consider the much publicized issue of immigration of foreign labor to the United States. How many people enter the United States legally and illegally each year? What are the economic ramifications of this inflow of people?

UNIONISM IN AMERICA

Some 17 million workers—16 percent of the employed labor force—now belong to labor unions. Statistics, however, may understate the importance of unions. The wage rates, hours, and working conditions of nonunionized firms and industries are influenced by those determined in organized industries. Unions are clearly important economic institutions of American capitalism.

As Figure 36-1 shows, the great growth of unionism occurred in the last half of the 1930s and during World War II (1939–1945). Prior to the 1930s employers and the courts were both hostile to unions. For example, employers often required **yellow-dog contracts** wherein workers were forced to agree to remain nonunion as a condition of employment. Workers often had little choice but to sign such contracts —no contract, no job. Violation of a yellow-dog contract exposed a worker to a lawsuit by his employer,

the result of which might be a court-imposed fine or even imprisonment. Furthermore, the courts readily issued **injunctions** prohibiting unions from enforcing their demands by striking, picketing, and boycotting. Stripped of these weapons, unions were relatively powerless to obtain the status and rights they sought.

AFL and "Business Unionism"

Despite this antiunion environment, a diverse group of unions gained a foothold in America. But it was not until 1886 with the creation of the **American Federation of Labor (AFL)** that the current union structure began to evolve. Under the leadership of Samuel Gompers, labor charted a conservative course which has been very influential to the present. Appropriately honored as "the father of the American labor move-

---

[1]Instructors may choose to treat the three topics in this chapter selectively.

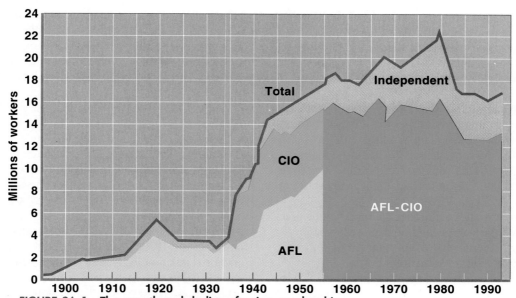

FIGURE 36-1   The growth and decline of union membership
Most of the absolute growth in organized labor has occurred since 1935. However, organized labor
has been declining as a percentage of the labor force for some time and, in recent years, the absolute
number of union members has also diminished. (U.S. Bureau of the Census and Bureau of Labor Statistics.)

ment," Gompers preached three fundamental ideas:
(1) practical business unionism, (2) political neutrality for labor, and (3) the autonomy of each trade or
craft.

1   Business Unionism   Gompers was convinced
that "safe and sane" **business unionism** was the only
course for American labor to follow. Gompers rejected
long-run idealistic schemes aimed at overthrow of the
capitalistic system. He spurned intellectuals and the-
orizers and believed unions should be concerned with
practical short-run economic objectives—higher pay,
shorter hours, and improved working conditions.

2   Political Neutrality   Gompers cautioned organized labor not to align itself with any political party.
Preoccupation with long-run political goals, he argued, causes labor to lose sight of the short-run economic objectives it should seek. Gompers admon-
ished organized labor to reward labor's friends and
punish its enemies at the polls regardless of political
affiliation.

3   Trade Autonomy   Gompers was firmly convinced that "autonomy of the trade," that is, unions or-

ganized on the basis of specific crafts, was the only
permanent foundation for the labor movement.
Unions composed of many different crafts lack the cohesiveness essential to strong, hard-hitting, business
unionism. These **craft unions** should then be affiliated in a national federation. "One union to each trade,
affiliated for one labor movement."

This philosophy—conservative business unionism, political "neutrality," and the craft principle of
union organization—was destined to dominate the
AFL and the entire labor movement for the next half-
century.

Union Growth: 1930s and 1940s

Two developments in the 1930s provided a stimulus
to union growth (Figure 36-1).

Prolabor Legislation of the 1930s   Against the
background of the depressed thirties, the Federal
government enacted two decidedly prolabor acts.

Norris-La Guardia Act of 1932   The **Norris-La
Guardia Act of 1932** did much to clear the path for

union growth by outlawing two of the more effective antiunion weapons. Specifically, the act:

1 Made it more difficult for employers to obtain injunctions against unions

2 Declared yellow-dog contracts unenforceable

Wagner Act of 1935 Three years later, in 1935, the Federal government took other positive steps to encourage union growth. The **Wagner Act of 1935** (officially the National Labor Relations Act) guaranteed the "twin rights" of labor: the right of self-organization and the right to bargain collectively with employers.

The act specified a number of "unfair labor practices" on the part of management. Specifically it:

1 Forbade employers from interfering with the right of workers to form unions

2 Prohibited antiunion discrimination by employers in hiring, firing, and promoting

3 Outlawed discrimination against any worker who files charges or gives testimony under the act

4 Obligated employers to bargain in good faith with a union duly established by their employees

The Wagner Act was "labor's Magna Charta."

A **National Labor Relations Board (NLRB)** was established by the act and charged with the authority to investigate unfair labor practices occurring under the act, to issue cease-and-desist orders in the event of violations, and to conduct worker elections in deciding which specific union, if any, workers might want to represent them.

The Wagner Act was tailored to accelerate union growth and was extremely successful in achieving this goal. The protective umbrella provided to unions by this act along with the Norris–La Guardia Act played a big role in increasing the ranks of organized labor from about 4 million in 1935 to 15 million in 1947.

The CIO and Industrial Unionism The second stimulus to union growth was a change in the organizational focus of the labor movement itself. The AFL comprised skilled crafts and ignored the hundreds of thousands of unskilled and semiskilled workers associated with emerging mass production industries. Under the leadership of John L. Lewis, the **Congress of Industrial Organizations (CIO)** was established on the principle of **industrial unionism.** Industrial unionism attempts to organize all workers—both skilled and unskilled—in a given industry or group of related industries, for example, all workers assem-

bling automobiles or making automobile components.[2] The CIO met with startling success in organizing the automobile and steel industries in the 1930s. By 1940 total union membership was approximately 9 million workers, up from about 3.5 million in 1930. *(Key Question 1)*

Curbing Union Power

As unions gathered strength—both numerical and financial—it became increasingly evident they could no longer be regarded as the underdog in negotiations with management. Just as the growing power of business monopolies brought a clamor for public control in the 1870s and 1880s, the upsurge of union power in the 1930s and 1940s brought a similar outcry for regulation. Aggravated by a series of postwar strikes which were perceived as fueling inflation, government moved to contain union power.

Taft-Hartley Act of 1947 This detailed piece of legislation (1) outlawed certain "unfair practices" by unions; (2) limited union status and security; and (3) provided for the handling of strikes imperiling the health and safety of the nation.

1 Unfair Union Practices The unfair union practices, which constitute some of the most controversial sections of the act, are: (*a*) Unions are prohibited from coercing employees to become union members. (*b*) **Jurisdictional strikes** (disputes between unions over the question of which has the authority to perform a specific job) are forbidden, as are **secondary boycotts** (refusing to buy or handle products produced by another union or group of workers) and certain **sympathy strikes** (strikes designed to assist some other union in gaining employer recognition or some other objective). (*c*) Unions are prohibited from charging excessive or discriminatory initiation fees or dues. (*d*) **Featherbedding,** a form of extortion where the union or its members receive payment for work not actually performed, is outlawed. (*e*) Unions cannot refuse to bargain in good faith with management.

2 Union Security Unions might enjoy differing degrees of recognition from management. Listed in or-

---

[2]Figures 28-6 and 28-7 compare the techniques employed by craft and industrial unions in attempting to raise wages.

der of the union's preference are (1) the closed shop, (2) the union shop, and (3) the open shop.

The closed shop would afford the greatest security to a union. Under a **closed shop** a worker must be a member of the union before being hired. A **union shop** permits the employer to hire nonunion workers but provides that these workers must join the union in a specified period—say, thirty days—or relinquish their jobs. Under the **open shop,** management may hire union or nonunion workers. Those who are nonunion are not obligated to join the union; they may continue on their jobs indefinitely as nonunion workers.

The Taft-Hartley Act outlawed the closed shop for workers engaged in interstate commerce and allows the states to ban the union shop by enacting so-called **right-to-work laws.** Some twenty states now have such laws which make compulsory union membership, and therefore the union shop, illegal. The status, security, and power of unions were curtailed by Taft-Hartley.

3   "Health and Safety" Strikes   The Taft-Hartley Act outlines a procedure for avoiding strikes which might disrupt the entire economy and imperil the health or safety of the nation, for example, a nationwide strike of port workers. According to this procedure, the President may obtain an injunction to delay such strikes for an 80-day "cooling off" period. Within this period striking workers are polled by the NLRB on the acceptability of the last offer of the employer. If the last offer is rejected, the union can then strike. The government's only recourse—one of questionable legality—is seizure of the industry.

Landrum-Griffin Act of 1959   Government regulation of the internal processes of labor unions was the focus of the **Landrum-Griffin Act of 1959.** The act regulates union elections by requiring regularly scheduled elections of officers and the use of secret ballots; restrictions are placed on ex-convicts and Communists in holding union offices. Furthermore, union officials are now held strictly accountable for union funds and property. The act is also aimed at preventing autocratic union leaders from infringing on the individual worker's rights to attend and participate in union meetings, to vote in union proceedings, and to nominate union officers. In addition, the act permits a worker to sue the union if it denies him or her these rights.

UNIONISM'S DECLINE

In 1955 unity was formally reestablished in the American labor movement with the merger of the AFL and CIO. This unification was prompted by legislative setbacks in the form of Taft-Hartley and Landrum-Griffin, but more specifically by the slowing of membership growth.

But despite the AFL and CIO merger, union membership has failed to keep pace with the growth of the labor force. While 25 percent of the labor force was organized in the mid-1950s, currently only some 16 percent are members. Indeed, in recent years the absolute number of union members has declined significantly. Over 22 million workers were unionized in 1980, falling to only about 17 million in 1993.

Let's consider two possible explanations for this drop.

Structural Changes   The **structural-change hypothesis** is that structural changes unfavorable to the expansion of union membership have occurred both in our economy and in the labor force.

1   Consumer demand and therefore employment patterns have shifted away from traditional union strongholds. Generally, the industry-mix of domestic output has been shifting away from manufactured goods (where unions have been strong) to services (where unions have been weak). This change in industry-mix may be reinforced by increased competition from imports in highly unionized sectors such as automobiles and steel. Growing import competition in these industries has curtailed domestic employment and therefore union membership.

2   An unusually large proportion of the increase in employment in recent years has been concentrated among women, youths, and part-time workers, groups allegedly difficult to organize because of their less firm attachment to the labor force.

3   Spurred by the soaring energy costs of the 1970s, the long-run trend for industry to shift from the Northeast and Midwest where unionism is "a way of life" to "hard to organize" areas of the South and Southwest may have impeded expansion of union membership.

4   An ironic possibility is that the relative decline of unionism may in part reflect the success unions have had in gaining a sizable wage advantage over nonunion workers in the United States and abroad. Confronted with high union wages, we would expect union employers to substitute machinery for workers, subcon-

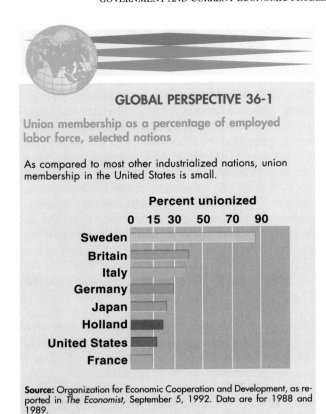

Percent unionized

Sweden
Britain
Italy
Germany
Japan
Holland
United States
France

Source: Organization for Economic Cooperation and Development, as reported in *The Economist*, September 5, 1992. Data are for 1988 and 1989.

tract more work to nonunion suppliers, open nonunion plants in less industrialized areas, or have components produced in low-wage nations. These actions reduce the growth of employment opportunities in the union sector compared to the nonunion sector. Perhaps more important, we would also expect output and employment in low-cost nonunion firms and industries to increase at the expense of output and employment in higher-cost union firms and industries. Union success in raising wages may have changed the composition of industry to the disadvantage of union employment and membership.

Managerial-Opposition Hypothesis Another view is that intensified **managerial opposition** to unions has deterred union growth. It is argued that the wage advantage which union workers enjoy in comparison to nonunion workers causes union firms to be less profitable than nonunion firms. The managements of unionized firms have therefore become more aggressive in their opposition to unions. One managerial strategy has been to employ labor-management consultants who specialize in mounting

aggressive antiunion drives to dissuade workers from unionizing or, alternatively, to persuade union workers to decertify their union. Finally, confronted with strikes by union workers, management has increasingly hired *permanent strikebreakers*. These nonunion workers later vote to decertify the union.

It is also alleged there has been a sharp increase in the use of illegal antiunion tactics. In particular, it has become increasingly common to identify and dismiss leading prounion workers even though this is prohibited by the Wagner Act.

COLLECTIVE BARGAINING

Despite the decline of unionism, collective bargaining remains an important feature of labor-management relations. Nearly 1900 major collective bargaining agreements—those involving 1000 or more workers—cover 8.2 million workers in the United States. Many million other workers are covered under collective bargaining agreements in small firms.

The Bargaining Process

In bargaining the union usually assumes the initiative, presenting its demands. These take the form of specific adjustments in the current work agreement. The merits and demerits of these demands are then debated. Typically, a compromise solution is reached and written into a new work agreement. Strikes, picketing, and violence are the exception and not the rule. About 95 percent of all bargaining contracts are negotiated without resort to work stoppages. In recent years less than one-fifth of 1 percent of all working time has been lost each year from work stoppages resulting from labor-management disputes. *Labor and management display a marked capacity for compromise and agreement.* Strikes and labor-management violence are newsworthy, whereas peaceful renewal of a work agreement hardly rates a page 5 column.

The Work Agreement

Collective bargaining agreements assume many forms. Some are brief, covering two or three typewritten pages; others are highly detailed, involving 200 or 300 pages of fine print. Some agreements involve only a local union and a single plant; others set wages, hours, and working conditions for entire industries. There is no such thing as an "average" or "typical" collective bargaining agreement.

At the risk of oversimplification, collective bargaining agreements usually cover four basic areas: (1) the degree of recognition and status accorded the union and the prerogatives of management, (2) wages and hours, (3) seniority and job opportunities, and (4) a procedure for settling grievances.

Union Status and Managerial Prerogatives

Because the closed shop was effectively outlawed by the Taft-Hartley Act, unions prefer the security and status associated with a union shop to an open shop.

The other side of the union-status coin is the issue of *managerial prerogatives*. Most work agreements contain clauses outlining certain decisions which are to be made solely by management. These managerial prerogatives usually cover such matters as size and location of plants, products to be manufactured, types of equipment and materials used in production, and production scheduling. Frequently the hiring, transfer, discipline, discharge, and promotion of workers are decisions made solely by management but are subject to the principle of seniority and to challenge by the union through the grievance procedure.

Wages and Hours

The focal point of any bargaining agreement is wages and hours. Both labor and management tend to be highly pragmatic and opportunistic in wage bargaining. The criteria, or "talking points" most frequently invoked by labor in demanding (and by management in resisting) wage boosts are (1) "what others are getting," (2) ability to pay, (3) cost of living, and (4) productivity. If a given firm's wage rates are below those of comparable firms, the union is likely to stress that wages should be increased to bring them into line with what workers in other firms are getting. Similarly, if the firm has had a very profitable year, the union is likely to demand high wages on the ground that the company is able to grant such increments. Unions have often achieved success in tying wages to the cost of living. About 28 percent of all union workers are covered by some kind of *cost-of-living adjustment* (COLA). Finally, unions bargain for their "fair share" of the additional revenues associated with increases in productivity.

Hours of work, overtime pay, holiday and vacation provisions, and **fringe benefits**—health plans and pension benefits—are other "economic" issues which must be addressed in the bargaining process.

Seniority and the Control of Job Opportunities

The uncertainty of employment in a market economy, coupled with the fear of antiunion discrimination on the part of employers, have made workers and their unions "job-conscious." The explicit and detailed provisions covering job opportunities which most work agreements contain reflect this concern. Unions stress **seniority** as the basis for worker promotion and for layoff and recall. The worker with the longest continuous service has first chance at relevant promotions, is last to be laid off, and first to be recalled from a layoff.

In recent years unions have become increasingly sensitive to losing domestic jobs to overseas workers. Unions sometimes seek restrictions on a firm's ability to import product components from abroad or to relocate production facilities overseas.

Grievance Procedure

Even the most detailed and comprehensive work agreement cannot anticipate all the issues and problems which might occur during its life. What if workers show up for work on a Monday morning to find that for some reason—say, a mechanical failure—the plant is closed down? Should they be given "show-up" pay amounting to, say, two or four hours' pay? Or management and the union may disagree as to whether the worker with the most seniority has the ability to perform the job to which he or she wants to be promoted. Such events and disagreements cannot be anticipated by even the most detailed collective bargaining contracts and therefore must be ironed out through a *grievance procedure*. Virtually all bargaining agreements contain a grievance procedure to handle disputes which arise during the life of an agreement.

QUICK REVIEW 36-1

■ Prior to the 1930s, the hostility of businesses and the courts inhibited union growth.

■ In the 1930s and 1940s union membership grew rapidly due to *a* prolabor legislation (the Norris–La Guardia and Wagner Acts) and *b* the emergence of industrial unionism (the CIO).

■ The Taft-Hartley and Landrum-Griffin Acts regulated union tactics and their internal operations.

■ The decline of unionism in recent decades has been attributed to *a* changes in the structures of the economy and the labor force, and *b* growing managerial opposition to unions.

■ Collective bargaining agreements determine *a* union status and managerial prerogatives, *b* wages and hours, *c* control of job opportunities, and *d* the resolution of grievances.

Given the historical and legislative background of the labor movement and some understanding of collective bargaining, let's now consider the economic implications of unions.

ECONOMIC EFFECTS OF UNIONS

Are the economic effects of labor unions positive or negative? We will respond to this issue by examining several questions: Do unions raise wages? Do they increase or diminish economic efficiency? Do they make the distribution of earnings more or less equal? You should be forewarned there is considerable uncertainty and debate regarding the answers to these questions.

The Union Wage Advantage

The three union models of Chapter 28 (see Figures 28-5, 28-6, and 28-7 and the accompanying discussions) all imply that unions have the capacity to raise wages. Has unionization caused higher wage rates?

Empirical research overwhelmingly suggests that *unions do raise the wages of their members relative to comparable nonunion workers,* although the size of the union wage advantage varies according to occupation, industry, race, and gender. The consensus estimate is that the overall union wage advantage is about 15 percent.

This estimate of the union wage advantage tends to be an understatement because union workers enjoy substantially larger *fringe benefits* than nonunion workers. Union workers are more likely to have private pensions, medical and dental insurance, and paid vacations and sick leaves than nonunion workers. Where such benefits are available to both union and nonunion workers, their magnitude is greater for union workers. Thus the total compensation (wage rates plus fringe benefits) advantage of union workers is greater than the previously indicated 15 percent.

Economists also generally agree that *unions have probably had little or no impact on the average level of real wages received by labor—both organized and unorganized—taken as a whole.* At first, these two conclusions—that unions gain a wage advantage but do not affect the average level of real wages—may seem inconsistent. But they need not be if the wage gains of organized workers are at the expense of unorganized workers. As we will see (Figure 36-2), higher wages in unionized labor markets may cause employers to move back up their labor demand curves

and hire fewer workers. These unemployed workers may seek employment in nonunion labor markets. The resulting increase in the supply of labor will depress wage rates in these nonunion markets. The net result may be no change in the average level of wages.

The tight relationship between productivity and the average level of real wages shown in Figure 28-1 correctly suggests that unions have little power to raise real wage rates for labor as a whole. But Figure 28-1 is an average relationship and therefore compatible with certain groups of (union) workers getting higher relative wages if other (nonunion) workers are simultaneously getting lower real wages.

Efficiency and Productivity

Are unions a positive or negative force insofar as economic efficiency and productivity are concerned? While there is much disagreement as to the efficiency aspects of unionism, let's consider some of the ways unions might affect efficiency both negatively and positively. We will consider the negative view first.

Negative View There are three means by which unions might exert a negative impact on efficiency.

1 Featherbedding and Work Rules Some unions have undoubtedly diminished productivity growth by engaging in "make-work" or "featherbedding" practices and resisting the introduction of output-increasing machinery and equipment. These productivity-reducing practices often arise against a backdrop of technological change. Labor and management may agree to a crew size which is reasonable and appropriate at the time the agreement is concluded. But labor-saving technology may then emerge which renders the crew too large. The union is likely to resist the potential loss of jobs. For many years the Brotherhood of Locomotive Firemen and Engineers retained a fireman on train crews, even though his function was eliminated by the shift from steam to diesel engines.

Similarly, union painters sometimes eschewed the use of spray guns and in some instances limited the width of paint brushes. In more recent years, typographer unions resisted the introduction of computers in setting type. Historically, the musicians' union insisted on oversized orchestras for musical shows and required that a union standby orchestra be paid by employers using nonunion orchestras.

More generally, one can argue that unions are responsible for the establishment of work rules and practices which impede efficient production. For example, under seniority rules workers may be promoted in accordance with their employment tenure, rather than in terms of who can perform the available job with the greatest efficiency. Also, unions may impose jurisdictional restrictions on the kinds of jobs workers may perform. Sheet-metal workers or bricklayers may be prohibited from performing the simple carpentry work often associated with their jobs. Observance of such rules means, in this instance, that unneeded and underutilized carpenters must be available. Finally, it is often contended that unions constrain managerial prerogatives to establish work schedules, determine production targets, and to make freely the decisions contributing to productive efficiency.

2 Strikes A second way unions may adversely affect efficiency is through strikes. If union and management reach an impasse in their negotiations, a strike will result and the firm's production will cease for the strike's duration. The firm will forgo sales and profits; workers will sacrifice income.

Statistics on strike activity suggest strikes are rare and the associated aggregate economic losses are minimal. In 1993, 669 major collective bargaining agreements—those covering 1000 or more workers —were negotiated. Strikes occurred in only 35 of these instances. Furthermore, many strikes last only a few days. The average amount of work-time lost each year because of strikes is only about one-fifth of 1 percent of total work-time. This loss is the equivalent of 4 hours per worker per year, which is less than 5 minutes per worker per week!

Economic costs associated with strikes may be greater or less than suggested by the amount of work-time lost. Costs may be greater if production of non-struck firms is disrupted. An extended strike in the steel or rail transportation industries could have serious adverse repercussions for production and employment in many other industries and sectors of the economy.

On the other hand, costs may be less than implied by workdays lost by strikers as nonstruck firms increase their output to offset the loss of production by struck firms. While the output of General Motors will fall when its workers strike, car buyers may shift their demand to Ford and Chrysler which respond by increasing their employment and outputs. While GM and its employees are hurt by a strike, society as a whole may experience little or no decline in employment, real output, and income.

3 Labor Misallocation A more subtle avenue through which unions might adversely affect efficiency is the union wage advantage itself. In Figure 36-2 we have drawn (for simplicity) identical labor demand curves for unionized and nonunion sectors of the labor market for some particular kind of labor.[3] If there were no union initially, the wage rate which would result from the competitive hire of labor would be, say, W_n. Now assume a union comes into being in sector 1 and succeeds in increasing the wage rate from W_n to W_u. As a consequence, $N_1 N_2$ workers lose their jobs in the union sector. Assume they all move to nonunion sector 2 where they are employed. This increase in labor supply in the nonunion sector depresses the wage rate from W_n to W_s.

Recall that the labor demand curves reflect the marginal revenue products (MRPs) of workers or, in other words, the contributions workers make to domestic output. This means that the shaded areas $A + B + C$ in the union sector represent the *decrease* in domestic output caused by the $N_1 N_2$ employment decline in that sector. This $A + B + C$ area is the sum of the MRPs—the total contribution to domestic output—of the workers displaced by the W_n to W_u wage increase achieved by the union. The reemployment of these workers in nonunion sector 2 results in an *increase* in domestic output indicated by the shaded areas $D + E$. Because area $A + B + C$ exceeds area $D + E$, there is a net loss of domestic output. More precisely, because $A = D$ and $C = E$, the *net* loss attributable to the union wage advantage is equal to area B. Since the same amount of employed labor is now producing a smaller output, labor is being misallocated and inefficiently used.

From a slightly different perspective, *after* the shift of $N_1 N_2$ workers from the union to the nonunion sector has occurred, workers will be paid a wage rate equal to their MRPs in both sectors. But the MRPs of the union workers will be higher than the MRPs of the nonunion workers. The economy will always benefit from a larger domestic output when any given type of labor is reallocated from a low MRP use to a high MRP use. But, given the union's presence and its ability to maintain the W_u wage rate in its sector, this reallocation from sector 2 to 1 will *not* occur.

---

[3]Technical note: Our discussion assumes pure competition in both product and resource markets.

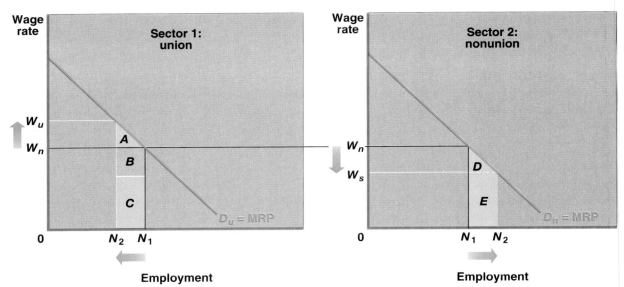

FIGURE 36-2 **The effect of the union wage advantage on the allocation of labor**
The higher wage W_u which the union achieves in sector 1 causes the displacement of $N_1 N_2$ workers. The reemployment of these workers in nonunion sector 2 reduces the wage rate there from W_n to W_s. The associated loss of output in the union sector is area $A + B + C$, while the gain in the nonunion sector is only area $D + E$. The net loss of output is equal to area B. This suggests that the union wage advantage has resulted in the misallocation of labor and a decline in economic efficiency.

Attempts to estimate the output loss due to the allocative inefficiency associated with union wage gains suggest the loss is small. One study assumed a 15 percent union wage advantage and estimated that approximately 0.14 percent—only about one-seventh of 1 percent—of the domestic output was lost! Similarly, a more recent estimate indicates that union wage gains cost the economy 0.2 to 0.4 percent of domestic product. In 1994 this cost would amount to about $13 to $27 billion or $50 to $103 per person. *(Key Question 7)*

Positive View Other economists take the position that on balance unions make a positive contribution to productivity and efficiency.

1 Managerial Performance: The Shock Effect
The *shock effect* is the idea that a wage increase imposed by a union may induce affected firms to adopt improved production and personnel methods and become more efficient. We may carry Figure 36-2's analysis of labor misallocation one step further and argue that the union wage advantage will prompt union firms to *accelerate* the substitution of capital for labor (Chapter 27) and *hasten* the search for cost-reducing (productivity-increasing) technologies. When

faced with higher production costs due to the union wage advantage, employers will be pushed to reduce costs by using more machinery and by seeking improved production techniques using less of both labor and capital per unit of output. In fact, if the product market is reasonably competitive, a unionized firm with labor costs 10 to 15 percent higher than nonunion competitors will not survive unless productivity can be raised. In short, union wage pressure may generate managerial actions which increase national productivity.

2 Reduced Worker Turnover Unions may also contribute to raising productivity within firms through their effects on worker turnover and worker security. Unions function as a **collective voice** for members in resolving disputes and improving working conditions. If a group of workers is dissatisfied with its conditions of employment, it can respond in two ways: the "exit mechanism" and the "voice mechanism."

The **exit mechanism** refers to the use of the labor market—leave or exit your present job in search of a better one—as a means of reacting to "bad" employers and "bad" working conditions.

The **voice mechanism** involves communication by workers with the employer to improve working conditions and resolve worker grievances. It might be risky for *individual* workers to express their dissatisfaction to employers because employers may retaliate by firing them as "troublemakers." But unions can provide workers with a *collective* voice to communicate problems and grievances to management and to press for their satisfactory resolution.

More specifically, unions may help reduce worker turnover in two ways.

1   Unions provide the voice mechanism as a substitute for the exit mechanism. Unions are effective in correcting job dissatisfactions which would otherwise be "resolved" by workers through the exit mechanism of changing jobs.

2   The union wage advantage is a deterrent to job changes. Higher wages make unionized firms more attractive places to work. Several studies suggest that the decline in quit rates attributable to unionism is substantial, ranging from 31 to 65 percent.

A lower quit rate increases efficiency in several ways. First, lower turnover means a more experienced and, hence, more productive labor force. Second, fewer quits reduce the firm's recruitment, screening, and hiring costs. Finally, reduced turnover makes employers more willing to invest in the training (and therefore the productivity) of their workers. If a worker quits or "exits" at the end of, say, a year's training, the employer will get no return from the higher worker productivity attributable to that training. Lower turnover increases the likelihood that employers will receive a return on any training they provide, thereby making them more willing to upgrade their labor forces.

3   *Seniority and Informal Training*   Much productivity-increasing training is transmitted informally. More-skilled workers may explain their functions to less-skilled workers on the job, during lunch, or during a coffee break. However, a more-skilled senior worker may want to conceal his or her knowledge from less-skilled junior workers *if* the latter can become competitive for the former's job. Because of union insistence on the primacy of seniority in such matters as promotion and layoff, worker security is enhanced. Given this security, senior workers will be more willing to pass on their job knowledge and skills to new or subordinate workers. This informal training enhances the quality and productivity of the firm's work force.

Mixed Research Findings   Many studies have measured the impact of unionization on productivity.

These studies attempt to control for differences in labor quality, the amount of capital equipment used per worker, and other factors aside from unionization which might contribute to productivity differences. Unfortunately, evidence from these studies is inconclusive. For every study which finds a positive union effect on productivity, another study using different methodology or data concludes that there is a negative effect. Hence, at present there is no generally accepted conclusion regarding the overall impact of unions on labor productivity.

Distribution of Earnings

Labor unions envision themselves as institutions which enhance economic equality. Do unions reduce the inequality with which earnings are distributed? The most convincing evidence suggests they do.

Increasing Inequality   Some economists employ Figure 36-2's analysis of labor misallocation to conclude that unions increase earnings inequality. They contend that, in the absence of the union, competition would bring wages into equality at W_n in these two sectors or submarkets. But the higher union wage realized in sector 1 displaces workers who seek reemployment in the nonunion sector. In so doing they depress nonunion wages. Instead of wage equality at W_n, we have higher wage rates of W_u for union workers and lower wages of W_s for nonunion workers. The impact of the union is to increase earnings inequality. Furthermore, the fact that unionization is more extensive among the more highly-skilled, higher-paid blue-collar workers than among less-skilled, lower-paid blue-collar workers also suggests that the obtaining of a wage advantage by unions increases dispersion of earnings.

Promoting Equality   There are other aspects of union wage policies which suggest that unionism promotes greater, not less, equality in the distribution of earnings.

1   *Uniform Wages within Firms*   In the absence of unions employers are apt to pay different wages to individual workers on the same job. These wage differences are based on perceived differences in job performance, length of job tenure, and, perhaps, favoritism. Unions traditionally seek uniform wage rates for all workers performing a particular job. In short, while nonunion firms tend to assign wage rates to *individual workers,* unions—in the interest of worker allegiance and solidarity—seek to assign wage rate to *jobs*. To the extent that unions are successful, wage and earnings differentials based on supervisory judgments of individual worker performance are eliminated. A side effect of this standard-wage policy is that wage discrimination against blacks, other minorities, and women is likely to be less when a union is present.

2 Uniform Wages among Firms In addition to seeking standard wage rates for given occupational classes *within* firms, unions also seek standard wage rates *among* firms. The rationale is that the existence of substantial wage differences among competing firms may undermine the ability of unions to sustain and enhance wage advantages. For example, if one firm in a four-firm oligopoly is allowed to pay significantly lower wages to its union workers, the union is likely to find it difficult to maintain the union wage advantage in the other three firms. To avoid this kind of problem unions seek to "take wages out of competition" by standardizing wage rates among firms, thereby reducing the degree of wage dispersion.

Net Effect What is the *net* effect of unionism on the distribution of earnings? Although the issue remains controversial, one authoritative study concludes that the wage effects indicated in Figure 36-2 *increase* earnings inequality by about 1 percent, but the standardization of wage rates within and among firms *decreases* inequality by about 4 percent. The net result is a 3 percent decline in earnings inequality due to unionism. Because only a small proportion of the labor force is unionized, this 3 percent reduction in inequality is substantial.

QUICK REVIEW 36-2

■ Union workers receive average wage rates 15 percent higher than comparable nonunion workers.

■ Union work rules, strikes, and the misallocation of labor associated with the union wage advantage are ways unions may reduce efficiency.

■ Unions may enhance productivity through the shock effect, by reducing worker turnover, and by providing the worker security prerequisite to informal on-the-job training.

■ On balance, unions probably reduce wage inequality by achieving wage uniformity within and among firms.

With this survey of unionism and collective bargaining complete, we now consider two additional factors affecting American labor markets—discrimination and immigration.

DISCRIMINATION

In Chapter 34 we noted that blacks, Hispanics, and women bear a disproportionately large burden of poverty. Their low incomes are a consequence of the operation of the labor market. So we must consider the labor market aspects of discrimination.

Economic discrimination occurs when female or minority workers, who have the same abilities, education, training, and experience as white male workers, are accorded inferior treatment with respect to hiring, occupational access, promotion, or wage rate. Discrimination also occurs when females or minorities are denied access to education and training. Table 36-1 provides evidence suggesting the presence of racial discrimination. Similar data imply discrimination on the basis of gender. For example, the weekly earnings of full-time female workers is only about 75 percent that of males.

Dimensions of Discrimination

As Table 36-1 and our definition both suggest, discrimination may take several forms. Our discussion is in terms of racial and gender discrimination, but these remarks also generally apply to discrimination based on age, religion, or ethnic background.

1 Wage discrimination occurs when black and other minority workers are paid less than whites for doing the same work. This kind of discrimination is declining because of its explicitness and the fact that it clearly violates Federal law. But, as this chapter's Last Word demonstrates, wage discrimination can be very subtle and difficult to detect.

2 Employment discrimination means that unemployment is concentrated among minorities. Blacks are frequently the last hired and the first fired. The unemployment rate for blacks has been roughly double that for whites (Table 36-1).

3 Human-capital discrimination occurs when investments in education and training are lower for blacks than for whites. The smaller amount (Table 36-1) and inferior quality of the education received by blacks have cost them the opportunity to increase their productivity and qualify for better jobs. Unfor-

TABLE 36-1   Selected measures of discrimination and inequality of opportunity, 1993

Selected measure	Whites	Blacks
Income		
Median income of families	$39,300	$21,542
Percent of families in poverty	9.4	31.3
Percent of families with incomes of $75,000 or more	16.6	6.6
Employment		
Unemployment rate (percent of civilian labor force)		
All males	6.2	13.8
All females	5.7	12.0
Teenage[†] males	17.6	40.1
Teenage[†] females	14.6	37.5
Education		
Percent of population 25 years and over completing 4 years of high school or more	81.5	70.4
Percent of population 25 years and over completing 4 years of college or more	22.6	12.2
Occupational distribution (percent of total civilian employment)		
Managerial and professional occupations	28.1	17.6
Service occupations	12.6	23.5

[†]Males and females, 16–19 years old.
Sources: Statistical Abstract of the United States, 1994; Economic Report of the President, 1994; and Employment and Earnings, January 1994.

tunately, a vicious circle seems to exist here. Many blacks are poor because they have acquired little human capital. Being poor, blacks have less financial ability to invest in education and training. They also have less economic motivation to invest in human capital. Facing the very real possibility of wage, employment, and occupational discrimination, blacks tend to receive a lower rate of return on their investments in education and training.

Differences in education do not fully explain earnings differences. For example, in 1991 a black male with a bachelor's degree earned $31,346 as compared to $45,699 for a white male college graduate. A black female with a bachelor's degree earned $28,986, almost identical to the earnings of a white male high school graduate!

4 Occupational discrimination means minority workers have been arbitrarily restricted or prohibited from entering the more desirable, higher-paying occupations. Black executives and salespeople, as well as black electricians, bricklayers, and plumbers, are relatively few and far between. Historically, many craft

unions effectively barred blacks from membership and hence from employment.

Occupational Segregation: The Crowding Model

This latter form of discrimination—**occupational segregation**—is particularly apparent in our economy. Women are disproportionately concentrated in a limited number of occupations such as nursing, public school teaching, secretarial and clerical jobs, and retail clerks. Blacks are crowded into a limited number of low paying jobs such as laundry workers, cleaners and servants, hospital orderlies, and other manual jobs.

Assumptions The character and income consequences of occupational discrimination can be revealed through a supply and demand model similar to the one used to analyze the efficiency consequences of unions. We make the following assumptions.

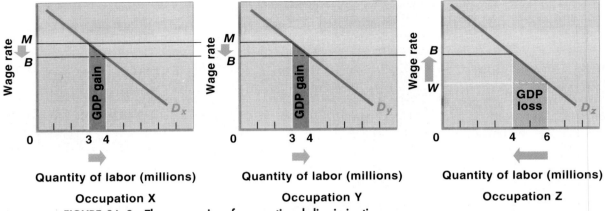

FIGURE 36-3 **The economics of occupational discrimination**
By crowding women into one occupation, men enjoy high wage rates of 0M in occupations X and Y
while women receive low wages of 0W in occupation Z. The abandonment of discrimination will equalize wage rates at 0B and result in a net increase in domestic output.

1 The labor force is equally divided between male and female (or white and black) workers. Let's say there are 6 million male and 6 million female workers.
2 The economy is comprised of three occupations, each having identical labor demand curves, as shown in Figure 36-3.
3 Men and women (whites and blacks) have identical labor force characteristics; each of the three occupations could be filled equally well by men or women.

Effects of Crowding Suppose as a consequence of discrimination, the 6 million women are excluded from occupations X and Y and crowded into occupation Z. Men distribute themselves equally among occupations X and Y so there are 3 million male workers in each occupation and the resulting common wage rate for men is 0M. (Assuming no barriers to mobility, any initially different distribution of males between X and Y would result in a wage differential which would prompt labor shifts from low- to high-wage occupation until wage equality was realized.)

Women are crowded into occupation Z and, because of this occupational segregation, receive a much lower wage rate 0W. Given the reality of discrimination, this is an "equilibrium" situation. Women *cannot,* because of discrimination, reallocate themselves to occupations X and Y in the pursuit of higher wage rates.

Eliminating Discrimination But now assume that through legislation or sweeping changes in social at-

titudes, discrimination disappears. Women, attracted by higher wage rates, will shift from Z to X and Y. Specifically, 1 million women will shift into X and another 1 million into Y, leaving 4 million workers in Z. At this point 4 million workers will be in each occupation and wage rates will be equal to 0B in all three occupations. Wage equality eliminates the incentive for further reallocations of labor.

This new, nondiscriminatory equilibrium is clearly to the advantage of women, who now receive higher wages, and to the disadvantage of men, who now receive lower wages. Women were initially harmed through discrimination to the benefit of men; the termination of discrimination corrects that situation.

There is also a net gain to society. Recall that the labor demand curve reflects labor's marginal revenue product (Chapter 27)—labor's contribution to the domestic output.[4] Hence, the shaded areas for occupations X and Y shows the *increases* in domestic output —the market value of the marginal or extra output— realized by adding 1 million women workers in each of those two occupations. Similarly, the shaded area for occupation Z shows the *decline* in domestic output caused by the shifting of the 2 million women workers from occupation Z.

The sum of the two additions to domestic output in X and Y exceeds the subtraction from domestic output in Z when discrimination is ended. Women work-

---

[4]Technical note: This assumes pure competition in product and resource markets.

ers are reallocating themselves from occupation Z, where their contribution to domestic output (their MRP) is low, to employments in X and Y, where their contributions to domestic output (their MRPs) are high.

Conclusion: *Society gains from a more efficient allocation of resources when discrimination is abandoned.* Discrimination influences the distribution of a *diminished* domestic output. Discrimination places the nation on a point inside of its production possibilities curve. *(Key Question 10)*

Costs of Discrimination

Given the diverse types of discrimination, the economic costs of discrimination are difficult to estimate. However, one estimate for racial discrimination is that if economic and social policies were successful in lowering the black unemployment rate to the level of the white rate, and if education and training opportunities were made available to the black labor force so that the average productivity of black labor became equal to that of white workers, the total output of the economy would rise by about 4 percent. For example, in 1994 the economic cost of racial discrimination alone would be about $270 billion. A more complex study has concluded that the elimination of gender discrimination would increase domestic output by almost 2.6 percent.

Addenda

We must consider two more aspects of discrimination.

Comparable Worth Doctrine The first involves public policy. The reality of pervasive occupational segregation has given rise to the issue of comparable worth. Legislation such as the Equal Pay Act of 1963 which forced employers to pay equal wages to men and women performing the same jobs was of no help to many women because occupational segregation limited their access to jobs held by men. The **comparable worth doctrine** says female secretaries, nurses, and clerks should receive the same salaries as male truck drivers or construction workers if the levels of skill, effort, and responsibility in these disparate jobs are comparable. The basic advantage of comparable worth is it is a means of quickly correcting perceived pay inequities.

While the concept of comparable worth has considerable appeal, there are objections. For example,

any comparison of the relative worth of various jobs is necessarily subjective and therefore arbitrary, opening the door to endless controversies and lawsuits. Second, wage setting by administrative or bureaucratic judgment, rather than supply and demand, does not bode well for long-run efficiency. To the extent that the calculated worth of specific jobs varies from their market or equilibrium value, worker shortages or surpluses will develop. Furthermore, increasing the wages of women could attract even more females to traditionally "women jobs" and prolong occupational segregation.

Nondiscriminatory Factors Not all the average income differentials found between blacks and whites *and* males and females are necessarily due to discrimination. Most researchers agree, for example, that some part of the male-female earnings differential is attributable to factors other than discrimination. For example, the work-life cycle of some married women who have children involves a period of work until birth of the first child. Then there may be a five- to ten-year period of nonparticipation or partial participation in the labor force related to childbearing and child care, followed by a more continuous period of work experience when the mother is in her late thirties or early forties. The net result is that, on the average, married women have accumulated less labor force experience than men in the same age group. Hence, on the average, females are less productive workers and are therefore paid a lower average wage rate.

Furthermore, family ties apparently provide married women with less geographical mobility in job choice than males. Married women may give up good positions to move with husbands who accept jobs elsewhere. And some married women may put convenience of job location and flexibility of working hours ahead of occupational choice. Women may have purposely crowded into such occupations as nursing and elementary school teaching because such occupations have the greatest carryover value for productive activity within the home. Finally, in the past decades more women have entered the labor force than have men. This large increase in the supply of female workers has acted as a drag on women's wages and earnings.

All this implies that some portion of the male-female earnings differential is due to considerations other than discrimination by gender. It also suggests that the male-female wage gap will narrow in the future, now that more women are attending college, working through their childbearing years, and pursuing higher-paying professional jobs.

QUICK REVIEW 36-3

■ Discrimination may mean *a* paying different wages to equally qualified workers, *b* higher unemployment rates for minorities, *c* less education and training for women and minorities, and *d* the concentration of minorities and women in a limited number of occupations.

■ The crowding model demonstrates how *a* men can increase their wages at the expense of women, and *b* occupational segregation diminishes the domestic output.

■ Comparable worth means females in one occupation should receive the same wages as males in another occupation if the levels of skill, effort, responsibility, and working conditions are comparable.

IMMIGRATION

The immigration issue has long been clouded in controversy and misunderstanding. Should more or fewer people be allowed to migrate to the United States? How should the much-publicized problem of illegal entrants be handled? We will illuminate these problems by (1) briefly summarizing United States' immigration history and policy, (2) presenting a bare-bones model of the economic effects of immigration, and (3) embellishing this simple model by considering some of the more subtle costs and benefits associated with the international movement of labor.

History and Policy

During the first 140 years of our history as an independent nation, immigration to the United States was virtually unimpeded. There is little question that the great infusion of foreign labor into our labor-scarce country was a major factor in our nation's economic growth. But the flood of immigrants which came to the United States in the quarter-century prior to World War I was sharply curtailed by the war itself and by a series of restrictive immigration laws enacted in the 1920s. After World War II, immigration policy was liberalized and the annual inflows of **legal immigrants** were roughly 250,000 in the 1950s, 320,000 in the 1960s, and 500,000 to 600,000 during the 1970s and

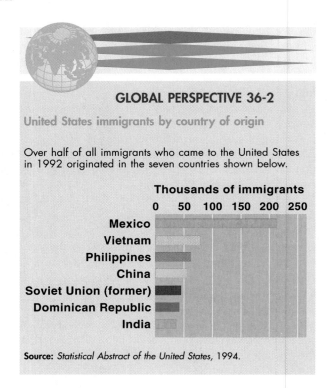

GLOBAL PERSPECTIVE 36-2

United States immigrants by country of origin

Over half of all immigrants who came to the United States in 1992 originated in the seven countries shown below.

Thousands of immigrants

Mexico, Vietnam, Philippines, China, Soviet Union (former), Dominican Republic, India

Source: *Statistical Abstract of the United States,* 1994.

1980s. In absolute terms the 1980s—when 7.3 million came to the United States—was the second largest decade of immigration in our history. About one-third of our population growth is the result of immigration.

Such data are imperfect, however, because they do not include **illegal immigrants.** The Census Bureau estimates that in the 1980s the net inflow of illegal aliens was about 200,000 per year, most coming from Mexico, the Caribbean, and Latin America. Therefore, it was not uncommon for total immigration (legal and illegal) to have exceeded 750,000 per year during the 1980s. This figure has risen to 1 million or more per year in the 1990s.

Despite the large annual influx of illegals, the total number of illegal aliens living in the United States may be only about 3 to 4 million. Many illegals come to the United States for a year or so to earn a "grubstake" and then return to their native countries.

Public concern over illegal immigration gave rise to the Immigration Reform and Control Act (IRCA), popularly known as the **Simpson-Rodino Act of 1986.** This law granted amnesty and legal status to undocumented individuals who had lived in the United States since 1982. It also made it illegal for em-

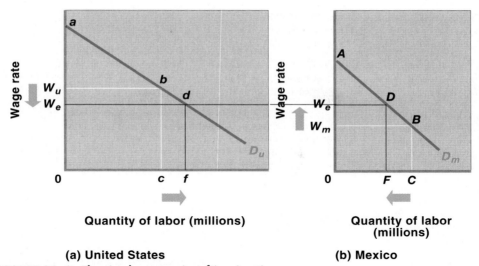

FIGURE 36-4   The simple economics of immigration
The migration of labor to high-income United States (a) from low-income Mexico (b) will increase the domestic output, reduce the average level of wages, and increase business incomes in the United States, while having the opposite effects in Mexico. The United States' domestic output gain of *cbdf* exceeds Mexico's domestic output loss of *FDBC;* thus, there is a net increase in world output.

ployers to hire undocumented workers. The idea behind the employer sanctions was to diminish or eliminate the demand for undocumented workers, thereby reducing their incentives to enter the country. But illegals have skirted the law by obtaining counterfeited documents and it is generally agreed that the law has failed to stem the flow of illegals.

Current legislation sets the number of legal immigrants at 700,000 per year. The legislation stresses family reunification by allowing United States citizens to bring in immediate relatives—spouses, children, and parents. But there has also been a substantial increase in the number of visas made available to highly skilled professionals such as researchers, engineers, and scientists. In addition, some 10,000 visas have been earmarked for wealthy immigrants who are willing to invest at least $1 million in the United States. Emphasis is clearly on the kinds of immigrants who are likely to make significant contributions to American economic growth.

Economics of Immigration

We can gain some insight into the economic effects of immigration using a variation of the crowding model of discrimination (Figure 36-3). In Figure

36-4 we portray the demand for labor in the United States as D_u in the left diagram and the demand for labor in Mexico as D_m in the right diagram. The demand for labor is greater in the United States, presumably because of more capital equipment and more advanced technologies which enhance the productivity of labor. (Recall from Chapter 27 that the labor demand curve is based on the marginal revenue product of labor.) Conversely, we assume machinery and equipment are scarce in Mexico and technology is less sophisticated; hence, labor demand is weak. We also assume that the premigration labor forces of the United States and Mexico are $0c$ and $0C$ respectively, *and* that full employment exists in both countries.

Wage Rates and World Output   If we further assume that (1) migration is costless; (2) it occurs solely in response to wage differentials; and (3) it is unimpeded by legislation in either country, workers will migrate from Mexico to the United States until wage rates in the two countries are equal at W_e. In this case some FC $(=fc)$ million workers will have migrated from Mexico to the United States before equilibrium is achieved. Although the average level of wage rates falls from W_u to W_e in the United States, the domestic output (the sum of the marginal revenue products of the labor force) increases from $0abc$ to $0adf$. In Mexico, average wage rates rise from W_m to W_e, but domestic output declines from $0ABC$ to $0ADF$.[5] Observing that the domestic output gain of $cbdf$ in the United States exceeds the $FDBC$ loss in Mexico, we conclude that the world's real output has increased.

Just as elimination of the barrier of sex or racial discrimination enhances economic efficiency within a country, so the elimination of legislative barriers to the international flow of labor increases worldwide economic efficiency. The world gains because freedom to migrate moves people to countries where they can make a larger contribution to world production. To repeat: Migration involves an efficiency gain. It enables the world to produce a larger real output with a given amount of resources.

Income Shares Our model also suggests this flow of immigrations will enhance business or capitalist incomes in the United States and reduce them in Mexico. We have just noted that the before-immigration domestic output in the United States is $0abc$. The total wage bill is $0W_ubc$—the wage rate multiplied by the number of workers. The remaining triangular area W_uab is "business" or capitalist income. The same reasoning applies to Mexico.

Unimpeded immigration will increase business income from W_uab to W_ead in the United States and reduce it from W_mAB to W_eAD in Mexico. American business benefits from immigration; Mexican businesses are hurt by emigration. This is what we would expect intuitively; America is receiving the "cheap" labor, Mexico is losing "cheap" labor. This conclusion is consistent with the historical fact that American employers have often actively recruited immigrants.

Complications and Modifications

Our model includes simplifying assumptions and omits several relevant considerations. Let's therefore release some of the more critical assumptions and in-

troduce omitted factors, observing how our conclusions are affected.

1 Cost of Migration The international movement of workers is not costless. Costs are not only the explicit or out-of-pocket costs of geographically moving a worker and his or her possessions, but also the implicit or opportunity cost of lost income during the period of movement and reestablishing that worker in the host country. Still more subtle costs are involved in adapting to a new culture, language, climate, and so forth. All such *costs* must be estimated by the potential immigrant and weighed against the expected *benefits* of higher wages in the host country. If benefits are estimated to exceed costs, it is rational to migrate. If costs exceed benefits, do not migrate.

In Figure 36-4 the existence of migration costs means that the flow of labor from Mexico to the United States will *not* occur to the extent that wages are equalized. Wages will remain higher in the United States than in Mexico. Furthermore, the world gain from migration will be reduced.

2 Remittances and Backflows Many migrants view their moves as temporary. Their plan is to move to a wealthier country, accumulate some wealth through hard work and frugality, and return home to establish their own enterprises. During their period in the host country, migrants frequently make sizable **remittances** to their families at home. This causes a redistribution of the net gain from migration between the countries involved. In Figure 36-4 remittances by Mexican workers in the United States to their relatives would cause the *gain* in the United States' domestic output to be less than shown and the *loss* to Mexican domestic output to also be less than shown.

Actual **backflows**—the return of migrants to their home countries—might also alter gains and losses through time. For example, if some of the Mexican workers who migrated to the United States acquired substantial labor-market or managerial skills and then returned home, their enhanced human capital might make a substantial contribution to economic development in Mexico. Evidence suggests, however, that migrant workers who acquire skills in the receiving country tend *not* to return home. At times the United States has been a beneficiary of "brain drains" as professional and other highly skilled workers have left Europe and Asia for higher wages and better job opportunities in the United States.

---

[5]What happens to the wage bill (wage rate multiplied by the number of workers) in each of the two countries depends on the elasticity of labor demand. If the demand for labor is elastic in the W_uW_e wage range in the United States, the absolute size of the wage bill will increase. Conversely, if labor demand is inelastic in the W_uW_e wage range, the absolute size of the wage bill will decline. A similar application of the total revenue (earnings) test for elasticity applies to Mexico.

3 Full Employment versus Unemployment Our model assumes full employment in both the sending and receiving country. Mexican workers presumably leave low-paying jobs to more-or-less immediately take higher-paying jobs in the United States. However, in many cases the factor that "pushes" immigrants from their homelands is not low wages, but chronic unemployment and underemployment. Many less developed countries are characterized by overpopulation and surplus labor; workers are either unemployed or so grossly underemployed that their marginal revenue product is zero.

Again, allowance for this possibility affects our discussion of gains and losses. Specifically, Mexico would *gain* (not lose!) by having such workers emigrate. These unemployed workers are making no contribution to Mexico's domestic output and must be sustained by transfers from the rest of the labor force. The remaining Mexican labor force will be better off by the amount of the transfers after the unemployed workers have migrated to the United States. Conversely, if the Mexican immigrant workers are unable to find jobs in the United States and are sustained through transfers from employed American workers, then the after-tax income of native American workers will decline.

4 Fiscal Aspects What impacts do immigrants have on tax revenues and government spending in the receiving country? Do immigrants go on welfare and become a drain on the national treasury? Or are they net contributors?

The conventional wisdom has been that the immigrant population is less likely to receive public assistance than the native population. Migrants were typically young, single males with some significant amount of education and labor force training. Thus they were readily employable. Furthermore, illegal immigrants would steer clear of the welfare system for fear of detection and deportation.

Recent research suggests, however, that since the late 1970s the situation is reversed and immigrants use the welfare system proportionately more than natives. The main factor in this turnabout is the changing mix of immigrants, with fewer skilled workers coming from Europe and large numbers of unskilled immigrants coming from Asia and Latin America. A generous welfare system may be drawing unskilled workers to America from some of the world's poorest nations. Also, immigrants (often with forged documents) may now be more informed as to how to use our welfare system. Thus immigrants made up 11 percent of Supplemental Security Income (SSI) rolls in 1992 as compared with only 3.3 percent a decade earlier. California's controversial Proposition 187, passed in 1994, denies illegal immigrants access to welfare programs and public education. *(Key Question 11)*

QUICK REVIEW 36-4

■ Current policy allows about 700,000 immigrants to enter the United States each year with preference being given to "priority workers" who have special education, training, and talents.

■ A country receiving immigrants will experience a larger domestic output, a lower average level of wages, and an increase in business incomes. The opposite effects will occur in the donor country.

■ The economic effects of immigration are complicated by the costs of migration, remittances, backflows of immigrants, employment conditions, and fiscal implications.

Immigration: Two Views

The traditional perception of immigration envisions young, ambitious workers seeking opportunity in America. They are destined for success because of the courage and determination they exhibit in their willingness to forgo their cultural roots to improve their lives. These energetic workers increase the supply of goods and services with their labor and simultaneously increase the demand for goods and services with their incomes and spending. A kind of benevolent cycle of growth unfolds which accrues, not only to the immigrants, but to the economy as a whole. In short, immigration is an engine of economic progress.

The counterview is that immigration is a socioeconomic drag on the host country. Immigrants compete with domestic workers for scarce jobs; pull down the average level of real wages; and burden our welfare rolls at taxpayers' expense. Furthermore, the currently high levels of legal and illegal immigration have effectively undermined the "melting pot" conception of America. The diversity of recent immigrants allegedly threatens America's cohesiveness, generates social and racial frictions, and challenges our culture and way of life.

LAST WORD

RACISM IN PROFESSIONAL BASKETBALL?

Although black players earn more than white players in the NBA, researchers have discovered evidence of wage discrimination against blacks.

Causal observation would suggest no racial discrimination in the National Basketball Association (NBA). Almost four-fifths of all NBA players are black. Teams are highly integrated. There are more black coaches in the NBA than in other professional sports. Many of the most highly paid players are black. Raw salary data for 1985–1986 show that black players earned $10,620 (2.7 percent) more than white players.

Yet recent research suggests that discrimination *does* exist. Sherer and Kahn[*] have adjusted 1985–1986 raw salary data for various measures of player performance (productivity) such as number of seasons played, games played per season, career points, field goal percentage, rebounds, assists per game, and so forth. These measures indicate that black players are superior to whites. Adjusting salaries to account for this superiority, Sherer and Kahn have concluded that black players earn about $80,000 or 20 percent *less* than white players.

What is the source of this discrimination? Sherer and Kahn reject the notion of racist attitudes on the part of team owners. By rejecting talented black players, racist owners would find themselves with less successful teams, declining revenues, and franchises

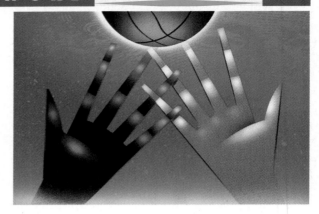

of lesser value. Furthermore, the fact that NBA teams are highly integrated suggests that fellow employees (white players) are not the source of discrimination. Sherer and Kahn found that team customers (fans) are the source of NBA discrimination. Their research shows that home game attendance increases with the number of white players on the team. Specifically, they estimate that a team's revenue may increase by about $115,000 to $131,000 per season per additional white player, and suggest that both white players and team owners gain by serving fans' preferences to watch white players. Sherer and Kahn conclude that "As long as fans prefer to see white players, profit-oriented teams will make discriminatory salary offers."[†]

[*]Peter D. Sherer and Lawrence M. Kahn, "Racial Differences in Professional Basketball Players' Compensation," *Journal of Labor Economics,* January 1988, pp. 40–61.

[†]Ibid., p. 60.

CHAPTER SUMMARY

1 The growth of labor unions was slow and irregular until the 1930s due to court and employer hostility.

2 The AFL dominated the American labor movement from 1886 until the CIO was formed in 1936. Its philosophy was essentially that of Samuel Gompers—business unionism, political neutrality, and craft unionism.

3 Union growth was rapid in the 1930s and 1940s. The shift toward industrial unionism, triggered by the formation of the CIO in 1936, was a significant factor in this growth. Equally important was the prolabor legislation passed by the Federal government in the 1930s.

4 The Norris La Guardia Act of 1932 rendered yellow-dog contracts unenforceable and sharply limited the use

of injunctions in labor disputes. The Wagner Act of 1935—"labor's Magna Charta"—guaranteed labor the rights to organize and to bargain collectively with management.

5 The Taft-Hartley Act of 1947 was designed to limit union power by **a** prohibiting certain "unfair practices" by unions, **b** outlawing the closed shop and permitting state "right-to-work" laws which make the union shop illegal, and **c** establishing procedures for handling "national health and safety" strikes.

6 The Landrum-Griffin Act of 1959 was designed to regulate the internal processes of unions—in particular the handling of union finances and the union's relationships with its members.

7 Unionism has declined relatively in the United States since the mid-1950s. Some labor economists attribute this to changes in the composition of domestic output and in the demographic structure of the labor force. Others contend that employers, recognizing that unionization results in lower profitability, have more aggressively sought to dissuade workers from being union members.

8 Labor and management "live together" under the terms of collective bargaining agreements. These work agreements cover: **a** union status and managerial prerogatives; **b** wages and hours; **c** seniority and job control; and **d** a grievance procedure.

9 Union workers currently enjoy wages which are about 15 percent higher than comparable nonunion workers. There is little evidence that unions have been able to raise the average level of real wages for labor as a whole.

10 There is disagreement whether the net effect of unions on allocative efficiency and productivity is positive or negative. The negative view cites **a** inefficiencies associated with featherbedding and union-imposed work rules; **b** loss of output through strikes; and **c** the misallocation of labor to which the union wage advantage gives rise. The positive view holds that **a** through the shock effect union wage pressure spurs technological advance and mechanization of the production process; **b** as collective voice institutions unions contribute to rising productivity by reducing labor turnover; and **c** the enhanced security of union workers

increases their willingness to teach their skills to less experienced workers.

11 Those who say unions increase earnings inequality argue that **a** unionization increases the wages of union workers but lowers the wages of nonunion workers and **b** unions are strongest among highly paid, skilled blue-collar workers but relatively weak among low-paid, unskilled blue-collar workers. But other economists contend that unions contribute to greater earnings equality because unions seek uniform wages both for given jobs within firms and among firms.

12 The incomes of blacks and other racial minorities are below those of whites, while the incomes of females are below males. In part, these differences arise because of wage, employment, human-capital, and occupational discrimination.

13 The crowding model of occupational segregation indicates how white males may gain higher earnings at the expense of blacks and women. The model also shows that discrimination causes a net loss of domestic output.

14 Supply and demand analysis suggests the movement of migrants from a poor to a rich country will **a** increase the domestic output, **b** reduce the average level of wages, and **c** increase business incomes in the receiving country. The opposite effects will occur in the sending country, but the world as a whole can be expected to realize a larger total output.

TERMS AND CONCEPTS

yellow-dog contract	Congress of Industrial	Landrum-Griffin Act of	wage, employment,
injunction	Organizations (CIO)	1959	human-capital, and
American Federation of	industrial unionism	structural-change and	occupational
Labor (AFL)	Taft-Hartley Act of 1947	managerial-opposition	discrimination
business unionism	jurisdictional strikes	hypotheses	comparable worth
craft unions	secondary boycotts	fringe benefits	doctrine
Norris La Guardia Act of	sympathy strikes	seniority	legal and illegal
1932	featherbedding	collective voice	immigrants
Wagner Act of 1935	closed shop	exit and voice	Simpson-Rodino Act of
National Labor Relations	union shop	mechanisms	1986
Board (NLRB)	open shop	occupational segregation	remittances
	right-to-work laws		backflows

QUESTIONS AND STUDY SUGGESTIONS

1 *Key Question* *Briefly explain the slow growth of unionism prior to the 1930s and its rapid growth in the 1930s and 1940s.*

2 It has been said that the Taft-Hartley Act was passed to achieve three major goals: **a** to reestablish an equality of bargaining power between labor and management to

maintain industrial peace; **b** to protect "neutrals," that is, third parties not directly concerned with a given labor-management dispute; and **c** to protect the rights of individual workers in their relations with unions. Review the Taft-Hartley provisions as outlined in this chapter, and relate each to these three major goals.

3 Use the structural-change and managerial-opposition hypotheses to explain the relative decline of organized labor in the United States. In your opinion which explanation is more convincing?

4 You are the president of a newly established local union about to bargain with an employer for the first time. List those points you would want covered explicitly in the work agreement. Assuming the economic climate which exists at this moment, what criteria would you use in backing your wage demands? Explain.

5 What is the estimated size of the union wage advantage? Explain: "Although unions get higher wages than nonunion workers, unions have not been successful in raising the average real wage of the American labor force."

6 Comment on each of the following statements:

a "By constraining the decisions of management, unions inhibit efficiency and productivity growth."

b "As collective voice institutions unions increase productivity by reducing worker turnover, inducing managerial efficiency, and enhancing worker security."

7 *Key Question* *"There is an inherent cost to society that accompanies any union wage gain. That cost is the diminished efficiency with which labor resources are allocated." Explain this contention.*

8 Describe the various avenues through which unions might alter the distribution of earnings. Evaluate: "Unions purport to be egalitarian institutions, but their effect is to increase earnings inequality among American workers."

9 Compare and account for differences in the economic status of whites and nonwhites. Distinguish between the various kinds of economic discrimination. Do you believe on balance that the distribution of education and training in our society alleviates, or contributes to, income inequality?

10 *Key Question* *Use supply and demand analysis to explain the impact of occupational segregation or "crowding" upon the relative wage rates and earnings of men and women. Who gains and who loses as a consequence of eliminating occupational segregation? Is there a net gain or loss to society as a whole? "Wage differences between men and women do not reflect discrimination, but rather differences in job continuity and rational decisions with respect to education and training." Do you agree?*

11 *Key Question* *Use a demand and supply model to determine the gains and losses associated with the migration of population from low- to high-income countries. Explain how your conclusions are affected by* **a** *unemployment,* **b** *remittances from the host country,* **c** *backflows of migrants to their home countries, and* **d** *the personal characteristics of the migrants. If the migrants are highly skilled workers, is there any justification for the sending country to levy a "brain drain" tax on emigrants?*

12 If you favor the free movement of labor within the United States, are you being inconsistent in favoring restrictions on the international movement of labor?

13 Evaluate: "If we deported 1 million illegal aliens who are in America, our total national unemployment would decline by 1 million."

14 Why did organized labor in the United States oppose the North American Free Trade Agreement (NAFTA) which is designed to remove trade barriers between the United States, Mexico, and Canada?

15 (Last Word) Black players numerically dominate the National Basketball Association and receive higher average salaries than white players. How can researchers argue there is wage discrimination against black players? What is the source of this discrimination?

PART

EIGHT

International Economics and the World Economy

37

INTERNATIONAL TRADE

NAFTA, GATT, trade deficits with Japan. Exchange rates, dumping, the European Union. The IMF, nontariff trade barriers, exchange rates. Official reserves, the G-7 Nations, currency interventions. Capital flight, brain drains, the ruble.

People across the globe are speaking the language of international economics—on television, in the newspapers, in corporate offices, in stores, and in union halls. A "foreign" language? Not if you have read Chapter 6 and now master the material in Chapters 37 through 40.

This chapter builds on Chapter 6, providing a more focused analysis of international trade and protectionism. First, we review salient facts about world trade. Second, we take a more advanced look at how international specialization based on comparative advantage can mutually benefit participating nations. Third, we use supply and demand analysis to examine equilibrium prices and quantities of imports and exports. Fourth, the economic impact of trade barriers such as tariffs and import quotas are examined. Fifth, we evaluate the arguments for protectionism. Finally, we discuss the costs of protectionism and some continuing controversies in international trade.

FACTS OF INTERNATIONAL TRADE

In Chapter 6 we developed a number of facts about international trade. Let's quickly review them and add a few others.

1 Our exports of goods and services are about 11 to 13 percent of American GDP. The percentage is greater in many other nations. Examples: Netherlands —52 percent, Germany—27 percent, New Zealand— 33 percent, Canada—30 percent (Table 6-1).

2 The United States leads the world in the volume of exports and imports. Currently, it provides about one-eighth of the world's exports, down from one-

third in 1947. Germany, Japan, France, and Britain follow in the list of top five merchandise exporters by volume (Global Perspective 6-1).

3 American exports and imports have increased in volume and more than doubled as a percent of GDP since 1965 (Figure 6-1).

4 In 1994 the United States had a $133 billion trade deficit—meaning that imports of goods exceeded exports of goods by this amount. But in that year America's exports of services exceeded its imports of services by $57 billion. Thus, as we will see in Chapter 38 (Table 38-1), the goods and services deficit was $76 billion.

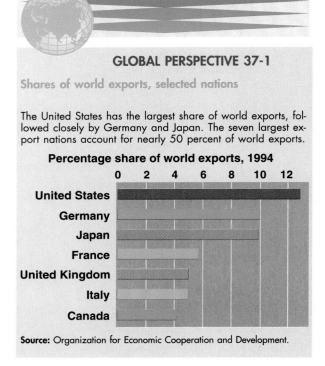

5 America's principal commodity exports are chemicals, computers, consumer durables, and aircraft. Its main imports are automobiles, petroleum, computers, and clothing (Table 6-2).

6 Like other advanced industrial nations, America imports some of the same categories of goods that it exports. Examples: Autos, computers, chemicals, semiconductors, and telecommunications equipment (Table 6-2).

7 The bulk of United States export and import trade is with other industrially advanced nations, specifically Canada, nations of western Europe, and Japan (Table 6-3).

8 Improved transportation and communications technologies, declines in tariffs, and peaceful relations among major industrial nations have all helped expand world trade since World War II.

9 Although trade is still dominated by the United States, Japan, and western European nations, several new "players" have greatly increased their roles (Global Perspective 37-1). The four "Asian tigers"—Hong Kong, Singapore, South Korea, and Taiwan—have expanded their share of world trade from 3 percent in 1972 to nearly 10 percent today. China has

emerged as a new international trader and the collapse of communism has led eastern European nations and Russia to look globally for new trade partners.

10 International trade has recently been at the center of international policy. Examples: The North American Free Trade Agreement (NAFTA), the conclusion of negotiations on the General Agreement on Tariffs and Trade (GATT), and United States–Japan negotiations on reducing the American trade deficit with Japan.

Keeping these facts in mind, let's take a closer look at the economics of international trade.

THE ECONOMIC BASIS FOR TRADE

In Chapter 6 we found that international trade is a way nations can specialize, increase the productivity of their resources, and realize a larger total output. Sovereign nations, like individuals and regions of a nation, can gain by specializing in products they can produce with greatest relative efficiency and by trading for goods they cannot produce efficiently. This rationale for trade is correct, but a more detailed understanding is needed. The more complete answer to the question "Why do nations trade?" hinges on two points.

1 The distribution of economic resources—natural, human, and capital goods—among nations is uneven; nations are different in their endowments of economic resources.

2 Efficient production of various goods requires different technologies or combinations of resources.

The character and interaction of these two points can be readily illustrated. Japan, for example, has a large, well-educated labor force; skilled labor is abundant and therefore inexpensive. Japan can produce efficiently (at low cost) a variety of goods whose design and production require much skilled labor; cameras, transistor radios, and video recorders are examples of such **labor-intensive** commodities.

In contrast, Australia has vast amounts of land compared with its human and capital resources and can inexpensively produce such **land-intensive** commodities as wheat, wool, and meat. Brazil has the soil, tropical climate, rainfall, and lots of unskilled labor needed for efficient low-cost production of coffee.

Industrially advanced nations are in a position to produce inexpensively a variety of **capital-intensive** goods, for example, automobiles, agricultural equipment, machinery, and chemicals.

The economic efficiency with which nations produce various goods can change. Both the distribution of resources and technology can change, altering the relative efficiency with which goods can be produced by various countries. For example, in the past few decades South Korea has upgraded the quality of its labor force and has greatly expanded its stock of capital. Although South Korea was primarily an exporter of agricultural products and raw materials a half-century ago, it now exports large quantities of manufactured goods. Similarly, the new technologies which gave us synthetic fibers and synthetic rubber drastically altered the resource-mix needed to produce these goods and changed the relative efficiency of nations in manufacturing them.

As national economies evolve, the size and quality of their labor forces may change, the volume and composition of their capital stocks may shift, new technologies will develop, and even the quality of land and quantity of natural resources may be altered. As these changes occur, the efficiency with which a nation can produce goods will also change.

COMPARATIVE ADVANTAGE: GRAPHICAL ANALYSIS

Implicit in what we have just discussed is the principle of comparative advantage, described in Chapter 6. Let's again look at that idea, now using graphical analysis.

Two Isolated Nations

Suppose the world economy is composed of just two nations, the United States and Brazil. Each can produce both wheat and coffee, but at differing levels of economic efficiency. Suppose the United States' and Brazilian domestic production possibilities curves for coffee and wheat are as shown in Figure 37-1a and b. Let's look at two characteristics of these production possibilities curves.

1 Constant Costs We have purposely drawn the "curves" as straight lines, in contrast to the concave-from-the-origin production possibilities boundaries introduced in Chapter 2. This means the law of increasing costs has been replaced with the assumption of constant costs. This simplification will make it easier for you to follow our discussion and will not impair the validity of our analysis and conclusions. We will consider later the effect of the more realistic increasing costs.

2 Different Costs The production possibilities lines of the United States and Brazil are different, reflecting different resource mixes and differing levels of technological progress. Specifically, the opportunity costs of producing wheat and coffee differ between the two nations.

United States In Figure 37-1a, with full employment, the United States can increase its output of wheat 30 tons by forgoing 30 tons of coffee output. That means the slope of the production possibilities curve is -1

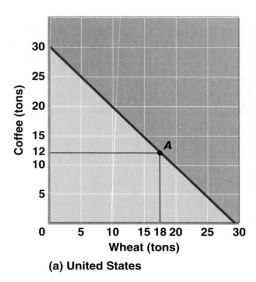

(a) United States

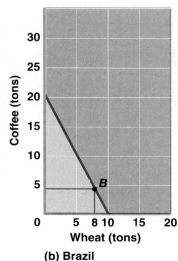

(b) Brazil

FIGURE 37-1 Production possibilities for the United States and Brazil The two production possibilities curves show the amounts of coffee and wheat the United States (a) and Brazil (b) can produce domestically. The production possibilities for both countries are straight lines because we are assuming constant costs. The different cost ratios—$1W = 1C$ for the United States and $1W = 2C$ for Brazil —are reflected in the different slopes of the two lines.

TABLE 37-1   International specialization according to comparative advantage and the gains from trade (in tons)

Country	(1) Outputs before special- ization	(2) Outputs after special- ization	(3) Amounts exported (−) and imported (+)	(4) Outputs available after trade	(5) = (4) − (1) Gains from special- ization and trade
United States	18 wheat 12 coffee	30 wheat 0 coffee	−10 wheat +15 coffee	20 wheat 15 coffee	2 wheat 3 coffee
Brazil	8 wheat 4 coffee	0 wheat 20 coffee	+10 wheat −15 coffee	10 wheat 5 coffee	2 wheat 1 coffee

(= −1/1), implying that 1 ton of wheat can be obtained for every 1 ton of coffee sacrificed. In the United States the domestic exchange ratio or **cost ratio** for the two products is 1 ton of wheat for 1 ton of coffee, or $1W = 1C$. The United States can "exchange" a ton of wheat for a ton of coffee domestically by shifting resources from wheat to coffee. Our constant-cost assumption means this exchange or cost ratio prevails for all possible moves from one point to another along the United States' production possibilities curve.

Brazil   Brazil's production possibilities line in Figure 37-1b represents a different exchange or cost ratio. In Brazil 20 tons of coffee must be given up to get 10 tons of wheat. The slope of the production possibilities curve is −2(= −2/1). This means that in Brazil the domestic cost ratio for the two goods is 1 ton of wheat for 2 tons of coffee, or $1W = 2C$.

Self-Sufficiency   If the United States and Brazil are isolated and self-sufficient, each must choose some output-mix on its production possibilities line. Assume point *A* in Figure 37-1a is the optimal output-mix in the United States. The choice of this combination of 18 tons of wheat and 12 tons of coffee is presumably made through the market system. Suppose Brazil's optimal product-mix is 8 tons of wheat and 4 tons of coffee, indicated by point *B* in Figure 37-1b. These choices are also reflected in column 1 of Table 37-1.

Specializing According to Comparative Advantage

With these different cost ratios, the way to determine the products in which the United States and Brazil should specialize is as follows: The **principle of comparative advantage** says that *total output will be greatest when each good is produced by that nation* which has the lower domestic opportunity cost. For our illustration, the United States' domestic opportunity cost is lower for wheat; the United States need only forgo 1 ton of coffee to produce 1 ton of wheat, whereas Brazil must forgo 2 tons of coffee for 1 ton of wheat. *The United States has a comparative (cost) advantage in wheat, and should specialize in wheat production.* The "world" (the United States and Brazil) clearly is *not* economizing in the use of its resources if a specific product (wheat) is produced by a high-cost producer (Brazil) when it could have been produced by a low-cost producer (the United States). To have Brazil produce wheat would mean that the world economy would have to give up more coffee than is necessary to obtain a ton of wheat.

Brazil's domestic opportunity cost is lower for coffee; it must sacrifice only $\frac{1}{2}$ ton of wheat in producing 1 ton of coffee, whereas the United States must forgo 1 ton of wheat in producing a ton of coffee. *Brazil has a comparative advantage in coffee, and should specialize in coffee production.* Again, the world would *not* be employing its resources economically if coffee were produced by a high-cost producer (the United States) rather than a low-cost producer (Brazil). If the United States produced coffee, the world would be giving up more wheat than necessary to obtain each ton of coffee. *Economizing—using fixed quantities of scarce resources to obtain the greatest total output—requires that any particular good be produced by that nation having the lower domestic opportunity cost, or the comparative advantage.* The United States should produce wheat and Brazil, coffee.

In column 2 of Table 37-1 we can verify that specialized production in accordance with the principle of comparative advantage allows the world to get more output from its fixed amount of resources. By specializing completely in wheat, the United States can produce 30 tons of wheat and no coffee. Brazil, specializing completely in coffee, produces 20 tons of coffee and no wheat. The world has more wheat—30 tons compared with 26 (= 18 + 8) tons—*and* more coffee—20 tons compared with 16 (= 12 + 4) tons—than when there is self-sufficiency or unspecialized production.

Terms of Trade

But consumers of each nation want *both* wheat and coffee. Specialization implies the need to trade or exchange the two products. What will be the **terms of trade?** At what exchange ratio will the United States and Brazil trade wheat and coffee?

Because $1W = 1C$ in the United States, the United States must get *more than* 1 ton of coffee for each ton of wheat exported or it will not pay the United States to export wheat in exchange for Brazilian coffee. The United States must get a better "price" (more coffee) for its wheat in the world market than it can get domestically, or else there's no gain from trade and it won't occur.

Similarly, because $1W = 2C$ in Brazil, it must get 1 ton of wheat by exporting some amount *less than* 2 tons of coffee. Brazil must be able to pay a lower "price" for wheat in the world market than it must pay domestically, or it will not want to trade. The international exchange ratio or *terms of trade* must lie somewhere between

$1W = 1C$ (United States' cost conditions)

and

$1W = 2C$ (Brazil's cost conditions)

But where will the world exchange ratio fall between these limits? The exchange ratio or terms of trade determines how the gains from international specialization and trade are divided between the two nations. The United States will prefer a rate close to $1W = 2C$, say, $1W = 1\frac{3}{4}C$. Americans want to get much coffee for each ton of wheat they export. Similarly, Brazil wants a rate near $1W = 1C$, say, $1W = 1\frac{1}{4}C$. Brazil wants to export as little coffee as possible for each ton of wheat it receives in exchange.

The exchange ratio between the two limits depends on world supply and demand for the two products. If overall world demand for coffee is weak relative to its supply and the demand for wheat is strong relative to its supply, the price of coffee will be low and the price of wheat high. The exchange ratio will settle near the $1W = 2C$ figure preferred by the United States. Under the opposite world supply and demand conditions, the ratio will settle near the $1W = 1C$ level favorable to Brazil. We will take up the topic of equilibrium world prices later in this chapter.

Gains from Trade

Suppose the international exchange ratio or terms of trade is $1W = 1\frac{1}{2}C$. The possibility of trading on these terms permits each nation to supplement its domestic production possibilities line with a **trading possibilities line.** This can be seen in Figure 37-2a and b (Key Graph). Just as a production possibilities line shows the options a full-employment economy has in obtaining one product by shifting resources from the production of another, so a trading possibilities line shows the options a nation has by specializing in one product and trading (exporting) its specialty to obtain the other product. The trading possibilities lines in Figure 37-2 are drawn on the assumption that both nations specialize based on comparative advantage—the United States specializes completely in wheat (point W in Figure 37-2a) and Brazil completely in coffee (point c in Figure 37-2b).

Improved Options Now, instead of being constrained by its domestic production possibilities line and having to give up 1 ton of wheat for every ton of coffee it wants as it moves up its domestic production possibilities line from point W, the United States, through trade with Brazil, can get $1\frac{1}{2}$ tons of coffee for every ton of wheat it exports to Brazil, so long as Brazil has coffee to export. Line WC' demonstrates the $1W = 1\frac{1}{2}C$ trading ratio.

Similarly, we can think of Brazil as starting at point c, and instead of having to move down its domestic production possibilities line, giving up 2 tons of coffee for each ton of wheat it wants, it can now export just $1\frac{1}{2}$ tons of coffee for each ton of wheat it wants by moving down its cw' trading possibilities line.

Specialization and trade create a new exchange ratio between wheat and coffee, reflected in a nation's trading possibilities line. This exchange ratio is superior for both nations to the self-sufficiency exchange ratio in the production possibilities line of each. By specializing in wheat and trading for Brazil's coffee, the United States can obtain *more than* 1 ton of coffee for 1 ton of wheat. By specializing in coffee and trading for United States' wheat, Brazil can get 1 ton of wheat for *less than* 2 tons of coffee.

KEY GRAPH

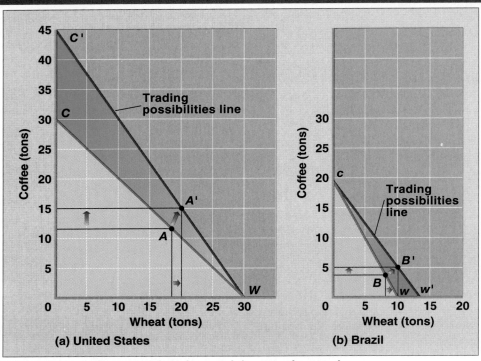

FIGURE 37-2 Trading possibilities lines and the gains from trade
As a result of international specialization and trade, the United States and Brazil can both have levels of output superior to those attainable on their domestic production possibilities curves. For example, the United States in (a) can move from point A on its domestic production possibilities line to point A' on its trading possibilities line; Brazil in (b) can move from B to B'.

Added Output By specializing according to comparative advantage and trading for those goods produced with the lowest efficiency domestically, both the United States and Brazil can realize combinations of wheat and coffee beyond their production possibilities boundaries. *Specialization according to comparative advantage results in a more efficient allocation of world resources, and larger outputs of both wheat and coffee are therefore available to the United States and Brazil.*

Suppose at the $1W = 1\frac{1}{2}C$ terms of trade, the United States exports 10 tons of wheat to Brazil and Brazil in return exports 15 tons of coffee to the United States. How do the new quantities of wheat and coffee available to the two nations compare with the optimal product-mixes that existed before specialization and trade? Point A in Figure 37-2a reminds us that the United States chose 18 tons of wheat and 12 tons of coffee originally. But, by producing 30 tons of wheat

and no coffee, and by trading 10 tons of wheat for 15 tons of coffee, the United States can enjoy 20 tons of wheat and 15 tons of coffee. This new, superior combination of wheat and coffee is shown by point A' in Figure 37-2a. Compared with the nontrading figures of 18 tons of wheat and 12 tons of coffee, the United States' **gains from trade** are 2 tons of wheat and 3 tons of coffee.

Similarly, we assumed Brazil's optimal product-mix was 4 tons of coffee and 8 tons of wheat (point B) before specialization and trade. Now, by specializing in coffee—producing 20 tons of coffee and no wheat—Brazil can realize a combination of 5 tons of coffee and 10 tons of wheat by exporting 15 tons of its coffee in exchange for 10 tons of American wheat. This new position is shown by point B' in Figure 37-2b. Brazil's gains from trade are 1 ton of coffee and 2 tons of wheat.

As a result of specialization and trade, both coun-

tries have more of both products. Table 37-1 is a summary statement of these figures. You should be sure you understand it.

The fact that points *A'* and *B'* are economic positions superior to *A* and *B* is extremely important. Recall from Chapter 2 that a nation can expand its production possibilities boundary by (1) expanding the quantity and improving the quality of its resources or (2) realizing technological progress. We have now explained another way—international trade—for a nation to circumvent the output constraint imposed by its production possibilities curve. The effects of international specialization and trade are the equivalent of having more and better resources or discovering improved production techniques.

Increasing Costs

To explain in a simple way the principles underlying international trade, we have made several assumptions. Our explanation was limited to two products and two nations. But multination and multiproduct examples yield similar conclusions. However, the assumption of constant costs is a more substantive simplification. Let's consider the significance of the law of increasing costs (concave-from-the-origin production possibility curves) for our analysis.

Suppose, as in our previous constant-cost illustration, that the United States and Brazil are at positions on their production possibilities curves where their cost ratios are initially $1W = 1C$ and $1W = 2C$ respectively. As before, comparative advantage indicates that the United States should specialize in wheat and Brazil in coffee. But now, as the United States begins to expand wheat production, its $1W = 1C$ cost ratio will *fall;* it will have to sacrifice *more than* 1 ton of coffee to get 1 additional ton of wheat. Resources are no longer perfectly shiftable between alternative uses, as the constant-cost assumption implied. Resources less and less suitable to wheat production must be allocated to the American wheat industry in expanding wheat output, and this means increasing costs—the sacrifice of larger and larger amounts of coffee for each additional ton of wheat.

Similarly, Brazil, starting from its $1W = 2C$ cost ratio position, expands coffee production. But as it does, it will find that its $1W = 2C$ cost ratio begins to *rise.* Sacrificing a ton of wheat will free resources which are only capable of producing something *less than* 2 tons of coffee, because these transferred resources are less suitable to coffee production.

As the American cost ratio falls from $1W = 1C$ and Brazil's rises from $1W = 2C$, a point will be reached where the cost ratios are equal in the two nations, for example, at $1W = 1\frac{1}{2}C$. At this point the underlying basis for further specialization and trade—differing cost ratios—has disappeared, and further specialization is therefore uneconomic. And most important, this point of equal cost ratios may be realized where the United States is still producing some coffee along with its wheat and Brazil is producing some wheat along with its coffee. *The primary effect of increasing costs is to make specialization less than complete.* For this reason we often find domestically produced products competing directly against identical or similar imported products within a particular economy. *(Key Question 4)*

The Case for Free Trade Restated

The case for free trade reduces to this one potent argument. *Through free trade based on the principle of comparative advantage, the world economy can achieve a more efficient allocation of resources and a higher level of material well-being.* The resource mixes and technological knowledge of each country are different. Therefore, each nation can produce particular commodities at different real costs. Each nation should produce goods for which its domestic opportunity costs are lower than the domestic opportunity costs of other nations and exchange these specialties for products for which its domestic opportunity costs are high relative to those of other nations. If each nation does this, the world can realize the advantages of geographic and human specialization. The world—and each free-trading nation—can obtain a larger real income from the fixed supplies of resources available to it. Protection—barriers to free trade—lessens or eliminates gains from specialization. If nations cannot freely trade, they must shift resources from efficient (low-cost) to inefficient (high-cost) uses to satisfy their diverse wants.

A side benefit of free trade is that it promotes competition and deters monopoly. The increased competition from foreign firms forces domestic firms to adopt the lowest-cost production techniques. It also compels them to be innovative and progressive with respect to both product quality and production methods, thereby contributing to economic growth. And free trade gives consumers a wider range of product choices. The reasons to favor free trade are the same reasons which endorse competition. That's why

INTERNATIONAL ECONOMICS AND THE WORLD ECONOMY

most economists embrace free trade as economically valid.

SUPPLY AND DEMAND ANALYSIS OF EXPORTS AND IMPORTS

Supply and demand analysis helps us see how equilibrium prices and quantities of exports and imports are determined. The amount of a good or service a nation will export or import depends on differences between the equilibrium world price and the domestic price. The equilibrium **world price** derives from interaction of *world* supply and demand; it is the price that equates quantity supplied and demanded globally. The equilibrium **domestic price** is determined by *domestic* supply and demand; it is the price which would prevail in a closed economy—one having no international trade. At this price there will be neither a domestic surplus nor shortage of the good or service.

Because of comparative advantages and disadvantages, no-trade domestic prices *may* or *may not* equal world equilibrium prices. When economies are opened for international trade, differences between world and domestic prices form the basis for exports or imports. Let's look at the international effects of these price differences in a simple two-nation world.

Supply and Demand in the United States

Suppose the world consists of just the United States and Canada, each producing aluminum. There are no trade barriers such as tariffs and quotas. Also, let's ignore international transportation costs to keep things simple.

Figure 37-3a shows the domestic supply and demand curves for aluminum in the United States. The intersection of S_d and D_d determines the equilibrium domestic price of $1 per pound and the equilibrium domestic quantity of 100 million pounds. The market clears at $1—there are no domestic surpluses nor shortages of aluminum.

But what if the United States' economy is opened to trade and the *world price* of aluminum is above or below this $1 domestic price?

United States Export Supply   If the world aluminum price exceeds $1, American firms will produce more than 100 million pounds and export the excess domestic output to the rest of the world (Canada). First, consider a world price of $1.25. We see from the supply curve S_d that American aluminum firms will produce 125 million pounds of aluminum. The demand curve D_d tells us Americans will purchase only 75 million pounds at $1.25. A domestic surplus or excess supply of 50 million pounds of aluminum results. American producers will export these 50 million pounds at the $1.25 world price.

What if the world price is $1.50? The supply curve shows that American firms will produce 150 million pounds of aluminum, while the demand curve tells us that American consumers will buy only 50 million pounds. The domestic surplus or excess supply of 100 million pounds will be exported.

In Figure 37-3b we plot on the horizontal scale the domestic surpluses—American exports—occurring at world prices above the $1 domestic equilibrium price. When the world and domestic prices are equal (= $1), the quantity of exports supplied is zero (point *a*). There is *no* surplus of domestic output to export. But when the world price is $1.25 American firms export 50 million pounds of surplus aluminum (point *b*). At a $1.50 world price, the domestic surplus of 100 million pounds is exported (point *c*).

The upsloping American **export supply curve** —found by connecting points *a, b,* and *c*—shows the amount of aluminum American producers will export at each world price above $1. This curve slopes upward, indicating a direct or positive relationship between the world price and amount of American exports. *When world prices rise relative to domestic prices, American exports increase.*

United States Import Demand   World prices below $1 in Figure 37-3a result in American imports. Consider a $.75 world price. The supply curve reveals that

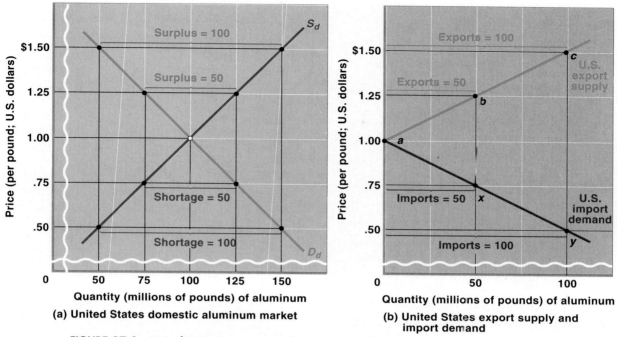

FIGURE 37-3 United States' export supply and import demand
In (a) world prices above the $1 domestic price create domestic surpluses of aluminum. As shown by the export supply curve in (b), these surpluses are exported. Domestic shortages occur when the world price is below $1 (a). These shortages are met by importing aluminum (b). The export supply curve shows the direct relationship between world prices and American exports; the import supply curve portrays the inverse relationship between world prices and American imports.

American firms can profitably produce and domestically sell 75 million pounds of aluminum. But we see from the demand curve that Americans want to buy 125 million pounds at this price. The result? A domestic shortage of 50 million pounds. To satisfy this shortage, 50 million pounds of aluminum imports will enter the United States.

At the lower $.50 world price, American producers supply only 50 million pounds. Because American consumers want to buy 150 million pounds, there is a domestic shortage of 100 million pounds. Imports flow to the United States to make up the 100 million pound difference. That is, at a $.50 world price American firms supply 50 million pounds and foreign firms supply 100 million pounds.

In Figure 37-3b we derive the American **import demand curve.** This downsloping curve shows the amount of aluminum imported at world prices below the $1 American domestic price. The relationship between world prices and imports is inverse or negative. Domestic output will satisfy American demand at a world price of $1; imports will be zero (point *a*). But

at $.75 Americans will import 50 million pounds of aluminum (point *x*); at $.50, they will import 100 million pounds (point *y*). Connecting points *a*, *x*, and *y* yields a downsloping American import demand curve. *When world prices fall relative to American domestic prices, American imports increase.*

Supply and Demand in Canada

Now we repeat our analysis in Figure 37-4 for Canada. [We have converted Canadian dollar prices to American dollar prices via the exchange rate (Chapters 6 and 38).] To begin, note that the domestic supply and demand curves for aluminum in Canada yield a domestic price of $.75, which is $.25 lower than the $1 American domestic price.

The analysis is identical. If the world price is $.75, Canadians will neither export nor import aluminum (point *q* in Figure 37-4b). At prices above $.75, Canadian firms will produce more aluminum than Canadian consumers will buy. The surplus or excess supply of aluminum represents Canada's supply of

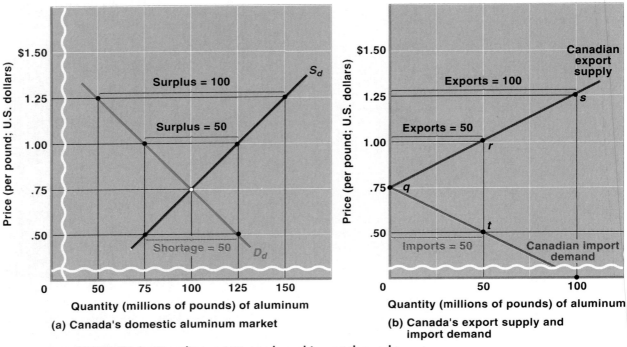

FIGURE 37-4 Canadian export supply and import demand
In (a) domestic production of aluminum in Canada exceeds domestic consumption at all world prices above the $.75 domestic price. These domestic surpluses result in Canadian exports (b). When the domestic price falls below $.75, domestic shortages occur (a) and imports flow to Canada (b). The Canadian export supply curve and import demand curve depict these relationships.

exports. At a $1 world price Canada will export a domestic surplus of 50 million pounds (point *r*). At $1.25 it will export a domestic surplus of 100 million pounds (point *s*). The upsloping Canadian *export supply curve* reflects the domestic surpluses and hence exports occurring when the world price exceeds the $.75 Canadian domestic price.

Domestic shortages occur in Canada at world prices below $.75. At a $.50 world price, Canadian consumers want to buy 125 million pounds of aluminum but Canadian firms can profitably produce only 75 pounds. The shortage or excess demand brings 50 million pounds of imports to Canada (point *t* in Figure 37-4b). The Canadian *import demand curve* represents the domestic shortages and thus Canadian imports occurring at world aluminum prices below the $.75 Canadian domestic price.

Equilibrium World Price, Exports, and Imports

We now have the tools to determine the equilibrium world price of aluminum and the equilibrium world

levels of exports and imports. Figure 37-5 combines the American export supply curve and import demand curve of Figure 37-3b and the Canadian export supply curve and import demand curve of Figure 37-4b. The two United States' curves proceed rightward from the $1 American domestic price; the two Canadian curves proceed rightward from the $.75 Canadian domestic price. *International equilibrium occurs in this two-nation model where one nation's import demand curve intersects another nation's export supply curve.* In this case the United States' import demand curve intersects Canada's export supply curve at *e*. There, the world price of aluminum is $.88. The Canadian export supply curve indicates Canada will export 25 million pounds of aluminum at this price. That means the United States will import 25 million pounds from Canada, indicated by the American import demand curve. The $.88 world price equates the quantity of imports demanded and the quantity of exports supplied (25 million pounds). This price reflects world demand and supply (Canada and the United States).

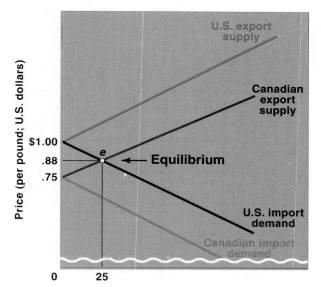

FIGURE 37-5 Equilibrium world price and quantity of exports and imports
In a two-nation world, the equilibrium world price (= $.88) is determined at the intersection of one nation's export supply curve and another nation's import demand curve. This intersection also decides the equilibrium volume of exports and imports. Here, Canada exports 25 million pounds of aluminum to the United States.

Note that after trade, the single $.88 world price will prevail in both Canada and the United States. *Only one price for a standardized commodity can persist in a highly competitive market.* With trade, all consumers can buy a pound of aluminum for $.88 and all producers can sell it for that price. This world price means that Canadians will pay more for aluminum with trade ($.88) than without it ($.75). The increased Canadian output caused by trade raises Canadian production costs and therefore the price of aluminum in Canada. Americans, however, pay less for aluminum with trade ($.88) than without it ($1). The American gain comes from Canada's comparative cost advantage in producing aluminum.

Why would Canada willingly send 50 million pounds of its aluminum output to America for consumption? Producing this output uses up scarce Canadian resources and drives up the price of aluminum for Canadians. Canadians are willing to export aluminum to the United States because they can gain the means—the earnings of dollars—to import other goods, say, computer software, from the United

States. Canadian exports enable Canadians to acquire imports that have greater value to Canadians than the exported aluminum. Canadian exports to America finance American exports to Canada. *(Key Question 6)*

TRADE BARRIERS

No matter how compelling the logic for free trade, barriers to free trade do exist. Let's look again at Chapter 6's list of trade impediments and see what we can add to our understanding of them.

1   *Tariffs* are excise taxes on imported goods; they may be imposed for purposes of revenue or protection.

Revenue tariffs are usually applied to products not produced domestically, for example, tin, coffee, and bananas in the case of the United States. Rates on revenue tariffs are modest; their purpose is to provide the Federal government with tax revenues.

Protective tariffs are designed to shield domestic producers from foreign competition. Although protective tariffs are usually not high enough to prohibit importation of foreign goods, they put foreign producers at a competitive disadvantage in selling in domestic markets.

2   **Import quotas** specify the maximum amounts of commodities which may be imported in any period. Import quotas can more effectively retard international commerce than tariffs. A product might be imported in large quantities despite high tariffs; low import quotas completely prohibit imports once quotas are filled.

3   **Nontariff barriers** (NTBs) refer to licensing requirements, unreasonable standards pertaining to product quality and safety, or unnecessary bureaucratic red tape in customs procedures. Japan and the European countries frequently require their domestic importers of foreign goods to obtain licenses. By restricting the issuance of licenses, imports can be restricted. Great Britain bars importation of coal in this way.

4   **Voluntary export restrictions** (VERs) are a trade barrier by which foreign firms "voluntarily" limit the amount of their exports to a particular country. VERs, which have the effect of import quotas, are agreed to by exporters in the hope of avoiding more stringent trade barriers. Japanese auto manufacturers agreed to a VER on exports to the United States under the threat of higher U.S. tariffs or the imposition of low import quotas.

Later in this chapter we will consider the specific arguments and appeals made to justify protection.

Economic Impact of Tariffs

Once again we use supply and demand analysis—now to examine the economic effects of protective tariffs. The D_d and S_d curves in Figure 37-6 show domestic demand and supply for a product in which the United States has a comparative *dis*advantage, for example, video cassette recorders (VCRs). (Disregard $S_d + Q$ for now.) Without world trade, the domestic price and output would be P_d and q, respectively.

Assume now that the domestic economy is opened to world trade and that the Japanese, who have a comparative advantage in VCRs, begin to sell their recorders in the United States. We assume that with free trade the domestic price cannot differ from the world price, which here is P_w. At P_w domestic consumption is d and domestic production is a. The horizontal distance between the domestic supply and demand curves at P_w reflects imports of ad. Thus far, our analysis is similar to the analysis of world prices in Figure 37-3.

Direct Effects Suppose now that the United States imposes a tariff of P_wP_t per unit on the imported VCRs. This will raise the domestic price from P_w to P_t and will have several effects.

1 Decline in Consumption Consumption of video recorders in the United States will decline from d to c as the higher price moves buyers up their demand curve. The tariff prompts consumers to buy fewer recorders; they reallocate a portion of their expenditures to less desired substitute products. American consumers are clearly injured by the tariff, since they pay P_wP_t more for each of the c units they buy at price P_t.

2 Increased Domestic Production American producers—who are *not* subject to the tariff—will receive a higher price of P_t per unit. Because this new price is higher than the pretariff or world price of P_w, the domestic VCR industry will move up its supply curve S_d, increasing domestic output from a to b. Domestic producers will enjoy both a higher price and expanded sales. This explains why domestic producers lobby for protective tariffs. But from a social point of view, the expanded domestic production of ab means the tariff permits domestic producers of recorders to bid resources away from other, more efficient, industries.

3 Decline in Imports Japanese producers will be hurt. Although the sales price of recorders is higher by P_wP_t, that increase accrues to the United States government, not to Japanese producers. The after-tariff world price, and thus the per unit revenue to Japanese producers, remains at P_w, while the volume of United States imports (Japanese exports) falls from ad to bc.

4 Tariff Revenue The shaded rectangle indicates the amount of revenue which the tariff yields. Total revenue from the tariff is determined by multiplying the tariff, P_wP_t per unit, by the number of imported recorders, bc. This tariff revenue is a transfer of income from consumers to government and does *not* represent any net change in the nation's economic well-being. The result is that government gains this portion of what consumers lose.

Indirect Effects There are subtle effects of tariffs beyond what our supply and demand diagram can show. Because of diminished sales of recorders in the

FIGURE 37-6 The economic effects of a protective tariff or an import quota
A tariff of P_wP_t will reduce domestic consumption from d to c. Domestic producers will be able to sell more output (b rather than a) at a higher price (P_t rather than P_w). Foreign exporters are injured because they sell less output (bc rather than ad) in the United States. The shaded area indicates the amount of tariffs paid by American consumers. An import quota of bc units will have the same effects as the tariff, with one exception: the shaded area will go to foreign producers rather than to the U.S. Treasury.

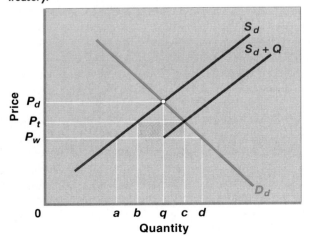

Quantity

United States, Japan will earn fewer dollars with which to buy American exports. American export industries —industries in which the United States has a comparative advantage—will cut production and release resources. These are highly efficient industries, as evidenced by their comparative advantage and ability to sell goods in world markets.

Tariffs directly promote the expansion of inefficient industries which do not have a comparative advantage and indirectly cause the contraction of relatively efficient industries which do have a comparative advantage. This means tariffs cause resources to be shifted in the wrong direction. Not surprising. We know that specialization and unfettered world trade based on comparative advantage would lead to the efficient use of world resources and an expansion of the world's real output. The purpose and effect of protective tariffs are to reduce world trade. Therefore, aside from their specific effects on consumers and foreign and domestic producers, tariffs diminish the world's real output.

Economic Impact of Quotas

We noted previously that an import quota is a legal limit placed on the amount of some product which can be imported each year. Quotas have the same economic impact as a tariff with one big difference: While tariffs generate revenue for the United States government, a quota transfers that revenue to foreign producers.

Suppose in Figure 37-6 that, instead of imposing a tariff of P_wP_t per unit, the United States prohibits any Japanese imports of VCRs in excess of bc units. In other words, an import quota of bc recorders is imposed on Japan. We have deliberately chosen the size of this quota to be the same amount as imports would be under a P_wP_t tariff, so we are comparing "equivalent" situations. As a consequence of the quota, the supply of recorders is $S_d + Q$ in the United States. This consists of the domestic supply plus the constant amount bc ($= Q$) which importers will provide at each domestic price. The $S_d + Q$ supply curve does not exist below price P_w because Japanese producers would not export recorders to the United States at any price *below* P_w when they can sell them to other countries at the world market price of P_w.

Most of the economic results are the same as with a tariff. VCR prices are higher (P_t instead of P_w) because imports have been reduced from *ad* to *bc*. Domestic consumption of VCRs is down from *d* to *c*.

American producers enjoy both a higher price (P_t rather than P_w) and increased sales (*b* rather than *a*).

The difference is that the price increase of P_wP_t paid by American consumers on imports of *bc*—the shaded area—no longer goes to the United States Treasury as tariff (tax) revenue, but flows to those Japanese firms which have acquired the rights to sell VCRs in the United States. For Americans, a tariff produces a better economic outcome than a quota, other things being the same. A tariff generates government revenue which can be used to cut other taxes or to finance public goods and services which benefit Americans. In contrast, the higher price created by quotas results in additional revenue for foreign producers.

In the early 1980s the American automobile industry with the support of its workers successfully lobbied for an import quota on Japanese autos. The Japanese government in turn apportioned this quota among its various auto producers. The restricted supply of Japanese cars in the American market allowed Japanese manufacturers to increase their prices and, hence, their profits. The American import quotas in effect provided Japanese auto manufacturers with a cartel-like arrangement which enhanced their profits. When American import quotas were dropped in the mid-1980s, the Japanese government replaced them with its own system of export quotas for Japanese automakers! *(Key Question 7)*

THE CASE FOR PROTECTION: A CRITICAL REVIEW

Although free-trade advocates prevail in the classroom, protectionists regularly reside in the halls of Congress. What arguments do protectionists make to justify trade barriers? How valid are these arguments?

Military Self-Sufficiency Argument

The argument here is not economic—it's political-military. Protective tariffs are needed to preserve or strengthen industries producing goods and materials essential for defense or war. It contends that in an uncertain world, political-military objectives (self-sufficiency) must take precedence over economic goals (efficiency in the use of world resources).

Unfortunately, there is no objective criterion for weighing the worth of the increase in national security relative to the decrease in economic efficiency accompanying reallocation of resources toward strategic industries when such tariffs are imposed. The economist can only point out that there are economic costs when tariffs are levied to enhance military self-sufficiency.

Although we might all agree that it is not a good idea to import our missile guidance systems from China, the self-sufficiency argument is nevertheless open to serious abuse. Nearly every industry can directly or indirectly claim a contribution to national security.

Aside from abuses, are there not better ways than tariffs to provide for needed strength in strategic industries? When achieved through tariffs, self-sufficiency creates costs in the form of higher domestic prices on the output of the shielded industry. The cost of enhanced military security is apportioned arbitrarily among those consumers who buy the industry's product. A direct subsidy to strategic industries, financed out of general tax revenues, would more equitably distribute these costs.

Increase Domestic Employment

Arguing for a tariff to "save American jobs" becomes fashionable as an economy encounters a recession. It is rooted in macro analysis. Aggregate demand in an open economy is comprised of consumption expenditures (C) plus investment expenditures (I_g) plus government expenditures (G) plus net export expenditures (X_n). Net export expenditures consist of exports (X) minus imports (M). By reducing imports, M, aggregate demand will rise, stimulating the domestic economy by boosting income and employment. But there are shortcomings associated with this policy.

1   Job Creation from Imports   While imports may eliminate some American jobs, they create others. Imports may have eliminated jobs of American steel and textile workers in recent years, but others have gained jobs selling Hondas and imported electronics equipment. While import restrictions alter the composition of employment, they may have little or no effect on the volume of employment.

2   Fallacy of Composition   All nations cannot simultaneously succeed in import restriction; what is true for *one* nation is not true for *all* nations. The exports of one nation must be the imports of another. To the extent that one country is able to stimulate its economy through an excess of exports over imports,

another economy's unemployment problem is worsened by the resulting excess of imports over exports. It is no wonder that tariff and import quotas to achieve domestic full employment are termed "beggar my neighbor" policies. They achieve short-run domestic goals by making trading partners poorer.

3   Retaliation   Nations adversely affected by tariffs and quotas are likely to retaliate, causing a competitive raising of trade barriers which will choke off trade to the end that all nations are worse off. The **Smoot-Hawley Tariff Act of 1930,** which imposed the highest tariffs ever enacted in the United States, backfired miserably. Rather than stimulate the American economy, this tariff act only induced a series of retaliatory restrictions by adversely affected nations. This "trade war" caused a further contraction of international trade and lowered the income and employment levels of all nations. As clarified by one of America's foremost international trade experts:

> A trade war in which countries restrict each other's exports in pursuit of some illusory advantage is not much like a real war. On the one hand, nobody gets killed. On the other, unlike real wars, it is almost impossible for anyone to win, since the main losers when a country imposes barriers to trade are not foreign exporters but domestic residents. In effect, a trade war is a conflict in which each country uses most of its ammunition to shoot itself in the foot.[1]

4   Long-Run Feedbacks   In the long run an excess of exports over imports is doomed to failure as a device for stimulating domestic employment. It is through American imports that foreign nations earn dollars for buying American exports. In the long run a nation must import to export. The long-run impact of tariffs is not to increase domestic employment but at best to reallocate workers away from export industries and toward protected domestic industries. This shift implies a less efficient allocation of resources.

In summary, the argument that tariffs increase net exports and therefore create jobs is misleading:

> Overall employment in an economy is determined by internal conditions and macroeconomic policies, not by the existence of trade barriers and the level of

---

[1]Paul Krugman, *Peddling Prosperity* (New York: W. W. Norton & Co., 1994), p. 287.

trade flows. The United States created [more than 18] million payroll jobs over the course of the [1982–1990] economic expansion, a period of U.S. trade deficits and relatively open U.S. markets. During the same period the European [Union (EU)] created virtually no net new jobs, even though they experienced trade surpluses. The same level of employment can be obtained in the total absence of free trade as when trade is completely free. But without foreign trade a nation will be worse off economically because, in effect, it will throw away part of its productive capability—the ability to convert surplus goods into other goods through foreign trade.[2]

Diversification for Stability

Highly specialized economies—for example, Saudi Arabia's oil economy or Cuba's sugar economy—are very dependent on international markets for their incomes. Wars, cyclical fluctuations, and adverse changes in the structure of industry will force large and painful readjustments on such economies. Tariff and quota protection is allegedly needed to promote greater industrial diversification and less dependence on world markets for just one or two products. This will help insulate the domestic economy from international political developments, depressions abroad, and from random fluctuations in world supply and demand for one or two particular commodities, thereby providing greater domestic stability.

There is some truth in this diversification for stability argument. There are also serious qualifications and shortcomings.
1 The argument has little or no relevance to the United States and other advanced economies.
2 The economic costs of diversification may be great; for example, one-crop economies may be highly inefficient in manufacturing.

Infant-Industry Argument

The infant-industry argument contends that protective tariffs are needed to allow new domestic industries to establish themselves. Temporarily shielding young domestic firms from the severe competition of more mature and more efficient foreign firms will give infant industries a chance to develop and become efficient producers.

This argument for protection rests on an alleged exception to the case for free trade. The exception is

that all industries have not had, and facing mature foreign competition, will never have, the chance to make long-run adjustments in the direction of larger scale and greater efficiency in production. Tariff protection for infant industries will correct a misallocation of world resources perpetuated by historically different levels of economic development between domestic and foreign industries.

Counterarguments Consider the qualifying points below to the logical validity of the infant-industry argument.
1 In the less developed nations it is difficult to determine which industries are the infants capable of achieving economic maturity and therefore deserving of protection.
2 Protective tariffs may persist even after industrial maturity has been realized.
3 Most economists feel that if infant industries are to be subsidized, there are better means than tariffs for doing it. Direct subsidies, for example, have the advantage of making explicit which industries are being aided and to what degree.

Strategic Trade Policy In recent years the infant-industry argument has taken a modified form in advanced economies. The contention is that government should use trade barriers to reduce the risk of product development borne by domestic firms, particularly products involving advanced technology. Firms protected from foreign competition can grow more rapidly and achieve greater economies of scale than unprotected foreign competitors. The protected firms can eventually dominate world markets because of lower costs. Supposedly, dominance of world markets will enable the domestic firms to return high profits to the home nation. These profits will exceed the domestic sacrifices caused by trade barriers. Also, specialization in high-technology industries is deemed beneficial because technology advances achieved in one domestic industry often can be transferred to other domestic industries.

Japan and South Korea, in particular, have been accused of using this form of **strategic trade policy.** The problem with this strategy and therefore this argument for tariffs is that the nations put at a disadvantage by strategic trade policies tend to retaliate with tariffs of their own. The outcome may result in higher tariffs worldwide, reductions in world trade, and loss of the gains from specialization and exchange.

---

[2]*Economic Report of the President, 1988,* p. 131. Updated.

Protection Against "Dumping"

The protection-against-dumping argument for tariffs contends that tariffs are needed to protect American firms from foreign producers which "dump" excess goods onto the American market at less than cost. Two reasons have been suggested as to why foreign firms might wish to sell in America at below cost.

1   Driving Out Competitors   Firms may use **dumping** to drive out American competitors, obtain monopoly power, and then raise prices. The long-term economic profits resulting from this strategy may more than offset the earlier losses which accompany the dumping.

2   Price Discrimination   Dumping may be a form of price discrimination—charging different prices to different customers. The foreign seller may find it can maximize its profits by charging a high price in its monopolized domestic market while unloading its surplus output at a lower price in the United States. The surplus output may be needed to obtain the overall per unit cost saving associated with large-scale production.

Because dumping is a legitimate concern, it is prohibited under American trade law. Where dumping occurs and is shown to injure American firms, the Federal government imposes tariffs called "antidumping duties" on the specific goods. But relative to the number of goods exported to the United States, documented cases of dumping are few. Dumping therefore does *not* justify widespread, permanent tariffs. Furthermore, allegations of dumping require careful investigation to determine their validity.

Foreign producers argue that dumping allegations and antidumping duties are an American method of restricting legitimate trade. The fact is that some foreign firms can produce certain goods at substantially less cost than American competitors, and what on the surface may seem to be dumping often is comparative advantage at work. If abused, the antidumping law can increase the price of imports and restrict competition in the American market. This reduced competition allows American firms to raise prices at consumers' expense. And even where true dumping does occur, American consumers gain from the lower-priced product—at least in the short term—much as they gain from a price war among American producers.

Cheap Foreign Labor

The cheap-foreign-labor argument says domestic firms and workers must be shielded from the ruinous competition of countries where wages are low. If protection is not provided, cheap imports will flood American markets and the prices of American goods—along with the wages of American workers—will be pulled down and our domestic living standards reduced.

This argument can be rebutted at several levels. The logic of the argument suggests it is *not* mutually beneficial for rich and poor persons to trade with one another. However, that is not the case. A low-income farm worker may pick lettuce or tomatoes for a rich landowner and both may benefit from the transaction. And don't American consumers gain when they buy a Taiwanese pocket radio for $12 as opposed to a qualitatively similar American-made radio selling for $20?

Also, recall that gains from trade are based on comparative advantage. Looking back at Figure 37-1, suppose the United States and Brazil have labor forces of exactly the same size. Noting the positions of the production possibilities curves, we observe that American labor is absolutely more productive because our labor force can produce more of either good. Because of this greater productivity, we can expect wages and living standards to be higher for American labor. Brazil's less-productive labor will receive lower wages.

The cheap-foreign-labor argument suggests that, to maintain our standard of living, America should not trade with low-wage Brazil. Suppose we don't. Will wages and living standards rise in the United States as a result? No. To obtain coffee America will have to reallocate a portion of its labor from its efficient wheat industry to its inefficient coffee industry. As a result, the average productivity of American labor will fall as will real wages and living standards. The labor forces of *both* countries will have diminished standards of living because without specialization and trade they will have less output available to them. Compare column 4 with column 1 in Table 37-1 or points A' and B' with A and B in Figure 37-2 to confirm this point.

A Summing Up

These many arguments for protection are not weighty. Under proper conditions, the infant-industry argument stands as a valid exception, justifiable on economic grounds. And on political-military grounds, the

GLOBAL PERSPECTIVE 37-2

Growth per capita and level of trade protection

Higher levels of trade protection in less developed nations are generally associated with lower levels of economic growth, as measured by average annual increases in output per person.

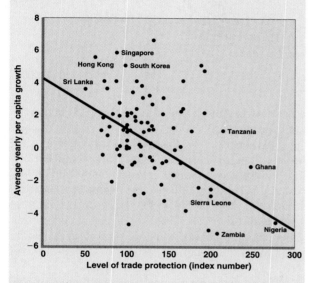

Source: David M. Gould, Graeme L. Woodbridge, and Roy J. Ruffin, "The Theory and Practice of International Trade," *Economic Review,* Federal Reserve Bank of Dallas, 4th Quarter, 1993, p. 3. Data are for 1976–1985.

this is a positive factor in the economic development of our nation.

2   Great Britain's shift toward freer international trade in the mid-nineteenth century was instrumental in its industrialization and growth at that time.

3   The creation of the Common Market in Europe after World War II has eliminated tariffs among member nations. Economists agree that creation of this free-trade area, now the European Union, has been an ingredient in western European prosperity.

4   The trend toward tariff reduction since the mid-1930s has been a stimulus to post-World War II expansion of the world economy.

5   The high tariffs imposed by our Smoot-Hawley Act of 1930 and the retaliation which it engendered worsened the Great Depression of the 1930s.

6   Studies of less developed countries overwhelmingly suggest that those which have relied on import restrictions to protect their domestic industries have had slow growth compared to those pursuing more open economic policies (see Global Perspective 37-2).

QUICK REVIEW 37-2

■ A nation will export a particular product if the world price exceeds the domestic price; it will import the product if the world price is less than the domestic price.

■ In a two-country model, equilibrium world prices and quantities of exports and imports occur where one nation's export supply curve intersects the other nation's import demand curve.

■ Trade barriers include tariffs, import quotas, nontariff barriers, and voluntary export restrictions.

■ A tariff on a product increases price, reduces consumption, increases domestic production, reduces imports, and generates tariff revenue for government; an import quota does the same, except that a quota generates revenue for foreign producers rather than the government imposing the quota.

■ Most arguments for trade protection are special-interest pleas which, if followed, would create gains for protected industries and their workers at the expense of greater losses for the economy.

self-sufficiency argument can be used to validate protection. Both arguments are susceptible to severe abuses, and both neglect other ways of fostering industrial development and military self-sufficiency. Most other arguments are semi-emotional appeals—half-truths and fallacies. These arguments see only the immediate and direct consequences of protective tariffs. They ignore the fact that in the long run a nation must import to export.

There is also compelling historical evidence suggesting that free trade has led to prosperity and growth and that protectionism has had the opposite effects. Several examples follow.

1   The United States Constitution forbids individual states from levying tariffs, making America a huge free-trade area. Economic historians acknowledge

COSTS OF PROTECTIONISM

How costly are existing American trade protections such as tariffs, quotas, and voluntary export restraints to Americans?

TABLE 37-2 The net costs of trade protection, eight industries

(1) Industry	(2) Annual loss to economy from barriers	(3) Net employment loss if barriers removed	(4) Annual cost per job saved
Textiles and apparel	$15.85 billion	71,639	$221,258
Maritime transport	3.09 billion	11,905	259,555
Dairy	847 million	2,195	385,877
Sugar	657 million	2,040	322,059
Peanuts	353 million	no estimate	—
Meat	177 million	928	190,733
Nonrubber footwear	170 million	1,377	123,456
Watches and clocks	101 million	no estimate	—

Source: Compiled from United States International Trade Commission data released in 1993. Data are for 1991.

Cost to Society

Figure 37-6 showed that tariffs and quotas impose costs on domestic consumers but confer gains to domestic producers and in the case of tariffs, revenue to the Federal government. The consumer cost of trade restrictions can be calculated by determining the effect they have on prices of protected goods. Protection will raise the price of a product in three ways.

1 The price of the imported product goes up (Figure 37-6).

2 The higher price of imports will cause some consumers to shift their purchases to higher-priced domestically produced goods.

3 The price of domestically produced goods will rise because import competition has declined.

Several studies indicate that costs to consumers of protected products substantially exceed gains to producers and government.[3] There is a sizable net cost or efficiency loss to society from trade protection. Most recently the United States International Trade Commission (USITC)—the agency which hears unfair trade complaints—has identified forty-four sectors of the American economy where trade barriers have boosted prices. These trade barriers resulted in

a net cost to Americans of more than $20 billion annually in the early 1990s.

Furthermore, net losses from trade barriers are greater than the losses reported in most studies. Tariffs and quotas produce myriad costly, difficult-to-quantify secondary effects. For example, import restraints on steel in the 1980s drove up the price of steel to all American buyers of steel—including the American automobile industry. Therefore, American automakers had higher costs than otherwise and were less competitive in world markets.

Finally, industries employ large amounts of economic resources to influence Congress to pass and retain protectionist laws. To the extent that these rent-seeking efforts divert resources away from more socially desirable purposes, trade restrictions impose another cost on society.

Conclusion: The gains which America's trade barriers create for protected industries and their workers come at the expense of much greater losses for the entire economy. The result is economic inefficiency.

Table 37-2 looks at efficiency losses for the eight industries where net costs of trade protection are greatest. It also shows the estimated reduction in domestic employment which would result if the Federal government eliminated trade barriers in these industries. Column 4 reveals how much trade restrictions cost per job saved (column 2 divided by column 3).

Two items stand out in the table.

1 Trade restrictions in the textile and apparel industries are especially costly to Americans. The Federal government has imposed import quotas on more

---

[3]United States International Trade Commission, *The Economic Effects of Significant U.S. Import Restraints,* November 1993; Cletus C. Coughlin et al., "Protectionist Trade Policies: A Survey of Theory, Evidence and Rationale," *Review* (Federal Reserve Bank of St. Louis), January/February 1988, pp. 17–18; and Gary C. Hufbauer and Kimberly A. Elliott, *Measuring the Costs of Protectionism in the United States* (Washington: Institute for International Economics, 1994), pp. 8–9.

than 3000 kinds of textile products. [These quotas eventually will be replaced with tariffs under the terms of the General Agreement on Tariffs and Trade (Chapter 6).]

2 The cost of saving jobs through trade protection is enormous. Because annual wages per job in these industries are only a fraction of these amounts, protectionism to save jobs is hardly a bargain. Moreover, it is clear from historical experience that eliminating trade barriers does not cause a *net* loss of jobs in America; it simply redistributes employment, and may even increase it.

The USITC estimates that removing trade barriers would reduce product prices in protected industries by an average of 3 percent. Prices of apparel products would fall by 11.4 percent; luggage prices by 9.1 percent; and sugar prices by 8 percent. Prices would also decline for footwear, watches, roller bearings, pressed and blown glass, costume jewelry, machine tools, frozen fruit and vegetables, ceramic tiles, and leather goods.

Impact on Income Distribution

Studies also show that import restrictions affect low-income families proportionately more than high-income families. Because tariffs and quotas act much like sales or excise taxes, these trade restrictions are highly regressive. That is, the "overcharge" associated with trade protection falls *as a percentage of income* as income increases. Example: Households on average pay an estimated extra $260 per year for clothing because of trade restrictions. Relative to their incomes, the burden of this protectionism is heavier for poorer households than for wealthier ones.

Also, items such as clothing and food, on which poor families spend a disproportionate amount of their incomes, have the most restrictive trade protection. Children's polyester sweaters face a 34.6 percent import duty, while mink coats can be imported duty-free. Trade protection lifts the price of domestic orange juice by 40 percent, but increases the price of French Perrier water by less than 1 percent. Cheap costume jewelry carries a 27.5 percent duty; gold necklaces, 6.5 percent.[4] *(Key Question 11)*

[4]James Bovard, "America's Unfairest Taxes: Tariffs and Quotas," National Center for Policy Analysis, Policy Report No. 171, June 1992.

AMERICAN INTERNATIONAL TRADE POLICY

In the past several years American international trade policy has been a mixture of generalized trade liberalization, aggressive export promotion, and bilateral negotiations on specific trade disputes.

Generalized Trade Liberalization

We discussed in Chapter 6 two recent regional and global agreements to reduce trade barriers.

North American Free Trade Agreement (NAFTA)
This widely debated accord, which took effect in 1994, eliminates tariffs and other trade barriers between Canada, Mexico, and the United States over a fifteen-year period. When fully implemented, the **North American Free Trade Agreement (NAFTA)** will constitute the largest geographical free-trade zone in the world. In late 1994, Chile was invited to apply for membership in NAFTA.

General Agreement on Tariffs and Trade (GATT)
In 1994 more than 120 of the world's nations successfully completed negotiation of the Uruguay Round of the **General Agreement on Tariffs and Trade (GATT).** GATT provisions to be implemented between 1995 and 2005 include:
1 Reduction of tariffs worldwide
2 Liberalization of rules which have impeded trade in services
3 Reduction of agricultural subsidies which have distorted the global pattern of trade in agricultural goods
4 New protections for intellectual property (copyrights, patents, trademarks)
5 A phasing out of quotas on textiles and apparel, to be replaced with gradually declining tariffs
6 Establishment of the **World Trade Organization** to oversee the provisions of the agreement and to resolve any disputes under the new rules

When completed in 2005, GATT will boost the world's GDP by an estimated $6 trillion, or 8 percent. Incidentally, it will also reduce American tariff revenues by $12 billion to $14 billion.

Aggressive Export Promotion

The Federal government recently has aggressively promoted American exports in a number of ways. Undoubtedly, the reason is that American exports generally support high-paying jobs and increases in exports are needed to end America trade deficits. Perhaps, too, the popular myth that the global marketplace is a battleground for economic supremacy has played a role. Japan wins; America loses. America wins; Germany loses. But trade is not like war, nor like a World Cup match, where one nation wins and the other loses. Every nation is both seller *and* buyer in the world market. Gains from trade come from the increased consumable output shared by the trading countries. Exports are *not* the end goal of international trade; they simply enable a country to pay for imports—goods which would cost the nation more to produce at home.

Here are some recent examples of export promotion policy at work.

1 Direct government advocacy of export interests of American producers. High American officials have hawked American goods throughout the world. Example: President Clinton and other administration officials directly lobbied King Fahd of Saudi Arabia to buy commercial aircraft from America's Boeing and McDonnell Douglas, rather than from Europe's Airbus.

2 Relaxation of **export controls.** In the past, national security and foreign policy objectives have restricted from export certain high-technology products such as computers and advanced communications equipment. Many of these controls have now been ended.

3 Increased government funding of America's **Export-Import Bank.** This government-funded "bank" provides interest-rate subsidies to foreign borrowers who buy American exports on credit. The result is a lower total product price (product price + interest on loan) and therefore increased exports.

4 Renewed emphasis on **industrial policy** consisting of government actions designed to expand specific firms or industries. When focused on international trade, this facet of strategic trade policy channels government subsidies to specific high-technology industries for development of products that bolster exports. These government payments are a type of **export subsidy** (Chapter 6), which reduce development or production costs. Thus, they lower the price of exported goods and enhance their sales in world markets.

Example: In 1994 the Clinton administration announced a $1 billion plan to help industry compete with Japan in developing advanced flat-panel com-

puter screens. The administration justified this massive subsidy as necessary for national defense. But this action had as much to do with competing with Japan in a burgeoning world export market as with ensuring national defense.

5 Controversial uses of retaliatory tariffs—or threats thereof—to force other nations to reduce their trade barriers against American products. By using American economic and political leverage American firms can obtain freer access to foreign markets. Since 1989 the United States has used retaliatory tariffs in addressing specific trade issues with Japan, Brazil, India, South Korea, Taiwan, France, and other nations. For example, in 1992 it tripled the import duty on French white wine to spur France to open its doors to more American soybean exports.

Bilateral Negotiations

Bilateral trade negotiations—discussions between two countries, rather than many—are another facet of American international trade policy. These negotiations have occurred directly between the United States and several other nations, including China, Japan, South Korea, and Canada. Usually these negotiations have focused on specific trade restrictions or on alleged dumping of specific goods. But negotiations with China and Japan have dealt with broader trade issues.

Renewal of China's Most-Favored-Nation Status
In 1994 the United States again renewed China's **most-favored-nation (MFN)** status, first conferred in 1980. MFN (which applies to most of America's trading partners) means imports from China will continue to face the lowest American tariffs. Also, any subsequent reductions in American tariffs negotiated with other nations will also apply to Chinese imports. These low tariffs are important to China, since the United States buys about 30 percent of all Chinese exports. American imports from China mainly include labor-intensive goods such as toys, shoes, and clothes. In 1994 the United States had a $28 billion trade deficit with China.

Renewal of MFN for China was controversial. The Clinton administration initially sought to link renewal of China's MFN status with improvements in China's human rights record. No decrease in political repression, no renewal of MFN status. China rejected this linkage as being an unacceptable interference in China's domestic affairs.

After a series of unsuccessful negotiations, America backed down on its threat. Weighing heavily in this decision was the argument that our international trade with China is *consistent* with our goal of improved Chinese human rights. International trade opens China to the outside world and exposes it to the personal and social benefits of economic freedom. Greater freedom in one sphere may whet the appetite for freedom in other spheres. Also, international trade expands the political influence of leaders in China's business sector. These business leaders are more reform-minded than the older political leadership and, in general, lack commitment to communist ideology —an ideology used to support dictatorship and political repression.

Despite renewal of MFN status, trade relations between America and China remain fragile. Example: In 1995 the United States temporarily invoked high tariffs against selected Chinese imports in retaliation for China's unwillingness to crack down on massive, unauthorized reproduction and sale of American-made software, videos, and recordings.

Negotiations with Japan   Much recent American bilateral negotiation has centered on America's annual $60 billion trade deficit with Japan. Specific goods for which there are large deficits are automobiles and parts, computers and office machines, electrical machinery and appliances, televisions and radios, and photo and optical gear.

America and Japan have held numerous, sometimes testy, negotiations on this deficit problem. The initial American position was that Japan needed to set numerical targets for increasing imports from the United States. The Japanese retorted that it vehemently opposed "managed trade" of this sort. The trade balance between two nations should be determined by market forces, say the Japanese. United States negotiators counter that the deficit is not totally a "market" deficit. Japan's widespread system of nontariff trade barriers impedes the working of the global market, contributing heavily to Japan's trade surplus. Also, the Japanese system of *keiretsu*—large groups of interlocked Japanese firms which buy and sell exclusively from one another—denies American firms access to Japanese markets. American negotiators have pointed out that even products such as cellular phones, which American firms produce in high quality and at low cost, have not made inroads in Japan. And while American firms hold about 45 percent of the global market for large-scale construction projects, their share in Japan is a minuscule 0.1 percent.

The Japanese have pointed out that in 1993 the average Japanese spent $150 more on American imports than the average American spent on Japanese imports. (The American trade deficit results from the far greater number of Americans.) Japan also points to its $13 billion annual *deficit* in *services* (as opposed to goods) with the United States. No one in the United States views that American *surplus* as a problem, say the Japanese. Nor did Americans view their historical trade *surplus* with Canada as a matter for concern. Why the concern with Japan's trade surplus with the United States?

While new trade agreements between the United States and Japan have been reached, the two nations will not end their trade imbalance soon. Elimination of *all* tariffs and nontariff trade barriers in Japan would increase American exports to Japan by only an estimated $9 billion to $18 billion, compared to the current $60 billion deficit.

CHAPTER SUMMARY

1   America is the world's largest international trader in terms of volume. Since 1965 our exports and imports have more than doubled as a percentage of GDP. Other major trading nations are Germany, Japan, the western European nations, and the newly industrialized Asia tigers (Hong Kong, Singapore, South Korea, and Taiwan).

2   World trade is based on two considerations: the uneven distribution of economic resources among nations, and the fact that efficient production of various goods requires particular techniques or combinations of resources.

3   Mutually advantageous specialization and trade are possible between any two nations so long as the domestic opportunity cost ratios for any two products differ. By specializing according to comparative advantage, nations can realize larger real incomes with fixed amounts of resources. The terms of trade determine how this increase in world output is shared by the trading nations. Increasing costs impose limits on specialization and trade.

4   A nation's export supply curve shows the quantity of exports it will supply when world prices exceed the domestic price—the price in a closed, no-international-trade economy. The import demand curve reveals the quantity of imports demanded at world prices below the domestic price. In a two-nation model, the equilibrium world price and the

LAST WORD

PETITION OF THE CANDLEMAKERS, 1845

The French economist Frédéric Bastiat (1801–1850) devastated the proponents of protectionism by satirically extending their reasoning to its logical and absurd conclusions.

Petition of the Manufacturers of Candles, Waxlights, Lamps, Candlesticks, Street Lamps, Snuffers, Extinguishers, and of the Producers of Oil Tallow, Rosin, Alcohol, and, Generally, of Everything Connected with Lighting.

TO MESSIEURS THE MEMBERS
OF THE CHAMBER
OF DEPUTIES.

Gentlemen—You are on the right road. You reject abstract theories, and have little consideration for cheapness and plenty. Your chief care is the interest of the producer. You desire to emancipate him from external competition, and reserve the *national market* for *national industry.*

We are about to offer you an admirable opportunity of applying your—what shall we call it? your theory? No; nothing is more deceptive than theory; your doctrine? your system? your principle? but you dislike doctrines, you abhor systems, and as for principles, you deny that there are any in social economy: we shall say, then, your practice, your practice without theory and without principle.

We are suffering from the intolerable competition of a foreign rival, placed, it would seem, in a condition so far superior to ours for the production of light, that he absolutely *inundates* our *national market* with it at a price fabulously reduced. The moment he shows himself, our trade leaves us—all consumers apply to him; and a branch of native industry, having countless ramifications, is all at once rendered completely stagnant. This rival . . . is no other than the Sun.

What we pray for is, that it may please you to pass a law ordering the shutting up of all windows, skylights, dormerwindows, outside and inside shutters, curtains, blinds, bull's-eyes; in a word, of all openings, holes, chinks, clefts, and fissures, by or through which the light of the sun has been in use to enter houses, to the prejudice of the meritorious manufactures with which we flatter ourselves we have accommodated our country,—a country which, in gratitude, ought not to abandon us now to a strife so unequal.

If you shut up as much as possible all access to natural light, and create a demand for artificial light, which of our French manufactures will not be encouraged by it?

If more tallow is consumed, then there must be more oxen and sheep; and, consequently, we shall behold the multiplication of artificial meadows, meat, wool, hides, and, above all, manure, which is the basis and foundation of all agricultural wealth.

The same remark applies to navigation. Thousands of vessels will proceed to the whale fishery; and, in a short time, we shall possess a navy capable of maintaining the honor of France, and gratifying the patriotic aspirations of your petitioners, the undersigned candlemakers and others.

Only have the goodness to reflect, Gentlemen, and you will be convinced that there is, perhaps, no Frenchman, from the wealthy coalmaster to the humblest vender of lucifer matches, whose lot will not be ameliorated by the success of this our petition.

Source: Frédéric Bastiat, *Economic Sophisms* (Edinburgh: Oliver and Boyd, Tweeddale Court, 1873), pp. 49–53, abridged.

equilibrium quantities of exports and imports occur where one nation's import supply curve intersects another nation's export demand curve.

5 Trade barriers take the form of protective tariffs, quotas, nontariff barriers, and "voluntary" export restrictions. Supply and demand analysis reveals that protective tariffs and quotas increase the prices and reduce the quantities demanded of affected goods. Foreign exporters find their sales diminish. Domestic producers, however, enjoy higher prices and enlarged sales. Tariffs and quotas promote a less efficient allocation of domestic and world resources.

6 The strongest arguments for protection are the infant-industry and military self-sufficiency arguments. Most of the other arguments for protection are half-truths, emo-tional appeals, or fallacies which emphasize the immediate effects of trade barriers while ignoring long-run consequences. Numerous historical examples suggest that free trade promotes economic growth; protectionism does not.

7 Protectionism costs American consumers substantial amounts annually. The cost to consumers for each job saved is far greater than the average salary paid. Consumer losses from trade restrictions greatly exceed producer and government gains, creating an efficiency loss to society.

8 Recent American international trade policy entails: **a** general liberalization of trade through NAFTA and GATT; **b** aggressive export promotion by government, and **c** bilateral negotiations over specific trade disputes, including the problem of the large American trade deficit with Japan.

TERMS AND CONCEPTS

labor- (land-, capital-) intensive commodity	world price	Smoot-Hawley Tariff Act of 1930	World Trade Organization
cost ratio	domestic price	strategic trade policy	export controls
principle of comparative advantage	export supply curve	dumping	Export-Import Bank
	import demand curve	North American Free Trade Agreement (NAFTA)	industrial policy
terms of trade	revenue and protective tariffs		export subsidy
trading possibilities line	import quotas	General Agreement on Tariffs and Trade (GATT)	most-favored-nation (MFN)
gains from trade	nontariff barriers		
	voluntary export restrictions		

QUESTIONS AND STUDY SUGGESTIONS

1 Quantitatively, how important is international trade to the United States relative to other nations?

2 Distinguish among land-, labor-, and capital-intensive commodities, citing an example of each. What role do these distinctions play in explaining international trade?

3 Suppose nation A can produce 80 units of X by using all its resources to produce X and 60 units of Y by devoting all its resource to Y. Comparative figures for nation B are 60 of X and 60 of Y. Assuming constant costs, in which product should each nation specialize? Why? Indicate the limits of the terms of trade.

4 *Key Question* The following are hypothetical production possibilities tables for New Zealand and Spain.

New Zealand's production possibilities table (millions of bushels)

Product	Production alternatives			
	A	B	C	D
Apples	0	20	40	60
Plums	15	10	5	0

Spain's production possibilities table (millions of bushels)

Product	Production alternatives			
	R	S	T	U
Apples	0	20	40	60
Plums	60	40	20	0

Using a graph, plot the production possibilities data for each of the two countries. Referring to your graphs, determine:

a *Each country's domestic opportunity cost of producing plums and apples.*

b *Which nation should specialize in which product.*

c *The trading possibilities lines for each nation if the actual terms of trade are 1 plum for 2 apples.*

d *Suppose the optimum product mixes before specialization and trade were B in New Zealand and S in Spain. What are the gains from specialization and trade?*

5 "The United States can produce X more efficiently than can Great Britain. Yet we import X from Great Britain." Explain.

6 *Key Question* *Refer to Figure 4-5. Assume the graph depicts America's domestic market for corn. How many bushels* of corn, if any, will the United States export or import at a world price of $1, $2, $3, $4, and $5? Use this information to construct America's export supply curve and import demand curve for corn. Suppose the only other corn-producing nation is France, where the domestic price is $4. Why will the equilibrium world price be between $3 and $4? Who will export corn at this world price; who will import it?

7 *Key Question* *Draw a domestic supply and demand diagram for a product in which the United States does not have a comparative advantage. Indicate the impact of foreign imports on domestic price and quantity. Now show a protective tariff which eliminates approximately one-half the assumed imports. Indicate the price-quantity effects of this tariff to* **a** *domestic consumers,* **b** *domestic producers, and* **c** *foreign exporters. How would the effects of a quota which creates the same amount of imports differ?*

8 "The most valid arguments for tariff protection are also the most easily abused." What are these arguments? Why are they susceptible to abuse? Evaluate the use of artificial trade barriers, such as tariffs and import quotas, as a means of achieving and maintaining full employment.

9 Evaluate the following statements:

a "Protective tariffs limit both the imports and the exports of the nation levying tariffs."

b "The extensive application of protective tariffs destroys the ability of the international market system to allocate resources efficiently."

c "Unemployment can often be reduced through tariff protection, but by the same token inefficiency typically increases."

d "Foreign firms which 'dump' their products onto the American market are in effect presenting the American people with gifts."

e "In view of the rapidity with which technological advance is dispersed around the world, free trade will inevitably yield structural maladjustments, unemployment, and balance of payments problems for industrially advanced nations."

f "Free trade can improve the composition and efficiency of domestic output. Only the Volkswagen forced Detroit to make a compact car, and only foreign success with the oxygen process forced American steel firms to modernize."

g "In the long run foreign trade is neutral with respect to total employment."

10 In 1981–1985 the Japanese agreed to a voluntary export restriction which reduced American imports of Japanese automobiles by about 10 percent. What would you expect the short-run effects to have been on the American and Japanese automobile industries? If this restriction were permanent, what would be its long-run effects in the two nations on **a** the allocation of resources, **b** the volume of employment, **c** the price level, and **d** the standard of living?

11 *Key Question* *What are the benefits and the costs of protectionist policies? Which are larger?*

12 What are NAFTA and GATT and how do they relate to international trade? What policies has the United States government recently used to promote American exports? What factors make it difficult for American firms to sell their goods in Japan? What actions do you think the United States should take to reduce America's trade deficit with Japan?

13 (Last Word) What point is Bastiat trying to make with his petition of the candlemakers?

EXCHANGE RATES, THE BALANCE OF PAYMENTS, AND TRADE DEFICITS

If you take an American dollar to the bank and ask to exchange it for United States currency, you will get a puzzled look. If you persist, you may get in exchange another dollar. One American dollar can buy exactly one American dollar. But, as of January 25, 1995, one United States dollar could buy 40,887 Turkish lira, 1.30 Australian dollars, .63 British pounds, 1.42 Canadian dollars, 5.23 French francs, 1.51 German marks, 99.63 Japanese yen, or 7.44 Swedish krona. What explains this seemingly haphazard array of exchange rates?

In Chapter 37 we examined comparative advantage as the underlying economic basis of world trade and discussed the effects of barriers to free trade. In this chapter we first introduce the monetary or financial aspects of international trade. How are currencies of different nations exchanged when import and export transactions occur? Second, we analyze and interpret a nation's international balance of payments. What is meant by a "favorable" or "unfavorable" balance of trade? Third, the kinds of exchange rate systems which trading nations have used are explained and evaluated. In this discussion we examine the polar extremes of freely flexible and fixed exchange rates and then survey actual systems which have existed historically. Finally, we explore the balance of trade deficits the United States has encountered over the past several years.

FINANCING INTERNATIONAL TRADE

One thing that makes international trade different from domestic trade is two different national currencies. When American firms export goods to British firms, the American exporter wants to be paid in dollars. But British importers have pounds sterling. They must exchange pounds for dollars to permit the American export transaction to occur.

This problem is resolved in *foreign exchange markets* where dollars can purchase British pounds, Japanese yen, German marks, Italian lira, and so forth, and vice versa. Sponsored by major banks in New York, London, Zurich, Tokyo, and elsewhere, foreign exchange markets facilitate American exports and imports.

American Export Transaction

Suppose an American exporter agrees to sell $30,000 worth of computers to a British firm. Assume the *rate of exchange*—the rate or price at which pounds can be exchanged for, or converted into, dollars, and vice

LONDON BANK	
Assets	Liabilities and net worth
	Demand deposit of British importer −£15,000 (a)
	Deposit of New York bank +£15,000 (c)

NEW YORK BANK	
Assets	Liabilities and net worth
Deposit in London bank +£15,000 (c) ($30,000)	Demand deposit of American exporter +$30,000 (b)

FIGURE 38-1   Financing a U.S. export transaction
American export transactions create a foreign demand for dollars. The satisfaction of this demand increases the supplies of foreign monies held by American banks.

versa—is $2 for £1. This means that the British importer must pay £15,000 to the American exporter. Let's track what occurs in terms of simple bank balance sheets (Figure 38-1).

a To pay for the American computers, the British buyer draws a check on its demand deposit (checking account entry) in a London bank for £15,000. This is shown by the −£15,000 demand deposit entry on the right-hand side of the balance sheet of the London bank.

b The British firm sends this £15,000 check to the American exporter. But the American exporting firm must pay its employees and materials suppliers, as well as its taxes, in dollars, not pounds. So the exporter sells the £15,000 check or draft on the London bank to a large American bank, say in New York City, which is a dealer in foreign exchange. The American firm is given a $30,000 demand deposit in the New York bank in exchange for the £15,000 check. Note the new demand deposit entry of +$30,000 in the New York bank.

c What does the New York bank do with the £15,000? It deposits it in a correspondent London bank for future sale. Thus, +£15,000 of demand deposits appear in the liabilities column of the balance sheet of the London bank. This +£15,000 ($30,000) is an asset as viewed by the New York bank. To simplify, we assume the correspondent bank in London is the same bank from which the British importer obtained the £15,000 draft.

Note these points.

1   *American exports create a foreign demand for dol-*

lars, and the satisfaction of this demand generates a supply of foreign monies—pounds, in this case—owned by American banks and available to American buyers.

2   The financing of an American export (British import) reduces the supply of money (demand deposits) in Britain and increases the supply of money in the United States by the amount of the purchase.

American Import Transaction

But why would the New York bank be willing to give up dollars for pounds sterling? As just indicated, the New York bank is a dealer in foreign exchange; it is in the business of buying—for a fee—and selling—also for a fee—pounds for dollars.

Let's now examine how our New York bank would sell pounds for dollars in financing an American import (British export) transaction. Suppose an American retail concern wants to import £15,000 worth of woolens from a British mill. Again, simple commercial bank balance sheets track what goes on (Figure 38-2).

a Because the British exporting firm must pay its obligations in pounds rather than dollars, the American importer must exchange dollars for pounds. It does this by going to the New York bank and purchasing £15,000 for $30,000—perhaps the American importer purchases the same £15,000 which the New York bank acquired in the previous American export transaction. In Figure 38-2, this purchase reduces the American importer's demand deposit in the New York

LONDON BANK		NEW YORK BANK	
Assets	**Liabilities and net worth**	**Assets**	**Liabilities and net worth**
	Demand deposit of British exporter +£15,000(b)	**Deposit in London bank −£15,000(a) ($30,000)**	**Demand deposit of American importer −$30,000(a)**
	Deposit of New York bank −£15,000(a)		

FIGURE 38-2   Financing a U.S. import transaction
American import transactions create an American demand for foreign monies. The satisfaction of that demand reduces the supplies of foreign monies held by American banks.

bank by $30,000 and the New York bank gives up its £15,000 deposit in the London bank.

b The American importer sends its newly purchased check for £15,000 to the British firm, which deposits it in the London bank where it is recorded as a +£15,000 deposit in the liabilities and net worth column of its balance sheet.

Here, you see that:

1 *American imports create a domestic demand for foreign monies (pounds sterling, in this case) and that fulfillment of this demand reduces the supplies of foreign monies held by American banks.*

2 An American import transaction increases the money supply in Britain and reduces the money supply in the United States.

By combining export and import transactions, a further point comes into focus. American exports (computers) make available, or "earn," a supply of foreign monies for American banks, and American imports (British woolens) create a demand for these monies. In a broad sense, *any nation's exports finance or "pay for" its imports.* Exports provide the foreign currencies needed to pay for imports. From Britain's point of view, its exports of woolens earn a supply of dollars, which are then used to meet the demand for dollars associated with Britain's imports of computers.

Postscript: Although our examples are confined to the exporting and importing of goods, we will find that demands for and supplies of pounds also arise from transactions involving services and the payment of interest and dividends on foreign investments.

Americans demand pounds not only to finance imports, but also to purchase insurance and transportation services from the British, to vacation in London, to pay dividends and interest on British investments in the United States, and to make new financial and real investments in Britain. *(Key Question 2)*

THE INTERNATIONAL BALANCE OF PAYMENTS

We now explore the variety of international transactions which create a demand for and generate a supply of a specific currency. This spectrum of international trade and financial transactions is reflected in the United States' international **balance of payments.** A nation's balance of payments statement records *all* transactions which take place between its residents (including individuals, businesses, and governmental units) and the residents of all foreign nations. These transactions include merchandise exports and imports, imports and exports of services, tourist expenditures, interest and dividends received or paid abroad, purchases and sales of financial or real assets abroad, and so on. *The United States' balance of payments shows the balance between all the payments the United States receives from foreign countries and all the payments which we make to them.* A simplified balance of payments for the United States in 1993 is shown in Table 38-1. Let's analyze this accounting statement to see what it reveals about our international trade and finance.

TABLE 38-1 The United States' balance of payments, 1993 *(in billions)*[*]

Current account		
(1) U.S. merchandise exports	$+457	
(2) U.S. merchandise imports	−589	
(3) Balance of trade		$−133
(4) U.S. exports of services	+185	
(5) U.S. imports of services	−128	
(6) Balance on goods and services		−76
(7) Net investment income	+4	
(8) Net transfers	−32	
(9) Balance on current account		−104
Capital account		
(10) Capital inflows to the U.S.	+180†	
(11) Capital outflows from the U.S.	−147	
(12) Balance on capital account		+33
(13) Current and capital account balance		−71
(14) Official reserves		+71
		$ 0

*Mathematical discrepancies in the table result from rounding.
†Includes a $21 billion statistical discrepancy which is believed to be comprised primarily of unaccounted capital inflows.
Source: Survey of Current Business, December 1994.

Current Account

The top portion of Table 38-1 summarizes the United States' trade in currently produced goods and services and is called the **current account.** Items 1 and 2 show American exports and imports of merchandise (goods) respectively in 1993. We have designated American exports with a *plus* sign because American merchandise exports (and other export-type transactions) are **credits.** They create or earn supplies of foreign exchange. As we saw in our discussion of how international trade is financed, any export-type transaction obligating foreigners to make "inpayments" to the United States generates supplies of foreign monies in American banks.

We have designated American imports with a minus sign. American imports (and other import-type transactions) are **debits;** they use up foreign exchange. Our earlier discussion of trade financing indicated that American imports obligate Americans to make "outpayments" to the rest of the world which draw down available supplies of foreign currencies held by American banks.

Trade Balance   Items 1 and 2 in Table 38-1 tell us that in 1993 our merchandise exports of $457 billion

did *not* earn enough foreign monies to finance our merchandise imports of $589 billion. The merchandise balance of trade or simply, the **trade balance** refers to the difference between a country's merchandise exports and merchandise imports. If exports exceed imports, the result is a *trade surplus* or "favorable balance of trade." If imports exceed exports, then there is a *trade deficit* or "unfavorable balance of trade" is occurring. We note in item 3 that in 1993 the United States incurred a trade deficit of $133 billion. The American trade balance is broken down by country or region in Global Perspective 38-1.

Balance on Goods and Services   Item 4 reveals that the United States not only exports autos and computers, but also sells transportation services, insurance, and tourist and brokerage services to residents of foreign countries. These service sales or "exports" totaled $185 billion in 1993. Item 5 indicates that Americans buy or "import" similar services from foreigners. These service imports were $128 billion in 1993.

The **balance on goods and services,** shown as item 6, is the difference between our exports of goods and services (items 1 and 4) and our imports of goods and services (items 2 and 5). In 1993 our exports of goods and services fell short of our imports of goods and services by $76 billion.

Balance on Current Account Item 7, net investment income, represents the excess of interest and dividend payments people abroad have paid us for the services of our exported capital over what we paid in 1993 in interest and dividends for foreign capital invested in the United States. Table 38-1 shows that our net investment income earned us $4 billion worth of foreign currencies for "exporting" the services of American money capital invested abroad.

Item 8 reflects net transfers, both public and private, from the United States to the rest of the world. Included here is American foreign aid, pensions paid to Americans living abroad, and remittances of immigrants to relatives abroad. These $32 billion of transfers are "outpayments" and exhaust available supplies of foreign exchange. Facetiously put, net transfers mean the importing of "goodwill" or "thank-you notes."

By taking all transactions in the current account into consideration we obtain the **balance on current account** shown by item 9. In 1993 the United States realized a current account deficit of $104 billion. This means that our current account import transactions (items 2, 5, and 8) created a demand for a larger dollar amount of foreign currencies than our export transactions (items 1, 4, and 7) supplied.

Capital Account

The **capital account** reflects capital flows in the purchase or sale of real and financial assets which occurred in 1993. For example, Honda or Nissan might acquire an automobile assembly plant in the United States. Or, the investments may be of a financial nature, for example, an Arabian oil sheik might purchase GM stock or Treasury bonds. In either event such transactions generate supplies of foreign currencies for the United States. They are therefore credit or inpayment items, designated with a plus sign. The United States is exporting stocks and bonds and earning foreign exchange. Item 10 shows that such transactions amounted to $180 billion in 1993.

Conversely, Americans invest abroad. General Electric might purchase a plant in Hong Kong or Singapore to assemble pocket radios or telephones. Or an American might buy stock in an Italian shoe factory. Or an American bank might finance construction of a meat processing plant in Argentina. These

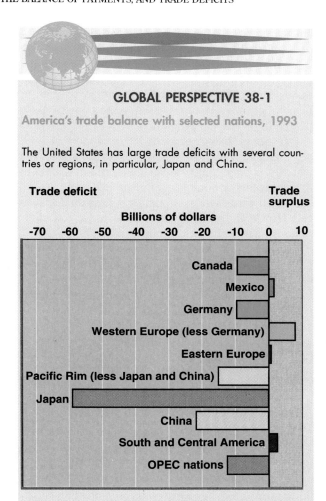

GLOBAL PERSPECTIVE 38-1

America's trade balance with selected nations, 1993

The United States has large trade deficits with several countries or regions, in particular, Japan and China.

Source: *Economic Trends,* Federal Reserve Bank of Cleveland, March 1994, p. 17.

transactions have a common feature—they all use up supplies of foreign currencies. So we attach a minus sign to remind us that these are debit or outpayment transactions. The United States is importing stocks, bonds, and IOUs from abroad. Item 11 reveals that $147 billion of these transactions occurred in 1993. When items 10 and 11 are combined, the **balance on the capital account** was a *plus* $33 billion—the United States enjoyed a capital account surplus of $33 billion in 1993.

Interrelationships

The current and capital accounts are interrelated; they are reflections of one another. The current account *deficit* means that American exports of goods and services were not sufficient to pay for our imports of goods and services. (We ignore transfer payments—item 8—in making this statement.) How did we finance the difference? The answer is that the United States must either borrow from abroad or give up ownership of some of its assets to foreigners as reflected in the capital account.

A simple analogy is useful here. Suppose in some year your expenditures exceed your earnings. How will you finance your "deficit"? You might sell some of your assets or borrow. You might sell some real assets (your car or stereo) or perhaps some financial assets (stocks or bonds) which you own. Or you might obtain a loan from your family or a bank.

Similarly, when a nation incurs a deficit in its current account, its expenditures for foreign goods and services (its imports) exceed the income received from the international sales of its own goods and services (its exports). It must finance that current account deficit by selling assets and by borrowing, that is, by going into debt. And that is what is reflected in the capital account surplus. Our capital account surplus of $33 billion (item 12) indicates that in 1993 the United States "sold off" real assets (buildings, farmland) and received loans from the rest of the world in that amount to help finance our current account deficit of $104 billion.

Recap: A nation's current account *deficit* will be financed essentially by a net capital *inflow* in its capital account. A nation's current account *surplus* would be accompanied by a net capital *outflow* in its capital account. The excess earnings from its current account surplus will be used to purchase real assets of, and make loans to, other nations.

Official Reserves

The central banks of nations hold quantities of foreign currencies called **official reserves** which are added to or drawn on to settle any *net* differences in current and capital account balances. In 1993 the surplus in our capital account was considerably less than the deficit in our current account so we had a $71 billion net deficit on the combined accounts (item 13). That is, the United States earned less foreign monies in all international trade and financial transactions than it used. This deficiency of earnings of foreign currencies was subtracted from the existing balances of foreign monies held by our central banks. The *plus* $71 billion of official reserves shown by item 14 represents this reduction of our stocks of foreign curren-

cies. The plus sign indicates this is a credit or "export-type" transaction which represents a supply of foreign exchange.

Frequently the relationship between the current and capital account is just the opposite of that shown in Table 38-1. That is, the current account deficit is less than the capital account surplus. Hence, our central banks would experience an increase in their holdings of foreign currencies. This would show as a *minus* item in the balance of payments; it is a debit or "import-type" transaction because it represents a use of foreign exchange.

The point here is that *the three components of the balance of payments statement—the current account, the capital account, and the official reserves account—must sum to zero.* Every unit of foreign exchange used (as reflected in our "minus" outpayment or debit transactions) in our international transactions must have a source (our "plus" inpayment or credit transactions).

Payments Deficits and Surpluses

Although the balance of payments must always sum to zero, economists and political officials speak of **balance of payment deficits and surpluses.** In doing so they are referring to the "current and capital account balance" shown as item 13 in Table 38-1. If this is a negative item, there is a balance of payments deficit as was the case in 1993 when the United States earned less foreign monies from all its trade and financial transactions than it used. The United States did not "pay its way" in world trade and finance and therefore depleted its official reserves of foreign monies. If the current and capital account balance were positive, then the United States would face a balance of payments surplus. The United States would have earned sufficient foreign exchange from its export-type transactions to pay for its import-type transactions. As we have just seen, it would add to its stocks of foreign monies—that is, increase its official reserve holdings.

A decrease in official reserves (shown by a positive official reserves item in Table 38-1) measures a nation's balance of payments deficit; an increase in official reserves (shown by a negative official reserves item) measures its balance of payments surplus.

Deficits and Surpluses: Good, Bad, or Ugly?

Are deficits bad, as the term implies? Is a surplus desirable, as that word suggests? The answer to both is "not necessarily." A large merchandise trade deficit such as the United States has been incurring in recent years is regarded by many as "unfavorable" or "adverse," as it suggests American producers are losing their competitiveness in world markets. Our industries seem to be having trouble selling their goods abroad and are simultaneously facing strong competition from imported goods. On the other hand, a trade deficit is *favorable* from the vantage point of American consumers who are currently receiving more goods as imports than they are forgoing as exports.

Whether a balance of payments deficit or surplus is good or bad depends on (1) the events causing them and (2) their persistence through time. For example, the large payments deficits imposed on the United States and other oil-importing nations by OPEC's runup of oil prices in 1973–1974 and 1979–1980 were very disruptive, forcing the United States to invoke policies to curtail oil imports.

Also, any nation's official reserves are limited. Persistent or long-term payments deficits, which must be financed by drawing down those reserves, would ultimately deplete reserves. In this case that nation would have to undertake policies to correct its balance of payments. These policies might require painful macroeconomic adjustments, trade barriers and similar restrictions, or changing the international value of its currency. *(Key Question 3)*

QUICK REVIEW 38-1

■ American *exports* create a demand for dollars and a supply of foreign currencies; American *imports* create a demand for foreign currencies and a supply of American dollars.

■ The current account balance is a nation's exports of goods and services less its imports of goods and services plus its net investment income and net transfers.

■ The capital account balance is a nation's capital inflows less its capital outflows.

■ A balance of payments deficit occurs when the sum of the balances on current and capital accounts is negative; a balance of payments surplus arises when the sum of the balances on current and capital accounts is positive.

FREELY FLOATING EXCHANGE RATES

Both the size and persistence of a nation's balance of payments deficits and surpluses and the adjustments it must make to correct these imbalances depend on the system of exchange rates being used. There are two polar options: (1) a system of **flexible** or **floating exchange rates** where the rates at which national currencies exchange for one another are determined by demand and supply, and (2) a system of rigidly **fixed exchange rates** by which governmental intervention in foreign exchange markets or some other mechanism offsets the changes in exchange rates which fluctuations in demand and supply would otherwise cause.

Freely floating exchange rates are determined by the unimpeded forces of demand and supply. Let's examine the rate, or price, at which American dollars might be exchanged for, say, British pounds sterling. Figure 38-3 (Key Graph) shows the demand for pounds as downsloping; the supply of pounds as upsloping.

The downsloping *demand for pounds* shown by D indicates that, if pounds become less expensive to Americans, British goods will become cheaper to Americans. Americans will demand larger quantities of British goods and therefore larger amounts of pounds to buy those goods.

The *supply of pounds* S is upsloping because, as the dollar price of pounds *rises* (that is, the pound price of dollars *falls*), the British will purchase more American goods. At higher and higher dollar prices for pounds, the British can get more American dollars and therefore more American goods per pound. American goods become cheaper to the British, inducing them to buy more of these goods. When the British buy American goods, they supply pounds to the foreign exchange market because they must exchange pounds for dollars to purchase our goods.

The intersection of the supply and demand for pounds will determine the dollar price of pounds. Here, the equilibrium rate of exchange is $2 to £1.

Depreciation and Appreciation

An exchange rate determined by free-market forces can and does change frequently. When the dollar price of pounds increases, for example, from $2 for £1 to $3 for £1, the value of the dollar has **depreciated** relative to the pound. Currency depreciation means that

KEY GRAPH

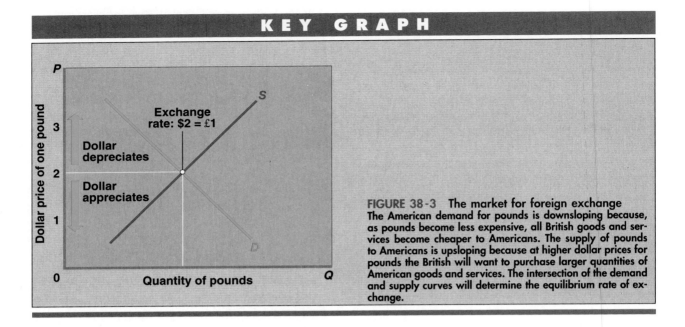

FIGURE 38-3 The market for foreign exchange
The American demand for pounds is downsloping because, as pounds become less expensive, all British goods and services become cheaper to Americans. The supply of pounds to Americans is upsloping because at higher dollar prices for pounds the British will want to purchase larger quantities of American goods and services. The intersection of the demand and supply curves will determine the equilibrium rate of exchange.

it take more units of a country's currency (dollars) to buy a single unit of some foreign currency (pounds).

When the dollar price of pounds decreases— from $2 for £1 to $1 for £1—the value of the dollar has **appreciated** relative to the pound. Currency appreciation means that it take fewer units of a country's currency (dollars) to buy a single unit of some foreign currency (pounds).

In our American-British illustrations, when the dollar depreciates the pound appreciates and vice versa. When the exchange rate between dollars and pounds changes from $2 = £1 to $3 = £1, it takes *more* dollars to buy £1 and the dollar has depreciated. But it takes *fewer* pounds to buy a dollar. At the initial rate it took £$\frac{1}{2}$ to buy $1; at the new rate it only takes £$\frac{1}{3}$ to buy $1. The pound has appreciated relative to the dollar. *If the dollar depreciates relative to the pound, the pound appreciates relative to the dollar. If the dollar appreciates vis-à-vis the pound, the pound depreciates vis-à-vis the dollar.* (You may want to review Figure 6-5.)

Determinants of Exchange Rates

Why are the demand for and the supply of pounds located as they are in Figure 38-3? What forces will cause the demand and supply curves for pounds to change, causing the dollar to appreciate or depreciate?

Changes in Tastes Any change in consumer tastes or preferences for the products of a foreign country will alter the demand for, or supply of, that nation's currency and change its exchange rate. If American technological advances in computers make them more attractive to British consumers and businesses, then they will supply more pounds in exchange markets in purchasing more American computers and the dollar will appreciate. If British tweeds become more fashionable in the United States, our demand for pounds will increase and the dollar will depreciate.

Relative Income Changes If the growth of a nation's relative income is more rapid than other countries', its currency is likely to depreciate. A country's imports vary directly with its level of income. As incomes rise in the United States, American consumers buy more domestically produced goods *and* more foreign goods. If the United States' economy is expanding rapidly and the British economy is stagnant, American imports of British goods—and therefore U.S. demand for pounds—will increase. The dollar price of pounds will rise, meaning the dollar has depreciated.

Relative Price Changes If the domestic price level rises rapidly in the United States and remains constant in Britain, American consumers will seek out low-priced British goods, increasing the demand for pounds. The British will purchase fewer American goods, reducing the supply of pounds. This combination of an increase in the demand for, and a reduction in the supply of, pounds will cause the dollar to depreciate.

Differences in price levels among nations—which reflect changes in price levels over time—help explain persistent differences in exchange rates. In 1995 an American dollar could buy .63 British pounds, 100 Japanese yen, or 40,887 Turkish lira. One reason for these differences is that the prices of British goods and services in pounds were far lower than the prices of Japanese goods and services in yen and the prices of Turkish goods and services in lira. For example, the same market basket of products costing $500 in the United States might cost 300 pounds in England, 50,000 yen in Japan, and 20 million lira in Turkey. *Generally, the higher the prices of a nation's goods and services in terms of its own currency, the greater the amount of that currency which can be obtained with an American dollar.*

Taken to extreme, this **purchasing power parity theory** holds that differences in exchange rates *equate* the purchasing power of various currencies. That is, the exchange rates among national currencies perfectly adjust to match the ratios of the nations' price levels. If a market basket of goods costs $100 in the United States and £50 in Great Britain, the exchange rate should be $2 = £1. Thus, a dollar spent on goods sold in Britain, Japan, Turkey, and other nations supposedly will have equal purchasing power. In practice, however, exchange rates depart significantly from purchasing power parity, even over long periods. Nevertheless, relative price levels are a determinant of exchange rates.

Relative Real Interest Rates What if the United States restricts the growth of its money supply (tight money policy), as it did in the late 1970s, early 1980s, and in 1994 to control inflation? As a result, *real* interest rates—nominal interest rates adjusted for the rate of inflation—rose in the United States compared to most other nations. Consequently, British individuals and firms found the United States an attractive place to make financial investments. This increase in the demand for American financial assets

TABLE 38-2 Determinants of exchange rates: factors which change demand or supply of a particular currency and thus alter the exchange rate

1 **Changes in tastes** Examples: Japanese autos decline in popularity in the United States (Japanese yen depreciates, American dollar appreciates); German tourists flock to the United States (American dollar appreciates, German mark depreciates)

2 **Changes in relative incomes** Example: England encounters a recession, reducing its imports, while American real output and real income surge, increasing American imports (British pound appreciates, American dollar depreciates)

3 **Changes in relative prices** Example: Germany experiences a 3 percent inflation rate compared to Canada's 10 percent rate (German mark appreciates, Canadian dollar depreciates)

4 **Changes in relative real interest rates** Example: The Federal Reserve drives up interest rates in the United States, while the Bank of England takes no such action (American dollar appreciates, British pound depreciates)

5 **Speculation** Examples: Currency traders believe France will have much more rapid inflation than Sweden (French franc depreciates, Swedish krona appreciates); currency traders think German interest rates will plummet relative to American rates (German mark depreciates, American dollar appreciates)

meant an increase in the supply of British pounds and the dollar therefore appreciated in value.

Speculation Suppose it is widely anticipated that the American economy will (1) grow faster than the British economy, (2) experience more rapid inflation than the British economy, and (3) have lower future real interest rates than Britain. All these expectations would lead us to believe that in the future the dollar will depreciate and the pound will appreciate. Holders of dollars will attempt to convert them into pounds, increasing the demand for pounds. This conversion causes the dollar to depreciate and the pound to appreciate. A self-fulfilling prophecy arises: The dollar depreciates and the pound appreciates because speculators act on the supposition that these changes in currency values will in fact happen. (Currency speculation is the subject of this chapter's Last Word.)

Table 38-2 provides additional illustrations to reinforce your understanding of the determinants of exchange rates.

Flexible Rates and the Balance of Payments

Proponents argue that flexible exchange rates have a compelling virtue: *They automatically adjust so as eventually to eliminate balance of payments deficits or surpluses.* We can explain this by looking at S and D in Figure 38-4 which restate the demand for, and supply of, pounds curves from Figure 38-3. The equilibrium exchange rate of $2 = £1 means there is no balance of payments deficit or surplus. At the $2 = £1 exchange rate the quantity of pounds demanded by Americans to import British goods, buy British transportation and insurance services, and pay interest and dividends on British investments in the United States equals the amount of pounds supplied by the British in buying American exports, purchasing services from Americans, and making interest and dividend payments on American investments in Britain. In brief, there would be no change in official reserves in Table 38-1.

Suppose tastes change and Americans buy more British automobiles. Or the American price level has increased relative to Britain, or interest rates have fallen in the United States compared to Britain. Any or all of these changes will cause the American demand for British pounds to increase from D to, say, D′ in Figure 38-4.

We observe that *at the initial $2 = £1 exchange rate* an American balance of payments deficit has been created in the amount ab. That is, at the $2 = £1 rate there is a shortage of pounds in the amount of ab to Americans. American export-type transactions will earn xa pounds, but Americans will want xb pounds to finance import-type transactions. Because this is a free competitive market, the shortage will change the exchange rate (the dollar price of pounds) from $2 = £1 to, say, $3 = £1; that is, the dollar has *depreciated.*

At this point it must be emphasized that *the exchange rate is a special price which links all domestic (United States') prices with all foreign (British) prices.* The dollar price of a foreign good is found by multiplying the foreign product price by the exchange rate in dollars per unit of the foreign currency. At an exchange rate of $2 = £1, a British automobile priced at £9000 will cost an American $18,000 (= 9000 × $2).

A change in the exchange rate alters the prices of all British goods to Americans and all American goods to potential British buyers. The change in the exchange rate from $2 = £1 to $3 = £1 will alter the relative attractiveness of American imports and exports so as to restore equilibrium in the balance of

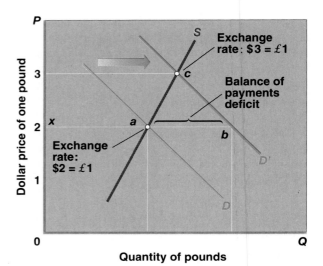

FIGURE 38-4 **Adjustments under flexible exchange rates, fixed exchange rates, and the gold standard** Under flexible rates an American trade deficit at the $2-for-£1 rate would be corrected by an increase in the rate to $3 for £1. Under fixed rates the ab shortage of pounds would be met out of international monetary reserves. Under the gold standard the deficit would cause changes in domestic price and income levels which would shift the demand for pounds (D′) to the left and the supply (S) to the right, sustaining equilibrium at the $2-for-£1 rate.

payments of the United States. From the American point of view, as the dollar price of pounds changes from $2 to $3, the British auto priced at £9000, which formerly cost an American $18,000, now costs $27,000 (= 9000 × $3). Other British goods will also cost more to Americans, and American imports of British goods and services will decline. Graphically, this is shown as a move from point b toward point c in Figure 38-4.

From Britain's standpoint the exchange rate—the pound price of dollars—has fallen (from £$\frac{1}{2}$ to £$\frac{1}{3}$ for $1). The international value of the pound has *appreciated.* The British previously got only $2 for £1; now they get $3 for £1. American goods are therefore cheaper to the British, and American exports to Great Britain will rise. In Figure 38-4 this is shown by the move from point a toward point c.

The two adjustments described—a decrease in American imports from Great Britain and an increase in American exports to Great Britain—are precisely those needed to correct the American balance of payments deficit. (You should reason through the operation of freely fluctuating exchange rates in correcting an initial American balance of payments *surplus* in its trade with Great Britain.)

In summary, the free fluctuation of exchange rates in response to shifts in the supply of, and demand for, foreign monies automatically corrects balance of payments deficits and surpluses. *(Key Question 6)*

Disadvantages of Flexible Rates

Even though freely fluctuating exchange rates automatically work to eventually eliminate payments imbalances, they may cause several significant problems:

1 Uncertainty and Diminished Trade The risks and uncertainties associated with flexible exchange rates may discourage the flow of trade. Suppose an American automobile dealer contracts to purchase ten British cars for £90,000. At the current exchange rate of, say, $2 for £1, the American importer expects to pay $180,000 for these automobiles. But if in the three-month delivery period the rate of exchange shifts to $3 for £1, the £90,000 payment contracted by the American importer will now be $270,000.

This increase in dollar price of pounds may turn the potential American importer's anticipated profits into substantial losses. Aware of the possibility of an adverse change in the exchange rate, the American importer may not be willing to assume the risks involved. The American firm may confine its operations to domestic automobiles, with the result that international trade does not occur in this item.

The same rationale applies to investment. Assume that, when the exchange rate is $3 to £1, an American firm invests $30,000 (or £10,000) in a British enterprise. It estimates a return of 10 percent, that is, it anticipates earnings of $3000 or £1000. Suppose these expectations prove correct in that the British firm earns £1000 the first year on the £10,000 investment. But suppose that during the year, the value of the dollar *appreciates* to $2 = £1. The absolute return is now only $2000 (rather than $3000) and the rate of return falls from the anticipated 10 percent to only $6\frac{2}{3}$ percent (= $2000 ÷ $30,000). Investment is inherently risky. The added risk posed by adverse changes in exchange rates may persuade the potential American investor to avoid overseas ventures.[1]

2 Terms of Trade A nation's terms of trade will be worsened by a decline in the international value of its currency. For example, an increase in the dollar price of pounds will mean that the United States must export more goods and services to finance a given level of imports from Britain.

3 Instability Freely fluctuating exchange rates may have destabilizing effects on the domestic economy as wide fluctuations stimulate and then depress industries producing internationally traded goods. If the American economy is operating at full employment and the international value of its currency depreciates as in our illustration, the results will be inflationary for two reasons. Foreign demand for American goods will increase—the net exports component of aggregate demand will increase and cause demand-pull inflation. Also, prices of all American imports will increase. Conversely, appreciation of the dollar would lower exports and increase imports, causing unemployment.

With regards to policy, floating exchange rates may complicate the use of domestic fiscal and monetary policies in seeking full employment and price stability. This is especially true for nations whose exports and imports are large relative to their GDPs (Table 6-1).

FIXED EXCHANGE RATES

At the other extreme nations have often fixed or "pegged" their exchange rates to circumvent the disadvantages associated with floating rates. To analyze the implications and problems associated with fixed rates, assume the United States and Britain agree to maintain a $2 = £1 exchange rate.

The problem is that a governmental proclamation that a dollar is worth so many pounds does *not* mandate stability of the demand for, and supply of, pounds. As demand and supply shift over time, government must intervene directly or indirectly in the foreign exchange market if the exchange rate is to be stabilized.

In Figure 38-4 suppose the American demand for pounds increases from *D* to *D'* and an American payments deficit of *ab* arises. This means the American government is committed to an exchange rate ($2 = £1) which is below the equilibrium rate ($3 = £1). How can the United States prevent the shortage of pounds—reflecting an American balance of payments deficit—from driving the exchange rate up to the equilibrium level? The answer is to alter market de-

---

[1]We will see in this chapter's Last Word, however, that a trader can circumvent part of the risk of unfavorable exchange rate fluctuations by "hedging" in the "futures market" for foreign exchange.

mand or supply or both so that they continue to intersect at the $2 = £1 rate of exchange. There are several ways to do this.

Use of Reserves

The most desirable means of pegging an exchange rate is to manipulate the market through the use of official reserves. International monetary *reserves* are stocks of foreign monies owned by a government. How do reserves originate? Let's assume that in the past the opposite market condition prevailed in which there was a surplus, rather than a shortage, of pounds, and the United States government had acquired that surplus. That is, at some earlier time the United States government spent dollars to buy surplus pounds which were threatening to reduce the $2 = £1 exchange rate to, say, $1 = £1. By selling part of its reserve of pounds, the United States government could shift the supply of pounds curve to the right so that it intersects D' at b in Figure 38-4, thereby maintaining the exchange rate at $2 = £1.

Historically nations have used gold as "international money" or as reserves. In our example the United States government might sell some of the gold it owns to Britain for pounds. The pounds acquired could be used to augment the supply of pounds earned through American trade and financial transactions to shift the supply of pounds to the right to maintain the $2 = £1 exchange rate.

It is critical that the amount of reserves be enough to accomplish the required increase in the supply of pounds. This is *not* a problem if deficits and surpluses occur more or less randomly and are about the same size. That is, last year's balance of payments surplus with Britain will increase the United States' reserve of pounds and this reserve can be used to "finance" this year's deficit. But if the United States encounters persistent and sizable deficits for an extended period, the reserves problem can become critical and force the abandonment of a system of fixed exchange rates. Or, at least, a nation whose reserves are inadequate must resort to less appealing options to maintain exchange rate stability. Let's consider these options.

Trade Policies

One set of policy options includes measures designed to control the flows of trade and finance directly. The United States might try to maintain the $2 = £1 exchange rate in the face of a shortage of pounds by discouraging imports (thereby reducing the demand for pounds) and by encouraging exports (thereby increasing the supply of pounds). Imports can be reduced by tariffs or import quotas. Special taxes may be levied on the interest and dividends Americans receive for foreign investments. Also, the United States government might subsidize certain American exports to increase the supply of pounds.

The fundamental problem with these policies is they reduce the volume of world trade and distort its composition or pattern away from that which is economically desirable. Tariffs, quotas, and the like can be imposed only at the sacrifice of some portion of the economic gains or benefits attainable from a free flow of world trade based on comparative advantage. These effects should not be underestimated; the imposition of trade barriers can elicit retaliatory responses from other nations which are adversely affected.

Exchange Controls: Rationing

Another option is exchange controls or rationing. Under exchange controls the United States government would handle the problem of a pound shortage by requiring all pounds obtained by American exporters be sold to it. Then the government allocates or rations this short supply of pounds (*xa* in Figure 38-4) among various American importers who demand the quantity *xb*. In this way the American government would restrict American imports to the amount of foreign exchange earned by American exports. American demand for British pounds in the amount of *ab* would be unfulfilled. Government eliminates a balance of payments deficit by restricting imports to the value of exports.

There are many objections to exchange controls.

1 Distorted Trade Like trade controls—tariffs, quotas, and export subsidies—exchange controls distort the pattern of international trade away from comparative advantage.

2 Discrimination The process of rationing scarce foreign exchange means discrimination among importers. Serious problems of equity and favoritism are implicit in the rationing process.

3 Restricted Choice Controls impinge on freedom of consumer choice. Americans who prefer Mazdas may be forced to buy Mercuries. The business opportunities of some American importers will be impaired because imports are constrained by government.

4 Black Markets There are likely to be enforcement problems. The market forces of demand and supply indicate there are American importers who want foreign exchange badly enough to pay *more* than the $2 = £1 official rate; this sets the stage or extralegal or "black market" foreign exchange dealings.

Domestic Macro Adjustments

A final means of maintaining a stable exchange rate is to use domestic fiscal and monetary policies to eliminate the shortage of pounds. Restrictive fiscal and monetary measures will reduce the United States' national income relative to Britain's. Because American imports vary directly with our national income, our demand for British goods, and therefore for pounds, will be restrained.

To the extent that these contractionary policies reduce our price level relative to Britain's, American buyers of consumption and investment goods will divert their demands from British to American goods, also restricting the demand for pounds.

Finally, a restrictive (tight) money policy will increase United States' interest rates compared to Britain and reduce American demand for pounds to make financial investments in Britain.

From Britain's standpoint lower prices on American goods and higher American interest rates will increase British imports of American goods and stimulate British financial investment in the United States. Both developments will increase the supply of pounds. The combination of a decrease in the demand for and an increase in the supply of pounds will eliminate the initial American payments deficit. In Figure 38-4 the new supply and demand curves will intersect at some new equilibrium point on the *ab* line where the exchange rates persists at $2 = £1.

This means of maintaining pegged exchange rates is hardly appealing. The "price" of exchange rate stability for the United States is falling output, employment, and price levels—in other words, a recession. Achieving a balance of payments equilibrium and realizing domestic stability are both important national economic objectives; but to sacrifice the latter for the former is to let the tail wag the dog.

QUICK REVIEW 38-2

■ In a system where exchange rates are free to float, they are determined by the demand for, and supply of, individual national currencies.

■ Determinants of freely floating exchange rates—factors which shift currency supply and demand curves—include changes in tastes, changes in relative national incomes, relative price level changes, relative real interest rate changes, and speculation.

■ Under a system of fixed exchange rates, nations set their exchange rates and then maintain them by buying or selling reserves of foreign currencies, establishing trade barriers, employing exchange controls, or incurring inflation or recession

INTERNATIONAL EXCHANGE RATE SYSTEMS

There have been three different exchange rate systems which nations have employed in recent history.

The Gold Standard: Fixed Exchange Rates

Over the 1879–1934 period—except for the World War I years—an international monetary system known as the gold standard prevailed. The **gold standard** provided for fixed exchange rates. A look at its operation and ultimate downfall helps us see the functioning and some of the advantages and problems associated with fixed-rate systems. Currently a number of economists advocate fixed exchange rates and a few even call for a return to the international gold standard.

Conditions A nation is on the gold standard when it fulfills three conditions. It must:
1 Define its monetary unit in terms of a certain quantity of gold
2 Maintain a fixed relationship between its stock of gold and its domestic money supply
3 Allow gold to be freely exported and imported

If each nation defines its monetary unit in terms of gold, the various national currencies will have a fixed relationship to one another. Suppose the United

States defines a dollar as worth 25 grains of gold and Britain defines its pound sterling as worth 50 grains of gold. This means that a British pound is worth $\frac{50}{25}$ dollars or, £1 equals $2.

Gold Flows   Now, ignoring costs of packing, insuring, and shipping gold between countries, under the gold standard the rate of exchange would not vary from this $2-for-£1 rate. No one in the United States would pay more than $2 for £1, because you could always buy 50 grains of gold for $2 in the United States, ship it to Britain, and sell it for £1. Nor would the British pay more than £1 for $2. Why should they, when they could buy 50 grains of gold in Britain for £1, send it to the United States, and sell it for $2?

In practice the costs of packing, insuring, and shipping gold must be taken into account. But these costs would only amount to a few cents per 50 grains of gold. If these costs were 3 cents for 50 grains of gold, Americans wanting pounds would pay up to $2.03 for a pound rather than buy and export 50 grains of gold to get the pound. Why? Because it would cost them $2 for 50 grains of gold plus 3 cents to send it to Britain to be exchanged for £1. This $2.03 exchange rate, above which gold would begin to flow out of the United States, is called the **gold export point.**

The exchange rate would fall to $1.97 before gold would flow into the United States. The British, wanting dollars, would accept as little as $1.97 in exchange for £1, because from the $2 which they could get by buying 50 grains of gold in Britain and reselling it in the United States, 3 cents must be subtracted to pay shipping and related costs. This $1.97 exchange rate, below which gold would flow into the United States, is called the **gold import point.**

Under the gold standard the flow of gold between nations would result in exchange rates which for all practical purposes are fixed.

Domestic Macro Adjustments   Figure 38-4 helps explain the kinds of adjustments the gold standard would produce. Initially the demand for and the supply of pounds are *D* and *S* and their intersection point at *a* coincides with the fixed exchange rate of $2 = £1 which results from the "in gold" definitions of the pound and the dollar. Now suppose for some reason American preferences for British goods increase, shifting the demand for pounds curve to *D'*. In Figure 38-4 there is now a shortage of pounds equal to *ab,* implying an American balance of payments deficit.

What will happen? Remember that the rules of the gold standard prohibit the exchange rate from moving from the fixed $2 = £1 relationship; the rate can *not* move up to a new equilibrium of $3 = £1 at point *c* as it would under freely floating rates. Instead, the exchange rate would rise by a few cents to the American gold export point at which gold would flow from the United States to Britain.

Recall that the gold standard requires participants to maintain a fixed relationship between their domestic money supplies and their quantities of gold. The flow of gold from the United States to Britain would bring about a contraction of the money supply in America and an expansion of the money supply in Britain. Other things equal, this will reduce aggregate demand and, therefore, lower real domestic output, employment, and the price level in the United States. Also, the reduced money supply will boost American interest rates.

The opposite occurs in Britain. The inflow of gold boosts the money supply, increasing aggregate demand, national income, employment, and the price level. The increased money supply will also lower interest rates in Britain.

In Figure 38-4 declining American incomes and prices will reduce our demand for British goods and services and therefore reduce the American demand for pounds. Lower interest rates in Britain will make it less attractive for Americans to invest there, also lessening the demand for pounds. For all these reasons the *D'* curve will shift to the left.

Similarly, higher incomes and prices in Britain will increase British demand for American goods and services and higher American interest rates will encourage the British to invest more in the United States. These developments all increase the supply of pounds available to Americans, shifting the *S* curve of Figure 38-4 to the right.

In short, domestic macroeconomic adjustments in American and Britain, triggered by the international flow of gold, will produce new demand and supply for pound curves which intersect at some point on the horizontal line between points *a* and *b.*

Note the critical difference in the adjustment mechanisms associated with freely floating exchange rates and the fixed rates of the gold standard. With floating rates the burden of the adjustment is on the exchange rate itself. In contrast, the gold standard involves changes in the domestic money supplies of participating nations which precipitate changes in price levels, real output and employment, and interest rates.

Although the gold standard boasts the advantages of stable exchange rates and the automatic correction of balance of payments deficits and surpluses, its drawback is that nations must accept domestic adjustments in such distasteful forms as unemployment and falling incomes, on the one hand, or inflation, on the other. In using the gold standard nations must be willing to submit their domestic economies to painful macroeconomic adjustments. Under this system a nation's monetary policy would be determined largely by changes in the demand for and supply of foreign exchange. If the United States, for example, was already moving toward recession, the loss of gold under the gold standard would reduce its money supply and intensify the problem. Under the international gold standard nations forgo independent monetary policies.

Demise   The worldwide Great Depression of the 1930s signaled the end of the gold standard. As domestic outputs and employment plummeted worldwide, the restoration of prosperity became the primary goal of afflicted nations. Protectionist measures such as the United States' Smoot-Hawley Tariff were enacted as nations sought to increase net exports and stimulate their domestic economies. And each nation was fearful that its economic recovery would be aborted by a balance of payments deficit which would lead to an outflow of gold and consequent contractionary effects. Indeed, nations attempted to devalue their currencies in terms of gold to make their exports more attractive and imports less attractive. These devaluations undermined a basic condition of the gold standard and the system broke down.

The Bretton Woods System

Not only did the Great Depression of the 1930s lead to the downfall of the gold standard, it also prompted erection of trade barriers which greatly impaired international trade. World War II was similarly disruptive to world trade and finance. Thus, as World War II drew to a close in the mid-1940s, the world trading and monetary systems were in shambles.

To lay the groundwork for a new international monetary system, an international conference of nations was held at Bretton Woods, New Hampshire, in 1944. This conference produced a commitment to an *adjustable-peg system* of exchange rates, called the **Bretton Woods system.** The new system sought to capture the advantages of the old gold standard (fixed exchange rates), while avoiding its disadvantages (painful domestic macroeconomic adjustments).

Furthermore, the conference created the **International Monetary Fund** (IMF) to make the new exchange rate system feasible and workable. This international monetary system, emphasizing relatively fixed exchange rates and managed through the IMF, prevailed with modifications until 1971. The IMF continues to play a basic role in international finance and in recent years has performed a major role in ameliorating debt problems of the less developed countries.

IMF and Pegged Exchange Rates   Why did the Bretton Woods adjustable-peg system evolve? We have noted that during the depressed 1930s, various countries resorted to **devaluation**—devaluing[2] their currencies to try to stimulate domestic employment. For example, if the United States was faced with growing unemployment, it might devalue the dollar by *increasing* the dollar price of pounds from $2.50 for £1 to, say, $3 for £1. This action would make American goods cheaper to the British and British goods dearer to Americans, increasing American exports and reducing American imports. This increase in net exports, abetted by the multiplier effect, would stimulate output and employment in the United States.

But every nation can play the devaluation game, and most did. The resulting rounds of competitive devaluations benefited no one; on the contrary, they contributed to further demoralization of world trade. Nations at Bretton Woods therefore agreed that the postwar monetary system must provide for overall exchange rate stability whereby disruptive currency devaluations could be avoided.

What was the adjustable-peg system of exchange rates like? First, as with the gold standard, each IMF member was obligated to define its monetary unit in terms of gold (or dollars), thus establishing par rates of exchange between its currency and the currencies of all other members. Each nation was further obligated to keep its exchange rate stable with respect to any other currency.

---

[2]A note on terminology: We noted earlier in this chapter that the dollar has *appreciated (depreciated)* when its international value has increased (decreased) as the result of changes in the demand for, or supply of, dollars in foreign exchange markets. The terms *revalue* and *devalue* are used to describe an increase or decrease, respectively, in the international value of a currency which occurs as the result of governmental, rather than market, action.

But how was this obligation to be fulfilled? The answer, as we saw in our discussion of fixed exchange rates, is that governments must use international monetary reserves to intervene in foreign exchange markets. Assume that under the Bretton Woods system the dollar was "pegged" to the British pound at $2 = £1. Now suppose in Figure 38-4 the American demand for pounds temporarily increases from D to D' so that a shortage of pounds of ab arises at the pegged rate. How can the United States keep its pledge to maintain a $2 = £1 rate when the new market or equilibrium rate would be at $3 = £1? The United States could supply additional pounds in the exchange market, shifting the supply of pounds curve to the right so that it intersects D' at b and maintains the $2 = £1 rate of exchange.

Where would the United States obtain the needed pounds? Under the Bretton Woods system there were three main sources.

1 Reserves The United States might currently possess pounds in a "stabilization fund" as the result of the opposite exchange market condition existing in the past. That is, at some earlier time the United States government may have spent dollars to purchase surplus pounds which were threatening to reduce the $2 = £1 exchange rate to, say, $1 = £1.

2 Gold Sales The United States government might sell some of the gold it holds to Britain for pounds. The proceeds would then be offered in the exchange market to augment the supply of pounds.

3 IMF Borrowing The needed pounds might be borrowed from the IMF. Nations participating in the Bretton Woods system were required to make contributions to the IMF on the basis of the size of their national income, population, and volume of trade. If necessary, the United States could borrow pounds on a short-term basis from the IMF by supplying its own currency as collateral.

Fundamental Imbalances: Adjusting the Peg A fixed-rate system such as Bretton Woods functions well so long as a nation's payments deficits and surpluses occur more or less randomly and are approximately equal in size. If a nation's payments surplus last year allows it to add a sufficient amount to its international monetary reserves to finance this year's payments deficit, no problems will arise. But what if the United States encountered a "fundamental imbal-

ance" in its international trade and finance and was confronted with persistent and sizable payments deficits? In this case it is evident that the United States would eventually run out of reserves and be unable to maintain its fixed exchange rate.

Under the Bretton Woods system, a fundamental payments deficit was corrected by devaluation, that is, by an "orderly" reduction in the nation's pegged exchange rate. Also, the IMF allowed each member nation to alter the value of its currency by 10 percent without permission from the Fund to correct a "fundamental" balance of payments deficit. Larger exchange rate changes required the sanction of the Fund's board of directors. By requiring approval of significant rate changes, the Fund guarded against arbitrary and competitive currency devaluation prompted by nations seeking a temporary stimulus to their domestic economies. In our illustration, devaluing the dollar would increase American exports and lower American imports, correcting its persistent payments deficits.

The objective of the adjustable-peg system was a world monetary system which embraced the best features of both a fixed exchange rate system (such as the old international gold standard) and a system of freely fluctuating exchange rates. By reducing risk and uncertainty, short-term exchange rate stability—pegged exchange rates—would presumably stimulate trade and lead to the efficient use of world resources. Periodic exchange rate adjustments—adjustments of the pegs—made in an orderly fashion through the IMF, and on the basis of permanent or long-run changes in a country's payments position, provided a mechanism by which persistent international payments imbalances could be resolved by means other than painful changes in domestic levels of output and prices.

Demise of the Bretton Woods System Under the Bretton Woods system gold and the dollar came to be accepted as international reserves. The acceptability of gold as an international medium of exchange was derived from its role under the international gold standard of an earlier era. The dollar became acceptable as international money for two reasons.
1   The United States emerged from World War II as the free world's strongest economy.
2   The United States had accumulated large quantities of gold and between 1934 and 1971 maintained a policy of buying gold from, and selling gold to, foreign monetary authorities at a fixed price of $35 per

ounce. The dollar was convertible into gold on demand; the dollar came to be regarded as a substitute for gold, or "as good as gold."

But the role of the dollar as a component of international monetary reserves contained the seeds of a dilemma. Consider the situation as it developed in the 1950s and 1960s. The problem with gold as international money was a quantitative one. The growth of the world's money stock depends on the amount of newly mined gold, less any amounts hoarded for speculative purposes or used for industrial and artistic purposes. Unfortunately, the growth of the gold stock lagged behind the rapidly expanding volume of international trade and finance. Thus the dollar came to occupy an increasingly important role as an international monetary reserve.

Economies of the world acquire dollars as reserves as the result of United States' balance of payments deficits. With the exception of some three or four years, the United States incurred persistent payments deficits throughout the 1950s and 1960s. These deficits were financed in part by drawing down American gold reserves. But mostly United States' deficits were financed by growing foreign holdings of American dollars which were "as good as gold" until 1971.

As the amount of dollars held by foreigners soared and as our gold reserves dwindled, other nations began to question whether the dollar was really "as good as gold." The ability of the United States to maintain the convertibility of the dollar into gold became increasingly doubtful, and so did the role of the dollar as generally accepted international monetary reserves. Thus, the dilemma was that to maintain the dollar as a reserve medium, the United States' payments deficit had to be eliminated. But elimination of the trade deficit would remove the source of additional dollar reserves for the system. The United States had to reduce or eliminate its payments deficits to preserve the dollar's status as an international medium of exchange. But success in this endeavor would limit the expansion of international reserves or liquidity and restrict the growth of international trade and finance.

This problem came to a head in the early 1970s. Faced with persistent and growing United States' payments deficits, President Nixon suspended the dollar's convertibility into gold on August 15, 1971. This suspension ended the thirty-seven-year-old policy to exchange gold for dollars at $35 per ounce. This new policy severed the link between gold and the international value of the dollar, thereby "floating" the dollar and allowing its value to be determined by market forces. The floating of the dollar withdrew American support from the old Bretton Woods system of fixed exchange rates and sounded its death knell.

The Managed Float

The present exchange rate system might best be labeled a system of **managed floating exchange rates** —floating exchange rates, accompanied by occasional currency interventions by central banks to stabilize or alter rates. It is recognized that changing economic conditions among nations require continuing changes in exchange rates to avoid persistent payment deficits or surpluses. Normally, the major trading nations allow their exchange rates to float to equilibrium levels based on supply and demand in the foreign exchange market. The result has been considerably more volatility in exchange rates than in the Bretton Woods era (see Global Perspective 38-2).

But nations also recognize that short-term changes in exchange rates—perhaps accentuated by purchases and sales by speculators—can disrupt and discourage the flow of trade and finance. Moreover, some longer-term moves in exchange rates may not be desirable. Thus, at times the central banks of the various nations intervene in the foreign exchange market by buying or selling large amounts of specific currencies. They "manage" or stabilize exchange rates by influencing currency demand and supply. Two examples:

1 *The 1987 G-7 Intervention* In 1987 the "Group of Seven" industrial nations **(G-7 nations)**— the United States, Germany, Japan, Britain, France, Italy, and Canada—agreed to stabilize the value of the dollar. In the previous two years the dollar had declined rapidly because of sizable American trade deficits. Although the United States' trade deficit remained large, these nations concluded that further dollar depreciation might disrupt economic growth in the G-7 economies. The G-7 nations therefore purchased large amounts of dollars to prop up the dollar's value. Since 1987 the G-7 has periodically intervened in foreign exchange markets to stabilize currency values.

2 *The 1994 Intervention* In 1994 the American dollar eroded in value relative to the Japanese yen and German mark. America's large, continuing trade deficit partly precipitated this depreciation. Another factor was that people from other countries began selling their holdings of American stocks and bonds, us-

GLOBAL PERSPECTIVE 38-2

Exchange rates in terms of dollars

The floating exchange rate system (managed float) introduced in 1971 has produced far more volatile exchange rates than in the earlier Bretton Woods era.

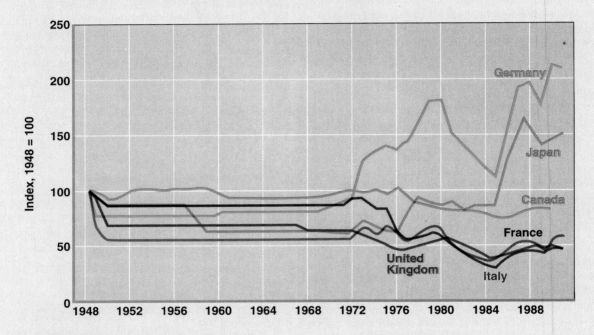

Source: *Economic Report of the President*, 1993, p. 287.

ing the dollar proceeds to buy other currencies to invest elsewhere.

Led by the United States, the central banks of sixteen nations countered this steep dollar depreciation by buying large amounts of dollars. These actions strengthened the demand for dollars and temporarily slowed the pace of the dollar's slide.

Actually, the current exchange rate system is more complicated than we just described. While the major currencies—German marks, American and Canadian dollars, Japanese yen, and the British pound—fluctuate in response to changing demand and supply conditions, some of the European Union nations attempt to peg their currencies to one another. Also, many less developed nations peg their

currencies to the dollar and allow their currencies to fluctuate with it. And, finally, some nations peg the value of their currencies to a "basket" or group of other currencies.

How well has the managed floating system worked? It has both proponents and critics.

Pros Proponents argue that the system has functioned well—far better than anticipated.

1 Trade Growth In the first place, fluctuating exchange rates have not reduced world trade and finance as skeptics had predicted. In real terms world trade has grown at about the same rate under the managed float as during the decade of the 1960s under the fixed exchange rates of the Bretton Woods system.

2 Managing Turbulence Proponents argue the managed float has weathered severe economic turbulence which might have caused a fixed exchange regime to have broken down. Such events as worldwide agricultural shortfalls in 1972–1974, extraordinary oil-price increases in 1973–1974 and again in 1979–1980, worldwide stagflation in 1974–1976 and 1981–1983, and large U.S. budget deficits in the 1980s and 1990s all generated substantial international trade and financial imbalances. Flexible rates facilitated international adjustments to these developments, whereas the same events would have put unbearable pressures on a fixed-rate system.

Cons But there is still much sentiment in favor of greater exchange rate stability. Those favoring stable rates see problems with the current system.

1 Volatility and Adjustment Critics argue that exchange rates have been excessively volatile under the managed float (Global Perspective 38-2). This volatility, it is argued, has occurred even when underlying economic and financial conditions of particular nations have been stable. Perhaps more importantly, the managed float has not readily resolved balance of payments imbalances as flexible rates are supposed to do. Thus the United States has run persistent trade deficits in recent years, while Germany and Japan have had persistent surpluses. Changes in the international values of the dollar, mark, and yen have not yet corrected these imbalances.

2 A "Nonsystem"? Skeptics feel the managed float is basically a "nonsystem"; the rules and guidelines circumscribing the behavior of each nation as to its exchange rate are not sufficiently clear or constraining to make the system viable in the long run. Nations will inevitably be tempted to intervene in foreign exchange markets, not merely to smooth out short-term or speculative fluctuations in the value of their currencies, but to prop up their currency if it is chronically weak or to manipulate the value of their currency to achieve domestic stabilization goals. There is fear that in time there may be more "managing" and less "floating" of exchange rates, and this may be fatal to the present loosely defined system.

The jury is still out on floating exchange rates in general and the managed float in particular. Floating

exchange rates have neither worked perfectly nor failed miserably. But this can be said for them: They *have* survived—and no doubt eased—several shocks to the international trading system. Meanwhile, the "managed" part of the float has given nations some sense of control over their collective economic destiny.

QUICK REVIEW 38-3

■ Under the gold standard (1789–1934), nations fixed exchange rates by valuing their currencies in terms of gold, by tying their stocks of money to gold, and by allowing gold to flow between nations when balance of payment deficits and surpluses occurred.

■ The Bretton Woods, or adjustable-peg, system of exchange rates (1944–1971) fixed or pegged short-run exchange rates, but permitted orderly long-run adjustments of the pegs.

■ The managed floating system of exchange rates (1971–present) relies on foreign exchange markets to establish equilibrium exchange rates. But it also permits central banks to buy and sell foreign currencies to stabilize short-term speculative changes in exchange rates or to correct exchange rate imbalances negatively affecting the world economy.

RECENT UNITED STATES TRADE DEFICITS

As shown in Figure 38-5, American trade deficits have been large since the early 1980s. The merchandise trade deficit for 1994 was $166 billion. In 1994 the goods and services deficit was $108 billion and the current account deficit, $156 billion.

Causes of the Trade Deficits

Two central factors have contributed to the large trade deficits.

The Rise of the Dollar Figure 38-6 shows that the international value of the dollar rose significantly between 1980 and 1985. An appreciated dollar means foreign currencies are cheaper to Americans and dollars are more expensive to people abroad. Therefore, foreign goods are cheap to Americans and our imports rise. Conversely, American goods are expensive to the

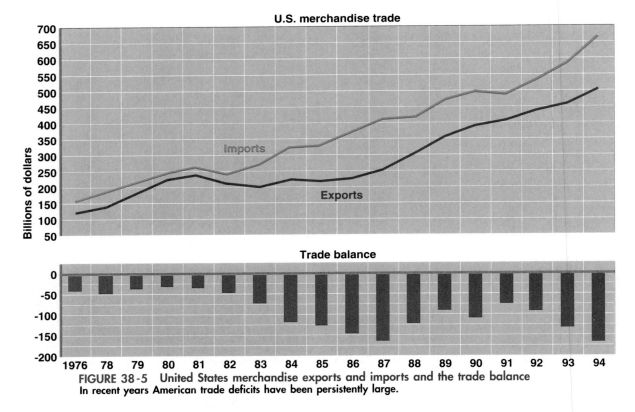

FIGURE 38-5   United States merchandise exports and imports and the trade balance
In recent years American trade deficits have been persistently large.

rest of the world and our exports decline. The pronounced appreciation of the dollar produced large American trade deficits.

Why did the value of the dollar surge between 1980 and 1985? The answer is that real interest rates —nominal interest rates less the rate of inflation— rose in the United States compared to other nations. These rises in real interest rates resulted from large Federal budgets deficits in the 1980s and a tight monetary policy early in that decade. Government borrowing to finance its deficits increased the domestic demand for money and boosted interest rates. The tight money policy directly increased interest rates by reducing the supply of money relative to its demand. Indirectly, the lower rate of inflation which resulted from the tight money policy kept the foreign demand for dollars high, because lower inflation meant higher real rates of return on investments in the United States.

By 1985 the dollar had reached record heights relative to other currencies. The major industrial nations then collectively pushed the dollar down by supplying dollars in the foreign exchange market. The purpose was to help correct the massive American trade deficits just discussed. Observe in Figure 38-6

that the dollar went into "free fall" during the next two years. This fall was aided by a sizable rise in the American demand for foreign currencies—an increase resulting from the expanded volume of United States imports.

Recall that in 1987 the G-7 nations halted the rapid decline in the value of the dollar. Meanwhile, as shown in Figure 38-5, American exports began to rise more rapidly than American imports, reducing somewhat the size of the trade deficit. The American recession of 1990–1991 contributed to a further decline in the American trade deficit. But what went up (the American trade deficit) when the dollar appreciated did not go down by the same amount when the dollar depreciated. We see from Figure 38-5 that large trade deficits remained.

One reason for the continuing overall trade deficit has been America's stubborn trade deficit with Japan (Global Perspective 38-1). Thus far this deficit has not declined as fast as the dollar has depreciated. Japanese firms have resisted increasing the dollar prices of their export goods by the same percentage as the decline in the value of the dollar. Instead, major Japanese exporters have accepted lower profit margins on goods sent to the United States.

Index, March 1973 = 1.0

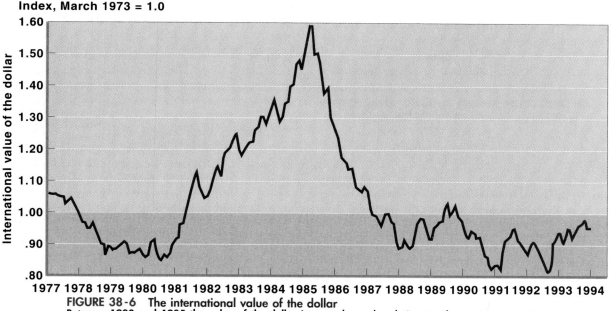

FIGURE 38-6   The international value of the dollar
Between 1980 and 1985 the value of the dollar increased greatly relative to other major currencies, tending to increase our imports and decrease our exports. The dollar fell sharply from 1985 through 1987 but trade deficits continued into the 1990s. (Here the value of the dollar is determined through comparison to ten major currencies and weighted by the amount of trade we carry on with each nation.)

American Growth   A second cause of the trade deficits is that the United States experienced a more rapid recovery from the 1980–1982 world recession than did its major trading partners. This is significant because, like domestic consumption, a nation's purchases of foreign goods (its imports) vary directly with its level of national income. Because our national income expanded more rapidly than the income of our major trading partners, our imports also increased more quickly.

Differences in growth rates also occurred in 1992–1994. Recession and slow growth in Japan and Europe meant that Japanese and European imports (our exports) grew only slowly. This disparity in economic growth kept the American trade deficit relatively high, even though the dollar had fallen in value relative to the yen and the mark.

Effects of American Trade Deficits

Are large trade deficits something that should concern us? There is disagreement on this issue, but most economists see both benefits and costs of trade deficits.

Increased Current Domestic Consumption   At the time a trade or current account deficit is occurring, American consumers benefit. A trade deficit means Americans are receiving more goods and services as imports from abroad than they are sending out as exports. Taken alone, a trade deficit allows us to operate outside our production possibilities curve, so it augments our domestic living standard. But there is a catch: The gain in present consumption will come at the expense of reduced future consumption.

Increased American Indebtedness   A trade deficit is considered "unfavorable" because it must be financed by borrowing from the rest of the world or selling off our assets. Our failure to "pay our way" in international trade has contributed to our net indebtedness to the rest of the world. Recall that current account deficits are financed primarily by net capital inflows to the United States. When our exports are insufficient to pay for our imports, we finance the difference by borrowing from foreign citizens—going into debt. The financing of our recent large trade deficits has enabled people abroad to accumulate a larger volume of claims against American assets than we have accumulated against foreign assets.

In 1985 the United States became a net debtor nation for the first time since 1914, and today it is the world's largest debtor nation. In 1994 foreign citizens abroad owned $600 billion more of American assets—corporations, land, stocks, and bonds—than Americans owned in foreign assets.

One implication: We can no longer look forward to our once-large net inflow of dividend and interest payments (see item 7 in Table 38-1's balance of payments) to help offset deficits in our goods and services trade. Another implication: If we want to regain ownership of these domestic assets, at some future time we will need to export more than we import. At that time domestic consumption will be lower, because we will need to send more of our domestic output abroad than we receive as imports. Therefore, the current consumption "gains" associated with trade deficits may mean consumption "losses" later.

There are other, more subtle "costs" of our large trade deficits. For example, these deficits have hurt industries which are most competitive with imports. Some of the problems faced by automobile manufacturers and steel producers in the 1980s, for example, were related to the strong dollar and the related trade deficits. These difficulties contributed to an upsurge in political pressure for protectionist policies. We know that such policies create efficiency losses for society. Moreover, our trade deficit with Japan and the bickering it has engendered have strained political relations between America and Japan. Finally, trade deficits have led to a series of aggressive Federal government policies to promote exports (Chapter 37), some of which perpetuate the myth that international trade is a battle against enemies rather than a source of mutual gain.

QUICK REVIEW 38-4

■ In the early and mid-1980s the United States experienced large and growing trade deficits, caused mainly by rapid appreciation of the dollar.

■ The dollar fell in value in 1986 and 1987 and the deficit declined somewhat. A recent cause of the continuing trade deficit is America's strong economic growth coupled with recession and sluggish growth in Europe and Japan.

■ American trade deficits benefit American consumers at the time of the deficits.

■ American trade deficits have increased American financial indebtedness to the rest of the world and will mean future "losses" to American consumers.

Reducing the Trade Deficit

Reducing the American trade deficit has been difficult. Nevertheless, economists suggest two ways for reducing future trade deficits: reduction of the Federal budget deficit and acceleration of economic growth abroad.

Reduction of the Budget Deficit   Many economists agree that reductions in our large annual Federal budget deficits will lower the government's borrowing, reducing real interest rates in the United States. Lower real interest rates make financial investments in the United States less attractive to people abroad. The demand for dollars by foreign citizens declines and the dollar depreciates. With a depreciated dollar, our exports eventually increase and imports eventually fall, reducing our trade deficit.

Because of the Budget Deficit Reduction Act of 1993 and economic growth, American budget deficits have recently been declining. Along with this decline, the dollar has significantly fallen in value against the Japanese yen and the German mark. This slide was so steep that in 1994 the United States and other nations tried to halt further declines. There is general agreement that the dollar is now sufficiently low in value to begin having a *major* impact in reducing our trade deficit, particularly with Japan. A dollar that bought 262 yen in 1985 bought only 80 yen in April 1995. Japanese producers have no further profit margins to squeeze as a way to resist the dollar price increases necessitated by the depreciated dollar. Japanese firms need more dollars for their exports because each dollar now buys fewer yen—yen needed to pay workers and secure other resources in Japan.

Economic Growth Abroad   Faster rates of growth among our major trading partners will also reduce the American trade deficit. Higher levels of foreign national income increase the demand for American exports. The G-7 group of industrial nations has recognized the importance of economic growth in nations with trade surpluses as a way to reduce these surpluses and lower the American trade deficit. Japan and Germany have established expansionary fiscal and monetary policies to bolster their national incomes. Faster economic growth in these nations should make a major impact on the stubborn American trade deficit.

Other "Remedies"   There are other possible "remedies" to the persistent United States' trade deficits.

Easy Money Policy Under appropriate circumstances, an easy money policy lowers real interest rates and reduces a trade deficit. The process works as follows. The decline in interest rates reduces the international demand for dollars, which results in a depreciation of the dollar. Dollar depreciation raises our exports and lowers our imports.

Protective Tariffs Protective tariffs can be used to reduce imports, but this strategy results in the loss of the gains from specialization and international trade. Furthermore, it may not be successful: Tariffs which reduce our *imports* foster retaliatory tariffs abroad which reduce our *exports*. Trade deficits do not disappear; instead, all trading partners suffer declines in their living standards.

Recession Recessions in the United States reduce disposable income and spending on all goods, including imports. Because exports are largely unaffected, the decline in imports trims the trade deficit. This is what happened in the United States during the recession of 1990–1991. But recession is an undesirable way to reduce trade deficits; it imposes higher economic costs (lost output) on society than the costs associated with the trade deficit itself. Also, unless the fundamental causes of the deficits have in the meanwhile been remedied, imports and thus trade deficits again rise when the economy recovers from recession.

Increased American Competitiveness American trade deficits can be reduced by lowering the costs of, and improving the quality of, American goods and services relative to foreign goods. Cost-saving production technologies, development of improved products, and more efficient management techniques each can contribute to a decline in the trade deficit by lowering United States demand for imported goods and increasing foreign demand for American goods.

Direct Foreign Investment Ironically, our persistent trade deficit has set off a chain of events which has begun to feed back to reduce the trade deficit itself. The vast accumulation of American dollars in foreign hands has enabled foreign individuals and firms to buy American factories or to build new plants in the United States. Furthermore, the fall in the value of the dollar has provided an incentive for foreign firms to produce in the United States rather than in their own nations.

In short, the trade deficit has resulted in increased *direct foreign investment* in the form of plant and equipment. Foreign-owned factories are turning out increasing volumes of goods that otherwise would have been imported. Hondas and Mazdas, produced in American factories, have replaced Hondas and Mazdas formerly imported from Japan. Other examples abound. The upshot is that the American trade deficit may shrink as imports are replaced with goods produced in foreign-owned factories in the United States. *(Key Question 13)*

CHAPTER SUMMARY

1 American exports create a foreign demand for dollars and make a supply of foreign exchange available to Americans. Conversely, American imports simultaneously create a demand for foreign exchange and make a supply of dollars available to foreigners. Generally, a nation's exports earn the foreign currencies needed to pay for its imports.

2 The balance of payments records all international trade and financial transactions taking place between a given nation and the rest of the world. The trade balance compares merchandise exports and imports. The balance on goods and services compares exports and imports of both goods and services. The current account balance considers not only goods and services transactions, but also net investment income and net transfers.

3 A deficit on the current account will be largely offset by a surplus on the capital account. Conversely, a surplus on the current account will be largely offset by a deficit on the capital account. A balance of payments deficit occurs

when the sum of the current and capital accounts is in deficit. A payments deficit is financed by drawing down official reserves. A balance of payments surplus occurs when the sum of the current and capital accounts is in surplus. A payments surplus results in an increase in official reserves. The desirability of a balance of payments deficit or surplus depends on its causes and its persistence.

4 Flexible or floating exchange rates are determined by the demand for and supply of foreign currencies. Under floating rates a currency will depreciate or appreciate as a result of changes in tastes, relative income changes, relative price changes, relative changes in real interest rates, and speculation.

5 Maintenance of fixed exchange rates requires adequate reserves to accommodate periodic payments deficits. If reserves are inadequate, nations must invoke protectionist trade policies, engage in exchange controls, or endure undesirable domestic macroeconomic adjustments.

LAST WORD

SPECULATION IN CURRENCY MARKETS

Contrary to popular belief, speculators often play a positive role in currency markets.

Most people buy foreign currency to facilitate buying goods or services of another country. An American importer buys Japanese yen to purchase Japanese-made automobiles. A British investor purchases marks to buy shares in the German stock market. But there is another group of participants in the currency market—speculators—who buy foreign currencies solely to resell for profit. A British pound bought for $1.50 earns a 10 percent return when sold for $1.65.

Speculators sometimes contribute to exchange rate volatility. The expectation of currency appreciation or depreciation can be self-fulfilling. If speculators expect the Japanese yen to appreciate, they sell other currencies to buy yen. The sharp increase in demand for yen boosts its value, which may attract other speculators—people expecting the yen to rise further. Eventually, the yen's value may soar too high relative to economic realities such as tastes, incomes, real interest rates, price levels, and trade balances. The "speculative bubble" bursts and the yen plummets.

But speculative bubbles are not the norm in currency markets. Changed economic realities, not speculation, usually are the cause of changing currency values. Anticipating these changes, speculators simply hasten the adjustment process. Most major adjustments in currency values persist long *after* spec-

ulators have sold their currency and made their profits or incurred their losses.

Speculation, in fact, has two positive effects in foreign exchange markets.

1 Lessening Rate Fluctuations Speculation smooths out fluctuations in currency prices. When temporarily slack demand or excess supply reduces a currency's value, speculators quickly buy it, adding to the demand and strengthening its value. When temporarily strong demand or weak supply increases a currency's value, speculators sell the currency. This selling increases the supply of the currency and reduces its value. In this way speculators smooth out supply and demand—and thus exchange rates—from

---

6 Historically, the gold standard provided exchange rate stability until its disintegration during the 1930s. Under this system, gold flows between nations precipitated sometimes painful changes in price, income, and employment levels in bringing about international equilibrium.

7 Under the Bretton Woods system, exchange rates were pegged to one another and were stable. Participating nations were obligated to maintain these rates by using stabilization funds, gold, or borrowings from the IMF. Persistent or "fundamental" payments deficits could be resolved by IMF-sanctioned currency devaluations.

8 Since 1971 a system of managed floating exchange rates has been in use. Rates are generally set by market forces, although governments intervene with varying frequency to alter their exchange rates.

9 The United States has experienced large trade deficits

in the 1980s and first-half of the 1990s. Causes include **a** a rapidly appreciating dollar between 1980 and 1985; and **b** faster American growth of national income during the early 1980s than in Europe and Japan, and again in 1992–1994, when Europe and Japan were struggling with recession and sluggish growth.

10 Trade deficits have produced current increases in the living standards of American consumers. However, these deficits have also increased our debt to the rest of the world.

11 Two paths to a reduced American trade deficit are **a** reductions in the Federal budget deficit and   **b** faster economic growth abroad. Other possible remedies—some desirable, some not—are an easy money policy, protective tariffs, recession, improved American competitiveness, and direct foreign investment in the United States.

period to period. We know that exchange rate stability facilitates international trade.

2   Absorbing Risk   Speculators aid international trade in another way: *They absorb risk which others do not want to bear.* International transactions are riskier than domestic transactions because of potential adverse changes in exchange rates. Suppose AnyTime, a hypothetical American retailer, signs a contract with a German manufacturer to buy 10,000 German clocks to be delivered in three months. The stipulated price is 75 marks per clock, which in dollars is $50 per clock at the present exchange rate of $1 = 1.5 mark. AnyTime's total bill will be $500,000 (750,000 marks).

But if the German mark would appreciate, say, to $1 = 1 mark, the dollar price per clock would rise from $50 to $75 and AnyTime would owe $750,000 for the clocks (750,000 marks). AnyTime may reduce part of the risk of unfavorable exchange rate fluctuations by hedging in the futures market. *Hedging is an action by a buyer or seller to protect against a change in future prices. The futures market is a market where items are bought and sold at prices fixed now, for delivery at a specified date in the future.*

AnyTime can purchase the needed 750,000 marks at the current $1 for 1.5 market exchange rate to be made available in three months when the German clocks are delivered. And here is where speculators arrive on the scene. For a price determined in the futures market, they agree to deliver the 750,000

marks to AnyTime in three months at the $1 = 1.5 mark exchange rate, regardless of the exchange rate then. The seller of the futures contract need not own marks when the contract is made. If the German mark *depreciates* to, say, $1 = 2 marks in this period, the speculator makes a profit. He or she can buy the 750,000 marks stipulated in the contract for $375,000, pocketing the difference between that amount and the $500,000 AnyTime has agreed to pay for the 750,000 marks.

If the German mark *appreciates,* the speculator —but not AnyTime—suffers a loss. The amount AnyTime will have to pay for this futures contract will depend on how the market views the likelihood of the mark depreciating, appreciating, or staying constant over the three-month period. As in all highly competitive markets, supply and demand determine the price of the futures contract.

Unfortunately, the futures market does not entirely eliminate exchange rate risks. Suppose the market depreciates in the three-month delivery period and a competing importing firm did *not* hedge its foreign exchange purchase. This means the competitive retailer will obtain its shipment of clocks at less than $50 per clock and can underprice AnyTime. But the futures market *does* eliminate much of the exchange rate risk associated with buying foreign goods for future delivery. With the full exchange rate risk, AnyTime might have decided against importing German clocks. The futures market and currency speculators greatly reduce that risk, increasing the likelihood the transaction will occur. *Operating through the futures market, speculation promotes international trade.*

TERMS AND CONCEPTS

balance of payments
current account
credits
debits
trade balance
balance on goods and
  services
balance on current
  account

capital account
balance on the capital
  account
official reserves
balance of payments
  deficits and surpluses
fixed exchange rates
flexible or floating
  exchange rates

depreciation and
  appreciation
purchasing power parity
  theory
gold standard
gold import and export
  points
Bretton Woods system

International Monetary
  Fund
devaluation
managed floating
  exchange rates
G-7 nations

QUESTIONS AND STUDY SUGGESTIONS

1 Explain how an American automobile importer might finance a shipment of Toyotas from Japan. Demonstrate how an American export of machinery to Italy might be financed. Explain: "American exports earn supplies of foreign monies which Americans can use to finance imports."

2 *Key Question* *Indicate whether each of the following creates a demand for, or a supply of, French francs in foreign exchange markets:*

a *An American importer purchases a shipload of Bordeaux wine*

b *A French automobile firm decides to build an assembly plant in Los Angeles*

c *An American college student decides to spend a year studying at the Sorbonne*

d *A French manufacturer exports machinery to Morocco on an American freighter*

e *The United States incurs a balance of payments deficit in its transactions with France*

f *A United States government bond held by a French citizen matures*

g *It is widely believed that the international value of the franc will fall in the near future*

3 *Key Question* *Answer the following questions on the basis of Alpha's balance of payments for 1996 as shown below. All figures are in billions of dollars. What is the balance of trade? The balance on goods and services? The balance on current account? The balance on capital account? Does Alpha have a balance of payments deficit or surplus?*

Merchandise exports	+ $40	Net transfers	+ $10
Merchandise imports	30	Capital inflows	+ 10
Service exports	+ 15	Capital outflows	− 40
Service imports	− 10	Official reserves	+ 10
Net investment income	− 5		

4 "A rise in the dollar price of yen necessarily means a fall in the yen price of dollars." Do you agree? Illustrate and elaborate: "The critical thing about exchange rates is that they provide a direct link between the prices of goods and services produced in all trading nations of the world." Explain the purchasing power parity theory of exchange rates.

5 The Swedish auto company Saab imports car components from Germany and exports autos to the United States. In 1990 the dollar depreciated, and the German mark appreciated, relative to the Swedish krona. Speculate as to how this hurt Saab—twice.

6 *Key Question* *Explain why the American demand for Mexican pesos is downsloping and the supply of pesos to Americans is upsloping. Assuming a system of floating exchange rates between Mexico and the United States, indicate whether each of the following would cause the Mexican peso to appreciate or depreciate:*

a *The United States unilaterally reduces tariffs on Mexican products*

b *Mexico encounters severe inflation*

c *Deteriorating political relations reduce American tourism in Mexico*

d *The United States' economy moves into a severe recession*

e *The Federal Reserve embarks on a tight money policy*

f *Mexican products become more fashionable to Americans*

g *The Mexican government encourages American firms to invest in Mexican oil fields*

h *The rate of productivity growth in the United States diminishes sharply*

7 Explain whether or not you agree with the following statements:

a "A country which grows faster than its major trading partners can expect the international value of its currency to depreciate."

b "A nation whose interest rate is rising more rapidly than in other nations can expect the international value of its currency to appreciate."

c "A country's currency will appreciate if its inflation rate is less than that of the rest of the world."

8 "Exports pay for imports. Yet in 1994 the rest of the world exported about $108 billion more worth of goods and services to the United States than were imported from the United States." Resolve the apparent inconsistency of these two statements.

9 Explain in detail how a balance of payments deficit would be resolved under **a** the gold standard, **b** the Bretton Woods system, and **c** floating exchange rates. What are the advantages and shortcomings of each system?

10 Outline the major costs and benefits associated with a large trade or current account deficit. Explain: "A current account deficit means we are receiving more goods and services from abroad than we are sending abroad. How can that be called 'unfavorable'?"

11 Some people assert that the United States is facing a foreign trade crisis. What do you think they mean? What are the major causes of this "crisis"?

12 Cite and explain two reasons for the decline in the international value of the dollar between 1985 and 1987. Why did the United States trade deficit remain high, even though the dollar fell in value?

13 *Key Question   Explain how a reduction in the Federal budget deficit could contribute to a decline in the United States trade deficit. Why do trade deficits fall during recessions? Is recession a desirable remedy to trade deficits?*

14 (Last Word) Suppose Winter Sports—a French retailer of snowboards—wants to order 5000 snowboards made in the United States. The price per board is $200, the present exchange rate is 6 francs = 1 dollar, and payment is due in dollars when the boards are delivered in three months. Use a numerical example to explain why exchange rate risk might make the French retailer hesitant to place the order. How might speculators absorb some of Winter Sports' risk?

GROWTH AND THE LESS DEVELOPED COUNTRIES

It is difficult for the typical American family, whose 1993 average income was $36,959, to grasp the fact that some two-thirds of the world's population lives at, or perilously close to, the subsistence level. Hunger, squalor, and disease are common in many nations of the world. The World Bank estimates that over 1 billion people—approximately 20 percent of the world's population—lives on less than $1 per day!

In this chapter we first identify the poor or less developed nations. Second, we seek to determine why they are poor. What are the obstacles to growth? Third, the potential role of government in economic development is considered. Fourth, international trade, private capital flows, and foreign aid are examined as vehicles of growth. Fifth, the external debt problems faced by many of the poor nations are analyzed. Finally, we present the demands of poor nations to establish a "new global contract" to improve their economies.

THE RICH AND THE POOR

Just as there is considerable income disparity among individual families within a nation (Chapter 34), so there also is great economic inequality among the family of nations. Table 39-1 shows the remarkable degree of income disparity in the world. The richest one-fifth of the world's population receives almost 83 percent of world income; the poorest one-fifth obtains less than 1.5 percent. The poorest 60 percent of the world population gets less than 6 percent of the world's income.

Table 39-2 helps to sort out rich and poor by identifying the following groups of nations.

1 Industrially Advanced Countries The **industrially advanced countries (IACs)** include the United States, Canada, Australia, New Zealand, Japan, and most of the nations of western Europe. These nations have developed market economies based on large stocks of capital goods, advanced production technologies, and well-educated labor forces. As column 1 of Table 39-2 indicates, these twenty-three economies have a high per capita (per person) GNP.

2 Less Developed Countries Most of the remaining nations of the world—located in Africa, Asia, and Latin America—are underdeveloped or **less developed countries (LDCs).** These 109 nations are unindustrialized with their labor forces heavily committed to agriculture. Literacy rates are low, unemployment is high, population growth is rapid, and exports consist largely of agricultural commodities (cocoa, bananas, sugar, raw cotton) and raw materi-

TABLE 39-1   Global income disparity

World population	Percentage of world income
Richest 20%	82.7
Second 20%	11.7
Third 20%	2.3
Fourth 20%	1.9
Poorest 20%	1.4

Source: United Nations Development Program, *Human Development Report 1992* (New York: Oxford University Press, 1992), p. 36.

als (copper, iron ore, natural rubber). Capital equipment is scarce, production technologies are typically primitive, and labor force productivity is low. About three-fourths of the world's population lives in these nations, which share the characteristic of widespread poverty.

In Table 39-2 we have divided the poor nations into two groups. The first group comprises sixty-seven "middle-income" LDCs with an average annual per capita GNP of $2490. The range of per capita GNPs of this diverse group is from $670 to $7510. The other group is made up of forty-two "low-income" LDCs with per capita GNPs ranging from $60 to $670 and averaging only $390. This group is dominated by India, China, and the sub-Saharan nations of Africa.

Several comparisons may bring global income disparities into sharper focus.

1   The United States' 1992 GDP was approximately $5.9 trillion; the combined GDPs of the 109 LDCs in that year were only $5.7 trillion.

2   The United States with only about 5 percent of the world's population produces one-fourth of the world's output.

3   The annual sales of many large U.S. corporations exceed the GDPs of many of the LDCs. General Motors' annual revenues are greater than the GDPs of all but twenty or so nations.

4   Per capita GNP in the United States is 387 times greater than in Mozambique, the world's poorest nation.

Growth, Decline, and Income Gaps

We need to append two other points to our discussion of Table 39-2.

1   Miracles and Disasters   There have been considerable differences in the ability of the various LDCs to improve their circumstances over time. On the one hand, a group of so-called newly industrialized economies—Singapore, Hong Kong, Taiwan, and South Korea—have achieved very high annual growth rates of real GNP of 6 to 7 percent over the 1960–1989 period. As a consequence, real per capita GNPs rose fivefold in these nations. In vivid contrast, many of the highly indebted LDCs and the very poor sub-Saharan nations of Africa have had *declining* real per capita GNPs during the past decade.

2   Growing Absolute Gaps   The income gap between rich and poor nations has been widening. To demonstrate this point, let's assume the per capita GNPs of the advanced and less developed countries have both been growing at about 2 percent per year. Because the income base in the advanced countries is initially much higher, the income gap grows. If per capita income is $400 a year, a 2 percent growth rate means an $8 increase in income. Where per capita in-

TABLE 39-2   GNP per capita, population, and growth rates

	GNP per capita		Population	
	(1) Dollars, 1992	(2) Annual growth rate, 1980–1992	(3) Millions, mid-1992	(4) Annual growth rate, 1980–1992
Industrially advanced countries: IACs (23 nations)	$22,160	2.3%	828	0.7%
Less developed countries: LDCs (109 nations)				
Middle-income LDCs (67 nations)	2,490	− 0.1	1,419	1.8
Low-income LDCs (42 nations)	390	3.9	3,191	2.0

Source: World Bank, *World Development Report, 1994* (New York: Oxford University Press), pp. 162–164, 210–211.

TABLE 39-3   Selected socioeconomic indicators of development

Country	(1) Per capita GNP, 1992	(2) Life expectancy at birth, 1992	(3) Infant mortality per 1000 live births, 1992	(4) Adult illiteracy rate, 1990	(5) Daily per capita calorie supply, 1990	(6) Per capita energy consumption, 1992*
Japan	$28,190	79 years	5	under 5	2,848	3,586
United States	23,240	77	9	under 5	3,666	7,662
Brazil	2,770	66	57	19	2,730	681
Mauritania	530	48	117	66	2,450	108
China	470	69	31	27	2,640	600
India	310	61	79	52	2,230	235
Bangladesh	220	55	91	65	2,040	59
Ethiopia	110	49	122	—	1,700	21
Mozambique	60	44	162	67	1,810	32

*Kilograms of oil equivalent.
Source: World Development Report, 1994.

come is $4000 per year, the same 2 percent growth rate translates into an $80 increase in income. Thus, the absolute income gap will have increased from $3600 (= $4000 − $400) to $3672 (= $4080 − $408). The LDCs must grow faster than the IACs to catch up.

In fact, the absolute income gap between rich and poor nations has widened significantly. The absolute difference in per capita income between the richest 20 percent and the poorest 20 percent of the world's population increased from $1854 in 1960 to $15,149 in 1989. *(Key Question 3)*

Implications

Mere statistics conceal the human implications of the extreme poverty characterizing so much of our planet:

> . . . let us examine a typical "extended" family in rural Asia. The Asian household is likely to comprise ten or more people, including parents, five to seven children, two grandparents, and some aunts and uncles. They have a combined annual income, both in money and in "kind" (i.e., they consume a share of the food they grow), of from $250 to $300. Together they live in a poorly constructed one-room house as tenant farmers on a large agricultural estate owned by an absentee landlord who lives in the nearby city. The father, mother, uncle, and the older children must work all day on the land. None of the adults can read or write; of the five school-age children, only one attends school regularly; and he cannot ex-

pect to proceed beyond three or four years of primary education. There is only one meal a day; it rarely changes and it is rarely sufficient to alleviate the childrens' constant hunger pains. The house has no electricity, sanitation, or fresh water supply. There is much sickness, but qualified doctors and medical practitioners are far away in the cities attending to the needs of wealthier families. The work is hard, the sun is hot and aspirations for a better life are constantly being snuffed out. In this part of the world the only relief from the daily struggle for physical survival lies in the spiritual traditions of the people.[1]

In Table 39-3 various socioeconomic indicators for selected LDCs are contrasted with those for the United States and Japan. These data confirm the major points stressed in the above quotation.

BREAKING THE POVERTY BARRIER

The avenues of economic growth are essentially the same for industrially advanced and less developed nations:

1   Greater Efficiency   Existing supplies of resources must be used more efficiently in the future. This means not only eliminating unemployment but

[1]Michael P. Todaro, *Economic Development in the Third World*, 5th ed. (New York: Longman, 1994), p. 4.

also achieving greater efficiency in the utilization of resources.

2   Resource Enhancement   Supplies of productive resources must be altered—typically, increased. By expanding supplies of raw materials, capital equipment, effective labor, and technological knowledge, a nation can push its production possibilities curve to the right.

Why have some nations been successful in pursuing these avenues of growth while others lag far behind? The difference is in the physical, human, and sociocultural environments of the various nations.

Natural Resources

There is no simple generalization as to the role of natural resources in the economic development of LDCs. This is because the distribution of natural resources among these nations is very uneven. Some less developed nations have valuable deposits of bauxite, tin, copper, tungsten, nitrates, and petroleum. Some LDCs have been able to use their natural resource endowments to achieve rapid growth and a significant redistribution of income from the rich to the poor nations. The Organization of Petroleum Exporting Countries (OPEC) is a standard example. On the other hand, in many cases natural resources are owned or controlled by the multinational corporations of industrially advanced countries, with the economic benefits from these resources largely diverted abroad. Furthermore, world markets for many of the farm products and raw materials which the LDCs export are subject to great price fluctuations which contribute to instability in their economies.

Other LDCs lack mineral deposits, have little arable land, and have few sources of power. Also, most of the poor countries are in Central and South America, Africa, the Indian subcontinent, and Southeast Asia where tropical climates prevail. The hot, humid climate is not conducive to productive labor; human, crop, and livestock diseases are widespread; and weed and insect infestations plague agriculture.

A weak resource base can pose a serious obstacle to growth. Real capital can be accumulated and the quality of the labor force improved through education and training. But the natural resource base is largely unaugmentable. It may be unrealistic for many of the LDCs to envision an economic destiny comparable with that of, say, the United States and Canada. But we must be careful in generalizing: Switzerland and

Japan, for example, have achieved high levels of living *despite* restrictive natural resource bases.

Human Resources

Three statements describe many of the LDCs' circumstances with respect to human resources:
1   They are overpopulated.
2   Unemployment and underemployment are widespread.
3   Labor force productivity is low.

Overpopulation   As column 3 of Table 39-2 makes clear, many of the LDCs with the most meager natural and capital resources have the largest populations to support. Table 39-4 compares population densities and population growth rates of a few selected nations with those of the United States and the world as a whole.

Most important for the long run is the vivid contrast of population growth rates: The middle- and low-income LDCs of Table 39-2 are now experiencing approximately a 2 percent annual increase in population compared with a 0.7 percent annual rate for advanced countries. Recalling the "rule of 70," the current rate suggests that the total population of the LDCs will double in about 35 years.

These statistics indicate why the per capita income gap between the LDCs and the IACs has widened. In some of the less developed countries rapid population growth actually presses on the food supply to the extent that per capita food consumption is pulled down to the subsistence level or below. In

TABLE 39-4   Population statistics for selected countries

Country	Population per square mile, 1994	Annual rate of population increase, 1980–1992
United States	74	1.0%
Pakistan	429	3.1
Bangladesh	2,421	2.3
Venezuela	60	2.6
India	801	2.1
China	331	1.4
Kenya	128	3.6
Philippines	606	2.4
World	112	1.7

Source: Statistical Abstract of the United States, 1994.

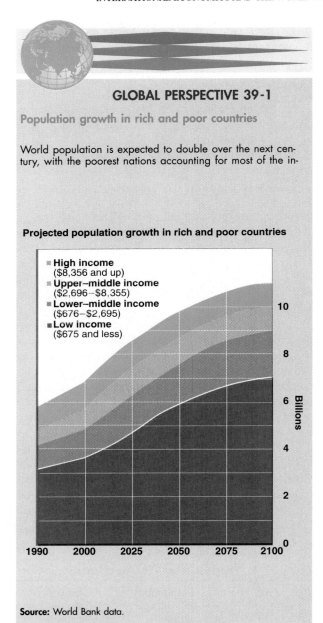

GLOBAL PERSPECTIVE 39-1

Population growth in rich and poor countries

World population is expected to double over the next century, with the poorest nations accounting for most of the increase.

Projected population growth in rich and poor countries

- **High income**
  ($8,356 and up)
- **Upper–middle income**
  ($2,696–$8,355)
- **Lower–middle income**
  ($676–$2,695)
- **Low income**
  ($675 and less)

(Billions)

10

8

6

4

2

0

1990 2000 2025 2050 2075 2100

Source: World Bank data.

the standard of living could be raised by boosting consumer goods—particularly food—production. But the problem is more complex than this, because any increase in consumer goods production which initially raises the standard of living is likely to induce a population increase. This increase, if sufficient in size, will dissipate the improvement in living standards, and subsistence living levels will again prevail.

But why does population growth in LDCs accompany increases in output? First, the nation's *death* or *mortality rate* will decline with initial increases in production. This decline is the result of (1) a higher level of per capita food consumption, and (2) the basic medical and sanitation programs which accompany the initial phases of economic development.

Second, the *birthrate* will remain high or may increase, particularly as medical and sanitation programs cut infant mortality. The cliché that "the rich get richer and the poor get children" is uncomfortably accurate for many LDCs. An increase in the per capita standard of living may lead to a population upsurge which will cease only when the standard of living has again been reduced to the level of bare subsistence.

In addition to the fact that rapid population growth can convert an expanding GDP into a stagnant or slow-growing GDP per capita, there are other reasons why population expansion is an obstacle to development.

1   Saving and Investment   Large families reduce the capacity of households to save, restricting the economy's ability to accumulate capital.

2   Productivity   As population grows, more investment is required to maintain the amount of real capital per person. If investment fails to keep pace, each worker will have fewer tools and equipment, reducing worker productivity (output per worker). Declining productivity implies stagnating or declining per capita incomes.

3   Resource Exploitation   Because most less developed countries are heavily dependent on agriculture, rapid population growth may result in overuse of limited natural resources such as land. The much-publicized African famines are partially the result of past overgrazing and overplanting of land caused by the pressing need to feed a growing population.

the worst instances, only malnutrition and disease and the high death rate they engender keep incomes near subsistence. This chapter's Last Word is relevant.

It would seem at first glance that, since

$$\text{Per capita standard of living} = \frac{\text{consumer goods (food) production}}{\text{population}}$$

4 **Urban Problems** Rapid population growth in the cities of the LDCs, accompanied by unprecedented flows of rural migrants, are generating massive urban problems. Substandard housing in impoverished slums, deteriorating public services, congestion, pollution, and crime are all problems worsened by rapid population growth. The resolution or lessening of these difficulties necessitates a diversion of resources from growth-oriented uses.

Most authorities advocate birth control as the most effective means for breaking out of this dilemma. And breakthroughs in contraceptive technology in recent decades have made this solution increasingly relevant. But obstacles to population control are great. Low literacy rates make it difficult to disseminate information on contraceptive devices. In peasant agriculture, large families are a major source of labor. Adults may regard having many children as a kind of informal social security system; the more children, the greater the probability of having a relative to care for you during old age. Finally, many nations which stand to gain the most through birth control are often the least willing, for religious and sociocultural reasons, to embrace contraception programs. Population growth in Latin America, for example, is among the most rapid in the world.

China—with about one-fifth of the world's population—adopted a harsh "one-child" program in 1980. The government advocated late marriages and one child per family. Couples having more than one child are fined or lose various social benefits. Even though the rate of population growth has diminished under this program, China's population continues to expand at about 100 million per decade. India, the world's second most populous nation, had a 103 million or 13 percent population increase in the 1986–1992 period. With a total population of 884 million, India has 16 percent of the world's population but less than 2.5 percent of its land mass.

Three Addenda But three additional points are worthy of note.
1 As with natural resources, the relationship between population and economic growth is less clear than one might expect. A high population density and rapid population growth do not necessarily mean poverty. China and India have immense populations and are poor; but Japan and Hong Kong are densely populated and relatively wealthy.
2 Population growth rates for the LDCs as a group have declined somewhat in recent decades. In the mid-1960s the annual population growth rate was about 2.35 percent. Currently it is about 2 percent and projections suggest further future declines.
3 The traditional view is that the reduction of population growth through the more widespread use of birth control techniques is the basic means for increasing per capita incomes in the LDCs. Reduce population growth in the denominator of our earlier equation and the standard of living will rise.

But there is a contrary view—known as the **demographic transition**—which reverses causation by arguing that rising incomes must first be achieved and only then will slower population growth follow. The demographic transition view observes that in low-income countries children are viewed as economic assets; they are a cheap source of labor and potentially provide financial support and security for their parents in their old age. Thus people in poor countries have high birthrates. But in wealthy IAC nations children are economic liabilities. Their care requires the sacrifice of high earnings or the need to purchase expensive child care. Also, children require extended and expensive education for the highly skilled jobs characteristic of IAC economies. Finally, the wealth of the IACs results in "social safety nets" which protect adults from the insecurity associated with old age and the inability to work. Thus people in the IACs recognize that high birthrates are neither necessary nor desirable, so they choose to have fewer children.

Note the differences in causation implied by the two views. The traditional view says reduced birthrates must come first and higher per capita incomes will follow; lower birthrates cause per capita income growth. The demographic transition view says higher incomes must first be achieved and lower rates of population growth will be the result; higher incomes are the cause of slower population growth. *(Key Question 6)*

Unemployment and Underemployment Reliable unemployment statistics for the LDCs are not readily available. But observation suggests that unemployment and underemployment are both quite high. **Unemployment** occurs when someone who is willing and able to work cannot find a job. **Underemployment** occurs when workers are employed fewer hours or days per week than they desire, work at jobs that do not fully use their skills, or spend much of the time on their job unproductively.

Many economists contend that unemployment is high—as much as 15 to 20 percent—in the rapidly growing urban areas of the LDCs. There has been substantial migration in most less developed countries from rural to urban areas, motivated by the *expectation* of finding jobs with higher wage rates than are available in agricultural and other rural employments. But this huge migration makes it unlikely that a migrant will in fact obtain a job. Migration to the cities has greatly exceeded the growth of urban job opportunities, resulting in very high urban unemployment rates. Thus, rapid rural-urban migration has given rise to urban unemployment rates which are two or three times as great as rural rates.

Underemployment is widespread and characteristic of most LDCs. In many LDCs rural agricultural labor may be so abundant relative to capital and natural resources that a significant percentage of this labor contributes little or nothing to agricultural output. Similarly, many LDC workers are self-employed as proprietors of small shops, in handicrafts, or as street vendors. A lack of demand means that small shop owners or vendors spend more time in idleness in the shop or on the street. While they are not without jobs, they are underemployed.

Low Labor Productivity Labor productivity tends to be very low in most LDCs. As we will see, the LDCs have found it difficult to invest in *physical capital*. As a result, their workers are underequipped with machinery and tools and are relatively unproductive. Keep in mind that rapid population growth tends to reduce the amount of physical capital available per worker which decreases labor productivity and real incomes.

In addition, most poor countries have not been able to invest sufficiently in their *human capital* (Table 39-3, columns 4 and 5); that is, expenditures on health and education have been meager. Low levels of literacy, malnutrition, absence of proper medical care, and insufficient educational facilities all contribute to populations ill equipped for economic development and industrialization. Attitudes may also play a role. In some countries hard work is associated with slavery, servitude, and inferiority. It is therefore to be avoided.

Particularly vital is the absence of a vigorous entrepreneurial class willing to bear risks, accumulate capital, and provide the organizational requisites essential to economic growth. Closely related is the dearth of labor prepared to handle the routine supervisory functions basic to any program of development. Ironically, the higher education systems of many LDCs are oriented heavily toward the humanities and offer little work in business, engineering, and the sciences. Some LDCs are characterized by an authoritarian view of human relations—often fostered by repressive governments—which generates an environment hostile to independent thinking, taking initiatives, and assuming economic risks. Authoritarianism discourages experimentation and change—the essence of entrepreneurship.

An additional irony is that, while migration from the LDCs has modestly offset rapid population growth, it has also deprived some LDCs of highly productive workers. Often the best-trained and most highly motivated workers—physicians, engineers, teachers, and nurses—leave the LDCs to seek their fortunes in the IACs. This so-called **brain drain** contributes to the deterioration in the overall skill level and productivity of the labor force.

Capital Accumulation

An important focal point of economic development is the accumulation of capital goods. There are several reasons for this.

1 All LDCs suffer from shortages of capital goods—factories, machinery and equipment, public utilities, and so forth. Better-equipped labor forces would greatly enhance their productivity and help boost the per capita standard of living. There is a close relationship between output per worker (labor productivity) and real income per worker. A nation must produce more goods and services per worker to enjoy more goods and services per worker as income. One way of increasing labor productivity is to provide each worker with more tools and equipment. Indeed, empirical studies for the LDCs confirm a positive relationship between investment and the growth of GDP. On the average a 1 percentage point increase in the ratio of investment to GDP raises the overall growth rate by about one-tenth of 1 percentage point. Thus an increase in the investment-to-GDP ratio from 10 to 15 percent would increase the growth of real GDP by one-half of 1 percentage point.[2]

2 Increasing the stock of capital goods is crucial because of the very limited possibility of increasing the supply of arable land. If there is little likelihood of increasing agricultural output by increasing the supply

---

[2]International Monetary Fund, *World Economic Outlook* (Washington, 1988), p. 76.

of land, an alternative is to use more and better capital equipment with the available agricultural work force.

3   Once initiated, the process of capital accumulation *may* be cumulative. If capital accumulation can increase output faster than population grows, a margin of saving may arise which permits further capital formation. In a sense, capital accumulation can feed on itself.

Let's first consider the prospects for less developed nations to accumulate capital domestically. Then we will examine the possibility of foreign capital flowing into them.

Domestic Capital Formation   A less developed nation—or any nation—accumulates capital through saving and investing. A nation must save (refrain from consumption) to release resources from consumer goods production. Investment spending must then absorb these released resources in the production of capital goods. But impediments to saving and investing are much greater in a low-income nation than in an advanced economy.

Savings Potential   Consider first the savings side of the picture. The situation here is mixed and varies greatly between countries. Some of the very poor countries such as Ethiopia, Bangladesh, Uganda, Haiti, and Madagascar save only from 2 to 5 percent of their domestic outputs. They are too poor to save a significant portion of their incomes. Interestingly, however, other less developed countries save as large a percentage of their domestic outputs as do advanced industrial countries. In 1992 India and China saved 22 and 36 percent of their domestic outputs, respectively, compared to 34 percent for Japan, 28 percent for Germany, and 15 percent for the United States. The problem is that the domestic outputs of the LDCs are so low that even when saving rates are comparable to advanced nations, the total absolute volume of saving is not large. As we will see, foreign capital inflows and foreign aid are means of supplementing domestic saving.

Capital Flight   Many of the LDCs have suffered **capital flight.** Citizens of the LDCs have transferred their savings to, or invested their savings in, the IACs. Citizens of many LDCs regard the risks of investing at home to be high compared to the industrially advanced nations. These risks include loss of savings or real capital due to government expropriation, taxation,

higher rates of inflation, or changes in exchange rates. If an LDC's political climate is volatile, savers may shift their funds overseas to a "safe haven" in fear that a new government might confiscate their wealth. Likewise, rapid or galloping inflation in an LDC would have similar confiscatory effects. The transfer of savings overseas may also be a means of evading domestic taxes on interest income or capital gains. Finally, financial capital may flow to the IACs where there are higher interest rates or a greater variety of investment opportunities.

Whatever the motivation, studies suggest the amount of capital flight from the LDCs is significant. One estimate suggested that the five largest Latin American debtors had capital outflows of $101 billion of private assets between 1979 and 1984. At the end of 1987 Mexicans are estimated to have held some $84 billion in assets abroad. Foreign asset holdings for Venezuelans, Argentinians, and Brazilians were $58, $46, and $31 billion, respectively. It is estimated that $6 to $10 billion flees Brazil every year. Brazilians are sending more money abroad as interest on foreign debt and capital flight than they receive as foreign investment and foreign aid. The critical point is that a significant portion of capital lending by the IACs to the LDCs is offset by LDC capital flights to the IACs. The World Bank estimates that the inflows of foreign aid and loans to Latin America were essentially negated by their capital flight in the 1980s.

Investment Obstacles   The investment side of capital formation abounds with equally serious obstacles. These obstacles undermine the rate of capital formation even when a sufficient volume of saving is available to finance the needed investment. Obstacles to investment fall into two categories: lack of investors and lack of incentives to invest.

Oddly, in some less developed countries the major obstacle to investment is the lack of business executives willing to assume the risks associated with investment. This is a special case of qualitative deficiencies of the labor force previously discussed.

But even if substantial savings and a vigorous entrepeneurial class are present, an essential ingredient in capital formation—the incentive to invest—may be weak. A host of factors may combine in an LDC to cripple investment incentives. We have just mentioned such factors as political instability and higher rates of inflation in our discussion of capital flight. Similarly, very low incomes mean a limited domestic market— a lack of demand—for most nonagricultural goods.

This factor is crucial when we recognize that the chances of successfully competing with mature industries of advanced nations in international markets are meager. Then, too, lack of trained administrative and operating personnel may be a factor in retarding investment, Finally, many LDCs simply do not have an adequate **infrastructure,** that is, the public capital goods, which are prerequisite to private investment of a productive nature. Poor roads and bridges, inadequate railways, little gas and electricity production, antiquated communications, unsatisfactory housing, and meager educational and public health facilities scarcely provide an inviting environment for investment spending. It is significant that approximately four-fifths of the investment of multinational companies goes to IACs.

The absence of an adequate infrastructure presents more of a problem than you might first surmise. The dearth of public capital goods means that much investment spending which does not *directly* result in the production of goods and which may not be capable of bearing profits must take place before, and simultaneously with, productive investment in manufacturing machinery and equipment. Statistics for advanced nations indicate that about 60 percent of gross investment goes for housing, public works, and public utilities, leaving about 40 percent for directly productive investment in manufacturing, agriculture, and commerce. These figures probably understate the percentage of total investment which must be devoted to infrastructure in emerging nations. The volume of investment required to initiate economic development may be much greater than it first appears.

One bright spot is the possibility of accumulating capital through *in-kind* or **nonfinancial investment.** With leadership and willingness to cooperate, capital can be accumulated by transferring surplus agricultural labor to improvement of agricultural facilities or the infrastructure. If each agricultural village allocated its surplus labor to the construction of irrigation canals, wells, schools, sanitary facilities, and roads, significant amounts of capital might be accumulated at no significant sacrifice of consumer goods production. Nonfinancial investment simply bypasses the problems inherent in the financial aspects of the capital accumulation process. Such investment does not require consumers to save portions of their money income, nor does it presume the presence of an entrepreneurial class anxious to invest. When leadership and cooperative spirit are present, nonfinancial investment is a promising avenue for accumulation of basic capital goods. *(Key Question 8)*

Technological Advance

Technological advance and capital formation are frequently part of the same process. Yet, there are advantages in treating technological advance—the discovery and application of new methods of producing—and capital formation, or the accumulating of capital goods, as separate processes.

The rudimentary state of technology in the LDCs puts them far from the frontiers of technological advance. There already exists an enormous body of technological knowledge accumulated by advanced nations which less developed countries *might* adopt and apply without expensive research. Crop rotation and contour plowing require no additional capital equipment, and may contribute significantly to productivity. By raising grain storage bins a few inches above ground, a large amount of grain spoilage can be avoided. Such changes may sound trivial to people of advanced nations. However, resulting gains in productivity can mean the difference between subsistence and starvation in some poverty-ridden nations.

In most instances application of either existing or new technological knowledge involves new and different capital goods. But, within limits, this capital can be obtained without an increase in the rate of capital formation. If the annual flow of replacement investment is rechanneled from technologically inferior to technologically superior capital equipment, productivity can be increased out of a constant level of investment spending. Actually, some technological advances may be **capital-saving** rather than **capital-using.** A new fertilizer, better adapted to a nation's topography and climate, might be cheaper than one currently employed. A seemingly high-priced metal plow which will last ten years may be cheaper in the long run than an inexpensive but technologically inferior wooden plow which requires annual replacement.

To what extent have LDCs transferred and effectively used available IAC technological knowledge? The picture is mixed. There can be no doubt that such technological borrowing has been instrumental in the rapid growth of such Pacific Rim countries as Japan, South Korea, Taiwan, and Singapore. Similarly, the OPEC nations benefitted greatly from IAC knowledge of oil exploration, production, and refining. Recently the former Soviet Union and the nations of eastern Europe have been seeking western technology to hasten their conversions to viable market-based economies.

At the same time, we must be realistic about the transferability of advanced technologies to less developed countries. In industrially advanced nations technologies are usually predicated on relatively scarce, highly skilled labor and relatively abundant capital. Such technologies tend to be capital-using or, alternatively stated, labor-saving. In contrast, less developed economies require technologies appropriate to *their* resource endowments—abundant unskilled labor and very limited quantities of capital goods. Labor-using and capital-saving technologies are appropriate to LDCs. Much of the highly advanced technology of advanced nations is inappropriate in the less developed countries; they must develop their own technologies. Recall, too, that many less developed nations have "traditional economies" and are not highly receptive to change. This is particularly true in peasant agriculture which dominates the economies of most LDCs. A potential technological advance which fails can mean hunger and malnutrition; therefore, there is a strong propensity to retain traditional production techniques.

Sociocultural and Institutional Factors

Economic considerations alone do not explain why an economy does or does not grow. Substantial social and institutional readjustments are usually an integral part of the growth process. Economic development means not only changes in a nation's physical environment (new transportation and communications facilities, new schools, new housing, new plants and equipment), but also changes in the way people think, behave, and associate with one another. Emancipation from custom and tradition is frequently a prerequisite of economic development. A critical but intangible ingredient in economic development is **the will to develop.** Economic growth may hinge on "what individuals and social groups *want,* and *whether they want it badly enough to change their old ways of doing things* and to work hard at installing the new."[3]

Sociocultural Obstacles Sociocultural impediments to growth are numerous and varied.

1 Some of the least developed countries have failed to achieve the preconditions for a national economic unit. Tribal and ethnic allegiances take precedence over national identity. Warring tribes confine all economic activity within the tribe, eliminating any possibility for production-increasing specialization and trade. The pathetic economic circumstances in Somalia, Sudan, Liberia, Zaire, and other sub-Saharan nations of Africa are due in no small measure to martial and political conflicts among rival clans.

2 The existence of a caste system—formal or informal—causes labor to be allocated to occupations on the basis of caste or tradition rather than on the basis of skill or merit. The result is a misallocation of human resources.

3 Religious beliefs and observances may seriously restrict the length of the workday and divert resources which might have been used for investment to ceremonial uses. In rural India total ceremonial expenditures are estimated at about 7 percent of per capita income.[4] Generally, religious and philosophical beliefs may be dominated by the fatalistic **capricious universe view,** that is, the notion that there is little or no correlation between an individual's activities and endeavors and the outcomes or experiences which that person encounters.

> If the universe is deemed capricious, the individual will learn to expect little or no correlation between actions and results. This will result in a fatalistic attitude. . . .
>
> These attitudes impinge on all activities including saving, investment, long-range perspective, supply of effort, and family planning. If a higher standard of living and amassing of wealth is treated as the result of providence rather than springing from hard work and saving, there is little rationale for saving, hard work, innovations, and enterprise.[5]

Other attitudes and cultural factors may impede economic activity and growth: emphasis on the per-

[3]Eugene Staley, *The Future of Underdeveloped Countries,* rev. ed. (New York: Frederick A. Praeger, 1961), p. 218.

[4]Inder P. Nijhawan, "Socio-Political Institutions, Cultural Values, and Attitudes: Their Impact on Indian Economic Development," in J. S. Uppal (ed.), *India's Economic Problems* (New Delhi: Tata McGraw-Hill Publishing Company, Ltd., 1975), p. 31.

[5]Ibid., p. 33.

formance of duties rather than the exertion of individual initiative; the focus on group rather than individual achievement; the notion of a preordained and unalterable universe; the belief in reincarnation which reduces the importance of one's present life.

Institutional Obstacles Political corruption and bribery are common in many LDCs. School systems and public service agencies are often ineptly administered and their functioning impaired by petty politics. Tax systems are frequently arbitrary, unjust, cumbersome, and detrimental to incentives to work and invest. Political decisions are often motivated by a desire to enhance the nation's international prestige, rather than to foster development.

Because of the predominance of farming in LDCs, the problem of achieving that institutional environment in agriculture most conducive to increasing production must be a vital consideration in any growth program. Specifically, the institutional problem of **land reform** demands attention in virtually all LDCs. But needed reform may vary tremendously between specific nations. In some LDCs the problem is excessive concentration of land ownership in the hands of a few wealthy families. This situation is demoralizing for tenants, weakening their incentive to produce, and is typically not conducive to capital improvements. At the other extreme is the absurd arrangement where each family owns and farms a minute fragment of land far too small for the application of modern agricultural technology. An important complication to the problem of land reform lies in the fact that political considerations sometimes push reform in that direction which is least defensible on economic grounds. For many nations, land reform may well be the most acute institutional problem to be resolved in initiating the process of economic development.

Examples: Land reform in South Korea undermined the political control of the landed aristocracy and made way for the development of strong commercial and industrial middle classes, all to the benefit of the country's economic development. In contrast, the prolonged dominance of the landed aristocracy in the Philippines has helped stifle the development of that economy.[6]

---

[6]Mrinal Datta-Chaudhuri, "Market Failure and Government Failure," *Journal of Economic Perspectives,* Summer 1990, p. 36.

QUICK REVIEW 39-1

■ About three-fourths of the world's population lives in the LDCs of Africa, Asia, and Latin America.

■ Natural resource scarcities and inhospitable climates restrict growth in many LDCs.

■ The LDCs are characterized by overpopulation, high unemployment rates, underemployment, and low labor productivity.

■ Low saving rates, capital flight, weak infrastructures, and lack of investors impair capital accumulation.

■ Sociocultural and institutional factors are often serious impediments to growth.

THE VICIOUS CIRCLE

Many of the characteristics of LDCs just described are simultaneously causes and consequences of their poverty. These countries are caught in a **vicious circle of poverty.** They *stay* poor because they *are* poor! Consider Figure 39-1. The fundamental feature of an LDC is low per capita income. Being poor, a family has little ability or incentive to save. Furthermore, low incomes mean low levels of demand. Thus, there are few available resources, on the one hand, and no strong incentives, on the other, for investment in physical or human capital. This means labor productivity is low. And, since output per person is real income per person, it follows that per capita income is low.

Many experts feel that the key to breaking out of this vicious circle is to increase the rate of capital accumulation, to achieve a level of investment of, say, 10 percent of the national income. But Figure 39-1 reminds us that the real villain for many LDCs—rapid population growth—may be waiting in the wings to undo the potentially beneficial effects of this higher rate of capital accumulation. Using hypothetical figures, suppose that initially an LDC is realizing no growth in its real GDP. But now it somehow manages to increase its saving and investment to 10 percent of its GDP. As a result, its real GDP begins to grow at, say, 2.5 percent per year. Given a stable population, real GDP per capita will also grow at 2.5 percent per year. If this persists, the standard of living will *double* in about 28 years. But what if population grows at the

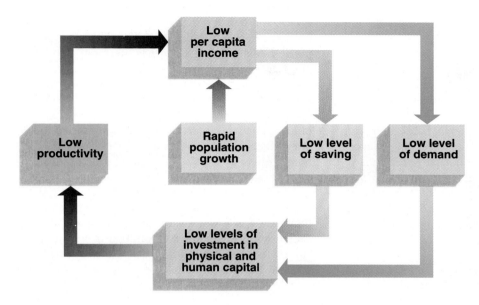

FIGURE 39-1 The vicious circle of poverty
Low per capita incomes make it extremely difficult for poor nations to save and invest, a condition that perpetuates low productivity and low incomes. Furthermore, rapid population growth may quickly absorb increases in per capita real income and thereby may negate the possibility of breaking out of the poverty circle.

Latin American rate of 2.5 percent per year? Then real income per person is unchanged and the vicious circle persists.

More optimistically, *if* population can be kept constant or constrained to some growth rate significantly below 2.5 percent, then real income per person will rise. This implies the possibility of still further enlargement in the flows of saving and investment, continued advances in productivity, and the continued growth of per capita real income. If a process of self-sustaining expansion of income, saving, investment, and productivity can be achieved, the self-perpetuating vicious circle of poverty can be transformed into a self-regenerating, beneficent circle of economic progress. The trick is to make effective those policies and strategies which will accomplish this transition. *(Key Question 14)*

ROLE OF GOVERNMENT

Economists do not agree on the appropriate role of government in seeking economic growth.

A Positive Role

One view is that, at least during initial stages of development, government should play a major role. The

reasons for this stem from the character of the obstacles facing LDCs.

1 Law and Order   Some of the poorest countries are plagued by banditry and intertribal warfare which divert both attention and resources from the task of development. A strong and stable national government is needed to establish domestic law and order and to achieve peace and unity. Research demonstrates that political instability (as measured by the number of revolutions and coups per year) is associated with slow growth.

2 Lack of Entrepreneurship   The absence of a sizable and vigorous entrepreneurial class, ready and willing to accumulate capital and initiate production, indicates that in many cases private enterprise is intrinsically not capable of spearheading the growth process.

3 Infrastructure   Many obstacles to economic growth center on deficiencies of public goods and services—an inadequate infrastructure. Sanitation and basic medical programs, education, irrigation and soil conservation projects, and construction of highways and transportation-communication facilities are all essentially nonmarketable goods and services yielding widespread spillover benefits. Government is the sole institution in a position to provide these goods and services in required quantities.

4 Forced Saving and Investment Government action may also be required to break through the saving-investment dilemma which impedes capital formation in LDCs.

It may be that only governmental fiscal action can provide a solution by forcing the economy to accumulate capital. There are two alternatives. One is to force the economy to save by increasing taxes. These tax revenues can then be channeled into priority investment projects. The problems of honestly and efficiently administering the tax system and achieving a high degree of compliance with tax laws can be great.

The other alternative is to force the economy to save through inflation. Government can finance capital accumulation by creating and spending new money or by selling bonds to banks and spending the proceeds. The resulting inflation is the equivalent of an arbitrary tax on the economy.

There are serious arguments against the advisability of saving through inflation. In the first place, inflation often distorts the composition of investment away from productive facilities to such items as luxury housing, precious metals and jewels, or foreign securities, which provide a better hedge against rising prices. Furthermore, significant inflation may reduce voluntary private saving as potential savers become less willing to accumulate depreciating money or securities payable in money of declining value. Inflation also induces "capital flight." Internationally, inflation may boost the nation's imports and retard its flow of exports, creating balance of payments difficulties.

5 Social-Institutional Problems Government is in the key position to deal effectively with the social-institutional obstacles to growth. Controlling population growth and land reform are problems which call for the broad approach that only government can provide. And government is in a position to stimulate the will to develop, to change a philosophy of "Heaven and faith will determine the course of events" to one of "God helps those who help themselves."

Public Sector Problems

But serious problems and disadvantages may exist with a governmentally directed development pro-

gram. If entrepreneurial talent is lacking in the private sector, can we expect leaders of quality to be present in the ranks of government? Is there not a real danger that government bureaucracy will impede, not stimulate, much-needed social and economic change? And what of the tendency of some political leaders to favor spectacular "showpiece" projects at the expense of less showy but more productive programs? Might not political objectives take precedence over the economic goals of a governmentally directed development program?

Development experts are less enthusiastic about the role of government in the growth process than they were thirty years ago. Government maladministration and corruption are common in many LDCs. Government officials often line their own pockets with foreign aid funds. Similarly, political leaders frequently confer monopoly privileges on relatives, friends, and political supporters. A political leader may grant exclusive rights to relatives or friends to produce, import, or export certain products. These monopoly privileges lead to higher domestic prices for the relevant products and diminish the LDC's ability to compete in world markets. Similarly, managers of state-owned enterprises are often appointed on the basis of cronyism rather than competence. Many LDC governments, particularly in Africa, have created "marketing boards" as the sole purchaser of agricultural products from local farmers. The boards buy farm products at artificially low prices, sell the output at higher world prices, and the "profit" ends up in the pockets of government officials. In recent years the perception of government has shifted from that of catalyst and promoter of growth to that of a potential impediment to development.

A Mixed Bag

It is possible to muster casual evidence on both sides of this question. Positive government contributions to development are evident in the cases of Japan, South Korea, and Taiwan. In comparison, Mobutu's Zaire, Somoza's Nicaragua, Marcos' Philippines, and Haiti under the Duvaliers are recognized examples of corrupt and inept governments which functioned as impediments to economic progress. Certainly the revolutionary transformations of the former Soviet Union and other eastern European nations away from communism and toward market-oriented economies makes clear that central planning is no longer recognized as an effective mechanism for development.

Many LDCs are belatedly coming to recognize that competition and individual economic incentives are important ingredients in the development process, and that their citizens need to see direct personal gains from their efforts to motivate them to take actions which will expand production.

ROLE OF ADVANCED NATIONS

What are the ways by which industrially advanced nations can help less developed countries in their quest for growth? To what degree have these avenues of assistance been pursued?

Generally, less developed nations can benefit from (1) an expanding volume of trade with advanced nations; (2) foreign aid in the form of grants and loans from governments of advanced nations; and (3) flows of private capital from more affluent nations.

Expanding Trade

Some authorities maintain that the simplest and most effective way the United States and other industrially advanced nations can aid less developed nations is by lowering international trade barriers, enabling LDCs to expand their national incomes through increased trade.

Though there is some truth in this view, lowered trade barriers are not a panacea. It is true that some poor nations need only large foreign markets for their raw materials to achieve growth. But the problem for many is not obtaining markets for utilizing existing productive capacity or the sale of relatively abundant raw materials, but the more fundamental one of getting the capital and technical assistance needed to produce something for export.

Furthermore, close trade ties with advanced nations are not without disadvantages. The old quip, "When Uncle Sam gets his feet wet, the rest of the world gets pneumonia," contains considerable truth for many less developed nations. A recession among the IACs can have disastrous consequences for the prices of raw materials and the export earnings of the LDCs. For example, in mid-1974 copper was $1.52 per pound; by the end of 1975 it had fallen to $.53 per pound! Stability and growth in industrially advanced nations are important to progress in less developed countries.

Foreign Aid: Public Loans and Grants

Foreign capital—both public and private—can supplement an emerging country's saving and investment and play a crucial role in breaking the circle of poverty.

Most LDCs are sadly lacking in infrastructure—irrigation and public health programs and educational, transportation, and communications systems—prerequisites to attracting either domestic or foreign private capital. Foreign public aid is needed to tear down this roadblock to the flow of private capital to the LDCs.

Direct Aid   The United States and other IACs have assisted LDCs directly through a variety of programs and through participating in international institutions designed to stimulate economic development. Over the last decade American aid to the LDCs—including both loans and grants—averaged $10–$14 billion per year. The bulk of this aid is administered by our Agency for International Development (AID). Some, however, takes the form of grants of surplus food under the Food for Peace program. Other advanced nations have also embarked on substantial foreign aid programs. In recent years foreign aid from all industrially advanced nations has been about $60 billion per year.

The aid programs of the IACs merit several additional comments. First, aid is typically distributed on the basis of political and military, rather than economic, considerations. Israel, Turkey, Egypt, and Greece are major recipients of American aid at the expense of Asian, Latin American, and African nations with much lower standards of living. Second, aid from the IACs only amounts to about one-third of 1 percent of the IAC's collective GDPs (Global Perspective 39-2). Finally, LDCs are increasingly concerned that the shift of the former Soviet Union and eastern Europe toward more democratic, market-oriented systems will make these nations "new players" as foreign aid recipients. The LDCs worry that IAC aid which formerly flowed to Latin America, Asia, and Africa may be redirected to, say, Poland, Hungary, and Russia. Similarly, there is the prospect of a substantially larger aid flow to the Middle East if the PLO-Israeli peace accord is durable.

The World Bank Group   The United States is a participant in the **World Bank,** whose major objective is assisting LDCs in achieving growth. Supported by

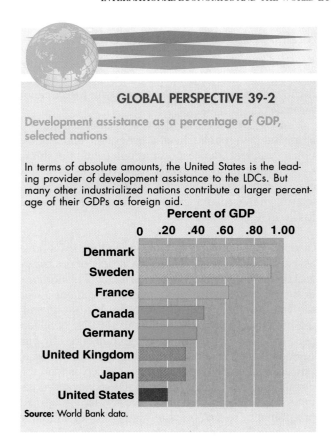

GLOBAL PERSPECTIVE 39-2

Development assistance as a percentage of GDP, selected nations

In terms of absolute amounts, the United States is the leading provider of development assistance to the LDCs. But many other industrialized nations contribute a larger percentage of their GDPs as foreign aid.

Percent of GDP

Source: World Bank data.

nearly 180 member nations, the World Bank not only lends out of its capital funds, but also (1) sells bonds and lends the proceeds, and (2) guarantees and insures private loans.

Several characteristics of the World Bank are noteworthy.

1 The World Bank is a "last resort" lending agency; its loans are limited to productive projects for which private funds are not readily available.

2 Because many World Bank loans have been for basic development projects—dams, irrigation projects, health and sanitation programs, communications and transportation facilities—it has been hoped that the Bank's activities will provide the infrastructure needed to encourage flows of private capital.

3 The Bank has played a role in providing technical assistance to the LDCs by helping them discover what avenues of growth seem appropriate for their economic development.

Two World Bank affiliates function in areas where the World Bank has been weak. The *International Fi-*

nance Corporation (*IFC*) has the primary function of investing in *private* enterprises in the LDCs. The *International Development Association* (*IDA*) makes "soft loans"—loans which may not be self-liquidating—to the poorest of the LDCs on more liberal terms than does the World Bank.

Foreign Harm? But foreign aid to the LDCs has been subject to criticism.

1 Dependency and Incentives A basic criticism is that, like domestic welfare programs, foreign aid may generate dependency rather than self-sustaining growth. It is argued that transfers of wealth from the IACs allow the LDCs to avoid the painful economic decisions, the institutional and cultural changes, and the alterations in attitudes regarding thrift, industry, hard work, and self-reliance which are needed for growth. Critics say that, after some five decades of foreign aid, the LDCs' demand for foreign aid has increased; if aid programs had been successful in promoting sustainable growth, demand should have fallen.

2 Bureaucracy and Centralized Government IAC aid is given, not directly to the residents and businesses of the LDCs, but rather to their governments. The direct consequence is that aid typically generates massive, relatively unproductive government bureaucracies and centralizes government power over the economy. The recent stagnation and collapse of the centralized economies of the Soviet Union and eastern Europe provide evidence that market-oriented economies are much more conducive to growth and development. Furthermore, not only does the bureaucratization of the LDCs divert valuable human resources from the private to the public sector, but it shifts the nation's focus from the *production* of output and income to its *redistribution*.

3 Corruption and Misuse Critics also allege that foreign aid is ineffectively used. Corruption is rampant in many LDCs and some estimates suggest 10 to 20 percent of aid is diverted into the pockets of government officials. Some of the wealthiest individuals in the world—for example, Zaire's Mobutu, the Duvaliers in Haiti, the Philippines' Marcos—are (or were) rulers of LDCs. Foreign aid may create an ironic and perverse incentive for LDC leaders to keep their populations poor so they continue to qualify for aid.

Also, IAC-based aid consultants and multinational corporations are major beneficiaries of aid programs. Some economists contend that as much as one-fourth or more of each year's aid is spent on expert consultants. Furthermore, because IAC corporations carry out most aid projects, they are major beneficiaries of, and lobbyists for, foreign aid.

Private Capital Flows

The LDCs have also received substantial flows of private capital from the IACs. These private investors for the most part are large corporations and commercial banks. General Motors or Chrysler might finance construction of a plant in Mexico or Brazil to assemble autos or produce auto parts. Or Citicorp or Bank of America may make loans to the governments of Argentina or the Philippines.

Although these private capital flows were modest in the 1950s and 1960s—ranging from $2 to $4 billion per year—they grew in the 1970s. Specifically, average annual private flows of capital to the LDCs in the decade of the 1970s was $28 billion. Then in the early 1980s an LDC debt crisis developed which caused private capital flows to the poor nations to fall precipitously.

THE LDC DEBT CRISIS

What is the magnitude of LDC debt? What are its causes? And effects? What has been done to resolve the debt problem?

The Debt and Its Growth

The external debt (debts owed to foreign governments, businesses, individuals, and financial institutions) of the LDCs increased thirteenfold in the past two decades, from $100 billion in 1970 to about $1350 billion in 1990.

Causes of the Crisis

We have noted that private capital flows—particularly from large IAC commercial banks—increased greatly in the 1970s. But in the 1970s and early 1980s a series of converging world economic events had serious adverse effects on the LDCs and created a debt crisis.

1   Soaring Oil Prices   The dramatic runup of oil prices by OPEC in 1973–1974 and again in 1979–1980 (raising the price of a barrel of oil from about $2.50 to $35) greatly increased the energy bills of the oil-importing LDCs. These nations were faced with growing current account deficits in their balance of payments which were financed largely by increased borrowing. Hence, the external debt of oil-importing LDCs grew from $130 billion in 1973 to $700 billion by 1982. Borrowed funds which could have been used for development were instead used to pay higher energy costs.

2   Tight Money Policy   In the early 1980s the IACs —and the United States in particular—invoked strong anti-inflationary monetary policies. These tight money policies triggered two adverse effects for the LDCs. On the one hand, growth of IAC national incomes slowed; in 1980–1982 the United States suffered its most serious postwar recession. As a result, IAC demands for the raw material and farm product exports of LDCs declined. This meant sharp reductions in the export earnings which the LDCs needed to pay interest and principal on their debts. On the other hand, tight money policies in the IACs resulted in much higher interest rates. This greatly increased the cost to the LDCs in servicing their debts.

3   Appreciating Dollar   The burden of LDC debt rose for another reason. Over the 1981–1984 period the international value of the dollar appreciated. This meant that LDCs had to pay more for their imports of American manufactured goods. And, because much LDC debt is denominated in dollars, it also meant that LDCs would have to export a larger amount of goods to acquire each dollar needed to pay interest and principal on their debts.

4   Unproductive Investments   In a number of LDCs the improper use of borrowed funds contributed to the debt crisis. Because of political corruption and economic mismanagement, LDC investment of loan funds was frequently unproductive. Returns on such investments were not sufficient to cover interest and principal payments, thereby generating loan defaults.

5   Mexican Crisis   In 1982 Mexico was on the verge of defaulting on its debt. Creditors were forced to reschedule that debt and make further loans to Mexico. This Mexican debt crisis precipitated an abrupt loss of confidence in the creditworthiness of many highly indebted LDCs. As a result, private voluntary lending to LDCs declined sharply. This was complicated by the fact that the United States was incurring very large Federal budget deficits during the 1980s. The sale of United States government bonds to finance these budget deficits absorbed a significant portion of the world's financial capital which might otherwise have been available to LDCs.

In short, higher prices on imported oil, declines in LDC export earnings, higher interest rates, appreciation of the dollar, unproductive investment by the LDCs, and declines in recent private lending to the LDCs all combined to create a debt crisis. By 1982 and 1983 many LDCs were unable to make scheduled payments on their external debts.

Economic Consequences

There has followed a period of "muddling through" during which creditor nations in cooperation with the International Monetary Fund attempted to deal with the LDC debt crisis on a nation-by-nation basis. The debts of many LDCs were rescheduled (stretched out over a longer period of time) to reduce the burden of annual interest and principal payments. In return for these concessions the LDCs had to agree to domestic austerity programs to improve their prospects for debt repayment. This meant that LDCs had to reduce their imports and increase their exports to realize more international trade earnings for debt repayment. But increased exports and reduced imports clearly imply a further impairment of living standards in the LDCs. Similarly, with net export earnings being used primarily for debt retirement little or nothing is left to invest in development projects. It is not by chance that, while the growth of real GDP for the LDCs as a group was 3.8 percent per year over the 1980–1989 period, the rate for highly indebted LDCs was only 1.9 percent.

The debt crisis has also had adverse repercussions in the IACs. IAC commercial banks have been forced to write off some LDC debt as uncollectible. In mid-1987 Citicorp increased its bad-debt reserves by $3 billion in recognition that as much as 25 percent of its loans to LDCs would not be repaid.

Reform and Revival

The 1980s was characterized by intensive negotiations between the IACs and the IMF, on the one hand, and the highly indebted LDCs, on the other, to resolve the debt crisis. The results included (1) restructuring of debt, that is, increasing the period of repayment and reducing interest rates; (2) writing-off or forgiving some of the debt; (3) making additional loans to the LDCs to help them make payments on existing debt; and (4) debt-equity swaps. **Debt-equity swaps** occur when LDC governments and businesses pay off debt by giving shares of stock (ownership claims to government-owned or private enterprises) to foreign creditors. The advantage of such swaps to LDCs is that no fixed interest or principal payments must be made to stockholders. The disadvantage to LDCs is that partial ownership of their businesses is transferred to foreigners. The advantage to lending IACs is that stock ownership is better than default.

Although private capital flows to the LDCs virtually ceased in the 1980s, there has been a modest revival in the 1990s. Two interrelated factors are involved.

LDC Economic Reforms As part of the debt negotiations, heavily indebted LDCs agreed to reform their economies so as to promote growth and avert future debt crises. At the macro level greater efforts are being made to reduce budget deficits and control chronically high levels of inflation. At the micro level many governments have privatized state-owned businesses and deregulated industry. Tariffs and other trade barriers, along with exchange rate controls, have been reduced. In general, the economic role of government has been lessened and that of free markets enhanced. These reforms have made the LDCs more attractive to foreign lenders.

Revived Investment The 1990s has witnessed a modest revival in private capital flows to the LDCs, particularly to those with reformed economies. However, the makeup of this revived investment flow is now different. First, private IAC firms and individuals, rather than commercial banks, are the primary lenders. Second, the loans are largely direct investment in LDC enterprises, rather than loans to LDC governments. The potential advantage of directly investing in LDC enterprises is that management skills and technological knowledge often accompany such capital flows.

Two words of caution. The revived flow of capital is highly selective. Most of the flow is directed toward the more affluent, reformed countries of Latin

America and not toward the extremely impoverished sub-Saharan nations of Africa. And it is premature to say that the LDC debt crisis has been resolved. Some LDC nations still face staggering debt burdens and there is no assurance that some combination of circumstances will not bring about future defaults. The debt crisis has been alleviated, not solved. Evidence: In early 1995 the United States, other G-7 Nations, and the IMF found it necessary to provide a $50 billion package of loan guarantees to offset the collapse of the Mexican peso. The immediate cause of the peso's dramatic fall was an expansion of Mexican debt in excess of its export earnings.

QUICK REVIEW 39-2

■ LDC governments may encourage growth by *a* providing law and order; *b* engaging in entrepreneurial activities; *c* improving the infrastructure; *d* forcing higher levels of saving and investing; and *e* resolving social-institutional problems.

■ The IACs can assist the LDCs through expanded trade, foreign aid, and private capital flows.

■ Many LDCs have huge external debts which have become an additional obstacle to growth.

TOWARD A NEW GLOBAL COMPACT[7]

As the income gap between the rich and the poor nations widens, spokespersons for the LDCs have put forth an agenda for reform which includes the following.

1 Sharing the Peace Dividend With the end of the Cold War, LDC leaders argue that IAC military spending can be reduced and the released resources shared with the poor nations. Specifically, all countries should reduce their military expenditures by at least 3 percent per year, making available a "peace dividend" of about $1.2 trillion in the IACs by the year 2000.

2 Reform of Foreign Aid The LDCs say foreign aid is (a) deficient quantitatively, (b) borne inequitably by donor nations, and (c) not allocated to the poorest nations.

Quantity While the governments of IACs "recycle" from 15 to 25 percent of their GDPs to alleviate income inequality internally, they only provide 0.35 percent of their GDPs in foreign aid to impoverished peoples around the world. The LDCs advocate that this figure should by doubled to the 0.7 percent level recommended by the United Nations.

Equity The LDCs would like to see foreign aid restructured to resemble a progressive tax so that the percentage of aid donated by each nation would increase the larger its GDP. Currently we find that superrich United States and Japan donate only 0.20 and 0.32 percent of their GDPs, respectively, as aid while less-affluent Sweden and Denmark give 0.90 percent or more. If the United States and Japan were to pay recommended progressive rates of approximately 0.80 percent, most of the aid shortfall between the current 0.35 and the recommended 0.70 percent of GDP would disappear.

Allocation Foreign aid is strongly influenced by political and military—not economic—considerations. The consequence is that LDCs do *not* receive aid in accordance with their needs or degree of destitution. Only a quarter of foreign aid goes to those ten countries whose populations constitute 70 percent of the world's poorest people. The most affluent 40 percent of the LDC world population receives over twice as much aid as the poorest 40 percent.

3 Debt Relief The LDCs have also sought debt relief. They say their present debt is so large that it constitutes a severe obstacle to LDC growth. Arguing that the prosperity of the IACs depends on the prosperity of the LDCs, LDCs feel that forgiving some portion of the debt would be mutually beneficial. One proposal suggests that as much as two-thirds of all existing LDC external debt be canceled and the remainder be rescheduled for payment over a twenty-five-year period.

4 Improving Global Markets The LDCs complain that their export earnings have been impaired because of deteriorating terms of trade and trade barriers.

Terms of Trade The long-term price trend of LDC commodity exports (such as coffee, sugar, cocoa, bauxite, tin, and copper) has been downward. For example, in the 1980s the price index for a group of

---

[7]This section is based primarily on the United Nations Development Program, *Human Development Report 1992* (New York: Oxford University Press, 1992).

LAST WORD

FAMINE IN AFRICA

The roots of Africa's persistent famines include both natural and human causes.

The recent famine in Somolia—documented by shocking photos of fly-tormented, emaciated children with bloated bellies—is not uncommon in sub-Saharan Africa. Before U.S. armed forces and U.N. aid arrived in Somalia in late 1992, severe famine had caused an estimated 2000 deaths each day. One out of four Somali children under the age of 5—about 300,000—are believed to have died. Similarly, despite an outpouring of aid from the rich nations, the 1983–1984 Ethiopian famine caused 1 million deaths. A number of African nations—including Ethiopia, Sudan, Angola, Liberia, Zaire, Mozambique, and Malawi—are persistently threatened by famine. Estimates put from 5 to 20 million Africans at risk. This tragedy is ironic because most African countries were self-sufficient in food at the time they became independent nations; they are now heavily dependent on imported foodstuffs for survival.

The immediate cause of this catastrophe is drought. But the ultimate causes of Africa's declining ability to feed itself are more complex, an interplay of natural and human conditions. Lack of rainfall, chronic civil strife, rapid population growth, widespread soil erosion, and counterproductive public policies, all contribute to Africa's famines.

1 Civil Strife Regional rebellions and prolonged civil wars have devastated some African nations. Both Ethiopia and Sudan, for example, have been plagued by decades of civil strife. Not only do these conflicts

divert precious resources from civilian uses, they also greatly complicate the ability of wealthy nations to provide famine and developmental aid. In the 1983–1984 famine the Ethiopian government denied food aid to areas occupied by rebel forces. Donated food is frequently diverted to the army and denied to starving civilians. During Ethiopia's 1973–1974 famine Haile Selassie sold much of the donated food on world markets to enrich his regime! In Somolia factional feuding has destroyed most institutions—schools, factories, and government ministries—and reduced the country to anarchy. Armed gangs steal water pumps, tractors, and livestock from farms and loot ports of donated foodstuffs.

2 Population Growth In Africa population is growing more rapidly than is food production. Population is increasing about 3 percent per year while food output is growing only 2 percent per year. This grim arithmetic suggests declining living standards, hunger, and malnutrition. The World Bank reports

thirty-three primary commodities (excluding oil) fell by almost one-half. Part of this decline is explained by the slow growth of demand relative to supply. Ironically, many LDCs stepped up production of their commodity exports to increase their foreign exchange earnings to meet interest and principal payments on their external debts. But these attempts were largely frustrated by the price declines which resulted from the increased commodity supplies. Product substitution has also contributed to falling commodity prices. Synthetic fibers have been substituted for cotton and

jute; glass fibers have supplanted copper in communications; corn syrup and other sweeteners have tended to reduce the demand for sugar.

In contrast, the LDCs import manufactured goods produced by the corporate giants of the advanced nations which have the market power to charge high prices. The LDCs argue that the **terms of trade** have shifted against them; the prices of their exports tend to be depressed while the prices of their imports tend to rise. Hence, it takes more of the LDCs' exports to purchase a given quantity of imports.

that during the 1980s the per capita incomes of the sub-Saharan nations fell to about three-quarters of the level reached by the end of the 1970s.

3 Ecological Degradation But apart from the simple numbers involved, population growth has contributed to the ecological degradation of Africa. With population pressures and the increasing need for food, marginal land has been deforested and put into crop production. In many cases trees which have served as a barrier to the encroachment of the desert have been cut for fuel, allowing the fragile topsoil to be blown away by desert winds. The scarcity of wood which has accompanied deforestation has forced the use of animal dung for fuel, thereby denying its traditional use as fertilizer. Furthermore, traditional fallow periods have been shortened, resulting in overplanting and overgrazing and a wearing out of the soil. Deforestation and land overuse have reduced the capacity of the land to absorb moisture, diminishing its productivity and its ability to resist drought. Some authorities feel that the diminished ability of the land to absorb water reduces the amount of moisture which evaporates into the clouds to return ultimately as rainfall. All of this is complicated by the fact that there are few facilities for crop storage. Even when crops are good, it is difficult to accumulate a surplus for future lean years. A large percentage of domestic farm output in some parts of Africa is lost to rats, insects, and spoilage.

4 Public Policies and Debt Ill-advised public policies have contributed to Africa's famines. In the first place, African governments have generally neglected investment in agriculture in favor of industrial development and military strength. It is estimated that African governments on the average spend four times as much on armaments as they do on agriculture. Over 40 percent of Ethiopia's budget is for the support of an oppressive military. Second, many African governments have followed the policy of establishing the prices of agricultural commodities at low levels to provide cheap food for growing urban populations. This low-price policy has diminished the incentives of farmers to increase productivity. While foreign aid has helped to ease the effects of Africa's food-population problems, most experts reject aid as a long-term solution. Experience suggests that aid in the form of food can only provide temporary relief and may undermine the realization of long-run local self-sufficiency. Foreign food aid, it is contended, treats symptoms and not causes.

All of this is made more complex by the fact that the sub-Saharan nations are burdened with large and growing external debts. The IMF reports that the aggregate debt of these nations rose from $21 billion in 1976 to $127 billion in 1990. As a condition of further aid, these nations have had to invoke austerity programs which have contributed to declines in their per capita incomes. One tragic consequence is that many of these nations have cut back on social service programs for children.

To summarize: The famine confronting much of Africa is partly a phenomenon of nature and in part self-inflicted. Drought, civil strife, overpopulation, ecological deterioration, and errant public policies have all been contributing factors. This complex of causes implies that hunger and malnutrition in Africa may persist long after the rains return.

Trade Barriers The LDCs lament that trade barriers are highest for the labor-intensive kinds of manufactured goods—textiles, clothing, footwear, and processed agricultural products—in which the LDCs have a comparative advantage. Some twenty of the twenty-four most industrialized nations are more protectionist than they were a decade ago. And, ironically, many tariffs increase with the degree of product processing—for example, tariffs on chocolate are higher than on cocoa—which effectively denies the LDCs the opportunity to develop processing industries. One estimate suggests that trade barriers reduce the gross domestic products of the LDCs by 3 percent, causing an annual loss of $75 billion in income.

5 Immigration There are both quantitative and qualitative aspects to the LDCs' immigration complaints. Too few people are allowed to move from the LDCs to the IACs and IAC policies tend to favor movement of the most productive LDC workers.

LDC spokespersons believe that the IACs should liberalize their immigration laws to enlarge the flow of unemployed and underemployed workers from the LDCs. While some nations—the United States and Canada, for example—have abolished discrimination by country of origin, several European nations are moving toward more restrictive stances with respect to potential LDC immigrants. Some pressure is building to repatriate unemployed migrants. Not only is migration an outlet for surplus LDC labor, but also a source of income in the form of migrant remittances. Currently aggregate remittances from emigrants back to the LDCs is about $25 billion per year.

The United States, Canada, and other IACs have rewritten their immigration laws to favor workers with high skill levels such as researchers, physicians, engineers, and scientists. This, of course, encourages the "brain drain" where LDCs lose human capital in which they have made substantial investments. To illustrate: Estimates indicate that Africa as a whole lost some 60,000 middle-and high-level managers to migration in the 1985–1990 period.

6 Neocolonialism A more general grievance is that, despite the realization of political independence, many LDCs feel an economic-based **neocolonialism** persists. Over four-fifths of the world's direct investment by multinational companies is received by IACs and the remaining one-fifth goes largely to those LDCs which are already better off. And most of the contracts, leases, and concessions which multina-

tional corporations of advanced countries have negotiated with the LDCs have benefitted the multinationals at the expense of the host countries. The poor countries argue that most benefits from the exploitation of their natural resources accrue to others. Furthermore, LDCs seek to achieve greater diversification and therefore greater stability in their economies. Foreign private capital, however, seeks out those industries which are currently the most profitable, that is, the ones now producing for the export market. In brief, while LDCs strive for less dependence on world markets, flows of foreign private capital enhance that dependence. Exxon, Alcoa, United Fruit, and the rest are after profits and allegedly have no particular interest in either the economic independence, diversification, or overall progress of the LDCs.

Whether the IACs will address these grievances, creating a "new global compact" with the LDCs is problematic. While the poor countries feel their proposals are egalitarian and just, many advanced nations see them as a demand for a massive redistribution of world income and wealth which is simply not in the cards. Many industrialized nations feel there is no "quick fix" for underdevelopment and that the LDCs must undergo the same process of patient hard work and gradual capital formation as did the advanced nations over the past two centuries.

CHAPTER SUMMARY

1 Most nations are less developed (low per capita income) nations. While some LDCs have been achieving quite rapid growth rates in recent years, others have realized little or no growth.

2 Initial scarcities of natural resources and the limited possibility of augmenting existing supplies may limit a nation's capacity to develop.

3 The large and rapidly growing populations in most LDCs contributes to low per capita incomes. Increases in per capita incomes frequently induce rapid population growth, again reducing per capita incomes to near subsistence levels. The "demographic transition" concept suggests that rising living standards must precede declining birthrates.

4 Most LDCs suffer from unemployment and underemployment. Labor productivity is low because of insufficient investment in physical and human capital.

5 In many LDCs both the saving and investment aspects of capital formation are impeded by formidable obstacles.

In some of the poorest LDCs the savings potential is very low. Many LDC savers transfer their funds to the IACs rather than invest domestically. The absence of a vigorous entrepreneurial class and the weakness of investment incentives are also impediments to capital accumulation.

6 Appropriate social and institutional changes and, in particular, the presence of "the will to develop" are essential ingredients in economic development.

7 The vicious circle of poverty brings together many of the obstacles to growth, saying in effect that "poor countries stay poor because of their poverty." Low incomes inhibit saving and accumulation of physical and human capital, making it difficult to increase productivity and incomes. Rapid population growth can offset otherwise promising attempts to break the vicious circle.

8 The nature of the obstacles to growth—the absence of an entrepreneurial class, the dearth of infrastructure, the saving-investment dilemma, and the presence of social-institutional obstacles to growth—suggests the need for government action in initiating growth. However, the corruption and maladministration which are quite common to the public sectors of the LDCs suggest that government may be ineffective as an instigator of growth.

9 Advanced nations can assist in development by reducing trade barriers and by providing both public and private capital. Critics of foreign aid say it **a** creates LDC dependency; **b** contributes to the growth of bureaucracies and centralized economic control; and **c** is ineffective because of corruption and mismanagement.

10 Rising energy prices, declining export prices, depreci-

ation of the dollar, the unproductive use of borrowed funds, and concern about LDCs' creditworthiness combined to create an LDC debt crisis in the early 1980s. External debt problems of many LDCs remain serious and inhibit their growth.

11 The LDCs seek a "new global compact" with the IACs which entails **a** a larger and better allocated flow of aid; **b** debt relief; **c** greater LDC access to world markets; **d** liberalized immigration policies; and **e** an end to neocolonialism.

TERMS AND CONCEPTS

industrially advanced
   countries (IACs)
less developed
   countries (LDCs)
demographic transition
unemployment and
   underemployment

brain drain
capital flight
infrastructure
nonfinancial
   investment
the will to develop

capital-saving and
   capital-using
technological
   advance
capricious universe
   view
land reform

vicious circle of
   poverty
World Bank
debt-equity swaps
new global compact
terms of trade
neocolonialism

QUESTIONS AND STUDY SUGGESTIONS

1 What are the characteristics of an LDC? List the avenues of economic development available to such a nation. State and explain obstacles which face LDCs in breaking the poverty barrier. Use the "vicious circle of poverty" to outline in detail steps an LDC might take to initiate economic development.

2 Explain how the absolute per capita income gap between rich and poor nations might increase, even though per capita GDP is growing faster in LDCs than it is in IACs.

3 *Key Question   Assume an LDC and an IAC currently have real per capita outputs of $500 and $5000 respectively. If both nations realize a 3 percent increase in their real per capita outputs, by how much will the per capita output gap change?*

4 Discuss and evaluate:

   a "The path to economic development has been clearly blazed by American capitalism. It is only for the LDCs to follow this trail."

   b "Economic inequality is conducive to saving, and saving is the prerequisite of investment. Therefore, greater inequality in the income distribution of the LDCs would be a spur to capital accumulation and growth."

   c "The IACs fear the complications from oversaving; the LDCs bear the yoke of undersaving."

   d "The core of development involves changing human

beings more than it does altering a nation's physical environment."

   e "America's 'foreign aid' program is a sham. In reality it represents neocolonialism—a means by which the LDCs can be nominally free in a political sense but remain totally subservient in an economic sense."

   f "Poverty and freedom cannot persist side by side; one must triumph over the other."

   g "The biggest obstacle facing poor nations in their quest for development is the lack of capital goods."

   h "A high per capita GDP does not necessarily identify an industrially advanced nation."

5 Explain how population growth might be an impediment to economic growth. How would you define the optimal population of a country?

6 *Key Question   Contrast the "demographic transition" view of population with the traditional view that slower population growth is a prerequisite for rising living standards in the LDCs.*

7 Much of the initial investment in an LDC must be devoted to infrastructure which does not directly or immediately lead to a greater production of goods and services. What bearing might this have on the degree of inflation which results as government finances capital accumulation through the creating and spending of new money?

8   *Key Question   Since real capital is supposed to earn a higher return where it is scarce, how do you explain the fact that most international investment flows to the IACs (where capital is relatively abundant) rather than to the LDCs (where capital is very scarce)?*

9   "The nature of the problems faced by the LDCs creates a bias in favor of governmentally directed as opposed to a decentralized development process." Do you agree? Why or why not?

10   What is the LDC debt crisis? How did it come about? What solutions can you offer?

11   What types of products do the LDCs export? Use the law of comparative advantage to explain the character of these exports.

12   Outline the main components of the "new global compact" proposed by the LDCs. Which of these demands do you feel are justified?

13   What would be the implications of a worldwide policy of unrestricted immigration between nations for economic efficiency and the global distribution of income?

14   *Key Question   Use Figure 39-1 (changing box labels as necessary) to explain rapid economic growth in a country such as Japan or South Korea. What factors other than those contained in the figure might contribute to growth?*

15   (Last Word) Explain how civil wars, population growth, and public policy decisions have contributed to periodic famines in Africa.

40

RUSSIA: AN ECONOMY IN TRANSITION

Arguably the most profound event of the past decade was the collapse of the Soviet Union in late 1991 and the decision by Russia and the other successor republics to transform themselves from centrally directed to market economies.

In this final chapter we examine the breakup of the Soviet Union and the problems the new republics now face. Specific questions are: What were the main characteristics and goals of the Soviet planned economy? Why did Soviet communism fail? What must be accomplished to achieve the transition to a market or capitalistic system? What role, if any, might the United States and other western nations play in this transition? What progress has been realized thus far? What problems remain?

The transition from central planning to markets has been widespread. Such eastern European nations as Poland, East Germany, Czechoslovakia, and Hungary, among others, preceded the former Soviet Union on this path. We focus on Russia because of its economic, political, and military importance. Russia encompasses about three-fourths of the territory of the former Soviet Union, and is two and one-half times larger than Canada, the world's second largest nation. Russia has about 150 million people, over half as many as were in the former Soviet Union. It also encompasses vast natural resources, including oil and gas, precious metals, diamonds, and timber.

IDEOLOGY AND INSTITUTIONS

To understand the planned economy of the former Soviet Union, we must look back at its ideology and institutions.

Marxian Ideology

The Communist Party was the dominant force in Soviet political and economic life. It viewed itself as a dic-

tatorship of the proletariat or working class. Based on Marxism-Leninism, the Communists envisioned their system as the inevitable successor to capitalism, the latter being plagued by internal contradictions stemming from the exploitation, injustice, and insecurity which it was thought to generate. To communists, the market system was chaotic, unstable, and inequitable. Markets bred inflation, unemployment, and an unfair distribution of income. In contrast, central planning was viewed as a means for rationally organizing the economy's resources, achieving macroeconomic stability, and providing greater equality.

Especially important for our purposes is the Marxian concept of a **labor theory of value**—the idea that the economic or exchange value of any commodity is determined solely by the amount of labor time required for its production. Thanks to the capitalistic institution of private property, capitalists own the machinery and equipment necessary for production in an industrial society. The propertyless working class is therefore dependent on the capitalists for employment and for its livelihood. Because of the worker's inferior bargaining position and the capitalist's pursuit of profits, the capitalists will exploit labor by paying a daily wage far below the value of the worker's daily production. The capitalist can and will pay workers a subsistence wage and expropriate the remaining fruits of their labor as profits, or what Marx termed **surplus value.** In the Soviet system, surplus value was to be extracted by the state as an agency of the working class and distributed in large part through subsidies to what we would call public or quasi-public goods, for example, education, transportation, health care, and housing.

The function of communism was to overthrow capitalism and replace it with a classless society void of human exploitation. The Communist Party viewed itself as the vanguard of the working class, and its actions were held to be in keeping with the goals of the working class. In fact, it was a strong dictatorship. Many westerners characterized the Soviet government as a dictatorship *over* the proletariat, not *of* the proletariat.

Institutions

The two outstanding institutional characteristics of the Soviet economy were: (1) state ownership of property resources, and (2) authoritarian central economic planning.

State Ownership   **State ownership** meant the Soviet state owned all land, natural resources, transportation and communication facilities, the banking system, and virtually all industry. Most retail and wholesale enterprises and most urban housing were governmentally owned. In agriculture many farms were state-owned; most, however, were government-organized collective farms—essentially cooperatives

to which the state assigned land "for free use for an unlimited time."

Central Economic Planning   **Central economic planning** meant that the Soviet Union had a centralized "command" economy functioning in terms of a detailed economic plan. The Soviet economy was government-directed rather than market-directed. Choices made through the market in the United States' economy were made by bureaucratic decision in the Soviet Union. Through the plan "all the manifold activities of the Soviet economy [were] coordinated as if they were parts of one incredibly enormous enterprise directed from the central headquarters in Moscow."[1]

CENTRAL PLANNING AND ITS PROBLEMS

The Soviet system of central planning was put in place in the late 1920s and early 1930s. Despite occasional reforms, the system remained fundamentally unchanged for almost seven decades.

Ends and Means

The following generalizations describe how Soviet planning functioned historically.

1   Industrialization and Military Strength   The economy of the former Soviet Union was a system of "totalitarianism harnessed to the task of rapid industrialization and economic growth." Planned goals stressed rapid industrialization and military strength. This was achieved through extensive investment in heavy industries—steel, chemicals, and machine tools—and the allocation of a large percentage of domestic output to the military. As a consequence, development of consumer goods industries, the distribution and service sectors, and the infrastructure were neglected.

2   Resource Overcommitment   Production increases sought in the various plans were ambitious; they overcommitted the economy's available re-

---

[1]Harry Schwartz, *Russia's Soviet Economy,* 2d ed. (Englewood Cliffs, N.J.: Prentice-Hall, Inc., 1954), p. 146.

sources. As a result, not all planning targets could be achieved. And planning priorities were to achieve those goals associated with heavy industry and the military at the expense of consumption.

3   Resource Mobilization Industrialization and rapid economic growth were initially achieved through mobilization of labor, capital, and raw materials. In the early years of planning there was substantial surplus labor in agriculture which the plans reallocated to industrial production. Similarly, a larger proportion of the population was induced or coerced into the labor force. Early Soviet growth was achieved through more inputs rather than using fixed amounts of inputs more productivity. In the 1930s and again in the early post-World War II era, this strategy produced growth rates greater than the United States and other industrialized nations.

4   Allocation by Directives Soviet central planners directed the allocation of inputs among industries and firms, thereby determining the composition of output. Planning directives were substituted for the market or price system as an allocational mechanism.

5   Government Price Fixing Prices were set by government direction rather than by the forces of demand and supply. Consumer good prices were changed infrequently and, as a matter of social policy, the prices of "necessities"—for example, housing and basic foodstuffs—were established at low levels. Rents on Soviet housing averaged only about 3 percent of income and did not change between 1928 and 1992! Input prices and the price of an enterprise's output were also governmentally determined and were used primarily as accounting devices to gauge a firm's progress in meeting its production target.

6   Self-Sufficiency The Soviet Union viewed itself as a single socialist nation surrounded by hostile capitalistic countries. Therefore, the central plans stressed economic self-sufficiency. Trade with western nations was greatly restricted because the ruble was not convertible into other currencies. Soviet trade was largely with the other communist nations of eastern Europe.

7   Passive Macroeconomic Policies The Soviet economy was a quantity-directed system with money and prices playing only a limited role in resource allocation. Unlike most market economies, monetary and fiscal policies were passive rather than active in the Soviet Union. In the United States and other market systems, monetary and fiscal policies are used to manipulate the aggregate levels of output, employment, and prices. Historically, unemployment in the Soviet Union was very low, perhaps 1 or 2 percent of the labor force. This was partly the result of ambitious planning targets and various admonitions to work. Low unemployment was also due to overstaffing (managers could not fire redundant workers), a disinterest in cost-minimization (gross output was the overriding objective), and a population whose growth rate was steadily diminishing. Similarly, government price determination was the primary device used to control the price level.

The Coordination Problem

The market system is a powerful organizing force which coordinates millions of individual decisions by consumers, resource suppliers, and businesses, and fosters a reasonably efficient use of scarce resources. It is not easy to substitute central planning as a coordinating mechanism.

Example: Suppose an enterprise in Minsk is producing men's shoes. Planners must establish a realistic production target for that enterprise and then see that all the necessary inputs—labor, electric power, leather, rubber, thread, nails, appropriate machinery, transportation—for production and delivery of that product are made available. When we move from a simple product such as shoes to more complex products such as television sets and farm tractors, planners' allocational problems are greatly compounded.

Because the outputs of many industries are inputs to other industries, the failure of any single industry to fulfill its output target will cause a chain of adverse repercussions. If iron mines—for want of machinery or labor or transportation inputs—fail to supply the steel industry with the required inputs of iron ore, the steel industry will be unable to fulfill the input needs of the many industries dependent on steel. All these steel-using industries—automobiles, tractors, and transportation—will be unable to fulfill their planned production goals. And so the bottleneck chain reaction goes on to all firms using steel parts or components as inputs. Bottlenecks and production stoppages occurred with alarming regularity in the 1980s and early 1990s.

COMMUNISM'S FAILURES

Diminishing economic growth, shoddy product quality, and the inability to meet consumer expectations all contributed to the Soviet system's collapse.

Declining Growth

Soviet economic growth in the 1950s and 1960s was impressive. In the 1950s Soviet real domestic output expanded at roughly 6 percent per year compared to about 3 percent for the United States. The Soviet economy continued to grow at about 5 percent per year in the 1960s. But growth fell to an annual rate of about $2\frac{1}{2}$ or 3 percent in the 1970s and further declined to 2 percent by the mid-1980s. In the last year or two before the system's breakdown, real output was falling sharply.

Poor Product Quality

Further evidence of economic failure was reflected in the quality of goods. In such vital manufacturing sectors as computers and machine tools, Soviet technology lagged some seven to twelve years behind the United States. Overall, the quality of most Soviet manufactured goods was far short of international standards. Consumer goods were of notoriously poor quality and product assortment was greatly limited. Durable goods—automobiles, refrigerators, and con-

sumer electronics products—were primitive by world standards. Furthermore, widespread shortages of basic goods, interminable shopper queues, black markets, and corruption in the distribution of products characterized the consumer sector.

Consumer Needs

The major contributing factor to the downfall of Soviet communism was its inability to efficiently supply the goods and services consumers wanted to buy. In the early decades of Soviet communism the government established a "social contract" with its citizenry to the effect that, by enduring the consumer sacrifices associated with the high rates of saving and investment necessary for rapid industrialization and growth, the population would be rewarded with consumer abundance in the future (Figure 2-5). The failure of the system to meet consumer expectations contributed to frustration and deteriorating morale among consumers and workers (Global Perspective 40-1).

Causes of the Collapse

Having chronicled the deteriorating performance of the economy of the former Soviet Union, we now consider causes of its collapse.

1   Military Burden   Large Soviet military expenditures of 15 to 20 percent of domestic output—compared to 6 percent for the United States—absorbed great quantities of resources which would otherwise have been available for the development and production of consumer and investment goods. During the cold war era it was the government's policy to channel superior management and the best scientists and engineers to defense and space research, which adversely affected technological progress and the quality (productivity) of investment in the civilian sector.

2   Agricultural Drag   By western standards agriculture in the former Soviet Union was something of a monument to inefficiency and a drag on economic growth, engulfing some 30 percent of the labor force and roughly one-fourth of annual investment. Furthermore, output per worker was only 10 to 25 percent of the United States' level. The low productivity of Soviet agriculture was attributable to many factors: relative scarcity of good land; vagaries in rainfall and length of growing season; serious errors in planning and administration; and, perhaps most important, the failure to construct an effective incentive system.

Once a major exporter of grain and other agricultural products, the Soviet Union became one of the world's largest importers of agricultural commodities. Agricultural imports were a serious drain on foreign currency reserves which its leadership wanted for financing imports of western capital goods and technology.

3   More Inputs versus Increased Efficiency Much of the former Soviet Union's rapid growth in the early decades of central planning resulted from using more labor, capital, and land in the production process—taking up "slack" in the economy. But in time this means of increasing real output was exhausted. Soviet labor force participation rates were among the highest in the world so there was little or no opportunity to recruit more workers. Furthermore, population and labor force growth slowed significantly. While the annual average increase in the labor force was about 1.5 percent in the 1970s, it slowed to about 0.6 percent in the 1980s. Similarly, the percentage of domestic output devoted to investment was comparatively high and could only be increased by reducing output devoted to consumption. Because of the low standard of living in the former Soviet Union, it was unpopular and politically difficult to further increase the output of capital goods at the expense of consumption. Also, natural conditions limited the availability of additional farmland. Occasional attempts to bring more land of marginal quality into crop production were counterproductive in that yields were minimal and the land lost to grazing.

The alternative to growth through the use of more inputs is to increase the productivity or efficiency of available inputs. But this is a more complex and difficult way of achieving economic growth. Productivity growth requires modern capital equipment, innovation and technological progress, and strong material incentives for workers and managers—none of which characterized the traditional Soviet planning system. Indeed, labor productivity in the former Soviet Union was estimated to be only 35 to 40 percent that of American workers.

4   Planning Problems The problem of centrally coordinating economic activity becomes much more difficult as an economy grows and develops. Early planning under Stalin in the 1930s and 1940s resembled the simple World War II planning of western cap-

GLOBAL PERSPECTIVE 40-1

Consumption and product availability: former Soviet Union and the United States, mid 1980s

Because the former Soviet Union allocated large quantities of resources to industrialization and the military, the availability of consumer goods was far below that found in the United States.

Product	United States	Soviet Union
Wheat (kilograms per capita)	329	322
Meat (kilograms per capita)	74	47
Automobiles (per 1000 persons)	555	42
Washing machines (% of households)	74	55
TVs (per 1000 persons)	815	396
Radios (per 1000 persons)	2123	306
Energy consumed (kilograms per capita)	9563	5549
Telephones (per 1000 persons)	501	120
Personal computers (per 1000 persons)	229	2

Source: *Statistical Abstract of the United States, 1988.*

italist nations. A few key production goals were established and resources were centrally directed toward fulfilling those goals regardless of costs or consumer welfare. But the past success of such "campaign planning" resulted in a more complex, industrially advanced economy. Products became more sophisticated and complex and there were more industries for which to plan. Planning techniques workable in the Stalinist era became inadequate and inefficient in the more advanced Soviet economy of the 1970s and 1980s. The Soviet economy outgrew its planning mechanisms.

5   Inadequate Success Indicators Market economies have a single, comprehensive success indicator—profits. Each firm's success or failure is measured by its profits or losses. Profits depend on consumer demand, production efficiency, and product quality.

In contrast, the major success indicator of a Soviet enterprise was its fulfillment of a quantitative production target assigned by the central planners. This generated inefficient practices because production costs, product quality, and product-mix became secondary considerations at best. Achieving least-cost production is nearly impossible without a system of genuine market prices accurately reflecting the relative scarcity or economic value of various resources. Product quality was frequently sacrificed by managers and workers who were awarded bonuses for fulfilling quantitative, not qualitative, targets. If meeting production goals of a television or automobile manufacturing plan meant sloppy assembly work, so be it.

Finally, it is difficult for planners to assign quantitative production targets without unintentionally producing ridiculous distortions in output. If the production target for an enterprise manufacturing nails is specified in terms of weight (tons of nails), it will tend to produce all large nails. But if its target is a quantity (thousands of nails), it will be motivated to use available inputs to produce all small nails. The problem is that the economy needs *both* large and small nails.

6 Incentive Problems Perhaps the main deficiency of central planning was the lack of economic incentives. The market systems of western economies have built-in signals resulting in the efficient use of resources. Profits and losses generate incentives for firms and industries to increase or decrease production. If a product is in short supply, its price and profitability will increase and producers will be motivated to expand production. Conversely, surplus supply means falling prices and profits and a reduction in output. Successful innovations in the form of either product quality or production techniques are sought because of their profitability. Greater work effort by labor means higher money incomes which can be translated into a higher real standard of living.

These actions and adjustments do not occur under central planning. The output-mix of the former Soviet economy was determined by the central planners. If their judgments as to the quantities of automobiles, razor blades, underwear, and vodka wanted by the populace at governmentally determined prices were incorrect, there would be *persistent* shortages and surpluses of products. But the managers who oversaw the production of these goods were rewarded for fulfilling their assigned production goals; they had no incentive to adjust production in response to product shortages or surpluses. And they did not have changes in prices and profitability to signal that more or less of each product was desired. Thus in the for-

mer Soviet Union many products were unavailable or in short supply, while other unwanted goods languished in warehouses.

Incentives to innovate were almost entirely absent; indeed, innovation was often resisted. Soviet enterprises were essentially governmentally owned monopolies. As a result, there was no private gain to managers or workers for improving product quality or developing more efficient production techniques. Historically, government-imposed innovations were resisted by enterprise managers and workers. The reason was that new production processes were usually accompanied by higher and unrealistic production targets, underfulfillment, and loss of bonuses.

Innovation also lagged because there was no competition. New firms could not come into being to introduce better products, superior managerial techniques, or more efficient production methods. Similarly, the Soviet goal of economic self-sufficiency isolated its enterprises from the competitive pressures of international markets. In general, over an extended period Soviet enterprises produced the same products with the same techniques, with both goods and techniques becoming increasingly obsolete by world standards.

Nor were individual workers motivated to work hard, because of a lack of material incentives. Because of the low priority assigned to consumer goods in the plans, there was only a limited array of low-quality goods and services available to Soviet workers-consumers. (The price of an automobile was far beyond the means of average factory workers, and for those able to buy, the waiting period was one to five years.) While hard work might result in promotions and bonuses, the increase in *money* income did not translate into a proportionate increase in *real* income. Why work hard for additional income if there is nothing to buy with the money you earn? As a Soviet worker once lamented to a western journalist: "The government pretends to pay us and we pretend to work."

The Gorbachev Reforms

The deteriorating Soviet economy of the 1970s and early 1980s prompted then-President Mikhail Gorbachev to introduce in 1986 a reform program described as **perestroika,** a restructuring of the economy. This economic restructuring was accompanied by **glasnost,** a campaign for greater openness and democratization in both political and economic affairs. Under *glasnost,* workers, consumers, enterprise managers, political leaders, and others were provided greater opportunity to voice complaints and make suggestions for improving the economy.

The **Gorbachev reforms** involved six interrelated elements: (1) the modernization of industry; (2) greater decentralization of decision making; (3) provision for a limited private enterprise sector; (4) improved worker discipline and incentives; (5) a more rational price system; and (6) an enlarged role in the international economy.

While *perestroika* had some initial success, it did not comprehensively address the systemic economic problems facing the Soviet Union. In retrospect, *perestroika* was more in the nature of traditional Soviet "campaigns" to elicit better performance within the general framework of the planned economy. It was *not* an overall program of institutional change such as those adopted by Poland and Hungary. Thus, in the late 1980s the Soviet economy was stagnating; some estimates put its growth rate at only 2 percent per year, while others indicated it did not grow at all. In late 1991 Gorbachev's successor, Boris Yeltsin, outlined a program of radical or "shock therapy" reform to move the economy from planning to a market system.

QUICK REVIEW 40-2

■ The failure of central planning in the former Soviet Union was evidenced by diminished growth rates, low-quality goods, and the failure to provide a rising standard of living.

■ The collapse of the Soviet economy in the 1980s was attributable to *a* a large military burden; *b* chronic inefficiencies in agriculture; *c* the need to expand real output by increasing input productivity rather than increasing the quantity of inputs; *d* the inability of traditional planning techniques to deal with the growing complexity of the Soviet economy; *e* inadequate success indicators; and *f* ineffectual incentives to produce, innovate, and work.

■ The Gorbachev reforms of the late 1980s centered on *perestroika* ("restructuring") and *glasnost* ("openness") but failed to provide major systemic change.

TRANSITION TO A MARKET SYSTEM

The former Soviet republics—particularly Russia—have committed themselves to making the transition to a market economy. What are the components of such a dramatic reform program?

Privatization

If entrepreneurship is to come into existence, private property rights must be established and protected by law. This means that existing government property—farmland, housing, factories, machinery and equipment, stores—must be transferred to private owners. It also means that new private firms must be allowed to form and develop.

Promotion of Competition

The industrial sector of the former Soviet Union consisted of large state-owned enterprises in which average employment exceeded 800 workers. Thirty to 40 percent of total industrial production was produced by single-firm "industries." When several enterprises produced a product, their actions were coordinated by the planning process to create a cartel. In short, most production took place under monopoly or near-monopoly conditions.

Realization of an efficient market economy requires the dismantling of these public monopolies and the creation of antitrust laws to sustain competition. Privatization without "demonopolization" will be of limited benefit to the economy. Existing monopolies must be restructured or split apart as separate, competing firms. For example, a tractor manufacturing enterprise with four plants could be separated into four independent and competing firms. The establishment and guarantee of property rights are prerequisite to the creation and entry of new firms into previously monopolized industries. Joint ventures between Russia and foreign companies provide a further avenue for increasing competition, as does opening the economy to international trade. Recent legislation has opened the door for foreign firms to invest directly in Russia.

Limited and Reoriented Role for Government

The transition to a market economy will curtail government's economic role. The government must reduce its involvement to those tasks associated with a market economy: providing an appropriate legal framework; maintaining competition; reducing excessive inequality in the distribution of income and wealth; making market adjustments where spillover costs or benefits are large; providing public goods and services; and stabilizing the economy (Chapter 5).

Many of these functions will be new to the Russian government, at least in the environment of a market system. Unemployment and overt inflation were controlled by central planning. Historically, ambitious production plans and overstaffing of enterprises yielded low unemployment rates while government price-setting controlled the price level. The task will be to develop monetary and fiscal policies—and institutional arrangements appropriate to their implementation—to indirectly provide macroeconomic stability. Restructuring will likely result in substantial short-run unemployment as inefficient public enterprises are closed or fail to be viable under private ownership. Thus, a priority goal will be to establish a *social safety net* for Russian citizens. In particular, a program of unemployment insurance must be established, not only on equity grounds but also to reduce worker resistance to the transition. Similarly, antitrust legislation of some sort will be needed to maintain competitive markets.

Price Reform: Removing Controls

Unlike competitive market prices, the prices established by the Soviet government bore no relationship to the economic value of either products or resources. In an effectively functioning competitive market system the price of a product equates, at the margin, the value consumers place on that good ("benefits") and the value of the resources used in its production ("costs"). When free markets achieve this equality for all goods and services, the economy's scarce resources are being used efficiently to satisfy consumer wants.

But in the former Soviet Union both input and output prices were fixed by government and in many instances were not changed for long periods of time. Because input prices did not measure the relative scarcities of resources, it was impossible for a firm to minimize real production costs. With fixed prices it is impossible to produce a unit of X in such a way as to minimize the sacrifice of alternative goods.

Example: High energy prices have caused firms in market economies to curtail its use. But energy was underpriced in the former Soviet Union (the world's largest producer of energy) and its industries used two to three times as much energy per unit of output as leading industrial countries.

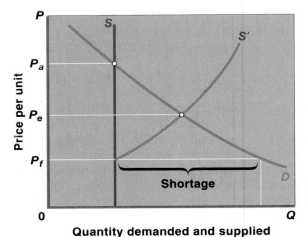

FIGURE 40-1   The effects of government price fixing
Central planners establish below-equilibrium prices such as P_f on many basic consumer goods to make them widely available to everyone. But in fact at such low prices quantity demanded exceeds quantity supplied and this shortage means that many consumers cannot obtain such goods. Assuming no privatization, abandonment of government price fixing would raise price from P_f to P_a. With privatization and an accompanying increase in output as price rises, price would increase from P_f to P_e. In either event, the decontrol of prices can be expected to be inflationary.

A difficult problem arises in making the transition from government- to market-determined prices because historically the prices of many basic consumer goods were fixed at low levels. The Soviet rationale for this was that low prices would ensure everyone access to such goods. As Figure 40-1 shows, this pricing policy helps explain the chronic product shortages and long lines which frustrated consumers in the former Soviet Union. The perfectly inelastic supply curve S reflects the fixed output of, say, shoes for which the plan provided. (Disregard supply curve S' for the moment.) The demand curve slopes downward as it would in a market economy. Given S, the equilibrium price would be P_a. But in an effort to make shoes accessible to those with lower incomes, the government fixed the price at P_f.

But not everyone who wanted shoes at price P_f could obtain them. At P_f quantity demanded was substantially greater than quantity supplied, so there was excess demand or, in other words, a shortage. This explains the long, impatient lines of consumers and the empty shelves we saw in television news clips of Soviet shoppers. Black markets—illegal markets where goods are sold at much higher prices than those fixed by the government—were widespread. *(Key Question 7)*

Joining the World Economy

The Soviet Union was largely isolated from the world economy for almost three-quarters of a century. A key aspect of transition is to open the economy to international trade and finance.

One basic task is to make the ruble a stable convertible currency, meaning that it is acceptable in exchange for other currencies. Convertibility and stability are necessary for Russia to achieve an enlarged role in international trade and finance. Firms cannot buy from or sell to Russia unless a realistic exchange rate is established for the ruble. Nor can western firms be expected to invest in the former Soviet Union unless they are certain that rubles can be exchanged for dollars and other "hard" currencies. American and other western firms want their profits in dollars, yen, pounds, and marks, not rubles.

Opening the Russian economy to world trade will be beneficial because world markets are sources of competition and a means of acquiring much-needed superior technologies from industrially advanced capitalist nations. Liberalized international trade will put pressure on privatized Russian firms to produce efficiently products which meet world quality standards. Also, free world trade will allow Russia to realize the benefits from production based on comparative advantage—income gains which its isolation has long denied it.

Macroeconomic Stability

The transition to free markets poses the possibility of high rates of inflation. Figure 40-1 is again relevant. As government price controls on shoes are eliminated, prices will rise from P_f to P_a. With privatization, this runup of prices will be dampened somewhat by the extra output induced by the rising prices. As shown by supply curve S' in Figure 40-1, private producers will respond to higher prices by increasing quantity supplied. Nevertheless, prices will rise substantially, as from P_f to P_e. Similarly, prices will also rise for butter, soap, meat, housing, vodka, and all other goods and services whose prices have been liberalized. An important need during the transition is to control inflationary pressures.

The worst scenario is hyperinflation, where there is a "flight from the currency" and the ruble ceases to function as an effective medium of exchange because businesses and consumers find it unacceptable. In these circumstances hoarding and speculation supplant production and the economy grinds to a halt. Rapidly and unevenly rising prices also create a hostile environment for microeconomic decision making. Achieving both least-cost production (productive efficiency) and production of the most desired output-mix (allocative efficiency) is predicated on a reasonable measure of price stability.

Finally, an environment of high and volatile inflation greatly complicates achieving other components of transition. The purchase of formerly public enterprises by private buyers, the establishing of a convertible ruble, and the encouragement of both domestic and foreign investment to modernize the economy are all more difficult with the uncertainties posed by a rapidly rising price level.

Public Support: Attitudes and Values

The reforms comprising the transition from planning to markets must have wide public support. Consider some of the difficulties.

1 Bureaucratic Resistance   The reforms threaten the jobs and status of many former party members and bureaucrats. These individuals continue in many instances to have positions of power and prestige and want to maintain the status quo. Ironically, those most likely to have access to formerly state-owned enterprises and other assets are those very same bureaucrats who formerly administered the failed system of central planning.

2 Worker Incentives   Under a system of capitalist incentives most workers and managers will be required to be more disciplined and to work harder and more productively. This may be difficult to accept in an economy which historically has served consumers-workers poorly. Money wage increases do not provide incentives without corresponding improvements in the quantity and quality of housing, food, and other consumer goods and services.

Some observers say that many citizens in the former Soviet Union and other communist nations have acquired work habits and personality traits which will only change slowly. These include working at a leisurely pace, avoiding responsibility, resistance to innovation and change, stressing output quantity over quality, and promotion based on connections and party affiliation rather than productive efficiency. It may be wishful thinking to assume that the populace possesses a strong work ethic and a latent entrepreneurial spirit, and that these attributes will emerge as the heavy hand of central planning is removed. The citizenry has been indoctrinated for some seventy years regarding the evils of private property, profits, and capitalist enterprise. The "mental residue" of communism may not be easily removed.

The Simultaneity Problem

A more subtle problem is that the reform components are interlinked. Not to move forward on all fronts may enhance the prospects for failure. Examples: Private ownership will do little to increase productive efficiency unless prices are reformed to accurately measure relative scarcities. Privatization—the selling off of state enterprises—may be helpful in reducing budget deficits. When market prices for inputs and output are unknown, it is difficult to determine the value of an enterprise when it is being privatized. The creation of a more competitive environment depends on the economy being opened to world trade and foreign investment. *(Key Question 8)*

ROLE OF ADVANCED NATIONS

The world's industrialized capitalistic nations can facilitate Russia's reforms in three ways: providing foreign aid; private investment in Russia by western firms; and helping to integrate Russia into the world economy.

Foreign Aid

Foreign aid can ease the painful transition process when planning is being abandoned and free enterprise has not yet been firmly established. In particular, foreign aid can help the Russian government avoid financing its deficits by money creation and thereby reduce the rate of inflation.

The United States and the other market democracies have a great economic stake in Russia's transition to democracy and capitalism. If the transition fails, the peace dividend associated with the end of the cold war may not be realized and the possibility of accelerated economic growth through expanded international trade with a free-market Russia will also be sacrificed. The political benefit is that a democratic Russia will isolate the last strongholds of communism—China, Cuba and North Korea—and perhaps force their leaders toward political and economic reform.

But there are serious reservations concerning aid to Russia. One is that aid is likely to be ineffectual and wasteful until the transition to market capitalism has been accomplished. Aside from humanitarian aid in the form of foodstuffs and medicine, economic aid is not likely to be of much help until capitalistic institutions are firmly in place.

A second contention is that Russia has not yet exploited the opportunity it now has to divert vast amounts of resources from the military to the civilian sector.

Finally, there is the hard political fact that foreign aid for a long-time cold war foe may not be popular among the voters of industrialized nations who see in their own countries unemployment, poor education, crime, poverty, and drug abuse.

The foreign aid issue involves a kind of chicken-or-egg problem. The west wants aid to be contingent upon a firm commitment to, or completion of, reforms; Russia contends that aid is necessary for reforms to be realized. Similarly, rapid inflation in Russia makes potential aid donors hesitant; but lack of aid forces Russia to finance its deficits with money creation, which fuels further inflation.

How much aid has been forthcoming? And in what forms? Table 40-1 shows that in 1992–1993 the west provided $23 billion in aid to Russia. International financial institutions made $3 billion available—$2.5 billion from the International Monetary Fund and $0.5 billion from the World Bank. The remaining $20 billion was bilateral or nation-to-nation aid. About $18 billion of this was in the form of export credits—government-subsidized credit—which allows Russia to buy a nation's exports via low-interest loans rather than paying cash. The remaining $2 billion is in the form of grants.

The United States' share in bilateral (nation-to-nation) aid is approximately $2 to $3 billion per year. In 1994 the United States pledged $2 billion in grants and almost $1 billion in credits.

Private Investment

As Russia moves toward a capitalistic system, will it be able to attract foreign investment to shore up its economy? In view of the vast potential market provided by some 150 million citizens, we would expect

TABLE 40-1   Foreign aid to Russia, 1992–1993

Type of aid		Amount (billions of dollars)
International financial institutions		$ 3
IMF	$2.5	
World Bank	0.5	
Bilateral aid		20
Export credits	$18	
Grants	2	
Total		$23

Source: International Monetary Fund.

the answer to be "Yes." These flows of private investment could be extremely helpful to the Russian economy, perhaps more so than public aid. In addition to providing real capital, profit-seeking private investors will bring in managerial skills, improved technologies, entrepreneurial behavior, and marketing connections.

But substantial obstacles face foreign firms doing business in Russia. One problem is determining who is in charge. Should you deal with the Trade Ministry in Moscow or regional officials or both? To whom does a foreign firm pay taxes, and with whom does one sign contracts? Who issues the necessary permits and licenses? Furthermore, the legislative underpinnings of commercial activities are often cumbersome, ambiguous, or simply nonexistent. In many cases reliable sources of inputs are not available. And the infrastructure—for example, communication and transportation systems—is primitive by western standards. Business taxes are among the world's highest. Racketeers regularly extort protection money from businesses and scam artists bilk investors. Bouts of hyperinflation create uncertainty and make private investors hesitant.

Membership in International Institutions

Historically the former Soviet Union distanced itself from the major international trade and financial institutions such as the International Monetary Fund (IMF), the World Bank, and the General Agreement on Tariffs and Trade (GATT). Membership in these institutions could benefit the Soviet Union. Russia was admitted to the IMF and World Bank in 1992 and, as we saw in Table 40-1, has received $3 billion in

aid from those institutions. Membership in GATT would result in lower tariff barriers for Russian exports.

A PROGRESS REPORT

What's the current status of Russia's reforms?

Accomplishments

On the positive side, several aspects of Russian economic reform have gone quite well.

1   Privatization   By late 1994 about 70 percent of the entire economy was privately held. About two-thirds of former state-owned enterprises have been privatized; 90 percent of small companies are privately owned; and 80 percent of service-sector companies are private.

The privatization process involved two phases. In the first phase the government gave vouchers, each with a designated monetary value, to 40 million Soviet citizens. Recipients could then pool these vouchers to purchase enterprises. The second phase, begun in 1994, allows state enterprises to be purchased for cash. This makes it possible for foreign investors to buy Russian enterprises and also provides much-needed capital to the enterprises.

Land reform, however, has progressed more slowly. Farmers fear the uncertainties and potential problems which might accompany privatization and free markets.

2   Price Reform   With some exceptions, government price fixing has been abandoned. In January 1992 the government decontrolled approximately 90 percent of all prices. The international value of the ruble was devalued to the current black market level and was allowed to float—that is, its value to be determined by demand and supply.

3   Low Unemployment   Despite vast structural changes and other dislocations associated with the transition to markets, massive unemployment has not yet occurred. In the spring of 1994 unemployment was slightly under 6 percent, close to full employment by international standards.

The downside of this is that many Russian workers have been forced to accept substantial wage cuts to save their jobs. The consequences have been sharply reduced living standards for such workers and growing wage inequality.

Problems

The problems Russia has encountered in its economic transition are substantial.

1 Inflation As column 2 of Table 40-2 shows, inflation in Russia has been enormous. The sources of this inflation are several.

First, prices were decontrolled in January 1992 and, as expected, prices on many products tripled or quadrupled almost overnight (Figure 40-1).

Second, Russian households stored massive amounts of currency and deposits at savings banks during years of waiting for scarce consumer goods to become more abundant. This **ruble overhang** helped fuel inflation once prices were decontrolled.

The third and most important source of inflation has been large government deficits financed by increases in the money supply. The deficits in turn have many roots. First, privatization of state enterprises has caused the government to lose an important source of revenue—firm profits. Second, the uncertainties inherent in the transition have led to widespread tax avoidance. Many local governments have withheld tax payments to the central government. Large numbers of privatized businesses have avoided the new 28 percent value-added (sales) tax. And, ironically, the government's anti-alcohol campaign has led to a loss of vodka-tax revenues. Third, the government has extended massive subsidy credits to both industry and agriculture and has increased welfare benefits to ease transition problems.

One dramatic side effect of Russia's inflation has been the plunging international value of the ruble. When the ruble was floated in early 1992, the exchange rate was 90 rubles (R) for 1 dollar (R90 = $1). By January 1994 the ruble had fallen to R1607 = $1 and plunged to R3926 = $1 in the fall of 1994 before recovering somewhat as the result of Russian Central Bank intervention. Such drastic changes in the ruble's international value are obviously detrimental to Russia's world trade.

2 Falling Output and Living Standards Real output began to fall in the 1980s, but its decline has accelerated during the reforms. Column 3 of Table

TABLE 40-2 Inflation and real GDP in Russia, 1991–1994

(1) Year	(2) Rate of inflation	(3) Growth of real GDP (percent)
1991	93	−13
1992	1353	−19
1993	896	−12
1994*	292	−12

*Estimate.

Source: International Monetary Fund and Russian authorities.

40-2 documents recent declines. Note that the fall in real GDP bottomed out in 1992 at 19 percent, and the government's program hopes to limit the drop to 12 percent in 1994.

Causes of these declines include: (1) rapid inflation, which created an uncertain environment for borrowing and investing; (2) the unraveling of Russia's international trade relationships with former communist-bloc nations of eastern Europe; (3) the bankruptcy and closing of many former state-owned enterprises which could not survive in a market environment; and (4) the massive reallocation of resources required by the reforms and the downgrading of the military.

We know that output is income. Declining real output has meant declines in Russian living standards. Farmers, government employees, and pensioners have been hard hit, and as we have noted, many workers have had to accept deep wage cuts to keep their jobs.

3 Inequality and Social Costs Economic inequality has increased during the transition. As noted, many farmers, pensioners, and state employees have been impoverished. A small enriched elite—some associated with honest entrepreneurship and others with corruption, illegal activities, and speculation—is also emerging. Considerable friction between gainers and losers fuels public doubts as to the desirability of a market economy. Greater economic insecurity exists; medical and educational services have deteriorated, and school enrollments have declined. So has life expectancy. In 1988 the life expectancy of Russian men was 65 years. It is currently 59 years, thirteen less than American males.

FUTURE PROSPECTS

There is widespread disagreement among experts as to the prospects for the success of Russia's transition to a market economy.

Destabilization and Collapse

The pessimistic view is that Russia is now plagued by highly volatile economic and political conditions which could undermine both economic reforms and democratization. In particular, the Russian government's persistent deficits, financed by money creation, pose the possibility of hyperinflation and collapse as inflation and government weaknesses feed upon one another. A weak and indecisive central government will find it difficult to impose and collect taxes. Businesses and political subdivisions will evade or withhold tax payments because the central government cannot effectively enforce collection. Widespread tax evasion means declining tax revenues, enlarged budget deficits, and therefore more inflation and financial instability. Declining tax revenues further weaken the government's ability to enforce tax laws, so a kind of vicious circle continues until political and economic collapse results. Declining revenues also cripple the central government's ability to perform other basic functions, such as maintaining law and order and providing a social safety net for its citizens. A longing may arise for the old political order and economic security of communism, leading to abandonment of economic reforms and democracy.

Muddling Through

A more optimistic view is that Russia's reform process is relatively new and that the most severe economic dislocations in the form of inflation and a declining real output may be behind it. As Table 40-2 suggests, while inflation and real GDP declines are still at serious levels, the rate of inflation is falling and production declines may be bottoming out.

More positively, the private sector is developing rapidly. Some 70,000 state enterprises have been at least partly privatized and about 18,000 new private firms have arisen. Financial and securities markets are beginning to emerge, and perhaps some of the estimated $40 billion which Russians hold abroad will return to fuel investment and growth. While Russia's central planning-to-markets transition might span another decade or so, with further hardships, collapse of its economic and political reforms and a return to socialism are unlikely.

CHAPTER SUMMARY

1　The labor theory of value is a central principle of Marxian ideology. Capitalists, as property owners, allegedly expropriate most of labor's value as profits or surplus value.

2　Virtually complete state ownership of property resources and central planning historically were the major institutional features of the Soviet economy.

3　Characteristics of Soviet planning included **a** emphasis on industrialization and military strength; **b** overcommitment of resources; **c** economic growth based on additional inputs rather than increased productivity; **d** allocation of resources by bureaucratic rather than market decisions; **e** economic self-sufficiency; and **f** passive macroeconomic policies.

4　The basic problem Soviet central planners faced was

LAST WORD

CHINA: EMERGING ECONOMIC SUPERPOWER?

The characteristics and consequences of China's reforms are quite different from those of Russia.

China has achieved a remarkable 8 to 9 percent growth of real output over the last decade. In 1992 its growth rate was a spectacular 12.8 percent! In terms of real GDP China has emerged as the world's third largest economy, behind only the United States and Japan. If the current 6 or $6\frac{1}{2}$ percentage point differential in the growth rates of China and America persist, China would become the world's largest economy shortly after 2010 (even though its per capita output will remain far below that of the major industrial nations because of its huge population).

The direction of reform in both China and Russia is the same—from central planning to markets. Why, then, has China done so well compared to Russia? While there is considerable disagreement among experts, the answer might lie in the different characteristics of China's reforms.

1 "Shock Therapy" versus Gradualism Russia pursued a rapid and radical "shock therapy" approach

to reform, seeking to institute privatization, price liberalization, competition, macroeconomic stability, and other elements of reform in a short time. China's reforms, begun in 1978, have been piecemeal and gradual.

2 Political and Economic Reform Russia believed its political apparatus—the Communist Party in particular—was an obstacle to economic reform. Political

achieving coordination or internal consistency in their plans to avoid bottlenecks and the chain reaction of production failures which they cause.

5 Diminishing growth rates, shoddy consumer goods, and the inability to provide a promised high standard of living were all outcomes of the failure of Soviet central planning.

6 Stagnation of the agricultural sector, a growing labor shortage, and the burden of a large military establishment contributed to the failure of the Soviet economy. However, the primary causes of failure were the inability of central planning to coordinate a more complex economy, the absence of rational success indicators, and the lack of adequate economic incentives.

7 The Gorbachev reforms attempted to restructure the economy and introduce greater political "openness," but did not address fundamental systemic deficiencies.

8 To change from central planning to a market economy, Russia must move from public to private ownership of property; establish a competitive environment for businesses; restructure government's role to activities appropriate to capitalism; abandon state-determined prices in favor of market-determined prices; integrate its system into the world economy; provide price level and employment stability; and sustain public support for the reforms.

9 Industrialized capitalist nations may assist Russia's transition by a providing foreign aid; b encouraging private firms to invest in Russia; and c facilitating Russian membership in international financial and tariff-determining institutions.

10 While progress has been made in privatization and price decontrol, Russia has experienced severe inflation and significant declines in real output and living standards.

TERMS AND CONCEPTS

labor theory of value	central economic	Gorbachev reforms	*glasnost*
surplus value	planning	*perestroika*	ruble overhang
state ownership			

reform or democratization preceded economic reform. China has sought economic reform under the strong guidance of its Communist Party. China's view is that the upsetting of the political system would generate endless debate, competition for power, and ultimate stagnation and failure of economic reforms. China feels communist dictatorship and markets are compatible; Russia does not.

3 Role of SOEs Russia focused most of its institutional reform on privatizing its state-owned enterprises (SOEs), which produce most of its GDP. China has protected the existence and development of its SOEs, while simultaneously encouraging the creation of competing private enterprises.

4 Ties to the World Economy Russia has sought to integrate itself into the world economy by floating the ruble, lowering international trade barriers, and seeking membership in international institutions such as the IMF. China established "special economic zones" along its coast which eliminated the government's monopoly on foreign trade and finance. The purpose was to attract foreign capital and foreign companies, along with their advanced technologies and business ex-

pertise. The result has been burgeoning growth in these zones, spearheaded by ethnic Chinese businesspersons in Hong Kong, Taiwan, and elsewhere in Asia.

Can China sustain its economic surge? Many experts are optimistic. The economy is highly competitive; saving rates are very high, encouraging the financing of industrial investment; rising agricultural productivity permits transfer of redundant farm labor to industry; the labor force has sufficient education and skills to support further industrialization; and its current low level of technology has the potential for substantial efficiency gains by adopting superior world technology.

Perhaps the main reason for pessimism is the widening gap between economic reform and political control. China remains a politically repressive society. As a rising standard of living permits its citizenry to make more economic choices, it may also decide it wants to choose the kind of government it wants and who will run that government. China's authoritarian capitalism may contain the seeds of upheaval, chaos, and even civil war, which bodes ill for continued economic progress.

QUESTIONS AND STUDY SUGGESTIONS

1 Compare the ideology and institutional framework of the former Soviet economy with that of American capitalism. Contrast the manner in which production was motivated in the Soviet Union compared to how it is motivated in the United States.

2 Discuss the problem of coordination which faced central planners in the former Soviet Union. Explain how a planning failure can cause a chain reaction of additional failures.

3 How was the number of automobiles to be produced determined in the former Soviet Union? In the United States? How are the decisions implemented in the two different types of economies?

4 What were the major characteristics and goals of Soviet central planning?

5 What was the evidence of the failure of Soviet planning? Explain why Soviet economic growth diminished after 1970.

6 Explain why the use of quantitative output targets as

the major success indicator for Soviet enterprises contributed to economic inefficiency.

7 *Key Question* *Use a supply and demand diagram to explain why persistent shortages of many consumer goods occurred in the former Soviet Union. Why has the transformation to a market economy been accompanied by inflation? Why were black markets so common in the Soviet Union?*

8 *Key Question* *What specific changes must be made to transform the Soviet economy to a market system? Why is it important that these changes be introduced simultaneously?*

9 What progress has Russia achieved in its transition to a market economy? What problems has it encountered?

10 Briefly assess the quantity and types of foreign aid which have been made available to Russia.

11 (Last Word) In what specific respects have Chinese economic reforms differed from Russia's? Do you believe these differences account for China's superior growth?

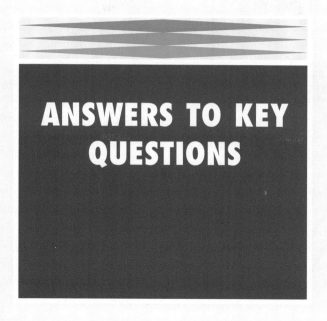

ANSWERS TO KEY QUESTIONS

Chapter 1

1-1 Effective policy must be based on sound theory—factually supported generalizations about behavior. Two methods are used to obtain sound economic theory: deduction and induction.

In *deduction,* the economist starts directly with an untested hypothesis. The hypothesis or theory is tested for accuracy by gathering and examining all relevant facts. If the facts support the hypothesis, the theory can be used for policy. The other approach is *induction,* in which the economist starts by gathering facts and then notes their relationship to each other. Eventually, the data may reveal a cause and effect pattern from which a theory results. From this theory, economic policy relevant to the real world can be formulated. Deduction and induction are complementary and often used simultaneously.

As for the quotation, the opposite is true; any theory not supported by facts is not a good theory. Good economics is empirically grounded; it is based on facts and highly practical.

1-5 (a), (d), and (f) are macro; (b), (c), and (e) are micro.

1-6 (a) and (c) are positive; (b) and (d) are normative.

1-9 (a) The fallacy of composition is the mistake of believing that something true for an individual part is necessarily true for the whole. Example: A single auto producer can increase its profits by lowering its price and taking business away from its competitors. But matched price cuts by all auto manufacturers will not necessarily yield higher industry profits.

(b) The "after this, therefore because of this" fallacy is incorrectly reasoning that when one event precedes another, the first event *necessarily* caused the second. Example: Interest rates rise, followed by an increase in the rate of inflation, leading to the erroneous conclusion the rise in interest rates caused the inflation. Higher interest rates slow inflation.

Cause and effect relationships are difficult to isolate because "other things" are continually changing.

1-13 This behavior can be explained in terms of marginal costs and marginal benefits. At a standard restaurant, items are priced individually—they have a positive marginal cost. If you order more, it will cost you more. You order until the marginal benefit from the extra food no longer exceeds the positive marginal cost. At a buffet you pay a flat fee no matter how much you eat. Once the fee is paid, additional food items have a zero marginal cost. You therefore continue to eat until your marginal benefit is also zero.

Appendix 1-2 (a) More tickets are bought at each price; the line plots to the right of the previous line. (b) and (c) Fewer tickets are bought at each price; the line plots to the left of the previous line.

Appendix 1-3 Income column: $0; $5,000; $10,000, $15,000; $20,000. Saving column: $−500; 0; $500; $1,000; $1,500. Slope = 0.1 (= $1,000 − $500)/($15,000 − $10,000). Vertical intercept = $−500. The slope shows how much saving will go up for every $1 increase in income; the intercept shows the amount of saving (dissaving) occurring when income is zero. Equation: $S = \$-500 + 0.1Y$ (where S is saving and Y is income). Saving will be $750 at the $12,500 income level.

Appendix 1-6 Slopes: at $A = +4$; at $B = 0$; at $C = -4$.

Chapter 2

2-5 Economics deals with the "limited resources–unlimited wants" problem. Unemployment represents valuable resources which could have been used to produce more goods and services—to meet more wants and ease the economizing problem.

Allocative efficiency means that resources are being used to produce the goods and services most wanted by society. Society is located at the optimal point on its production possibilities curve where marginal benefit equals marginal cost for each good. *Productive efficiency* means the least costly production techniques are being used to produce wanted goods and services.

Example: manual typewriters produced using the least-cost techniques but for which there is no demand.

2-6 (a) See curve *EDCBA* in the accompanying figure. The assumptions are full employment and productive efficiency, fixed supplies of resources, and fixed technology.

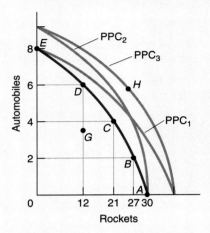

Rockets

(b) 4.5 rockets; .33 automobiles, as determined from the table. Increasing opportunity costs are reflected in the concave-from-the-origin shape of the curve. This means the economy must give up larger and larger amounts of rockets to get constant added amounts of automobiles—and vice versa.

(c) It must obtain full employment and productive efficiency.

2-9 The marginal benefit curve is downsloping; MB falls as more of a product is consumed. The first units of a good consumed yield greater additional satisfaction than subsequent units. The marginal cost curve is upsloping; MC increases as more of a product is produced. The opportunity cost of producing good A rises as resources increasingly better suited to other uses are used to produce A. The optimal amount of a particular product occurs where MB equals MC. If MC exceeds MB, fewer resources should be allocated to this use. The resources have more value in some alternative use (as reflected in MC) than in this use (as reflected in MB).

2-10 See the figure accompanying the answer to question 2-6. *G* indicates unemployment, productive inefficiency, or both. *H* is at present unattainable. Economic growth—through more inputs, better inputs, improved technology—must be achieved to attain *H*.

2-11 See question 2-6 figure. PPC$_1$ shows improved rocket technology. PPC$_2$ shows improved auto technology. PPC$_3$ shows improved technology in producing both products.

Chapter 3

3-2 Demand increases in (a), (c), (e), and (f); decreases in (b) and (d).

3-5 Supply increases in (a), (d), (e), and (g); decreases in (b), (c), and (f).

3-7 Data, from top to bottom: −13; −7; 0; +7; +14; and +21.
(a) $P_e = \$4.00$; $Q_e = 75{,}000$. Equilibrium occurs where there is neither a shortage nor surplus of wheat. At the im-

mediately lower price of $3.70, there is a shortage of 7000 bushels. At the immediately higher price of $4.30, there is a surplus of 7000 bushels.

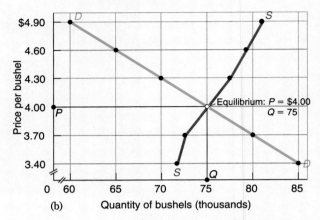

(b)   Quantity of bushels (thousands)

(c) Because at $3.40 there will be a 13,000 bushel shortage which will drive price up. Because at $4.90 there will be a 21,000 surplus which will drive the price down. Quotation is incorrect; just the opposite is true.

(d) A $3.70 ceiling causes a persistent shortage. Also, a black market (illegal sales above $3.70) might occur. Government might want to suppress inflation.

3-8 (a) Price up; quantity down; (b) Price down; quantity down; (c) Price down; quantity up; (d) Price indeterminate; quantity up; (e) Price up; quantity up; (f) Price down; quantity indeterminate; (g) Price up; quantity indeterminate; (h) Price indeterminate and quantity down.

Chapter 4

4-2 "Roundabout" production means using capital goods in the production process, enabling producers to obtain more output than through direct production. The direct way to produce a corn crop is to scatter seed about in an unplowed field. The roundabout way is to plow, fertilize, harrow, and till the field using machinery and then use a seed drill to sow the seeds in rows at the correct depth. The higher yield per acre will more than compensate the farmer for the cost of using the roundabout techniques.

To increase the capital stock at full employment, the current production of consumer goods must decrease. Moving along the production possibilities curve toward more capital goods comes at the expense of current consumption.

No, it can use its previously unemployed resources to produce more capital goods, without sacrificing consumption goods. It can move from a point inside to a point on the curve, thus obtaining more capital goods.

4-8 (a) Technique 2. Because it produces the output with least cost ($34 compared to $35 each for the other two). Economic profit will be $6 (= $40 − $34), which causes the industry to expand. Expansion continues until prices are competed down to where total revenue is $34 (equal to total cost).

(b) Adopt technique 4 because its cost is now lowest at $32.

(c) Adopt technique 1 because its cost is now lowest at $27.50.

(d) Increasing scarcity causes prices to rise. Firms ignoring higher prices will become high-cost producers and be competed out of business by firms switching to the less expensive inputs. The market system forces producers to conserve on the use of highly scarce resources. Question 8c confirms this because technique 1 was adopted because labor had become less expensive. The least-cost combination is *not* necessarily the one using the fewest inputs. The relative prices of inputs is important.

Chapter 5

5-2 The distribution of income is quite unequal. The highest 20 percent of the residents receive 10 times more income than the lowest 20 percent.

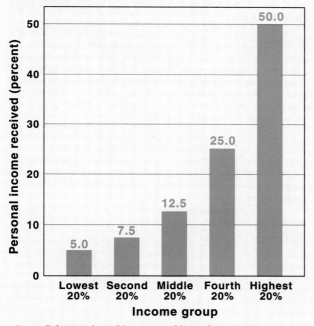

5-4 Sole proprietorship, partnership, and corporation.

Proprietorship advantages: easy to open and provides maximum freedom for the proprietor to do what she or he thinks best. Proprietorship disadvantages: limited financial resources; the owner must be a "Jack-or-Jill-of-all-trades"; and unlimited liability.

Partnership advantages: easy to organize; greater specialization of management; and greater financial resources. Disadvantages: financial resources are still limited; unlimited liability; possibility of disagreement among the partners; and precarious continuity.

Corporation advantages: can raise large amounts of money by issuing stocks and bonds; limited liability; and continuity.

Corporation disadvantages: red tape and expense in incorporating; potential for abuse of stockholder and bondholder funds; double taxation of profits; and separation of ownership and control.

The dominant role of corporations stems from the advantages cited, particularly unlimited liability and superior ability to raise money capital.

5-9 Public goods (a) are indivisible—they are produced in such large units that they cannot be sold to individuals and (b) the exclusion principle does not apply; once the goods are produced nobody—including free riders—can be excluded from the goods' benefits. The free-rider problem explains the significance of the exclusion principle. The government must provide public goods such as the judicial system, national defense, police protection, and weather warning systems since people can obtain the benefits without paying. Government must levy taxes to get revenues to pay for public goods.

5-10 If on the curve, the only way to obtain more public goods is to reduce the production of private goods (from *C* to *B*).

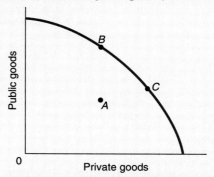

If operating inside the curve, it can expand the production of public goods without sacrificing private goods (from *A* to *B*).

5-15 Total tax = $13,000; marginal tax rate = 40%; average tax rate = 26%. This is a progressive tax; the average tax rate rises as income goes up.

Chapter 6

6-3 An export increases domestic output and revenues to domestic export firms. Because these firms would employ more resources, household income would rise. Households would then use part of their greater income to buy more imported goods.

United States exports in 1993 were $457 billion (flow 13) and imports were $590 billion (flow 16).

Flow 14 must equal flow 13. Flow 15 must equal flow 16.

6-4 (a) Yes, because the opportunity cost of radios is less (1R = 1C) in South Korea than in the United States (1R = 2C). South Korea should produce radios and the United States, chemicals.

(b) If they specialize, the United States can produce 20 tons of chemicals and South Korea can produce 30,000 radios. Before specialization South Korea produced alternative B and the United States alternative U for a total of 28,000 radios (24,000 + 4,000) and 18 tons of chemicals (6 tons + 12 tons). The gain is 2,000 radios and 2 tons of chemicals.

(c) The limits of the terms of trade are determined by the comparative cost conditions in each country before trade: 1R = 1C in South Korea and 1R = 2C in the United States. The terms of trade must be somewhere between these two ratios for trade to occur.

If the terms of trade are 1R = 1½C, South Korea would end up with 26,000 radios (= 30,000 − 4,000) and 6 tons of chemicals. The United States would have 4,000 radios and

14 tons of chemicals (= 20 − 6). South Korea has gained 2,000 radios. The United States has gained 2 tons of chemicals.

(d) Yes, the world is obtaining more output from its fixed resources.

6-6 The first part of this statement is incorrect. Our exports create a domestic *supply* of foreign currencies, not a domestic demand for them. The second part of the statement is accurate. The foreign demand for dollars (from our exports) generates a supply of foreign currencies to Americans.

A decline in American incomes or a weakening of American preferences for foreign goods would reduce our imports, reducing our demand for foreign currencies. These currencies would depreciate (the dollar would appreciate). Dollar appreciation means our exports will decline and our imports will rise.

6-10 GATT is the General Agreement on Tariffs and Trade. Its provisions apply to more than 120 nations, affecting people around the globe. The Uruguay Round of GATT negotiations produced an agreement which will reduce tariffs, liberalize trade in services, cut agricultural subsidies, protect intellectual property, reduce import quotas, and create the World Trade Organization.

The EU and NAFTA are free-trade blocs. GATT reduces tariffs and liberalizes trade for nearly *all* nations, not just countries in these blocs. The ascendancy of the EU and the passage of NAFTA encouraged nations to reach a new GATT agreement. No nation wanted to be disadvantaged by the formation of the trade blocs.

Chapter 7

7-2 Because the dollar value of final goods includes the dollar value of the intermediate goods. If intermediate goods were counted, then double (or triple or quadruple, etc.) counting would occur. The value of the steel used in autos is included in the price of the auto (the final product).

GNP is the dollar value of final goods and services produced by Americans within the United States and abroad. GDP is the value of final goods and services produced by Americans and others within the geographical borders of the United States.

NDP is GDP less depreciation—the physical capital used up in producing this year's output.

7-5 When gross investment exceeds depreciation, net investment is positive and the economy is said to be expanding; it ends the year with more physical capital. When gross investment equals depreciation, net investment is zero and the economy is said to be static; it ends the year with the same amount of physical capital. When depreciation is greater than gross investment, net investment is negative and the economy is said to be declining; it ends the year with less physical capital.

The first statement is wrong. Just because *net* investment was a minus $6 billion in 1933 doesn't mean the economy produced no new capital in that year. It simply means depreciation exceeded gross investment by $6 billion. Although gross investment was positive, the economy ended the year with $6 billion less capital.

The second statement is correct. If only one $20 spade is bought by a construction firm in the entire economy in a year and no other physical capital is bought, then gross investment is $20. This is true even though *net* investment will be highly negative, equaling the whole of depreciation less the $20 spade. If not even this $20 spade had been bought, then gross investment would have

been zero. But "gross investment can never be *less* than zero."

7-7 (a) GDP = $388; NDP = $361; (b) NI = $339; (c) PI = $291; (d) DI = $265.

7-10 In this hypothetical case, the GDP price index for 1974 was 0.65 (= $39/$60). Between 1974 and 1987, the price level rose by 53.85 percent [= (($60 − $39)/$39) × 100].

7-11 Values for real GDP, top to bottom of the column: $1930.5 (inflating); $2339.4 (inflating); $2687.4 (inflating); $3267.8 (inflating); $3702.7 (inflating); $4716.4 (deflating).

Chapter 8

8-1 The four phases of a typical business cycle, starting at the bottom, are: trough, recovery, peak, and recession. The length of a cycle varies from two to three years to as much as six or seven years or even longer.

Normally there will be a pre-Christmas spurt, followed by a slackening in January after post-Christmas sales. This normal seasonal variation must not be viewed as signaling a boom in the first case nor a recession in the second. From decade to decade the long-term, or secular, trend of the United States economy has been upward. If there is no growth of GDP over a period, this does not signal all is normal but rather the economy is functioning below its trend rate of output growth.

Because durable goods last, consumers can postpone buying replacements. This happens when people are worried about a recession and whether there will be a paycheck next month. And firms will soon quit producing what people are not buying. Durable goods industries therefore suffer large output declines during recessions.

In contrast, consumers cannot long postpone the buying of many nondurables such as food and therefore recessions only slightly reduce output.

8-3 GDP gap = 10 percent [= (9 − 5) × 2.5]; forgone output = $50 billion (= 10% of $500 billion).

8-5 Labor force = 230 [= 500 − (120 + 150)]; unemployment rate = 10% [= (23/230) × 100].

8-7 This year's rate of inflation = 10% [(121 − 110)/110] × 100.

Dividing 70 by the annual rate of increase of any variable (for instance, the rate of inflation or population growth) will give the approximate number of years for doubling of the variable.

(a) 35 years (= 70/2); (b) 14 years (= 70/5); (c) 7 years (= 70/10).

Chapter 9

9-6 Data for completing the table (top to bottom). Consumption: $244; $260; $276; $292; $308; $324; $340; $356; $372. APC: 1.02; 1.00; .99; .97; .96; .95; .94; .94; .93. APS: −.02; .00; .01; .03; .04; .05; .06; .06; .07. MPC: .80, throughout. MPS: .20, throughout.

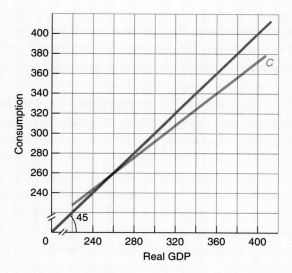

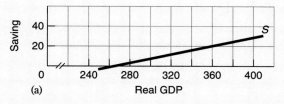

(a)

(b) Break-even income = $260. By borrowing or using past savings.

(c) Technically, the APC diminishes and the APS increases because these schedules have positive and negative vertical intercepts (Appendix to Chapter 1). MPC and MPS are measured by the *slopes* of the consumption and saving schedules; they relate to *changes* in consumption and saving as income changes. With straight-line consumption and saving schedules, these slopes do not change as the level of income changes; the slopes and thus the MPC and MPS are unrelated to the intercepts.

9-8 Aggregate investment: (a) $20 billion; (b) $30 billion; (c) $40 billion. This is the investment-demand curve because we have applied the rule of undertaking all investment up to the point where the expected rate of net profit, *r*, equals the interest rate, *i*.

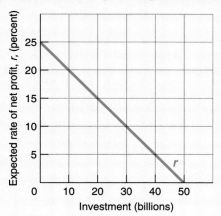

9-10 Saving data for completing the table (top to bottom): $−4; $0; $4; $8; $12; $16; $20; $24; $28.

Equilibrium GDP = $340 billion, determined where (1) aggregate expenditures equal GDP (*C* of $324 billion + *I* of $16 billion = GDP of $340 billion); or (2) where planned *I* = planned *S* (*I* of $16 billion = *S* of $16 billion). Equilibrium level of employment = 65 million; MPC = .8; MPS = .2.

9-11 At the $380 billion level of GDP, planned saving = $24 billion; planned investment = $16 billion (from the question). This deficiency of $8 billion of planned investment causes an unintended $8 billion *increase* in inventories—inventory investment. Actual investment is $24 billion (= $16 billion of planned investment *plus* $8 billion of unplanned inventory investment), matching the $24 billion of actual saving.

At the $300 billion level of GDP, planned saving = $8 billion; planned investment = $16 billion (from the question). This excess of $8 billion of planned investment causes an unintended $8 billion *decline* in inventories—inventory disinvestment. Actual investment is $8 billion (= $16 billion of planned investment *minus* $8 billion of an unplanned inventory disinvestment). Actual saving is also $8 billion.

When unintended investment in inventories occur, as at the $380 billion level of GDP, businesses revise their production plans downward and GDP falls. When unintended disinvestment in inventories occur, as at the $300 billion level of GDP, businesses revise their production plans upward and GDP rises. Equilibrium GDP—in this case, $340 billion—occurs were planned investment equals planned saving.

Chapter 10

10-2 The simple multiplier effect is the multiple by which the equilibrium GDP increases when any component of aggregate expenditures changes. The greater the MPC (the smaller the MPS), the greater the multiplier.

MPS = 0, multiplier = infinity; MPS = .4, multiplier = 2.5; MPS = .6, multiplier = 1.67; MPS = 1; multiplier = 1.

MPC = 1; multiplier = infinity; MPC = .9, multiplier = 10; MPC = .67; multiplier = 3; MPC = .5, multiplier = 2; MPC = 0, multiplier = 1.

Change in GDP = $40 billion (= $8 billion × multiplier of 5); change in GDP = $24 billion ($8 billion × multiplier of 3). The simple multiplier takes account of only the leakage of saving. The complex multiplier also takes account of leakages of taxes and imports, making the complex multiplier less than the simple multiplier.

10-5 (a) Equilibrium GDP for the closed economy = $400 billion.

(b) Net export data for column 5 (top to bottom): $−10 billion in each space. Aggregate expenditure data for column 6 (top to bottom): $230; $270; $310; $350; $390; $430; $470; $510. Equilibrium GDP for the open economy is $350 billion, $50 billion below the $400 billion equilibrium GDP for the closed economy. The $−10 billion of net exports reduces equilibrium GDP by $50 billion (= $400 billion − $350 billion) because the multiplier is 5. Since every rise of $50 billion of GDP increases aggregate expenditures by $40 billion, the MPC is .8, and the multiplier is 5.

(c) Net exports would fall by $10 billion and GDP would decline by $50 billion (= $10 billion × the multiplier of 5).

Net exports would increase by $10 billion and GDP would rise by $50 billion (= $10 billion × the multiplier of 5). Exports constant, increases in imports reduce GDP; decreases in imports, increase GDP.

(d) 5.

10-8 The addition of $20 billion of government expenditures and $20 billion of personal taxes increases the equilibrium GDP from $350 to $370 billion. The $20 billion increase in *G raises* equilibrium by $100 billion (= $20 billion × the multiplier of 5); the $20 billion increase in *T reduces* consumption by $16 billion (= $20 billion × the MPC of .8). This $16 billion decline in turn reduces equilibrium GDP by $80 billion (= $16 billion × multiplier of 5). The net change from adding government is $20 billion (= $100 billion − $80 billion.).

10-10 (a) Recessionary gap. Equilibrium GDP is $600 billion, while full employment GDP is $700 billion. Employment will be 20 million less than at full employment. Aggregate expenditures will have to increase by $20 billion at each level of GDP to eliminate the recessionary gap.

(b) Inflationary gap. Aggregate expenditures are excessive, causing demand-pull inflation. Aggregate expenditures will have to fall by $20 billion at each level of GDP to eliminate the inflationary gap.

(c) MPC = .8 (= $40 billion/$50 billion). MPS = .2 (= 1 − .8). Multiplier = 5 (= 1/.2).

Chapter 11

11-4 (a)

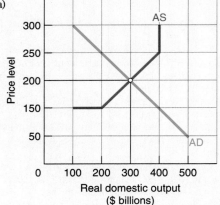

Equilibrium price level = 200. Equilibrium real output = $300 billion. No, the absolute full-capacity level of GDP is $400 billion, where the AS curve becomes vertical.

(b) At a price level of 150, real GDP supplied is a maximum of $200 billion, less than real GDP demanded of $400 billion. The shortage of real output will drive the price level up. At a price level of 250, real GDP supplied is $400 billion, which is more than real GDP demanded of $200 billion. The surplus of real output will drive down the price level. Equilibrium occurs at the price level where AS and AD intersect.

(c) Increases in consumer, investment, government, or net export spending shift the AD curve rightward. New equilibrium price level = 250. New equilibrium GDP = $400 billion. The intermediate range.

11-5 (a) Productivity level = 2.67; (b) Per unit cost of production = $.75; (c) New per unit production cost = $1.13. The AS curve would shift leftward. The price level would rise and real output would decrease; (d) New per unit cost of production = $0.375 [($2 × 150)/800]. AS curve shifts to the right; price level declines and real output increases.

11-7 (a) AD curve left; (b) AD curve right; (c) AS curve left; (d) AD curve right; (e) AD curve left; (f) AD curve right; (g) AS curve right; (h) AD curve right; (i) AS curve right; (j) AS curve left; (k) AD curve right; AS curve left; (l) AD curve left; (m) AS curve right.

11-9 (a) Price level rises and no change in real output; (b) price level drops and real output increases; (c) price level does not change, but real output rises; (d) price level does not change, but real output declines; (e) price level increases, but change in real output is indeterminate; (f) price level does not change, but real output declines.

Chapter 12

12-2 Increase in government spending = $5 billion. Decrease in taxes = $6.25 billion. (Initial new consumption spending would rise by $5 billion, because the MPC is .8.) Because part of the tax reduction ($1.25 billion) is saved, not spent. The multiplier applies only to that part of a tax cut which boosts consumption. Combination: a $1 billion increase in government spending and a $5 billion tax cut.

12-3 Reduce government spending, increase taxes, or some combination of both. See Figure 12-2 in the chapter. If the price level is flexible downward, it will fall. In the real world, the goal is to reduce *inflation*—to keep prices from rising so rapidly—not to reduce the *price level*. A "conservative" economist might favor cuts in government spending, since this would reduce the size of government. A "liberal" economist might favor a tax hike; it would preserve government spending programs.

12-7 The *full-employment budget* indicates what the Federal budgetary deficit or surplus would be if the economy were to achieve full employment throughout the year. This budget is a useful measure of fiscal policy. If the full-employment budget is moving toward deficit, fiscal policy is expansionary. If the full-employment budget is moving toward surplus, fiscal policy is contractionary. The *actual budget* simply compares G and T for the year and is an unreliable indicator of the government's fiscal policy. It does not account for shortfalls of tax revenues arising from less than full-employment output. A *structural deficit*—or a full-employment budget deficit—is the difference between G and T when the economy is at full employment. A *cyclical deficit* is the difference between G and T caused by tax revenues being below those accruing when the economy is at full employment.

At GDP_f, the structural deficit is *ab* and the cyclical deficit is zero. Government should raise T or reduce G to eliminate this deficit, but it may want to take this action over several years to avoid pushing the economy into recession.

12-9 It takes time to ascertain the direction the economy is moving (recognition lag), to get a fiscal policy enacted into law (administrative lag); and for the policy to have its full effect on the economy (operational lag). Meanwhile, other factors may change, rendering inappropriate a particular fiscal policy. Nevertheless, discretionary fiscal policy is a valuable tool in preventing severe recession or severe demand-pull inflation.

A political business cycle is the concept that politicians are more interested in reelection than in stabilizing the economy. Before the election, they enact tax cuts and spending increases even though this may fuel inflation. After the election, they apply the brakes to restrain inflation. The economy will slow and unemployment will rise. In this view the political process creates economic instability.

The crowding-out effect is the reduction in investment spending caused by the increase in interest rates arising from an increase in government spending, financed by borrowing. The increase in G was designed to increase AD but the resulting increase in interest rates may decrease I, thus reducing the impact of the expansionary fiscal policy.

The net export effect also derives from the higher interest rates accompanying fiscal policy. The higher interest rates make American bonds more attractive to foreign buyers. The inflow of foreign currency to buy dollars to purchase the bonds drives up the international value of the dollar, making imports less expensive for Americans and American exports more expensive for people abroad. American net exports decline, and like the crowding-out effect, diminish the expansionary fiscal policy.

It seems improbable to us that people respond to government budget deficits by reducing consumption and increasing saving in anticipation of a future tax increase tied to current budget deficits.

Chapter 13

13-5 $M1$ = currency (in circulation) + checkable deposits. The largest component of $M1$ is checkable deposits. If the face value of a coin were not greater than its intrinsic (metallic) value, people would remove them from circulation and sell them for their metallic content. $M2 = M1$ + noncheckable savings deposits + money market deposit accounts + small time deposits + money market mutual fund balances. $M3 = M2$ + large time deposits (those $100,000 or more). Near-monies include the components of $M2$ and $M3$ not included in $M1$ and, secondly, other less liquid assets such as Savings bonds and Treasury bills.

Near-monies represent wealth; the more wealth people have, the more they are likely to spend out of current income. Also, the fact that near-monies are liquid adds to potential economic instability. People may cash in their near-monies and spend the proceeds while the monetary authorities are trying to stem inflation by reducing the money supply. Finally, near-monies can complicate monetary policy because $M1$, $M2$, and $M3$ do not always change in the same direction.

The argument for including noncheckable savings deposits in a definition of money is that saving deposits can quickly be transferred to a checking account or withdrawn as cash and spent.

13-7   In the first case, the value of the dollar (year 2, relative to year 1) is $.80 (= 1/1.25); in the second case, $2 (= 1/.50). Generalization: The price level and the value of the dollar are inversely related.

13-8   (a) The level of nominal GDP. The higher this level, the greater the amount of money demanded for transactions. (b) The interest rate. The higher the interest rate, the smaller the amount of money demanded as an asset.

On a graph measuring the interest rate vertically and the amount of money demanded horizontally, the two demand for money curves can be summed horizontally to get the total demand for money. This total demand shows the total amount of money demanded at each interest rate. The equilibrium interest rate is determined at the intersection of the total demand for money curve and the supply of money curve.

(a) Expanded use of credit cards: transaction demand for money declines; total demand for money declines; interest rate falls. (b) Shortening of worker pay periods: transaction demand for money declines; total demand for money declines; interest rate falls. (c) Increase in nominal GDP: transaction demand for money increases; total demand for money increases; interest rate rises.

Chapter 14

14-2   Reserves provide the Fed a means of controlling the money supply. It is through increasing and decreasing excess reserves that the Fed is able to achieve a money supply of the size it thinks best for the economy.

Reserves are assets of commercial banks because these funds are cash belonging to them; they are a claim the commercial banks have against the Federal Reserve Bank. These reserves deposited at the Fed are a liability to the Fed because they are funds it owes; they are claims which commercial banks have against it.

Excess reserves = actual reserves − required reserves. Commercial banks can safely lend excess reserves, thereby increasing the money supply.

14-4   Banks create or add to checking account balances when they make loans; these checkable deposits are part of the money supply. People pay off loans by writing checks. Checkable deposits fall, meaning the money supply drops. Money is "destroyed."

14-8   Table data: Column (1) of Assets (top to bottom): $22,000; $38,000; $42,000. Column (2) of Assets (top to bottom): $20,000; $38,000; $42,000. Column (1) of Liabilities: $102,000. Column (2) of Liabilities: $100,000.

(a) $2000; (b) $2000; The bank has lent out its excess reserves, creating $2000 of new demand-deposit money. (c) See column (2) data; (d) Required reserves = $15,000 (= 15% of $100,000). Excess reserves = $7000 (= $22,000 − $15,000). When the bank lends out its excess reserves, the money supply increases by $7000.

14-13   (a) Required reserves = $50 billion (= 25% of $200 billion). Excess reserves = $2 billion (= $52 billion − $50 billion). Maximum amount banking system can loan = $8 billion (= 1/.25 × $2 billion). Column (1) of Assets data (top to bottom): $52 billion; $48 billion; $108 billion. Column (1) of Liabilities data: $208 billion. Monetary multiplier = 4 (1/.25).

(b) Required reserves = $40 billion (= 20% of $200 billion). Excess reserves = $12 billion (= $52 billion − $40 billion). Maximum amount banking system can lend = $60 billion (= 1/.20 × $12 billion). Column (1) data for assets after loans (top to bottom): $52 billion; $48 billion; $160 billion. Column (1) data for liabilities after loans (top to bottom): $260 billion. The decrease in the reserve ratio increases the banking systems' excess reserves from $2 billion to $12 billion and increases the size of the monetary multiplier from 4 to 5.

Chapter 15

15-2 (a) Column (1) data, top to bottom: (Commercial banks) $34; $60; $60; $150; $4; (Fed banks) $60; $4; $34; $3; $27.
(b) Column (2) data: (Commercial banks) $30; $60; $60; $147; $3; (Fed banks) $57; $3; $30; $3; $27.
(c) Column (3) data (top to bottom): $35; $58; $60; $150; $3; (Fed banks) $62; $3; $35; $3; $27.
(d1) Money supply (demand deposits) directly changes only in (b), where it decreases by $3 billion; (d2) See balance sheets; (d3) Money-creating potential of the banking system increases by $5 billion (a); decreases by $12 billion in (b) (not by $15 billion—the sale of $3 billion of bonds to the public reduced demand deposits by $3 billion, thus freeing $0.6 billion of reserves. Three billion dollars − $0.6 billion = $2.4 billion and this multiplied by the monetary multiplier of 5 = $12 billion); and increases by $10 billion in (c).

15-3 (a) Increase the reserve ratio. This would increase the size of required reserves. If the commercial banks were fully loaned up, they would have to call in loans. The money supply would decrease, interest rates would rise, and aggregate demand would decline.
(b) Increase the discount rate. This would decrease commercial bank borrowing from the Fed. Actual reserves of the commercial banks would fall, as would excess reserves and lending. The money supply would drop, interest rates would rise, and aggregate demand would decline.
(c) Sell government securities in the open market. Buyers of the bonds will write checks to the Fed on their demand deposits. When these checks clear, reserves will flow from the banking system to the Fed. The decline in reserves will reduce the money supply, which will increase interest rates and reduce aggregate demand.

15-4 The basic objective of monetary policy is to assist the economy in achieving a full-employment, noninflationary level of total output. Changes in the money supply affect interest rates, which affect investment spending and therefore aggregate demand.
(a) A steep demand for money curve makes monetary policy more effective since the steepness of the curve means that only a relatively small change in the money supply will be needed to produce large changes in interest rates. A relatively flat investment-demand curve means that only a small change in the interest rate will be sufficient to change investment sharply. (b) A high MPC (low MPS) yields a large income multiplier, meaning that a relatively small initial change in spending will multiply into a larger change in GDP.
The increase in GDP resulting from an easy money policy will increase the transactions demand for money, partially offsetting the reduction in the interest rate associated with the initial increase in the money supply. Investment spending, aggregate demand, and GDP will not rise by as much.

15-7 The Federal funds interest rate is the interest rate banks charge one another on overnight loans needed to meet the reserve requirement. The prime interest rate is the interest rate banks charge on loans to their most credit-worthy customers. The tighter the monetary policy, the fewer the excess reserves in the banking system and the higher the Federal funds rate.
The Fed wanted to reduce excess reserves, slowing the growth of the money supply. This would slow the expansion of AD and keep inflation from occurring. The prime interest rate went up.

15-8 The intent of a tight money policy would be shown as a leftward shift of the AD curve and a decline in the price level (or in the real world, a reduction in the rate of inflation). In an open economy, the interest rate hike resulting from the tight money policy would entice people abroad to buy American securities. Because they would need American dollars to buy these securities, the international demand for dollars would rise, causing the dollar to appreciate. Net exports would fall, pushing the AD curve farther leftward than in the closed economy.

Chapter 16

16-1 (a) Classical economists envision the AS curve as being perfectly vertical. When prices fall, real profits would not decrease because wage rates will fall in the same proportion. With constant real profits, firms would have no reason to change the quantities of output they supplied. Keynesians view the AS curve as being horizontal at outputs less than the full-employment output. Declines in aggregate demand in this range do not change the price level because wages and prices are assumed to be inflexible downward.
(b) Classical economists view AD as stable so long as the monetary authorities hold the money supply constant. Therefore inflation and deflation are unlikely. Keynesians view the AD curve as unstable—even if the money supply is constant—since investment spending is volatile. Decreases in AD can cause a recession; rapid increases in AD can cause demand-pull inflation.
Neither model—in these simple forms—is realistic. Wage rates and prices are not perfectly *flexible* downward as the classical vertical AS curve suggests; nor are they completely *inflexible* downward as implied by the Keynesian horizontal AS curve. A more realistic view of the economy would incorporate an AS curve having a horizontal, intermediate, and vertical range.
The Keynesian view of AD seems more realistic than the monetarist's view. Aggregate demand appears to be unstable, sometimes causing recession and other times causing demand-pull inflation.

16-5 (a) Keynesian mechanism: Change in monetary policy; change in commercial bank reserves; change in the money supply; change in the interest rate; change in investment; change in aggregate demand; change in nominal GDP (= PQ).
(b) Monetarists mechanism: Change in monetary policy; change in commercial bank reserves; change in the money supply; change in aggregate demand; change in nominal GDP (= PQ).
Because of the longer and more problematic chain in their transmission mechanism, Keynesians view monetary policy as less reliable than fiscal policy in achieving full-employment, noninflationary GDP. Monetarists believe there is a dependable link between the money supply and nominal GDP. The preferred monetary policy therefore is for the Fed to adhere to a monetary rule: increase the money supply at a constant 3 percent to 5 percent annual rate.

16-12 Refer to Figures 16-5a (Keynesian) and 16-5b (monetarism) and Figure 16-6 (rational expectations). Stabilization policy

—in this case, to increase AD—is highly effective in the Keynesian model; highly inflationary in the monetarist model; and totally ineffective in the rational expectations model.

In the RET model there is never any deviation from full-employment output—all changes in AD are fully anticipated. In the old classical model, there are temporary "lapses" from full employment until market adjustments are complete.

16-13 (b), (c), (d), and (e).

Chapter 17

17-1 To derive the Phillips Curve from the AD-AS model we accept that the AS curve has three ranges: horizontal (or near so), upsloping, and vertical. When the economy moves from its horizontal to upsloping range, there is a tradeoff between more output (or employment) and the price level. The economy can only have more output (and employment) if it is willing to accept a higher price level.

The 1970s saw a succession of supply shocks that destabilized the Phillips Curve and cast doubts on its existence. These included: the quadrupling of world oil prices; decreased agricultural production; depreciation of the dollar; the ending of wage-price controls; and a decline in productivity growth. All these factors shifted the AS curve to the left, causing stagflation—rising unemployment and inflation.

17-2 Check your answer against Figure 17-5 and its legend.

17-7 Check your answer against Figure 17-7a and b and its legend.

17-8 Guideposts are voluntary; controls have the force of law. Controls (1) cause product shortages, resulting in black markets; (2) lead to lowering of product quality to circumvent the controls; (3) result in an inefficient allocation of society's scarce resources.

The few economists who do favor controls see them as useful in ending the inflationary expectations which often propel rapid inflation. A highly credible wage-price control program can convince businesses and labor that large price and wage hikes are not warranted to keep up with inflation since "inflation is under control." Wage and price controls held down—or at least postponed—inflation during World War II. But guideposts and controls applied since then have been largely ineffective.

17-10 The major tenets of supply side economics are: (1) the tax-transfer system negatively affects incentives to work, invest, innovate, and assume entrepreneurial risks; (2) tax cuts can occur without loss of tax revenues; (3) business taxes such as payroll taxes cause higher business costs, reduced employment, and reduced GDP; (4) government regulation of business is excessive.

According to supply side economists, the basic cause of stagflation—leftward shifts of the AS curve—is rising costs and stagnating productivity. High taxes and excessive regulation reduce economic incentives and lower productivity. The AS curve shifts to the left, causing stagflation.

Refer to Figure 17-8. In the graph, the advocates of tax cuts contend the economy is somewhere above m (where tax revenue would be at their maximum). By lowering the tax rate from, say, n to m, the government would increase tax revenues. This increase would occur because the lower tax rate would increase incentives to produce output and earn income. Example: Suppose GDP in an economy is initially $100 billion. At an average tax rate of 30 percent, tax revenues will be $30 billion (= 30% of $30 billion). Now suppose government drops the tax rate to 20 percent and, as a result, the economy expands to $200 billion. The new tax revenue rises to $40 billion (= 20% of $200 billion). Aggregate supply would rise, simultaneously decreasing unemployment and prices. In two words: remedy stagflation.

Chapter 18

18-1 (a) There is practically no potential for using fiscal policy as a stabilization tool under an annually balanced budget. In an economic downturn, tax revenues fall. To keep the budget in balance, fiscal policy would require the government to reduce its spending or increase its tax rates, adding to the deficiency in spending and accelerating the downturn. If the economy were booming and tax revenues were mounting, to keep the budget balanced fiscal policy would have to increase government spending or reduce taxes, thus adding to the already excessive demand and accelerating the inflationary pressures. An annually balanced budget would intensify cyclical ups and downs.

(b) A cyclically balanced budget would be countercyclical, as it should be, since it would bolster demand by lowering taxes and increasing government spending during a recession and restrain demand by raising taxes and reducing government spending during an inflationary boom. However, because boom and bust are not always of equal intensity and duration, budget surpluses during the upswing need not automatically match budget deficits during the downswing. Requiring the budget to be balanced over the cycle may necessitate inappropriate changes in tax rates or levels of government expenditures.

(c) Functional finance pays no attention to the balance of deficits and surpluses annually or over the cycle. What counts is the maintenance of a noninflationary full-employment level of spending. Balancing the economy is what counts, not the budget.

18-3 Two ways of measuring the public debt: (1) measure its absolute size; (2) measure its size as a percentage of GDP.

An internally held debt is one where the bondholders live in the nation having the debt; an externally held debt is one where the bondholders are citizens of other nations. Paying off an internally held debt would involve boosting taxes or reducing other government spending and using the proceeds to buy the government bonds. This would present a problem of income distribution, because holders of the government bonds generally have higher incomes than the average taxpayer. But paying off an internally held debt would not burden the economy as a whole—the money used to pay off the debt would stay within the domestic economy.

In paying off an externally held debt people abroad would use the proceeds of the bonds sales to buy goods from the country paying off its external debt. That nation would have to send some of its output abroad to be consumed by others (with no imported goods in exchange).

Refinancing the public debt simply means rolling over outstanding debt—selling "new" bonds to retire maturing bonds.

18-7 Economists do not view the large public debt as a burden for future generations. Future generations not only inherit the public debt, but they inherit the bonds which constitute the public debt. They also inherit public capital goods, some of which were financed by the debt.

There is one way the debt can be a burden to future generations. Unlike tax financing, debt financing may drive up interest rates, since government must compete with private firms for funds in the bond market. Higher interest rates will crowd out some private investment, resulting in a smaller stock of future capital goods and thus a less productive economy for future generations to inherit.

18-8   Cause and effect chain: Government borrowing to finance the debt competes with private borrowing and drives up the interest rate; the higher interest rate induces an inflow of foreign money to buy the now higher-return American bonds; to buy the bonds, the foreign financiers must first buy dollars; the demand for dollars rises and the dollar appreciates; American exports fall and American imports rise; an American trade deficit results.

The public often blames our large trade deficits on the trade policies of other countries—particularly Japan. But, as noted in the scenario just described, a substantial portion of our large *trade* deficits may have resulted from our policy of running large *budget* deficits for the past decade or more.

The controversial Ricardian equivalence idea contradicts this view. People supposedly anticipate that debt-financed increases in government spending will require higher future taxes. In response, they reduce their present consumption and increase their saving. Because this increase in saving perfectly offsets the increase in government borrowing, the interest rate does not rise and crowding out does not occur. Because interest rates do not change, exchange rates are not affected, and the link between budget deficits and trade deficits is broken.

Chapter 19

19-2   There are four supply factors, a demand factor, and an efficiency factor in explaining economic growth. (1) Supply factors: the quantity and quality of natural resources; the quantity and quality of human resources; the stock of capital goods; and technology. (2) Demand factor: full employment. (3) Efficiency factor: productive and allocative efficiency.

In the long run, a nation must expand its production capacity in order to grow (supply side). But aggregate demand must also expand (demand side) or else the extra capacity will stand idle. Economic growth depends on an enhanced ability to produce *and* a greater willingness to buy.

The supply side of economic growth is illustrated by the outward expansion of the production possibilities curve, as from *AB* to *CD* in Figure 19-1. The demand side of economic growth is shown by the movement from a point on *AB* to an optimal point on *CD*, as from *a* to, say, *b* in the figure.

19-3   Growth rate of real GDP = 4 percent (= $31,200 − $30,000)/$30,000). GDP per capita in year 1 = $300 (= $30,000/100). GDP per capita in year 2 = $305.88 (= $31,200/102). Growth rate of GDP per capita is 1.96 percent = ($305.88 − $300)/$300).

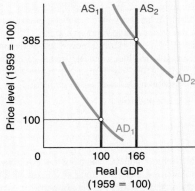

"One Possible Graphical Solution"

In the graph, AD$_1$ and AS$_1$ intersect for 1959 at a price level of 100 and GDP of 100. The 1993 AD$_2$ and AS$_2$ intersect at a price level of 385 (an increase of 285 percent) and at a real GDP of 166 (an increase of 66 percent).

19-5   Increase in labor inputs: 32 percent; increase in labor productivity: 68 percent.

Refer to Table 19-2. Productivity increasing factors in descending order: (1) Technological advance—the discovery of new knowledge which results in the combining of resources in more productive ways. (2) The quantity of capital. (3) Education and training. Since 1940 the proportion of those in the labor force with a high school education has doubled from 40 to 80 percent. And those with a college education have more than doubled from under 10 percent to 20 percent. (4) Economies of scale and (5) improved resource allocation. Workers have been moving out of lower productivity jobs to higher productivity jobs. Part of this is associated with the increased efficiency often derived from production in larger plants where specialization of labor and productivity-increasing methods are possible.

19-8   (1) Investment as percentage of GDP has been relatively weak. (2) A rapid increase in the labor force caused by the surge of women workers enabled firms to expand output without raising output per worker. (3) Average labor quality declined as more inexperienced workers moved into the labor force and as the rate of increase of educational attainment slowed. (4) Expenditures on research and development as a percentage of GDP dropped, slowing technological progress. (5) Adversarial relationships between workers and firms impeded advances in labor productivity.

Consequences of the slowdown: (1) a slower rise in the standard of living; (2) higher inflation; and (3) a decline in American competitiveness overseas.

There are several reasons for optimism about future productivity growth: (1) the most recent productivity growth rates are double the averages of the slowdown years; (2) inflation is now more under control than in the 1970s and stagflation and its investment-depressing effect have not returned; (3) some business taxes have been reduced and some regulatory controls relaxed; (4) R&D has increased as a percentage of GDP; (5) the baby boom flood of labor-force entrants is over and the boomers themselves are now well integrated into the labor force; and (6) labor relations have improved, with a greater emphasis on profit sharing and improved wages through training.

(d) Column (2) data, top to bottom: 0; 0; 5; 6; 7; 8; 9. Column (3) data, top to bottom, in dollars: −60; −60; −55; −39; −8; +63; +144. Column (4) data, top to bottom: 0; 0; 7,500; 9,000; 10,500; 12,000, 13,500.

(e) The firm will not produce if $P <$ AVC. When $P >$ AVC, the firm will produce in the short run at the quantity where $P (=$ MR$)$ is equal to its increasing MC. Therefore, the MC above the AVC curve is the firm's short-run supply curve. It shows the quantity of output the firm will supply at each price level. See Figure 23-6 for a graphical illustration.

(f) Column (4) data, top to bottom: 17,000; 15,000; 13,500; 12,000; 10,500; 9,500; 8,000.

(g) Equilibrium price = $46; equilibrium output = 10,500. Each firm will produce 7 units. Loss per unit = $ 1.14, or $8 per firm. The industry will contract in the long run.

23-8 See Figures 23-8 and 23-9 and their legends. See Figure 23-11 for the supply curve for an increasing cost industry. The supply curve for a decreasing cost industry is below.

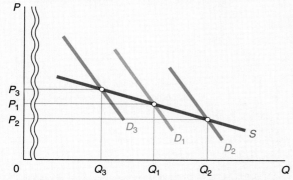

23-10 The equality of P and minimum ATC means the firm is achieving *productive efficiency*. It's using the most efficient technology and employing the least-costly combination of resources. The equality of P and MC means the firm is achieving *allocative efficiency*. It's producing the right product in the right amount based on society's valuation of marginal cost and marginal benefit.

Chapter 24

24-4 The TR curve is derived at each output level by multiplying $P \times Q$. Because TR is increasing at a diminishing rate, MR is declining. When TR turns downward, MR becomes negative. Four units sell for $5.00 each, but three of these four could have been sold for $5.50 had the monopolist been satisfied to sell only three. Having decided to sell four, the monopolist had to lower the price of the first three from $5.50 to $5.00, sacrificing $.50 on each for a total of $1.50. This "loss" of $1.50 explains the difference between the $5.00 price obtained on the fourth unit of output and its marginal revenue of $3.50. The demand curve is elastic from $P = 6.50 to $P = 3.50, a range where TR is rising. The curve is of unitary elasticity at $P = 3.50, where TR is at its maximum. The curve is inelastic from then on as the price continues to decrease and TR is falling. When MR is positive, demand is elastic. When MR is zero, demand is of unitary elasticity. When MR is negative, demand is inelastic. If MC is zero, the monopolist should produce 7 units where MR is also zero. It would never produce where demand is inelastic because MR is negative while MC is positive.

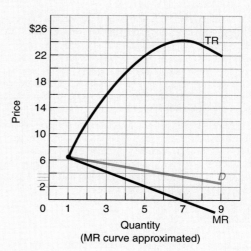

(MR curve approximated)

24-5 Total revenue data, top to bottom, in dollars: 0; 100; 166; 213; 252; 275; 288; 294; 296; 297; 290. Marginal revenue data, top to bottom, in dollars: 100; 66; 47; 39; 23; 13; 6; 2; 1; −7.

   Price = $63; output = 4; profit = $42 [= 4($63 − 52.50)]. Your graph should have the same general appearance as Figure 24-4. At $Q = 4$, TR = $252 and TC = $210 [= 4($52.50)].

24-6 Perfect price discrimination: Output = 6. TR would be $420 (= $100 + $83 + $71 + $63 + $55 + $48). TC would be $285 [= 6($47.50)]. Profit = $135 (= $420 − $285).

   Your single diagram should combine Figures 24-7a and 24-7b in the chapter. The discriminating monopolist faces a demand curve which is also its MR curve. It will sell the first unit at f in Figure 24-7b and then sell each successive unit at lower prices (as shown on the demand curve) as it moves to Q_2 units, where D (= MR) = MC. Discriminating monopolist: Greater output; total revenue, and profits. Some consumers will pay a higher price under discriminating monopoly than with nondiscriminating monopoly; others, a lower price. Good features: greater output and improved allocative efficiency. Bad feature: more income is transferred from consumers to the monopolist.

24-14 No, the proposal doesn't consider that the output of the natural monopolist would still be at the suboptimal level where $P >$ MC. Too little would be produced and an underallocation of resources would result. Theoretically, it would be more desirable to force the natural monopolist to charge a price equal to marginal cost and subsidize any losses. Even setting price equal to ATC would be an improvement over this proposal. This fair-return pricing would allow for a normal profit and ensure a larger production than in the proposal.

Chapter 25

25-2 (a) Less elastic than a pure competitor; (b) more elastic than a pure monopolist. Price is higher and output lower for the monopolistic competitor. Pure competition: $P =$ MC (allocative efficiency); $P =$ minimum ATC (productive efficiency). Monopolistic competition: $P >$ MC (allocative inefficiency) and $P >$ minimum ATC (productive inefficiency). Monopolistic competitors have excess capacity, meaning that fewer firms operating at capacity (where $P =$ minimum ATC) could supply the industry output.

25-6 Traditional view: Advertising is persuasive rather than informative; it enhances monopoly power (makes firms' demand curves less elastic); it creates an entry barrier; and it is the source of waste and inefficiency. New perspective: Advertising is a low-cost source of information for consumers; it increases competition by adding to consumer awareness of substitutes (makes firms' demand curves more elastic); makes entry of new firms easier; and improves economic efficiency.

25-9 Effect (1): Advertising may increase demand, allowing the firm to expand output and achieve economies of scale, meaning a lower ATC. Effect (2): Advertising is a business expense, implying a higher ATC. If (1) > (2), ATC will fall and consumers may benefit through lower prices. If (1) < (2), per unit cost will rise and consumers will likely face higher prices.

Chapter 26

26-3 A concentration ratio of 60 percent means the largest four firms in the industry account for 60 percent of sales; a concentration ratio of 90 percent means the largest four firms account for 90 percent of sales. Shortcomings: (1) they pertain to the nation as a whole, although relevant markets may be localized; (2) they do not account for interindustry competition; (3) the data are for American products—imports are excluded; and (4) they don't reveal the dispersion of size among the top four firms.

26-4 Herfindahl index for A: 2400 (=900 + 900 + 400 + 100 + 100). For B: 4300 (= 3600 + 625 + 25 + 25 + 25). We would expect Industry A to be more competitive than Industry B, where one firm dominates and two firms control 85 percent of the market.

26-5 The matrix shows the four possible profit outcomes for each of two firms, depending on which of two price strategies each follows. Example: If C sets price at $35 and D at $40, C's profits will be $59,000, and D's $55,000.

(a) C and D are interdependent because their profits depend not just on their own price, but also on the other firm's price.
(b) Likely outcome: Both firms will set price at $35. If either charged $40, they would be concerned the other would undercut the price by charging $35. At $35, C's profit would be $55,000; D's, $58,000.
(c) Through price collusion—agreeing to charge $40—each firm would achieve higher profits (C = $57,000; D = $60,000). But once both firms agree on $40, each sees it can increase its profits even more by secretly charging $35 while its rival charges $40.

26-6 Assumptions: (1) Rivals will match price cuts; (2) Rivals will ignore price increases. The gap in the MR curve results from the abrupt change in the slope of the demand curve at the going price. Firms will not change their price because if they do their total revenue and profits will fall. Shortcomings of the model: (1) It does not explain how the going price evolved in the first place; (2) it does not allow for price leadership and other forms of collusion.

Chapter 27

27-2 Marginal product data, top to bottom: 17; 14; 12; 10; 7; 5. Total revenue data, top to bottom: $34; $62; $86; $106; $120; $130. Marginal revenue product data, top to bottom: $34; $28; $24; $20; $14; $10.

(a) Two workers. Because the MRP of the first worker is $34 and MRP of second worker is $28, each MRP exceeding the $27.95 wage. Four workers. Because the MRP of workers 1 through 4 have MRPs exceeding the $19.95 wage. But the fifth's workers MRP is only $14, and will not be hired.
(b) The demand schedule consists of the first and last columns of the table in the question.

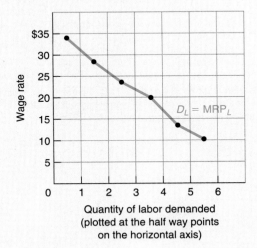

Quantity of labor demanded
(plotted at the half way points
on the horizontal axis)

(c) Reconstruct the table. New product price data, top to bottom: $2.20; $2.15; $2.10; $2.05; $2.00; $1.95. New total revenue data, top to bottom: $37.40; $66.65; $90.30; $108.65; $120.00; $126.75. New marginal revenue product data, top to bottom: $37.40; $29.25; $23.65; $18.35; $11.35; $6.75. The second demand curve is less elastic. Here, MRP falls because of diminishing returns *and* because product price declines as output (and inputs of labor) increase. A decrease in the wage rate will produce less of an increase in the quantity of labor demanded, because the output from the added labor will reduce product price.

27-4 Four factors: the rate at which MP declines; the ease of resource substitutability; elasticity of product demand; and labor cost to total cost ratio.

(a) Increases the demand for C. (b) The price increase for D will increase the demand for C through the *substitution effect,* but decrease the demand for all resources—including C—through the *output effect.* The net effect is uncertain; it depends on which effect outweighs the other. (c) Increases the elasticity of demand for C. (d) Increases the demand for C. (e) Increases the demand for C through the output effect. There is no substitution effect. (f) Reduces the elasticity of demand for C.

27-5 (a) 2 capital; 4 labor. $MP_L/P_L = 7/1$; $MP_C/P_C = 21/3 = 7/1$.
(b) 7 capital and 7 labor. $MRP_L/_L = 1$ (= 1/1) = $MRP_C/P_C = 1$ (= 3/3). Output is 142 (= 96 from capital + 46 from labor). Economic profit is $114 (= $142 − $28).
(c) Yes, least-cost production is part of maximizing profits—the profit-maximizing rule includes the least-cost rule.

27-7 (a) More of both; (b) less labor and more capital; (c) maximum profits obtained; (d) less of both.

Chapter 28

28-3 See Figure 28-3 and its legend.

28-4 Total labor cost data, top to bottom: $0; $14; $28; $42; $56; $70; $84. Marginal resource cost data: $14, throughout.

    (a) The labor supply curve and MRC curve are shown as a single horizontal line at the market wage rate of $14. The firm can employ as much labor as it wants, each unit costing $14.

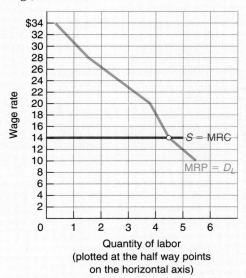

    (b) Equilibrium wage rate = $14; equilibrium level of employment = 4 units of labor. From the tables: MRP exceeds MRC for each of the first four units of labor, but MRP is less than MRC for the fifth unit. Graph: equilibrium is at the intersection of the MRP and MRC curves. (MRP is again plotted half-way between each unit of labor.)

28-6 The monopsonist faces the market labor supply curve S—it is the only firm hiring this labor. MRC lies above S and rises more rapidly than S because all workers get the higher wage rate which is needed to attract the added worker. Equilibrium wage = $12; equilibrium employment = 3. The monopsonist can pay a below-competitive wage rate by restricting its employment.

28-8 The union wage rate becomes the firm's MRC, which we would show as a horizontal line from Wc to S. Each unit of labor now adds only its own wage rate to the firm's costs. The firm will employ Qc workers, where MRP = MRC (= W_c), an increase from the Qm workers it would employ if there were no union.

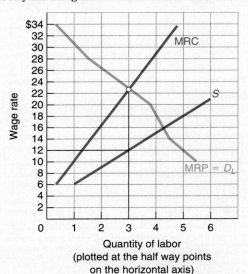

Chapter 29

29-2 Land is completely fixed in total supply. As population expands and the demand for land increases, rent arises and grows. From society's perspective this rent is a surplus—a payment unnecessary for ensuring the land is available to the economy as a whole. If rent declined or disappeared, the same amount of land would be available. If it increased, no more land would be forthcoming. Thus, rent has no incentive function.

    But land does have alternative uses. To get it to its most productive use, individuals and firms compete and the winners are those who pay the highest rent. To the high bidders, rent is a cost of production which must be covered by the revenue gained through the sale of the commodities produced on that land.

29-4 Level of nominal GDP; the interest rate. See Figure 13-2 and its legend. Although the interest rate is an equilibrium price, it is "administered" by the monetary authorities through their ability to establish the location of the money supply curve.

29-6 The nominal interest rate is the interest rate stated in dollars of current value (unadjusted for inflation). The real interest rate is the nominal interest rate adjusted for inflation (or deflation). The real interest rate is relevant for making investment decisions—it reflects the true cost of borrowing money. It is compared to the expected return on the investment in the decision process. Real interest rate = 4 percent (= 12 percent − 8 percent). They saved because if they simply kept their money out of saving accounts, they would have earned no nominal interest at all and the value of their savings would have declined at the full rate of inflation. With inflation at 12 percent and the interest on their savings at, say, 7 percent, these people were losing 5 percent a year. Not good, but better than losing the full 12 percent.

29-8 Business profits (accounting profits) are what remains of a firm's total revenues after it has paid all its explicit costs, these being payments to the factors of production employed by the firm, but not to the resources owned by the business itself. Economists also take into consideration implicit costs—what the owners could have received using the resources they own in some other way. The economist adds these implicit costs to the accountant's explicit costs to arrive at total costs. Subtracting these total costs from total revenue results in a smaller profit (economic profit) than the accountant's business profit.

    Sources of economic profits: (1) uncertainty and risk; (2) uncertainty and innovations; and (3) monopoly.

    (a) Profits from assuming the risks and uncertainties of innovation, as well as the monopoly profits from the patent. (b) Monopoly profits arising from its locational advantage. (c) Profits from bearing the uninsurable risk of a change in demand (the change could have been unfavorable).

Chapter 30

30-1 (a) Private good, top to bottom: $P = \$8$, $Q = 1$; $P = \$7$, $Q = 2$; $P = \$6$, $Q = 4$; $P = \$5$, $Q = 7$; $P = \$4$, $Q = 10$; $P = \$3$, $Q = 13$; $P = \$2$, $Q = 16$; $P = \$1$, $Q = 19$. (b) Public good, top to bottom: $P = \$19$, $Q = 1$; $P = \$16$, $Q = 2$; $P = \$13$, $Q = 3$; $P = \$10$, $Q = 4$; $P = \$7$, $Q = 5$; $P = \$4$, $Q = 6$; $P = \$2$, $Q = 7$; $P = \$1$, $Q = 8$. The first schedule represents a horizontal summation of the individual demand curves; the second schedule represents a vertical summation of these curves. The market demand curve for the private good will determine—in combination with market supply—an actual price-quantity outcome in the marketplace. Because individual preferences are not revealed in the market by potential buyers of public goods, the collective demand curve for the public good is hypothetical or needs to be determined through "willingness to pay" studies.

30-2 Optimal quantity = 4. Because at price $10 the collective willingness to pay for the final unit of the good (= $10) matches the marginal cost of production (= $10).

30-3 Program B, since the marginal benefit no longer exceeds marginal cost for programs which are larger in scope. Plan B is where net benefits—the excess of total benefits over total costs—are maximized.

30-4 Spillover costs are called negative externalities because they are *external* to the participants in the transaction and *reduce* the utility of affected third parties (thus "negative"). Spillover benefits are called positive externalities because they are *external* to the participants in the transaction and *increase* the utility of affected third parties (thus "positive"). See Figures 30-3 and 30-4. Compare (b) and (c) in Figure 30-4.

30-7 The low marginal benefit from reducing water flow from storm drains would mean the MB curve would be located far to the left of where it is in the text diagram. It will intersect the MC curve at a low amount of pollution abatement, indicating the optimal amount of pollution abatement (where MB = MC) is low. Any cyanide in public water sources could be deadly. Therefore, the marginal benefit of reducing cyanide would be extremely high and the MB curve in the figure would be shifted to the extreme right where it would intersect the MC curve at or near 100 percent.

30-13 Moral hazard problem: (b) and (d). Adverse selection problem: (a), (c), and (e).

Chapter 31

31-2 The paradox is that majority voting does not always provide a clear and consistent picture of the public's preferences. Here the courthouse is preferred to the school and the park is preferred to the courthouse, so we would surmise that the park is preferred to the school. But in fact the school is preferred to the park.

31-3 Project B (small reservoir wins). There are no "vote order" problems here and B is the preference of the median voter. The two voters favoring No reservoir and Levees, respectively, will prefer Small reservoir—project B—to Medium or Large reservoir. The two voters preferring Large reservoir or Medium reservoir will prefer Small reservoir to Levees or No reservoir. The median voter's preference for B will prevail. However, the optimal size of the project from an economic perspective is C—it would provide greater net benefits to society than B.

31-6 The electorate is faced with a small number of candidates, each of whom offers a broad range or "bundle" of proposed policies. Voters are then forced to choose the individual candidate whose bundle of policies most resembles their own. The chances of a perfect identity between a particular candidate's preferences and those of any voter are quite slim. As a result, the voter must purchase some unwanted public goods and services. This represents an inefficient allocation of resources.

Government bureaucracies do not function on the basis of profit, reducing the incentive for public servants to hold down costs. Because there is no market test of profits and losses, it is difficult to determine whether public agencies are operating efficiently. Nor is there entry of competing entities to stimulate efficiency and develop improved public goods and services. Also, wasteful expenditures can be maintained through the self-seeking lobbying of bureaucrats themselves, and the public budgetary process can reward rather than penalize inefficiency.

31-9 Average tax rates: 20; 15; and 13.3 percent. Regressive tax.

31-11 The incidence of an excise tax is likely to be primarily on consumers when demand is highly inelastic and primarily on producers when demand is elastic. The more elastic the supply, the greater the incidence of tax on consumers.

The efficiency loss of a sales or excise tax is the net benefit society sacrifices because consumption and production of the taxed product are reduced below the allocatively efficient level which would occur without the tax. Other things equal, the greater the elasticities of demand and supply, the greater the efficiency loss of a particular tax.

Chapter 32

32-2 Sherman Act: Section 1 prohibits conspiracies to restrain trade; Section 2 outlaws monopolization. Clayton Act (as amended): Section 2 outlaws price discrimination; Section 3 forbids exclusive or tying contracts; Section 7 prohibits mergers which substantially lessen competition; Section 8 prohibits interlocking directorates. The acts are enforced by the Department of Justice and Federal Trade Commission. Also, private firms can bring suit against other firms under these laws.

32-5 (a) They would block this horizontal merger (violation of Section 7 of the Clayton Act). (b) They would charge these firms with price fixing (violation of Section 1 of the Sherman Act). (c) They would allow this vertical merger, unless both firms had very large market shares. (d) They would allow this conglomerate merger.

32-10 Industries composed of natural monopolies subject to significant economies of scale. Regulation based on "fair-return" prices creates disincentives for firms to minimize costs, since cost reductions lead regulators to force firms to charge a lower price. Regulated firms may also use "creative" accounting to boost costs and hide profits. Because regulatory commissions depend on information provided by the firms themselves and commission members are often recruited from the industry, the agencies may in effect be controlled by the firms they are supposed to oversee. Also, industrial regulation sometimes is applied to industries which are not natural monopolies. Because the calculation of a fair return is based on the value of the firm's capital, there is an incentive for regulated natural monopolies to increase allowable profits by uneconomically substituting capital for labor.

32-12 Unlike industrial regulation—which concentrates on prices and service in specific industries—social regulation deals with the broader impact of business on consumers, workers, and third parties. Benefits: increased worker and product safety; less environmental damage; reduced economic discrimination. Two types of costs: administrative costs and compliance costs. Regulations must be administered by costly government agencies. The firms must increase spending to comply with the regulatory rules.

32-14 Industrial policy consists of direct government actions to promote technological advance and economic growth through subsidies to specific firms or industries. Antitrust, industrial, and social regulation restrict the conduct of firms, often increasing their costs or reducing their revenues. In contrast, industrial policy enhances profits—targeted firms view it favorably. Example: $1 billion Federal government plan to help American firms compete with Japan in developing flat-panel computer screens. Proponents contend industrial policy strengthens critical industries, speeds development of new technologies, increases labor productivity, and strengthens international competitiveness. Opponents charge that industrial policy substitutes the whims of politicians and bureaucrats for the hard scrutiny of entrepreneurs and business executives. They also point to failures of past industrial policies.

Chapter 33

33-1 First sentence: the supply curve is shifting (*a change in supply*) along a relevant inelastic demand curve, producing a large change in equilibrium price and a modest change in equilibrium quantity. Second sentence: the demand curve is shifting along a relevant inelastic short-run supply curve, causing a large change in price and a small change in *quantity supplied*.

Being volatile from one year to the next, exports increase the instability of demand for farm products.

33-3 (a) Because the demand for most farm products is inelastic, the frequent fluctuations in supply brought about by weather and other factors have relatively small effects on quantity demanded, but large effects on equilibrium prices of farm products. Farmers' sales revenues and incomes therefore are unstable. (b) Technological innovations have decreased production costs, increased long-run supply for most agricultural goods, and reduced the prices of farm output. These declines in prices have put a downward pressure on farm income. (c) The modest long-run growth in the demand for farm products has not been sufficient to offset the expansion of supply, resulting in stagnant farm income. (d) Because the number of producers in most agricultural markets is high, it is difficult if not impossible for producers to collude as a way to limit supply and lessen fluctuations in prices and incomes or halt their long-run declines.

33-8 Parity ratio = .73 (= 120/165). This ratio shows that prices received by farmers relative to prices paid by them have decreased on average by just over one quarter since the base period used to construct the price indexes. If farm output were the same in the base period, farmers' real income would also have declined by 27 percent.

33-9 Price supports benefit farmers, harm consumers, impose costs on society, and contribute to problems in world agriculture. Farmers benefit because the prices they receive and the output they produce will both increase, expanding their gross incomes. Consumers lose because prices they pay for agricultural goods rise and quantities purchased decline. Society as a whole bears several

costs. Surpluses of farm products will have to be bought and stored, leading to a greater burden on taxpayers. Domestic economic efficiency is lessened as the artificially high prices of farm products leads to an overallocation of resources to agriculture. The environment suffers: the greater use of pesticides and fertilizers contributes to water pollution; farm policies discourage crop rotation; and price supports encourage farming of environmentally sensitive land. The efficient use of world resources is also distorted because of the import tariffs or quotas which such programs often require. Finally, domestic overproduction leads to supply increases in international markets, decreasing prices and causing a decline in the gross incomes of foreign producers.

Chapter 34

34-2 In this simple economy each person represents a complete income quintile—20 percent of the total population. The richest quintile (Al) receives 50 percent of total income; the poorest quintile (Ed) receives 5 percent.

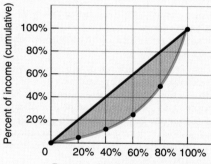

34-5 There are three broad reasons for income inequality: unequal personal endowments; differences in individual character; and external social factors. The first is largely a matter of luck—some people possess high intelligence, particular talents, or physical dexterity which allow them to earn high incomes. Also, they may inherit property or be aided by the social status and financial resources of their parents. The second reason involves personal initiative—individuals may be willing to undergo costly training, accept risk, or tolerate unpleasant working conditions in the expectation of higher pay. They may also show high personal initiative on the job. The third factor relates to society as a whole. Market power and discrimination are two important social determinants of income inequality.

A high IQ normally does not lead to high income unless it is combined with personal initiative and favorable social circumstances. Inherited property—as long as it is competently managed—provides income irrespective of one's character and personal attributes. Both factors are largely a matter of luck to the recipient.

34-11 (a) Plan 1: Basic benefit = $4,000; benefit-reduction rate = 50 percent; break-even income = $8,000 (= $4,000/.5). Plan 2: Basic benefit = $4,000; benefit-reduction rate = 25 percent; break-even income = $16,000 (= $4,000/.25). Plan 3: Basic benefit = $8,000; benefit-reduction rate = 50 percent; break-even income = $16,000 (= $8,000/.5).
(b) Plan 3 is the most costly. Plan 1 is the least costly. Plan 3 is most effective in reducing poverty (although it has a higher benefit-reduction rate than Plan 2, its basic benefit is higher). Plan 1 is least effective in reducing poverty. Plan

3 has the strongest disincentive to work (although it has the same benefit-reduction rate as Plan 1, its higher basic benefit discourages work). Plan 2 has the weakest disincentives to work (its basic benefit level and benefit-reduction rate are low).

(c) The only way to eliminate poverty is to provide a basic benefit high enough to lift everyone from poverty, including people who cannot work or choose not to work. But this large basic benefit reduces the incentive to work, expands the number of people receiving income supplements, and substantially boosts the overall program costs.

Chapter 35

35-2   The "twin problems" are rising costs for all and limited access (lack of insurance) for about 15 percent of the population. The problems are related since rising costs make insurance unaffordable for many individuals and families and make it difficult for some businesses to insure their workers.

35-7   Income elasticity is 1.0, suggesting that health care spending will rise proportionally with incomes. Price elasticity is only 0.2, meaning higher prices for health care services will increase total health care spending.

35-10   Health care insurance removes or greatly lessens a person's budget constraint at the time health care is purchased, causing an overconsumption of health care. (See Figure 35-3b.) Insurance reduces the price of health care at the time of purchase from P_u to P_i, increasing the quantity consumed from Q_u to Q_i. At Q_i the marginal cost of health care is $Q_i b$ which exceeds the marginal benefit of $Q_i c$, indicating an overallocation of resources. The efficiency loss is area *cab*.

Chapter 36

36-1   The growth in union membership before the 1930s was restricted by the strong antiunion sentiments of business and the judiciary. The business community was allowed to use antiunion techniques such as yellow-dog contracts which forced workers to agree to permanent nonunion status.

In the depression years of the 1930s, unions were encouraged through the Norris-LaGuardia and Wagner Acts. The first restricted the use of injunctions and the second guaranteed the right to organize and bargain collectively, and forbade specific antiunion activities by management. Also, in the 1930s and 1940s unions successfully organized major mass production industries such as autos and steel. Total union membership surged from 3.5 million in 1930 to more than 16 million in 1950.

36-7   The higher wages which unions achieve reduce employment, displace workers, and increase the marginal revenue product in the union sector. Labor supply will increase in the nonunionized sector, reducing wages and decreasing marginal revenue product there. Because of the lower marginal revenue product, the workers added in the nonunion sector will contribute less to GDP than they would have in the unionized sector. The gain of GDP in the nonunionized sector will not offset the loss of GDP in the unionized sector, causing an efficiency loss.

36-10   See Figure 36-3. Discrimination against women in two of the three occupations will crowd women into the third occupation. The labor supply curve in the "men's occupations" (X and Y) shift to the left, making them high-wage occupations. The labor supply curve in the "women's occupation" (Z) shifts to the right, creating a low-wage occupation.

Eliminating occupational segregation would entice women into the high-wage occupations, increasing labor supply there and reducing it in the low-wage occupation. The wage rates in the three occupations would converge to B. Women would gain, men would lose. Society would gain, because the increase in GDP in the expanding occupations would exceed the loss of GDP in the contracting occupation.

Decisions relating to education and job duration have differed for men and women because of the larger role women traditionally have played in child-rearing. On average, men have higher levels of education and more years of work experience than women. Therefore, part of the pay gap between men and women reflects different choices.

36-11   See Figure 36-4. Migration of labor from the low- to high-income country increases labor supply in the high-income country and decreases it in the low-income country. Wages are equalized at W_e. Output and business income increase in the receiving country; decline in the sending country. World output increases—the GDP gain in the receiving country exceeds the GDP loss in the sending country.

(a) The gains to the receiving country will not materialize if the migrants are unemployed. (b) Remittances to their home country will decrease the income gain in the receiving country and reduce the income loss in the sending country. (c) If migrants who return to their home country have enhanced skills, their temporary departure might be to the long-run advantage of the home country. (d) Besides increasing income in the receiving country, young skilled migrants will likely be net taxpayers in the receiving country. Older or less skilled workers who are not so easily assimilated could be net recipients of government services.

In view of the sometimes large investments which sending countries have made in providing education and skills, there is a justification for levying a departure tax on such migrants. But if this tax were too high, it would infringe with a basic human right —the right to emigrate.

Chapter 37

37-4   (a) New Zealand's domestic opportunity cost of 1 plum = 4 apples (or 1 apple = $\frac{1}{4}$ plum). Spain's domestic opportunity cost of 1 plum = 1 apple (or 1 apple = 1 plum).

(b) New Zealand should specialize in apples; Spain in plums.

(c)

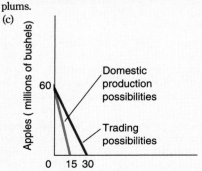

(a) New Zealand

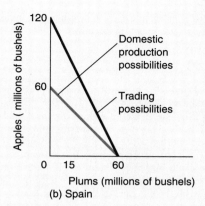

(b) Spain

(d) Before specialization and trade: 40 apples (20 + 20) and 50 plums (10 + 40). After specialization and trade: 60 apples and 60 plums. Gain = 20 apples and 10 plums.

37-6 At $1: import 15,000. At $2: import 7,000. At $3: no imports or exports. At $4: export 6,000. At $5: export 10,000.

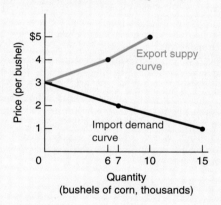

(bushels of corn, thousands)

The world price must be between the $3 American domestic price and the $4 French domestic price. The United States will export corn to France.

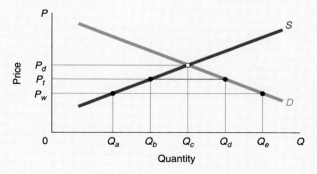

37-7 The world price Pw is below the domestic price Pd. Imports will reduce the price to Pw, increasing consumption from Qc to Qe and decreasing domestic production from Qc to Qa. A tariff of $PwPt$ (a) harms domestic consumers by increasing price from Pw to Pt and decreasing consumption from Qe to Qd; (b) aids domestic producers through the increase in price from Pw to Pt and

the expansion of domestic production from Qa to Qb; (c) harms foreign exporters by decreasing exports from $QaQe$ to $QbQd$.

An import quota of $QbQd$ would have the same effects as the tariff, but there would be no tariff revenues to government from these imports; this revenue is in effect transferred to foreign producers.

37-11 The major portion of the costs of trade protection is borne by consumers through price increases. Prices of imported goods rise, decreasing levels of competition for domestic firms producing similar goods and allowing them to increase their prices. Prices of products using these goods as inputs also rise. Prices of all other goods increase as consumer spending patterns change. Also, resources are reallocated from more-efficient to less-efficient domestic industries.

The main benefit of protectionist policies is greater profits for the protected firms. Government also benefits from the tariff revenues. But empirical studies find that costs of protectionism greatly exceed benefits, resulting in a large net cost—or efficiency loss—to society.

Chapter 38

38-2 A demand for francs is created in (a), (c), and (f). A supply of francs is created in (b), (d), (e), and (g).

38-3 Balance of trade = $10 billion surplus (= merchandise exports of $40 billion minus merchandise imports of $30 billion). Balance of goods and services = $15 billion surplus (= $55 billion of exports of goods and services minus $40 billion of imports of goods and services). Balance on current account = $20 billion surplus (= credits of $65 billion minus debits of $45 billion). Balance on capital account = $30 billion deficit (= capital inflows of $10 billion minus capital outflows of $40 billion). Balance of payments deficit of $10 billion (= $10 billion decrease in official reserves).

38-6 The American demand for pesos is downsloping when the dollar price of pesos is used as the relevant exchange rate. As the peso depreciates relative to the dollar, Americans find that Mexican goods and services are less expensive in dollar terms and purchase more of them, demanding a greater quantity of pesos in the process. The supply of pesos to Americans is upsloping because as the peso appreciates relative to the dollar, American goods and services become cheaper to Mexicans in peso terms. Mexicans buy more dollars, supplying a larger quantity of pesos.

The peso appreciates in (a), (f), (g), and (h) and depreciates in (b), (c), (d), and (e).

38-13 A decline in the Federal budget deficit will cause real interest rates to fall (the crowding-out effect in reverse), decreasing foreign financial investment in the United States, and reducing the international value of the dollar. This depreciation eventually will increase American exports and reduce imports, diminishing the size of the merchandise trade deficit.

Trade deficits fall during recessions because national income declines and consumers buy fewer domestic and imported goods. Our exports do not decline; they depend on other nations' income, not our own. The result of the decline in imports is a lower trade deficit. Economists would not propose a recession as a remedy for trade deficits. This "cure" is worse than the "disease."

Chapter 39

39-3 Rise in per capita output gap = $135 (= 3% × $5000 − 3% × $500).

39-6 Demographic transition view: Expanded output and income in LDCs will result in lower birthrates and slower growth of population. As incomes of primary family members expand, they begin to see extra children as "liabilities," not "assets." The policy emphasis should therefore be on economic growth. Traditional view: Less developed nations should reduce population growth as a first priority. Slow population growth enables the growth of per capita income.

39-8 Capital earns a higher return where it is scarce, *other things equal*. But, when comparing investment opportunities between IACs and LDCs, other things aren't equal. Advanced factories filled with specialized equipment require a productive work force. IACs have an abundance of educated, experienced workers; these workers are scarce in LDCs. Also, IACs have extensive public infrastructures which increase the returns on private capital. Example: a network of highways makes it more profitable to produce goods which need to be widely transported. Finally, investment returns must be adjusted for risk. IACs have stable governments and "law and order," reducing the risk of capital being "nationalized" or pilfered by organized crime.

39-14 To describe countries such as Japan and South Korea, we would need to change labels on three boxes, leading to a change in the "results" boxes. "Rapid" population growth would change to "low" rate of population growth; "low" level of saving would change to "high" level of saving; "low" levels of investment in physical and human capital would change to "high" levels of investment in physical and human capital. These three changes would result in higher productivity and higher per capita income, which would produce a rising level of demand. Other factors: stable national government; homogeneous population; extensive investment in infrastructure; "will to develop"; strong private incentives.

Chapter 40

40-7 See Figure 40-1 in the text. Because prices were set by government and not allowed to change as supply or demand shifted, prices were below the market equilibrium for most goods and services. When the fixed price, *Pf*, is below the equilibrium price, *Pe*, there will be a shortage since the quantity demanded will exceed the quantity supplied. As fixed prices are abolished, they will rise to their significantly higher equilibrium levels, contributing to rapid inflation. Black markets are common where prices are fixed below equilibrium levels. People can buy goods at the fixed government prices (or pay off clerks to save such goods to sell to them), and because of the shortages at the low fixed price, resell these goods at a much higher price to those unable to find the goods in the government stores at controlled prices. Official attempts to interfere with the market mechanism often lead to an unofficial market system which is called the black market.

40-8 Privatization of state-owned property and enterprises; promotion of competition by "demonopolizing" the huge state-run enterprises; reduction of the government's role as owner, manager, price-setter, and production planner; removal of price controls; joining the global economy; achieving macroeconomic stability; and altering entrenched anticapitalist attitudes. Because these changes are interlinked, they need to be accomplished more or less simultaneously. Example: If price controls are lifted without competition or privatization, there is no incentive for producers to expand output. Rather there is incentive to behave like monopolists and take the higher price without expanding supply. Second example: Greater competition requires opening the economy to world trade and foreign investment.

GLOSSARY

A

Ability-to-pay principle The belief that those who have greater income (or wealth) should be taxed absolutely and relatively more than those who have less.

Abstraction Elimination of irrelevant and noneconomic facts to obtain an economic principle.

Acreage-allotment program The program which determines the total number of acres to be used in producing various agricultural products and allocates these acres among individual farmers who are required to limit their plantings to the number of acres allotted if they wish to obtain the support price for their crops.

Actual budget The amount spent by the Federal government (to purchase goods and services and for transfer payments) less the amount of tax revenue collected by it in any (fiscal) year; and which can *not* reliably be used to determine whether it is pursuing an expansionary or contractionary fiscal policy. Compare (*see*) the Full-employment budget.

Actual deficit The size of the Federal government's Budget deficit (*see*) actually measured or recorded in any given year.

Actual investment The amount which business Firms do invest; equal to Planned investment plus Unplanned investment.

Actual reserves The funds which a Member bank has on deposit at the Federal Reserve Bank of its district (plus its Vault cash).

Adaptive expectations theory The idea that people determine their expectations about future events (for example, inflation) on the basis of past and present events (rates of inflation) and only change their expectations as events unfold.

Adjustable pegs The device used in the Bretton Woods system (*see*) to change Exchange rates in an orderly way to eliminate persistent payments deficits and surpluses: each nation defined its monetary unit in terms of (pegged it to) gold or the dollar, kept the Rate of exchange for its money stable in the short run, and changed (adjusted) it in the long run when faced with international disequilibrium.

Adverse selection problem A problem arising when information known to one party to a contract is not known to the other party, causing the latter to incur major costs. Example: Individuals who have the poorest health are more likely to buy health insurance.

AFDC (*See* Aid to families with dependent children.)

Aggregate demand A schedule or curve which shows the total quantity of goods and services demanded (purchased) at different price levels.

Aggregate demand–aggregate supply model The macroeconomic model which uses Aggregate demand and Aggregate supply (*see* both) to determine and explain the Price level and the real Domestic output.

Aggregate expenditures The total amount spent for final goods and services in the economy.

Aggregate expenditures–domestic output approach Determination of the Equilibrium gross domestic product (*see*) by finding the real GDP at which aggregate expenditures are equal to the Domestic output.

Aggregate expenditures schedule A schedule or curve showing the total amount spent for final goods and services at different levels of GDP.

Aggregate supply A schedule or curve showing the total quantity of goods and services supplied (produced) at different Price levels.

Aggregation Combining individual units or data into one unit or number. For example, all prices of individual goods and services are combined into a Price level, or all units of output are aggregated into Real gross domestic product.

Agricultural Adjustment Act The Federal act of 1933 which established the Parity concept (*see*) as the cornerstone of American agricultural policy and provided Price supports for farm products, restriction of agricultural production, and the disposal of surplus output.

Aid to families with dependent children (AFDC) A state-administered and partly federally funded program in the United States which provides aid to families in which dependent children do not have the support of a parent because of his or her death, disability, or desertion.

Alcoa case A 1945 case in which the courts ruled the possession of monopoly power, no matter how reasonably that power had been used, was a violation of the antitrust laws; and which overturned the Rule of reason (*see*) applied in the U.S. Steel case (*see*).

Allocative efficiency The apportionment of resources among firms and industries to obtain the production of the products most wanted by society (consumers); the output of each product at which its Marginal cost and Price or Marginal benefit are equal.

American Federation of Labor (AFL) The organization of affiliated Craft unions formed in 1886.

Annually balanced budget The equality of government expenditures and tax collections during a year.

Anticipated inflation Inflation (*see*) at a rate equal to the rate expected in that period of time.

Applied economics (*See* Policy economics.)

Appreciation of the dollar An increase in the value of the dollar relative to the currency of another nation; a dollar now buys a larger amount of the foreign currency. For example, if the dollar price of a British pound changes from $3 to $2, the dollar has appreciated.

"Asian tigers" The newly industrialized and rapidly growing nations of Hong Kong, Singapore, South Korea, and Taiwan.

Asset Anything of monetary value owned by a firm or individual.

Asset demand for money The amount of money people want to hold as a Store of value (the amount of their financial assets they wish to have in the form of Money); and which varies inversely with the Rate of interest.

Asymmetric information A situation where a seller (buyer) has much more information about a product or service than does the buyer (seller).

Authoritarian capitalism An economic system in which property resources are privately owned and government extensively directs and controls the economy.

Average fixed costs A Firm's total Fixed cost (*see*) divided by output (the quantity of product produced).

Average product The total output produced per unit of a resource employed (total product divided by the quantity of a resource employed).

Average propensity to consume Fraction of Disposable income which households spend for consumer goods and services; consumption divided by Disposable income.

Average propensity to save Fraction of Disposable income which households save; Saving divided by Disposable income.

Average revenue Total revenue from the sale of a product divided by the quantity of the product sold (demanded); equal to the price at which the product is sold so long as all units of the product are sold at the same price.

Average tax rate Total tax paid divided by total (taxable) income; the tax rate on total (taxable) income.

Average total cost A Firm's total cost divided by output (the quantity of product produced); equal to Average fixed cost (*see*) plus Average variable cost (*see*).

Average variable cost A Firm's total Variable cost (*see*) divided by output (the quantity of product produced).

B

Backflows The return of workers to the countries from which they originally migrated.

Balanced-budget amendment Proposed constitutional amendment which would require Congress to balance the Federal budget annually.

Balanced budget multiplier The effect of equal increases (decreases) in government spending for goods and services and in taxes is to increase (decrease) the Equilibrium gross domestic product by the amount of the equal increases (decreases).

Balance of payments deficit The sum of the Balance on current account (*see*) and the Balance on the capital account (*see*) is negative.

Balance of payments surplus The sum of the Balance on current account (*see*) and the Balance on the capital account (*see*) is positive.

Balance on current account The exports of goods (merchandise) and services of a nation less its imports of goods (merchandise) and services plus its Net investment income and Net transfers.

Balance on goods and services The exports of goods (merchandise) and services of a nation less its imports of goods (merchandise) and services.

Balance on the capital account The Capital inflows (*see*) of a nation less its Capital outflows (*see*).

Balance sheet A statement of the Assets (*see*), Liabilities (*see*), and Net worth (*see*) of a firm or individual at some given time.

Bank deposits The deposits which banks have at the Federal Reserve Banks (*see*).

Bankers' bank A bank which accepts the deposits of and makes loans to Depository institutions; a Federal Reserve Bank.

Bank reserves Bank reserves held at the Federal Reserve Banks (*see*) plus bank Vault cash (*see*).

Barrier to entry Anything that artificially prevents the entry of Firms into an industry.

Barter The exchange of one good or service for another good or service.

Base year The year with which prices in other years are compared when a Price index (*see*) is constructed.

Benefit-cost analysis Deciding whether to employ resources and the quantity of resources to employ for a project or program (for the production of a good or service) by comparing the marginal benefits with the marginal costs.

Benefit-reduction rate The percentage by which subsidy benefits in a Negative income tax plan (*see*) are reduced as earned income rises.

Benefits-received principle The belief that those who receive the benefits of goods and services provided by government should pay the taxes required to finance them.

Big business A business Firm which either produces a large percentage of the total output of an industry, is large (in terms of number of employees or stockholders, sales, assets, or profits) compared with other Firms in the economy, or both.

Bilateral monopoly A market in which there is a single seller (Monopoly) and a single buyer (Monopsony).

Board of Governors The seven-member group that supervises and controls the money and banking system of the United States; formally, the Board of Governors of the Federal Reserve System; the Federal Reserve Board.

Brain drain The emigration of highly educated, highly skilled workers from a country.

Break-even income The level of Disposable income at which Households plan to consume (spend) all of their income and to save none of it; also denotes that level of earned income at which subsidy payments become zero in an income maintenance program.

Break-even point Any output which a (competitive) Firm might produce at which its Total cost and Total revenue would be equal; an output at which it has neither an Economic profit nor a loss.

Bretton Woods system The international monetary system developed after World War II in which Adjustable pegs (*see*) were employed, the International Monetary Fund (*see*) helped to stabilize Foreign exchange rates, and gold and the dollar (*see*) were used as International monetary reserves (*see*).

Budget deficit The amount by which the expenditures of the Federal government exceed its revenues in any year.

Budget line A line which shows the different combinations of two products a consumer can purchase with a specific money income.

Budget restraint The limit the size of the consumer's income (and the prices that must be paid for the goods and services) imposes on the ability of an individual consumer to obtain goods and services.

Budget surplus The amount by which the revenues of the Federal government exceeds its expenditures in any year.

Built-in stability The effect of Nondiscretionary fiscal policy (*see*) on the economy; when Net taxes vary directly with the Gross domestic product, the fall (rise) in Net taxes during a recession (inflation) lessens unemployment (inflationary pressures).

Business cycle Recurrent ups and downs over a period of years in the level of economic activity.

Business unionism Labor unionism which concerns itself with such practical and short-run objectives as higher wages, shorter hours, and improved working conditions.

C

Capital Human-made resources (machinery and equipment) used to produce goods and services; goods which do not directly satisfy human wants; capital goods.

Capital account The section in a nation's International balance of payments (*see*) in which are recorded the Capital inflows (*see*) and the Capital outflows (*see*) of that nation.

Capital account deficit A negative Balance on the capital account (*see*).

Capital account surplus A positive Balance on the capital account (*see*).

Capital flight The transfer of savings from less developed to industrially advanced countries to avoid government expropriation, taxation, and high rates of inflation or to realize better investment opportunities.

Capital gain The gain realized when securities or properties are sold for a price greater than the price paid for them.

Capital goods (*See* Capital.)

Capital inflow The expenditures made by the residents of foreign nations to purchase real and financial capital from the residents of a nation.

Capital-intensive commodity A product which requires a relatively large amount of Capital to produce.

Capital outflow The expenditures made by the residents of a nation to purchase real and financial capital from the residents of foreign nations.

Capital-saving technological advance An improvement in technology that permits a greater quantity of a product to be produced with a specific amount of Capital (or the same amount of the product to be produced with a smaller amount of Capital).

Capital-using technological advance An improvement in technology that requires the use of a greater amount of Capital to produce a specific quantity of a product.

Cartel A formal written or oral agreement among Firms to set the price of a product and the outputs of the individual firms or to divide the market for the product geographically.

Causation A cause-and-effect relationship; one or several events bring about or result in another event.

CEA (*See* Council of Economic Advisers.)

Cease-and-desist order An order from a court or government agency (commission or board) to a corporation or individual to stop engaging in a specified practice.

Ceiling price (*See* Price ceiling.)

Celler-Kefauver Act The Federal act of 1950 which amended the Clayton Act (*see*) by prohibiting the acquisition of the assets of one firm by another firm when the effect would be to lessen competition.

Central bank A bank whose chief function is the control of the nation's money supply.

Central economic planning Government determination of the objectives of the economy and the direction of its resources to the attainment of these objectives.

***Ceteris paribus* assumption** (*See* "Other things equal" assumption.)

Change in amount consumed Increase or decrease in consumption spending that results from an increase or decrease in Disposable income, the Consumption schedule (curve) remaining unchanged; movement from one row (point) to another on the same Consumption schedule (curve).

Change in amount saved Increase or decrease in Saving that results from an increase or decrease in Disposable income, the Saving schedule (curve) remaining unchanged; movement from one row (point) to another on the same Saving schedule (curve).

Change in the consumption schedule An increase or decrease in consumption at each level of Disposable income caused by changes in the Nonincome determinants of consumption and saving (*see*); an upward or downward movement of the Consumption schedule.

Change in the saving schedule An increase or decrease in Saving at each level of Disposable income caused by changes in the Nonincome determinants of consumption and saving (*see*); an upward or downward movement of the Saving schedule.

Checkable deposit Any deposit in a commercial bank or Thrift institution against which a check may be written; includes Demand deposits and NOW, ATS, and share draft accounts.

Checking account A Checkable deposit (*see*) in a Commercial bank or Thrift institution.

Circular flow of income The flow of resources from Households to Firms and of products from Firms to Households accompanied in an economy using money by flows of money from Households to Firms and from Firms to Households.

Classical economics The Macroeconomic generalizations accepted by most economists before the 1930s which led to the conclusion that a capitalistic economy would employ its resources fully.

Clayton Act The Federal antitrust act of 1914 which strengthened the Sherman Act (*see*) by making it illegal for business firms to engage in certain specified practices.

Clean Air Act of 1990 Legislation to deal with air pollution, urban smog, motor vehicle emissions, ozone depletion, and acid rain.

Closed economy An economy which neither exports nor imports goods and services.

Close-down case The circumstance in which a Firm would experience a loss greater than its total Fixed cost if it were to produce any output greater than zero; alternatively, a situation in which a firm would cease to operate when the price at which it can sell its product is less than its Average variable cost.

Closed shop A place of employment where only workers who are already members of a labor union may be hired.

Coase theorem The idea that Externality problems may be resolved through private negotiations of the affected parties.

Coincidence of wants The item (good or service) which one trader wishes to obtain is the same as another trader desires to give up and the item which the second trader wishes to acquire is the same as the first trader desires to surrender.

COLA (*See* Cost-of-living adjustment.)

Collection of checks The process by which funds are transferred from the checking accounts of the writers of checks to the checking accounts of the recipients of the checks; also called the "clearing" of checks.

Collective voice The function a union performs for its members as a group when it communicates their problems and grievances to management and presses management for a satisfactory resolution.

Collusion A situation in which Firms act together and in agreement (collude) to set the price of the product and the output each firm will produce or to determine the geographic area in which each firm will sell.

Collusive oligopoly Occurs when the few firms comprising an oligopolistic industry reach an explicit or unspoken agreement to fix prices, divide a market, or otherwise restrict competition; may be a Cartel (*see*), Gentleman's agreement (*see*), or Price leadership (*see*).

Command economy   An economic system (method of organization) in which property resources are publicly owned and Central economic planning (*see*) is used to direct and coordinate economic activities.

Commercial bank   Firm which has a charter from either a state government or the Federal government to engage in the business of banking.

Commercial banking system   All Commercial banks and Thrift institutions as a group.

Communism   (*See* Command economy.)

Comparable worth doctrine   The belief that women should receive the same salaries (wages) as men when the levels of skill, effort, and responsibility in their different jobs are the same.

Comparative advantage   A lower relative or Comparative cost (*see*) than another producer.

Comparative cost   The amount by which one product must be reduced to increase the production of another product; Opportunity cost (*see*).

Compensating differences   The differences in the Wages received by workers in different jobs which compensate for nonmonetary differences in the jobs.

Compensation to employees   Wages and salaries paid by employers to workers plus Wage and salary supplements (*see*).

Competing goods   (*See* Substitute goods.)

Competition   The presence in a market of a large number of independent buyers and sellers and the freedom of buyers and sellers to enter and leave the market.

Competitive Industry's short-run supply curve   The horizontal summation of the short-run supply curves of the Firms in a purely competitive industry (*see* Pure competition); a curve which shows the total quantities offered for sale at various prices by the Firms in an industry in the Short run (*see*).

Competitive labor market   A market in which a large number of (noncolluding) firms demand a particular type of labor supplied by a large number of nonunion workers.

Complementary goods   Goods and services for which there is an inverse relationship between the price of one and the demand for the other; when the price of one falls (rises) the demand for the other increases (decreases).

Complex multiplier   The Multiplier (*see*) when changes in the Gross domestic product change Net taxes and Imports, as well as Saving.

Concentration ratio   The percentage of the total sales of an industry made by the four (or some other number) largest sellers (Firms) in the industry.

Conglomerate combination   A group of Plants (*see*) owned by a single Firm and engaged at one or more stages in the production of different products (of products which do not compete with each other).

Conglomerate merger   The merger of a Firm in one Industry with a Firm in another Industry (with a Firm that is neither supplier, customer, nor competitor).

Congress of Industrial Organizations (CIO)   The organization of affiliated Industrial unions formed in 1936.

Constant-cost industry   An industry in which the expansion of the Industry by the entry of new Firms has no effect on the prices the Firms in the industry pay for resources and no effect, therefore, on the cost curves.

Consumer goods   Goods and services which satisfy human wants directly.

Consumer price index (CPI)   An index which measures the prices of a fixed "market basket" of some 300 consumer goods bought by a "typical" consumer.

Consumer sovereignty   Determination by consumers of the types and quantities of goods and services produced from the scarce resources of the economy.

Consumption of fixed capital   Estimate of the amount of Capital worn out or used up (consumed) in producing the Gross domestic product; depreciation.

Consumption schedule   A schedule showing the amounts Households plan to spend for Consumer goods at different levels of Disposable income.

Contractionary fiscal policy   A decrease in Aggregate demand brought about by a decrease in Government expenditures for goods and services, an increase in Net taxes, or some combination of the two.

Copayments   Requirement that an insured individual pay a certain percentage of (say, health care) costs while the insurer pays the remainder.

Corporate income tax   A tax levied on the net income (profit) of Corporations.

Corporation   A legal entity ("person") chartered by a state or the Federal government which is distinct and separate from the individuals who own it.

Correlation   Systematic and dependable association between two sets of data (two kinds of events); does not necessarily indicate causation.

Cost-of-living adjustment   An increase in the incomes (wages) of workers which is automatically received by them when there is inflation and guaranteed by a clause in their labor contracts with their employer.

Cost-plus pricing   A procedure used by (oligopolistic) Firms to determine the price they will charge for a product and in which a percentage markup is added to the estimated average total cost of producing the product.

Cost-push inflation   Inflation resulting from a decrease in Aggregate supply (from higher wage rates and raw material prices) and accompanied by decrease in real output and employment (and by increases in the Unemployment rate).

Cost ratio   The ratio of the decrease in the production of the product to the increase in the production of another product when resources are shifted from the production of the first to the second; the amount the production of one product decreases when the production of a second increases by one unit.

Council of Economic Advisers A group of three persons which advises and assists the President of the United States on economic matters (including the preparation of the economic report of the President to Congress).

Craft union A labor union which limits its membership to workers with a particular skill (craft).

Credit An accounting notation that the value of an asset (such as the foreign money owned by the residents of a nation) has increased.

Credit union An association of persons who have a common tie (such as being employees of the same Firm or members of the same Labor union) which sells shares to (accepts deposits from) its members and makes loans to them.

Cross elasticity of demand The ratio of the percentage change in Quantity demanded of one good to the percentage change in the price of some other good. A positive coefficient indicates the two products are Substitute goods; a negative coefficient indicates Complementary goods.

Crowding model of occupational discrimination A model of labor markets that assumes Occupational discrimination (*see*) against women and blacks has kept them out of many occupations and forced them into a limited number of other occupations in which the large Supply of labor (relative to the Demand) results in lower wages and incomes.

Crowding-out effect The rise in interest rates and the resulting decrease in planned investment spending in the economy caused by increased borrowing in the money market by the Federal government.

Currency Coins and Paper money.

Currency appreciation (*See* Exchange rate appreciation.)

Currency depreciation (*See* Exchange rate depreciation.)

Current account The section in a nation's International balance of payments (*see*) which records its exports and imports of goods (merchandise) and services, its net investment income, and its net transfers.

Current account deficit A negative Balance on current account (*see*).

Current account surplus A positive Balance on current account (*see*).

Customary economy (*See* Traditional economy.)

Cyclical deficit A Federal Budget deficit which is caused by a recession and the consequent decline in tax revenues.

Cyclical unemployment Unemployment caused by insufficient Aggregate expenditures (or by insufficient Aggregate demand).

Cyclically balanced budget The equality of Government expenditures and Net tax collections over the course of a Business cycle; deficits incurred during periods of recession are offset by surpluses obtained during periods of prosperity (inflation).

D

Debit An accounting notation that the value of an asset (such as the foreign money owned by the residents of a nation) has decreased.

Debt-equity swaps The transfer of stock in private or government-owned enterprises of Less developed countries (*see*) to foreign creditors.

Declining economy An economy in which Net private domestic investment (*see*) is less than zero (Gross private domestic investment is less than Depreciation).

Declining industry An industry in which Economic profits are negative (losses are incurred) and which will, therefore, decrease its output as Firms leave the industry.

Decrease in demand A decrease in the Quantity demanded of a good or service at every price; a shift of the Demand curve to the left.

Decrease in supply A decrease in the quantity supplied of a good or service at every price; a shift of the Supply curve to the left.

Deductibles Requirement that an insured individual pay a certain sum of (for example, health care) costs before the insurer pays.

Deduction Reasoning from assumptions to conclusions; a method of reasoning that first develops a hypothesis (an assumption) and then compares the conclusions to which it leads with economic facts.

Defensive medicine The notion that physicians might recommend more tests and procedures than warranted medically to protect themselves from malpractice suits.

Deficit Reduction Act of 1993 Federal legislation intended to reduce the budget deficit by about $500 billion over five years by increasing taxes and cutting expenditures.

Deflating Finding the Real gross domestic product (*see*) by decreasing the dollar value of the Gross domestic product produced in a year in which prices were higher than in the Base year (*see*).

Deflation A fall in the general (average) level of prices in the economy.

Demand A Demand schedule or a Demand curve (*see* both).

Demand curve A curve showing the amounts of a good or service buyers wish to purchase at various prices during some period of time.

Demand deposit A deposit in a Commercial bank or Thrift against which checks may be written; a Checking account or checking-account money.

Demand-deposit multiplier (*See* Monetary multiplier.)

Demand factor The increase in the level of Aggregate demand which brings about the Economic growth made possible by an increase in the productive potential of the economy.

Demand management The use of Fiscal policy (*see*) and Monetary policy (*see*) to increase or decrease Aggregate demand.

Demand-pull inflation Inflation resulting from an increase in Aggregate demand.

Demand schedule A schedule showing the amounts of a good or service buyers will purchase at various prices during some period of time.

Dependent variable A variable which changes as a consequence of a change in some other (independent) variable; the "effect" or outcome.

Depository institution A Firm that accepts the deposits of Money of the public (businesses and persons); Commercial banks, Savings and loan associations, Mutual savings banks, and Credit unions.

Depository Institutions Deregulation and Monetary Control Act Federal legislation of 1980 which, among other things, allowed Thrift institutions to accept Checkable deposits and to use the check-clearing facilities of the Federal Reserve and to borrow from the Federal Reserve Banks; subjected the Thrifts to the reserve requirements of the Fed; and provided for the gradual elimination of the maximum interest rates that could be paid by Depository institutions on Savings and Time deposits.

Depreciation (*See* Consumption of fixed capital.)

Depreciation of the dollar A decrease in the value of the dollar relative to another currency; a dollar now buys a smaller amount of the foreign currency. For example, if the dollar price of a British pound changes from $2 to $3, the dollar has depreciated.

Derived demand The demand for a good or service which is dependent on or related to the demand for some other good or service; the demand for a resource which depends on the demand for the products it can be used to produce.

Descriptive economics The gathering or collection of relevant economic facts (data).

Determinants of aggregate demand Factors such as consumption, investment, government, and net export spending which, if they change, will shift the aggregate demand curve.

Determinants of aggregate supply Factors such as input prices, productivity, and the legal-institutional environment which, if they change, will shift the aggregate supply curve.

Determinants of demand Factors other than its price which determine the quantities demanded of a good or service.

Determinants of supply Factors other than its price which determine the quantities supplied of a good or service.

Devaluation A decrease in the governmentally defined value of a currency.

DI (*See* Disposable income.)

Diagnosis-related-group system (DRG) A program by which hospitals are paid a fixed amount for Medicare patients based on one of 468 diagnostic categories.

DIDMCA (*See* Depository Institutions Deregulation and Monetary Control Act.)

Differentiated oligopoly An Oligopoly in which the firms produce a Differentiated product (*see*).

Differentiated product A product which differs physically or in some other way from the similar products produced by other Firms; a product such that buyers are *not* indifferent to the seller from whom they purchase it when the price charged by all sellers is the same.

Dilemma of regulation When a Regulatory agency (*see*) must establish the maximum legal price a monopolist may charge, it finds that if it sets the price at the Socially optimal price (*see*) this price is below Average total cost (and either bankrupts the Firm or requires that it be subsidized) and if it sets the price at the Fair-return price (*see*) it has failed to eliminate fully the underallocation of resources that is the consequence of unregulated monopoly.

Directing function of prices (*See* Guiding function of prices.)

Directly related Two sets of economic data that change in the same direction; when one variable increases (decreases) the other increases (decreases).

Direct relationship The relationship between two variables which change in the same direction, for example, product price and quantity supplied.

Discount rate The interest rate which the Federal Reserve Banks charge on the loans they make to Depository institutions.

Discouraged workers Workers who have left the Labor force (*see*) because they have not been able to find employment.

Discretionary fiscal policy Deliberate changes in taxes (tax rates) and government spending (spending for goods and services and transfer payment programs) by Congress to achieve a full-employment noninflationary Gross domestic product and economic growth.

Diseconomies of scale Forces which increase the Average total cost of producing a product as the Firm expands the size of its Plant (its output) in the Long run (*see*).

Disinflation A reduction in the rate of Inflation (*see*).

Disposable income Personal income (*see*) less personal taxes; income available for Personal consumption expenditures (*see*) and Personal saving (*see*).

Dissaving Spending for consumer goods and services in excess of Disposable income; the amount by which Personal consumption expenditures (*see*) exceed Disposable income.

Division of labor Dividing the work required to produce a product into a number of different tasks which are performed by different workers; Specialization (*see*) of workers.

Dollar votes The "votes" which consumers and entrepreneurs in effect cast for the production of the different kinds of consumer and capital goods, respectively, when they purchase them in the markets of the economy.

Domestic capital formation Adding to a nation's stock of Capital by saving and investing part of its own domestic output.

Domestic output Gross (or net) domestic product; the total output of final goods and services produced in the economy.

Domestic price The price of a good or service within a country, determined by domestic demand and supply.

Doomsday models Computer-based models which predict that continued growth of population and production will exhaust available resources and the environment, causing an economic collapse.

Double counting Including the value of Intermediate goods (*see*) in the Gross domestic product; counting the same good or service more than once.

Double taxation Taxation of both corporate net income (profits) and the dividends paid from this net income when they become the Personal income of households.

Dumping The sale of products below cost in a foreign country.

Du Pont cellophane case The antitrust case brought against du Pont in which the U.S. Supreme Court ruled (in 1956) that while du Pont (and one licensee) had a monopoly in the narrowly defined market for cellophane, it did not monopolize the more broadly defined market for flexible packaging materials, and was not guilty of violating the Sherman Act.

Durable good A consumer good with an expected life (use) of three years or more.

Dynamic progress The development over time of more efficient (less costly) techniques of producing existing products and of improved products; technological progress.

E

Earned Income Tax Credit A Federal tax credit for low-income working families designed to encourage labor force participation.

Earnings The money income received by a worker; equal to the Wage (rate) multiplied by the quantity of labor supplied (the amount of time worked) by the worker.

Easy money policy Expanding the Money supply.

EC European Economic Community. (*See* European Union.)

Economic analysis Deriving Economic principles (*see*) from relevant economic facts.

Economic concentration A description or measure of the degree to which an industry is monopolistic or competitive. (*See* Concentration ratio.)

Economic cost A payment that must be made to obtain and retain the services of a resource; the income a Firm must provide to a resource supplier to attract the resource away from an alternative use; equal to the quantity of other products that cannot be produced when resources are employed to produce a particular product.

Economic efficiency The relationship between the input of scarce resources and the resulting output of a good or service; production of an output with a specific dollar-and-cents value with the smallest total expenditure for resources; obtaining the largest total production of a good or service with resources of a specific dollar-and-cents value.

Economic growth (1) An increase in the Production possibilities schedule or curve that results from an increase in resource supplies or an improvement in Technology; (2) an increase either in real output (Gross domestic product) or in real output per capita.

Economic integration Cooperation among and the complete or partial unification of the economies of different nations; the elimination of the barriers to trade among these nations; the bringing together of the markets in each of the separate economies to form one large (a common) market.

Economic law (*See* Economic principle.)

Economic model A simplified picture of reality; an abstract generalization.

Economic perspective A viewpoint which envisions individuals and institutions making rational or purposeful decisions based on a consideration of the marginal benefits and marginal costs associated with their actions.

Economic policy Course of action intended to correct or avoid a problem.

Economic principle Generalization of the economic behavior of individuals and institutions.

Economic profit The Total revenue of a firm less all its Economic costs; also called "pure profit" and "above normal profit."

Economic regulation (*See* Industrial regulation.)

Economic rent The price paid for the use of land and other natural resources, the supply of which is fixed (perfectly inelastic).

Economic resources Land, labor, capital, and entrepreneurial ability which are used in the production of goods and services.

Economics Social science concerned with using scarce resources to obtain the maximum satisfaction of the unlimited material wants of society.

Economic theory Deriving economic principles (*see*) from relevant economic facts; an Economic principle (*see*).

Economies of scale   The forces which reduce the Average total cost of producing a product as the Firm expands the size of its Plant (its output) in the Long run (*see*); the economies of mass production.

Economizing problem   Society's material wants are unlimited but the resources available to produce the goods and services that satisfy wants are limited (scarce); the inability to produce unlimited quantities of goods and services.

Efficiency factors in growth   The capacity of an economy to combine resources effectively to achieve the growth of real output which the Supply factors (*see*) make possible.

Efficiency loss of a tax   The loss of net benefits to society because a tax reduces the production and consumption of a taxed good below the economically efficient level.

Efficiency wage   A wage which minimizes wage costs per unit of output.

Efficient allocation of resources   That allocation of the resources of an economy among the production of different products which leads to the maximum satisfaction of the wants of consumers; producing the optimal mix of output.

Elastic demand   The Elasticity coefficient (*see*) is greater than one; the percentage change in Quantity demanded is greater than the percentage change in Price.

Elasticity coefficient   The number obtained when the percentage change in Quantity demanded (or supplied) is divided by the percentage change in the price of the commodity.

Elasticity formula   The price elasticity of demand (supply) is equal to

$$\frac{\text{percentage change in quantity demanded (supplied)}}{\text{percentage change in price}}$$

Elastic supply   The Elasticity coefficient (*see*) is greater than one; the percentage change in Quantity supplied is greater than the percentage change in Price.

Emission fees   Special fees that might be levied against those who discharge pollutants into the environment.

Employment Act of 1946   Federal legislation which committed the Federal government to the maintenance of economic stability (a high level of employment, stable prices, and Economic growth); established the Council of Economic Advisors (*see*) and the Joint Economic Committee (*see*); and provided for the annual economic report of the President to Congress.

Employment and training policy   Policies and programs involving vocational training, job information, and antidiscrimination which are designed to improve labor-market efficiency and lower unemployment at any level of aggregate demand.

Employment discrimination   Higher-than-average unemployment rates for a particular group after adjusting for differences in education and experience.

Employment rate   The percentage of the Labor force (*see*) employed at any time.

Entitlement programs   Government programs such as Social security, Food stamps, Medicare, and Medicaid (*see all*) which guarantee particular levels of Transfer payments (*see*) to all who fit the programs' criteria.

Entrepreneurial ability   The human resource which combines the other resources to produce a product, makes nonroutine decisions, innovates, and bears risks.

Equality versus efficiency tradeoff   The decrease in Economic efficiency (*see*) which may accompany a decrease in Income inequality (*see*); the presumption that an increase in Income inequality is required to increase Economic efficiency.

Equation of exchange $MV = PQ$, in which M is the Money supply (*see*), V is the Velocity of money (*see*), P is the Price level, and Q is the physical volume of final goods and services produced.

Equilibrium gross domestic product   The Gross domestic product at which the total quantity of final goods and services produced (the Domestic output) is equal to the total quantity of final goods and services purchased (Aggregate expenditures); the real Domestic output at which the Aggregate demand curve intersects the Aggregate supply curve.

Equilibrium position   The point at which the Budget line (*see*) is tangent to an Indifference curve (*see*) in the indifference curve approach to the theory of consumer behavior.

Equilibrium price   The price in a competitive market where the Quantity demanded (*see*) and the Quantity supplied (*see*) are equal; where there is neither a shortage nor a surplus; and where there is no tendency for price to rise or fall.

Equilibrium price level   The price level at which the Aggregate demand curve intersects the Aggregate supply curve.

Equilibrium quantity   The Quantity demanded (*see*) and Quantity supplied (*see*) at the Equilibrium price (*see*) in a competitive market.

European Common Market   (*See* European Union.)

European Union (EU)   The association of European nations initiated in 1958 to abolish gradually the Tariffs and Import quotas that exist among them, to establish common Tariffs for goods imported from outside the member nations, to allow the eventual free movement of labor and capital among them, and to create other common economic policies. (Earlier known as "European Economic Community" and the "Common Market.")

Excess capacity   A situation where an imperfectly competitive firm produces an output less than the minimum average total cost output, thereby necessitating a higher product price than a purely competitive firm would charge.

Excess reserves   The amount by which a bank or thrift's

Actual reserves (see) exceed its Required reserves **(see)**; Actual reserves minus Required reserves.

Exchange control (*See* Foreign exchange control.)

Exchange rate The Rate of exchange **(see)**.

Exchange rate appreciation An increase in the value of a nation's money in foreign exchange markets; an increase in the Rate of exchange for foreign monies.

Exchange rate depreciation A decrease in the value of a nation's money in foreign exchange markets; a decrease in the Rate of exchange for foreign monies.

Exchange rate determinant Any factor other than the Rate of exchange **(see)** that determines a currency's demand and supply in the Foreign exchange market **(see)**.

Excise tax A tax levied on the expenditure for a specific product or on the quantity of the product purchased.

Exclusion principle The exclusion of those who do not pay for a product from the benefits of the product.

Exclusive unionism The policies employed by a Labor union to restrict the supply of labor by excluding potential members to increase the Wages received by its members; the Policies typically employed by a Craft union **(see)**.

Exhaustive expenditure An expenditure by government resulting directly in the employment of economic resources and in the absorption by government of the goods and services these resources produce; a Government purchase **(see)**.

Exit mechanism Leaving a job and searching for another one to improve the conditions under which a worker is employed.

Expanding economy An economy in which Net private domestic investment **(see)** is greater than zero (Gross private domestic investment is greater than Depreciation).

Expanding industry An industry in which economic profits are obtained by the firms in the industry and which will, therefore, increase its output as new firms enter the industry.

Expansionary fiscal policy An increase in Aggregate demand brought about by an increase in Government expenditures for goods and services, a decrease in Net taxes, or some combination of the two.

Expectations What consumers, business Firms, and others believe will happen or what conditions will be in the future.

Expected rate of net profit Annual profit a firm anticipates it will obtain by purchasing Capital (by investing) expressed as a percentage of the price (cost) of the Capital.

Expenditures approach The method which adds all the expenditures made for Final goods and services to measure the Gross domestic product.

Expenditures-output approach (*See* Aggregate expenditures–domestic output approach.)

Explicit cost The monetary payment a Firm must make to an outsider to obtain a resource.

Export controls The limitation or prohibition of the export of certain high-technology products on the basis of foreign policy or national security objectives.

Export-Import Bank A Federal institution which provides interest-rate subsidies to foreign borrowers who buy American exports on credit.

Exports Goods and services produced in a nation and sold to customers in other nations.

Export subsidies Government payments which reduce the price of a product to foreign buyers.

Export supply curve An upsloping curve showing the amount of a product domestic firms will export at each World price **(see)** above the Domestic price **(see)**.

Export transactions A sale of a good or service which increases the amount of foreign money held by the citizens, firms, and governments of a nation.

External benefits (*See* Spillover benefit.)

External cost (*See* Spillover cost.)

External debt Private or public debt **(see)** owed to foreign citizens, firms, and institutions.

Externality (*See* Spillover.)

F

Face value The dollar or cents value stamped on a coin.

Factors of production Economic resources: Land, Capital, Labor, and Entrepreneurial ability.

Fair-return price The price of a product which enables its producer to obtain a Normal profit **(see)** and which is equal to the Average total cost of producing it.

Fallacy of composition Incorrectly reasoning that what is true for the individual (or part) is therefore necessarily true for the group (or whole).

Fallacy of limited decisions The false notion that there are a limited number of economic decisions to be made so that, if government makes more decisions, there will be fewer private decisions to render.

Farm Act of 1990 Farm legislation which reduces the amount of acreage that is covered by price supports and allows farmers to plant these uncovered acres in alternative crops.

Farm problem Technological advance, coupled with a price inelastic and relatively constant demand, has made agriculture a Declining industry; also, the tendency for farm income to fluctuate sharply from year to year.

FDIC (*See* Federal Deposit Insurance Corporation.)

Featherbedding Payment by an employer to a worker for work not actually performed.

Federal Advisory Committee The group of twelve commercial bankers which advises the Board of Governors (*see*) on banking policy.

Federal Deposit Insurance Corporation (FDIC) The Federally chartered corporation which insures the deposit liabilities of Commercial banks and Thrift institutions.

Federal funds rate The interest rate banks and other depository institutions charge one another on overnight loans made out of their excess reserves.

Federal Open Market Committee (*See* Open Market Committee.)

Federal Reserve Bank Any one of the twelve banks chartered by the United States government to control the Money supply and perform other functions. (*See* Central bank, Quasi-public bank, *and* Banker's bank.)

Federal Reserve Note Paper money issued by the Federal Reserve Banks.

Federal Trade Commission (FTC) The commission of five members established by the Federal Trade Commission Act of 1914 to investigate unfair competitive practices of business Firms, to hold hearings on the complaints of such practices, and to issue Cease-and-desist orders (*see*) when Firms were found to engage in such practices.

Federal Trade Commission Act The Federal act of 1914 which established the Federal Trade Commission (*see*).

Feedback effects The effects which a change in the money supply will have (because it affects the interest rate, planned investment, and the equilibrium GDP) on the demand for money which is itself directly related to the GDP.

Fee-for-service payments Traditional payment system in the health care industry where physicians and other providers are paid a fee for each service provided.

Female labor force participation rate The percentage of the female population of working age in the Labor force (*see*).

Fewness A relatively small number of sellers (or buyers) of a good or service.

Fiat money Anything that is Money because government has decreed it to be Money.

Final goods Goods which have been purchased for final use and not for resale or further processing or manufacturing (during the year).

Financial capital (*See* Money capital.)

Financing exports and imports The use of Foreign exchange markets by exporters and importers to receive and make payments for goods and services they sell and buy in foreign nations.

Firm An organization that employs resources to produce a good or service for profit and owns and operates one or more Plants (*see*).

Fiscal federalism The system of transfers (grants) by which the Federal government shares its revenues with state and local governments.

Fiscal policy Changes in government spending and tax collections designed to achieve a full-employment and noninflationary domestic output.

Five fundamental economic questions The five questions which every economy must answer: what to produce, how to produce, how to divide the total output, how to maintain Full employment, and how to assure economic flexibility.

Fixed cost Any cost which in total does not change when the Firm changes its output; the cost of Fixed resources (*see*).

Fixed exchange rate A Rate of exchange which is prevented from rising or falling.

Fixed resource Any resource employed by a firm in a quantity which the firm cannot change.

Flexible exchange rate A rate of exchange determined by the international demand for and supply of a nation's money; a rate free to rise or fall.

Floating exchange rate (*See* Flexible exchange rate.)

Food for peace program The program established under the provisions of Public Law 480 which permits less developed nations to buy surplus American agricultural products and pay for them with their own monies (instead of dollars).

Food stamp program A program permitting low-income persons to purchase for less than their retail value, or to obtain without cost, coupons that can be exchanged for food items at retail stores.

Foreign competition (*See* Import competition.)

Foreign exchange control The control a government may exercise over the quantity of foreign money demanded by its citizens and business firms and over the Rates of exchange in order to limit its outpayments to its inpayments (to eliminate a Payments deficit, *see*).

Foreign exchange market A market in which the money (currency) used by one nation is used to purchase (is exchanged for) the money used by another nation.

Foreign exchange rate (*See* Rate of exchange.)

Foreign purchases effect The inverse relationship between the Net exports (*see*) of an economy and its Price level (*see*) relative to foreign Price levels.

45-degree line A line along which the value of the GDP (measured horizontally) is equal to the value of Aggregate expenditures (measured vertically).

Fractional reserve A Reserve ratio (*see*) which is less than 100 percent of the deposit liabilities of a Commercial bank.

Freedom of choice Freedom of owners of property resources and money to employ or dispose of these resources as they see fit, of workers to enter any line of work for which they are qualified, and of consumers to spend their incomes in a manner which they deem appropriate (best for them).

Freedom of enterprise Freedom of business Firms to employ economic resources, to use these resources to produce products of the firm's own choosing, and to sell these products in markets of their choice.

Freely floating exchange rates   Rates of exchange (*see*) which are not controlled and which may, therefore, rise and fall; and which are determined by the demand for and the supply of foreign monies.

Free-rider problem   The inability of potential providers of an economically desirable but indivisible good or service to obtain payment from those who benefit, because the Exclusion principle (*see*) is not applicable.

Free Trade   The absence of artificial (government imposed) barriers to trade among individuals and firms in different nations.

Frictional unemployment.   Unemployment caused by workers voluntarily changing jobs and by temporary layoffs; unemployed workers between jobs.

Fringe benefits   The rewards other than Wages that employees receive from their employers and which include pensions, medical and dental insurance, paid vacations, and sick leaves.

Full employment   (1) Using all available resources to produce goods and services; (2) when the Unemployment rate is equal to the Full-employment unemployment rate and there is Frictional and Structural but no Cyclical unemployment (and the Real output of the economy is equal to its Potential real output).

Full-employment budget   What government expenditures and revenues and its surplus or deficit would be if the economy were to operate at Full employment throughout the year.

Full-employment unemployment rate   The Unemployment rate (*see*) at which there is no Cyclical unemployment (*see*) of the labor force (*see*); and because some Frictional and Structural unemployment is unavoidable, equal to about 5.5 to 6 percent.

Full production   The maximum amount of goods and services which can be produced from the employed resources of an economy; occurs when both Allocative efficiency and Productive efficiency are realized.

Functional distribution of income   The manner in which national income is divided among those who perform different functions (provide the economy with different kinds of resources); the division of National income (*see*) into wages and salaries, proprietors' income, corporate profits, interest, and rent.

Functional finance   Use of Fiscal policy to achieve a full-employment noninflationary Gross domestic product without regard to the effect on the Public debt (*see*).

G

G-7 Nations   A group of seven major industrial powers (the United States, Japan, Germany, United Kingdom, France, Italy, and Canada) whose leaders meet regularly to discuss common economic problems and try to coordinate economic policies.

Game theory   A theory which compares the behavior of participants in games of strategy, such as poker and chess, with that of a small group of mutually interdependent firms (an Oligopoly).

GATT   (*See* General Agreement on Tariffs and Trade.)

GDP   (*See* Gross domestic product.)

GDP deflator   The Price index (*see*) for all final goods and services used to adjust the money (or nominal) GDP to measure the real GDP.

GDP gap   Potential Real gross domestic product less actual Real gross domestic product.

General Agreement on Tariffs and Trade   The international agreement reached in 1947 in which twenty-three nations agreed to give equal and nondiscriminatory treatment to the other nations, to reduce tariff rates by multinational negotiations, and to eliminate Import quotas. Now includes 124 nations.

Generalization   Statistical or probability statement; statement of the nature of the relation between two or more sets of facts.

Gentleman's agreement   An informal understanding on the price to be charged among the firms in an Oligopoly.

Glasnost   A Soviet campaign of the mid-1980s for greater "openness" and democratization in political and economic activities.

GNP   (*See* Gross national product.)

Gold export point   The rate of exchange for a foreign money above which—when nations participate in the International gold standard (*see*)—the foreign money will not be purchased and gold will be sent (exported) to the foreign country to make payments there.

Gold flow   The movement of gold into or out of a nation.

Gold import point   The Rate of exchange for a foreign money below which—when nations participate in the International gold standard (*see*)—a nation's own money will not be purchased and gold will be sent (imported) into that country by foreigners to make payments there.

Gorbachev's reforms   A mid-1980s series of reforms designed to revitalize the Soviet economy. The reforms stressed the modernization of productive facilities, less centralized control, improved worker discipline and productivity, more emphasis on market prices, and an expansion of private economic activity.

Government purchases   Disbursements of money by government for which government receives a currently produced good or service in return; the expenditures of all governments in the economy for Final goods (*see*) and services.

Government transfer payment The disbursement of money (or goods and services) by government for which government receives no currently produced good or service in return.

Grievance procedure The methods used by a Labor union and the Firm to settle disputes that arise during the life of the collective bargaining agreement between them.

Gross domestic product (GDP) The total market value of all Final goods (*see*) and services produced annually within the boundaries of the United States, whether by American or foreign-supplied resources.

Gross national product (GNP) The total market value of all Final goods (*see*) and services produced annually by land, labor, and capital, and entrepreneurial talent supplied by American residents, whether these resources are located in the United States or abroad.

Gross private domestic investment Expenditures for newly produced Capital goods (*see*)—machinery, equipment, tools, and buildings—and for additions to inventories.

Guaranteed income The minimum income a family (or individual) would receive if a Negative income tax (*see*) were adopted.

Guiding function of prices The ability of price changes to bring about changes in the quantities of products and resources demanded and supplied. (*See* Incentive function of price.)

H

Health maintenance organization (HMO) Health care providers which contract with employers, insurance companies, labor unions, or governmental units to provide health care for their workers or insurees.

Herfindahl index A measure of the concentration and competitiveness of an industry; calculated as the sum of the squared market shares of the individual firms.

Homogeneous oligopoly An Oligopoly in which the firms produce a Standardized product (*see*).

Horizontal axis The "left-right" or "west-east" axis on a graph or grid.

Horizontal combination A group of Plants (*see*) in the same stage of production which are owned by a single Firm (*see*).

Horizontal merger The merger of one or more Firms producing the same product into a single Firm.

Horizontal range Horizontal segment of the Aggregate-supply curve along which the price level is constant as real domestic output changes.

Household An economic unit (of one or more persons) which provides the economy with resources and uses the money paid to it for these resources to purchase goods and services which satisfy material wants.

Human-capital discrimination The denial to blacks (and other minority groups) and women of the same quality and quantity of education and training received by white males.

Human-capital investment Any action taken to increase the productivity (by improving the skills and abilities) of workers; expenditures made to improve the education, health, or mobility of workers.

Hyperinflation A very rapid rise in the price level.

I

Illegal immigrant A person who unlawfully enters a country.

IMF (*See* International Monetary Fund.)

Immobility The inability or unwillingness of a worker or another resource to move from one geographic area or occupation to another or from a lower-paying to a higher-paying job.

Imperfect competition All markets except Pure competition (*see*); Monopoly, Monopolistic competition, and Oligopoly (*see all*).

Implicit cost The monetary income a Firm sacrifices when it employs a resource it owns to produce a product rather than supplying the resource in the market; equal to what the resource could have earned in the best-paying alternative employment.

Import competition Competition which domestic firms encounter from the products and services of foreign suppliers.

Import demand curve A downsloping curve showing the amount of a product which an economy will import at each World price (*see*) below the Domestic price (*see*).

Import quota A limit imposed by a nation on the quantity of a good which may be imported during some period of time.

Imports Spending by individuals, Firms, and governments for goods and services produced in foreign nations.

Import transaction The purchase of a good or service which decreases the amount of foreign money held by citizens, firms, and governments of a nation.

Incentive function of price The inducement which an increase (a decrease) in the price of a commodity offers to sellers of the commodity to make more (less) of it available; and the inducement which an increase (decrease) in price offers to buyers to purchase smaller (larger) quantities; the Guiding function of prices (*see*).

Incentive pay plan A compensation scheme which ties worker pay directly to performance. Such plans include piece rates, bonuses, commissions, and profit sharing.

Inclusive unionism A union which attempts to include as members all workers employed in an industry.

Income approach The method which adds all the incomes generated by the production of Final goods and services to measure the Gross domestic product.

Income effect The effect of a change in price of a product on a consumer's Real income (purchasing power) and thus on the quantity of the product purchased, after the Substitution effect (*see*) has been determined and eliminated.

Income elasticity of demand The ratio of the percentage change in the Quantity demanded of a good to the percentage change in income; it measures the responsiveness of consumer purchases to income changes.

Income inequality The unequal distribution of an economy's total income among persons or families.

Income-maintenance system The programs designed to eliminate poverty and to reduce inequality in the distribution of income.

Incomes policy Government policy which affects the Nominal incomes of individuals (the wages workers receive) and the prices they pay for goods and services and alters their Real incomes. (*See* Wage-price policy.)

Income velocity of money (*See* Velocity of money.)

Increase in demand An increase in the Quantity demanded of a good or service at every price; a shift in the Demand curve to the right.

Increase in supply An increase in the Quantity supplied of a good or service at every price; a shift in the Supply curve to the right.

Increasing-cost industry An Industry in which expansion through the entry of new firms increases the prices the Firms in the Industry must pay for resources and, therefore, increases their cost schedules (shifts their cost curves upward).

Increasing returns An increase in the Marginal product (*see*) of a resource as successive units of the resource are employed.

Independent goods. Goods or services for which there is no relationship between the price of one and the demand for the other; when the price of one rises or falls the demand for the other remains constant.

Independent variable The variable causing a change in some other (dependent) variable.

Indifference curve A curve showing the different combinations of two products which give a consumer the same satisfaction or Utility (*see*).

Indifference map A series of Indifference curves (*see*), each representing a different level of Utility; and which together show the preferences of the consumer.

Indirect business taxes Such taxes as Sales, Excise, and business Property taxes (*see all*), license fees, and Tariffs (*see*) which Firms treat as costs of producing a product and pass on (in whole or in part) to buyers of the product by charging them higher prices.

Individual demand The Demand schedule (*see*) or Demand curve (*see*) of a single buyer.

Individual supply The Supply schedule (*see*) or Supply curve (*see*) of a single seller.

Induction A method of reasoning which proceeds from facts to Generalization (*see*).

Industrially advanced countries (IACs) Countries such as the United States, Canada, Japan, and the nations of western Europe which have developed Market economies based on large stocks of technologically advanced capital goods and skilled labor forces.

Industrial policy Any policy in which government takes a direct and active role in promoting specific firms or industries to expand output and achieve economic growth.

Industrial regulation The older and more traditional type of regulation in which government is concerned with the prices charged and the services provided the public in specific industries; in contrast to Social regulation (*see*).

Industrial union A Labor union which accepts as members all workers employed in a particular industry (or by a particular firm).

Industry A group of (one or more) Firms which produce identical or similar products.

Inelastic demand The Elasticity coefficient (*see*) is less than one; the percentage change in Quantity demanded is less than the percentage change in Price.

Inelastic supply The Elasticity coefficient (*see*) is less than one; the percentage change in Quantity supplied is less than the percentage change in Price.

Inferior good A good or service of which consumers purchase less (more) at every price when their incomes increase (decrease).

Inflating Finding the Real gross domestic product (*see*) by increasing the dollar value of the Gross domestic product produced in a year in which prices are lower than in the Base year (*see*).

Inflation A rise in the general (average) level of prices in the economy.

Inflation premium The component of the nominal interest rate which reflects anticipated inflation.

Inflationary expectations The belief of workers, business Firms, and consumers that there will be substantial inflation in the future.

Inflationary gap The amount by which the Aggregate-expenditures schedule (curve) must decrease (shift downward) to decrease the nominal GDP to the full-employment noninflationary level.

Inflationary recession (*See* Stagflation.)

Infrastructure The capital goods usually provided by the Public sector for the use of its citizens and Firms (e.g., highways, bridges, transit systems, wastewater treatment facilities, municipal water systems, and airports).

Injection An addition of spending to the income-expenditure stream: Investment, Government purchases, and Exports.

Injunction   A court order directing a person or organization not to perform a certain act because the act would do irreparable damage to some other person or persons; a restraining order.

In-kind investment   Nonfinancial investment (*see*).

In-kind transfer   The distribution by government of goods and services to individuals and for which the government receives no currently produced good or service in return; a Government transfer payment (*see*) made in goods or services rather than in money.

Innovation   The introduction of a new product, the use of a new method of production, or the creation of a new form of business organization.

Inpayments   The receipts of (its own or foreign) money which the individuals, Firms, and governments of one nation obtain from the sale of goods and services, investment income, Remittances, and Capital inflows from abroad.

Insurable risk   An event—the average occurrence of which can be estimated with considerable accuracy—which would result in a loss that can be avoided by purchasing insurance.

Interest   The payment made for the use of money (of borrowed funds).

Interest income   Income of those who supply the economy with Capital (*see*).

Interest rate   The Rate of interest (*see*).

Interest-rate effect   The tendency for increases (decreases) in the Price level to increase (decrease) the demand for money; raise (lower) interest rates; and, as a result, to reduce (expand) total spending in the economy.

Interindustry competition   Competition or rivalry between the products of one Industry (*see*) and the products of another industry (or of other industries).

Interlocking directorate   A situation where one or more members of the board of directors of a Corporation are also on the board of directors of a competing Corporation; and which is illegal under the Clayton Act.

Intermediate goods   Goods which are purchased for resale or further processing or manufacturing during the year.

Intermediate range   The upsloping segment of the Aggregate supply curve lying between the Horizontal range and the Vertical range (*see both*).

Internally held public debt   Public debt (*see*) owed to (United States government securities owned by) American citizens, Firms, and institutions.

International balance of payments   Summary statement of the transactions which took place between the individuals, Firms, and governments of one nation and those in all other nations during the year.

International balance of payments deficit   (*See* Balance of payments deficit.)

International balance of payments surplus   (*See* Balance of payments surplus.)

International Bank for Reconstruction and Development   (*See* World Bank.)

International economic goal   Assumed to be a current-account balance of zero.

International gold standard   An international monetary system employed in the nineteenth and early twentieth centuries in which each nation defined its money in terms of a quantity of gold, maintained a fixed relationship between its gold stock and money supply, and allowed the free importation and exportation of gold.

International Monetary Fund   The international association of nations which was formed after World War II to make loans of foreign monies to nations with temporary Payments deficits (*see*) and to administer the Adjustable pegs (*see*).

International monetary reserves   The foreign monies and such assets as gold a nation may use to settle a Payments deficit (*see*).

International value of the dollar   The price that must be paid in foreign currency (money) to obtain one American dollar.

Interstate Commerce Commission   The commission established in 1887 to regulate the rates and monitor the services of the railroads in the United States.

Interstate Commerce Commission Act   The Federal legislation of 1887 which established the Interstate Commerce Commission (*see*).

Intrinsic value   The market value of the metal in a coin.

Inverse relationship   The relationship between two variables which change in opposite directions, for example, product price and quantity demanded.

Investment   Spending for (the production and accumulation of) Capital goods (*see*) and additions to inventories.

Investment curve (schedule)   A curve (schedule) which shows the amounts firms plan to invest (along the vertical axis) at different income (Gross domestic product) levels (along the horizontal axis).

Investment-demand curve (schedule)   A curve (schedule) which shows Rates of interest (along the vertical axis) and the amount of Investment (along the horizontal axis) at each Rate of interest.

Investment in human capital   (*See* Human-capital investment.)

Invisible hand   The tendency of Firms and resource suppliers seeking to further their self-interests in competitive markets to further the best interest of society as a whole (the maximum satisfaction of wants).

J

JEC   (*See* Joint Economic Committee.)

Joint Economic Committee   Committee of Senators and members of Congress which investigates economic problems of national interest.

Jurisdictional strike   A Labor union's withholding of its labor from an employer because of the union's dispute with another Labor union over which is to perform a specific kind of work.

K

Keynesian economics   The macroeconomic generalizations which lead to the conclusion that a capitalistic economy does not always employ its resources fully and that Fiscal policy (*see*) and Monetary policy (*see*) can be used to promote Full employment (*see*).

Keynesianism   The philosophical, ideological, and analytical views pertaining to Keynesian economics (*see*).

Kinked demand curve   The demand curve for a noncollusive oligopolist which is based on the assumption that rivals will follow a price decrease and will ignore a price increase.

L

Labor   The physical and mental talents (efforts) of people which can be used to produce goods and services.

Labor force   Persons sixteen years of age and older who are not in institutions and who are employed or are unemployed and seeking work.

Labor force participation rate   The percentage of the working-age population which is actually in the labor force.

Labor-intensive commodity   A product which requires much Labor to produce.

Labor-Management Relations Act   (*See* Taft-Hartley Act.)

Labor-Management Reporting and Disclosure Act   (*See* Landrum-Griffin Act.)

Labor productivity   Total output divided by the quantity of labor employed to produce the output; the Average product (*see*) of labor or output per worker per hour.

Labor theory of value   The Marxian notion that the economic value of any commodity is determined solely by the amount of labor required to produce it.

Labor union   A group of workers organized to advance the interests of the group (to increase wages, shorten the hours worked, improve working conditions, etc.).

Laffer curve   A curve showing the relationship between tax rates and the tax revenues of government and on which there is a tax rate (between zero and 100 percent) where tax revenues are a maximum.

Laissez faire capitalism   (*See* Pure capitalism.)

Land   Natural resources ("free gifts of nature") used to produce goods and services.

Land-intensive commodity   A product requiring a relatively large amount of Land to produce.

Landrum-Griffin Act   The Federal act of 1959 which regulates the elections and finances of Labor unions and guarantees certain rights to their members.

Law of conservation of matter and energy   The notion that matter can be changed to other matter or into energy but cannot disappear; all production inputs are ultimately transformed into an equal amount of finished product, energy, and waste (potentially pollution).

Law of demand   The inverse relationship between the price and the Quantity demanded (*see*) of a good or service during some period of time.

Law of diminishing marginal utility   As a consumer increases the consumption of a good or service, the Marginal utility (*see*) obtained from each additional unit of the good or service decreases.

Law of diminishing returns   When successive equal increments of a Variable resource (*see*) are added to the Fixed resources (*see*), beyond some level of employment, the Marginal product (*see*) of the Variable resource will decrease.

Law of increasing opportunity cost   As the amount of a product produced is increased, the Opportunity cost (*see*)—Marginal cost (*see*)—of producing an additional unit of the product increases.

Law of supply   The direct relationship between the price and the Quantity supplied (*see*) of a good or service during some period.

Leakage   (1) A withdrawal of potential spending from the income-expenditures stream; Saving (*see*), tax payments, and Imports (*see*); (2) a withdrawal which reduces the lending potential of the Commercial banking system.

Leakages-injections approach   Determination of the Equilibrium gross domestic product (*see*) by finding the GDP at which Leakages (*see*) are equal to Injections (*see*).

Least-cost combination rule (of resources)   The quantity of each resource a Firm must employ if it is to produce an output at the lowest total cost; the combination at which the ratio of the Marginal product (*see*) of a resource to its Marginal resource cost (*see*) (to its price if the resource is employed in a competitive market) is the same for all resources employed.

Legal cartel theory of regulation   The hypothesis that industries want to be regulated so that they may form legal Cartels (*see*) and that government officials (the government) provide the regulation in return for their political and financial support.

Legal immigrant   A person who lawfully enters a country.

Legal reserves (deposit)   The minimum amount a Depository institution (*see*) must keep on deposit with the Federal Reserve Bank in its district, or in Vault cash (*see*).

Legal tender   Anything that government has decreed must be accepted in payment of a debt.

Lending potential of an individual commercial bank The amount a single Commercial bank can safely increase the Money supply by making new loans to (or buying securities from) the public; equal to the Commercial bank's Excess reserves (*see*).

Lending potential of the banking system The amount the Commercial banking system (*see*) can increase the Money supply by making new loans to (or buying securities from) the public; equal to the Excess reserves (*see*) of the Commercial banking system multiplied by the Monetary multiplier (*see*).

Less developed countries (LDCs) Most countries of Africa, Asia, and Latin America which are characterized by a lack of capital goods, primitive production technologies, low literacy rates, high unemployment, rapid population growth, and labor forces heavily committed to agriculture.

Liability A debt with a monetary value; an amount owed by a Firm or an individual.

Limited liability Restriction of the maximum loss to a predetermined amount; for the owners (stockholders) of a Corporation, the maximum loss is the amount they paid for their shares of stock.

Limited-liability company An unincorporated business whose owners are protected by Limited liability (*see*).

Line-item veto A proposal to give the President the power to delete specific expenditure items from spending legislation passed by Congress.

Liquidity Money or things which can be quickly and easily converted into Money with little or no loss of purchasing power.

Loaded terminology Terms which arouse emotions and elicit approval or disapproval.

Loanable funds theory of interest The concept that the supply of and demand for loanable funds determines the equilibrium rate of interest.

Logrolling The trading of votes by legislators to secure favorable outcomes on decisions to provide public goods and services.

Long run A period of time long enough to enable producers of a product to change the quantities of all the resources they employ; in which all resources and costs are variable and no resources or costs are fixed.

Long-run aggregate supply curve The aggregate supply curve associated with a time period in which input prices (especially nominal wages) are fully responsive to changes in the price level.

Long-run competitive equilibrium The price at which Firms in Pure competition (*see*) neither obtain Economic profit nor suffer losses in the Long run and the total quantity demanded and supplied at that price are equal; a price equal to the minimum long-run average total cost of producing the product.

Long-run farm problem The tendency for agriculture to be a declining industry as technological progress increases supply relative to an inelastic and relatively constant demand.

Long-run supply A schedule or curve showing the prices at which a Purely competitive industry will make various quantities of the product available in the Long run.

Lorenz curve A curve showing the distribution of income in an economy; and when used for this purpose the cumulated percentage of families (income receivers) is measured along the horizontal axis and cumulated percentage of income is measured along the vertical axis.

Loss-minimizing case The circumstances where a firm loses less than its Total fixed cost; when the price at which the firm can sell its product is less than Average total cost but greater than Average variable cost.

Lotteries Games of chance where people buy numbered tickets and winners are drawn by lot; a source of state and local government revenue.

Lump-sum tax A tax which is a constant amount (the tax revenue of government is the same) at all levels of GDP.

M

M1 The narrowly defined Money supply; the Currency and Checkable deposits (*see*) not owned by the Federal government, Federal Reserve Banks, or Depository institutions.

M2 A more broadly defined Money supply; equal to *M*1 (*see*) plus Noncheckable savings deposits, Money market deposit accounts, small Time deposits (deposits of less than $100,000), and individual Money market mutual fund balances.

M3 Very broadly defined Money supply; equal to *M*2 (*see*) plus large Time deposits (deposits of $100,000 or more).

Macroeconomics The part of economics concerned with the economy as a whole; with such major aggregates as the household, business, and governmental sectors and with totals for the economy.

Managed floating exchange rate An Exchange rate allowed to change (float) to eliminate Payments deficits and surpluses and is controlled (managed) to reduce day-to-day fluctuations.

Managerial-opposition hypothesis The explanation that attributes the relative decline of unionism in the United States to the increased and more aggressive opposition of management to unions.

Managerial prerogatives The decisions—often enumerated in the contract between a Labor union and a business Firm—that the management of the Firm has the sole right to make.

Marginal analysis Decision making which involves a comparison or marginal ("extra" or "additional") benefits and marginal costs.

Marginal cost   The extra (additional) cost of producing one more unit of output; equal to the change in Total cost divided by the change in output (and in the short run to the change in total Variable cost divided by the change in output).

Marginal labor cost   The amount the total cost of employing Labor increases when a Firm employs one additional unit of Labor (the quantity of other resources employed remaining constant); equal to the change in the total cost of Labor divided by the change in the quantity of Labor employed.

Marginal product   The additional output produced when one additional unit of a resource is employed (the quantity of all other resources employed remaining constant); equal to the change in total product divided by the change in the quantity of a resource employed.

Marginal productivity theory of income distribution   The contention that the distribution of income is equitable when each unit of each resource receives a money payment equal to its marginal contribution to the firm's revenue (its Marginal revenue product).

Marginal propensity to consume   Fraction of any change in Disposable income spent for Consumer goods; equal to the change in consumption divided by the change in Disposable income.

Marginal propensity to save   Fraction of any change in Disposable income which households save; equal to change in Saving (*see*) divided by the change in Disposable income.

Marginal rate of substitution   The rate (at the margin) at which a consumer is prepared to substitute one good or service for another and remain equally satisfied (have the same total Utility); and equal to the slope of an Indifference curve (*see*).

Marginal resource cost   The amount the total cost of employing a resource increases when a Firm employs one additional unit of the resource (the quantity of all other resources employed remaining constant); equal to the change in the Total cost of the resource divided by the change in the quantity of the resource employed.

Marginal revenue   The change in the Total revenue of the Firm which results from the sale of one additional unit of its product; equal to the change in Total revenue divided by the change in the quantity of the product sold (demanded).

Marginal-revenue–marginal-cost approach   A method which determines the total output where Economic profit (*see*) is a maximum (or losses a minimum) by comparing the Marginal revenue (*see*) and the Marginal cost (*see*) of each additional unit of output.

Marginal revenue product   The change in the Total revenue of the Firm when it employs one additional unit of a resource (the quantity of all other resources employed remaining constant); equal to the change in Total revenue divided by the change in the quantity of the resource employed.

Marginal tax rate   The fraction of additional (taxable) income which must be paid in taxes.

Marginal utility   The extra Utility (*see*) a consumer obtains from the consumption of one additional unit of a good or service; equal to the change in total Utility divided by the change in the quantity consumed.

Market   Any institution or mechanism which brings together the buyers (demanders) and sellers (suppliers) of a particular good or service.

Market demand   (*See* Total demand.)

Market economy   An economy in which only the private decisions of consumers, resource suppliers, and business Firms determine how resources are allocated; the Market system.

Market failure   The failure of a market to bring about the allocation of resources which best satisfies the wants of society (that maximizes the satisfaction of wants). In particular, the over- or underallocation of resources to the production of a particular good or service (because of Spillovers or informational problems) and no allocation of resources to the production of Public goods (*see*).

Market for externality rights   A market in which the Perfectly inelastic supply (*see*) of the right to pollute the environment and the demand for the right to pollute would determine the price a polluter would have to pay for the right.

Market-oriented income stabilization   The proposal to shift the goal of farm policy from the enhancement to the stabilization of farm prices and incomes; allow farm prices and incomes to move toward their free-market levels in the long run; and have government stabilize farm prices and incomes from year to year by purchasing farm products when their prices fall below and by selling surplus farm products when their prices rise above their long-run price trend.

Market period   A period in which producers of a product are unable to change the quantity produced in response to a change in its price; in which there is Perfect inelasticity of supply (*see*); and where all resources are Fixed resources (*see*).

Market policies   Government policies designed to reduce the market power of labor unions and large business firms and to reduce or eliminate imbalances and bottlenecks in labor markets.

Market socialism   An economic system (method of organization) in which property resources are publicly owned and markets and prices are used to direct and coordinate economic activities.

Market system   All the product and resource markets of the economy and the relationships among them; a method which allows the prices determined in these markets to allocate the economy's scarce resources and to communicate and coordinate the decisions made by consumers, business firms, and resource suppliers.

Median-voter model   The view that under majority rule the median (middle) voter will be in the dominant position to determine the outcome of an election.

Medicaid   A Federal program in the United States which helps finance the medical expenses of individuals covered by the Supplemental security income (*see*) and the Aid to families with dependent children (*see*) programs.

Medicare   A Federal program which is financed by Payroll taxes (*see*) and provides for (1) compulsory hospital insurance for senior citizens and (2) low-cost voluntary insurance to help older Americans pay physicians' fees.

Medium of exchange   Money (*see*); a convenient means of exchanging goods and services without engaging in Barter (*see*); what sellers generally accept and buyers generally use to pay for a good or service.

Microeconomics   The part of economics concerned with such individual units within the economy as Industries, Firms, and Households; and with individual markets, particular prices, and specific goods and services.

Minimum wage   The lowest Wage (rate) employers may legally pay for an hour of Labor.

Mixed capitalism   An economy in which both government and private decisions determine how resources are allocated.

Monetarism   An alternative to Keynesianism (*see*); the macroeconomic view that the main cause of changes in aggregate output and the price level are fluctuations in the money supply; advocates a Monetary rule (*see*).

Monetary multiplier   The multiple of its Excess reserves (*see*) by which the Commercial banking system (*see*) can expand the Money supply and Demand deposits by making new loans (or buying securities); and equal to one divided by the Required reserve ratio (*see*).

Monetary policy   Changing the Money supply (*see*) to assist the economy to achieve a full-employment, noninflationary level of total output.

Monetary rule   The rule suggested by Monetarism (*see*); the Money supply should be expanded each year at the same annual rate as the potential rate of growth of the Real gross domestic product; the supply of money should be increased steadily at from 3 to 5 percent per year.

Money   Any item which is generally acceptable to sellers in exchange for goods and services.

Money capital   Money available to purchase Capital goods (*see*).

Money income   (*See* Nominal income.)

Money interest rate   The Nominal interest rate (*see*).

Money market   The market in which the demand for and the supply of money determine the Interest rate (or the level of interest rates) in the economy.

Money market deposit account (MMDA)   Interest-earning accounts at banks and thrift institutions which pool the funds of depositors to buy various short-term securities.

Money market mutual funds (MMMF)   Interest-bearing accounts offered by brokers which pool depositors' funds for the purchase of short-term securities; depositors may write checks in minimum amounts or more against their accounts.

Money supply   Narrowly defined (*see*) $M1$, more broadly defined (*see*) $M2$ and $M3$.

Money wage   The amount of money received by a worker per unit of time (hour, day, etc.); nominal wage.

Money wage rate   (*See* Money wage.)

Monopolistic competition   A market in which many Firms sell a Differentiated product (*see*), into which entry is relatively easy, in which the Firm has some control over its product price, and in which there is considerable Nonprice competition (*see*).

Monopoly   A market in which the number of sellers is so small that each seller is able to influence the total supply and the price of the good or service. (Also *see* Pure monopoly.)

Monopsony   A market in which there is only one buyer of a good, service, or resource.

Moral hazard problem   The possibility that individuals or institutions will change their behavior as the result of a contract or agreement. Example: A bank whose deposits are insured against loss may make riskier loans and investments.

Most-favored-nation (MFN) clause   A clause in a trade agreement between the United States and another nation which provides that the other nation's Imports into the United States will be subjected to the lowest tariff levied then or later on any other nation's Imports into the United States.

MR = MC rule   A Firm will maximize its Economic profit (or minimize its losses) by producing the output at which Marginal revenue (*see*) and Marginal cost (*see*) are equal—provided the price at which it can sell its products is equal to or greater than Average variable cost (*see*).

MRP = MRC rule   To maximize Economic profit (or minimize losses) a Firm should employ the quantity of a resource where its Marginal revenue product (*see*) is equal to its Marginal resource cost (*see*).

Multinational corporations   A firm which owns production facilities in other countries and produces and sells its products abroad.

Multiplier   The ratio of the change in the Equilibrium GDP to the change in Investment (*see*), or to the change in any other component of Aggregate expenditures or Aggregate demand; the number by which a change in any component of Aggregate expenditures or Aggregate demand must be multiplied to find the resulting change in the Equilibrium GDP.

Multiplier effect   The effect on Equilibrium gross domestic product of a change in Aggregate expenditures or Aggregate demand (caused by a change in the Consumption schedule, Investment, Government expenditures, or Net exports).

Mutual interdependence   Situation in which a change in price (or in some other policy) by one Firm will affect the sales and profits of another Firm (or other Firms) and any Firm which makes such a change can expect the other Firm(s) to react in an unpredictable (uncertain) way.

Mutual savings bank   A Firm without stockholders which accepts deposits primarily from small individual savers and which lends primarily to individuals to finance the purchases of residences.

Mutually exclusive goals   Goals which conflict and cannot be achieved simultaneously.

N

National bank   A Commercial bank (*see*) chartered by the United States government.

National health insurance (NHI)   A program through which the Federal government would provide a basic package of health care to all citizens at no direct charge or at a low cost-sharing level. Financing would be out of general tax revenues.

National income   Total income earned by resource suppliers for their contributions to the production of the Gross domestic product (*see*); equal to the Gross domestic product minus the Nonincome charges (*see*) minus Net foreign factor income earned in the United States (*see*).

National income accounting   The techniques employed to measure the overall production of the economy and other related totals for the nation as a whole.

National Labor Relations Act   (*See* Wagner Act.)

National Labor Relations Board   The board established by the Wagner Act (National Labor Relations) Act (*see*) of 1935 to investigate unfair labor practices, issue Cease-and-desist orders (*see*), and to conduct elections among employees to determine if they wish to be represented by a Labor union and which union they wish to represent them.

Natural monopoly   An industry in which Economies of scale (*see*) are so great the product can be produced by one Firm at a lower average total cost than if the product were produced by more than one Firm.

Natural rate hypothesis   The idea that the economy is stable in the long run at the natural rate of unemployment; views the long-run Phillips Curve (*see*) as vertical at the natural rate of unemployment.

Natural rate of unemployment   (*See* Full-employment unemployment rate.)

NDP   (*See* Net domestic product.)

Near-money   Financial assets, the most important of which are Noncheckable savings accounts, Time deposits, and U.S. short-term securities and savings bonds, which are not a medium of exchange but can be readily converted into Money.

Negative income tax   The proposal to subsidize families and individuals with money payments when their incomes fall below a Guaranteed income (*see*); the negative tax would decrease as earned income increases. (*See* Benefit-reduction rate.)

Negative relationship   (*See* Inverse relationship.)

Net capital movement   The difference between the real and financial investments and loans made by individuals and Firms of one nation in the other nations of the world and the investments and loans made by individuals and Firms from other nations in a nation; Capital inflows less Capital outflows.

Net domestic product   Gross domestic product (*see*) less that part of the output needed to replace the Capital goods worn out in producing the output (Consumption of fixed capital, *see*).

Net export effect   The notion that the impact of a change in Monetary policy (Fiscal policy) will be strengthened (weakened) by the consequent change in Net exports (*see*). For example, a tight (easy) money policy will increase (decrease) domestic interest rates, increasing (decreasing) the foreign demand for dollars. The dollar appreciates (depreciates) and causes American net exports to decrease (increase).

Net exports   Exports (*see*) minus Imports (*see*).

Net foreign factor income earned in the United States   Payments of resource income to the rest of the world minus receipts of resource income from the rest of the world; the difference between GDP (*see*) and GNP (*see*).

Net investment income   The interest and dividend income received by the residents of a nation from residents of other nations less the interest and dividend payments made by the residents of that nation to the residents of other nations.

Net private domestic investment   Gross private domestic investment (*see*) less Consumption of fixed capital (*see*); the addition to the nation's stock of Capital during a year.

Net taxes   The taxes collected by government less Government transfer payments (*see*).

Net transfers   The personal and government transfer payments made to residents of foreign nations less the personal and government transfer payments received from residents of foreign nations.

Net worth   The total Assets (*see*) less the total Liabilities (*see*) of a Firm or an individual; the claims of the owners of a firm against its total Assets.

New classical economics   The theory that, although unanticipated price level changes may create macroeconomic instability in the short run, the economy is stable at the full-employment level of domestic output in the long run because of price and wage flexibility.

New Global Compact A reform agenda by which Less developed countries (*see*) seek more foreign aid, debt relief, greater access to world markets, freer immigration, and an end to neocolonialism.

New perspective view of advertising Envisions advertising as a low-cost source of consumer information which increases competition by making consumers more aware of substitute products.

NIT (*See* Negative income tax.)

NLRB (*See* National Labor Relations Board.)

Nominal gross domestic output (GDP) The GDP (*see*) measured in terms of the price level at the time of measurement (unadjusted for changes on the price level).

Nominal income The number of dollars received by an individual or group during some period of time.

Nominal interest rate The rate of interest expressed in dollars of current value (not adjusted for inflation).

Nominal wage The Money wage (*see*).

Noncash transfers Governmental Transfer payments (*see*) in the form of goods and services rather than money; for example, housing assistance and job training.

Noncheckable savings account A Savings account (*see*) against which a check can *not* be written.

Noncollusive oligopoly An Oligopoly (*see*) in which the firms do not act together and in agreement to determine the price of the product and the output each Firm will produce or to determine the geographic area in which each Firm will sell.

Noncompeting groups Groups of workers in the economy who do not compete with each other for employment because the skill and training of the workers in one group are substantially different from those in other groups.

Nondiscretionary fiscal policy The increases (decreases) in Net taxes (*see*) which occur without Congressional action when the gross domestic products rises (falls) and which tend to stabilize the economy; also called Built-in stability.

Nondurable good A Consumer good (*see*) with an expected life (use) of less than three years.

Nonexhaustive expenditure An expenditure by government which does not result directly in the employment of economic resources or the production of goods and services; *see* Government transfer payment.

Nonfinancial investment An investment which does not require households to save a part of their money incomes; but which uses surplus (unproductive) labor to build Capital goods.

Nonincome charges Consumption of fixed capital (*see*) and Indirect business taxes (*see*).

Nonincome determinants of consumption and saving All influences on consumption spending and saving other than the level of GDP.

Noninterest determinants of investment All influences on the level of investment spending other than the rate of interest.

Noninvestment transaction An expenditure for stocks, bonds, or second-hand Capital goods.

Nonmarket transactions The production of goods and services not included in the measurement of the Gross domestic product because the goods and services are not bought and sold.

Nonprice competition The means other than decreasing the prices of their products which Firms employ to increase the sale of their products; and which includes Product differentiation (*see*), advertising, and sales promotion activities.

Nonproduction transaction The purchase and sale of any item which is not a currently produced good or service.

Nontariff barriers All barriers other than Tariffs (*see*) which nations erect to impede international trade: Import quotas (*see*), licensing requirements, unreasonable product-quality standards, unnecessary red tape in customs procedures, etc.

Normal good A good or service whose consumption increases (decreases) when income increases (decreases); price remaining constant.

Normal profit Payment that must be made by a Firm to obtain and retain Entrepreneurial ability (*see*); the minimum payment (income) Entrepreneurial ability must (expect to) receive to induce it to perform the entrepreneurial functions for a Firm; an Implicit cost (*see*).

Normative economics That part of economics pertaining to value judgments about what the economy should be like; concerned with economic goals and policies.

Norris-LaGuardia Act The Federal act of 1932 which made it more difficult for employers to obtain Injunctions (*see*) against Labor unions in Federal courts and which declared that Yellow-dog contracts (*see*) were unenforceable.

North American Free Trade Agreement (NAFTA) A 1993 agreement establishing a trade bloc (*see*) comprising Canada, Mexico, and the United States. The goal is to establish free trade between the three nations. In late 1994 Chile was invited to apply for membership.

NTBs (*See* Nontariff barriers.)

O

OASDHI (*See* Old age, survivors, and disability health insurance.)

Occupational discrimination The arbitrary restrictions which prevent blacks (and other minority groups) or women from entering the more desirable and higher-paying occupations.

Occupational licensure The laws of state or local governments which require a worker to obtain a license from a licensing board (by satisfying certain specified requirements) before engaging in a particular occupation.

Official reserves   The foreign monies (currencies) owned by the central bank of a nation.

Okun's law   The generalization that any one percentage point rise in the Unemployment rate above the Full-employment unemployment rate will increase the GDP gap by 2.5 percent of the Potential output (GDP) of the economy.

Old age, survivors, and disability heath insurance   The social program in the United States financed by Federal Payroll taxes (*see*) on employers and employees and designed to replace the Earnings lost when workers retire, die, or become unable to work.

Oligopoly   A market in which a few Firms sell either a Standardized or Differentiated product, into which entry is difficult, in which the Firm has limited control over product price because of Mutual interdependence (*see*) (except when there is collusion among firms), and in which there is typically Nonprice competition (*see*).

Oligopsony   A market in which there are a few buyers.

OPEC   An acronym for the Organization of Petroleum Exporting Countries (*see*).

Open economy   An economy which both exports and imports goods and services.

Open Market Committee   The twelve-member group which determines the purchase-and-sale policies of the Federal Reserve Banks in the market for United States government securities.

Open-market operations   The buying and selling of United States government securities by the Federal Reserve Banks.

Open shop   A place of employment where the employer may hire either Labor union members or workers who are not (and need not become) members of the union.

Opportunity cost   The amount of other products which must be forgone or sacrificed to produce a unit of a product.

Optimal amount of externality reduction   That reduction of pollution or other negative externality where society's marginal benefit and marginal cost of reducing the externality are equal.

Organization of Petroleum Exporting Countries   The cartel formed in 1970 by thirteen oil-producing countries to control the price and quantity of crude oil exported by its members, and which accounts for a large proportion of the world's export of oil.

"Other things equal" assumption   Assuming that factors other than those being considered are constant.

Outpayments   The expenditures of (its own or foreign) money which the individuals, Firms, and governments of one nation make to purchase goods and services, for Remittances, as investment income, and Capital outflows abroad.

Output effect   The change in labor input resulting from the effect of a change in the wage rate on a Firm's cost of production and the subsequent change in the desired level of output, after the Substitution effect (*see*) has been determined and eliminated.

P

Paper money   Pieces of paper used as a Medium of exchange (*see*); in the United States, Federal Reserve Notes (*see*).

Paradox of voting   A situation where voting by majority rule fails to provide a consistent ranking of society's preferences for public goods or services.

Parity concept   The notion that year after year a specific output of a farm product should enable a farmer to acquire a constant amount of nonagricultural goods and services.

Parity price   The price at which a specific amount of an agricultural product would have to be sold to enable a farmer to obtain year after year money income needed to purchase a constant total quantity of nonagricultural goods and services.

Parity ratio   The ratio (index) of the price received by farmers from the sale of an agricultural commodity to the (index of the) prices paid by them; used as a rationale for Price supports (*see*).

Partnership   An unincorporated business Firm owned and operated by two or more persons.

Patent laws   The Federal laws granting to inventors and innovators the exclusive right to produce and sell a new product or machine for a period of seventeen years.

Payments deficits   (*See* Balance of payments deficit.)

Payments surplus   (*See* Balance of payments surplus.)

Payroll tax   A tax levied on employers of Labor equal to a percentage of all or part of the wages and salaries paid by them; and on employees equal to a percentage of all or part of the wages and salaries received by them.

Perestroika   The essential feature of Mikhail Gorbachev's mid-1980s reform program to "restructure" the Soviet economy; included modernization, decentralization, some privatization, and improved worker incentives.

Perfectly elastic demand   A change in the Quantity demanded requires no change in the price of the product or resource; buyers will purchase as much of a product or resource as is available at a constant price.

Perfectly elastic supply   A change in the Quantity supplied requires no change in the price of the product or resource; sellers will make available as much of the product or resource as buyers will purchase at a constant price.

Perfectly inelastic demand   A change in price results in no change in the Quantity demanded of a product or resource; the Quantity demanded is the same at all prices.

Perfectly inelastic supply A change in price results in no change in the Quantity supplied of a product or resource; the Quantity supplied is the same at all prices.

Per se violations Collusive actions, such as attempts to fix prices or divide a market, which are violations of the antitrust laws even though the actions are unsuccessful.

Personal consumption expenditures The expenditures of Households for Durable and Nondurable consumer goods and services.

Personal distribution of income The manner in which the economy's Personal or Disposable income is divided among different income classes or different households.

Personal income The earned and unearned income available to resource suppliers and others before the payment of Personal taxes (*see*).

Personal income tax A tax levied on the taxable income of individuals (households and unincorporated firms).

Personal saving The Personal income of households less Personal taxes (*see*) and Personal consumption expenditures (*see*); Disposable income not spent for Consumer goods (*see*).

Phillips Curve A curve showing the relationship between the Unemployment rate (*see*) (on the horizontal axis) and the annual rate of increase in the Price level (on the vertical axis).

Planned economy An economy in which government determines how resources are allocated.

Planned investment The amount which business firms plan or intend to invest.

Plant A physical establishment (Land and Capital) which performs one or more of the functions in the production (fabrication and distribution) of goods and services.

"Play or pay" A means of expanding health insurance coverage by requiring employers to either provide insurance for their workers or pay a special payroll tax to finance insurance for uncovered workers.

$P = MC$ rule A firm in Pure competition (*see*) will maximize its Economic profit (*see*) or minimize its losses by producing the output at which the price of the product is equal to Marginal cost (*see*), provided that price is equal to or greater than Average variable cost (*see*) in the short run and equal to or greater than Average total cost (*see*) in the long run.

Policy economics The formulation of courses of action to bring about desired results or to prevent undesired occurrences (to control economic events).

Political business cycle The tendency of Congress to destabilize the economy by reducing taxes and increasing government expenditures before elections and to raise taxes and lower expenditures after elections.

Positive economics The analysis of facts or data to establish scientific generalizations about economic behavior; compare Normative economics.

Positive relationship The relationship between two variables which change in the same direction, for example, product price and quantity supplied.

Post hoc, ergo propter hoc fallacy Incorrectly reasoning that when one event precedes another the first event is the cause of the second.

Potential competition The possibility that new competitors will be induced to enter an industry if firms now in that industry are realizing large economic profits.

Potential output The real output (GDP) an economy is able to produce when it fully employs its available resources.

Poverty An existence in which the basic needs of an individual or family exceed the means to satisfy them.

Poverty rate The percentage of the population with incomes below the official poverty income levels established by the Federal government.

Preferred provider organization (PPO) An arrangement by which participating doctors and hospitals agree to provide health care to insured individuals at rates negotiated with the insurer.

Premature inflation Inflation (*see*) which occurs before the economy has reached Full employment (*see*).

Price The quantity of money (or of other goods or services) paid and received for a unit of a good or service.

Price ceiling A legally established maximum price for a good or service.

Price-decreasing effect The effect in a competitive market of a decrease in Demand or an increase in Supply upon the Equilibrium price (*see*).

Price discrimination The selling of a product to different buyers at different prices when the price differences are not justified by differences in production costs; a practice made illegal by the Clayton Act (*see*) when it reduces competition.

Price elasticity of demand The ratio of the percentage change in Quantity demanded of a product or resource to the percentage change in its price; the responsiveness or sensitivity of the quantity of a product or resource demanded to a change in the price of a product or resource.

Price elasticity of supply The ratio of the percentage change in Quantity supplied of a product or resource to the percentage change in its price; the responsiveness or sensitivity of the quantity of a product or resource supplied to a change in the price of a product or resource.

Price floor A legally determined price above the Equilibrium price.

Price guidepost A government exhortation that the price charged by an industry for its product should increase by no more than the increase in the Unit labor cost (*see*) of producing the product.

Price increasing effect   The effect in a competitive market of an increase in Demand or a decrease in Supply on the equilibrium price.

Price index   An index number which shows how the average price of a "market basket" of goods changes through time. A price index is used to change nominal output (income) into real output (income).

Price leadership   An informal method which Firms in an Oligopoly (*see*) may employ to set the price of their product: one firm (the leader) is the first to announce a change in price and the other firms (the followers) quickly announce identical (or similar) changes in price.

Price level   The weighted average of the Prices paid for the final goods and services produced in the economy.

Price level surprises   Unanticipated changes in the price level.

Price maker   A seller (or buyer) of a product or resource which is able to affect the product or resource price by changing the amount it sells (buys).

Price support   The minimum price which government allows sellers to receive for a good or service; a legally established or maintained minimum price.

Price taker   A seller (or buyer) of a product or resource who is unable to affect the price at which a product or resource sells by changing the amount it sold (or bought).

Price-wage flexibility   Changes in the prices of products and in the Wages paid to workers; the ability of prices and Wages to rise or to fall.

Price war   Successive and continued decreases in the prices charged by the firms in an oligopolistic industry by which each firm hopes to increase its sales and revenues and from which firms seldom benefit.

Prime interest rate   The interest rate banks charge their most credit-worthy borrowers, for example, large corporations with impeccable financing credentials.

Principal-agent problem   A conflict of interest which occurs when agents (workers) pursue their own objectives to the detriment of the principal's (employer's) goals.

Private good   A good or service subject to the Exclusion principle (*see*) and which is provided by privately owned firms to those who are willing to pay for it.

Private property   The right of private persons and Firms to obtain, own, control, employ, dispose of, and bequeath Land, Capital, and other Assets.

Private sector   The Households and business firms of the economy.

Product differentiation   Physical or other differences between the products of different Firms which result in individual buyers preferring (so long as the price charged by all sellers is the same) the product of one Firm to the Products of the other Firms.

Production possibilities curve (table)   A curve (table) showing the different combinations of two goods or services that can be produced in a Full-employment (*see*), Full-production (*see*) economy where the available supplies of resources and technology are constant.

Productive efficiency   The production of a good in the least costly way; occurs when production takes place at the output where Average total cost is at a minimum and where Marginal product per dollar's worth of each input is the same.

Productivity   A measure of average output or real output per unit of input. For example, the productivity of labor may be determined by dividing hours of work into real output.

Productivity slowdown   The recent decline in the rate at which Labor productivity (*see*) in the United States has increased.

Product market   A market in which Households buy and Firms sell the products they have produced.

Profit   (*see*) Economic profit and Normal profit; without an adjective preceding it, the income of those who supply the economy with Entrepreneurial ability (*see*) or Normal profit.

Profit-maximizing case   The circumstances which result in an Economic profit (*see*) for a Firm when it produces the output at which Economic profit is a maximum; when the price at which the Firm can sell its product is greater than the Average total cost of producing it.

Profit-maximizing rule (combination of resources)   The quantity of each resource a Firm must employ if its Economic profit (*see*) is to be a maximum or its losses a minimum; the combination in which the Marginal revenue product (*see*) of each resource is equal to its Marginal resource cost (*see*) (to its price if the resource is employed in a competitive market).

Progressive tax   A tax such that the Average tax rate increases as the taxpayer's income increases and decreases as income decreases.

Property tax   A tax on the value of property (Capital, Land, stocks and bonds, and other Assets) owned by Firms and Households.

Proportional tax   A tax such that the Average tax rate remains constant as the taxpayer's income increases and decreases.

Proprietors' income   The net income of the owners of unincorporated Firms (proprietorships and partnerships).

Prosperous industry   (*See* Expanding industry.)

Protective tariff   A Tariff (*see*) designed to protect domestic producers of a good from the competition of foreign producers.

Public assistance programs   Programs which pay benefits to those who are unable to earn income (because of permanent handicaps or because they are dependent children) which are financed by general tax revenues, and which are viewed as public charity (rather than earned rights).

Public choice theory   Generalizations that describe how government (the Public sector) makes decisions for the use of economic resources.

Public debt   The total amount owed by the Federal government (to the owners of government securities) and equal to the sum of its past Budget deficits (less its budget surpluses).

Public finance   The branch of economics which analyzes government revenues and expenditures.

Public good   A good or service to which the Exclusion principle (*see*) is not applicable; and which is provided by government if it yields substantial benefits to society.

Public interest theory of regulation   The presumption that the purpose of the regulation of an Industry is to protect the public (consumers) from the abuse of the power possessed by Natural monopolies (*see*).

Public sector   The part of the economy that contains all its governments; government.

Public-sector failure   The failure of the Public sector (government) to resolve socioeconomic problems because it performs its functions inefficiently.

Public utility   A Firm which produces an essential good or service, has obtained from a government the right to be the sole supplier of the good or service in the area, and is regulated by that government to prevent the abuse of its monopoly power.

Purchasing power parity   The idea that exchange rates between nations equate the purchasing power of various currencies; exchange rates between any two nations adjust to reflect the price level differences between the countries.

Pure capitalism   An economic system in which property resources are privately owned and markets and prices are used to direct and coordinate economic activities.

Pure competition   (1) A market in which a very large number of Firms sells a Standardized product (*see*), into which entry is very easy, in which the individual seller has no control over the price at which the product sells, and in which there is no Nonprice competition (*see*); (2) a market in which there is a very large number of buyers.

Pure monopoly   A market in which one Firm sells a unique product (one for which there are no close substitutes), into which entry is blocked, in which the Firm has considerable control over the price at which the product sells, and in which Nonprice competition (*see*) may or may not be found.

Pure profit   (*See* Economic profit.)

Pure rate of interest   (*See The* rate of interest.)

Q

Quantity-decreasing effect   The effect in a competitive mar-

ket of a decrease in Demand or a decrease in Supply on the Equilibrium quantity (*see*).

Quantity demanded   The amount of a good or service buyers wish (or a buyer wishes) to purchase at a particular price during some period.

Quantity-increasing effect   The effect in a competitive market of an increase in Demand or an increase in Supply on the Equilibrium quantity (*see*).

Quantity supplied   The amount of a good or service sellers offer (or a seller offers) to sell at a particular price during some period.

Quasi-public bank   A bank which is privately owned but governmentally (publicly) controlled; each of the Federal Reserve Banks.

Quasi-public good   A good or service to which the Exclusion principle (*see*) could be applied, but which has such a large Spillover benefit (*see*) that government sponsors its production to prevent an underallocation of resources.

R

R & D   Research and development; activities undertaken to bring about Technological progress.

Ratchet effect   The tendency for the Price level to rise when Aggregate demand increases, but not fall when Aggregate demand declines.

Rate of exchange   The price paid in one's own money to acquire one unit of a foreign money; the rate at which the money of one nation is exchanged for the money of another nation.

Rate of interest   Price paid for the use of Money or for the use of Capital; interest rate.

Rational   An adjective which describes the behavior of any individual who consistently does those things enabling him or her to achieve the declared objective of the individual; and which describes the behavior of a consumer who uses money income to buy the collection of goods and services yielding the maximum amount of Utility (*see*).

Rational expectations theory   The hypothesis that business firms and households expect monetary and fiscal policies to have certain effects on the economy and take, in pursuit of their own self-interests, actions which make these policies ineffective.

Rationing function of price   The ability of a price in a competitive market to equalize Quantity demanded and Quantity supplied and to eliminate shortages and surpluses by rising or falling.

Reaganomics   The policies of the Reagan administration based on Supply-side economics (*see*) and intended to reduce inflation and the Unemployment rate (Stagflation).

Real-balances effect   The tendency for increases (decreases) in the price level to lower (raise) the real value (or purchasing power) of financial assets with fixed money values; and, as a result, to reduce (expand) total spending in the economy.

Real capital (*See* Capital.)

Real gross domestic product Gross domestic product (*see*) adjusted for changes in the price level; Gross domestic product in a year divided by the GDP deflator (*see*) for that year expressed as a decimal.

Real income The amount of goods and services an individual or group can purchase with his, her, or its Nominal income during some period of time. Nominal income adjusted for changes in the Price level.

Real interest rate The rate of interest expressed in dollars of constant value (adjusted for inflation); and equal to the Nominal interest rate (*see*) less the expected rate of inflation.

Real rate of interest The Real interest rate (*see*).

Real wage The amount of goods and services a worker can purchase with his or her Nominal wage (*see*); the purchasing power of the Nominal wage; the Nominal wage adjusted for changes in the Price level.

Real wage rate (*See* Real wage.)

Recessionary gap The amount by which the Aggregate expenditures schedule (curve) must increase (shift upward) to increase the real GDP to the full-employment noninflationary level.

Reciprocal Trade Agreements Act of 1934 The Federal act which gave the President the authority to negotiate agreements with foreign nations and lower American tariff rates by up to 50 percent if the foreign nations would reduce tariff rates on American goods and which incorporated Most-favored-nation clauses (*see*) in the agreements reached with these nations.

Refinancing the public debt Paying owners of maturing United States government securities with money obtained by selling new securities or with new securities.

Regressive tax A tax such that the Average tax rate decreases (increases) as the taxpayer's income increases (decreases).

Regulatory agency An agency (commission or board) established by the Federal or a state government to control the prices charged and the services offered (output produced) by a Natural monopoly (*see*).

Remittance A gift or grant; a payment for which no good or service is received in return; the funds sent by workers who have legally or illegally entered a foreign nation to their families in the nations from which they have migrated.

Rental income Income received by those who supply the economy with Land (*see*).

Rent-seeking behavior The pursuit through government of a transfer of income or wealth to a resource supplier, business, or consumer at someone else's or society's expense.

Required reserve ratio (*See* Reserve ratio.)

Required reserves (*See* Legal reserves.)

Reserve ratio The specified minimum percentage of its deposit liabilities which a Member bank (*see*) must keep on deposit at the Federal Reserve Bank in its district, or in Vault cash (*see*).

Resolution Trust Corporation (RTC) A Federal institution created in 1989 to oversee the closing and sale of failed Savings and loan institutions.

Resource market A market in which Households sell and Firms buy the services of resources.

Retiring the public debt Reducing the size of the Public debt by paying money to owners of maturing United States government securities.

Revaluation An increase in the governmentally defined value of a currency.

Revenue tariff A Tariff (*see*) designed to produce income for the (Federal) government.

Ricardian equivalence theorem The idea that an increase in the public debt will have little or no effect on real output and employment because taxpayers will save more in anticipation of future higher taxes to pay the higher interest expense on the debt.

Right-to-work law A law which has been enacted in twenty states that makes it illegal in those states to require a worker to join a Labor union in order to retain his or her job with an employer.

Roundabout production The construction and use of Capital (*see*) to aide in the production of Consumer goods (*see*).

Ruble overhang The large amount of forced savings formerly held by Russian households due to the scarcity of consumer goods; these savings fueled inflation when Russian prices were decontrolled.

Rule of reason The rule stated and applied in the U.S. Steel case (*see*) that only combinations and contracts unreasonably restraining trade are subject to actions under the antitrust laws and that size and the possession of monopoly are not themselves illegal.

Rule of 70 A method for determining the number of years it will take for the Price level to double; divide 70 by the annual rate of inflation.

S

Sales tax A tax levied on expenditures for a broad group of products.

Saving Disposable income not spent for Consumer goods (*see*); equal to Disposable income minus Personal consumption expenditures (*see*).

Savings account A deposit in a Depository institution (*see*) which is interest-earning and which can normally be withdrawn by the depositor at any time.

Savings and Loan association (S&L) A Firm which accepts deposits primarily from small individual savers, and lends primarily to individuals to finance purchases of residences.

Saving schedule Schedule which shows the amounts Households plan to save (plan not to spend for Consumer goods, *see*) at different levels of Disposable income.

Savings institution A Thrift institution (*see*).

Say's law The (discredited) macroeconomic generalization that the production of goods and services (supply) creates an equal Aggregate demand for these goods and services.

Scarce resources The fixed (limited) quantities of Land, Capital, Labor, and Entrepreneurial ability (*see all*) which are never sufficient to satisfy the virtually unlimited material wants of humans.

Schumpeter-Galbraith view (of oligopoly) The belief shared by these two economists that large oligopolistic firms are necessary for rapid technological progress (because only this kind of firm has both the means and the incentive to introduce technological changes).

Seasonal variation An increase or decrease during a single year in the level of economic activity caused by a change in the season.

Secondary boycott The refusal of a Labor union to buy or to work with the products produced by another union (or a group of nonunion workers) which is having a dispute with another employer.

Secular trend The expansion or contraction in the level of economic activity over a long period of years.

Self-interest What each Firm, property owner, worker, and consumer believes is best for itself and seeks to obtain.

Seniority The length of time a worker has been employed by an employer relative to the lengths of time the employer's other workers have been employed; the principle which is used to determine which workers will be laid off when there is insufficient work for them all and who will be rehired when more work becomes available.

Separation of ownership and control Difference between the group that owns the Corporation (the stockholders) and the group that manages it (the directors and officers) and between the interests (goals) of the two groups.

Service That which is intangible (invisible) and for which a consumer, firm, or government is willing to exchange something of value.

Sherman Act The Federal antitrust act of 1890 which made monopoly, restraint of trade, and combinations and conspiracies to monopolize or to restrain trade criminal offenses; and allowed the Federal government or injured parties to take legal action against those committing these offenses.

Shirking Attempts by workers to increase their Utility or well-being by neglecting or evading work.

Shortage The amount by which the Quantity demanded of a product exceeds the Quantity supplied at a particular (below-equilibrium) price.

Short run A period of time in which producers of a product are able to change the quantity of some but not all of the resources they employ; in which some resources—the Plant (*see*)—are Fixed resources (*see*) and some are Variable resources (*see*); in which some costs are Fixed costs (*see*) and some are Variable costs (*see*); a period of time too brief to allow a Firm to vary its plant capacity but long enough to permit it to change the level at which the plant capacity is used; a period of time not long enough to enable Firms to enter or to leave an industry (*see*).

Short-run aggregate supply curve The aggregate supply curve relevant to a time period in which input prices (particularly nominal wages) remain constant when the price level changes.

Short-run competitive equilibrium The price at which the total quantity of a product supplied in the Short run (*see*) by a purely competitive industry and the total quantity of the product demanded are equal and which is equal to or greater than the Average variable cost (*see*) of producing the product.

Short-run farm problem The sharp year-to-year changes in the prices of agricultural products and in the incomes of farmers.

Short-run supply curve A curve which shows the quantities of a product a Firm in a purely competitive industry (*see* Pure competition) will offer to sell at various prices in the Short run (*see*); the portion of the firm's short-run Marginal cost (*see*) curve which lies above its Average variable cost curve.

Simple multiplier The Multiplier (*see*) in an economy in which government collects no Net taxes (*see*), there are no Imports (*see*), and Investment (*see*) is independent of the level of income (Gross domestic product); equal to one divided by the Marginal propensity to save (*see*).

Simpson-Rodino Act of 1986 Immigration legislation which provided amnesty to qualified illegal aliens; included penalties for employers who knowingly hire illegal aliens; and allowed temporary migrants to harvest perishable crops.

Single-tax movement The attempt of a group which followed the teachings of Henry George to eliminate all taxes except one which would tax all Rental income (*see*) at a rate of 100 percent.

Slope of a line The ratio of the vertical change (the rise or fall) to the horizontal change (the run) in moving between two points on a line. The slope of an upward sloping line is positive, reflecting a direct relationship between two variables; the slope of a downward sloping line is negative, reflecting an inverse relationship between two variables.

Smoot-Hawley Tariff Act Passed in 1930, this legislation established some of the highest tariffs in United States history. Its objective was to reduce imports and stimulate the domestic economy.

Social accounting (*See* National income accounting.)

Socially optimal price The price of a product which results in the most efficient allocation of an economy's resources and which is equal to the Marginal cost (*see*) of the last unit of the product produced.

Social regulation The type of regulation in which government is concerned with the conditions under which goods and services are produced, their physical characteristics, and the impact of their production on society; in contrast to Industrial regulation (*see*).

Social security programs The programs which replace the earnings lost when people retire or are temporarily unemployed, which are financed by Payroll taxes (*see*), and which are viewed as earned rights (rather than charity).

Sole proprietorship An unincorporated business firm owned and operated by a single person.

Special-interest effect Effect on public decision making and the allocation of resources when government promotes the interests (goals) of small groups to the detriment of society as a whole.

Specialization The use of the resources of an individual, a Firm, a region, or a nation to produce one or a few goods and services for which there is a Comparative advantage.

Speculation The activity of buying or selling with the motive of then reselling or rebuying to make a profit.

Spillover A benefit or cost from production or consumption, accruing without compensation to nonbuyers and nonsellers of the product (*see* Spillover benefit and Spillover cost).

Spillover benefit A benefit obtained without compensation by third parties from the production or consumption of other parties. Example: A bee keeper benefits when the neighboring farmer plants clover.

Spillover costs A cost imposed without compensation on third parties by the production or consumption of other parties. Example: A manufacturer dumps toxic chemicals into a river, killing the fish sought by sport fishers.

SSI (*See* Supplemental security income.)

Stabilization policy dilemma The use of monetary and fiscal policy to decrease the Unemployment rate increases the rate of inflation, and the use of monetary and fiscal policy to decrease the rate of inflation increases the Unemployment rate.

Stagflation Inflation accompanied by stagnation in the rate of growth of output and a high unemployment rate in the economy; simultaneous increases in both the Price level and the Unemployment rate.

Standardized product A product such that buyers are indifferent to the seller from whom they purchase it so long as the price charged by all sellers is the same; a product such that all units of the product are perfect substitutes for each other (are identical).

State bank A Commercial bank chartered to engage in the business of banking by a state government.

State ownership The ownership of property (Land and Capital) by government (the state); in the former Soviet Union by the central government (the nation).

Static economy (1) An economy in which Net private domestic investment (*see*) is zero—Gross private domestic investment (*see*) is equal to the Consumption of fixed capital (*see*); (2) an economy in which the supplies of resources, technology, and the tastes of consumers do not change and in which, therefore, the economic future is perfectly predictable and there is no uncertainty.

Store of value Any asset (*see*) or wealth set aside for future use; a function of Money.

Strategic trade policy The use of trade barriers to reduce the risk of product development by domestic firms, particularly products involving advanced technology.

Strike The withholding of their labor services by an organized group of workers (a Labor union).

Structural-change hypothesis The explanation that attributes the decline of unionism in the United States to changes in the structure of the economy and of the labor force.

Structural deficit The difference between Federal tax revenues and expenditures when the economy is at full employment.

Structural unemployment Unemployment caused by changes in the structure of demand for Consumer goods and in technology; workers who are unemployed because their skills are not demanded by employers, they lack sufficient skills to obtain employment, or they cannot easily move to locations where jobs are available.

Subsidy A payment of funds (or goods and services) by a government, business firm, or household for which it receives no good or service in return. When made by a government, it is a Government transfer payment (*see*).

Substitute goods Goods or services for which there is a direct relationship between the price of one and the Demand for the other; when the price of one falls (rises) the Demand for the other decreases (increases).

Substitution effect (1) The effect which a change in the price of a Consumer good would have on the relative expensiveness of that good and the resulting effect on the quantity of the good a consumer would purchase if the consumer's Real income (*see*) remained constant; (2) the effect which a change in the price of a resource would have on the quantity of the resource employed by a firm if the firm did not change its output.

Superfund Law of 1980 Legislation which taxes manufacturers of toxic products and uses these revenues to finance the cleanup of toxic-waste sites; assigns liability for improperly dumped waste to the firms producing, transporting, and dumping that waste.

Superior good   (*See* Normal good.)

Supplemental security income   A program federally financed and administered which provides a uniform nationwide minimum income for the aged, blind, and disabled who do not qualify for benefits under the Old age, survivors, and disability health insurance (*see*) or Unemployment insurance (*see*) programs in the United States.

Supply   A Supply schedule or a Supply curve (*see both*).

Supply curve   A curve showing the amounts of a good or service sellers (a seller) will offer to sell at various prices during some period.

Supply factor   An increase in the availability of a resource, an improvement in its quality, or an expansion of technological knowledge which makes it possible for an economy to produce a greater output of goods and services.

Supply schedule   A schedule showing the amounts of a good or service sellers (or seller) will offer at various prices during some period.

Supply shock   One of several events of the 1970s and early 1980s which increased production costs, decreased Aggregate supply, and generated Stagflation in the United States.

Supply-side economics   A view of macroeconomics which emphasizes the role of costs and Aggregate supply in explaining Inflation, unemployed labor, and Economic growth.

Supply-side view   The view of fiscal policy held by the advocates of Supply-side economics which emphasizes increasing Aggregate supply (*see*) as a means of reducing the Unemployment rate and Inflation and encouraging Economic Growth.

Support price   (*See* Price support.)

Surplus   The amount by which the Quantity supplied of a product exceeds the Quantity demanded at a specific (above-equilibrium) price.

Surplus value   A Marxian term; the amount by which the value of a worker's daily output exceeds his daily wage; the output of workers appropriated by capitalists as profit.

Sympathy strike   Withholding labor services from an employer by a Labor union which does not have a disagreement with the employer but wishes to assist another Labor union that does have a dispute with the employer.

T

Tacit collusion   Any method used in a Collusive oligopoly (*see*) to set prices and outputs which does not involve outright (or overt) collusion (formal agreements or secret meetings); and of which Price leadership (*see*) is a frequent example.

Taft-Hartley Act   The Federal act of 1947 which marked the shift from government sponsorship to government regulation of Labor unions.

Tangent   The point where a line touches, but does not intersect, a curve.

Target dilemma   A problem arising because monetary authorities cannot simultaneously stabilize both the money supply and the level of interest rates.

Tariff   A tax imposed by a nation on an imported good.

Tax   A nonvoluntary payment of money (or goods and services) to a government by a Household or Firm for which the Household or Firm receives no good or service directly in return.

Tax incidence   The income or purchasing power different persons and groups lose as a result of a tax after Tax shifting (*see*) has occurred.

Tax shifting   The transfer to others of all or part of a tax by charging them a higher price or by paying them a lower price for a good or service.

Tax subsidy   The subsidization of individuals or industries through favorable tax treatment; for example, employer-paid health insurance is exempt from Federal income and payroll taxes.

Tax-transfer disincentives   Decreases in the incentives to work, save, invest, innovate, and take risks which allegedly result from high Marginal tax rates and Transfer-payment programs.

Tax "wedge"   Such taxes as Indirect business taxes (*see*) and Payroll taxes (*see*) which are treated as a cost by business firms and reflected in the prices of their products; equal to the price of the product less the cost of the resources required to produce it.

Technology   The body of knowledge which can be used to produce goods and services from Economic resources.

Terms of trade   The rate at which units of one product can be exchanged for units of another product; the Price (*see*) of a good or service; the amount of one good or service given up to obtain one unit of another good or service.

Theory of human capital   Generalization that Wage differentials (*see*) are the result of differences in the amount of Human-capital investment (*see*); and that the incomes of lower paid workers are increased by increasing the amount of such investment.

The rate of interest   The Rate of interest (*see*) which is paid solely for the use of money over an extended period of time and which excludes the charges made for the riskiness of the loan and its administrative costs; and which is approximately equal to the rate of interest paid on the long-term and virtually riskless bonds of the United States government.

Thrift institution   A Savings and loan association, Mutual savings bank, or Credit union (*see all*).

Tight money policy   Contracting, or restricting the growth of, the nation's Money supply (*see*).

Till money   (*See* Vault cash.)

Time deposit   An interest-earning deposit in a Depository institution (*see*) which the depositor can withdraw without a loss of interest after the end of a specific period.

Token money   Coins having a Face value (*see*) greater than their Intrinsic value (*see*).

Total cost   The sum of Fixed cost (*see*) and Variable cost (*see*).

Total demand   The Demand schedule (*see*) or the Demand curve (*see*) of all buyers of a good or service.

Total demand for money   The sum of the Transactions demand for money (*see*) and Asset demand for money (*see*); the relationship between the total amount of money demanded, nominal GDP, and the Rate of Interest.

Total product   The total output of a particular good or service produced by a firm (a group of firms or the entire economy).

Total revenue   The total number of dollars received by a Firm (or Firms) from the sale of a product; equal to the total expenditures for the product produced by the Firm (or firms); equal to the quantity sold (demanded) multiplied by the price at which it is sold—by the Average revenue (*see*) from its sale.

Total-revenue test   A test to determine whether Demand is Elastic (*see*), Inelastic (*see*), or of Unitary elasticity (*see*) between any two prices: Demand is elastic (inelastic, unit elastic) if the Total revenue (*see*) of sellers of the commodity increases (decreases, remains constant) when the price of the commodity falls; or Total revenue decreases (increases, remains constant) when its price rises.

Total-revenue–total-cost approach   The method which finds the output at which Economic profit (*see*) is a maximum or losses a minimum by comparing the Total revenue and the Total costs of a Firm at different outputs.

Total spending   The total amount buyers of goods and services spend or plan to spend. Also called Aggregate expenditures.

Total supply   The Supply schedule (*see*) or the Supply curve (*see*) of all sellers of a good or service.

Total utility   The total amount of satisfaction derived from the consumption of some particular amount of a product.

Trade balance   The export of merchandise (goods) of a nation less its imports of merchandise (goods).

Trade bloc   A group of nations which lower or abolish trade barriers among members. Examples include the European Union (*see*) and the North American Free Trade Agreement (*see*).

Trade controls   Tariffs (*see*), Export subsidies, Import quotas (*see*), and other means a nation may employ to reduce Imports (*see*) and expand Exports (*see*).

Trade deficit   The amount a nation's imports of merchandise (goods) exceed its exports of merchandise (goods).

Tradeoffs   The notion that one economic goal or objective must be sacrificed to achieve some other goal.

Trade surplus   The amount a nation's exports of merchandise (goods) exceed its imports of merchandise (goods).

Trading possibilities line   A line which shows the different combinations of two products an economy is able to obtain (consume) when it specializes in the production of one product and trades (exports) this product to obtain the other product.

Traditional economy   An economic system in which traditions and customs determine how the economy will use its scarce resources.

Traditional view of advertising   The position that advertising is persuasive rather than informative; promotes industrial concentration; and is inefficient and wasteful.

Transactions demand for money   The amount of money people want to hold to use as a Medium of exchange (to make payments); and which varies directly with the nominal GDP.

Transfer payment   A payment of money (or goods and services) by a government or a Firm to a Household or Firm for which the payer receives no good or service directly in return.

Tying agreement   A promise made by a buyer when allowed to purchase a product from a seller that it will make all of its purchases of certain other products from the same seller; and a practice forbidden by the Clayton Act (*see*).

U

Unanticipated inflation   Inflation (*see*) at a rate which was greater than the rate expected for that period of time.

Underemployment   Failure to produce the maximum amount of goods and services that can be produced from the resources employed; failure to achieve Full production (*see*).

Undistributed corporate profits   After-tax corporate profits not distributed as dividends to stockholders; corporate or business saving.

Unemployment   Failure to use all available Economic resources to produce goods and services; failure of the economy to employ fully its Labor force (*see*).

Unemployment compensation   (*See* Unemployment insurance).

Unemployment insurance   The insurance program which in the United States is financed by state Payroll taxes (*see*) on employers and makes income available to workers who are unable to find jobs.

Unemployment rate   The percentage of the Labor force (*see*) unemployed at any time.

Uninsurable risk   An event—the occurrence of which is uncontrollable and unpredictable—which would result in a loss that cannot be avoided by purchasing insurance and must be assumed by an entrepreneur (*see* Entrepreneurial ability); sometimes called "uncertainty."

Union shop   A place of employment where the employer may hire either labor union members or nonmembers, but where nonmembers must become members within a specified period of time or lose their jobs.

Unitary elasticity   The Elasticity coefficient (*see*) is equal to one; the percentage change in the quantity (demanded or supplied) is equal to the percentage change in price.

Unit labor cost   Labor costs per unit of output; equal to the Nominal wage rate (*see*) divided by the Average product (*see*) of labor.

Unlimited liability   Absence of any limit on the maximum amount which may be lost by an individual and which the individual may become legally required to pay; the amount which may be lost and which a sole proprietor or partner may be required to pay.

Unlimited wants   The insatiable desire of consumers (people) for goods and services which will give them satisfaction or Utility.

Unplanned investment   Actual investment less Planned investment; increases or decreases in the inventories of business firms resulting from production greater than sales.

Unprosperous industry   (*See* Declining industry.)

Uruguay Round   The eighth and most recent round of trade negotiations under GATT (*see*).

U.S. Steel case   The antitrust action brought by the Federal government against the U.S. Steel Corporation in which the courts ruled (in 1920) that only unreasonable restraints of trade were illegal and that size and the possession of monopoly power were not violations of the antitrust laws.

Usury laws   State laws which specify the maximum interest rate at which loans can be legally made.

Utility   The want-satisfying power of a good or service; the satisfaction or pleasure a consumer obtains from the consumption of a good or service (or from the consumption of a collection of goods and services).

Utility-maximizing rule   To obtain the greatest Utility (*see*) the consumer should allocate Money income so that the last dollar spent on each good or service yields the same Marginal utility (*see*); so that the Marginal utility of each good or service divided by its price is the same for all goods and services.

V

Value added   The value of the product sold by a Firm less the value of the goods (materials) purchased and used by the Firm to produce the product; and equal to the revenue which can be used for Wages, rent, interest, and profits.

Value-added tax   A tax imposed on the difference between the value of the goods sold by a firm and the value of the goods purchased by the firm from other firms.

Value judgment   Opinion of what is desirable or undesirable; belief regarding what ought or ought not to be (regarding what is right or just and wrong or unjust).

Value of money   The quantity of goods and services for which a unit of money (a dollar) can be exchanged; the purchasing power of a unit of money; the reciprocal of the Price level.

Variable cost   A cost which in total increases (decreases) when the firm increases (decreases) its output; the cost of Variable resources (*see*).

Variable resource   Any resource employed by a firm which can be increased or decreased (varied) in quantity.

VAT   Value-added tax (*see*).

Vault cash   The Currency (*see*) a bank has in its safe (vault) and cash drawers.

Velocity of money   The number of times per year the average dollar in the Money supply (*see*) is spent for Final goods and services (*see*).

VERs   (*See* Voluntary export restrictions.)

Vertical axis   The "up-down" or "north-south" axis on a graph or grid.

Vertical combination   A group of Plants (*see*) engaged in different stages of the production of a final product and owned by a single Firm (*see*).

Vertical intercept   The point at which a line meets the vertical axis of a graph.

Vertical merger   The merger of one or more Firms engaged in different stages of the production of a final product.

Vertical range   Vertical segment of the Aggregate supply curve along which the economy is at full capacity.

Vicious circle of poverty   A problem common to the less developed countries where their low per capita incomes are an obstacle to realizing the levels of saving and investment requisite to acceptable rates of economic growth.

Voice mechanism   Communication by workers through their union to resolve grievances with an employer.

Voluntary export restrictions   The limitations by firms of their exports to particular foreign nations to avoid the erection of other trade barriers by the foreign nations.

W

Wage   The price paid for Labor (for the use or services of Labor, *see*) per unit of time (per hour, per day, etc.).

Wage and salary supplements   Payments made by employers of Labor into social insurance and private pension, health, and welfare funds for workers; and a part of the employer's cost of obtaining Labor.

Wage differential   The difference between the Wage (*see*) received by one worker or group of workers and that received by another worker or group of workers.

Wage discrimination   The payments to women or blacks (or other minority groups) of a wage lower than that paid to whites for doing the same work.

Wage guidepost A government exhortation that wages *(see)* in all industries in the economy should increase at an annual rate equal to the rate of increase in the Average product *(see)* of Labor in the economy.

Wage-price controls A Wage-price policy *(see)* which legally fixes the maximum amounts Wages *(see)* and prices may be increased in any period.

Wage-price guideposts A Wage-price policy *(see)* which depends on the voluntary cooperation of Labor unions and business firms.

Wage-price inflationary spiral Increases in wage rates which bring about increases in prices and in turn result in further increases in wage rates and in prices.

Wage-price policy Government policy that attempts to alter the behavior of Labor unions and business firms to make their Wage and price decisions more nearly compatible with the goals of Full employment and a stable Price level.

Wage rate (*See* Wage.)

Wages The income of those who supply the economy with Labor *(see)*.

Wagner Act The Federal act of 1935 which established the National Labor Relations Board *(see)*, guaranteed the rights of Labor unions to organize and to bargain collectively with employers, and listed and prohibited a number of unfair labor practices by employers.

Wealth effect (*See* Real balances effect.)

Welfare programs (*See* Public assistance programs.)

Wheeler-Lea Act The Federal act of 1938 which amended the Federal Trade Commission Act *(see)* by prohibiting and giving the commission power to investigate unfair and deceptive acts or practices of commerce (false and misleading advertising and the misrepresentation of products).

(The) "will to develop" Wanting economic growth strongly enough to change from old to new ways of doing things.

Workfare plans Reforms of the welfare system, particularly AFDC, designed to provide education and training for recipients so that they may move from public assistance to gainful employment.

World Bank A bank which lends (and guarantees loans) to less developed nations to assist them to grow; formally, the International Bank for Reconstruction and Development.

World price The international price of a good or service, determined by world demand and supply.

World Trade Organization (WTO) An organization established in 1994 by GATT *(see)* to oversee the provisions of the Uruguay Round *(see)* and resolve any disputes stemming therefrom.

X

X-inefficiency Failure to produce any given output at the lowest average (and total) cost possible.

Y

Yellow-dog contract The (now illegal) contract in which an employee agrees when accepting employment with a Firm that he or she will not become a member of a Labor union while employed by the Firm.

INDEX